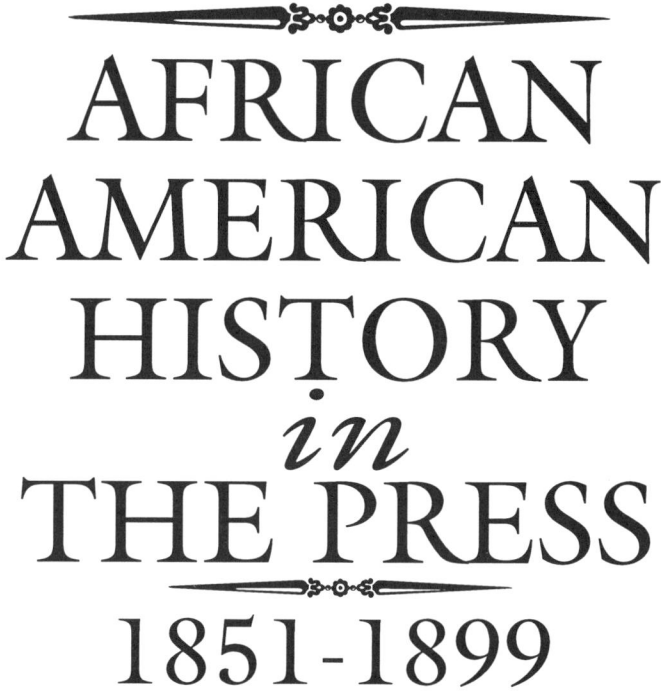

AFRICAN AMERICAN HISTORY *in* THE PRESS 1851-1899

From the Coming of the Civil War to the Rise of Jim Crow as Reported and Illustrated in Selected Newspapers of the Time

About the Book

African American History in the Press, 1851-1899 *offers readers the opportunity to witness the positive and negative portrayal of African Americans in more than 1,200 articles and editorials and over 470 cartoons and engravings as depicted in thirteen major newspapers of the nineteenth century. Newspapers include* Frank Leslie's Illustrated Newspaper, Harper's Weekly, *the* New York Times, *and the* Richmond Enquirer. Harper's Weekly *featured such artists as Frederic Remington and Thomas Nast and such journalists as George Curtis, who helped Henry David Thoreau build his cabin at Walden Pond.*

Readers will find first-hand reports as they were originally presented in the newspapers of the day, including abolitionist activities of John Brown, the Civil War, and the Supreme Court's Plessy v. Ferguson *decision upholding the separate but equal doctrine. Each chapter begins with an introductory overview written by an historian. News articles were reprinted without editorial corrections or censorship. For example "[i]ndorse," "characteri[s]ed," and "M'Donald" were reprinted using the spelling of the times.*

African American History in the Press, 1851-1899 *is based on the Schneider Collection of illustrated nineteenth century newspapers relating to the African American experience. The collection of 3,326 original items was assembled by Richard C. Schneider over a period of 35 years. Approximately 200 news articles from various regions of the country were chosen to supplement the Schneider Collection to offer regional perspectives on and related to African Americans. In addition, a timeline notes important dates in American history, with particular emphasis on milestones in African American history. A map from 1861 shows the United States around the start of the Civil War. Special sections on all newspapers used in* African American History in the Press: 1851-1899 *are provided: one gives biographical background on the newspapers and the other, an index, shows the dates of those issues of the papers used in the book. Finally, a subject index quickly leads users to important people, places, events, and institutions cited within the newspaper articles.*

AFRICAN AMERICAN HISTORY *in* THE PRESS
1851-1899

From the Coming of the Civil War to the Rise of Jim Crow as Reported and Illustrated in Selected Newspapers of the Time

Volume 2: 1870-1899

The Schneider Collection

ADVISORS

Robert L. Harris, Jr.
Africana Studies and Research Center, Cornell University

David Dennard
East Carolina University

Cynthia Neverdon-Morton
Coppin State College

Jacqueline Rouse
Georgia State University

GALE

DETROIT • NEW YORK • TORONTO • LONDON

Gale Research Staff

Marie Ellavich, Kenneth Estell, *Developmental Editors*
Camille Killens, *Associate Developmental Editor*
Lawrence W. Baker, *Managing Editor*
With thanks to Jolen M. Gedridge, Andrea Kovacs, and Jessica Proctor

Mary Beth Trimper, *Production Director*
Evi Seoud, *Assistant Production Manager*
Shanna Heilveil, *Production Assistant*
Cindy Baldwin, *Product Design Manager*

Tracy Rowens, *Art Director*
Barbara Yarrow, *Graphic Services Manager*
Randy Bassett, *Image Database Supervisor*
Pamela A. Hayes, *Photography Coordinator*
Mikal Ansari, *Imaging Specialist*
C.J. Jonik, *Desktop Publisher*

Front cover images reproduced from *Frank Leslie's Illustrated Newspaper* and *Harper's Weekly*.

Library of Congress Cataloging-in-Publication Number: 96-15384.

While every effort has been made to ensure the reliability of the information presented in this publication, Gale Research Inc. does not guarantee the accuracy of the data contained herein. Gale accepts no payment for listing; and inclusion in the publication of any organization, agency, institution, publication, service, or individual does not imply endorsement of the editors or publishers.

This publication is a creative work copyrighted by Gale Research and fully protected by all applicable copyright laws, as well as by misappropriation, trade secret, unfair competition, and other applicable laws. The authors and editors of this work have added value to the underlying factual material herein through one or more of the following: unique and original selection, coordination, expression, arrangement, and classification of the information.

Gale Research will vigorously defend all of its rights in this publication.

Copyright © 1996 Richard C. Schneider

Published by
Gale Research
835 Penobscot Bldg.
Detroit, MI 48226-4094

All rights reserved including the right of reproduction in whole or in part in any form.

∞™ This book is printed on acid-free paper that meets the minimum requirements of American National Standard for Information Sciences--Permanence Paper for Printed Library Materials, ANSI Z39.48-1984.

ISBN 0-8103-9555-x (set)
ISBN 0-8103-9556-8 (volume 1)
ISBN 0-8103-9557-6 (volume 2)
Printed in the United States of America
10 9 8 7 6 5 4 3 2

This book is dedicated to the sacred memory of America's sons and daughters of African descent who lived and died under the inhuman, immoral, and degrading conditions of slavery, bigotry, oppression, prejudice, and racial intolerance.

This book is also dedicated to us, the living of all racial, ethnic, social, and religious backgrounds. Hopefully, within its pages we may find truth and understanding to help guide us in our personal efforts to free ourselves from ourselves. Perhaps if the past is truly a prologue, then this book can introduce a new light of truth to help us further understand how far we have come and how far we must go on our own personal journey to freedom.

"Right is of no sex, truth is of no color, liberty is the birthright of all and all men are brothers."
Frederick Douglass

"When we were the political slaves of King George, and wanted to be free, we called the maxim that 'all men are created equal' a self-evident truth, but now, when we have grown fat, and have lost all dread of being slaves ourselves, we have become so greedy to be masters that we call the same maxim a 'self-evident lie.'"
Abraham Lincoln

"If a race has no history, if it has no worthwhile tradition, it becomes a negligible factor in the thought of the world, and it stands in danger of being exterminated."
Carter G. Woodson

"Slavery's impact touches more than black, but white as well, the shame of it, the lasting pain of it, the bewilderment of it, and the guilt too for having let slavery happen. It has left all of us less than whole."
Eddy L. Harris
South of Haunted Dreams

"I am the farmer, bondsman to the soil. I am the worker, sold to the machine. I am the Negro, servant to you all. I am the people, humble, hungry, near-hungry yet today despite the dream. Beaten yet today—O, Pioneers! I am the man who never got ahead, the poorest worker bartered through the years, yet I'm the one who dreamt our basic dream...."
Langston Hughes
"Let America Be American Again"

Contents

Introduction ix
Advisors xv
Acknowledgements xvii
Map xviii
Timeline xxi

Volume 1: 1851	1	**1874**	739
1852	15	**1875**	779
1853	23	**1876**	827
1854	33	**1877**	869
1855–56	43	**1878**	891
1857	53	**1879**	903
1858	77	**1880**	943
1859	95	**1881**	993
1860	145	**1882–83**	1009
1861	169	**1884**	1037
1862	217	**1885–86**	1053
1863	263	**1887**	1087
1864	317	**1888**	1109
1865	363	**1889**	1129
1866	417	**1890**	1141
1867	483	**1891–92**	1159
1868	535	**1893–94**	1187
1869	591	**1895**	1203
Volume 2: 1870	619	**1896**	1219
1871	649	**1897**	1233
1872	673	**1898**	1247
1873	719	**1899**	1265

Newspaper Histories 1285
Newspaper Index 1291
Keyword Index 1299
Illustrations Index 1323

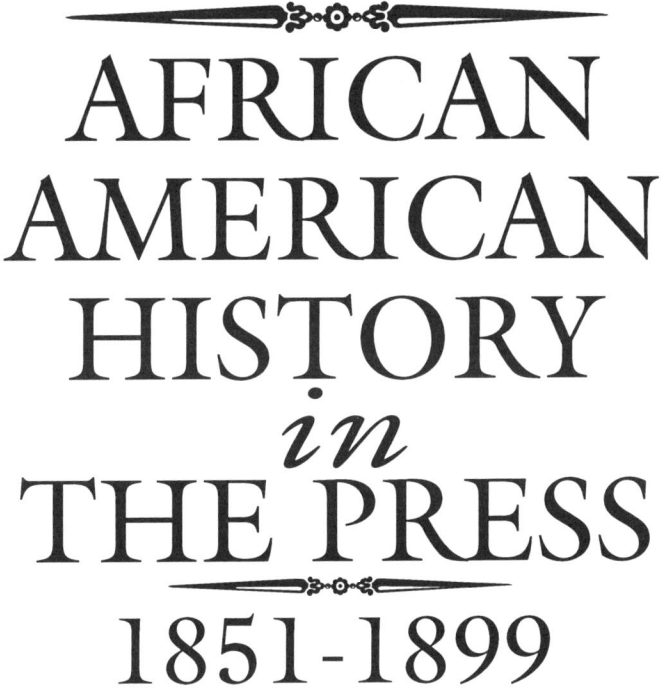

From the Coming of the Civil War to the
Rise of Jim Crow as Reported and
Illustrated in Selected Newspapers of the Time

1870

After the close of the Civil War in 1865 the Thirteenth, Fourteenth, and Fifteenth Amendments were passed to provide civil rights for African Americans. In 1870 ratification of the Fifteenth Amendment to the Constitution guaranteeing all citizens the right to vote was significantly reported on by journalists.

The Fifteenth Amendment forbade federal and/or state governments to deny or abridge the right to vote "on account of race, color, or previous condition of servitude." Northern and Southern journalists were divided on the effects this legislation would have on the African American voters. In May 1870 additional legislation was passed to support the Fifteenth Amendment, making it a felony for two or more persons to enter into a conspiracy or disguise themselves in order to deny anyone the right to vote. Additionally under the law, the president was given the authority to use military forces, if necessary, to enforce this legislation.

In the South, most local, state, and federal elected officials were members of the Democratic party, which had supported slavery and states' rights and continued to believe that giving African Americans equal rights after the war was folly.

Many Republicans and Northerners believed the Fifteenth Amendment, and reconstruction acts, would provide African Americans equal rights under the U.S. Constitution. Journalists supported the idea that life for all citizens in a democracy is best protected by the ballot and not by military force. Those who were opposed to the amendment created voting regulations to ensure that African Americans could not vote, including: poll taxes, grandfather clauses (requiring that one's grandfather had voted), and "white primaries" held prior to the general election and open only to white voters.

For journalists above and below the Mason-Dixon line, the novelty of African Americans in state supreme courts, the United States Congress, and other institutions of power played out in the news. Jonathan J. Wright, in South Carolina, was elected as associate justice of the state supreme court in 1870, a post that he held for six years. Hiram Revels was elected to the U.S. Senate in 1870. Harper's Weekly *(19 February 1870) reported this event as "a living symbol of the victory of equal rights which has been achieved should appear in the Senate of the United States in the person of Mr. Revels, the colored Senator from Mississippi." Not all journalists viewed the election of Revels as a positive step for democracy.* Harper's Weekly *(2 April 1870) reported the newspaper* New York World *as publishing the following: "To-day's session of the Senate was signalized . . . by the first speech ever delivered by the lineal descendant of an orang-outang in Congress. . . ." Also, few journalists missed the irony of Revels as the senator from Mississippi: former president of the Confederacy, Jefferson Davis, had been the senator from Mississippi prior to the start of the Civil War in 1860.*

In 1870 news regarding African Americans also focused on equality and civil rights. One group determined to eliminate African American equality was the Ku-Klux Klan. This group was established in 1865 to reassert white supremacy in the South. The Ku-Klux Klan waged war across the South, particularly to annul the votes of African Americans. As reported by Harper's Weekly *(20 August 1870), the governor of North Carolina imposed martial law on several counties to establish peace because "the comparative smallness of the colored population promised that a rigorous system of terror and coercion would practically annul the vote." The Ku-Klux Klan continued to flourish, however, through intimidation and violence against people of color and sympathetic whites.*

Robert L. Harris, Jr.
Cornell University

MISSISSIPPI POLITICS

HARPER'S WEEKLY
January 1, 1870, p. 2

The result of the late elections in Texas and Mississippi, if, as now seems to be the fact, Mr. Davis is elected Governor of Texas, is very agreeable to those who see in it the evidence of a really Republican party in those States. It was a favorite theory of Governor Andrew of Massachusetts that the real work of reconstruction at the South must be done by native or long-resident Southern white men. He foresaw the immigration from the Northern States; but he was not satisfied that it would be composed altogether of those who could do the work that was essential. This was a view shared by many thoughtful persons, who have been waiting to see if there were any signs of the appearance of such men. They would be those of whose coming our experience made us despair—Southern men who fought for the Confederacy, and who honestly and honorably accepted the defeat, and the consequent situation. In the nature of the case there could be few such men; but Governor Alcorn, the newly-elected Governor of Mississippi, seems to be one of them.

He did not conceal before the election that he had been a rebel; that he had served in the rebel army, and lost a son in it; that he had been a slave-owner, and was a large property-holder in the State where he had lived for twenty-five years, and with which he was entirely identified. But General Alcorn seems to have been able to understand the logical consequences of the utter fall of the Confederacy and of emancipation. He saw also that Congress represented the supreme and resistless power of the victorious Government, and that to defy it was merely to dash his head against the wall. Looking around him, he saw that the hatred of the negro in consequence of emancipation threatened his annihilation, with the loss of the laboring population and endless woes. He saw also that the negro could not best be defended by a military force, but by the ballot. The old masters were, so to speak, the natural leaders of the freedmen. But they cursed the new citizens, who were obliged to seek leadership elsewhere, and they turned to the Northern settlers, many of whom were educated, and had various social and property ties to the South. But others were, as was to be expected, mere adventurers who would stop at nothing that might secure their selfish advantage.

The leadership of the new citizens by such men was for every reason not desirable, and in 1867 Mr. Alcorn called upon the white people of the South to accept the situation in good faith, and not to pout and sulk against the inevitable. He was universally denounced by them in consequence. But when a policy of general proscription was proposed in the State of Mississippi it failed. Then the Republican party of Mississippi was founded upon the platform of an intelligent union of all who heartily accepted the Republican national policy, including amnesty, and of this party General Alcorn was the candidate in the late contest with Judge Dent. The latter was the candidate of the irreconcilables—the "Conservatives" of every kind—as they are absurdly called, as if it were conservatism to refuse to rise out of the ruins of your wagon when it has been upset. The former was the candidate of the Radicals, the intelligent and perceptive part of the community. In his address before the election Governor Alcorn said:

"The reconstruction to which I go forward is a reconstruction which will make rich and poor equal in *fact* before the law. I move on with it, guiding a harnessed revolution over the ruins of an oligarchy, to the erection of a government by the people and for the people. I go forward, fellow-citizens, to build up in accordance with the spirit of the age, in accordance with the will of the nation, a party new to the history of Mississippi—a party determined, while raising the State from her prostrate position under the foot of power, to erect it, not upon its point, but upon its base—the masses of the citizens."

But he knows that the interests of all are inseparable. He grants that in the old day the oligarchy of slaveholders, of which he was one, controlled the voters of the State. Among his declarations, therefore, this is very significant:

"The 50,000 poor voters who have been dominated in the past by a wealthy class will strike now for their independence. The small farmer who had been dragooned formerly by an insolent oligarchy will refuse to vote any more in the interests of the few. The small trader finds his interests now with the masses. He is justified no longer in declining to assert his independence because of the terrors of a rich man's frown. The party I am laboring to form will unite these several classes of the whites with the masses of the tillers of the soil; and, hurling the dotards of a dead system from their seats, will go forward with me to the erection of a government based on education, prompt payment, equality before the law, and a general system of legislation, having its foundation in strict justice to the rich and to the poor!"

The Republican party in Mississippi polled fully a fourth of the white vote. But the majority for General Alcorn and his intelligent platform was so immense that many of those who voted against him will not necessarily remain opposed to an administration which, by insisting upon equal rights, will plainly promote peace and prosperity. For ourselves, however, we do not expect that the old rebel element of the Southern States will become a safe and valuable power. The very fact that General Alcorn and a very few others stand alone among their old associates, reveals the hopelessness of the position of the latter. They will be an obstruction. But there is no reason to suppose that the party in the State, which has shown such strength upon the declaration of so just and generous a policy, will decline. It has comprehended the situation. It has found a leader who could truly express its faith and its purpose; and a man who, under the circumstances that surrounded him, has done what General Alcorn has done, will naturally not wish to undo it.

DOMESTIC INTELLIGENCE

HARPER'S WEEKLY
January 29, 1870, p. 67

General News Items

The Tennessee Constitutional Convention assembled at Nashville, January 10, sixty-one delegates present. John C. Brown, formerly a Confederate general, was chosen President. On the 11th the members and officers took an oath to support the Constitution of the United States. Amendments to the State Constitution were submitted, forbidding slavery and involuntary servitude.

The Fifteenth Amendment was ratified by the Senate of the Rhode Island Legislature January 10: by the

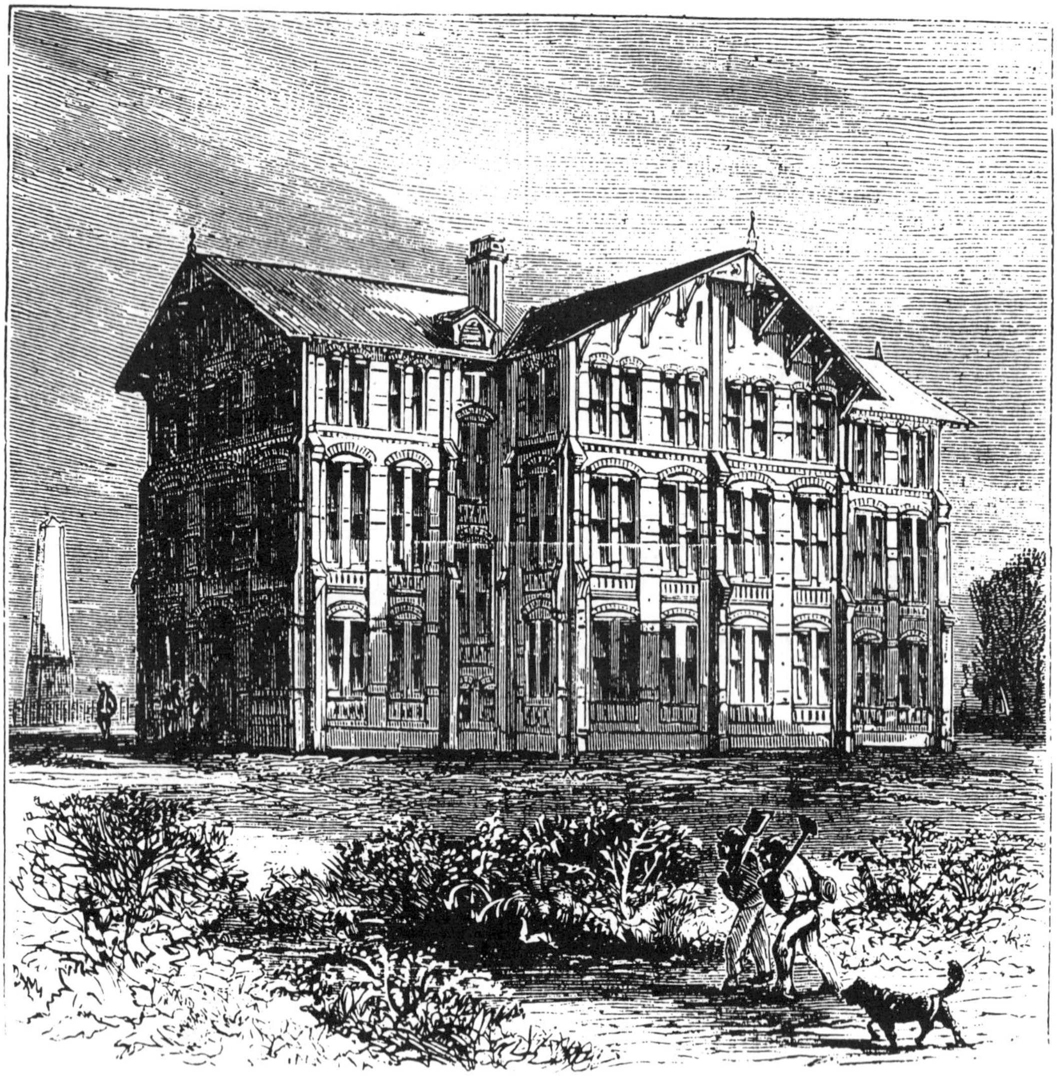

NORMAL AND AGRICULTURAL INSTITUTE, HAMPTON, VIRGINIA.

Harper's Weekly, January 29, 1870, p. 77.

Ohio Senate on the 14th; and by the Kansas Senate on the 13th.

THE HAMPTON, VIRGINIA, NORMAL AND AGRICULTURAL INSTITUTE

HARPER'S WEEKLY
January 29, 1870, p. 77

This institution, of which a view will be found on this page, is located in Hampton, Virginia, within sight of Fortress Monroe. It was established in 1868, under the auspices of the American Missionary Association, for the purpose of preparing youth of the South, without distinction of color, for the work of organizing and instructing schools in the Southern States. The extreme poverty of those who needed such an institution, and the value of self-help as a means of culture and true manhood, induced the Association to purchase a farm of one hundred and twenty acres and provide it with all appliances of profitable labor. The farm lies upon Hampton Roads. The school and home buildings, valued at $50,000, occupy a beautiful site upon the shore. They are so furnished and arranged as to offer to the students the helps to right living which belong to a cultivated Christian home. In the farm-work, under the constant direction of an educated practical farmer, the graduates of this institution will have learned both the theory and practice of the most profitable methods of agriculture. The female students do all the house-work of the boarding department. Thus in the home, on the farm, and in the school-room the students have the opportunity to learn the three great lessons of life—how to live, how to labor, and how to teach others. There are at present about 80 pupils at the Institute. The terms of tuition are merely nominal; and, to meet the necessities of the Institute, the managers solicit temporary endowments for scholarships yielding $85 for males, and $100 for females. All labor performed on the farm by the inmates is paid for at rates varying from four to twelve cents an hour.

[UNTITLED]

CHARLESTON DAILY COURIER
February 2, 1870

By the new Constitution of the State it is prescribed, by Section 3 of Article 4, that there shall be elected by the Legislature a Chief Justice for six years, and two Associate Justices, one of whom shall hold office for four years, and one for two years; and that the Legislature, by a *viva voce* vote, should determine which of the Associate Justices thus elected should hold for four, and which for two years. On the 30th July, 1868, Mr. A. J. Willard was elected an Associate Justice, receiving 90 votes out 136 votes cast. Mr. S. L. Hoge was also elected an Associate Justice, by a vote of 76 out of 131 votes cast.

The Legislature on the same day went into a *viva voce* vote to determine the length of their respective terms. By a vote of 91 to 28, Mr. Willard was elected for the long term and Mr. Hoge for the two years term. Mr. Hoge resigned, so as to become a candidate for Congress, and thus created a vacancy. The Legislature yesterday elected J. J. Wright, simply because he was a black man, as his successor, for the abort term expiring in 1870.

WHERE HAVE THEY GONE!

DETROIT FREE PRESS
February 2, 1870

The census of Kentucky for 1860 shows the colored population of that State to have been 236,167. The Louisville *Courier-Journal* states that by the State Auditor's report for 1869 the total colored population is shown to be but 140,445. If this is a correct statement of the condition of affairs in that State, and we have no doubt it is, the Radical party will gain little in Kentucky by the adoption of the fifteenth amendment. The entire voting power of the freedmen will fall below 39,000, and this will hardly overcome the immense Democratic majority in that State, even if these people were all to vote the Radical ticket, which they will by no means do. But where have the Kentucky freedmen gone? Many of them have immigrated to the North, and many have gone to the Gulf States, but more of them have died from exposure and disease, and a consequent want of that care which has heretofore been bestowed upon them by others, and from indulgences which have proved so fatal to their race all over the South. What is true of the diminution of these people in Kentucky is true of nearly all the old slave-holding States. North Carolina, Virginia, Tennessee and Maryland, all tell the same story. "Passing away."

SOUTH CAROLINA LEGISLATURE

CHARLESTON DAILY COURIER
February 3, 1870
[Reported for the Courier]
Columbia, S. O., February 1, 1870
The Election of Associate Justice
There has been really but little of interest today beyond the election of J. J. Wright to fill the vacancy on the Supreme Bench, occasioned by the withdrawal of Congressman Hoge. The excitement has been up to the highest pitch. Last night the friends of Wright and Whipper both held caucuses, and both parties felt sanguine of success. This morning the Democrats also held a caucus to discuss the propriety of casting their vote in favor of either of the two prominent candidates most acceptable to them and their constituents. They decided to support Wright.

To-day when the two Houses met in joint assembly, almost every vacant seat on the floor and in the galleries of the House of Representatives was already occupied. The Hall for the first time this session was over crowded. . . .

Recapitulation.—J. J. Wright, 72; W. J. Whipper, 57; J. L. Orr, 3; S. McGowan, 1; Thomas Thompson, 1. Whole number of votes given, 134 Necessary to a choice, 68.

The President announced that J. J. Wright having received a majority of the whole number of votes given, was duly elected an Associate Justice of the Supreme Court for the unfinished term ending 30th July, A.D. 1870.

VIRGINIA AND CONGRESS

HARPER'S WEEKLY
February 5, 1870, p. 82

The debate in the Senate upon the admission of Virginia was very acrimonious, and ended in a passage of peculiar bitterness between Senators Trumbull and Sumner. Mr. Trumbull declared that Mr. Sumner persisted in statements after they had been disproved, and in general undertook to brow-beat the Senate very much in the manner of the old slave-masters. Mr. Sumner retorted that Mr. Trumbull had opposed all efforts to help the colored citizen, and was the representative of the Ku-Klux Klan; and, moreover, that he made a technical argument to screen the criminal Andrew Johnson. Both Senators were called to order by the Chair for unparliamentary language; and the speeches of both were in a temper which is not, theoretically, senatorial. After they had spoken the question was taken, and the bill was passed by a strict Republican vote. It will, probably, have been considered by the House before this paper is issued.

SENATOR REVELS

HARPER'S WEEKLY
February 19, 1870, pp. 114–15

It is a curious and interesting fact that with the adoption of the Fifteenth Amendment, and the close of the great series of measures of reconstruction which formally end the war, a living symbol of the victory of equal rights which has been achieved should appear in the Senate of the United States in the person of Mr. Revels, the colored Senator from Mississippi. It is no less striking and significant that the papers which always toadied the great slave-drivers in Congress gibe and sneer at the new Senator, not because of any want of capacity, any fault of character, or any defect of manner, but solely because of color. If Mr. Revels shall prove to be as shallow as Mr. Wigfall, as arrogant as Mr. Toombs, as false to his country as Mr. Jefferson Davis; and if, like those ancient Democratic Senators and all their brethren, he shall devote all his energies to the perpetuity and extension of the most un-American, the most disastrous, and the most inhuman policy that was ever proposed in the Legislature of a civilized nation, we shall agree that the Democratic gibes are well deserved.

If, on the other hand, he shall modestly and steadily continue to support the great principles to which his life has been devoted—if he shall continue to do all that he can to elevate and enlighten the most unfortunate class of American citizens, to establish securely that policy of equal rights among the people which is alone truly American and democratic, to cultivate universal sympathy and fraternity, and to hold the Union to the great and humane purposes for which it is declared in the Constitution to be established—if he proves by his Senatorial course his faith in popular government, in liberty, in justice, as the best guarantees of civilization and progress, and the greatest good of the greatest number, he will do what neither Mr. Wigfall, nor Mr. Toombs, nor Mr. Slidell, nor Mr. Mason, nor Mr. Jefferson Davis, nor any of the Democratic Senators ever did, and will commend himself, as they certainly never did, to the grateful remembrance and honor of his fellow-citizens.

HON. H. R. REVELS

HARPER'S WEEKLY
February 19, 1870, pp. 116–17

On this page will be found the portrait of Hon. H. R. Revels, Senator elect from Mississippi. Mr. Revels was born in North Carolina, in 1822, of free colored parents. He was educated at a Quaker Seminary in Indiana, and became a Methodist minister. At the breaking out of the war he was settled in Baltimore, and from that time took an active part in the management of freedmen's affairs. In 1864 he went to Vicksburg, in pursuance of this mission, and assisted in the organization of schools and churches among the liberated slaves. He passed the next two years in Kansas and Missouri, preaching and lecturing on moral and religious subjects; returned to Mississippi the following year, and has since resided in Natchez. He is presiding elder of his Church for the southern portion of the State. Since July last he has been a member of the City Council, and has served in that capacity with credit. A short time since he was elected to the State Senate by a handsome majority, and has now been selected by the Legislature as a proper man to represent the State in the Senate of the United States.

Mr. Revels is a tall, portly man, of light complexion; has benevolent features, a pleasant voice, and cultivated manners. He is thoroughly respected by his own people, and by the whites.

HON. H. R. REVELS, UNITED STATES SENATOR ELECT FROM MISSISSIPPI.

Harper's Weekly, February 19, 1870, p. 116.

HIRAM R. REVELS, UNITED STATES SENATOR-ELECT FROM MISSISSIPPI.—FROM A PHOTOGRAPH BY BRADY.

Frank Leslie's Illustrated Newspaper, February 26, 1870, p. 401.

THE CASE OF SENATOR REVELS

DETROIT FREE PRESS
February 25, 1870

The Mississippi subject was their taken up, the question being upon the motion of Mr. Stockton to refer the credentials of Mr. Revels to the Judiciary Committee.

Mr. Saulsbury supported the proposed reference upon the ground entertained by his political associates in the Senate, that under the Constitution Revels was not eligible to a seat in the Senate.

Mr. Drake, during the remarks of Mr. Saulsbury, made a statement that Mr. Revels was neither a negro nor a mulatto, but an octoroon, and that he made the statement out of compassion for the mental sufferings of his friend (Saulsbury), upon the probability of being compelled to associate in the Senate with a jet black negro.

Mr. Wilson asked unanimous consent to enter a motion to reconsider the vote by which the House amendment to the Political Disability bill was concurred in.

Mr. Fowler objected, and the motion was deferred until tomorrow.

Mr. Howard believed the proof of Revels election conclusive, and that the only issue now was upon the acceptance or rejection of him on account of color. He (Howard) maintained that every person born in the United States who had not been a slave was a citizen He would carry this doctrine so far as to assert that even a black man, born a slave, was to be held a citizen from his birth. The Dred Scott decision, in his opinion, had sunk into eternal decision and contempt.

Mr. Williams remarked that Chief Justice Taney expressly limited the Dred Scott decision to those with pure African blood in their veins, and whose ancestors had been sold as slaves. It appeared that Revels was a man with a large proportion of white blood, and it followed necessarily that some of his ancestors were not slaves. Upon the whole, in view of all authorities, legal and otherwise, Mr. Revel—had always been a citizen of the United States.

Mr. Cameron narrated the particulars of an interview between himself and Jefferson Davis just prior to the war and before the latter had left the Senate, during which he declared to Davis his own conviction that slavery would have ceased from the moment the first gun was fired upon the flag of the country, and that his (Davis) seat would some day, in the justice of God, be occupied by a negro. He considered the attempt of the Senator from Oregon to argue that this man had more of white than black blood in his veins unworthy of any Senator, in view of the great services of the colored soldiers. Without action upon the subject, the Senate adjourned.

HIRAM R. REVELS, U. S. SENATOR-ELECT FROM MISSISSIPPI

FRANK LESLIE'S ILLUSTRATED NEWSPAPER
February 26, 1870, p. 401

The "revenges of time" have never been more severely exemplified than in the rapid social and political changes which have, in the past decade, marked the progress of society in the states that, in 1860, in order to more firmly establish a system of thraldom, to which the unbiased sense of Christendom was obnoxious, arrayed themselves in arms against the integrity of the Republic.

The struggle was for freedom, equality on one side; slavery, degradation on the other. It was the Battle of the Giants—the Dying Past with the Young Present; and the Past, with many a ghastly wound on his darkened brows, went to his grave. Behold the result! Ten years ago, the head and front of the best organized and most audacious rebellion Wrong ever confronted against Right, sat in the councils of the Republic as the Voice of Mississippi. He there wielded an influence that ought to have satisfied his ambition; but, like Lucifer, from that pride of state which Slavery engendered, he fell. Ten years have rolled away, and we find elected to fill his seat, by Mississippi, a representative of the very race he unwisely sought to make forever in the fertile fields of the South, the "chattel" of his economy. This representative is Hiram R. Revels, who is said to be a man of much energy of character, with excellent and well developed mental qualifications. In his person is centred one of the grandest thoughts of the nineteenth century—the equality of all men before the law.

Mr. Revels was not born a slave, although he first saw the light, forty-seven years ago, in the county of Cumberland, North Carolina. He remained in his native town of Fayette until the year 1844, when he immigrated to Liberty, Union County, Indiana. He was there entered a student in the Friends' Seminary, where he mastered the elements of an English education. Two years later he removed to Ohio, and, completing a full theological course at college, was ordained a minister in the African Methodist Church. At the breaking out of the war, Mr Revels removed to Baltimore, where he was entrusted with the conduct of a high school for negro students. While residing in Baltimore, he assisted in organizing colored regiments, and, accepting the chaplaincy of one, was at Vicksburgh and other points on the Mississippi.

At the close of the war Mr. Revels located at Natchez, and since then has been Presiding Elder of the African Methodist Episcopal Church for the Southern District of the State. He was appointed a member of the City Council of Natchez by General Ames, and was elected to the State Senate by a large majority over his competitor.

This body quite recently returned him for the short term, as the coadjutor of General Adelbert Ames, to the Senate of the United States, and as the successor of Jefferson Davis.

The personal appearance of Mr. Revels is decidedly prepossessing. He is five feet ten inches in height, weighs one hundred and eighty pounds, and is about three-fourths white. His features are regular, but prominent, and, with his broad expansive brow, indicate large intelligence. In manner he is easy and affable, and takes the honor conferred upon him as humbly and thankfully as General Grant did the Presidency.

JUDGE J. J. WRIGHT, OF SOUTH CAROLINA

HARPER'S WEEKLY
March 5, 1870, p. 151

The Honorable J. J. Wright, recently elected to a seat in the Supreme Court of South Carolina, whose portrait we give on page 149, was born in Luzerne County, Pennsylvania, and is now about thirty-one years of age. When

HON. J. J. WRIGHT, JUDGE OF THE SUPREME COURT OF SOUTH CAROLINA.
PHOTOGRAPHED BY WEARN AND HIX, COLUMBIA, S. C.—[SEE PAGE 151.]

Harper's Weekly, March 5, 1870, p. 149.

he was about six years old his parents removed to Montrose, Susquehanna County, in the same State, where for several years he attended the district school during the winter months, working for the neighboring farmers the rest of the year. Having saved up a small sum of money he entered the Lancasterian University, at Ithaca, in New York State; and after a thorough course of study there returned to the village where his parents resided, and entered the office of a law firm, where he read law for two years, supporting himself by teaching. He subsequently entered the office of Judge Collins, in Wilkesbarre, Pennsylvania, with whom he read law for another year. Feeling himself qualified for the legal profession, he now applied for admission to the Bar; but so great was the existing prejudice against colored men that the Committee refused to examine him.

In April, 1865, he was sent by the American Missionary Society to Beaufort, South Carolina, as a teacher and laborer among the freedmen. He remained in Beaufort until after the Civil Rights Bill had passed, when he returned to Montrose, Pennsylvania, and demanded an examination. The Committee found him qualified, and recommended his admission to the Bar. He was admitted August 13, 1865, being the first and only colored man ever admitted to practice law in Pennsylvania. In April, 1866, he was appointed by General O. O. Howard legal adviser for the freedmen in Beaufort, and acted in that capacity until he was elected

to the Constitutional Convention of South Carolina. He was soon afterward elected Senator from the county of Beaufort, and acted as such until February 1, 1870, when he was elected to the Supreme Bench of the State, and immediately entered upon the discharge of his duties as Judge.

"THE HISTORY OF TEN YEARS."

HARPER'S WEEKLY
April 2, 1870, p. 211

It is just ten years ago that Jefferson Davis, then a Senator from Mississippi, proposed in the Senate a series of resolutions which were passed by a strict party vote of the Democratic majority in that body, excepting Mr. Pugh of Ohio. The resolutions were elaborately and ingeniously drawn. Their intention was, first, to brand Mr. Douglas's squatter sovereignty as a party heresy; and second, to nationalize human slavery. The Democratic majority, sternly ruled by Mr. Davis and his friends, did not hesitate. One Senator ventured to move that it was not meant that Congress should provide a complete system of laws for slavery. But Mr. Davis looked at him, and the poor Senator—it was Mr. Clingman—had no supporting Democratic vote but the same Mr. Pugh. So vast was the crime against human nature and American liberty proclaimed by the Democratic party.

A year from that time, on the 21st of January, 1861, Jefferson Davis, still a Senator, and his conspiracy being ripe, gravely argued, in the highest legislative body of this government, the right of a few citizens, at their pleasure, to destroy a nation; in the Senate that grew out of the Declaration of Independence asserted that the Declaration, when it alleged that *all* men were created equal, meant *some* men; and after a little rhetoric about solemn separation, departed to do his best to destroy the American Union, and perpetuate African slavery upon the American continent. At the end of nine years the American Union is impregnable; African slavery is abolished; and a Senator from Mississippi rises in the place of Jefferson Davis to address the Senate, and that Senator, intelligent and self-possessed, is one of the enslaved race.

No wonder that a paper which represents the ridiculous theory that the glory of the country departed when Jefferson Davis and his accomplices left the Capi-

"A BROWN STUDY."—By the late William Hunt.—[See Page 155.]

Harper's Weekly, March 5, 1870, p. 152.

tol says of his successor's speech (see the New York *World*): "To-day's session of the Senate was signalized ... by the first speech ever delivered by the lineal descendant of an orang-outang in Congress.... During the morning hour ... Revels himself sat at his desk, tranquilly pawing his lower visage and beard with hands resembling claws, and eying the assemblage aloft with a greasy and complacent smile.... In the United States Senate sat to-day Sumner, Wilson, and the other Radicals who helped to bring on a bloodier revolution than the French, still so drunk with the vindictive spirit of the conflict and its issues that it seemed to them a fine

1870

WASHINGTON, D.C.—ADMINISTERING THE OATH TO HIRAM REVELS, COLORED SENATOR FROM THE STATE OF MISSISSIPPI, IN THE SENATE CHAMBER OF THE UNITED STATES, ON FRIDAY, FEBRUARY 25, 1870.—SKETCHED BY OUR SPECIAL ARTIST.—SEE PAGE 431.

Frank Leslie's Illustrated Newspaper, March 12, 1870.

thing to foist this African into false equality with themselves and their betters, among American statesmen to raise this mulatto idol, stuffed with vapid argumentation and sentimental logic." It is the very comedy of impotent hate.

NOTES

HARPER'S WEEKLY
April 2, 1870, p. 211

The first speech of Senator Revels began most fitly, under the circumstances, by a generous and earnest vindication of the part played by the colored population in the war inaugurated by his predecessor to enslave them and their posterity forever:

> "While the Confederate army pressed into its ranks every white male capable of bearing arms, the mothers, wives, daughters, and sisters of the Southern soldiers were left defenseless and in the power of the blacks, upon whom the chains of slavery were still riveted, and to bind those chains the closer was the real issue for which so much life and property were sacrificed. And now, Sir, I ask, how did that race act? Did they, in those days of Confederate weakness and impotence, evince the malignity of which we hear so much? Granting, for the sake of argument, that they were ignorant and besotted, which I do

629

AFRICAN AMERICAN HISTORY IN THE PRESS, 1851-1899

XVth AMENDMENT. — "*Shoo Fly, don't Bodder me!*"

Harper's Weekly, March 12, 1870, p. 176.

not believe, yet, with all their supposed ignorance and credulity, they, in their way, understood as fully as you or I the awful import of the contest. They knew if the gallant corps of national soldiers were beaten bad, and their flag trailed in the dust, that it was the presage of still heavier bondage. They longed, too, as their fathers did before them, for the advent of that epoch over which was shed the hallowed light of inspiration itself. They desired, too, with their fathers, to welcome the feet of the strangers, shod with the peaceful preparation of good news. Weary years of bondage had told their tale of sorrow to the court of Heaven. In the councils of the Great Father of all they knew the adjudication of their case, albeit delayed for years, in which patient suffering had nearly exhausted itself, would in the end bring the boon for which they sighed—God's most blessed gift to his creatures—the inestimable boon of liberty. They waited, and they waited patiently. In the absence of their masters they protected the virtue and chastity of defenseless women. Think, Sir, for a moment what the condition of this land would be today if the slave population had risen in servile insurrection against those who, month by month, were fighting to perpetuate that institution which brought them all the evils of which they complained. Where would have been the security for property, female chastity, and childhood's innocence? The bloody counterpart of such a story of cruelty and wrong would have been paralleled only in those chapters of Jewish history as recorded by Josephus, or in the still later atrocities of that reign of terror which sent the unfortunate Louis XVI, and Marie Antoinette to the scaffold. Nay, the deeds in that drama of cold-blooded butchery would have out-Heroded the most diabolical acts of Herod himself."

It is a truth that should silence forever the political touters against the colored citizens of this country.

DOMESTIC INTELLIGENCE

HARPER'S WEEKLY
April 2, 1870, p. 211

General News Items
The Richmond (Va.) City Council, appointed by Governor Walker under the Enabling Act of the State Legislature on the 9th of March, elected Henry K. Ellison Mayor, but Mayor Cahoon, the incumbent under military rule, declined to recognize the new Mayor, and, having possession of the lower station-house, immediately proceeded to swear in 150 special constables to maintain his right. Mayor Ellison thereupon swore in 200 constables, and surrounded the station-house, intending to starve out the garrison. Mayor Cahoon made an appeal to Governor Walker, and was advised by him to seek judicial redress. General Canby ordered a company of troops into the city to preserve order. The conflict continued several days, and at last accounts the situation was unchanged. A negro had been killed by some of Mayor Ellison's police for refusing to "move on" when ordered.

SOUTHERN SCENES

FRANK LESLIE'S ILLUSTRATED NEWSPAPER
May 21, 1870, p. 157

The engravings in this issue, of Southern scenes, accurately illustrate the life and social *status* of the negro on the Ashley and Cooper rivers, and the Sea Islands particularly those within the jurisdiction of South Carolina. No longer held in a state of abject servitude, these cultivators of small arable tracts of land seem to labor with an industry and persistency which markedly contrasts with the indolence they displayed anterior to the rebellion. Their "garden patches" are sources of great profit, and very many cultivators are known to be among the richest of the laboring classes. The old theory, that negroes, without a master and the whip of the overseer, would relapse into barbarism, and become a burden to the whites, has been exploded. They are now acknowledged, even by the most prejudiced of the late "ruling classes," to be in the main industrious and frugal—saving up money against a rainy day. As a free, peasant population, they are infinitely more profitable to the South than they were when accounted "chattels" and in intelligence ranked but one or two removes from the brute creation. To-day they are the chief reliance of the whites in the cotton States; and this fact, not unknown to them, doubtless incites them to appear to the very best advantage among their "political compeers" of the Caucasian race, whose good-will they naturally and ardently seek. The sketches are truthful, and represent, first, early morning on the Ashley river; and, second, taking vegetables by land to Charleston. On the Ashley and Cooper rivers, scows are rowed down-stream, laden with such garden products as are salable in Northern ports. When the vegetables are taken to the market, or to the wharves at Charleston, they are readily disposed of to speculators. A small percentage only is purchased by the citizens, the rest being shipped in sloops, schooners, and steamers to Baltimore, Philadelphia, and New York. Baltimore is considered the best market, as the "truck" is not there so stale or wilted as when taken to more distant marts. Possibly, one advantage which the present generation of the colored population of the South has over the white, rests in the fact, that the women are quite as strong and devoted to labor as the men. Thirty or forty years hence, this may not be the case. The young negro girls of that day will doubtless be desirous of imitating their white sisters in all manners and fashions; and when they do, their husbands, brothers, and fathers, like those of the pale-faces of their era, will have all the work for their share of life's "toil and trouble."

OUR WASHINGTON CORRESPONDENCE

CHARLESTON DAILY COURIER
June 2, 1870
[From Our Own Correspondent]

Washington, May 30
... The Southern people who come to this city and visit the capital invariably enquire first about the negro Senator from Mississippi. They are hardly yet accustomed to the idea of a negro sitting in the seat of Jefferson Davis, and can scarcely realize the change as a fact. But those who visit the Senate lobby or galleries for this purpose are generally disappointed, for Revels is seldom in his seat, or even in the city. He is in great demand in all the towns and cities North and West of us, as a public lecturer, and he receives three hundred dollars for each lecture. He has nothing to say except of the merest common-place; but to exhibit himself, as a signal example of the extent of the Federal triumph is all that is required of him. So far as his relations with the

THE PROMISES OF THE DECLARATION OF INDEPENDENCE FULFILLED

AN ALLEGORICAL PICTURE COMMEMORATIVE OF THE PASSAGE OF THE FIFTEENTH AMENDMENT TO THE FEDERAL CONSTITUTION.—"ALL MEN EQUAL BEFORE THE LAW."—See page 13.

Frank Leslie's Illustrated Newspaper, March 19, 1870, p. 8-9.

"TIME WORKS WONDERS."
IAGO.(JEFF DAVIS.) "FOR THAT I DO SUSPECT THE LUSTY MOOR HATH LEAP'D INTO MY SEAT: THE THOUGHT WHEREOF DOTH LIKE A POISONOUS MINERAL GNAW MY INWARDS." — OTHELLO.

Harper's Weekly, April 9, 1870, p. 232.

THE OTHELLO OF TO-DAY.

Iago (*Democratic Politician*). "The Moor is of a free and open nature, that thinks men honest that but seem to be so, and will as tenderly be led by the nose as asses are."

Harper's Weekly, April 23, 1870, p. 272.

body or with individual Senators are concerned, they are not intimate, nor disagreeable. Revels believes himself with modesty and propriety, and assumes nothing upon the strength of the adulation he receives from Northern negrophilists. I have heard Southern men say that they would treat Revels with more regard than they would some of the carpet-baggers.

It is not probable that the Southern States will send another colored citizen to the Senate, and, so far, the House is destitute of such a significant work of Republican triumph. The Republican party has made nearly all the use of the colored man that it required, and now will drop him. He must even here, in Maryland and Virginia, look hereafter to his old neighbors and sources as his true and most serviceable friends. —LEO.

The engraving on the first page is from a sketch taken by the artist while passing through a street in Charleston to the Battery. "Aunty"—for by such familiar phrase is the old colored woman of the South ordinarily addressed—has, in all their "seductive beauty," if such a term may be addressed to the members of the genus Cancer, spread her boiled soft-shell crabs, decorated with seaweed, on a wooden tray. When everything is properly prepared, the old woman, in a low and peculiarly sweet voice, which, however, is heard at a considerable distance, informs the lovers of crustacean fish that—"Heah's yer sof-shell crabs, only a penny apiece. Dey's jus' de ting." The negroes are great lovers of fish, and aunty's patrons are mostly from her own people. It is not uncommon thing to pass in the evening colored men and women near the stands of venders, industriously at work demolishing the crabs—which, to tell the truth, are very tooth-some—and, between mouthfuls, laughing at some joke which one of their number has uttered.

Leaving aunty and her tray of soft-shell crabs, "ebery one ob dem pure beauties, sah," we invite our readers to the eighth page, where are two fine illustrations of ebon-skinned disciples of Isaak Walton, under influences that show the negro fisherman in his leading mental characteristics.

"Tide Out" and "Tide In" tell their own stories. Words are useless here. We may not gild refined gold; nor can we heighten, by verbalisms, the effect of a really fine picture which tells everything. In "Tide Out" and in "Tide In" the artist has made his figures prominent, full of character and genuine humor. Look at that sleeper lying on his back! Can those peculiar muscular contractions of the nostrils, cheek and mouth, which give the impression of the loudest of snores, be more perfect?

The sleeper's nose is a study, and we have no doubt that all who scan these companion-pictures will thoroughly enjoy it. Mr. Sheppard has succeeded in all his negro portraitures, but we are persuaded that in the recumbent figure, with the face turned upward, and in the nasal organ, in which sonorousness is so markedly expressed, he has surpassed himself.

SOUTHERN SCENES

FRANK LESLIE'S ILLUSTRATED NEWSPAPER
July 16, 1870, p. 277

We present, in this number of the ILLUSTRATED NEWSPAPER, three sketches of the ex-slave as seen to-day in the South in all the glory of freedom and *insouciance*.

A SCENE IN A SAVANNAH MARKET

FRANK LESLIE'S ILLUSTRATED NEWSPAPER
July 30, 1870, p. 311

Hot weather, except in its tendency to somnolency, does not affect Sambo if of genuine African descent, in

1870

NEW YORK CITY.—DEMONSTRATION OF THE COLORED INHABITANTS OF NEW YORK IN HONOR OF THE ADOPTION OF THE FIFTEENTH AMENDMENT TO THE CONSTITUTION OF THE UNITED STATES—FRIDAY APRIL 8, 1870.

Frank Leslie's Illustrated Newspaper, April 30, 1870, p. 105.

the days of the dog-star. On the contrary, he rather likes it. Even in the equatorial regions of his ancestors it is said he is not averse to a comfortable fire at which he may "warm his hands and roast his shins" when Night lets her curtain fall upon the earth. The negro north of Mason and Dixon's line is a poor specimen of the "gemman" who vegetates south of it. And, if one would look on the Southern-born in all his glory—the genuine Georgia representative of the race that erst was "contraband"—one must pass a morning-hour in the principal market of Savannah, which our artist, during his recent Southern tour, visited, and where he rapidly sketched the scene so rich in humor and character that graces our first page. The counter around which the negroes gathered, and feasted on greasy edibles, had a "fan" placed over it, which a boy, much given to sleep, was employed to operate. The little fellow, notwithstanding that the flies, which swarmed in hungry thousands upon the viands and the group, would crawl into his mouth, nose, and ears, could not keep his eyes open or his arm in motion sufficiently to "pull dat yer string," and so agitate the air, for the benefit of the sweat-covered customers. Many times had his mother, with a shake and a slap, brought her son out of his lethargic slumbers; but it would be only for the moment. At last, losing all patience, she seized a stick, and, with an objurgation peculiarly Southern and negro, "made fo' de chile." This incident the artist has graphically and pleasantly depictured.

Nothing could be more characteristic—nothing more genuine of negro life as it is seen in the South, particularly in its "Empire State." Every figure in the illustration tells a story—every one, from the pompous "gemman" who is seen "argumfyin; wid de cullud lady," to the "moque" who rejoices in the huge doughnut he holds in his right hand, and which will presently be engulfed in his capacious mouth.

THE NORTH CAROLINA TROUBLES

HARPER'S WEEKLY

August 20, 1870, p. 530

There has been in certain quarters, notorious for sympathy with the late rebels and rebellion, such a vehement denunciation of Governor Holden, of North Carolina, as

SOUTHERN SCENES.—ON THE ROAD—MEN AND WOMEN CARRYING VEGETABLES TO THE CHARLESTON, S. C., MARKET.—FROM A SKETCH BY OUR SPECIAL ARTIST.

Frank Leslie's Illustrated Newspaper, May 21, 1870, p. 157.

a peculiarly malignant "satrap," who was waging fiendish war upon "the people" of North Carolina, that it is well to understand the facts. The organization of the Ku-Klux Klan has been especially vigilant in that State, where the comparative smallness of the colored population promised that a rigorous system of terror and coercion would practically annul their vote. To this end the efforts of the Ku-Klux have been directed. Of the existence and operations of this body there is no question. We have ourselves received details of its proceedings from the most "conservative" authority. It is the natural result of the war. It is a sucker from the root of the rebellion.

That there must be disturbances of all kinds in the States of the rebellion there was, of course, no question. That great care and forbearance would be necessary upon the part of the civil authorities was evident; and that it was very desirable to restore the normal condition of society as soon as practicable was unquestionable from the first. It was the duty of the civil officers of those States to postpone appeals to military interference to the last possible moment; and this was most desirable, not only in itself and upon general principles, but, for the Republican party, upon partisan grounds. For it was clear that an appeal to force would injure the party in two ways: first, it would suggest the suspicion that it was, as has been alleged of the present difficulty in North Carolina, oppression for party purposes; and, in the second place, it would be cited as proof of the inefficiency of Republican reconstruction. For every reason, therefore, it was most desirable that the civil authority should be every where paramount.

But it was equally evident that in the condition of society which the war left in the States of the rebellion there must necessarily be such occasional disturbances of the peace, so organized, so persistent, so formidable, that the ordinary civil processes would not avail. It was unreasonable to expect that the disordered States would be restored to a normal situation without very serious troubles, in which military interference would be wholly justified. And precisely this is the case in North Carolina. The crimes of the Ku-Klux defied the civil means of repression. The Governor, who is the responsible executive officer, states, as a fact, what all the probabilities confirm, that the organized ruffians and assassins laughed at proclamations, exhortations, and the civil process, and he was compelled either to tolerate anarchy in the State or to use military force. He decided not to surrender to the rebels, and placed certain counties under martial law, and invoked, as the Constitution authorizes, the assistance of the national power, which was promptly granted. Governor Holden did what Governor King, of Rhode Island, did in the "DORR war" in that State in 1842.

Of course, a Governor is to be held responsible if he invokes national aid before it is necessary; if he does not exhaust the lawful resources of the State before this

AN OLD SCHOLAR.

"There is a negro school at Meherrin Station, on the Richmond and Danville Railroad, where the teachers receive scholars of all ages and both sexes. Mr. ARVINE, of Lunenberg, had an old cook, 71 years of age, who took it into her head to learn to speak and write the English language correctly; so she entered the school, and bringing her ten cents per day and regularly paying it over to the teachers, she got along very well until, perhaps, at the end of the second week, she missed her lesson, and *was kept in in play time*. The idea! an old negro seventy-odd years of age kept in in play time."—*Danville (Va.) Times*.

Harper's Weekly, May 21, 1870, p. 336.

final appeal; and if he permits any abuse of the military interference when it becomes indispensable. But the passionate assertion of his partisan opponents can not be accepted as evidence of his guilt. We have the testimony of the Chief Justice of the State, that the power of the civil process was exhausted. And while there is unquestionably exaggeration in all the reports, no one who has been a faithful student of the spirit and methods of the Ku-Klux Klan will believe that the action of the Governor has been merely a partisan trick to carry the election.

FIRST MUNICIPAL ELECTION IN RICHMOND SINCE THE END OF THE WAR—REGISTRATION OF COLORED VOTERS.—[DRAWN BY W. L. SHEPPARD.]

Harper's Weekly, June 4, 1870, p. 365.

BURNING OF DARIEN, GEORGIA

HARPER'S WEEKLY
September 3, 1870, p. 563

Robert F. Clute, Rector, and W. Robert Gignilliat, Senior Warden of St. Andrew's Church, Darien, Georgia, have published an appeal "to the members of the Episcopal Church and all other friends of religion and education in the United States," asking relief for their parish.

This appeal begins by a statement concerning a young officer in the service of the United States who subsequently fell, at the head of his regiment, in the assault upon Fort Wagner. It is in these words:

> "June 11, 1863, without an engagement, the town of Darien, Georgia, was taken and burned by the United States colored troops, Colonel Shaw, Fifty-fourth Massachusetts Regiment, commanding."

This statement is incorrect in so far as it refers to Colonel Shaw, Colonel Montgomery having been the officer in command.

Colonel Shaw's opinion respecting the burning of Darien may be learned from the following extracts from letters written by him at the time, which we publish as an act of justice toward all concerned in that affair:

> "ST. SIMON'S ISLAND, *June* 14, 1863.
> "*His Excellency* John A. Andrew, *Governor of Massachusetts:*
> "DEAR SIR,—... On the 10th and 11th inst. we took part in an expedition under Colonel Montgomery. We met no enemy, and our only exploits were the capture of 85 bales of cotton, and the burning of the town of Darien. The latter performance disgusted me exceedingly. I never knew before of a town being burned to the ground without some good reason, especially when it contained only old men, women, and children."
>
> "*June* 12, 1863.—... About noon we came in sight of Darien.... Montgomery said to me, 'I shall burn this town.'... I told him that I did not want the responsibility, and he was only too happy to take it all on his own shoulders; so the pretty little place was burned to the ground.... One of my companies assisted, because he ordered them out, and I had to obey.... The reason he gave me for destroying Darien was that the Southerners must be made to feel that this was a real war, and that they were to be swept away by the hand of God like the Jews of old. In theory this may seem all right to some; but when it comes to

1870

SOUTHERN SCENES.—THE CRAB-VENDER IN CHARLESTON, S. C.—FROM A SKETCH BY JOSEPH BECKER.—SEE PAGE 277.

Frank Leslie's Illustrated Newspaper, July 16, 1870, p. 273.

being made the instrument of the Lord's vengeance, I myself don't like it. Then he says: 'We are outlawed, and therefore not bound by the rules of regular warfare.' But that makes it none the less revolting to wreak our vengeance on the innocent and defenseless. . . . I have not yet made up my mind as to what I ought to do. Besides my own distaste for this barbarous kind of warfare, I am not sure that it will not be very injurious to the reputation of black troops and of those connected with them. For myself, I have gone through the war

639

Frank Leslie's Illustrated Newspaper, July 16, 1870, p. 280.

so far without dishonor, and I do not like to degenerate into a plunderer and a robber; and the same applies to every officer in my regiment. If it were the order of our government to overrun the South with fire and sword, I might look at it in a different light, for then we should be carrying out what had been decided upon as a necessary policy. As the case stands, we are no better than 'Semmes,' who attacks and destroys defenseless vessels.

"Montgomery, from what I have seen of him, is a conscientious man, and really believes what he says: 'That he is doing his duty to the best of his knowledge and ability.'

"There are only two courses for me to pursue: To obey orders and say nothing, or to refuse to go on any such expeditions, and be put under arrest—probably court-martialed—which is a serious thing."

"*June* 13, 1863.—I am going to write to General Hunter's Assistant Adjutant-General; for, unless Montgomery has orders from headquarters to lay the country in ruins, I am determined to refuse to obey his orders in that respect."

"*June* 22, 1863.—Montgomery returned from Hilton Head this morning. . . . He found General Gillmore, who has relieved General Hunter, very friendly and anxious to second him in every way, with the exception of the burning business—so that is satisfactorily settled. Montgomery now tells me that he acted entirely under orders, and was at first very much opposed to it himself, but finally changed his mind."

"*June* 28, 1863.—. . . I think now, as I did at the time of the burning of Darien, that such wanton destruction is cruel, barbarous, impolitic, and degrading to ourselves and our men; and I shall always rejoice that I expressed myself just as I did. . . . It is rather hard that my men, my officers, and myself should have to bear part of the abuse for that affair, when they—the officers, at least—all felt exactly as I did about it."

"ST. SIMON'S ISLAND, *June* 14, 1863.

"*Lieut.-Col.* Halpine, *A. A. G. 10th A. C. & Dep. of the South:*

"*Dear Sir,*—Will you allow me to ask you a private question, which, of course, you are at liberty to answer or not?

"Has Colonel Montgomery orders from General Hunter to burn and destroy all towns and dwelling-houses he may capture? On the 11th inst., as you know, we took the town of Darien without opposition, the place being occupied, so far as we ascertained, by non-combatants. Colonel Montgomery burned it to the ground, and, at leaving finally, shelled it from the river. If he does this on his own

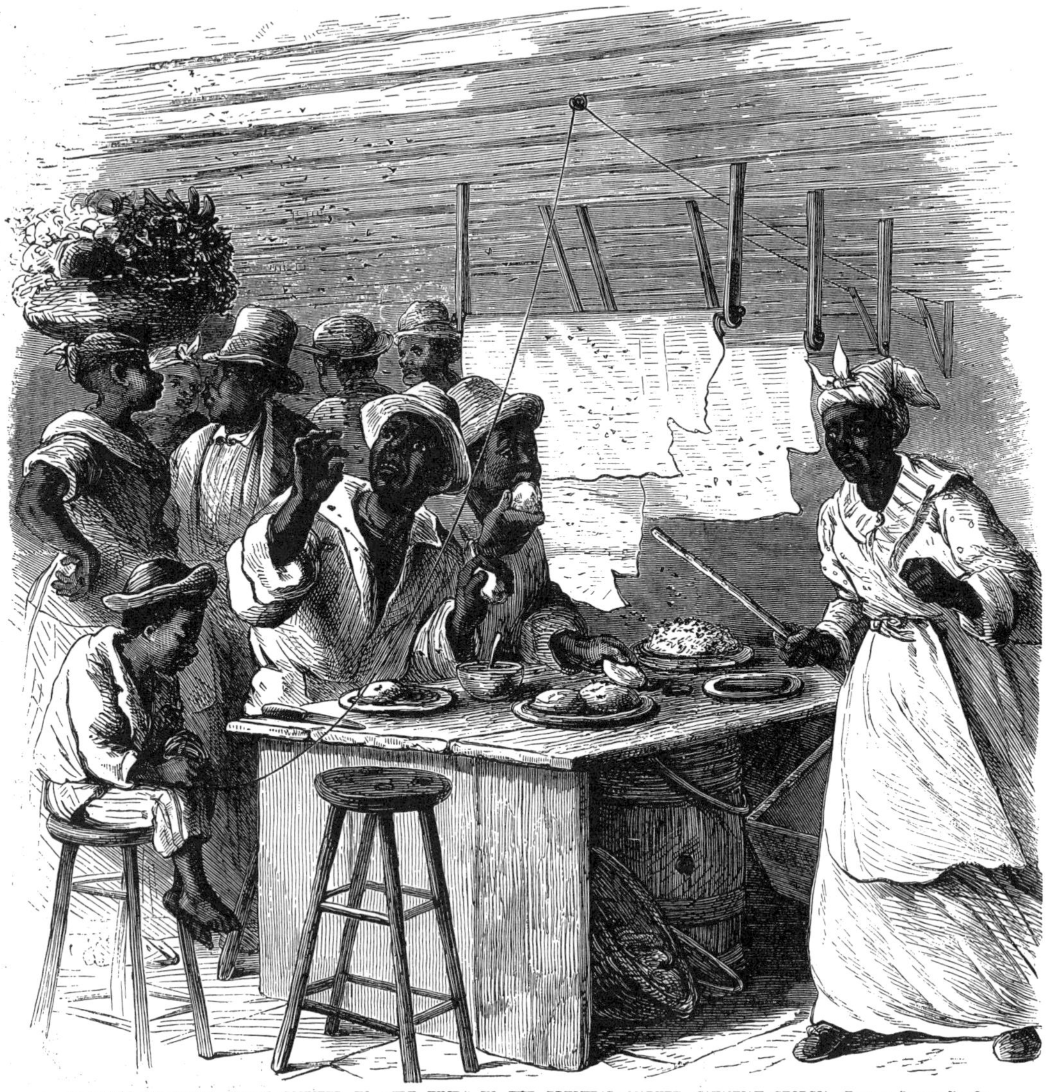

SOUTHERN SCENES.—A LUNCH COUNTER IN "FLY TIME," IN THE PRINCIPAL MARKET, SAVANNAH, GEORGIA.—FROM A SKETCH BY OUR SPECIAL ARTIST.—SEE PAGE 311.

Frank Leslie's Illustrated Newspaper, July 30, 1870.

responsibility, I shall refuse to have a share in it, and take the consequences; but, of course, if it is an order from headquarters, it is a different matter; as in such case I suppose it to have been found necessary to adopt that policy. He ordered me, if separated from him, to burn all the planters' houses I came across.

"Now I am perfectly ready to burn any place which resists, and gives some reason for such a proceeding; but it seems to me barbarous to turn women and children adrift in that way; and if I am only assisting Colonel Montgomery in a private enterprise of his own, it is very distasteful to me.

"I am aware that this is not a military way of getting information, and I hope you will feel that I shall not be hurt if you refuse to answer my question.

"Believe me, very truly yours,
"Robert G. Shaw,
"Colonel Commanding Fifty-fourth Massachusetts Regiment."

NOTES

HARPER'S WEEKLY

September 3, 1870, p. 563

In an old book of travels, which may be found in almost every library, there is a curious account of the ludicrous prejudices of one of the tribes in the interior of New

Holland. Thus, if a bald-headed foreigner suddenly appears among them, the savages of the tribe, after one look at him, close their doors and refuse to receive him, as if he were accursed. We who are civilized, and especially those of us who wear wigs, know, however, that a bald-headed man is as good as the rest of us. But in the interior of New Holland they have a great deal to learn. Upon reflection, however, it was not New Holland, it was New York, that the book must have described. For we find the following paragraph in the latest newspaper:

> "The steamship *Palmyra,* from Liverpool, *via* Queenstown, brought to this port, among other passengers, President Roye of the Liberian Republic in Africa, and his private secretary. They applied for admission at several well-known hotels, but were not permitted to enter on account of their color."

THE OLD SERPENT

HARPER'S WEEKLY
September 24, 1870, p. 611

The tenacious refusal of the Democratic party to recognize any of the fundamental changes wrought by the war, or, more truly speaking, made evident by the war, is extraordinary. But it is not to be regretted, as it reveals more plainly the tendency and policy of the party. If the bloody attempt at secession might have been supposed to prove any thing, it is that the people of this country will not tolerate the old theory of State sovereignty. Any effort to recuperate that doctrine is necessarily anarchical. That the Union is paramount; that the States, equal as they constitutionally are, have no right, upon any pretense whatever, to disturb the Union, which is the guarantee of that common equality, has been settled finally and forever. The attempt, therefore, to insinuate the old dogma, and under obscure phrases to renew the declaration of the State authority as supreme, is merely a reopening of the whole angry discussion.

Thus the Democratic party of Georgia, not daring to assert openly that the State reserves the right to withdraw from the Union if it chooses, but wishing to foster as ugly and hostile a feeling as possible, has just resolved:

> "That the Democratic party of the State of Georgia stand upon the principles of the Democratic party of the Union, bringing into special prominence, as applicable to the present extraordinary condition of the country, the unchangeable determination that this is a Union of States, and the indestructibility of the States, and of their rights, and of their equality with each other, is an indispensable part of our political system."

This is part of the whole policy of the non-acquiescence of the Democratic party in the results of the war and in reconstruction. It is not satisfied with the decision in the field, nor with the repeated judgments of the country. It is not content with the election of 1868, which was an appeal to the people upon the validity of Republican reconstruction, which proceeded upon views wholly irreconcilable with the Democratic dogmas. Indeed, the Democratic party knows only too well that the moment it leaves its old ground of injustice to the negro, and concedes that every citizen should be civilly and politically equal, and that the States form a really national Union, and not a confederacy at the pleasure of a packed vote of its weakest member, that moment it is irretrievably lost. It coheres as a party because it is the organization of all the disaffected to the Government upon every ground, and of all who still cherish the theories which hard experience has exposed and refuted.

It is for the people of the country to decide whether its peace and progress are likely to be promoted by a party which steadily insists that the Union is a mere league of sovereign States—the dogma of Calhoun, and inevitably the root of endless jealousy and confusion.

"THE BURNING OF DARIEN, GEORGIA."

HARPER'S WEEKLY
October 1, 1870, p. 627

We publish with great pleasure the following letter, and remind our readers that subscriptions may be sent either to the senior warden, to the Rev. Robert F. Clute, rector, or to the Rt. Rev. John W. Beckwith, Bishop of Georgia.

> *"To the Editor of Harper's Weekly:*
>
> "Sir,—Through several copies sent to me my attention has been called to an editorial in your issue of September 3, 1870, with the above caption. You publish parts of Colonel Robert G. Shaw's letters, written shortly after the event, to prove that he was not responsible for the burning of Darien. You not only make out a clear case of the Colonel's blamelessness, but also of his abhorrence of the act, which now seems, by these extracts, to be fixed upon General Hunter and Colonel Montgomery.
>
> "Be this as it may, as one of the authors of the appeal for aid for St. Andrew's Church, addressed 'to the members of the Episcopal Church, and all other friends of religion and education in the United States,' which has

called forth the above-named editorial, I desire to state in your columns that the object of the circular was simply to set forth, in as concise a manner as possible, the sad historical fact of the destruction of the town, including church and academy, and the other grounds upon which assistance was asked. It was not intended to reflect, even by implication, upon the memory of any one, as you will readily observe by reference to the inclosed copy. Yet I have been informed that such a construction had been placed upon the circular, to the injury of the cause it was intended to advance.

"The impression prevailed in this community that Colonel Shaw commanded the troops by whom Darien was plundered and destroyed. Before issuing the circular I asked one of the few citizens who remained in the vicinity at the time—a gentleman of intelligence—if he could give me any information on this point. In answer to my request he handed me a card which he had taken from an old mill, left standing, upon his going into Darien a few hours after the Federal gunboats had retired. That card is before me. I extract from it the following: 'June 11, 1863. Stuart W. Woods, Company I, Fifty-fourth Regiment Massachusetts Volunteers, in command of Colonel Shaw, Captain G. Pope, First-Lieutenant Heginson Second-Lieutenant Tucker.' When it is remembered that there were no other Federal sources of information at hand it will be readily understood why the above was accepted as satisfactory evidence.

"But the members of St. Andrew's parish are truly glad that the memory of Colonel Shaw—who certainly proved to the world at Wagner that he was a gallant soldier, even as these published fragments of his letters evince him to have been a Christian gentleman—has been exculpated from the disgrace of burning a defenseless town, 'which contained only old men, women, and children,' who were then, while they still stood around the smouldering ruins of their homes, 'finally shelled from the river.' His opinion of the transaction is expressed in his own language, as published by you: 'I think now, as I did at the time of the burning of Darien, that such destruction is cruel, barbarous, impolitic, and degrading to ourselves and our men, and I shall always rejoice that I expressed myself as I did.' Will not Northern friends, taking the simple appeal of the members of the parish in connection with this expression of opinion, deem the rebuilding of St. Andrew's Church a fit subject for their generosity, and *act* upon the feeling?

"Respectfully yours,

"W. Robert Giguilliat, *Senior Warden.*

"Darien, *September* 9, 1870."

THE HON. EDWARD J. ROYE, PRESIDENT OF LIBERIA, W.A

FRANK LESLIE'S ILLUSTRATED NEWSPAPER
October 15, 1870, pp. 69–70

The fifth President of the Republic of Liberia, West Africa, Hon. Edward J. Roye, was inaugurated on Monday, January 3, 1870 at Monrovia.

President Roye was born in Newark, Licking County, O., February 3, 1815, his father, John Roye, being a native of Kentucky, but a pure descendant of one of the oldest African tribes—the Eboe. He died in 1829, and left his son Edward, in addition to some personal property, 640 acres of land and a few town lots in and near Vandalia, Ill.

Among the few colored children admitted to the schools of Ohio at that period was the subject of this sketch. His thirst for knowledge soon became apparent, and he made such rapid progress in his elementary studies, that he was admitted into the High School, after quite a brief period. During the time that young Roye attended this institution, it was taught by Mr. Chase, the present Chief-Justice of the United States.

Having succeeded in the necessary preparatory studies, he entered the University at Athens, O., in the spring of 1832, where he spent three years, leaving at the close of the fall term of 1835.

After leaving the University, Mr. Roye taught school for a few years in the city of Chilicothe. With that provident forecast and prudence with which his life has been marked, he saved money enough to enable him to enter upon business.

In 1840, the leaders of the colored people began to discuss their condition, and to hold conventions for the purpose of adopting measures for their elevation. Mr. Roye, whose education and refinement made him unpleasantly sensitive to the burdens and deprivations of his race, attended these conventions to learn if anything could possibly be done for his people in the United States; but he soon became satisfied that the remedial measures proposed were partial and defective, and must be powerless to effect their purpose as long as the negro remained in this country. He saw that the prejudices of race, the competition of labor, and the rivalry of a superior wealth and education, would never accord him an equal chance in the United States. He accordingly made up his mind to emigrate to Hayti; but, while residing at Oberlin, whither he had gone to study the French language, to prepare for his residence in his

THE HON. E. J. ROYE, PRESIDENT OF THE LIBERIAN REPUBLIC.

Frank Leslie's Illustrated Newspaper, October 15, 1870, p. 69.

new home, he changed his mind, and concluded to go to Liberia.

On the 2d of May, 1846, he embarked in New York for Liberia, reaching his destination June 7th. On his arrival at Monrovia, being much pleased with the appearance of things, and the encouraging prospects for the future, he concluded to make Africa his home.

Mr. Roye has filled various positions of influence and usefulness in the Republic of Liberia. In 1849 he was Speaker of the House of Representatives, and he served as Chief-Justice from the beginning of 1865 to the beginning of 1868. He has been a candidate three times for the Presidency, as leader of the True Whig party, and has always received large majorities in his own country.

His administration is looked forward to with great hopes by the masses of the people. Prominent among his most ardent supporters is Ex-President Warner. His policy is progressive. Among the measure which he proposes to carry out, are a complete financial reconstruction, a general education of the masses, an improved system of roads for interior communication, and alliances with powerful nations.

For the efficient execution of his plans, it is proposed to add to the existing executive officer a Secretary of the Interior and a Secretary of Education.

For several weeks President Roye has been in this country, looking after the interests of the young Republic.

A part of his mission was, if possible, to secure a vessel from the United States authorities for use in Liberian waters, for the protection of the coast, and the collection of the revenue. He succeeded in obtaining the steamer *Rescue,* for which bonds are to be filed to the amount of $11,000, after which the vessel will be forwarded to Liberia. The *Rescue* is ninety-two feet long, eighteen feet beam, and her capacity 111 tons. She was purchased nine years ago by the United States, and is a stanch and seaworthy vessel. President Roye is well pleased with his treatment wherever he has gone, and hopes to make Liberia such a place as will draw shiploads of his race to it. As soon as he finishes his business in New York, connected with the improvement of Liberia's communication with her interior, he will sail for England, and from there to his own country, in time to be present at the opening of the Liberian Congress.

THE FIFTEENTH AMENDMENT IN OPERATION

HARPER'S WEEKLY
November 5, 1870, p. 707

The autumn elections show that the colored vote is true to the party which proposed and carried the Fifteenth Amendment. It would be very strange if it were not so. If the citizens who have been so long disfranchised or disabled should vote against those who have fought and won their battle, and in favor of the party which has steadily derided and oppressed them, it would only prove how utterly degraded that oppression had made them. The case was put so strongly by ex-Governor Orr, of South Carolina, in his letter of the 15th of August, when speaking of the new vote in the Southern States, that we are glad to repeat what he said:

"The colored vote is, and has been from 1867, nearly a unit for the Republican party; and have they acted unwisely or unpatriotically in their ardent devotion to the Republican party? Suppose our conditions—the white race—were reversed; that we and our ancestors had been slaves for two hundred years; that a party had made war to give us freedom; that it had succeeded; that the same party had periled its own supremacy by guaranteeing to us civil rights; and that, above all, the ballot, the effectual weapon of preserving those rights, had been secured to us by solemn constitutional enactment by the same party, and we were, in the face of all this, appealed to by those who had opposed all these great boons, to join with them in overthrowing the party of our deliverance and redemption, would any white man tolerate with patience any such proposition?" And Mr. ORR asks most conclusively, "Is it strange the colored Republican should be cautious, and adhere with tenacity to his party? Can we justly hope to exercise that political influence over him which we now constantly do in all the other relations and duties of life, until he is convinced that we intend in good faith to protect him equally with the whites, not only in his person and property, but in all his civil and political rights?"

These questions, so obvious to every sagacious politician, have, of course, suggested themselves to the Democratic party chiefs in the Northern States. But they had so long prospered by pandering to the contempt and hatred of the colored population that they could not suddenly turn to flatter and cajole them without alienating their followers. They have, therefore, lost all chance of securing any considerable part of the new vote, and their aim is to bully it from the polls if they can. This was tried in Philadelphia at the late election, but the United States Marshal had made provision of military force which awed the bullies and protected the voters. In the city of New York, the *World,* the organ of what it calls shameless corruptionists, openly suggests to the repeaters and ballot-stuffers to go armed to the polls. Such advice is, of course, to be expected from those who are used to carrying elections by fraud and violence, and who truckle to ignorance and crime. But the honest voters are, fortunately, still in the majority; and although the present Mayor, like his predecessor, Mr. John T. Hoffman, should strive to protect frauds, and the Governor—the same Mr. Hoffman—should sustain the Mayor's attempts, honest voting will still be practicable so long as the superior national authority is in Republican hands.

No good citizen, whose purposes are honest, will object to the most stringent protection of legal voting, nor to the summary exposure and the severest punishment of illegal. But nobody, of course, who believes the organ of the Ring, believes an honest election to be practicable under the Ring auspices. For what chance of a fair election could there possibly be from gentlemen who, as we are told by the *World,* "cut down below its level the rightful vote of the electors of Horatio Seymour?" If they cut down the vote for a candidate whom they do not like, they will certainly not hesitate to "pile it up" for one whom they favor. If the *World* is to be trusted, the honest voters are defrauded at the polls, and ought to be protected. How glad the *World* must be to know that the Government is resolved that they shall be!

A STRAW THAT SHOWS THE WIND

HARPER'S WEEKLY
November 19, 1870, p. 739

At a recent political meeting in Norfolk, Virginia, at which the Secretary of the Navy and other gentlemen were present as speakers, a disturbance began while Professor Langston, a colored citizen, was addressing the audience, which ended in a riot which the police were powerless to quell. Fire-arms were freely used. The next morning one colored man was found gashed and dead in an alley near by, and John T. Daniel, a well-known white Republican, was seriously wounded. Of course nobody supposes that it was the Republicans who disturbed their own meeting, and shot and murdered their own friends. It was an ebullition of the hatred and jealousy which still agitate the public mind in the late rebel region. And what does such an incident suggest?

Nothing is truer than that trouble must for a long time be expected in that part of the country. We have constantly insisted in these columns that nothing was more foolish than to suppose that, because actual hostilities in the field were over, all the amenities of peace had returned. The Democratic candidate for Governor of Massachusetts at the late election said that of course there were disturbances in the Southern States, and of course they would continue. That is the undoubted fact. Ex-Governor Orr says that the late rebel leaders do not co-operate with the means of peace offered by Congress. Let us make no more of the fact than it will honestly bear, but do not let us assume that it is not a fact, and act accordingly. Ostrich statesmanship is the most intolerable of all.

What the late rebel States really want more than any thing else is the conviction that the people of the country have a steady policy in regard to the whole subject of political equality and reconstruction. If the ugly element in those States knows that the government—that is, the people—is friendly to that equality, and will support it to the last, and with all its power, that element will become less and less pernicious and incendiary. If, on the other hand, it knows that the government is hostile, and heartily hates the political equality established by reconstruction, that element will be the dominant influence in the Southern States, and endless agitation must follow. When the Democratic organs feebly hint to their fellow-partisans that the party ought to cease its open warfare upon the political equality of all citizens, the persuasive argument is, in substance, that if, under pretense of acquiescence, the party at large could only gain the national control, then the party in the various States might treat the colored citizens as it pleased, and the Democratic central power would be sleeping or gone upon a journey; in any case it would not see nor interfere.

Mr. Gerrit Smith, in urging the colored voters to support the anti-dram-shop ticket at the late election in New York, said that it was "insulting as well as nonsensical" to tell them that if the Democratic party triumphed the freedmen would be re-enslaved or disfranchised. Mr. Gerrit Smith is a true friend of the colored citizen, but is it insulting as well as nonsensical to say that if the Democratic party could obtain national power, such riots as that at Norfolk would become very common; that the exercise of the right of voting and of free discussion in public would become extremely difficult for the colored citizens; that terror can disfranchise as well as law; and that while slavery might not be restored, the spirit of slavery would affect the conduct of the ugly

HOLIDAY SCENES AT RICHMOND, VA.—"THE CAKE WALK."—DESIGN BY W. L. SHEPPARD.—SEE PAGE 261.

Frank Leslie's Illustrated Newspaper, **December 31, 1870, p. 265.**

element of which we have spoken? Could there fail to be immense excitement and agitation, a feeling of insecurity upon the part of the colored citizens, and of triumph upon that of the worst classes of the population? And what possible benefit would this be to any human being? On the contrary, would it not be a very grave disaster for the whole country?

When, therefore, we read the story of such a riot as that at Norfolk, let us reflect that if such things are to be naturally expected, as we admit, even under the Republican national ascendency, what might be naturally expected should the Democratic party come into power?

GOOD SENSE IN POLITICS

HARPER'S WEEKLY
December 17, 1870, p. 810

There is a remark constantly made by those who were not really opposed to the rebellion, and which is much too often echoed by those who supported the government with all their hearts, that the old issues are settled. We are exhorted to believe that there is no possible relation between yesterday and to-day, and that those who half a dozen years ago were either forcibly attempting the overthrow of the government or quietly conniving at it may be now safely trusted with its control. There is no profounder error, nor one which the country will more bitterly rue if it should become more general. The old issues are not settled, simply because the old spirit survives. The action of Governor Walker, of Virginia, in regard to the President's Thanksgiving proclamation, and the Ku-Klux demonstrations in Kentucky, show decisively, if any proof were needed, that just in the degree that the Democratic party in the Northern States apparently gains, the ugly spirit at the South makes itself felt. That it would attempt the restoration of slavery need not be supposed, but that it would be as mischievous as it could be can not be doubted. It would keep the country in perpetual agitation. It would abuse the colored population in every practicable way. It would threaten and swagger in the old manner; and the country would most seriously deplore having treated the situation theoretically and not practically.

There is one thing, and one thing only, which is the sure guarantee of that national confidence which is now imperatively necessary, and that is the constant conviction upon the part of all disaffection that the country fully understands what it did in the war, and means to secure it to the utmost. To insist that the old issues are settled, that the rebellion was suppressed five years ago, that slavery is abolished, and the reconstruction acts are law, and that, therefore, it is wise to elect Jefferson Davis to the Senate, or to take Toombs into the cabinet, or to turn over the country to a Copperhead administration, because some of its members hold certain opinions upon certain other subjects, is to trifle with the very gravest peril. Those Republicans, therefore, who, upon a theory that revenue reform is the most vital and paramount of all issues, would willingly bring in the Democratic party, under cover of voting for Democratic free-traders against Republican protectionists, assume a very heavy responsibility. Suppose a representative denies the validity of the amendments, shares the Democratic hostility to the negro and hatred of the Southern Union men, and winks at the revival of the old Southern spirit of jealousy of the Union, and of the principles and tendency of the Republican party, how is he less desirable or dangerous because he may be a free-trader?

"THE CAKE WALK."
A Richmond Christmas Festival.

FRANK LESLIE'S ILLUSTRATED NEWSPAPER
December 31, 1870, p. 261

The negroes certainly deserve the palm for inaugurating novel festivities and keeping in lively remembrance customs that have become traditional from their remotest ancestors. Every season has its peculiar holiday, and it is safe to say that no class of people enters into the noise and fun and excitement of these occasions with more zest than the colored population of our Southern States.

During Christmas week their amusements take a variety of forms that would puzzle many a more sober head, but we know of none more laughable than the "Cake Walk." This *fête* is peculiar to the colored race, and the amount of side-stitching they owe to it is sufficient to make one wonder that they live so long as they do. They laugh, elongate and collapse by turns, and never seem to be satisfied.

A house is chosen having a large room with substantial floor, for the pedestrians are selected without regard to weight. Somehow, one of the shortest, heaviest females is always nominated for the contest, while another person, that might be pardonably mistaken for a lamp-post, is placed beside her on the list. Around the room are ranged tables loaded with seasonable fruit, while at the four points of the compass are displayed tooth-some delicacies, the second collection richer than the first, the third than the second, and the fourth than the third. In case one of the walkers grows weary, a few winks at one of these tables causes a nervous telegram to proceed to the stomach to inquire if supplies are needed, but the eye, catching the next table with its superior attractions, urges the feet forward. Thus round after round is frequently made, the innocent walkers totally unconscious of the length of their tramp. Everything being in readiness, we will step aside and witness this unique entertainment.

For a moment all is silence; than a hundred heads are strained; hats fall from hands; chairs are eagerly mounted and quickly upset; coarse throats and shrill voices commence the shout, "Hi, ho! here they come!" and two females set off on the walk for one of the prize cakes.

It is impossible to repress a smile as these ages dames elevate their turbaned heads, and, striving to throw all the youthfulness possible into their carriage, hasten around the room. One cannot help remembering the story of the little old woman who swept the sky with her broom, and half believing that, if two broomsticks were produced, these antiquated specimens of humanity would seize upon them, and fly away through the air. But as everything has been placed in "apple-pie order," not a broomstick is visible, and the little dusky-faced pedestrians reach the goal amid a burst of laughing applause. Breathlessly they resume their seats, and their places are taken by three young colored maidens. One of these damsels is a tall, slender girl, seemingly strung upon wires; another is short and pretty-faced, and the third exceedingly stout. Perhaps yellow dresses with red flounces, and decked with green bows, would not be considered in good taste by some ultra-fashionable feminine judges of the matter; but tastes differ, and certainly, from the self-satisfied, half-coquettish air of these competing damsels, it is easily to be perceived that each one considers herself quite *au fait*.

1871

The Ku-Klux Klan dominated the news relating to African Americans in 1871. Southern newspapers such as the Charleston Daily Courier (7 April 1871) published the Ku-Klux manifesto, ostensibly to demonstrate the benevolent nature of the Klan. This view of the Klan was further espoused in the Charleston Daily Courier (20 April 1871) in an article purportedly written by an "unbiased witness." The witness claimed: "Wherever the Klan has made itself evident, their vengeance has been direct, not against the officers and men of the United States army, nor even against the civil Federal authorities in the State, but always against either criminals or individuals who have made themselves obnoxious for public theft or private perfidy."

Congress enacted laws signed by President Grant (known as the Ku-Klux Klan Acts), making interference with voting a federal offense and putting elections of congressmen under federal control. The Klan activities moved from intimidation and violence due to political affiliation to intimidation and violence for being black, being white and sympathizing with black citizens, or working with blacks, as school-teachers did. In March of 1871 Grant requested Congress to enact legislation supporting the Fourteenth Amendment through the Ku-Klux Klan Bill. The Fourteenth Amendment, ratified in 1868, established the concept of "equal protection" for all citizens under the United States Constitution. The Ku-Klux Klan Bill also outlawed terrorist conspiracies and authorized the president to use military force to enforce the law and suspend the writ of habeas corpus. The issue of amnesty for supporters of the Confederacy was closely linked to the Ku-Klux Klan Bill. An Amnesty Bill was killed by the Senate Republican caucus, however. Newspaper commentaries from both the North and South believed the two issues were inextricably linked. The Ku-Klux Klan Bill would provide greater protection of equality for minorities while the Amnesty Bill would return rights lost during the Civil War to those individuals who had supported the Confederacy.

Journalists from the South viewed the Ku-Klux Klan Bill as a pretext to interfere in southern affairs and another attempt at reconstruction under "the bayonet and the sword." Northern journalists from papers such as Harper's Weekly viewed the bill as a measure to end the lawlessness committed by the Klan. Harper's Weekly (29 April 1871) reported, "What the Ku-Klux can do in preventing voting was shown in the State of Louisiana at the last Presidential election. In certain parishes or counties where the aggregate registered colored vote was hundreds, and even thousands, only one or two Republican votes—in some no Republican votes at all—was cast." In this same article the writer questions "whether, in the light of experience and common sense, a national election in this country is likely to be fairer with national supervisors and bayonets to support them, or with the Ku-Klux terror and ballot-box stuffers."

After a series of Ku-Klux Klan campaigns in South Carolina, events deteriorated to the point where the governor requested assistance from the federal government. President Grant sent a detachment of infantry, cavalry troops, and several pieces of artillery to quell the disturbance by the Klan.

Occasionally arising throughout the year are news reports regarding incidents based solely on color, such as the troubles of the "colored cadet" at West Point or the number of African Americans serving in Congress.

Twenty-two black men received appointments to West Point between 1870 and 1899, but only three survived racial hostility at the academy. Henry Ossian Flipper became the first black graduate of West Point in 1877, followed by John Hanks Alexander in 1887 and Charles Young in 1889. It would be 47 years before another African American graduated from West Point.

Robert L. Harris, Jr.
Cornell University

A CHRISTIAN HERO

HARPER'S WEEKLY
February 18, 1871, p. 139

A true American hero lately died, over whom no elaborate eulogies will be spoken, but whose name will long be fondly cherished as that of a most faithful friend by the most unfortunate class of American citizens. It is fifteen years since we saw in Wilmington, Delaware, a hearty, cheery Quaker, whom every body knew, and who, in that Slave State, was famous for aiding the escape of fugitive slaves. He was, indeed, the chief agent of the underground railroad. He was a conspicuous, uncompromising abolitionist—that is to say, a sincere American. The sentiment of his neighborhood was un-American, medieval, and barbarous. There were scarcely a dozen persons who cared to have it known that they sympathized with him. But Thomas Garrett was of a sturdy, stalwart frame—a man of invincible bravery, hearty, humorous, and frank; and as you looked at him, and thought of the sullen hatred and inhumanity and ignorant prejudice around him, his brawny shoulders and the indomitable heart that smiled in his eyes seemed an impregnable bulwark of freedom.

Thomas Garrett was an iron-monger, and established one of the largest houses of that kind in Wilmington. But while his industry and sagacity in business were well rewarded, his delight was to help the helpless and succor the forlorn. He was, of course, suspected, hated, watched; but he worked in secret only so far as was necessary to elude the vigilance of the slave-catchers. The masters came to him, and stormed and threatened; but, with oaths and revolvers and bowie-knives, they never frightened him. While Mr. Webster was calling upon Massachusetts to conquer its prejudices, and consent to kidnapping; while the New York merchants hastened to Castle Garden, and resolved that the compromises of the Constitution must be respected, even if the self-respect of honorable men was annihilated; while, on the one hand, eloquent men were exposing the evils and infamies of slavery, and on the other there was a loud chorus that it was indeed horrible, but that nothing could be done about it—Thomas Garrett did something about it. The slave stole from the lash and the block, trusting to God, and seeking the north star and Thomas Garrett; and before President Lincoln, in the name of the loyal nation, emancipated all the slaves, the Delaware Quaker had sent forward twenty-seven hundred into freedom.

When he was nearly sixty years old he was tried before Chief Justice Taney for abducting certain persons who had no rights which white people were bound to respect, and the damages awarded against him swept away all his property. But Thomas said to the crowd in the court-room that he should only work harder than ever to save his fellow-creatures from slavery; and he kept his word. He began business, also, anew, and was again prosperous. But his hand and heart never relaxed their labor for the oppressed; and when, a year ago, the colored people of Wilmington celebrated the great release of their race, Thomas Garrett was borne in an open carriage, surrounded by his faithful friends, who carried banners inscribed, "Our Moses." His years increased, but his heart never grew old, and his interest in all generous and humane movements was unabated. Had he lived until next August he would have lived eighty-two years; but on the 11th of January of this year he wrote, renewing his subscription to *The Woman's Journal:* "I now must own up that I am an old man—the machinery has not rusted out, but worn out. . . . I have been favored to keep cheerful, but feel that my work here is nearly done." The old man was right. He died after a few days, and, as he had promised when they asked him a year before, men of the race he had so faithfully served bore him to his grave.

Who are the Christian heroes? Are they not those of whom it is written, "And the King shall answer and say unto them, Verily I say unto you, inasmuch as ye have done it unto one of the least of these my brethren, ye have done it unto me?"

THE KU-KLUX

HARPER'S WEEKLY
April 1, 1871, p. 282

The Ku-Klux question has become very serious. Before the war a citizen of the United States who believed in the Declaration of Independence, and said so, was outlawed, harried, and liable to be murdered in half the country. It was safer for a free-tongued American, who held to the rightful equality of all men, to travel in Central Africa than in South Carolina under the flag of the United States. Now that the war is ended, no conspicuous Union man, and no colored citizen who takes an active and positive position in sympathy with the Union, is safe from assault or murder in a large part of the old Slave States. If he complains, he is told that the local courts are open to him. If he replies that the mob holds the courts, and that he has the same protection that the Abolitionist in the interior of Mississippi had against the slavery assassins fifteen years ago, he is told that he has the ballot, and he must right himself at the polls. If he replies that the mob, which is supreme, prevents his voting, he is told that that is his misfortune, but that the United States authority can only interfere in a State upon the requisition of the governor. If he says that the governor is the Ku-Klux, he is told that it is a pity; but that the principle of the government requires that every State must protect its citizens. And he is asked, in turn, if the United States should interfere at its pleasure in every State by a mere resolution of Congress, how would it be with him if his friends should lose power, and the friends of the Ku-Klux come in? To which he would, of course, reply that it would certainly be no worse for him—and it would not. But how would it be elsewhere and hereafter?

The question is undeniably a very grave and difficult one. The States rights answer, however, is very short and simple. The Southern States, it says, from an unnatural fostering of slavery and the inevitable consequences of war, have lapsed into quasi-barbarism, and they must work themselves clear. They must learn by experience. They must civilize themselves. This answer would be more satisfactory if the barbarians were not voters in a common Union, and adherents of a great party which contests its government. In view of that fact the practical question immediately is, whether that situation of things could be changed by legislation. And if it could, if the protection of those whom the Ku-Klux keeps from the polls by terror would prevent the national government falling into the hands of the Ku-Klux party, ought they not to be protected and the government saved?

Granting, as every sensible man must, that the process of reconstruction has been altogether too swift, and that the States in rebellion should, under the peculiar circumstances, have been much longer directly held by the national authority, shall nothing be done to avoid the ill effects of the haste, even to the control of the government by its open enemies? For every man knows what spirit would animate a Democratic national administration. Every body remembers that the last Democratic Convention was swayed by rebel chiefs rejoicing in their rebellion, and that a great portion of the party see with satisfaction now the very barbarism of which we speak. If our political system really be one which forbids the government to protect its own citizens when voting for its officers, and which requires the country to look on passively while mobs controlling various State authorities harry those voters, it will certainly be necessary to reconsider some of our raptures over the infinite superiority of the American to all other possible systems of government. But if the United States authority will amply protect its citizens at the national polls, and secure the equal liberty which it guarantees, it will, perhaps, solve the problem. For then its military force would be large enough in every disaffected State, without superseding the local authority, to give heart to good citizens.

ANOTHER AFRICAN IN CONGRESS

CHARLESTON DAILY COURIER
April 5, 1871

Distinctions on account of color are being rapidly obliterated in Congress. The House of Representatives contains five colored members, and yesterday that body deposed a white boy acting as a page or messenger and appointed a negro youth in his place. This is the first instance in which a colored boy has been appointed a page in Congress.

SUMTER

CHARLESTON DAILY COURIER
April 7, 1871

The *Watchman* publishes the following Ku-Klux manifesto which it says came into its possession in such a way as to induce the conviction that it is a genuine emanation from the mysterious (yet no longer to be disputed, powerful) organization known as the Ku-Klux-Klan:

"K. K. K."
Head Quarters, 54th Division.
"We have been misrepresented. It must stop. Once for all it is announced:
I. That the Union League gave us birth.
II. That taxation without representation, fed and nurtured us during our weakness and infancy.
III. That the vices and enormities of our rulers and legislators—their ignorance, their recklessness, their depravity, their corruption their viciousness, gave us strength.
IV. The determination of the Governor to accomplish our destruction, and the ruin of ourselves and of our families, as shown by his arming the negroes and disarming the whites, gave us determination.
V. We cannot live longer under this misrule and these enormities, and we are determined to right them or perish in the effort.
VI. The good and virtuous have nothing to fear from us. We are their friends. Let the vile and vicious beware. We are their enemies.
VII. We strike in self-defence, and for equal rights and justice to all.
By order of the Grand Chief,
K. O. Secretary.

AMERICAN LIBERTY AND THE SO-CALLED KU-KLUX BILL

CHARLESTON DAILY COURIER
April 8, 1871

By a vote of one hundred and eighteen to ninety-one, the House of Representatives has attempted another reconstruction of the South, under the pretext of a Ku-Klux Bill. The real object is simply the perpetuation of party power. Some pretence was needed. This was found more suitable than any other to blind and mislead the public judgment. It has, therefore, been seized upon for the purpose of further aggressions on the rights and liberties of the people. There can be no other conclusion. The necessity of the hour requires peace and not hostile legislation. But the majority seem entirely to have ignored the public welfare. They have acted from the first upon the theory that they constitute the United States of America, and that, to the assertion of this end, they are invested with absolute power.

There is neither any individual, or any bodies of individuals at the South, who have any idea of overthrowing the Government, or levying war against the

United States. Nor is there any such intention or combination in any section of the country. No such instance, since the close of hostilities, can be pointed out. It is the wildest assertion, without the slightest foundation, in fact. And yet this is gravely recited as the cause and origin of a Bill which, at one swoop, erects military power in the place of civil right.

The Bill is one of false pretences. It is a blow at free institutions, under carefully covered and deceiving words.

Again, under the Constitution, the United States can only interfere in the affairs of the respective States in case of invasion, or of domestic violence, and only then on the application of the Legislature, or, when that cannot be convened, on the application of the Executive. There is certainly no invasion, and, as to what is meant in the Constitution by domestic violence, the very best exposition is the view of those who, at the time, voted for the insertion of the clause. This shews that invasion meant an attack by armed forces from without, and domestic violence, an attempt by arms from within the State, to overthrow the Government.

Mr. Luther Martin, was of opinion that it should be left to the States to suppress rebellions themselves. Mr. Gorham, combated this view and favored the clause guaranteeing to each State a Republican form of government, and its protection against foreign and domestic violence, and spoke as follows: "It would be strange that a rebellion should be known to exist, and the General Government be restrained from interposing to subdue it. At this rate, an enterprising citizen might erect *the standard of monarchy,* in a particular State, might gather together partisans from all quarters, might extend his views from State to State, and threaten to establish a tyranny over the whole, and the General Government be compelled to remain an inactive witness of its own destruction. With regard to different parties in a State, as long as they confine their disputes to words, they will be harmless to the General Government, and to each other. If they appeal to the sword, it will then be necessary for the General Government, however difficult it may be, to decide on the merits of their contest, and put an end to it." It is clear, therefore, that by domestic violence, was intended an *appeal to the sword, and an actual and existing rebellion by arms, from within a State.*

But more than this, the original power of suppression, in this extreme case, which has no existence or color of existence at the present, was only granted upon the application of the Legislature, in its hour of extreme need, or when it could not, by reason of force or other causes be convened on the application of the Executive, who found himself powerless in the presence of an armed insurrection, or, as it is termed, domestic violence.

In the face of the fact that no such domestic violence exists, the majority in the House have, by the Bill passed, deliberately set aside this wise safeguard and provision of the Constitution. They propose, in effect, that the party now in power and which has constituted itself into the Government, may determine when domestic violence exists, and in case the Legislature or the Executive should *not* apply to the President for aid it shall be lawful for the President to employ the national forces to suppress such disorders and to arrest offenders.

Thus, President Grant may at any moment, in any State, where there is a Democratic Governor or Legislature, whenever it may be necessary for his party to constitute a case of domestic violence, send the national forces there for the suppression of free opinion and popular franchise. These are not the words, but they present the meaning. To this it amounts. It in fact renders the military independent of, and superior to the civil power.

But again, if there is one right more than all others necessary for the protection of freedom, it is that of the *Habeas Corpus* Act. Without this and there at once exists the most absolute of tyrannies. The Constitution expressly provides that its privileges shall not be suspended, except in two cases.

1. Of rebellion or of open revolt against the Government by arms.
2. Of invasion or the entrance of a hostile army into a country for the purpose of conquest or plunder.

To these two cases the suspension of the writ, under the fundamental law, is limited. This is the extent of the grant as against the people. But by this proposed Act the President is made superior to all Constitutions. He is empowered to suspend the writ of *Habeas Corpus* whenever, *in his opinion,* unlawful combinations exist in any State, or when, in his view, the *State authorities shall be in complicity with such combination.*

Such powers are as dangerous as they are without warrant or legal title. These at once dispose of a Republican character of government, and establish party as the State, with no appeal from its power and its sway. Laws like these may subject and enthrall the South, but they have a wilder and as certain a sweep. They undermine the liberties of all sections, and open up the path to universal absolutism.

A WORD TO CONGRESS

HARPER'S WEEKLY
April 8, 1871, p. 306

The President, at the request of the Governor of South Carolina, who is unable to keep order in the State, has summoned the illegal combinations—known as the Ku-Klux—to disperse within twenty days; and he has also sent a message to Congress asking for such legislation as may effectually secure life, liberty, and property in all parts of the United States. We gather from the context that this request is designed not to supersede the local authorities, but to provide for those cases of which the United States has constitutional cognizance, such as offenses against mail-carriers and revenue collectors. The report of the committee which was appointed to consider the recommendations of the message will, of course, open debate upon the whole subject. We beg the Republicans in the House of Representatives to remember that this debate will make an issue of the most vital importance for the Presidential campaign. Any error would be disastrous; and as opinion in the party upon the subject is not unanimous, there must be the greatest care that the policy recommended can be justified at every point before the people.

If the Constitution empowers the United States to keep the internal peace of a State without the requisition of the State authorities, let it be done at all hazards. But let the constitutional provision which authorizes it be made plain. To the question whether the United States may not rightfully defend the lives of its citizens the reply is conclusive: "Yes, in the way its fundamental law provides." But if the reader of these lines in the State of Iowa is injured in his person or property when not officially acting for the United States, does he appeal to the State or to the national courts? Is he willing that the United States should decide just when the local authorities are unable to protect him? Indeed, does not the Constitution expressly forbid the national government to decide that question by providing that the State authorities shall call for assistance if they wish it? If those authorities are themselves lawless, and refuse to ask assistance of the nation, the United States have still the right and the power of protecting their own agents and functions, and defending them at all costs.

Meanwhile, also, the Government of the United States has the indisputable constitutional right of enforcing the Fifteenth Amendment. It has made large numbers of persons in the Southern States voters, and it is bound to protect their political rights to the last. But in doing this with the amplest force, let Congress consider the essential disadvantage of continuing any kind of proscription, and by a general amnesty remove forever the feeling of injustice which is the fruitful source of so much evil. By a declaration of amnesty, and by a vigorous and ample provision for the defense of rights which nobody questions the duty of the Government to defend, Congress will do what the best and most earnest Republicans desire—Republicans who can not but feel that there must yet be great disorder in parts of the Southern States, disorder which only time and moral influences can restrain, and who believe that the policy which we suggest would be conclusive evidence that the party does not repose upon its victories, but carries its old spirit of constitutional liberty into the new issues of the hour.

FROM WASHINGTON
Confirmations—Ku-Klux Bill Passed—Deficiency Bill.

CHARLESTON DAILY COURIER
April 15, 1871

Washington, April 14

The President has abandoned his California trip until the Fall. The reference question from the High Commission and the enforcement of the Ku-Klux Bill keeps him here.

Nominations: P. R. Cowan, Assistant of the Interior, H. H. Manning, Collector of the Fourth Texas District.

Both Houses meet to-morrow at 11 o'clock.

The Senate passed the Ku-Klux Bill with the amendments proposed by the Judiciary Committee, which amendment strikes out the repeal of the test oath for United States jurors, leaving the law as at present; and another by Sherman, as follows: that if any house, tenement, cabin, shop, building, barn or granary shall be unlawfully or feloniously demolished, pulled down, burned or destroyed, wholly or in part, by any persons riotously or tumultuously assembled together, or if any person shall unlawfully, and with force and violence be whipped, scourged, wounded or killed by any persons, riotously or tumultuously assembled together, and if such offence was committed to deprive any person of any right, conferred upon him by the Constitution and laws of the United States, or deter him from, or punish him for exercising any such right, or by reason of his race color or previous condition of servitude, in every such case, the inhabitants of the county, city or parish in which any of the said offences shall be committed shall be liable to pay a full compensation to the person or persons demnified by such offence, if living, or legal representative of the dead, and such compensation may be recovered by such person or his representative by a suit in any Court of the United States of competent jurisdiction in the district in which the offence was committed, to be in the name of the person injured, or his legal representative, and against such county, city or parish; and the execution may be issued on a judgment rendered in such suit, and may be levied upon any property, real or personal, of any person in said county, city or parish, and the said county, city or parish which may have satisfied said judgment, or the person out of whose property said judgment shall have been satisfied, as the case may be, he may recover the full amount of said judgment, costs and interest from any person engaged as principal or accessory in such riot, in an action in any Court of competent jurisdiction; and the person out of whose property such judgment shall have been satisfied, shall in such case have contribution as at common law, and the Circuit Court of the United States for the proper district shall have jurisdiction of such action. The Bill passed by 45 to 19, Hill, Robertson, Shurz, Tipton and Trumbull voting nay.

THE LOYAL KU-KLUX

CHARLESTON DAILY COURIER
April 15, 1871

There are serious grounds for Federal interference in the affairs of the loyal city of Cincinnati. Colonel Wm. Travis, a colored gentleman, who slings a graceful razor, digs out a corn or bunion with neatness and dispatch, and is, withal, no slouch in military affairs, saw fit, in the exercise of his rights and privileges as a freeman, to vote for a Democrat. On Monday night, while peacefully sitting on his doorstep smoking a segar and revolving various schemes for the redemption and regeneration of his race, Mr. Travis was "yanked" into the street by a body of colored Ku-Klux, and most foully and inhumanly mauled. The midnight assassins smote him in the ribs, barked his shine, punched his head, tweaked as much of his nose as they could get hold of, and put mice under his eyes. In the meantime the police watched the proceedings from a neighboring corner, and turned a deaf ear to poor Travis' roars of anguish. We call upon Congress to do something for Cincinnati and for Travis. Of what benefit is the privilege of suffrage to an African if he cannot vote for whom he pleases?

THE KU-KLUX BILL

HARPER'S WEEKLY
April 15, 1871, p. 330

No one who was familiar with the unspeakable horrors of slavery, or who knew its degrading, demoralizing, dehumanizing effect upon the master class, will doubt that the stories of the Ku-Klux atrocities are substantially true. They may be exaggerated in number. They may be misrepresented in certain cases. But the political and social hate from which they spring will not be denied. Citizens of the United States, because they are black, or because, being white, they sympathize with the black citizens, and both black and white because they are loyal to the Union and of the Republican party, are exposed to violence of every kind and degree; so that in one State—South Carolina—the Governor has appealed to the President for aid. From other States the cries of individual sufferers have reached Congress, imploring protection, and a committee has reported a bill designed to relieve the lawlessness of the States in question.

We are very sure that nobody who is conversant with the course of this paper during the war and the epoch of reconstruction has any doubt of our sympathy with the victims of the Ku-Klux, nor of our desire to do whatever can be done to succor them, short of doing greater evil. But the first fact that we encounter is this—that the Constitution of the United States guarantees every State, "on application of the Legislature, or of the Executive (when the Legislature can not be convened), against domestic violence." The second fact is that the Governors of many of the States which the Ku-Klux ravage are in political sympathy with the President, and with the Republican majority in Congress. If the domestic violence in those States is beyond the control of the Governors, why do they not, with the Governor of South Carolina, require the President's aid, as the Constitution authorizes? So long as they refrain from the demand—they whose information if immediate and ample—is there any good reason for extraordinary legislation?

The proposed bill, in its fourth section, provides that whenever in any State the unlawful organizations violently set at defiance the constituted authorities, the President may interfere. But that is precisely what the Constitution already provides, upon the sole condition that the Legislature, or the Executive, testifies the inability of the local authority to deal with the disorder. But the bill, omitting this condition, leaves to the President to determine when the State authority is insufficient. Is that, upon reflection, a wise change in the system; and if it be, can it be made by an act of Congress? And again, if it be wise, and if it can be made by Congress, why should it be a provision which is to expire on the first day of June, 1872, as the same section provides? The peril is always possible; ought not the law, therefore, if unquestionably constitutional, to be permanent? These are grave questions, as our fellow-Republicans will see.

The bill proceeds, in the same section, to declare that if the constituted authorities themselves, instead of asking aid of the national government, become accomplices in the disorder, the situation shall be deemed a rebellion, and the President may suspend the privilege of the writ of habeas corpus, and suppress the difficulty by arms. This, again, makes the President the sole and final judge of the complicity of the State authorities in a conspiracy, and empowers him practically to supersede them. There is a riot in Boston, for instance. The President, with or without reason—for no system of evidence is mentioned—decides that it is the work of an armed and numerous combination, with which the State authorities are unable to deal, or with which they are in league, and thereupon marches troops to restore order. This is the scope of the bill. This is the grant of power until the 1st of June, 1872. Is it wise? Is it desirable that the Republican party should make it? Is it safe for liberty that it should be made? If it be, ought the power to expire next year?

That there are emergencies in which even the fundamental law must be disregarded to save both itself and the country is true. That there was no folly so criminal as that of the assertion that armed and summary resistance to secession was unconstitutional, is unquestionable. But with Republican Governors in many disordered States, and a constitutional provision empowering them to ask aid against insuperable domestic violence, is there any necessity for suspending the fundamental law? It will not be forgotten that in 1866, while the legislation of reconstruction was proceeding, and before the lately rebel States were restored, the project of an amendment to the Constitution, expressly providing that Congress should have power to secure "to all persons in the several States equal protection in the rights of life, liberty, and property," was, upon motion of Mr. Conkling, postponed, and not called up for consideration. If at that time, and under those circumstances, it was thought necessary—if such an object were desirable—to provide for the purposes of the present bill by an amendment of the Constitution, upon which it was not deemed wise to take action, can it be desirable now to aim at that object by a mere act of Congress? Or will it be alleged that the proposed amendment of 1866 was not called up because the power conferred by it was believed to be included in the Fourteenth Amendment? Mr. Bingham, indeed, says that he drew the amendment, and that the power was meant to be conferred. It is certainly most unfortunate, then, that the first form was not retained.

The deplorable and menacing condition of some of the Southern States can, perhaps, hardly be exaggerated. If we were to heed feelings only, all loyal and orderly citizens would resort to the most summary measures. Indeed, when great crimes are committed any where, the instinct is to demand instant vengeance. Reason and experience, however, insist that "the due process of law" shall be observed for the common safety, knowing that "order" is always the plea of despotism. In the same way regard for the general liberty, for all those guarantees which defend us from tyranny and ruthless ambition, requires that the plain conditions of the fundamental law shall be rigidly respected, and changed only as itself provides. We are not now saying that so essential and vital a change in the system of the Union as this bill contemplates is unwise; but surely it should be the result not of an act of Congress, under a challenged and doubtful interpretation, but of an express and explicit constitutional amendment.

THE SOUTH CAROLINA KU-KLUX

CHARLESTON DAILY COURIER
April 20, 1871

Views of a United States Army Officer—The K. K. Not a Political Association—The Testimony of an Unbiassed Witness—General Amnesty Recommended.

A correspondent of the New York *World,* an officer of the United States army, has written a letter to that paper from Charleston, under date of the 12th instant, which may be commended to the Revolutionists in Congress. Without comment we print the testimony of this officer upon the situation in this State. He says:

It is impossible that a correct understanding of affairs in this and other States similarly situated can be arrived at while such statements as are frequently made in the Tribune and repeated from time to time on the floor of Congress, relative to the political character of the organization known as the Ku-Klux Klan are authoritatively asserted and believed. I have thought that it would not be uninteresting to you to have a fair, candid, and reliable showing from an impartial outsider of the condition of things, political and economical, in this State.

The Ku-Klux Klan is not primarily a political organization. It may be compared much more truthfully to the Vigilance Committee of the early 'Frisco days, and the best proof of this is to be found in their published utterances and the record of their acts, unlawful, violent, and unjustifiable as they are. Wherever the Klan has made itself evident, their vengeance has been directed, not against the officers and men of the United States army, nor even against the civil Federal authorities in the State, but always against either criminals or individuals who have made themselves obnoxious for public theft or private perfidy.

That these acts of lawlessness should seem to exhibit an antagonism to Republicans is solely due to the fact that the Republicans are in control of the State Government, and the thieves and robbers who are so untiring and desperate in their attacks upon the public Treasury, naturally announce themselves of that party, and find support and shelter in the cry of outrages to loyal men on account of their loyalty, the truth being that loyalty or disloyalty has nothing whatever to do with the question, which is solely one of honesty or dishonesty. That the Klan is supposably composed of native white men does not detract from the force of this statement, since natives are found on both sides, and especially because the absorbing interest of all classes in the State is directed solely to their own affairs, and national politics possess scarcely a passing interest. Relief from the troubles that overwhelm them is not anticipated from any change in the political majority in Congress, since even a Democratic President and Government cannot deprive the negroes of votes or alter their majority of 30,000. The key to the whole difficulty is in this very majority, which controls legislation, levies taxes, and disburses them when collected, through their representatives—ignorant, rapacious, and utterly dishonest. The spectacle of these legislators, arrayed in "purple and fine linen," driving handsome turnouts and spending large sums of money, is not particularly improving to their constituents, whose cupidity, a new sensation to them, is likewise awakened, and the barbarous taste for personal adornment and display, so well known in the negro, is cultivated and intensified.

The record of the present administration may be briefly summed up as follows: The State debt increased from five to sixteen millions, taxation five times what it was in 1860, while taxable property is about one-third its valuation in the same year by the loss of slaves and by depreciation.

These statements, undoubtedly nearly correct, are taken from the speech of Mr. R. Lathers in support of his resolution before the Board of Trade the other night. In addition to these facts should be presented the legislation compelling the taxes for 1870 and 1871, amounting to four millions, to be collected this year; the secret being that the present Legislature holds a final session next winter, and is desirous of having the largest possible amount of money in the treasury. Remembering that the whites pay the taxes, while the negro majority, who do not furnish a dollar towards the support of either State or Federal Government, have the disbursement of them. You will readily perceive that the only termination of the present rule, if allowed to go on, will be in the utter ruin of the property holders.

This downward course must be stopped or the whites will be compelled to sell out and emigrate while they have anything to sell. In the up-country the so-called Ku-Klux Klan has endeavored to stay the avalanche of ruin by intimidating the prominent men concerned in this wholesale robbery, but their efforts being guided probably by men of small intelligence, and unable to act except against individuals, and only in the country districts, are utterly ineffectual, and only result in precipitating an anarchy worse than the evils they seek to cure. You see I make no apology for them, but have said enough to disprove the reiterated statements of politicians relative to their political character. Among the more intelligent and temperate men of the cities especially, the great question, "what shall we do to be saved?" is seriously engaging their almost undivided attention. What the Klan, with rude, blind, and useless violence, seeks to accomplish in the thinly settled up-country, the combined wealth, intelligence, and honesty of the State are devising some plan to attain peacefully and without bloodshed.

The only method of doing this that possesses the merit of immediate application and avoidance of force is to fail to pay the taxes imposed for this year and next, and so let the State Government fall to pieces by removing the cohesive power of money, as sands would fall from the pole of a magnet were the magnetism suddenly destroyed. The action of the Chamber of Commerce and the Board of Trade is taken in accordance with this view, and the inefficiency and uselessness of any Ku-Klux legislation by Congress may be made perfectly apparent when viewed in the light of these facts. The Federal Government is pouring troops into South Carolina. The troops will meet almost a welcome.

In conclusion it might be desirable to point out some method of curing the evils so keenly felt, and which have been eating into the very heart of these people as the fotters gnaw into the flesh of the prisoner. But this is not so easy to do. A complete and perfect country should be the first measure. This would give property-holders an opportunity to use their full influence. Minority representation would have the effect of measurably purifying the political atmosphere of the Legislature, and without, abridgment of the rights of the negroes, would aid to protect the white man, who in this State, is the down-trodden and oppressed. The condition of affairs being perfectly understood North, the tremendous moral effect of the universal sympathy of the whole country for this unfortunate State must make itself felt for good, and, perhaps, the increased flow of business and gradual reacquisition of some degree of wealth would finally accomplish, beneath the auspices of an honest and economical government, the regeneration so essential, and the absence of which is now a blot upon our civilization and a reproach to the institutions under which we live.

THE COLORED CADET

His Troubles at West Point.

CHARLESTON DAILY COURIER
April 20, 1871

A correspondent of a Northern exchange, writing from West Point, expatiates on Smith, the colored cadet and his troubles, as follows:

Said a cadet to me some days ago; "We do not refuse to associate with cadet Smith on account of his having negro blood in his veins. I was brought up with darkies for my playfellows. His color is nothing; it is the fellow himself whom we dislike and despise. He is low in his tastes, evil-tempered, malicious and a liar!"

These were strong words, but careful enquiry and the sincerest intention possible to be fair, have led me to the conclusion that they are perfectly justifiable and not a whit too strong. In my previous letter hence you have had some account of the degree to which the canker of falsehood had eaten its way into the vitals of the Military Academy. Now, while the wholesale propagation of this vice cannot be charged upon Smith, there is no reasonable doubt that the example of his obtaining immunity for indulgence in conspicuous inexactness has done much to influence weak minded plebes to follow his example. But alas for them! They have, ere this, learned by sad experience the futility of white blood to keep them from coming to grief.

I have referred to Smith's color as not being the reason why he is shunned by his fellow-cadets; and to illustrate this more plainly I cannot do better than give the words of one of the instructors here.

"Why, sir," he said to me, only this morning, "it's ridiculous to think of Smith's being cut because of his having negro blood. The fault lies with himself and his own evil nature. When he came here for the first time there came with him a pure darkey, black as the ace of Spades. This latter failed to pass the preliminary examination, but during the short while he was here became a general favorite, and had he staid would have been a kind of pet to the boys. He was jolly, lively, full of fun, showing his teeth from ear to ear on the shortest notice; and though of course very many jokes were cracked about his skin, he took them all in good part, and became the friend of everybody. But he was a real darkey, no coffee-colored mulatto, who, by the way, usually possess the worst traits of both races."

Smith is much to be pitied on account of the unfortunate position in which the misjudged advice of his protectors has placed him. When Mr. Clark, of New Haven, (Smith's "guide, philosopher and friend") had him in training preparatory to entering the Academy, he made the mulatto eat with his footman and coachman, never, by any chance, admitting him to his own table. And now this gentleman sends him to the Academy, and is very much astonished that gentlemen's sons will not associate with him. In addition to this, Smith has received so many letters and papers from Radicals all over the country exhorting him to "stand firm and uphold the good cause," &c., that he actually fancies himself to be the representative of a principle, and consequently acts accordingly.

It is doubtful if he be more than demerited for his last offense, and meanwhile we have the spectacle of the fifteenth amendment grossly set aside, and a discrimination made in color, by allowing to Smith that for which a white boy would have been expelled.

FIFTEENTH AMENDMENT CELEBRATION AT RICHMOND

CHARLESTON DAILY COURIER
April 22, 1871

Richmond, April 21
The colored people celebrated the Fifteenth Amendment anniversary by a procession, at the head of which was carried a rooster. They were addressed by George F. Downing, colored, of Washington, who denounced the Administration for its treatment of Sumner. The crowd gave three cheers for Sumner, and then cheered for Grant.

AMNESTY REFUSED AND ANOTHER RECONSTRUCTION ENACTED

CHARLESTON DAILY COURIER
April 22, 1871

There were two measures before the Congress of the United States at its present session. The one was a measure of peace; the other of fresh war, under false pleas, upon the people and liberties of the South. The first was the Amnesty Bill; the second the so-called enforcement of Re-construction. The common sense of the country has long since settled the question of amnesty. To hold any portion of the American people under pains and disabilities is to that extent a declaration against their citizenship and freedom. It places them beyond the pale of complete right, and thus inculcates ostracism and oppression. There can be no freedom where there is a deprivation of equality and right. The common welfare, the nature of the Government, and the public concord and interests, all alike with one voice, proclaim for the entire and absolute removal of all disabilities and the restoration of every citizen to a perfect citizenship.

The Radical caucus at Washington has decided against this plain and wise course. Senator Robertson, of South Carolina, introduced the subject, and urged the passage of this measure. It was advocated by Senator Sawyer, of this State, and Senator Stewart, of Nevada, but under the opposition of Senator Chandler, of Michigan, who advocated the late war, on the ground that the country needed a little "blood-letting," of Senator

Morton, of Indiana—President Grant's man Friday—and of Senators Conkling, of New York, and Edmunds, of Vermont, it was determined to lay the whole matter on the table. And this extreme and party Radicalism carried the day, in defiance of the general sentiment and the general welfare. Even the Washington *Chronicle,* which has been decided in its opposition to the re-instatement of the South, "regrets the action of the Senate in postponing the Amnesty Bill to next autumn." But there stands the fact, and it reveals not only the partisan nature of the rule, but that this rule is deaf to all audience on the part of the South or of right and concord.

But while thus refusing all measures of relief to the South, there is passed, under the form of a Ku-Klux Bill, a new and additional reconstruction for the South, under the power of the bayonet and the sword. Amnesty is refused, and fresh oppressions exacted. But yet, though often disheartened, we are not in despair. We rest in the faith and hope that the darkness of night cannot always cover the land, and that at last the sun of self-government must dawn. All that we can do is to work for this end.

As to the character of this course of wrong, we know not what we can do better than quote the following words from the Hon. Gideon Welles, the Secretary of the Navy, during the administration of President Grant. Speaking of the further reconstruction of the Southern States, he says:—

"I have no respect for those who claim that it is necessary for Massachusetts or for others to supervise Virginia and to take care of the people of that and other States in their local concerns. If the people are incapable of self-government, our system is a failure. If the people of the States respectively cannot make and execute their own laws, but are to be governed and controlled in their local and municipal affairs by a central power, then American Democracy and American Republicanism are mere shams and delusions. The Union of these States can be preserved only by maintaining the reserved and guaranteed rights of the States. If the Federal Government is not restrained by constitutional limitations, it is a central despotism of unlimited power and authority.

"The laws of Congress giving the President authority to introduce military at the elections, and all schemes by which the Central Government assumes to take cognizance of and to punish offences by Ku-Klux organizations, or by others in the States, are like almost every act in what is called re-construction, unwarranted, unconstitutional, centralizing and revolutionary. Punishment for crimes against a State committed within the jurisdiction of a State belongs exclusively to a State and not to the General Government. I am aware that the attempted justification for these usurpations is necessary —always the tyrant's plea for crime, oppression and wrong—the sham excuse which was set up for the wrongs inflicted in Kansas, and for the greater wrongs since inflicted on Georgia and other States of the South.

While not disposed to obtrude my opinions upon others, I desire not to be misunderstood. I fully recognize necessity of party as a means to sustain essential principles, but let the means be subordinate to the ends.

"I am a Republican, but not an exclusionist, who would exclude States from their rightful representation in Congress, deny them the right to frame their fundamental laws, the right to regulate their own domestic affairs, or deny them their reserved and undoubted exclusive right and authority to punish offenses committed within their respective jurisdictions. This doctrine of exclusion is incompatible with a Federal union, inconsistent with and in violation of the constitution, and subversive of the Government. I, therefore, oppose the Grant administration."

OUR WASHINGTON CORRESPONDENCE

[From Our Own Correspondent.]

CHARLESTON DAILY COURIER
April 22, 1871

Washington, April 19, 1871

The Ku-Klux Bill has finally passed and the President will promptly sign it. The Committee of Conference gained every point contended for the Senate Radicals, the House yielding every thing of importance. True, the Sherman clause rendering the property of all people of a county or town liable for the outrages of the Ku-Klux was modified, so that the damages will fall not upon private property, but upon the public property of a county, or city, or town. Thus, if the amount of damages cannot be collected from the offenders, it must be levied on the public property, such as the money in the County Treasury, or the jail, courthouse, market house, school houses, alms houses, streets, or any possession of the municipality.

It was contended by Mr. Sherman that this was the most efficient remedy in the Bill for all the evils complained of, and that it had been found indispensible in England and other countries, and had been engrafted on the laws of a number of our States. In the State of Maryland such a law has existed, and under it Reverdy Johnson was paid for his house, destroyed by a mob. Under the ruling of Judge Taney, the claim of Duffy against the city of Baltimore for the destruction of a house in a riot, was decided in favor of the defendant, as the claim came within the exceptions laid down.

One of the worst provisions of the Bill is that the juries that are to act in these cases are required to take the iron-clad oath, thus excluding from the juries nine of ten of the intelligent citizens of a county. Then again the House concurred in the Senate amendment, limiting the existence of the law till the end of the next session of Congress, instead of the first of next June. It is alleged that the law is to be made use of for the purposes of the Republican party in regard to the next Presidential election. It will be observed that Senators Schurz and Sprague voted against the Bill. The last named Senator, though a Republican, is also a property holder in South Carolina, and probably failed to see the benefits derivable from the Bill.

The Amnesty Bill was killed in the Senate Republican caucus. It was decided that the subject should not be considered at this session. There was a majority of the Senate, including the Democrats, for the Bill, but there was evidently no chance to carry it, as the House had done, by a vote of two-thirds. The party has made a mistake in this matter, as will be found to its cost.

The Democratic members of Congress will agree upon an address to the people of the United States upon the public issues of the day, and it will be of a character well calculated to influence public opinion.

THE SAN DOMINGO MESSAGE

HARPER'S WEEKLY
April 22, 1871, p. 354

The message of the President, accompanying the Report of the San Domingo Commission, has made the most favorable impression upon the country. It is the simple statement of a man in whose honesty there is entire confidence, and with whose judgment the report offers the strongest evidence of sympathy. The President briefly recounts the circumstances under which his attention was drawn to the subject of annexation. His function is that of initiation, and he believed that his evident duty was to negotiate a treaty, and to leave its ratification to the proper authority. But as a cloud of personal aspersion obscured the whole subject as soon as it was made public, and, as he thought, seriously affected the action of the Senate, it seemed to him most desirable, as well as just to those who had been accused, that a Commission of the highest character should investigate the whole subject, and report through him to the country. Congress agreed with him, and the Commission has now laid its conclusions before the final tribunal.

And with this result, the President adds, all his personal solicitude upon the subject ends, although his opinion of the advantages of annexation remain unchanged. The final paragraph of the message will, perhaps, be regretted by many persons, and we wish that the President had spared the remark about "disappointed men." But the charges of corruption against him have been so malignant, that it is certainly not surprising that he should have wished to complete the final appeal to the country by a warm declaration of his consciousness of honest purpose. It was not, indeed, necessary, but it was certainly natural; and it will not harm him with the popular heart.

The subject of the annexation of San Domingo is now, as we hoped it would be, left to the country. With this disposition of the matter we hope and we believe that occasion of vehement dissent from the executive action will also disappear, and that Senators, without renouncing any conviction whatever, will remember the paramount necessity to the country of Republican dominance, and the impracticability of that dominance if a friendly spirit does not prevail. We hope that it will not be forgotten that no party in this country can succeed which alienates its best members from hearty co-operation. The tendency has, perhaps, been to be unmindful of this truth, and to forget that what the Republican party needs is the union which comes alone from a comprehensive and progressive policy. Senator Morton speaks truly in saying that the great issue of 1872 will evidently be the maintenance of the Union upon the Republican settlement; but he is less wise in belittling civil service reform and in not seeing what an element of strength to the party a positive policy upon that subject would be. For while we maintain the great loyal Republican line against the last sullen assault of baffled slavery, it would be madness to despise the opening and alarming fire of corruption which succeeds it as the national foe. The Republican host should move upon this enemy's works immediately.

THE SWORD AND THE OLIVE-BRANCH

HARPER'S WEEKLY
April 22, 1871, p. 355

The Ku-Klux bill, which has passed the House of Representatives by a strictly party vote, is very little changed from that upon which we commented last week, and for the reasons which we then gave we consider it a profound mistake. The President is authorized at his discretion to decide when the State authority is unable, or refuses, to keep the peace, and when the situation may be deemed a rebellion. Has Congress really measured the scope of such a bill? It is a power which every one knows, indeed, that General Grant will not abuse, but which might be used to subvert all liberty. It would have been very easy to qualify it; to require, for instance, the certificate of a District Judge of the United States that unlawful combinations obstructed the courts; but the bill provides no restraint whatever upon the executive discretion. There is no excuse for not having made the language of the Fourteenth Amendment so plain as to render misconception impossible.

And now more than ever is amnesty imperative. Mr. De Long, a colored representative from South Carolina, cogently declared in the House that while intelligent and influential men are disfranchised they have no interest in maintaining order, and they can not reasonably be expected to support vigorously a system which politically outlaws them. He demanded general amnesty. We observe also that at a recent meeting of Ohio Republicans interested in the Cincinnati declaration both General Cox and Mr. Clark, a prominent colored Republican, urged, amidst great applause, the necessity and good policy of amnesty. And if the Ku-Klux bill is passed by the Senate the President can do no more signal and sagacious service to the country and to his party than to sign a message strongly recommending general amnesty at the same time that he signs the bill.

THE KU-KLUX AND AMNESTY

HARPER'S WEEKLY
April 29, 1871, p. 378

It is comparatively unimportant whether the Ku-Klux is a purely political organization or not. It is enough that it has necessarily a direct political bearing. It springs confessedly from hostility to the colored citizens. Out of one hundred and thirty cases specifically and by name reported in North Carolina, eighty-nine were colored, and forty-one white; and the white were victims because of their sympathy with the colored citizens. Now, as the colored citizens are almost exclusively of one party, and all the Ku-Klux, without exception, of the other, and as one of the alleged excuses of the crimes is the political rights conferred upon the colored citizens, the necessary political influence of the whole conspiracy is evident, even if it were not very fully established.

Obviously, therefore, the duty of the dominant party in the government is plain. It is, first of all, to ascertain what actual cause of dissatisfaction there is. An honest effort of this kind would undoubtedly show that there is a great deal of ignorance and incapacity and rascality in the Southern State governments, as we all know there is in the State of New York; that a large class of the most intelligent and influential citizens are disfranchised, and therefore apathetic, or venomously hostile, constantly chagrined and indignant with the consciousness of their inability to remedy misgovernment. Is it wise to continue this source of discontent? Can it be extinguished by force? If the number of the disabled be large, the discontent is natural. If it be insignificant, nothing can be gained by excluding them. The advantage of the punishment is lost in the disadvantage of bitter hostility to a policy which, since it can effect no actual result, inevitably seems to be wanton. Mr. Hale's amnesty excepts a thousand or two, perhaps, in the Southern States. But such a number is merely a thorn which pricks a million. The bill gives to each one of the proscribed the power of a martyr. The discontent is not according to the number. It is the sense of wrong, not its extent, which tells. A century ago Lord North said that he would not tax America heavily, but he would declare the right of taxing. And so, said Mr. Webster, the Revolution was fought upon a preamble. The argument for any amnesty is conclusive for a complete amnesty.

Meanwhile we have no sentimental expectations from an amnesty. The old slave-holding class that led the rebellion—men like Davis, Hampton, and Toombs—will hate the Union, and the party and principles that maintained it, as heartily as the old English Cavaliers hated Cromwell, or as the Jacobites hated the house of Hanover. They will work and vote against Republican ascendency. But so they work against it now, and the exclusion of a thousand or two does us no good, and only gives them a plausible cry—that is to say, it helps them, and hurts us. Mr. Wendell Phillips declares that the demand for amnesty is a "coward and blundering anxiety for party success," and that it will dig the grave of the Republican party. Now we confess that it is a desire for party success, based upon the profound conviction that the success of the party is indispensable to the national welfare, which leads us to urge an amnesty. It certainly is not to propitiate the Ku-Klux Democracy, but it is to baffle them. Amnesty is not cowardly, but heroic, and it is the soundest policy for the Republican party. Should we have been really stronger, and the country more peaceful, if the States had been restored with the entire ex-rebel population disfranchised? Is it not wise, or is it cowardly, to do what is practicable to soften, since we can not extinguish, the necessary ill feeling between the old and the new citizens in the Southern States?

One of Mr. Phillips's finest passages is a denunciation of the English policy in Ireland a hundred years ago. Remembering that, we see three things that ought to be done in the disturbed part of the Union. First, the pretense of what is called "negro ascendency"—a pretense which rests upon the fact that all the disfranchised are white, and which disappears the moment that all are made politically equal—should be removed by a general amnesty. Then the people of the Union should require the government to secure the widest education in every State. And the government, simultaneously with amnesty, should take ample care that those whom it has made citizens are perfectly protected in voting. What the Ku-Klux can do in preventing voting was shown in the State of Louisiana at the last Presidential election. In certain parishes or counties where the aggregate registered colored vote was hundreds, and even thousands, only one or two Republican votes—in some no Republican vote at all—was cast. In Caddo parish there were 777 registered white votes, and 2987 colored; and 2895 votes were polled for Seymour, and 1 for Grant. In De Soto there were 620 registered white votes, and 1700 colored; and there were 1260 for Seymour, and none for Grant. In sixteen parishes the aggregate registered colored vote was more than 33,000; and there were 1188 Republican votes polled against nearly 50,000 for Seymour. Had the election been decided by the vote of Louisiana the result would have been as evidently fraudulent as the election of Hoffman in this State in 1868. And if the next Presidential election should be very close, and decided by the vote of a State in which the Ku-Klux terror prevailed, it could not be accepted as valid. On the other hand, what the government can do was shown in the city of New York last autumn; and not a single honest voter was hindered from voting or forced to vote against his will.

The alternative is very simple. It is whether, in the light of experience and common sense, a national election in this country is likely to be fairer with national supervisors and bayonets to support them, or with the Ku-Klux terror and ballot-box stuffers. And it is not for the masked Ku-Klux, murdering indiscriminately at midnight, nor for Tammany repeaters, nor for their apologists and accomplices, to appeal to the old English law removing soldiers two miles from the polls. That law is now changed, and merely retains the soldiers in their barracks, as ours were retained last autumn. Meanwhile the rule of common sense is to guard against the most obvious danger. Let every good citizen ask himself this question: Is an honest election more threatened by the Ku-Klux and repeaters, or by the military force that may be summoned to hold them in check?

GENERAL GRANT.—"Who has been Mutilating this Tree?"
KU-KLUX.—"Mr. President, I can not tell a lie—that Nigger done it."

Harper's Weekly, April 29, 1871, p. 387.

HOME AND FOREIGN GOSSIP

HARPER'S WEEKLY
May 6, 1871, p. 407

An uncompromising slave-holder of Tennessee could not bring his mind to live in the United States after the abolition of slavery. He migrated to Brazil, and became a South American citizen; but, unfortunately for him, became bankrupt, and, in accordance with the laws of that country, his two daughters have been sold into slavery to pay his debts. Such strange recompense is sometimes meted out to men. Steps have been taken to place the amount of the debt—$1200 in gold—in the hands of the father.

FROM WASHINGTON

CHARLESTON DAILY COURIER
May 19, 1871

A Military Order—Regular Troops to Aid the Civil Authorities in Suppressing Ku-Klux Outrages.

Washington, May 18

An order has been issued from the War Department containing the President's Ku-Klux Proclamation. It concludes: The President directs that whenever occasion shall arise the regular forces of the United States stationed in the vicinity of any locality where offences described by the Act approved April 20th, 1871, may be committed, shall, in strict accordance with the provisions of the said Act, be employed by their commanding officers in assisting the authorized civil authority of the United States in making arrests of persons accused under the Act; in preventing the rescue of persons arrested for such cause; in breaking up and dispersing bands of disguised marauders, or armed organizations against the power and quiet of the lawful pursuits of the citizens in any S[t]ate.

Whenever troops are employed in the manner indicated in this order, the commanding officer will, at the earliest opportunity, make a full report of his operations to the proper superior authority.

THE KU-KLUX DOWN SOUTH.
"WE CORDIALLY INVITE IMMIGRATION."

Harper's Weekly, May 6, 1871, p. 407.

THE REAL ISSUE

HARPER'S WEEKLY
May 20, 1871, p. 450

The Mobile *Register,* which, after fiercely upholding human slavery as the corner-stone of free institutions, and struggling to the last to overthrow a mild and equable government which promised to curtail in the Territories of the United States the precious right of the Southern gentleman of selling at the auction-block the mother of his colored children, with her offspring—which cherished a system that was the degradation of slave and slave-holder together, and the foul stench and disgrace of the American name—which was utterly foiled in its hope of destroying the Constitution and government of the republic of the United States, to rear upon its ruins an empire of slavery—now begs its Democratic friends and allies not to oppose the "wonderful institution" known as Tammany, but to turn all their guns "on the Jacobin tyrant who sits enthroned at Washington to the terror of all patriots, and to the peril of free government." This is its description of the modest and honest soldier who finally frustrated the plans of the Mobile *Register* and its fellow-rebels, and who, by the will of the loyal and intelligent friends of the Union and of equal liberty—who are a great majority of the American people—is to-day in very truth, and to the joy of every honest believer in equal rights, "the terror" of such patriots as the Mobile *Register,* and "the peril" of the freedom of the Ku-Klux, the Mobile *Register's* friends.

The precise feeling of the Southern element of their party, upon which the Democratic leaders rely for success, is shown in the ardent appeals of the *Register* for harmony. Its one fond remembrance is the rebellion. Its one passionate hope is the destruction of the results of the Union victory. All its illustrations spring instinctively from its most familiar associations. Be friends! be friends! it cries to its allies. Don't underrate the power of Tammany. "Tammany is the right bower of the Democratic strength. . . . We fire no shots into Tammany while it stands a bulwark of strength, an adamantine wall, betwixt the Empire State and the Jacobin traitor to the Constitution of his country. *What would have been thought of* Lee's *men firing into Stonewall* Jackson's Blücher *corps when it came up to sweep the gray-coats on to victory on the Chickahominy?*. . . The Democratic press and politicians would do far better to imitate Tammany . . . than in making war upon *this Stonewall wing of the grand Democratic party."*

This is no insignificant newspaper, nor uncertain sound. It is the voice of what Democratic authority calls "the most influential journal now published in the State." Americans! Republicans! it is with the same old rebel cries and aims, it is by gladly and proudly identifying itself with the lost cause, that the Democratic party enters upon the Presidential campaign. We appeal to every intelligent man of every party in the land, what advantage to the peace and prosperity of the country can be hoped from its success? The policy of disturbing the settlements is the only policy it proposes. Those who demand it are those who have always dominated the party, who will contemptuously leave to Tammany and its lackeys the plunder which they desire, and to whom Tammany and its lackeys will be absolutely subservient. "Its voice," says the *World,* speaking of the Mobile *Register,* "will be heard and heeded in the councils of the conservative men. . . ." Certainly it will. It was precisely the same voice that was heard and heeded in the Democratic National Convention of 1868, and which then, as now, declared the settlements of the war to be "revolutionary, unconstitutional, and void."

DOMESTIC INTELLIGENCE

HARPER'S WEEKLY
May 20, 1871, p. 451

President Grant has taken steps to protect the citizens of South Carolina from further outrages by the Ku-Klux by sending a strong body of cavalry, a detachment of infantry, and several pieces of artillery to Charleston and Columbia, for use in any counties where the civil authorities are powerless to give protection.

ANOTHER OUTRAGE

CHARLESTON DAILY COURIER
May 22, 1871

We regret to state that a diabolical outrage was committed near Gist's station, in this county, last Saturday night in which a peaceable and quiet colored man was killed and his step-daughter badly whipped, by a gang of disguised men. The reported circumstances which surround this outrage are of such a character that we cannot, as yet, prudently publish them; but we are free to state that if the report to us be true, the occurrence grew out of a personal and private difficulty; but avenged under the convenient disguise of the Ku-Klux.

We are pleased to learn that the neighbors feel much incensed at the deed, and are making every exertion to ferret out the perpetrators.

When will these terrible deeds have an end? Our heart sickens at the frequency of their occurrence, and we sometimes give up all hope of seeing peace and order restored among us. We sincerely hope the people in the neighborhood of Gist's station will persevere in hunting up the perpetrators of the foul outrage and have them brought to a just punishment. It is a duty they owe to themselves, the county and the State, and we call upon them to perform that duty faithfully and fearlessly.

Unionville Times.

THE LESSON OF THE KU-KLUX

HARPER'S WEEKLY
May 27, 1871, p. 474

Those who persistently deny the truth of the Ku-Klux stories, or ridicule them as mere tales of rawhead and bloody-bones, should remember that, whatever the explanation may be, the testimony is conclusive. And the presumption in favor of the general truth of the reports is decided. Just before the rebellion Mr. F. L. Olmsted, a remarkably sagacious traveler, made a journey through the Slave States, carefully observing and noting every thing that he saw. He did not write as an Abolitionist, nor as a partisan of any kind; and he did for the Slave States what Arthur Young did for France just before the great revolution of '89—he gave a faithful and detailed picture of their condition. It represented a kind of medieval state of society. There was great wealth in a few hands; luxury of a certain kind; enormous estates; and upon the other side immense ignorance, squalor, and barbarism. Mrs. Stowe's story of "Uncle Tom's Cabin," like Smollett's novels in England in the last century, also depicted the aspects of society in that region with a vividness for which the historian will be grateful.

Harper's Weekly, May 27, 1871, p. 479.

A DISTINCTION WITH A DIFFERENCE.

The probable truth of the Ku-Klux reports rests upon two considerations. The great proprietors, who had poisoned the minds of their dependents with every kind of false theory and passionate appeal, at last dragged them into a war, in which they were utterly defeated, amidst the desolation of the country, the paralysis of industry, and the uprooting of all local social, political, and industrial traditions and organizations. The end of active hostilities was followed by the incursion of all kinds of useful and useless persons into the disordered region. The situation was perplexed by political uncertainties at Washington. False hopes rose for a moment in minds brooding upon revenge, and their extinction did not extinguish bitterness and jealousy. This ill feeling was fostered and sustained by the hope of ultimate advantage from political alliances in other parts of the Union. And when the military presence of the successful government was withdrawn, nothing under the circumstances was so probable as constant ebullitions of anger and lawlessness. Had there been no emancipation and no equal suffrage, the condition of a population, ignorant, impoverished, and baffled in the frantic effort to reverse the course of civilization, would have been one of agitation and insecurity.

But to all this there was added in the Southern States a peculiar presumption that there would be such disturbance as we see. The war had freed the slaves, to confirm whose bondage the Southern chiefs had provoked it; and those slaves had become, from the necessity of the case, the political equals of the master class, and in many places they were the majority. To understand the probable feeling of an ignorant population, whose color alone was the sign of absolute social and political superiority, when they suddenly found those whom they had despised as pariahs their equals, and often their official superiors, it is only necessary to read Mr. Olmsted's book. Just as this population, when it thought it was to have all the power after the war, endeavored by black codes to retain all that was possible of slavery, so, when it finds that the power has passed from its hands, vents its rage in outrages, which it hopes may inspire so deep and general a terror that the power may be recovered even under the new conditions.

Therefore, both for this general and this particular reason, a disordered and almost barbarous situation was to be expected in many parts of the Southern States. And that impatience and indignation have been often justified in those States we do not doubt. That the new voters were, as a rule, ignorant, and that the new governments have often been as extravagant and corrupt as the old governments often are in other States, is not to be denied. We offer no excuse for political knavery any where. But we are speaking of public order; and we repeat that those who deny the disorder in many parts of the Southern States, or affect to laugh it away, are sneering at all experience. In his interview with the delegates from the Tax-payers' Convention in South Carolina, Governor Scott said that the embarrassment of the State was mainly due to the disturbed condition of the public mind, and to the sense of insecurity to life and property. So Governor Alcorn, of Mississippi, asked from the Legislature a mounted patrol to assist in keeping the peace. Certainly experience and common-sense teach that the surest method of permanently restoring order in that region is not to encourage every element of disorder, but to show that the general policy of equality, against which all the disturbance is a protest, is the fixed and final policy of the American people.

GESSLER'S CAP IN NEW YORK

HARPER'S WEEKLY
July 29, 1871, p. 690

The Democratic party formerly surrendered the American right of free speech at the command of the slave-masters; and now in the city of New York it surrenders the right of peaceful assembly at the summons of a religious mob. A party bred in abject subservience to slavery has no conception of the principles of liberty or of the fundamental rights of freemen. While the Democratic newspapers affect to deny the existence of the Ku-Klux in the Southern States, the Democratic municipal authorities in the great city of the continent carefully foster a Ku-Klux to which they command American citizens to yield. The tyrant Gessler at Altorf put his cap upon a pole, and ordered the Swiss to bow before it. The Democratic authorities of New York elevate the Pope's tiara, and warn American citizens that they will refuse to honor it at their peril! And this is the party that beseeches the people of the United States to give it control of the national government!

The circumstances of the recent prohibition of the parade of the Orange or Protestant Irishmen in the city of New York will serve, perhaps, to show to the country two things: one is the absolute alliance of the Democratic city government with political Romanism; and the other is that, in consequence of that alliance, the indisputable rights of American citizens are deliberately sacrificed. The facts are very few and simple. The Orangemen resolved to celebrate the anniversary of the battle of the Boyne by a public parade in the streets of the city. Certain Roman Catholic associations thereupon resolved that they would attack them if they did; and as they did attack them last year, and killed several of the Orangemen, there was no doubt that they would keep their word. The Roman Catholic party having thus distinctly announced that they would make a riot if the procession took place, the city authorities surrendered, and forbade the procession. The surrender was made under the absurd pretext that processions in the streets are not matters of right, but of toleration, and that they may be forbidden when the peace is likely to be broken!

That is to say, that every public parade of peaceable citizens through the streets may rightfully be forbidden if a band of desperadoes and assassins announce that they do not choose to favor the procession, and will attack it if it appears. Upon this principle, if some French *cercle* had declared that it would assault the Germans if they paraded on Easter-Monday, the authorities might rightfully have prohibited the celebration! Of course, in the present instance, every body knows that if the circumstances had been reversed, and the Orangemen had declared that they would attack a Roman Catholic procession, they would have been sternly warned that their blood would be upon their own heads, and the Roman Catholic parade would not have been prohibited. Nor is the talk about the celebration of foreign events and the feuds and animosities of other lands less absurd. If there were Italians in New York who chose to perpetuate the strife of Guelfs and Ghibellines, and to parade in honor of their respective heroes and events, their right to do so would be indisputable, and equally indisputable would be the duty of the authorities to protect those Italians peaceably parading.

The principle laid down in this ridiculous proceeding is that the right of American citizens peaceably to assemble may be arbitrarily annulled by a police superintendent upon the threat of unlawful disturbance of the meeting. The truth is that the police and the whole military force of the State exist for the protection of that right and similar rights. In the very culmination of events before the war and in the week following the execution of John Brown a speech was announced in Philadelphia upon the then situation of the antislavery movement. The friends of slavery instantly resolved that it should not take place. They placarded the walls with virtual invitations to a riot. They appealed in the papers to the most inflamed passions. Large numbers of what were called respectable citizens waited upon the mayor and told him that the hall would be demolished and the streets would run with blood if he did not stop the speech. But the mayor—it was Alexander S. Henry—replied that although he deprecated the speech as much as any body, and wished with all his heart that it might not be delivered, yet that the right of the speaker was a fundamental right of an American citizen, and that he, the mayor, was officially bound under his oath to protect him to the last gasp, if it took all the police and all the militia at his command, and that he should certainly do his duty. There was a tremendous riot; but the mayor did his duty, and the rioters were conquered.

PERSONAL

HARPER'S WEEKLY
August 5, 1871, p. 715

For the first time in this country, perhaps in any country, a negro has been appointed a college professor. The new educator is Lawrence Minor, and the institution is Alcorn University, Mississippi, which was founded two years ago, and an endowment fund of $50,000 per annum appropriated for its support. This sum is to be paid annually for five years, after which it is expected to be self-supporting. Professor Minor was born in Louisiana, the son of a rich bachelor, a planter. His mother had also another son and a daughter by the same person. The daughter is now living in Cleveland, and has a son who is private secretary to Lieutenant-Governor Dunn. Before the death of Minor's father he was importuned by the female members of his family to give his children a thorough education, to which he consented, and engaged a private tutor for that purpose. Dying, he left a will manumitting the mother and children, and making provision for their education. Lawrence entered Oberlin College in 1846, and proved an apt scholar. In 1850 he went to New Orleans, taught school for four years, and was then obliged, in order to support his family, to become porter on one of the river steamers, where his conduct was excellent, and where he remained until this professorship was given to him, which insures him a salary of $2500 per annum. He is a strikingly handsome man for one of his color, tall, stout, and dignified; his conversation is fluent and pleasant, and by all who know him he is regarded as a remarkable man.

AN EXTRAORDINARY ILLUSION EXPOSED

HARPER'S WEEKLY
August 19, 1871, p. 762

In the beginning of May, 1850, the sixteenth anniversary of the American Anti-slavery Society was held at the Broadway Tabernacle, in New York. All the conspicuous leaders—Mr. Garrison, Mr. Phillips, Mrs. Lucretia Mott, Mr. Furness, and the rest—were present. The church was crowded, and the feeling, as usual, was intense. After a prayer and the reading of the Bible, and the transaction of the formal business of the occasion, Mr. Garrison left the chair and addressed the meeting. His characteristic manner was singularly bland and calm and measured. The impression he always made upon his peculiar platform was that of thorough comprehension of his subject, of indomitable resolution, and of the most perfect self-possession. In the course of his speech he alluded to the hostile attitude toward the Antislavery movement of the ecclesiastical organizations; and, proceeding to details, he stated that even certain priests and members of the Roman Catholic Church held slaves. Suddenly a voice from the gallery—and it is here that the illusion begins—cried out to know if that was the only Church of which the remark could be made. Mr. Garrison, without the slightest change of manner, replied that if the inquirer would wait a moment his question would be answered, and he went on to state the same truth of many of the other sects.

General Taylor was then President, and Mr. Garrison presently spoke of him as what was called a Christian, and yet, he said, the General holds and buys slaves, and his Christianity—quoting a current phrase—did not prevent him from "giving the Mexicans hell." Upon this the stranger in the gallery interrupted the speaker still more violently, and, surrounded by a body of men, members of the "Empire Club," he pressed up to the platform, vociferating that Mr. Garrison must stick to his text, and not insult the government. The whole audience arose in the utmost confusion, and the proceedings stopped. Colonel Kane, son of the late Judge Kane, of Philadelphia, a young man who had been drawn by sympathetic curiosity to the meeting, and who stood upon the platform, immediately planted himself by the side of the ringleader of the disturbers, and said, quietly, his hands in his overcoat pockets, "I shall shoot this man if he lays a finger upon any body." "This man" was Captain Isaiah Rynders. The members of the society appealed to the Chief of Police, Mr. Matsell, for protection. He replied that he should do nothing until Rynders struck somebody. The Hutchinsons attempted to allay the tumult with a song. But it was in vain.

Captain Rynders virtually took command of the meeting. The great mass of the audience, evidently friendly to Mr. Garrison and his cause, called for Mr. Furness, of Philadelphia. There were also calls for Dr. Grant, a friend of Captain Rynders. It was agreed that Mr. Furness should speak if he would not take all the time, and he proceeded, incessantly interrupted and insulted by Captain Rynders. Then Dr. Grant spoke, asserting that science showed negroes to be baboons. When he ended there was a cry for Frederick Douglass. Douglass appeared amidst a temp test of applause. When it subsided he was about to begin, when Captain Rynders, who with his followers, still stood upon the platform, declared that he would knock him down if he said a word against the government or country. "Dr. Grant," began Mr. Douglass, "says that science shows the negro to be a baboon. Look at me and answer. Am I a monkey or a man?" The response from the audience was a tempest of applause. "Pooh!" said Captain Rynders; "you are not a negro; you are half white." "Then I am your half-brother," instantly retorted Douglass, and the church rang again. Captain Rynders still interrupted Douglass as he proceeded, but more cautiously, so trenchant were Douglass's replies. As he ended, Douglass called his friend Ward to the platform—a man six feet high, and of the blackest skin. "Am *I* black enough?" began Ward, and he spoke so brilliantly and wittily that he was scarcely interrupted.

The Tabernacle had been secured for one meeting only, and the adjournment was to Hope Chapel. At the hour appointed Captain Rynders and the Empire Club had taken possession of that hall. The antislavery orators, Mrs. Mott, Mr. Phillips, Mr. Garrison, were not permitted to speak. Presently the owner of the hall sent word to them that they might do with themselves what they chose, but that the hall should not be exposed to violence, and they must therefore leave. The meeting was thus dispersed by Captain Rynders and his mob; it "ran away," as the newspapers said; and the mob sealed their victory by cheers for the *Herald,* the *Globe,* the Constitution, and the Church. And so absolute was the triumph of the mob that for two years the American Antislavery Society held no meeting in New York, because nobody dared to let a hall for the purpose.

This is the story. It is familiar to thousands of persons, and is implicitly believed by them as well as by those who were present. The English readers were not more firmly persuaded that the apparition of Mrs. Veal appeared at Canterbury than these persons are convinced that Captain Rynders and his mob appeared at the Tabernacle, and drove the Antislavery Society from Hope Chapel. And such was their faith in what they had seen and heard that it affected others. The illusion passed into history. The Rynders mob was regarded as no less a fact than the Sacheverel mobs in De Foe's own time. But it is the part of a free and independent press to scatter illusions and to correct history. We are now enabled to tell the truth. The persons at the antislavery meeting saw no mob and no rioters. Mrs. Mott, Mr. Garrison, Mr. Phillips, Mr. Furness, Colonel Kane, and the vast numbers who have always believed otherwise will think better of human nature when they learn that they are all mistaken. For twenty years they have been imagining a vain thing. There was no mob, no riot. The scene on the platform at the Tabernacle, the dispersion at Hope Chapel, were both an illusion, and if the members of the society only knew it, they held their meetings and departed undisturbed; and to say that Captain Rynders and his mob silenced Mrs. Mott is libelous.

THE TRUTH TOLD IN GEORGIA

HARPER'S WEEKLY
September 2, 1871, p. 811

It was always claimed that one of the good results of emancipation would be the relief of intelligent and honorable men in the Southern States from that relentless tyranny of opinion which made it personally dangerous in a Slave State to express the instincts of reason and humanity. A very striking illustration both of the tyranny and of the independence is found in a late address of the Hon. B. H. Hill, of Georgia, and some of the criticisms upon it. With a distinctness and vigor which are doubly refreshing when we remember that he spoke in Georgia, Mr. Hill said in his address: "The primal cause of our failure as a people is the fact that our system of labor was slavery. From this, as from a disturbed den of vipers, have crawled out the innumerable and poisonous evils that have lamed our energies and polluted our blood." Who believed, twenty years ago, that the time would ever come in this century when a conspicuous public man in Georgia would tell such plain truths to his neighbors and friends, and be sure of some, if not of general, hearty sympathy and approval? And yet what Mr. Hill said was only what Oglethorpe and the first trustees of the Georgia Company believed when they forbade slavery in the colony at its settlement.

That Mr. Hill would be severely criticised was certain. One of the most poisonous evils of the system he denounced was the moral and intellectual perversion which it produced, and which does not readily disappear. One paper gravely disputes his assertion, and declares that "slavery was never allowed to perfect its mission and develop its full effects upon the civilization of the South." But would the editor of this paper assert with equal gravity that the effect of slavery while it existed was elevating, refining, humanizing, and progressive both for the subject and master classes? If he would not, another would, for a correspondent of Mr. Alexander H. Stephens's *Sun* has the hardihood to say that under slavery "we"—that is, the Southern whites—"had reached a higher degree of cultivation, refinement, moral elevation, and intellectual power in the aggregate than any nation on earth." We do not believe that there are a hundred intelligent men in the Southern States, outside of the lunatic asylums, who think so. They may have thought that they must make the best of it, that there was no way to shake it off, and that they would fight to the death any body who should interfere; but that common-sense, intelligence, humanity, and experience were powerless with them we do not believe.

But Mr. Hill fitly deals with this kind of maundering. After a caustic description of the absolute dependence of the late Slave States upon the Free, he concludes:

> "Our politicians strut like condescending Jupiters to the hustings with Northern hats on their heads, Northern shoes on their feet, and Northern coats on their backs, and prove to gaping crowds their unequaled fitness for office in straining their lungs, as the thunder-gust doth the yielding clouds, with noisy denunciations of Northern weakness and greed, and climactic eulogies on Southern power and independence!"

Then in a serious and sincere strain he says what the heart and mind of every thoughtful man and woman in the Southern States must heed and ponder:

> "If my humble voice could be heard by the Southern people, I would urge them to do many things which these very derided Northern people have done. Endow first-class universities, provide for polytechnic schools in those universities, honor labor, and make the callings of the miner, the manufacturer, the metallurgist, the machinist, the agriculturist, and the mechanic as learned and as honorable as are the learned professions of law, medicine, and theology. We can not live by bread alone. We can not grow great, or rich, or independent by planting alone. Let us find in our own children that skilled labor which was impossible in the ignorant negro slave, and with that skilled labor let us utilize the unsurpassed natural physical elements of power with which God has filled almost every portion of our heretofore neglected country. If we do these things promptly, vigorously, and liberally, it will soon be that the sun in his cycles will not let fall his rays on a greater or more prosperous people. If we do not these things, we shall grow weaker until we be despised as contemptible."

If, instead of listening to the flattery of Northern Democratic demagogues, and to the rhetoric of their own local leaders who have so fearfully betrayed them, American citizens in the Southern States would hear and meditate the truths, disagreeable though they be, which their own life-long neighbors, like Mr. Hill, speak to them, all the old roots of bitterness would gradually disappear.

OCTAVIUS V. CATTO

HARPER'S WEEKLY
October 28, 1871, p. 1005

We give on this page the portrait of Mr. Octavius V. Catto, a worthy colored citizen of Philadelphia, who was shot by a ruffian on the night of the late election in that city. He was master of the Institute for Colored Youth, and was highly esteemed by all who knew him. Shortly after three o'clock on election day, having closed his school, he was quietly proceeding homeward, when he was rudely accosted by a white man, who leveled a pistol at his head. Mr. Catto endeavored to pass on, taking advantage of the shelter afforded by a passing street-car, but was again accosted by the same ruffian, who then fired at him three times. One ball took effect in his left breast, passing through the heart; another struck him in the left shoulder. He fell immediately. Several citizens carried him into a station-house, where he died a few minutes afterward. Mr. Catto was a quiet, well-educated man, and the murder was entirely unprovoked.

THE CONVENTION OF COLORED CITIZENS

HARPER'S WEEKLY
November 18, 1871, p. 1074

The recent convention of the colored people of the Southern States, in Columbia, South Carolina, was notable and interesting as another demonstration of the earnest wish of that class of citizens to promote the best understanding of their feelings and purposes. In a little pamphlet called "Indices," which Mr. Sinclair Tousey has recently published, containing many brief papers indicating the current of patriotic feeling during the war and just after it, there is a letter of Mr. H. J. Raymond in reply to one from Mr. Tousey, in which Mr. Raymond said, "The interest of any one class, black or white, whatever might be their condition, would always be of secondary interest to me." Mr. Raymond meant nothing unkind. He thought that the objections to class legislation, as it is called, covered the question of special care of the freedmen, and that they must take their chance with the rest. But the abnormal condition of that class, which had been produced by the government, rightfully demanded, and for the highest reasons of justice and the public welfare, that there should be a special treatment, and that fact was recognized in the continuance of the Freedmen's Bureau.

Since that time the special care has ceased, but the peculiar hardship of the colored population has contin-

1871

President Grant and Why They Don't Like Him.

- He won't let me steal — THE POLITICIAN.
- Daily Calumniator. He won't give me all the best offices.
- He won't let us bull gold. U.S. GOLD.
- He makes me pay my taxes. U.S.C.
- He won't let me hang niggers. THE KU-KLUX.
- He won't let us destroy the Union. CONSTITUTION OF THE UNITED STATES NORTH SOUTH.
- He killed the Copperheads. DEMOCRACY.

THE DEBT HAS BEEN DIMINISHED, TAXATION REDUCED, THE UNION RESTORED, FOREIGN DIFFICULTIES SETTLED, AND THE GOVERNMENT WAS NEVER SO RESPECTED NOR SO STRONG AT HOME.

HOWARD

Harper's Weekly, September 16, 1871, p. 873.

OCTAVIUS V. CATTO.—[PHOTOGRAPHED BY MESSRS. BROADBENT & PHILLIPS, PHILADELPHIA.]

Harper's Weekly, October 28, 1871, p. 1005.

ued. The great truth of their position is well stated in the report of their Columbia convention. After saying that they do not ask to be treated with peculiar favor, the report continues. "While we have, as a body, contributed our labor in the past to enhance the wealth and promote the welfare of the community, we have, as a class, been deprived of the acquisition of labor and experience, the return that civilization makes for the labor of the individual." It is a cruel injustice to forget this. The slaves were freed in the midst of war. They had no education, no money, no land. They were ignorant and dependent children, and their old masters regarded them bitterly as the cause of their humiliation, and the living monuments of the Yankee triumph. The black codes at the end of the war showed what the feeling was toward them; and against every kind of opposition, despised and contemned, they began their exodus from slavery and degradation toward the promised land of civilization and equality.

That they have borne themselves well, no one will deny. That, with every disadvantage and discouragement, the slaves of yesterday have shown themselves to be citizens more orderly and valuable than the majority of the master race that sneered at them, is indisputable. That to-day the anarchy which undermines society in many of the Southern States is not due to them, but to the "enlightened" and "conservative" and "superior" master class, is notorious. Indeed, they are the objects of the malignant hatred of the Ku-Klux. The "chivalry" that sold babes and mothers at the auction block now wreaks its expiring vengeance upon the colored race because of its loyalty to the government that gave it freedom. One of the Ku-Klux, whom the late action of the government persuaded to surrender himself, said that an order one day came to him and others to take out a certain negro and shoot him. The victim was tied to a sapling, and the man who told the story begged for his life as he would have asked for that of a favorite dog. But it was useless, and the negro was shot: and the man who vainly tried to save him told the story as coolly as if he had been describing the drowning of a day-old kitten.

Every colored man in those States knows that if he conspicuously aids the party which the old master class hates as that of its victors, he is in peril of his life. We have heard enough in authentic ways to satisfy us that the situation is not exaggerated. And in the midst of it all the colored people gravely and calmly ask by their representatives in convention that they, in common with the laboring whites, may have such facilities of education as Congress may upon inquiry think expedient, and they invoke the aid of the American people to destroy the prejudice which excludes them from an equal chance in the various mechanical industries. And knowing that every race suffers when any part of it is degraded, they pray that the influence of the country may be directed to the abolition of slavery wherever it lingers.

Naturally the convention asked a word from Charles Sumner, which he gladly sent. He urged the colored people to insist always and every where upon their equal rights, guaranteed by law. He said, "It is in vain to teach equality if you do not practice it." It is well said, and it indicates the duty of every honorable man to do what he can to destroy the prejudice. If public opinion permitted the same kind of discrimination against any other class of equal citizens that it tolerates against this, the sentiment of justice would be obscured, and equality become a name. If, for instance, the Irish or the Germans were excluded from hotels and schools and public conveyances because they were Germans or Irish, the stigma could not fail to hurt them and to harm the rest of us. It would introduce and perpetuate the feeling of caste, which is cruel to a class and fatal to popular government. That feeling is the great foe of the colored population. They are conscious of it, as the appeal of their Southern convention shows. And every honest white American citizen will help to dispel it.

THE SOUTHERN STATES

HARPER'S WEEKLY
December 23, 1871, p. 1194

The President says that "the condition of the Southern States is, unhappily, not such as all true patriotic citizens

CHRISTMAS IN VIRGINIA—A PRESENT FROM THE GREAT HOUSE.—[Drawn by W. L. Sheppard.]

Harper's Weekly, December 30, 1871, p. 1220.

would like to see." It is, in fact, what such citizens sincerely dislike to see. But the problem is not so simple as some intelligent critics assume. Of course the talk of the old guard of slavery about the frightful overthrow of liberty in those States by the "ignoble incubus" and "usurper," whom they used to call with the same propriety "butcher," troubles the country very little. It sustains him by increasing majorities, wisely deeming liberty somewhat safer with those who abolished slavery than with those who strove to perpetuate it. There is a very plain logic upon this subject in the American mind; and the Democratic critics, although too dull to see it, would yet help their cause by changing their point and method of assault.

We say that the problem is not simple. When the war ended we were of those who thought the better policy was to maintain for some time the complete national supremacy in the Southern States. But another policy prevailed, and we have to deal with its results. There were three classes of persons in those States—the old slave-holding proprietors, the poor whites, and the freedmen. The first two classes had been rebels, and the last had been honestly loyal. The first class comprised the persons of property and education, the traditional political leaders; the other two classes were ignorant and poor. The state of feeling was, of course, deplorable. The old proprietors and the poor whites were morbid with hate of the Yankee, and bitterly humiliated by their defeat. The easy contempt of the first for the late slaves had changed into a feeling of aversion, and a resolution, which was not surprising, to do what was possible still to hold them as inferiors. The jealousy which the poor whites felt for a class from which they were separated only by caste became hatred when caste disappeared.

The first attempt of the proprietary class was to recover political control of their States, and to remand the freedmen to virtual slavery. This could not be allowed; and by laws of prohibition, of disfranchisement, and ineligibility on the one hand, and of equal civil and political rights upon the other, it was defeated. The operation of these laws was necessarily deplorable in many ways, but the alternative was still more deplorable. Political power was taken from the old proprietors and given to the new men; but had it remained with the old proprietors, the condition of the new men would unquestionably have been such that the United States could not have tolerated it, and would have peremptorily changed the situation. Indeed, that was really very much the course of events, the original settlement being milder than that which followed. The Ku-Klux was, as the *Nation* says, naturally developed from this situation. Hate of the victorious Union, and of the freedmen who represented it, with the indignation at laws which were believed to submit the whites to the blacks, took expression in secret conspiracies which aimed at the control of the blacks and their friends by terror; and in certain parts of the Southern States the Ku-Klux has unquestionably produced anarchy.

Meanwhile the disabilities have been gradually removed, and the President now suggests that they be made to disappear entirely. But in the degree that this has taken place the situation has become worse in the Southern States. It is alleged that the exclusion of part of the old proprietary class from political power and from office has thrown the conduct of affairs into the hands of ignorant knaves, white adventurers, and ductile blacks. But the number of those actually disfranchised has long been very small, and the explanation does not suffice. Then it is said that where knaves legislate we must expect the Ku-Klux, and that it is useless to hunt the Ku-Klux if honest men do not control the government. But is it gravely meant that the United States must patiently see its citizens harried, whipped, murdered, and terrorized in certain States until honest men are elected to office there? If the difficulty is that there are dishonest and ignorant men in the Legislature, and if disabilities are removed and there is equal suffrage, so that the ordinary chances of a free government are provided for all, must honest citizens submit to be scourged and shot upon the plea that where Legislatures are corrupt public disorders must be expected? What can any honest citizen, white or black, do except vote for honest representatives? And if he and his friends can not carry the election, are they to be murdered because they have not been successful, while the United States tranquility remark that the principles of free government require the sacrifice?

Nothing more preposterous can be imagined. If the old proprietors and the poor whites, all disabilities being removed, can elect honest officers, we shall all rejoice; but if they can not, they really must not expect to be allowed to shoot their political opponents. We have long favored the completion of amnesty. But amnesty has been for some time practically a fact, and it will be found that the completion will not remove the trouble: it will remove only one of the excuses of the trouble. A wise government will avoid every reasonable pretense for disorder; it will do what it can to secure equal rights; and it will then take care that disorder is not tolerated.

PERSONAL

HARPER'S WEEKLY
December 30, 1871, p. 1219

There are five colored members of the House of Representatives: De Large, Rainey, and Elliott, of South Carolina; Turner, of Alabama; and Walls, of Florida.

1872

The year 1872 began much the way 1871 ended as the attention of journalists was focused on the Ku-Klux Klan. In 1871 most of the coverage was on the Ku-Klux Bill in Congress and in 1872 the focus was on prosecution of Klan members. Newspapers such as Harper's Weekly had continually deplored the crimes committed by the Ku-Klux Klan. In January 1872, Harper's reported on events in North Carolina:

> "At the end of September ten noted gentlemen, among who was Mr. Bragg, former Governor and Senator of the State, wrote to Judge Bond, asking that the further prosecution of those who were charged with Ku-Klux offenses should be postponed until November. These gentlemen admit that 'the fact that a secret, unlawful organization called the Ku-Klux, or Invisible Empire exists in certain parts of the State has been manifested in the recent trials before the court over which you preside.'"

Conservatives who had previously turned a blind eye to the activities of the Klan were now willing to "enlist the 'law-loving citizens' to suppress the organization." Questions were raised as to whether they would even try or what means they would use to suppress the activities of the Klan. Later during the year the Charleston Daily Courier published a plea from the Grand Jury of Chester County, South Carolina, to "His Excellency, the President of the United States" for a pardon for Ku-Klux members "in prison abroad, under sentence of violating the Enforcement Act of Congress."

While a great deal of attention was focused on the Klan, journalists were also preoccupied with the upcoming presidential election in the fall of 1872. Conservatives, who were largely Democrats, together with the Ku-Klux Klan, continuously worked to defeat Reconstruction and the

Republicans. President Grant faced a strong reelection challenge from Horace Greely, editor of the New York Tribune. Although Greely had joined the Republican party in 1854 and had been an abolitionist, he ran as the nominee of the Liberal Party, which was endorsed by the Democrats. Greely ran on a platform of civil service reform and called for an end to Reconstruction. Debates in the news focused on whether voters could trust Greely to remain committed to Reconstruction, suffrage, and equal rights, particularly for African Americans. Harper's Weekly (20 July 1872) reported:

> "...the present policy of the Democratic candidate for Presidency, to take the Democratic tone in speaking of Reconstruction. It says that the chief offices in the Southern States 'were the prizes of conquest that fell right to the disbanded army, and the Southern people were to be treated as idiots and children who must be taken care of by their betters. . . .'"

An ardent supporter of equal rights for African Americans, Senator Charles Sumner came out in support of Greely's presidential bid after African American voters asked him which candidate would support their "political and social rights." Journalists questioned how African Americans could possibly believe the conversion of the Democratic party to equal rights as the Democratic party supported "black codes." Southern legislatures enacted the codes to limit freedmen's economic and social opportunities. The codes included requiring African Americans to sign yearly labor contracts, declaring unemployed blacks vagrants available to be hired out to white landowners, and apprenticing black children to white employers without consent.

A minor campaign issue had to do with free public education. Harper's Weekly (3 August 1872) reported, "not over one-third of the people of the South could read and write, and perhaps even a less proportion. Four million of the colored race were forbidden by law to learn any thing—a law the most odious and unnatural known to the history of man." President Grant established an education system in the South to remedy this condition.

Journalists also continued the discussion of amnesty for Civil War supporters. The issue of general amnesty had continually surfaced after the war—it comprised a general forgiveness by the federal government for those who had supported the Confederacy and a waiver from prosecution for the rebellion. In May 1872 Congress passed a general amnesty, excepting people such as senators and congressmen from the Thirty-seventh Congress, judges, military officers, and other governmental personnel who had supported the Confederacy.

The close of 1872 was fraught with controversy in Louisiana.

The political firestorm began when the lieutenant governor died while in office and Pinckney Benton Stewart Pinchback, president pro tem of the state senate, won the battle for the office. Pinchback, the son of a free woman of mixed ancestry and a white planter, was vaulted into a larger struggle when the governor, Henry Warmoth, was impeached by the legislature. Warmoth claimed William Kellogg, in supporting Pinchback, wanted to turn the state over to "Negro control."

The controversy went through the courts before finally being settled in December, when U.S. Attorney General George Williams wrote to Pinchback informing him the president recognized him as the "lawful executive of Louisiana." Pinchback served as governor for five weeks. The Charleston Daily Courier *(16 December 1872) quoted the* New Orleans Times *as reporting:*

". . . a vicious and depraved mulatto, a former waiter or scullion in the low gambling den, was foisted into the seat once occupied by Claiborne, a Robertson, a Roman and a Meuton. It was by virtue of that maudlin signature that a Legislature, composed largely or brutal negroes, was called into existence to rule a State, founded by the chivalry of France and nourished into wealth and power by the best representatives of the Caucassian race!"

William Kellogg, who had supported Pinchback, ran for the governorship and won. The Democratic challenger, John McEnery, was supported by Warmoth, the impeached Republican governor.

Robert L. Harris, Jr.
Cornell University

KU-KLUX IN NORTH CAROLINA

HARPER'S WEEKLY
January 6, 1872, p. 2

Those who have sneered at the assertion of the existence of the Ku-Klux, or who have excused it upon the ground that in so disturbed a region and under such miserable governments there must be some kind of voluntary organization against offenders, will be interested in the correspondence between certain prominent citizens of North Carolina and Judge Bond. At the end of September ten noted gentlemen, among whom was Mr. Bragg, former Governor and Senator of the State, wrote to Judge Bond, asking that the further prosecution of those who were charged with Ku-Klux offenses should be postponed until November. These gentlemen admit that "the fact that a secret, unlawful organization called the Ku-Klux, or Invisible Empire, exists in certain parts of the State has been manifested in the recent trials before the court over which you preside." They denounce them, and declare it to be the duty of all good citizens to suppress them, adding that no man can deny or palliate their crimes. If the trials were adjourned, they thought that they could enlist all good citizens to make an earnest effort to restore good order, and obliterate an evil which brings nothing but calamity. They conclude by solemnly protesting that the violations of order and justice must cease.

The judge, in reply, thanked them for their letter, but as the city was full of witnesses who had been staying at large cost, and could not properly be required to go home and return with nothing done to make their journey safe, he declines to postpone the trials. He adds, that gentlemen who have expressed so warm a wish to relieve North Carolina of so disgraceful and infamous an association will not remit their labors to suppress it because the Court sits for a week or two longer to help them. The letter of the eminent gentlemen, however, proposes an extraordinary method of dealing with what they call criminals. If the courts will close, they think that they can enlist the "law-loving citizens" to suppress the organization. But whether they will try, if the Court does not postpone the trials, or by what means outside of the law they intend to deal with the criminals, they do not say.

There is but one presumption from such a letter. The Ku-Klux is an organization of political terrorism. Its crimes and the calamities it causes are undeniable. But these gentlemen believe that they can prevail upon the criminals to stop. They must intend to prevail by moral suasion. But could they hope to prevail except upon members of their own party? and all the gentlemen are Democrats. It is foolish to deny in the presence of such facts that there is a Ku-Klux, and that it is a political organization to prevent, by terror, by scourging, and murder, the exercise of their political rights by Republican citizens. And why, it would be interesting to know, have ex-Senator Bragg, and Attorney-General Shipp, and ex-minister to Spain Barringer, and ex-Judge Battle, and the other gentlemen who sign—why have they waited until there was some prospect of bringing offenders to justice before they began their efforts to suppress the crimes of organizations so notorious every where else in the country? and why do they make the suspension of the trials the condition of their efforts? Or was the first knowledge which these gentlemen had of the Ku-Klux derived from the trials? The President was upon the point of enforcing the law against the criminals before these worthy gentlemen had discovered that there was any trouble. They found, fortunately, however, that in writing to Judge Bond they were not writing to the marines. The judge, in the excellent Irish phrase, was able for them; and promised to their vigorous efforts to suppress the "Invisible Empire" the support of his court. How far, as Artemus Ward might have said, these excellent gentlemen have got in their suppression does not appear. But, jesting aside, if such gentlemen are in earnest, and every where in the Southern States would, in their words, "use all the means in our power to absolutely suppress this organization," they would show a spirit which they might be very sure would be recognized and appreciated every where.

EQUAL RIGHTS

HARPER'S WEEKLY
January 20, 1872, pp. 50–51

Senator Sumner, whose life and powers have been so largely consecrated to the elevation of the colored race to an equality before the law with all other races, will undoubtedly press his supplementary Civil Rights bill with all his customary tenacity in a good cause, nor do we see why Republican Senators should oppose it. It is strictly the completion of the Civil Rights bill of 1866. There are, however, two classes of objectors: those who think that it compels every body to associate with colored people; and those who think that under existing laws the colored citizen has the same rights and resources with all other citizens. A story will dispose of the first objection, which is the more common and powerful. A New Englander was talking with a Virginian of the proposition of Senator Sumner, and the Virginian was troubled by what he supposed was a law to force disagreeable guests upon his table, if not worse. The New Englander replied that he thought there was no just ground of fear; that Irishmen had long been upon perfect equality with every body else in his State, but that he had never been obliged to chum with a hod-carrier in his life. Social equality is not to be determined by law, nor does Senator Sumner propose it. He proposes that the equality before the law which we profess shall be secured to every citizen.

The original Civil Rights bill provides that all persons born in the United States, and not subject to any foreign power, excluding Indians not taxed, shall have in every State and Territory the same rights with white citizens to inherit, hold, and convey property, to give evidence, and to the full and equal benefit of all laws and proceedings for the benefit of persons and property. The statute is limited by its definitions, but its object and spirit are unmistakable. They are to provide perfect equality in all the rights which are regulated by law. Elsewhere, possibly—in England, for instance, where the Somerset decision was rendered—it might be safely supposed that the law would be most generously interpreted in its just spirit. But in this country, where the prejudice arising from slavery must long survive the extinction of slavery, it is most desirable to define precisely and to guard securely that equality before the law which it is the constant tendency of the tradition of slavery to despise and disregard. It is by no means clear that the courts under an act worded like the original Civil Rights act would defend every right, and it is to remove that uncertainty that Senator Sumner introduced his bill.

It declares that all citizens are entitled to the equal enjoyment of every accommodation furnished by common carriers, by innkeepers, by managers of public entertainments licensed by law, by the officers of common schools and other institutions of learning, by the trustees of church organizations, cemetery associations, and benevolent institutions, and provides that the right shall not be denied or abridged on any pretense of color or previous condition of servitude. And the fifth section of the act provides that every law, State or national, which discriminates against any person by the use of the word white, is repealed and annulled. Actions are to be brought in the United States courts; and any person convicted of violating the law shall be fined not less than five hundred nor more than one thousand dollars, and shall be imprisoned not less than thirty days, nor more than a year; and any chartered body so convicted shall forfeit its charter.

This is simply the completion of the original Civil Rights bill. If that was right, this is right; and if that was right, it is a halting and defective right without this. All that the supplementary bill states is implied in the original bill; and every argument that justified that confirms this. It is the one act of legislation necessary to finish and round the civil work of the war. When this is accomplished, all that law can do for the race so long oppressed by the acquiescence of law is done. What remains of unjust and belittling hostility will slowly disappear before a more and more enlightened public opinion. But as long as we hesitate or fail amply to secure the equal right of every citizen, rich or poor, white or colored, so long we discredit our manhood and disgrace our national principle.

THE KU-KLUX

HARPER'S WEEKLY
January 27, 1872, p. 73

We give on this page an illustration, engraved from a photograph from life, showing three members of a band of Mississippi Ku-Klux, who are now under indictment in that State for the attempted murder of a family by the name of Hunicutt. These men were captured last September in Tishamingo County, Mississippi, by G. W. Wells, United States Attorney for the Northern District of that State, assisted by United States Marshal J. H. Pierce, and his deputy, John M'Coy. The illustration is doubly interesting as showing the disguises actually worn by these miscreants. They are not, however, always so elaborate in their brigand toilet. A white blanket or sheet thrown over the head, with holes for the eyes, is usually sufficient.

It is gratifying to know that the government is putting forth efficient exertions to bring to justice these miscreants in every part of the South troubled by their presence. While there is evidence that the better portion of the Southern people discountenance the outrages committed by the Ku-Klux bands, it is no less evident that nothing short of the most energetic and summary measures on the part of the general government can bring them to an end, and give protection to peaceful citizens, black and white. The outrages committed in Kentucky, Mississippi, and the Carolinas by these brigands are too notorious for denial. In the recent trials at Columbia, South Carolina, one of the counsel for the prisoners, the Hon. Reverdy Johnson, felt compelled by the evidence to use this extraordinary language toward his own clients:

"Neither my distinguished friend Mr. Stanbery nor myself are here to defend, or justify, or palliate any outrages that may have been perpetrated in your State by the association of Ku-Klux. *I have listened with horror to some of the testimony which has been brought before you. The outrages proved have been shocking to humanity; they admit neither of justification nor excuse; they violate every obligation which law and nature impose upon men.* These men appear to have been alike insensible to the obligations of humanity and religion; but the day will come, however, if it has not already arrived, when they will deeply lament it. Even if justice should not overtake them, there is another tribunal from which there is no escape. It is their own conscience, that tribunal which sits in the breast of every living man, that still small voice that thrills through the heart, and as it speaks gives happiness or torture—the voice of conscience—the voice of God."

Had this language come from the lips of a "Federal judge" or a "military satrap," it might have been characterized as exaggerated, or suspected of violent partisanship; but forced by irresistible evidence from the lips of the prisoners' own counsel, it must be accepted as conclusive testimony to the truth of the charges against these lawless disturbers of the South.

Recent intelligence from Kentucky shows that the government can not be too prompt and energetic in its measures of protection. On the night of the 2d inst. a band of twenty Ku-Klux made a raid upon some negroes near Frankfort, in that State, whipping one of them and ordering the others to leave the neighborhood on pain of death. One farmer was warned to employ none but white laborers. It is the declared purpose of these outlaws to drive the negroes from the county. But the day is past when such threats can be carried out. These outlaws will speedily be taught that the government will protect peaceable citizens in the full enjoyment of their rights, life, and property, if it takes the whole military power of the nation to do it.

WOOD-SELLERS IN RICHMOND

HARPER'S WEEKLY
January 27, 1872, pp. 73–74

Mr. Sheppard's characteristic sketches in the Richmond markets will remind the traveled reader of almost similar scenes in European cities, especially those of Italy, where the smaller industries have not yet been superseded by organized capital. There is something quaint and primitive in these figures. They give Northern eyes a glimpse of quite a different life from the bustling, busy existence which we are accustomed to behold. These poor people, black and white, must make a shift to live. They do a little farming, a little fishing, a little hunting,

MISSISSIPPI KU-KLUX IN THE DISGUISES IN WHICH THEY WERE CAPTURED
[FROM A PHOTOGRAPH.]

Harper's Weekly, January 27, 1872, p. 73.

and when they want a trifle of money they cut a little wood and take it to some town for sale. Some of them make long journeys of ten or fifteen miles to dispose of a few shillings' worth of wood or a basket of vegetables.

But these characteristics of Southern life are gradually disappearing with other remnants of slavery and the war. As fast as the disturbing elements give way before the establishment of civil order, the industry of the South will find itself elevated to a higher position than it ever held in the most palmy days of the old plantation regime. It rests with the South itself to say whether this shall be a rapid or a slow process. Let civil order be maintained every where, the Ku-Klux bands dispersed, and the immigration of thrifty and industrious farmers and artisans encouraged, and a new order of things will soon prevail.

THE FIRST RESPONSE TO THE CINCINNATI CALL

HARPER'S WEEKLY
February 24, 1872, p. 155

A significant sign of the times is the adoption by the Democratic Convention of Connecticut of two resolutions of the Missouri "Liberal Republicans." But the Connecticut platform and the proceedings are of a very different character from those of the same party during the war, when all its energies and eloquence were devoted to paralyzing the efforts of the Government. There is no consciousness of life or power in this latest manifesto. It begins by declaring that the Democrats of Connecticut regard emancipation and the equality of civil rights as established facts, although the Democrats of Connecticut have always done their best to prevent their becoming so. They "repudiate with scorn" the idea that the Democracy of Connecticut are in favor of repudiating any portion of the public debt, although the Democracy of Connecticut at the last national convention of their party acquiesced in virtual repudiation. The Democracy of Connecticut are also anxious for the people to rise and sweep selfish men from power.

If those people, in Connecticut or elsewhere, who during the war did what they could, without taking up arms, to destroy the Union, who before the war labored to perpetuate and extend slavery, and who since the war have striven to retain all of the consequences of slavery possible, have at last seen that their course was un-American and inhuman, it is good both for them and for the country. But their case presents two considerations. It is just possible that they are not so much persuaded of their error as of the necessity of seeming to be so persuaded, in order to recover power. If that be so, the fleece of the sheep is not large enough. If, on the other hand, they are really convinced that their policy has been wrong, upon what grounds do they ask for public confidence or for preference over those who have done what Democrats themselves now confess to be right?

The Democrats of Connecticut say that they recognize emancipation and equality of civil rights as established facts; but at the very moment in which they spoke the Democratic Senators in Congress were refusing to guarantee the protection of those rights. What security could the people of the United States possibly have that the Democrats would carefully guard rights which they have always despised, and for defending which the Republicans rose to power? That will be the omnipresent question in the campaign now opening. That is the question for all "Liberal Republicans" to consider. That is the question, as we said last week, which those who are invited to Cincinnati are morally bound to weigh.

The Democrats retain their name and their organization. They assent formally to incontestable facts. But they are the same men, with the same traditions and the same convictions, with whom the loyal men of this country have constantly dealt since 1860. If they have truly repented, let us all rejoice. But let us also reflect a little upon human nature and history before we insist that what are flippantly called "old issues" have wholly passed away, and that, therefore, a victory which the Ku-Klux would hail is desirable for the country.

DOMESTIC INTELLIGENCE

HARPER'S WEEKLY
February 24, 1872, p. 155

In the House of Representatives, February 5, the validity of the Thirteenth, Fourteenth, and Fifteenth amendments was indorsed by a heavy vote.

VISIT OF THE KU-KLUX

HARPER'S WEEKLY
February 24, 1872, p. 157

The artist, on page 160, pictures an outrage of frequent occurrence in some of the most turbulent districts of the Southern States. The scene is the interior of a negro cabin, where the little family—fearing no evil—is gathered after the work of the day is over. Suddenly the door is opened, and a member of the Ku-Klux Klan appears, with gun in hand, to take the life of the harmless old man who sits at the fire-place, and whose only "crime" is his color. It is to be hoped that under a rigorous administration of the laws these deeds of violence will soon cease forever.

THE KU-KLUX REPORTS

HARPER'S WEEKLY
March 9, 1872, p. 187

Both the minority and majority reports upon the Ku-Klux in the Southern States leave no doubt whatever of the actual situation in that part of the country. The minority or Democratic report enlarges upon the corruption of the governments and the condition of society, and there is an unpleasant suggestion of justification of much of the violence in that region as necessitated by the conduct of the government. A frank and manly confession of the fact that in many parts of those States fidelity to the Union is an offense not to be forgotten or forgiven would have been better than the attempted plea. If the crimes are exaggerated, there are nevertheless crimes, and of the most atrocious kind. They are directed against a certain class, both white and colored, the distinction of which is its loyalty. The object of the Ku-Klux is both revenge and intimidation. Those who were true to the government must pay for it, and those who would sustain the party that saved the country must be prevented from voting.

"The men in the South who stood by the government," said one of the most eminent of them recently, "have had a hard fate." There was a pathos in his words which these reports explain. The old hatreds and passions are not readily extirpated, and for many a year the bitter memories of the war will disturb the States upon which its hand fell heaviest. The majority report, the conclusions of which are amply sustained by the evidence, recommends amnesty. It will be the removal of the last pretext of complaint. The rest is the natural and inevitable result of the social convulsion, which the dominant sentiment of those States invited. The duty of the government meanwhile is plain. It is to defend the rights of all citizens of the United States, and to defend them effectively, and to show that rage and fury can not prevail against the national purpose. It must endure to be called a despotism. But the men, whether in the Northern or the Southern States, who so describe the policy which has required no executions, no fines, no imprisonments, no vindictive confiscations, show only the impotent malice of mere party spirit.

WOOD-SELLERS, RICHMOND, VIRGINIA.—[Drawn by W. L. Sheppard.]

Harper's Weekly, January 27, 1872, p. 73.

DOMESTIC INTELLIGENCE

HARPER'S WEEKLY
March 9, 1872, p. 187

The Richmond (Virginia) City Railroad Company have resolved to permit negroes to ride in all their cars hereafter....

The State Republican Convention of South Carolina met at Columbia, February 19, to nominate delegates to the National Republican Presidential Convention. Nearly 200 delegates were present, nearly four-fifths of whom were negroes. Of the fourteen delegates chosen, seven were white and seven colored. Governor Orr was among the number. The platform heartily indorsed the administration of President Grant, thanked Congress for the Ku-Klux act, and advocated civil rights measures and general amnesty.

PERSONAL

HARPER'S WEEKLY
March 16, 1872, p. 203

President Roberts, recently inaugurated President of Liberia under the new constitution, received a good common-school education at Fredericksburg, Virginia, and went to Monrovia in 1829. He was appointed

Governor of Liberia by the American Colonization Society in 1841. In 1847 he was elected the first President. In 1861 he was appointed president of the Liberia College. He is a tall gentleman, dignified, affable, and intelligent.

DOMESTIC INTELLIGENCE

HARPER'S WEEKLY
March 16, 1872, p. 203

In the New York State Senate, February 26, a bill amending the military law by striking out the word "white," so as to make negroes liable for duty, was passed to a third reading.

THE FIFTEENTH AMENDMENT

HARPER'S WEEKLY
April 20, 1872, p. 308

The 3d of April, the anniversary of the passage of the Fifteenth Amendment, was celebrated by our colored fellow-citizens throughout the country. In this city the display was remarkably fine; the procession contained over 3000 persons, and the streets were thronged by interested spectators. Among the most noticeable features was the Colfax Club, the members of which were handsomely dressed, and mounted on fine horses. The largest organization was the Saloon Men's Association, who mustered in great force, and immediately became the cynosure of all eyes, and were heartily cheered. The Willett Pioneer Club was also a feature in the procession. The members wore tall bear-skin hats. There was a large wagon draped with American flags, drawn by four horses, in which were seated fifteen little girls tastefully dressed in blue and white. The tallest stood in the centre and represented the Goddess of Liberty. A large escort of police accompanied the procession along the whole route; but the rowdy element in our population has learned that all classes of citizens are under the protection of our laws; and there was no necessity to repeat the lesson. The procession had an undisturbed march through the streets, and made an excellent impression.

THE COLORED CITIZENS

HARPER'S WEEKLY
May 11, 1872, p. 363

The Convention of colored citizens at New Orleans was a significant assembly, and, immediately followed as it was by the celebration in Washington of the tenth anniversary of emancipation in the District of Columbia, furnishes the means of ascertaining the political tendencies of the new citizens. The New Orleans platform very plainly expresses the conviction that "as all roads out of the Republican party lead into the Democratic camp, we pledge our unswerving devotion to support the nominee of the Philadelphia Convention." It also contains an exuberant and glowing tribute to the services of Senator Sumner, and of gratitude to President Grant and to Vice-President Colfax. Beside this declaration of continued fidelity to the Republican party and its Administration and leaders, there is also a solemn appeal to the country in favor of the Civil Rights bill, which simply removes the last lingering inequality before the law. Social relations must settle themselves. They are not the creation of law. But there can be no excuse for the abuses to which these equal citizens are subject.

The members of the Convention pronounced against all who voted for the defeat of the Civil Rights bill, and pledged their efforts to elect successors more favorable to equality. But while they declared their unshaken fidelity to the Republican party, they did not insist upon the incorporation of civil rights in the platform at Philadelphia as the condition of their support. This was wisely done; for while there will undoubtedly be a strong feeling in the Convention favorable to including the substance of the bill in the platform, the proposition may fail, and it would be very foolish for that reason to do any thing for the advantage of the heredity enemies of all the rights of the colored race. Indeed, it is a mistake to make the support of a party which is preferable upon all general grounds depend upon its adoption of a single measure, and all the more when that measure is one which the party is sure presently to sustain. Mr. Frederick Douglass very truly said in his speech that the colored citizens owed their gratitude to the nation, not to the States; and that the Cincinnati movement should be suspected because its force must be derived from those who, under the plea of State rights, had so long degraded his race.

The day after the New Orleans platform was adopted was a holiday in the District of Columbia. The sun shone brightly, and about noon the procession passed before the White House. It was a marvelous spectacle. The city was Washington, which, twelve years ago, in that same White House, Democratic conspirators in possession of the government were plotting to make the capital of a slave empire. And now, amidst inspiring peals of patriotic music, band following band,

VISIT OF THE KU-KLUX.—Drawn by Frank Bellew.—[See Page 157.]

Harper's Weekly, February 24, 1872, p. 160.

marched long columns of the late enslaved race, trained soldiers of the most manly bearing; and the President of the United States—the great captain in the war which gave them their manhood and the nation its salvation—stood, surrounded by his cabinet, and modestly saluted them as they passed by. It was all festival and joy. But nine years ago, at Wagner, at Fort Pillow, and in how many unknown spots and untold ways, the same race were bravely charging and dying, or faithfully guiding and concealing their friends, helping the quiet man before whom their brethren were now gayly marching to win his great victory. It was a spectacle never to be forgotten. No man who saw it, and who had taken any part in the political movements which restored their long-lost manhood to a race, but must have resolved anew not to rest until the great political organization which proposed to rob them of that manhood forever was as effectually vanquished and dispersed as the armies of the rebellion.

Later in the day an immense crowd was addressed by Mr. Elliott, a colored Representative in Congress from South Carolina. The poetic justice was complete. Mr. Elliott responded to the words and to the convictions of Mr. Douglass at New Orleans:

> "If the Republican party goes down, freedom goes down with it. But it will not go down, for it stands to-day triumphant, with a vast majority in nearly all the States, and with an unbroken front. Though personal dissensions may arise and widen our ranks temporarily, they will close up when the long roll of battle is sounded, and we will all march together to victory."

It is the well-grounded faith of the colored citizens that their friends are of the Republican party, and they may count upon the steady effort of those friends to secure the absolute equality of all citizens before the law.

PERSONAL

HARPER'S WEEKLY
May 11, 1872, p. 363

Robert B. Elliott, the colored member of Congress from South Carolina, was born in Massachusetts and educated in England. In 1853 he entered High Holborn Academy, in London, where he prepared for Eton College, which he entered in 1855, and graduated in 1859. He afterward studied law, and practices his profession. He was a member of the State Constitutional Convention in

LINCOLN, THE EMANCIPATOR.—[Drawn by C. S. Reinhart.]

Harper's Weekly, April 20, 1872, p. 308.

1868, a member of the Legislature of that State from 1868 to 1870, and Assistant Adjutant-General until elected to the present Congress. He is a ready speaker, and has none of the accent peculiar to his race. He has made a fortune within the past few years, lives in considerable style, drives a fine span of horses, and spends his money freely. —Mr. De Large, another colored member from the same State, is a short, olive-complexioned man, of not much talent, moderately educated, and a farmer. —Josiah T. Wallis, colored member from Florida, was born in Virginia thirty years ago, and claims to be a planter. He is conspicuous for neatness of apparel and stunning neck-ties. —Benjamin S. Surner, colored member from Alabama, is a large, broad-shouldered man, forty-seven years old, born a slave, educated himself clandestinely, and has some reputation among the Republicans for good sense and political sagacity.

NEGRO LIFE AT THE SOUTH

HARPER'S WEEKLY
May 18, 1872, p. 391

Mr. Sheppard's admirable sketches on page 388 exhibit two characteristic phases of negro life in the Southern States. In one there is the slave, apparently the property of a kind-hearted wealthy planter, whose mansion looms up in the distance. The day's work is over, the wife is preparing supper, and the old man sits down to cheer himself and the children a few minutes with some

Harper's Weekly, May 18, 1872, p. 388.

lively scraping on the fiddle. None of them appear to take any thought of the future or any interest in any thing but the music, with a thought, perhaps, on the coming supper.

The other sketch shows the effect of emancipation on the negro. He becomes another character; he wants to learn; his children go to school; and when the day's work is over they read the paper to him. In short, he has changed from a slave to a man.

PERSONAL

HARPER'S WEEKLY
June 8, 1872, p. 443

Judge Colt, of Pittsfield, Massachusetts, who recently returned from a Southern trip, visited a court in Charleston, South Carolina, where judge, jury, lawyers, and all were negroes, and engaged in trying a white man!

MR. GREELEY AND THE COLORED CITIZENS

HARPER'S WEEKLY
June 15, 1872, p. 467

In replying to a statement made by Mr. Voorhees, and in recommending Mr. Greeley to the support of the Democratic party, the *Tribune* shows that he is not favorable to Mr. Sumner's Civil Rights bill. Its little effort was timely, for it was made on the day after the Democrats in the House of Representatives had voted solidly even against Mr. Carpenter's bill, which Mr. Sumner called an emasculated substitute for his own. The coincidence and the fact we commend to the most thoughtful consideration of such original antislavery Republicans as may have been inclined to Cincinnati. They will not forget that Frederick Douglass, William Lloyd Garrison, Wendell Phillips, Gerrit Smith, and Henry Ward Beecher oppose Mr. Greenly as a candidate for the Presidency, and that Charles Sumner declined, notwithstanding the most powerful pressure, to declare for the Cincinnati movement, because he feared it might lead to the restoration of Democratic control of the government, which he knows would be most hostile to the chance of fair play for the race whose rights he has so long defended. It is plain, therefore, what these old antislavery chiefs think of the relations of Cincinnati to the prospects of the colored citizens.

The *Tribune*, in its effort to show that Mr. Greeley need not be unacceptable to the enemies of equal rights before the law, quotes from the speech which he made to the colored people in Poughkeepsie. Mr. Greeley, in that speech, hopes that the time will come when no man's color will exclude him from any kind of association with other people. But he says, "If the majority chose that the minority should be educated in separate schools, I would say, 'Gentlemen, be it as you please: I have no choice in the matter.'" The difficulty with this statement is, that upon the vital point it is not clear. Does Mr. Greeley mean that in a community which guarantees equal rights before the law he would favor laws for separate schools, or that he would leave the matter to individual taste? The latter is all that Mr. Sumner's bill contemplates. He would not have the law recognize color among citizens. That we have always understood to be Mr. Greeley's position also. But if it be, that is the very point to which Mr. Voorhees takes exception; and Mr. Greeley can escape the exception only by renouncing the principle.

However, as Mr. Greeley's career for nearly forty years has been one of uncompromising hostility to every cardinal principle and measure of the Democratic party, it is a waste of time for his supporters to attempt to show his agreement upon some detail. Yet it is none the less painful to see the New York *Tribune* commending Horace Greeley to the support of the life-long enemies of the colored race upon the plea that he is not so much their friend as some Democrat had represented, or in the particular way to which some Knight of the Golden Circle may have objected.

PERSONAL

HARPERS'S WEEKLY
June 15, 1872, p. 467

Colonel Forney, speaking of the intellectual progress of the colored man, says, "If you were to compare the chiefs of the freedmen with the chief slave-holders, knowing them as I do, you would soon realize that John M. Langston, Professor of the Law Department of the Howard University, is as thorough a lawyer as Pierre Soulé in his best days; that Robert Brown Elliott is a better scholar and speaker than Lawrence M. Keitt; and that Benjamin Sterling Turner, of Selma, Alabama, a self-educated slave, is as practical a business man as George S. Houston.

THE PRESIDENT AND THE COLORED CITIZENS

HARPER'S WEEKLY
June 22, 1872, pp. 482-83

It is stated in Mr. Sumner's speech that the President has never "exhibited to the colored people any true sympathy;" and in proof of this assertion Mr. Sumner quotes from the letter of the President to the meeting of the colored people at Washington in favor of equal civil rights. In that letter the President said: "I beg to assure you, however, that I sympathize most cordially in any effort to secure for all our people, of whatever race, nativity, and color, the exercise of those rights to which every citizen should be entitled." Mr. Sumner calls this "a meaningless juggle of words entirely worthy of the days of slavery," and says that, of course, every body is in favor of the rights to which every citizen should be entitled.

Mr. Sumner misquotes the President's words, and then calls them a meaningless juggle. The President does not say that he is in favor of the rights to which every citizen should be entitled. What he does say is that he cordially favors the exercise of the rights to which every citizen is entitled; and every citizen, under the Constitution, is equal. It is not easy to understand how Mr. Sumner avoided the plain and necessary meaning of the words. He quotes them in illustration of the President's want of sympathy with colored citizens; and he couples with them the treatment of Frederick Douglass by the President as another illustration. Yet of the very letter which Mr. Sumner quotes to alienate the colored people from the President Frederick Douglass's own paper, the *New National Era,* says: "We entirely misapprehend the character of the colored citizens, North and South, if they do not accept this letter as the fullest assurance that, so far as General Grant is concerned, they are certain to have their just and equal rights, whenever those rights can be secured to them by law. Abraham Lincoln said and did many good things while he was President of the United States, but nothing like this letter ever came to colored men even from him."

So the National Convention of colored men at New Orleans, while expressing its profound regard for Mr. Sumner, also resolved that "our thanks are due and hereby tendered to President Grant for overriding the precedents of prejudice in the better recognition of the services of men without regard to color." And at the same convention Frederick Douglass made the speech from which we have before quoted a remarkable figure, which is an argument in itself, "For colored men the Republican party is the deck—all outside is the sea," which was received with "tremendous enthusiasm." In the same speech Mr. Douglass stated his admiration and regard for Mr. Sumner, and said, "Messrs. Trumbull and

Schurz are falling back into the party of reaction.... They are honorable men. Nothing must be said against them for their past record; but they are upon a path that would lead the colored man to ruin.... All the laws and all the amendments can not protect the colored man if his enemies get control of the government;" and he declared that he should vote for General Grant. The speeches of the colored delegates to the Philadelphia Convention repeat the conviction and the determination of Mr. Douglass.

This is the instinct of every colored citizen. Since his speech was delivered Mr. Sumner was called upon by a deputation of colored voters. The *Tribune*'s dispatch says that he urged them to vote against Grant. But the music of Douglass's eloquence was ringing in their hearts. On one side they saw Grant and their life-long friends, on the other side Greeley and their life-long enemies. The Senator could not persuade them. "For colored men the Republican party is the deck—all outside is the sea."

DOMESTIC INTELLIGENCE

HARPER'S WEEKLY
June 22, 1872, p. 483

The Methodist General Conference adjourned finally June 4, after a session of five weeks. The last day was spent chiefly in discussing the question of separating the colored and white members of the denomination in the South. By an almost unanimous vote, however, it was decided to make no distinction of race or color in the Church. The decision was greeted with applause.

RECONSTRUCTION

HARPERS'S WEEKLY
July 20, 1872, p. 562

It is the present policy of the New York *Tribune*, in its support of a Democratic candidate for the Presidency, to take the Democratic tone in speaking of reconstruction. It says that the chief offices in the Southern States "were the prizes of conquest that fell by right to the disbanded army, and the Southern people were to be treated as idiots and children who must be taken care of by their betters.... The reconstruction and disfranchisement laws had all been framed under similar principles. The educated and experienced men of the South had been carefully excluded from places of trust," etc.

Now whatever the reconstruction laws were, they were zealously supported by the *Tribune;* and when, for his plain intention of thwarting the will of Congress in regard to the late rebel States, Andrew Johnson was impeached, no paper in the country was more indecently clamorous for his conviction than the *Tribune,* which did not hesitate virtually to charge Senator Trumbull with being bribed, sneered at Senator Fessenden, and compared Senator Grimes, one of the justest and purest of men, to Judas Iscariot receiving his thirty pieces. And last year, when the Ku-Klux laws, as they are called, were passed—laws of which "the South," that is, the late rebel element, complains most bitterly—the editor of the *Tribune,* Mr. Horace Greeley, said: "I therefore, on every proper occasion, advocated and justified the Ku-Klux act. I hold it especially desirable for the South; and if it does not prove strong enough to effect its purpose, I hope it will be made stronger and stronger." And the *Tribune* in May, 1870, said of the same act: "The law applies only to Presidential and Congressional elections, though we heartily wish it could be made to apply to all others." If the laws of which "the South" now complains are harsh and cruel, they are, nevertheless, laws for which, within its sphere, the New York *Tribune* is as responsible as Congress.

The facts in regard to the reconstruction laws are well known. There were two theories upon which they might have been founded. The late rebels might have been authorized to reconstruct their States; or Congress might have decided who should vote, and under what conditions. The latter course was adopted, and for the reason that it was perfectly evident that the power, exclusively confided to the white population, would be abused. Equal suffrage was a necessity. But there was nothing vindictive, cruel, or unjust in the laws as adopted. Indeed, not the least glory of the Republican party is its settlement of the results of the war which it had so triumphantly conducted and closed. It is charged with the unhappiness of much of the Southern section, but only as it was charged with deluging the South with blood. The responsibility of the war did not rest with the Republican party; nor is it guilty of the misfortunes that have followed. The black codes, the treachery of Andrew Johnson, the dangerous attitude of the Democratic party at the North, taught the necessity of vigorous and radical measures. But they were never revengeful; and as late as 1867 Thaddeus Stevens exclaimed, despondingly, "The punishment of traitors has been wholly ignored by a treacherous Executive and by a sluggish Congress."

There has been no man in that section criminally punished for a political offense; the equal suffrage of which complaint is made was necessitated by the conduct of those who make the complaint; the disfranchisement of certain classes was temporary, and to-day, with the exception of a few scores of chief rebels who are ineligible to office—an exception which has always seemed to us unwise—the people in the Southern States are upon an absolute equality with those in the other parts of the country. There is no hostile feeling upon the part of the Republican party toward any class in the Southern States; but there is a very profound conviction that the highest welfare of every part of the country requires that the government should still remain under the control of those who saved it. Equality being secured, the great necessity of the Southern section is tranquility and stability, that industry may revive and prosper. To this end, also, Republican success is essential. A Democratic victory would imperil not only the tranquility and stability, but the equality also.

GRANT AND EDUCATION

HARPER'S WEEKLY
August 3, 1872, pp. 593–94

One excellent result of the peaceful administration of General Grant has been the founding of a system of popular education at the South. Of all nations nominally civilized the Southern States, under the rule of the slave-holders, were the in most ignorant. Even Italy and Spain were progressive and enlightened compared to that utterly barbarous population that, spreading from the Potomac to the Rio Grande, formed the ruling section of the American Union. Not over one-third of the people of the South could read and write, and perhaps even a less proportion. Four millions of the colored race were forbidden by law to learn any thing—a law the most odious and unnatural known to the history of man. Of the whites the larger part were left in starting ignorance. It was admitted that they were often more degraded than the blacks. No teacher reached them; no schoolhouse cheered the pines of Georgia or the swamps of the Mississippi. The only education the poorer classes of the South received was gleaned from their coarse and barbarous politicians, who spoke to them at public meetings, who used the people as the instruments of their own misdeeds, and scoffed at their ignorance if not their simplicity; from the gross examples of corrupt slave-holders, and the degrading vices of a terrible oligarchy. Except in papal Rome, under its Jesuit rulers, there was no population within the limits of civilization that was so rigorously shut out from the light of modern progress as that which was inclosed within the domain of Jefferson Davis.

By a series of vigorous blows Grant and the Union armies broke down this dreadful barrier, and let in the sunlight of knowledge. Every barbarous law, every unnatural restriction upon the human intellect, faded away; and it is touching to notice with what eager and enthusiastic joy the colored race at least hailed the approach of the teacher. When in 1865 the United States troops took possession of Wilmington, North Carolina, it was announced at once that the teachers of the Freedmen's Bureau would meet the children at nine o'clock in the morning at the church vestry. By seven o'clock the church-yard and even the street were filled with the throng of parents bringing their children to be enrolled as scholars. One thousand pupils were soon provided; no age, sex, or color was excluded; and it was not long before a considerable proportion of the colored people of North Carolina were, for the first time, enabled to read the Bible. More than three centuries had passed since Luther had planted free schools in Germany, that its people might study the Scriptures. His example had at last conquered the barbarism of the South as well as that of papal Rome. In South Carolina the restrictions upon knowledge had begun even earlier than in its sister States. It was the fiercest of the enemies of the teacher. In 1740 it prohibited every person from teaching its slaves to read and write under heavy penalties; in 1800 it decreed twenty lashes to every slave or free negro who sought "mental instruction" from sunset to sunrise; but in 1834 it completed its guilty pre-eminence by imposing fines and heavy whippings upon the teachers and the taught, free or slave. This barbarous law was repealed alone by the Union armies. The teacher followed the soldier; schools sprang up at the first landing of the troops; and already a large part of the colored people of South Carolina are rising rapidly to an equality in general information with their former masters, if not to a plain superiority. Virginia, until 1860, had punished every attempt to educate the slave. In September, 1861, securely nestled beneath the guns of Fortress Monroe, not far from the spot where the first cargo of African slaves had been landed on our soil, sprang up a little school of freedmen, the first gleam of the new civilization that was to break over the South.

While the colored race thus eagerly seized upon the first opportunities for self-improvement, and even amidst the din and alarms of actual war learned spelling and writing, the white population of the rebellious States seem to have discovered, on the return of peace, that education was at least of some value, that it would be necessary for them to do something for the advance of knowledge. The crash of the Union guns had awakened notions of progress even in the swamps of Mississippi. The influence of Northern intelligence has made itself felt in distant Texas; and the colored legislators who, after Richmond fell, began to take part in the rule of the Southern States were nearly all advocates of public instruction. Bitterly as the slave-holders had always hated the teacher, successfully as they had labored to keep their poorer classes in extreme ignorance, the arms of Grant and the influence of the new voters drove them into the path of progress. Nearly every Southern State at the close of the war, and upon the election of President Grant, began to provide schools for the education of its white children. The change was startling; the conversion was universal. Even Tennessee and Kentucky provided common-school systems, or Georgia imposed a poll-tax to educate its frightful mass of ignorance. South Carolina was forced to open com-

AFRICAN AMERICAN HISTORY IN THE PRESS, 1851-1899

HARPER'S WEEKLY.
A JOURNAL OF CIVILIZATION.

Vol. XVI.—No. 809.] NEW YORK, SATURDAY, JUNE 29, 1872. [SINGLE COPIES TEN CENTS. $4.00 PER YEAR IN ADVANCE.

Entered according to Act of Congress, in the Year 1872, by Harper & Brothers, in the Office of the Librarian of Congress, at Washington.

THE SAGE OF CHAPPAQUA.

Uncle Tom. "I say, Uncle Sam, Massa Horrors Greedey will find it a Tough Job when he tries his Hand at this Tree."

Harper's Weekly, June 29, 1872, p. 505.

WHAT H. G. KNOWS ABOUT THRÆSHING.

And now "He comes among us to ask that we adopt *Him* as our Party Chief!"—*New York World*, June 6, 1872.

THE DEATH-BED MARRIAGE.
THE DAUGHTER OF DEMOCRACY HAS AT LAST MARRIED A "NIGGER!" (A RADICAL BLACK REPUBLICAN)—July 10, 1872.

Harper's Weekly, July 27, 1872, p. 584.

mon schools. Even Texas passed a free-school law. No sooner, indeed, was the peace of the country assured by the election of President Grant than over all those districts through which his armies had passed victoriously, and whence it had once been excluded by barbarous laws, the general education of the people became for the first time a leading object of policy, and the school-house sprang up in the track of the advancing troops.

Yet we are assured by the various superintendents of education in the Southern States that nothing but the vigorous support of the general government can preserve their new systems of public instruction from utter ruin. The opposition party every where retains its bitter hostility to knowledge and the teacher. In several States where it has gained the control of affairs it has at once checked the progress of the common schools. The system has been abandoned or the school funds withheld. It was the favorite aim of the marauders of Mississippi to burn school-houses and whip teachers. That secret association which has recently been vigorously repressed in the Carolinas, by the said of the United States officials and the national troops, was never weary of its incessant outrages upon innocent school-masters. In Mississippi Northern women, accomplished, devoted, and taken from the best classes of society, are still treated with singular indignities because they consent to teach in the colored schools. No Southern woman will receive them in her house; they can find no lodging except among the blacks; they are shut out from all the kindly offices of neighborhood and society; their Southern sisters turn away from them, when they meet, with marks of contempt and aversion; and so painful are the conditions upon which they pursue their useful labors the only a deep and generous sense of duty retains them in their difficult position.

Of Texas we are told that, for the first time in its history, public free schools in the fall of 1871 were opened to its people. Protected alone by the Union armies, the teacher has made his way into that vast, populous, and productive State. The common schools are looked upon as yet with doubt, hostility, and even terror, as the portents of a new era: they are slowly rising in vigor and importance. The Freedmen's Bureau has even provided schools for the colored race, which the Legislature appears to have wholly overlooked, and the adventures of its teachers seem often to resemble those of missionaries among savages and bishops in New Zealand. Not long since the master of a colored school in Bastrop County was taken from his home at night, tied to a tree, and whipped nearly to death, and his school-house burned: many school-houses and many teachers have suffered a similar fate. A bitter hatred and even jealousy of the colored race prevail among the ruder Texans, which can only be restrained, we are told by the superintendent, "by the strong arm of the government," which can only be removed by the slow growth of knowledge.

It is easy to conceive what must be the swift reaction in the Southern States should the opposition party elect its President: it is plain that the whole of that broad system of popular education which as been established under the peaceful rule of Grant will be at once overthrown. The enemies of Grant and the Union are necessarily the enemies of knowledge. Every rioter and assassin, every blind and brutal politician who in Texas drags out school-masters at night to whip them until they are nearly dead, who in South Carolina, masked and cowardly, tortures poor negroes and honest white men with torments not surpassed under the Inquisition, is raging for the removal of that vigorous hand that alone checks his course of crime. Should this desperate faction succeed, not a school-house would be left, at least for the colored children, from Charleston to San Antonio; no Northern woman would any longer dare to teach poor blacks in Mississippi; no Union man would venture to speak of common schools in Texas; a whole region would be thrown back into moral and mental darkness, and the rising prospects of Southern civilization be forever destroyed.

All the enemies of the common schools, indeed, seem to have formed an alliance to defeat General Grant. The men who burn school-houses in Texas are cheered on by the men who assail the public schools in New York. The extreme papist joins the extreme secessionist—the one threatens the life of the teacher, as at Hunter's Point; the other whips him in the still midnights of the South. In this remarkable alliance the Romish priest, the Texas brigand, and the Mississippi rebel join in a common assault upon the teacher and the teacher's friend, would check the spread of that knowledge which they hate, and bring upon free America the ignorance and barbarism of Italy and Spain. Nor is it the common schools, the administration, or the Bible at which they really aim their united blows. Their true object is to destroy the Union. The wild marauder of Texas or South Carolina abhors the restraints of an intelligent government; the Jesuit aims his sharpest arrows against that free civilization which he is pledged to destroy; both are the vigorous supporters of a Greeley or of any partisan who suits their purpose: both are resolved, by force and fraud, by gross calumnies and restless intrigues, by a union of the vicious and depraved, the ignorant and fanatical, to overthrow freedom in America.

Yet since General Grant's election the great army of teachers have obtained their most wonderful triumphs. They have overrun the South, defied the bitter opposition of rebels and of priests, and are swiftly extending the vast fabric of a common-school system from the borders of Canada to the California Gulf. Under the administration of President Grant our country stands far in the front of all civilized communities. It is the first of the nations to expend more money upon the education of its people than upon fleets and armies. Such a condition of affairs is altogether unprecedented in the annals of man, and may well seem the dawn of a happy age of rational reform. Since the close of the war the zeal of our people for the instruction of all classes has risen to a wonderful height. Money, labor, intellect, are all poured out in the great cause with unexampled liberality. The amount expended each year by the various States for educational purposes is nearly $60,000,000. New York leads in the path of intelligence, having given during the past year $10,000,000 to its public schools, besides the interest on its school property and the sums expended for private tuition. In 1850 the outlay for its public schools was only $2,000,000. New England pays annually for education at least $10,000,000; Pennsylvania, $8,000,000; Ohio and Illinois, about $7,000,000 each. The national government has given 60,000,000 acres of land to the States and Territories, at different periods, for school purposes. The amount required for the army and navy for the present year is about $48,000,000—a sum inferior to that which will be expended upon the growing army of teachers; and with the re-election of General Grant, and four years more of progress and repose, the power of knowledge will bind together the various sections of the country in a lasting union, will expel brigandage from Texas or South Carolina, and shield our foreign population from the intrigues of corrupt politicians and envious priests.

By Eugene Lawrence

A NEGRO CAMP-MEETING IN THE SOUTH

HARPER'S WEEKLY
August 10, 1872, p. 623

American life, usually so devoid of the picturesque, offers in the camp-meeting, or Southern "short," some food for the imagination. The negro mind has an insatiable craving for excitement, which finds its gratification chiefly in the varied scenes of the camping ground. Here, under the shadow of the mighty forest trees, singing sweet, weird melodies, and in the wild exaltation of religious devotion, the poor creature finds some compensation for the bitter, thankless toil of daily life. Nor is it surprising that these feelings, driven into this single channel, should overleap all bounds, and find expression in strange and extraordinary modes. To a calm observer it seems very like desecration, but at the bottom there is doubtless true devotion; it is the answer to nature's demand for something higher, the satisfying of those deeper feelings which are native to every human soul.

We have here in our illustration on page 620 the mingling of these two elements. See that gray-haired old negro shouting with such evident sincerity; he is certainly no pretender, his religion is real to him. He doubtless sees the golden streets, and feels in imagination the joy that awaits his toil-worn frame. But the pickaninny, solemnly munching her bit of corn-bread, is evidently "taking notes" for future use. She watches with a knowing air the coquettish damsel who is "posing" with natural grace, and doing her religion most becomingly. The small pupil will be able to do the same thing when she gets big enough, for the negroes are apt scholars.

The scene portrayed in our illustration is one of these characteristic gatherings. The negroes have come from all parts of the adjacent country, some, doubtless, walking twenty or thirty miles in their eagerness to join the worshipers. They rarely wear their good clothes at these times, but don their commonest work-day attire, for, as one of them explained to me, "Soon's Lucy begins to shout I jes pulls off her bunnit, and takes off her cuffs and collar and all her nice things; for when she gits goin' she jes t'ars every thin' right off her!"

It is not many months since the writer attended a camp-meeting in one of our Southern States, and a description of it may interest the readers of the Weekly. I had been spending a few weeks, together with another lady friend, in the little village of M———, which lies in a spur of the Alleghany Mountains. Our landlord, a staid, hospitable man of the small-farmer stamp, invited us one pleasant Sunday morning to accompany him to the meeting. We gladly accepted his invitation, and seating ourselves in the roomy, stout-built wagon, drawn by two lively little mules, we drove off. The way led for the most part through the mountains. Magnificent tulip-trees, with other varieties, waved over our head, and the pretty sprays of sauer-wood blossoms, dropped gracefully among the shining leaves, while the dark, rich foliage of the calico plant gave an almost tropical aspect to the scene. Far away in the dim distance we could see the grand old mountains of the distant ranges.

Our host left us, and we found seats under an old pine-tree. Then from the distance welled up, in low and solemn tones at first, then swelling to a mighty chorus, the wild, sweet notes of the "Trumpet Call" and "Passing over Jordan." From all sides the refrain was caught up and echoed back till the old woods rang again. The tunes they sang that day were seldom the gay, rollicking ones we had expected to hear, but were melancholy, dirge-like airs, born of a race that had come through "great tribulation."

The meeting opened quietly, but soon the negroes began to get excited. Their shouts could be heard for miles, and the excitable Lucy, having exhausted herself with leaping, shouting, and singing, was at last seen completely used up and done for, being jumped up and down by two stout men.

"Hyar you, Car'line!" shouts some one from a distant corner. "Gift up, dar; you're sittin' on your best-bunnit!"

"I don't car'," cries Caroline back, defiantly. "I'm bound to git religion to-day, if I spiles every thing I's got on. Glory hallelujah!"

Suddenly, while we were all in the full tide of devotion, our landlord reappeared, running swiftly toward us. Without uttering a word of explanation, but simply exclaiming, "Run! run!" he seized us each by an arm, and lifting us from our seats, forced us into a run with him. Our sole idea was that our respected host had become suddenly insane, and our only course seemed to be to humor him in his designs, whatever they were. So on we dashed as fast as our feet could carry us, over hillocks and stones, grazing past big rocks, and through reeds and over roots. My companion was large and fat, but very plucky; I was small and swift. How our host kept us so well in hand and up to time I could never explain. At length, when we were dead beat, and could go no farther, we were gladdened by the sight of the mules and wagon. Our host let go his hold, and we sank exhausted on the ground. As soon as I could get breath I said to him, "Please explain all this." We then learned that while we were listening to the services a party of roughs had come from town with the intention of breaking up the meeting. They had attacked the negroes indiscriminately, and the fight rapidly became general. Four men had already been killed when our host came to our rescue. But for his presence of mind, we, confiding strangers, would in a few moments have been in the midst of a bloody fight.

MR. SUMNER'S LETTER

HARPER'S WEEKLY
August 17, 1872, p. 634

By his letter to the colored citizens of Washington Mr. Sumner has done as much as he could do to reverse the work of his life. It has been his honorable pride, as it will be hereafter his glory, to have been the friend of the colored race. His abilities, his accomplishments, and his character have been steadily devoted to the service of the oppressed. He has been bitterly slandered and hated by those who were not wise enough to know that without justice there can be no permanent peace or prosperity in this country, and the brutal personal assault upon him during the Kansas debate is one of the significant events of our later political history. During the twenty-one years that he has served in the Senate—of which he is the oldest member—not a breath of suspicion has stained the purity of his character, and it is not the least of his services to his country that he has shown that a good man may pass unscathed through the fiery tempest of political and public life. The lackeys of slavery who now shout his praises can not understand

and do not admire that which is the true glory of Charles Sumner.

Yet it is Mr. Sumner who, on the eve of an election in the State which has been harried by the Ku-Klux, writes a letter which makes the Ku-Klux laugh with glee, and confounds their victims. With what incredulity and dismay must the colored voters of North Carolina have learned that Charles Sumner had declared for the party which is the traditional enemy of equal rights, and which sought by the most desperate and bloody war to make slavery absolute and hopeless! They could have learned only the fact, for there was not time to read the letter. And it was a cruel chance that they were astounded by the knowledge of his conclusion, yet were not able to see how shadowy and utterly inadequate were the reasons that he alleged for it.

His letter is a campaign document, addressed to the colored voters of the United States, in reply to a letter from some of them asking him which of the candidates will, if elected, "enforce the requirements of the Constitution and laws respecting our civil and political rights with the most heart-felt sympathy and the greatest vigor." Mr. Sumner answers that in his opinion Mr. Greeley, supported by the late rebels and Copperheads, with the rest of the Democratic party and a few Republicans, is more likely to respect justice and equality, and enforce the amendments which they have steadily denounced as unconstitutional, than General Grant with the Republican party, which was born of liberty, and whose fundamental principles are incorporated in the amendments. And Mr. Sumner's reasons for this conclusion are that the Democratic party says that it will do so, and has nominated Mr. Greeley.

He compares Mr. Greeley and General Grant as men and as Republicans, but he is too sagacious not to see that the key of the position is not the personality of the candidates, but the spirit and tendency of their supporters. He knows that when he advises the colored citizens to vote with the Democratic party, it is not enough to say that he prefers the candidate, and he therefore deliberately declares that the Democratic party has become Republican. "They may continue Democrats in name, but they are in reality Republicans *by the same title* that those who sustain Republican principles are Republicans." A more astounding statement of the kind was never made. The very dead soldiers in their graves, Gettysburg, Shiloh, Fort Wagner, the Wilderness, protest against the monstrous assertion. Answer, Republicans, who sustained Fremont, and Lincoln twice, and Grant, and through the terrible war stood faithful, is your title to your name the declaration upon the eve of an election of a creed which you have always spurned! And you, Charles Sumner, answer, is the title of your Republicanism a parrot lip-service of yesterday, or the sincere and profound faith of your mind and heart and conscience, attested by the acts and words of your life? In the name of the immeasurable sorrow and ruin of the struggle, in the name of reason and truth, answer, is Toutant Beauregard a Republican by the same title with William Lloyd Garrison!

And that is the whole argument of the letter. Those who yesterday in the Southern States were devising black codes to retain the substance of slavery will stand by the colored race with more "heart-felt sympathy" and greater vigor than those with whom equal liberty is a religion—because the Democratic Convention adopted the Cincinnati platform! Those who to the day of the adjournment of Congress railed at Mr. Sumner's own Civil Rights bill as preposterous will respect more truly the rights which it was intended to protect than those who have always defended them! Why, then, is the colored vote banded as a virtual unit against the Democrats? Is the instinct of an oppressed race of no weight as against Mr. Sumner's hostility to the President? The colored voters are to support Mr. Greeley because the Democratic party has become Republican. Yet while Mr. Sumner accepts the mere declaration of a party convention as proof of the conversion of the whole Democracy to Republicanism, he finds no evidence in the career of the President that he has any sympathy whatever for Republican principles.

But this Democratic conversion, upon which the letter turns, is not a fact. In the papers which published the letter of Mr. Sumner was one from Mr. Groesbeck, who says, "I differ in politics" from Mr. Greeley. Senator Thurman, Senator Bayard, both say the same thing. The *World*, in publishing the letter, denies the conversion, and we mention elsewhere that the Georgia Democracy are so far from converted that they would not even put Liberal Republican names upon their electoral ticket. Mr. Sumner thinks that the profession of the Democratic party, longing to return to power, is a surer security to the colored race than the whole history and all the deeds of the Republican party. And he adds the extraordinary remark, that if valued friends differ from him, it is because they regard men more than principles! Nothing is wanting to the sorrowful character of this letter, for in the face of this assertion Mr. Sumner withdraws from the Republican party because of one man, and accepts the Democratic party as more Republican because of another! The whole election with him turns upon a man. All the tendencies, logic, necessities, facts, principles of the Republican party avail nothing with him, because he does not like the candidate. The whole moral drift of the Democratic party does not dismay him, because the candidate is agreeable to him. Does he charge others with preferring men to principles?

Yet while the colored citizens hear Mr. Sumner advising them to join the Democracy and a few Republicans in supporting Mr. Greeley, they will not forget that Frederick Douglass and their own most representative and trusted leaders, with Garrison, Phillips, Beecher, Gerrit Smith, and others not less honored, counsel them to trust those the sincerity of whose friendship has been tried as by fire, rather than the sweetest promises of foes whose selfish motive in promising is plain enough. Not without deep regret will those who have always stood by the side of Charles Sumner in the good fight of progressive freedom now see him turn away. Nor, as they watch him recede from the line which his presence has inspired, will they believe him any less sincere, or doubt for a moment the purity of his intention. But Liberty is greater than any of her champions, and those who aim to serve her in the state will learn that it is a service costing many a personal pang. What Mr. Sumner said to a friend whose views of duty differed from his own may now be said to himself: "You have taken a tremendous responsibility; God keep your conscience clear!"

FREDERICK DOUGLASS UPON MR. SUMNER'S LETTER

HARPER'S WEEKLY
August 24, 1872, p. 651

That nothing may be wanting to the completeness of the reply to Mr. Sumner's unhappy letter, Frederick Douglass, who is perhaps the most eminent man of his race in the country, and who is a personal friend of Mr. Sumner, but an earnest supporter of General Grant, says:

> "Aside from his purpose to support the Democratic candidate for the Presidency, Mr. Sumner has added but little of either fact or argument to his previous utterances. To his fierce, bitter, sweeping, and unqualified impeachments of U. S. Grant we oppose the sober, unimpassioned, and just record in other columns setting forth General Grant's military and political course toward the colored people of the United States during the last ten years. We appeal from the power of invective to the power of simple, unadorned truth. Judged by this standard, U.S. Grant stands triumphantly vindicated as a wise, firm, and consistent friend of the just rights of man, without regard to race, color, or previous condition of servitude, and every way worthy of the support of colored citizens and of the whole nation."

THE SPEEDIEST WAY

HARPER'S WEEKLY
August 24, 1872, p. 651

The late Attorney-General Akerman, of Georgia, who knows the Ku-Klux thoroughly from long investigation, and who understands the real feeling of the Southern States, states the case admirably in a late letter. Speaking of the disturbing spirit in that section, he says:

> "Owing to the action of the Government of the United States it is now checked, but it is not yet extirpated. Should Grant be re-elected, the offenders will cease to hope for impunity in crime, and will betake themselves to better ways or to other countries. Should Greeley be elected, they will feel that their side has triumphed, and in the intoxication of victory will break out in violence the fiercer from long restraint. No matter how earnestly Mr. Greeley might exert himself to suppress them, it would be long before he could put them where Grant has them now. The speediest way to give permanent tranquility to the South is to re-elect General Grant."

ECHOES FROM THE FIELD

HARPER'S WEEKLY
August 31, 1872, p. 666–67

In a recent eloquent speech advocating the re-election of General Grant, Mr. Shellabarger, of Ohio, one of the purest and ablest representatives in Congress, said: "I declare, and in response to those who accuse him of infidelity to the black race, that one single sentence of that inaugural which to the shout of fifty thousand people I heard him utter from the east porch of the Capitol, and which is in these words, 'I entertain the hope and express the desire that it [the right of the colored man to vote] may be settled by the ratification of the Fifteenth Article of amendment to the Constitution,' did more for the colored man than all the acts in the lives of all his traducers put together."

Frederick Douglass, in a fervent appeal to his race, says: "Are we prepared to vote for the nominees of the Democratic party, whose hearts never have changed toward us, who kept us in slavery as long as they had the power, and who, if they had the power again, would (to say the least of it) do their very utmost to restrict our liberties and oppress us as of old? Mr. Sumner may

"IT IS ONLY A TRUCE TO REGAIN POWER ("PLAYING POSSUM").
H. G. "Clasp hands over the bloody chasm."
C. S. "Freely accept the hand that is offered, and reach forth thine own in friendly grasp."

Harper's Weekly, August 24, 1872, p. 652.

deceive himself; he can not deceive us. . . . With Grant our security is unquestionable—our happiness will be made lasting."

General Garfield, speaking in Kansas, says: "It is the old fight—the slavery fight. The old minority contests. Dare any one lead one of these newly enfranchised citizens into the Democratic camp and tell him that with it is peace and security for his rights?. . . 'Tis the same old party that confronted us in 1864. They are the men that resisted the war, that forgot to be glad when our arms triumphed, and forgot to be sad when they wavered."

THE KU-KLUX PRISONERS

HARPER'S WEEKLY
August 31, 1872, p. 667

Mr. Gerrit Smith, always a philanthropist, wrote to the President for clemency to some of the Ku-Klux convicts in the Albany Penitentiary; and the President directed Colonel Whitley, the chief of the Secret Service, to go to the prison and report whether, in his judgment, any of the prisoners should be pardoned. About forty examinations were made, none of the men knowing that any one else had been called out, nor the official character of Colonel Whitley, nor the object of his visit. His report is brief, but very interesting.

The answers of the prisoners fully expose the infamous character of the Ku-Klux conspiracy. Colonel Whitley says that in reply to the general inquiry into the objects of the association the answer almost invariably was: "When we joined the order we supposed it to be a society established for mutual protection, but after having been fully initiated discovered it to be for a political purpose, which purpose was embodied in an oath in which we swore to oppose the radical party in all its forms, and prevent the negroes from voting. It was this great deception that misled us, and which has brought us into our present condition." They spoke also of crimes which they had committed, but into the commission of which they claim to have been betrayed by unscrupulous and designing men of more enlightened minds.

Indeed, their story only confirms the truth that has been amply established by the immense body of evidence collected by the Congressional committee of

HUMORS OF THE DAY.

ECLIPSE IN NORTH CAROLINA—WILL BE VISIBLE THROUGHOUT THE UNITED STATES NOVEMBER 5, 1872.

Harper's Weekly, August 31, 1872, p. 675.

investigation upon this subject. "Reconciliation," it will not be forgotten, means repeal of the laws of the United States for the defeat and punishment of this conspiracy. Colonel Whitley recommends a number of the convicts to Executive clemency; and his report comes opportunely to remind the country of a condition of society that it can not safely forget.

PERSONAL

HARPER'S WEEKLY
August 31, 1872, p. 667

Mr. James C. Napier has been promoted to a position in the Sixth Auditor's office. He is a graduate of Howard University, and the first colored person in the government service at Washington to receive promotion under the new civil service rules.

Professor Blyden, an educated gentleman of color, and an accomplished Arabic scholar, now on an exploring expedition to the interior of Africa, writes from a town eighty miles from Freetown, Sierra Leone, that he has found a Mohammedan university with about a thousand persons connected with it, among them a large number of girls studying Arabic. The teachers were glad to get the Arabic Bible published by the American Bible Society, and not unwilling to admit it as a textbook.

THE CASE CANDIDLY STATED IN GEORGIA

HARPER'S WEEKLY
September 14, 1872, p. 714

The Georgia Democrats are an interesting study for "Liberal Republicans." In that State, and, indeed, in all the Southern States, there is no mincing. The feeble cry of "reform" which is occasionally attempted by the Northern Republican allies of the Democrats is not heard from the South. There the campaign is precisely what it was in 1868—an effort to restore the Democratic party and to undo as much of reconstruction as possible; and Mr. Greeley is supported because he is the regular Democratic candidate.

At a recent meeting in Georgia General H. L. Benning, late of the rebel army and now a Greeley elector at large, made a very intelligible speech. It is worth considering, as a fair statement of the views of the Southern Democracy, which is the strongest wing of the party to which the people are asked to intrust the government.

General Benning began by asking whether Democrats should support Greeley and Brown. He thought they should, "because their election will expel the party in power to substitute the Democratic party.... It will restore the South to her place before the war, and offers some hope that she will receive some compensation for her losses, and it is the best thing we can do."

He then proceeded:

"If Greeley and Brown are elected, the contest will result in a Democratic House of Representatives, and subsequently of a Senate.... The Democrats being the strongest power, will merge into their members the Liberal element. The creek flows to the river, not the river to the creek. The Chattahoochee ought not to complain because the creek empties into it. The Liberals can do nothing but fuse with us.... All the offices of profit are held by radicals. The election of Greeley will give the bulk of them to Democrats. It will tend to the establishment of a fraternal feeling between the South and North. This will tend to indemnify us for heavy losses sustained otherwise than by the freeing of slaves, and gives a hope we may receive something for them.... The election of Greeley and Brown will produce reconciliation between the South and North, and tend greatly to our advantage.... Their election will restore the South to her weight in the government. Before the war our Representatives were incorruptible, and though in a minority, controlled to a great extent the

1872

This is a white man's government.
Auction block.
Hunting down with blood-hounds.
A negro has no rights which a white man is bound to respect.
Slavery.
Whipping-post.
New York riots.
Negroes hung at lamp-posts.
Attempt to introduce pestilence in the North.
Attempt to burn Northern cities.
Burning of colored orphan asylum.
New Orleans and Memphis massacres.
Belle Isle and Andersonville atrocities.
Assassination of Lincoln.
Ku-klux outrages to Unionists, white and black.
Burning of Freedmen's schools.
Whipping and shooting of teachers.
Repudiation.
Fort Pillow massacre, approved by Congress of Confederate States of America.

KU-KLUX.

THE RULE OF TAMMANY RING.
WHOLESALE FRAUD.
CORRUPTION.
NO CITIZEN HAD ANY RIGHTS THAT A TAMMANY ROUGH WAS BOUND TO RESPECT.
CORRUPT JUDICIARY—CARDOZO, BARNARD, AND M'CUNN.
FRAUDULENT AND ILLEGAL VOTING.
BRIBERY.
COUNTING OUT THE VOTES OF CITIZENS.
RIOT AND BLOODSHED.

NAMES NOT TO BE FORGOTTEN:
TWEED, SWEENY, CONNOLLY, and HALL.

SLAVERY.

THE WHITED SEPULCHRE.
COVERING THE MONUMENT OF INFAMY WITH HIS WHITE HAT AND COAT.

Harper's Weekly, September 7, 1872, p. 692.

government.... We will be stronger now, because we will go as a unit."

General Benning denied that any Democratic principle had been surrendered, and denounced the third party movement. He continued:

> "The great Democratic principle is State rights. Does not Greeley profess the same opinion on this subject as the Democrats of the North?... He occupied an almost identical position [upon the slavery question] with that of Douglas, only he insulted the owner. He was in favor of the secession of the South if a majority of the people wished to do so. When war came he went with his section, as the Northern Democrats did. During the war he was an advocate of peace. After the Gettysburg fight he advocated liberal terms.... Altogether he has the best record of any Northern man.... We took Seymour and Blair in 1868. If Seymour hadn't pushed forward reinforcements, Lee would have won Gettysburg.... This contest is not a duel between Greeley and Grant, but a battle between the Republicans and the Democrats. If the battle is won, what difference does it make about the leader? The great contest is, which party is to rule. Is it not best to honor Greeley a little, and gain a party victory?... The amendments to the Constitution may be susceptible to change. The people at the elections four years ago decided as regards them for the present."

This is plain, practical talk. It states precisely what the Southern Democrats mean by their support of Mr. Greeley. It shows exactly how much they respect the platform upon which they propose to stand, and just what is meant by reconciliation. Yet this speech illustrates what Mr. Sumner calls "conversion." It is of General Benning and the Georgia Democrats that Mr. Sumner says, "They may continue Democrats in name, but they are in reality Republicans by the same title that those who sustain Republican principles are Republicans." The perilous delusion of such an assumption is every day exposed. The Georgia Democrats, with the Democratic leaders in the Northern States, distinctly abjure Mr. Sumner's theory. "A victory will not give us every thing at once," says Judge Black, in Pennsylvania, implying that it will be a good beginning. And General Benning in Georgia responds in the same spirit: "Is it not best to honor Greeley a little, and gain a party victory?... The amendments to the Constitution may be susceptible to change." And while these words, still freshly uttered, with a sincerity that can not be questioned, are in our ears and minds, General Banks says at Lynn that General Benning and his friends "now accept the result readily and joyfully,... sacrifice their prejudices, and... stand before the country in support of the great principles on which the government was established."

Here are the new Northern allies of the Democratic party telling us that the Southern brethren are only anxious to show how fully they accept every thing, and how sweetly they will administer the government and protect equal rights; while the Southern brethren themselves say, frankly, "We mean to get power if we can by voting for Mr. Greeley, and State sovereignty will take care of the rest." It is probable that General Benning and his friends know their purposes quite as well as Mr. Sumner and General Banks.

MR. R. H. DANA, JUN., AND FUGITIVE SLAVES

HARPER'S WEEKLY
September 21, 1872, p. 730

The force of the letter of Richard H. Dana, Jun., to some colored citizens of Boston has been shown by the fury with which it was received by the supporters of Mr. Greeley, and the falsehood with which they answer it. Those amiable brethren in Greeley, the New York *Tribune* and the New York *World*, especially fell upon Mr. Dana with laughable ferocity. But his character and career effectually dispose of more misrepresentations. Mr. Dana's opinion was naturally asked by his colored fellow-citizens, for his brilliant services in behalf of fugitive slaves are well known, and the high regard felt for him by the colored citizens is shown in the letter to which his is a reply. Alluding to the Fugitive Slave bill, the letter to Mr. Dana says: "While this repulsive measure seemed to overawe the bar of Massachusetts, we are happy to know that there remained still a few of the members true to humanity, foremost of whom to tender their services in our defense was your honored self, as the records of the courts from time to time attest."

Such testimony is something of which a man may well be proud, and therefore his enemies instinctively hawk at it. Mr. Dana writes that he thinks that "such a Chief Magistrate as Mr. Greeley, and such a combination as would use and control him," would be perilous; and with incisive brevity he declares, "President Grant will be elected, and surrounded by those forces of society which, with his powerful aid, have saved the Union, abolished slavery, extended equal rights to freedmen, enacted and enforced laws against barbarism at the South, secured the debt from repudiation, preserved the public credit, done justice to the Indian, avoided foreign war with honor and given new scope and dignity to arbitration among nations." These are trenchant truths; and the *Tribune* and the *World* have no reply but that Mr. Dana was largely paid—they even mention a sum—for defending fugitive slaves.

The statement is wholly untrue. Mr. Dana never received pay for defending a fugitive slave. It is, indeed, no credit to have declined, but it is a discredit to be thought to have sold such service. And this circumstantial assertion is another illustration of the wanton way in which the fair fame of eminent citizens is assailed in this campaign. But it is a campaign which began in personality, in personal hostility to the President, not upon any principle or policy; and the aim of which is to make enmity to the President the means of defeating his party. Mr. Dana's letter is so powerful a blow at the wretched plot that he is, of course, assailed by the familiar weapon of the adversary, defamation.

ANOTHER

HARPER'S WEEKLY
September 21, 1872, p. 730

We have received many letters from all parts of the country asking if it be true that General Grant said, during the war, that if it was waged for emancipation, he would carry his sword to the South. And the New York *Tribune* quotes a Missouri paper, which states that General Grant made the remark in "Ringo's banking house," in Mexico, Missouri. We hope that "Ringo's banking house" is innocent of issuing this false coin. The *Tribune* remarks: "He hadn't much to do there at that time, and might well have been walking about and making just such observations in offices and elsewhere." That is the manner in which the *Tribune* tries to imply a belief of the story. Then, as if aware that a quotation from the Randolph *Citizen* specifying "Ringo's banking house" as the very place in which General Grant made the remark was not very conclusive, the *Tribune* adds: "We give our authority, and we have no doubt of the substantial truth of the story."

Nevertheless, it is totally false. It is sheer invention. The President never said any thing that could be tortured into such a remark, because he had never such a thought. Nor is the story new. It is one of the Copperhead relics of 1868, and it is precisely one of the inventions which are most easily made. Now it is in "Ringo's banking house" that General Grant is reported to have made the remark to "a sterling Union man." But in 1868 it was reported as a speech to his regiment! He was always such an inveterate speech-maker! Four years ago, in June, 1868, Mr. E. B. Washburne wrote, in allusion to the same story: "It is idle for the loyal men of the country to attempt to deny the rebel and Copperhead lies now being put in circulation against General Grant.... The whole thing is false, there not being the 'shadow of a shade' of foundation for it."

This letter the *Tribune* publishes, as it says, "for what it is worth." Perhaps it does not consider the word of the President's intimate friend worth as much as the anonymous slander of the Randolph *Citizen*. But whether the story proceed from "Ringo's banking house" or elsewhere, it is wholly false.

MR. GREELEY'S SUPPORTERS IN GEORGIA

HARPER'S WEEKLY
September 28, 1872, pp. 757–58

The interior life of the Southern States, and the character and designs of those "liberal" politicians to whom we are invited by the opposition party to commit the control of the national government, may well be studied interest at he present moment; and the example of Georgia will serve to show a condition of disorder, misrule, and utter barbarism such as can scarcely be paralleled in any country within the limits of civilization. Georgia by a plain usurpation has fallen into the hands of the Democratic party. For a brief period it was controlled by the Republicans. Then the Democracy, or rather the former slave-holders, drove the colored members from the Legislature, expelled its Republican Governor, banished the Republican voters from the polls, and now rule by force and fraud over the unhappy State. A reign of terror has been perfectly established. When the colored and white Republicans in 1868 would have voted for General Grant, they were met at the polls by bands of armed men, and driven away with blows and terrible threats. The Republican sheriff of Augusta was murdered; the Republican mayor assaulted and nearly killed. In one county the managers of the election refused to receive the votes of the colored citizens "unless they were given for Seymour and Blair." Of seven hundred in another county only three persons were allowed to vote. At Savannah they were set upon by a mob and driven to their homes. In Lincoln County, "to escape death, nearly all the colored and some of the white Republicans voted the Democratic ticket." The election throughout the State was controlled by the worst portion of the population. To save their lives the honest citizens resigned their right of suffrage, and Georgia, which had once been Republican, gave Seymour and Blair a majority of 30,000. In 1870 the Republicans were again every where defeated, the Democrats triumphant; the same means were employed, and still more barbarous deeds enacted. Republican voters were shot, beaten, or maltreated; leading politicians were assassinated on their way to public meetings; the colored voters were stabbed, set upon by dogs, cut with knives, torn with slung-shot; and the horrible details of the savage cruelty of the Democratic party in every part of Georgia are certainly without a parallel in any civilized country. Yet it is this murderous faction in the South that has nominated Mr.

Greeley, professes to deserve the compassion of the nation by its unmerited woes, and is overwhelmed with the ready sympathy of Seymour, Kernan, and Blair.

Mr. Stearns, from whose interesting work on "The Black Man of the South and the Rebels," recently published, these details are taken, went to Georgia in 1866 and purchased a plantation near Augusta. He was an enthusiast, and hoped by mildness and forbearance to disarm the malice of the Southern whites, to teach by example and precept the colored laborers. He opened a school for his workmen, and succeeded in winning their attention and regard. With many faults, the results of generations of oppression, the colored population seem at least to have been grateful and loyal. Mr. Stearns became a leading Republican politician, and was elected ordinary of his county by the colored vote; but when he attempted to take possession of his office was set upon by a Democratic mob, was in danger of his life, and was forced to resign. "They then seized me," he relates of his expulsion from office, "dragged me to the top of the stairs, and hurried my departure from the halls of justice by pushing and kicking me until I had reached the bottom of the long flight of stairs, some of them crying out, 'Let's put him into the creek.'" His narrative of his dangers and sufferings as a Southern planter throws no doubtful light upon the degraded condition of the great body of the people. Such cruel and desperate men, plunged in utter ignorance, such uncleanly and intolerable women as seem to abound in the interior districts of Georgia, can hardly be imagined without actual observation. Of a certain Mrs. Loving, "a poor white," we are told, "her presence at the breakfast-table was enough to considerably lessen the cost of feeding one's family, so uncouth and uncleanly was she in appearance." Of the politeness of Southern men Mr. Stearns seems to have received no agreeable impression. He was constantly assailed by gross language, vile epithets, and the coarsest abuse; their humanity was shown in attacking his house when he lay ill with a fever, in terrifying his family, and shooting revolvers under his windows. That there are many intelligent and cultivated people at the South is not to be doubted, but they can scarcely belong to the Democratic party. Though a man of peace, unoffending and blameless, he was compelled to sleep with his rifle under his pillow; saw the Union men around him treated with horrible severity; heard of murders and outrages every where; and declares that had Seymour and Blair been elected, every Republican in Georgia would have been assassinated or driven from the country. If Greeley and Brown are more fortunate, it is easy to see what will be the unbounded rule of the Democrats and the fate of the loyal citizens of the South.

It was the *Ku-Klux* that committed most of the enormities with which Mr. Stearns became familiar during his stay in Georgia; to this secret association of assassins was due the success of the Democrats and the sudden check to the progress of the State. Nor is the Ku-Klux composed of disbanded soldiers alone, or the ignorant as well as the vicious. We are told that it embraces many of the wealthy and perhaps "respectable" class, the sons of planters and leading politicians. Its first aim seems to have been to terrify and subject the blacks, to arouse their native superstition, and convert them to Democracy by apparitions and ghostly sounds. Its members, the "respectable" class of the South, clothed themselves in grotesque gowns and masks, gathered in church-yards, followed at night the more influential colored men, assailed them with menaces, cries, groans, warnings, and chased them to their cabins. But very soon, if not at once, this association of "liberal" politicians sank into crimes so dreadful as can not be told here. Their nightly rides over the country became orgies of license and horrible brutality. Their numbers increased; they ruled all Georgia; no negro hut was safe from these "pests of society;" no language can paint too severely the outrages committed under their secret shelter. "Lincoln County," says the author, "is emphatically 'the valley of the shadow of death' for the poor colored man;" and he relates how three prominent colored Republicans were taken to a mill-dam by the Democratic club to be shot or drowned. They were offered the alternative. At a signal from these "repentant" Democrats they leaped into the water. The Democrats fired at them. Two were shot dead; one escaped, severely wounded, to relate the fearful story. And this is only a single instance of the incessant outrages of the Democratic Ku-Klux. The courts took no notice of their misdeeds, and Democratic politicians led or tolerated the crimes of their indispensable allies. It was this class of the Southern gentlemen that crowded around the house of Mr. Stearns when he lay ill of a fever, and fired their revolvers to deprive him of sleep, from whose bullets he scarcely preserved the lives of his wife and daughter; who assailed him with blows and coarse language when he attempted to exercise his official powers; who shot down the colored voters, and renewed the rebellion in Georgia. The condition of the negroes, Mr. Stearns assures us, is almost unendurable. Often they were on the brink of revolt, ready to rise against their persecutors, and lay the towns and cities of the Ku-Klux in ashes. Yet they have restrained themselves. Thus far the conduct of the colored people has shown a startling contrast to that of the barbarous and licentious whites. In the midst of the unpunished outrages upon their families or themselves, the negroes—often in a vast majority, and not unpracticed in military affairs—have spared the plantations and the towns of their oppressors, have shown a humanity that may well touch the hearts of their fellow-citizens. From the spectacle of the general lawlessness around him Mr. Stearns addresses an appeal to his countrymen. He claims their help to repress the "villains" who prey upon Southern society. He urges the utmost severity of legislation to save the Republicans of Georgia, and avert the ruin of that extensive territory. Nothing but the aid of the national government, he asserts, can protect the freedmen, stay the brutality of the Democratic leaders, and restore to civilization the wasted borders of the State. He warns every man—and he wrote but a year ago—to vote steadily against those politicians who would weaken the force of the Ku-Klux law, or who would place any confidence in the rebellious leaders of the South. He calls upon the nation to rise with unprecedented unanimity, and show to the Ku-Klux and the Southern Democracy that they are resolved to protect the white and black Republicans in all the rights of freemen; that they have heard of the dreadful enormities committed in the South, and are resolved to redress them; and he foretells, in case of the election of an opposition President, a general rising of the colored race against their tyrants, a frightful period of anarchy and of civil war.

Facts like those related by Mr. Stearns, and which he supports by the affidavits of numerous witnesses, white as well as colored, sometimes by the touching narratives of the sufferers themselves, and often by official documents, must arouse a natural indignation in every part of the nation, and serve to throw a terrible light upon the designs of those Southern politicians who are attempting to delude the public mind with professions of peace and of reconciliation. They have already established a despotism in Georgia, and probably in many other sections of the South, founded upon bloodshed, and covered with gross deception. In that State alone their murdered victims are numbered by thousands. During the past five years they have exercised cruelties upon the unoffending negroes that disgrace human nature, that even the Communists of Paris shrank from approaching, and they have labored with no common success to hide their guilt from the eyes of their countrymen. The Southern press is silent; the Southern courts refuse to punish or even notice their misdeeds: the only hope of the white and colored Republicans is in the protection of the general government. For the less shocking offenses of the Democratic leaders we have scarcely room. That they have broken up the schools provided for the colored race and striven to spread every where ignorance and vice, have discouraged or neglected the education of the poorer classes of the whites, strive to check the progress of the people, and would perpetuate the moral and mental degradation produced by generations of slavery, may well be imagined; and it is plain that the prevalence of the Democratic rule will throw back the South into a new barbarism, and check forever all hope of its reform. To these enemies of education and of progress, to the Ku-Klux and the politicians who rule by terror and crime, Mr. Greeley hopes to owe his election. The vote of Democratic Georgia is confidently counted upon by the opposition party as one of their surest supports. But it is not difficult to see that whoever sustains Mr. Greeley and his policy places himself on the side of the persecutors of the white and black voters of Georgia, and lends his countenance to all those enormities that have marked the Democratic rule in that unfortunate State. It is impossible, indeed, to believe that any humane politician would consent to profit by an election gained by means so cruel as those described by Mr. Stearns, or that even a Seymour or a Kernan, a Greeley and a Sumner, would not blush to hold an office that had been won by the oppression of the innocent negro and the infamous orgies of the Ku-Klux canvass.

Some improvement in the condition of Georgia has followed the passage of the Ku-Klux laws of 1871. So long as the general government interposed, the life of the colored voter was safe, or his assassins were punished; the white Republicans for the past year have escaped personal violence from their Democratic neighbors. But a usurping minority still rules in the State, the partisans of Greeley and the allies of Sumner, of Kernan, and Buckalew; the Ku-Klux law has already been so amended as to deprive it of some of its most effective traits: upon the success of the Democracy it would be wholly swept away. This is the chief aim of the Southern leaders. They cry out for the withdrawal of all interference in the affairs of their State by the general government. A minority whose crimes terrify humanity demands from the nation not only amnesty, but permission to perpetrate new offenses unchecked and unseen. A minority that drove the South into rebellion is once more ruling in Georgia. It sends its armed bands to the polling places; it governs the mechanic and the small farmer, the colored and the white voter—the rising intelligence of the State—by blows and nightly raids upon negro cabins. If the arm of the general government were lifted, if Greeley and Kernan and Buckalew ruled at the North, the guilty minority would rage unrestrained in every Southern State, the atrocities painted by Mr. Stearns would be renewed, the whole South would be transformed into a cruel despotism, and its guilty leaders would once more dream of independence and of vengeance upon the prosperous North.

The chief question to be decided in the approaching Presidential election is, whether this condition of affairs shall be permitted to continue at the South, whether a cruel and desperate minority shall be allowed to renew its outrages upon the rights and the welfare of the whole people under the shelter of Mr. Greeley's supporters, or whether it shall be crushed and broken down by the firm rule of the Republican party and of President Grant. The opposition party count upon securing the vote of nearly all the Southern States. The example of Georgia shows, in its recent elections, by what means they will proceed to effect their purpose. There whole counties have been disfranchised; the majority has been ruled by the minority; the Republican voters have been the victims of their murderous opponents; the Ku-Klux is preparing to commence once more its career of infamy and terror. Let, then, the people rise with unprecedented unanimity, rescue Georgia and the South from their tyrants, and crush with a mighty hand the last struggle of the slave-holders, rebellion.

By Eugene Lawrence

MURDER OF A NEGRO AT MRS. CARTER'S HOUSE.

Harper's Weekly, October 12, 1872, p. 796.

THE PATENBURG MASSACRE

HARPER'S WEEKLY
October 12, 1872, p. 798

An obscure settlement called Patenburg, on the Muthockaway Creek, Hunterdon County, New Jersey, has just been the scene of an outrage which, although of less extent, recalls by its unprovoked atrocity the New Orleans riots of 1866, and the draft riots in our own city. Full illustrations of the scenes and incidents of the outrage are given on page 796. The facts, briefly stated, were as follows:

In the neighborhood of Patenburg the railroad now building from Easton to Perth Amboy is to run through the Musconetcong Mountain by a tunnel which will be a mile in length. Work is in progress in this tunnel at both ends. The approach to the tunnel from the east is by a deep cut, on which large gangs of laborers are now employed, some white and others black. The negroes work in gangs separate from the whites, and were quartered in log-houses on the south side of the cut, the quarters of the whites being on the opposite side. Immediately at the village of Patenburg, half a mile from the tunnel, the road skirts a mill-pond formed by a dam across the Muthockaway Creek. Here some heavy rock cutting is required to be done, and other gangs of laborers, all whites, are employed. About a mile further east, on the farm of a Mrs. Carter, there is some heavy earth-work in progress, upon which several gangs of colored men have been employed, who were quartered in shanties in that vicinity. In all there were about one hundred and fifty negroes and between two and three hundred white laborers, mostly Irish, employed about the tunnel.

On Saturday, September 21, the laborers were paid off, and, retiring to their repective quarters, spent the evening in great jollity. The white laborers appear to have drank a good deal of whisky; whether the negroes did is not known. Late in the evening a party of the latter went to the village on a serenading expedition, and on their return fell in with a party of Irish laborers, by whom they were violently assaulted. They succeeded in driving off their assailants, and retired to their own quarters.

The negroes immediately collected reinforcements, and, to the number of fifteen or twenty, advanced toward the scene of the first conflict. They were met near the same spot by a still larger party of Irishmen, armed with pistols and clubs, and, after a sharp fight, were discomfited, cut off from their quarters, and forced

THE MURDER OF POWELL.

Harper's Weekly, October 12, 1872, p. 796.

back to Mrs. Carter's farm. Here they obtained further help, and then endeavored to save the cabins of the first party, which had been already attacked by their assailants. The Irish, better armed and more numerous, fired upon them across a deep cut and drove them off. The abandoned cabins were pillaged, and the money which the poor fellows had received the day before, and which was mostly deposited in sachels left in the quarters, was stolen. The Irishmen then fired the cabins, and immediately got into a row among themselves, during which one of their number, named Colls, was killed, and his body left near the cabins.

During the night the Irishmen collected reinforcements, and next morning renewed the fight. By spreading the report that Colls had been murdered by the negroes, they roused their countrymen to the utmost frenzy, and a party of about 150 made an attack on the negroes of Mrs. Carter's farm just at daybreak. Roused from sleep by the firing, the poor fellows fled in terror and confusion, closely pursued by the infuriated Irishmen. One of the negroes, Denis Powell, was shot, and left dying by the road. A portion of the fugitives sought refuge in the out-buildings around Mrs. Carter's house, under the porch, and elsewhere about the premises. The Irish demanded admission to the house, and when the brave woman refused, they beat in the door. Just at that moment a poor old negro was discovered crouching under the porch. He was immediately shot, dragged out, and beaten to death with clubs. After searching the premises, and finding no one, they retired. On their way back they found Powell still alive, and falling upon him, beat out his brains with clubs and stones. Spying another fugitive, Oscar Bruce, in the act of climbing a fence, they shot him down, and then, jumping upon his prostrate form, stamped it and beat it with clubs until it was unrecognizable as the remains of a human being.

This murder ended the bloody work. The butchers withdrew to their quarters and disbanded. The leaders of the mob fled. To the disgrace of New Jersey, no determined effort was made by the authorities to arrest and punish the perpetrators of these horrible outrages. Inquests were held on the bodies of the murdered men; but the magistrates appear to be afraid to move vigorously, and the murderers are not only still at liberty, but seem likely to remain so. The Irish openly defy the sheriff, who dares not make his appearance among them. Five days after the massacre Governor Parker offered the paltry sum of $500 reward for the arrest and conviction of the murderers, but meanwhile the opportunity passed. As *three colored fugitives* from the massacre have been arrested, while the main body of their assailants remain at large, it is reasonable to conclude that nothing but the pressure of public opinion will compel the authorities of New Jersey to do any thing toward bringing to justice the authors of this horrible outrage.

"PILE UP THE ASHES!"—Charles Sumner.

"There is heat enough yet in the dead ashes of my country to bring forth the Phenix of its Restoration, if Horace Greeley is made President."—*Speech which was delivered by Mr. Shorter, of Alabama, one of the Visitors to Chappaqua.*

Harper's Weekly, October 12, 1872, p. 800.

THE GEORGIA ELECTION

HARPER'S WEEKLY
October 19, 1872, p. 803

Evidences multiply that the large Democratic majority in Georgia by which Mr. James M. Smith was re-elected Governor was obtained by fraud, outrage, and violence. Telegrams, letters, and special messengers from all parts of the State show that where the negroes were not driven from the polls, other means were taken to reduce the Republican vote.

In Macon the colored men were driven away from the polls by pistol-shots and brickbats, two of their number being murdered outright, and others severely wounded. In Dougherty County more than a thousand Republican votes were polled, and but three hundred returned by the Democratic managers. In Liberty County the vote of two strong Republican precincts was thrown out upon a trivial pretext by the Democratic managers, disfranchising 600 Republican voters. Burke County, with an actual Republican majority of 1500, has been Ku-Kluxed into showing a Democratic majority of 800.

The Democratic Legislature had changed the time of holding the election from November to October, and required the production of a receipt for the poll-tax of 1871 as a condition precedent to voting. This was done because it was known that the negroes would be very likely to have lost the tax receipt of the previous year, and could only obtain a duplicate of it from Democratic officials. To carry out more effectively their scheme of disfranchisement, the polling places were made few in number—in Savannah, for example, only four were provided for a vote of 8000, and these all in the same building. The polls were surrounded by armed Democrats, and the roads were patrolled by Democratic "sabre clubs" to overawe the negroes. The voters were required by the election officers not only to produce the receipts required by law, but to swear that they had paid a poll-tax every year since emancipation. In some cases the day before election the bondsmen of the tax-collector surrendered their bonds, leaving no one qualified to give the necessary receipts. In view of these outrages, we are not surprised to learn that, as the New York *Tribune* mildly puts it, many of the negroes "concluded to wait for November before voting at all!" How they were driven to this conclusion is abundantly shown by the foregoing facts; while the spirit of the Democratic party in the South and their "Liberal" allies in the North is strikingly illustrated in Mr. Nast's powerful cartoon on page 804.

DOMESTIC INTELLIGENCE

HARPER'S WEEKLY
October 19, 1872, p. 803

A serious riot took place at Macon on the 2d inst., during the progress of the Georgia election. The whites sought to drive the blacks from the polls, and a fight ensuing, two negroes and one white man were killed, and several negroes wounded.

THE KU-KLUX CONSPIRACY

HARPER'S WEEKLY
October 19, 1872, pp. 805–6

An English traveler who has recently visited the Southern States describes with enthusiasm their boundless resources and attractive clime. Almost endless acres of productive soil remain yet to be brought under cultivation; an immense population might be sustained on the fertile fields reaching from the Ohio to the Gulf of Mexico. Forests and woodlands, mines and mineral wealth, the varied products of the hot or the temperate zone, corn and cotton, tropical fruits—a rich and never-failing harvest of all the rarest gifts of nature—allure immigration and invite the hand of industry. Laborers, indeed, Mr. Somers assures us, already abound: the colored population is rapidly learning to work well, and to save the results of their toil; the white farmers may yet

"H. G." "LET US CLASP HANDS OVER THE BLOODY CHASM."—[SEE PAGE 803.]
"A Great Victory has been won in Georgia..... The verdict in Georgia is certainly conclusive."—*New York Tribune*, October 3, 1872.

Harper's Weekly, October 19, 1872, p. 804.

throw off their languor and improvidence; and the day is not perhaps far distant when Georgia or Alabama shall be as thickly settled and as prosperous as Ohio or Massachusetts. Coal-fields, we are told, and never-failing streams provide all the requirements of manufactures; the wealth of the mountains has never yet been explored, the untouched forests of pine, the unopened quarries, and the undiscovered ores lie ready for the mechanic and the engineer; and nothing but a liberal and stable government is wanting to complete the prosperity of this fortunate land. But this the Southern States have never known. Under the rule of the slaveholders all their wealth was neglected, or was gradually thrown away. The mechanic, the manufacturer, and the white artisan avoided a land where labor was despised; the richest plantation, under the improvident culture of slavery, soon lost its productiveness; the barbarous ignorance of the workman and the tyranny of the master, the intellectual decay that followed the vicious system of government, left the resources of nature unexplored, and covered with an unnatural blight the land that might have teemed with unprecedented wealth. Since the rebellion some improvement is visible. The small farms are increasing; the colored people labor with new zeal; even the white population is more industrious, less improvident, and less wasteful. Yet still the South wants a settled government; lawlessness and disorder drive off the settler, and diminish the value of its soil; its farms can be purchased for prices that seem insignificant and incredible to the inhabitants of the more quiet States; its people still linger in self-chosen ignorance; capital and commerce avoid its dangerous borders; and the merchant or the mechanic approaches almost as timidly the home of the Ku-Klux as if it were the chosen retreat of brigands and the hunting-ground of savages.

The Congressional reports on the Ku-Klux conspiracy show the real causes of the decline in the value of every kind of property in the Southern States, and the dangers that threaten the future of their industry and trade. The Democratic party has fallen under the control of a murderous faction: its more intelligent and prudent members have not sufficient courage to free themselves from the tyranny of robbers and assassins; the colored population and the white. Republicans, the industrious and the honest, in many parts of the South are disfranchised by intimidation and open violence; the governments of several States are plain usurpations; a minority of lawless men rule over the powerless majority, and once more threaten rebellion, defy the national government, and bring ruin upon their fellow-citizens. The Ku-Klux conspiracy has extended its mysterious links through every Southern State: it has usually flourished before and after every election with a sudden vigor, and has then sunk into obscurity until the hour for new efforts arrived; its measures are always the same, whether in Texas or Missouri; its members ride around at night in strange disguises; their victims are white and colored Republicans, their wives and children, honest working-

AFRICAN AMERICAN HISTORY IN THE PRESS, 1851-1899

"ONE VOTE LESS."—*Richmond Whig.*

Harper's Weekly, October 19, 1872.

men, teachers, and active Baptist or Methodist ministers; sometimes United States officials or State judges and Senators have fallen before their rifles; sometimes the clergyman has been shot in his pulpit or the lawyer in his court-house; but oftener they are content to rob and burn the negro cabin, to seam the backs of its unlucky tenants with pitiless lashes, or leave the husband and the father bleeding and dying in the midst of his horror-stricken family. The pitiless cruelty of these Southern Democrats—for the chief object of the Ku-Klux assassins is always to insure the election of the Democratic officials—surpasses the barbarity of the savage.

Charlotte Fowler, an aged colored woman, thus relates the story of the murder of her husband, whose head was white as snow. "Tell how he was killed," said one of the Congressional Committee to her. We give the narrative in her own touching words. "The night he was killed—I was taken sick on Wednesday morning, and I laid on my bed Wednesday and Thursday. I didn't eat a mouthful; I couldn't do it, I was so sick. So he went out working on his farm. We still had a little grandchild living with me—my daughter's child. He had two little children living with him on the farm, but that little child staid with me. He kept coming backward and forward to the house to see how I got, and what he could do for me. I never ate nothing until Thursday night. When he came home he cooked something for me to eat, and said, 'Old woman, if you don't eat something you will die.' Says I, 'I can't eat.' Says he, 'Then I will eat, and feed the little baby.' That is the grandchild, he meant. I says, 'You take that little child, and sleep in the bed. I think I have got the fever, and I don't want you to get it.' He said, 'No, I don't want to get the fever, for I have too much to do.' He got up, and pulled off his clothes and got in bed. He came and called the grandchild, Tody—she is Sophia—

and he says, 'Tody, when you are ready, come to bed; come, and grandmother will open your frock, and you can go to bed.' So he lay there for about half an hour, and then I heard the dogs. I was only by myself now, for the children were all abed. Then I got up, and went into the room to my bed. I reckon I had not laid in bed half an hour before I heard somebody by the door; it was not one person, but two—ram! ram! ram! at the door. Immediately I was going to call him to open the door; but he heard it as quick as lightening, and he said to them, 'Gentlemen, do not break the door down; I will open the door;' and just as he said that they said, '——— you, I have got you now.' I was awake, and I started and got out of the bed, and fell down on the floor. I was very much scared. The little child followed its grandfather to the door. You know, in the night it is hard to direct a child. When he said, '——— you, I have got you now!' and he said, 'Don't you run!' And just then I heard the report of a pistol, and they shot him down; and this little child ran back to me before I could get out, and says, 'Oh, grandma, they have killed my poor grandpappy!' He was such an old gentleman, I thought they just shot over him to scare him; but, sure enough, as quick as I got to the door I raised my right hand and said, 'Gentlemen, you have killed a poor innocent man!' my poor old man! Says he, 'Shut up!' I never saw but two of them, for by that time the others had vanished."

The murderer was masked. The victim had been a firm Republican, but had never been an active one. The aged wife screamed and called in vain for help; in the dim moonshine she saw the body of her husband lie bleeding before the cottage door, and his assassins ride swiftly away: nor in the long line of the touching tragedies of all ages will there be found one more full than this of saddening contrasts between the innocence of the victims and the dreadful guilt of the destroyers, between the love and tender impulses that reigned in the negro cabin and the horrible passions that raged in the breasts of the white Carolinians. In several of the counties of South Carolina the Ku-Klux ruled for a long period unchecked; hundreds of persons suffered from their unparalled malignity; the sick, the aged, and the feeble were torn from their beds at night, whipped, tortured, or shot; women were often the express objects of their cruelty. Scarcely a year ago, disguised with masks, horns upon their heads, long dresses, and fantastic ornaments, these representatives of the fallen chivalry dashed along the roads of South Carolina in the depth of night, committed their atrocities upon the harmless and the innocent, and tormented the helpless and the weak. They openly declared to their bleeding victims that they must promise to vote for the Democratic party, or they would return and kill them. Many, after severe whippings, yielded to their dreadful argument. The newspapers were filled with the recantations of white and black Republicans, who had been converted to Democratic principles by stripes and wounds. One aged victim, beaten and bruised, crawled to the court-house steps, and there pronounced in faltering words his abjuration of Republican heresy. And if for a moment the murderous association seems suppressed in South Carolina, there can be no doubt that it would at once renew its outrages should the national government fall into the hands of its friends.

In Alabama the rage of the Democratic politicians seems chiefly turned against school-teachers, Methodist and Baptist preachers, and white Republicans who strive to elevate the colored race. The Ku-Klux labors have proved successful: a Democratic Governor has been elected (Lindsay), who denies the existence of any Ku-Klux conspiracy, and will see nothing of the brutal system of intimidation by which he has won an office; the State is ominously quiet. Governor Lindsay boasts of his power over the colored voters; the Democratic politicians assert that they are fast winning the negroes to their side—by what means who can fail to see? and that it can not be by any known train of argument is shown from the open assertion of leading Democrats that, had they the power, they would take from the colored population the right to vote at all.

The measures employed by the Democrats to recruit their party from the Republican side is best shown in the testimony of the Rev. Mr. Lakin, and his narrative of the fearful deeds of the Ku-Klux in Alabama is sustained and made probable by the long series of their similar crimes in every Southern State. Mr. Lakin was sent to Alabama by Bishop Clark, of Ohio, to renew the Methodist Episcopal Church in that State. He seems to have been unusually successful. He traveled over nearly all the counties of the State. He numbered seventy ministers or teachers among his assistants; he was presiding elder of his district, and was gladly welcomed in many humble cottages on the mountains, and in every negro cabin. He was chosen president of the State university. But in 1868 the Ku-Klux were awakened by the approaching election, and by the cheering words of their friends in the North, of Seymour, Buckalew, Kernan, and Wood; they drove the Rev. Mr. Lakin from the university; they threatened death to every Republican student. In the *Independent Monitor,* of Tuscaloosa, Alabama, appeared a leading article warning the new president to leave the State at once, and a cut was given, in which the Rev. Mr. Lakin was represented as hanging from the limb of a tree. It was also suggested that the end of "negroism" was near, and that three was room on the same limb for every "Grant negro." The Ku-Klux now renewed their terrible career, nor have we space even to allude to the details of their frightful deeds. Judge Thurlow was shot at Hunstville, where the disguised assassins had ridden in openly and in "line of battle;" Judge Charlton, another active Republican, was pursued and shot; a band of Ku-Klux rode into the town of Eutaw, in irresistible strength, seized a Mr. Boyd in his room at the hotel, and murdered him. The Rev. Mr. Lakin was threatened, shot at, and finally driven to take refuge in the mountains. The fate of many of his assistant preachers revives the image of the persecutions of Decius or Diocletian. A Mr. Sullivan was barbarously whipped; the Rev. J. A. M'Cutchen, a presiding elder, was driven from Demopolis; the Rev. James Buchanan, and the Rev. John W. Tailly, another presiding elder, were expelled by force; the Rev. Jesse Kingston was shot in his pulpit; the Rev. James Dorman whipped; Dean Reynolds whipped and left nearly dead, with both arms broken; a colored preacher and his son where murdered on the public road; the Rev. Mr. Taylor severely beaten; six churches were burned in one district; school-houses were every where destroyed, and the teachers, male or female, driven away or infamously ill treated; while in many a negro cabin disguised assassins murdered the unoffending inmates, and spread terror beyond conception in all the colored population of Alabama. Such were the means by which Alabama was converted to Democracy, and by which Mr. Greeley and his associates must hope to gain the Southern vote.

The Ku-Klux sprang up almost at the same moment through all the Southern States. It terrified and subdued Louisiana; it swept over Texas; mounted and disguised ruffians rode through Mississippi in 1871, breaking up the colored schools, and driving away preachers and teachers; they covered Western Tennessee; they murdered, whipped, and tormented in North Carolina. In Georgia, we are told by Mr. Stearnes, whole counties of colored voters are disfranchised by the terrors of their fearful orgies. Not even the Congressional Committee has been able to pierce the depths of this widespread conspiracy. The Democratic leaders of the South, who profit by its secret influence, endeavor to hide in doubt and obscurity the means by which they forced Republican States to vote for Seymour and Blair, and by which they hope again to drive them to vote for Greeley and the Democracy. They pretend that the period of license is past; that a year of the rigid intervention of the national government has suffered to dissolve forever the wide spread conspiracy which in 1871 was active in its enormities in every Southern State; that every colored citizen may vote safely in Alabama, and every white Republican till his plantation in Georgia in peace. He may; but it is on the condition that he will support the Democratic candidates and the Democratic policy. Whatever be the opinion of Northern or Southern politicians, the colored and the white Republicans of the South know that the Ku-Klux conspiracy is not dissolved; that the men who rode last year in masks and grotesque disguises over Georgia and Mississippi are more ready now than they were then to murder an aged Fowler almost in the arms of his wife ("He was so old a gentleman," she said, "that she did not think they could do it"); to shoot Methodist ministers in their pulpits; to whip Republican voters until they profess Democracy, and drive them to proclaim their shame, in faltering accents, on the steps of a court-house, or in the public papers; to disfranchise counties and States. And he can scarcely deserve the confidence of honest men who professes to believe that because the Ku-Klux has hidden from justice, it is not yet firmly united, pledged to rebellion, resolute to effect its aim; that it has not its allies at the North as cruel and as barbarous as in its own section; that an organized conspiracy does not still exist in every Southern State, laboring to provoke civil war and to destroy the Union. We might learn in every negro family, and in the home of every true Republican at the South, the universal terror of the midnight assassins by which the Democracy has risen to power.

Yet Mr. Greeley and Mr. Schurz wander through the country repeating their delusive dreams of reconciliation and of peace. "The colored man at the South," exclaims the former, "has now the same rights as every other citizen." Does he not know that in many sections of the South the colored man is forced to vote the Democratic ticket, or often heroically proclaims his loyalty to the Union at the peril of his life? And still Mr. Greeley grasps the blood-stained hands of the Southern Democratic leaders, and calls it reconciliation! For Mr. Greeley there is no excuse; with Mr. Schurz ignorance is probably bliss. He has never heard nor cared to hear the simple tales of the suffering negroes, nor studied the fate of the Republican voters in Georgia and Alabama. Even in his own State, Missouri, the secret assassins a few weeks ago renewed their nightly raids, their whippings, and their murders; and still Mr. Schurz persists in forgetting the reign of terror that has never ceased at the South.

It is certain that a large majority of the Southern people would rejoice to see these "pests of society" swept away forever by the rigorous hand of the government. The merchant and the mechanic, the farmer and the laborer, had they dared, would long ago have suppressed the infamous association. But they are terrified into silence. It is not improbable that most of the honest Democrats have no sympathy with their murderous allies. And the whole colored population awaits, in prayerful silence, the result of the approaching election. From a Greeley or a Schurz they have no sympathy and no hope; but with the success of the Union party and the re-election of President Grant an assurance of a free government and of progressive prosperity will be given to all that fertile and fortunate region which has so long endured the blight of anarchy and disorder. Immigration will begin, commerce, industry, and trade revive; the rich products of the mines and the coal-fields will be unfolded by engineering skill; the errors or the frauds in its financial management will be amended or punished; peace and reconciliation must accompany the return of good order; and the brigands of the Carolinas or Alabama, of Texas and Missouri, will no longer be suffered to hold great communities in awe, and establish their usurping governments in the centre of American freedom. What freeman is there but will give his vote against that faction whose only hope of success lies in ruling the Southern States by violence and fraud? What honest man but will labor with ceaseless energy to set free the South from these enemies of industry, knowledge, liberty, and Union?

An election has just been held in Georgia, the centre of the Ku-Klux conspiracy. In Geogia Mr. Stearns has told us how whole counties are disfranchised, and colored and white Republicans held in a terrible bondage. In Georgia the Ku-Klux have once more triumphed over the oppressed majority, and insolent fraud and rebellion rule over the unhappy State. Let the freemen of the North as well as the South reply to the unblushing traitors of Georgia with indignant unanimity, and show that they will permit no governments founded upon usurpation, terror, and bloodshed to exist within the bounds of the American Union.

By Eugene Lawrence

NOTES FROM WASHINGTON

Another Letter of Horace Greeley of Interest to Colored Men.
Heartless and Impertinent Interference with a Scheme of Benevolence Toward Colored Women—The Senate Committees To Be Reformed.
Special Dispatch to the New-York Times.

NEW-YORK TIMES
October 25, 1872

Washington, Oct. 24.—Another letter from Mr. Greeley has been unearthed, which, considering the circumstances under which it was written, will go far to offset the fulsome assurances which he has taken pains to give to every colored person who has called upon him for an expression during the present campaign. The *Woman's Campaign,* a Republican sheet which is issued here, will tomorrow contain the following letter, the original of which is in Mr. Greeley's unmistakable handwriting. It should be stated in explanation that the lady to whom it is addressed, Mrs. J. S. Griffing, was engaged at the time in raising funds to send the unemployed colored women of the District to places where they could be employed. She had been engaged in this benevolent and humane work for several years, under the original approval of Secretary Stanton and with the help of Congress, which granted her several small appropriations to aid her work. Just previous to the time named in this letter, she had issued a public appeal for funds to prosecute her purpose. In responses and entirely unsolicited, Mr. Greeley wrote the following letter:

New York Tribune
New-York, Sept. 7, 1870.
Mrs. Griffing: In my judgment, you and others who wish to befriend the blacks crowded into Washington do them great injury. Had they been told years ago, "You must find work, go out and seek it," they would have been spared much misery. They are an easy, worthless race, taking no thought of the morrow, and liking to lean on those who befriend them. Your course aggravates their weakness, when you should raise their ambition and stimulate them to self-reliance. Unless you change your course speedily and signally, the swarming of blacks to the District will increase, and the argument that slavery is their natural condition will be measurably strengthened. So long as they look to others to calculate and provide for them, they are not truly free. If there be any woman capable of earning wages, who would rather some one else than herself should pay her passage to the place where she could have work, then she needs reconstruction and awakening to honest self-restraint. Yours, Horace Greeley.
To Mrs. J. S. Griffing, Washington, D. C.

A PLEA FOR THE KU-KLUX

Presentment of the Grand Jury of Chester County.

CHARLESTON DAILY COURIER
November 2, 1872

The Grand Jury of the Circuit Court of Chester County, made the following presentment during its last session, concluded on the 27th October:

State Of South Carolina, Chester County, October 26th, 1872.
To His Honor T. J. Mackey, Judge of the Sixth Circuit of South Carolina:
The Grand Jury, before closing their labors for the year, desire to beg leave of this Honorable Court, to appeal most earnestly and respectfully to His Excellency, the President of the United States, to grant a pardon to such citizens of this County who are now in prison abroad, under sentence of violating the Enforcement Act of Congress, and to accord amnesty to those heretofore charged or now chargeable with having violated said Act in the year 1870–'71, except in cases of persons charged with the crime of murder, incident to their violation of said Act, if any such there be. The Grand Jury are sensible that in making this appeal, they are passing beyond the sphere of their prescribed duties, but they trust that they will not be deemed intrusive for exhibiting in this, the only mode available to them, their deep interest in a matter that involves the personal and material interests of possibly a very large number of their fellow citizens.
The Grand Jury forbear comment on the causes that tended to incite the armed violence

which manifested itself in this county, happily however, but on one occasion, in March, 1871.

They do not intend to justify or excuse any infraction of the laws of the land, or any invasions of the rights of the humblest citizen; believing that the courts are adequate to remedy all wrongs either to person or property, and that the safety of the citizen and the welfare of the community rests upon a rigid obedience to the laws, both State and Federal.

The undersigned, members of the grand jury, holding themselves loyal citizens of the United States, while they thus invoke the timely and merciful exercise of Executive clemency, have no hesitation in saying that henceforth the good people of the county will actively exert themselves, whenever necessary, for the maintenance of peace and order, and the supremacy of law in this county; and especially to secure to every citizen the free, safe and unquestioned exercise of his political rights and privileges, whenever the same shall be assailed.

The Grand Jury therefore respectfully ask that your Honor will endorse this appeal, and transmit His Excellency the President of the United States, through His Excellency the Governor of South Carolina, whose kind offices in furtherance of its object, are hereby most earnestly invoked.

 E. T. Atkinson.
 John C. Fleniken.
 G. W. Jones.
 T. A. Lee.
 F. M. Torbit.
 J. B. Linebarger.
 J. J. Lee.
 Jomn C. McFadden.
 his
 Nathan (X) McAliley.
 mark.
 his
 John (X) Cornwell.
 mark.
 his
 Levi (X) McClerkin.
 mark.
 his
 Solomon (X) Johnson.
 mark.
 his
 Jordan (X) Peden.
 mark.
 Alexander Wise.
 W. J. Latham.

"THE SOUTH."

HARPER'S WEEKLY
November 2, 1872, p. 843

The situation of the Southern States and the state of public opinion there are problems that will long tax the best political sagacity of the country. The cry of reconciliation is merely confusing and knavish, because it is raised as a declaration that the Government in some way persecutes the Southern States, and that there is monstrous inequality in the national laws. This is wholly untrue, and it necessarily diverts public attention from the real question. There is now, as there was before the war, deplorable ignorance of the actual state of feeling in both parts of the country. And this ignorance is carefully cultivated. The Greeley orators represent the Southern States as full of prostrate and ruined brothers sighing for fraternal reconciliation, and the Northern States as haughty and tyrannical, insolently insisting upon holding their hapless associates under an iron heel. The mischief which has been done in this way by those who affect to be peculiarly anxious for "reconciliation" is incalculable. It is like the old Democratic policy of representing the slave-holders as the victims of incendiaries in the free States who would insist upon repeating the Declaration of Independence, and who were sowing the seeds of hate and distrust. That the sum of all cruelties and evils might possibly tend to sow alienation, and that the barometer was not responsible for the weather, were not suggested by the Democratic doctors.

Those who know the actual situation of the Southern States feel most strongly the necessity of the continuance of Republican administration. The tyranny of opinion in those States is still most powerful. The old Southern element is represented by those who hesitate at nothing, and the ignorance and passions necessarily bred in a society ruled by the slave interest still govern by brute fear and force as in the older day. There are many counties in the Southern States in which no man dares to betray that he is a Republican; and there are large numbers of respectable persons who are absolutely terrorized, and who conform to the prevailing despotism even to voting. Republican meetings are held with difficulty and even with danger in many parts of those States. The memories of the lost cause are carefully cherished. Many of the old military organizations of that cause are still maintained, and the feeling is, of course, regretful and bitter.

Certainly we would not deal with such a state of things by sharp and harsh laws. But with equal certainty we would not try to persuade ourselves or any reader

PREPARING FOR SCHOOL.   VIRGINIA SKETCHES.   CANVASSING FOR VOTES.

Harper's Weekly, November 2, 1872, p. 849.

that any sentimental gushing about "reconciliation" will help the matter. The first step toward radical and final pacification in the Southern States is the universal conviction that Republican ascendency will be maintained, and then that it will not adopt hard nor unequal measures. And the earnest of the future is the past. There is not one thoughtful man of that part of the country who can truthfully say that the policy of the Republican party has ever been a vindictive policy. Not a life has been taken, not a dollar confiscated, in penalty of the war. Political and civil rights have been made equal, and all that has been required is that they shall be respected. But so long as the despotic class, the old "South," believes that there is a chance of the return of the Democratic party, its party, to power, so long final pacification is impossible.

It is the hope of this chance that rallies this class to the support of Mr. Greeley. If it could succeed, the condition of the known Union men in the Southern States would be intolerable. Even now the Ku-Klux virtually sits upon the bench in many places, and the triumph of the Democracy with Mr. Greeley would make justice toward Union men of any color a farce. Human nature in the Southern States is just what it is in the Northern, and every where else. The way to peace is through, and not backward. A sincere conviction that the national policy will not be changed, and an evident care that it shall be a just and firm and humane policy, are the two springs of hope for the Southern situation.

REPUBLICANISM, PAST AND FUTURE

The Good Time Come.

HARPER'S WEEKLY
November 23, 1872, p. 910

In the moment of victory the Republican party may well look back to the story of its earlier labors, and survey the past. It began as a protest against the enormous strides of slavery, and the dominion of an indolent and decaying caste, and boldly stood forward the defender of honest and honorable industry against its persecutors in every land. It demanded from the slave-holder some limitation to the spread of his noxious institution; it declared that the fair fame of transatlantic freedom should not always be tainted with an ineffaceable stain; it spoke firmly of the rights of man. Yet it offered no forcible measures, nor ever threatened violence. It besought the slave-holders to fall peacefully into the swift current of modern progress, to abandon a system of labor upon which all other cultivated nations looked with abhorrence, and to admit the light of education and of humanity into that sombre region over which they had raised unnatural barriers, and which they had imprisoned in a strange barbarism. Yet no Republican had ever dreamed of civil war, or had ever hoped to remove the national shame by any but legal and constitutional processes. But slavery had already produced its necessary consequences; the national disease could admit of none but a sharp, severe remedy. In the Slave States the indolent and the vicious ruled with a bitter tyranny. The industrious and the virtuous were terrified into obedience; a Toombs or a Davis led the desperate band of politicians who had resolved upon rebellion, and the plot against the Union, which had been the favorite theme of the Southern leaders, was suddenly executed. Of the insolence or the open robberies and intentional violence of the conspirators it is needless to tell. They made the election of Lincoln their pretext; they seized upon forts, ships, arms, and military stores within their territories; they plunged the nation in civil war; and almost in a moment sprang up a powerful slave empire from the Potomac to the Rio Grande, united, vigorous, terrible, whose single aim was to ravish away the rights of man, and to cover land and sea with a fearful despotism. . . .

In the moment of its triumph, too, the Republican party will look to its future with hope, yet not without a rational alarm. It bears with it the destiny of freedom. It stands at the front of human progress. The freemen of every advancing nation will be affected by its example, and are listening to its voice. We believe that the chief and favorite labor of Republicanism will be to educate the people. Governments in the future must become school-masters if they would continue to exist, and every free government has the right to compel all the members of the community to learn the duties of citizenship. Rigid compulsory education can alone dissipate that vast mass of foreign ignorance and prejudice which has made the city of New York a centre of fraud and of political danger, the instrument in the hands of foreign priests. A just and thorough scheme of compulsory education must be devised to raise the population of the Southern States into a higher grade of civilization, to banish brigandage and assassination, the duelist and the bravo, to teach all men the duty of labor, and to insure to every man a peaceful enjoyment of the fruits of his toil. A compulsory system of education, spreading from the Atlantic to the Pacific, can alone produce that mental equality which is the true foundation of union: the golden links of the common-school system must chain together that congeries of minds which is to provide for the freedom and elevation of coming generations. In its future, as in its past, we believe that the Republican party will be faithful to the highest impulses of freedom; that modesty, charity, and firmness will be its guides, and that in all its education it will never fail to trace the hand of that good Providence to whose glory all education tends. In this way only can every nation be made a school-house of virtue, and a just knowledge become as free to all as the light from heaven.

By Eugene Lawrence

AFTER ELECTION IN THE SOUTHERN STATES

HARPER'S WEEKLY.
December 7, 1872, p. 947

One of the most candid of Republicans in the Southern States, who was born and has always lived in that part of the country, and is the type of the men to whom we must look for the completion of the work of reconciliation, writes as follows:

"You have but little idea how much my *respectability* has been increased by the election. From being a scalawag, a representative of the party of hate, a traitor to my State, and other such flattering appellations, I am again recognized as a gentleman by the upper-tendom. I trembled for the consequences of Greeley's election. While not in a position to render direct aid to General Grant, we were in the position of the temperance lecturer's 'frightful example,' and perhaps rendered good service in that way. For I am told that the outrageous frauds and murders and riots and frightening from the polls did good in solidifying our friends North, and perhaps in this way did more good for Grant than we could have done in any other way.

". . . But what are our people to do? The colored men are timid, and in many counties are not allowed to vote. Where they are more intelligent, and attempt to assert their rights, they are shot down and driven off, as in Macon, Georgia, in October, where I learn that fifteen were killed. The governments of the Old World are strong enough to protect all their subjects. How is it in the United States, when citizens are not allowed to perform the duties of citizens? Is the fault in the system of government? We boast that it is the best in the world, and yet large numbers are virtually disfranchised. We are in a dilemma here; for if we move in the matter of having the Federal government interfere, we fall under the hatred and persecutions of the ruling class among us. As it is, our people are not free. I confess that I do not know what is best. To submit is to yield and give up the right of suffrage so far as the colored man is concerned, or nearly so. To attempt to get aid from Federal legislation is to incur still further odium, for the worst thing our adversaries can say to bring odium upon us is to charge us with aiding to enforce the Enforcement laws."

HOME AND FOREIGN GOSSIP

HARPER'S WEEKLY
December 7, 1872, p. 951

The horrors of the East African slave-trade are well known; but they have been exemplified anew by the recent capture of a slave dow, of which an account is given in the *Times of India*. In addition to the terribly crowded condition of the slaves and the fearfully foul state of the hold, the miseries of the poor creatures were complicated by the presence of small-pox. Thirty-five were discovered on board, at the time of the capture, in various stages of the disease, of whom a great part subsequently died; and it turned out on inquiry that at the first outbreak of the epidemic the Arab crew had endeavored to stamp it out by the simple process of throwing overboard all infected. Forty perished in this manner, but afterward the disease gained such a head that the attempt to check it was abandoned, and it was allowed to take its course among the slaves. A large portion of the cargo were children, many of them not more than three years old, and "most of them bearing marks of the brutality of the Arabs." The London *Court Journal*, in speaking of this case, says: "Hitherto the exertions of our cruisers on the east coast of Africa have been in a great measure futile, because a certain license has been given to the coasting trade in slaves, and the illicit traffic has been sheltered and encouraged by that which we permitted. Obviously the only remedy is root-and-branch destruction."

THE TROUBLES IN NEW ORLEANS

CHARLESTON DAILY COURIER
December 11, 1872

New Orleans, December 10
The Custom House Legislature passed a resolution impeaching Warmouth by a vote of 58 to 6. A Committee was appointed to inform the Senate. Pinchback qualified and took possession of the Governor's office.

Warmouth is suspended, pending the impeachment proceedings.

Pinchback exculpates C. A. Weed from participation in an attempt to bribe him. Pinchback says: I owe it to myself and Mr. Weed to state that he was not present at the meeting, as in my heat I had first stated. He was in an entirely separate room, and the doors were closed between us. He came to the house with Mr. Warmouth, but was not present.

Pinchback proclaims his assumption of the Governorship, and asks the support of all good citizens.

Warmouth has petitioned the Eighth District Court against Pinchback's assuming the Governorship. The petition nominates Pinchback as a wrong-doer and trespasser. The Court issued the injunction prayed for by warrant.

Washington, December 10
It was stated on the street that the Cabinet has decided to support Pinchback as Governor pro tem. of Louisiana.

AFFAIRS IN LOUISIANA

CHARLESTON DAILY COURIER
December 13, 1872

New Orleans, December 12
The Kellogg Legislature abolished the Seventh and Eighth District Courts, and created a Superior Court with exclusive jurisdiction in injunctions where the State, City or Municipal Board are concerned. They placed Longstreet in command of the militia. The officers refuse to obey Longstreet. Warmouth commands by proclamation that the Sheriffs, Tax Collectors and other officers disregard the Kellogg Legislature, promising the full power of the State for their protection. The militia who refuse to obey Longstreet are guarding their armory.

The following explains itself:

State of Louisiana, Executive Department, New Orleans, December 12, 1872
To the People of Louisiana:

It is my duty to make known that the President of the United States has formally and officially recognized the State Government of Louisiana, to the head of which I have been called under the Constitution of Louisiana.

The following dispatch has been received, and is published for the information of all law abiding citizens of the State, to wit:

Washington, December 12

To Acting Governor Pinchback, New Orleans:—
Let it be understood that you are recognized by the President as the lawful Executive of Louisiana, and the body assembled at Mechanic Institute as a lawful Legislature, and it is suggested that you make a proclamation to that effect, and also that all necessary assistance will be given to you and the Legislature herein recognized to protect the State from disorder and violence.

(Signed) Geo. H. Williams,

Attorney-General.

Now, therefore, I, P. B. S. Pinchback, Lieutenant-Governor, and acting Governor of the State, do issue this, my proclamation, counseling and commanding all citizens to recognize, support, and give obedience to the Government of the State. So recognized, I counsel and command all persons who may be participating in any illegal assembly, claiming to be the Legislature of the State, assembled elsewhere than at the State House or the Mechanic's Institute, to disperse. I request all citizens to aid in maintaining peace and order, and obedience to law and fully constituted authorities. And, furthermore, in the discharge of the Executive duties of the State, I warn all parties or combinations, or whatever pretense or authority that they may allege as their acting, that they will be held to a strict account for their conduct in the premises, and be punished to the utmost extent of law for the violation of good order of society, or in disregard of the dignity and peace of the State, and I now command and will enforce obedience to all laws which may have been enacted, or may be enacted, by the General Assembly of the State now in session at the State House, Mechanics' Institut.

Given under my hand, and seal of the State offixed, at New Orleans, this twelfth day of December, 1872, and of the independence of the United States the ninety-seventh.

By the Governor. P. B. S. Pinchback,

Acting Governor of Louisiana.

E. Bovee, Secretary of State.

DOMESTIC INTELLIGENCE

HARPER'S WEEKLY
December 14, 1872, p. 971

A colored delegation, representing the Equal Rights League of Philadelphia, waited upon President Grant recently with an appeal for "more rights." They went away with the assurance that all voters in the United States should be treated with equal fairness.

THE 'COON HUNT

HARPER'S WEEKLY
December 14, 1872, p. 974

All who are familiar with the sports and customs of the "old Virginny nigger," as he existed in "ante-bellum" days, associate his memory with the hoe-down, the corn-shucking, and the "'coon and 'possum hunt." With the change of his condition the last named of these sports has lost none of its ancient vigor. A favorite mode of conducting the hunt is this: A few hours after darkness sets in, when the wary game has wandered far from his place of refuge in search of his scanty fare, the party, provided with axes, dogs, matches, and bags, repair to the woods. In some wild spot a blazing dry-wood fire is built, where the hunters gather in a circle and pass the hour of waiting in tale-telling or song. When the dogs, trained to their work, announce by their barking that the game is "treed," fire-brands and axes are seized, and the tree in which the 'coon has taken refuge felled to the ground, the game captured and bagged, and the dogs sent out again, while the happy party return to their fire. When the hunt is finished the night's sport is wound up with tales wilder still, in which "Mr. Coon" often figures as a prominent character. Our illustration on page 972 shows this jolly point of the game. When the cider jug has been exhausted, and the dogs have been fully rested, the exhilarated party disperse to their homes, where their captives must pine and fatten before the cabin fire, unconscious of their doom.

SEEING THE CIRCUS PASS

HARPER'S WEEKLY
December 14, 1872, p. 974

In one of his rambles in the Old Dominion in search of picturesque subjects for his pencil our artist stumbled upon the merry group represented in the lower illustration on page 972. A large circus was passing along the road, and the pasture bars were completely covered with a motley crowd of white and black children, all intent upon seeing the grand display. The effect, as the sketch shows, was ludicrous in the extreme.

ENSLAVED LOUISIANA

CHARLESTON DAILY COURIER
December 16, 1872

Judge Durell, of Louisiana, has destroyed Republican liberty in the United States if the action which he has taken as United States District Judge should be sustained. If a United States Judge can destroy the results of an election and defeat the popular will by a stroke of his pen; if he can enjoin Governors, improvise Legislatures, declare elections, without even taking the trouble to have votes counted, then the sooner the States are

THE 'COON HUNT—TELLING STORIES ROUND THE CAMP FIRE.—Drawn by R. N. Brooke.—[See Page 974.]

Harper's Weekly, December 14, 1872, p. 972.

destroyed the better it will be. People will at least then understand that they have no rights, and be able to adapt themselves to their condition. At present the name of liberty is a mockery. A reckless, unprincipled man can make his individual will the law of the land, and can compel Federal bayonets to execute his orders.

How infamous the order of Judge Durell is, may be seen in the following paragraph, taken from the New Orleans *Times*. That paper, in speaking of him, says:

Encouraged by this submissiveness, he has capped the climax of his infamy by attempting, through a judicial order, to destroy the government of a State, and to degrade the honest, intelligent and virtuous of our population into serfs of their former slaves. To do this he has played traitor to his own Government, and by false pretences and representations procured the aid of the regular military of that Government to enforce his decrees. At midnight he scrawls an illegible signature to an order prepared for him by his soberer companions, and by this order the soldiers of the United States are directed to march against the State House, to expel the officers of the State, and to hold possession of the building until his negro legislators can be assembled, to declare themselves the rulers of the State. By his order and authority a bogus returning board is permitted to count in a Legislature composed of an overwhelming majority of negroes, nearly every one of whom was beaten in the election. And, this Legislature is further authorized to declare all the officers returned, and even those who have been qualified, no longer officers of the State, and to induct their opponents in their places.

It also says, in another place, in speaking of the order:

"Under this order, a vicious and depraved mulatto, a former waiter or scullion in a low gambling den, was foisted into the seat once occupied by a Claiborne, a Robertson, a Roman and a Meuton. It was by virtue of that maudlin signature that a Legislature, composed largely of brutal negroes, was called into existence to rule a State, founded by the chivalry of France and nourished into wealth and power by the best representatives of the Caucassian race!"

Elsewhere, speaking of him and his action, it says:

The chief agent and instrument in this revolting act has been this worthy son of a New Hampshire keeper of a cross-roads tavern.

His main object and consideration have been the elevation of his associate, his boon companion and favorite, E. C. Billings, a plausible and crafty Connecticut attorney, to the Senate of the United States, and to secure the Governorship for that Aminidab Sleek of carpet-baggers, William Pitt Kellogg.

SEEING THE CIRCUS PASS—A VIRGINIA SKETCH.—Drawn by R. N. Brooke.—[See Page 974.]

Harper's Weekly, December 14, 1872, p. 972.

We are at a loss to conceive the slightest ground on which Judge Durell can rest his claim to the right which he has claimed to exercise. It certainly is not to be found in the Constitution, nor in any law passed by Congress. It is simply a stretch of power which threatens to destroy the freedom of the people. It is an invitation to revolution, an attempt at destruction of the form of government and subversion of every principle on which our institutions are founded. The New York *Herald* forcibly comments on this disgraceful usurpation of power as follows, in speaking of the Enforcement Act under which Judge Durell pretended to act:

In the face of the recent events in Louisiana and Alabama, no one will deny the evils of the present political condition of the South, and the necessity of a speedy reform. In one of these States, through what President Grant calls a "miserable scramble for office," the City of New Orleans has been brought to the verge of civil war. Riot and bloodshed have only been averted by a surrender of all the rights of the State. If Judge Durell did not strain the law, and exceed his powers in handing over the Executive Office and the State Legislature to the Kellogg party then the Enforcement Act really destroys Republican institutions, and surrenders the States to the arbitrary will of the Federal Government. The Act in question gives large powers to the United States Courts. If any colored citizens are denied the right of registration or voting, solely "on account of race, color or previous condition of servitude," and by reason of such denial a candidate for any office except for Presidential elector, member of Congress or of the State Legislature, shall be defeated, the United States Circuit or District Court, "concurrently with the State Courts," is given the power to count the votes thus excluded, and if they are sufficient to elect the minority candidate, to award him the office. Acting under this provision of the law, Judge Durell granted injunctions against the State Board of Canvassers from discharging its functions, placed a new Board in power and thus declared Governor Kellogg and the Republican State Legislature elected. Neither Judge Durell nor the Kellogg Board of Canvassers has possession of a single election return; no co-operation has been bad with any State Court; no evidence has been taken or offered to substantiate the affidavits of thousands of negroes as to the rejection of their voice, and there is not a particle of proof that any citizens were disfranchised on account of race, color or previous condition of servitude. We repeat, if the Enforcement Act has been properly interpreted by Judge Durell the Southern States are at the present moment stripped of all their constitutional rights and holding their liberties only at the mercy of Federal bayonets. At any time, after any election, the popular verdict may be set aside by any political aspirants who can command the services of a Federal Judge and Federal troops. The ballot is a mere farce—the Constitution of the United States nothing more than waste paper—while each an Act stands upon the statute books.

The Enforcement Act is bad enough, but it can only be interpreted as Judge Durell has seen fit to interpret it, by one who desires to destroy liberty and to disregard the rights of the citizen.

1873

The political firestorm at the close of 1872 in Louisiana surrounding the governorship was settled in January 1873 when William Kellogg was inaugurated as governor. Kellogg had led the forces supporting Pinckney Benton Steward Pinchback as lieutenant governor and then again as governor after the former Republican governor had been impeached. The Democratic candidate for governor, John McEnery, and Kellogg both claimed victory. Kellogg was declared the victor by the official election board and the courts. Meanwhile forces loyal to McEnery armed themselves and attacked the Kellogg faction. Many of McEnery's loyal forces were members of the White League, the Louisiana "brother" to the Ku Klux Klan. In response Kellogg requested federal troops to suppress the uprising.

White Leaguers in Louisiana, like the Ku Klux Klan, flourished using intimidation and violence to disenfranchise citizens, particularly African Americans. However, the disenfranchisement of citizens was just one goal of these groups as depicted in a Harper's Weekly (10 May 1873) news report of a massacre of African Americans in Grant Parish, Louisiana.

Northern journalists provided scant attention to the conditions of African Americans except in the South. While newspapers such as Harper's Weekly provided commentary on the atrocities committed by the Ku Klux Klan or the progress of African Americans socially and culturally, newspapers such as the Richmond Whig (11 November 1873) provide commentary on the "triumph of Conservatism in the recent election." The Whig states "The colored people knew that their struggle was for race supremacy, and not for the success of any political system or principles."

In spite of the efforts of the Ku Klux Klan, African Americans were casting their ballots at the polls. John Lynch was the first African

American from the state of Mississippi elected to Congress. Lynch was the son of a former slave and a white Louisiana planter.

Although African Americans were constantly being terrorized politically, socially, and economically, they continued to demonstrate a commitment to education as a means to improve conditions for the race. Harper's Weekly *(13 September 1873) quoted an African American clergyman, the Rev. M. Johnson in Eatonton, Georgia, as saying the lesson taught by Independence Day is "education for the masses."* Harper's Weekly *continues that: "The Eatonton newspaper notices Mr. Johnson's speech, and remarks with a rude sneer that the colored people must never hope to rise to a level with the white, that they can never look to equal the virtues of their former masters." Richard T. Greener, the first black graduate of Harvard in 1870, became professor of mental and moral philosophy at the University of South Carolina in 1873. He held this faculty position until 1877 when the legislature barred African Americans from the school.*

Robert L. Harris, Jr.
Cornell University

THE CHRISTMAS DINNER GONE!

HARPER'S WEEKLY
January 4, 1873, p. 1

Mr. Sheppard's humorous and graphic picture suggests its own story so well that the reader's imagination can easily fill in the missing links—the tramp through the snowy woods to the trap, the too eager haste of the younger party, the disappointed hopes of a good Christmas dinner, the sulky march homeward, and the shrill scolding at the cabin when the unlucky sportsmen return empty-handed. The Virginia negroes, we may add, call the rabbit "he-yar," and the trap a "gum."

LOUISIANA

HARPER'S WEEKLY
March 22, 1873, p. 219

The persistent efforts of the Democratic politicians—or at least the rebellious element of the Democracy—to destroy the prosperity of the Southern States, to drive capital from the country, to check the growth of commerce, force the merchant and the farmer to bankruptcy, depreciate the value of land, and stop the tide of immigration, can not fail at last to bring upon them the general indignation of the people. Every Ku-Klux murder, every assault upon the supremacy of the law, every threat of violence and of usurpation, tends to produce infinite loss to the country, and helps to reduce to poverty and decay a region fitted by nature to teem with material wealth, and support in affluence an immense population. Lands in various portions of the Southern States that under a peaceful government would prove more productive than the rich fields of Minnesota are left idle and untilled. Farms are sold at prices so low as to seem incredible to Northern cultivators. The mineral resources of the mountain chains are left untouched. Railroads that would open up wide districts of country to foreign immigration are stopped in their progress because the capitalist is afraid of spoliation and open robbery. The commerce of the Southern cities languishes, while the cities of the great West press on with unprecedented strides. The merchant, the honest laborer, the mechanic, and the investor shrink from the home of the Ku-Klux, and avoid a region where life and property are threatened by brigands and revolutionists.

Louisiana has suffered as severely as any of its sister States from the cruel deeds of its rebellious faction. The great majority of its people, no doubt, desire repose; but their Democratic leaders will not suffer them

1873

THE CHRISTMAS DINNER GONE!
"Dar now! I done tole you so fust."

Harper's Weekly, January 4, 1873, p. 1.

to rest. The recent riots in New Orleans are only the latest of a long series of outrages. The same faction that has never ceased to threaten and ill treat Republican voters and peaceful colored men has at last covered the streets of New Orleans with bloodshed. They have been the first to shed the blood of their fellow-citizens. They have not only defied the authority of the State and national courts, but have endeavored to seize the government by armed violence.

The particulars of this contest deserve a general attention. Two governments existed in Louisiana, each

A STEP IN THE DARWINIAN DEVELOPMENT.
GENTLEMANLY STOREKEEPER. "Wa'al, what do you want?"
PROGRESSIVE BUYER. "I don't want nuffin; dis yere Lady wants a *Chignon.*"

Harper's Weekly, February 27, 1873, p. 160.

claiming to represent the majority of the people. The Warmoth and M'Enery faction, supported by the rebel leaders, and composed of many men who had served in the rebel armies, assert that at the fall election they had a large majority of the votes. The Kellogg party, embracing all the Republicans, insist that the majority was on their side. The question as to the validity of either claim was submitted to the Supreme Court of New Orleans, and also to the United States judge, Durell. Both courts decided in favor of Kellogg and his associates. They were declared elected by the highest legal decision. They entered upon their offices, took possession of the public buildings, organized the police, proceeded to discharge their proper duties, and the national Administration, as it was obliged to do, respected the decision of the courts, and acknowledged the State government of the Kellogg party. It could have done nothing else; it was forced to follow the ruling of the courts; and, besides, the Kellogg government was in existence *de facto* as well as *de jure.* It was the only one known to the law.

Meantime the M'Enery party also organized a government, assembled a Legislature, and proceeded to perform various acts annoying and obstructive to its opponents. It next, as was most proper, appealed to the President and to Congress. The President had no power to interfere, but Congress, perhaps, might have determined the controversy. It would seem, however, rather a question for the Supreme Court; and even Congress would scarcely care to reverse the decision of the New Orleans judges. But however this may be, the plain duty of the M'Enery party, if they found themselves aggrieved, was to commence such legal proceedings as might expose the errors of their opponents and obtain justice for themselves. They should have awaited the operation of the law. Instead of this they armed themselves, prepared a large military force, and made an attack upon their opponents, which ended in the loss of several lives and the wounding of fifteen or twenty persons. Their object, it seems, was to seize the court-houses and reinstate their own judges: they might thus gain a show of legality on their side, which is now wholly wanting. The rebels fought with courage; but their plans had been revealed to the Kellogg officials, and General Longstreet, by his prudent disposition of the armed police, saved the court-houses. General Emory, the United States officer in command, next ordered the rioters to disperse, and, obeying the instructions of President Grant, aided in restoring order in New Orleans. For this the President has been assailed with extraordinary bitterness by the friends of Warmoth and M'Enery, by the opposition press of the North, and the enemies of the public peace. The people of the whole country, however, will probably approve of his conduct, and show the rebellious portion of the Southern population that they are resolved to check at once their constant tendency toward bloodshed and crime.

The chief sufferers from the violence of Warmoth and M'Enery, next to the dead and the wounded, to whose fate they have been accessory, will be the merchants, mechanics, and farmers of Louisiana. Business has long been inactive at New Orleans, owing to the fear of riots and the political disturbances. Republicans and the colored citizens are naturally alarmed for their lives when they see their enemies armed parading in the streets, and when they remember the long series of outrages which have been inflicted upon them by a small but desperate faction of the opposition. Louisiana, rich in natural advantages, requires capital to repair its levees, drain its swamps, renew its productiveness; and New Orleans must insure good order among its citizens before it can hope for the revival of its trade.

Let, therefore, the intelligent people of Louisiana of all parties unite to repair the evils that have been inflicted upon them. Let them discourage every attempt to violate the law; let them select for office moderate, honest men, who are willing to do justice to all; let them punish with imprisonment and hard labor the desperate politicians, who are the enemies of industry and peaceful progress; and New Orleans will once more assume the appearance of a commercial city. Nor will the whole South ever recover its prosperity until it has pursued a similar course—has proved to the world that the rule of rapine and disorder, which has so long impoverished many of its fairest districts, has passed away forever, and that the life and property of the immigrant, the Republican voter, and the foreign capitalist are as safe in North Carolina and Georgia as they are in Minnesota or Nebraska.

LOUISIANA MURDERS

HARPER'S WEEKLY
May 3, 1873, p. 362

By the amendments to the Constitution the nation pledged itself, by the Enforcement laws it provided the means, to secure to the white and colored population of the Southern States equal rights and a general tranquillity. To aid in the effort to preserve the peace of the country and give freedom to the colored race the Democratic leaders at the South had plighted their honor, and promised obedience to the law. Many of them have kept their word; others have violated it. And the recent accounts of horrible outrages inflicted in all parts of the Southern States show that with the perjured and unscrupulous portion of the Democracy neither humanity nor good faith is any longer regarded. From Kentucky to Louisiana the whole country seems penetrated by a secret association of the lawless portion of the population, who are bound by no pledges, however solemn, who scoff at the Constitution, and defy the laws. Nowhere except in the States where the Republicans rule is there any safety for life and freedom. It seems a fixed purpose on the part of the Democratic politicians to prevent the restoration of peace at the South, and in this policy they are unhappily encouraged by the Democratic and Liberal Republican leaders at the North. Both hope to keep up their party organization by inciting insurrections in Louisiana, and by charging upon the Administration these scenes of fatal discord which have sprung from their own evil promptings.

That the recent shocking events in Louisiana owe their origin in great part to the intrigues of selfish and cruel politicians in all parts of the country might easily be shown. And if the Ku-Klux association has been able to maintain its existence in every Southern State with even more than its early ferocity, this too is due to the open countenance it has received from Democrats and Liberal Republicans. When Georgia was overridden by the Ku-Klux, and the vast majority of its voters driven from the polls at the last Presidential election, when the opposition ticket was chosen by violence and fraud, every Liberal Republican and every intolerant Democrat expressed unbounded joy. They accepted the labors of the Ku-Klux as their own, and gave their countenance to the league of murders. At the same time the Ku-Klux in Louisiana renewed its outrages. There too it drove the white and colored Republicans from the polls, scoffed at the constitutional provisions or the Enforcement act, and deprived a large part of the population of their votes. It endeavored to force the M'Enery government, elected by such lawless usurpation, into office; and when it was defeated by the resolution of the honest portion of the citizens, it refused to obey the decisions of the courts, and began an ineffectual rising in New Orleans. M'Enery and Warmoth began a period of bloodshed. They were secretly or openly encouraged by the Liberal Republican and Democratic politicians of the North. Their guilty courage rose, and their latest exploit, or that of their imitators, is the burning of a hundred negroes at Colfax, the murder of as many more, and the infliction of such a calamity upon Louisiana as a generation can scarcely repair.

But the question of permitting disorder and violence at the South must now be taken from the control of cruel and selfish politicians, and be committed to the decision of the whole people. It is a question that belongs to the community, and we believe the community will now sweep aside the frivolous logic of political leaders, the outcries of faction, and the clamors of the unwise. It will proceed to do its duty. The nation is bound by the Constitution to secure the equal rights of the colored citizen in Georgia or Louisiana, to afford security to the white voter, and to repress every lawless association. The Executive is bound by his position to enforce the Constitution to its utmost limit. The people will demand the punishment of every political outlaw, however noted his name, or however he may be sheltered under the patronage of the Liberal Republican or Democratic leaders; and if the Liberal Republicans and the Democrats persist in their alliance with the Ku-Klux association, they will soon be swept away before the general rage of the nation. For we believe it is the intention of the people in every section, with no party distinctions, to insist on the preservation of good order in the Southern States, and to make them all at last the home of a free and prosperous population.

STRAIGHTENING THE CROOKED TREE

HARPER'S WEEKLY
May 3, 1873, p. 368

One of the most remarkable and encouraging features attending the emancipation of the colored race in our Southern States is the eagerness to learn displayed from

STRAIGHTENING THE CROOKED TREE.—[DRAWN BY R. N. BROOKE.]

Harper's Weekly, May 3, 1873, p. 368.

the earliest moment of freedom. Old and young crowded to the schools opened for the benefit of the freedmen; and it was not uncommon to see men and women who had nearly reached the allotted term of life poring over the spelling-book with all the eager interest of children.—Slowly and painfully, against every kind of discouragement, they would master the A, B, C, and learn to pick out simple words, until they could read in the book, which thousands of them knew already by heart, the Bible. The younger learned readily, not only to read but to write, and to comprehend the elementary principles of arithmetic.

Our illustration on this page shows a simple-hearted old colored woman poring intently over the alphabet, and trying to master its difficult mysteries, while her young instructor leans on her shoulder ready to assist and explain. The poor old woman may never be able to do more than painfully spell out a few sentences in her Bible, but even this will be a comfort and consolation in her declining years.

THE LOUISIANA MURDERS

HARPER'S WEEKLY
May 10, 1873, p. 396

The official report of Colonels William Wright and T. W. De Klyne, of General Longstreet's staff, who were sent to Grant Parish, Louisiana, to investigate the late massacre of colored people there, shows that the first reports of that atrocity were not exaggerated. Between one hundred and fifty and two hundred colored men had been killed by the whites. The former had intrenched themselves about the court-house at Colfax, inclosing a space of about 200 yards square with a slight earthwork, with ditch inside. This ditch was from ten to eighteen inches in depth, and the breastwork in front of it from twenty to thirty inches in height, and was protected in front by two-and-a-half-inch planking. On the lower side of the court-house the greater portion of the breastwork was composed of planking alone, laid in zigzags, and without ditches. They were poorly armed, and had rigged up a couple of guns by fastening lengths of gas-pipe on rafter timbers, blocking up one end with a pine plug, and drilling a touch-hole. One of these was burst while trying it, some days before the fight, and the other has not the appearance of having been used. The attacking party had in their possession a small cannon, taken from a steamboat in the river, with which they bombarded the court-house.

During the fight the negroes were driven from their breastworks into the court-house, one end of which was without windows, nor had the besieged prepared loop-holes. The leader of the whites, a man named Nash, caused the court-house to be fired, and the negroes "were shot down like dogs" as they fled from the burning building. The report, describing the atrocities of the massacre, says:

"Many were shot in the back of the head and neck. One man still lay with his hands clasped in supplication; the face of another was completely flattened by blows from a broken stock of a double-barreled gun, lying on the ground near him; another had been cut across the stomach with a knife after being shot; and almost all had from three to a dozen wounds. Many of them had their brains literally blown out. It is asserted by the colored people that after the fight thirty-four prisoners who were taken before the burning of the court-house were taken to the river-bank two by two, executed, and hurled into the river. We caused to be buried in the ditch near the ruins of the court-house the remains of fifty-four colored men, three of whom were so badly burned as to be unrecognizable. There were inside the court-house the charred bones of one other, and five bodies we gave to their friends for interment elsewhere. We saw also twelve wounded colored men, two of whom will certainly die, and others of whom are very unlikely to recover. We are informed that since the fight parties of armed men have been scouring the country surrounding Colfax, taking the mules and other property of the colored people."

Near the court-house the commissioners met a party of colored men and women carrying away a wounded colored man upon a sled. At a little distance in the field were the dead bodies of two colored men. About two hundred yards nearer the court-house were three dead bodies of colored men, and from that point to the court-house and its vicinity the ground was thickly strewn with dead. A general feeling of insecurity prevails among the colored people of Louisiana, and hundreds are seeking safety in the swamps and forests.

GOVERNOR KELLOGG AND THE ASSASSINS

HARPER'S WEEKLY
May 24, 1873, p. 434

The moderation and good feeling, prudence and forbearance, with which Governor Kellogg and his supporters have controlled the affairs of disordered Louisiana have been repaid by the lawless portion of the population with unprecedented crimes. That Governor Kellogg represents the majority of the people, that if a free election could be held in the State to-day he would receive a still larger support than before, few can doubt. But the worst elements of the rebel faction, the vicious and indolent remnant of the party of slavery, have resolved to make Louisiana the seat of a new insurrection. In every Southern State exists this class of depraved and worthless characters, too indolent or too proud for labor, yet ready for any act of violence, maddened with whisky and accustomed to bloodshed, who are feared, hated, or despised by every honest merchant or mechanic, and from whom the South can only rid itself by patient severity. To this class is due the enormities that have been recently committed in Louisiana, as well as in

NEGROES HIDING IN THE SWAMPS OF LOUISIANA.

Harper's Weekly, May 10, 1873, p. 396.

several other Southern States. It has filled the country with riot and bloodshed. It has attempted an insurrection. It incited its allies at Colfax to their horrible deeds. It would bring upon New Orleans the guilt and perhaps the fate of Charleston. It has plundered the gun shops, beaten respectable citizens on the public streets, and completed its crimes by attempting the life of the Governor. It is plainly no better than a band of assassins claiming to be a political party.

Less and less tolerable are the accounts that come to us of the Colfax massacre, and the horrors of the dreadful scene make it worthy to stand beside the most shameful acts of human barbarity. From Colonel Wright's report, a member of General Longstreet's staff, we have some accurate details. The negroes had retreated to the court-house from the rude barriers which they had formed to defend themselves from the murderous rebels. It was Easter-Sunday, and they resisted successfully every assault until evening. Then Nash, the rebel chief, forced a colored man to hold a pine torch to the side of the building where there was no window. The fire spread, and the brave garrison, conscious that they must fly from the flames, waved white handkerchiefs, and made every symbol of submission. But as they poured out of the burning building, no longer thinking of resistance, and begging for life, they were shot down by the merciless Louisianians as if they had been dogs. No honorable enemy but is willing to accept the submission of a suppliant foe, but these barbarians were intent only upon extermination. Many of the colored people fled back into the court-house, and perished in its ashes. Many fell by the knives or bullets of the assailants. No quarter was given. Beneath the floor of the building, near the river, were found the bodies of six persons who had been shot in their hiding-place. One man lay not far off, dead, his hands clasped in supplication. Some were hacked and hewn to pieces.

And yet we have among us apologists for M'Enery and his followers, who would even intrust Louisiana to their care, and expose every white or colored Republican to a fate like that of the garrison at Grant Parish! It is difficult indeed to understand so strange a delusion, or to read with any calmness the studied arguments that are offered to maintain it. No one can be unfamiliar with the long series of similar though perhaps less terrible deeds perpetrated by the brutal associations at the South. There is no one who does not know that in 1868 the colored and white voters were driven from the polls by the same miscreants; that on every succeeding election they have resorted to the same method of terrorism; or that, on the last, they had nearly succeeded in establishing their brutal tyranny over Louisiana. Whatever be the venial errors of the Kellogg government, it is stained by no acts of frightful massacre, and has striven to rule with humanity and moderation.

The insurgents on their way to their victims seized upon a Mr. Colhoun, a wealthy planter, who has always been an active Republican, and carried him away with

THE LOUISIANA MURDERS—GATHERING THE DEAD AND WOUNDED.—[SEE PAGE 396.]

Harper's Weekly, May 10, 1873, p. 397.

them, intending, no doubt, to kill him. But reflection alarmed them; they released him after a painful imprisonment, and he escaped to New Orleans. No white Republican is safe from their murderous aim. No Union man can hope to live secure in the rural parishes so long as these lawless bands are permitted to wander over the State. The sooner they are suppressed by the most rigid and severe punishment, the better for the peace of the community, the honor of the nation. And we suspect the feeling that is being aroused in all parts of the country will never be satisfied until full justice has been awarded to every one of the authors of the Louisiana massacres. We think it likely, however, that the majority of the people of that State will join cordially in aiding the Kellogg government to search out and punish them; it is the plain duty of the wiser citizens to hasten to relieve themselves from the stain of complicity in the horrible deed. It will be dangerous indeed for Louisiana, fatal to its welfare, destructive to all its hopes of future progress, to pause for a moment in the course of punishment for all the guilty; and if it can be proved that M'Enery and his followers had any direct share in the massacre, they should be the first to suffer. That they are indirectly its chief cause no one can avoid seeing. They had already set the example of defying the law. Nor can Louisiana ever hope to see its levees renewed, its great resources developed, its port filled with lucrative trade, until it has driven into obscurity the enemies of all industry, who teach lawlessness, and thrive upon the misery of their fellow-citizens. Scarcely will the Democracy of Louisiana ever again recover from the odium of this fearful massacre.

PERSONAL

HARPER'S WEEKLY
May 24, 1873, p. 435

Mr. Richard T. Greener, the first colored graduate of Harvard (1870), has joined the editorial staff of Mr. F. Douglass's *New Era* newspaper at Washington. . . .

Henry Ossian Flipper (good name, the first two-thirds), a colored boy of Atlanta, Georgia, has been appointed to a cadetship at West Point. The Atlanta *Sun* says of him: "This is the son of 'Flipper,' the well-known boot-maker of Atlanta. He has been at school here for five years, and has studied Latin and Greek, and the first six books in geometry, and at this time stands first in the class. He is tall, stout, intelligent-looking, and converses very well, and is far above the average of his race. He is an octoroon, with light eyes. He solicited the appointment, and as there was no other applicant, he had an easy thing of it."

COLOR IN POLITICS

HARPER'S WEEKLY
June 7, 1873, p. 482

The Richmond Enquirer assures its readers that the chief aim of the radical party in that State is to insure the supremacy of the colored population over the white. The Virginian conservative is eager to begin a faint imitation of that war of races which the Democracy of Louisiana have striven to excite, but which will probably be closed forever in the universal horror awakened by the massacre at Colfax. Yet it scarcely required that fatal event to show that the colored race have always been the victims and not the perpetrators of cruelty at the South, that they have never aspired to political power with any extraordinary effort unless where it was plainly necessary for the preservation of their lives and the safety of their families. The history of the African at the South has shown a general humanity and an abstinence from all tendency to pitiless deeds that forms a touching contrast to the intolerant annals of their masters. In the period of slavery the negro bore with signal patience such evils as have seldom fallen to the lot of man. He was forced to see his children torn from him; to separate from wife and friends at every new sale; to bear the lash, the chain, the prison. Yet, when the rebellion came, it is admitted by the most rigid conservative at the South that the conduct of the colored population was admirable. When the plantations were deserted by their owners, who were fighting to bind anew the bonds of the escaping slaves, when none but women and children were found in the lonely mansion or the unprotected village, the colored people, conscious to a remarkable degree of the true meaning of the contest, yet abstained from all deeds of violence. They waited patiently for the result. They still performed their household or plantation duties with perhaps more than ordinary care. They watched over the white women and children tenderly. And only when the Union armies approached the solitary plantation or the fallen city did the slave proclaim that he was free.

His fidelity and forbearance were repaid with pitiless ingratitude by the lawless portion of the Southern whites. Scarcely was the war over when they formed an association to control the colored vote by terror and by acts of rare cruelty. Instead of rewarding the generosity and the humanity of the former slaves by teaching them the kindly arts of civilization, the worst class of the Southern population, always apparently the masters of the rest, began that series of horrible outrages known as the Ku-Klux conspiracy. It was against the inoffensive and often industrious and deserving negro that all this childish paraphernalia and all the excess of wickedness were directed. For five years the colored population in almost every Southern State have been made the victims of midnight raids and mysterious crimes; have suffered untold oppression at the hands of the Southern conservatives. Yet they have rarely returned a blow. No inhumanity is ever laid to their charge. Where they hold the political power, life is safe, and violence discountenanced. They ask only the privilege of labor, and when they take part in politics it is with the conviction that only by exercising the right of suffrage can they secure themselves from the pitiless cruelty of men like those who drove their victims from the polls at Colfax, and then burned them in the court-house or flung them into the river.

We trust that the large majority of the white population at the South have already become shocked and indignant at the cruelty of their lawless companions. There is, indeed, but one course for the Southern whites to adopt toward the new citizens that can insure peace and progressive ease to their fertile territory. It is to protect the right of every citizen to vote with the utmost freedom; to defend the privileges of the colored population as they would their own; to punish with exemplary severity every desperate politician who strives to rule by terror; to repay the humanity of their former slaves by giving them a liberal education; to win their votes, if necessary, by the exhibition of equity and justice. Let the Southern whites drive from power every politician who has joined in the desperate deeds of the Ku-Klux or profited from its labors, and a liberal share of immigration and commerce will soon blend together the united community. In such a course they will have the aid of the honest of every color or sect, and it will be found that the white and the black races are both capable of producing good men and patriotic officials.

If the Southern whites had pursued a moderate and kindly policy toward the colored citizens, they might long ago have won easily their confidence and support. They might have ruled in the States where they are now in a poor minority. But they chose to encourage the lawless outrages of the Ku-Klux. They carried the elections of Georgia by violence, and hoped to rule Louisiana or Arkansas by the same means. Their Democratic and Liberal Republican allies at the North helped to confirm them in their error, and strove to profit by the merciless deeds of Southern outlaws and the miseries of the colored race; and the fatal results of the pitiless intrigues of the opposition politicians and journals may be seen in the disorder and decay, the deserted farms and wasted trade, of too many of the Southern States.

GOING INTO THE SWAMP—A CHECK ON THE TOW.

Harper's Weekly, June 14, 1873, p. 504.

THE PRESIDENT'S PROCLAMATION AND LOUISIANA

HARPER'S WEEKLY
June 14, 1873, p. 498

The madness of the Louisiana Democracy is of such a nature as to admit of no easy cure. To those who remonstrate with them in all kindness upon the imprudence of their course, who would stop them in that cruel policy which is destroying the poor remains of their commerce and wealth left by the rebellion, whose only desire is to secure them ease and prosperity, they reply with insults, and reject their friendly counsel with scorn. They seem resolute to persecute the colored race, who are the only resource for the cultivation of their land, and to drive off Northern capital and enterprise, which can alone save Louisiana from ruin. It is stated that they have made the visit of the Congressional committee to New Orleans so uncomfortable by their bad manners and childish petulance as to hasten its departure, that they met the Congressmen with insolent remarks, and gave them such a welcome as can not fail to leave no friendly recollections behind it. Yet Louisiana is a persistent applicant for the bounty of the whole country. A low, marshy strip of land seated along the mouths of the Mississippi, thinly peopled, impoverished, and decaying, its only hope of improvement or even of preservation lies, we are told in the message of one of its Governors, in the repair of its levees. These embankments that line the river alone save the State from complete submersion. They require constant repairs. Many millions have already been expended upon them since the war. But their condition is still dangerous: they crumble away with each rising flood; they are threatened with a total destruction; nor is it incredible that should they still remain neglected they may be wholly swept away, and the richest land of Louisiana be sunk beneath the Mississippi. In such an event, the Governor's message assures us New Orleans might still be saved, although even this he thinks not altogether certain.

To provide help to secure their levees, therefore, the planters are begging aid from the national government. Another project for which New Orleans is asking assistance from the North and West is the deepening of the month of the Mississippi. The Father of Rivers, it seems, brings down annually immense masses of mud, and is filling up the only outlet for the commerce of the Crescent City. A huge bar is forming in the channel, often changing its form, embarrassing navigation, and threatening the ruin of the port. To dredge the entrance to the city is now a favorite speculation of the New Orleans merchants. They are asking aid every where to enable them to remove the vast mass of deposit that is gradually growing year by year. Yet it is believed that

TIMBER CUTTERS GOING INTO THE SWAMP.

Harper's Weekly, June 14, 1873, p. 505.

the project is altogether hopeless. The wealth of the nation might be readily exhausted in the vain attempt, and the only plan that can be devised to save the larger part of its trade is that of a ship-canal from New Orleans through the lakes to the sea.

Such is the condition of this unlucky State. With an extravagant debt, a heavy taxation, small resources, and no help from immigration, instead of giving all its energies to peaceful labor, the madness of its Democratic politicians has nearly plunged it in a civil war. The origin of this contest is one of the most shameful passages in our history. Those—and we fear they are too few—who have studied carefully the Congressional reports on the Ku-Klux conspiracy will find there the source of the woes of Louisiana. In 1868 the "White Brotherhood," or the Ku-Klux, began their murderous attempt to convert the Republican population to Democracy. In the spring of that year the elections showed a large Republican majority; in the autumn, so successful had been the efforts of the murderous associations that but a few thousand votes in the whole State were given for General Grant. In one parish, where the Republican majority was large, no Republican vote was offered. The State was almost unanimous for Seymour and Blair. Yet the horrible means by which the victory was achieved might well bring a blush to the cheek of every Northern supporter of the opposition candidates. Two thousand negroes were murdered or maimed to secure the terrible result. The sworn testimony of many witnesses proves the number and the crime. The "Knights of the White Camellia" rode through the rural parishes inflicting atrocities that are altogether unparalleled. In the famous Bossier negro hunt alone it is shown that nearly two hundred peaceable colored men were killed in one raid. The desired effect was gained. No colored man in many districts dared vote for Grant and Colfax. But from that moment a stain has rested upon Louisiana that not all the floods of the Mississippi can ever wash away.

The outrages were continued with varying intensity through the succeeding elections. We do not believe that many of the merchants or the planters looked upon them with any thing but horror and dread, yet they made no effort to save the colored population. They have never dared even to rebuke the murderers; and in the last election of 1872, we are told, whole parishes were carried for the Democracy by similar acts of violence. Even Mr. Carpenter was forced to admit that had the vote been fairly taken, Kellogg would have been chosen by a large majority; and the real question now to be decided in Louisiana is not whether Kellogg or M'Enery is the legal Governor, but whether the supporters of M'Enery are not actual rebels who have endeavored to deprive their fellow-citizens by violence of the right of voting, and who under the Constitution and the Enforcement act have become outlaws and the enemies of the nation.

If the party of M'Enery obtained a nominal majority at the recent election by means as desperate and unlawful as those employed by Seymour and Blair in 1868, when two thousand victims suffered in order that the rights of the people might be overridden and destroyed; if, as the colored citizens told Mr. Carpenter, they were afraid to vote; if the massacre at Colfax properly represents the impulses of that desperate faction which is laboring for the ruin of Louisiana, and seeks to place M'Enery in power—we think the safety of the colored population and the honor of the Union demand the retention of the Kellogg government. Rejecting the fraudulent returns and the returns of parishes where no free election could be held, Kellogg was certainly chosen. No decision of Congress or of courts could confer legality on the blood-stained election of his opponent. The employment of violence or intimidation in politics is a crime so great as to be inexpiable. We trust that the people of Louisiana will soon learn to think it so. If the white population of that State have not sufficient courage to protect the liberties of all their people, we hope the aid of the national government will not prove ineffective.

THE DISMAL SWAMP

HARPER'S WEEKLY
June 14, 1873, p. 504-5

The genius of popular nomenclature was never better evinced than in the aptness of the name bestowed upon the great swamp of the Atlantic coast. Lying partly in Virginia and partly in North Carolina, it extends north and south some thirty miles, with a mean breadth of ten miles. It is elevated eighteen feet above the level of the Chesapeake Bay, and five navigable rivers and many creeks take their rise in it. It is covered for the most part with a dense growth of timber, cypress, juniper, gum, and pine, and upon the dryer ridges which intersect it the beech and oak grow to great size. Its soil is composed for a great depth of peat, which may, and probably will, at some time be turned to good account. . . .

The productions of the Dismal consist chiefly in the various forms of lumber—ship timber, boards, shingles, staves, railroad ties, and fire-wood. In the labor of preparing this lumber of market a large force is employed during the dryer season of the year.

The tourist who would see the swamp and the "swampers" in all their glory should embark, say in March, upon a steamer on the Dismal Swamp Canal, which is taking to the scene of their labors a merry and noisy crew of lumbermen. Picked up about Norfolk and Portsmouth, and often hired for the season, these men are full of their coming exploits with axe and saw, the elders swelling with self-importance, the younger gaping, awe-struck, to hear the wonderful yarns of the "camps." Reaching the "store" (pronounced "sto") of their employer, the gang debarks, each man to spend all he can of his summer's wages. No women are among them, and if you ask them why, they will tell you that women once went with a party, and "a man was killed dar." It is in their camps—of brush-wood often, or of cypress bark, open on all sides but one—that the true negro character comes out. They are a sleepless race, these "swampers," and after working all day they drone half the night away in religious discussions containing the longest words, conducted with the utmost gravity, and leading to absolutely no conclusion, each party gravely assenting to or denying the positions of the other, while neither, it is plain, knows his own meaning nor that of the other. Their work is severe, they are always in mud or water, and their diet consists almost solely of bacon and the traditional "ash-cake;" yet, strange to say, their health is good, and they love the life they lead. The regular "swamper," however, is often a boatman as well as axe man, and the canal is seldom without the sight of a heavy laden lighter, long and narrow, propelled by its two "trackers" (from the low Dutch "treck"), pushing against long poles fastened, as seen in the sketch, at the bow and stern. The love of subordination is innate in the negro, and of this crew of two one is invariably the skipper, the other the common sailor, and discipline is always observed.

FLORIDA'S DEBT

HARPER'S WEEKLY
July 26, 1873, p. 643

If every embarrassed Southern State would imitate the course of Florida, there would at least be no doubt as to the condition of its finances. Florida has just published an account of its debt. We presume that it is perfectly accurate, and it shows that the whole liability of the State is under $5,000,000. Of this amount $3,000,000 are bonds guaranteed for railway objects. If the railway succeeds, the State will not be obliged to pay the interest. Hence the actual debt is less than $2,000,000, while the valuation of the State at a low figure is over $30,000,000. The result is not discouraging for a community that for ten years has been ravaged by a violent rebellion, by a long reign of Ku-Klux outrages, and a resolute persistence on the part of the Democracy to ruin the reputation and the prosperity of the State. Nowhere were the acts of the Democratic associations more infamous or more bloody than in Florida. Human nature will forever blush at the unheard-of immoralities and cruelties of many of its young men. But we believe this period of disorder is passing away, that some sense of shame has reached even the most corrupt of the opposition leaders, and that an immigration of wiser and better men will at last bring to the State industry, decency, and humanity.

THE "COURIER-JOURNAL" ON THE KU-KLUX

HARPER'S WEEKLY
August 23, 1873, p. 738

We are glad to hear one voice from the Southern States denouncing the secret labors of the Ku-Klux. The Louisville *Courier-Journal* has at last ventured to break the silence in which the Southern editors have usually watched the course of this barbarous association. For eight years the Southern press has been chained by its prejudices or its terrors, and has looked upon the destroyers of its people with complacency or with submission. In Georgia, we believe, no newspaper is permitted to exist that is not willing to hear of barbarous deeds which it is afraid to mention, to hide the persecutions of white and colored Republicans, and to aid a policy of tyranny that is driving labor and industry from the State. The misfortunes of Louisiana may be traced to the same source. It is overspread with journals and editors who are the sure instruments of the Ku-Klux, who are duelists and bravoes, the friends and allies of noted assassins, the companions and defenders of the class of men whom the Louisville *Courier* paints so distinctly, the enemies of education, intelligence, and humanity, and from whom have come the disasters that have driven away the trade of New Orleans, and left thousands of its buildings tenantless, that reduced the planters to bankruptcy, and made Louisiana that ruined State over which Beauregard and his companions now raise their ineffectual cry of despair.

The Louisville *Courier-Journal* has at last spoken of the Ku-Klux in language such as we have frequently used, but which has never before been permitted or heard in Kentucky. It is well known that this infamous society is often composed of the young men of the wealthier class at the South, that it is highly popular with the former secessionists, that when seized and brought before the tribunals its guilty members are sometimes caressed by politicians of the fair sex, and supported by all the discontented of the sterner, and that their crimes are never told. Their crimes are committed in disguise and under the shelter of night, and they are such as the day might blush to see. But the *Courier-Journal* can no longer keep silence. It seems that the house of Mrs. Mason Brown, the step-mother of Governor Gratz Brown, the Liberal candidate for the Vice-Presidency, was visited at night because Mrs. Brown had chosen to employ negro labor. A colored man was brutally murdered, his property destroyed, and various other acts of barbarism were committed the same night that scarcely can be tolerated even in Kentucky.

Nothing that we or any Northern journal have ever said can exceed the force with which our contemporary now denounces the Ku-Klux. They are "bandits," "lynchers;" they have never done a day's honest work, and give their lives to whisky and gambling; they deserve the detestation of all good citizens; their "ruffianism covers the cheek with the blush of shame;" the Bender murderers and the Iowa railroad robbers are criminals of no deeper dye; they are pests of the commonwealth; they blight its dearest interests, drive off useful citizens, lower the value of land, repel capital, banish education, and impoverish and desolate Kentucky. Such are some of the epithets and objurgations which the *Courier-Journal* applies to the society, and adds, with a new sense of justice, that the humblest and most ignorant negro who toils for an honest living is, in every respect, the superior of men who terrify and ill-treat defenseless women, and pretend to decide what kind of laborers the farmers of Kentucky shall employ to tend their crops. "Their presence," it exclaims, "is insufferable;" they should be treated with "short shrift and a long rope." The "devilish fraternity" is dead to every generous feeling, and "the State must meet them with the halter in its hand."

This certainly is instructive language, and shows that Kentucky, which has suffered as much as any other Southern State from the terrors of the Ku-Klux, is gathering up sufficient courage to treat them as they deserve. Yet what can now be said of those Democratic or Liberal politicians, who on the last election and through many previous elections were in close alliance with the secret associations, who carried Kentucky and several other Southern States by their aid, who rejoiced over their victory in Georgia with extravagant triumph, though they knew well how it had been won, and who have coldly defended the Ku-Klux of Louisiana in the midst of its enormities! If the courage and good sense of the *Courier-Journal* find a general support in its own and other depressed Southern States, it seems likely that the Northern allies of the Ku-Klux will not win many more elections, even with the aid of what the *Courier* calls "the pests of society."

A COLORED ORATOR

HARPER'S WEEKLY
September 13, 1873, pp. 794–95

At Eatonton, Georgia, on the last Fourth of July, a colored clergyman, the Rev. Mr. Johnson, was permitted to address the "Canaan Union School" of his countrymen. He felt perhaps that they had nearly reached the land of refuge out of the house of bondage, yet his

HAVING IT OUT.

Harper's Weekly, November 8, 1873, p. 985.

eloquence was evidently tempered by the fear of the Ku-Klux and the hatred of the dominant power. But his address was one of the most sensible of the Fourth-of-July orations. It must, indeed, be with only the most rigid self-restraint that the colored race can suppress its impetuous joy on Independence-day, and speak of freedom in the heart of Georgia with chained lips. Our orator delicately avoids all the perilous limits of his theme. "The lesson taught by the mighty celebration of this day," he said, "is education for the masses." It is, indeed, remarkable with what passionate earnestness the colored race demands knowledge. One of the pledges

AN INTERESTED LISTENER.

Harper's Weekly, December 6, 1873, p. 1085.

AT THE COUNTRY STORE.

Harper's Weekly, December 6, 1873, p. 1085.

given by each member of the North Carolina Union (colored) League was that he would educate his children. We are told by Mr. Gibbs, Superintendent of Education in Florida, that his people are eager to be instructed. They are anxious to learn cleanliness, order, propriety, to rise in the scale of civilization, to rival their former masters in knowledge, and perhaps surpass them in all the higher traits of humanity and forbearance.

But our colored orator offers advice to his people that can not fail to give them prosperity if followed. He urges them to work patiently, to save, and to accumulate. "Why leave Georgia?" he exclaims to those who would emigrate from their ill-governed State. "Here," he urges, "we have the control of the production of cotton, and cotton must always rule; here work will be master, and the idle must sink into decay." Evidently he has no fear that the colored race will not be able to defend itself against oppression, that it will not deserve success by its industry, and make itself an honorable name in the annals of freedom. It will, no doubt, have much to contend against and to bear. The Eatonton newspaper notices Mr. Johnson's speech, and remarks with a rude sneer that the colored people must never hope to rise to a level with the white, that they can never look to equal the virtues of their former masters. But Mr. Johnson thinks that "the door of liberty is open to the colored race in Georgia;" that Georgia will always be the centre of the cotton trade; that they are gradually becoming land-holders of tenants of land; and that, with patience, temperance, and education, they will need no better home than they can find in their native State.

There seems, indeed, no foundation for the notion that the two races can not live together in the fertile South and share in its productiveness. The colored people profess and have shown already a sincere resolution to forget the sorrows of the past, and to labor faithfully for the planter wherever they are honestly paid and kindly treated. We believe a better feeling is rising up toward them among the whites, and that the Southern merchants and farmers are anxious to eradicate those murderous associations that have so long disturbed the peace of society, and brought ruin upon all their material interests. They should at once unite to preserve good order. Georgia, which has inflicted the worst outrages upon the colored people, should now take the lead in insuring them all their civil rights and the prosperity which they have so well deserved. The moment it does so the war of races will cease. It is not likely that the colored people will aspire to political power, or to any larger share of it than their own safety and progress demand. If treated with justice and humanity, they will probably prefer to be ruled by white men who are their friends, and who are the supporters of union and of peace. They will require Republican leaders, and must not be expected to respect or to obey those whom they can not trust. The persecutors, the bigoted, and the cruel will be driven from office, but with Republican rulers who are worthy of confidence and sincerely anxious to promote the welfare of both races, the

THROUGH THE PINE WOODS AT NIGHT.

Harper's Weekly, December 6, 1873, p. 1085.

Southern States may easily rise to extraordinary prosperity, and attract a limitless stream of wealth, of trade, of immigration and capital, of refinement and progress, to their abundant territory.

A deputation of distinguished colored men, political leaders and private citizens, from Louisiana, are about to relate to the people the history of the recent disorders in that State. It is a fortunate circumstance. The colored race has never yet been permitted to tell its wrongs. We fear their narrative will not lessen the catalogue of Democratic cruelties and crimes in Louisiana, but it will no doubt prove of singular interest.

FRANK MOSS

RICHMOND WHIG
November 4, 1873

Frank Moss, the negro Radical candidate for the Legislature from Buckingham county, the other day in a speech in that county said that if they got into power, he for one would never rest until they had mixed schools, mixed marriages, mixed everything, until in short, he, a black negro, could lead a white bride to the altar! How do you like that doctrine, white men? —*Lynchburg News*

HAVING IT OUT

HARPER'S WEEKLY
November 8, 1873, p. 985

Mr. Sheppard's graphic sketch tells its own story so well as almost to preclude the necessity of comment. The belligerents are certainly "having it out" in a very stormy and vigorous manner, greatly to the amusement of the placid saloon-keeper who leans on the window-sill in an attitude of complacent neutrality. It matters little to him which side wins. The sedate old colored man, standing behind one of the angry antagonists, is evidently trying to pour oil on the troubled waters, and with soothing words to bring the quarrel to an end. He is very likely a preacher, and is scandalized that two members of his flock should engage in such an unseemly brawl in a public thoroughfare. But their blood is up, and each one being determined to have the last word, his efforts will probably have no effect until one of the belligerents descends into her cellar fortress and closes the door against her enemy. The artist gives us no hint as to the cause of the dispute. It may have originated in the saloon, where "cool lager-beer" is sold; for it is well known that "cooling" summer beverages, unless taken in very moderate quantities, often produce the very opposite effect upon the temper. Whatever the cause of the wrangling, Mr. Sheppard has caught the real spirit of the scene, and depicted the quarrel and its incidental accessories with great humor and effect.

THE COLORED PEOPLE

RICHMOND WHIG
November 11, 1873

The triumph of Conservatism in the recent election settles, we hope forever, the race question as a political issue in Virginia. The full effect will not probably be developed at once. Time must be allowed for excitement to subside and for disappointment and mortification to heal. It will be two years before we shall have an election to choose members of the General Assembly, and four years before another gubernatorial election will take place. The colored people will thus have ample opportunity to ponder calmly the lessons to be drawn from the late contest and its results. They were formed by their leaders into a race organization and taught to vote as a unit. This organization thus formed was called a Republican organization in order to command sympathy and support from the administration and the Northern Republican party. The colored people were assured by their leaders that they would succeed—that the administration would stand by them with all its influence and power, and that money and sympathy would pour in from the North.

The name, Republican, assumed by them imposes upon nobody—not even themselves. The colored people knew that their struggle was for race supremacy, and not the success of any political system or principles. That attempt has been battled in so decided a manner as to leave them without any hope as a mere negro party, for the future. They were not aided in the election, as far as we can learn, by Northern money, nor have we any evidence that they were backed up by Presidential ininfluence. Those two sources of help promised by their leaders, failed them—just as every thing has failed them that has been promised.

But no assistance of money or influence could have given them the victory. The white people of Virginia, drawn together by the race issue chosen by their adversaries, stood as solidly and unitedly almost as they did. Discerning the danger they were determined to meet and disarm it. Money could not have swerved them from the line of rectitude; nor could any amount of Federal influence have deterred or seduced them from the discharge of their duty.

One lesson the negroes will have to learn is this: That having been made citizens and voters the white people of the North and the government of the United States feel that they have done their duty towards them. No ism lasts long, and negroism, like all the rest, must sooner or later come to an end. The war and its results pushed the black race into undue prominence. They are now beginning to recede to their proper level. The white Northern race cannot be expected to form a perpetual alliance with them for the political subjugation of the whites of the South. It is not in reason—not in the nature of things that they should do so. The shrewd Northern mind has already become convinced that negro rule means material ruin, and the Northern people desire that affairs in the South shall be so administered as to make that large and productive region tributary to the general prosperity.

The only course for the negroes to pursue, if they wish to be respected and desire to become useful citizens, is to do as other citizens do—to rise above mere race and color and make principles their guide. As the first step towards this let them cast off their selfish leaders.

A NEGRO FAIR.
SOMETHING NEW UNDER THE SUN

[From Turf, Field and Farm.]

RICHMOND WHIG
November 14, 1873

At Lexington, the very centre of Kentucky aristocracy, and the home of white wealth and culture, the blacks own a beautiful tract of land, which they have converted into a fair ground. The place is well improved, and it always presents a neat and striking appearance to those who view it from their carriage windows driving along the public highway. In the purchase and construction of these grounds the blacks have had the assistance of the whites for the whites recognize the importance of cultivating habits of thrift and industry among those who only a few short years ago were in a state of vassalage. And in the management of the colored fairs the whites are always ready to lend a helping hand. They freely grant their servants and tenants the privilege of taking their finest specimens of cattle and their best horses to the exhibition, and therefore it is a common thing to find on the grounds of those colored fairs animals of princely pedigree and of national fame. There is no partisan feeling in the movement. The leading white citizens, regardless of political faith, unite to encourage the blacks to become good and useful citizens. The broadest spirit of liberality pervades the management of the fairs. In many of the Northern States, where so much said about the wrongs which the Southern people have inflicted upon the negro, the white man refuses to drive in a ring with the black man, and this refusal is sustained by the judges in power. At the colored fair which was

HARPER'S WEEKLY.
A JOURNAL OF CIVILIZATION.

Vol. XVII.—No. 887.]   NEW YORK, SATURDAY, DECEMBER 27, 1873.   [WITH A SUPPLEMENT. PRICE TEN CENTS.

Entered according to Act of Congress, in the Year 1873, by Harper & Brothers, in the Office of the Librarian of Congress, at Washington.

BOND AND FREE.—[SEE PAGE 1158.]

Harper's Weekly, December 27, 1873, p. 1153.

held at Lexington in the last days of September, in the contest for the largest purse offered for trotting horses two of the drivers were white and two were colored, and in the judges' stand were two white gentlemen, prominent citizens of the community. In the many carriages driving about the grounds and surveying with curious eyes the scene, were gentlemen and ladies who had been slave owners; and among the distinguished of the gentler sex were the families of Federal and Confederate officers in the late struggle, the wife of the ex-Confederate Secretary of War, and the daughter of and ex-Governor of the State. The blacks seemed to be grateful for the attention shown them by those whose slaves they had been, and good feeling prevailed on all sides. There was a vast crowd on the grounds, but it was quiet and orderly. Great interest was taken in every feature of the exhibition. We remember one old woman who was made as proud as a queen by receiving the first premium for the best loaf of bread, and her happiness would not have been complete had she not been able to carry a portion of that loaf home and place it on the table of the family in which she served as cook.

NORTH CAROLINA SKETCHES

HARPER'S WEEKLY
December 6, 1873, p. 1085

The illustrations on this page are from the pencil of an American artist, Miss Mary L. Stone, who passed several months in the mountain districts of North Carolina for the purpose of studying the characteristics of the people of that section of our country. They represent, as may be seen at a glance, only the poorer classes of whites, impoverished by the war, and some phases of negro character.

In many of the mountain districts of the "Old North State" the women are compelled to do a great deal of out-door work and drudgery. They not only cultivate the fields, but carry the scanty produce to market in bags, or "pokes," as they call them. This is hard work, and to avoid it they will often tackle dogs to a small cart. A young steer and a donkey make an elegant turn-out, as represented in our illustration.

The negro population of these districts alone display any cheerfulness and jollity. Their irresponsibility, the heritage of slavery, still clings to them, and a day's work that brings them pork and coffee and tobacco, and leaves the evening free for their religious gatherings, is all that can be expected of them. Every evening after eight o'clock they go trooping through the pine woods, with candles or torches, to spend hours in the log-house which serves for a church, in dancing, shouting, singing, and praying. When physically worn out with these fervent exercises, they creep away to sleep by the nearest fire until daylight, or drop in their tracks while on their way home, and slumber off their weariness. They have a constitutional aversion to hard work, and do as little of it as possible.

Here and there by the roadside may be seen a rough schoolhouse, in which white and black urchins gather to be taught by a white teacher. The task, it must be confessed, is not particularly encouraging. The children are slow to learn, and, with rare exceptions, seldom get beyond the very rudiments of reading and writing.

Yet, even in these wild mountain districts, intelligence and education are gradually making their way. The dawn of a brighter day for both races is at hand. Every year the means of transportation are improved, the lands show better cultivation, the schools are more largely attended. And as poverty and ignorance die out, as the circulation of books and newspapers increases, as good highways and railroads open up these regions to settlers, and bring them into closer connection with the outside world, we shall find the characteristics shown in these illustrations fading out, until they are lost in the clear light of a true American civilization. They belong entirely to the past, and can not survive the better influences of the present.

BOND AND FREE

HARPER'S WEEKLY
December 27, 1873, p. 1158

Our readers can not have forgotten the indignation recently aroused against the Italian "padrones" for their cruel treatment of the boys and girls they kidnap or buy at home and bring over to this country. The efforts made on behalf of these waifs of humanity, and the dread of punishment, compelled the hard-hearted taskmasters to relax their cruelties, for a time at least, and to treat the little street musicians with a little kindness; but no doubt the children are still subject to many hardships which do not come to light, and the title to Mr. Sheppard's sketch on our first page is not a misnomer. The sad-faced young musicians, ignorant of our language, and held in harsh subjection by the "padrone" for whose benefit they are sent out to roam the streets, enjoy far less freedom than the gay young "contraband" who is dancing to their music.

1874

Issues pertaining to civil rights dominated the news in 1874. Senator Charles Sumner of Massachusetts proposed a supplementary civil rights bill in the U.S. Senate. The bill was intended to further support the Fourteenth Amendment. In 1868 the Fourteenth Amendment, providing equal protection to all citizens under the U.S. Constitution, was ratified. The supplementary bill forbade discrimination based on color in hotels, public schools, theaters, steamers, and railways.

Support for the bill came from a Republican base seeking to elevate the status of African Americans in the nation. Rarely were the conditions of African Americans' lives in the North reported on in newspapers. However, newspapers such as Harper's Weekly *supported the bill by commenting on African Americans in New York City being discriminated against due to race. Journalists who supported the bill believed just as it was absurd to deny a man equality based on height or eye color, it was absurd to deny equal rights based on skin color. Southerners opposed the bill because the law would require integration, particularly in schools. Objections to the bill included the idea that it is useless to legislate against bigotry, prejudice, and the superiority of the white race. Although journalists gave little attention to the issue of educating minorities, it was a paramount issue to African Americans.*

Under slavery most states had laws against African Americans learning to read and write. African Americans saw education as a crucial factor to the success of the race. The nation appeared to view education of the masses as the road to good citizenship and good government. Out of New York, Harper's Weekly *(13 June 1874) published:*

"The House of Representatives has passed a very brief and significant bill, prohibiting any person who can not read or write from sitting

upon a jury in any United States court. In this State Governor Dix has signed the Compulsory Education Bill. New Jersey has passed a similar law, and in several States like bills passed one House during the winter."

Southerners saw the bill as creating a race war by allowing "mixed marriages," "mixed" schools, and general mixing of the races.

Harper's Weekly *(30 May 1874) reported:*

"We observe that the State Superintendent of Public Instruction in Tennessee thinks that the passage of the bill by 'mixing' the schools would close them, and put an end to public education. The school levies would cease, and the colored people would find that while in law they could enter any public school whatever, there would be no schools to enter."

Not to be forgotten in this equation was the Ku-Klux Klan. Julia Hayden, a seventeen-year-old African American school teacher, was brutally murdered in Tennessee for the "crime" of providing education to other African Americans.

Politics and the Ku-Klux Klan in Louisiana were again center stage in the newspapers. Harper's Weekly *(3 October 1874) reports that "the New Orleans* Picayune *edited by a duelist's blood stained hand, commanded the White Leaguers 'to shoot down like a dog' every white or black Republican. . . ."*

In September 1874 the White Leaguers and the metropolitan police of New Orleans were engaged in a bloody battle; the police retreated. Louisiana Republican governor William Kellogg called in federal forces to return order. In 1872, Kellogg and his Democratic challenger, John McEnery, had both claimed victory of the governorship. Kellogg was declared the winner in court and finally recognized by the federal government. McEnery led the White Leaguers' rebellion in New Orleans.

Robert L. Harris, Jr.
Cornell University

COLOR AND LAW

HARPER'S WEEKLY
January 10, 1874, p. 27

The Supplementary Civil Rights bill which Mr. Sumner has introduced in the Senate is intended to protect the rights guaranteed by the Fourteenth Amendment. Its object is to prevent a State from depriving any citizen of rights conferred by the United States. This was distinctly stated by General Butler in introducing his bill in the House. The purpose is plain, and should be approved by all patriotic and sensible men. The bill merely proposes that the equality of citizens before the law shall be maintained, and that color shall no longer incapacitate a citizen. Mr. Beck, of Kentucky, opposed General Butler's bill upon the ground of State rights, and seems to have supposed that the bill is an attempt to force social equality upon certain States. That he really thinks so can not be supposed, because he knows as well as the rest of us that such is not the fact. He also knows as well as the rest of us, and as his colored colleague, Mr. Rainey, of South Carolina, trenchantly said, that there is a feeling against the negro in the Southern States which is most injurious and persistent. It was expressed in Mr. Beck's speech, and it is precisely that feeling which inspires the hostility to the colored citizen from which the bill would defend him. It is the spirit which made the black codes after the war, and which would now make a lower caste of the colored race if it could.

It is constantly said that feeling can not be changed by legislation. But this is not precisely true. The feeling for a race which is stigmatized by the law is very different when the stigma is removed. The change of the law, indeed, may precede the change of feeling, for the word here means social feeling, which does not at once alter, although a sense of justice may reform the law. But the feeling will follow. That the British Tory party should bring a gentleman whom a Tory once called "a Jew novelist" to be Prime Minister of England seemed quite as impossible as that Mr. Rainey should be Mr. Beck's colleague in Congress. And having raised to citizenship a class hitherto stigmatized and contemned, it is our duty to do all that law can do to release them from the results of a prejudice due to their old condition. If hotels and restaurants may turn respectable guests away because they are of the colored race, and theatres and cars, all doing business by legal license, may refuse them entrance for the same reason, it is plain that the law fosters the prejudice and distinction which all good citizens are interested in allaying and removing. The moment the law enables the colored guest to call the offending host to account, and the host is taught that he can enforce no whimsical distinctions among proper guests, the prejudice will begin to wane. There is an immense amount of twaddle about the "instinctive repugnance" to colored persons. It is touching to observe of how much repugnance some persons are conscious, and how very "instinctive" they think it toward a quiet colored neighbor in a car or elsewhere, who are not in the least "instinctively" troubled by the neighborhood of the most offensive persons of another color. A man, as Mr. Rainey said, may choose his companions as he will, but the law in this country must see no difference between equal citizens.

DOMESTIC INTELLIGENCE

HARPER'S WEEKLY
January 10, 1874, p. 27

John S. Hopkins, who was reputed the wealthiest citizen of Baltimore, died December 24, in the seventy-ninth year of his age. In March last he donated property valued at $4,000,000 to found a free hospital in the city

THE HON. ROBERT BROWN ELLIOTT, OF SOUTH CAROLINA.
FROM A PHOTOGRAPH BY GARDNER, WASHINGTON, D. C.—[SEE PAGE 150.]

Harper's Weekly, February 14, 1874, p. 149.

for the indigent sick and poor, without regard to sex, age, or color, and also a training school for nurses.

THE HON. ROBERT B. ELLIOTT

HARPER'S WEEKLY
February 14, 1874, p. 150

The South Carolina district that for many years sent John C. Calhoun to Congress is now represented in that body by the Hon. Robert Brown Elliott, who is of unmixed African blood. He was born in Boston, Massachusetts, in 1842, received his primary education at private schools, and afterward studied at Eton College, England, where he graduated in 1859. From Massachusetts he went to Charleston, South Carolina, in 1866, and began his new career there as a type-setter in the office of a newspaper edited by his present colleague, Mr. Ransier. He has a natural gift for oratory, which has been cultivated by large experience on the stump. "His voice," says one who has listened to his oratory, "is full and agreeable, and in his pronunciation he displays far less of the peculiarities of the negro dialect than many of the Southern white members. His sentences are constructed with an obvious regard for euphonious sound, and if any fault were to be found in his manner of speaking, it would be that he falls into too much of a cadenced delivery."

Mr. Elliott's name was brought into prominence by his speech on the Civil Rights Bill, delivered on the 6th of January, in reply to Mr. Harris, of Kentucky. Those who heard him declared the speech to be the most remarkable effort yet made by a colored member of Congress. He read his remarks from manuscript, but this did not detract from their force as from that of Mr. Stephens's speech of the day before, for he made use of all the orator's art, voice, and gesture. He got a much more attentive hearing from the House than did the great Georgian, and was more than once applauded by the members, whose hand-clappings were at once echoed from the galleries, packed with colored people. When he sat down the applause was deafening, and many members rushed forward to shake his hand and congratulate him. A portrait of Mr. Elliott is given on the preceding page.

TAKING IN LIVE STOCK

HARPER'S WEEKLY
March 14, 1874, pp. 240–41

A correspondent with the English expedition against the Ashantees thus pleasantly describes the scene depicted in our illustration: "After being accustomed for some years to the natives of Bengal, with their scowling faces and impassible manner, beneath which it is extremely difficult to penetrate so as to discover their real sentiments, it is quite a pleasure to get among the negroes of West Africa. They have their faults, it is true; though many of them, especially the Kroomen, are magnificent in their muscular development, so as to be fit models for a Hercules in ebony, they have not much of that adventurous gentleman's pluck, but are apt to start off and run as soon as they hear a shot fired in anger. Nor are they always to be relied on as bearers of burdens; they will labor for a short time, but as soon as they have received enough pay for their immediate necessities they do not hesitate to leave you and your baggage in the lurch in the midst of a dense forest, and with a scorching sun overhead. Lastly, like all members of their race, they are highly odoriferous, so that on board ship we were compelled to pass an edict that no officer should have his servant to wait on him, for a couple of dozen of these fellows behind our chairs would have rendered the atmosphere of the already highly heated cabin perfectly unendurable. So we restricted the blacks to the deck, and there, I must say, they displayed the most amiable qualities, for, in spite of occasional qualms of seasickness, and some heavy deluges of rain, which drenched them to the skin, they were perpetually laughing; and when the weather cleared and the sun shone out they sang, they asked riddles, they yah-yahed—in fact, they went on so wonderfully like a certain distinguished body of performers at St. James's Hall that it was difficult to believe that they were not a troupe of professional minstrels come down to the west coast for a pleasure trip.

"But our sable friends came out more strongly than ever when we arrived at Jellah Koffee for the purpose of taking live stock on board. Any one who has been by the Overland Route has seen the Maltese boys who pester the Peninsular and Oriental passengers with their 'For dive, Sir—for dive, Sir;' but they were nothing compared to our jolly Kroomen, who plunged into the water on the slightest pretext, like a pack of Newfoundland dogs. A biscuit was enough to tempt them, and they seemed especially to enjoy eating their prize in the sea. Matters reached a climax when the period for shipping the live stock came. Live stock is apt to be obstinate on such occasions, and to object strongly to embarking for a sea-voyage; consequently a Babel of sounds filled the air—goats bleating, sheep baaing, pigs squealing, poultry cackling, and, above all, negroes shouting and yelling to an extent beyond the power of most white men's lungs. It was nearly as bad as the noise on the Paris Bourse. Then the animals, warned, apparently, by instinct that they are about to be consigned to a floating prison, make themselves as disagreeable as possible, and produce all sorts of comic incidents. Pigs run between the legs of corpulent men, and lay them prostrate; unconscious sable gentlemen find the horns of an enraged goat where their own coat tails ought to be if they had any; fowls dodge their pursuers in the cleverest fashion—in fact, the whole scene resembles an ebony pantomime, saving that every body, quadruped or biped, uses his lungs to the utmost. The scene is most provokingly ludicrous, and helps greatly to relieve the monotony of our daily life."

Jellah Koffee, referred to in the foregoing account, is a small port lying between Accra and Lagos, latitude 5 deg. 35' north, longitude 0 deg 7' east. It has a limited trade, principally British, French, and American, with a few Portuguese vessels. The population is about 5000.

APING BAD EXAMPLES

HARPER'S WEEKLY
March 14, 1874, p. 242

If we may trust the following report, taken from a recent number of the Charleston *News,* some of the colored members of the South Carolina Legislature must be men of very different stamp from the cultivated and able gentleman who represents that State in the Congress of the United States. During a recent debate in the House on the appropriation for the penitentiary, a motion for a reduction of the amount named in the bill led to the following scene:

> Minort (*colored*). "The proposed appropriation is not a whit too large."
>
> Humbert (*colored*). "The institution ought to be self-sustaining. The member only wants a grab at the money."
>
> Hurley (*coming to Minort's relief*). "Mr. Speaker, I rise—"
>
> Humbert (*to Hurley*). "You shet you mouf, Sah." (Roars of laughter).
>
> Greene (*colored*). "That thief from Darlington." (A delicate allusion to Humbert.)
>
> Humbert. "If I have robbed any thing, I expect to be Ku-Kluxed by just such highway robbers as the member [Greene] from Beaufort. If I get in the penitentiary, I won't ask for $65,000 to support me."
>
> Greene (*to Hurley*). "You know as much about it as you do the Governor's contingent fund."
>
> Hurley. "At least no one has been able, or ever attempted, to refute my charges against the Governor, and his Excellency will not dare deny them."
>
> Greene (*colored*). "No; but if the Governor were not such a coward, he would have cowhided you before this, or got somebody else to do it."
>
> Hurley. "If the gentleman from Beaufort [Greene] would allow the weapon named to be sliced from his cuticle, I might submit to the castigation."

The next day Mr. Greene attempted to explain that he did not mean to say Governor Moses was a coward.

> Greene (*rising to a question of privilege*). "It was not the Governor to whom I referred, but his aids. What I said was that if the Governor's aids were not cowards, they would have cowhided Hurley, and if I were a member of the Governor's staff, I would have done it before this."
>
> Hurley (*rising to a counter-question of privilege*). "Nobody on the Governor's staff, nobody he could put on there, not the doughty gentleman from Beaufort, nor the valiant Governor himself, dare undertake to cowhide me."

This, says the Charleston *News,* "is the usual style in which the business of law-making and money-grabbing is conducted in the South Carolina Legislature. The radical members call each other thieves, liars, and rascals without any provocation, and do not appear to have any idea that they are insulting any body, or that they are not telling the Gospel truth. Roars of laughter on the part of the House and an increased consumption of pea-nuts follow these outpourings of fish-fag rhetoric; but for the honest citizens of the State the farce threatens to have a tragic ending." The moral to be drawn from this is indicated in Mr. Nast's cartoon on our front page. These ignorant and incompetent legislators must give place to those who will more faithfully represent the worth and intelligence of the people of the State, both white and colored. But it must be confessed that the colored members of the South Carolina Legislature could point to very unsavory precedents as to manner and language among white legislators of Southern and Northern States.

CHARLES SUMNER

HARPER'S WEEKLY
April 4, 1874, p. 289

No event since the assassination of President Lincoln has more deply touched the heart of the American people than the death of Charles Sumner, and nowhere was this feeling more expressively shown than at Washington. When the body of the deceased Senator was removed, on Monday, March 16th, from his residence to the Rotunda of the Capitol, the streets were filled with thousands of people, moved not by curiosity, but by a deep and sincere grief. No pomp, civic or military, attended the removal of the remains, but it was a touching spectacle when three hundred colored men, moved by a common impluse to do honor to one who had done so much for their race, joined the procession as it left the house, and wound its way through the streets to the Capitol. A large crowd of people had already assembled there when the procession arrived. Black drapery had been hung over each entrance to the Rotunda, upon the main columns that support the main portico of the Capitol, over the entrances to the Senate-chamber, around the galleries in the hall, along the corridor leading to the east door of the Senate wing, and upon the columns of its front. Mr. Sumner's chair in the Senate-chamber was hung with crape, and a modest bouquet of delicate white flowers and violets was upon his desk.

The procession entered the Rotunda a little after ten o'clock. The casket was placed upon a low catafalque in the centre of the Rotunda, under the dome, the lid removed, and the floral offerings placed upon the glass. There preparations completed, the people were admitted to take a last look at the remains. The colored men who had taken part in the procession were first admitted, and as they passed the coffin many of them were unable to restrain their grief. For about two hours the throng of people poured in and out, and in that time probably ten thousand persons, half of them colored people, took their last look at the face of the dead Senator. It had become somewhat discolored since embalmment, but the expression was calm and majestic. The body was dressed in a plain black suit, the hands resting on the breast.

AFRICAN AMERICAN HISTORY IN THE PRESS, 1851-1899

TAKING IN LIVE STOCK FOR THE ASHANTEE EXPEDITION—SCENE ON BOARD SHIP AT JELLAH KOFFEE.

Harper's Weekly, March 14, 1874, p. 229.

The funeral serives in the Senate-chamber took place at noon. Among those present, besides the Senate, were President Grant, Generals Sherman and M'Dowell, Admiral Porter, the Cabinet, the Supreme Court of the United States, the diplomatic corps, the members of the House of Representatives, and many others. The room was densely crowded, and hundreds unable to obtain admission lingered in and around the Capitol.

The service was simple but impressive, consisting of reading appropriate passages of Scripture and prayer by the chaplain of the Senate. The coffin, which had been brought in from the Rotunda, was then removed, followed by the committees appointed by the Senate and House to accompany the remains to Boston. The coffin was placed on board a special train, which started at three o'clock in the afternoon.

Our illustrations on page 292 represent the scene at the death-bed of Mr. Sumner, the procession leaving the house when his body was taken to the Capitol, and the library, which as our sketch will show is adorned with paintings, engravings, statues, casts, and tasteful specimens of ornamental art. The room opening from the library is the dining-room. Above the library is the study, where the Senator was wont to pass much of his time. Opening from the Study is the rook in which Mr. Sumner breathed his las, and whence his body was carried to the Rotunda.

MR. SUMNER'S CIVIL RIGHTS BILL

HARPER'S WEEKLY
April 11, 1874, p. 310

The last thoughts and the last words of Mr. Sumner were for his Civil Rights Bill, which he regarded as the completion of the great work to which his life had been chiefly devoted. And he was right in believing its passage to be a duty which the country could not honorably neglect. When the Amnesty Bill was offered in the Senate in 1871, he proposed his bill as an amendment. He was entreated not to press it, because, as a two-thirds vote was required, his amendment would only defeat the bill, as many Senators would vote for amnesty who would not vote for the civil rights. His reply was, "Justice with generosity: let us be just to our friends while we are generous to our late enemies." In a private letter written on the 30th of December, 1871, Mr. Sumner said: "My bill is an application on the national theatre of an argument made by me in Boston as long ago as 1849, where I first employed the term Equality before the Law. Its theory is that in all institutions, functions, or privileges created or regulated by law there shall be no discrimination on account of color. Now is the time to secure this

744

HARPER'S WEEKLY
JOURNAL OF CIVILIZATION

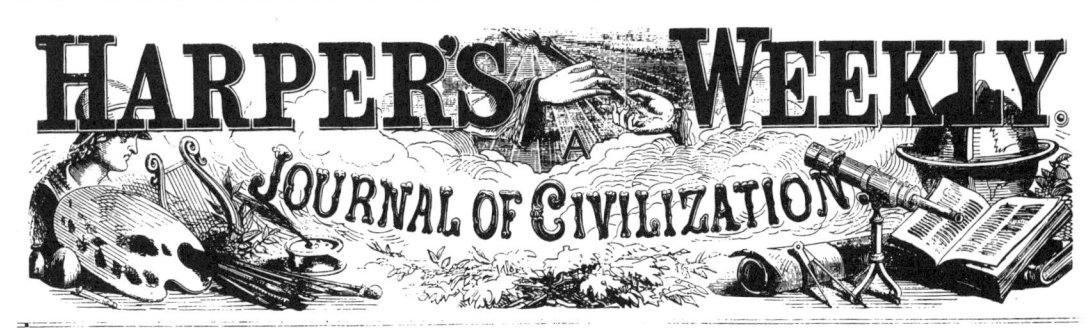

Vol. XVIII.—No. 898.] NEW YORK, SATURDAY, MARCH 14, 1874. [WITH A SUPPLEMENT. PRICE TEN CENTS.

Entered according to Act of Congress, in the Year 1874, by Harper & Brothers, in the Office of the Librarian of Congress, at Washington.

COLORED RULE IN A RECONSTRUCTED (?) STATE.—[SEE PAGE 242.]
(THE MEMBERS CALL EACH OTHER THIEVES, LIARS, RASCALS, AND COWARDS.)
COLUMBIA. "You are Aping the lowest Whites. If you disgrace your Race in this way you had better take Back Seats."

Harper's Weekly, March 14, 1874, p. 229.

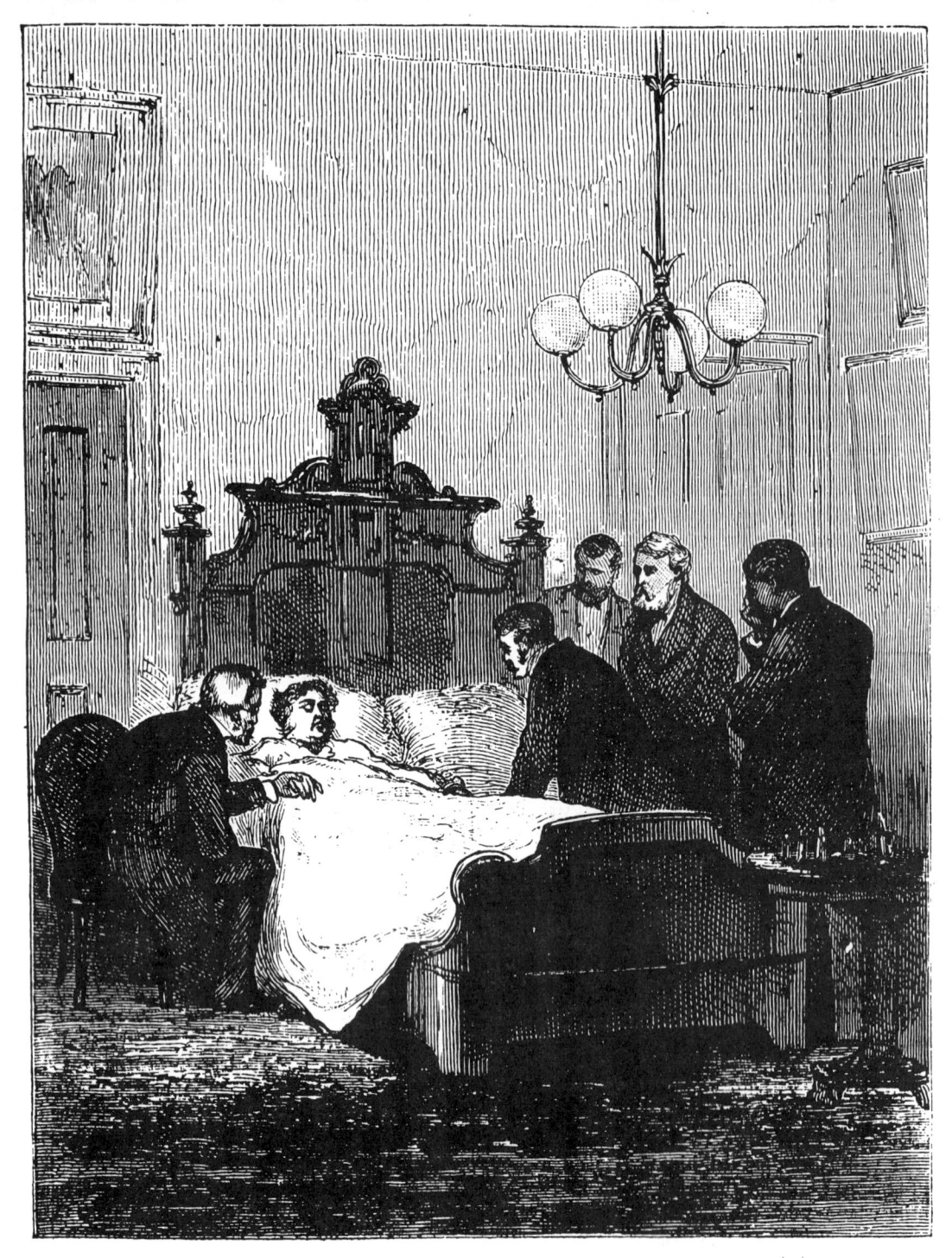

AFRICAN AMERICAN HISTORY IN THE PRESS, 1851-1899

THE DEATH OF CHARLES SUMNER.—Drawn by Theo. R. Davis.—[See First Page.]

Harper's Weekly, April 4, 1874, p. 292.

immense boon, which is the final fulfillment of the promises of the Declaration of Independence."

The bill forbids hotels, public schools, theatres, steamers, and railways to discriminate against orderly and proper persons on account of color. It is the completion of the promise of equal civil rights which we have already made, and it is resisted only by the old prejudice. It is declared to be inexpedient, because the feeling about the colored race can not be affected by legislation. This argument is not only too late, but it is unfounded in fact. The moment that political and civil

REMOVING THE BODY TO THE CAPITOL.—DRAWN BY THEO. R. DAVIS.—[SEE FIRST PAGE.]

Harpers's Weekly, April 4, 1874, p. 292.

disability ceases to stigmatize color, the prejudice against it begins to disappear. The "instinct" of dislike is founded in legal injustice. If the Irish were held as slaves for generations, and sold like cattle at the shambles, and robbed of every human right, there would be plenty of people to insist that they had an "instinctive aversion" to the Irish brogue. And so long as the prejudice against color is legalized, so long it will continue, and be urged as an argument against justice. But having declared that political and civil disability by reason of color shall cease, we are bound to take care that it does cease, and to see that the equality which we have proclaimed shall be secured. The other evening an orderly person was refused admittance to Mrs. Conway's theatre, in Brooklyn, because of the color of his skin. He could as properly, under the general guarantee of the Civil Rights Bill, have been refused because of the color of his clothes.

Honest legislation upon the subject will not at once remove all prejudice, but it will clear the way for its disappearance. While the law fails to protect their equality, trouble will remain. It is often said that they prefer to associate with each other, to have their own schools and churches, and to frequent hotels where the guests are of their own color. So far as this is voluntary there is no complaint from any quarter. But when separate public schools are maintained for them by law, however equal in every convenience to all other schools, and while they can not go to any hotel which they may prefer, they are stigmatized, and the spirit of the original Civil Rights Bill, to which Mr. Sumner's is supplementary, is outraged and violated. The real intent of Republican legislation in regard to political and civil equality was the removal of all legal disability or inequality upon account of color; and the passage of Mr. Sumner's bill is, therefore, a moral obligation upon the party.

SOUTH CAROLINA

HARPER'S WEEKLY
April 18, 1874, p. 330

The memorial of the tax-payers of South Carolina which has been laid before Congress, and the statements made by the delegation to the President, are of the utmost importance, and deserve the most serious consideration. We are unwilling to believe the report that in the interview the President made the speech of a foolish orator in the tax-payers' convention a pretext for virtual indifference to the representations of the committee. For the condition of South Carolina is undoubtedly deplorable, and if the Administration and Congress can properly do any thing to relieve it, they are bound by every patriotic and humane consideration not to delay. But the situation seems to be hopeless when the committee themselves go to General Butler to invite his assistance, because it shows that they are not aware that he is the chief representative of the very spirit and method which they oppose. Of course the appeal of the State is at first considered to be anomalous and absurd, and the reply swiftly offered is that South Carolina must work out her own salvation. But South Carolina is an integral part of the Union. When she cherished human slavery, every State was hurt, and at last the nation went to war. Now that she cherishes ignorance and corruption, every State is imperiled. The foot and the hand are separate members, but a wound in either may destroy the whole body. What, then, is the situation in South Carolina, and what is the remedy?

The State is governed by a combination of shrewd and unprincipled white men, some native and others strangers, who control the enormous colored vote, which they hold as representatives of the national Republican party, to which the colored citizens owe their political rights. This combination preys upon the State by laws

CHARLES SUMNER'S LIBRARY.—Drawn by Theo. R. Davis.—[See First Page.]

Harpers's Weekly, April 4, 1874, p. 292.

which under the form of taxation virtually confiscate the income of property.

RELIGIOUS INTELLIGENCE

HARPER'S WEEKLY

April 25, 1874, p. 359

The statistics of the Southern Methodist Episcopal Church for 1873 have appeared. They show a total of 35 annual conferences, 3134 traveling and 5344 local preachers, 237 superannuated preachers, 659,677 white, 3429 colored, and 4779 Indian members, making the aggregate of members 676,600. The total increase of members for the year is 22,441. The number of Sunday schools is 7019, with 321,572 scholars. The total of collections for the worn-out preachers' fund was $64,013; for missions, $96,644. The former colored members of this Church have been organized into a separate body, known as the "Colored Methodist Episcopal Church in America."

THE CIVIL RIGHTS BILL

HARPER'S WEEKLY

May 9, 1874, p. 391

We recently mentioned the case of a citizen of Brooklyn who was denied admission to a theatre in that city by reason of his color. The other day a man of the same race—intelligent, cultivated, courteous, who had been a slave, and who many years ago was one of those who had the courage to make his way, in the face of the terrible consequences of detection, to the North and freedom—went into an oyster-house in the Sixth Avenue, and seated himself at a table. As a waiter passed, the guest asked for oysters. The waiter told him that he could not have them. The guest—guilty of a darker skin—asked the reason, which he yet very well knew. "Have you no oysters?" "Yes." "Do you think that I will not pay for them?" "No." "Why, then, do you not bring them?" The waiter paused a moment: "Because we do not serve colored people. I have no objection; but it is the rule of the house." The guest arose, and moved toward the door. "Would you like to see the proprietor?" asked the waiter. "Certainly not," replied the guest; "why should I wish to see so mean a man?"

Is it surprising that the colored citizens of this country are profoundly and painfully anxious for the passage of Mr. Sumner's Civil Rights Bill? That bill, as he said, is supplementary, but it is indispensable. It defines certain common, universal, familiar rights, and it provides a remedy for their violation. It says in effect, and simply, that the United States mean to keep their word. It declares that solemn guarantees shall not be disregarded under the plea of natural prejudice. Why, in the name of common-sense, should one citizen of this country be allowed to gratify his prejudices against another in circumstances which the law can regulate? An innholder, for instance, keeps a house for public accommodation under the law. A guest arrives, late, weary, ill, and the landlord refuses him shelter solely because he has gray eyes or a blue coat, and the landlord has a natural prejudice against gray eyes and blue coats. Shall the guest have no remedy, and shall we say that it is useless to legislate against a prejudice? The reply does not answer the question. Here is the equal right of a citizen invaded. Prejudice may be as bitter as possible. But shall the citizen have no remedy? The next man may have a prejudice against his carrying a pocket-book. Shall it be taken from him without redress?

The short and sure way to deal with this kind of prejudice against the colored citizen is to make it unlawful to gratify it. So long as the indulgence is tolerated, the prejudice will continue. It is a matter of education and of habit; it is not natural. Children of all colors play together, nor know any aversion on account of color. Seamen of every hue sail together, and make one family. All that the colored citizens ask is that they shall have the equal protection of the laws. They do not demand favors. They desire that the law may strike at a custom which is allowed to set the law aside. Is their request unreasonable? Is it unnecessary? Personal preference, social intercourse, they know, quite as well as the rest of us, are beyond law; and certainly they have never shown the slightest disposition to disregard common good feeling and courtesy. Indeed, there is something very dignified in such conduct as that we have described in the oyster-house. Is there not also a powerful appeal in it? Shall honest, intelligent, industrious, useful, and orderly citizens be obliged to submit to such treatment? The insults of bullies they must endure as they can. But will the law refuse to guard them against outrage? The Senate has just warmly eulogized Mr. Sumner. But could his noble form, so long familiar in the Capitol, have re-appeared but for a moment in his place as the music of those kind words died away, his voice would have rung through the chamber, "Senators, do not let the Civil Rights Bill fail!"

DOMESTIC INTELLIGENCE

HARPER'S WEEKLY
May 16, 1874, p. 411

During the speech of Mr. Parker in the House on the 29th, in favor of elevating the Indian race to citizenship, a colored Representative, for the first time in our history, occupied the Speaker's chair. This honor was borne by Mr. Joseph H. Rainey, of South Carolina, who was formerly a slave in the South.

PREJUDICE AND EQUAL RIGHTS

HARPER'S WEEKLY
May 23, 1874, pp. 430–31

The question of equal civil rights, like that which it succeeds, slavery, will insist upon debate until it is settled. The Louisville *Courier-Journal* says that it is perhaps the gravest subject before Congress. Certainly it is one which should be fully understood by the country. The present bill embraces the substance of that which was offered by Mr. Sumner, and upon which he made the last of his great speeches upon the subject with which his name will be always most gratefully associated. It is acceptable to the citizens who are most interested, and it is to be considered in its object and in its method. Its object is to establish equality among American citizens by abolishing laws that stigmatize a certain class, and by affording a sure legal remedy against the violation of laws that establish equality. As long as prejudice against a certain class is fortified by law, the equality guaranteed by the United States is an idle pretense. Mr. Frelinghuysen well said, on introducing and explaining the bill, "If we did not intend to make the colored race full citizens, if we purpose to place them under the ban of any legalized disability or inferiority, and there to hold them, we should have left them slaves." The bill touches no law in regard to inns, theatres, schools, cemeteries, supported in whole or in part by general taxation, except to abrogate all discrimination on account of race, or color, or previous servitude. Innholders, for instance, hold a public license, and the law makes certain requirements of them. This bill adds to them that there shall be no such discrimination. Its purpose is simply the equality of citizens before the law. The common argument that it aims to establish social equality is of the same value as that conclusive appeal against human liberty which was so familiar in the old days of slavery—"How would you like your daughter to marry a nigger?" That powerful argument was properly dealt with by Mr. Lincoln when Mr. Douglas unwarily ventured upon it in the famous oratorical contest in which the rail-splitter pulverized the Little Giant.

Next as to its methods. The act provides that the United States courts shall have cognizance of violations of the law, and this is opposed as an overthrow of legitimate State authority. Now the Thirteenth Amendment secures freedom, the Fifteenth secures the suffrage, and the Fourteenth declares, "Nor shall any State deny to any person within its jurisdiction the equal protection of the laws." But the Fourteenth Amendment goes beyond the old Constitution, as Mr. Frelinghuysen says, in making United States citizenship primary, and State citizenship derivative. The citizen of the United States comes under the protection of the national government for his fundamental rights. Now how are the United States to protect the privileges of their citizens in the States? They can not compel the States to pass laws and furnish protection; they can only deal with the offenders who violate those rights. In certain States equal protection under the law is now denied to citizens of the United States, as in the classification by color in the common schools; and the bill gives original action in the national courts against offenses under the law which the amendment has forbidden.

We observe that the State Superintendent of Public Instruction in Tennessee thinks that the passage of the bill by "mixing" the schools would close them, and put an end to public education. The school levies would cease, and the colored people would find that while in law they could enter any public school whatever, there would be no schools to enter. This is an admission that the public-school system of Tennessee is based upon a total disregard of the Fourteenth Amendment of the Constitution of the United States. And how soon does the superintendent suppose that the equality guaranteed by the nation would be established if its deliberate outrage by the laws or practices of the States is permitted? If there may be separate schools and inns and theatres and conveyances and cemeteries for one class of American citizens, if they are to be stigmatized and separated like lepers in other lands, if at every point they are to be told that they are inferior and degraded and unworthy, why were they made citizens? why did we not have leave them to be sold like sheep and swine? There are many persons who have "an antipathy," a "natural prejudice," against all foreigners: against the Irish, the Germans, the French, the English. What if the State of New York should establish separate schools for the Germans, and refuse to establish any for the Irish; what if the Germans should be turned away from the hotels they sought, and the Irish from the theatres in which they wished to find amusement, should they have no remedy under the authority which has guaranteed their equal rights? And shall any other class of citizens be deprived of the same protection against the same offense? "It punishes," says Senator Conkling, speaking of the bill, "only the man who indulges in assault, in opprobrium, in injury, of his fellowman, merely because he cherishes a lawless prejudice, merely because he carries in his heart a base and paltry hate insulting to the spirit and civilization of the age—a hate which has been trampled out on this continent in blood, and it is to be hoped forever." We wish Mr. Sumner could have heard Mr. Conkling say those words.

GENERAL HOWARD

HARPER'S WEEKLY
May 30, 1874, p. 451

There have been for a long time stories in circulation prejudicial to General Howard, late of the Freedman's Bureau. He was a brave and conspicuous soldier of the war, he had been eminent in the good work of the freedmen, and he was a member of the Church. To blacken his name, therefore, was to stigmatize several good things, and the dirty work has been zealously prosecuted in what were known when General Howard was leading an army corps and losing an arm as "Copperhead" circles, his chief opponent being Fernando Wood. Some time since the Secretary of War sent certain statements to the House of Representatives, and a court-martial was ordered, upon charges involving General Howard's personal and official character. The court has sent its decision to the President, and as it is known to be favorable, the expiring effort of malice was to insinuate that there were serious differences of judgment in the court. But the counsel of General Howard telegraphed to Mr. Edgar Ketchum that the court was unanimous upon the statement of facts, also upon all matters affecting his character as an officer and a gentleman, and also in commending his conduct as Commissioner—a decision which will be cordially welcomed by the country.

AN UNDOUBTED RIGHT

HARPER'S WEEKLY
May 30, 1874, p. 451

There is one kind of civil right which the strictest constitutional interpretation will not deny to the colored citizens of the Southern States, and that is the right of educating their own children at their own expense, assisted by the voluntary aid of others. This is what William Craft, whose story was very familiar during the Fugitive Slave Act excitement twenty-three years ago, proposes to do in South Georgia. His object is to give the poor country colored children a chance at the rudiments of education. Mr. Craft and his wife and son have bought a plantation or farm of 1800 acres about twenty miles from Savannah, to which families with children will remove, hiring part of the land and paying a portion of the crop toward the school, while the children will work upon the land to raise grain and vegetables for their own use. Mr. Craft in 1871 tried a similar experiment upon another spot, advanced the money, and secured a good crop; but the Ku-Klux destroyed the buildings and the harvest. Several gentlemen in Boston, in New York, and elsewhere have subscribed to further a project which is in such capable hands; and whoever is disposed may address Mr. Craft at 252 West Twenty-sixth Street, New York.

SOME NEW BOOKS

HARPER'S WEEKLY
May 30, 1874, p. 451

In the last number of our paper we made a reference to that portion of Dr. Schweinfurth's *Heart of Africa* relating to the rediscovery of the Pygmies, always considered fabulous when mentioned in the pages of Herodotus and the older poets. The other great features of his work are his contributions to the hydrography of Central Africa, and the light which he throws on the slave-hunting system, and the work begun for the Egyptian government by Sir Samuel Baker. In regard to the question of the Nile, it may be briefly stated that Schweinfurth crossed the western water-shed of that river, and having arrived where the Lualaba must come—if it come northward at all, and not into the Nyanza—he found the Welle, the Keebaly, the Gadda, and all the streams of the land flowing westward, and probably to the Shary. This does not "settle the Lualaba," but it proves the existence of a separate river system where Livingstone and Stanley thought there might be found the continuous channel of the Bahr-el-Ghazal. Besides seeing the Pygmies, Dr. Schweinfurth gives us distinct and interesting accounts of other tribes with whom we have had little previous acquaintance. The Monbuttoos and the Niam-niams, among whom the doctor lived for a long-time, are confirmed cannibals; and one of the most curious points of the description is to show that this unpleasant foible is not incompatible with marked advance in social arts and manners. For instance, those man-eaters, the Niam-niams, are affectionate husbands and wives, and will surrender the most cherished possession to buy back one of their household if captured by the slave-hunters or by a hostile tribe. Dr. Schweinfurth has unquestionably taken rank as a leading African explorer, and the present work, published in two volumes by Messrs. Harper & Brothers, with profuse and interesting illustrations, will more than justify the position assigned him by scientific men.

SIGNS OF THE TIMES

HARPER'S WEEKLY
June 13, 1874, p. 490

The House of Representatives has passed a very brief and significant bill, prohibiting any person who can not read or write from sitting upon a jury in any United States court. In this State Governor Dix has signed the Compulsory Education Bill. New Jersey has passed a similar law, and in several States like bills passed one House during the last winter. And Senator Stewart, of Nevada, has proposed an amendment to the Constitution of the United States in these words:

> "Article 16. If any State shall fail to maintain a common-school system, under which all persons between the ages of five and eighteen years, not incapacitated for the same, shall receive, free of charge, such elementary education as Congress may prescribe, the Congress shall have power to establish therein such a system, and cause the same to be maintained at the expense of such State."

These events are all signs that a truth which has been hitherto treated as rhetorical and ceremonial is coming to be regarded as very vital to the existence of freedom and good government in this country. The Rev. James Freeman Clarke, of Boston, a singularly candid and judicious man, has lately spent some time in the Southern States, and he said to his congregation upon his return: "There are now about twenty white men in the South Carolina Legislature. The remainder are colored men, most of whom can not read or write. I saw one colored man, who is now a candidate for the next Legislature, who not only can not read and write, but who maintains it as a proposition that no one who can write ought to be allowed in the Legislature. This man is also trustee and superintendent of schools in a certain district of the State."

This is no reason for refusing to sustain the Civil Rights Bill, but it is the best reason in the world for considering ignorance in its relations to government. Let us not, however, suppose ignorance to be confined to South Carolina. We have known a justice not a hundred miles from New York who was elected by the vote of a great party, and who could with difficulty write his name. But all generalization upon such data is very rash. There are plenty of colored men in South Carolina and elsewhere who see and deplore the consequences of ignorance, and who are quite ready to unite in any effort to remove and obviate them. Mr. Clarke gladly testifies that there are large numbers of such men, thrifty, industrious, decorous, and honest; as, for instance, on the island of St. Helena, where there are six thousand black men, and among them not a single pauper or beggar; and he believes, what will be heartily wished by every intelligent man, that within five or six years the sensible, good people of both races will be working harmoniously together.

But for the future of the country every where nothing is more indispensable than the requirement of education. If it could be made a condition of the electoral franchise, so much the better; and we know colored citizens even in South Carolina who are of that opinion. However, one thing is practicable, and that is for every State to adopt substantially the system that is to be tried in New York after the 1st of next January, and for every citizen to reflect whether an amendment of the general scope of that proposed by Senator Stewart is not desirable. The menacing evil of the country being corruption in various forms, the practical methods of withstanding it are a reform of the civil service, which, under the old system, furnishes the machinery and means of corruption, and education, which gives every body the chance, at least, of knowing what he is doing. Laws like the new one of New York are in operation in Michigan and New Hampshire, in Massachusetts and Connecticut. The principle is well known in many European countries, and the statistics of the condition of those countries are most encouraging. We shall recur to the details of the New York law, which, if it is honestly enforced, and modified as experience may wisely suggest, can not fail to be of the greatest service.

THE CIVIL RIGHTS BILL

HARPER'S WEEKLY
June 27, 1874, p. 534

The other day in the House, upon the motion to suspend the rules and take up the Civil Rights Bill, which has passed the Senate, the vote was 136 yeas to 86 nays. This was not a two-thirds vote, and the rules were not suspended; so that there is an impression that the bill will not be reached, and is lost for this session. We are very sorry, because it is desirable that the "negro question" should be settled, and because it is not settled, and will be constantly and properly agitated until all citizens of the United States are made equal under the laws, as they are not now. There is no more signal error than the supposition that the defeat of this bill tends to settle any thing. It is baffled by the party and the influence which have never comprehended and never will comprehend the real feeling of the country upon the subject, and which oppose the Civil Rights Bill upon the same general grounds and with the same hopelessness that they opposed the antislavery agitation and the Republican policy. The slavery should not go into the Territories—that having tried to destroy the government, it should be abolished—and that the colored race, being made citizens, should be defended as equal citizens, are parts of the same purpose; and happily very little is now wanting of its perfect accomplishment.

Mr. Lynch, a colored Representative from Mississippi, said in the late Republican Congressional caucus that he did not take it much to heart that Congress had refused to pass the bill, for the Republican party had been true to his race in the past, and would continue to be so in the future. But he also said that it mattered little to the colored race in the South about the dishonesty of leaders, for if the Republican governments had stolen money, the Democrats proposed to steal rights. Mr. Lynch leans upon a broken reed. Does he not know that without honesty in administration neither he nor his race have any real ground of hope? A thief is a thief. A party which steals money to-day will steal rights to-morrow. The men whom he defends sustain him to-day because they think that they can "make most" in that way. They will throw him over the instant they think that they can make more. A dishonest party is the least to be trusted of any; and Mr. Lynch and his friends may more safely confide themselves to the mercy of honest opponents than of dishonest friends.

Fortunately that alternative is not offered. The Republican party, as such, is honestly the friend of equal rights, and will persist in the effort to secure them. The Democrats will oppose, instinctively and traditionally; for what is called the Democratic party in this country is and always has been, as Mr. Adams so well showed in his discourse upon Mr. Seward, an aristocratic conspiracy. It has never respected the people, although it has constantly pandered to the mob. The bill now goes over, perhaps, to another session, but it will constantly reappear until the engagement of the country is fulfilled, as the financial agitation will continue until the holder of the United States note receives the dollar which it promises to pay.

AN OLD LANDMARK

HARPER'S WEEKLY
June 27, 1874, p. 545

Another relic of the olden time is about to disappear from the face of the earth. The members of the First African Church, Richmond, Virginia, with true American lack of veneration for old things and old buildings, are preparing to demolish and rebuild their ancient house of worship, the oldest colored church in America, if not in the world.

1874

INTERIOR OF THE CHURCH, FROM THE WESTERN WING.
THE FIRST AFRICAN CHURCH, RICHMOND, VIRGINIA.—[Drawn by W. L. Sheppard.]

Harper's Weekly, June 27, 1874, p. 545.

It stands on Broad Street, a few blocks above the Chesapeake and Ohio Railroad Depot, and is a long, low, irregular building of gray brick, with little in its architecture or surroundings to attract attention. Built in 1802, it was the first Baptist church erected in Richmond. Previous to the Revolution the Baptists were a proscribed sect in Virginia, and the preaching of their doctrines was a crime to be punished with stripes or imprisonment; consequently they have no church edifices of earlier date than the removal of this proscription in 1785. This one was owned at first by a white congregation, and John Courtney, more widely known as Father Courtney, one of the pioneers of the Baptist denomination in Virginia, was its first pastor. Years afterward its white members, increasing in wealth and numbers, moved a couple of squares up town, and built the First Baptist Church, at the corner of Broad and Twelfth streets, leaving the old edifice to the colored communicants of the same congregation. It was deemed best for the interests of the church that it should be as far as possible self-supporting, and the lot and building were sold at a nominal price instead of being given to the colored people. They were to pay for it by installments as they were able, and the debt has long ago been discharged.

Meantime it was regarded as an offshoot from the white church; and as, under the laws of Virginia, slaves, who composed the bulk of its congregation, could hold no property independently of their masters, the title to church and lot was vested in a board of trustees, composed of prominent members of the parent church, who held the property in trust for its colored congregation.

After the Southampton insurrection, in 1831, all assemblages of slaves, religious or otherwise, were prohibited by law unless at least two responsible white persons were present. These trustees, therefore, in turn attended all services held in the church until after the evacuation of Richmond and its occupation by the Federal troops in 1865.

In 1811, when the theatre on the square above it was destroyed by fire with such fearful loss of life, this building gave shelter to the dead and dying, and on its bare benches and uncarpeted floors were laid the sufferers rescued from the flames. Its size and convenient location have made it play an important part as the scene of political gatherings. Here it was that Jefferson Davis made his last speech in the Confederate capital as President of the Confederate States, and here that the first Republican Convention held in Virginia assembled in 1865. It is often used for political mass-meetings, and the negroes show their respect for the sanctity of the edifice by opening all such gatherings with hymnsinging and prayer—a practice which has become a stock subject for jest with fun-loving newspaper reporters.

The present pastor, Rev. James Holmes, is a colored man born in Richmond. He has considerable talent

753

THE REV. JAMES HOLMES.

Harper's Weekly, June 27, 1874, p. 545.

and a fair education, is of some repute as an orator, and a man of note among his own people. A corps of colored deacons assist him in his pastoral duties, and attend to the secular affairs of the congregation. These visit the sick, conduct prayer-meetings and minor funerals, and see that church members conform to the rules of the church—help much needed in a congregation in which nearly four thousand names are upon the list of communicants—a congregation, next to Spurgeon's, perhaps the largest in the world. The congregational singing and the colored choir who lead it have long been famous in Richmond, and when the multitude of negro worshipers who throng the house every Sunday unite in singing the weird hymn tunes of their race the effect is very fine, and the scene impressive in its solemnity.

A great revival has recently taken place among the colored people of Richmond, and this church has counted the additions to its membership by hundreds. They hold the creed of their color, which places dancing among the cardinal sins, and a score of communicants were not long since expelled at one time for this offense.

In spite of repeated additions to the church edifice, it is still much too small for its immense congregation, and the plans for the new building which is to rise upon its site are already in the hands of the builder.

THE CIVIL RIGHTS BILL

HARPER'S WEEKLY
August 1, 1874, p. 630

The veteran Truman Smith, ex-Senator from Connecticut, and now eighty-three years old, but apparently with his natural force unabated, has written a letter to Senator Brownlow, of Tennessee, sympathizing with his opposition to the Civil Rights Bill. Mr. Smith is a good representative of a sturdy New England sagacity, and his opinions are well worth considering. Moreover, like Mr. Brownlow, he is a Republican. His argument, indeed, is from the view of party policy, and asserts that the bill is an attempt to extirpate a prejudice by legislation, and must inevitably have the effect of closing the schools in the Southern States, and of alienating the whole white population, so that ignorance will be perpetuated, the colored race and the poor whites will tend to relapse into barbarism, and the whole mass of the whites will politically unite with the Democrats against the Republicans, and increase the chances of a return of the Democratic party to power in 1876. Should that event occur, Mr. Smith argues from the fact of the election of Mr. Eaton as Democratic Senator from Connecticut, and from his speech after his election, in which he defined his position, what the Democratic policy toward the colored citizens would doubtless be. The national purpose in regard to them is shown in the Fourteenth and Fifteenth amendments, which gave the care of their rights and interests as a separate class to the national government by authorizing Congress to enforce the articles by suitable legislation. Now Mr. Eaton has much to say of State rights and Federal despotism; and the meaning of his remarks, in Mr. Smith's opinion, is that under Democratic ascendency the necessary legislation for the enforcement of the protection guaranteed by the amendments would cease, and while chattel slavery could not be restored, the Democratic doctrine that the colored race have no rights which white men are bound to respect would become the rule, with evil results that may be imagined. Thus the Civil Rights Bill, designed for the proper protection of the colored citizens, would prove, in Mr. Smith's judgement, their ruin.

In sympathy with his view we have a letter from an eminent Republican in the State of Georgia, who says:

"I am not aware that history records the fact of two races living together happily and prosperously, upon terms of perfect equality, for any very long time.... If the Supplementary Civil Rights Bill become a law, the public common-school system of Georgia, as well as of most of the Southern States, will be abandoned, in my opinion. It is immaterial what the sentiment of opposition may be called, whether prejudice, fanaticism, aristocracy, or whatever: it exists and it can not be overcome

EXTERIOR OF THE CHURCH.

Harper's Weekly, June 27, 1874, p. 545.

during the present generation. The opposition is stronger among the poor whites and that class embraces most of the Republicans, than among the rich, who can educate their own children. No law so odious as this can be enforced among a people so hostile to it. Massachusetts was perhaps more law-abiding than the Southern States, and the Fugitive Slave Law could not be enforced there without producing riots and bloodshed. My judgment is that there is but little to be gained by the colored man by the passage of the law, and he will lose infinitely by it. No man can be sustained in the Southern States who approves it, except by the colored voters, and the strong tendency of such a state of things must be to produce a party based exclusively on race—a result greatly to be deplored by both, but more especially by the colored man. I think that the bill will defeat one if not two of the Republican members of Congress from this State this fall. The whites can't approve it, and the blacks can't succeed without whites to lead, and if some can be found to lead, they will lead colored men only."

This is the view of a very sagacious native of the region from which he writes, a gentleman who was not writing for publication, but to state privately his sincere convictions. He expresses strongly what is felt also by many Republicans in this part of the country. But the situation seems to us plain and imperative. It is the intention of the amended Constitution to make the new citizens perfectly equal with the old citizens before the law. Of that there is no doubt whatever. If, therefore, they have now, all circumstances considered, the same safeguards of those rights that the older citizens have, they have all that the Civil Rights Bill claims, and as there will be no change, the evil results which are anticipated can not arise. But if these citizens have not those safeguards, upon what possible grounds of principle or policy, of humanity or patriotism, is it urged that the laws of the United States shall authorize a prejudice of race, or deliberately secure civic inequality among citizens? The Civil Rights Bill is denounced as visionary, theoretical, impracticable legislation. But this objection, even if it were valid, comes too late. The folly, if it exists, was in granting the citizenship, not, certainly, in defending it when it is granted. The logical position, and the only tenable one, of those who oppose the bill is to demand the repeal of the original grant.

The objection, as stated, is that it is useless to legislate against a prejudice. That is not the point. The question is whether it is useless to assert and maintain the equality of American citizens before the law. The present consequences of enforcing that equality may be unfortunate to the schools in some parts of the country. But that is only a theory, and if it prove to be a fact, the evil is in its nature temporary. But deliberately to estab-

A BAPTIZING.
Harper's Weekly, June 27, 1874, p. 545.

lish injustice in the law is a degradation which is permanently fatal to the national character. It is said that the prejudice must be left to time and various influences. But in the mean while what will you do about legal injustice? Is that also a prejudice? Is that to be left to time? Moreover, if you recognize the prejudice at one point, why not at another? If the legal rights of a citizen in a hotel or in the cars are to be abandoned at the demand of prejudice, why not abandon his legal rights at the polls if prejudice requires? And we ask those who think that a prejudice is to be conquered by allowing it to dictate the laws, how soon and in what manner they expect it to disappear? The sure way to foster it is to recognize it in the law, as the sure way to begin its extinction is to outlaw it. When the war began, and colored troops were proposed, there were wiseacres who said that if the whites could not do the necessary fighting, the government might as well be destroyed. Suppose that the prejudice had then been recognized by refusing colored soldiers, would it have been weaker or stronger to-day? There are those who say, and will continue to say, that they have a natural prejudice against colored persons. But can any good purpose be served by strengthening that prejudice by law?

Mr. Smith argues that to pass the bill would be a party blunder, because it would help the Democrats into power. But since the Republicans passed the amendments, and since the bill is merely carrying the amendments into effect, they can not reject it without a fatal confession that they do not really trust their own principles and policy, a confession which would of course defeat them. If the Republican party has any duty plainer and more pressing than that of establishing the equality of American citizens before the law, we do not know what it is. It is true that had the question not been raised, its decision might wait upon the general ground that the necessity of legislation or of declaration had not arisen. But it has been raised. Some kind of action is imperative; and that action which maintains the constitutional and conceded rights of the citizen will withdraw the negro, as such, from politics, and will leave prejudice only its own folly to feed upon.

COLOR AND RIGHTS

HARPER'S WEEKLY
August 22, 1874, p. 690

The resolutions of the Alabama Democratic Convention undoubtedly express the real feeling of the Democratic party toward the colored citizens—a feeling which is strongly expressed in the platform of the Indiana Democracy, and which constantly appears in Democratic speeches and newspapers. It deserves careful consideration amidst the general chorus that the past is past, that old issues are dead, and that he is a madman and no patriot who tries to rekindle exhausted fires. The Alabama Democratic platform asserts the essential superiority of the white race, denounces the colored citizens as an ignorant and barbarous race, which is justly excluded from social intercourse with the higher, offers the right hand of fellowship to whites every where, and invites them cordially to settle in the State. Politically this is a substantially revolutionary declaration. Logically carried out, it would end in civil war. It is as unjustifiable as a similar assertion upon religious grounds would be. It is as intolerable in American politics as a wholesale denunciation of citizens of foreign birth. So far as it is a resolution of opposition to the Civil Rights Bill, it is based upon wholly illegitimate grounds, as if a party should resolve against the election of General Grant because he is a Methodist. The Constitution which defines citizenship makes all citizens equal, and knows nothing of their color, their religious faith, or their place of birth.

The Alabama resolutions, indeed, state that "the rights of all classes of men" under the Constitution must be maintained, but protests that no law can constitutionally enforce social equality. What does a Democratic or any other American Convention mean by "classes of men under the Constitution?" There is but one class known to the Constitution—the class of perfectly equal citizens. It recognizes no ignorant or barbarous, or rich or poor, or white or black class. And upon all citizens it confers equal rights, and those rights of all citizens the government under the Constitution is equally and expressly bound to protect. The Alabama and Indiana Democratic Conventions declare that they regard with abhorrence the attempt of the Federal Government to

Harper's Weekly, July 11, 1874, p. 581.

"take control of the schools, colleges, churches, hotels, railroads, steamboats, theatres, and grave-yards for the purpose of establishing negro equality." The words are the same in both platforms. Upon no other point is there more hearty Democratic accord. But the Federal Government is making no attempt to take such control. It has it already, under the Constitution. It is proposing to assert its power because equal rights are not protected. Nor does it propose to establish "social" equality in the sense of forcing negroes or any body else to what the Alabama resolutions call "equal participation with our families in our social institutions." The Civil Rights Bill provides that no "institution" which exists by authority of law made by the citizens shall recognize any distinction among those citizens founded upon color. It proposes that there shall not be a legal class of pariahs among equal American citizens. The declaration of the Alabama resolutions that the common law of the State provides for the protection of civil rights is a simple mockery. Even political rights which the resolutions declare must be kept inviolate are notoriously denied. Mr. King, in a late number of *Scribner's Magazine,* says that of the ninety thousand colored voters in Georgia scarcely thirty thousand vote, and that the most honorable Georgian Republicans state that the negroes are still grossly intimidated.

We are not discussing the wisdom of negro suffrage, nor denying the terrible ignorance and consequent wretchedness of the voting population of many of the Southern States. Nor it is necessary to revert to the general question of reconstruction. It is the duty of every good citizen in Alabama, as in every other State, to acquiesce honorably and co-operatively in the new provisions of the Constitution, or to attempt honorably their repeal. So long as all citizens, black and white, are equal under the law, the true policy of Alabama is to maintain and defend that equality. It is not defended, however, if a defensive law is a dead letter upon the statute-book. Laws, indeed, which are hostile to public sentiment, whether a sentiment founded upon a prejudice or a moral conviction, can not readily, sometimes can not at all, be enforced. That is a good reason for considering the wisdom of a change in the law. But while a just statute, like that of maintaining the equality of citizens before the law, remains, no constitutional effort should be omitted to enforce it. Those who oppose it really oppose equality, and their attempt should be to abolish it.

A party which seeks power to make the laws, under a declaration that an immense body of its political equals are ignorant, barbarous, and unfit for association with the rest, when that party is composed of late slave-masters, and the denounced class of their late slaves, will certainly not make or enforce equal laws. In this country it is that party, and that alone, which blows amidst the ashes to revive smouldering embers. It is resolutions like those of the Democratic Conventions of Alabama and Indiana which postpone indefinitely a real reconstruction. For while no reasonable man in the Northern States denies the unhappy situation in which so many of the Southern States are plunged, and is ready with the utmost sympathy to do what he can to remove the difficulties, nothing is plainer than that a party which plants itself upon the single plank of a white man's government is a party which would re-open a controversy that may introduce prolonged bitterness and trouble, but can have but one result.

EQUAL RIGHTS

HARPER'S WEEKLY
August 29, 1874, p. 710

The Louisville *Courier-Journal,* a Democratic journal in Kentucky, says:

> "The Civil Rights Bill may be passed, and signed by the President. If it does, there will be a war of races, a revolution, the overthrow of universal suffrage, and a military government at Washington. If the North is ready for this, so is the South: we have touched bottom, and can go no further. We have reached the point where gravitation stops and turns back. But the intermediate stage is to be avoided if possible, and we would avoid it, even if we have to back General Grant for a third term, or for life. He may veto the Civil Rights Bill, and being made sure of a re-election, may startle the country by refusing to run. If so, let him dictate his successor, and the South will accept him."

The *World,* a Democratic journal in New York, says:

> "The talk about a general war of races is too preposterous to receive serious attention. Neither race wants that; but the time seems to have fully come when the question must be peacefully decided at the polls whether the whites are to rule or the negroes to ruin the Southern States."

The Indiana Democratic Convention

> "views with abhorrence the attempt on the part of the Federal government to take control of all schools, colleges, churches, hotels, railroads, steamboats, theatres, and graveyards for the purpose of establishing negro equality, and enforcing it under numerous penalties of fines, damages, and imprisonments."

The Alabama Democratic Convention denounces the colored citizens as an "ignorant and barbarous race," and repeats the words of the Indiana resolution. And Mr. Eaton, just elected to the United States Senate by the Democratic Legislature of Connecticut, announces that he "shall try with other honest Senators to take away the Federal bayonets from our brothers," meaning that he shall try to commit the blacks in the Southern States to the care of the whites.

The situation in the Southern States, bad as it is, is mainly due to the Democratic party. It is not the result of the policy of reconstruction, but of the conditions and circumstances which shaped reconstruction. If the Democratic party had had absolute control of those States from the surrender of Lee to this moment, the situation would have been different, but it would have been very much more threatening, because injustice would have been organized upon the largest scale, and the monstrous consequences of such a policy to the moral tone of the whole country were shown in the influence of slavery for seventy years. And yet at the end of the war had the white leaders in the Southern States shown themselves equal to the situation, had they learned of Governor Orr and General Longstreet, they might have controlled affairs. But they sulked and defied and protested, and passed the most infamous black codes, with the full sympathy of the Democratic press in the Northern States, which openly sneered at General Longstreet and all the late Confederates who showed signs of sense and of statesman-like instincts.

Two courses were open to Congress: one was to hold the recovered States in a Territorial condition, the other was to restore them as rapidly as possible to practical relations in the Union. Public opinion scarcely permitted the first course to be considered; and in adopting the second, Congress, instructed by the overwhelming facts, having the completest evidence of the revolting spirit and intolerable policy with which the colored population were to be treated if the old Democratic ascendency in the States should be suffered to reorganize the governments at its pleasure, justly took all the risks, and made both races equal citizens. That great confusion, much misgovernment, and injustice in many ways have followed is not to be denied; and the only consolation is that much and much more permanent evil must have resulted from adopting any other course. If, by any unhappy chance, the Democratic party could have obtained possession of the government, the condition of the colored population under black codes and vagrant laws, and at the mercy of Democratic ex-slave-holding State-sovereignty legislation, would have been only a less shame to humanity and civilization than the slavery which under another form it would have perpetuated.

Plainly the wise and patriotic, the peaceful and necessary, course for the country to pursue is to maintain the equal rights of all citizens in the fullest and completest manner. This can not and will not be done by the Democratic party. It declares, indeed, that the rights of the colored citizens must be protected. But it "abhors" an equality which it calls social, but which is not social, being merely legal. It speaks with Mr. Eaton of "our brothers" in the Southern States, meaning those who denounce the colored race as barbarous. Its animating spirit is one of hostility to the policy that gave political and civil rights to the colored people. It is traditionally servile to the class that held them in slavery; and while the Democratic party does not declare that the colored race should be deprived of the suffrage, the manner in which it would protect that right can be inferred from every Democratic journal and orator and convention, while Democratic contempt of equal civil rights is openly and vehemently expressed. But equality of citizenship and the disappearance of prejudice against that equality are simply impossible when the law stigmatizes any class of citizens.

This is the very time to insist that the policy which has been adopted shall not be abandoned. To hesitate, to retreat, to attempt to undo this work, would be the height of folly. The Louisville *Courier-Journal* ought to know that its threats of civil war and revolution are obsolete. There was a time when they had force, and when a timid "North" trembled. That time is gone forever, and we wish that the *Courier* could understand the unspeakable contempt with which the new generation, the new "North," hears a menace of revolution should the legal equality of American citizens be every where maintained. From the first moment in the first Congress that the question of the colored race in the Union challenged attention down to the present moment, every proposition of amelioration of its condition has been met with the same assertion, that it was unnatural, monstrous, unchristian, and would surely end in universal massacre and anarchy. The event has uniformly belied the prediction; and had the Democratic warning been heeded and the counsel followed, this nation would have been absolutely subjugated by the slave power, the power of injustice and inhumanity.

Since, then, the Democratic party, always the foe of equal liberty, returns to its vomit, it is the duty of all intelligent citizens to understand what is involved in a victory of that party, under whatever pretense it may be won, and to take care that exasperation with whatever venality and misconduct may be detected in Republican administration, and the hope of advantage from change, shall not cause them to aid in establishing Democratic ascendency. For no intelligent observer can doubt that it would lead to a policy of oppression toward the colored race, and an angry and indefinite prolongation of that cause of national trouble. To avert this result the Democratic party must be defeated now, as it has been necessary for fourteen years to defeat it, in the interest of liberty, intelligence, and civilization. And to this end it is indispensable that secondary issues of every kind be patriotically postponed, and that the best men be nominated by the Republicans. We hope especially that the Republican Conventions of New York and Massachusetts will remember the real issue at stake.

FREEDOM, JUBILEE, AND PARDON

HARPER'S WEEKLY
August 29, 1874, p. 715

According to statistics given by the Charleston *News,* the number of pardons granted by Governor Moses, of South Carolina, from December 12, 1872, to July 22, 1874, a period of only nineteen months, was four hundred and twenty-one, an average of about twenty-two a month. The offenses of which the parties pardoned were convicted are shown in the following table:

Murder	21
Manslaughter	25
Rape	16
Infanticide	5
Burglary	33
Forgery	4
Arson	24
Highway robbery	3
Perjury	4
Larceny	110
Bigamy	6
Assault and battery	107
Horse and mule stealing	6
Libel	1
Kidnapping	1
Abduction	1
Trespass	4
Miscellaneous	38
Official misconduct and malfeasance in office	12
Total	421

This list, says the *News,* is exclusive of twenty-five or thirty criminals who were discharged in a batch, and of whose pardon there is no record. These details, obtained by the *News* from the office of the South Carolina Secretary of State, furnish a startling *expose* of

AFRICAN AMERICAN HISTORY IN THE PRESS, 1851-1899

HARPER'S WEEKLY
A JOURNAL OF CIVILIZATION

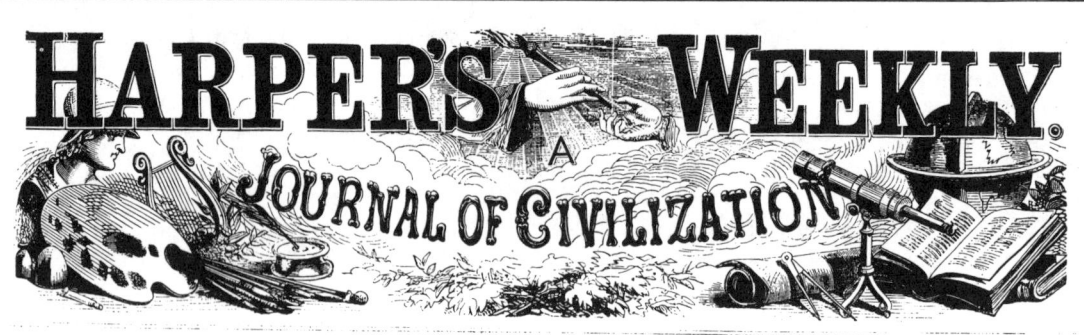

Vol. XVIII.—No. 922.] NEW YORK, SATURDAY, AUGUST 29, 1874. [WITH A SUPPLEMENT. PRICE TEN CENTS.

Entered according to Act of Congress, in the Year 1874, by Harper & Brothers, in the Office of the Librarian of Congress, at Washington.

FREEDOM, JUBILEE, AND PARDON.—[SEE PAGE 715.]
HE IS DOING UNTO OTHERS AS HE WOULD HAVE DONE UNTO HIM.

Harper's Weekly, August 29, 1874, p. 709.

the abuse of the pardoning power in that State. It is the general belief that the Governor is working for his "second term." The negroes have great confidence in him, because, as the Nation well puts it, they believe "that Grant stands by him, and that he represents freedom, jubilee, and the pardoning power."

LOUISIANA

HARPER'S WEEKLY
October 3, 1874, p. 811

Before this paper is issued the national government will undoubtedly have subdued the insurrection in New Orleans, and it will be heartily sustained by every intelligent citizen. The outbreak has thoroughly aroused the country, which will demand why Congress, after a report of its special committee of inquiry that Kellogg was not lawfully elected Governor, declined all action. The situation has been wretched, nor can all the blame be laid upon one party. Kellogg, whom the Congressional committee virtually declared to be a usurper, had apparently laid his plans to secure absolute control of the next election, which, under the form of a republican government, would thus have destroyed its substance. An appeal of the reputable people of all parties in Louisiana to Congress to consider whether there was no remedy for the situation in the constitutional authority to guarantee to each State a republican form of government would, under such circumstances, be very powerfully supported by the best opinion of the country. But one of the most pacificatory measures that could be adopted would be the appointment of national officers in the spirit of the President's civil service scheme, that is to say, the appointment of collectors, marshals, judges, and others who are known not to be political intriguers, and who would take the lead in opposing and exposing such political knaveries as have been notoriously perpetrated in Louisiana without remonstrance from Washington. If the Administration were represented in all the troubled States by men who are personally respected, however they may be politically opposed, there would be the beginning of a good understanding.

Meanwhile, we repeat, prompt and absolute suppression of Penn's insurrection is the most imperative duty of the Government; and careful reflection upon the situation that produced the insurrection is the equally imperative duty of all good citizens.

PERSONAL

HARPER'S WEEKLY
October 3, 1874, p. 811

It is said that Cadet Smith, the colored young man who failed to pass his examination at West Point, is writing a book upon the abuses at the Military Academy, and proposes to disclose certain things.

LOUISIANA AND THE RULE OF TERROR

HARPER'S WEEKLY
October 3, 1874, pp. 813–14

Julia Hayden, the colored school-teacher, one of the latest victims of the White Man's League, was only seventeen years of age. She was the daughter of respectable parents in Maury County, Tennessee, and had been carefully educated at the Central College, Nashville, a favorite place for the instruction of youth of both sexes of her race. She is said to have possessed unusual personal attractions as well as intelligence. Under the reign of slavery, as it is defined and upheld by Davis and Toombs, Julia Hayden would probably have been taken from her parents and sent in a slave-coffle to New Orleans to be sold on its auction block. But emancipation had prepared for her a different and less dreadful fate. With that strong desire for mental cultivation which has marked the colored race since their freedom, in all circumstances where there is an opportunity left them for its exhibition, the young girl had so improved herself as to become capable of teaching others. She went to Western Tennessee and took charge of a school. Three days after her arrival at Hartsville, at night, two white men, armed with guns, appeared at the house where she was staying and demanded the school-teacher. She fled, alarmed, to the room of the mistress of the house. The White Leaguers pursued. They fired their guns through the door of the room, and the young girl fell dead within. Her murderers escaped, nor is it likely that the death of Julia Hayden will ever be avenged, unless the nation insists upon the extermination of the White Man's League. The fearful association extends through every Southern State, and one of its chief objects is to prevent the education and elevation of the colored race. It whips, intimidates, or murders their teachers from the Ohio to the Gulf, and its terrible outrages have already surpassed the horrors of the most vindictive civil war.

Yet the colored people have already made a remarkable progress. Their faithful labors have nearly restored the usual productiveness of the South. The

THE COMMANDMENTS IN SOUTH CAROLINA.
"We've pretty well smashed that; but I suppose, Massa Moses, you can get another one."

Harper's Weekly, September 26, 1874, p. 792.

THE LOUISIANA OUTRAGES—PRESIDENT GRANT DEMANDS "UNCONDITIONAL SURRENDER."—[SEE PAGE 813.]

Harper's Weekly, October 3, 1874, p. 812.

most respectable planters even of Louisiana attest their industry and good conduct. Wherever they have been able they have planted schools, cultivated farms, entered into trade, and in the brief course of eight years have risen from abject slavery to an honorable and useful freedom. No cruelty is laid to their charge even by their enemies—no massacres and frightful deeds like those of the White Man's League. It is only the followers of Toombs and Davis who have brought upon us the shame of assassinations and midnight murders, who shoot down Republican voters in the open day, and murder young lady school-teachers in the excess of their insanity. The aim of these Thugs of the South is the total extermination of the colored race. Davis and Toombs, M'Enery and Penn, are no more than the chiefs of a band of assassins, and their Democratic allies of the North encourage them (it may be hoped unconsciously) in their policy of blood. A very remarkable statement is made in one of the morning papers of a conversation held with an eminent Democratic lawyer, in which he avows his belief that the only remedy for the disorders at the South is the "extirpation" of the colored race. Yet the same arguments which Mr. O'Conor employs to convince himself of so dreadful a necessity were used by the Norman and Saxon oppressors of Ireland in their war of extermination against his own countrymen. The Roman Catholic priests and monks of the Norman period taught that it was no crime to kill an Irishman. The Protestant rulers, Elizabeth and even Cromwell, followed their barbarous example. The Irish kerns were massacred with as little remorse by the English soldiers of the sixteenth century as are the negroes of Louisiana by M'Enery and Penn. It was a contest of races, and the weaker and more abject received no different treatment from their masters than that which Democratic politicians now prepare for the laboring people of the South. Happily, at least for Ireland, the founders of our republic began a new period of humanity. The cruel superstition of a savage age they threw aside forever. They opened a fair and happy home for the Irish kern and German peasant. The Irish race, which in its own land seemed only worthy of extirpation or of extreme oppression, was received with generous liberality in that of Jefferson and Adams. Its chains were torn off, its sorrows amended, and the only return our people ask from the once oppressed but now prosperous Irish is that the pity that was bestowed upon them they should show to others, and that they prove their gratitude to freedom and to Protestantism by avoiding every act that may endanger the peace of the republic in which they have found a shelter.

But can Mr. O'Conor say that they have done this so long as he and his countrymen lend aid to the rebellion at the South, or would introduce into the New World that hatred and contempt for any one class of our citizens, founded upon the difference in race, from which they themselves have been the chief sufferers in the Old? Scarcely, indeed, can it be said that Mr. O'Conor has set his people a good example. During the rebellion

MISS JULIA HAYDEN, THE MURDERED SCHOOL-TEACHER.—[FROM A PHOTOGRAPH.]

Harper's Weekly, October 3, 1874, p. 813.

he was the ally of Davis and Toombs, the foe of the Union cause; at its close he became the friend and supporter of all those desperate men who are laboring to destroy the peace of the Southern States. He is now apparently an advocate for the "extirpation" of the negro, and his last words will be eagerly seized upon by the White Man's League, as incentives to further enormities. The strange, unaccountable hatred of the Irish Catholics for the negro can only be removed by the gradual influence of an American education. It was, no doubt, upon the principles advocated by Mr. O'Conor that in 1863 they hung unlucky colored men to the lamp-posts of New York, or burned an orphan asylum filled with colored children, that they gave their votes uniformly to disunion throughout the war, and that their leaders, with some honorable exceptions, strove to destroy the government to whose friendly shelter they had fled from their native island. It may be hoped that the future of the Irish race will be marked by more honorable traits of conduct, that they will study the teachings of Washington and Jefferson, and learn in the common school the duties of an American citizen.

Louisiana, now torn and dismembered by a new insurrection, has been the chief victim of the White Man's League. Rich, prosperous, the centre of the most hideous features of the Southern slave-trade, it flung itself madly into rebellion without a cause, and staked its whole welfare upon the maintenance of slavery. It came out from the war ruined and covered with woe. Poverty and even extreme want stalked through the streets of New Orleans, and its people were fed by the charity of the nation they had sought to destroy. Its merchants were bankrupt, its levees crumbling into ruin, and but for the aid of the too lenient North, the Mississippi might have flowed over its richest lands, and its capital fallen into a blighted waste. But the Free States lent it their aid; its people pledged their honor to obey the laws; the prosperity of Louisiana seemed about to revive; the colored population labored once more with new assiduity as free men. It was at this moment that the White Man's League began its outrages, and the new progress of Louisiana suffered a fatal check. In 1867 it had given a Republican majority; in 1868 so fearful had been the system of terrorism established by the Ku-Klux that only five thousand Republicans ventured to vote for Grant and Colfax. From that time the State has been the scene of constant assassinations, outrages, violence, disorder. The life of no Republican, white or black, has been safe. And the people who had sworn obedience to the constitution and the laws have violated every principle of honor. Capital and industry have fled from the terrified community. The shops and houses of New Orleans have stood silent and empty. The Mississippi has broken over the crumbling levees, and a large part of the people of the State have once more lived upon the alms of the nation. The White Man's League has affected the ruin of a community that might have been slowly benefited by Northern capital and enterprise, and has at last completed its crimes by rising in a new rebellion. Nothing but severe and austere justice should now be awarded to this infamous association. The murderers who in 1868 drove all the Republican voters from the polls, who in 1872 burned nearly a hecatomb of colored people in Grant Parish, and who have recently slaughtered the United States officials at Coushatta, whose offenses are enormous and indescribable, have presumed to seize upon the city of New Orleans, and defy the will of the people. Living upon the alms of the government, they have yet found money, it seems, to purchase muskets; covered with crime, they appeal to the country for sympathy. But the strong arm of the nation has already reached them, and they will find that the period of mercy is past. Rebellion and disunion must be crushed to atoms in every Southern State, and so strict a guard kept for the future that our country will offer no asylum for traitors in the guise of a White Man's League.

Such a policy would be sustained by a majority of the peaceful citizens of the South as well as the North. The White Man's League has no strength except where it rules by force. Even Georgia would give a vast majority against disunion and the profligate Toombs if its people were allowed to vote freely. It was only terror that held New Orleans in subjection to Penn. The New Orleans *Picayune*, edited by a duelist's blood-stained hand, commanded the White Leaguers "to shoot down like a dog" every white or black Republican who was seen attempting to excite an opposition to its murderous rule. There is no disguise there. The citizens of the North and West have been insulted upon its streets, and shot like dogs. And they have been scarcely better treated in Georgia and Alabama. The condition of the Southern States has been for a long time a shame to freedom and to civilization. Let the people rise with stern unanimity from ocean to ocean to strike down the rebels and their Northern abettors, and insist that the life of the humblest citizen of Maine or Minnesota shall be inviolable even in New Orleans. Before a united people the rebellion will be crushed to atoms in a moment.

The sudden surrender of the rebels and their late repentance can afford no palliation for their guilt. For eight years they have wasted the resources of Louisiana and destroyed its prosperity, have covered it with terror, bloodshed, and shame. The President has never more clearly represented the will of the people than when he declared that there should be no compromise with rebellion. Whatever may have been the errors of the Kellogg government—and it is worthy of notice that the only testimony against the Republican Governor comes from men stained with murder, and to whom falsehood is more familiar than truth—it is not for the assassins of Coushatta or Grant Parish to speak of justice, nor will they find any sympathy or support, except perhaps among their natural allies in Tammany Hall. The people demand their punishment. The majesty of the law must be asserted in every part of the South. Impunity only excites the outlaws to new violence; nor will the nation be satisfied until free speech and perfect liberty of thought and action are enforced from the Ohio to the Gulf. —Eugene Lawrence.

THE PRESIDENT AND LOUISIANA

HARPER'S WEEKLY
October 10, 1874, p. 831

Notwithstanding all the sharp censure of the President in many quarters for his original recognition of Kellogg in Louisiana, his duty in the late events was perfectly plain. It was to suppress the revolution promptly and peremptorily. The one thing that was evident was that we were threatened with the beginning of a Mexican method in our politics. Had it received the slightest countenance, or any thing but the short and summary summons of General Grant, with the instant movement of troops, the mischief would have been incalculable. The doctrine of "home rule" might have perplexed a less sound head than that of the victor over "home rule" organized as secession and rebellion; while the telegrams sent to Washington by Penn and various bodies in New Orleans argued gravely that because not many officers of the law had been killed, the insurrection should be acknowledged. In the Rhode Island case Dorr showed an undisputed majority of votes in favor of his constitution, but the whole proceeding was irregular, and the Administration did not hesitate to sustain the actual Governor.

The situation in Louisiana has been most wretched; but let the President be judged by the facts. After the election in 1872 both Kellogg and M'Enery claimed to be Governor, and two Legislatures assumed to be valid. Appeal was made to the President, but he declined to interfere until resistance was made to judicial process. The President says, nor is there any reason to suppose that he deliberately tells a falsehood in a state paper, that he did not think that he had any right to review the judgment of the court. This seems to us a most serious error, not only because the Constitution in the review of the Supreme Court makes him the sole judge, but because under the act of 1870 he was made responsible for using the whole force of the Union, and it was clearly his duty not to use it until he was satisfied that it ought to be used. Under the circumstances, the judgment of a court should not have satisfied him. But there is no doubt that he acted in perfect good faith. The courts having decided the Lynch returning board to be lawful, and action being imperative, the President recognized Kellogg.

This he did, so far as has been shown, with entire honesty, and the proof of it is that when further investigation developed every kind of fraud, and threw the whole question into the utmost uncertainty, he referred the whole question to Congress, stating frankly that if it did nothing he should adhere to the government that he had already recognized. Congress declined to act, notwithstanding his urgent request, and its refusal was regarded by him as a virtual approval of his action. From that moment, obliged to consider one of the contestants as Governor, he sustained Kellogg; and an insurrection against the Kellogg administration was "the domestic violence" against which the United States guarantees every State. Meanwhile a committee of Congress reported, after investigation, that Kellogg had not been lawfully elected, but Congress refused to order a new election. It has been a wretched business from the beginning, for which Congress is mainly responsible. But the Mexican solution sought by the M'Energy men and the White League made it only worse, and it has been most satisfactorily and properly disposed of.

Of course the only remedy is an honest election; but Kellogg holds his office for two years more. The President, we presume, will now insist upon Congressional attention to Louisiana. He may justly remind Congress that his previous message was not uncalled for. And as even he, who recognized Kellogg, presently said that it was doubtful whether he were elected, and as the Congressional committee declared that he was not elected, and as the insurrection has shown how slight a popular support he has, it may be quite worth while to consider whether there is nothing to do for Louisiana but to uphold a Governor whom nobody believes to

THE LOUISIANA OUTRAGES—ATTACK UPON THE POLICE IN THE STREETS OF NEW ORLEANS.

Harper's Weekly, October 3, 1874, p. 813.

have been elected, and who is apparently sustained solely by the national power.

THE LOUISIANA OUTRAGES

HARPER'S WEEKLY
October 10, 1874, p. 842

We give on our first page a series of illustrations relating to the recent outbreak of the White Leaguers in New Orleans. The three sketches, all from the pencil of Mr. R. Lawrence, will give the reader a graphic idea of the appearance of the city while the streets were under the control of these desperate men. Owing to the prompt and decisive action of President Grant, the insurrection was quelled before it could attain dangerous headway. Mr. M'Enery and Mr. Penn quietly surrendered their usurped and brief authority, and the regular State officers were as quietly reinstated.

The portraits on the same page will also be studied with interest. Governor William Pitt Kellogg was born in Vermont in 1830. He was educated at Norwich University, removed to Illinois in 1848, and was admitted to the bar in that State in 1853. In 1861 he was appointed Chief Justice of Nebraska by President Lincoln, but resigned the same year and accepted the colonelcy of the Seventh Illinois Cavalry. He served under General Pope in Missouri, and had command of a cavalry brigade until the evacuation of Corinth. In April, 1865, Mr. Kellogg was appointed Collector of the port of New Orleans, and held that position until July, 1868, when he was elected to the Senate of the United States. At the election in November, 1872, he was chosen Governor of Louisiana.

Colonel John M'Enery, Democratic candidate for Governor in 1872, is a native of Louisiana, and served during the war in the Confederate ranks. It is unnecessary here to recapitulate the details of the recent attempt to place him and Mr. Penn, who was candidate for Lieutenant-Governor on the same ticket, in possession of the State government. General Longstreet's career is familiar to all. He was one of the bravest and most capable of the Confederate generals during the war, but at the close he accepted the situation, and devoted all his energies to the work of pacification and union. This brought upon him a weight of undeserved obloquy such as few men could bear. He was called a renegade to the South, and socially ostracized, and all his efforts to bring about a better understanding between the North and the South have been scornfully repelled by his old friends. General Badger, who commanded the Metropolitan Police of New Orleans at the beginning of the recent outbreak, and was severely wounded in the first day's fighting, served in the Union army during the war,

A DEAD FAILURE.

Harper's Weekly, October 3, 1874, p. 814.

and enjoyed a high reputation for bravery and capability. The portraits are engraved from photographs by W. W. Washburn, of New Orleans.

THIS IS A WHITE MAN'S GOVERNMENT

HARPER'S WEEKLY
October 17, 1874, p. 858

"The White Man's Party embraces nearly all the intelligence and wealth of the State."—New York *Tribune*.

However desirous our peaceable citizens may be of placing a more hopeful construction upon the condition of the Southern States than the events of the past few months will allow, the letters that are constantly received from the friends of the Union in that section show that they, at least, share in no such agreeable delusion. They steadily assert that the disunion faction is active in every part of the South, and that the political leaders who have assumed the name of Democrats are no better than traitors in disguise. In the neighborhood in Alabama where Mr. Billings was recently assassinated a reign of terror exists, we are told, that is "simply appalling." The Ku-Klux, masked and armed, in companies of two or three hundred, have resumed their nightly rides. They are composed of "the vilest and lowest" of the population, but they are supplied with money and horses, and supported by the countenance of the Democratic leaders, who hope by their aid to control the elections. They are determined, it seems, to force the negroes into insurrection; and the negroes, who, we are told, "are quiet and peaceable, and have no more idea of insurrection than an infant," are subjected to such horrible outrages as no other race has ever borne so patiently. Every night the murderers chase them from their cabins to the woods and swamps, where they hide in hopeless terror. Some are shot down as they fly; all live in fear of their lives, in a condition of misery that no language can describe. Meanwhile, our informant continues, "these villains—White Leaguers—march in hundreds by (I have seen them), making night hideous with their demoniac yells." No Republican dares to sleep in his own house in this district of Alabama, where the Mobile *Register* insists that all is peace and order. But it is against the white Republicans, whether native or Northern born, that the Democrats show their deadliest hatred. Mr. Billings, one of their most recent victims, was an amiable and excellent man, "a noble Northern gentleman, against whom not a word of reproach could be uttered." He was a moderate Republican, but careful never to introduce political topics in conversation, possessing a wide information, and a welcome visitor in every household "not prejudiced by passion." None of his friends dreamed of his assassination. He was shot down in the night by a troop of the masked and demoniac League. The Southern-born Unionists are no more secure than the Northern. Unless speedy help is given them they will be murdered like the patriot Billings. "I beg you in God's name," exclaims one of them, "to heed my cry for help, and spare no effort to have these murderers brought to justice."

These simple words, this cry for help, indicate what must be the true policy of our government and people. The justice of the nation should at once fall upon the murderers. In no country can such a condition of society be safely tolerated for a moment; in no country can it be suffered to prevail long without a total destruction of the moral sense of the people. These infamous associations should be extirpated with so firm a hand that their leaders and abettors may learn in future to dread the laws they now openly contemn. If any part of the Southern people have wrongs to complain of, let them do so peaceably and properly, and the nation will do them justice. They know that the chief desire of the whole country is to bring back prosperity and good order to their unhappy section. But when any part of the Southern people become assassins and open murderers, join in treasonable leagues, and defy the government, they can look for nothing but the strict punishment of their crimes; and however that punishment may apparently be delayed, it will come at last with redoubled severity. Coushatta and Grant Parish and the long list of murders and outrages at the South have yet to be atoned for by those who have been engaged in them. But that the government should suffer wild gangs of murderous villains to ride through the inland districts of Alabama, Texas, or Tennessee, hunting the white and black Republicans from their homes to swamps and

AFRICAN AMERICAN HISTORY IN THE PRESS, 1851-1899

HARPER'S WEEKLY
JOURNAL OF CIVILIZATION

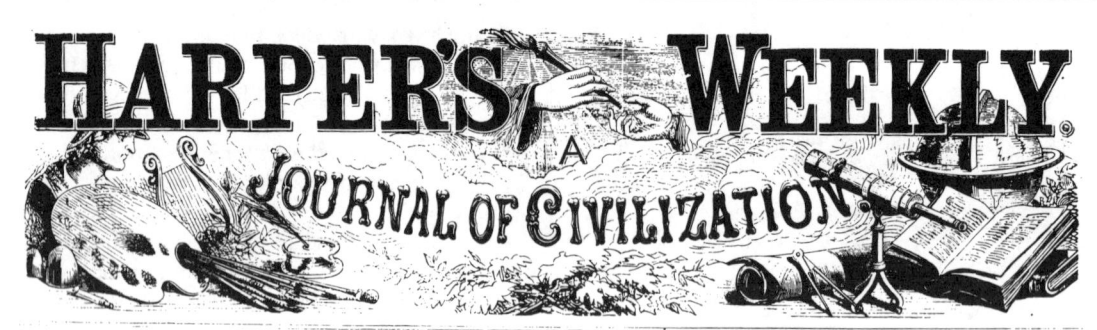

Vol. XVIII.—No. 928.] NEW YORK, SATURDAY, OCTOBER 10, 1874. [WITH A SUPPLEMENT. PRICE TEN CENTS.

Entered according to Act of Congress, in the Year 1874, by Harper & Brothers, in the Office of the Librarian of Congress, at Washington.

RENDEZVOUS OF WHITE LEAGUERS.

GOVERNOR KELLOGG.

WHITE LEAGUERS GUARDING A LEVEE.

GENERAL LONGSTREET.

JOHN F. M'ENERY.

D. B. PENN.

GENERAL BADGER.

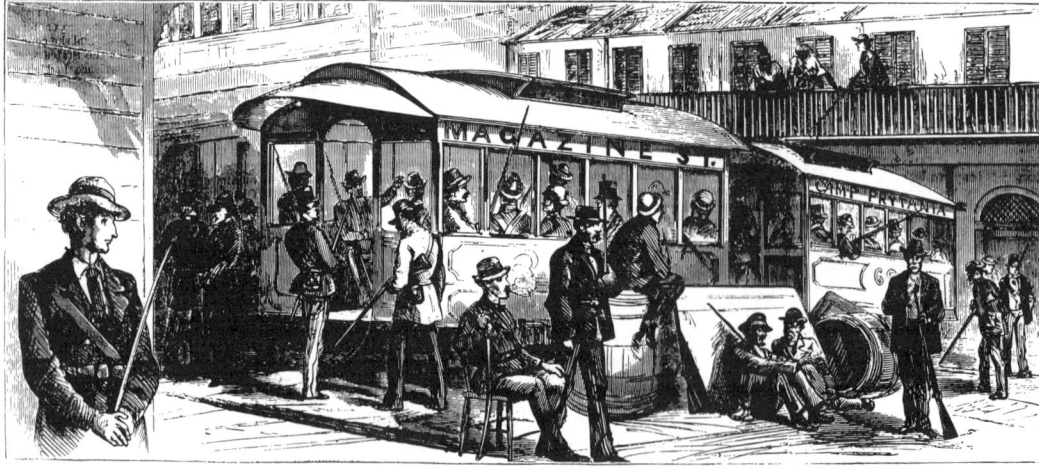

A STREET BARRICADE, GUARDED BY WHITE LEAGUERS.
THE LOUISIANA OUTRAGES.—[SEE PAGE 842.]

Harper's Weekly, October 10, 1874, p. 829.

THIS IS A WHITE MAN'S GOVERNMENT.
"The White Man's Party embraces nearly all the intelligence and wealth of the State."—New York *Tribune*.

Harper's Weekly, October 17, 1874, p. 858.

forests, destroying the first principles of free government, forcing free citizens to abstain from voting by terror, committing barbarous murders and crimes that exceed the horrors of the Paris Commune or an Irish insurrection, is what the Southern leaders can no longer look for, and if they persist in rebellion, they must encounter a united nation. Their allies of Tammany Hall can no longer save them. The cry for help from the despairing Unionists has been heard by the people.

The class of the population at the South from which the White Leaguers come is said to be the "worst and vilest," the idle, dissipated, and worthless, who would gladly live by robbery rather than honest labor, and who even plunder the poor cabins of the negroes from which they have just driven the industrious inmates. Slavery has created in the Southern States a "dangerous class" less easily controlled than that of any other land. They terrify the moderate; they rule over society. But they have a wholesome respect for Northern justice and power, and nothing but the sympathy shown them by the Northern Democracy has supplied them with sufficient courage to seize upon New Orleans, or to massacre the United States officials at Coushatta. They hate the United States government, no doubt, intensely, but they have a clear sense of its power. It was the encouragement given by the Democratic press and leaders in the North to the party of M'Enery that led them to begin the insurrection at New Orleans. The White League would never have dared to show itself openly, even in Louisiana, if it had not hoped that the arm of the government would have been palsied by Democratic interference. The White Leaguers have evidently been misled by their Northern allies into the belief that they are objects of real sympathy and interest to their fellow-countrymen, that their nightly raids and midnight murders are looked upon with congenial interest by their Democratic brethren at the North, who long to join even in the poor pilfering of a negro cabin. But they will find, we believe, that there are not many native-born citizens either North, or West, or East who are not ready to listen to the appeal of the Southern Unionists and avenge their wrongs. The brigands of Georgia and Alabama can look for no different fate from those of Italy and Spain. Massachusetts is not accustomed to suffer her citizens to be murdered with impunity, nor is the great Northwest any longer willing to look patiently upon the outrages of the South.

To the revival of the prosperity of the Southern States the existence of these White Leagues and incessant disturbances has proved nearly fatal. While all over the North and West the swift tide of immigration and the rapid progress of trade have repaired the ravages of four years of warfare, and founded new nations in the wilderness, the unhappy South lies shrunken and wasted, covered with debt, the centre of hopeless poverty. The emigrant turns away from a land where the demoniac yells of the White League are heard in every district; where life is constantly in peril, or free speech and free thought banished by a rigid tyranny; where schools are neglected, and even churches burned down lest they might teach Republicanism and enforce good order. No settler ventures within reach of the Alabama Ku-Klux, or even cares to renew the rich lands on the Tennessee. Nor are capital and trade less timid. It is credibly asserted that but for the ceaseless crimes of the Leaguers even New Orleans might once more have become a flourishing port. It is certain that what Louisiana most wants is a chain of prosperous settlements like Coushatta, full of enterprise and thrift; but the White League has closed for many a year all hope of Northern aid to the fallen State, and in the midst of its madness the trade of New Orleans has probably been forever diverted. Debt, dishonor, and decay hang over all the Southern States where the White League rules. Even Texas is so impoverished as to have reached a virtual bankruptcy. Its Democratic Legislature robs the public schools, and its people tremble before the Ku-Klux. The fate of the Southern States under the rule of the White Man's League is so plainly indicated as to escape no observation. Diseased and decaying, they cling to the vigorous and progressive nation, perishing in the midst of their boundless strength and unimproved resources. Knowledge flies from their borders, and a nearly universal ignorance weighs down their people. Commerce and capital shrink from their disordered communities. The policy of murder and violence, the outrages of the White Man's League, have produced their necessary results, and population, intelligence, and wealth avoid the lawless land. Meanwhile the Free States grow with a swiftness that is unparalleled. They already surround the decaying South with a chain of powerful communities. Life, property, and liberty are secure even amidst the peaks of the Rocky

Mountains, and the free school and the church are the harbingers of limitless prosperity.

The wiser class of the Southern leaders may well profit from the contrast. Nature has supplied them with all the elements of progress; freedom and peace, wealth and plenty, lie within their grasp. But so long as they tolerate murder and riot within their midst, they must remain impoverished and fallen. Their first aim should be to establish good order every where. Let them consign their White Leaguers to the nearest penitentiary, and their vagabond population that disturb the night with demoniac yells to the work-house. Let them protect their colored population from all harm, and no country will have more assiduous laborers. That the negroes have become politicians is due to their danger in part. Fear has driven them often to seek office, for they knew that should their enemies—the M'Enerys and Penns—seize upon power, they could look for no safety from robbery and assassination. With kind treatment and a careful education, the colored people will easily yield to a white man's government that obeys the law of humanity and of equal rights; but no outrages and no terrors can convert them into rebels. In fact, the white leaders of the Southern people must cease to be the dupes or the abject slaves of their assassins and murderers, must reject the mad counsels of their Democratic allies at the North, must respect the rights of every citizen, and punish rebellion and disorder, if they would bring back hope and prosperity to their fallen land. And in such a course they would have the support and sympathy of the East, West and North. But, on the other hand, it has become the duty of the people of the whole country to provide for the safety of the despairing Unionists. Let their cry for help be heard in the coming elections. Let each citizen remember that every vote given for a Democratic candidate is an implied approval of the murders and assassinations of the White Man's League; that every victory of the Democracy will be met with shouts of joy by the Alabama Ku-Klux, and spread a deadly terror in every loyal heart from Georgia to the Rio Grande. —Eugene Lawrence.

DOMESTIC INTELLIGENCE

HARPER'S WEEKLY
October 24, 1874, p. 871

The following report has reached Washington from the special agent sent to investigate the murder of a colored post-office employe by the Ku-Klux in Alabama last month: "I have just had warrants issued against nine of the murderers to Thomas Iney, including the sheriff of his county, and will proceed to make the arrests immediately. The reign of terror existing in this county at present far exceeds any thing of the kind I have ever

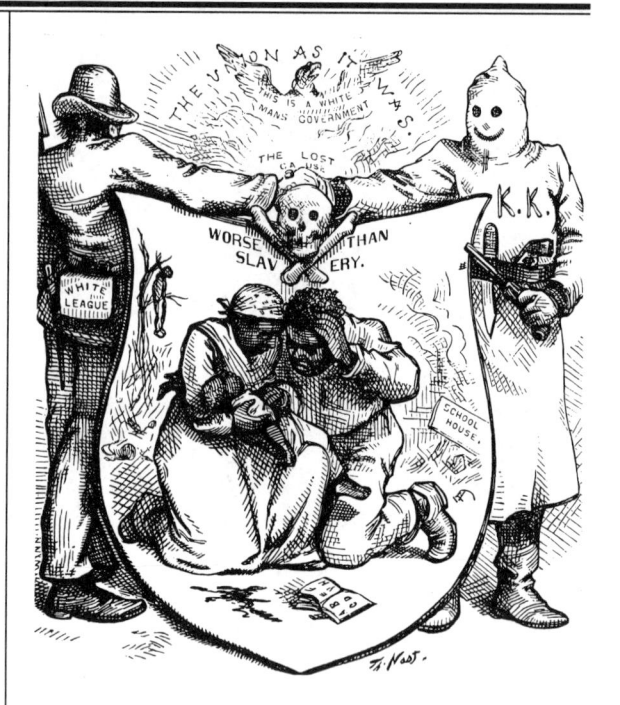

Harper's Weekly, October 24, 1874, p. 878.

seen. Armed bodies of men are riding over the country, and the colored people are afraid to go into the fields to save their crops from waste and ruin. The right of free speech is denied them, and many desire to return to slavery." The agent dates the letter "In the woods, near Livingston, Sumter County, Alabama, September 29."

JUDGE BALLARD'S CHARGE

HARPER'S WEEKLY
October 31, 1874, p. 890

The recent charge of Judge Ballard, of the United States District Court in Kentucky, is very important, and deserves the most serious attention. After describing the crimes upon the negroes known as Ku-Klux outrages, which he does not deny, but admits to be "extremely grievous," and a disgrace to the State and to civilization, he says that the United States have no jurisdiction over them whatever. In other words, he declares that in his opinion the Enforcement Acts are unconstitutional. He does not admit that ordinary crimes, such as murder, assault, robbery, etc., are punishable by the United States, but that the State governments must deal with them. He recognizes, of course, the principle laid down by Judge Grier, of the Supreme Court of the United States, and quoted by the Attorney-General in his letter to Governor Brown, of Tennessee, that the same act may in certain cases be an offense both against the State and the United States, and punishable by both. But

Judge Ballard evidently relies upon the opinion announced by Justice Bradley, of the Supreme Court, in the Grant Parish case, that Congress is not authorized to make laws punishing ordinary crimes and offenses against colored citizens or any others. Judge Bradley's words are, "All ordinary murders, robberies, assaults, thefts, and offenses whatsoever are cognizable only in the State courts, unless, indeed, the State should deny to the class of persons referred to the equal protection of the laws."

Judge Ballard holds that, as Congress could not authorize the United States courts to punish such offenses as those of the Ku-Klux if they were committed openly, the fact that they are done secretly and in disguise does not change their nature, and therefore that they are not cognizable by the national courts. The Enforcement Acts, moreover, it is said, are to protect citizens in the right of voting; and if the Ku-Klux outrages, or such a murder as that of Billings, three months before an election, is to be regarded as political intimidation, then all breaches of the peace against the negroes may be so considered, and every such case may be removed from the jurisdiction of the State. This, it is claimed, can not have been the intention of the amendments upon which the Enforcement Acts are based.

But there is no doubt what the purpose of Congress was. Having freed the slaves, it meant to protect them; and it adopted the amendments and passed the laws because it knew that there was a necessity for protecting them. That necessity arose from the general hostility to them of the dominant race in most of the late Slave States, which deprived the colored people of a just hope of fair treatment. A community which held them to be an inferior race, and had striven, by black codes and vagrant laws and disabling acts, to reduce them again to practical slavery and to extinguish the hope and the effort toward self-respect and self-support, was not very likely to reverence rights conferred, as they believed, vindictively and unwarrantably. From the perception of this state of things came the amendments and the laws enforcing them. And the only question under Justice Bradley's ruling is, When may a State be held to deny to the colored people the equal protection of the laws? Is it only when it passes a literally unequal law, or when the ruling sentiment of the State, its controlling public opinion, practically nullifies laws which are verbally equal? The latter is plainly the view entertained by Congress in passing the Enforcement Laws. The treatment of the colored people amounted to a general intimidation, which was sustained by public opinion, and of course prevented them, and was doubtless intended to prevent them, from exercising the right to vote.

If to-day the national government is powerless and the State government is unwilling to protect the negro as it does the white man, what becomes of the liberty given to the colored race and guaranteed by the United States? In a community which naturally spawns the Ku-Klux and the White League, what reasonable hope is there of justice to the negro? He is a citizen of the United States as well as of the State, and all the circumstances of the situation must be carefully considered. Such consideration can not fail to show that it would be a cruel injustice to hold, with Judge Ballard, that the United States courts are powerless in the Ku-Klux cases.

"EVERYTHING POINTS TO A DEMOCRATIC VICTORY THIS FALL."—SOUTHERN PAPERS

HARPER'S WEEKLY
October 31, 1874, pp. 901–2

Nine years have passed since Louisiana, wasted, ruined, and depraved by slavery and by rebellion, came out from a contest in which, had only the guilty suffered, it had been punished not half so severely as it deserved. Its slave-traders had forced it among the earliest into revolt. The very thought of a limitation upon their dreadful traffic filled them with unreflecting rage. The election of Lincoln seemed to menace the slave-trade on the Mississippi; the auction-blocks of New Orleans might no longer be supplied from Kentucky and Tennessee with human chattels; and the desperate leaders of the violent faction forced the small yet wealthy community to rise in arms against the government. With a population of perhaps seven hundred thousand, more than half of whom were colored, all Unionists in life and death, while of the whites it is not probable that a majority were ready for the mad measures of the slave-traders, the State soon felt the results of its folly, and fell again into the hands of the government. At the close of the rebellion Louisiana was impoverished with an excess of poverty to which not even South Carolina had reached. A large proportion of its white population were paupers, maintained by the alms of the national government. Its lucrative slave-trade was stopped forever; its colored people were free. There was no money to pay its taxes, no resources to maintain its levees; no hope of rescue from its fallen condition except the aid of the national government and the Northern capitalists. Of this, so generously offered, the State freely availed itself, and commerce once more began to revisit the deserted wharves of New Orleans. So fertile is its land, and so favorable the site of its metropolis, that a few years of peace would soon impart to Louisiana new elements of progress; and, as the centre of Western trade, and the home of Western merchants, New Orleans might rise to a high rank among the sea-ports of the world.

But this the fallen rebels were resolved to prevent. Malice ruled in their counsels of such a depth of depravity as could only be born of the poisonous remnants of slavery. They formed secret associations, not, as one

"EVERY THING POINTS TO A DEMOCRATIC VICTORY THIS FALL."—SOUTHERN PAPERS.

Harper's Weekly, October 31, 1874, p. 901.

might suppose, to restore agriculture, to enlarge trade, to preserve good order, and invite the commerce and emigration of the West, but to insult and terrify honest negro laborers, to drive off white settlers who were Republicans, and at last murder both; to hold the State in miserable poverty and force the people to live still on the alms of the government. The reports of the Ku-Klux Committee for 1871–72 show how successfully the White Leaguers of four or five years ago overawed or ill-treated their miserable fellow-citizens; how in 1868 scarcely a Republican ventured to vote in many parishes, and what perpetual bankruptcy and poverty ruled in the small community. Two thousand persons were murdered by the White Leaguers in a population not much larger than that of Brooklyn.

The fact that the Ku-Klux or the White League began its reign of terror in Louisiana immediately after the war, and has continued it ever since, until it rose into the recent rebellion, or that the Democratic leaders, M'Enery and Penn, owe all their political strength to its prevalence, is what the chiefs of the lawless faction in the State would now willingly conceal. Having spread a deadly terror through all the Republican population, they are now satisfied, and they labor to hide from the Northern press and people by all their arts the means by which they hope to control all future elections. Yet it is plain to the whole Northern public that it is not any misgovernment on the part of the Kellogg rule that brought the White League into existence, since it appeared at once upon the close of the rebellion; nor is it the fault of the Federal officials that the assassins have ravaged the State under the names of Knights of the White Camellia or of a White Man's Party for the past nine years. It is not the State but the Federal government against which the outrages have been aimed. It was the lingering fires of rebellion that blazed up anew in unlucky Louisiana; and it is certain that no government favorable to the Union would satisfy these supporters of M'Enery and Penn. They will have nothing but an ascendency of the rebel interests.

Our White Leaguers who were only a few days ago urging that every one who opposed their rule in New Orleans should be "shot down like a dog," are now complaining of "misrepresentation" and of the harsh construction put upon their actions by the more observant part of the Northern press. We think their actions are not unworthy of their words, and that they are not unknown to the history of the times. Never did so small a community as Louisiana in so-few years exhibit such a succession of horrors. In 1868 we have the raids on the negro voters detailed in the Ku-Klux reports, when the White Camellias dominated in the streets of New Orleans. In 1869–71 fear kept them in tolerable quiet. In 1872 they re-appear. In 1873 they burned or shot down sixty or seventy negroes at Grant Parish, and attempted an insurrection in New Orleans. In 1874 they have murdered the United States officials at Coushatta and a large number of negroes; they have risen in rebellion in New Orleans and shot thirty or forty Unionists in a deadly contest. They are still importing large quantities of arms, and are evidently preparing for further massacres whenever the eye of the law is withdrawn. That such men should complain that they are "misrepresented" is an excess of effrontery; that they should find any portion of the Northern Democracy willing to believe any thing they choose to affirm against the Republican government is not a little remarkable. It is ridiculous to suppose that the murderers and revolutionists of 1874 are in any way to be disconnected from those of 1868 or 1873, or that M'Enery and Penn are not the chiefs of a band of assassins and outlaws of whom the white as well as the colored population of Louisiana would rejoice to be able to rid themselves.

There is evidently a strong desire entertained by the people of the whole country to bring back peace and prosperity to all the Southern States that are still suffering from the terrors of the White Man's League or the lingering penalties of the rebellion, and to lend aid to their merchants and farmers to rise from their temporary depression. They want capital and labor to extend their means of internal communication, and a large immigrant population to add to the value of their lands; they want public schools and churches, a free press, and liberty of speech and action to relieve them gradually from the influence of their dangerous classes, to diffuse knowledge, and increase the results of labor. But none of these can they hope to obtain in the midst of their civil convulsions. Insurrection is the most costly of political measures, and Louisiana is the most unlucky of all the States, because it has been tormented by a horde a traitors. While Charleston flourishes in peace and has become already an opulent sea-port, New Orleans is the scene of a lamentable decay. Galveston and Mobile draw away its commerce, and the Western merchants turn away in alarm from the home of the White Man's League. Even Florida, where peace has been maintained and the Ku-Klux apparently suppressed forever, has made a rapid progress, while Savannah languishes and Georgia is losing its population. If, therefore, the Northern and Western press are desirous of aiding in developing the natural advantages of the Southern States, it is plain that their first duty is to point out the causes that have led to their decay. Publicity and a perfect information of the real condition of the country are the earliest steps in its future advance. If there are outlaws in any of the States, or any reign of disorder, the truest friends of the South are those who expose and denounce them. Secrecy only increases the evil, and bad men hide their ill deeds in darkness.

The question is now fairly before the people, How can life and liberty be secured to all classes of our citizens in the Southern States, and those enormities prevented in the future that have made the name of Democracy in Tennessee and even Kentucky, in Alabama, Georgia, Louisiana, and Arkansas, odious to the instincts of civilization? Modern progress abhors the notion of murder and of inhumanity, and it would be well for our people to place the mark of their disapprobation upon the party that hopes to profit by these cruel measures at the South with so conclusive a condemnation as shall show how deeply they detest them.

It is quite certain that the Southern Democratic leaders have not begun as yet an era of peace. Every part of their section has shown traces of a war intimidation against the Union party. It is only a short time ago that the Louisville papers related the outrages of the White Man's League almost in the suburbs of that city. Tennessee has recently been the scene of frightful massacres. The colored and white Republicans of the South, in many districts, vote with the fear of death before them. Their courage has been tested by nine years of perilous devotion to good order and peace. Will their countrymen now desert them? —Eugene Lawrence.

SOUTH CAROLINA POLITICS

HARPER'S WEEKLY
November 7, 1874, p. 911

Mr. Chamberlain, the regular Republican candidate for Governor in South Carolina, has written a letter to the New York *Tribune* denying certain statements against him made by an anonymous correspondent of that paper. As we have mentioned the same allegations, which have been long current and familiar, we give Mr. Chamberlain the benefit of mentioning his denial. He says explicitly that the notorious acts for the increase of the debt were not only not drawn by him, but that he was not consulted about them, and knew nothing of them until they were published. He states also that the acts, which are described as "cunningly worded" and "opening the door to fraud," are simply literal copies from the acts of Congress authorizing the present bonded debt of the United States—acts which are understood to have been drawn by Chief Justice Chase. Mr. Chamberlain points out a material mistake of the correspondent as to the date of the Conversion Bond Act, which was passed in March, 1869, instead of February, 1872, as alleged, and denies that he prepared the act. He says also that Mr. Kimpton, although an old college friend of his, was appointed not upon his recommendation, but upon that of eminent financial gentlemen in New York. Mr. Chamberlain offers, if the correspondent will sustain his assertions by evidence, to establish what he says by incontestable proofs. As the case stands, his denial must be accepted as against an anonymous assertion.

We have also had put into our hands a letter written by Mr. Chamberlain in May, 1871, when, we believe, he was still Attorney-General of the State, and published in the papers at that time, which disposes of the assertion that he made no protest against the frauds of the ring which then controlled the government of South Carolina. It is a long letter, addressed to Colonel W. L. Trenholm, of Charleston, in which Mr. Chamberlain not only exposes and denounces the situation, but proposes a remedy. He begins by a review of the circumstances under which reconstruction began, the whites holding aloof, the blacks inexperienced and ignorant, and mainly dependent upon leaders who had drifted into South Carolina from other States. He says that every sensible man must have seen that the elements which went to compose the dominant party were not such as produce public virtue or even long secure public order, and that at the time in which he wrote, three years after the new system went into effect, "incompetency, dishonesty, corruption in all its forms, have 'advanced their miscreated fronts,' have put to flight the small remnant that opposed them, and now rule the party which rules the State." "I am a Republican," he adds, "by habit, by conviction, by association; but my Republicanism is not, I trust, composed solely of equal parts of ignorance and rapacity." Mr. Chamberlain then proposes a system of minority representation which, properly applied in the cumulative form, would at once have given—what is now known as the tax-payers' interest—forty-seven members in the Lower House of the Legislature, against seventy-seven of the dominant party. Such a body, representing, as he says, character, intelligence, and property, would have been of the best influence. He then states the reforms which he deems indispensable, and among them an absolute prohibition of any further increase of the public debt except under the most stringent safeguards and conditions, a reduction of the public expenditure by two-thirds, and the immediate removal of incompetent and dishonest tax-collectors. The hope of the State, he says, lies solely in itself. The national government may repress crime, but permanent reform "can come only through ourselves."

As for his silence in the matter of the "conversion bonds," his friends state that the law imposed the duty of exchanging the outstanding bonds and stocks upon the Treasurer alone, and it was he alone who, without making the exchange, put them upon the New York market, and Mr. Chamberlain had no opportunity of knowing the fact sooner than any other member of the Republican party, nor was it his duty to know it. We state these things in justice to Mr. Chamberlain. That Governor Moses supports him is explained by the fact that he is a candidate for the Legislature, and knows that the colored vote, upon which he relies for his election, is generally faithful to Mr. Chamberlain. But there is no doubt of the very bitter hostility to him upon the part of many who desire honest government, and who, although they are largely Democrats, have pledged themselves to support any candidate who is beyond suspicion. That they are in earnest is shown by their hearty adoption of Judge Green, who is a "civil rights" Republican, and stands upon the platform of the regular Republican Convention. Judge Green has not renounced his Republicanism in the least degree; and since the tax-payers are willing to support such a man, and proved it by waiting to see if the regular Republican Convention would not nominate some one of that kind, it was a fatal error to select a candidate who was one of the corrupt administration, and who, if really innocent, was covered with suspicion. There are undoubtedly many Democrats who would rather see the State ruined than peaceful and prosperous under a Republican administration. Such gentlemen are seriously disconcerted by the recent action of the Republican State Committee in selecting four respectable Democrats to act with four Republicans in equalizing the State taxes. But the more honest

Democrats hail it as the sign of a better day which it is plain is now dawning in South Carolina.

THEORY AND PRACTICE

HARPER'S WEEKLY
November 14, 1874, p. 930

The special committee of the trustees of the Peabody School Fund are of opinion that the Civil Rights Bill would destroy the public-school system in the Southern States. Senator Schurz has expressed the same opinion in a speech in St. Louis. It is, in fact, the only serious argument that has been urged against the bill. The plea is that the white citizens of the Southern States will not consent to mixed schools, and that wherever they control legislation they will lay no tax for the support of schools, or if they can not do that, they will refuse to allow their children to attend. The consequence will be, it is alleged, that there will be no schools whatever for the poorer classes, and that only the children of the rich will be educated. Moreover, it is asserted by the opponents of the bill that equal rights do not demand mixed schools, but only schools of equal excellence. This last suggestion is puerile. Every man of common-sense knows that in a community where color prejudice is so strong as to abandon the whole school system rather than to provide for schools in common, schools of equal excellence are simply impossible. It might as reasonably be expected that where the same prejudice condemned the colored citizens to the deck of steamers and to the freight cars of railroad trains, there would be "equal excellence" of accommodation provided.

But while the Peabody committee and others make the assertion, what is the fact? Has the experiment been tried? and how did it work? Mr. Thomas W. Conway, Superintendent of Education in Louisiana from 1868 to 1872, has answered this question. The Louisiana constitution of 1868 required that the public schools should be opened to black and white alike. The usual clamor was raised. The ruin of the school system was foretold as it is now. The opposition was rancorous and intense. Mr. Conway, in considering the practicability of the project, found that it would be no easy matter to draw the line between the colors. Should children half white and half black be excluded? Should quadroons and octoroons be admitted? Should he recur to the old slave code of Louisiana to decide what children of free and equal citizens should be taught in the public schools? Of course he did not hesitate, and when he publicly announced the opening of the schools to all, he was assailed on every hand with threats of assassination. At first some of the white children were kept away by their parents, for there was no antagonism among the children themselves; but very soon they returned, and "the year actually closed with a larger number of white pupils in the schools than ever before."

Mr. Conway adds:

"A little over a year ago, when in New Orleans, I took pains to visit some of the largest and best schools of the city, then under the charge of the Hon. Mr. Brown, my successor. I saw some of the children of the best white citizens of the city sitting alongside of colored children, and I may add that the latter were as neatly clad and as well behaved as the former. I ascertained that there were colored pupils in every school in New Orleans, and that there was no trouble whatever from that source."

While this is the situation in Louisiana, Judge Green, who, although a Civil Rights Republican, was supported by the Democrats for Governor of South Carolina, says that in that State the system of mixed schools is practically in force already. As for the insuperable prejudice, Mr. Conway truly says that the white "Conservatives" of the Southern States are as good authority upon the subject as any body at the North, and he quotes the declaration of General Beauregard and four other Democrats in New Orleans in July, 1873, taking the strongest position in detail upon every point covered by the Civil Rights Bill, and saying distinctly:

"We shall further recommend that no distinction shall exist among citizens of Louisiana in any of our public schools or State institutions of learning, or in any other public institution supported by State, city, or parishes."

All this seems to us to be very much more to the point than speculations at a distance upon the force or the probable consequences of a prejudice. That the prejudice exists, like the prejudice against the Irish, against Hebrews, against Roman Catholics, is very true; but if Congress, because of prejudice, should deliberately sanction the doctrine that there might be caste and classes among the citizens of the United States, the government would have ceased to be one of equal laws.

The objection that it is foolish and impracticable to contend with the prejudice against color is urged too late. No one who supported the amendments freeing the slaves and clothing them with equal political and civil rights can logically deride the proposition to enforce that equality as "impracticable" and "ideal." And no one, again, who wishes to take the negro out of politics forever can consistently insist upon stigmatizing him as an inferior in any relation which is regulated by law and not by individual choice. All these objections were valid against the amendments, but they are impotent against a bill which is intended solely to enforce and carry out the amendments. If absolute equality of citizenship be unwise because of a bitter prejudice, then let us repeal the fundamental law which establishes it. But while we insist upon the law, let us not try to shirk its consequences.

MR. WILSON'S HISTORY OF THE SLAVE POWER

HARPER'S WEEKLY
November 28, 1874, p. 971

Two volumes of Vice-President Wilson's *Rise and Fall of the Slave Power in America* have been published, and the third and last volume will appear next year. It is, we believe, a "subscription" book, and may not, therefore, fall under the eyes of many of our readers; but there are few American historical books that merit a more universal perusal. It is a complete cyclopedia of its subject, prepared with conscientious care and research, and written with simplicity and force. It has this farther value, that its author was a witness and actor in much of the most exciting and important portion of his story, which has thus a vivid freshness that it must otherwise have wanted. Mr. Wilson's work begins with the planting of slavery in this country, and follows its course with singular and satisfactory minuteness step by step. The legislation of every kind, with the debates upon the slave taxes and fugitive laws and the slave-trade; the movements of protest and of emancipation; negotiations and relations with foreign powers growing out of the subject; the Indian policy, as entangled with slavery; the compromises and the great Missouri contest; every form of antislavery society and of colonization; the story of colored schools, and the bitter hostility to freedom; the Florida war and all the famous "cases," the *Prigg*, the *Creole*, the *Amistad*, the *Pearl*, and the *Garner*; the Liberty party and the Texas plot; the Wilmot Proviso and the Mexican War; the black laws; the Free-soil movement, with all its details, its conventions, and combinations; the Kansas iniquity; the plots against Cuba; the Dred Scott decision; John Brown, and the designs of Jefferson Davis, Mason, Toombs, and their fellow-conspirators; the uprising of the people, and the election of Abraham Lincoln. The next volume will treat of the war and of emancipation.

It is essentially a political history, for the aggressions of slavery were made and resisted under the forms of law, except by the Abolitionists; and it is an amazing and incredible story. That for fifty years the central point around which our politics moved should have been human slavery is one of the most humiliating facts that an American can consider. It destroyed the Whig party. And that the party organization by whose servility the successes of slavery were gained should now have recovered power in so many States, and under so many of the leaders who served their party while it served slavery, is a fact full of significance. The next Senator

WHITE LEAGUE INTIMIDATION.

ONE of the means employed by the White League in the intimidation of Republican voters at New Orleans we give above. The following is an extract from the letter which accompanied it:

"I was on duty in New Orleans on the night of November 3, when it was reported to me by a captain of police that during the morning incendiary and threatening documents of various kinds had been distributed over the city by the White Leaguers. On my asking him to get me a sample copy, he handed me the inclosed."

When we reflect that employers in Louisiana formed leagues that pledged themselves to discharge every negro laborer who did not vote for the Democratic ticket, that others are said to have driven their workmen before them to the polls, that the secret menaces of the White Leaguers, armed and powerful, may well have terrified every Republican voter whether white or black into submission, it seems extraordinary that so many Republicans were so courageous as to vote at all.

Harper's Weekly, November 28, 1874, p. 975.

from New York is very likely to be Horatio Seymour, who was educated to palliate and defend the encroachments of slavery upon freedom in this country, and who, when slavery undertook the overthrow of the government, asked whether "successful coercion by the North is less revolutionary than successful secession by the South," while Mr. James S. Thayer, another leading Democrat, following Mr. Seymour, said that if Mr. Lincoln's administration should try to coerce the Southern States, "we will" make "those who would inaugurate a reign of terror the first victims of a national guillotine."

These are the natural sentiments and appeals of those who, educated under the great contest between Liberty and Slavery which Mr. Wilson describes, threw themselves against humanity, justice, and all the noblest instincts and monitions of the conscience and the heart. No man of intelligence and ability like Mr. Seymour can accustom himself through a long political career to the debasing sophistries and mean quibbles upon which slavery relied without necessarily becoming untrue to the highest humane and American principle. Appealing always with studied moderation to the vilest passions and the worst prejudices of the ignorant, as every advocate of the domination of slavery was compelled to do, Mr. Seymour is no more capable of representing the intelligent, liberty-loving convictions and purposes of New York than Paul Cassagnac, the thick-and-thin apologist of Louis Napoleon, could have properly represented the republic of Laboulaye. No man who gave the prime of his life and the fullness of his powers to the task of perpetuating human slavery in America can be a true American statesman. "The test of the health of a people," says a wise observer, "is to be found in the utterances of those who are its spokesmen, and in the action of those whom it accepts or chooses to be its chiefs." This is a truth to be borne in mind by every student of Mr. Wilson's most interesting and instructive history. It is the political memoir of the last generation. In reading it it is clear how the election of Abraham Lincoln showed the surviving fidelity of the American people to the great principles from which our government sprang, for he was true to them every one, and gave his life for them. It is equally clear why the success of a party of which Horatio Seymour is still a leader, and by whom he will probably be placed in the Senate, is, should the elections prove to show a preference of Democratic rule, an indication of moral reaction. Mr. Wilson's work is indispensable to every one who would truly understand the political history of the country, and who would justly measure the significance and probable result of Democratic ascendency for another generation.

A FREEDMEN'S SCHOOL IN VIRGINIA

HARPER'S WEEKLY
December 12, 1874, p. 1015
Holley School, Lottsburgh, Northumberland County, Virginia, *November 23, 1874*
Mr. Harper:

Dear Sir,—Our school owes you an unspeakable debt of gratitude for your gift, nearly six years ago, through Miss Holley, of a set of the "Object Lesson Charts."

These beautiful charts were our constant and valuable aid in instruction until last June, when the rebel hate and persecution of our work of education of these freedmen culminated in the destruction of these charts, and all our books, maps, etc., which were torn down from the walls and thrown away. The school-house was seized by this mob violence from its rightful owners, the freedmen, and our excellent school broken up.

With a fund contributed by a few noble-hearted Northern friends Miss Holley and I have succeeded in building a better school-house on our own lot. And we shall soon be able to re-open school to our eager pupils.

We shall so sadly miss the charts that I do not see how we can possibly do without them, and I am moved to venture to appeal to your benevolent kindness to ask if you will not make a donation of another set that we may hang upon our new walls, for the delight and improvement of these colored children and their parents, who are always wonderfully attracted and learning from them.

Many of these white Virginians, too, who visit our school, and attend its celebrations of national holidays, are indirectly enlightened and benefited by the sight of these "Object Lessons."

I earnestly hope you will generously repair our desolation by sending us again the charts, that we may go on with our mission—as we hope we shall—more vigorously and prosperously than ever.

We shall continue to cherish your name here as among our chief benefactors so long as we gratefully see and remember the vast usefulness of the charts to hundreds of minds about us.

I inclose the address by which a package will reach us.

Very sincerely and respectfully,

Caroline F. Putnam.

The charts have been sent. H. & B.

CIVIL RIGHTS

HARPER'S WEEKLY
December 19, 1874, p. 1038

If the Civil Rights Bill is to be rejected, let it be upon its merits, and not upon persistent misrepresentations. It is constantly alleged to be a law to enforce social equality. But it is not. It is a bill to enforce the civil equality secured by the amendments to the Constitution, and the argument which opposes it condemns those amendments. Prejudice can not be abolished by law, we are told, and have been told ever since the antislavery movement began. But we have hitherto failed to discover those persons who are leveling laws at prejudice. Certainly the supporters of the Civil Rights Bill are not. They say only that the Fourteenth Amendment forbids any State to "abridge the privileges or immunities of citizens of the United States," or to "deny to any person within its jurisdiction the equal protection of the laws," and they hold that State laws which forbid certain citizens to serve upon juries by reason of their color, and which for the same reason exclude them from public inns, conveyances, cemeteries, and schools, common to all other citizens, violate that amendment. And as Congress has authority to enforce it, Congress may pass a law forbidding the States to deprive any citizen of the equality which the amendment has guaranteed, and enforcing the amendment by providing a remedy for aggrieved persons. Nor does such a law enforce "social equality." Blacklegs and drunkards, and men and women of every degree of personal and moral repulsiveness, are admitted to every hotel and steamboat and railroad car in the country, as in former days slave-drivers and people who bought and sold children at the auction block were allowed in them. Are the other guests forced into "social equality" with them? But if the prejudice which all honorable persons feel for such people does not authorize their exclusion by law from the common inns and the common conveyances, why should the prejudice against color authorize such laws? There is no more forcing of social equality in the one case than in the other.

Does a law which stigmatizes a class of citizens on account of color violate the equality which the Constitution guarantees? This is the question, and the Slaughterhouse decision answers it. "The existence of laws in the States where the newly emancipated negroes resided which discriminated with gross injustice and hardship against them as a class, was the evil to be remedied by this clause, and by it such laws are forbidden. If, however, the States did not conform their laws to its requirements, then, by the fifth section of the article of amendment, Congress was authorized to enforce it by suitable legislation." The laws here spoken of were those which discriminated against certain citizens on account of color. Does or does not a law which excludes an orderly citizen from a jury-box, a hotel, a public conveyance, on account of color, discriminate against him for that reason? If it does, the Supreme Court holds that Congress may legislate upon the subject. And if to remedy the grievance is to enforce social equality, it is the Constitution which does it. If there be any fault or folly in the matter, it is that of so framing the Constitution.

The practical objection to the bill which has been most generally urged is that the prejudice against the colored citizens is so strong in many States that, should the bill pass, such States would abandon their public-school system. In other words, if the rights and immunities of citizens which are expressly guaranteed by the fundamental law are maintained, the result will be general ignorance and consequent vice. But if the rights guaranteed by the fundamental law are deliberately violated, what then? The amended Constitution declares that there shall be no legal discrimination on account of color. The objection merely says that there must be and shall be. The Supreme Court of Indiana, indeed, has just decided that equality of rights does not necessitate "mixed schools" more than teaching of both sexes in the same schools, or keeping different grades of scholars in the same school. The reply to this is that any distinction or classification for any legitimate school purpose may be made which is not based upon color. Practically, whenever distinctions are made upon grounds of prejudice, equality in the sense contemplated becomes impossible. What in such a case does prejudice mean but unwillingness to treat the negroes as legal equals? If prejudice against the Irish, or the Germans, or the Hebrews, or the Roman Catholics, or the Baptists, or the Freemasons, or the Martha Washingtonians, were strong enough in any State to cause them and their children to be confined to separate inns, conveyances, and schools, no man who knows human nature or the meaning of words would contend that the guarantee of equality was satisfied. When exclusion from the street cars on account of color was abolished, was social equality enforced by law? The amended Constitution secures civil as well as political equality to every citizen of the United States. Let us have that security enforced; and if any State fails to enforce it, let us not leave the aggrieved person without remedy, in face of the explicit declaration that Congress shall have power to enforce it.

1875

In 1875 the press devoted considerable attention to the civil rights legislation working its way through Congress and the reaction it was causing outside the halls of Congress. The pending legislation was intended to prevent racial discrimination in places of public accommodation, including inns, public transportation, and public amusements, such a theaters. However, the ideal of prohibiting discrimination and the definition of public accommodation continued to be challenged. The press did not think that the passage of a civil rights bill possible, and opponents claimed that such a bill would serve only to stigmatize African Americans. Opponents to the bill on these grounds asserted that "If . . . we can not abolish prejudice by law, we are certainly not called upon to perpetuate it by law."

Congress debated the bill's provisions for some time. Earlier versions of the civil rights bill contained provisions for "mixed schools" that were stricken out of later versions, and many considered the deletion of the "mixed schools" provision an authorization for the establishment of separate educational accommodations for African Americans. In the light of the tacit approval of separate educational accommodations, opponents saw separation in public accommodations a logical extension. Harper's Weekly *(January 9) reported: "If the prejudice against color is to be respected in the school-house, why not in the theatre and the tavern and the railroad car?" Debate continued for some as to what establishments were covered by the act. Were drinking establishments covered by act? Were barber shops and like services covered? Slowly facilities and services once considered public became private. As expressed in* Harper's Weekly *(April 24) "The white race may have at least this one superior privilege to the colored man, that they can drink in bar-rooms and saloons . . ." Similarly it was expressed that "a barber has a right to shave whom he pleases as much as a jeweler has a right to repair a watch for whom he pleases, or a blacksmith to shoe such colored horses as he pleases. In other words, these are not public employments, but private business, in which the law does not interfere."*

Southerners clearly were uncomfortable with the implied integration required by the civil rights act. It was an outrage for many to think that such a law was being used "to promote fraternity among men." Harper's Weekly (July 24) reports a well dressed black man, who had insisted upon being admitted into the first-class passenger coach of a train in Georgia, being spit upon by white passengers. Such behavior was not uncommon.

In its final form, the civil rights act provided that "all persons within the jurisdiction of the United States . . . be entitled to the full and equal enjoyment of the accommodations, advantages, facilities, and privileges of inns, public places, conveyances . . . and other places of amusement." According to the new law, it was essential for government to recognize the equality of all men before the law. However, despite its intent, the law was eventually challenged in the United States Supreme Court.

Robert L. Harris, Jr.
Cornell University

DEMOCRATIC "HOME RULE."

HARPER'S WEEKLY
January 2, 1875, p. 3

At the time of the negro massacre of 1865 in New Orleans it was announced in the Northern Democratic papers as a riot and slaughter by negroes, and the utmost efforts were made to inflame Northern sentiment against them. The fact was that it was a wanton and murderous assault upon them. There has just been a similar slaughter in Vicksburg, which was carefully telegraphed as an attack upon that city by the negroes, although the report admitted that the result was the massacre of sixty or a hundred negroes and no white man. The simple fact is that a white mob attempted to compel the resignation of certain colored officers, among whom was the sheriff, Crosby. All the officers fled except Crosby, and he signed a resignation. "No one," says the Cincinnati *Commercial,* which is an independent and not a Republican journal, "concealed what his fate would be if he had not done so. He would have been hanged on the spot." Crosby escaped and saw the Governor, who ordered him to return and take possession of his office, and summon the people to sustain him. He did so, and the Cincinnati *Commercial,* which sent a correspondent to the scene to investigate, tells the sequel:

"He sent news to the country for the negroes to come in Monday and report to the Court-house. They came, were met at the city limits, and slaughtered—simply slaughtered and butchered. They were chased through the woods and fields and shot down like dogs. Many were shot after they gave up, and some were shot on their knees while begging for mercy. The spirit of demons was in the people. It was not safe for any one not in full accord with them to be on the street. One poor old negro by the name of Ambrose Brown was ordered off the street by Captain Cowan, a former rebel battery commander, and being tardy in going, Cowan deliberately shot him. Many prisoners were taken and kept in the Court-house, and taken out in the morning. With winks and nods, and laughter and jest, it was reported that three of the most obnoxious made their escape, which means they have simply been murdered while prisoners. This is unquestionably the truth of the massacre, and the people of the nation should fully recognize all its enormities. The worst of it is that the persons who have been guilty of this wholesale murder fully justify themselves upon the statement of facts that we have given, and, we are bound to add, they are animated by the conviction that there has been a political revolution in the North, and that their time has come."

The last words of this extract are very significant. Nine years ago, when it was thought that Andrew Johnson would favor the Democratic party, the negroes were slaughtered at New Orleans; and now when the result of the autumn elections seems to show a general reaction and Democratic restoration, the negroes are slaughtered at Vicksburg. We presume that no well-informed person supposes that this Vicksburg massacre would have occurred had the Democratic party been as generally defeated as it was successful in the elections. The moral needs no enforcement. The facts show us what is to be expected under Democratic "home rule."

All that is wanted in the national policy toward the Southern States is that practical common-sense which is the characteristic of the American and English political genius. It is not an inflexible indifference nor a scorn of facts. It is a policy of administration that is wanted; but the administration of friends, not of foes. There is something comical in the air with which the Democrats propose what they call "home rule," a phrase borrowed from the Irish friends of a separate Parliament, the impracticability of which Mr. Freeman has conclusively exposed. The Democrats mean by "home rule" State sovereignty, and they say with truth there would have been no Southern question had they been in power. There would have been no Southern question, just as order reigned in Warsaw. "Home rule," we are now informed, requires that the States should have reconstructed themselves. And what that was the country saw. It was the practical restoration of all of slavery but the name. It was vagrant laws, apprentice laws, black codes, non-ownership of the land by the negroes, their exclusion from all civil rights, and in general the same legislation which made General Terry say in Virginia that the condition of the freedmen was worse than that of the slaves. Should the Democrats return to power in the national government, their policy would be what it would have been had they controlled the government at the end of the war. They already announce that "home rule" is the remedy for all Southern ills, meaning by "home rule" the supremacy of the spirit whose manifestations made the amendments necessary. They will repeal the laws enforcing them, and leave the amendments to shift for themselves.

No reasonable man could complain of this if it promised to give the negro fair play or an equal chance with other citizens. "Let him be treated like the rest of us, and don't cocker him and hold him up. If he can't stand, let him fall." Certainly; so say we all. Let him be treated like the rest of us. But don't knock him down, and then say that he can't stand. The difficulty is that he is not treated like the rest of us, and the ill treatment comes from those who stigmatize him and brand him with odium in every way. In such a situation "home rule" is a sound policy only when the national power is in the hands of his friends, not of his enemies. "Look," says one of the colored leaders of his people in Georgia—"look how we are summarily tried and convicted for trivial charges before jurors who assert that 'they will be d—d if they will acquit a negro, guilty or not, for if a negro is not guilty, he ought to be.' You might as well try a frog for his life before a hungry snake."

The colored citizens are an eighth of the population. They can not be colonized nor expatriated. They are native Americans, and they are equal citizens under the supreme law; nor will that law be changed. They are in large part ignorant, like the poor whites of the South and a great proportion of the foreign-born population of the North. But no "home rule," no removal of the Federal sword from "our brothers of the South," no repeal of enforcement laws, no exhortations that they cease to regard themselves as wards of the nation, will remedy the difficulty. The colored problem will remain a difficulty and the colored race a disturbance until their immediate white neighbors do them the same justice that they do each other, and cease to persist in disgracing them with a stigma of inferiority. The American negro will not go out of politics, and ought not to go out of politics, until he has justice. As long as his equal civil rights are not maintained and protected with those of white men, he has not justice; and while they are denied, his equal political rights will not be really respected. The Republican party has made mistakes in dealing with the subject, and rascals, under the cloak of humanity and justice, have advanced themselves. But there is no folly so absolute as the supposition that Democratic hatred, contempt, impatience, and despair will secure that justice which can alone solve the problem.

PERSONAL

HARPER'S WEEKLY
January 2, 1875, p. 3

A few days since at the dinner-table at Willard's Hotel, in Washington, were seated at adjacent tables ex-Senator Clingman, of North Carolina, and Senator-elect Pinchbeck (colored), of Louisiana. On the 4th of March next there will be in the United States Senate a colored man, Mr. Bruce, of Mississippi, who nine years ago was a slave....

Speaking of John Brown's execution, the Springfield (Massachusetts) *Republican,* writing on the fifteenth anniversary of that event, says: "His comrades have nearly all passed away too, except the surviving members of his own family, none of whom have died since 1859. A daughter of one of his colored followers—Lewis Leary, who was slain at Harper's Ferry—is now a school-girl completing her education, and an appeal is made to the friends of Brown to raise a small sum for that purpose. The object is a worthy one, and the anniversary is suggestive of the propriety of doing something of the kind. Any contributions for this object sent to F. B. Sanborn, at Concord, Massachusetts, will be devoted to the object above named. It is time also to be talking about a monument to Brown himself, at Harper's Ferry or elsewhere.

DOMESTIC INTELLIGENCE

HARPER'S WEEKLY
January 2, 1875, p. 3

The Judiciary Committee of the House reported, December 16, the Supplementary Civil Rights Bill. It is substantially the Senate bill of the last session, but with the mixed school section stricken out, and a provision inserted requiring equal school facilities for the children of both races. It further changes the penalty to a choice between civil and criminal. The bill was ordered to be printed and recommitted. In the Senate, on the 14th, Mr. Morton presented a petition from the colored men of Indiana protesting against the recent decision of the Supreme Court of that State excluding colored children from the common schools. This, they claim, deprives them of the rights of citizenship, and their children of the benefits of an education; they therefore ask that the Attorney-General be directed to appeal the case to the Supreme Court of the United States.

AN ACT TO CONFIRM PREJUDICE

HARPER'S WEEKLY
January 9, 1875, p. 26

The probability of the passage of a civil rights bill is not great, but that is no reason for the introduction of such an act as has been presented to the House by the Judiciary Committee. If, as the opponents of the bill constantly declare, we can not abolish prejudice by law, we are certainly not called upon to sustain and perpetuate it by law. Yet this is what the proposed bill does. It is an act to stigmatize a class of American citizens on account of color and previous condition of servitude. This it does by authorizing any State to maintain separate schools or institutions with equal facilities in all respects to all classes entitled thereto. But as separate schools are demanded only on account of color, this is the authority to establish them. Of course such a provision makes the whole bill ridiculous, as any shrewd Democrat could instantly show by moving to amend by making the provision which applies to schools apply also to "inns, public conveyances on land and water, theatres, and other places of public amusement." If the prejudice against color is to be respected in the school-house, why not in the theatre and the tavern and the railroad car? It is no harder for a white child to sit beside a colored child at school than for a white parent to sit beside a colored parent in a car or at a public table or in a theatre. The distinction is without a difference. The bill as reported is an insult to every intelligent colored citizen, as it is a humiliation to every white citizen who remembers that the Constitution guarantees to all the equal protection of the laws—a guarantee which is deliberately violated when the law stigmatizes any class of innocent citizens under any pretense whatever.

The folly of such a rule was shown by Mr. Conway's letter describing his experience as Superintendent of Schools in Louisiana, and by the daily reports from New Orleans, which state that "the color line in schools promises to be the momentous question, as it is difficult to settle who are colored." As for the alleged prejudice, it is now frankly confessed that before the war the lighter-colored children—quadroons and others—were admitted to the schools, and no issue was raised; while it is perfectly well known that some of the most refined, cultivated, courteous, and wealthy citizens in that city were "tainted" with color. But not only is it impracticable to decide who is "colored," but even if every child who is to be stigmatized by this law were coal-black, so that no question could arise, the mischief lies in the obloquy thus cast by law upon certain citizens to whom the Constitution secures equality. Suppose any other class against whom there is a similar feeling should be selected for this leper-like segregation, its enormity and injustice would be at once conceded.

THE DANGEROUS CLASSES AT THE SOUTH

HARPER'S WEEKLY
January 9, 1875, pp. 37–38

The latest exploit of the dangerous class at the South is one of the most horrible of all. The Vicksburg massacre seems to have been wholly without a cause, and the result of that rage for violence and bloodshed that marks the depraved and profligate young men of a land of ignorance and barbarity. No State, indeed, had heretofore shown clearer traits of reviving prosperity than Mississippi, and nowhere had life and person been apparently more secure. A republican government, mild, tolerant, and not inequitable, had slowly produced harmony among all its people; the productiveness of the State had returned; Vicksburg and Natchez had risen from their ruins; the laboring class worked cheerfully; and good morals, education, and religion were swiftly placing Mississippi in a high rank of civilization compared with disordered Louisiana or Arkansas. In fact, we had received from one of its white citizens, apparently an honest and intelligent witness, an indignant reproof because we had denounced the White League of the South in no gentle phrases. He denied that it existed. He described the happy condition of his own county, where the whites were in the majority, yet where the colored

SHALL WE CALL HOME OUR TROOPS?
"We intend to beat the Negro in the battle of life, and defeat means one thing—EXTERMINATION."—*Birmingham (Alabama) News.*

Harper's Weekly, January 9, 1875, p. 37.

children went freely to their schools; where the teachers were well paid, both white and colored; where "three out of five of the Board of Supervisors were black men;" where the two races lived together in perfect friendship and peace, and nothing remained to mar the work of reconstruction. "When I witness all these things," our correspondent added, "and reflect that we are only an average Southern community, I am indignant and insulted at the slanders referred to." We had never; indeed, alluded to Mississippi, and had spoken only of States in which the White League ruled. But unhappily the prosperity and good fortune of Mississippi have excited the malice of the secret assassins, and the dreadful deeds they have committed in Louisiana and Arkansas have been surpassed by the massacre of Vicksburg. The White Leaguers are evidently resolved that the harmony and progress described by our correspondent shall exist no longer. They have brought bloodshed and war into the hapless community. They have sown the seeds of endless enmity. The same demoniac wickedness which marked them at Coushatta or Grant Parish, in Texas and Alabama, Kentucky and Tennessee, has risen to an extraordinary excess in Mississippi, and they have shot down helpless and harmless colored people as they begged for mercy or fled terrified to their homes.

The story, indeed, is so shocking as to be incredible if it had not been told by the latest appliances of modern civilization. Such horrible monsters apparently do not exist upon the earth as these "blood-bespattered young men of the South," to use the epithet of the *Times* correspondent. The White Leaguers had planned their bloody deed with that low cunning that every where marks them. They procured the indictment of the colored officials of Vicksburg, it is stated, by intimidation, for various offenses. They called a meeting of the white citizens, and declared that the time for action had come. They went to the colored Sheriff, Crosby, the School Superintendent, Cardoza, and others, and ordered them to resign their offices, and threatened to hang them if they resisted. The colored men fled from the town; but Governor Ames denounced the conduct of the rioters, and a considerable number of colored people from the country approached Vicksburg to defend the men whom they had elected to office. Yet they had made no hostile demonstration, nor had apparently designed any. But the White Leaguers had now the opportunity they desired. They began at once the massacre of the negroes. Their first victim was a colored Presbyterian clergyman, whom they seem to have murdered in the street in an excess of malice. They then pursued the colored people into the country, and butchered them without mercy. Some were shot as they knelt in prayer, some as they fled from their pursuers. It is not pretended that the negroes made any resistance, and scarcely that they gave the least provocation. The number killed is stated at from one to two hundred, but it is probable, as in the similar massacres in Louisiana or Alabama, that the true number of the victims will never be known. The assassins next called a meeting of the citizens of the town, prepared an address to the people of the country, in which they confess their own violation of the laws, and which was signed by presidents of banks and other "leading" men of the place—we trust not of their own free-will—and assured the country that peace once more reigned in Vicksburg. The associated telegraph company, so often the apologist for the murderers of Alabama and Louisiana, gave the first news of the massacre to the North in the chosen words of the conspirators against the peace of Mississippi. But Governor Ames and various trustworthy eye-witnesses of the terrible scene attest its horrors and the innocence of the colored officials. It is stated that detachments from the White League of Louisiana lent the aid of their experience to their allies in Mississippi, and shared their guilt. It is probable that the whole infamous association is every where planning mischief.

We suggested some months ago that the success of the Democratic party at the North must encourage the dangerous classes in the Southern States to new outrages, and endanger the lives of the white and colored Republicans, not because we thought that the more intelligent members of the Democracy were willing to share in the crimes of the White Leaguers, but because the White Leaguers were so ignorant as to believe them capable of doing so. They evidently fancy that the recent election was an implied approval of all their acts, and have begun a war against all the Republican governments at the South. To this degree the Democracy must be held responsible for the recent disorders and massacres in the Southern States, and it would seem their especial duty to show in some plain way their abhorrence of such methods of gaining political power, so shameful and so perilous to freedom. But still more is it the duty of Republicans to rise from their lethargy and re-assert that strength which they really possess in every Northern State. Let the people show their hatred for murder and violence in all the new elections. Nothing but the defeat of Republicanism has made New Orleans rebellious and Vicksburg a scene of bloodshed. Nor can any thing restore peace to Mississippi, Arkansas, or Louisiana but a perfect union of the North, East, West, in a resolute policy toward the Southern maranders. In their own section there is nothing that can resist them. Their press is dumb; the wiser majority in every Southern State, who, no doubt, fear and abhor the murderous company, are powerless before it. This desperate class of men drove the South into rebellion fourteen years ago, and left it shorn of its wealth and honor, plunged in intolerable poverty, and clamorous for the national aid.

The White League of 1860 was composed of the same elements of cruelty and ignorance that now mark its successor of 1874. And the people of the South were driven into the civil war often with the knives of the assassins at their breasts. At its close, when peace and repose might have restored a new prosperity to the fair land from the Potomac to the Rio Grande, the White League once more interfered. In the form of the Ku-Klux it spread terror and bloodshed through every Southern State, and checked that influx of immigration and capital which was alone needed to make Georgia and Mississippi as prosperous and as happy as the great Northwest. Its fatal influence was strikingly apparent in Louisiana. During the period from the close of the rebellion to the year 1868 a remarkable prosperity seemed to have dawned upon the State. Its fertile lands were eagerly sought for; a tide of immigration flowed in upon it; New Orleans was full of commercial activity, and its shops and warehouses, hotels and private buildings, could scarcely contain the growing population or the active trade. In 1867 the Ku-Klux association began its assassinations and outrages, and capital, immigration, and commerce fled at once from the distressed community. Since 1868 the fear of its dangerous class and the constant insecurity of life and property have made New Orleans no attractive place for merchants and mechanics. Its shops and houses are untenanted, or let for only a meagre return; its streets have been the scene of frequent conflicts between the White Leaguers and their opponents; and in the maddest of their recent outbreaks, when they held the city for two or three days, the lives of the most conspicuous Democrats who counseled moderation and compromise were in plain danger from their murderous allies. The majority were forced to follow the guidance of the most violent and least reputable of their own party, and countenance a scene of massacre and woe. The New Orleans *Times,* a paper strongly Democratic, yet apparently opposed to riot and murder, seems to have felt itself in danger. It was threatened with suppression, yet it bravely defied the White Leaguers in the midst of their brief power. It denounced the "braggart and boasting Bobadils of the ultra-Southern journals," and warned New Orleans of the perils of treason. Yet the dangerous classes have evidently overpowered the moderate opposition in Louisiana and Mississippi, and their reign of terror has reached at last to Vicksburg. They are unifed, unsparing, of savage cruelty, yet need but to be resisted to be overthrown.

The moderate Democracy at the South has plainly lost all control over the violent members of its party, and it is quite impossible to say where this spirit of massacre may not reach. The whole people may soon be forced to interfere in order to save the South from utter ruin. Yet it is with natural regret that one must survey the fate of this fair territory, reaching from the Potomac to the Rio Grande, so full of the finest attributes of nature, so fitted to make millions happy and prosperous, suddenly checked in its new career of progress, deprived of education, peace, repose, turned back into a savage barbarism, and ruled by a class of men whose brutality, ignorance, and cruelty seem doubly monstrous in the light of a general civilization. It is only in the return to republican principles and a severe enforcement of good order that the Southern States can hope for an escape from the control of their criminal classes.

Recent reports from the neighborhood of Shreveport show that that whole section of country has fallen into a kind of anarchy. General Merrill, a brave and cultivated officer, noted for having suppressed the Ku-Klux of South Carolina, has re-established order in the town itself, but through all the inland districts of Northwestern Louisiana there is neither law nor justice, no safety for human life nor security for property. The White Leaguers hunt the negroes from their farms and homes to the woods, and shoot them as they formerly shot fugitive slaves. A newspaper in Shreveport directs the assassinations, and advocates a war of races. The same bitter hostility, we are told by the colored people, who seem to have but scanty means of relating their wrongs to the public, prevails through Georgia and Alabama. The courts deny them justice, the White Leaguers rob them of their wages. They plan a general emigration, but scarcely know where to go. The plots of the White League already threaten the peace of the Carolinas and the Virginias. Anarchy and ruin hang over the South, and the lawless deeds of a small minority of its population have made land almost valueless in Georgia, and threaten to leave Louisiana in great part an uncultivated waste.

To remedy these disorders is the first step in restoring the prosperity of the Southern States, and in this labor public opinion will have a large share. There is a general desire that every official at the South who betrays his trust should be punished; that every white or colored man who is a peculator or a thief should feel all the severity of the law. But the massacres of the White Leaguers are evidently done not to enforce law, but to destroy it. Their pretenses are falsehoods, their aim the general ruin. Against them the press may well direct all its weapons. Already they are beginning to feel the force of public opinion, and Kentucky, Tennessee, and Virginia labor honestly to repress crime. Such horrible deeds as that at Vicksburg, or the endless outrages in Louisiana and Alabama, show the need of some vigorous and resolute action. The colored people will make quiet and valuable citizens if protected in all their rights. On their industry and progress rests the chief productiveness of the South. To suffer them to be destroyed would bring commercial disaster to St. Louis and New York; and already the malicious deeds of the White League have cost the country untold millions, besides fixing a lasting stain upon its humanity.

Eugene Lawrence

LOUISIANA

HARPER'S WEEKLY
January 16, 1875, p. 50

The report of the committee which has gone to New Orleans to investigate the situation in Louisiana will be a very valuable paper, because the members of the committee are able, intelligent, and honest. Mr. Wilson is a positive Republican, and Mr. Potter is an equally positive Democrat, while Mr. Phelps is a peculiarly independent and candid public man. None of them, however, will stoop to mere party chicanery, and undoubtedly the actual situation can be more correctly gathered from their report than from any other representation whatever. The vehement assertions of newspapers which have prejudged the case and taken a side to support are of no importance. Before the election was held it was evident that certain papers had decided that the Democrats would certainly succeed, and that any other result must be the consequence of fraud. The ease with which the Kellogg government was overthrown in September was held to be conclusive proof that his party was a minority, and the suspicious character of the laws under which the returning board was organized and renewed was thought sufficient evidence of contemplated fraud.

The suspicion arising from this last fact we pointed out at the time of the September revolution. But the apparent numerical weakness of the Kellogg party was undoubtedly due to the fact that it is largely composed of the colored voters, and that they are unquestionably intimidated by the White League. Mr. Marr, the chairman of the New Orleans Committee of Seventy, and one of the Democratic leaders, says, with great simplicity, to a New York reporter, that General Ogden, the commander of the White League, has declared it to be the purpose of that organization to "guarantee and, if necessary, protect the colored race in every civil and political right." It is for that reason, probably, that the editor of one of the organs of the White League attacked ex-Governor Warmoth for insisting that the old practice of excluding negroes from the street cars should not be revived.

The simple truth is that the White League and the Democratic party, by sedulously calling themselves "the people of Louisiana," in accordance with the old Democratic tradition that "the people" means the white class, strive to impress upon the country the idea that in supporting the existing government of Louisiana the Administration is defying the will of the inhabitants of the State and terribly oppressing "the people." It is probably true that if the national power were withdrawn or were withheld, as it would be under a Democratic Administration, the White League would overthrow the government of the State and establish itself in authority. But that is merely to say, what is not denied, that the Republican party, largely composed of the colored people, could be readily overcome by the whites. It by no means establishes, however, the fact that the White League represents the only or the true "people of Louisiana," or that the Republicans alone are guilty of fraud and misconduct.

We have a right to expect from the committee now in New Orleans some authentic statement upon points which are now subjects of mere heated assertion. The President has earnestly requested Congress to deal with the difficulty; and if its committee now declares that Kellogg is evidently not the rightful Governor, and that the late returns have been fraudulently counted by the board, we trust that the Republicans in Congress will insist that Kellogg shall retire, and that the Democratic Legislature shall organize itself in peace. Meanwhile the constitutional duty of the Administration is plain, and there is no doubt that it will be fully discharged. Mr. Marr, who seems to be a droll gentleman, says that General Sheridan did not make himself socially acceptable when he was last in New Orleans. He certainly did not, and no other loyal officer of the United States would have been socially acceptable there. The sentiment of New Orleans "society" was, and apparently is, hostile to the United States and its government, and that feeling, quite as much as radical fraud and oppression, is the spring of the troubles in Louisiana. One of the organs of the White League covers Sheridan with ribald insults in the worst spirit of the war, and that, we suppose, is the voice of "the people" of Louisiana. These things following upon the elections are significant. Already they arrest public attention. The real tendencies of the situation are not to be studied in the rhetoric of the Manhattan Club supper-table in New York, but in events in the late slave and rebel States, and in the spirit manifested wherever the rebel party has obtained ascendency.

GERRIT SMITH

HARPER'S WEEKLY
January 16, 1875, p. 50

The active antislavery movement in this country began forty years ago, and it is not surprising that many of its most famous champions have already gone or are departing in a ripe and honorable age. Gerrit Smith was one of that band of moral heroes, and he was also one of the few Americans who may be called public men although not in official position, and who have a signal and influential individuality. He was born seventy-seven years ago, and his long life, his great riches, and his admirable talents were devoted to the relief and elevation of the forlorn and friendless and oppressed, and in a large and generous sense to the service of humanity. He was essentially a noble man. His advocacy of reforms was so strenuous and uncompromising that he seemed often fanatical and impracticable, but his great heart so overflowed with goodness and sympathy that no one who knew him could be his enemy, and in Congress, where nobody was more radical or more positive, no one was more heartily liked, even by his bitterest opponents....

Gerrit Smith was one of the men whose service to this country was not inferior to that of the fathers of the Revolution. As the earlier patriots made the nation independent, their later brethren made it free and just. When Gerrit Smith began to take an interest in public affairs it was doubtful whether the American republic would not soon end in a huge slave empire. There was no national flag in Christendom so disgraced as ours, for no other was prostituted to an internal slave-hunting which was worthy of Dahomey. Mr. Smith was one of those whose voice did not spare the infamy and its abettors, and who by their courageous eloquence and action aroused the dormant heart and conscience of America, until the people threw off the tyranny which was destroying them. For his part in this great service his name will be cherished and honored; and if those who know with him the perils that still menace our peace can not think without sorrow that the noble heart and lion port and uncompromising conscience of Gerrit Smith have now become only a memory, they will not forget that they are also an inspiration.

EVENTS IN LOUISIANA

HARPER'S WEEKLY
January 23, 1875, p. 70

It is the happy fortune of this country that we live under a government of laws and not of men, and that there is a universal and prompt awakening of the public mind whenever the authority of law is transcended. The late events in New Orleans have produced a more general and painful excitement than any thing that has recently occurred, and the consequences will undoubtedly be far-reaching and most important. The Louisiana question is no longer one of party under the government, but of the fundamental guarantees of American liberty. The condition of the State, indeed, has long been deplorable, and it is one of the chief offenses of Congress that after the report of its own committee, revealing the anarchy that prevailed, it refused to take action. A large share of the responsibility for the late events, therefore, belongs to Congress. But while this is true—while the situation may be all that has been represented by the most heated partisan—while all may be true that General Sheridan stated in his first dispatch, although he could hardly have known it to be so—while all that is charged as to the murderous and unlawful designs of the White League may be correct—while all that was said in the Senate of assassination, Ku-Klux, and rebellion may be well founded—while all that is alleged of the irregularity and illegality of the organization of the Legislature may be conceded, the action of the Republican government upon the assembling of the Louisiana Legislature has no precedent whatever in American constitutional history, except the Democratic crime against Kansas, and painfully recalls King Charles's fatal and foolish arrest of the five members.

We will take the facts from the chief actor, Mr. Kellogg, in his statement to the reporter of the *Herald,* and they are confirmed by the mass of testimony. The general election took place in November, and the result for the Lower House of the Legislature was very close. The Returning Board, which is the lawful body to declare the result, gave a majority of two or three to the Republicans, and left some seats in doubt, to be settled by the Legislature. The Legislature met, and, like all legislative bodies, was the sole judge of the qualifications and election of its members.

It is claimed that persons not legally returned as elected took part in the organization, and that there was great disorder. Upon this fifty-two members—"a clear majority" of those legally returned as elected—waited upon the Governor, and told him that a mob was in possession of the legislative hall, obstructing the action of the Legislature. Undoubtedly, if there was dangerous disorder, it was the duty of the Governor, in the last extremity, to maintain the peace. He immediately ordered a body of police to the spot, and fearing, from the appearance of things, a riot, he requested the officer commanding the United States troops to send soldiers to his assistance, to be marched into the building to aid the police, "orders being given," and of course by his authority, "that no member returned as elected, nor any regular officer of the Legislature, should be interfered with, but that the mob, and persons not returned as elected, should be removed from the floor of the House."

This is the Governor's own statement. Now he is not authorized to employ the United States troops to keep the peace until he has made a requisition upon the President, and such is the jealous regard of the Constitution for the people as represented in the Legislature that he can not do that except "when the Legislature can not be convened." But it appears that the Governor made no request to the President, while, by his own statement, there was a lawful quorum of the Legislature upon the spot. If, as the Governor claims, a clear majority of the lawful Legislature waited upon him, the simple, obvious, lawful course was that they should organize, and then, with the Governor, if they thought the peril imminent, call for necessary aid. But there was and would have been no peril. There would have been two bodies claiming to be the Legislature—one composed, according to the Governor's statement, of a minority of those lawfully declared to be elected, the other of a lawful majority, and recognized by him. If necessary, an appeal could then have been made to Congress. The gravity and the menace of this case we can better understand by making it our own. Suppose that the election had left the New York Legislature as closely divided between the parties as that of Louisiana, and half a dozen Republicans, claiming to be elected, but thrown out by the canvassers, had taken part in the organization and the House so constituted had chosen a Republican Speaker, what should we have thought if Governor Tilden had sent a file of United States soldiers with orders that "persons not returned as elected should be removed from the floor of the House?" Mr. Thurman stated in the Senate that some years ago the Legislature of Ohio was engaged for a fortnight in a desperate wrangle over organization, but from whatever cause the trouble may have arisen, he said that if President Van Buren had sent the army to settle the difficulty, the army would not have left Columbus again. Sam Adams would have said very much the same thing a hundred years ago.

A very great wrong, as it seems to us, has been committed in New Orleans, and with the acquiescence of the Administration. Republican as we are, we are so only because we believe the equal rights of all Americans are safer with the intelligence and conscience that make the inspiration, and have in general directed the policy, of the Republican party. But we do not excuse or justify, in this or in any other case, what seems to us a flagrant and fatal disregard of those guarantees which are indispensable to free popular government. And because we are Republican, and contemplate with profound apprehension the possibility of the restoration of the Democratic party to power, we see with the utmost amazement, incredulity, and pain that measures are approved by the Administration which can have but one result, and that is the total destruction of the party that was called into active and triumphant life by the aggressions of human slavery and the wrongs of Kansas.

We trust that the Congress of the United States will no longer evade its duty; but its action, whatever it may be, can not wholly undo the wrong that has been done, nor altogether heal the wound which the great party of liberty, order, and equal rights has received in the house of its friends. The report of the Louisiana committee will perhaps be submitted before this paper is issued. It will be awaited with intense interest, and should it be, as we hope it will be, unanimous, it will unquestionably be accepted by the country as the best attainable statement of the situation in that unhappy State. Meanwhile there is the remedy that never fails. There is no need of rhetorical fury or brute force. Either our whole American system is wrong, or the intelligent vote of the country will peaceably settle this question.

MORE SIGNS

HARPER'S WEEKLY
January 23, 1875, p. 71

Those who are interested in studying the probable results of Democratic ascendency in this country will watch every sign with great attention. In Missouri a Democratic Senator is to be elected, and there are those who have seriously urged the return of Mr. Schurz, as if the fact that he is the ablest expounder of what a part of the Democratic party professes to profess gave him the least chance of an election. Those who suppose that in some inscrutable manner the Democratic party has become a party of reform and of patriotic administration may wisely consider these words from the Missouri *Democrat*:

> "Democracy in this State is at heart in favor of repudiation as well as reaction, and hates Schurz the more bitterly because he not only opposes them, but will not stoop to any hiding of his convictions for the sake of any office. To every sensible man of either party in this State the fact has been known for a long time that Senator Schurz would have no more chance with a Democratic Legislature in Missouri than Jeff Davis would have with a Republican Legislature in Massachusetts. One thing the election will demonstrate, whatever else happens, namely, that Democracy in this State, when it feels strong enough to show its real character, is as irreconcilably hostile to all that moderate independent reform element which in other States it tries to cajole as it is to Republicanism of the most unlovely type. Senator Schurz denounces men like Kellogg. But Kellogg himself could be elected by Democrats of Missouri more easily than Schurz."

As the commander-in-chief of the White League in Louisiana says that its object is self-defense, defense against the aggressive and sanguinary colored people, another sign of the reviving spirit of the Democratic party may be seen in this extract from the Logan *Sentinel* in Kentucky. It is an unimportant paper, but the Democratic sentiment of the cross-roads in Kentucky is much better worth studying than that of the Manhattan Club in New York as a controlling influence upon party action:

> "We will have a National Convention of all the States to revise and amend the Constitution of the United States, and there will be no niggers in that Convention. The Constitution as revised will be the Constitution as it was in 1860, except in the matter of slavery. State laws and State constitutions will be made to conform to the reformed Constitution; so will the Federal laws. We will have the niggers free, as they are, but no more. This will leave them on the footing of unnaturalized foreigners, and of our mothers, wives, daughters, and sisters. This is enough. More than that they have no right to, and more than that they never will get from us. That is what we propose to do with the niggers."

Meanwhile the Louisville *Courier-Journal*, one of the most devoted Democratic papers, says that upon a careful study of the party since the election it concludes that the Democratic want is a want of brains. It sees reaction every where, and not the promise of reform. Mr. Eaton has been elected Senator in Connecticut; Messrs. Voorhees and Jerry Black are the prominent Senatorial candidates in Indiana and Pennsylvania; in Missouri Mr. Schurz is thrown aside for candidates whose claim is that they were uncompromising rebels, not that they are faithful patriots; and Fernando Wood is the probable Speaker of the Democratic House. Did the honest and disgusted Republicans who, hating Butler and Butlerism, voted the Democratic ticket, think that a reformed, economical, intelligent, and honorable administration of the government lay in that direction?

LOUISIANA
General Sheridan's Report.

HARPER'S WEEKLY
January 23, 1875, p. 71

Head-Quarters Military Division of the Missouri, New Orleans, Louisiana, *January 8*
To Hon. W. W. Belknap, Secretary of War, Washington:

I have the honor to submit the following brief report of affairs as they occurred here in the organization of the State Legislature of January 4, 1875. I was not in command of this military department until nine o'clock at night on the 4th inst., but I fully indorse and am willing to be held responsible for acts of the military as conservators of the public peace upon that day. During the few days in which I was in the city prior to the 4th of January the general topic of conversation was the scenes of bloodshed that were liable to occur on that day, and I repeatedly heard threats of assassinating the Governor, and regrets expressed that he was not killed on the 14th of September last; also threats of the assassination of Republican members of the House, in order to secure the election of a Democratic Speaker. I also know of the kidnaping by the banditti of Mr. Cousin, one of the members elect of the Legislature.

In order to preserve peace, and to make the State-house safe for the peaceable assembling of the Legislature, General Emory, upon the requisition of the Governor, stationed troops in the vicinity of the building. Owing to these precautions the Legislature assembled in the State-house without any disturbance of the peace. At 12 o'clock William Vigers, the Clerk of the last House of Representatives, proceeded to call the roll, as according to law he was empowered to do. One hundred and two legally returned members answered to their names. Of this number fifty-two were Republicans and fifty Democrats. Before entering the house Mr. L. A. Wiltz had been selected in caucus as the Democratic nominee for Speaker, and Michael Hahn as the Republican nominee.

Mr. Vigers had not finished announcing the result when one of the members, Mr. Billien, of Lafourche, nominated Mr. L. A. Wiltz for temporary Speaker. Mr. Vigers promptly declared the motion out of order at that time, when some one put the question, and amidst cheers on the Democratic side of the House, Mr. Wiltz dashed on to the rostrum, pushed aside Mr. Vigers, seized the Speaker's chair and gavel, and declared himself Speaker. A protest against this arbitrary and unlawful proceeding was promptly made by members of the majority, but Mr. Wiltz paid no attention to these protests, and on motion from some one on the Democratic side of the House, it was declared that one Trezevant was nominated and elected Clerk of the House. Mr. Trezevant at once sprang forward and occupied the Clerk's chair amidst the wildest confusion over the whole house.

Mr. Wiltz then again, on another nomination from the Democratic side of the House, declared one Flood elected Sergeant-at-Arms, and ordered a certain number of assistants to be appointed. Instantly a large number of men throughout the hall, who had been admitted on various pretexts, such as reporters and members' friends and spectators, turned down the lapels of their coats, upon which were pinned blue ribbon badges, on which were printed in gold letters the words "Assistant Sergeant-at-Arms," and the Assembly was in the possession of the minority, and the White League of Louisiana had made good its threat of seizing the House, many of the assistant Sergeants-at-Arms being well known as captains of White League companies in this city.

Notwithstanding the suddenness of this movement, the leading Republican members had not failed to protest again and again against this revolutionary action of the minority, but all to no purpose, and many of the Republicans rose and left the House in a body, together with the clerk, Mr. Vigers, who carried with him the original roll of the House as returned by the Secretary of State. The excitement was now very great, and the acting Speaker directed the Sergeant-at-Arms to prevent the egress or ingress of members or others, and several exciting scuffles, in which knives and pistols were drawn, took place, and for a few moments it seemed as if bloodshed would ensue.

At this juncture Mr. Dupre, a Democratic member from Orleans Parish, moved that the military power of the general government be invoked to preserve the peace, and that a committee be appointed to wait on General De Trobriand, the commanding officer of the United States troops stationed at the State-house, and request his assistance in clearing the lobby. The motion was adopted. A committee of five, of which Mr. Duper was made chairman, was sent to wait upon General De Trobriand, and soon returned with that officer, who was accompanied by two of his staff officers.

As General De Trobriand walked down to the Speaker's desk, loud applause burst from the Democratic side of the House. General De Trobriand asked the acting Speaker if it was not possible for him to preserve order without appealing to him to preserve order as a United States army officer. Mr. Wiltz said it was not, whereupon the general proceeded to the lobby, and, addressing a few words to the excited crowd, peace was at once restored. On motion of Mr. Dupre, Mr. Wiltz then, in the name of the General Assembly of the State of Louisiana, thanked General De Trobriand for his interference in behalf of law and order, and the general withdrew.

The Republicans had now generally withdrawn from the hall, and united in signing a petition to the Governor, stating their grievances and asking his aid, which petition, signed by fifty-two legally returned members of the House, is in my possession.

Immediately subsequent to the action of Mr. Wiltz in ejecting the Clerk of the old House, Mr. Billien moved that two gentlemen from the parish of De Soto, one from Winn, one from Bienville, and one from Iberia, who had not been returned by the Returning Board, be sworn in as members, and they were accordingly sworn in by Mr. Wiltz, and took their seats on the floor as members of the House. A motion was now made that the House proceed with its permanent organization, and accordingly the roll was called by Mr. Trezevant, the acting Clerk, and Wiltz was declared Speaker and Trezevant Clerk of the House.

Acting on the protest made by the majority of the House, the Governor now requested the commanding general of the department to aid him in restoring order, and enable the legally returned members of the House to proceed with its organization according to law. This request was reasonable, and in accordance with law. Remembering vividly the terrible massacres that took place in this city on the assembling of the Constitutional Convention in 1866, at the Mechanics' Institute, and believing that the lives of the members of the Legislature were, or would be, endangered in case an organization under the law was attempted, the posse was furnished, with the request that care should be taken that no member of the Legislature returned by the Returning Board should be ejected from the door.

This military posse performed its duty under directions from the Governor of the State, and removed from the floor of the House those persons who had been illegally seated, and who had no legal right to be there; whereupon the Democrats rose and left the House, and the remaining members proceeded to effect an organization under the State laws.

In all this turmoil, in which bloodshed was imminent, the military posse behaved with great discretion. When Mr. Wiltz, the usurping Speaker of the House, called for troops to prevent bloodshed, they were given him; when the Governor of the State called for a posse for the same purpose and to enforce the law, it was furnished also, Had this not been done, it is my firm belief that scenes of bloodshed would have ensued.

(Signed) P. H. Sheridan, Lieutenant-General.

A REPUBLICAN VIEW OF THE SITUATION

HARPER'S WEEKLY
January 30, 1875, p. 90

Events in Louisiana, and even a rupture of the cabinet, should it occur, do not change the point of view from which the political situation in the country should be regarded. Indeed, the participation of some Republicans in the New York meeting, and the emphatic protest of the stanchest Republican papers in the country against the conduct of affairs in New Orleans, show only the more plainly the truth of what we say. If the action in Louisiana had been justified by the party, and could therefore be regarded as the deliberate party policy, it is evident that those who instinctively suspect even lawful military interference in politics, however well intentioned, as the beginning of radical and fatal trouble, could no longer trust a control of affairs which appealed unlawfully to force. This is the position in which the Democratic opposition would like to place the Republicans. It declares that the Republican party is in power, and must take responsibility of administrative acts. The proceedings in New Orleans are under Republican auspices, and they will prove a Nessus shirt to consume the party if the Democrats can compass it.

We do not deny that the party in power is responsible for the Administration, and we agree that the military interference in New Orleans was a great wrong, which can only tend to imperil the country by throwing the national government into Democratic hands. But while this is true, it is no less true that if the weight of the party, its best opinion, its leading men and journals, condemn a course for which it is formally responsible, every good citizen who sympathizes with the general character and spirit of the party will decline to array himself with the organized opposition, but will wait to see whether that better element will not correct and control the party action, or, if that is improbable, whether a new combination to secure the just objects of that party is not possible. If we are asked whether we believe that the Republican party can recover its lost ground, and repair the consequences of the blunders that have been committed, we reply that the great objects which every patriotic man in this country should desire seem to us impossible of attainment under Democratic ascendency. It is not because we think that parties can not change, nor because of any theory whatever, but it is from the observation of very simple and evident facts.

The first and most striking of these facts is that the leadership of the Democratic party is practically unchanged. In the State of New York, for instance, Horatio Seymour, Governor Tilden, Judge Church, Mr. Kernan, Mr. Henry C. Murphy, Fernando Wood, Mr. Belmont, and Mr. John Kelly are the Democratic chiefs. The last name is comparatively new. It is that of the present director of Tammany Hall, the most powerful local organization in the party. But Mr. Kelly's efforts are for the promotion of old party leaders; and what is there in the name or career of any of those that we have named which should make any man who has acted with the Republican party for the last ten or fifteen years suppose that the purposes and principles which he most warmly cherishes will be respected or safe in their hands, or with the party in which they are leaders? Take with this another conspicuous fact, that the white population of the Southern States, which has grown up in a social system of human slavery, which is essentially a system of violence and injustice, necessarily hostile to liberty and equal rights, the corner-stones of the American political system, is not, and can not be, in any just sense republican, unless caste is republican. Yet this population, aristocratic in instinct and training and prejudice, and with all the want of general enlightenment which belongs to states in which there has been no efficient system of free schools, is the chief dependence of the Democratic party in its hope of return to power.

We certainly do not say this in any other than a perfectly friendly spirit, or with the least wish to rekindle "smouldering fires," or to re-open "closed gulfs." But it is not an answer to plain statements of fact to say that we ought to conciliate, nor does it dispose of an argument based upon knowledge common to all intelligent men to shout that it is "the gospel of hate," just as it is not the part of good sense or of good citizenship when a friendless negro is wantonly persecuted and murdered to sneer at "the grist of the outrage mill." What is most wanted in the country is an honest administration of the government in cordial and actual sympathy with the radical changes that have been made in the fundamental law, and in direct and stern opposition to the policy and spirit of the Democratic party upon the great questions that convulsed the Union for a generation, and finally brought it to civil war. In view of the fact that the leadership of that party is substantially unchanged, as we see in New York, and that the late slave-holding population, which is necessarily the most hostile of all to the new spirit of the Constitution and government, and the least essentially republican in feeling, is the mainstay of that party, nothing is plainer than that the government can not safely be intrusted to it.

In the actual situation, therefore, even if the Administration of General Grant should be conceded to have failed in fulfilling properly the purposes of the Republican party, the failure should not be regarded as a justification of a Democratic restoration by any Republican, unless he thinks that those purposes are more likely to be achieved by the Democrats. If any Lincoln Republican or any sincere Union man of '64 thinks that the amendments will be more faithfully observed, that the equal rights of whites and blacks will be more honestly protected, that the authority of the national government will be more firmly maintained, or the just rights of the States more truly respected by the party, still unchanged

in its leadership, and with the following that we have described, which so long defied humanity and reason and conscience, which prostituted the power of the national government to strangle Kansas because, and only because, it sought to be a Free State—the party which made the national power a masked battery against liberty, and with the aid of the Supreme Court sought to impose slavery upon free soil as a national institution, guaranteed and protected by the national flag—if any Republican, if any intelligent American, thinks this, he will properly sustain the party which hopes by the errors of Republicans to make its way to power. The things that we describe were not of the last century; they were of yesterday, in the time of men not yet old; and in the defense and maintenance of these things the present Democratic leaders were trained. Republicans have made many mistakes. But in politics as in all action, disappointment and despair are the worst of counselors. If the Administration of General Grant has failed to satisfy Republicans, their duty to themselves, to their country, and to humanity demands that they secure one that will, not that they intrust the government to those who acquiesce in the gains and guarantees of liberty only because they could not prevent them.

THE LOUISIANA MESSAGE

HARPER'S WEEKLY
January 30, 1875, p. 90

The President's message clearly relieves him of the responsibility of ordering the troops to interfere for any purpose in Louisiana. He knew nothing of events there until he read of them in the papers of the next day. No communication had passed between him and Governor Kellogg since the early part of December, when he told the Governor that it would be time for the United States to interfere when it was found that the State authorities were likely to be overpowered. He says, further, that the suggestion of General Sheridan was of a kind that could not be adopted, and he deprecates the interference of troops in a State under any circumstances.

All this in the message is excellent, and disposes of a great deal of foolish talk about the purposes of the President, and the overthrow by this "tyrant" of the Legislature of a "sovereign State." But having described the situation in New Orleans, and shown that Governor Kellogg had no more authority, under the circumstances, to call upon the national troops than any other citizen of the State, he does not distinctly reprove his conduct, but says that it is "debatable" whether his action was justifiable. This is a very perilous position, and can not be sustained. There was no reason whatever that the lawful Assembly should not have organized, and if the danger was imminent, and the State means of defense

THE PRESIDENT'S MESSAGE ON LOUISIANA AFFAIRS.

To the Senate of the United States:

.... I have heretofore urged the case of Louisiana upon the attention of Congress, and I can not but think that its inaction has produced great evil......... The task assumed by the troops is not a pleasant one to them; the army is not composed of lawyers capable of judging at a moment's notice of just how far they can go in the maintenance of law and order, and it was impossible to give specific instructions providing for all possible contingencies that might arise. The troops were bound to act upon the judgment of the commanding officer upon each sudden contingency that arose, or wait instructions which could only reach them after the threatened wrongs had been committed which they were called on to prevent. It should be recollected, too, that upon my recognition of the KELLOGG Government I reported the fact, with the grounds of recognition, to Congress, and asked that body to take action in the matter, otherwise I should regard their silence as an acquiescence in my course. No action has been taken by that body, and I have maintained the position then marked out. If error has been committed by the army in these matters, it has always been on the side of the preservation of good order, the maintenance of the law, and the protection of life. Their bearing reflects credit upon the soldiers, and if wrong has resulted, the blame is with the turbulent elements surrounding them. I now earnestly ask that such action be taken by Congress as to leave my duties perfectly clear in dealing with the affairs of Louisiana, giving assurance at the same time that whatever may be done by that body in the premises will be executed according to the spirit and letter of the law, without fear or favor.

U. S. GRANT.

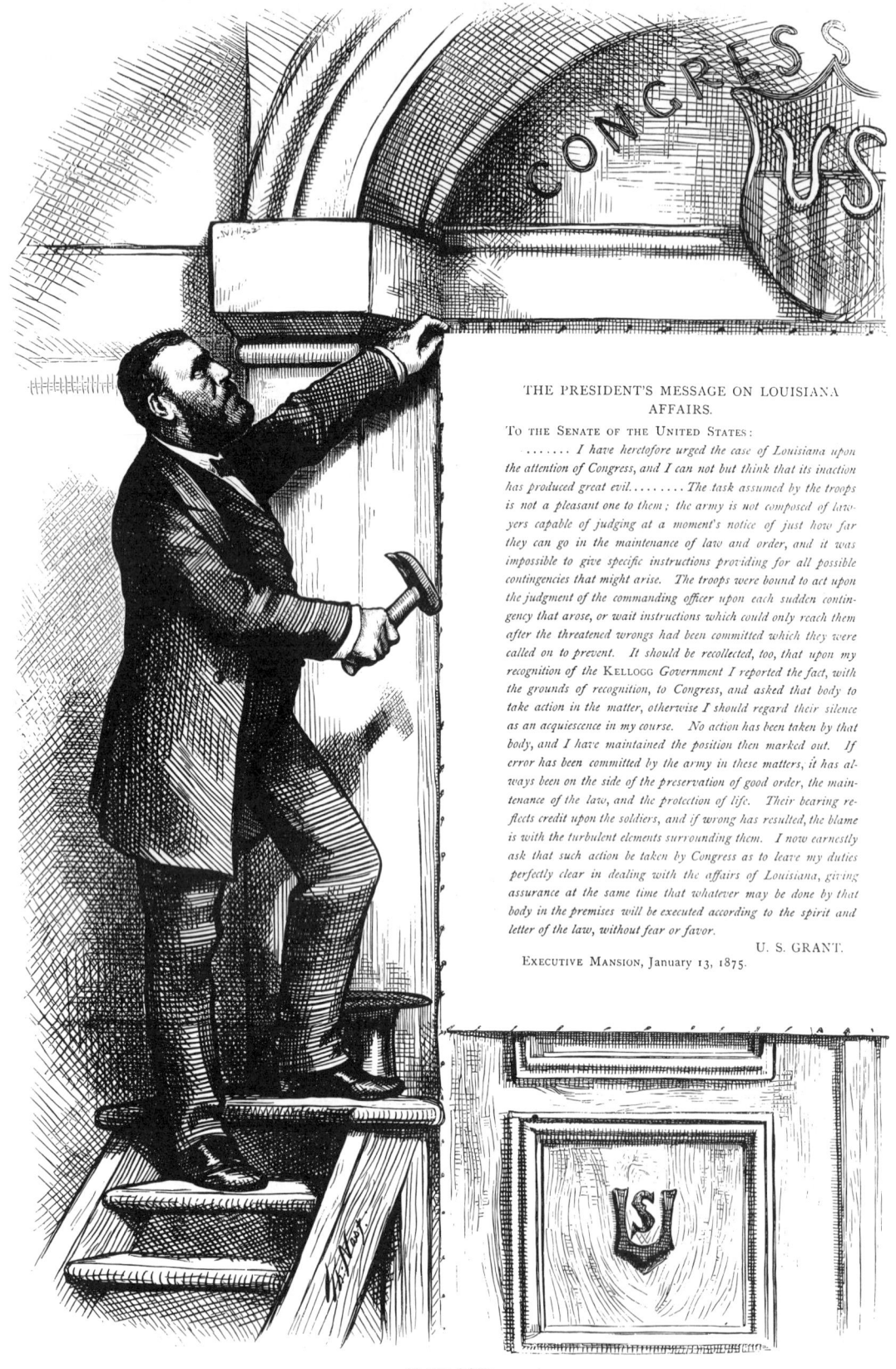

EXECUTIVE MANSION, January 13, 1875.

AT THE DOOR.
U. S. G. "If I hammer long enough, perhaps they'll wake up."

Harper's Weekly, January 30, 1875, p. 92.

hopeless, that the Legislature should not call, in the constitutional method, for aid. It is the extenuation and palliation of Kellogg's conduct that weaken the message.

The President shows by his explanation that the interference was in no sense the Republican policy; but it is equally the Republican policy to condemn such interference promptly, plainly, and trenchantly, and that the President has not done. The strength of the party is in its strict adhesion to constitutional rights. This can not be too constantly remembered. The friendless negro who cowers in dread of the White League, or of a Colfax or Coushatta massacre, can be outraged by nothing so much as by a deliberate disregard of the Constitution. With its amendments it is the sheet-anchor of his welfare. But if we, his friends, the Republicans, violate it in one part to help him, how can we complain of the Democrats if they violate it in another to hurt him? If we contemn a plain provision of its original text, we invite the Democrats to trample upon the amendments.

SHERIDAN'S JUSTIFICATION.

HARPER'S WEEKLY
January 30, 1875, p. 91

"Lieutenant-General Sheridan was requested by me to go to Louisiana to observe and report the situation there, and, if in his opinion necessary, to assume the command, which he did on the 4th inst., after the legislative disturbances had occurred—at 9 o'clock P.M.—a number of hours after the disturbance. No party motives or prejudices can reasonably be imputed to him; but, honestly convinced by what he has seen and heard there, he has characterized the leaders of the White Leaguers in severe terms, and suggested summary modes of procedure against them, which, though they can not be adopted, would, if legal, soon put an end to the troubles and disorders in that State. General Sheridan was looking at facts, and possibly not thinking of proceedings which would be the only proper ones to pursue in a time of peace, and thought more of the utterly lawless condition of society surrounding him at the time of his dispatch, and of what would prove a sure remedy. He never proposed to do any illegal act, nor expressed a determination to proceed beyond what the law in the future might authorize for the punishment of the atrocities which have been committed, and the commission of which can not be denied. It is a deplorable fact that political crimes and murder have been committed in Louisiana which have gone unpunished, and which have been justified or apologized for, which must rest as a reproach upon the state and country long after the present generation has passed away."—*President Grant's Message.*

RELIGIOUS INTELLIGENCE

HARPER'S WEEKLY
January 30, 1875, p. 99

The Rev. Charles New, of the Methodist Mission in East Africa, reports that, despite the lately made treaty, slavery flourishes on that side of the continent as much as ever before. Under date of November 2 he writes: "The institution among the native population remains untouched, except as regards the open sale of slaves in the market. Any trader can sell as many as he pleases upon his own land, provided he surrounds it with a fence of some kind. Wherever I go I see and hear the same horrors that prevailed years ago—chained gangs, manacled and fettered individuals, the clank, clank, clank of irons, the grip of the stocks, the thud of the stick. The screams of the afflicted fall on the ear every day.... Zanzibar is as well stocked with slaves as ever, and it is likely to be so, the circumstances being such as they are."

PRESIDENT GRANT AND HIS ASSAILANTS

HARPER'S WEEKLY
January 30, 1875, pp. 101–2

Ten years ago the armies of the people were closing around Richmond, and amidst a general clamor of rage and despair from all the adherents of slavery and rebellion, the patience and the courage of Grant and Sheridan were steadily sapping the last defenses of treason. No pretext had been left untried, no threats nor open defiance spared, to draw them off from their approaching victory. The opposition press teemed with calumny and detraction, and opposition leaders encouraged resistance at Richmond, and labored to stir up riot and disorder in the North. There were great meetings held to denounce General Grant, to cut off the supplies of the army, to menace the administration, and to shake the credit of the nation. The most noted Republican journal of New York, under some occult influence, began to speak of compromise even to the perpetuation of slavery. There was doubt and even despair in many timid but still patriotic minds. Many noted opposition leaders now in office plainly desired the success of Davis, and the revival of that barbarous and cruel aristocracy which had driven the Southern States into a ruinous rebellion. A secret association had been formed, with agents in most of the Northern cities, pledged to excite a counter-revolution, and resolute to bring fire and the sword into the heart of New York or Cincinnati. There were threats

HARPER'S WEEKLY.
JOURNAL OF CIVILIZATION.

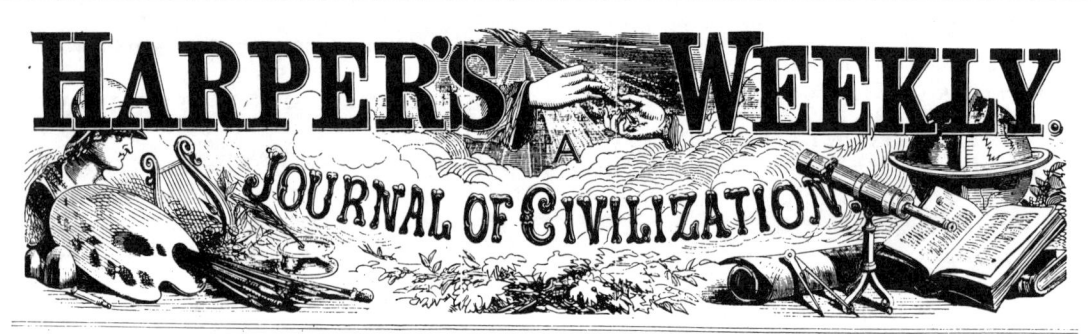

Vol. XIX.—No. 944.] NEW YORK, SATURDAY, JANUARY 30, 1875. [WITH A SUPPLEMENT. PRICE TEN CENTS.

Entered according to Act of Congress, in the Year 1875, by Harper & Brothers, in the Office of the Librarian of Congress, at Washington.

HEAD-QUARTERS OF THE
MILITARY DIVISION OF THE MISSOURI,
NEW ORLEANS, LA., January 4, 1875.

Hon. W. W. BELKNAP, Secretary of War, Washington, D. C.:

It is with deep regret that I have to announce to you the existence in this State of a spirit of defiance to all lawful authority, and an insecurity of life which is hardly realized by the general government or the country at large. The lives of citizens have become so jeopardized that unless something is done to give protection to the people, all security usually afforded by law will be overridden. Defiance to the laws and the murder of individuals seem to be looked upon by the community here from a stand-point which gives impunity to all who choose to indulge in either, and the civil government appears powerless to punish or even arrest.

I have to-night assumed control over the Department of the Gulf. P. H. SHERIDAN, Lieutenant-General.

HEAD-QUARTERS OF THE
MILITARY DIVISION OF THE MISSOURI,
NEW ORLEANS, LA., January 5, 1875.

Hon. W. W. BELKNAP, Secretary of War, Washington, D. C.:

I think the terrorism now existing in Louisiana, Mississippi, and Arkansas could be entirely removed, and confidence and fair dealing established, by the arrest and trial of the ring-leaders of the armed White Leagues. If Congress would pass a bill declaring them banditti, they could be tried by a military commission. This banditti, who murdered men here on the 14th of last September, also more recently at Vicksburg, Mississippi, should, in justice to law and order and the peace and prosperity of this Southern part of the country, be punished. It is possible that, if the President would issue a proclamation declaring them banditti, no further action need be taken, except that which would devolve upon me.

P. H. SHERIDAN, Lieutenant-General U. S. A.

GENERAL SHERIDAN STANDS BY HIS DISPATCHES.—[SEE PAGE 91.]

"He is a soldier, and does not hesitate to do his duty......He is also prudent and discreet, and will do nothing to complicate matters or precipitate events......That is the kind of man SHERIDAN is."—GENERAL SHERMAN.

CONGRATULATORY.—Drawn by C. S. Reinhart from a Sketch by W. H. Caldwell.—[See Article, "President Grant and his Assailants," Page 101.]

Patrick Kelley (loq.). "Me worthy friends, three for yez! Divil a bit more right has the Prisidint to interfare wid the byes in New Orleans than he had wid us here in '63. Faith, we're moighty encouraged to kill a Naygur this night. Glad to see yez, ould gintlemin, here; yez were niver wid us before."

Harper's Weekly, January 30, 1875, p. 100.

of assassination, and men prepared for any desperate extremity. And the most bitter and dangerous foes of Lincoln and Grant were no longer the perishing and disheartened Confederates within the lines of Richmond, but their active adherents without, who labored to divert the nation from the support of its armies in the field. Yet one sure reliance General Grant found never to fail him amidst the clamor and the calumnies of a thousand assailants: the people felt that he was their truest friend. They had watched his conduct with approbation; they gave their treasures and their lives lavishly to his support. Richmond fell amidst the acclamations of the working-men of Europe and America, the republic was saved, and the progress of the New World assured.

Never was a victory more generously used, or a fallen rebellion more tenderly treated. To the generous but misguided Lee and his soldiers the victors strove to seem only brothers in arms. No punishment awaited the most active and guilty insurgent; no painful retribution such as European governments are accustomed to impose in similar events. The nation turned at once to heal the woes of civil war by an unbounded charity, to feed the starving South from its own diminished resources, to build up its cities, to revive its trade, renew its productiveness, and to forget that a momentary strife had divided those who were still the members of a common family of freemen. Nor has this liberal and natural policy ever been departed from through the brief period that has fled so rapidly by since Richmond fell and Grant restored the vigor of the republic. There has been a constant effort on the part of the general government to win the rebellious district to a better spirit by forbearance and almost excessive moderation. It has looked on patiently while a violent and mischievous minority in almost every Southern State has violated all the duties of good citizenship, and driven away knowledge, progress, and reform; it has been forced to see without redress the rights and lives of its supporters placed in peril from the Ohio to the Gulf; it has watched silently while "banditti"—for no name can be more appropriate to such deeds and such men—and troops of assassins for nearly ten years have covered Kentucky and Tennessee with deeds of violence, established a pure tyranny in Georgia, and filled Louisiana with a succession of horrors. In the latter State only has the government interfered, because there the rebels chose to raise the question of the right of the nation to interfere, and have made the case of Louisiana a test case for all the Southern States. For the points involved in this matter are exactly those that were supposed to have been decided at Richmond. Portions of the State, as General Sheridan plainly shows, have fallen into the hands of real "banditti." The ruffians of Shreveport seek to control the government. The Shreveport *Times* inspires their movements, and if the national arm was withdrawn, Louisiana would be an independent community ruled by the murderers of Coushatta or Grant Parish. In other words, the question raised in Louisiana is whether a band of rioters may seize upon a State government by violence and intimidation, and defy the United States officers when they insist upon obedience to the law.

"Perfidy and cruelty," says a great historian, "are the distinguishing traits of a barbarous race." Of the cruelty of the dangerous classes at the South the last ten years have given fearful proofs; of their perfidy it should be the first aim of sensible men to beware. They profess to obey the national government, but who can trust the professions of those to whom murder is a common pastime, and obedience to the law unknown? It is the extravagant error of some of our Northern contemporaries to look upon the less civilized Southern States as communities resembling our own, and capable of being governed with equal mildness; those who have examined the real condition of Louisiana or Georgia know that it resembles rather society as it may have existed five hundred years ago in England, or as it lives to-day in portions of Italy and Spain. That sacredness of human life which has ever been the chief mark of advancing civilization is nowhere to be found in lands where slavery has corrupted the people, and it will be many years before education and the force of public opinion shall have wholly eradicated from the South its dangerous class. A reluctant witness, one of the correspondents of the New York *Times,* writing from Columbus, Georgia, confirms at last what has often been stated in these articles of the painful condition of Southern society, and says, "In Georgia and Alabama, at least in that section bordering on the Chattahoochee River, it is not usual to keep a white murderer in jail." He adds that within the past eighteen months fourteen white men have been murdered in the neighborhood of Columbus alone. The murderers were at once released on bail, were received as usual in society, and all escaped punishment through the influence of family connections or the venality of the courts. But if the murder of white men is looked upon as so venial an offense in these lawless districts, it is easy to conceive that the tortures and death of a multitude of harmless negroes would scarcely be noticed by the superior race. It is plain that the massacre of Coushatta would be to the people of Shreveport only a morning's sport.

Connected with the savage cruelty of this ruling class at the South is their shameless and audacious cunning. They deny every thing, spread false rumors, talk of oppression, claim the sympathy of the Northern Democracy, fill the newspapers with calumnies against Republican Governors, and assail the President and the administration with a ferocious bitterness that indicates both their hatred and their fear. Yet the murderers of Coushatta and Grant Parish, of Teche Parish and New Orleans, must hear almost with a grim smile that their rude cunning and daring falsehoods have found any credence in the more civilized part of the country; that their violent attempt to seize on the government of Louisiana has been countenanced by any honest or humane men; that a great meeting has been held in the city of New York to sustain them in their new rebellion; and that respectable citizens have been so far deluded by their pretenses as to look upon them as the victims of Republican oppression, and join in a fierce denunciation of the tyranny of Grant and Sheridan. With what peals of ribald laughter must they learn that their rude inventions are repeated by respectable journals; that the Northern Democracy is willing to assume the responsibility of their crimes, and shield them from a swift justice; that a venerable poet is prepared to chant their praises as the martyrs of freedom; that astute lawyers uphold their usurpations, and Irish judges defend the cause of rampant murder; that even some reputable Germans have been deceived by their hypocritical complaints; and that all the followers of Tweed and Sweeny have once more crept out into the public eye from their hiding-places, no longer conscious of the general detestation, to join in the assault upon the nation's defenders!

The patience and kindliness which President Grant and his administration have shown in all their conduct toward the rebellious South through their whole term of office—their careful abstinence from all military interference in the revolted States, except where actual murder and riot forced them to intervene—their generosity to unhappy Louisiana in its recent disasters, when a large part of its people were fed by the public charity—their willingness to confer offices and emoluments on every loyal native of the South—their firmness and discretion, will, we think, be remembered by the nation, if not by enraged and rival politicians; and it is certain that the judgment of future ages will decide that no policy could have been devised more likely to heal the wounds of the suffering section than those plans of education and internal improvement which Republican legislators have impressed deeply upon the Southern States. In response to this lenient treatment, what return have the Republican party and President Grant received? Future ages will hear with shame and sorrow the reply. His life is openly threatened by the assassins of the South whom he has striven to tame and subdue. A journal in New York plainly demands his assassination. He is called tyrant or dictator, and assailed with all the ribald terms the White League of the South or their Northern allies can devise. He on whose life once rested the fate of freedom before Richmond, whose arm saved the nation in the midst of a thousand foes, who is the defender of the rights of the workingmen of every land, is now assailed once more by the terrible minions of slavery at home and abroad, and by their deluded followers at the North and South. At the recent meeting in New York, when Grant's name was mentioned, there was a cry, "Hang him!" "Hang him!" And grave men sat looking on, and made no remonstrance! And for what? Why do they [s]eek his life? Because he has labored earnestly to protect the weak and the suffering in Louisiana, and is firmly resolved that the murderers of Coushatta and Colfax shall neither escape a just punishment nor bring utter ruin to their perishing State. If this is an error, it is so venial a one that it will probably be shared by the great majority of his countrymen. The people can not be deceived, and should the ruffians of Coushatta or any of their Northern allies proceed to execute their threats, a living wall of faithful hearts and manly breasts will gather around their country's chief defender, reaching from Maine to Oregon, and from the Lakes to the Gulf, that not all the rage of the White League nor the fiercest shafts of rival politicians can pierce.

It is instructive to review the histories of many of the men who gathered at the recent meeting in New York to assail the fame and threaten the ruin of the conqueror of Richmond. Many of them were the same violent partisans who ten years ago were laboring to starve the national armies in the field and snatch the Confederacy from the grasp of Grant and Sheridan. There were noted reactionary politicians to whom slavery was once dear, and who had now come together to avenge its fall; there were the chiefs of the ultramontane faction in New York; there were noted rebels who were once fighting against the armies of the republic; there was the secretary of Jefferson Davis, now pensioned by its Mayor upon the diminished revenues of our city; there, possibly, was Quincy, the former keeper of the Libby prison, who is also maintained at the cost of New York; there was an array of much that must have shocked every patriotic heart; there Kernan declared that he was present in spirit—an assurance scarcely needed; and there in spirit were present every Ku-Klux and every ruffian of the South. There, listening to the subtle denunciation of the President by a practiced advocate, whose argument would have been more effective had it been founded upon facts, sat a thick array of the Crokers and Kellys of Tammany Hall. There were many honest and just men, misled, no doubt, by the daring fictions of the Southern Leaguers. But one thing was wanting: the heart of the people was not there. It still beats full of grateful confidence for him whom the country owns as its truest friend since Washington, and in whose honesty and sincerity, foresight and prudence, it trusts as firmly now as it did when, ten years ago, it shielded him from the hatred of a thousand foes until Richmond fell.

Eugene Lawrence

THE SUB-COMMITTEE UPON LOUISIANA

HARPER'S WEEKLY
February 6, 1875, p. 110

The sub-committee that went to New Orleans to investigate the situation, and whose report has been published, was composed of three gentlemen who were well known as of the highest character and acknowledged ability, and their report was eagerly and confidently awaited. Mr. Foster and Mr. Phelps are Republicans, and Mr. Potter is a Democrat, yet they made a unanimous report. Their visit was short, their investigation necessarily limited, and, as they state, they merely "took such proof as the opportunity offered" upon the general subject of outrage and intimidation and fraud. This shows that the committee do not offer the results of their inquiry as an exhaustive statement, although they frankly declare their view of the general situation in the State. That view is, in brief, that there is "a general want of confidence" both in the validity and integrity of the existing Kellogg government, a profound business depression, an increase of taxation amounting almost to confiscation, a general demoralization of the rural negro population, and a pervading distress which has carried the people beyond any mere partisan lines. The White League, they state, is an armed military organization, ostensibly for "protection;" but the committee being sensible men, and knowing that the significance of such bodies is to be determined by the circumstances, distinctly say that "such organizations may be dangerous, and are very rarely to be justified." The committee, in closing their report, record their personal observation of the events of the 4th of January, which confirms the illegality of the organization, which was, in fact, as was evident to any one who had closely followed the proceedings in the State since September, a mere Democratic *coup d'etat,* skillfully attempted and illegally frustrated.

The report is very clear and candid, and shows no heated feeling of any kind. It is a plain statement of fact, and not an argument, and makes no recommendation. Indeed, the committee were but a body sent to gather information, and to lay it before the full committee; and having heard the report, the full committee have submitted it to the House, and the other members have decided to go to Louisiana and satisfy themselves that the statements are correct. The exact situation, then, of the Louisiana question is this: A Republican committee of the Senate reported two years ago that Kellogg, the present Governor, was not lawfully elected, and their view was sustained in his speech of last winter by Mr. Carpenter: another Republican sub-committee, from the House, have now reported that the apparent Republican majority in the Lower House of the present Legislature was obtained by fraud, and that, in the absence of the army, the Democratic Governor would be restored without a struggle. This is not, however, a declaration that the M'Enery partisans are a majority; they may be only more determined, like the secessionists in Virginia in 1861, who were exhorted by James M. Mason to make short work of those who voted against them. If the rest of the committee who have now gone to New Orleans should reach the same general conclusion as that of their associates, there could no longer be reasonable grounds of doubt. The four members of that committee who are now in Louisiana are not less able, patriotic, and sincere than Messrs. Foster, Phelps, and Potter; and

Mr. George F. Hoar, of Massachusetts, Mr. W. A. Wheeler, of New York, Mr. W. P. Frye, of Maine, and Mr. S. S. Marshall, of Illinois, are men whose statements will not be less worthy of careful consideration than those of their predecessors. If their report should also be unanimous, it would have great weight with the country; but if Mr. Marshall, who is a Democrat, should offer a dissenting report in accord with that of the sub-committee, the force of his colleagues' statement would be weakened, and the present report would virtually become that of the majority of the committee. The sub-committee's report is a very important contribution to our knowledge of the condition of Louisiana, and leaves very little doubt of the fraudulent action of the Returning Board.

THE NEGRO VOTE

HARPER'S WEEKLY
February 6, 1875, pp. 110-11

There are certain general convictions arising from the nature of the case, and from human nature itself, which must affect a correct estimate of the situation in Louisiana. The white population of the State is largely French in descent, and, from the old system of black slavery, is aristocratic in feeling. That such a population, having thrown the State into a civil war which ended by ruining them, and by making their late slaves not only free, but equal citizens and voters with themselves, should be disposed to recognize that equality frankly and fairly is not only absolutely improbable in itself, but the recent history of the State shows the fact that it was not so. The appearance of the "carpet-baggers," the conduct of many of the national office-holders in the State, and the undoubted ignorance and venality of many of the new citizens, with consequent dishonest legislation, have certainly not tended to correct the disposition of which we speak. Yet the white population, and especially its leaders, are chiefly to blame for the wretched condition of the State. Had they been wise enough to accept a bad situation, which they owed to themselves, and to make the best instead of the worst of it, the woes of Louisiana might have been avoided. But their present demand, and that of their allies elsewhere, that the State "be left to itself," is founded upon their consciousness that, although probably the numerical minority, they could coerce the majority, which is largely composed of negroes. This intimidation may be very simple and quiet, yet very effective. Every employer and every country neighborhood understands that. We presume there are very few intelligent persons who suppose that the right of the negro to vote would not be practically "denied or abridged" in all but three or four of the late slave-holding States if the power of the general government were controlled by the Democrats. The object of the attempted coup in Louisiana, and the purpose elsewhere of the party of those who made it, is to obtain control of the State governments, so as to secure a Democratic electoral vote in 1876.

The degree of good order of the late election in Louisiana upon the Conservative side, as certified by the sub-committee, certainly does not signify that the Democrats are more favorable to the colored vote or tolerant of it, nor that they mean fair play to the negro. It means, and means only, that their leaders were quite shrewd enough to know that their great hope of final success in their plan depended upon the appearance of a quiet and fair election. Last September, when they overthrew the Kellogg Administration, they were warned publicly and privately by their friends elsewhere that open resistance to the national authority, or any evident and general intimidation, or any conduct or policy that was not ostensibly fair and peaceful, would imperil the Democratic reaction which had begun, and which, if not checked, would secure all that they wished. They generally followed this advice. So far as the sub-committee can ascertain, there was very little open coercion of the negro vote. Indeed, they say that "no general intimidation of Republican voters was established," but they are evidently inclined to think that there was considerable intimidation of the Democratic vote by marshals and the military force. We shall be asked, then, whether, so far as the report is authority, it is not plain that in a free and fair election the Democrats are in the majority? We reply that the subcommittee also report that "throughout the rural districts of the State the number of white Republicans is very few. It hardly extends beyond those holding office and those connected with them;. . . applications to the United States Commissioners . . . because of alleged threats of discharge and non-employment, or other interference with political preference, were frequent;" and upon this statement, in the light of what every intelligent man knows to be the necessary situation in Louisiana, we say that the moral intimidation which must necessarily exist under the circumstances described by the committee forbids the supposition that the Democrats are in the numerical majority, while it may be conceded that they carried the election.

The conclusion to be fairly drawn is that the only hope even of a tolerable respect for the rights of the negro voters lies in the Republican control of the national government. For if now, with a friendly Republican Administration, with the national forces in the State, with the intimidation which the committee say was in some places produced among the white voters by the fear of the marshals and the troops, and with the obvious necessity of a fair election to the purposes of the Democrats, there was yet a certain amount of open coercion besides the universal moral intimidation which the white must long exercise over the black, what would be the condition of the negro voter in the interior of Louisiana if the Democrats should regain power? We are not saying that the States should be occupied by soldiers, nor that elections should be held under military supervision. We are alleging that the effective protection of the negro vote to-day in all but three or four of the late Slave States is a moral support derived from the knowledge that the national authority is in the hands of his friends, and not of his enemies, and to be used upon proper occasion, while the Democratic demand that the State be left to itself is a demand for the practical paralysis of that vote in those States. Every good citizen wishes that the State, and every State, be "left to itself." But it makes all possible difference in the situation of the Southern States whether they are left to themselves by a government hostile or friendly to the new voter, and the purpose of the late amendments.

PLEAS FOR KELLOGG

HARPER'S WEEKLY
February 6, 1875, p. 111

The late military interference in New Orleans, which *Harper's Weekly* has unequivocally condemned, is defended upon three grounds, and three only; and of these one only has even an apparent reason. It is said—and Mr. Wendell Phillips in his eloquent and striking speech in Faneuil Hall has put it as strongly as we have seen it— that the troops were lawfully used under the call of September; for, as "W. M. D." argues in the Cincinnati *Commercial,* in reply to what we have said, the rebellion of September 14 continued. The simple and conclusive reply is that the President says in his message that after the troops had been sent under the call of Kellogg in September, "no other disturbances seemed imminent," that is to say, the September summons was exhausted; but the troops were left in a convenient position, should another occasion, as was probable, arise, in which case they could be employed, provided, and only provided, another lawful requisition had been made. Indeed, so far is the President from agreeing with the view of Mr. Phillips, and of "W. M. D.," that he says distinctly, "Whether it was wrong for the Governor . . . to use such means as were in his power [namely, the United States troops] . . . is perhaps a debatable question." It seems to us, on the contrary, that, under the circumstances, there was never one less debatable. But nothing is plainer than that, if the President could possibly have said that Kellogg's action was lawful under the call of September, he would not have said that it was debatable.

Moreover, Kellogg's own conduct shows that he did not act upon the theory which is now suggested. On the 9th of December he telegraphed to the President that the White League meant to attack the Statehouse. If the troops were already under his command from the requisition of September, his dispatch was needless. And that the President did not consider that the troops were under Kellogg's control, but did consider that this was a new requisition, is shown by his reply deprecating the use of the soldiers "in anticipation of danger," and stating that if the authorities were molested, "the question will be determined whether the United States is able to maintain law and order." Did he mean that Kellogg was to determine? Nothing could show more conclusively that neither the Administration nor Kellogg himself considered the troops to be subject to his order under his September call.

The other forms of defense of his conduct are that the Democrats first called in General De Trobriand, and that there are a very ugly spirit and a great many political murders in Louisiana. Such pleas are only contemptible. That Democrats are lawless does not justify the lawlessness of a Republican Governor; and if political murders are committed, the law provides a remedy. Ours is a government of laws, not of men, and we have hitherto boasted that in this republic the law is adequate for the protection of every citizen. Are we ready to renounce that faith because Mr. Kellogg was outwitted by shrewder and bolder schemers?

A WARNING

HARPER'S WEEKLY
February 6, 1875, p. 111

It is very evident that the Democratic party relies now, as heretofore, upon its vote in the Southern States. The spirit that animates that vote may be better studied in the Southern Democratic papers than any where else; and we invite attention to the following expressions of feeling in regard to the late events in Louisiana. Is any thoughtful man of opinion that it would be wise to call this spirit to the control of the government?

The Memphis *Appeal* says:

"New Orleans has been as fatal to him [Sheridan] as to Beast Butler, the spoon thief. Hereafter he will be known as Superserviceable Liar Sheridan, to be continued in the army only until a Democratic Congress shall order him before a committee, presided over by Senator Gordon, to whom he shall surrender his commission as a disgraced soldier, with the ineffaceable brand of 'liar' burned to his very heart."

The *Daily Times* of Shreveport, Louisiana, says:

"Some time during the day yesterday the little blackguard and barnburner, ycleped Phil, got in with 'General Order No. 1,' issued from 'Head-quarters Military Division of the Mis-

THE TARGET.

"* * * They (Messrs. PHELPS & POTTER) seem to regard the White League as *innocent as a Target Company.*"—*Special Dispatch to the "N. Y. Times," from Washington, Jan. 17, 1875.*

LITTLE PHIL'S EXTINGUISHER

"Would, if legal, soon put an end to the troubles and disorders."—U. S. GRANT.

Harper's Weekly, February 6, 1875, p. 124.

souri, New Orleans, January 4, 1875.' This, notwithstanding the unnecessary lies he has been telling—unnecessary, because no one believed him. . . . We can not pretend to say what action will be taken by our friends in New Orleans. That they feel outraged beyond patient endurance we can well suppose, but it seems that no effort will be made to resist the infamy by force of arms. Knowing the vindictiveness and meanness of Grant, and the unscrupulous character of the thieves whom he affiliates with and protects, we can not say that we are greatly surprised at the result."

The Louisville *Courier-Journal*:

"General Sheridan fears assassination—
'If the assassination
Could trammel up the consequence, and catch
With his surcease success'—
but there's De Trobriand and Merrill and all the small fry—too many to pick off in that way."

The Atlanta (Georgia) *News*:

"To confront the danger which threatens the country—to kill Caesarism before Caesar can cross the Rubicon—we believe it necessary to repel force with force. If the people of Louisiana take up arms and drive Sheridan into the Mississippi River, an overwhelming majority of the American people will justify the act."

The St. Louis *Despatch*:

Harper's Weekly, February 6, 1875, p. 124.

"Kellogg, in eclipse, has fallen back on the Legislature; Sheridan, with his puffed and bloated face, appears on the horizon as the rounded disk of a moon struggling through clouds. The old Romans had the habit of paying their devoirs to the rising and not the setting sun; and if it really is to be Ceasarism, then all hail, Sheridan! True, he is a low squat swash; true, he was content to see stolen from a gallant brother officer in the Valley laurels that all the world knows he had no more right to than the dog to the lion's mane; true, that on neither side can fifty soldiers be found who will declare Sheridan could ever whip any body, man to man, or two even to one; true, that he is immense in plans that circumvent Indians with the plague, that break by violent arrest the legal powers of Representatives, that beleaguer a State-house and overthrow a Legislature; but did a *real* Caesar any of these things? Instead of Ceasar, it is Ceasarion."

The Memphis *Avalanche*:

"General Sheridan has disgraced humanity, disgraced the name of America, disgraced the army, but he has not disgraced himself. This it was not possible for him to do. . . . He wants to restore peace to Louisiana as it was once restored to Warsaw. Remember, he carried to Louisiana 'sealed instructions' prepared in the White House. He is but executing a programme whereon is written '1876.' A President is to be elected that year. It is not desirable that the votes of many Southern States should appear in the Electoral College."

The Memphis *Appeal:*

> "If there is any independence left in the present Congress, it will see to this immediately upon its assembling on Monday next, and cite both Sheridan and De Trobriand, and, if necessary, bring Grant to the bar of the House to answer for a crime against the nation that we are at a loss to account for, *unless it is that he consented to it at a moment when yet in a maudlin condition from one of his beastly debauches.*"

The New Orleans *Picayune:*

> "We know that a military commission means death by the rope or the musket. But why should the Lieutenant-General trouble himself with this superfluous formality? He is familiar with speedier ways of dealing with defenseless people."

Hundreds of innocent and helpless men, women, and children have been persecuted, tortured, and murdered by the partisans of these organs of opinion, and they have been silent, or, with their Northern allies, have spoken only to sneer and jeer at the "outrage mill." Now General Sheridan impetuously describes the ringleaders of those among whom these crimes are committed as banditti who should be summarily dealt with—a passionate military appeal which can not be justified, and should never have been made or published—and the same organs burst into a chorus of long-concealed hate and rage with one of the illustrious soldiers of the Union. These things will be marked and remembered.

COLOR IN THE NEW ORLEANS SCHOOLS

HARPER'S WEEKLY
February 13, 1875, pp. 147-48

The Superintendent of the Common Schools of Louisiana, the Hon. William G. Brown, is a colored man of unusual attainments, energy, and refinement. He was born in the British West Indies, where the strife of races has long ceased, and was carefully educated in an English school. Afterward he emigrated to New Orleans, became a public teacher, was then an editor, and next, in 1872, was elected to his present office. Before his election his opponents were accustomed to represent him as "an ignorant, brutal, plantation negro." Since he became State Superintendent the public has discovered, and even some of his former defamers admit, that he is admirably fitted for his difficult position. Fearless, impartial, intelligent, he has given a new impulse to public education in Louisiana, and has been particularly useful in advancing the intellectual welfare of his own race. It is even asserted that the colored children of New Orleans are more intelligent than the white, and the colored schools more zealous in the search for knowledge than those of their former superiors. It is indeed to be hoped that in this generous rivalry the latter will resort to no unscholarly expedients to win the race. But, unfortunately for the peace of the schools of New Orleans, a question of color has sprung up, excited by the general violence of political feeling in the city, and even the children of the place have formed their own "White League" to expel all colored pupils from the schools attended by the whites.

This is a plain violation of the law. Like their elder examples at Coushatta or Vicksburg, our young crusaders are too impetuous to await the slow action of legislation, or even to regard that which exists, and have essayed to purge the public schools of every shade of the offensive tinge. The constitution of Louisiana, however, provides that there shall be no distinction of color in the schools, and that they shall be open to all children of proper age. In New Orleans there are over seventy schools, about one-third of which are used almost exclusively by the whites, another third by the colored children, and the remainder by a mixture of all shades and colors, including Indians and even Chinese. Color is not alluded to in the law, nor has it had any practical influence upon the course of education. All classes have united in pleasing themselves as to the choice of the schools where they would educate their children. But the law forbids any teacher from rejecting any scholar who applies for admission, and makes it a misdemeanor to do so, and hence colored parents have the right to send their children to the schools where the purest Caucasian tint is alone supposed to prevail. They have not, however, done so, and have in general preferred the mixed or colored schools, which are said to be better taught and managed than the white. Yet it was reported that the white schools for girls were not altogether free from the obnoxious tinge, and a disorderly band of boys, apparently with no more discretion and commonsense than most of the White League leaders of New Orleans, went round from school to school to select and drive out the colored pupils. Rude, careless in dress, sometimes armed with sticks, and possibly knives, like their amiable exemplars, the young "regulators" broke into a number of the female schools, but soon found that they had entered upon a task that might have puzzled the keenest observer. It is insufficient to say that they were baffled at every step. They gave up their crusade in shame. The question of color was one that not even the sharpest inquiry could decide. Indignant parents, noted in the gay society of New Orleans, frowned at the insult that had been put upon their children; young maidens of the purest blood were frequently the objects of the mistaken ardor of the young crusaders, and were forced to prove that they were white. From one school the intruders were expelled by a courageous teacher and

EDUCATION IN SENEGAL—A SCHOOL FOR BOYS.—[See Article, "Color in the New Orleans Schools," on next page.]

Harper's Weekly, February 13, 1875, p. 146.

the friends of his pupils; and the latest crusade of the White Leaguers in the cause of unmixed schools has ended in general ridicule. It throws new light upon their extreme folly and violence.

Nowhere, indeed, would it be so difficult, so invidious, to establish a government founded upon a distinction of color as in New Orleans. Here all shades and tints are blended in harmonious confusion. The dark bronze of the creole inhabitants, the descendants of French and Spanish blood, is sometimes of a deeper shade than the traits of negro descent. Of these there are every degree and every hue. Even the pure Caucasian, white and red from the misty climate of England, grows tawny and atrabilious beneath the sun, the habits, and the dissipations of New Orleans; and there are persons of negro descent apparently so purely white as to surpass in this particular the emigrants from New York and Connecticut. Color has never, in fact, been a badge of division at New Orleans. There are families of African descent of great respectability and wealth, and some of the most valuable citizens have been of that just now unlucky race, so that when the young White Leaguers penetrated into the female schools to drive out their colored sisters, a series of laughable or painful incidents met them at every step of the inquiry. In one of the schools they ordered an intelligent little girl of about eleven years old to leave at once. Of her guilt there could be no mistake, they thought, for the offensive tinge mantled on her cheek.

"Do you know who I am?" said the young girl, with natural indignation.

"No," said the captain of the White League, "nor do I desire to know you. You are a negro, and must leave this school."

"A negro!" cried the young girl, with all the pride of color swelling at her heart. "I am the daughter of your leader. My name is Miss P———."

They made no further attempt to eject her, and retired in confusion. But they went to other schools and drove out children and even fair young women of sixteen, bathed in tears or glowing with indignation. Their threats and their lifted sticks made resistance impossible. Several Jewish maidens, touched with the olive tint of an Orient clime, it is said, were included among those who were expelled. In fact, the coarse manners and rude conduct of the leaders of the movement toward the gentler sex in their foolish crusade have left them few friends among the mothers of New Orleans. If there is anything particularly noticeable in this whole affair of the White League in Louisiana, both of the young and old, it is the total want of intelligence shown by its leaders. Such dull and half-stupefied intellects, such extreme mental weakness, could only have been brought into public notice by its extraordinary wickedness. The "platform" of the White League of New Orleans, which it has recently published to defend its useless cruelty and bloodshed, reads like the drivel of

EDUCATION IN SENEGAL—A SCHOOL FOR GIRLS.

Harper's Weekly, February 13, 1875, p. 147.

idiots. It speaks of "brutal violence stalking at midnight in the draggled shroud of judicial authority;" it paints the colored people in language that every one will naturally apply to its own acts alone. It would seem not unlikely that the sensible people of all colors in New Orleans must at last unite to throw off the yoke of stupid violence, and settle its affairs in a way that will be satisfactory to all colors and races, and this is to do justice to all.

Mr. Conway, who from 1868 to 1872 was the able State Superintendent of the Common Schools in Louisiana, and on whom fell the duty of first publishing the order throwing them open to children of all colors, relates that when he had issued it he received many letters threatening his life, commanding him to leave the State, and showing the bitter hostility of a part of the people against the new regulation. But he was not intimidated, and persevered. The law was obeyed. The number of white children attending the schools was soon larger than ever before; the irrational rage of their opponents subsided; all races and classes were mingled in the mixed schools, or divided, according to their tastes or nationality, as they chose; and it was not until the recent foolish outbreak of the White League, young and old, that any danger threatened the course of education in New Orleans. Even General Beauregard in 1873 lent his aid to the extinction of the race-quarrel, and a wiser spirit seemed about to animate the people. Since then a White League of twenty-five hundred men has assumed the control of New Orleans, and nearly completed the ruin of the divided city. . . .

In connection with the colored schools at New Orleans our artist has given sketches of schools for natives established by French Protestant missionaries in the heart of the tropics, at Senegal, in Western Africa. There the African race seems to be in a condition almost savage. Yet they are said to be very intelligent, and to learn quickly the common branches of knowledge. The teachers are whites, and French, but a kind of normal school, or the germs of one, have already been laid. In that hot climate, only sixteen degrees above the equator, where the inhabitants have long been corrupted by the slave-trade and slavery, it is yet found that knowledge is powerful, and that it expels cruelty, and teaches honesty even to the uncultivated negro. There the colored race is in a condition resembling that of our ancestors of the German forests, but they easily learn the elements of civilization. The rapid progress which the African has shown himself capable of making of late may well excite the whites to emulation. In humanity the negroes at the South seem often far in advance of their former masters.

This, indeed, is a trait which the early travelers in Africa unite in ascribing at least to the native women, and Mungo Park's touching story of the negro mother who, when every one else refused to give him a shelter from starvation and the wild beasts of the forest, took him into her hut and fed and nursed him, while her attendants sang to him a plaintive song of his parents and his home, is familiar to us from childhood, and has served to soften many a heart to the voice of charity. Our travelers relate that they never in all their distresses met with a cold look or an unkind word from the African women, that they fed them, when hungry, with their best food, and always gave from their own small stores with a generous smile. The love of the African mother for her child is said to be strong beyond expression; the child returns it with equal devotion; and the poor slaves who traveled in the coffle with Mungo Park, to become perhaps the parents of a race of slaves in South Carolina, in their deepest woes would remember their mothers with an undying affection. "Strike me, but spare my mother's memory," was the cry of the poor captives. This trait of tenderness and humanity has not been eradicated by generations of slavery in our own country.

During the rebellion it is admitted even by their former masters that the negroes protected their families while they were fighting the battles of slavery, and that scarcely an outrage occurred. "Since the close of the war," we are told by Senator J. B. Gordon, in his testimony before the Congressional committee (Ku-Klux Com., i. p. 53) "they" (the colored people) "have behaved so well that the remark is not uncommon in Georgia that no race on earth, relieved from servitude under such circumstances as they were, would have behaved so well." How they have been repaid in Georgia and other States for this humane and generous conduct may well be remembered with shame by those who have chiefly benefitted by it—the mothers and fathers of families at the South. And it would seem their duty to intervene at once to save the colored race from their oppressors.

Let all those who have been fed and tended by the negroes during the rebellion unite in a White League to soften and amend their lot, to educate, defend, and elevate them, and we need fear no war of races nor another Coushatta in Louisiana.

Eugene Lawrence

LAZZARONI

HARPER'S WEEKLY
February 20, 1875, p. 150

In the late Congressional debates the Democratic speakers spoke often of "the South," and the same phrase constantly occurs in the Democratic newspapers. It always means one thing. When we are told that "the South" is suffering, that "the South" is oppressed, that "the South" is a martyr, and patiently bears its wrongs, only a certain part of the people of the Southern States is meant—the white population. Before the war the Democratic slave Senators spoke of "the people of the South," and attempted to justify secession as a unanimous act of "the people." What people? The slave-holding class and their white dependents. In Louisiana, Mississippi, and South Carolina "the people" were not half of the population, and in all the other Southern States those who were not included in that term were a very large proportion of all. It is the spirit shown in these phrases, with the meaning attached to them, which is one of the reasons why the Democratic party can not safely be trusted with the government.

Mr. Cox is an amiable man, but a vehement partisan, and in the late debate upon the rules, smarting under the sarcasm of the Speaker that he had offered his resignation from the Committee on the Rules for dramatic effect, he exclaimed that the term was not applied to General Butler when he went into the Clerk's desk and spoke to the lazzaroni in the galleries. That is his honest feeling. It is the feeling of his party. The colored people are lazzaroni; they are beggars, idle, shiftless, indolent, ignorant, good for nothing. They need a good master and a strong hand. However this may be in fact, the contemptuous generalization is the natural view of those who have been bred to regard a large class of human beings as cattle, and yet suppose themselves to be democrats, or believers in the rights of man. There is nothing at once more ludicrous and revolting in history than the spectacle of the old slave aristocracy, with its Northern lackeys, sitting in the Capitol, calling itself a Democratic party, and stretching and straining the power of the government to extend and perpetuate human slavery. This is what Mr. Cox and Mr. Randall and their party associates were trying to do but yesterday, shouting themselves hoarse about "freedom" and the "land of liberty" and "the home of the oppressed." And to-day they wish to administer a government in which the men whom they dealt with as property, as swine, as things without rights, are their equal citizens. They struggle to show that they may be trusted. They "acquiesce," and by-gones are to be by-gones. But the cat transformed into a seeming lady leaped for the mouse on the floor, and to the "Democrat," as this country knows him, "the South" means a class, and the colored people are "lazzaroni" and niggers.

But the question of these people is the most important of all before us, and its treatment will be confided to one of the two parties at the next election. It is alleged that the Republicans have failed in dealing with it, and that the Democrats should be allowed to try. But the Southern situation, whatever it is, is largely due to the Democrats, as every man knows who seeks facts and not forms. And what is it that the Democrats propose to do? If the Republicans have failed, what is the Democratic policy? Of course echo answers, What? The New Hampshire Democratic Convention, the first of the year, says, "The people of each State to regulate their own domestic affairs in their own way, subject only to the Constitution of the United States." Certainly: so say we all; and that plank, therefore, in itself foreshows no policy, inasmuch as the essential question is, What does the Constitution authorize? The Democratic policy is to be inferred from the character and antecedents of the party and from the expressions of its leaders. These all foreshow passivity. The party would grant Jeff Davis's prayer at the beginning of the rebellion and leave "the South" alone. This would mean the reduction of the colored population to a pariah class, and then the question would be whether the general intelligence and good sense of the whites could be trusted to avoid what in the changed condition of the Southern States would always threaten them, an internecine war.

There is another consideration. The ruling political sentiment among the whites of the Southern States is not, in the American sense, republican. The Southern orators always appealed to Greece and Rome, because the democracy of Athens rested upon slavery, and the freemen were a very inconsiderable number of the population. But American republicanism asserts individual equal rights, and demands the suffrage as their guarantee. In this sense the sentiment of the white class in those States is anti-republican. It is a sentiment of caste. It calls itself democratic, as when it openly maintained slavery; but should it gain power in all the Southern States, they would be a unit of hostility to the American principle of equal rights. And this hostility would only be confirmed were the national government in Democratic hands. In the worst sense, therefore, a Democratic restoration would be a reaction. It could not hasten the settlement of questions that can not be evaded, and which are imminent. If the negro, as an equal citizen, in States where he is half the population, suggests the important question of the situation, ought the answer to be intrusted to his friends or to his enemies? It is not a conclusive reason for taking it from his friends that they have made mistakes, unless it can be shown—and it can not be—that those mistakes must necessarily be continued and maintained.

SIGNS OF THE TIMES

HARPER'S WEEKLY
February 27, 1875, p. 170

More than three months have passed since the autumn elections. It is time to consider what evidence there is from the acts and deeds of the Democratic party since the victory in its name at the polls that it is a party with a new spirit and purpose, and not the same old organization that sustained slavery, plunged the country into war, and resisted the guarantees of equal rights in reconstruction. The first thing that is observable is the fact of a very general alarm at the prospect of a Democratic victory in 1876, and an alarm which is not in the least relieved, but greatly increased, by what are seen to be mistakes of policy upon the part of the Republicans. The alarm springs from the perception that while the Democratic party insists upon conciliation, it aims only to conciliate the late disaffected class in the Southern States; that while it preaches the golden rule and brotherly love, it sees the negro hunted and harried without protest; and that it chiefly honors those who were known during the war as Copperheads or Confederates. The fact that they may be its ablest men is not reassuring in view of other facts.

The Democrats have returned one hundred and twelve ex-Confederate soldiers to Congress. The Southern States, with Maryland, Delaware, and Kentucky, elect one hundred and thirty-eight members. Of these all but twenty-six are from the late Confederate army. This fact alone disposes of the Democratic assertion that the Republican policy is one of hatred and revenge, and that the party rejects conciliation and insists upon tyranny. When the war ended it was left in absolute control of the government. It could have dictated any terms, and the country would have acquiesced. But not a drop of blood did it shed in vengeance. It established no system of confiscation. It merely made every man free and a citizen, and embodied his rights in the fundamental law. This was not very iniquitous. It was a magnanimity unparalleled in history; and had it been met in the same spirit by the Democratic party, the peace and happiness of the country would have been assured.

But that party, bent upon its own interest and not upon the welfare of the country, sought in every way to perplex reconstruction and bring it to naught. The recent story of the Southern States is familiar. If the Republicans have committed great errors, if frauds and military coercion can be urged against them, equal frauds, with political murder and terrorism—the Ku-Klux, the White League, massacres, and open bloody revolution in New Orleans last September—can be truthfully alleged against the Democratic party. That under absolute Democratic domination in the Southern States a Republican would be no safer now than an abolitionist before the war is asserted in a private letter printed in the New York *Times,* and in the state of Southern society such as a late number of the *Nation* described, nothing is more probable. Meanwhile, in other parts of the country the Democratic party sends typical Copperheads, like Mr. Eaton, of Connecticut, to the Senate, and supersedes Mr. Schurz, the apostle of the Democracy as it pretends to be, by a gentleman of whom nothing is known but that he was an uncompromising Confederate general. We do not recall such facts reproachfully. The more sincere were the convictions of these gentlemen, the less should they be intrusted with the control of the government.

Simultaneously events in Louisiana have elicited from the press and orators of the Democratic party a vituperation of the Administration, and especially of General Sheridan, the ferocious tone of which shows

THE VALENTINE.
"Golly, Mommy! I 'most wrote sumfin dat time."

Harper's Weekly, February 20, 1875, p. 149.

that it is the outburst of a long-pent hatred of that officer, who owes all his distinction to his illustrious service in the war. We have certainly not justified his "banditti" dispatch. But we have never doubted that it was the indignant outburst of an honest soldier plainly unfit for civil administration. But never by any Democratic newspaper or orator were the treachery of Davis and Lee and the wretched Twiggs, or the unspeakable infamies of Andersonville and Belle Isle, or the massacres of innocent men at New Orleans in 1865, at Coushatta, and at Colfax, so denounced as the dispatch of General Sheridan. Mr. Bayard, of Delaware, declared in the Senate that this gallant soldier, who has done more than the whole Democratic party to keep this republic free, was "unfit to breathe the free air of the republic," as reported in the papers, but, according to the *Record*, "Who shall say whether he is even fit to breathe the air of a republican government?" Who is Mr. Bayard, of Delaware, who thus denounces Sheridan and extols freedom? He is the Senator of a State in which he and his political friends maintained human slavery as long as they could, and a leader of the party whose sole policy for more than a generation was to make this a slave republic.

Meanwhile, in the session of Congress now closing, the conduct of the Democrats, who have a majority in the next House, shows the old tone—the tone which Democratic success would restore to the government. The episode of Mr. John Young Brown's performance, for which he received the censure of the House through the Speaker, and the earnest efforts of the Democratic party to shield him from that censure after his plain prevarication, show the fire of the old feeling still burning—a fire which is not likely to ripen concord and tranquillity should it by success extend and obtain the mastery. Where in all the orations and resolutions and leading articles of the Democratic party for the last ten years is found any word of hearty American satisfaction that the rebellion of slavery was defeated, and that every man within the national domain is free?

PERSONAL

HARPER'S WEEKLY
February 27, 1875, p. 171

A recent issue of the Nashua (New Hampshire) *Telegraph* gives the particulars of the alleged murder in Louisiana of two graduates of Dartmouth College. These two young men, it seems, were college-mates—one, A. B. Long, talented, strong-hearted, resolute, graduated in

1858; the other, Frank Perkins, was still in college when the rebellion broke out, and at the first call for troops enlisted in the Twentieth Regiment to fight for his country. He was the first soldier Dartmouth sent to the war. When the war closed, Long, having read law and been admitted to the bar, was in New Orleans, and for a time his friends at the North heard of him as justifying all the bright promise of his college days. Afterward he was appointed to a judicial position in the city. Still later came the news that he had committed suicide by cutting his throat in his own office. This report reached his old friend Perkins, who, by his ability and integrity, had come to be the agent of a line of steam-ships running between St. Louis and New Orleans, and he went to New Orleans to investigate the affair. There he learned that Long, instead of committing suicide, had been murdered by a band of White Leaguers, to whom he had given offense by some of his judicial decisions, that no attempt had been made to discover his murderers, and that the whole White League exulted over the fate of the noted radical. Perkins at once published a card offering $5000 for the arrest and conviction of the persons who had committed the crime; but within less than a week he was himself pursued, shot down, and his body flung into the street. Such is the story told by the New Hampshire paper of the fate of the two Dartmouth graduates.

SHILLY-SHALLY

HARPER'S WEEKLY
March 6, 1875, p. 190

The Senate has practically refused to seat Mr. Pinchback, and as Mr. Morton had pressed it upon the ground that it would be a final recognition of the Kellogg government, the action of the Senate is a refusal to recognize Mr. Kellogg as Governor of Louisiana. If he is not Governor, who is? If there is no Governor, there is no proper Executive, for the fraud which vitiates him vitiates his colleagues. There is, then, no lawful government in the State. But the United States are bound by the Constitution to guarantee a republican form of government to every State. They may, then, argue Mr. Stoughton and Mr. Edmunds, order an election in Louisiana. This is one of the methods proposed for settling the difficulty in that State. Another method is the compromise which is still pending as we write, and which could have no better negotiator than Mr. Wheeler, one of the ablest, most experienced, and purest men now in public life. But the time is short. The 4th of March is at hand, and it is very doubtful if any thing will be done by Congress.

If not, the situation will still be what it has been for two years, with this essential difference, that the action of the Senate in virtually rejecting Pinchback, after the prolonged and passionate partisan discussion of Louisiana affairs, is a distinct declaration that the Governor whom the President recognizes and sustains is not a lawful Governor. That is to say, the army is supporting a fraud in Louisiana, which is a very serious business. Of course neither the action of the Senate nor the reports of the committees imply or assert that M'Enery was elected, or that he ought to be recognized. The Carpenter committee were of opinion that the whole election was void for fraud. But should Congress, in the most cowardly manner, refuse to act, the President will be compelled to decide between the claimants, both of whom are branded as fraudulent by the Senate committee, and both of whom the Senate refuses to acknowledge. The President will, of course, sustain the Governor whom he has sustained, and the Republican party will pay the piper.

The Democrats and their allies insist that in any case the troops should be withdrawn. If they were, is there any doubt that the existing authorities would be overturned by domestic violence? And has the national government a moral right to do what in all human probability would produce a situation against which it is bound to protect the State? We ask the question to show the scope of the proposition that the State should be left alone. The "Conservative" policy for Louisiana is revolution—not endurance of a fraudulent election, such as New York endured in the return of Hoffman, and, if the White League party is really the majority, showing it at the polls at the next election, but a violent overthrow of the existing authorities by the White League, as in September, knowing, as we all know, that an armed and organized and unscrupulous minority like the White League could easily overbear even a large adverse majority mainly composed of colored voters.

If Congress should fail to deal with the Louisiana question, it will have betrayed its most pressing trust, and have gone far to show that the Republican party is unequal to the responsibility of the hour.

THE MINORITY LOUISIANA REPORT

HARPER'S WEEKLY
March 13, 1875, p. 210

We advise every voter to read carefully the report of the minority of the Louisiana committee. It is long, but a fair

"A REPUBLICAN FORM OF GOVERNMENT, AND NO DOMESTIC VIOLENCE."

BANDITTI. "The Northern and Southern Democratic Party *command you to suffer*, as it will place the United States Government in our hands. So what are you going to do about it?"

Harper's Weekly, March 6, 1875, p. 192.

statement of the situation could not be very short. That situation is lamentable, and indeed it could hardly be otherwise. Slavery had utterly poisoned the State, and the laws of 1865 and the massacres and corruptions since that time are but the anarchy to be expected. It is simply ridiculous to suppose that in the condition of society which exists in Louisiana there is not necessarily an intimidation of the colored vote. The knowledge of the organization of the White League throughout the State, an armed conspiracy of the late master class, is itself a permanent intimidation, as the Ku-Klux was. Nor have we seen it any where urged that the spirit which led to the Dostie massacre, and that of Coushatta and Colfax, has seriously changed, or that there is any reason that it should change. Does any intelligent man believe that the negro in Louisiana, or in many parts of the Southern States, votes, or can vote, with the same fearlessness that the Irishman votes in the Northern States? We do not say, indeed, that the fact justifies the suspension of the *habeas corpus,* but it is foolish to deny that it is a fact. That there was false registration, as the majority report asserts, is undoubtedly true, but that does not disprove intimidation. It is also true that it may have been the interest of the Conservatives not to frighten the colored vote at the last election; but the interest of the master to treat the slave well did not secure his good treatment, and it is the general feeling and practice, not the policy at a particular election, which determine intimidation.

Yet after making this powerful presentation of the sad condition of affairs, the report does not recommend the Force Bill, although Messrs. Hoar and Frye are supposed to favor it. This is a very important point, for in endeavoring to understand the Southern situation it must not be forgotten that a large part of the ill feeling toward the negro is due to the conviction that he is the power that sustains fraud in the State administration, and that with all this ill feeling and half anarchy there is no evidence of rebellious spirit against the United States. Undoubtedly there are fools and fanatics and men who worship "the lost cause," and undoubtedly also there is a general desire among the whites, who are Democrats, that their party should obtain control of the national government. But there is no object to be gained by the Southern whites in open rebellion or in warring upon the Union; and not only are they without an object, but they are absolutely without resources, and they would now find a terrible and desperate enemy at home.

The minority report says very truly that the two great parties in the Northern States are largely responsible for the situation in Louisiana. If the Democrats had sternly repelled all political complicity with murder, and the Republicans with fraud, the Southern difficulty would have been greatly lessened. It is evident, however, that the bayonet alone is no more a remedy for the trouble in the Southern States than it has been in Ireland; and if by the passage of the Force Bill the Republicans should proclaim the bayonet as their policy, they would soon discover how monstrous and fatal a blunder they had committed.

THE FOURTH OF JANUARY

HARPER'S WEEKLY
March 13, 1875, p. 211

We invite those Republicans who complained of our assertion that Governor Kellogg had no legal right to order the troops into the State-house in New Orleans on the 4th of January to observe that not only did the President not assert that right in his message, nor Senators Frelinghuysen and Conkling in the debate, but that Mr. Hoar's report, which took the most favorable view of the affair possible, does not affirm the legality of Governor Kellogg's action, saying of General De Trobriand that "whether the officer had warrant for his action or not," etc.—a phrase which shows that, as lawyers and good citizens, the committee knew that he had not. The plea that the Governor could command the troops under the requisition of September is not made by the President nor by the committee, both anxious to say all that could be said. Indeed, the plea could not be truthfully made, for on the 13th of December General Emory asked the precise question whether, in case of trouble, he was to regard the September instructions as in force, or "await the result of another application from Governor Kellogg to the President?" This question was evaded in Washington, although, if the September requisition was then considered in force, there is no conceivable reason that the Government should not have said so. Its refusal to take that ground in reply to the direct inquiry is conclusive evidence that it did not think the September requisition still valid. And it is for that reason that the President did not say that it was so in his message, but, on the contrary, said, expressly, "No orders nor suggestions were ever given to any military officer in that State upon that subject [the interference] prior to the occurrence."

Mr. Hoar's report states, what has been alleged in many speeches and articles, that the Governor's illegal action prevented a scene of blood. That is possible; but not only was there no need that the Republicans should remain in the room (for they should have withdrawn and organized elsewhere), but if military interference was necessary to save bloodshed, there was no reason that it should not have been made legal, as General Emory had especially, and with a view to the very event that occurred, requested. Moreover, it now appears by the statement of Mr. Hoar's report that the danger of trouble arose solely from the illegal action of the Returning Board, so that the final truth is, by consent of all parties, that Governor Kellogg illegally employed United States troops to enforce the illegal decision of the Returning Board. All the testimony, therefore, the message of the President, the speeches in the Senate, Republican as well as Democratic, the documents submitted to the Senate from the War Department, and the reports of both of the committees of investigation, fully justify what we said at the time, upon the statement of Governor Kellogg himself, that a great wrong had been committed in Louisiana with the apparent approval of the Administration. We shall be very glad if Mr. Wheeler's compromise be adopted and the irritation somewhat allayed.

THE LOUISIANA COMPROMISE

HARPER'S WEEKLY
March 20, 1875, p. 230

The opposition of the Democrats to the resolution recognizing Mr. Kellogg as Governor of Louisiana shows their desire to keep open the difficulties in that State. The resolution does not declare that Mr. Kellogg was elected beyond question, but that, upon the whole, and as the election of M'Enery is quite as much tainted with irregularity and fraud, the person who has held the office for two years, and whom the President has recognized, shall be declared Governor *de facto*. Whatever we may have thought, there seems to be no alternative. To order a new election raises constitutional and practical questions not easy to settle. To recognize M'Enery is to overturn the existing order without any more reason than that order offers for itself. To do nothing is to prolong the evident mischief of uncertainty. To abandon the State to violent revolution is a violation of plain duty. To recognize Mr. Kellogg and to condemn the Board of Registration is apparently the only practicable course.

The weightiest reason for adopting it is that it is the substance of the Wheeler compromise, which has been approved by a majority of the caucus of M'Enery's partisans. This fact should be conclusive with all good citizens, even if they have doubted whether, under any circumstances, the Kellogg Administration should be acknowledged. It is this approval also which makes the Democratic action in the House more significant. That action was determined by the protesting White League minority of the caucus. Thus once more the Democratic party in the Northern States, by the virtually unanimous action of its representatives in Congress, shows all its old servility to the extreme fire-eating Southern sentiment. And this is the point which all intelligent men should ponder. It is not Governor Tilden, and such Democrats as Mr. Thompson, who succeeds General Butler, who represent the spirit and tendency of the Democratic party. It is the White League, and gentlemen like Mr. John Young Brown, who show what may be expected of Democratic ascendency. It was not the Girondists, the mild, honorable, judicious men of the French Revolution, who controlled it, but Robespierre, Danton, and Marat.

This country has seen something of the Democratic party, when its cabinet in the White House was a nest of traitorous conspiracy; when its ex-President, Pierce, wrote that the blood of the war would flow in Northern streets; when its Mayor of New York, Fernando Wood, tried to smuggle arms to rebels; when its Governor of New York, Horatio Seymour, in the midst of war, denounced the Administration, and warned it that the doctrine of public necessity could be proclaimed by a mob as well as by a government—a direct incitement, under the circumstances, of the mob that nine days afterward ravaged the city: the country, we say, has seen something of the Democratic party, and knows that it has been always controlled by its most reckless and desperate element. And now it is with the White League, with the determination that in the unfortunate exigency in Louisiana no kind of compromise or settlement shall be made save that of a revolutionary overthrow of the existing authorities, that the Democrats in the House ally themselves. This they do when they are upon their good behavior, when their policy is to play the part of Christian conciliation. The tendency is irresistible; and when they control the House, the same servility to the violence of their party will betray itself still more.

The danger to the repose and prosperity of the country in the ascendency of a party whose most vital and resolute element is composed of those who most relentlessly hate the settlements of the war needs no emphasis. It is not necessary to suppose that they will take up arms. Should they acquire control of the government, that would be needless. We have but to ask the man of any party who sincerely wishes the honest observance of the amendments what he thinks the condition of the colored citizens would be in the Southern States with a Democratic Administration in Washington, coerced by the White League sentiment that rejects the Wheeler compromise and dictates the policy to which the Democratic members even now bow down.

ARKANSAS

HARPER'S WEEKLY
March 20, 1875, p. 230

On the 8th of February the President sent a message to the Senate upon affairs in Arkansas, in which he said, "I earnestly ask that Congress will take definite action in the matter to relieve the Executive from acting upon the questions which should be decided by the legislative branch of the government." He was himself of opinion that Brooks should be recognized as Governor, and that the new Constitution of the State should be set aside. The special committee, of which Judge Poland was chairman, simultaneously reported that there was no reason for interference, and on the 2d of March, two days before the end of the session, the House, by a vote of 149 to 80, passed this resolution:

> "*Resolved,* That the report of the special committee on Arkansas be accepted, and, in the judgment of this House, no interference with the existing government in that State by any department of the government of the United States is advisable."

THE DEMOCRATIC PARTY

HARPER'S WEEKLY
March 27, 1875, p. 254

The Democratic party has not advanced in public favor since the autumn elections. During the late session of Congress the two questions that most commanded public attention were those of the Louisiana Legislature and the Force Bill. But the most striking speech against the Louisiana policy was made by Senator Schurz, who refuses to join the Democratic party, and the significant opposition to the Force Bill was that of more than thirty of the most eminent Republicans, including almost every representative and influential leader in the House. And the Republican press throughout the country, in its most powerful representatives, from the Boston *Advertiser* to the Chicago *Tribune,* agreed with the Congressional leaders. The really significant opposition to the objectionable policy has thus proceeded from the Republican party, and has been so efficient that the winter has demonstrated that there is a sentiment in the party which is the guarantee to the country of the results which good citizens desire.

But the late session has shown something else which every honest and loyal American will ponder. It is that the most important Democratic leaders in both Houses of Congress are Southern men and late Confederates. The most marked Democratic member of the House of Representatives is Mr. Lamar, of Mississippi; and General Gordon, of Georgia, is equally prominent in the Senate. Both these gentlemen were summoned to New Hampshire by the Democratic State Committee to take part in the campaign. The tone of the speeches of each, whether in New Hampshire or in Congress, was equally cool, moderate, restrained, conciliatory, and both are able men. They represent admirably the kind of policy and of leadership which is most serviceable to their party. It is a party with the worst possible name, yet seeking the confidence and support of the country. It must therefore be immensely plausible, and by every means disarm and placate opposition. Mr. Nast's cartoon, representing Messrs. Fernando Wood and S. S. Cox trying to pull down and silence Mr. John Young Brown because the time had not come to roar and strike, exactly depicts the situation.

That Southern men should be the chief Democratic leaders, as they have been for a generation, is natural, and is due to the same causes. They were the chiefs of the party before the war because they had an object of vital importance, the protection of slavery, which the Northern Democrats had not. The Northern men wanted party power, but they had no absorbing purpose to which that power was essential, and the party was therefore managed by the Southern wing, and when the strain became too severe, the break occurred at the North, while the South remained intact and more united than ever. The situation is not changed. The Southern Democrats have a paramount object which the Northern wing has not, and can not have. The Southern Democrats wish the subordination of the colored population, but Tammany Hall wants plunder. The Southern men will therefore again be leaders, and the Northern wing followers. There is not a word said by a Democratic politician in Congress or in the Northern States which is not intended to please the Southern Democratic heart, and the Northern Democratic press has the same abject servility of tone toward the "gallant gentlemen" which is ludicrously familiar from the days when the same gentlemen took secession snuff, and the entire Democratic press sneezed from Maine to California.

When Mr. Lamar and General Gordon say that the spirit of the Southern States is misunderstood, and that they desire only friendly reunion and tranquil government, that nothing is further from their thoughts than any interference with equal rights or any disturbance of the settlements of the war, the reply is evident, that to secure such results a restoration of the Democratic party is not necessary, and the union of Messrs. Lamar and Gordon and their followers with the best Republican sentiment will surely obtain what they desire. While, as the Democratic party includes all those who do not wish friendly reunion, or tranquil government, or equal rights, or have respect for the settlements, its success certainly could not be accepted as a guarantee of those good things. The practical question for the country is, whether peace and equal rights and respect for the settlements are more likely to be maintained by those who have always favored them or by those who have not. A Republican defeat in 1876 would mean the restoration of the old Democratic party under the old Southern leadership, not with the intention of rebellion or disunion, but, as Andrew Johnson said in his *Herald* interview, of putting "the negro in his proper place." Whether such a policy would promote peace, friendly union, and the national millennium is for the Republicans of '56, of '60, and of '64 to consider, for it can not be carried out without their consent.

SOUTH CAROLINA

HARPER'S WEEKLY
April 10, 1875, p. 295

The administration of Governor Chamberlain in South Carolina is thus far justifying all that was prophesied by his friends and supporters. He has grappled with some of the most powerful of the corrupt cliques, and his frank and decisive veto of the Floating Debt Bill seems to be as bold as it is wise and honorable. In his efforts to expose and defeat frauds and to secure to his State, recently so sadly misgoverned, order, economy, and confidence, he deserves the most cordial support of honest men every where; and he seems to be receiving it, for the Charleston *News and Courier*, the leading Democratic paper in the State, warmly sustains him.

We state also, and with great pleasure, that the State Treasurer, Mr. Cardozo, who has been a constant and stanch friend of the Governor, and who was charged in the Legislature with fraud, has made a clear and conclusive explanation—so decisive, indeed, that the address asking for his removal has been emphatically rejected by both Houses of the Legislature. It is a result upon which the Treasurer is to be sincerely congratulated. Even the *News*, which can be suspected of no partisan sympathy with him, says: "The Treasury is in safe hands, and the result of the investigation into the operations of that important department must be an increased confidence in the ability and inflexibility of the Treasurer."

THE LOUISIANA RESOLUTION

HARPER'S WEEKLY
April 10, 1875, p. 295

The Senate, just before adjourning, passed the resolution approving the conduct of the President in defending Louisiana against civil violence in sustaining the government of Kellogg. It was, however, very careful not to say that he had been lawfully elected, but it recognized his *de facto* character, as the compromise in the House had already done. Neither did it approve Kellogg's action in January, of which the President, as he says, knew nothing until it was past, and which he did not justify, saying that it was questionable whether it was or was not lawful. The resolution in a very much more stringent form would have been more agreeable to Senator Morton, but the general sentiment of the Republicans was against him, and the moderate resolution was adopted. The debate furnished an opportunity for several Senators to present or to repeat their views upon the general subject. But the Senate merely expressed the universal judgment that was passed upon the conduct of the President last September, when the White League rose in arms in New Orleans. To have done nothing, to have acquiesced, as the League, through its Lieutenant-Governor Penn, demanded, would have been to recognize violent revolution as a legitimate method of changing the government in a State, notwithstanding the Constitution makes it the duty of the United States to protect the States against domestic violence.

That there was no evidence of the lawful election of Mr. Kellogg the Senate committee two years ago and the President himself had acknowledged. But neither was there evidence that his opponent had been lawfully elected. These facts, however, did not affect the duty of the President, in the absence of Congress, to defend the State against domestic violence. And there can be no question that the armed and bloody action of the White League was domestic violence. The Senate says that the President did his duty, and those who thought so last September have probably not changed their opinion.

It is, however, to be presumed that the Democrats, who voted solidly against the resolution, would have approved a different course. It must, from their votes and speeches, be assumed that had there been a Democratic President and the difficulty had arisen, there would have been total inaction upon the part of the Government, and an acquiescence in the revolution. It is no answer to say that had there been a Democratic President there would have been no trouble. The question is not what would have been done in a case that did not arise, but in one that did. There was domestic violence in Louisiana, the Governor *de facto*, the officer who had discharged the duties of the office for two years, called upon the President, and there was armed violence in the streets. That was the case. The President, under the Constitution, interfered. The Republican Senate said that he did his duty. The Democrats deny it. It is another illustration—and the Democrats are furnishing them abundantly—of the policy that may be expected should the Democratic party return to power.

PERSONAL

HARPER'S WEEKLY
April 17, 1875, p. 315

Beverly Nash is a colored statesman who pervades the Legislature of South Carolina, and a person of influence

THE GOOD (PURE WHITE) SHEPHERD.

It was known here Sunday morning that the Civil Rights Bill had passed both Houses of Congress, and needed only the signature of the President to become a law. On that very morning, in Manchester, just across the river from Richmond, a negro woman marched into the Meade Memorial Episcopal Church, just before the services began, and took a front seat beside a lady. The lady at once rose, went into the vestry-room, and informed the rector, Rev. Mr. SAMMS. Mr. SAMMS considered the situation for a few moments, and then determined that, as the easiest way out of the difficulty was perhaps the best way, he would dismiss the congregation without having any services, which he did promptly.—*New York Times.*

Harper's Weekly, April 3, 1875, p. 277.

in that body. He was formerly a slave of William C. Preston; afterward boot-black in a hotel. "He handles them all," said an enthusiastic admirer of the sable Senator, "and the lawyers have learned to let him alone. They know more of the law and some other things than he does, but he studies them all up and then comes down on them with a good story or an anecdote, and you better believe he carries the audience right along with him." The other day, in the South Carolina Senate, Nash got off a joke on the colored State Tresurer, Cardozo. The Legislature have been investigating the accounts of Cardozo with a view to impeachment, and

THE JUBILEE, 1875.
"Hi, Massa Peter, you can't objec' to open de gates fo' me now."
N. B. Pure White Churches please take notice.

Harper's Weekly, April 3, 1875, p. 288.

the friends of the treasurer stigmatized the investigators as "Chadbands," in derision of their professed desire to get at facts. Senator Nash arose, and producing a twenty-five-cent copy of Bleak House, read the following description of Mr. Chadband: "Mr. Chadband is a large, yellow man, with a fat smile, and a general appearance of having a good deal of train-oil in his system." The point of the joke is that Cardozo is himself a large, oily-looking man, of the color of a new saddle, with a fat smile, and a manner as oleaginous as his person. The audience saw the point at once, and the resolution was agreed to.

THE LOUISIANA REPORT, BY MESSRS. HOAR, WHEELER, AND FRYE

HARPER'S WEEKLY
April 17, 1875, p. 316

Danger of the Condition of Affairs
In our judgment, this condition of things is fraught with the greatest peril to the whole country. That the people of any State should be unwilling or unable to determine by peaceful and legal means the result of their election, and that the President should be compelled to interpose the military force of the government to prevent civil war, is itself a terrible misfortune....

Masters and Slaves
"The people of the States which engaged in the rebellion were composed in large part of two classes—a dominant race of slave-holders and those who approved of slavery, and a subject race of slaves. Each of these classes possessed the virtues and the faults which might be expected from its condition. The dominant class were domineering, impetuous, impatient of restraint, unwilling to submit to any government which they did not themselves control easily, and moved to fierce anger. They never had learned to respect human rights as such, or to tolerate the expression of opinions which differed from their own, or to see dignity in manhood beyond their own class. It was such a people that engaged in the rebellion.... They had submitted to the constitutional amendments, which rendered their former slaves their equal in all political rights, not because they would, but because they must. The passions which led to the war and the passions which the war excited were left untamed and unchecked except so far as their exhibition was restrained by the arm of power. On the other hand, the negro was, in his ordinary condition, gentle, patient, docile, affectionate, and grateful. His confidence was easily won. The fear of the whites and habits of submission had been implanted in him by ages of slavery. The virtues of frugality, of honesty, of respect for justice either in private or public concerns, had never been exhibited toward him by his superiors, and he was not likely to be an example of them in himself, or to be very exacting in demanding them in those whom he regarded as his friends...."

Laws of Labor
"After the war closed, the whites of Louisiana were permitted to elect a Legislature, which met during the years 1865–66–67. They enacted a series of laws which must have been designed to restore the negro to a state of political servitude. Statute 1865, chapter 10, provided that, under penalty of fine and imprisonment, no person shall carry fire-arms on to the premises or plantation of any citizen without the consent of the owner, thus depriving the great mass of the colored laborers of the State of the right to keep and bear arms, securely prized and guarded by his white employer. Statute 1865, chapter 11, punishes by fine and imprisonment the entry upon any plantation without the permission of the owner, thus preventing any person from seeking any interview with the negro for the purpose of giving political or other information except such as his master should approve. Statute 1865, chapter 12, authorizes any justice of the peace, on complaint that any person is a vagrant, on summary process to require such person to give bond for his good behavior and future industry for the period of one year. On failing to give such bond, the justice shall issue his warrant to the sheriff, and hire out such person for the term of twelve months, under such regulations as may be made by the municipal authorities: provided that if the accused be a person who has abandoned his employer before his

REQUIRED TO LIVE UNDER A NEW ORDER OF THINGS.

F. F., Esq. "During Slavery, I ruled supreme; while Know-Nothingism lasted, I killed Foreigners; in the War, I killed Yankees; and since then, both White and Black Niggers; but now you are taking away all my Privileges, what shall I do?"

"......If the history of the South for these ten years could be written in all its horrible details, it would present one of the blackest pages in the peaceful annals of the civilized world...... Men of the South, there is a road to peace, and there is but one road. It is the peaceful solution of all our difficulties. Whether you pursue it or not is a matter of your own free choice. It is a highway on which if you do but walk, you will have speedy and enduring peace and unexampled prosperity. Men of all parties can commend it, for it is obstructed by no constitutional doubts, but is paved with the Federal compact. It is this: Strip the hideous masks from your outlaw Ku-Klux; disband your White Leagues; visit swift and condign punishment on your unarrested and untried felons; enforce State and United States laws with a firm hand; give to human life security, and to property protection; recognize the equality of all men before the law, and their right to the fullest guardianship; put out the fires of your burning churches and school-houses; make the freedom of the ballot so secure that voters shall not be intimidated; let free speech reign; let ostracism be unknown; renew your allegiance to the government; extend a generous welcome to Northern labor and Northern capital; abandon all hope of the lost cause—in a word, accept the situation in good faith, and you will have a peace that will reign supreme. Do this, and your barren fields will stir with new life, your desolate streets will echo with the hum of returning industry, your spacious harbors will choke with the tide of commerce—do this, and the whole South will spring from her baptism of blood into the fullness of a new life, redeemed and regenerated forever. All hail that auspicious day!"

HON. JULIUS C. BURROWS, of Michigan.

Harper's Weekly, April 17, 1875, p. 316.

contract expires, the preference shall be given to such employer of hiring the accused—thus putting it into the power of any local magistrate on summary process to remand the laborer to a condition of practical slavery. Statute 1865, chapter 16, enacts that any person who shall persuade or entice away, feed, harbor, or secrete any person who leaves his employer without permission, shall be subject to a fine of not more than $500, or imprisonment of not more than twelve months, or both. Thus no laborer can leave his employer without permission without becoming an outcast, to whom food and shelter must be denied by all mankind. . . .

Conclusions

"Charges of corruption are made by the Conservatives against Republican officials without the slightest discrimination. They assume that the acceptance of office is a badge of fraud. No matter how high the position hitherto occupied socially, how spotless the reputation, the moment of acceptance of office witnesses an entire reverse. The gentleman suddenly becomes a blackguard, the honest man a thief. Four or five cases of defalcation were clearly shown to be mistakes during our session. That there was great wrong and corruption, that much bad legislation was enacted, that grievous monopolies were created, during Governor Warmoth's term of office, is undeniable. That the Democrats purchased him at the earliest possible moment for the purpose of converting to their own use his powers of corruption, his skill and cunning in manipulating the machinery of election, was asserted by some witnesses of their own; that there has been a decided improvement under Governor Kellogg all admit. . . .

"The President and Congress are bound to recognize, and if need be to support, the true government of Louisiana against all usurpers, and the American people will abandon their rights and flinch from the performance of their duties when they leave questions to be settled either by the mob or the assassin. . . .The white who kills a negro goes unpunished; a fearful vengeance overtakes the negro who snaps a cap at a white man. In parish after parish the whites turn out public officers whom they dislike by force, and no punishment follows: the assembling of a body of negroes at the command of the sheriff to maintain his lawful authority is followed by the Colfax massacre. . . .

"In a republic you can not long or permanently check their manifestation by the exercise of national power. Until the great body of the white people of Louisiana shall learn to obey the law, to submit to the Constitution, to respect labor, to base their institutions on liberty, equality, and justice, they can enjoy neither prosperity nor peace.

"The history of their State must be made up of exhibitions of tumult, violence, and crime, alternating with extraordinary exertions of national authority to repress them. . . . That people should understand that all the authority lodged in the general government to preserve republican government and to protect the rights of all its citizens will be kindly but fearlessly and steadily exerted, and that no party in this country will accept the alliance of men who are seeking power by such methods as we have been compelled to describe. Unless this can be done, the free institutions of the whole United States will not long survive the destruction of those in the South. . . ."

THE UNION AND THE STATES

HARPER'S WEEKLY
April 24, 1875, p. 334

The Methodist *Advocate*, of Atlanta, Georgia, in a long and careful article upon the situation in the Southern States, says:

"To leave the States to manage their own affairs, without restriction or interference from the central power, is simply to put them mostly into the hands of those who were and now are bitter and persistent enemies of the government, of national union, and of universal freedom and education."

Again it says that when certain papers urge

"That Republicans in the South, being in the majority, ought and must take care of themselves, their advice implies one of two things, viz., that they must submit to the tyranny of the cruel minority, steeped in secession, covered with blood, and ever seeking to destroy the nation, or to adopt such measures for mutual protection as will inevitably lead to violence and civil war. Submission to countless wrongs, or retaliation, are the only alternatives they have when thus left to themselves. They must accept the one or adopt the other."

The rest of the article is devoted to detailed illustration of the conclusions here stated, the whole showing that popular republican government is impracticable in the Southern States. There is, says the *Advocate*, little respect for law, or regard for the will of the numerical majority. "The slave-holding, aristocratic element has always governed here absolutely" in behalf of its own interest. The *Advocate*'s conclusion is that the only way to secure government by the people in the Southern States is to defend the majority against the minority, the loyal against the disloyal, the peaceful against the "banditti," by the power of the national government.

The *Advocate* assumes that the alternative is absolute State sovereignty or equally absolute centralization. But it is not so. Our Republican system is composite, not simple. Every citizen is subject to two governments, and the interference of the higher with the lower is specifically provided for; the occasion and the methods are all designated and arranged. But practical government is largely a matter of experience, and it is demonstrated—it is not open to discussion—that the result of a constant and familiar forcible supervision of the lower government by the higher is the destruction of that self-reliance and spirit of independence which are indispensable to successful popular republican government. We certainly do not deny much of the statement of the *Advocate*. We have no doubt of the ignorance among the white "banditti;" their degradation; their contempt of equal rights, of laws, of majorities; their hatred and jealousy of the negro, and their determination to hold him in subjection. Nor do we question the ignorance, timidity, and venality—the natural fruit of the cruel injustice of slavery—among many of the negroes themselves. The mistake of the *Advocate* is in the supposition that an army is a good remedy for such difficulties. "You are to be hanged," said the judge to the horse-thief, "not because you stole a horse, but that horses may not be stolen." Our problem is not how to protect a negro or a white man in his rights, but how free institutions, which are the guarantee of all rights, are best to be maintained.

The *Advocate*'s statement doubtless expresses a quite general feeling. But it involves the very grave

CIVIL RIGHTS. (?)
Waiting for a Five-Hundred-Dollar Kick.

Harper's Weekly, April 17, 1875, p. 328.

consideration that in a very large part of the country the American principle of government has failed. The American principle is that of government by the lawful majority. But if the majority must be permanently protected from the minority by another power, the whole system is brought into contempt. The vote was given to the emancipated class that it might defend itself. But if the result be what the *Advocate* asserts, it would be much better promptly to reduce the States in question to Territories than to hold them under the form of self-governing States, but really as military dependencies of the Union. There is, indeed, no constitutional authority to change the status of States, but that authority should be assumed rather than that the very substance of a popular government should be eaten out in the way that the *Advocate* proposes.

The *Advocate* says that the object of the white intimidation of the colored vote is Democratic control of the national government. We have no doubt of it. But will the *Advocate* consider that the policy which it favors, of incessant and direct national control of the States, has so alarmed the republican instinct of the most intelligent part of the country that the chances of Democratic success have been visibly increased? And if the disaster should occur, and that party come into power, the *Advocate* and its friends will have taught it to use all that power against the negro and in favor of the White League, and will have closed their own mouths against all protest. The first necessity of the Southern situation is not, indeed, to leave the amendments practically void and inoperative, and to tip the wink to the White League, with the Democrats, that it may do as it will; but it is certainly not the least pressing duty of all sincere friends of the colored race to teach them self-depend-

ence and the essential character of the government under which they are citizens and voters. If, as the *Advocate* virtually says, the Southern States are not fit for republican government, we deplore the fact; but if they are fit, they can dispose of the "bullying, blustering minority" as New York disposed of Tweed and his Ring. Our system contemplates the interference of the national government only upon extraordinary emergencies. If the actual emergency be constant, it is either because there is really a state of war, for which the Constitution provides, or because a republican government in the American sense is impossible.

LETTER FROM THE REV. MR. SAMS

HARPER'S WEEKLY
April 24, 1875, p. 335

We are glad to be assured of the falsity of the report referred to in the following letter from the Rev. Mr. Sams, rector of the Meade Memorial Episcopal Church in Manchester, Virginia. We very cheerfully publish Mr. Sams's explicit contradiction, and regret that we were led, by the correspondence in the New York *Times,* into doing him and his church an injustice:

"Manchester, Virginia, *April* 6, 1875.
"Dear Sir,—Your *Weekly* of the 3d of April contained a caricature which was based on a statement that appeared in the New York *Times* reflecting on myself as rector of the Meade Memorial Church of this place. That statement was *purely imaginary.* The colored person who entered my church on the occasion *remained to the very close of the exercises.* Her presence caused not the *least interruption.* If my church was large enough, as many colored persons would be welcome as might wish to worship with us. I am continually receiving through the Post-office copies of your caricature. For the sake of truth, and as a matter of justice to myself, you ought to undo, as far as you can, the false impression produced by your caricature. Probably thousands read *Harper's Weekly* who read nothing else. I ask you to make the correction as early as possible, and to be kind enough to send me one of the issues in which you make it.
"Most respectfully, J. Julius Sams,
"Rector Meade Memorial Church."

"TO THINE OWN SELF BE TRUE."

"THESE FEW PRECEPTS IN THY MEMORY."

Beware of entrance to a quarrel: but, being in,
Bear it that the opposer may beware of thee.
Give every man thine ear, but few thy voice:
Take each man's censure, but reserve thy judgment.

Costly thy habit as thy purse can buy,
But not express'd in fancy; rich, not gaudy:
For the apparel oft proclaims the man.
*   *   *   *

This above all,—To thine own self be true;
And it must follow, as the night the day,
Thou canst not then be false to any man.
SHAKSPEARE.

Harper's Weekly, April 24, 1875, p. 336.

GEN. BUTLER ON THE CIVIL RIGHTS BILL

HARPER'S WEEKLY
April 24, 1875, p. 336

Washington, *March* 18, 1875

Sir,—I have the pleasure to acknowledge receipt of yours of the 14th, containing expressions of appreciation of my efforts in behalf of the Civil Rights Bill, for which accept my thanks. You further ask, "Will you be kind enough to inform me if colored men are entitled to the privileges of saloons and barber shops under its provisions?"

An Unenvied Privilege

To this I answer: I understand by "saloons" you mean drinking saloons, and am happy to say that the Civil Rights Bill does not give any right to a colored man to go into a drinking saloon without the leave of the proprietor, and am very glad that it does not. I am willing to concede, as a friend to the colored man, that the white race may have at least this one superior privilege to the colored man, that they can drink in bar-rooms and saloons, and I never shall do any thing to interfere with the exercise of that high and distinctive privilege. I would not advocate a bill which should give that right to the colored man. If I were to vote for any bill on this subject at all, it would be one to keep the colored man out of the drinking saloons; and I hope no bar-keeper will ever let a colored man have a glass of liquor at any bar open for drinking. Indeed, I should be glad, whenever a colored man should go into a drinking saloon for the purpose of drinking at the bar, if somebody would at once take him and put him out, doing him as little injury as possible. He could do the colored man no greater kindness.

Privacy of a Barber Shop

As to the other branch of your question, in reference to barber shops, let me say that the trade of a barber is like any other trade, to be carried on by the man who is engaged in it at his own will and pleasure, and the Civil Rights Bill has nothing to do, and was intended to have nothing to do, with its exercise. A barber has a right to shave whom he pleases as much as a jeweler has a right to repair a watch for whom he pleases, or a blacksmith to shoe such colored horses as he pleases. In other words, these are not public employments, but private business, in which the law does not interfere.

The Colored Man's Rights at Common Law

From time immemorial all men have had equal rights at the common law in places of public amusement, in public conveyances, and in inns or licensed taverns, because all such business was for the public,

A PRIVILEGE?

WIFE. "I wish *you* were not allowed in here."

Harper's Weekly, April 24, 1875, p. 336.

under special privileges granted by the government. The theatre and like public amusements were licensed by the public authorities and protected by the police. The public conveyances used the king's highway. The public inn had the special privilege of a lien or claim upon the baggage or other property of any traveler using it for his keep; and if any man was refused, while behaving himself well and paying his fare, a seat in any place of public amusement, or carriage by public conveyance, or shelter in a public inn, he had at common law a right of action against the party so refusing. The Civil Rights Bill only confirms these rights of all citizens to the colored man in consideration of the prejudice against him and an attempt in certain parts of the country to interfere with the exercise of those common-law rights, and has enacted a penalty as a means of enforcing the right in his behalf in consideration of his helpless and dependent condition. The Civil Rights Bill has not altered the colored man's rights at all from what they were before under the common law applicable to nearly every State in the Union. It has only given him a greater power to enforce that right to meet the exigency of combined effort to deprive colored citizens of it; and all idea that the Civil Rights Bill allows the colored man to force himself into any man's shop, or into any man's private house, or into any eating-house, boarding-house, or establishment other than those I have named, is simply an exhibition of ignorance as well as, in some cases, of insufferable prejudice and malignity. And while I would sustain any colored man in firmly and properly insisting upon his rights under the Civil Rights Bill, which were his at common law, as they were the right of every citizen, yet I should oppose to the utmost of my power any attempt on the part of the colored men to use the Civil Rights Bill as a pretense to interfere with the private business of private parties. It is beneath the dignity of any colored man so to do, and all acts such as shutting him out from drinking saloons may be well left to the ignorant and generally vicious men who keep them, as a badge of their superiority to the colored race. I have the honor to be, etc.,

Benjamin F. Butler.

Robert Harlan, Esq., Cincinnati, Ohio.

CIVIL RIGHTS

HARPER'S WEEKLY.
July 24, 1875, p. 595

The following story, which we find in the Savannah *Morning News,* is illustrative of a spirit which is not confined to the State of Georgia, and to which it hardly seems worth while to commit the enforcement of the amendments. We do not expect by force of law to

SOUTHERN SKETCHES—A GENTLEMAN OF COLOR.—From the Water-color Painting by T. W. Wood.—[See Page 629.]

Harper's Weekly, July 31, 1875, p. 631.

promote fraternity among men nor to make people like each other. But this is a kind of outrage of personal rights for which in this part of the country the law supplies a remedy and redress. Possibly it does in Georgia. But we apprehend that the victim in this case would learn something of the law's delay should he appeal to it. We do not suppose that such conduct as is here described is universal, or that the persons who are guilty of it are recognized as "gentlemen" by those who properly bear that name in Georgia and elsewhere. Nevertheless, it is the sign of a wide-spread feeling that is not as sternly rebuked as it should be in the part of the

SOUTHERN SKETCHES—A POOR WHITE.—From the Water-color Painting by T. W. Wood.—[See Page 629.]

Harper's Weekly, July 31, 1875, p. 630.

country where it chiefly manifests itself; and what we do say and expect is that the people of the United States will understand that in this kind of conduct there is neither peace nor conciliation, and that they will take good care to cast their votes in a way that will not encourage such "gentlemen" as figure in this story.

"If you have ever been of the opinion that the people along the line of the Central road didn't know how to put down any manifestation of civil rights, you were very much mistaken. The Irwinton *Southerner* gives an example. On Thursday morning last a negro,

"THE REPUBLIC IN DANGER."

SPRING CHICKEN (*cackling to Centennial Eagle*). "Dear Mr. Eagle, I am seriously alarmed for your safety. Your *Constitution* is in danger of breaking down; and even if that Blackbird does not destroy you, I am afraid that my Father on the opposite Cliff will peck you to pieces. You had better take refuge under the Shelter of My Wing."

Harper's Weekly, May 1, 1875, p. 356.

dressed *à la mode*, presented himself at the door of the passenger coach of the up train, at Millen, conducted by Mr. Marlow, one of the best conductors in the State, and demanded admission. Mr. Marlow informed him that a splendid coach forward for persons of color would receive him. He demurred, and said that he had paid first-class fare, and would put up with nothing less than a seat with the white folks. Mr. Marlow, seeing that the negro's object was to bring a suit under the Civil Rights Law against the company, admitted him, and

A TOUGH CASE OF CIVIL RIGHTS.

Harper's Weekly, August 7, 1875, p. 648.

he took his seat. There were a few ladies and half a dozen gentlemen in the car when he entered. In a few minutes the gentlemen simultaneously took seats around the civil righter, and commenced chewing tobacco and spitting upon him. He applied to Mr. Marlow for protection, who informed him that he had as much as he could do to protect himself. Sullenly and silently he bore the indignity until his face, coat, vest, and pants were discolored by the saliva which was squirted upon him from the mouths of his tormentors. Finally one of them arose, and proceeding to the water-cooler, filled his capacious mouth with a half gallon of the fluid, and marching slowly and solemnly in front of the negro, he, with the force of a fire-engine, squirted it into the face and bosom of the man and brother. This was more than he could bear, and he left for the car set apart for people of his color. There was scarcely a word uttered all the time, and it was a cool and effective way to defeat the Civil Rights Bill."

SOUTHERN SKETCHES

HARPER'S WEEKLY
July 31, 1875, p. 629

On our opening pages we give engravings from two characteristic water-color paintings by Mr. T. W. Wood, which attracted much attention in the Water-color Exhibition at the New York Academy of Design last winter. Mr. Wood is a realist in art. He slights nothing, but paints the accessories in his pictures with all the care bestowed upon the principal object. The picture of the "Poor White" is an excellent specimen of his manner of working. If he has not painted every wisp in the haymow, every thread in the man's clothing, and every crack and knot-hole in the beams and boards, he gives the impression that he has done so. This almost photographic minuteness of finish finds many admirers.

Mr. Wood generally chooses subjects from common life, preferring also the country to the city, perhaps as affording more picturesque material of the kind that pleases his fancy. The two pictures we engrave present a strange and almost pathetic contrast—the "Poor White" of the South, a type of humanity which must disappear with the advance of education and industry, and the smart "Gentleman of Color" stepping gayly along the street, perfectly satisfied with himself and the world in general.

THE GEORGIA "NEGRO PLOT."

HARPER'S WEEKLY
September 11, 1875, p. 734

The character of the colored race in this country is so well established as gentle, inoffensive, and much-enduring, that the report of a frightful and bloody plot of universal extermination of the whites in the Southern States does not seriously startle the public mind. Indeed, it is no longer politically profitable even for the bitterest opponents of emancipation and the most positive advocates of negro inferiority to cite every instance of outbreak or trouble as final proof of the frightful lapse toward barbarism due to enfranchisement. The negroes have not only been more inhumanly degraded and oppressed, they have been also more contemptuously mistrusted, than any class or race. Yet their history in this country is not such as should cause them any shame—whatever it may cause the whites—and day by day they are justifying the faith and hope of the few who have sought to do them justice, not from political but from moral reasons. While they were slaves, more wretched

THE COLORED CREEDMOOR—"Jist watch de Captin of dis Team knock de Bull's-Eye Black and Blue!"

Harper's Weekly, August 28, 1875, p. 697.

than any slaves save those of Dahomey, victims of a slavery more monstrous than any other, because maintained by a nation of such enormous pretension as the American, they were docile and harmless. When there were rumors and apprehensions of insurrection, the ghastly terrors were not in the fact, but in the consciences of the master class. They knew, with Jefferson, that God has no attribute that could take sides with the slave-holder, and hence the unspeakable dread when they thought that their victims were about to settle the long-accumulated arrears of vengeance. But there was never any serious insurrection; and even had John Brown succeeded in establishing himself in the Southern mountains, the slaves would not have gathered to his camp.

The late report of the Georgia insurrection was read with universal incredulity. No paper—not even those which ten years ago represented the massacre of the blacks at New Orleans as a negro riot—cared to parade head-lines of horror. There was general distrust that it was probably a political trick, and a profound conviction that if there was any foundation whatever for the rumor, the story as told was a gross exaggeration. There was also a very disagreeable feeling that, as such rumors and real or affected panics have always been improved by the whites for wholesale slaughter of the negroes, there might be similar consequences now. The Governor authorized the use of the local militia only. Mr. Rivers, a South Carolina colored politician, was mentioned in a newspaper as a leader in the conspiracy. But he wrote instantly to the paper that published the slander, conclusively denying every statement, and saying what many white men in his section will do well to ponder: "I desire to set myself aright as a man and law-abiding citizen—that no encouragement of violence has ever been advised by me, and that all people, white or black, must obey the law of the land." The truth seems to be that under an old law an educational poll-tax is levied in Georgia, and that the vote of any man who has not paid all his taxes may be successfully challenged. This payment the negroes in certain counties have very generally neglected until the arrears of the tax, with the interest, have reached a sum so large for them that they are virtually disfranchised, and consequently in many parts of the State the minority governs. It was with some vague idea of remedying this evil that a queer call for a convention was issued; and some kind of scrawl, purporting to be a call, by order of Rivers, to a general massacre of the whites, was said to have been found. Out of this grew the whole story. It was a causeless fright. But it has had the good effect of showing that now that the negroes are free, every rumor of their rising does not throw the white population into a murderous panic. And this incident is but another illustration of the truth that nothing in the character or history of the colored race in this country, as they have been heretofore

A SECRET MEETING IN THE SOUTH.
Look out for another Insurrection.

Harper's Weekly, October 2, 1875, p. 808.

known, justifies the suspicion of conspiracy for massacre or mischief, or the least disposition to retort in kind for the fearful wrongs of slavery and the Ku-Klux.

FREDERICK DOUGLASS'S VIEW

HARPER'S WEEKLY
October 2, 1875, p. 795

Mr. Frederick Douglass was recently interviewed, and, according to a report in the Washington *National Republican,* he said:

"My idea is that but little advice is needed to the colored people. They are a docile and peace-loving race. They committed no outrages upon the hearths and homes of their late masters when the war gave them a chance to do it with impunity. Human nature is not changed in an instant. They are the same peace-loving people to-day that they were during the war, and it would be a terrible responsibility for any man to counsel violence on their part; nevertheless, they are men, and being men, they can not and ought not to be expected to submit tamely to violence and murder. My own impression is that when the Government will not or can not protect the black man, he ought to and will finally try to protect himself. There are scoundrels, midnight murderers, who have respect for no moral consideration. They are scarcely to be called human. They are wolves and tigers in human form, and to slaughter one of them is no more a crime than to slay a real tiger when his fangs are in one's flesh. My experience as a slave impressed upon me this lesson—that he is whipped oftenest who is whipped easiest, and that as long as the negro will tamely submit to be killed unresistingly there will be blood-thirsty cowards enough in the South to kill him. If the negroes must die at the South, my advice to them is to sell their lives as dearly as possible. Let it be seen by those cowardly mobocrats that in attempting to slaughter black men they invite the knife to their own throats and fire and rapine to their own hearth-stones, and they will cease."

In saying this Mr. Douglass says only what every self-respecting white man would say of his own race, that when the Government can not or will not protect them, they will and should protect themselves. There is no more reason that the colored people of any county in Mississippi or Georgia should acquiesce in perpetual terror and harrying because of their color than that the white citizens of Wayne or Chautauqua County in New York should do the same thing. Mr. Douglass has the profoundest contempt for the "rose-colored statements and gushing assurances" of the old Southern aristocracy and of Northern correspondents that the ex-slave-holding sentiment has accepted the situation. He holds such a result to be impossible within so short a time, and that many years of protection by the Government will be indispensable before the colored people will acquire the manly independence becoming freemen.

The opinion of Frederick Douglass upon such a question is entitled to very great consideration and respect. He alone in the country speaks with most authority for those who are most concerned. His voice is that of the intelligent colored race. More than any other man he is their representative, and what he says is thoughtful and reasonable. His conclusion—and it must be that of all sagacious men—is that the party of the old slave-drivers and their abettors should not be trusted with the defense of the new rights of the late slaves, but that that defense should remain with those who have always shown their fidelity to equal rights. This fidelity, while it should be, as the New York Republican platform demands, just, should be also generous and forbearing, that is to say, it should regard all the circumstances. It certainly does not require such representatives as Marshal Packard and Collector Casey and others, who have had regard solely to party interests. For nothing is plainer than that if the local national officers in the Southern States had been as truly wise and patriotic as they have been partisan, continued Republican ascendency would be less imperiled than it is. The party has been wounded by friends rather than by enemies. Yet every sign shows that its better sentiment, conscious of this fact, is rapidly resuming the control. This is a happy augury for the future; for we agree with Mr. Douglass that Democratic restoration would be an inexpressible calamity to his race, and therefore a disaster to the country.

1876

Regaining political control of the presidency and reestablishing home-rule were of primary concern to Southerners. In the congressional election of 1874 Democrats won a majority of the seats in the United States House of Representatives and a near-majority in the Senate. However, without the solid support of all Southern states, no Democratic candidate could hope to reach the presidency. Southern Democrats were so determined to regain political power that it was said that battles with Republicanism would be "fought over again at Vicksburg and Mobile and Richmond," and they were convinced that change could come only with the restoration of the Democratic party.

In the South the Democratic party held tight control over local politics. "Within ten years from the suppression of the rebellion the rebels once more hold the political control of nearly all the vast territory that was rescued from them . . . " (Harper's Weekly, June 24). Rebels often resorted to terrorism to control political and social opposition. This terrorism was not only directed toward African Americans, but white Republicans as well. Harper's Weekly reported that "no one can live safely and at ease in many districts of the South who is an ardent advocate of Republican principles, who insists that all the people shall be educated, and the right of suffrage be secured to all."

As devastating as the violent attacks on African Americans and Republican supporters were, the economic climate created by tensions was just as bad. Few Northern capitalists would invest in the region and land was almost valueless. "A general cry of distress arose and still rises from all its people," reported Harper's. Some observers blamed Democratic politicians in the North, including New York's William Marcy "Boss" Tweed and the Tammany Hall political machine, for the political and economic chaos in the South.

One of the biggest questions the press debated was the effect the rebels within the Democratic party were having on the upcoming presidential election.

The Republican party nominated Rutherford B. Hayes as its candidate for president of the United States, and he selected William A. Wheeler as his running mate. The Republican party platform called for vigorous enforcement of the Civil War amendments, the reestablishment of a sound fiscal policy, and the creation of national harmony. The hope of the party was that "of whatever race, country, name, or creed, all who hold the principles of 1776, who are resolved to be in all things Americans, who abhor cruelty, tyranny, and crime . . . will give their votes to Hayes." During the Radical Reconstruction the Republican party had depended heavily on the support of African American voters. Hayes' dream, however, was to build a strong Republican party that was not dependent upon the support of African Americans and "Carpetbaggers," and Reconstruction policies clearly stood in his way.

The Democratic party, on the other hand, nominated Samuel J. Tilden of New York as its candidate for president. Tilden ran on a platform of "retrenchment and reform." It was felt by many that Tilden could be elected only with the support of the "solid South" and old Democratic allies in the North. It was also felt, as Harper's Weekly *reported (October 21) that the old Democratic party was an obstruction to reconciliation between the North and the South. Although Tilden himself was a Northerner, most Southerners believed that his success would mean a return of power to the South.*

In most Southern states, the proportion of black voters to white voters was about the same; in Louisiana black voters outnumbered white voters 104,192 to 84,167. Of the white voting population, ninety-five percent voted Democratic; of African American voters, it was believed that ninety-nine percent would have voted the Republican ticket if given the chance. At the polls, African Americans were often the subject of terrorism; they faced intimidation, violence, and even murder. In other instances, black access to the polls was limited. In Savannah, Georgia, for example, there was only one polling place, and it was "arranged as to exclude the colored voters." It is reported that white citizens organized rifle clubs and other organizations to intimidate blacks and participants at Republican meetings. It was even reported that Democratic party members and supporters participated in the election fraud in the South and in other parts of the country.

The initial returns in the presidential election of 1876 were favorable for the Democrats. Tilden won a majority of popular votes. However, Republicans challenged the electoral votes from several states. At dispute were electoral votes from Florida, Louisiana, South Carolina, and Oregon. Each of the states in question sent dual returns, each purported to be valid. Both the Democratic and Republican parties claimed the disputed votes and sent "visiting statesmen" to review the situation. The crisis that ensued continued until a compromise was reached in 1877 and an electoral commission declared Hayes president.

Robert L. Harris, Jr.
Cornell University

HOME AND FOREIGN GOSSIP

HARPER'S WEEKLY
January 15, 1876, p. 51

It is strange what weak, silly, and contemptible prejudices are carried even to the grave. Last September the managers of Mount Moriah Cemetery, in Philadelphia, refused to receive the body of Henry Jones, a noted colored caterer, for burial. It seems that a lot had long before been purchased by Jones, and improved to the amount of two or three thousand dollars; but the managers had not allowed the purchase deed to be recorded when they learned that Jones was a colored man. So when the widow brought an action, the managers held that the sale was not valid, because not recorded. The Court of Common Pleas decided in favor of the plaintiff; but the matter will be carried to the Supreme Court, because it is believed that "the knowledge that a colored person is interred in the cemetery will deter others from buying lots, and thus depreciate the value of the property!"

"THE BLOODY SHIRT."

HARPER'S WEEKLY
February 26, 1876, p. 162

The press is called the organ of public opinion. But the remark must be accepted with care and discrimination. The newspapers seldom agree even in the statement of a simple fact, if it has any political significance. It is seen through party spectacles and reported with party partiality. There are also many questions which are privately and generally discussed by all intelligent persons, and many positive opinions entertained and expressed, which yet find no expression in the organs of public sentiment. The New York *Times* the other day cited as an instance the growing feeling among intelligent persons that the suffrage should be restricted to the educated—a proposition which the President is the first public man to put forth in its simple form. So, in regard to municipal government, it is a wide-spread conviction that the suffrage for municipal purposes exclusively should be confined to the taxpayers. If we are not mistaken, this is the latent theory of Governor Tilden's message proposing the commission upon the general subject of city government which he has lately appointed. But there is very little public and direct discussion of such opinions, because they are thought to be un-American—opinions whose expression would be exceedingly unbecoming the Centennial year; not only giving cause for exultation to the effete monarchies of Europe, but fatal to any party which should be suspected of holding them.

The press, also, often misrepresents the actual situation by insisting that a certain public opinion exists which is wholly imaginary, but the existence of which the papers may sincerely desire. Nothing is easier than for a newspaper writer to state his own wishes as public opinion. We constantly read in the papers that "the people" are all going this way or that. But every man corrects the assertion by his personal knowledge of his neighbors' opinions. Thus it might be supposed, if there were no other source of knowledge than the papers, that "the bloody shirt" was both an obsolete and a wicked delusion; that there were not and never had been any "outrages" upon the colored people in the Southern States; that nothing could well be more beautiful than the fraternal relations which exist between the races; that those who have been educated to believe the black man the son of a cursed race, designed by Heaven to be the slave of the white, have suddenly changed their minds, and are now anxious to secure to him every equality, especially upon juries in Georgia; and that any body in this Centennial year—this hundredth year since the Declaration, whose great doctrine we have so sedulously respected in this country—who does not confine himself to rejoicing over our happy reunion, but looks to see the facts, is an apostle of hate, delighting to dabble his fingers in the gore of the bloody shirt which he wickedly shakes in the pained eyes of peaceful brethren. Yet every man knows that the newspapers do not represent public opinion upon this subject. There is a very general conviction that the offenses and the system of hostility typified by the bloody shirt are very positive and ghastly facts, which no statesman and no patriot can safely disregard. It does not necessarily follow that force laws, as they are called, are desirable—laws are matters of expediency; but it does follow that the people should be watchful and alert to maintain what they won in the war.

The papers which suppose that there is no wide and deep interest in such facts as Mr. Morton states in his late speech are wholly mistaken. They are not new, indeed, but they are not the less true. The *Nation* remarks that nobody has any faith in the sincerity of any thing that Mr. Morton says. But, so far as that is concerned, Mr. Morton does not ask for belief because of his own assertion. In his recent speech he cites official reports. And when, leaving details, he speaks as follows of a certain political policy, he says what vast numbers of people believe, not because of his assertion, but of their own observation of events and knowledge of history and human nature:

> "In many of the Southern States the policy is openly avowed of seizing all power into the hands of the white race, and depriving the colored people of their political and civil rights. With this policy, commonly known as the white line, it is believed the Democracy sympathize in every Southern State, and I fear to a considerable extent in the Northern States. State after State has been conquered from the majority by violence, and we are no longer left in doubt as to the purpose thus to establish a solid South in the interest of the Democratic party; and when they shall have obtained the control of the national government, to reconstruct the Southern States upon the white man's basis, and to destroy the Republican party by making it impossible for men of Republican principles to enjoy and express their opinions in peace and safety. Then, as before the rebellion, the Republican party will be banished from the South, and it will be to them as a foreign country. When we consider how fearfully rapid the progress has been in that direction even under Republican administration, we can understand how it might be accelerated and consummated with a Democratic President, elected chiefly by the Southern Democracy, and necessarily sympathizing with them in their aspirations. Lest it be said that I do injustice to the Northern Democracy, I beg leave to remind the Senate that before the war the Northern Democracy not only connived at the oppressions upon the Republican party and its exclusion from the Southern States, but made merry over and defended the outrages committed in the South upon Abolitionists; and that now and ever since the war the Democratic party either deny, justify, or excuse the dreadful atrocities committed upon the white and black Republicans in the Southern States."

We add an extract from a Washington letter of the Springfield *Republican*—a newspaper which can not be accused of fondness for shaking the bloody shirt, but whose correspondent confirms the words of Mr. Morton and the feeling of the intelligent North:

> "I protest, however, against the idea that the issues of the war can not be re-opened for discussion. This is to padlock the lips, to stifle discussion. Besides, here is the South expecting to govern the country through its Northern allies, the Democrats. It becomes absolutely necessary to show the people what manner of men these are, what style of civilization they believe in. It is of vital importance that men of the North, who are humane and refined, should see the 'Confederates' as they are. They still despise the negro, they still defend the cruelties of the war—some of them, at least; in short, they are totally unfit to rule the country. How is this shown better than by the speeches of men like Ben Hill?"

The actual situation of the country, the state of opinion and feeling, undeniable facts and tendencies in the various States, will necessarily be a cardinal issue in the election of this year, whether it be called the gospel of hate and the bloody shirt, or common-sense and patriotic sagacity.

THE TRUE SOUTHERN QUESTION

HARPER'S WEEKLY
March 4, 1876, p. 182

In a recent speech in the House, Mr. Lynch, of Mississippi, a colored Representative, said some things which deserve to be pondered by a larger audience than that which heard the speech or which reads the *Record*. Mr. Lynch's colleague, Mr. Singleton, a white Representative, reported the bill under discussion from the committee, and remarked in his speech that he was a Southern man, every inch of him, from the crown of his head to the sole of his foot. To this Mr. Lynch observed that he could have no objection, for he, too, was a Southern man by birth, education, inclination, and interest, although he knew that the word was generally applied to those white persons who lived south of Mason and Dixon's line before the rebellion. In reply to Mr. Singleton's remarks upon the taxes imposed by adventurers and carpet-baggers in the Southern States, Mr. Lynch said that his colleague could not have meant to include the State which in part he so ably represented, for he presumed his colleague knew that nine-tenths of the offices in the State of Mississippi are now, and ever since the war have been, held by Southern men to the manor born. Mr. Singleton interrupted the speaker to say that he knew exactly to the contrary. Mr. Lynch, undisturbed, and with perfect courtesy, remarked, amidst the laughter of the House, that he regretted his colleague was not better informed, and proceeded to show that the taxation which his colleague so deeply deplored, and which required the relief to be afforded by abolishing a few consulates, was very much less in 1875 under Republican than it was in 1865 under Democratic control.

But the significant part of his speech was that in which Mr. Lynch told his colleague what he believed to be the true remedy for the evils complained of in the Southern States. That remedy, he said, is a public opinion which will crush out mob law and enforce obedience to the laws of the country. "What we want in the South," said Mr. Lynch—and his testimony is of the highest value as a native of that section—"what we want in the South is a public opinion that will cause every man, wherever he may have been born, whatever may be his color, whatever his politics, to feel perfectly safe and secure in the exercise of his rights and privileges as an American citizen." What we want, he continued, is a public sentiment that will make White Leagues and Ku-Klux Klans and all such organizations impossible. The good men of the South of both races, he declared, must unite so as to render impossible the elevation to power of a class of men who create confusion, stir up strife, and keep the country unsettled. He insisted that Mr. Singleton's party must tolerate an honest difference of opinion upon political questions. In a word, the summed up the political necessity in the Southern States by saying, forcibly, "We want his party to pursue a policy that will convince the colored voters that their identification as a mass with any one political organization is no longer a matter of necessity."

These words are worthy of careful attention. If immigrants will not turn to the Southern States, if capital is reluctant to place itself there, if there is a constant cry of depression and of oppression, how can any man wonder? Without confidence there can be no general and real prosperity, and how can there be confidence without a general sense of security? This is the real Southern question. And the test of Southern manhood is its capacity to deal with it, and to establish and maintain that security. If the better part of the white population in the Southern States can not see the cause of the difficulty, or cope with it with energy and intelligence, the difficulty will remain. The theory that "Federal interference," or carpet-baggery, or the Republican party, is chiefly responsible for the situation is futile. It was not the Revolution of '93 in France that was responsible for the guillotine; it was the long *régime* of injustice that made the Revolution which was responsible. And in the Southern States it is the feeling which Mr. Lynch describes, that identification with Republicans is a matter of necessity for the colored race, that produces the trouble.

And what is responsible for that feeling? Nothing but the treatment which ever since the war, more or less general, more or less cruel, the colored race has received, and which the old white element of the States has done so little to correct. If Mr. Singleton and his friends had been as furious with the White League and the Ku-Klux as they have been with the carpet-baggers, the situation would have been very much better than it is. Mr. Bruce, the colored Senator from Mississippi, has sharply declared that the Republicans have played false with his race; and unquestionably the conduct of many Republican politicians in the Southern States justifies his words. But even he would not suppose that the condition and prospects of that race would be improved under Democratic ascendency. The problem is not one to be settled easily, and it can be settled wisely only by those who hold, with Mr. Lynch, that "white men must be allowed to disagree upon political questions without being socially ostracized and destroyed in business; colored men must be convinced that they too can divide in political matters without running the risk of losing their rights and privileges under the government." It is because the conduct of the Democratic party shows that it does not hold that view that Republican prospects, if the party is wise, are so constantly brightening.

NO MISAPPREHENSION WHATEVER

HARPER'S WEEKLY
March 18, 1876, p. 222

In a late speech at Atlanta, General Gordon, one of the Senators from Georgia, said that what "the South" has to fear in the elections of this year is the groundless apprehension of "the North." He also declared that Republican legislation for "the South" was tyranny. Does General Gordon consider the refusal of the Republican Congress to justify General Sheridan's action in Louisiana last year, or its rejection of the President's proposed policy in Arkansas, "tyranny?" "Force laws" were directed against the Ku-Klux and White League, and what have General Gordon or his friends done to suppress those organizations? There has undoubtedly been unspeakable tyranny in the Southern States; but upon reflection Senator Gordon will probably agree that it was not, upon the whole and in any great degree, the work of Republicans. In the very Georgia in which he made his speech, colored citizens are virtually excluded from juries. There is no tyranny more absolute than that of which this is an illustration, and such an illustration implies a feeling and a system. Is the Republican party responsible for such tyranny? In the county of Chatham, in Georgia, there are more than ten thousand voters, of whom six thousand are colored. On election day these votes are required to be deposited at one polling-place in the city of Savannah. The purpose is plain. It is practically to disfranchise a large part of the voters, who must come into town from the country. Is that a Republican form of tyranny? Three weeks before Senator Gordon spoke, Robert Toombs spoke in the same place, and said that he gloried in having defrauded voters at the polls. Is that also Republican tyranny? These things are done, and things of which these are but illustrations, under the national ascendency of the Republican party. But if, with the full knowledge of them, the country should intrust the control of the national government to the party whose success is earnestly desired by Robert Toombs and Jefferson Davis and the public opinion which ostracizes the colored citizen from the jury-box and crowds him from the ballot-box, does Senator Gordon—does any man in his senses—suppose that these things would cease?

The general says that "the South" has to fear groundless misapprehensions at the North. But he is mistaken. There is no misapprehension in this part of the country, and there is, notwithstanding the most vehement denunciation of Northern hate and tyranny, no vindictive feeling whatever. The people of this part of the country are as friendly to those of the Senator's part as they are to the North. As we have heretofore said, Mr. Blaine is quite as conciliatory in feeling as Mr. Lamar. Nobody here desires any injustice or harsh dealing with ex-Confederates. General Gordon himself has seen this part of the country, and he knows that it is so. There is no misapprehension, no ill-feeling, no "hate." Northern men and Republicans are not hyenas. They do not misapprehend the sincere wish of many intelligent Southerners to have done as soon as may be with the war and all that belongs to it. They will cordially co-operate for a union of hearts as well as hands. But they are sagacious enough to know the significance of all that they observe, and they do not believe that the welfare of the Union or of its white and colored citizens demands that the Democratic party should return to power. We assure General Gordon that there is not the slightest misapprehension upon that point. There was the recent case of Hambleton, for instance. It leaked out that the clerk of the chief committee in the Democratic House, appointed by the Democratic leader, had named a child for the assassin of Mr. Lincoln. The story was lustily denied, but it was very soon put beyond question. The father was also notorious before the war by his black list of antislavery merchants in New York—a kind of black-mail in the interest of slavery. These were small things. But why is it that in the first Democratic House since the old slavery days—a House full of "conciliation" and "reform" and "fraternal love"—the leader should have appointed as clerk of the chief committee a man who had been conspicuously offensive for devotion to slavery, and who so honored the assassin of Abraham Lincoln as to give his name to his son? It was, we say, a little thing, and

so is a dried leaf. But a dried leaf shows the way that the wind blows. The Democratic party nominates for Governor in New Hampshire a man known only as a virulent Copperhead. It sends from Missouri as Senator another man with no other claim whatever than that he was a Confederate officer. Every thing, little and large, shows the instinctive direction of Democratic sympathy. It is not toward liberty and the Union, and their friends and defenders and policy. It is against them. No man whom the Republicans could by any possibility have appointed to any position whatever could have named a son for Abraham Lincoln's assassin. We can assure General Gordon that there is not the least misapprehension upon these points here at the North. There is no vindictiveness toward the South. But there is a very general conviction that it is not desirable to put at the helm those whom the admirers of Mr. Lincoln's assassin would like to see there.

This is a plain, practical feeling. It is an instinct, and it will elect a Republican President this year. Far from being elected under a misapprehension, he will be the conclusive proof of the clear and sound apprehension of the country. His election will show that the country feels the importance of retaining the government in hands whose honesty and patriotic fidelity are unquestioned and unquestionable; and that it sees that a sound financial policy and imperative reforms are not necessarily to be expected from a party which has tried within the year to carry two of the great States for soft money, and which includes every kind and degree of Hambleton.

PHILADELPHIA STREET CHARACTERS

HARPER'S WEEKLY
April 8, 1876, p. 294

One of our artists, in search of the picturesque in Philadelphia, came across the quaint characters rendered in the spirited sketches on page 292. The first of the large sketches is the "Catfish Woman," generally an elderly person, sharpfaced, sallow, shrewd, from Kensington, or "Fishtown." She is voluble, and has great powers of endurance, making her appearance by earli-

1876

PHILADELPHIA STREET CHARACTERS.—Drawn by F. H. Schell.—[See Page 294.]

Harper's Weekly, April 8, 1876, p. 292.

est daylight in the street, with her fish already cleaned and ready for cooking. Then comes the "Crab Man," with his cry of "Cra-a-abs! crab all alive! crabby! Centennial crabs! crab-a-rab-dab! all alive! spiteful fellows! some a-walkin', some a-talkin'! one of 'em can lick a man!" In the next sketch we have the "Hominy Man," who in this case happens to be a benevolent-looking negro. As he trudges along, he cries, "De hominy ma-a-an come out dis cold and frosty mornin' wid his good homin-y-y-y! Oh, it's good fo' de chile! good as de red cow's milk fo' de little babe!" Last of all, we have the sketch of the "Pepperpot Woman," whose cry

833

of "Pep-pree-ee-ee pot, all hot!" is sure of attracting a crowd of hungry, freezing customers on a cold winter morning, to whom a tin cup full of the well-peppered tripe, smoking hot, is a most welcome and tempting breakfast.

"THE SOUTH" AND THE PARTIES

HARPER'S WEEKLY
June 3, 1876, p. 443

"Eight colored men have been shot dead, four hanged, and about twenty wounded. No whites were killed.... Twenty colored men are reported to be held as prisoners. Their fate is uncertain, but the supposition is they will be killed. It is also said the number of negroes killed will never be ascertained. Precautions have been taken to remove the dead secretly. The number of Regulators under arms is said to be 500, from East Baton Rouge and East and West Feliciana, and Wilkinson County, Mississippi. The colored people are said to be arming for self-protection."

This was the first account of the latest Louisiana massacre. Every such story has the same ending—"No whites were killed." In this case, it is alleged that the trouble began by the negroes calling out a white man and riddling him with bullets. But the facts always show that the provocation did not come from the negroes. Whatever the explanation of the present trouble may be, this incident will recall public attention to the Southern question. It is not the least of the practical issues of the election. It is an old issue, indeed, but it is still vital, and it will be vital so long as the Democratic party shows itself anxious only to put the negro in the wrong, and to excuse or justify white terrorism under the plea of carpet-baggery and ignorance and rascality. If the Democratic party had ever said or had ever wished that "outrages" upon the negroes in the Southern States should cease, they would have ended. If that party had ever opposed the Ku-Klux and the White League as it has opposed "scalawags" and "Federal satraps," the situation in the Southern States would have been peaceful, and the Democratic party would have had a large and important colored vote.

Republicans are constantly taunted with the charge that their only voters in the Southern States are the negroes. They are told that the superior race, the intelligence, the character, the property, are all Democratic and opposed to them. They are held to the strictest account for Moses and Whipper and the colored Legislatures. But does it lie in the mouth of a murderer to accuse a thief? If the Republicans are responsible for the rascalities of Moses and Whipper, so are the Democrats responsible for the murder of Dostie and the massacre of Coushatta. We do not defend, nor have we defended, Republican offenses in the Southern States; but what shall be said of the Democrats who, claiming all the intelligence and virtue and superiority in that section, are yet responsible for the blackest and bloodiest of crimes? The deep and persuasive argument against a Democratic restoration is the universal distrust of the party upon the Southern question. The people of the United States will be very slow to commit the national power to a party which sends Hill and Tucker to Congress, which contains the spirit and furnishes the men for negro terrorism, and which has never made a single energetic protest against the crimes of its partisans.

In his recent letters upon the situation, Mr. F. W. Bird, of Massachusetts, an original Sumner and Andrew Republican, truly says that he had some share in creating the distrust of the Democratic party when it was well founded, and he adds that he thinks the worst Democrat whose nomination at St. Louis is possible is safer for the country than the best Republican whose nomination is possible at Cincinnati. But the distrust which he helped to create has not passed away. While the great mass of patriotic Americans, as we believe, demand political reform and purification with enthusiasm, they demand also such a care of the Southern question as no Democrat can give, because he would have no party conviction and conscience upon the subject behind him. The enthusiasm of the campaign will be for reform, but there will be no forgetfulness of the rights of those whom the Republicans made citizens, and whose citizenship the Democrats opposed. The Democratic party could not give the country administrative reform, nor a sound currency, nor equal rights at the South. Should it regain power, it would retain it for a generation. Yet in the present condition of the public feeling such a calamity can not be avoided merely by the nomination of a Republican who has stolen nothing and has run steadily with the machine. To borrow a term from the politics of France, the candidate must be a Republican of to-day as well as of yesterday. The plain condition of Republican success, which alone can repress the spirit of the Ku-Klux and protect the new citizen, is to heed the demand in the party for a nomination which shall be the earnest of reform.

THE KU-KLUX AND THE COLORED VOTERS

HARPER'S WEEKLY
June 24, 1876, p. 510

The Southern wing of the Democracy forms more than one-third, and possibly very nearly one-half, its strength.

"THE LION AND THE UNICORN FIGHTING"—AGAIN (?)
BRITISH LION (to Lord D—Unicorn). "What! give up the Fugitive Slave, and NOT the Criminal Fugitive!"

Harper's Weekly, June 17, 1876, p. 496.

In the South, if any where, it must win the control of the Union. Its battles with Republicanism are to be fought over again at Vicksburg and Mobile and Richmond. Without the solid support of nearly all the Southern States no Democratic candidate can have any rational hope of reaching the Presidency, no Congress or Senate would ever exhibit a Democratic preponderance. Repelled by that papal and Irish Catholic element on which the Northern Democratic leaders chiefly rely for success, shocked at its frauds, ignorance, barbarity, indignant that a foreign priest and the European enemies of the republic should presume to dictate the course of

BLOOD MONEY.

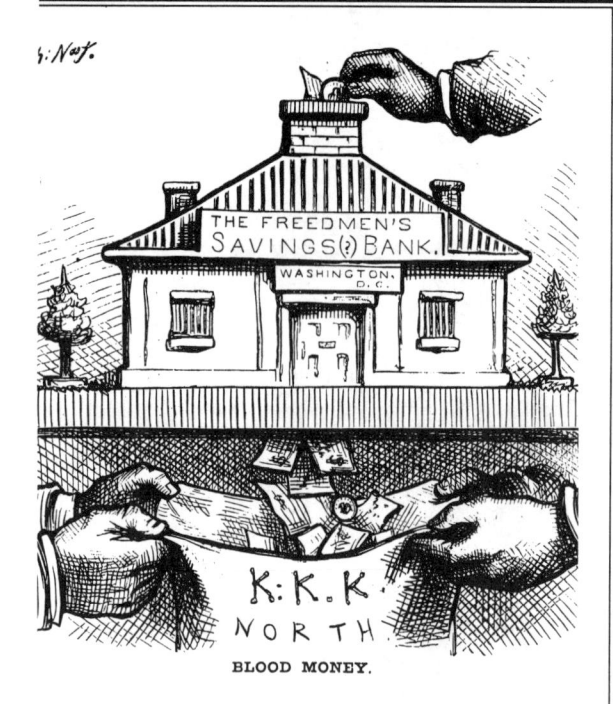

Harper's Weekly, June 17, 1876, p. 500.

American politics, the people of the North and West will in 1876 present an almost unbroken array in opposition to the candidate of the Roman Catholic faction. Protestantism is apparently resolved that no priests and cardinals, no Pope nor Jesuit, shall rule among us in the guise of Tilden and Kelly. Even the Germans, who have so often in New York joined with the ultramontanes to support the Democracy, seem at last about to separate from the enemies of their native land. It is doubtful if any honest Germans in 1876 can be misled so far as to vote for the candidate of the Irish Catholic Democracy. They are slowly escaping from the guidance of their untrustworthy politicians. The clamors, the scandals, the slanders, of the papal press can not any longer hide from them the imminent danger to which an ultramontane and Confederate cabinet at Washington might expose freedom in both Europe and America. It is only in New York or Connecticut that the Roman Catholic Democracy can hope for any success at the North, and even here they will probably be met by a general uprising of the non-sectarian part of the people.

But in the Southern States the Democratic leaders seem to hold a rigid control. They hope to bring over in a united body the whole of the recently rebellious section to the support of some reactionary candidate, and by the help of a fraudulent vote in New York or Connecticut, to win a sufficient majority. They have reduced to subjection Arkansas, Mississippi, and Florida. They even hope to overawe and conquer South Carolina. The tactics they have adopted through all the South have proved singularly successful. Within ten years from the suppression of the rebellion the rebels once more hold the political control of nearly all the vast territory that was rescued from them at the fall of Richmond and by the arms of Grant. They profess, it is true, Union principles; they obey for the present the laws of the nation; and the revolution at New Orleans was suppressed by a few gun-boats and the presence of Sheridan. But their real purpose is shown in the way in which they govern the timid majorities of their own section, terrify and oppress white Republicans, torture, massacre, intimidate, the colored voters, drive, away capital, emigration, and labor, and preserve a kind of isolation that reminds one of the despotism of Dr. Francia. No one can live safely and at ease in many districts of the South who is an ardent advocate of Republican principles, who insists that all the people shall be educated, and the right of suffrage be secured to all. Should he avow such opinions, he is liable to be shot at from lonely places, like Billings and Ivey in Alabama, or assailed openly, like Twitchell and King in Louisiana; he will be driven from his farm by threats of whipping, and silenced by a rule of terror. In Ireland it has long been the custom of the natives to shoot down unpopular landlords from behind hedges, or burn them in their houses. But over a large part of Ireland a state of siege extends, and the people are forbidden to carry arms. In Georgia, Alabama, and Mississippi no protection apparently is extended to the peaceful citizen. The armed ruffians ride over the country, and in the midst of a terrified community strike down whom they please in open day. The recent instance of Twitchell and King shows the disturbed condition of the Coushatta District of Louisiana. The massacre of two years ago is not enough, and two conspicuous Republicans, while crossing a river in a boat, where shot by an unknown person, who escaped without difficulty. He fired his musket until his ammunition was exhausted, and no one interfered. He even shot twice at a negro who kindly attempted to save one of his victims from drowning. He then rode away, probably to assure his Democratic associates of his success, and to boast, with ribald laughter, of the slaughter of an active and eminent Republican. Such are the most effective Democratic politicians at the South, and it is with this class of brutal, uncultivated natures in all parts of the Union that the people will contend in all the elections of 1876.

Even in the Southern States it can not be supposed that any more than a small minority is employed in these deeds of violence and inhumanity. Americans are not naturally cruel. Nowhere has freedom produced a more rapid advance in the elements of morals. But in the South the barbarous and terrible minority rules over society. It planned the rebellion; it drove the reluctant community into a wild reign of bloodshed. It was nearly successful in its designs. It was crushed, for the moment, by the victories of Grant. Then once more it planned a new subjugation of the Southern States by means of secret associations pledged to drive the Republican voters from the country and to terrify the colored population into submission. Soon after the fall of Richmond the Democratic leaders in New York boasted openly that the Ku-Klux would soon rule the South, and Democracy find its chief strength in the regions of reconstruction. They evidently relied upon the fierce and brutal minority who had so long governed in Georgia and Mississippi to establish once more their reign of terror. No State, before 1860, had been more plainly opposed to secession than Georgia. Its working-men, mechanics, and artisans had always contemned the agitators of South Carolina, were ruled by the instincts of humanity and common-sense. Even in the summer of 1865, according to the correspondence of the New York *Times*, it was asserted at political meetings in Georgia "that a majority of the citizens of the State were strongly opposed to secession, but by trickery and fraud and violence were beguiled or dispossessed of their rights." But the desperate minority had now once more projected the subjugation of Georgia and all the South, and with the apparent sanction of the corrupt Democratic leaders of the North, formed what is known as the Ku-Klux Association. By this secret machinery they planned the expulsion or death of every Republican, the complete reconquest of the territory from Maryland to Mexico. Within ten years they have almost gained their object. The governing class in nearly all the Southern States is the wild and savage men, maddened with whiskey and frenzied with vice, who ride over the country to shoot Republicans like partridges, and from whom the colored voters hide as if from an evil spirit.

A private correspondent relates that as he rode recently along the highways of Mississippi, he was surprised to see the negroes, whenever they caught sight of him, fall down on their faces in the grass and creep away on their hands and knees beyond the reach of a rifle-shot. The poor people, he thinks, supposed that he was a Democratic politician on an electioneering tour. They fancied every mounted man a political assassin. The anecdote seems hardly credible, yet its authenticity can not be doubted. In Mississippi at the last election no voting was allowed in many districts where the colored Republicans possessed an enormous majority. Georgia, Alabama, Texas, Kentucky, Tennessee, have long been held in bondage in a similar way by savage troops of Democratic politicians. In 1865, '66, and '67 Republicanism had made rapid progress in all the Southern States; the small farmers, mechanics, and even the laboring whites seemed anxious to invite immigration, plant free schools, and cultivate a land already half desolated by slavery. The rebellion had always been odious to this class of the white population; they seem in 1865 to have won the control of their section. But the Ku-Klux began now its silent atrocities. Hundreds of the colored people, we are assured, were murdered daily. "These unfortunate creatures are being hunted down like dogs," we are told as early as August, 1865; and the Raleigh *Progress* relates that even in North Carolina negroes were killed without provocation and without punishment. At the close of the war the project of exterminating the colored race seems at once to have been disclosed by a thousand barbarous deeds. Yet still the Northern settlers advanced into the disturbed country, allured by the promises and the hopes of the more rational part of the population, bought plantations in Georgia and Alabama, invested money in Southern railroads, founded free schools, projected vast improvements, and might have filled the Southern States with a rapid and lasting progress. Even Virginia might have been roused from its lethargy, and Kentucky cultivated into humanity and peace. Republicanism ruled for a few years at the South, and its traces are seen in lines of railways that have opened up vast districts to agriculture and trade, and a scheme of universal education that still lingers amidst the barbarous reaction.

For almost at once the secret association upon which the corrupt Democracy of the North had so confidently relied began its war upon Republican progress, and the nightly atrocities of its masked ruffians were heard of from Virginia to the Rio Grande. It was no longer the poor negroes, but the white settler, the Republican voters, and every man of mark and note, upon whom these bands of assassins inflicted horrible outrages. The story of the Ku-Klux in the Southern States is one of those passages in the annals of men on which memory refuses to dwell, and of which the dark outline need only be recalled. But its political effect was disastrous to the South beyond conception. State after State fell into the hands of robbers and assassins. The railroads were stopped, their bonds repudiated, the foreign capitalists were plundered, honesty was banished forever. Georgia was among the first to submit to the rule of the Ku-Klux. It repudiated its debt; it kept its railroads. It robbed the capitalists who had trusted it; it drove out Republicans who had invested their money in its wasted soil; it closed its common schools. Virginia soon followed in repudiation and Democracy. Alabama resisted for a time the rule of bloodshed and dishonesty, and has at last fallen amidst a disgraceful scene of robbery. Wherever the Ku-Klux have succeeded, their first aim has been to defraud the English and American capitalists who had trusted in the honor of a State and the wealth of the nation. But still more fatal to the Southern section has been that sudden check which was given to industry, emigration, and trade. The Democratic Ku-Klux, who terrified peaceful citizens by midnight murder and endless persecutions, soon completed the ruin of a large part of the South. Its credit was lost, its honor gone. No capitalist would any more lend money to repair its railways or rebuild its cities. Its lands were often almost valueless. A general cry of distress arose and still rises from all its people. Louisiana is a scene of anarchy. In Texas every progressive or reform movement for education and peace is certain to be broken up by deeds of bloodshed and by the savage emissaries of the Democracy. The Ku-Klux were nominally suppressed by the legislation of 1870–72. But the same cruel minority still pursued its silent action, and Republican cultivation, capital, intelligence, fled from the afflicted South. It is probable that the larger part of its population were sensible of the imprudence and the wickedness of their political leaders, that no honest farmer or mechanic but shuddered at the horrible crimes of the Ku-Klux, that every man of humanity and patriotism was ashamed of the evil renown brought upon his country by a band of miscreants and robbers. Yet in 1869–70 moderation at the South was crushed by the fierce and the vindictive. Humanity perished from the land. The chief Republican leaders were silenced, banished, or sometimes assassinated under the eyes of the nation. The victory of the Ku-Klux was complete in Georgia, Texas, Kentucky, Tennessee. Alabama was still in doubt. Mississippi was yet free. But the Democratic club at Tammany Hall promised its followers a final triumph by the aid of the rifle and the bowie-knife, and Democratic politicians rode swiftly at night over the doubtful districts, engaged in deeds that history blushes to remember.

And Democratic politicians in New York, the Seymours, the Tweeds, and the Tildens, knew of these horrible orgies, and prepared to profit by the successes of their barbarous allies.

Eugene Lawrence.

THE KU-KLUX DEMOCRACY

HARPER'S WEEKLY
July 15, 1876, p. 575

The question to be determined at the approaching election is, Shall the Ku-Klux select the next President of the United States? Shall a system of intimidation extending over a large part of the South defeat the will of the whole people? The Democratic leaders, it is plain, have no scruples in this matter. They were willing in 1872 to accept the aid of the worst class of Southern politicians and to profit from their excesses. They owe their control of the present House of Representatives to the frauds and intimidation practiced in several of the Southern States—Kentucky, where the activity of the Ku-Klux has been notorious for many years; Texas, where opposition to a Democratic rule has been perfectly effaced; Georgia, which permits no opposition; Mississippi, recently won to the Democratic side by a barbarous massacre; Missouri, overrun once more by Confederates and ultramontanes; Alabama, Louisiana, Virginia, and Tennessee make up that active majority of the House which, under the guidance of the Democratic leaders, are laboring to embarrass commerce, check emigration, and maliciously wound by a pretended economy the best interests of the nation. The Ku-Klux select the members of Congress at the South; they are encouraged to aim at the nomination and election of a President. What, then, is the Ku-Klux?

Louisiana is the State in which these merciless politicians have committed their worst deeds, and to its strangely revolutionary and uncertain condition we may best turn to discover the real meaning of the Ku-Klux.

That not any kind of government, even the best, would content them, except their own imperious rule, that their only aim is the destruction of all government, the ruin of their fellow-citizens, is plain from the history of that unhappy State. They complain, slander, revolt, sometimes appear as humble suppliants for redress, sometimes claim it with menacing gestures, the Bowie-knife, the rifle; but their purpose is always the same. They are steeped in the blood of their fellow-citizens, and would bring war and desolation, had they the power, to the whole nation. To those who would palliate these fearful cruelties of the Ku-Klux that for ten years past have startled and terrified the country, who would innocently attribute them to bad government, to Northern injustice, it may be well to ask, Why do they ever occur at all? Why resort to horrible murders, when peaceful means of redress are always at hand? Why not use the courts, the government protection, the easy rule of the whole nation, to suppress disorder and amend the wrong? What sufficient excuse has been offered for any one of the political murders that have covered all the South? Why resort to bloodshed in Louisiana any more readily than in New York? Bad government prevails every where, but is that any palliation for Grant Parish, Coushatta, or the murderous risings in New Orleans? How, indeed, wise and humane men can have listened so often to the cant of the Ku-Klux, the whine, the broad hypocrisy, the transparent falsehood, and lent any countenance to their hideous crimes, it is impossible to discover; yet it is by the aid of Northern politicians and editors that they have won their chief victories. The force of public opinion has been too often invoked to shield the murderer and suppress the commonest instincts of humanity.

An eye-witness and a private correspondent, who was present at one of the earliest and the most terrible of these political massacres, relates with new force the particulars of the startling scene. It was at New Orleans in 1866. It was therefore the result of no official interference from Washington; yet it was the opening of that inexpiable war which the Ku-Klux has carried on against all the supporters of the national government in every Southern State, and which it seems resolved to pursue, if unopposed, to some desperate conclusion. In the hot days of July, 1866, a convention of Republicans assembled at the Mechanics' Institute in New Orleans. Its proceedings were conducted with moderation and dignity; a large crowd outside watched with curiosity and interest the unusual scene; but no trace of disorder seemed to disturb the peaceful occasion. Suddenly a detachment of the police, then in the hands of the rebels, moved up Cannon Street. Without any apparent provocation, our informant saw them open a fire with their revolvers upon the thick mass of men, women, and children. A terrible panic followed. "I saw," says the eye-witness, "policemen leave the ranks, run after colored men, and shoot them down." "The firing was like that of a battlefield. Meanwhile the Convention was besieged by the White League; the doors of the building

THE NATION'S BIRTHDAY.—"ONE TOUCH OF NATURE MAKES THE WHOLE WORLD KIN."

were opened upon a treacherous promise of safety; the Ku-Klux fired upon the crowd of delegates, and white and colored men fell in a confused heap of slain. One clergyman, the Rev. Mr. Horton, was shot while on his knees praying. Dr. Dostie was cut and torn with penknives. The dead and dying were carried out in carts, and their bodies hidden. The number killed has never been told. Such was the first exploit of the Ku-Klux in New Orleans in 1866, and it explains with terrible clearness the real meaning of Coushatta, Grant Parish, the New Orleans rising, the Vicksburg massacre. All belong to the same secret association, the same desperate cause. Every humane citizen at the South deplores and shudders, no doubt, at these acts of lawlessness. Three-fourths of the laboring and mercantile classes in Louisiana or Mississippi would be rejoiced to see the men of blood and violence banished from the land, for they know that they bring ruin to all the best interests of the State; but they seem powerless. Even in Kentucky, on the brink of the intelligence of the Great West, the State government fails to give protection to the Northern settler. In Texas, a recent correspondent writes that he is obliged to conceal his Republican opinions, lest his neighbors may betray him. Life in Texas, he says, is held at the mercy of every ruffian. Another relates the way in which Republican meetings in that State are broken up and overawed. In a thickly settled Republican district a few hundred voters had gathered to discuss the political wants of the community and perhaps to nominate candidates. Good order and moderation marked all the proceedings. No harsh words were used. The Democracy was even complimented upon its general fairness. But a party of the Ku-Klux broke in upon the unarmed assembly; one Republican was killed, another cruelly beaten in the midst of his helpless companions. The murderers, who are well known, laugh at the instruments of justice, threaten violence to all who oppose them, and have effectually overawed a large Republican majority and carried all the elections. In Texas, it is said, the party of progress is large, respectable, intelligent; is able, if left untrammeled, to control the State. It might teach humanity to the people, check lawlessness, punish crime. But the least reputable part of the Democracy rule by violence, and retain the community in a condition of actual barbarism.

To every patriot, to every humane and republican intellect, it must seem singularly shameful that any part of the American Union should in the hundredth year of its existence be deprived of a free expression of opinion and of a free election by a general reign of lawlessness, that life should seem less secure in Mississippi or Kentucky in 1876 than it was in England under Saxon or Norman rule, and that this desperate class of our people should not only go unpunished, but even aim at the control of the whole country, should be taken under the protection of noted Democratic politicians, and be made use of by aspirants for office. The small but cruel and overbearing faction at the South which hates education and closes the common schools, drives away Northern settlers, plunders the public creditors, destroys trade, discourages industry, treats human life as valueless and freedom as an empty vision, is that part of the Southern people on which alone the Democracy relies for its success in the coming election. It is easy to see why the Democracy has the hearty sympathy of the Tory leaders in England, of the ultramontanes in Europe and America. It opposes to the will of the people a rule of force; it would condemn the people to perpetual ignorance; it would harry them by a Ku-Klux or hide from them their commonest rights. No Democratic editor has ever ventured to call for the punishment of the assassins of Vicksburg or Grant Parish, has reproved the Ku-Klux rulers of Georgia or Texas for closing the common schools, or spoken one word of hope to the suffering people who would be glad to live honest and reputable lives in Kentucky or Alabama, but are driven away because they are Republicans. One word from some noted Democratic leader, we are assured, condemning barbarous murder at the South, would have been the means of saving countless lives. One remonstrance against the harsh treatment of Northern settlers, against repudiation or fraud, would have been of infinite service. A strong appeal from a Democratic Convention against the cruelty of the Ku-Klux in Georgia or Texas might have made their people free. But of this nothing has ever been heard. In the hundredth year of the Union we are threatened by a faction which finds its chief strength in the open tyranny of the Ku-Klux and in the secret plottings of the papal priests, which closes the common schools at the South, betrays them at the North, and which is so dead to the common impulses of humanity as to hear of the cruelties of its adherents without a blush. But fortunately the heart of the American people is still true to the higher instincts of human nature. The Democratic leaders will soon discover that they have ceased to represent the wishes or opinions of their countrymen. It is stated that already the better class of Southern Democrats are anxious to break away from the restraints of the Ku-Klux, to repress crime, to educate the people, and, by joining with the Republicans in a friendly compromise, to establish a new epoch of progress and hope.

It is certain that the struggle of the progressive party at the South against the Ku-Klux Democracy will have the sympathy of every humane and honest intellect. The country has been too long shocked and horrified by the incessant return of these tragic occurrences, that seem to belong to some dark and forgotten age, that are too terrible for belief, and yet have all been done to secure the tyranny of an imperious and unpopular faction. To win the political control of the South, what have not its Democratic party leaders done? What are they not capable of? From the massacre of the Mechanics' Institute, in 1866, through a long succession of St. Bartholomews, the revolutionary faction has made its way. Its victims shake their gory locks in vain before the eyes of Tilden and Seymour and Kelly. But already it endangers freedom, it threatens the Union. If these political murders are tolerated and encouraged in New Orleans and Vicksburg, how long will it be before they are imitated in Washington or New York? To destroy the Ku-Klux Democracy is essential to the safety of the nation, of life and property every where. And happily the means of doing it are not difficult to find.

The Republican party—the party of the people—presents to the nation as its candidates for the high offices of President and Vice-President two men, honorable, moderate, just, and resolute. It presents Messrs. Hayes and Wheeler to the country as the symbols of honest and liberal progress, of education and humanity. Around such men in 1876 may well rally every friend of good order, of the Constitution and the law. Of whatever race, country, name, or creed, all who hold the principles of 1776, who are resolved to be in all things Americans, who abhor cruelty, tyranny, and crime, the politics of a foreign priesthood, the intrigues and vices of our European foes, will give their votes for Hayes and Wheeler. And if the papal Democracy at the North and the Ku-Klux Democracy at the South combine to resist the will of the people by force and fraud, they must be easily overthrown.

Eugene Lawrence.

PARTY UNITY

HARPER'S WEEKLY
August 5, 1876, p. 630

A careful study of the Democratic speeches and newspapers thus far in the canvass shows that the whole force of their argument lies in the assertion that while Governor Hayes is undoubtedly an honorable man, without a doubtful or suspicious point in his "record," yet that he must, as President, depend upon the Republican party, and that the very demand of reform proceeding from that party proves its incompetency. In a word, the only hope of "reform" lies in change, and change is possible only with the restoration of the Democratic party. There is some apparent reason in this statement, but it is apparent only because of an evident fallacy. It seems, however, almost conclusive to many persons. This is a party government, they say, and what can you do when one party fails but put in the other? Now if a party were a unit in the sense that such an argument implies, the argument would be sound. But it is not a unit. How far from it is seen in the situation of the Democratic party itself. In order to have any chance of success whatever, the party Convention selects two candidates who represent exactly opposing financial principles and policies. Mr. Nast's picture of the tiger with a head at each end, and of course going nowhere, is a true picture of the absurdity of the Democratic nominations.

Now the reason that the party is justly represented in the picture is that it is not a unit. Upon a vital and fundamental question it is divided. There are hard-money Democrats and soft-money Democrats, and should the Democratic party come into power, its financial policy would be what its demand of the repeal of the resumption clause is said to be—a compromise. That is to say, as a party it has no common financial principle or policy whatever. How, then, would "a change" give us "reform" in the currency, or any kind of financial reform? Take another instance. On the late Centennial Fourth of July the American flag was insulted by Democrats in Missouri and Kentucky, who preferred the flag of secession and rebellion. In other States, again, Democrats united heartily with Republicans in honoring the flag. What is the explanation? It is simply that the Democratic party is not a unit in patriotic feeling. It was divided into three parts during the war: war Democrats, who are now generally Republicans; Copperhead Democrats, like Mr. Tilden, Mr. Seymour, Vallandigham, and Fernando Wood; and rebels, like Davis, Toombs, Benjamin, Slidell, Mason, and the rest. It now comprises all those in the Southern States who compose the Ku-Klux Klans and White Leagues, men like Butler and his confederates, who massacred the black militia at Hamburg, South Carolina, the other day, the whole mass of those who secretly hate the Union, and are resolved that the colored people shall be "put down," and together with these all in the Northern States, like Mr. Tilden and Mr. Bayard, who now acquiesce and wish by-gones to be by-gones. The Democratic party is no more a unit in its patriotic feeling, its respect for the flag, and its regard for constitutional equal rights than it is for hard money or a sound financial policy. The only point upon which the party seems to be most nearly united is hostility to administrative reform, the evidence of which is found in the action of the Democratic majority in the House of Representatives, and in the States in which it has had power. So resolute in this hostility that in the State of New York, where Governor Tilden has pursued the canal contractors, the party has split upon the question, and he has been most bitterly opposed by the most conspicuous party leaders.

These illustrations show, what is so often forgotten, that a political party in this country is not a unit in the sense of uniformity of conviction and purpose. Reasoning based upon that assumption must therefore be largely fallacious. The only sound basis is the general drift and spirit of a party, and these are to be gathered only from careful observation and comparison. For instance, at this moment every intelligent student of public affairs knows that nothing would be more preposterous than the assertion that the Republican party is responsible for recent acts of the President. It may, indeed, be said that he is the Executive chosen by the party, and that it must bear the penalty of his misconduct. But that argument would have held the party for the performances of Andrew Johnson. The party itself has just declared in favor of the course of officers whom the President has since dismissed, and it has proclaimed as its guides principles which the President disregards. This is known to be the result of a contest which has long been waged within the party, and in which the reform element, as it is called, has been victorious. To hold the Republican party as a whole responsible for the things which it has censured and proposes to change, is practically absurd. To say, therefore, that Governor Hayes, however honest a reformer, can not reform, because he must depend upon the party, is equally absurd, because the party has just shown that its reformers are in the ascendant.

If it be said that the same reasoning applies to the Democratic party, we merely arrive again at the conclusion we have already stated, and it is that upon which the result of the campaign depends, namely, that the character, antecedents, principles, intelligence, patriotism, and present attitude of the Republican party, with the frank, sagacious, and courageous letter of its Presidential candidate announcing a policy which his career and the character of his chosen advisers prove that he will enforce, offer by far the surest guarantee to the country of a swift return to hard money, thorough administrative reform, and just and efficient constitutional protection of equal rights every where in the land.

It is to that point that the Democratic argument must be held, because there it utterly fails. If Governor Hayes must depend upon his party, not less must Governor Tilden upon his; and what possible evidence has been or can be presented to show that the reform element is either actually or probably stronger in the Democratic than in the Republican organization? So far as administrative reform, or sound financial doctrine, or respect for equal rights under the Constitution is concerned, we challenge a comparison. The one solitary point that the Democrats can make is Governor Tilden's nomination. But against that there is the nomination of Governor Hayes by the cooperation of the Bristow Republicans, Bristow's instant and unreserved support of him, the wise, patriotic, and unequivocal declaration of Governor Hayes, and the universal, joyful consciousness, not to be denied nor concealed, upon the part of the great mass of loyal American citizens, who were sincerely reluctant to take the desperate step of seeking reform by calling Copperheads and late Confederates to the control of the government, that no such necessity exists, and that those who saved the government are anxious and resolved to purify and strengthen it.

THE KU-KLUX

HARPER'S WEEKLY
August 5, 1876, p. 631

It is very easy, under cover of sneering at the bloody shirt, to do a very great and cruel wrong. Democrats like General M. C. Butler, of the Hamburg massacre, are very willing to hear any allusion to the brutal treatment of colored citizens in the Southern States reviled and belittled as a shaking of the bloody shirt, and Northern Democrats are very anxious to have no allusions made to it whatever, and to insist that the only question before the country is "reform." One reform is certainly indispensable, and that is reform of the spirit that displayed itself at Hamburg, as it has constantly shown itself in the Southern States for the last ten years. General Butler in his statement says that "the collision was the culmination of the system of insulting and outraging of white people which the negroes have adopted there for several years." These negro slaughters are undoubtedly very common and familiar in the late Slave States, and there may be those who believe that they are due to a negro system of insult and outrage. We believe, on the contrary, and from a careful study of many of the massacres, that the negro slaughters, and every kind and degree of Ku-Kluxery, are not due to negro insults and outrages, but to the deep and deadly contempt and hatred of the negroes upon the part of brutalized whites, intensified by the war and its consequences. We remember that the wanton and terrible Dostie massacre in New Orleans was called "a negro riot" in Northern Democratic newspapers. It was precisely as much a riot as Herod's slaughter was an insurrection of the innocents, and this slaughter at Hamburg is merely another outbreak of Ku-Kluxery.

One thing, indeed, until Mr. Lamar's speech in the House on the Hamburg crime, we had yet to see, and that was a hearty, indignant condemnation of the Ku-Klux spirit and conduct by any Democratic "statesman," orator, or newspaper. Had the Democratic party done its duty in this respect, the condition of the Southern States would now be very different. Nor are we unmindful of the extreme difficulty of the situation. Slavery, and Northern Democratic servility to it, fostered ignorance and virtual barbarism among great masses of the people in the Southern States. The complete social convulsion produced by the war, and the bitter feelings that naturally remained between the races, demanded of the more intelligent race a policy and conduct to which it has been steadily hostile, and this hostility has been sedulously encouraged by the Democratic party at the North. "Carpet-baggery," undoubtedly, has been a mischievous evil, but that was not the root of the trouble. The late Confederates seem, as a rule, to have abandoned themselves to awaiting the possible return of the Democratic party to power as an opportunity of "putting the negro into his place." The Southern States, of course, are full of such young men as the two who were "insulted" by the colored militia of Hamburg. They are supported by the general white sentiment of the communities in which they live, and the natural consequences are such massacres as this. The victims "were murdered in cold blood after they had surrendered and were utterly defenseless," says Governor Chamberlain. Who murdered them? The spirit and the men that demand the election of Mr. Tilden—not because he would personally connive at any wrong, but because they are of his party. The country sees what crimes are possible when the friends of the colored race are in control of the national government. What would it be with the political friends of General M. C. Butler in control?

The situation, we repeat, is difficult. It demands both forbearance and firmness. We do not say that the negroes are always right; we insist only that they are not always wrong. Above all, we are sure that nothing could be more unfortunate for both races and for the whole country than the transfer of the national government to the party which the Ku-Klux spirit supports. Nor can there be found wiser, more generous, more timely, views upon the whole subject than those of Governor Hayes:

> "The condition of the Southern States attracts the attention and commands the sympathy of the people of the whole Union. In their progressive recovery from the effects of the war, their first necessity is an intelligent and honest administration of government which will protect all classes of citizens in their political and private rights. What the South most needs is 'peace,' and peace depends upon the supremacy of the law. There can be no enduring peace if the constitutional rights of any portion of the people are habitually disregarded. A division of political parties resting merely upon sectional lines is always unfortunate, and may be disastrous. The welfare of the South, alike with that of every other part of this country, depends upon the attractions it can offer to labor and immigration and to capital. But laborers will not go and capital will not be ventured where the Constitution and the laws are set at defiance, and distraction, apprehension, and alarm take the place of peace-loving and law-abiding social life. All parts of the Constitution are sacred, and must be sacredly observed—the parts that are new no less than the parts that are old. The moral and national prosperity of the Southern States can be most effectually advanced by a hearty and generous recognition of the rights of all by all—a recognition without reserve or exception. With such a recognition fully accorded, it will be practicable to promote, by the influence of all legitimate agencies of the general government, the efforts of the people of those States to obtain for themselves the blessings of honest and capable local government. If elected, I shall consider it not only my duty, but it will be my ardent desire, to labor for the attainment of this end.
>
> "Let me assure my countrymen of the Southern States that, if I shall be charged with the duty of organizing an Administration, it will be one which will regard and cherish their truest interests—the interests of the white and of the colored people both and equally—and which will put forth its best efforts in behalf of a civil policy which will wipe out forever the distinction between North and South in our common country."

THE SOUTHERN QUESTION

HARPER'S WEEKLY
August 12, 1876, p. 651

The Hamburg massacre, and the deep and universal interest and horror that it has awakened, show that the Southern question is still one of the most vital and important subjects of public attention. It certainly is not so because of any wish or effort upon the part of Republicans in the Northern and Western parts of the country. In their State and National Conventions they have insisted only upon the honest constitutional protection of equal rights, and in New York last year they demanded "a just, generous, and forbearing policy in the Southern States." Nothing could be more baseless than the ill-timed and testy jesting of Mr. Cox, that the late troubles at Hamburg, in South Carolina, are in some way designed for political effect. As General Garfield truly and gravely said, murder is not to be laughed out of such occurrences. His question, indeed, goes to the root of the matter. Are such events in the Southern States sporadic, like the late Newark slaughter in New Jersey, or do they show a general feeling hostile to the equal rights of colored citizens? The history of those States for the last half century supplies the answer to his question. Nearly four millions of colored persons, who, with their ancestors, had been held in the most inhuman form of slavery for more than two hundred years, were suddenly freed and elevated to equal citizenship with the master class, as a consequence of the insurrection of that class against the Union, and of its total and ruinous

DECLARATION OF EQUALITY.—Justice. "Five more Wanted."

Harper's Weekly, August 12, 1876, pp. 656–57.

defeat. The general feeling of that class can only be one of contemptuous incredulity and distrust of the equality of those whom it had not considered or treated as human beings; and while many of them would not openly manifest their discontent, it is inevitable that there should be a large and reckless number who would not conceal their feelings nor hesitate at the most heinous crimes for its gratification.

This is precisely what has occurred. The Southern situation has constantly presented two facts: the most cruel and bloody outrage, terrorism, and massacre of the colored population, and a white public opinion that practically approved by declining to protest or to act with any vigor or efficiency. This is not a theoretical observation or abstract inference. In reply to General Garfield's direct question, Mr. Lamar, of Mississippi, said that the occurrence at Hamburg was not sporadic, although unnatural; it was the effect of a morbific element that he thought would disappear under good government. The Richmond *Whig* says that while it believes the great mass of the people in the Southern States to be peaceably inclined, "the misfortune is that public opinion is not outspoken enough to discourage these bad men from such acts against the weak," adding that the negroes are sometimes exasperating. And Colonel Higginson, calling attention to the fact that even the colored magistrate at Hamburg, before whom the case was brought, and whom he personally knows as a brave and loyal man, was also forced to fly for his life, speaks for thousands of intelligent and patriotic men in this part of the country in a letter to the New York *Times*:

> "Of all the Southern outrages since the war, there is no one more sure to have an important influence than this Hamburg atrocity. There is no conflict of testimony about it. It occurred in broad day, was utterly unprovoked, was attended by peculiar circumstances of barbarism, and included the armed invasion of a neighboring State. For one, I have been trying hard to convince myself that the Southern whites had accepted the results of the war, and that other questions might now come uppermost. So far from being a bigoted Republican, I took part in the 'Fifth Avenue Political Conference,' and should certainly have refused to support the Republican nominee had he not commanded my confidence. As it is, I am more than ever grateful for the influences which secured the nomination of Hayes and Wheeler. Of what use are all our efforts to lay aside the issues of the war, if they are still to be kept alive by our white fellow-citizens of the South? The spirit that sends armed men across the South Carolina border to-day may just as easily send them across the Pennsylvania border next year, if it secures the aid of a Democratic national Administration. For one, I do not propose to acquiesce in this."

Here is a question not to be shuffled aside by the cry that Democrats have accomplished reform by cutting down the army and reducing the salary of some foreign minister. Who commit these undeniable crimes against the very order and existence of society? Democrats. Who condone those crimes by silence, by incredulity, by calling them "negro riots," or by sneering at the bloody shirt? Democrats. Is it, then, to Democrats, to a party which counts for success in the election upon the votes of all in the Southern States who actively or passively connive at these constant and monstrous crimes, that the government of the country can be wisely intrusted?

THE HAMBURG BUTCHERY

HARPER'S WEEKLY
August 19, 1876, p. 671

President Grant, on the 1st inst., sent to the Senate a message concerning the recent massacre of negroes at Hamburg, South Carolina, and with it a copy of the following letter to Governor Chamberlain:

> "Executive Mansion,
> "Washington, D.C., *JULY 26,* 1876.
> "Dear Sir,—I am in receipt of your letter of the 22d of July, and all the inclosures enumerated therein, giving an account of the late barbarous massacre of innocent men at the town of Hamburg, South Carolina. The views which you express as to the duty you owe to your oath of office and to citizens to secure to all their civil rights, including the right to vote according to the dictates of their own consciences, and the further duty of the Executive of the nation to give all needful aid, when properly called on to do so, to enable you to insure this inalienable right, I fully concur in. The scene at Hamburg, as cruel, blood-thirsty, wanton, unprovoked, and uncalled-for as it was, is only a repetition of the course which has been pursued in other Southern States within the last few years, notably in Mississippi and Louisiana. Mississippi is governed to-day by officials chosen through fraud and violence such as would scarcely be accredited to savages, much less to a civilized and Christian people. How long these things are to continue, or what is to be the final remedy, the Great Ruler of the universe only knows; but I have an abiding faith that the remedy will come, and come speedily; and I earnestly hope that it will come peacefully. There has never been a desire on the part of the North to humiliate the South. Nothing is claimed for one State that is not freely accorded to all others, unless it may

be the right to kill negroes and Republicans without fear of punishment and without loss of caste or reputation. This has seemed to be a privilege claimed by a few States. I repeat again that I fully agree with you as to the measure of your duties in the present emergency, and as to my duties. Go on, and let every Governor where the same dangers threaten the peace of his State go on in the conscientious discharge of his duties to the humblest as well as the proudest citizen, and I will give every aid for which I can find law or constitutional power. A government that can not give protection to life, property, and all guaranteed civil rights—in this country the greatest is an untrammeled ballot—to the citizen is in so far a failure, and every energy of the oppressed should be exerted, always within the law and by constitutional means, to regain lost privileges and protection. Too long denial of guaranteed rights is sure to lead to revolution—bloody revolution, where suffering must fall upon the innocent as well as the guilty. Expressing the hope that the better judgment and co-operation of citizens of the State over which you have presided so ably may enable you to secure a fair trial and punishment of all offenders, without distinction of race or color or previous condition of servitude, and without aid from the Federal government, but on the promise of such aid on the conditions named in the foregoing, I subscribe myself, very respectfully, your obedient servant,

"U. S. Grant.

"To Hon. D. H. Chamberlain, Governor of South Carolina."

MR. TILDEN'S FRIENDS AS RIOTERS, 1863

HARPER'S WEEKLY
September 2, 1876, p. 715

It was upon the ultramontane population of New York that the indiscreet utterances of the Democratic leaders in Congress or in their public and private meetings produced their most dangerous effect, and roused them to a sudden act of rebellion, which, had it been successful, would have shaken to its centre the shattered republic. Could an armed body of insurgents have held even for a few days the command of the metropolis, they might have plundered it of its wealth or burned it to the ground. And it was this disaster that had nearly fallen upon us from the draft riots of 1863. Incited by the violent language of the Democratic leaders, encouraged by their imprudent policy, ignorant, barbarous, cruel, the Irish immigrants had been stirred by the emissaries of rebellion to an insane rage against the national government; they were prepared for riot, filled with insubordination.. On one occasion, long before the draft was begun, they had been seen gathered in crowds before their homes, murmuring against their rulers, threatening violence. For a time they were restrained by their leaders; but when at last the drafting was actually begun, when nearly all the forces of the nation were hurrying to Gettysburg, and only a small body of troops could be found in the ungarrisoned city, the ultramontanes rose with a fatal unanimity. So sudden and unlooked-for was the riot that New York awoke one morning to find itself in the hands of an enemy. Those who saw that troubled period, so full of doubt and terror, will remember the strange sensations with which they passed streets deserted by all save bands of plunderers; by houses, banks, and shops barred and guarded; beside the blazing ruins of fine buildings and the wrecks of stately manufactories; in the midst of fierce mobs who chased unfortunate colored men whenever they saw them, and hanged them ruthlessly to the nearest lamp post; through a forlorn and terrified city whose officials and chief rulers were believed to be in sympathy with the rioters and with rebellion, and who had been placed in power by the same wild mob that was now bent upon the ruin and plunder of New York. If the men who incite disorder are more guilty than even their blind adherents, it is to Messrs. Kernan, the two Woods, Brooks, Cox, Tilden, and Seymour that the nation owes this peril, from which it was only saved by a Republican police and a few United States soldiers.

On the morning of the 13th of July, 1863, no city could have been worse prepared for a sudden attack than was New York; and if we admit the theory of premeditation and of a well-concerted conspiracy, no moment could have been chosen more favorable for its foes. The swift, desperate, and brilliant movement of Lee toward Philadelphia had summoned away all the militia of the city. A barbarous inroad was to be met on the banks of the Delaware and the Potomac. The only protection of the metropolis was its police. But between the Governor of the State, Seymour, and the Police Commissioners a violent dispute existed, and the Governor had ordered their removal—would hold no communications with them. The Mayor, Opdyke, was loyal; the Common Council doubtful, and timid even to cowardice. The uncultivated Irish ruled in the elections, and to them Governor Seymour owed his place and power. If, as is reported, he called the rioters his "friends," it was only a proper recognition of their services. On the morning of Monday, the 13th, they rose in a vast multitude in the upper wards of the city, and came sweeping down the avenues in a resistless tide that seemed to meet no impediment. Every moment the concourse grew in strength. It was noticed by an observer to be twenty minutes in passing a single point, and reached from side to side of the street. The vast crowd set fire to

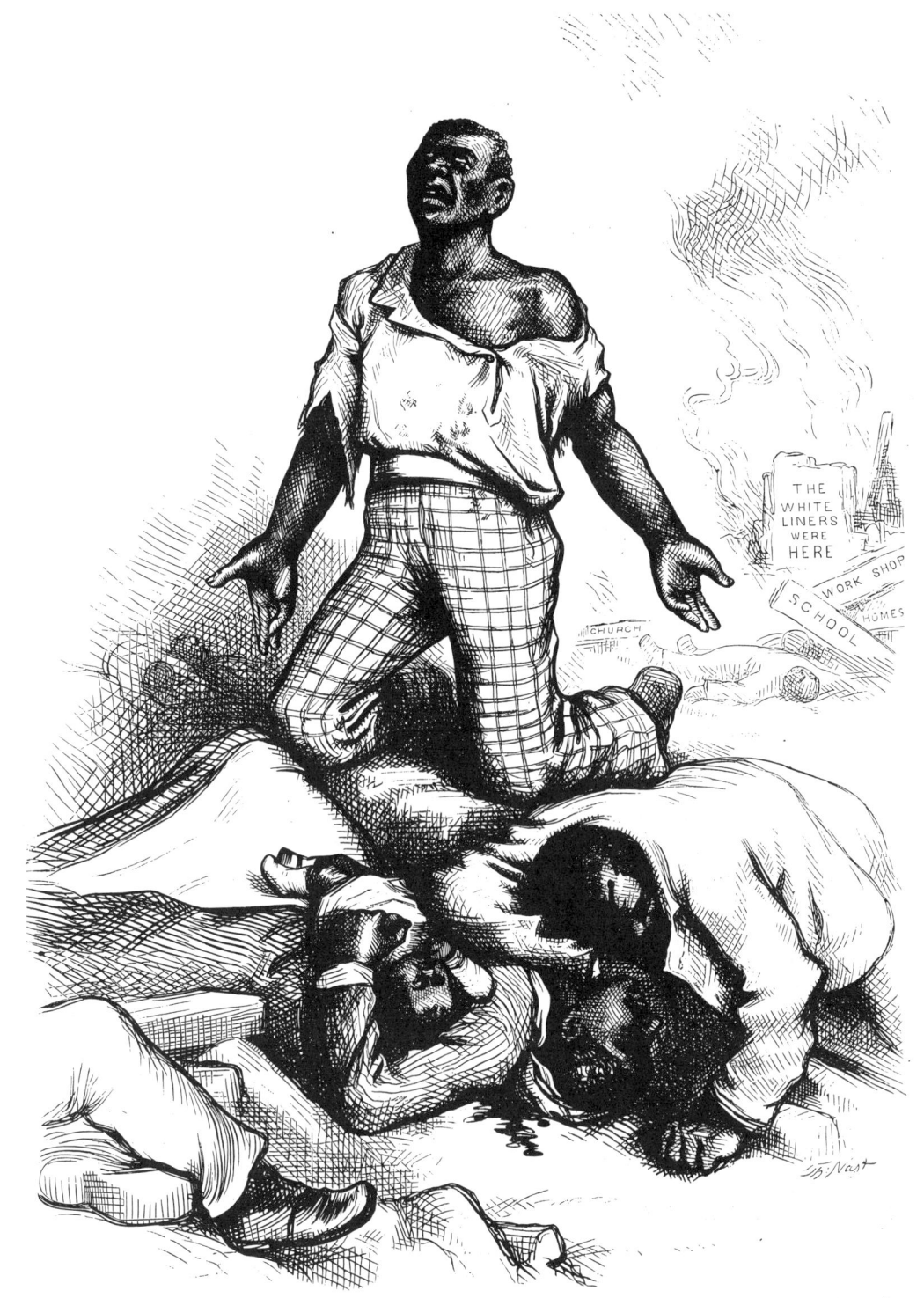

"IS *THIS* A REPUBLICAN FORM OF GOVERNMENT? IS *THIS* PROTECTING LIFE, LIBERTY, OR PROPERTY? IS *THIS* THE EQUAL PROTECTION OF THE LAWS?"
Mr. Lamar (*Democrat, Mississippi*). "In the words of the inspired Poet, 'Thy Gentleness has made thee Great.'" [Did Mr. Lamar mean the Colored Race?]

Harper's Weekly, September 2, 1876, p. 712.

the drafting places, beat back the police, and nearly killed its Superintendent, Kennedy. They chased him, half dead with wounds and bruises, through the streets; he leaped into a pond near Forty-seventh Street, and escaped to do good service in the later part of the affray. All that day the mob, composed chiefly of the Irish, ruled the city. They drove back and dispersed the Invalid Corps; they set fire to great blocks of buildings; they murdered harmless negroes; and on Monday night, except where the police and the few soldiers kept guard, or private buildings were protected by their owners, New York lay at the mercy of the insurgents, blazed with incendiary fires, and saw murder and rapine prevail in all its quarters.

The next morning, Tuesday, the rioters proceeded in a more regular manner; as if to secure their conquest they tore up the railroad tracks, and cut off all communication with the country. They seemed resolved to hold New York island, and had Lee been able to spare them a few troops and officers, might have beaten off the returning soldiers. They had supplied themselves with arms. They were mad with rapine and bloodshed. The secret dens of the secluded streets were filled with rich plunder, and in every part of the city might be seen the bodies of hapless negroes swinging from lamp posts, or lying bruised and mangled on the public way. The irrational hatred of the Irish for the harmless colored people was shown in acts of unparalleled barbarity. They murdered a lame son in the arms of his mother. "Save my mother," he cried, "if you kill me." Two ruffians seized him, a third struck him on the head with a heavy iron bar. Colored men chased by the mob plunged into the river, and sometimes saved themselves by swimming. Women and children were treated with equal severity. Often three or four negroes were found hanging together. Wild Irishmen were seen dancing around the corpses of their victims. A great number of houses occupied by colored people were sacked or burned. The Colored Orphan Asylum was burned to the ground. Its troop of children, often too young to know their danger, were moved in a sad procession, guarded by the police, to the river-side and carried to a safe retreat. Robbery went on unchecked in all our streets. The fine mansions on the avenues were laid under contribution. The blaze of a succession of fires terrified the city, civil war raged in its midst, and the second day of the riot seemed more disastrous than the first.

It was to the United States soldiers and General Brown, the commander of the troops in the harbor, that the rescue of the city was chiefly due. Governor Seymour had appeared early on the scene, had issued a strong proclamation, had made his memorable speech, but could do no more. He would hold no communication officially with the Police Commissioners he had striven to depose; it was well known that his sympathies were not with the national cause. The brave Acton, the head of the Commission, and his admirable police did all that their strength and numbers allowed to save the city; they fought successfully against immense odds, and clove the vast multitude of rioters like a fiery torrent. But it was not until General Brown and his well-trained soldiers came into action that the insurgents were made to feel that they had failed. The whole city was now in insurrection; the telegraph told of riot, murder, and devastation from the Park to Harlem River, and the seven hundred regulars, aided by the police, patrolled the island with incessant activity. They attacked the rioters on the east side, swept them away with cannon, pursued them into the houses, and flung them headlong from tall roofs upon the pavement below. In the Eighth Avenue a strong barricade had been formed between Thirty-seventh and Forty-third streets by lashing together carts, wagons, and telegraph poles with the telegraph wires. The side streets were also fortified. Against this strong position a detachment of regulars marched, aided by the police; they covered its defenders with a rapid fire of musketry, tore away barricade after barricade, and shot down the wild marauders as they fled madly along the streets. On Wednesday the fighting was renewed. On Thursday General Putnam, with the regulars, won a real but bloody victory over the rioters on East Twenty-ninth Street. Yet the struggle was now over; the various city regiments began to return from Gettysburg or Philadelphia; and the wild, fierce mob of Irish, who had been roused into fury by the arts of the Democratic leaders, were crushed into submission. The Germans, when the danger was at its height, sent word to the authorities that they would take care of their own section of the city and preserve the public peace.

By the Irish citizens of New York this unhappy episode can never be remembered without shame. But it must be said in palliation of their crime that they were ignorant, violent, untaught in the plainer rules of civilization, that they had been excited to madness by the imprudent suggestions of their Democratic leaders, and by violent appeals against abolitionists and Republicans. The Democratic meetings throughout the autumn of 1862 had been filled with the class of persons who led the riots and robbed the city. Seymour, Kernan, Cox, and Wood had never grown weary of denouncing the draft and defending the existence of slavery. These topics were the chief staple of every Democratic speech. Nor had the priest been more cautious. Always the leader of a compact Roman Catholic party, Archbishop Hughes openly expressed his condemnation of the draft in the midst of the flames of New York and the peril of the nation. The *Tribune* had suggested that he was in favor of a draft. In reply the archbishop pronounced the statement "a malignant lie." In a long and singularly Jesuitical letter he labored to show that he had been misunderstood, that he meant something else, or nothing at all; but no one could read that wary and verbose production without seeing where lay his sympathies and those of all his ultramontane party. They were not with the republic. He closed, however, his long letter with an appeal to all Roman Catholics to cease from unlawful proceedings and keep the peace. With one voice he incited to rebellion, with another he feebly inculcated submission. And the whole ultramontane press followed his example, and excused the violence it had labored to arouse.

Such in 1863 was the savage rage of that party in New York which must be hereafter known as the ultramontane, which has sedulously followed the guidance of Mr. Tilden and his friends, to whose support he owes all his political advancement, and from whose aid he hopes to win the control of the nation. The rioters who sacked and burned the city were nearly all Roman Catholics, and all Democrats. When they rose in rebellion, they only carried to an extreme those suggestions which they had so often heard from the lips of Hendricks, Cox, Wood, or Tilden. In their irrational hatred for the colored race they only anticipated the fearful deeds of the Ku-Klux Democracy. But every intelligent and patriotic Irishman and Roman Catholic, while he blushes for the mad violence of his countrymen, should labor to win them back to honesty and reason, should teach them to make reparation to the republic and the free institutions they have so often striven to overthrow. If in 1863 they were made the tools of the rebellion, if in 1868 they were the chief agents in the plunder of New York, let them in 1876 show their sincere penitence by becoming in heart and principle Americans. Let them leave forever their corrupt Democratic leaders and the murderous Ku-Klux of the South. Let them join the great party of education, progress, humanity, reform. In this way alone can Irishmen redeem their race from a lasting degradation, and win an honorable renown in every land.

Eugene Lawrence.

"THE SOUTH."

HARPER'S WEEKLY
September 9, 1876, p. 731

The report of the Senate's special committee upon the Mississippi troubles is a curious commentary upon Mr. Lamar's assertion that the late rebel partisans, who are now the force of the Democratic party in the Southern States, have honestly, fully, and finally acquiesced in reconstruction. This report considers, among other points, the election of the Legislature which chose Mr. Lamar to the Senate, and finds that it was accomplished by force and fraud. It asserts that the evidence of the general open arming of the Democrats, and of their frank declaration of an intention to carry the election "anyhow," is incontestable, and that the violence was mainly confined to the Republican counties, because those were the very places where it was necessary to overcome majorities. This is an illustration of the general conclusions of the report. That there is a great deal of negro terrorism at the South can not fairly be denied. It is equally true that there is a great deal of misgovernment. The disorder and violence are not unnatural. The reasons of the situation are obvious, and they must long continue. Meanwhile assertions of every kind will be made with vehemence and reason upon both sides.

We have, for instance, lying before us a letter from Texas and one from Kentucky. The Kentucky letter says that the troubles always occur in the States controlled by the "friends of the colored race," and it proceeds:

> "Your statesmen, when sincere, have not been philosophers on this subject. They have constantly said to the South, 'Stop these bloody occurrences, and we will stop meddling.' They ought to know that, so long as human nature remains as it is, the communities are practically powerless to stop them so long as the meddling continues. There have been several bloody riots and massacres of the Chinese in California. Suppose the United States Government were to send troops there for the avowed purpose of protecting the Chinese 'against the savage and uncivilized brutality' of the natives, what would a Chinaman's life be worth? Suppose, further, that they were as numerous, or more so, than the 'Mellicans,' that they had a general idea that they were possessed of an enormous amount of 'rights,' principal among which was the right to be offensive in any way they chose to be, and suppose the Government—to use a homely illustration—were to put this Chinaman on the 'Mellican's' shoulder or head, and dare him to knock the heathen off, would you like to insure that heathen's life? That's precisely what has been done toward the South all these weary years, and in this you may find the reasons for the fact that the State governments controlled by the Southern natives have been able to stop these disorders almost without an effort."

This is a letter written in good faith by a business man. But its tone reveals precisely the feeling toward the colored people from which the troubles spring. It says that they are due to outside interference, and that they do not occur where the "native people"—that is, the whites—have control. But that is the order of Warsaw. Georgia is controlled by the "native people." But the exodus of negroes from Georgia is greater than from any other State, and the simplest rights, such as jury duty, are denied them. The question of the method of keeping order is hardly less important than that of order. It is not denied that if the "white line" or White League or the Ku-Klux obtained absolute control, there would be "order" of a certain kind. When the negroes were absolutely enslaved there were few massacres like those of Hamburg and New Orleans. But that was a poor argument for slavery. The assertion that the massacres shall or will continue until the Butlers are allowed to manage matters as they choose, is a mere defiance. And our correspondent will observe that he differs radically from Mr. Lamar.

On the other hand, the Texas letter says:

> "The leading spirits of the Democracy here boast *an undivided South* for Tilden. An undivided South! when, without the presence

of the six-shooter as a hydra of intimidation to the timorous and peaceful black man, the Republican ticket would be *bound* to carry the Carolinas, Florida, Alabama, Mississippi, and Louisiana. These facts are based on correct estimates of the number of *colored* voters in those States, even though no whites should vote the Republican ticket—which, of course, can not be conceded. What, then, is meant by an undivided South for Tilden? Does it not plainly augur the pursuit of the old, old policy of the past—the intimidation of the black men from the polls? Most undoubtedly it does. I hereby warn the Northern Democrat that he does not know the heart of his brother in the South. Democracy in the North is not Democracy in the South. Here the term means only those who actively affiliated or deeply sympathized with the cause of secession during the war. Many noble citizens in the North, being justly indignant at the grave errors of men in the Republican party, have, in the name of reform, erroneously united themselves to the Democracy.... Again, I solemnly warn my fellow-citizens of the North and East that the spirit of 1861 is a flame smothered but not extinguished. To prove this, 'let facts be submitted to a candid world.' They have repeatedly claimed immunity for their emancipated slaves, thus seeking to ingulf the republic in fraudulent financial ruin. They still secretly hope, by a change of the national Administration in their favor, to obtain that immunity. In the name of justice and reform, they would grasp without shame and pocket without remorse the Treasury of this nation. They only accept the recent amendments to the Constitution on compulsion. They form a party of aristocracy and exclusion. Their motto is *death to negroes*; and they are constantly seeking, by every chicanery of local legislation, to deprive them of the right of franchise, under cover of educational and property qualification acts of their State Legislatures. They will not elect a Northern-raised man, though a Democrat, to the simplest office in their gift. A man's qualification for the most important offices is based upon his Confederate record. Coke, of Texas, was but recently elected to a seat in the national Senate over Hancock, a man acknowledged by both press and people to be vastly his superior as a statesman, because he was an ex-Confederate soldier, and Hancock was not, though both were Democrats of the strictest sect. They boast that they will use the Northern Democracy as a stepping-stone to power. Could they secure the election of Tilden in November, their next move would be to elect an ex-Confederate Democrat to the Presidency in 1880....All over the South secret bands are being drilled and organized, calling themselves Tilden *minute-men of '76*. This means a strong concert of action on the part of the Democracy to leave not a stone unturned in the South. The Democracy here also count heavily on the vote of the Pacific States, based on the explicit clause in their platform upon the Chinese question.... In many counties of these States they have gained majorities at the polls, when the census showed two colored to one white. Every colored man in these States is a Republican. They have accomplished this by the murder of our orators at political gatherings, and a regular armed and disguised *system* of terrifying the colored man from the ballot.... They have murdered the teachers of the black man's children. They protect each other, by the mockery of trial by *packed* juries, from punishment for any murder committed on Republicans in these States, thus hoping to destroy by bloodshed a spirit of loyalty to the Federal Union which neither force nor violence can extinguish. Is it possible, in view of all these facts, that the Northern Democrats will assist these men to power? God forbid!"

This is quite as good and conclusive evidence as to the situation as the other letter, and its tone of earnest conviction is obvious. The conclusion that we draw is, not that the Mississippi report suggests a wise policy, and certainly not that the party which the negro-butchers support, and which the Kentucky letter says can not manage them, should be brought into power, but that common-sense dictates that the Republican party, with the spirit and policy indicated by Governor Hayes's letter, should still control the government.

AFFAIRS IN SOUTH CAROLINA
"Riots" at Robbins on the Port Royal Railroad—
Blacks and Whites Reported Killed and Wounded—
The Whites Arming for Another "Riot."

NEW-YORK TIMES
September 21, 1876

Augusta, Sept. 20.—A portion of the Federal troops from Aiken are at Rouse's Bridge, and a portion at Ellenton. On Tuesday night the negroes burned the gin-house and other buildings on the plantation of Joseph Ashley, four miles from Robbins, on the Port Royal Railroad. The whites then attacked the negroes and a fight ensued. It is known that several were seriously wounded on both sides, and it is reported that some were killed. The negroes bushwhacked Deputy Sheriff Patterson, of Barnwell County, and seriously wounded him. Three hundred armed whites arrived at Steel Creek to-day, and a riot is expected. It is known that John Williams and Robert Williams (white) were killed by the negroes. Reports as to the number of negroes killed in the various battles differ.

"THE SOUTH."

HARPER'S WEEKLY
September 23, 1876, p. 770

The Republican party is held responsible for the condition of the Southern States. It is asserted that it ought to have pacified them and established harmony, and that the Southern situation is the reproach of Republican statesmanship. Now we concede all that may fairly be urged against the party. We do not defend the extraordinary report of Mr. Boutwell, nor any of the proved delinquencies and rascalities of any Republican officer, nor the extravagance and corruption of much legislation in some of the Southern States. But the responsibility of the Southern situation rests mainly with the Southern whites and with the Democratic party both in the Northern and Southern States. When the war ended, the entire moral and mental mastery of the position was in the hands of the Southern master class. This has always been evident to any one who reflected upon the subject. But the late speech of Mr. Lamar, the only really able Southern Representative, if accepted as a correct statement, would put it beyond question. He involves himself, indeed, in a logical absurdity by the effort to use his own statement against its necessary conclusion, but his evidence is decisive.

In speaking of the slaves and masters, Mr. Lamar said:

"Harmony, friendship, and confidence existed between these two races. Indescribable sympathies, old memories, kindly services mutually rendered, ties of childhood, of youth, of manhood, days of labor, days of battle, nights of watching, nights of anguish, had so intertwined the lives of that generation of Southern men and women, white and black, that at the close of the war there was scarce a black man, woman, or child who did not have some endearing relation with a white man, woman, or child, and was not also the object of a reciprocal attachment."

This, then, according to Mr. Lamar, was the relation between the races when the slaves were emancipated. But if it were so, it is not conceivable that the docile, dependent, affectionate blacks whom Mr. Lamar describes would instantly have deserted those with whom they were living in such endearing relations, to ally themselves with utter strangers. Yet the fact of the desertion is undeniable, and it can have, upon Mr. Lamar's theory, but one explanation. It is that the freedmen suddenly distrusted the master class.

What was the reason of this distrust upon the part of those who had been upon such "endearing" terms with the whites? Mr. Lamar insists that the government inspired distrust by assuming the hostility of the whites. But had the relation been what he describes, no government could possibly have accomplished such a result. From his own argument the conclusion is irresistible that it is the intelligent Southern whites and not the ignorant blacks who have drawn the color line. For if in any State the spirit of the master class had been truly friendly; if the first State legislation after the war had not been an oppressive black code; if the tone of the press had been sensible and sympathetic instead of cruel and scornful; if labor contracts had been reasonable and honestly enforced; if schools had been liberally encouraged; if political co-operation had been sincerely sought; if white public opinion had made the Ku-Klux impossible by its summary repression; if the press had denounced it, and the courts and juries and all local legal authorities had pursued and punished it; if, indeed, there had been any where among any considerable part of the white population a solitary sign of really friendly interest, or care, or desire of making the best instead of the worst of the situation, there would have been no white line, no considerable Ku-Klux, no Southern question.

The troubles of that question are not, as is constantly alleged, mainly due to the Republican party, but to the sullen folly which has always insisted upon one thing, and one only—that the Southern whites should be left to do with the blacks as they choose. This is what is meant by "home rule," and this is what Mr. Lamar and the Democratic party hope to accomplish by the election of Mr. Tilden. The Republicans are responsible for many mistakes and offenses in the Southern States, but the greatest of all for the country would be to abandon them in despair. There is quite enough intelligence and patriotism among Republicans to pursue a policy that could not be stigmatized as that of the carpet-bag or the bayonet. It is that foreshadowed by Mr. Hayes; while that of the Democrats must necessarily be that of Mr. Lamar and of Jefferson Davis in 1861, "Let us alone." They wished to be let alone then to secure slavery out of the Union, and they wish to be let alone now to secure practical political subjection of the negro within the Union. This is a policy sure to follow Democratic success, and no less sure to keep the country indefinitely disturbed, because the conscience and common-sense of the American people who freed the slaves will not endure the injustice involved in such a situation. The final settlement of the question lies, and lies only, in the defeat of that Democratic party to whose success "the

South" looks to "get even" with the negroes and the Republicans, and in the triumph of that just, generous, and forbearing policy, under Republican auspices, which the election of Governor Hayes will secure.

"THE SOUTH" IN THE CANVASS

HARPER'S WEEKLY
October 21, 1876, p. 846

It is not surprising that the immediate and general peril involved in a Democratic restoration—in other words, in the surrender of the administration to a combination of the old rebel and Copperhead interest—should precede all special issues in the campaign. The Democrats had so skillfully used Republican offenses, and had so sedulously declared that there was but one issue, and so many Republicans had become disheartened, that there was a general disposition when the canvass opened to forget that to-day can not be entirely dissevered from yesterday, and that the rules of common-sense and common prudence can not be more safely disregarded in public than in private affairs. It was the hitherto unconsidered fact that Mr. Tilden, if successful, could be elected only by the "solid South" with the aid of its old Democratic allies in the North, and that his administration would represent the defeat of the sentiment of the "loyal Union" States, which has suddenly and within a month startled the good sense of the country. It asks whether, conceding all that can fairly be charged against Republican administration, the individual offenses of Belknap and others, and all for which Republicans may justly be held responsible in the Southern States, is it advisable, in view of the powerful reform element in the Republican party and of the issues that are involved in the election, to call to the administration the unchanged Democratic party, with its controlling force now as always in the Southern States? Under any circumstances, and without the least partisan malice or unreason, can "the South," at this time and in the midst of late events, be supposed to be the seat of such patriotism, such love of the Union, such desire of reform, such devotion to the national faith and honor, such loyalty to the Stars and Stripes, before which the Confederate ensign went down ten years ago, that it would be wise to confide to it the government of the Union?

No allegation that "the South" has "acquiesced with dignity," that carpet-baggers and scalawags and negro Legislatures have devastated the land, should for an instant cloud the good sense of the country. The Republican party, whatever its failures, can not fairly be held to account for the inevitable consequences of slavery and of emancipation justified by the necessity of national existence. To intrust the protection of the rights guaranteed to the new citizens to the late master race, humiliated and exasperated as they are known to be, and not unnaturally, would offer the country the alternative of submitting tranquilly to the practical destruction of the rights conferred by the amendments, or of resisting. Certainly it is not an alternative that promises peace. This situation is not affected by the declarations of Mr. Wade Hampton that he will protect all rights and all persons, nor by the appeals of Mr. Isham G. Harris that he and his friends wish only peace. It is not their promises and professions on the stump, it is all experience, knowledge of human nature, the history of every land and of the last ten years in the Southern States, that must determine the action of the country. When in all those ten years has Mr. Hampton or Mr. Harris raised a voice or a hand to stay the terror that the Ku-Klux began? What have they and their friends practically done but hold aloof and pray and vote for a Democratic restoration? They were really masters of the situation. They might have readily acquired the control of the negro vote and the support of negro sympathy. In South Carolina Governor Chamberlain had made a stand against the Republican rascals. Why did not Mr. Hampton and his party strengthen the Governor's hands? The Convention that nominated Mr. Hampton was besought not to be guilty of the fatal folly of nominating him as against Chamberlain, and so forcing the Republicans to unite. He and his friends persisted. Why? Because they believed in a Democratic success in November, and did not wish to be entangled.

The Republican party is held responsible for the Southern situation; but if no scalawag or bummer had ever entered a Southern State, if every thing had been left to Hampton and Harris, if Andrew Johnson's policy had prevailed, would there have been any change in the situation of those States from the old time, except that upon the ruins of their prosperity peonage and the system of black codes would have taken the place of slavery? This does not seem to us the way of peace or of real union. The victorious country would have felt that it was cheated of the hardly won gains of the war. Now the Democratic policy tends precisely to that result. And as it is a result in which the country will not and should not acquiesce, it is to be resolutely avoided. Once abolish in the Southern mind the hope of a Democratic restoration, by which the negro will be "put down"—once compel the most reluctant to feel that they must make the best instead of the worst of the situation—and the best and most friendly Republican sentiment, that which is represented by Hayes and not by Butler, would at once control the national policy in the South. The Democratic party is the obstruction to pacific union now as it was the obstruction to pacific freedom twenty years ago. Nor can there be any real political re-organization until the old Democratic party of Seymour and Tilden, of Hampton and of Harris, disappears.

THE SOUTH

HARPER'S WEEKLY
November 4, 1876, p. 886

There is nothing more significant in the canvass than the Democratic talk about conciliation and fraternity in the Southern States. The country now sees distinctly that Mr. Tilden can be elected only by the virtual solidity of "the South." His warmest friends do not deny that the deliberate judgment of the States that saved the government would be against him. His success would be the return of the South to power. Two things, therefore, become imperative in his canvass—one is that his managers shall show the peculiarly lamb-like character of Southern sentiment and practices, and the other that any exposure of the truth of the situation in the Southern States shall be derided as unfraternal and hostile. But there is no necessity more pressing than that of preventing the diversion of public attention from the facts. And no greater evil could befall us than to suffer weariness of the Southern question to blind us to its controlling importance.

Many parts of the Southern States are practically camps. The whites, who have never shown any hesitation in the pursuit of their purposes, are resolved upon the virtual suppression of the colored vote. To this end they have established a terror. Their newspapers exhort the voters to refuse to deal with Republican tradesmen. The Charleston *News and Courier,* for instance, publishes the following:

> "The colored butchers in the Charleston market are Radicals, with, we believe, one exception. They are a well-to-do class, and contribute liberally to the Radical campaign fund at every election. Every dollar paid to them by the supporters of Hampton and Simpson is an indirect contribution to the election of Chamberlain and Elliott. And these Radical butchers get the bulk of the business. There are plenty of butchers in the market who are known Democrats, men who are thoroughly with us. These are the men to deal with and encourage in every possible way. And what is true of the butchers is true of those engaged in many other pursuits."

This being the spirit and method of the most reputable Democratic organs in the cities and amidst a more responsible public opinion, it is not difficult to understand what it is in the remoter districts. The whites have formed rifle clubs and other military organizations, which parade at Republican meetings and take possession of them, insisting upon a division of time with Democratic speakers. In Georgia, which is cited as the most peaceful of the Southern States, the negroes are excluded from juries; and in the election precinct of Savannah there is but one polling place, which is so arranged as to exclude the colored voters. It is not surprising that the negro exodus from Georgia is very great. The best private as well as public accounts leave no doubt whatever that by such means the white Democrats in the Southern States mean to carry them solid for Tilden and reform—in other words, for white Southern-supremacy in the government.

The effect of this kind of terrorism is easily conceivable. It effectually frightens the colored voter, and the reason the Democrats exult so loudly over their lean success in Indiana, and are so dumb over their eighty or a hundred thousand majority in Georgia, is that they know that a little severer pressure of their terror would have given them a virtually unanimous vote. In certain counties in Southern States where there is an undoubted colored Republican vote of more than two thousand, there have been polled sometimes about a dozen votes. This is the way by which "Tilden and Reform" are to be brought in, and the quality of the reform may be inferred from the methods and the men. No man of common-sense and comprehension of the American character can suppose that this is any more a solution of the question of the South than it is of that of reform. The Democratic party simply asks the country to suffer the system and principle of reconstruction to be overthrown. That party has already declared it to be void, and it hopes now to make it so. And of necessity this question commands the canvass, and it is a question raised not by the Republicans, but by the Democrats.

If Mr. Tilden and his friends wished to concentrate the attention of the country upon the financial issue or that of administrative reform, their policy was to secure fair play in the Southern States. They did not attempt it. Why? Because they knew that fair play would prevent a solid South, and destroy all chance of Mr. Tilden's election. The Democratic leaders could readily prevent the harassing of Republican meetings and the harrying and terrifying of negroes every where in the Southern States. They could have prevented the Ku-Klux and the massacres. They could have prevented the drawing of the white line. They are responsible for the situation. Mr. Tilden and his friends, the Democratic leaders of the North, had but to say that the terror must cease, and it would have ceased. They have not said so. They have contented themselves with denying what every body knew to be the truth, and they have done it, as usual, for their party advantage, and not for the public welfare. They knew that if the full colored vote was cast in the Southern States without coercion, there could be no doubt of Republican success.

If the Democrats desire conciliation and fraternity, let them show that disposition in the Southern States. Conciliation does not parade in arms at the meetings of political opponents, and fraternity does not use the Derringer as a political weapon. Home rule means the hopeless intimidation of the Southern colored vote and the practical overthrow of reconstruction. Will that poli-

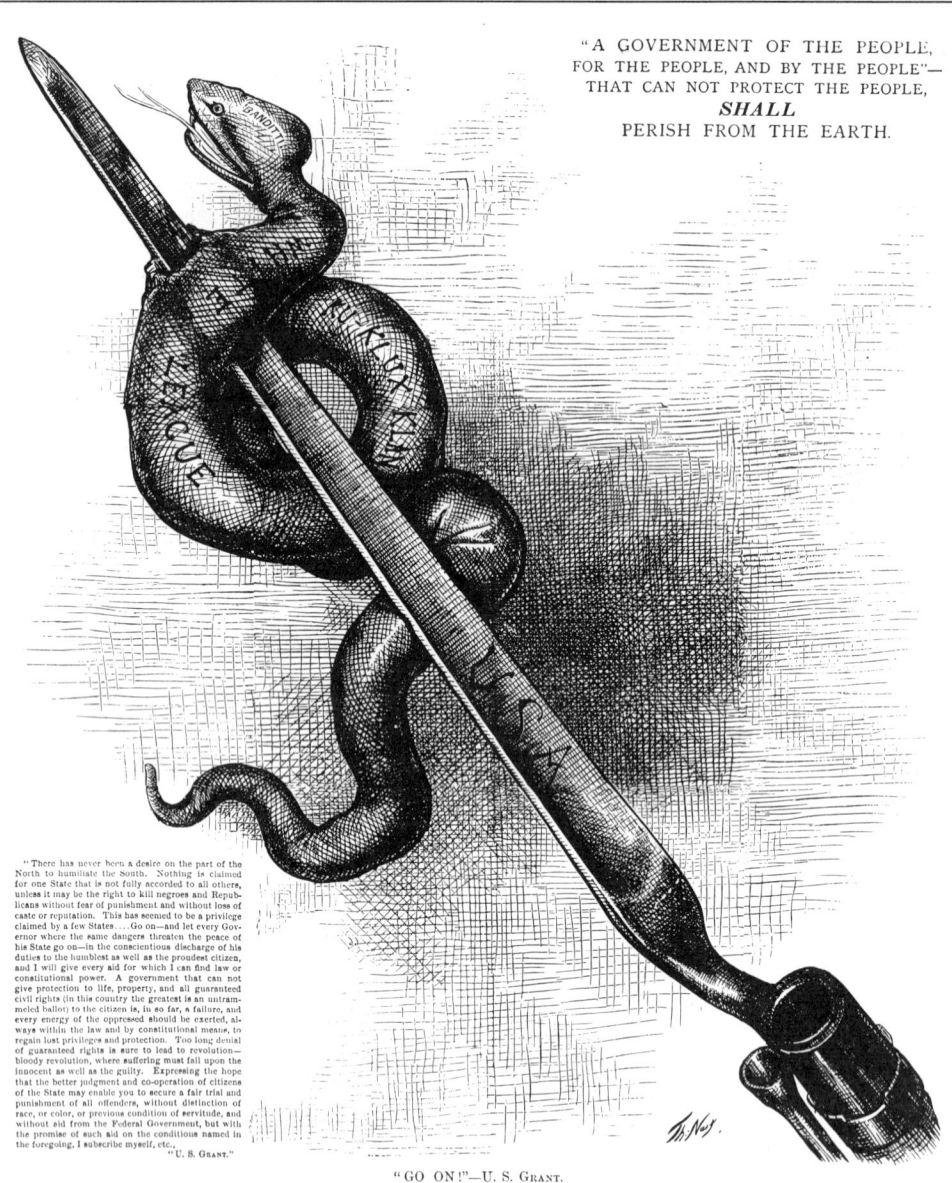

"A GOVERNMENT OF THE PEOPLE, FOR THE PEOPLE, AND BY THE PEOPLE"— THAT CAN NOT PROTECT THE PEOPLE, **SHALL** PERISH FROM THE EARTH.

"There has never been a desire on the part of the North to humiliate the South. Nothing is claimed for one State that is not fully accorded to all others, unless it may be the right to kill negroes and Republicans without fear of punishment and without loss of caste or reputation. This has seemed to be a privilege claimed by a few States.... Go on—and let every Governor where the same dangers threaten the peace of his State go on—in the conscientious discharge of his duties to the humblest as well as the proudest citizen, and I will give every aid for which I can find law or constitutional power. A government that can not give protection to life, property, and all guaranteed civil rights (in this country the greatest is an untrammeled ballot) to the citizen is, in so far, a failure, and every energy of the oppressed should be exerted, always within the law and by constitutional means, to regain lost privileges and protection. Too long denial of guaranteed rights is sure to lead to revolution—bloody revolution, where suffering must fall upon the innocent as well as the guilty. Expressing the hope that the better judgment and co-operation of citizens of the State may enable you to secure a fair trial and punishment of all offenders, without distinction of race, or color, or previous condition of servitude, and without aid from the Federal Government, but with the promise of such aid on the conditions named in the foregoing, I subscribe myself, etc.,
"U. S. GRANT."

"GO ON!"—U. S. GRANT.
THE CONSTITUTION OF THE UNITED STATES MUST AND SHALL BE PRESERVED—**AND PROTECTED**

THE ORDER TO GENERAL SHERMAN.

WAR DEPARTMENT, WASHINGTON CITY, *August* 15, 1876.
To General W. T. SHERMAN, *commanding United States Army*:

SIR,—The House of Representatives of the United States, on the 10th inst., passed the following preamble and resolution, viz. (SCOTT LORD, Dem., N. Y.):

Whereas, The right of suffrage prescribed by the Constitution of the United States is subject to the Fifteenth Amendment of the Constitution of the United States, which is as follows:
"ARTICLE XV.—SECTION 1. The right of citizens of the United States to vote shall not be denied or abridged by the United States or by any State on account of race, color, or previous condition of servitude.
"SECTION 2. The Congress shall have power to enforce this article by appropriate legislation."
And whereas, The right of suffrage so prescribed and regulated should be faithfully maintained and observed by the United States and the several States and the citizens thereof; and
Whereas, It is asserted that the exercise of the right of suffrage is in some of the States, notwithstanding the efforts of all good citizens to the contrary, resisted and controlled by fraud, intimidation, and violence, so that in such cases the object of the amendment is defeated; and
Whereas, All citizens, without distinction of race, or class, or color, are entitled to the protection conferred by such article; therefore,
Be it resolved by the House of Representatives, That all attempts by force, fraud, terror, intimidation, or otherwise to prevent the free exercise of the right of suffrage in any State should meet with certain, condign, and effectual punishment; and that in any case which has heretofore occurred or that may occur hereafter in which violence or murder has been or shall be committed by one race or class upon the other, the prompt prosecution and punishment of the criminal or criminals in any court having jurisdiction is imperatively demanded, whether the crime be one punishable by fine or imprisonment or one demanding the penalty of death.

The President directs that, in accordance with the spirit of the above, you are to hold all the available force under your command, not now engaged in subduing the savages on the Western frontier, in readiness to be used, upon the call or requisition of the proper legal authorities, for protecting all citizens, without distinction of race, color, or political opinion, in the exercise of the right to vote, as guaranteed by the Fifteenth Amendment, and to assist in the enforcement of "certain, condign, and effectual punishment" upon all persons who shall "attempt by force, fraud, terror, intimidation, or otherwise to prevent the free exercise of the right of suffrage," as provided by the law of the United States, and have such force so distributed and stationed as to be able to render prompt assistance in the enforcement of the law. Such additional orders as may be necessary to carry out the purpose of these instructions will be given to you from time to time after consultation with the law officers of the government.
Very respectfully your obedient servant,
J. D. CAMERON, Secretary of War.

Harper's Weekly, September 30, 1876, p. 801.

cy pacify Northern as well as Southern sentiment? Will that policy take the negro out of politics? Will it put an end to agitation upon the subject? No man in his senses believes it. Peace and order in the Southern States can not be fully reached until the white line is rubbed out. And that is not possible so long as the Derringer policy prevails. So long as the Democrats of that part of the country look for a Democratic reaction in the national administration, the present state of things will continue. When that hope is lost, they will understand that the only chance of real pacification lies in union with that Republican sentiment which sympathizes with the con-

THE CHRISTIAN (?) TURKS.
"Reforming" colored voters South.

Harper's Weekly, October 14, 1876, p. 840.

dition of the Southern States, but which is absolutely resolved upon maintaining the principle of reconstruction.

THE REBEL SENTIMENT
Specimen Extracts from a Mississippi Tilden Paper.

NEW-YORK TIMES
November 16, 1876

The following paragraphs are taken from the Meridian (Miss.) *Mercury* of the 11th inst.:

"It is just possible that the Northern Republicans who, in their rage, threaten that Tilden, if elected, will not be permitted to: be inaugurated, count largely, in case of a resort to arms to prevent it, on the negro element being in the way of throwing the weight of the South's strength in favor of the right. If their folly should provoke an appeal to arms, it will be attended with at least one result. They will learn that a "solid South" in peace is far more so in war. There will be no masters then to be interfering with the more perfect use of the thews and sinews of the negroes, which the governing race will then command most absolutely. The turbulent manifestations observed now, in war would cease altogether, because in war laws are silent, and the most silent of all the ridiculous statutes of reconstruction would be those laws which now tempt foolish negroes to turbulence, and such foolish ventures as at Artesia on Wednesday."

"The Radical ticket distributed among the negroes yesterday was headed 'Hold the Fort!' It had a picture with 'Father Abraham' as the principal figure. The darkeys stuck them deep down in their pockets and held them with a grip. It is not certainly known what white man distributed the tickets among them, but it was done clandestinely. They didn't hold the fort."

"The negroes didn't 'hold the fort' much in this county. Now that it is all over, we would give a pretty good sum to know who printed those tickets headed 'Hold the Fort,' and who distributed them. We suggest to them that the better policy, in future, is to print their tickets openly and distribute them openly, like white men. In other words, we recommend to our Radical friends to be as bold as a sheep in all of their election tricks. That is the way to put up the value of the wool as a factor in a popular election."

"There got out an impression yesterday that there was a Government United States Marshal and spy about. A drummer came into the crowd and was a looker-on in Vienna, and soon fell under suspicion. He was very soon interviewed, but with all due politeness. His references were satisfactory. We do not suppose he takes our inquisitiveness unkindly at all, as most gentlemanly apologies were tendered for interrupting his quiet observations."

VIRGINIA THREATS TO NEGROES
From the Petersburg Index-Appeal, Nov. 14.

NEW-YORK TIMES
November 16, 1876

Black folks are said to be "powerful uncertain." We had some instances of colored inconstancy in this district. The North Carolina papers are publishing the names of negroes in that State who promised their white friends solemnly to vote for Tilden, and then went treacherously to the polls, and deposited their ballots for Hayes and Wheeler. Among these scoundrels was a colored barber of Halifax, by the name of John Dabney. The hope is expressed in our North Carolina exchanges that these knaves will be spotted and treated as their perfidy deserves. The men who vote deliberately against the rights, the peace, the interests, and the liberties of the Southern people have no claim to be supported by the

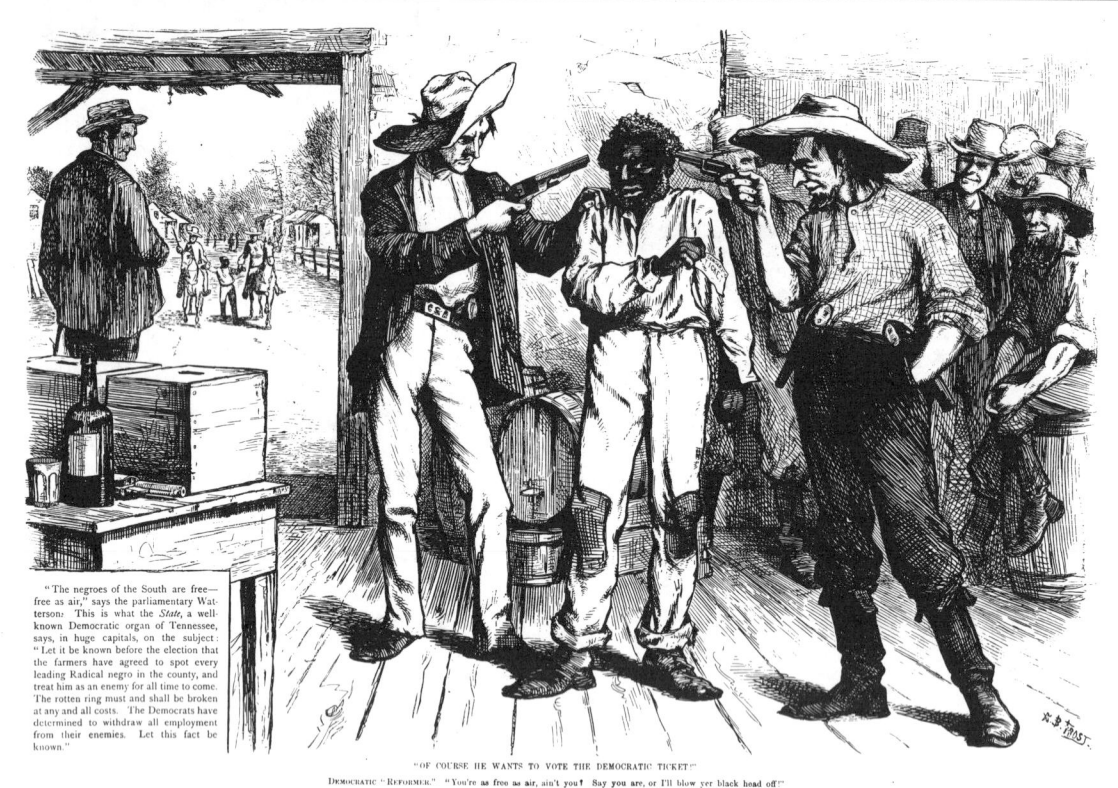

AFRICAN AMERICAN HISTORY IN THE PRESS, 1851-1899

"The negroes of the South are free—free as air," says the parliamentary Watterson: This is what the *State*, a well-known Democratic organ of Tennessee, says, in huge capitals, on the subject: "Let it be known before the election that the farmers have agreed to spot every leading Radical negro in the county, and treat him as an enemy for all time to come. The rotten ring must and shall be broken at any and all costs. The Democrats have determined to withdraw all employment from their enemies. Let this fact be known."

"OF COURSE HE WANTS TO VOTE THE DEMOCRATIC TICKET!"
DEMOCRATIC "REFORMER." "You're as free as air, ain't you? Say you are, or I'll blow yer black head off!"

Harper's Weekly, October 21, 1876, p. 848.

patronage of the citizens of this section. They will never be brought to reason except by short, sharp, and decisive measures. Let them be left without patrons and without friends, and they will soon enough find out where their interest be, and will vote accordingly. It may seem beneath the dignity of gentlemen to concern themselves about the politics of those who serve them; but this is no ordinary political issue, and those who oppose us are warring on the very liberties of our children, and on the bread which goes into their mouths. We cannot make it too warm for these [ ], and the sooner the policy of making them responsible for their iniquitous course is inaugurated, the better it will be for all parties interested.

INTIMIDATION IN GEORGIA

NEW-YORK TIMES
November 16, 1876

The Washington, (Wilkes County, Ga.,) *Gazette* says, that the vote there was 1,139 for Tilden and 2 for Hayes, and then talks thus plainly: "The above shows this old county to be still true to the Democracy. At the State election last month there was not a single Radical vote polled in the county. In the voting last Tuesday there were two voted at this precinct, by whom is unknown; and it is well, perhaps, that the two creatures who attempted to dim our bright [cutcheon] should remain unknown. The two Radical votes may have been polled by negroes, but we do not know. About 10 o'clock a large number of negroes, about two hundred in all, marched into town from the negro settlement in procession. They came, doubtless, with the intention of voting the Radical ticket. They marched up to the railing around the Court-house and halted. They stood around for about half an hour, looking confused and sheepish. They were no doubt ashamed of themselves. A few white men went among them and talked with them, but could get nothing out of them. Some of the crowd had a curiosity to see a Hayes and Wheeler ticket, and tried to find one among these negroes, but they failed, as not a darky would show his ticket. Finally they withdrew in good order, but looking very foolish."

WHIPPING-POST AND PILLORY

HARPER'S WEEKLY
November 18, 1876, p. 938

On the preceding page we give a picture representing scenes around the whipping-post and pillory at George-

"HE WANTS A CHANGE TOO."

Harper's Weekly, October 28, 1876, p. 872–73.

"IN SELF-DEFENSE."
SOUTHERN CHIV. "Ef I hadn't-er killed you, you would hev growed up to rule me."

Harper's Weekly, October 28, 1876, p. 880.

town, Sussex County, Delaware, which took place during the October court sessions. The chief incident was the whipping of a white tramp who had been convicted of larceny. A negro, convicted of the same crime, was standing in the pillory during the execution of the sentence, and appeared to witness the spectacle with great relish. The negro woman standing in the pillory underwent that punishment for the crime of housebreaking. Quite a large number of culprits were sentenced during the October sessions, some to be whipped only, others to both pillory and whipping, and others to stand in the pillory for periods varying with the degrees of the offenses of which they were convicted.

MORE LIGHT

How the Negroes Vote When They Have a Chance—Effect of the Presence of Soldiers—A Lady at the Ballot-box—A Fair Vote and a Fair Count, with the Result.

NEW-YORK TIMES
November 25, 1876

The following is an extract from a letter written by a lady teacher in South Carolina to a friend in the North. It will be found thoroughly worthy of perusal. How the negroes vote when they are allowed to do so freely, is very graphically set forth in the lady's communication:

My Dear G—**** The whites tore away about the soldiers being sent down, but let me tell you, where they thought the soldiers could help *them* they were in hot haste to avail themselves of them. For instance, on Monday afternoon, before election, up comes a squad of soldiers, under the command of a Lieutenant, to my school-house, accompanied by two native whites. I gave them the recitation-room in the school-house. They (the whites) represented to the General that there were a great many colored men who wanted to vote the Democratic ticket, but their lives were threatened in case they did. Not long after the soldiers came the news spread over the island like wild-fire, and the clans began to gather. On they came—on horse-back, mule-back, and "foot-back," and wanted to know of me "what dis yere ting mean?" and "how do rebel bring hem?" Their first thought was to put them off the island. Of course I set them all right, and told them all violence would only damage ourselves. In the meantime, seeing the gathering, the Lieutenant came up, told them when they saw the *blue* it was all right. One man said, "I know de blue cloths. Sir, but dese are tricky times, and de rebs can buy blue cloths." The Lieutenant smiled at the idea of tricky times. Well, next morning the polls opened at 6 o'clock—before daylight. The whites came with everything cut and dried. They said to the only sharp colored man, "We want you to be Chairman of the board, and Mr. S. here to be clerk of the board." (There are three managers, two colored and one white, and they choose the clerk.) "Oh, no!" said the person addressed. "I want Miss S. to be clerk of the board." All objections were overruled and at 6 A.M. I was sworn Clerk of the Board. That was a decided advantage to us, as two years ago with a much smaller vote, there were sixty-five more votes than names on the poll list; consequently they were thrown out. Well, the result at our poll was 585 solid Republican votes and only sixteen Democratic votes. Oh, but we had fun counting them—the poor forlorn votes. The last one I took out of the box was a Democrat. I held it up and began to sing "'Tis the Last Rose of Summer," and there the soldiers stood to see their magnificent pile of sixteen votes, and we only lacked fifteen of 600. During the day one fellow that the Democrats had been trying to persuade to vote their ticket, and as an argument laid all the hard times to the Republican Party, as he put his ticket in the box said: "There goes a straight Republican ticket, if I have to eat hay the next six months." Another old man hobbled along, and as he put in his ticket said: "There goes a good 'Publican ticket, and may de Lord prosper him!" "Amen!" said I, in good Methodistic fashion. Oat doors you could hear them say: "I tell you news; de ting is going right when you see Miss S. dere." No votes to throw out that day. We insisted on them keeping their own count, so there was no unfairness the whole day. But the whites were a sick crowd. They claim the State;

also that Tilden is elected. We have carried the State, and, of course, I believe Hayes is elected. You will know all about the election before you get this. We have carried this county by over 6,000 majority. The women went to the polls to see how their husbands voted. At one place a woman saw her husband about to put in a Democratic vote, and she sprang on him like a tiger and dragged his shirt off his back. The "brudder" left for repairs, and didn't vote that day. The News and Courier now complains that the women intimidated the men.

THE VOTE OF THE SOUTH

*Questions that the North Must Decide.
From Our Special Correspondent.*

NEW-YORK TIMES
November 30, 1876

Shall the Country Be Governed by Force or by Law?—How the Cotton States Obtain a Double Vote—Facts that Cannot Be Disputed—The Views of a Shrewd Observer—"Put Yourself in His Place."

New-Orleans, Saturday, Nov. 25, 1876

There are 84,167 white voters and 104,192 black voters in the State of Louisiana, and in the other cotton States of South Carolina, Florida, Alabama, and Mississippi the white and colored citizens are divided in about the same proportion. Of the white citizens ninety-five out of every hundred vote the Democratic ticket, and out of every hundred of the black citizens ninety-nine would vote the Republican ticket if they were permitted to freely exercise the rights which were guaranteed to them by the reconstruction acts and the amendments to the National Constitution. But the black citizens are not permitted to freely exercise those rights. By intimidation, by violence, by outrage, by murder, by the most unhuman cruelties, by proscription, and by glaring frauds the Democrats prevent them from voting as they desire to vote; and it is because they have been so prevented that Florida, South Carolina, and Louisiana did not give the Republican candidates for President and Vice President an unquestioned majority among from four to thirty thousand votes. Aside from the Presidential question, however, the political situation in this part of the Union presents many features which must be considered at this time, many problems which must now be definitely settled, if the peace and prosperity of the nation is to continue.

The foremost question and the one which most pressingly demands an answer is, shall the two political parties in the South be allowed to exist upon the same terms and conditions that they exist in other parts of the country, in other words, and to be more explicit, shall the right of every citizen, of every voter, to participate in the National and State Governments on election day, to assist and actively co-operate with the societies, clubs, and other organizations of this political party, be recognized and guaranteed absolutely, so that whether a man be a white Democrat or a black Republican he shall be allowed, in perfect security and with perfect freedom, to join and act with such political associations as his own interests, prejudices, or wishes may dictate? If this question receives an affirmative answer from the people of the United States, if the laws, as they exist, are properly executed and enforce; if the black men are protected; if the political murderers and cut-throats of the South are punished swiftly, surely, and at no matter what cost, then the country has heard the last of "a solid South," with all the dangers which the term implies; but if, on the other hand, the present condition of affairs is allowed to continue; if what some one has aptly called "the banditti vote" of Mississippi and Louisiana be allowed to control those States; if political massacres go unpunished; if the law-abiding masses of the country will stand quietly by and allow men, women, and children to be shot or starved to death for opinion's sake, then until another war frees it from the yoke the nation may expected to be governed more absolutely and completely by the "solid white South" than Louisiana was in the palmy days of the slave empire. And just here there is one act which must not be lost sight of. The Southern States have 138 votes in the Electoral College. Were it not for negro suffrage, those same States would have only about ninety votes in the Electoral College. Louisiana has eight Electoral votes, but if the law did not allow the black men to vote, if the negroes were legally disfranchised, the State would have only four votes in the College. As it is, the black citizens who give the State this increased influence in the nation are illegally and by violence kept away from the polls, and virtually every white man, every Democrat, casts two votes. So in nearly all the cotton States, the white Democrats have double representation in the Electoral College, and twice as much voice in the election of a President as have the citizens of New York or California. Should this state of things be allowed to exist?

Regarding the means which the Democrats employ to influence and intimidate the negroes. It is not necessary to speak at this time. All their terrible practices have been already fully detailed, and yet there is reason to believe that the people of the North have never quite realized the dangers of the Southern situation. In the words of Judge Hugh J. Campbell, one of the shrewdest political observers in this State, to fully understand what Southern Republicans have to endure, to understand why there is not one Republican vote cast in countries where there are two thousand Republican voters, the citizen of New-York or New-England must imagine for

THE CENTENNIAL—VISIT OF THE "SMALL BREED" FAMILY.—[Drawn by Sol Eytinge, Jun.]

Harper's Weekly, November 4, 1876, p. 904.

a moment that "the Mississippi plan" of carrying elections prevailed at the north. To carry out the Judge's idea, suppose, for instance, that Tom McEwen or Sam Hammond, the leading Democrats of Geneva, N. Y., were taken out of their beds some twelve months before the last election and hanged in the public square of the town. And suppose that Bob McLean, another leading Democrat, while on a visit to Albany had been kidnapped by a mob of Republican ruffians and had been bound hand and foot, tied to a horse and driven out into the woods; then suppose that he was met by a dozen masked men who cut him loose from the horse, tied him to a tree, and shot him to death with a hundred bullets. And after all this, suppose that the Republicans of Geneva and all the surrounding country had organized themselves into secret political societies, commanded by military officers, and armed with rifles and navy revolvers. Suppose, then, that these societies had driven every Democratic official out of the county; suppose that these Republican rifle clubs, or "bull-dozers," had ridden in armed bands through all the country about Geneva, nightly, for three months before the election. Suppose that during these rides they had shot twenty or thirty Democrats, whipped a couple of hundred, and warned the rest that they would surely be killed if they voted the Democratic ticket. Suppose these men had broken up every Democratic club in the district. Suppose they had burned the houses of a dozen Democrats. Suppose at the same time that these Republican cutthroats owned all the property, the stores, the houses, the banks, the railroads, the telegraph, the newspapers, the schools, the everything; and, suppose that all the Democrats except those who had been killed or driven away, were ignorant and poor, so poor, indeed, that they depended for every mouthful of bread upon the Republican "bull-dozers"—let the citizen of New-York suppose all these things, and then let him ask himself the question. "After such a campaign, how many votes would the Democratic ticket receive in Geneva!" This picture is not over-drawn. It is in the manner described that the Parish of East Feliciana, in this State, was carried for Tilden and Reform.

WAR ON THE FREE SCHOOLS

Southern Democratic Opposition to Educating the Negroes—They Should be Kept in their True Sphere Manual Labor.

NEW-YORK TIMES
December 1, 1876

The Macon (Ga.) *Telegraph and Messenger,* a Democratic paper, prints conspicuously a communication in

THE WHIPPING-POST AND PILLORY IN DELAWARE.—From a Sketch by A. Stierle.—[See Page 938.]

Harper's Weekly, November 18, 1876, p. 937.

which the writer says: "Our popular fellow-citizen, Col. Thomas Hardemau, was applauded to the very echo on the night of the 7th inst. when he boldly declared 'that though in the past he had talked, written, and spoken in behalf of our public schools, after the day's exhibition of the negro's continued enmity to the white race, voting solidly against their best and truest interests, eagerly following the suggestions of the bitterest foes of him and his people, so help him God, he would never again use his voice to urge the appropriation of white people's money to educate their most inflexible and determined enemies.' Let us beware how we vote money to raise up and educate in our midst those who will, by reason of their smattering of an education, refuse to do the work now done by their ignorant parents, and cause them to unite more intelligently in their efforts to extort money out of the whites to educate their own [ ] race, as well as to work the more zealously to injure their benefactors and educators in political matters. We should not be forced unjustly and unwillingly to surrender our money to educate and exalt our national and social enemies. It is a cruel wrong to expend large sums wrung by a grinding taxation from the oppressed whites, who really contribute a hundred times more to support the public schools than the negroes—upon a pretended education of freed slaves, when the State is burdened with huge debts it cannot pay except by ruinous taxation. The State and people must be just before they are generous. Very many of our white fellow-citizens before the war independent and intelligent, are now prevented from educating their own children properly, because they are compelled to keep them in the corn-field, laboring from year's end to year's end to raise taxes to give a pretended education to the brats of the black paupers, who are loafing around their plantations, stealing a part of the scanty crops and stock their poor struggling boys have worked to raise. This is a burning wrong upon the white race. This fatal [i]nnovation of negro suffrage and education was thrust upon us by the Radicals. The negroes do not, except in rare instances, possess any taxable property, hence they have no responsibility, no patriotic interests, no tax burdens to bear. They are driven and controlled like herds of sheep by our Radical slanderers and enemies. They are mere slaves to a party which is the relentless enemy of our most sacred rights and dearest interests. Educate these unfriendly blacks, and you teach them to seek a living without work, for a little learning [unfits] them for their true sphere—manual labor—and they will grow up to restive, surly, and insolent toward the whites. The carpet-bagger and white Radical have already inflicted grievous injury upon us by indoctrinating evil ideas into their woollyheads, and we should not join them in their unholy work of educating them to be lazy, trifling, and insolent. Voting and free schools awaken in the idle young negro foolish and absurd aspirations, which will surely engender much trouble and evil. Education makes the negro fickle, unreliable, and insolent; then let us not, in future, waste our hard-earned money in bringing up a race which seek to oppress and degrade us, while enjoying privileges which we confer. Let both races educate themselves, and each man his own off[ ]."

THE PRESIDENT

HARPER'S WEEKLY
December 9, 1876, p. 987

The conduct of the President during the suspense that followed the election has been universally commended by good citizens. His reasonable and admirable order to General Sherman at once steadied public sentiment, and reminded us that the head of the executive department is a firm, quiet, and patriotic man, who knows his duty, and will not hesitate to perform it. We have often criticised the Administration, but, in common with all who have had opportunity of observation and knowledge, we have always gladly testified to the perfect integrity and patriotism of the President. Those who talk about "the military" and "the army" and "the bayonet" and "despotism" may safely be challenged to show a single act in the eight years of General Grant's administration which indicates an improper ambition or an eagerness to resort to military methods. Even Democratic candor, could it escape the heats of party zeal, would probably agree that the President has never shown himself unmindful of the just restraints of the civil law.

The late disposition of troops at Washington was a simple measure of precaution, which it would have been unpardonable negligence in the President not to take. We believe that there are very few persons in the country who condemned the precaution, except those who would gladly see an opportunity of trouble left open. Professor Sumner, of Yale College, upon his return from Louisiana, wrote a letter in which he said that "the Federal arms are still enforcing the wrong." What is the meaning of his words? Do rational men, in the face of experience and of testimony, suppose that if the national arms were not present, the board would not be overthrown by the mob of New Orleans if they did not do what it wished? There is no question now of the misdeeds of carpet-baggers, scalawags, and unworthy agents of the government, which are unquestionably to be remedied. But does Professor Sumner mean that the law creating the Returning Board is a bad law, and therefore its action should not be regarded? He says that "the law which commands obedience because it is the will of the governed, is one thing. The law which the people who live under it never consented to and never made, is another thing." If this means any thing to the purpose, it is that the government and laws of Louisiana, not having been made by the consent of the people, are mere tyranny and unconstitutional, and all action under them, including the late election, is practically void.

On the other hand, nobody believes that the vote in the Feliciana parishes, as returned, expresses the will of the people of those parishes. And if not, what has interfered and prevented? Is it possible that an intelligent man can suppose that the situation in Louisiana is due solely to "Federal interference," or that there is any safe solution of the problem which men of all parties acknowledge to exist there, except under existing forms of law? Certainly no good citizen would wish an outbreak any where at this time. And all that the President has done is to provide for keeping order under the law. Those who denounce this as Federal interference merely encourage disorder.

THE LOUISIANA RETURNING BOARD

HARPER'S WEEKLY
December 9, 1876, p. 988

On Thursday, the 16th November, all the absent members of the Returning Board having arrived in New Orleans, the members performed the initial act of their administration by taking their oaths of office. This ceremony took place before Judge Alfred Shaw, of the Superior Criminal Court. Judge Shaw has been connected with the Louisiana bar for a long time as an active practitioner in some branches of the law, particularly in State and city cases, but his experience has been varied by occupancy of several important offices, having been successively clerk of the United States District Court, sheriff of the parish of Orleans, and Administrator of Public Accounts of the city. He is not classed as an active politician, his pursuits having been more of a literary and legal nature. The members qualified were four in number, there having been one vacancy to fill after organization. First and foremost is the president, ex-Governor James Madison Wells. Mr. Wells is a native of the State, and has led a very active political life. He was an Old-line Whig as long as such a designation had a meaning. Previous to and during the war he was of as strong a type of Union men as existed or could exist in the Red River district in Louisiana. The class of men to whom he belonged opposed the ultra-Confederate school as violently as was consistent with safety; and when the opportunity invited, Mr. Wells left the Confederate lines to assist in the reorganization of the State under General Banks. He was elected Lieutenant-Governor, and when Governor Hahn was elected to represent the State in the United States Senate, became Governor. When Andrew Johnson became President, Governor Wells adopted the policy of the new administration, which seemed to please the Conservatives, or Democrats, so well that he was re-elected Governor by a large majority. When, however, President Johnson's policy was fully developed, Governor Wells relapsed into his former sympathy with Republicanism. He was a member of the Returning Board of 1872 and 1874; is a man of firmness and courage, hated and threatened by the Ku-Klux Democracy on that account.

Thomas C. Anderson is another man of mark in Louisiana. He has sat in the Legislature in both branches, and held other and high State positions for twenty-two years. He was formerly a Democrat, and was evidently so considered when elected in 1872. He is a man of large means and enterprise in his section of the State (St. Landry), and has often been elected by the people when on the minority ticket. He is a Virginian by birth, and, like other Southern men who have adopted Republicanism, has been the object of much vituperation and abuse, which have, indeed, only proved his marked and salient character. In the recent contest for the Republican nomination for Governor he was the next in strength to Packard.

Gardane Casanave is an undertaker of the city of New Orleans, a light colored man, free before the war, and possessing a well-cultured mind. He is considered well off in means, and represents well the ancient free colored population.

Louis M. Kenner is also a colored man of light type; has been a member of the Legislature, and is a man of intelligence and very good clerical capacity, matters requiring which have been mainly referred to his management in previous administrations of the Returning Board.

GOING BEHIND THE RETURNS

HARPER'S WEEKLY
December 16, 1876, p. 1006

Some surprise has been expressed that the Returning Board of any State should have power to go behind the actual returns and to throw out votes under any circumstances whatever. But in the States where such authority was granted, the situation was exceptional. Slavery had been abolished as a result of war and as a condition of reconstruction, and the freedmen were made equal citizens. But they were absolutely dependent. They were entirely ignorant, homeless, landless, without money, or thrift, or habits of industry. Their total enfranchisement was part of the national policy, upon which there has been much difference of opinion. But it was adopted, and we do not now argue the question. The white population among which the new citizens lived comprised the old slave-holding class, or the aristocracy, and the "poor whites," "white trash," "clay-eaters"—a kind of population which has no parallel as a class in this part of the country, and of which there are vivid glimpses in Mr. Olmsted's invaluable books of Southern travel and experience before the war.

The feeling of the slave-holding class, surrounded by the ruin of the war, the devastation of property, the radical change of the social, political, and industrial situation, humiliated by their utter defeat in the field and by the sudden elevation of the race they had despised to civil and political equality with themselves, it is not difficult to imagine. Nor, could that class but know it, has there ever been wanting the truest sympathy for them among those in this part of the country who had always politically opposed them, and who fought them most bravely in the field. That sympathy still exists, and it is the action of the Southerners themselves which holds Northerners politically arrayed against them. It was, however, evident that under the circumstances in the Southern States the suffrage of the freedman would be either won to the side of the old master class by kindness and the habit of obedience, or organized against it by other influences. The last is what happened. For some time the old master class held aloof, and the Ku-Klux harried the negroes and threw them under the influence of a new class of whites. This situation was largely due to Andrew Johnson, whose administration persuaded the old masters that under Democratic ascendency the negro could soon be reduced to "his place." The master class thus lost the opportunity of gaining the colored voters, and the color line was drawn.

Nothing is plainer than that in such a situation, when the old political class again took an active interest in politics, the colored vote in remote counties of the old Slave States would be exposed to every kind of improper influence—to fear, force, and fraud in every form; and that if the returns were to be conclusive, without power to investigate further and to annul results proved to be due to fraud or force, the new vote would soon be paralyzed or turned improperly to strengthen the old. Such considerations led to the conferring of judicial as well as ministerial functions upon the final Board of Canvassers. And the power is not only as valid as that of counting the votes, but it is as mandatory. If the board is satisfied that there has been fraud or force in any district sufficient to throw the whole return under suspicion, it may throw it out. This is certainly a great power. It gives a dishonest board control of the result. But the wrong is no greater that one body rather than another should have such control. It is obviously better that an official board should exercise such authority rather than that it should be conceded to an irresponsible mob at a local poll. The members of the official boards in the disputed States who are not Democrats are described as rascals by the Democratic papers. But they are probably no more rascals than the Ku-Klux, or those who act in the Ku-Klux spirit. Let those who think that the board in Louisiana, for instance, should not have revisory powers, read the testimony of the negro woman Eliza Pinkston, of Ouachita Parish, and then say whether "the face of the return" from a precinct in which such atrocities were

AFRICAN AMERICAN HISTORY IN THE PRESS, 1851-1899

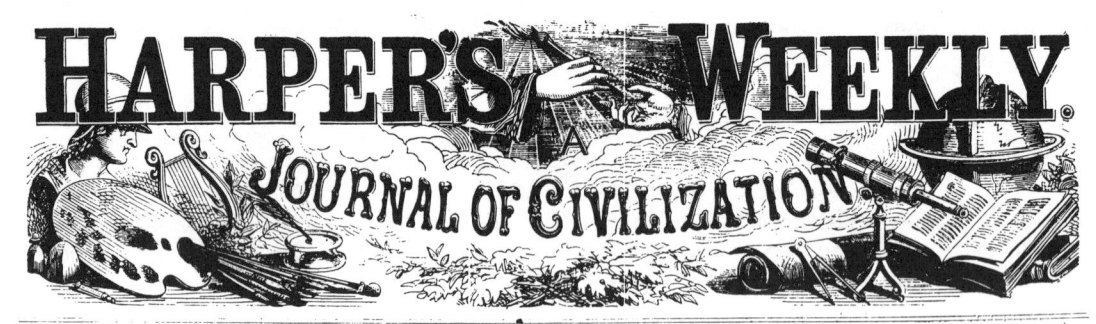

HARPER'S WEEKLY.
JOURNAL OF CIVILIZATION.

Vol. XX.—No. 1041.] NEW YORK, SATURDAY, DECEMBER 9, 1876. [WITH A SUPPLEMENT. PRICE TEN CENTS.

Entered according to Act of Congress, in the Year 1876, by Harper & Brothers, in the Office of the Librarian of Congress, at Washington.

THE IGNORANT VOTE—HONORS ARE EASY.

Harper's Weekly, December 9, 1876, p. 985.

General T. C. Anderson. Gardane Casanave. Judge Alfred Shaw. Governor J. M. Wells. L. M. Kenner.
THE LOUISIANA RETURNING BOARD—TAKING THE OATH.

Harper's Weekly, December 9, 1876, p. 988.

practiced ought to be accepted as final. The story is frightful. It describes deeds done by Americans in Louisiana that would have disgraced Turks in Bulgaria. No wonder that ex-Governor Palmer and ex-Senator Trumbull, of the Democratic Northern committee, were sickened and appalled, and that Mr. G. W. Julian, an old-time abolitionist, but of the same committee, refused to look at the woman's wounds. We believe that these gentlemen will not hesitate to say, in common with all honest and humane Americans, that there ought to be some authority to reject returns made by such means.

THE CONSPIRACY AGAINST FREEDOM

HARPER'S WEEKLY
December 16, 1876, p. 1011

The more closely the traits of the recent election are examined, the more distinctly does it appear a most sad and disheartening event for every lover of freedom. That any American should seek to win and hold a high office by means such as those employed by Mr. Tilden's friends at the South is an ominous circumstance; that he should be upheld in his usurpation of the rights of the people by many men apparently respectable, is still more alarming. Happily, we are no longer to be led away by mere names or reputation at the North; we judge for ourselves; we trust only the common test of experience; and in New York experience has shown that our most noted, active, or wealthy citizens are often least to be relied upon to shield us from the assaults of public thieves. Nor can the fact that Mr. Tilden has secured the services of several persons of this class hide from the people the real nature of that conspiracy against freedom to which he seems to have lent himself in nearly all the Southern States. The contrast, indeed, between the two parties who have contested the control of the Union is one that can bring only sincere satisfaction to those who have advocated the election of Mr. Hayes, for they have carried with them the free suffrages of the great mass of the nation. It is not to universal suffrage that the perils of the moment are due, but to the want of it. It is because hundreds of thousands of voters have been driven from the polls that we are threatened with a disputed election, and an administration sustained in the North by superstition, in the South by murder.

But for the papal priests and ultramontanism, Mr. Tilden would have lost every Northern State; but for that wide reign of violence and insecurity which has so long prevailed in all the Southern section, he would have been left in an insignificant and appropriate minority. Almost in a solid and imposing body the educated and industrious people of the North and West gave their suffrages for Republicanism and progress; free schools and humanity. No stain of blood rests upon their hands, no foreign superstition blinded them to the interests of freedom. The immense majorities for Republicanism in New England, in the interior of New York State, and the safe stability of Pennsylvania, were answered by the enormous and unequaled free votes in Iowa, Kansas, and Minnesota, and by the unbroken unity of the new States and the Pacific coast. Through all this vast region the election was carried on with perfect fairness and good order. No rifle clubs, as at Edgefield District, South Carolina, had scoured the country to intimidate voters, or formed a close circle around the polls, through which an opening for the brave white and colored Republicans was only made by the efforts of a few United States soldiers. No horrible massacre had happened or could happen in Iowa or Nebraska like that of Hamburg. In all the Republican States the people kept ruffians in check. In the Southern, it seems to have been scarcely possible for the Republicans in many districts to vote at all. From one town in Alabama comes a strange picture of the condition of Southern life, and of the utter loss of a free suffrage. The Democratic officials, intoxicated, shameless, ride around the district, threatening violence to white and colored Republicans, and a considerable white population is deprived of its vote. In Kentucky for ten years a reign of violence has continued in many districts; and the State government has in vain striven to secure the lives and property of its citizens. The condition of Mississippi is such that one can scarcely any longer look upon it as a part of the Union. It is in a state of semi-rebellion. Its defiance of all law is notorious. Georgia has long been in a similar condition. That any free election has been held in these States or in Alabama or Texas it is absurd to urge. The right of free voting has been violated at every step; the people have nowhere been allowed to signify their wishes. To compare an election in Georgia with one in Kansas or Nebraska is to mark the difference between a free state and a despotism. In the one, every citizen declares his preferences without molestation; in the other, he is harassed, intimidated, or wholly driven from the polls. The members of Congress who profess to represent Georgia or Mississippi, the candidate who claims his office by the vote of these semi-insurgent districts, are usurpers and intruders, and to suffer them to rule over the free and progressive States of the North and West, where good order prevails and the laws are observed, would be to submit to a total overthrow of all the principles of freedom. We should become the scoff of every enemy of free institutions, the subjects of a dangerous and probably ruinous tyranny.

There is a plain necessity for a rigid inquiry into all the circumstances of the recent election. If the Southern States have shown themselves unfit for self-government by allowing murderers and rioters to elect their officials, by refusing to their people the free exercise of the right of suffrage, no reputable Democrat will desire that they shall ever again control a Presidential canvass. This is the charge made against the Southern leaders, and this is the question to be determined by the action of the whole people. The moment seems favorable for such an inquiry. The Centennial year can not be better employed than in establishing the right of universal suffrage. It is not a party question, it is one that relates to the stability of the government. If Democratic Representatives are apparently elected by an illegal vote in the Southern States, by a denial of the right of voting to a large section of the people, by an actual abrogation of universal suffrage, the whole nation is concerned to see that they shall not be permitted to assume a position they have never won; if they are honestly elected, no one will object to their control. If members of Congress are chosen in Georgia or Mississippi by violence, no reputable Democrat will desire to see them admitted to office; if those elections were fair and orderly, they will meet no opposition from Republicans. But let us not in the Centennial year, full of its patriotic and honored memories, fail in our duty to the Constitution and the people. Let so just and rigid a scrutiny of the disputed districts be made as shall satisfy the humane and patriotic men of both parties. Then, if the Southern leaders, as they fiercely assert, have been unjustly assailed, they will stand unblemished in the eyes of their countrymen. If they are really guilty of the barbarities and acts of violence charged against them in the Edgefield District, in Mississippi, Louisiana, Georgia, Florida, and even Delaware, they will receive their punishment from the hands of the people.

To Congress belongs the right to determine whether its own members have been fairly chosen. The elections, therefore, in the Southern States will become a proper subject of its inquiry. If necessary, the new Congress may be called together at the close of the present session, and on no subject could it more properly exercise its intelligence and its candor than in a calm judicial inquiry into the validity of the Southern elections. The cries of the oppressed voters at the South, the shocking condition of society said to exist in many of its districts, the intense ignorance of its people, the corruption of its courts, the dishonesty of many of its Legislatures, the general insecurity of life and property, demand the attention of the Representatives of the people; and possibly even the present Congress may be able to give some time from its angry personalities to the high aim of saving a falling republic. For of the danger of the moment every one should have a clear conception. There is no doubt a conspiracy among us to usurp by force the control of the Southern elections, and that class of men who in 1861 rose in rebellion, were beaten, pardoned, began at once new treason, waited their time of action, have nearly reached their aim of seizing the national government. They have repaid the imprudent leniency of the people by gross dishonesty and ingratitude. They have nearly fulfilled the prediction of Mr. Stevens in 1866, that a general amnesty for the South would soon transfer the government into the hands of traitors. They have won the countenance of noted Democrats at the North to their deeds of blood, have joined with the ultramontanes to betray Protestantism, and are prepared for any desperate adventure. By the aid of the papal priests, they have nearly attained their aim, and the hand of the foreign Church, which has brought bloodshed and ruin to almost every other American republic, has at last reached our own.

The two pressing dangers of the nation, the fanatical intrigues of the papal priesthood and the secret plots of the wild Southern leaders, have now at last been brought into so clear a light, are so well understood, threaten such terrible consequences if unchecked, that no one can any longer overlook or disregard them. It has been too much the habit of the people to look too leniently on the designs of both. At last they are awakened by a terrible shock. They see that a part at least of the Southern people have never ceased to meditate a new insurrection; that they have risen with arms in their hands to seize upon the government; that they are eager for bloodshed, ready for civil war; that the political murders and outrages which have so long ruled over Georgia or Mississippi, these Southern politicians are already anxious to transfer to Washington or New York; that every papal priest is in league with the Southern rebellion. Such is the revelation which the disputed election of 1876 has brought to us. Happily we possess a President whose patriotic decision has already saved the nation in many a perilous moment; we have elected another President who will not deviate from the honorable path of his predecessor. We have a new Congress which, if all the claims of universal suffrage are respected, will be Republican by a large majority. We have the great mass of thoughtful, intelligent people every where rising to save the country from the conspiracy of priests and rebels.

The election of Mr. Hayes and the success of Republican principles will insure the triumph of humanity in the New World. The Democratic atrocities in all the Southern States have too long horrified the public mind. For ten years that unhappy section has been ruled by savages worse than Turkish raiders, by barbarities as shocking and infinitely more numerous than the briefer outrages in Bulgaria. The hour of retribution is at hand. Let the assassins be exterminated in every Southern State, and humanity, justice, knowledge, education, rule in all the limits of the Union.

Eugene Lawrence.

1877

Election fraud and polling irregularities were not new, and by start of 1877 the results of the 1876 presidential race between Rutherford B. Hayes and Samuel J. Tilden had not been validated. An economic depression and the Radical Reconstruction in the South combined to give Democrat Tilden a popular majority. However, at dispute were electoral votes from Florida, Louisiana, South Carolina, and Oregon. Each of the states in question sent dual returns, each alleged to be valid. Both parties claimed the disputed votes and sent "visiting statesmen" to review the situation. Meanwhile, in Congress the two parties debated over who had the power to count the electoral votes. Although the Constitution stated that the president of the Senate in a joint session of the House and Senate should open the votes, it did not specify who was to count the votes. Both parties realized that whoever possessed to authority to count the votes could declare the winner of the election. If the president of the Senate, who was a Republican, was allowed to count the votes he could choose to count the disputed Republican returns; if the Speaker of the House, who was a Democrat, was allowed to count the votes he could choose to count the disputed Democratic votes. As a solution to the problem, Congress placed the decision in the hands of an electoral commission. Three days before the scheduled inauguration in March, the commission ruled in favor of Hayes. Democrats, upset with the decision, threatened to disrupt proceedings in Congress and prevent Hayes from assuming the presidency. A compromise was reached.

As a part of what later became known as the Compromise of 1877, Hayes made a number of commitments to moderate Southerners. He agreed to withdraw federal troops from areas in the South still occupied and appointed Southerners to federal positions, thereby bring an end to the era of Reconstruction. In addition, Hayes agreed not to intervene in elections in the South, ensuring the Democratic party complete return to power, and made financial appropriations for the economic development of the South. This action was received with relative optimism. As Harper's Weekly reported on May 12,

> The action of the Administration has shown the intelligent people of the Southern States, what they have not hitherto believed, that the Republican sentiment of "the North," as such, is not a hostile and vindictive feeling. The truth is that the real Republican sentiment was very much more considerate, generous, and friendly than the spirit of many of the recognized Republican leaders. By enabling this to be seen, President Hayes has done a great service both to "the North" and "the South."

Despite the lack of political power wielded by blacks, during the late nineteenth century a great many black cultural and self-help organizations came into existence. The thrust of most of these groups was toward education, betterment, and religious training. In early 1877, the New-York Times reported the success of numerous black organizations: "The colored men are doing a great deal, according to their means, to help themselves in this matter." The African Methodist Episcopal Church, with some 200,000 members, contributed over $42,000 for the purpose of education and missions; the African Methodist Episcopal Zion Church constructed an educational facility at Fayetteville, North Carolina, and at West Middletown, Pennsylvania; and the Colored Methodist Episcopal Church was in the process of forming a school for religious education at Louisville, Kentucky. The Times reported on February 26:

> "The schools are designed mainly for theological training. But such training presupposes competent literary qualification, and the schools are forced to confer this upon their pupils. Nearly all of the schools give prominence to normal instruction. Their pupils expect to become teachers as well as preachers, and, in the aggregate, represent a strong force, which is or will be engaged in diffusing instruction among colored people in all quarters of the South."

Like black churches, white churches and organizations also contributed assistance; included among them were the Freedmen's Aid Society of the Methodist Episcopal Church and the American Baptist Home Missionary Society.

Robert L. Harris, Jr.
Cornell University

COERCION OF CONGRESS

HARPER'S WEEKLY
January 27, 1877, p. 62

The Democratic meetings on the 8th of January were chiefly notable for the absence of conspicuous Democratic leaders. In the Indiana assembly, which was the largest and most fervent, the chief speaker was George W. Julian, an old Abolitionist, who has been a member of Congress, but who has never been distinguished for sound judgment or the qualities of a popular leader. His speech was violent, denunciatory, and extravagant. It could have nothing but a mischievous effect, for the real question is of the best provision for a case not constitutionally provided for. The same thing is to be said of General Ewing's speech in Ohio. This gentleman has not commended himself to the confidence of the country by his rag-money doctrines, nor by any evidence of sober sagacity. He is merely a violent partisan. Mr. Joseph Pulitzer and Mr. Henry Watterson, who were the Washington orators, can hardly be supposed to speak with the authority or weight of Senators Thurman or Bayard. Mr. Pulitzer was, we believe, recently connected with a German paper in St. Louis, and came to the Democratic party by the way of the "Liberalism" of 1872, the same road by which Mr. George W. Julian travelled. His opinions are those of an individual only, and are in no sense representative. Mr. Watterson is the editor of the Louisville *Courier-Journal,* and is now a Representative in Congress from Kentucky. He served against the government during the war.

All these orators declared that Mr. Tilden had been unquestionably elected, and that "the people" would insist upon his inauguration. Now we can assume to speak for "the people" quite as authoritatively as these gentlemen, and more especially for "the people" of the States in which there was a fair and free election, and which gave an enormous Republican majority; and we say that "the people" will insist upon the inauguration of the man who shall be lawfully declared President. Messrs. Julian and Watterson went to Louisiana as members of a partisan committee, and saw apparently only what they wished to see. They have, so far as we are aware, shown no disposition whatever to allay public and party excitement, to look simply for the facts, and to see Democratic as well as Republican excesses and offenses. Their object and that of all of the promoters of the meetings was the increase of agitation and disturbance. The purpose of these Democratic meetings was the purpose of the Democratic Ku-Klux Klan and the Democratic White League and the Democratic bulldozers: it was intimidation and menace; it was to frighten the timid and to coerce Congress. The meetings were another revelation of the spirit, the character, and the methods of the Democratic party, and are another evidence of the immense misfortune for the country, for liberty, and for orderly government inevitably involved in the success of that party.

There was evidently a common understanding among some of the managers in regard to a mass-meeting or national convention of Democrats in Washington on the day that the votes are to be counted. What would be the purpose of such a meeting? Ostensibly to petition Congress to do its duty, but really to overawe it to execute the will of a few demagogues. The meeting would be called an assembly of citizens laying their own petition before Congress. The pretense is familiar. It was known perfectly well in Paris during the terror of '93, and it has been tried in London. Such a meeting would be merely a mob menacing Congress. It would demand a declaration of Tilden's election. But what would it do if Congress should not obey its instructions? Would it peaceably disperse and go home? If so, why should it assemble? But if Congress, should act under such intimidation, what would have become of free representative government? The meetings of the 8th January were, politically, blunders. There are a great many Republicans in the country who admit that there are questions in connection with the late election to be carefully considered in a patriotic and unpartisan spirit. But such consideration implies an equal and corresponding disposition among Democrats. It is manifestly impossible, if one side truculently insists that there is no question to be considered, but that under undisputed forms of law, and according to State and national statutes, and strictly under the plain provisions of the Constitution, Mr. Tilden has been elected. Such a proposition is absolutely preposterous, but such is the general Democratic proposition. It holds that the Democratic candidate was unquestionably elected, and can be kept from the office only by fraud.

There are, we say, very many Republicans who accept in their fullest sense the few weighty words spoken by Senator Conkling in presenting the New York petition. But the position and the character of such Republicans should not be misunderstood. They are men who represent, as we believe, both the conviction and the courage from which the Republican party sprang. They are those who maintained the long debate with slavery, and with the same unshrinking resolution sustained the war. They are men of reason, of conscience, of intelligence, of industry, of proved heroism and endurance, representative of the character and qualities that have really made and developed the country; men of the civilization of the Northwest and of New England rather than of that of Mississippi and Louisiana, and who cast at the polls the great Republican majorities of the old Free States. They are open to reason, to fair discussion, and they are devoted to the adjustment of differences under the forms of law. But they despise bluster and swagger, and their good sense at once pierces the fine pretenses and sounding phrases under which reckless demagogues mask their selfishness and crime. The Republicans who are disposed to regard the situation as patriots and not as partisans are the very last people in the country to be frightened by threats, or "Committees of Safety," or mass conventions to overawe Congress. They have seen service in the field, and they have the reticence of courage. The entire performance of the 8th of January, so far as they are concerned, totally defeats its own purpose, and makes a reasonable and just settlement more difficult, because it confirms the suspicion that the dominant desire with many of the Democratic leaders is not a lawful adjustment, but a partisan advantage at all costs and by any means. But we have still profound confidence in the patriotism of Congress.

THE SOUTHERN QUESTION

HARPER'S WEEKLY
February 17, 1877, p. 122

As slavery was the commanding question of our politics for a generation before the war, so the "Southern question" which grows out of reconstruction will long be the most important of all our political problems. The first step in its wise and peaceful solution is knowledge of the situation. A late article upon South Carolina by a South Carolinian, in the *Atlantic Monthly,* is one of the most important and suggestive reports yet made upon the subject. The general view of this article is confirmed by two letters which we print elsewhere upon these pages. One is from a "Native Southerner," a Kentuckian, and the other from a Louisianian; and taken in connection with the account of the South Carolinian, they show that the Southern question is not settled simply by leaving every thing to the armed white population. The Southern States, with the exception of Louisiana and South Carolina, in which the State government is disputed, have now passed absolutely under Democratic control, and they send to Congress as Senators and Representatives men who have been conspicuous chiefly by their active hostility to the Union and the government. In Congress, indeed, their tone is patriotic, but in their addresses at home they appeal mainly to the sectional Southern feeling, which shows their consciousness of the dominant sentiment.

This is certainly not surprising. The present generation of active white men in the Southern States was educated in hatred of the North, and in hostility to the Union as a national bond. The war and its results of every kind have not tended to foster any gentler feelings, and statesmanship must deal with the actual situation. It is obvious that the immediate result of the Democratic ascendency in those States will be the practical extinction of the colored vote, the ostracism of Republicans, the intense sectionalism, the Democratic unity secured by terror and crime, and the virtual discord of the two parts of the country which preceded the rebellion. This is not a condition of affairs which can be satisfactorily treated with an army alone. Nor is it enough to insist that the Southern whites have brought it all upon themselves. They are mainly responsible, but the present question is not one of causes, except so far as they properly affect the consideration of remedies. Recrimination is useless, for it merely imbitters the difference and postpones real amity. But "the South" must not suppose that suppression of the colored vote settles the question.

Democratic leaders in the Southern States like Senators Hill, Gordon, and Lamar, ought to understand that the first duty of their white constituents is to prove by deeds that there is an influential sentiment among them which condemns and resists the political policy of murder and torture toward the blacks. The election of a man like "Hamburg" Butler as a Democratic Senator from South Carolina is an insult and a challenge to every humane and loyal American citizen. And not until the leaders in such massacres are seized, tried, and punished by white Democrats, where they control the government, will the real, "North" which is Republican and not Democratic, believe that there is any ground in the Southern States upon which an actual reconstruction of the Union can be based. The more intelligent Southern whites permitted their great opportunity to slip from them when they abstained from securing control of the new vote. Their true policy was to use it, not to attempt to extinguish it. It is by their own conduct that it is now massed against them by means which have also massed against them the judgment and conscience of the North. If such men as we have mentioned are, as we would believe, something more than disappointed enemies who bide their time, they do not like such a situation. If they have, as we should be sorry to doubt, the generous instinct of American citizens, they know that "a solid South," on the sole basis of suppression of the negro vote, merely prolongs the *status quo*. They and their Democratic retainers will vainly look for a dissolution of the Republican party so long as the terror of the blacks by Democratic means, and with Democratic tolerance or denial, continues.

The Republican majorities in the Northern States at the last election were, as we have before stated, diminished as compared with those of 1872, when a large Democratic vote was withheld from Mr. Greeley. But the actual Republican vote was largely increased. General Grant in 1872 received 3,597,070 votes, Governor Hayes in 1876 received 4,033,295. The apprehen-

Harper's Weekly, February 17, 1877, p. 132.

sion that the Bourbon Republicans had entirely overpowered the party, which alienated a great many essentially Republican votes from Hayes, has rapidly vanished in the light of many recent events.

Our correspondents, however, who represent the best Southern Republican sentiment, will see that they concede that the Republican State governments in the South can be upheld only by the national power. Now a State government which does not even pretend or endeavor to maintain itself is at variance with the fundamental American principle. For such inaction implies that the government has neither the moral nor the physical support of the majority. The Constitution undoubtedly contemplates cases of invasion and domestic violence in the States in which the national power may re-inforce that of the State. But would either of our correspondents assert that the constitutional amendments that followed the war contemplated as a national policy the creation of State governments of the freed slaves, like that described by a South Carolinian in the *Atlantic,* so repugnant and odious to the white population that they could be maintained only by the military power of the Union? We do not say that such governments of actual majorities of equal citizens should not be maintained as against violent revolution. But this is the very gravity of the question. It will tax the national principle, courage, and patience to the utmost. One thing only is clear. The problem presented by the Southern situation is not to be settled by rifle clubs on one side and the army on the other, nor by affidavits of lamentable and indisputable disorder, but by the same wise and patriotic intelligence which has settled the Presidential dispute.

SOUTHERN VIEWS OF THE SOUTH

HARPER'S WEEKLY
February 17, 1877, pp. 122–23

We subjoin the letters of which we speak elsewhere in these columns. They were addressed to us in reply to some recent remarks of ours upon the situation in Louisiana, in which we asked what local efforts were made to repress disorder. The first letter is from Louisiana.

> "This secret league of white men which makes its existence apparent at every election, changing its name as the emergency appears to require, and to-day called 'Nicholls Militia,' extends through the whole State, and it may be truthfully charged with the manipulation of the white vote.

"Note its progress. There was the Mechanics' Institute riot in 1866, when it was feared the adjourned Convention of 1864 would set up a Free State Constitution.

"The Presidential campaign of 1868 was a continuous massacre, from beginning to close, of Republican leaders and voters.

"The reconstruction government was inaugurated in defiance of organized ex-rebel resistance, under the protection of the commander of the Union forces.

"Without making detailed specifications of the mobs wielded by the 'Citizens' Committees,' the 'Carter Rebellion,' the Democratic control of the election laws in 1872 (making violence unnecessary), the White League revolution in 1874, the main point deduced from these events is that the government established under reconstruction has only existed because of the superior military power of the United States government.

"The White League has preserved the color line throughout, as it is natural to expect of them, by virtue of their teachings espoused sincerely and with genuine American energy.

"All who are not for this League and its aim—to re-unite and solidify the South by the nullification of laws established by a conquering power—are placed under the social ban. Proscription follows in society, business, the courts, and the press.

"A murder in broad daylight, where political ends are subserved, is *not witnessed*. There is no affidavit preferred by one member of the White League against another, and Republicans may make one at their peril, or, making out a case, may witness the disagreement of a mixed jury, or the vacillation of an intimidated judge. There is no press to chronicle the naked truth and arouse the sympathies of the just in the sections where majorities must be annihilated, and the manufactured testimony of the League, eagerly proclaimed by the Associated Press, often passes current in the nation.

"Remember, the Governor within the State must base his action upon legal forms, judges must declare an inability to administer justice, the Legislature must provide a militia and appropriate the money to maintain it. Now a judge will naturally look to his self-protection in a state of society where he may not hope to call on adequate power to his assistance, and the love of life outweighs the consideration of duty. No legal form is certified to the Governor, and the latter is powerless in its absence. The Legislature of Louisiana authorized the Metropolitan Brigade; and in every emergency when it has appeared, in the performance of the duties assigned to it in the execution of the laws under the command of the Governor, it has been confronted, attacked, menaced, or captured and disarmed by a superior body of armed, drilled, duly officered and organized ex-rebels. The arsenal of the State was sacked in 1874, and the property of the State never restored. The Legislature under the Wheeler compromise never voted a dollar for militia, and hence Governor Kellogg *had none at his command during the last campaign,* because soldiers do not fight without pay; the Governor could give no guarantee of future pay, and the White League bankers do not volunteer funds or loans to Republican Governors.

"The struggle here from the first has been to maintain the existence of the Republican party, surrounded by all the influences of wealth, intelligence, and enmity of the national government, of whose decrees it is the representative. The wonder is not that in the midst of revolutionary and violent political crises the robber reaps a profit, but that reconstruction has been planted here so strongly. Men in the midst of a drawn battle do not stop to discriminate as to the moral calibre of comrades.

"What is also singular is the perversity of many, who should have pierced the thin veil of sophistry, in ascribing to the outbreaks of the secret league the character of a spontaneous uprising of legitimate forces of society, and even defense of valued liberties. The White League counts upon the *habitual fairness or timidity of Northern Republicans* as an assurance of the triumph of the policy of violence. Having annihilated majorities and forced certain others by intimidation, they sent boldly and unblushingly before the Returning Board records which they knew the letter of the law would not allow to be counted, accompanied with threats of violence if they should not be counted. These fraudulent records array figures to give Tilden and Nicholls the State as against a fair poll of the voters. To back up these records the secret leagues can furnish evidence in any quantity, of any character desired without a scruple of conscience, to influence public opinion outside of the State.

"You would not think of approving or dealing leniently with the July mob that ruled New York city in defiance of the national draft. Yet every argument possible to array against that mob applies equally to the kid-gloved gentry who boldly defy in an unlawful way the possibility of a success of national rule in Louisiana, unless national bayonets shall disperse and hold them in subjection."

The following letter upon the same subject is from Kentucky, and also from a native Southerner. It was written wholly without knowledge of the other letter.

"1. When the war closed, nine-tenths of the white people of the far South were fully allied with the Democratic party.

"2. When the Republican party gave suffrage to the negroes, it did so in good faith, and with an honest desire that colored voters might choose such rulers as their judgment dictated.

"3. No Republican government can exist in such States as South Carolina, Mississippi, Louisiana etc., unless elected by a vote that is nine-tenths colored.

"With these premises, what follows? Either the existing State government of Louisiana is the product of the votes of the white masses or of the colored masses; and if of the latter, it is according to the will of the Republican party of the United States. I presume, of course, as is the fact, that the colored vote is largely Republican. The Republican party ought not—it can not, in good faith—reject the Republican government of any Southern State simply because it rests on a basis of colored votes; if it does, then it is guilty of a great inconsistency, if not a grave crime. It has cruelly deceived the trusting black man. It has equally deceived the white Republicans of the South.

"Accepting Governor Kellogg, then, as the late lawful Governor of Louisiana, in the judgment and will of the Republicans of the nation, the question is, Did he discharge his duty in maintaining law and order in the State prior to the Presidential election?

"Disorders were of twofold nature: (1) there were individual acts of violence, occurring in detached localities and at intervals of time; (2) there were general acts of intimidation, caused by movements of the rifle clubs, by mobs, and by night excursion of squads of evil-disposed men.

"Both these lawless methods were the product of the determination of the white Democrats of the South that no government shall exist among them resting on colored votes as a basis. Northern Republicans may doubt this assertion in view of the St. Louis platform and the professions of Democratic conventions, newspapers, and leaders, but it is nevertheless a fixed truth. Living daily in a Southern atmosphere, *I know it to be so.*

"*An act of violence committed upon a negro at the South for political ends can not be punished. The perpetrator may be arrested; he may be tried before the courts. But, with few exceptions, the entire white community of Democrats is a solid element to commit perjury in his behalf and prove an alibi.* Respectable citizens, who would scorn to tell a lie concerning any personal or business matter, will boldly swear to a falsehood to screen a fellow-Democrat from punishment for injury to negroes. It is deemed in the South a political duty, and is justified under some indefinable law of self-defense, in which all Democrats are estimated as one person. (The Eliza Pinkston case, I have no doubt, affords an example of this depravity.) This is a sad, an awful, condition of social morals, and exhibits how debasing was human slavery.

"On the one side, then, are the oaths of white persons, on the other are the oaths of negroes. Southern sentiment dare not permit a verdict of guilty under such circumstances. The jury dare not convict on negro testimony against white testimony. It they did, they would be subjected to similar treatment as the murdered, or else the accused would be rescued by force of arms. An experience of over thirty years in Kentucky has never shown me a case where a white man was ever executed or suffered severe punishment for murdering a negro.

"Governor Kellogg surely can not be blamed because this character of violence becomes frequent from immunity from punishment. He could not force legal conviction.

"The second class of violence represents mob law. It terrorizes a whole community. The negro, accustomed from slavery to subjection under white rule, educated in the belief that he must obey law and make no resistance to violence, easily subject to panic under danger, becomes a non-voter, and often a refugee. Every effort at self-defense is construed and published as an insurrectionary uprising against the whites. Without money, without arms, without property of any extent, without intelligent means of communication, he is, in the face of mob law and a rifle rule, helpless. If he resists, and kills or wounds his assailant, the mob hangs or shoots him; if he submits and is murdered, his murderer goes free.

"Ordinarily there are two ways to suppress mob law. In one case, the police power of the community exerts itself, aided by the *posse comitatus;* in the other, the Governor uses the military.

"Where nearly all the whites of a community are *particeps criminis,* and probably half are fully armed, it will be seen how helpless are the local officers of the law. The latter are most likely, if troublesome, to be driven away or killed, as was done at Colfax and other points.

"The only local military force accessible to Governor Kellogg would have consisted of negroes. In open war, officered by whites and aided by white troops, negro soldiers are brave and efficient. As an element to suppress mobs or rifle clubs, they are uncertain and liable to panic. Besides, their use would have caused excessive excitement, produced a state of war wherever sent, been attended by complaints that Governor Kellogg had begun a war of races, and made the occasion for arousing the basest passions of men. This was demonstrated in the use of negro troops by Governor Chamberlain just prior to the Hamburg massacre.

"There was left, then, an appeal to the President for aid—for Federal troops. These would have arrested all parties accused under warrants. They would have been tried, and by false testimony acquitted. Prosecuting witnesses would have been driven away, or terrified into concealing the truth. (I follow a sad experience uniformly resulting under my own eyes in Kentucky.) This was done in many cases in Louisiana, where prosecutions occurred in Federal courts. Need any better proof of the futility of this mode of proceeding occur than is presented in the status of the parties arrested for the Hamburg murders? Look at Butler! A very hero and martyr.

"The facts and argument undoubtedly show a state of temporary helplessness in the State government of Louisiana—a condition originating either from inexcusable violence on the part of the white Democrats, or from Republican crime in giving to the negro the right of suffrage. It is either the one or the other. If the former; it ought to be condemned, and, by all capable powers of law and morals, be extinguished. To crown it with success, resulting from acquiescence in its fruits, is to put a premium on rebellion and disorder, and to play the hypocrite to the innocent negro. If the latter, then the Republican party ought to be manly and honest, and repeal the Suffrage Act.

"There really exist two remedies for the Violence done in Louisiana: (1) to educate the national mind to declare abhorrence to its outrages, and by moral pressure to subdue the evils practiced in local limits; (2) to declare marital law, and stamp out the plague in the same effectual manner practiced toward the Ku-Klux in North Carolina. Rifle clubs are but Ku-Klux with the mask off."

COMPROMISE

HARPER'S WEEKLY
February 24, 1877, p. 142

The plan of settlement of the Presidential dispute has been condemned and derided as a compromise, and members of Congress and others have declared that compromises are always fatal to those who favor them. There have been, also, copious references to the old slavery compromises, and to the rejection of compromise by the Republicans in 1860 and 1861, after the election of Mr. Lincoln, until it is quite clear that the vehement objectors are unfamiliar with two things—one, that compromise is not in itself wrong; and the other, that in the present adjustment there is no comprise whatever of acknowledged rights. There is simply a reference to arbitration of a dispute for which, by common consent of both sides, no remedy existed. The settlement is a provision adopted by agreement. It is an arbitration of differences. So far it is a compromise. But there is nothing culpable in that. The reference of the *Alabama* dispute between the United States and England to the Geneva Tribunal was a compromise in the same sense. But it was a compromise showing the highest courage and wisdom and humanity. It was not a surrender of moral principle or undoubted right. It was merely the surrender of a resolution to insist upon our own way, because it was our own way, as the only right way. Such a compromise is a commanding duty, but it is possible only to great and wise and heroic natures and nations.

The Crittenden compromise, and all the wretched make-shifts to avoid the inevitable, which preceded the war, were propositions of a deliberate surrender of undoubted and unquestionable legal and moral rights. Nobody doubted that Mr. Lincoln had been constitutionally elected. But it was urged that his election was thought in the Slave States to endanger their property, so that they meant to secede and make trouble, and, in order to placate this apprehension, the Free States were besought to agree to surrender free territory to the chances of slavery. But this was the very point of the controversy that had created the Republican party. The non-extension of slavery was the great question upon which the country had been asked to pronounce. It had decided by a clear and conceded constitutional majority that slavery should not be extended. And the defeated party then proposed, as a condition of its acquiescence in the lawful and unquestioned result, that slavery should be extended. This was the compromise offered in 1860 and 1861, and it was most righteously refused. But had the present case then arisen, had there been a dispute as to the lawful election of Mr. Lincoln, with no provision in the Constitution or the laws to settle it, and only the claim of one party that the House could decide, and of the other that the President of the Senate, in the absence of legislation, must, from the necessity of the case, decide all questions, then a mutual agreement to refer the decision to a tribunal, the most respectable and impartial and able that the country could furnish, would have been a compromise, indeed, but a compromise which every brave and patriotic man would have been morally bound to support. For what would have been the issue had there been a flaw in the title of President Lincoln? Or what the consequence if Breckinridge had had the sole and final power to decide every question in regard to the electoral vote?

Those who denounce the settlement as a compromise, meaning a cowardly and base surrender of undoubted and unquestionable rights, forget that the Constitution not only does not provide for, but does not even contemplate, the dispute that has arisen. The glory of the settlement is that it proves the highest capacity of the American people for self-government by their subordination, in a critical moment, of party passion to patriotism. If the Republicans had merely insisted that Hayes was elected, and that if any question arose, the President of the Senate must, from the necessity of the case, decide it finally; and the Democrats had insisted that Tilden was elected, and that the decision of the President of the Senate could not bind the House—what moral principle, what right, would have been at stake? What would there have been but opposing theories upon a trouble for which by common consent from the beginning the Constitution does not provide? If any body thinks that the harmonious agreement of both sides to leave a question which neither could satisfactorily settle to an arbitration in which both should acquiesce is a cowardly or unnecessary compromise, it is because he doubts the justice of his own side or his ability to establish it, or the courage of the other side to maintain its convictions.

The compromises with slavery were always wounds of liberty. They gained nothing, and did not avert the war. But they were wrong not because they were compromises, but because they were sacrifices of moral right, of justice and humanity. Naturally, therefore, the word compromise has become odious to those who were trained in the politics of the last thirty years, and the word applied to the Presidential settlement seems to them to stigmatize it. They have but to look, however, and they will see that there has been no sacrifice of any principle or right, none of justice or conscience. They may recall the words of Burke, with the happy consciousness that "the immediate jewel" is safer than ever: "All government is founded upon compromise and barter.... But in all fair dealing the thing bought must bear some proportion to the purchase paid. None will barter away the immediate jewel of the soul." In this instance the thing bought is lawful provision against a limitless danger without existing relief. The price paid is the renunciation of a disputed assertion. The jewel secured is the triumph of the principle of popular government and its peaceful continuity.

SCHOOLS FOR COLORED CITIZENS

NEW-YORK TIMES
February 26, 1877, p. 2

The importance of securing education to the negroes has been made more manifest than ever before in the midst of the confusion that has prevailed in political affairs since the November elections. The question of what is being done to render them intelligent and capable has become a pressing one. The answer to it is that much is being done. The public schools, such as they are, are established and opened to them, in name at least, by the law. The schools have suffered much in the political crash, and are obstructed by the interference of the roughs who seem to control Southern politics, and would be likely to go down, so far as the negro is concerned, but for his irrepressible determination to learn. They are, moreover, supplemented by certain helps which the Confederate cross-road rulers cannot control, the influence of which will go far toward diffusing knowledge "where it will do the most good." These helps are given by the Church missionary schools, which nearly every leading denomination has established on a systematic plan throughout the Southern States.

The colored men are doing a great deal, according to their means, to help themselves in this matter. They show much liberality in their contributions and energy in their efforts to build up good schools for themselves. They sustain four large Church organizations and several smaller ones, through which their efforts are mainly directed. The African Methodist Episcopal Church, with about 200,000 members, last year contributed over $42,000 for purposes connected with education, literature, and missions. It has undertaken thirteen schools, of which five are already in successful operation. The principal one is Wilberforce University, near Xenia, Ohio. It is designed for a college of high rank; it has ten Professors and teachers, and property worth $65,251 48, and reports 600 students in the last four years. The schools at Atlanta, Ga.; Galveston, Texas; Washington County, Texas, and Cokesbury, S.C., make returns of seven teachers and about 380 scholars. Other schools are projected at Louisville, Ky.; Baton Rouge, La.; Greensboro, La.; Hagerstown, Md.; in Florida, Arkansas, and Tennessee, and a mission is to be established in Hayti.

The African Methodist Episcopal Zion Church, a body of about the same numbers as the African, is building up institutions for higher education at Fayetteville, N. C., and West Middletown, Penn. The Colored Methodist Episcopal Church, a Southern organization, with not quite a hundred thousand members, and only six years old, is building up a school for the education of ministers at Louisville, Ky., which it designs making its central university. It has also in hand the establishment of a school for the education of young women. It is helped and encouraged by the white Methodists, North and South. The Consolidated American Baptist Missionary Convention is a large organization of colored Baptists. Its people use the schools which the Northern white Baptists have opened in the South, and are trying to establish institutions of their own. The Conventions of Georgia and Alabama have determined to combine to erect a school at Atlanta, Georgia, in which they expect to be helped by the American Baptist Home Missionary Society, and the Alabama Convention has resolved to establish a theological class at Marion, in connection with Lincoln University, and to hold Ministers' Institutes in different parts of the State.

The leading part in the work done by the white Churches for the education of the colored people has been taken by those of the North. The Southern Churches observe the work approvingly, without apparent jealousy, help in it some, do some like work in their own way, and plead poverty as their excuse for not doing more. Some, as the Baptists, confessed early that they could not accomplish much in this matter, and invited their Northern brethren to go down and perform what was a manifest duty. Others were later in reconciling themselves to the situation.

The American Missionary Association (Congregational) expended during its last year $198,985 35 in its Southern work, and added 665 members to its 56 churches. It sustains fourteen high schools and colleges, some of which have gained a wide reputation, and six common schools; employs 147 teachers; has 6,175 pupils under instruction, and claims that seventy thousand pupils were taught during the last year by teachers who had been instructed in its higher institutions.

The Freedmen's Aid Society of the Methodist Episcopal Church has in nine years spent $582,006 90 for purposes connected with colored education. It sustains thirteen high, normal, and Biblical schools, so placed as to have one in nearly every Southern State, and owns more than two hundred thousand dollars' worth of school property in the South. It raised and expended in its last year $58,204 75, supported sixty teachers, and taught over three thousand pupils, a majority of whom will preach or teach. It estimates that last year forty thousand children were taught by persons who had been instructed in its schools.

The American Baptist Home Missionary Society supports seven high-schools and colleges in the South, in which 926 students were taught in 1876. It also gives aid to the Southern Baptists and the (colored) Consolidated Missionary Convention, the value of which was handsomely acknowledged by their delegates as the last annual meeting of the society. The Southern Baptist (white) Convention in 1875 recommended the holding of Ministers' Institutes, under the direction of its Home Mission Board, for the instruction of colored ministers and the more intelligent colored brethren in doctrine and advised that missionaries be appointed to the colored people whenever the means were afforded, and that their Sunday-schools be helped. These recommendations were repeated in 1876.

The Northern Presbyterian Church spends about sixty thousand dollars a year on its missions to the freedmen. It sustains five high schools in North and South Carolina, in which are 903 students; 39 day schools, with 65 teachers and 3,776 scholars, and 107 Sunday-schools, with 7,009 scholars. In the Southern Presbyterian Church special attention is given in many Presbyteries to evangelistic work among the colored people. The General Assembly has decided to establish an institution for the education of colored ministers at Tuscaloosa, Ala. The Reformed (Dutch) Church in America is doing its work for the colored people in co-operation with this body, and has made an appropriation in aid of its school at Tuscaloosa.

The United Presbyterian Church has opened a normal and mission training-school at Knoxville, Tenn., the institution beginning with a fund of $12,389. The Associate Reformed Synod of the South, a small but active body, is co-operating with it.

The Protestant Episcopal Church spent last year $14,266 38 on its missions to the colored people. It has normal and high schools at Raleigh, N. C., Petersburg, Va., and Charleston, S. C., which together have furnished 119 teachers to the general field and several smaller schools, which have also furnished their quota of teachers.

The Disciples of Christ, (or Campbellites,) have missions among the colored people in Kentucky, Alabama, Mississippi, and Texas. A Bible school has been in operation three years at Louisville, Ky. Some ten or twelve young men who have been instructed in it have since done good service as missionaries and teachers. Another school is projected in Mississippi, and a charter has been obtained for it. Local Bible schools for colored ministers are contemplated to be built up in as many Southern States as possible.

The Unitarians have been helping the African Methodist Episcopal Church with books and money. Bishop Payne, of the African Church, acknowledged at the last National Conference of Unitarian Churches that Wilberforce University had in eight years received $4,600 from two of their societies.

The Roman Catholics have begun to carry out a plan of general mission work among the colored people, but there is no definite report of the extent to which their operations have been prosecuted. Prof. Day, of Howard University, estimates that they have two hundred thousand colored children in their schools, or under their influence. The estimate seems a very wild one.

The schools are designed mainly for theological training. But such training presupposes competent literary qualification, and the schools are forced to confer this upon their pupils. Nearly all the schools give prominence to normal instruction. Their pupils expect to become teachers as well as preachers, and, in the aggregate, represent a strong force, which is or will be engaged in diffusing instruction among colored people in all quarters of the South. The fact of the capacity of the negroes for scholarship is no longer in dispute. They have proved themselves interested in study, quick to learn, and able to make a good use of their culture. The colored teachers are full of energy, they make the elevation of their race a matter of personal pride, and go out prepared to do all they can to promote it. If their work is not stopped by the White Leagners, they will effect a great improvement in the intellectual and moral condition of the next generation of their people.

A SOUTHERN DEMOCRATIC VIEW

HARPER'S WEEKLY
March 17, 1877, p. 202
Petersburg, Virginia, *February*

To the Editor of Harper's Weekly:

I have been gratified to see that the Southern question is receiving consideration at your hands, in articles which evidently aim at a judicial spirit, and which seek in an unusual degree—in view of the avowed political status of your paper—to discard the tone and feeling of sectionalism. Permit me to say, however, that even your treatment of the Southern question, mild and just as it is compared with the average character of articles on that subject in Republican papers, is one-sided, and based on incorrect information, conducting, of course, to false and injurious conclusions. It can hardly be that the two correspondents quoted in a late number of the *Weekly* are any better informed with respect to the real condition of affairs in the Southern States than the correspondents of such papers as the New York *Herald*, the Philadelphia *Times*, and the Cincinnati *Commercial*, who have devoted whole weeks and months to the investigation of alleged Southern abuses, and who have been compelled to admit that the stories of Southern murders and whippings, and of nameless and numberless wrongs on the colored people, were but part of the machinery by which admitted knaves have maintained a wrongful and usurped ascendency. Allowing all that is put forward by you in behalf of these gentlemen's personal character, it demands to be said that the general reputation and record of the Southern white Republican, whether domestic or imported, are such that whatever they assert requires a liberal season of the salt of discount.

Republicans who are not native doubtless think they have good ground of grievance against the people of the South. They are, no doubt, often made to feel the social exclusion which is habitual in the South toward all strangers except such as come well introduced, and especially toward such as appear in the company and under the wings of the carpet-bag office-holding class. Let me remind you just here, however, that this ostracism is based not on the politics which these people profess, but on the bad character which the South has heretofore found, to her sorrow, to accompany the kind of politics known as truly loyal. Nor do these charges depend on the suspicious or slanders of the ex-rebel element. We have but to take the carpet-baggers at their own word to believe them devoid of every claim of decency and recognition. Thus in Louisiana Warmoth exposes Kellogg, and Kellogg Warmoth. When the opportunity of party advantage (I will not say personal plunder) is afforded, these people, lately enemies to the knife, become bedfellows to the depth of three or more. But the South, which is simple and earnest, like the satyr in the fable, does not understand this kind of thing, believes very naturally that all of these fellows are knaves, and holds up her skirt in no affected dignity and disgust as she withdraws from the disgrace of their very contact. Is there any thing in such an attitude that calls for "more troops" for its suppression and punishment? We hardly expect a "journal of civilization" to approve the scourging of people for the sin of despising fraud.

The assertion that the people of the South are banded together as White Leaguers and White Liners, and militia and rifle clubs, and the like of that, seems to me absurd in the extreme degree. Rest assured, Sir, there is no more organization in the South than there is among the people of the North. Men are excited and swayed by great popular waves of feeling, and need no *mot d'ordre* to give edge and direction to their action. The suspicion of any other more tangible, distinct source of action, the theory which refers such movements to the issuance of orders from mysterious head-quarters like those of Rex Felix on Shrove-Tuesday, is the emanation of ignorance, or, worse, the policy of interested slander. *Harper's Weekly* is neither ignorant nor slanderous, and therefore it can not espouse such fictions.

Here is a mere hint for your candid consideration: Conceding that the South *is* to blame for not having captured the colored vote when the right of suffrage was first conferred on the colored citizen, are her people to sit quiet forever under that disadvantage? I see no reason in such an assumption. I do not believe, indeed, that the late dominant class could, by any course of behavior, have won the political confidence of the late servile class. The South could not have outbid the fellows who offered the forty acres and mule. Still, the mistake the South made, if a mistake was made, can not be expected to endure forever. Her people have means, experience, political aptitude, the love of independence, the aspiration of power. Are they to employ none of these advantages which the God of nature has put in their power to prevent the shame and ruin of such administrations as negro votes would erect above them, to the prostration of every interest, social, material, and educational? If *Harper's Weekly* says yes, it will prove quite different from the champion of civilization which it claims to be.

Who shall venture to assert that the disposition of the South toward the negro will be made any more amiable by the sense of his proving the agent for the defeat of her hopes of recuperation and deliverance? I do not threaten. I believe the negro is safe in the hands of his former master, and that his rights will be sacredly protected against all invasion and spoliation. But this I do mean to say, most frankly: that the Northern people and the radical party can only bring trouble on the head of the negro by the attempt to coerce any prescribed method for his treatment, any exact limits for his rights, any inexorable rule for his recognition as a citizen and member of society.

But I may already have abused, if not exceeded, your patience. I shall be gratified to see that these frankly taken exceptions have met with consideration at your hands.

E.S.G.

THE SOUTHERN QUESTION

HARPER'S WEEKLY
March 31, 1877, p. 242

The attack upon the President was premature. When he was nominated, he stated in his letter of acceptance the principles that would guide his administration should he be elected. When he was inaugurated, he simply repeated and amplified the statement. Why should those who supported him after his letter, have insinuated that a repetition of it was proof of his treachery to any man or to any cause? Mr. Blaine was one of the most conspicuous figures in the late campaign. He was received every where with enthusiasm, and every where warmly advocated the election of Mr. Hayes. In so doing he advocated a thorough reform of the civil service system, equal protection of the rights of all citizens every where, and the promotion, by the "influence of all legitimate agencies of the general government,. . . .of the blessings of honest and capable local government" in the Southern States. These were the words of Mr. Hayes, and they are certainly humane and American principles. There could be no sounder or better grounds of appeal to the country. He was elected. As President he said no word implying that he had changed his views. Yet on the very first day of his administration, and before his cabinet was confirmed, he was covertly attacked as a renegade to his own convictions and to Republican principles. There is nothing in his character, nothing in any of his words or deeds, to justify such an imputation.

The President, in common with all thoughtful men, sees that the Southern question is difficult and not to be summarily settled. No man can be satisfied with the present condition of affairs in many parts of the Southern States, and nobody should be satisfied with that condition since the war. It is easy enough to see that the real original cause of the situation was the great wrong of slavery. But it is not easy to apportion responsibility for the existing condition. On the one hand, every humane and just man must detest the terror of the Ku-Klux and the White League; on the other hand, no such man but must recoil from forcibly subjecting States of the Union to semi-barbarous and corrupt governments. Undoubtedly the white race in the Southern States made a fatal mistake in not obtaining control of the new colored vote. But it is not surprising that it made the mistake. It would have been astonishing if it had not. On the other hand, it is certainly not surprising that intelligent and superior men can not see without protest local government becoming practically highway robbery, nor that they prefer the military authority of the Union to the rule of an ignorant and venal majority. There are ignorance and corruption in all the States—in the State of New York. But the worst days of Tweed were not as bad as much that was called government in some of the Southern States. Yet if Tweed had been imposed upon us by the army of the United States, we might well have been in despair. We can understand, therefore, the feeling of intelligent men at the imposition upon them by force of such government as is described in a late article in the *Atlantic*.

We do not for that reason say, nor does the President say, nor does any honorable man say, that the colored citizens in the Southern States must be abandoned to the Ku-Klux and the shot-gun. We say only that the Southern question is not disposed of by the assertion that the whites oppress the blacks. That was true under the military policy. The accounts from the Feliciana and other parishes in Louisiana show that there is ill treatment of the colored population; the massacre of New Hamburg and the murder of the Collector Weber are proofs of the angry and dangerous feeling that exists. But such facts necessarily raise the question whether a different policy might not produce better results. If the course that has been pursued has not produced the results desired, it is plain that a change of policy might secure them. Under the system which may be called the military policy all the Southern States but two have been recovered from the Republicans, and those two are now in doubt. Assume that the result has been produced by oppression of the colored citizens, then the national armed force was powerless to prevent it, or it was brought about in a manner with which that force could not legitimately deal. Mississippi is alleged to have been stolen from the Republicans by an organized terror and intimidation of the blacks. Assume that it is so. Are there Republicans who would propose to raise a national army and overthrow the existing government in Mississippi? And if there are such, could they probably carry a single State in the Union for such a policy? And, again, if they could not, would they be justified in asserting that the negro had been abandoned? Nobody can be justly reproached for saying that a policy which has lost to the Republicans every Southern State, which has not effectually protected the negro, and which has imbittered the jealousies of classes and of race, however indispensable it may have been when adopted, is not a wise permanent policy. A policy may have been wise and unavoidable twelve years ago, which it is now wise to modify in order to secure more surely the results for which it was originally adopted. There can be no doubt that if the freedmen had been abandoned at the end of the war to the "local self-government" of the old slaveholding class and the "white trash," they would have been reduced to a condition little better than slavery. That danger has in great measure passed away. Twelve years have taught the new citizens their power, and the old citizens the necessity, for their own safety, of friendly relations. And, above all, whatever wrongs may be done any where in the country to any citizen, the remedy is to be sought under the law, and under the law only. There can not be one kind of national protection in one State and another kind in another State. If the army may be a police any where, it may be so every where.

American statesmanship must trust American principles. American principles declare equal rights and demand equal protection. The problem of detail is how that equal protection shall be afforded most certainly. This is the question that meets the new Administration at the outset, and which is not to be settled in any summary way. It is not the interest of a single class or race that is to be considered, but the welfare and harmony of all the people in the State. If one class is to be protected from bulldozing, another is not less to be defended from the venality which stimulates bulldozing. The question is one for patriotic statesmanship, not for party passion; and therefore we have reason to believe that the measures which will be taken by the Administration will be such as the humanity and intelligence and national sense of justice will approve.

STREET SKETCHES

HARPER'S WEEKLY
March 31, 1877, p. 253

These characteristic sketches, drawn from real life by a gifted draughtsman of Philadelphia, find their counterpart in every large city. Let any one walk at night or early in the morning through Fulton Market, through the Bowery, or almost any of the streets near either side of New York, and he will meet with just such scenes as these....

As for the street politicians, neither the Senate nor the House of Representatives at Washington ever witnessed more earnest discussions of the affairs of the nation than can be heard about the coffee stands where working men congregate at night or early in the morning. One would imagine, listening to their arguments, that the decision of affairs depended entirely upon them; and as they are generally readers of newspapers, their views are often intelligent, and their arguments right to the point. Worse arguments may not unfrequently be heard in legislative halls. To be sure, no one ever convinces his opponent. The Republican sticks to what he has read in the Times or the Tribune, and the Democrat to the utterances of the Sun; but the same thing may be said of the debates in Congress, which were never known to convince any body on the opposite side.

The lower sketch is quite melancholy in its contrasts.

THE SOUTHERN QUESTION

HARPER'S WEEKLY
April 14, 1877, p. 282

The root of trouble in the South is hostility of race, with great ignorance and the alienation due to slavery and the war. How soon, by any reasonable calculation, would that sentiment of alienation and that hostility be removed by forcibly sustaining governments of adventurers and newly enfranchised freedmen? It is impossible to read the reports of this winter upon the Southern situation without perceiving that the outrages were of a kind sure to be produced by a policy of "crushing" by the armed hand. We hold the intelligent white population of the South largely responsible, as we have often said, for the color line. They could have done much to prevent the unhappy condition of the last ten years. They have tolerated the Ku-Klux and the White League and the outrages upon the negroes. But they have felt that under the sword, which represented to them, as they imagined, the vindictive hatred of the North and its determination to "crush," all means were fair, and they have been compelled to regard the Democratic party as their only hope. Nothing so surely disarms hostility and weakens hate as the magnanimity of power. A Republican administration—an administration of the almost solid North, which is known to be supported by the conscience, the intelligence, and the conviction of the industrious masses of the Republican party, which should show sincere confidence in the honest purpose of the

DISCUSSING THE POLITICAL SITUATION.

Harper's Weekly, March 31, 1877, p. 253.

intelligent citizenship of the South—would more effectually protect the negro and reconcile the country than an army quartered in every Southern State and holding every Southern capital.

THE PRESIDENT AND THE SOUTHERN POLICY

HARPER'S WEEKLY
April 21, 1877, p. 302

It is not surprising that there should be differences of opinion among Republicans as to the Southern policy of the Administration. Those who regard it as a betrayal and abandonment of the helpless and oppressed will naturally denounce it vehemently. Those who politically thrive by fostering hostility of race will condemn it with equal warmth. There are many, also, who, admitting the practical failure of military possession of some of the Southern States, and conceding the wisdom and necessity of a change of policy, yet fear that if national control of Louisiana and South Carolina be relinquished, it can not be readily resumed. Thus in the active or passive opposition to a change of methods there is both just and humane apprehension and contemptible selfishness. The opposition is, however, negative. It does not propose any other policy than the *status quo*. Sincere and frank opponents, like Mr. Garrison and Mr. Phillips, assert a continuing irrepressible conflict, a tireless hate that can be tamed only by force. The form that this force should take is apparently the maintenance of

HUNGRY.
RANDOM STREET SKETCHES IN PHILADELPHIA.—[Drawn by S. G. M'Cutcheon.]

Harper's Weekly, March 31, 1877, p. 253.

what is practically a government of the least intelligent and the most venal over the rest of the population. This is the first class of opponents. The political traders who care nothing for the negro, or for political principles, or for honest government, would have their personal interests secured at all hazards. The other class that we have mentioned, much the largest of the three, is merely reluctant and uncertain, disliking to venture into the water until it has learned to swim.

The only distinct reason for the permanent maintenance of State governments by the national arm that we have seen is that of Comptroller-General Dunn, of South Carolina, as stated by him to a correspondent of the *Tribune:* "He acknowledged the evils of negro government, and wanted to see the color line broken down, but he thought the way to break it down is for the Administration to uphold the Southern Republicans until their opponents divide." This is at least an intelligible policy. But it is not new. It has been tried for twelve years. And what is the result? Has there been any division of opponents? Has not the color line been more and more strongly drawn, until the Republican vote has almost come to be estimated by the census of the colored citizens? Has not State after State been withdrawn from Republican control? If it be said that this is because troops have not been freely used, is it not true that they have not been used because public opinion condemned such use, and that the Republican party was rapidly declining in popular confidence because of its supposed purpose of constant military interference? It seems to us evident that the same causes which have changed the political aspect of the other Southern States would inevitably affect Louisiana and South Carolina, and that the Democratic party in the South would certainly not "divide" so long as the national arm constantly interfered for the Republicans. It is that interference which holds the South solid upon the color line. It is that which inflexibly prevents the "division." So long as the situation is, on one side, the negroes plus the United States government, there will be a hopelessly united white citizenship on the other. How does such a situation help the negro? How does it hasten the day of mutual good understanding? How does it foster and develop the conditions under which alone orderly and peaceful State government is possible?

When the exterior pressure upon the States is withdrawn, it is fair to assume that the ordinary course of politics will have play. When the colored vote is no longer massed by an external force against the whites, the natural political differences of the whites will seek to gain the support of the colored vote. It is a factor altogether too important to be disregarded or abolished. In all the Southern States the colored vote is undoubtedly largely repressed by intimidation. There is unquestionably a great deal of hostility of race. There are immense ignorance and corruption and petty crimes. In a word, there are active elements of disorder and trouble. The very first necessity, therefore, is the promotion of better feeling between the races, and that will be effected very much more certainly by a policy which makes natural relations between them more practicable. If the negro is abandoned in South Carolina by the policy of President Hayes, he has been abandoned in all the other Southern States by President Grant. Grant did not think it necessary to interfere in Georgia, in Alabama, in Mississippi. Of course, if wrong was done in those States, it is no argument for the same wrong elsewhere. But if wrong was done there, it was reason for denunciations that have not been heard, and for appeals that should not have been spared.

The national bayonet, under existing circumstances, is merely a thorn of exasperation; it is certainly not a prop of peace. Did it prevent bulldozing, or the murder of Eliza Pinkston's husband, or the Hamburg massacre? Is it not, indeed, a question whether it did not promote them? The argument that non-interference in the police of the State will but multiply Hamburg massacres, is not only discredited by presumption, but by experience. The treatment of the negroes has been worst where military occupation was most stringent; and time, which has accustomed the white to the civil and political rights of the negro, has also taught the negro his power. We do not deny—we have often asserted—the enormity of the crimes in the Southern States. But there are two efficient and reasonable policies of treatment only. One is to occupy these States with troops enough to secure protection to every citizen; the other is to quarter troops in them only as they are quartered in New York and Virginia, and to leave to the State, under the Constitution, the maintenance of its own order. A policy of fretting, a protection that does not protect, is neither humane nor constitutional.

The Administration could not discharge its high trust without taking risks, and it has not taken them without long deliberation and deep conviction upon the President's part. Nothing has been done which was not fairly foretold by his letter of acceptance. The firmness with which he took the first step of selecting a cabinet which a powerful element of his party did not approve, and the tranquil deliberation with which he has proceeded to carry out his convictions in the treatment of the Southern question, are the auguries of an independence which is not ignorance, and a courage to which the patriotism of the country will not fail to respond.

FREDERICK DOUGLASS

HARPER'S WEEKLY
April 21, 1887, pp. 305–6

No man in America has had a more remarkable career than the new Marshal of the District of Columbia, whose portrait is given on this page. He was born at Tuckahoe,

FREDERICK DOUGLASS.—[PHOTOGRAPHED BY GENTILE.]

Harper's Weekly, April 21, 1877, p. 305.

Talbot County, Maryland, about the year 1817. Reared as a slave, he taught himself secretly to read and write while employed in a ship-yard in Baltimore. While very young he formed a resolution to escape from slavery, but it was not until 1838 that he found the opportunity to run away. In September of that year he fled, made his way to New York, and thence to New Bedford, where he married, and supported himself for three years by working on the wharves and in various shops. He was known to be intelligent and trustworthy; but his genius as an orator was first displayed at an antislavery convention held at Nantucket in 1841, where he made a speech so eloquent and stirring that he was offered the agency of the Massachusetts Antislavery Society. For nearly four years thereafter Mr. Douglass lectured constantly in Massachusetts and other New England States, rousing public sentiment against slavery, and gaining great distinction as an orator.

In 1845 Mr. Douglass published an autobiography, and in the same year made a visit to England, and lectured to enthusiastic audiences in every part of the United Kingdom. His freedom was purchased by his English friends, in order to insure him against legal annoyance in his labors. After remaining two years abroad, Mr. Douglass returned to this country, and established at Rochester, New York, a weekly journal, under the title of *The North Star,* afterward changed to *Frederick Douglass's Paper.* During the height of the excitement produced by John Brown's celebrated raid, Governor Wise, of Virginia, endeavored to have Mr.

Douglass arrested for supposed complicity in that movement, and he deemed it prudent to go abroad again. After an absence of a few months, Mr. Douglass returned to Rochester, and continued the publication of his paper.

When the civil war broke out in 1861, Mr. Douglass strongly advocated the use of colored troops and the emancipation of the slaves in the South. When permission was given, in 1863, to employ such troops, he assisted in the work of enlisting colored men, and was especially active in organizing the Fifty-fourth and Fifty-fifth Massachusetts regiments. Slavery having been abolished, Mr. Douglass discontinued the publication of his paper, and applied himself to lecturing, in which he was remarkably successful. His powers of oratory are unexcelled, and no man possesses greater influence over an audience. In 1870 he removed to Washington, D. C., and became the editor of the *New National Era*. The following year he was appointed secretary to the Santo Domingo Commission; and on his return the President appointed him one of the Territorial Council of the District of Columbia. In 1872 he was elected Presidential elector at large for the State of New York, and was appointed to carry the electoral vote of the State to Washington.

Soon after the inauguration of President Hayes, Mr. Douglass was nominated to the important and responsible position of United States Marshal for the District of Columbia, and was confirmed by the Senate with very little opposition. He has resided for several years in Washington, where his high personal character and great abilities have won universal recognition and esteem.

THE REV. JOSIAH HENSON

HARPER'S WEEKLY
April 21, 1877, p. 306

On the same page with the portrait of Frederick Douglass, we give that of the Rev. Josiah Henson, the original of "Uncle Tom" of Mrs. Stowe's celebrated novel. He has reached the venerable age of eighty-seven. He was the son of slave parents, and was born in Charles County, Maryland, June 15, 1789. When he was a mere infant he lost his father by forcible separation. The slave-husband on one occasion beat a brutal overseer for an attempted outrage on the slave-wife, and for this "offense" received a hundred lashes, had one of his ears cut off, and was sold south. The wife and children never saw him again, and never received any tidings of his fate.

Some years afterward, Josiah's elder brothers and sisters were sold away, but he, being a very small boy,

THE REV. JOSIAH HENSON—THE ORIGINAL OF "UNCLE TOM."—[SEE PAGE 306.]

Harper's Weekly, April 21, 1877, p. 305.

remained with his mother on the plantation of Mr. Isaac Riley, in Montgomery County, till he grew up to manhood. His mother, a sincere Christian woman, instilled religious principles into the boy's mind, and he grew up in the love of truth and the fear of God. His master was wild and dissipated, and Josiah, being bright and trustworthy, and at the same time high-spirited and athletic, was selected by him as his body-servant. In this service he often protected his master from harm in tavern brawls and affrays. At length Riley became bankrupt, and fearing that his negroes would be sold for his debts, he persuaded Josiah to lead them to Kentucky, to be kept by his brother, Amos Riley, on Big Blackford's Creek. Josiah safely conducted the whole party, consisting of eighteen persons besides his own wife and two children, a distance of nearly a thousand miles. He remained three or four years with Amos Riley, cultivated his religious faith, and, though still untaught to read, became a regular preacher of the Methodist Episcopal Church.

In 1830 he made his escape from slavery with his wife and four children, and after innumerable hardships and perils, found a place of refuge in Canada. He settled in a town now called Camden, in Upper Canada. His children were sent to school, and he himself was taught by his eldest son to read and write. He took an active part in the "underground railroad," and assisted in the escape of many slaves. In this noble service of liberty and humanity Josiah Henson more than once risked his life by venturing into the State of Kentucky for the rescue of his less fortunate brethren. At the same time he was engaged in founding an industrial settlement, with missions and schools, landed estate, buildings, and sawmills for the colonial timber trade. He travelled repeatedly, on business, through all the British American Provinces and the New England States.

At the London Universal Exhibition of 1851 there was a show of Canadian black-walnut from the sawmills of Dawn, as Camden was then called, in his charge. He arrived there with letters of introduction to statesmen from the Sumners and Lawrences of Massachusetts, from Sir Allan M'Nab and other eminent men of Canada, and with credentials to the chief Non-conformist ministers in London. He was invited to occupy the best Dissenting pulpits, was received by the Archbishop of Canterbury, and dined with the Prime Minister, Lord John Russell. Upon his return to America he wrote and published the story of his own life, that its sale might provide for the purchase of his elder brother's freedom in Georgia. Mrs. Stowe read the autobiography, and made the acquaintance of its writer, shortly before composing her famous romance, *Uncle Tom's Cabin.*

Mr. Henson is now in England for the second time. By her Majesty's special desire he was presented at Windsor Castle, and he was a guest at many distinguished houses.

"THE NORTH" AND "THE SOUTH."

HARPER'S WEEKLY
May 12, 1877, p. 362

A remarkable article, under the title of "The Final Test of Southern Statesmanship," recently appeared in the New York *Express.* It is entirely different in tone from any article upon the same general subject that we remember to have seen in that paper. The article proposes to answer the question, "What is to be the future political status of the negro? Is he to be citizen or serf? Is he to be denied a voice in the making of the laws of the Southern States? Is he to be denied representation in the American Congress?" The answer to these questions must come, it thinks, from "the negro-majority States of South Carolina, Florida, Mississippi, and Louisiana;" and if the problem is solved wisely, the *Express* holds that it "necessarily involves a fusion between the Confederates and the negro power in those States in the interest of peace and good government." The true policy, in the view of the *Express,* is to recognize the negro power in the States

SEEDY APPLICANT. "G'mornin'. I seed your advertisement in de paper, and kinder thought dat 'd like to come 'round and 'ply fur de situation."
PROPRIETOR. "G'long! Can't hire no fellah looks like dat, in no sich costume as you got on."
SEEDY APPLICANT. "Well, tell de trufe, my tailor's gone back on me. I've been huntin' all 'round to git anudder, but can't find any one jis zacly suit."

Harper's Weekly, April 21, 1877, p. 316.

named by giving it an equal share in representation, both State and national. It proceeds to say—and there is no more positive Democratic paper in the country—

> "It is needless to point out to Southern men the utter impossibility of reorganizing the American Union as a purely white man's government, based on negro serfdom as its corner-stone. Such a step backward is just as impracticable as is the reorganization of the old Whig party. Such a settlement, even if made, could not last. It would foment fanatical agitation. It would produce race discontent and race conflict at the South. It would in due time breed war."

The result of such a policy, in the judgment of the *Express,* would be the immediate dissolution of "the party of hate" in the North, the moral support and strengthening of Northern Democrats, and a solid South that could not be broken. But viewed partywise, the policy recommended by the *Express,* which is sound and sensible, would be the highest conceivable Republican triumph. For it would be the adoption by the Democratic party of the extremest Republican principle. Not only would the slave have been freed, not only would he have been made a citizen, but his political equality would have been assured by the willing action of his late master. Nothing less than this, however, is to be expected from the wise policy of the Administration. From the moment that the exterior pressure which has held the white political sentiment of the South firmly united is removed, that union will be relaxed. Inevitable differences of opinion will divide the white citizens, and the colored vote will be invoked by both sides. This was

THE FIRST OF MAY IN BLACKVILLE.—[Drawn by Sol Eytinge, Jun.]
"Got to go dis time. De Lan'lode 'buses to put in de Gas-Works."

Harper's Weekly, May 12, 1877, p. 364.

the exact situation contemplated by Republican reconstruction. The result of this practical recognition of the colored vote will be the selection of colored citizens for office. When this point is reached, however, the old party lines will have become exceedingly indistinct. When Messrs. Gordon, Lamar, and Hampton, for instance, have freely accepted the course so earnestly recommended by the *Express,* it will not be easy to see why they should call themselves Democrats, or why they should hesitate to unite with Republicans for great national purposes. The cardinal difference between Republicans and "the South" sprang from slavery. Free trade, State sovereignty, and secession were questions that had their root in slavery. When slavery has disappeared, and secession has no purpose, and the limitations of State sovereignty have been defined by the sword, and the equality of the Southern colored citizen is freely recognized by the Southern white, what does "Democracy" mean to "the South?" When these have ceased to be questions, what real interests remain to "the South" which are not as likely to be favored by Northern Republicans as by Northern Democrats?

We certainly anticipate no sudden millennium. The consequences of slavery and the feelings resulting from the war will only gradually be ameliorated. Hostility to the Republican party, as the party of Union and emancipation and the war, will long continue in "the South." But while this is true, such a sentiment, which in the nature of things can look forward to no gratification, will be constantly weakened by the pressure of actual necessities. Real motives, great principles, and practical conduct will take precedence of a vain sentiment. The intelligence and industry and enterprise of "the South," no longer under a local and resistless perversion, will instinctively seek a natural alliance with the intelligence and industry of "the North." Now, under the existing political nomenclature, "the North" is Republican. The characteristic popular elements and forces in this part of the country are politically Republican. With slavery and the questions springing from it settled, the natural sympathies of such men as Lamar and Hill and Gordon are with those who are known as Republicans, rather than with Democrats. They have no national views which require the success of the Democratic rather than that of the Republican party.

Undoubtedly, with their present party connections, if these men saw that "the South" could direct the Democratic party, they would prefer to see that party dominant. But we doubt whether Mr. Cox, who has been travelling through the Southern States, seems to such men the kind of party leader that they would wish to follow. In the great and dangerous emergency at the close of the late session, when if vengeance and discord were their real desires, the Southern Democrats could have easily gratified them, they showed an independence and a patriotism which no Republican, at least, can forget. The conduct of the Administration since the inauguration of President Hayes has not tended, probably, to make them less independent. It would not be surprising if some of them should be found in friendly accord with Republicans upon question that may arise during the extra session. Certainly, if the State policy recommended to them by the *Express* should be adopted by them they would find cordial sympathy from most patriotic and, as we believe, the truest Republicans.

The action of the Administration has shown the intelligent people of the Southern States, what they have not hitherto believed, that the Republican sentiment of "the North," as such, is not a hostile and vindictive feeling. The truth is that the real Republican sentiment was very much more considerate, generous, and friendly than the spirit of many of the recognized Republican leaders. By enabling this to be seen, President Hayes has done a great service both to "the North" and "the South." He has disclosed the healing truth that the deep solid sentiment of this party of the country approves and supports a policy which contemplates national harmony by justice and confidence. If it has shown that some of those who very recently seemed to be approved Republican leaders misrepresented the feeling of "the North," it is only the more heartily to be commended. If that general policy should be seriously attacked by Republicans in Congress, the depth and strength of its support in the country would be only he more plainly revealed.

RACE PREJUDICE

HARPER'S WEEKLY
July 7, 1877, pp. 518–19

Judge Hilton probably perceives that he has made a serious mistake, although there is no reason to doubt his statement that the Grand Union Hotel at Saratoga did not decline to receive Mr. Seligman because he was of the Hebrew religious faith. But whatever explanation may be offered, the action illustrates and confirms a prejudice which is simply monstrous. Judge Hilton said to a reporter of the *Times* that there was no religious question involved in any degree, and that the affair was simply "a question of what class of guests is wanted at a hotel." But what class of guests is excluded? Israelites, Hebrews, Jews. Not disorderly or drunken persons, or those who in any way violate the ordinary social proprieties of hotels, of whatever faith, or race, or nativity, but simply Jews, Hebrews, Israelites. Now as they are all mainly of one religious faith, and as few except of their race hold their faith, the exclusion is, in the first place, practically a religious exclusion. We do not suppose, however, that Judge Hilton views the subject from the religious point. His view is strictly commercial. His reasoning is that, right or wrong, there is a prejudice against Jews; that they are clannish among themselves and disagreeable to others; and as he has learned by experience that the kind of guests which he desires at his hotel will not come to it if Jews come, Jews must not be admitted. . . . .

Quite beyond all this, however, it is a great moral and social wrong to stigmatize an entire class against which a wretched prejudice already exists. There are undoubtedly disagreeable Hebrews or Jews, as there are disagreeable people of all other races, but undoubtedly, also, in every age and country there are Jews who have been masters in every sphere. To exclude Jews as Jews is as monstrous as to exclude English as English or Californians as Californians. Judge Hilton volunteers a distinction between "Seligman Jews" and a superior class of Hebrews. But that is a purely arbitrary discrimination of his own, which he has no lawful authority to impose upon those who seek accommodation at his inn. If what is called "vulgarity" is to exclude, the rule must be enforced against a great many other guests than those known as Jews, while to exclude Jews as a class because of vulgarity is preposterous. The action of Judge Hilton has had at least the good effect of showing how sincere and universal is the protest against the indulgence of a race prejudice against white skins. We beg to remind the protestants that a race prejudice against black skins is quite as despicable.

PERSONAL

HARPER'S WEEKLY
July 7, 1877, p. 519

Inman Edward Page, a colored student at Brown University, has succeeded in every respect better than his brother Flipper at West Point. While a rigid non-intercourse law was for four years maintained between Flipper and the nascent warriors at the Military Academy, Page has lived in the largest-leaved clover at Brown, and in the Senior year just closed was chosen Class-day Orator—a position so much coveted among students ambitious for class honors that it is ranked by many even higher than the Salutatory or the Valedictory. Page has throughout been treated by his classmates as one of themselves. He is a good writer and speaker, though not noticeably better than some of his classmates. His conduct had been uniformly modest but self-respectful, and he had won the esteem of professors as well as students. The deportment of his class toward him is in high and honorable contrast with that pursued by the less manly students supported by the government at West Point, who may have already learned that the "plain people" of the country are with Flipper.

SIX AND HALF A DOZEN

HARPER'S WEEKLY
July 14, 1877, p. 539

The universal protest against the exclusion of respectable guest from a Saratoga hotel because of race to which they belong and the consequent attempted identification of that race with repulsive vulgarity, is to that degree a gratifying proof of the just instinct of the American people. It is not denied that there are many persons of that race, as of all races, who are exceedingly disagreeable, nor that some hotels, especially at summer resorts, have found that their entertainment of such persons has led to a gradual abandonment of the hotels by many desirable guests; but that a whole race should be stigmatized for causes not peculiar to it is justly and unanimously condemned. We say that this condemnation is to that degree gratifying. But we must not flatter ourselves too much. When we are fluttering and bristling about Saratoga, a moment's attention may wisely be devoted to West Point. If we are all up in arms because Mr Seligman was refused lodgings at Judge Hilton's hotel Saratoga, why are we so passive over the fact—as reported in the newspapers—that the colored cadet Flipper, although duly admitted and instructed at our own military school at West Point, was virtually sent to Coventry during his course by his classmates because of his color?

It will be said that all we can do is to secure he equal chance in study; we can not regulate the social tastes and preferences of the students. That is unquestionably true. But it does not meet the point. We are abstractly indignant with Judge Hilton because he decided that Jews were not desirable associates for the other guests in his house, and we ought logically to be angry with the white cadets at West Point for deciding that colored youth were not desirable associates for their classmates. The trouble is the race prejudice, not Judge Hilton's or any other expression of it. If the guests who were not Jews at the Grand Union sent the guests who were Jews to Coventry, or, *vice versa,* if the Jews for the same reason avoided those who were not Jews, the offense would be precisely the same as it is with Judge Hilton. Indeed, Judge Hilton would have said nothing about it, and would have had no occasion to say any thing, except for the existence of the prejudice. Nobody denies that it exists; and the reproach of Judge Hilton is not that he has it—for individually, perhaps, he has it not—but it is that he was willing to recognize its existence in others so far as to exclude "the Seligman Jew" from his hotel.

The Grand Union Hotel at Saratoga declines to entertain Jews because they are Jews, and the newspapers from Maine to California shout with wrath at the miserable race prejudice. Yet we have known an educated and accomplished gentleman, a diplomatic representative from his government to ours, compelled to eat alone at a separate table in a Newport hotel because he was a colored man; and although the fact was published in the papers, there was entire resignation to the race prejudice. The indignation with the action of the Grand Union Hotel is unquestionably righteous; but we wish to point out that our sainthood is not quite perfect. The denunciation of face prejudice against Jews is just, and can not be too strongly expressed. But we propose a problem for the taxed intellects of hotel piazzas: If it is wrong to insult one man because of his race, how right is it to insult another because of his color?

DOMESTIC INTELLIGENCE

HARPER'S WEEKLY
July 14, 1877, p. 539

A special election for seventeen members of the South Carolina Legislature, to represent Charleston County, took place on the 26th ult. The Democratic ticket containing the names of fourteen whites and three blacks was elected. The Republicans did not run any ticket.

THE NEW GEORGIA CONSTITUTION

HARPER'S WEEKLY
September 22, 1877, p. 739

It was the expectation of the most thoughtful advocates of "the reconstruction policy" that the natural result of enfranchising the colored people, and so creating an immense constituency in every old Slave State, would be an attempt on the part of the white population to secure the new votes. Such, however, was not the immediate operation of the policy. The absolute social division of the races, the bitter feeling that naturally followed the war, the intrigues of unprincipled politicians, and the spirit of the Ku-Klux divided the two classes into two political camps. This has been a misfortune, but the original anticipation was still reasonable, although its fulfillment was deferred. It was tolerably clear that when the political dominance of one race had been definitely established, the old party lines would begin to fade, because projects within the party would instinctively seek the alliance of the other vote, and thus produce new political combinations. How this result would be accomplished it was utterly impossible to foretell. But in Georgia circumstances have suddenly made it probable. The old Constitution of the State was

The President's Policy has had the Effect of disbanding Illegal Organizations and inaugurating an Era of Peace and Good-Fellowship.

Harper's Weekly, October 13, 1877, p. 812.

THE COLOR LINE IS BROKEN.

Harper's Weekly, December 8, 1877, p. 972.

repugnant to many persons, and in the spring a vote was taken upon calling a Convention to frame a new one. The project was opposed by the Republicans, and although carried, it was carried by a majority which showed no very positive feeling upon the subject, and the Convention met in the summer, reframed the Constitution, and adjourned.

In the new instrument there is no offensive assertion of State sovereignty, as it was apprehended there might be, nor any discrimination on account of color, except in the schools. This is a blot upon the instrument, for such a distinction should not be lodged in the fundamental law. It is ordained that the social status of the citizen shall never be the subject of legislation, and the whipping-post and imprisonment for debt are prohibited. The public-school system, with the distinction already mentioned, is confirmed, with a larger revenue, and the range of studies limited to the English elementary branches. It was in the suffrage clause that the harsh treatment of the negro might be expected. But it is not there. A voter must have lived in the State for a year, and in the county for six months, and he must pay before voting all taxes due at the time he offers to vote. These are stricter conditions than those of the old Constitution, but they are not unreasonable. The required residence was formerly six months in the State and three in the county, and the required tax payment was merely of taxes of the year previous. There is also a strict system of registration. In these last provisions the essential difference in Democratic doctrine and practice between the Northern and Southern States will be noted. These guards of the suffrage, far from being extravagant or unjust, tend both to purify the ballot and to settle the population.

1878

Although the "back-to-Africa" movement had its origins in the seventeenth century, and maybe as early as the sixteenth century, the emigration of blacks from the South to Liberia captured a great deal of attention in 1878. Prior to 1878, a number of abolition organizations had been advocates of the resettlement of freed blacks. Included among such organizations was the American Society for Colonizing the Free People of Color in the United States, better known as the American Colonization Society. The society benefited greatly from the support of prominent white citizens, and by 1830 the organization had successfully settled 1,420 freed blacks in Liberia. In addition to organizations that devoted time and resources to resettlement, a number of freed African Americans, including Paul Cuffe, were advocates of the return of freed blacks to Africa. In 1815 Cuffe, a sea captain from New Bedford, Massachusetts, transported 38 blacks to Africa with his own resources.

The nation of Liberia was founded by freed black slaves and became an independent republic on July 26, 1847. The first settlement was located on Providence Island near the present capital city of Monrovia. Between 1822 and 1892 an estimated 16,400 former slaves settled in Liberia.

White confidence in the movement was not strong. Harper's Weekly reported: "It is not likely, nor in anyway desirable, that this movement will ever gather sufficient headway to reduce to any considerable extent the colored population of the South. . . ."

Between the years 1876 and 1914, a number of new resettlement movements were organized in the United States. The most prominent of these movements was the "back-to-Africa" movement, organized under the leadership of African Methodist Episcopal bishop Reverend Dr. Henry

McNeal Turner. On March 21, 1878, the ship Azor *was christened at Charleston, South Carolina, marking the beginning of what would be the repatriation of black Americans to Africa. The mission to Liberia had both religious and economic goals. Of the mission Turner said "it was not only to bear to Africa a certain number of her sable sons and daughters, it was not only to bear a load of humanity, but to take back the culture, education, and religion acquired here"* (Harper's Weekly, April 20). *To accomplish this mission, funds had to be raised, and it was claimed that 25,000 people throughout the South invested in the Liberian Joint-stock Steamship Company and over 160,000 enrolled to make the trip to Africa. However, only those who had the means to support themselves in Liberia for six months without assistance were taken. Many African Americans were desperate to escape racial violence and oppression in the South. Although enough emigrants for six trips to Liberia signed on, the Azor made only one trip and had to be sold for debts two years later due to the chicanery of its white ship captain.*

Robert L. Harris, Jr.
Cornell University

FOR LIBERIA

HARPER'S WEEKLY
April 20, 1878, p. 309

The consecration of the Liberian ship *Azor* at Charleston, South Carolina, March 21, may prove to be the beginning of an extensive movement among the colored people of our Southern States to seek new homes in a free African state. It is not likely, nor in any way desirable, that this movement will ever gather sufficient headway to reduce to any considerable extent the colored population of the South, but the strengthening of Liberia by the accession of an industrious and intelligent population, accustomed to self-government and tolerably well trained in mechanical pursuits, will greatly aid in the work of civilizing the continent, and opening up its mighty rivers and lakes to commerce.

The religious element is so strong in the nature of the negro that in giving the new movement toward Liberia the character of a missionary enterprise, it appealed to numbers that might have looked indifferently upon a scheme that had no further end than simply the bettering of their worldly condition. The colored man in America is easily persuaded to liken himself and his people to the ancient Israelites who were held in bondage in Egypt, and now the prospect of returning to his home in Africa may naturally appear like a Heaven-directed exodus toward the Promised Land. Indeed, this was the tone taken by all the speakers on the occasion depicted in our engraving. First one clerical brother of sable complexion and then another called attention to the missionary aspect of the case. The Rev. Mr. B. F. Porter explained that "the consecration or dedication of a ship was a little unusual, but the colored race was one that eminently believed in God, and was learning to believe in the evangelization of the millions of their people who now sat in darkness." Bishop Brown also gave his testimony to the effect that "the ship had been purchased by Christian men led forward by Christian ministers. They had so far succeeded in their object, which was to carry Christian men and women to aid in Christianizing Africa, and carrying on the work of civilization in her midst." The Rev. Dr. Henry M. Turner informed the multitude that "the object of this assemblage was to consecrate to the service and care of God this vessel which was about to cross the trackless ocean. It was not only to bear to Africa a certain number of her sable sons and daughters, it was not only to bear a load of humanity, but to take back the culture, education, and religion acquired here. The work inaugurated then would never stop until the blaze of Gospel truth should glitter over the whole broad African continent."

To turn, however, from the religious side of the enterprise to the business part of it, we find that the new scheme is under the charge of a stock company, whose object it is to arrange for the transportation of such portions of the colored population of our Union as may desire to colonize on the shores of their native Africa. Only those will be taken who have means to support themselves in Liberia for six months without assistance. It is claimed that 25,000 people through the South have invested in the Liberian Joint-stock Steam-ship Compa-

THE LIBERIAN SHIP "AZOR."—[Photographed by G. N. Barnard, Charleston, South Carolina.]

Harper's Weekly, April 20, 1878, p. 309.

ny, and that over 160,000 are enrolled to go when occasion offers. The *Azor*, however, has accommodations only for 250. After landing her passengers, the vessel is to return immediately for more, bringing back a cargo of African products. This method of transportation is to be continued until the company secures funds enough to purchase a steamship, when a regular line is to be established between this port and Monrovia for carrying over emigrants and bringing back produce. The officers of the company claim to have on hand now, after paying for the *Azor*, nearly sufficient funds to pay the first installment on the steamship. Every stockholder has a right to one passage to Monrovia when his turn comes. There are 30,000 shares of stock, at $10 per share.

Should the present enthusiasm for emigration continue, it would appear that in course of time the presence of the black man in our midst would be, like that of the Indian, little more than a memory. It is to be hoped that those who are among the first to venture will not be overwhelmed with the trial and discouragement that usually await emigrants to a new and unfamiliar country.

THE GREAT SUNDAY-SCHOOL CONVENTION

HARPER'S WEEKLY
May 18, 1878, p. 397

The meeting of the delegates to the International Sunday-school Convention that took place during the

INJURED INNOCENCE.—[Drawn by C. M. Coolidge.]
"I hain't seen nuffin of yer Chickens! Do you took me for a Thief? Do you see any Chickens 'bout me? Go 'way dar, white man! Treat a boy 'spectable, if he am brack!"

Harper's Weekly, February 9, 1878, p. 108.

month of April at Atlanta, Georgia, was characterized by unusual interest and enthusiasm, one incident only having occurred that might in any way cast a shadow upon the general harmony of the occasion. This was the exclusion of the colored brother whose portrait accompanies the present article. The Rev. B. W. Arnett is the pastor of a church in Ohio, and was regularly commissioned by the Sunday-school Union of that State to attend the Atlanta Convention as a delegate. Objection was, however, made to his presence, it having been decided by the officers of the Convention that the time was not yet arrived when such action might be taken without detriment to the cause of religion in the South. It is to be regretted that such is the condition of affairs, for certainly a religious body should be the last to insist upon distinctions of race that are not recognized by the State. The exhibition of feeling contained in the request that their single delegate should not attend the Convention, on account of his color, can not fail to impress the African Methodists with a sense of injury received at the hands of their white brethren.

A GOOD WOMAN

HARPER'S WEEKLY
July 6, 1878, p. 527

Mrs. Adelaide Butler, for twenty-five years the matron of the Colored Orphan Asylum in New York, recently

HARD TO PLEASE THE "WHITE TRASH."

U. S. "I hate the 'Nigger' because he is a citizen, and I hate the 'Yellow Dog' because he will not become one."

Harper's Weekly, April 6, 1878, p. 280.

died, and her name deserves to be remembered among those who have faithfully served their kind. It is the hard fate of every person of her race to be born into a society that associates them with servility and inferiority. The moral depression that such consciousness produces is incalculable. Gerrit Smith said that the representatives from the Slave States used to argue, in proof of the natural inferiority of the colored race, that while the colored and white children seemed to be in every way equal, there came a time, when they were a little older, at which the colored child drooped and sank into conscious subordination. Yes, said Mr. Smith in reply, and if the white child were born in a servile and despised class, he would sink and droop whenever he was old enough to perceive it. It is not a natural but an artificial phenomenon. Charles Lenox Remard, an intelligent colored man in Massachusetts, who was educated in England, and who died young, harried and chagrined, used to say that he would be flayed alive willingly, if the torture would give him a white skin.

All the more admirable is the patient well-doing of those who are born to the burden of this discouragement. Mrs. Butler was born in Virginia, and came to the North a quarter of a century ago. Widowed and childless, her care of the children in her charge was most tender and maternal, and the Rev. Mr. Garnett says that during the twenty-five years of her service as matron of the Asylum it had never once been necessary to suggest to her the performance of any duty devolving upon her. During the fierce draft riots of the war, when the mob, with its usual cowardly cruelty, fell upon the most helpless victims, it directed its fury against an asylum for poor colored orphan children. That fact alone stamped the true character of the riot which some of the papers

THE REV. B. W. ARNETT.—[Photographed by L. Hunster.]

Harper's Weekly, May 18, 1878, p. 397.

foully insulted all honorable men by calling a movement of "the people." The mob set fire to the building, and as if all the poor little waifs and strays were her own children, Mrs. Butler shielded them bravely from the white scoundrels, and, with the police, prevented a frightful massacre. The raging mob turned upon her, and she was saved only by being covertly carried to the station-house.

The crime of this country toward the colored race is the more marked because of the constant heroism and patience and nobility of character that illustrate their story. It is pitiful, and it is almost incredible, to reflect that only a quarter of a century ago men and women passed almost literally through fire and water, hungering, thirsting, tortured, nailed up in boxes, harried by bloodhounds, enduring agonies worse than St. Paul suffered, to escape from States in which they were treated more cruelly than brutes, only because they were of a black skin. They followed the north star, but they learned to their cost that they must often follow it out of the world if they would be safe, for the "superior" race was every where in league to drive them back into the hopeless pit from which they were struggling. It was a monstrous crime, for which a terrible reckoning has been made. Mrs. Butler was but fifty-five years old when she died two or three weeks ago. To the last, says Mr. Garnett, until her voice grew so faint that its accents could not be caught, she hummed the words of a familiar hymn:

"That gate ajar stands free for all

"Oh, why does the white man follow my path?"

Harper's Weekly, May 4, 1878, p. 360.

Who seek through it salvation;
The rich and poor, the great and small,
Of every tribe and nation."
"She fell asleep singing that verse like a lullaby."

FREEDOM OF ELECTIONS

HARPER'S WEEKLY
July 27, 1878, p. 586

Senator Bayard, of Delaware, is a Democrat whom his Republican opponents have been accustomed to regard as one of the men of his party who are sincerely anxious for something better than mere partisan politics. His opinions upon many practical public questions are those of patriotic and intelligent men in both parties, and his position upon the Electoral Bill was that of a wise statesman. He is, perhaps, the one conspicuous Democrat who as a candidate for the Presidency would most command the real respect of his political opponents. But when this was recently said to a prominent Democrat, he replied: "Yes, Mr. Bayard is a gentleman, and an able and experienced public man, holding many sound views; but he is a Bourbon. His personal and political associations are with the old South, and were he President, there would be an old Southern Administration." His letter to the Tammany Committee on the Fourth of July is surprising, because, while it demands a free election as the first end to be sought, there is no evidence in it that the writer suspects, what every body else knows, that interference with freedom of elections has always proceeded from the Democratic party.

The three great illustrations of this interference, before the present alleged Louisiana frauds in the Returning Board, were the Slidell Plaquemine frauds in Louisiana, the Tweed frauds in New York in 1868, and the vast Ku-Klux and later intimidation in the Southern States. Even in Louisiana the Democratic suppression of freedom of election at the polls is more distinctly proved than fraud by the Returning Board. We know ourselves of the declaration of a prominent Democratic leader in Georgia that the negroes would be permitted to vote so far and so long as they did not endanger the supremacy of the whites. A Raleigh Democratic paper, in North Carolina, lately announced that negro ascendency would not be tolerated there; and Governor Wade Hampton's speech to his Democratic friends on the Fourth of July in South Carolina shows very distinctly that he knows and condemns a Democratic purpose virtually to abolish negro citizenship. Now we have no more disposition than Senator Bayard to see ignorance and venality governing intelligence, and we can perfectly understand the feeling of educated Americans of the English-speaking race subordinated to the colored freedmen of the plantations. All that is very intelligible. It is not surprising in this point of view that freedom of elections should be assailed even by well-meaning and intelligent people, who see no other escape from monstrous misrule. But these people are generally Democrats. Notoriously it is they who attack this freedom, not the Republicans. There has never been any serious complaint that Democrats were prevented from voting by the Republicans. It is confessedly the Democrats who suppress the free vote of Republicans, and argue that it is mere human nature to do so. But Senator Bayard gravely writes a letter to the effect that Republicans are the sinners, and that the Democrats would protect freedom of elections—an assertion which is totally disproved by the facts. Mr. Bayard is right, of course, in saying that there should be such freedom. But if it were enforced at all hazards, it would be against his own party.

We offer no apology for Republican crimes. Let them be exposed and punished. But the candor of leading public men is a common interest, and their pandering to the basest party prejudice is no less an offense to political morality than that of their associates in destroying by terror the freedom of elections, or false counting of the votes. The three propositions which Mr. Bayard suggests, in conclusion, are admirable in themselves, but they are ludicrous as suggestions to Tammany and the Democratic party. The Senator seems to be unpleasantly aware of this, for he says that they should be sustained by just-minded men of every party—in which we heartily agree with him. The propositions are freedom of elections, undisturbed by "Federal interference, civil or military;" an honest count; and the destruction of any man or party that withstands them. But we remind Mr. Bayard, as a patriot and a Democratic leader, that his first and immediate duty in furtherance of his admirable suggestions is to secure that freedom where it is now most threatened, not by a Republican national Administration, but by Democratic coercion in the Democratic Southern States.

A SOUTHERN DUTY

HARPER'S WEEKLY
September 21, 1878, p. 747

There has been a great deal of sincere sympathy among the most intelligent citizens of the Northern States with the condition in which many Southerners were left by the war. It is a sympathy which does not refer to the merits or the causes of the contest, but is none the less genuine. The unhappy situation in many part of the Southern States has been made still more difficult by the apparent reversal of a rational order of society, and the apathy of humane and intelligent Southerners toward certain crimes and criminals has hardly seemed astonishing. But, for all that, this indifference has been one of the strongest arguments for distrust of that part of the country. When poor and defenseless colored families were hunted and harried, when blameless colored men were taken from their beds at night by masked scoundrels and scourged and tormented, when peaceful colored people were shot down in sheer wantonness, and the public opinion of the neighborhood was apparently unmoved, and the best citizens took no steps to punish or prevent the crimes, and the local authorities, with seeming sullenness, left all efforts of redress to the national courts and officers, it can not be surprising, certainly to reasonable Southerners that Northern public opinion and humanity itself were indignant, and half believed that slavery and the war had completely barbarized that part of the Union.

This distrust, under the circumstances was natural, but unfortunately it was reciprocal. To those who sat imbittered amid the total wreck of the Confederacy the attitude of the North, occasioned by the Ku-Klux enormities and the previous black codes, seemed remorseless, cruel, and unnatural. The local governments under Northern influences did not win, but repelled, the support of more intelligent Southerners. Southern politics became a movement to overthrow the Republican party, which was truly the party of "the North," and gradually the control of the Southern States was recovered by the old political interest which controlled them before the war. During all this time the strong popular Republican argument was distrust of the Southern treatment of the negro. It was not fear of "rebel claims" nor renewed rebellion, but it was suspicion of injury to the new colored citizen. This was an appeal that every body could understand and feel, and it has been generally successful.

It must be evident, therefore, to intelligent and patriotic Southerners who, without further argument as to the past, sincerely desire a good common understanding with the same class in other parts of the Union, that their first duty is to remove this distrust by showing that is has little reason. This can be done in very obvious ways. When want wanton crimes against colored men because they are Republicans are diligently pursued and punished by the local authorities, stimulated by local opinion, it will be believed that they are not willingly winked at. But such belief is impossible so long as such paragraphs as the following represent local opinion. An "up-country" paper in South Carolina, speaking of the organization of colored Republicans clubs, says:

> "As for *us,* we say this: People of Edgefield, watch this thin narrowly, ceaselessly, jealously, and if you discover any ring, or any fellow, trying to work this game, *seize them and hang them.* Do not be satisfied with abusing and ostracising them, *but seize them and hang them!* In Edgefield let us have no more of the negro in politics."

The same paper also names two Republicans, and adds:

> "If those named, and others, ever dare to inaugurate political schemes in Edgefield again, let us hang them. Not only our own self-respect but our safety demands it, and that without masks or disguise."

There are other Democratic papers in the State which say the same things. While they are unrebuked in the most stringent tone by the press and public opinion, the State is justly regarded as semi-barbarous, and no sensible white man in it can wonder that Northern indignation can be readily and rightfully aroused against it. Such expression, if not at once challenged on the spot, can be easily and reasonably represented as showing the general Southern sentiment. And for the suspicion, the jealousy, and the sectional hostility which inevitably ensue, not "Northerns" but "Southerners" are responsible who do no sternly repress such savagery, and rigorously punish the crimes that spring from it.

A SLANDER EXPOSED

HARPER'S WEEKLY
October 5, 1878, p. 787

There have been some unpleasant stories of the conduct of colored people in the yellow fever districts, and there is a very general disposition to believe any such report. The Washington *Post* published an interview with a physician who had just returned from Memphis, and who said that he had been "authentically informed" that colored men nurses had taken advantage of their helpless white victims, especially women. So monstrous a tale should not have been lightly repeated, for the prejudice of race would give it wide circulation and credit. It is fortunate that the slander was immediately exposed. Mr. Keating, editor of the Memphis *Appeal*, brands the falsehood with a generous emphasis which we gladly record:

> "No man, white or black, would be allowed to breathe a second breath after such a crime became known. No such crime has been committed, and white women have not been reduced to the necessity of taking negro men for nurses. The statement is a libel upon the negroes of Memphis. All honor to them! They have done their duty. They have acted by us nobly, as policemen and as soldiers, as well as nurses. They have responded to every call made upon them, in proportion to their number, quite as promptly as the whites. A few of them threatened trouble at one time about food, but they were at the moment suppressed by a company of soldiers of their own color. The colored people of Memphis, as a body, deserve well of their white fellow-citizens. We appreciate and are proud of them."

The frosts have been long delayed, and relief from the terrible pestilence has been very slow in coming. Meanwhile the sympathy of the whole North has been thoroughly aroused, and there has been a universal contribution for the comfort of the stricken Southerners. In every little village, as well as in the capitals and great cities, every church and society and trade has done something for the good work. The Republican Convention of New Hampshire passed a resolution of sympathy with the suffering communities in the Southern States. All this can not fail to have an effect beyond that of the immediate occasion. Prompt succor and hearty good feeling every body can understand, and it is hard to teach people to hate those who show a sincere sympathy. Indeed, all circumstances—the political situation, and now the destructive plague by the feeling that it develops—tend to bring the country closer together, and to promote that common good understanding which is the thing most to be desired.

THE NEW KU-KLUX

HARPER'S WEEKLY
November 16, 1878, p. 906

The forcible interruption of Republican meetings in South Carolina by armed Democrats is not a subject which loses its importance with the sunset of election-day. It is a question for the grave consideration of all good citizens every where. Among intelligent and patriotic men of every party in the Northern States there is a very strong desire that all reasonable grounds of mere sectional difference should be removed, and a good common national feeling restored as fast as possible. This is not a sentimental gush of shaking hands over the bloody chasm, but a wise and patriotic conviction that sectional politics are essentially revolutionary. It is evident that the only point of danger to this consummation is the treatment of the new citizens in the Southern States. If it should appear that the common equal rights of citizens were respected as much in South Carolina as in Wisconsin, the only real source of trouble would be removed. There has been good reason to suppose that this might be the case, because it was plain that there were two kinds of Democrats in the Southern States—the old-fashioned fire-eaters and Bourbons, like Gary and his school, and the more intelligent citizens, like Governor Hampton. If the latter should obtain control, the restoration of common good feeling was assured. Or if, failing to control, they should hold an attitude of strong and steady remonstrance—if, when gross offenses were committed or outrageous practices were proposed, they should be the first to protest, and were firm to maintain their protest—then there would be a general feeling that "the South" was to be restored in the only way possible—by itself.

Events in South Carolina have disappointed the expectation of such a situation. The Ku-Klux has been revived under the name of Red Shirts, and with the tacit approval or acquiescence of the better class of Democrats. The Charleston *News and Courier,* as we said last week, defends the armed Democratic disturbance of Republican meetings. Governor Hampton sees the most precious rights of citizens destroyed, and utters no word of warning to the criminals or of succor to the victims. The crimes themselves can not be denied. They can not be put down as radical lies. For the reports upon which we found our remarks are published in the News and Courier itself. They describe scenes which if they should occur in Northern States would not be completed without the bloodiest contests, and which are infinitely despicable as the conduct of armed white mobs over cowering negroes. There is no doubt that the attitude of Governor Hampton and of a paper like the *News and Courier* toward this new form of the Ku-Klux has done more to justify the estimate of "the South" as a nest of hopeless barbarism than any recent event.

The best friends of "the South" in the Northern States are those Republicans who, in full communion with their party, see clearly the only possible conditions of good sectional understanding, and aim to attain them. Those at the North who say, "What can you expect?" or Democrats who "go with their party," or critics who sneer that a pyramid can not be made to stand on its apex, or the shakers of "the bloody shirt" in and out of season, are not the real allies of patriotic Southern citizens. Those who see that the Republican party politically represents the North, and that the controlling public opinion of the country demands fair play every where, are the friends whom the better sentiment of the South should recognize and heed. These are the allies who are embarrassed by the Red Shirt revival of the Ku-Klux. It is true that no sensible man expects to see the same political good order in South Carolina that he sees in Maine or Iowa. He knows the vital difference of the conditions. Every sensible man also knows that the Republican party is one thing in South Carolina and entirely another in Massachusetts. He regrets that Republicanism undoubtedly and even truthfully in many quarters represents to intelligent Southerners an alliance of rascality and ignorance. He knows that Republicanism is responsible in some places in Southern States for local judges who could neither read nor write, controlled by white scoundrels, and sitting in judgment upon property. Intelligent Southern men ought to understand that the situation in regions which are wholly at the mercy of the new vote, directed by knaves, is perfectly understood by intelligent men at the North, and that it has great weight in the formation of opinion. But it must not be forgotten by such Southerners that government by ignorance controlled by venality is not unknown in many parts of the Northern States, and that property is attacked here too under every outrageous pretense. But even in such places systematic interference with the meetings of political rascals is unknown, and would be at once resented by the whole decent community. It is a great mistake to suppose, as so many Southerners evidently do, that as a Democratic victory in 1880 is only to be obtained by a solid South, a solid South must be obtained at any cost. A South solidified by barbarous outrage and defiance of law must reckon upon a North solidified by just indignation. We repeat that sensible men at the North expect friction and trouble and disorder in the South. They do not suppose that the vast upheaval of the war will not long manifest itself. But if they see no Southern protest against crime, the revival of the Ku-Klux applauded, and all the leaders who had been urging peace and harmony silent, and aiding by silence, while a political party is practically stifled, because its members see that resistance is hopeless, such men will gladly forego all minor differences in their party to unite in the defense of justice and humanity and the essential conditions of free popular government.

SUPPRESSED VOTES

HARPER'S WEEKLY
November 23, 1878, p. 926

It is a curious fact that while the proposed restriction of the municipal suffrage in New York was denounced especially by the Democratic party, the same party in States which it absolutely controls does not hesitate practically to disfranchise an immense minority of voters. The exact situation, therefore, is that Democrats insist in New York that the most ignorant non-taxpayers shall vote upon the city expenses, while in Delaware they enact that failure to pay the poll tax, from any cause, shall disfranchise a citizen from all elections for a year. The reason of the inconsistency is that in New York the Democrats wish to count the Irish vote, and in Delaware they wish to reject the colored vote. In the farther Southern States the colored vote is suppressed by open terror. Armed bodies of white men in red shirts surround the meetings of colored Republicans, insisting upon "dividing the time"—in other words, controlling the meetings as they choose—so that, with the bitter experience of past years, the colored vote is largely destroyed. To those Republicans at the North who think that President Hayes is morally responsible for this situation it is enough to say that in all the Southern States but three this became the situation under President Grant, the military policy, and the absolute national supremacy of the Republican party. The present state of things is no worse than it was before the Presidency of Mr. Hayes, and there was no constitutional action open to him which would have changed it. He has had no other "Southern policy" than strict obedience to his constitutional duty, and there is no doubt that President Grant would have enforced the principle of his latest telegrams to Louisiana before his retirement, which is the principle of the constitutional action of President Hayes.

The question which the political situation in the Southern States opens is, whether there is any national remedy at law for the suppression of the votes of a minority, or even of a majority, when local opinion refuses State relief. If armed Democrats in South Carolina attend a Republican meeting and practically disperse it, there are two courses for Republicans to pursue—one is to fight it out on the spot; the other, to appeal to the authorities. Evidently to adopt the first would be to invoke tremendous odds, and resort to the last is a doubtful remedy, because the Democrats control all the courts and fill all the offices. Under these circumstances can the United States interfere? The Constitution provides, in the old and familiar words, for the case of invasion and domestic violence, on application of the Legislature, or of the Executive when the Legislature can not be convened. Further than this, it provides in the Fourteenth Amendment that no State shall deny to any person within its jurisdiction the equal protection of the laws, and authorizes Congress to enforce the provision by legislation. The relevancy of this amendment and the power it confers to the case in question were clearly defined by Chief Justice Waite in the Ellenton conspiracy trial. He said:

"That a number of citizens of the United States have been killed there can be no question, but that is not enough to enable the government of the United States to interfere for their protection. Under the Constitution that duty belongs to the State alone. But when an unlawful combination is made to interfere with any of the rights of national citizenship secured to citizens of the United States by the national Constitution, then an offense is committed against the laws of the United States, and it is not only the right but the absolute duty of the national government to interfere, and afford to its citizens that protection which every good government is bound to give."

This is the view that applies to this case. In every instance a conspiracy must be proved, and it must be proved to a jury of the vicinage. Practically, therefore, there is no national remedy at law for the suppression of the Republican vote in the Southern States.

That, however, need not discourage exposure and discussion. Slavery was conceded to be wholly a State concern, but it was nevertheless overthrown by the discussion from which the Republican party sprang, and by the refusal of the slave power to submit to law. The suppression of an immense vote, the total denial to a vast minority, and even to a majority in certain States, of the fundamental and most sacred right of American citizens, is an appeal to the sense of justice and fair play in the country which can not fail of success. Such a suppression is practicable only in the Southern States, and there only because of the character of the voters who are suppressed. They were lately slaves, and they have not that sense of equality and the determination to resist injustice which would make bulldozing and red-shirting and Ku-Kluxery of every kind impossible on a great scale in the Northern States. Moreover, the disfranchising law in Delaware operates mainly through the want of alert and intelligent leadership and organization among Republicans. Such organization would take care that every voter was duly apprised of the time and place of payment of his dues. The real hope of the situation lies, however, as we have often said, in the good sense of intelligent and patriotic Southerners, and in the courage and efficiency of the Southern authorities. Governor Hampton's reply to Mr. Swails in South Carolina, dated the 24th of October, asserts positively that whenever a disturbance arises in which he can properly act he will use all his official authority; and he ordered through a Republican solicitor an inquiry into the conduct of the trial justice of whom Mr. Swails complained. Since our article of last week warmly censuring Governor Hampton was written, we have seen his speech at Beaufort, denying that he had failed to do his duty, and appealing to facts for his justification. The speech shows how hard it is to ascertain the truth of such occurrences. But speeches and letters are not enough. In Louisiana Governor Nicholls states unreservedly that the law officers will be made to understand that offenders must be brought to justice, and that, if necessary, the whole militia force will be called out. When any one offender—any bulldozer, or red-shirt, or Ku-Klux of any name—is actually arrested, tried, condemned, and punished by the local Democratic authorities, it will be proof to the country that the evil is in a way to be normally and effectively remedied. But until such an event good citizens in the Southern States can not be surprised by a Northern feeling of general distrust of the Democratic party, which has emphatically expressed itself in the autumn elections.

THE SOUTHERN ELECTION FRAUDS

HARPER'S WEEKLY
December 14, 1878, p. 986

The practical disfranchisement of the colored citizens in the Southern States is a matter of national concern, because it involves the possible decision of the Presidential election by violence and fraud. It is, however, an evil for which there is no immediate legal national remedy, and it is one, moreover, which in its nature is remediable mainly by other than legal methods. The President's Message will probably be published by the time this paper is issued. It is reported that he will point out the perils to be apprehended from such disfranchisement, and that he will urge Congress to secure the free exercise of the suffrage as far as it can. It may, however, be assumed that the present Democratic House will do nothing upon the subject, and will be disposed to regard the suggestion as an effort to revive an old cry. That is a foolish ground for the Democratic House or the Democratic press to take. The renewed interest in the Southern question is not the result of any Republican "scalawaggery," but of Democratic stupidity and crime. Nor is the evidence of that folly and rascality doubtful or partisan. It comes from Democratic sources. The most conclusive exposure of the lawless spirit and fraudulent scheme of the Democratic managers in South Carolina is that of an old unquestionable Democrat— James B. Campbell. It will not be enough, in reply to his assertions, to try to blacken his character; it will be necessary to disprove his statements of fact.

At the late election Mr. Campbell was an independent Democratic candidate for the State Senate in the Charleston district, and four days before the election he published a letter to the Democratic voters of Charleston County. He plainly exposes the Democratic ring which manages the party, and which he describes as a close corporation ruling with a political tyranny hitherto unsurpassed. He describes the legislation procured by this ring, which reduced the number of voting-places by one-third in the city and by two-thirds in the country, compelling poor laboring-men to go generally from five to fifteen miles, and in some instances even forty miles, to vote; and he plainly denounces the frank repudiation by this managing ring of good faith and justice toward the colored voters. Mr. Campbell offered himself to the voters as a Hampton Democrat, holding that Governor Hampton had advocated a fair and frank policy of good faith and justice toward all voters. But the special correspondent of the *Herald*—a gentleman who has no Republican prejudices—says that when Governor Hampton came to Charleston to speak, he betrayed his friend and spoke for the managing ring against him, lest he should lose a chance of election as Senator of the United States. And the correspondent justly asks why the State authorities, from Governor Hampton down, do not take cognizance of these crimes, instead of trying to shield the criminals and punish the victims. "The ruling spirits who govern us," says Mr. Campbell, in his letter," do not wish, will not allow, the colored vote." The dominant Democratic policy in South Carolina and elsewhere could not be more trenchantly or truly stated.

This is the policy and these are the crimes which have re-opened a question that all patriotic and honorably conservative men believed to be in a fair way of settlement. But it is not, fortunately, a bloody-shirt re-opening, and the position of Mr. Campbell and the support he received from the colored voters are among the most cheering signs of the situation. It shows that the true course of patriotic citizens is not a wholesale vituperation of the South and of Southerners, but a clear recognition of the fact that there are Southern Democrats who are both patriotic and courageous, and who are to be sustained in their contest with the dominant ring. A party, however, will be judged by the character of its control. If the spirit of the Executive Committee which Mr. Campbell describes dictates the course of the party in South Carolina, or in any other Southern State, the good sense and patriotism of the North in both parties will conclude and vote accordingly. And if the Democratic press in the Northern States—as now seems probable—proposes to justify fraud and violence in Southern States as necessary to keep the control in the hands of the intelligent white men of property, it will only the more surely promote the close and hearty union of all men of all parties at the North to secure the national government against such control. Southern leaders like Senators Lamar and Gordon ought to learn without delay that if they and the more intelligent citizens of their section are afraid either to speak or to act in the presence of such flagrant and unquestionable offenses, they will forfeit all respect from honorable men in this part of the country who earnestly desire that sectional politics shall disappear. They should know better than any that the sure way to relieve all reputable citizens in their part of the country from the ignominy of these wrongs, which are indisputable, is to see that the most thorough action is promptly taken by the State authorities, and that the protest of men like Mr. Campbell, who are known to represent an honorable class, shall be supported.

ONION-SKIN BALLOTS

HARPER'S WEEKLY
December 21, 1878, p. 1006–7

The calm and temperate tone in which the President discusses in his Message the election frauds in some of the Southern districts shows the spirit in which the matter should be treated. The offenses were confined to certain points, and the President's remarks are such as might be made and should be made by a Chief Magistrate of any party, and by every good citizen. The frauds that have been committed in the districts concerned are not essentially different from those with which we were familiar in New York under Tweed. Their purpose is not the same, but fraud to secure plunder or to obtain power is the same thing. The o[u]trageous tampering with the voting districts is only a form of gerrymander, and the bold stuffing of the boxes is an ancient crime. Indeed, the local limitation of the offense and its character show how far we have advanced from the first form of the Ku-Klux, and justify the conclusion of the President, which is that of other intelligent observers, that the condition of the Southern States is gradually improving. The frauds are like the gallows which the shipwrecked sailor saw upon a strange coast, and which caused him to thank God that he was at least in a Christian country.

It is evident, and it is a most fortunate fact, that the Republican press in this part of the country generally agrees with the President that the remedies for the Southern trouble are civil and judicial. And it is among the real achievements of the Administration that its course has given opportunity to the country for a more reasonable view of the whole Southern question. The key-note of wise statesmanship now is that "the South" must be allowed to work out her own salvation. That of course does not mean that any wrong for which there is a national remedy shall not be pursued vigorously and punished promptly, but that it shall be seen and conceded that no coercive national legislation and no army or navy can possibly make South Carolina what Massachusetts is, or give to Mississippi the intelligent order of Minnesota. This is the view urged very strongly by "An Old Abolitionist" in the Boston *Advertiser*, and it is the opinion of a great many old abolitionists, one of whom, Mr. T. W. Higginson, has plainly and cogently stated it. The social and political situation in the Southern States is due chiefly to slavery. "A community in which one half of the people own the other half must necessarily be found on a very low moral plane," and when the slaves are forcibly emancipated by a civil war, and made equal citizens with the master class amid the universal material ruin and the morbid passions of total defeat, a condition might be anticipated compared with which that of the Southern States is a miracle of order and peace. The improvement within the last ten years, despite much mistaken policy, is very remarkable, and the more so because, as "An Old Abolitionist" truly says, "so far down in the political scale are some half dozen Southern States that if the whole thirty-eight were like them, this Union could not hold together, nor could they, when separated, govern themselves in accordance with any known principles of free government. They would inevitably fall a prey to faction, and the strongest faction would rule despotically."

Such communities can not be lifted into peace and order and intelligence by the power of the national government, and any man or any party that wishes really to help them will begin with a conciliatory temper, however conciliation may be derided, and will seek and develop the really intelligent and patriotic tendency among them. The North can help the South by moral influence and appeal, but it can not help it by a bitter and jealous and contemptuous sectional hatred. Reasonable citizens every where, in the South as well as in the North, can see that just as opinion in the North practically united during the war, and against the Territorial aggressions of slavery, so it would unite against a political dominance obtained and maintained by the whip of the Ku-Klux, the shot-gun of the Regulator, the interference of the Red Shirt, or the fraud of the tissue ballot. The feeling produced among the most conservative of citizens in this part of the country by the late audacious frauds in South Carolina is not at all akin to a bloody shirt revival. It is like that which was aroused by the Plaquemine frauds in Louisiana, and by the border ruffians in Kansas. The political prospect has recently and suddenly changed, because the cipher dispatches, the tampering with the public faith, and the election frauds have shown that while under the Hayes Administration the Republican party has recovered something of its old tone, and is more and more the party of honesty and justice, the Democratic party is the sheltering name of every public danger of the hour. There is a host of independent Northern men who will gladly aid well-disposed Southerners to improve the prospects of their States. But such Southerners will see that the condition of sympathy and aid is evidence that there is in those States a sincere desire for honesty and a respect for law.

RELIGIOUS INTELLIGENCE

HARPER'S WEEKLY
December 21, 1878, p. 1015

The recent consecration of the St. Mark's Protestant Episcopal Church of Charleston was a memorable occasion. This is a church of colored people, and has always held a high position, having been filled before the war largely with free people of color. All the white Episcopal clergymen of Charleston attended, with the exception of one who was ill. Bishop Howe performed the consecration service. This church has been the occasion of a lively discussion in the Diocesan Convention, the Convention having so far refused to admit its delegates on an equal footing with other delegates.

1879

By 1879 the African American exodus to Kansas had caught the attention of the white press, although blacks had been attempting for years to escape the South. The earliest migration from the South took place in the flight of fugitive slaves to Canada, and in 1869 there was an organized movement in Tennessee and Kentucky to settle western and northern states.

The primary motive behind the initial migration of African Americans from the South was the need for social and economic freedom and the promise of their own land. Between 1875 and 1881, an estimated sixty thousand blacks left the South for Kansas; it was reported that between February and September of one year seven thousand people migrated. Papers reported of a group 107 settlers arriving at Kinsley, Kansas, in 1878. The town's location was selected in 1877 by a committee representing the settlers. Harper's Weekly of May 17 reported: "Emigrants from the South continue to arrive. They all tell the same story of extortion, oppression, and murder. They bring with them their wives and children, destitute and panic-stricken. They seek lands and homes where laws are administered with impartiality." The general view of the white population was that the African American population was a dependent class that needed to be kept dependent. Clearly, after fifteen years of freedom African Americans in the South still felt oppressed.

Of particular importance is the Southern response to the migration. As a result of the rapid and unexpected loss of labor, in parts of the South measures were taken to prevent blacks from leaving. Many blacks who might have wanted to leave were faced with intimidation from white planters and employers. Planters refused to make arrangements for raising crops due to the uncertainty of the labor force.

Even in light of the exodus, Southerners refused to recognize the discontentment of blacks. In a letter published in Harper's Weekly, *July 5, ex-senator James L. Alcorn of Mississippi claimed that "Competition for labor guarantees to good negroes on plantations the best of treatment. . . . Outside the voting places, aside from politics, the negro is kindly treated. Before the courts, on the plantations, in the family, I doubt if in all the broad land the negro can find more tender and sympathizing whites."*

In parts of Missouri and Kansas measures were taken to encourage settlers to return to the South, since migration strained resources. A number of cities and towns became black refugee camps. As reported in the press, "The cities of Kansas see a pauper population about to be thrust upon them, and, although desirous of emigrants in reasonable numbers, know not how to dispose of this overwhelming tide. Appeals are going forth on all sides for assistance, while the cities that have suffered the most from the inundation are casting about for means wherewith to give food and shelter" (Harpers' Weekly, *May 17).*

Upon arriving in Kansas, African Americans who were not assigned to specified localities were forwarded to Topeka, where buildings had been secured and transformed into barracks. In an attempt to improve the situation, the Anchor Line steamship company promised free transportation to any black wishing to return "home." However, once in Kansas few African Americans desired to return to the South. The Reverend Dr. R. S. Rust of the Methodist Episcopal Freedmen's Aid Society reported that most would have rather faced death than such a return.

Benjamin Singleton, president of the Tennessee Real Estate and Homestead Association, was responsible for encouraging many of the "Exodusters" and for the founding of several towns in Kansas, including Dunlap, Nicodemus, and Singleton. Originally the association's purpose was to facilitate the purchase of small farms in Tennessee. This endeavor, however, failed. Upon visiting Kansas, Singleton and others found that cheaper land could be found there. The first black settlers sent favorable reports back to the South and encouraged others to make the trip westward. The migration caught the attention of blacks all over the South. At a "convention of colored men" in Richmond, Virginia, it was agreed that if conditions in that state did not improve for blacks, they would organize a society to aid in the migration westward. Similar organizations were formed in other parts of the South.

Many of the first African American settlers in Kansas lived in dugouts and burros. Although they were plagued by crop failures and other natural disasters, their communities survived.

Robert L. Harris, Jr.
Cornell University

RELIGIOUS INTELLIGENCE

HARPER'S WEEKLY
January 25, 1879, p. 71

The colored Baptists are very numerous in Richmond, Virginia, and they are very prosperous. The "Old First Church," which has a great fame, reports for 1878 1115 baptisms. There are eight or nine other churches of colored Baptists in that city. Their ministers are men of energy and character. Among them is the Rev. John Jasper, usually known as "the philosopher," who stands firmly to his faith that "the sun does move." On this topic he has preached and lectured copiously.

RELIGIOUS INTELLIGENCE

HARPER'S WEEKLY
March 29, 1879, p. 247

While political animosities are so bitter in the South, it is pleasing to observe that Christian feeling is triumphing over sectionalism and race prejudice. Late in February Louisiana held its first State Sunday-school Convention. Among the Northern men present were Messrs. Peltz, of the *Sunday-school Times,* Ralph Wells, of New York, and E. Payson Porter and B.F. Jacobs, of Chicago. Dr. B.M. Palmer, of the Presbyterian Church, and Bishop Keener, of the Methodist Church South, participated actively in the proceedings. The Sunday-schools of the colored people were represented, and a colored delegate, the Rev. Mr. Newman, who is pastor of a Baptist church in New Orleans, was invited to address the Convention. Two colored pastors were placed on the Executive Committee of the State Association. The number of Sunday-school scholars in Louisiana was reported to be 70,000.

THE FLIGHT OF COLORED LABORERS

HARPER'S WEEKLY
April 26, 1879, p. 322

The emigration of colored laborers from Mississippi, Louisiana, and Texas to Kansas is a significant illustration of the situation. Some of the Southern papers very justly perceive that such a movement is alarming, and will result in great losses if it is not arrested. The colored people are the laboring class, and there are none to replace them. The question why they are going is one of peculiar interest, and the first fact shown by the movement is that they are greatly discontented. They are not a nomadic race, and they are satisfied with little. So general a flight shows that they are seriously suffering, or seriously alarmed. Obviously, if they had good wages and employment, and felt secure of all their rights, they would stay at home. It is, indeed, surprising how hard it is to ascertain the actual condition of the colored people in the Southern States. The letters in the newspapers have to be dismissed generally as written for a partisan purpose. Mr. T.W. Higginson and other old antislavery men and Union soldiers give a rather favorable account, and among foreign observers Sir G. Campbell, in the last number of the *Fortnightly Review,* writes a very interesting summary of the condition of the late slave class.

He says that in educational capacity they are apparently behind, but not very far behind. They have as yet, he says, shown very little mercantile skill of any kind, and are not as yet noted for energy or force under difficulties, nor do they show themselves to be superior artisans. But they are admirable laborers when under proper supervision, and he notes a disposition upon the part of proprietors and leaders to rely upon colored labor as a conservative element. The colored people are not very thrifty, however, and methods of labor are often loose and unsatisfactory. But Sir G. Campbell's general conclusion is one of agreeable surprise that the position of the colored people is so good, and their industrial relations with the whites so little strained and difficult. He thinks them in a fair way to become a comfortable, well-to-do population. The whites, he says, certainly can not do without them, while the whites are indispensable to them. He wisely sums up the whole matter by saying, "My advice would certainly be, to the blacks in America, 'Stay at home and make the best of an excellent situation;' to the whites, 'Do all you can to keep these people; conciliate them and make the most of them.'" This he is sure can be done if the political situation does not prevent, and that he means to consider in another paper.

The Southern States are undoubtedly very poor. Every observer reports that fact. But they certainly have not more labor than is wanted. The emigration of great bodies of laborers, therefore, means that they feel insecure. They would not feel so had their treatment been fair, and the movement beyond the Mississippi is an unmistakable impeachment of the conduct of the whites. Mr. Lamar is from Mississippi, and he must admit that if the assertions of his recent article in the *North American* were accurate, if the colored people felt sure of fair wages and fair play at the polls in Mississippi, they would certainly not go by hundreds to Kansas. He and all the intelligent white leaders in the States concerned are arraigned by this great exodus. Why have they not

AFRICAN AMERICAN HISTORY IN THE PRESS, 1851-1899

THE COLOR LINE STILL EXISTS—IN THIS CASE.

Harper's Weekly, January 18, 1879, p. 52.

cultivated a public opinion which would have made all kinds of Ku-Kluxery impossible, and would have assured the colored people that they need not look North for their best friends? Agents and knaves and demagogues may have promised mules and forty acres and a charming climate, but they would have been vain allurements against fair play at home. The remedy of the situation is not in Southern denunciation of the North, or in Northern talk about rebels and Confederates and slave-drivers: it is in the perception of honorable Southerners that their paramount duty is to regain the confidence of the colored people, which they have lost. This

HARPER'S WEEKLY
JOURNAL OF CIVILIZATION

Vol. XXIII.—No. 1158.] NEW YORK, SATURDAY, MARCH 8, 1879. [WITH A SUPPLEMENT. PRICE TEN CENTS.

THE CIVILIZATION OF BLAINE.
JOHN CONFUCIUS. "Am I not a Man and a Brother?"

Harper's Weekly, March 8, 1879, p. 181.

THE FREEDMENS (SAVINGS) BANK.

CLOSED
1873.
STILL "WINDING UP,"
TO DATE.
MARCH—1879.

THEY WILL KEEP ON "WINDING UP" TILL THE LAST DROP OF BLOOD IS GONE. AND EVERY BONE PICKED DRY.

THE FIRST SAVINGS OF THE EMANCIPATED SLAVE EMBEZZLED HERE,

BY MEN THAT "TRIED TO DO SOME GOOD."

"THE BANK DIRECTORS ARE ALL HONORABLE MEN."

1900 A.D.
THE LAST POOR DEPOSITOR WAITING FOR THE "FINAL WIND UP."

CONVICTED
GLASGOW BANK DIRECTORS PLEASE TAKE NOTICE HOW WE DO THINGS IN A FREE COUNTRY.

WAITING.
A DEBT THAT THE REPUBLICAN PARTY OUGHT TO WIPE OUT.

Harper's Weekly, March 29, 1879, p. 248.

DIFFICULT PROBLEMS SOLVING THEMSELVES.

Harper's Weekly, March 29, 1879, p. 256.

will be a work of time and of good sense. But there is no other course, and it must be heartily supported by all patriotic citizens.

SOUTHERN POLITICIANS

HARPER'S WEEKLY
April 26, 1879, p. 326

... The Southern politicians of the ruling caste are of all politicians the most absurd. They have no thought of progress, no projects of national usefulness, no desire to cultivate the intellect of their people or extend over their decaying section those common conveniences and advantages that science offers to the educated man. Their cities and towns are left unsewered and pestilential, the seats of perpetual disease; their roads and railroads are neglected; the Mississippi flows over broken levees and deserted plantations; law is powerless to protect property and life. Georgia and South Carolina teem with acts of violence; immigration turns away from the rich fields of Alabama and Louisiana; and amidst a country of unexampled fertility and native wealth, a blight of poverty rests upon the land. How easily, with a peaceful, progressive government, might Georgia and Alabama be converted into hives of busy industry, and the energy and intellect of their people spring up together! How soon would an intelligent administration change the whole face of the South! how easily might a tolerant and just one insure rest and progress to all its people! But this is never the aim of the Southern politician. He seems to forget that there is a people to be benefited, a country to be educated and improved. To his own section he brings only a ceaseless succession of disasters. He leaves behind him fear, violence, hate, the malediction of the poor, the deserted plantations of Georgia, the flying laborers of Louisiana—a land wasted by the ravages of a war kindled by his own stupid bigotry. His only aim in politics is despotic power. He has abandoned in adversity none of his prejudices. His knowledge seems only abridged by the lessons of defeat. He would fix his rule over the North. Having ruined his own section of the country, he has a malicious hatred for all the others. He proposes to reign over New York as he reigns at Charleston, and cover with his reactionary doctrines and practices the liberal West. It is easy to see that a continued rule of this class of Southern politicians would bring with it the decay of education, knowledge, liberal manners, polished arts, and crush the people with an intolerable burden.

It is time, indeed, for the people to see that they are in real peril. The Southern politician is secretive, and has a definite aim, remorseless in his measures, persistent in his designs. The man who would carry elections by violence in South Carolina would be still more ready to carry them in the same way in New York; the repudiator, revolutionist, the destroyer of his own section, would show little tenderness for the welfare and rights of freemen any where. The Southern politician of this class is dangerous, and must be looked upon with constant suspicion. He is a tiger to be chained and muzzled; and the longer this process is put off, the more difficult must prove its execution. Nothing but a general union of the people of the North will now have any effect upon these unscrupulous agitators, and only in a close and united party can the Republicans and the Unionists once more save their country. The people of the North have forgotten politics. Occupied with their factories and farms, their railroads, improvements, they have neglected their duty as citizens. The enemy has stolen upon them in their slumber. Already he rules the government. Should he continue to control it, their factories and farms, their railroads and improvements, will prove of little value, and the danger to the country can only be estimated by the height of prosperity from which it must fall.

Three Republican members of Congress alone are left from the great district of country recently in rebellion. Yet one of these, in a vivid, daring speech, asserts that throughout all the conquered States there is still a Republican majority, that with free elections it would drive from office the disloyal and violent, that the people are anxious for peace, and weary of their restless politicians. No one has a better opportunity of studying the wants, the condition, of that section than Mr. Houk. He is almost the last of the Republicans at the South. He stands on a frail eminence, still unconquered by the violent inroads of rebellious storms. It is certainly encouraging to be told that the majority of the Southern

AFRICAN AMERICAN HISTORY IN THE PRESS, 1851-1899

HARPER'S WEEKLY.
JOURNAL OF CIVILIZATION

Vol. XXIII.—No. 1165.] NEW YORK, SATURDAY, APRIL 26, 1879. [WITH A SUPPLEMENT. PRICE TEN CENTS.

Entered according to Act of Congress, in the Year 1879, by Harper & Brothers, in the Office of the Librarian of Congress, at Washington.

HE (THE SOLID SOUTH) WILL SOON BE "*LET ALONE.*"

"Massa, I leave you because you '*kill us with* KINDNESS.' There is *too much* FREEDOM *at the Polls*, and I am going where the '*bad Yankees*' live, and where there is 'WICKED BAYONET RULE.' Niggers can't stand so much '*Kindness*;' it makes them 'Impudent' and 'Ungrateful.'"

Harper's Weekly, April 26, 1879, p. 321.

people are opposed to their present rulers, that they have been driven by force from the polls, and may yet rebel against the policy of Toombs and Davis. It is mortifying to believe that ours is the only country, nominally a free one, that is ruled by violence, in which a savage and cruel minority has seized upon the chief control of a great people, that the majority in Congress have no more right to their seats than a band of usurpers and outlaws. It seems that our government has ceased to be a free one. —Eugene Lawrence.

BAYONETS AT THE POLLS

HARPER'S WEEKLY
May 10, 1879, p. 363

Patriotic Democrats like Mr. Bayard, who argue the pending question of defense of the ballot-box as if it were an abstract proposition, apparently forget the important facts. The demand for prohibiting national protection of voters at the polls comes from those who are themselves responsible for unlawfully and forcibly excluding voters from the polls, and for stuffing the boxes with tissue ballots. These persons naturally desire to be free from any control. They feel that they are justified in using any means to escape negro domination. When they demand the exclusion of the national authority, they propose that the States shall take care of the elections. But *they* are the States. Why did not the States suppress the Ku-Klux? Why did not the States arrest and punish the bulldozers? Because these very persons who decry the bayonet at the polls compose the rifle clubs at the polls, and the juries who try alleged offenders, and the public opinion which lies behind all. The most recent and impartial evidence upon this point is the second paper of Sir George Campbell, M.P. He says—and it is the general opinion of observers—that violence and disturbance in the Southern States since the war have been due to the white minority, not to the freedmen. The rifle clubs, he says, are an armed political organization outside of the militia, and the excuse for its terrorization has been that negro or carpet-bag rule was so wicked as to justify any kind of redress. But he was unable to find that the "black Legislatures" made bad laws, and the real trouble was general corruption. Sir George says distinctly that it was well understood that "the Democrats were determined to win every thing in the South." He states that there was perfect frankness in speaking of the way in which things were managed in the election of last autumn, and he was there at the time. "There was not a very great amount of violence or intimidation." "Great Democratic majorities were obtained by the simple process of what is called 'stuffing the ballot-boxes.'" Nobody pretended that the tissue ballots were designed for any other purpose than that of fraud. In one district, where not more than a thousand persons voted, there were more than three thousand ballots in the box. In other districts the number of polling-places was so reduced that it was impossible for all to vote who wished. At other polls the inspectors kept away. "In short," says this perfectly unprejudiced observer, "I have no hesitation in saying, as matter within my own knowledge, that if these elections had taken place in England, there were irregularities which must have vitiated them before an election judge a hundred times over."

Now when ballot-box stuffers by their representatives demand the repeal of existing national safeguards of the ballot-box, on the ground that it is incompatible with free government, and unconstitutional, and that the States will take care of the matter, we say, and every sensible man will say, that it is a mere pretense, and that the demand really is one for unrestricted cheating. The vital point is a free and fair election; but no one who demands the repeal of the safeguards has shown any interest in that point. If arms at the polls are so obnoxious, why is all the protest levelled against the arms of the United States, which are not even charged with intimidation, and not a word against those of rifle clubs and "red shirts," which are confessedly present to intimidate? If the party which inveighs so loudly against bayonets at the polls were not the very party which brings them there, and for an unlawful purpose, it might expect that its position would be respected, and its plea of redressing grievances and of threatened liberty would be heard with patience. But who have grievances in this matter? The whites or the blacks? Who threatens liberty? The whites or the blacks? The constitutional question is not properly raised by those who raise it to secure immunity for bulldozing. When it is raised, the Constitution, if doubtful, is to be interpreted favorably to liberty. Sir George Campbell, in commenting upon the seats in Congress obtained by fraud in the late election in the Southern States, says (and it is but the common-sense of the question, which we commend to the attention of Mr. Bayard and his friends): "Not only are nearly balanced parties much affected, but in case of a struggle over the next Presidential election, these votes might just turn the scale, and the question whether there is any remedy practically available to redress wrongs which are, I may almost say, admitted, puts in issue the wider question whether the Fifteenth Amendment of the United States Constitution, securing equal electoral rights to the blacks, is really to be enforced, or whether it may be set aside in practice by the action of individual States. Is, in fact, the settlement at the end of the war to be maintained or surrendered?" And he adds, what every intelligent American also sees: "There never can be peace, quiet, and safety in the United States till a mode of settling disputed elections is arranged, and this question of the black vote is definitively laid at rest."

In a word, experience has shown that the elections in certain States are unfair, and that the controlling opinion of those States does not wish them to be fair. If, therefore, every form and degree of national supervision be withdrawn from those States, the knowledge of the country that the election of a majority in Congress or a President has been determined by such States would inevitably produce a situation which no good citizen wishes to see. It is true, as Senator Davis says, that we need rest from sectional passion. But if our statement be correct, can he or any other honorable man assert that the States in question are not responsible for arousing those passions?

THE GREAT NEGRO EXODUS

HARPER'S WEEKLY
May 17, 1879, p. 386

Our illustration on page 384 has reference to the great movement now being made by the negro race from their accustomed homes in the South to the more tranquil region west of the Mississippi. Fugitives from injustice and oppression, these people are fleeing northward and westward, as others of their race formerly fled from the horrors of slavery. Deprived of their civil rights, they are now in their own section of our country nearly as far from the enjoyment of the privileges granted them by the Constitution as they were in their days of bondage. Apparently with one accord they have arrived at the conclusion that the only remedy for the ills from which they suffer lies in their removal to some region where no prejudice exists against their race; and thus a hegira is in progress which threatens to flood certain States of our Union with a population for which they can not provide, and to leave others without laborers wherewith to develop their resources.

The objective point of the negroes in almost every case is Kansas, few having turned their faces in any other direction. The reason probably is that this State has been more thoroughly advertised than any other, on account of the early struggles which established freedom in it when a Territory, and as having been the scene of the exploits of John Brown and other martyrs of freedom. Kansas is also the ground which finally became the field of operations of the society known as the Tennessee Real Estate and Homestead Association. The original objects of this society, which was formed in Nashville as early as 1869, were the purchase of small farms in Tennessee, and the encouragement of the freedmen in the farming districts to become owners of the land they should cultivate. It was soon found that no headway could be made in the undertaking, and, after holding a State Convention over the subject, a committee was appointed to visit Kansas, to see if cheaper homes could not be found among a more friendly people than in the land of their former bondage. The report brought back was favorable to the scheme, but on a second delegation being sent out, accounts were given of recent disasters affecting the prosperity of the State; and as most of the freedmen preferred remaining in the land of their birth, little progress was made in the scheme. Finally, however, a few families went to Kansas, and the letters sent back encouraged others to make the experiment. In 1873, Benjamin Singleton, the president of the association, went out to take a look at Kansas. His report was so favorable that a company of two or three hundred gathered, and Singleton brought them out that year, locating them in Cherokee County, in the southeast corner of the State. From that time the railroad agents over various routes have been stimulating the emigration by offers of low fares. They bring companies from Nashville to Topeka at $10 a head. The association has continued to keep up active operations. Emigrants desiring to come are by its agency thrown into companies, placed under competent leaders, and cheap rates of transportation are secured. Some half dozen different parties, numbering from one hundred to three hundred each, have come out under the auspices of this association. Most of the parties have come to Topeka, and from thence have gone to different parts of the State. Several hundred of them have gone to Barton County, in the Arkansas Valley, and some to other frontier counties.

With Mr. Singleton was associated Columbus M. Johnson—an intelligent colored man, and agent at Topeka of the association in question. In 1877 these two spent much time in obtaining information from government and other land officers, and in investigating the properties of the soil in different districts. Mr. Johnson remains permanently at Topeka, while Mr. Singleton conducts the affairs of the association at Nashville. Among other colonies which they have established is one in Morris and Lyon counties, called the Singleton Colony. This is upon some lands purchased by the government from the Kansas tribe of Indians, and which is to be sold to the settlers at a low price—at from one to five dollars per acre, it is said—and on long time. Other companies have also gone out besides those organized by this society, some from Tennessee and some from Kentucky, and many of the emigrants have scattered through the older counties, where they rent land, farm on shares, or work for wages. In some instances they are able to buy improved farms or small unimproved tracts at from five to ten dollars an acre. These emigrants are nearly all agricultural laborers, and few have any thing save their own hands to enable them to gain a living in a strange country. Many of those who have gone out to the frontier upon homestead or cheap railroad lands in the first instance subsist by working for wages on the farms of the more prosperous white emigrants, afterward doing something for themselves.

This comparatively successful start made by their brethren naturally turned the attention of the negroes of the South toward Kansas. Unfortunately, however, what should have taken the form of well-considered emigration has assumed the character of a vast exodus. At the time of writing it is estimated that nearly 9000 emigrants have arrived at St. Louis, only 2400 of that number having been possessed of sufficient means to pay their fare to Kansas. The others have been furnished with free transportation by the Colored Immigrant Relief Committee. Nearly every day there are fresh arrivals, and at all times groups of colored people can be seen upon the levee. About two weeks ago the Relief Committee entered into a contract with the Missouri River Packet Company, the terms of which were that when immigrants arrive they shall be proffered the use of the company's wharf boat until they depart for Kansas, and that the charges for transportation shall be $3 for each adult, $1 50 for each person between the ages of twelve and twenty-one years, and nothing for children less than twelve years old, from St. Louis to Wyandotte. In accordance with this agreement, the immigrants are landed on the company's wharf boat by the lower river packets on which they come. Their "plunder," as they call their household goods, is piled up by the roustabouts in the middle of the wharf boat. Wood and provisions are given them. They build fires with this wood on the levee and cook their food, using for the purpose such utensils as they can get possession of. After a boat has arrived the levee presents an animated appearance, the dusky people moving to and fro in the fire-light singing, or dancing, or prophesying, and the 'long-shoremen rushing from the boat with goods of various descriptions. When tired, they wrap themselves up in their rags and lie down to sleep upon the cold hard deck. The women are shown great respect by the men, who allow them to choose the best places for sleeping.

Naturally an exodus of such proportions as this is a cause of great alarm both to the section receiving such a rapid and unexpected increase in its population, and to that which through the same cause finds itself deprived of a large part of its laboring class. On the one hand efforts are being made to persuade the negroes to return, and on the other the most severe measures are being taken to prevent their departure. At St. Louis the Anchor Line of steamers has offered free transportation to all who are willing to go back, but in most cases the offer is rejected with indignation. In the mean time the alarm at the South is provoking the most terrible outrages. It appears that already the planters are becoming alarmed at the loss of the laborers by whom alone their fields can be cultivated, and are employing all kinds of repression and restriction. The steamboat companies have three or four times raised their rates of fare, in the expectation that the negroes could not obtain the means of transportation. Armed bands have assembled on the shores of the river to prevent the emigrants from embarking, and not less than twenty cases of deliberate murder have been reported. In one instance the wife of a man who had departed was visited by an armed mob in the night-time, who asked her where her husband was, and she replied that he had gone to Kansas. They asked her if it was her intention to follow him, and upon her reply in the affirmative, they took her out and hanged her to a neighboring tree. These statements appear to be well authenticated, and many of them have been published in the newspapers of Missouri and Kansas. They seem to establish the fact that the worst revelations that have hitherto been made have fallen far short of the truth in regard to the relations between the whites of the South and the enfranchised slaves. The movement, therefore, toward the North is simply an effort of this suffering people to escape from the grossest wrong and oppression. There is also one curious fact about this movement of the negroes. The people are of all ages, sizes, sexes, colors, and degrees. It is confined to no particular class. All Southern negroes have evinced a desire to leave their homes, and all who could have done so. The others are deterred from leaving by their want of means and their fear of the white planters, who threaten to kill them if they attempt to quit the South.

In the mean time there is great suffering among the negroes, who, accustomed to pass their days in one spot, know nothing of the difficulties of travel or of making new homes for themselves in a strange country. The cities of Kansas see a pauper population about to be thrust upon them, and, although desirous of emigrants in reasonable numbers, know not how to dispose of this overwhelming tide. Appeals are going forth on all sides for assistance, while the cities that have suffered most from the inundation are casting about for means wherewith to give food and shelter to the unfortunate visitors they are forced to entertain. On the 25th of April the Relief Committee of Wyandotte, Kansas, met with a similar board in the city of St. Louis, to consider the problem of providing for the negroes. The result was a thorough consideration of the situation, and the following touching appeal from what is called the "Committee of Twenty-five:"

> "Emigrants from the South continue to arrive. They all tell the same story of extortion, oppression, and murder. They bring with them their wives and children, destitute and panic-stricken. They seek lands and homes where laws are administered with impartiality.
>
> "Our committee has sheltered, fed, clothed, and transported 5000 colored emigrants to Kansas, but on account of their destitution they became burdens upon the infant and struggling communities of the young commonwealth. They need clothing, food, transportation, lands, and implements of husbandry.
>
> "Kansas extends her liberal hand, and we throw ourselves upon the sympathies of the charitable and liberty-loving throughout the republic, believing that loyal men will not forget that those men who are now refugees from grinding extortion and a bloody terrorism were the companions in arms of soldiers, piloted the Union armies, and fed and clothed escaping Union prisoners in the great war for Union and liberty, and by centuries of unrequited toil planted and gathered the great Southern staples of our foreign and domestic

commerce, built up great States, and by their labor poured untold millions into the Federal and individual purse of the nation.

"It would be some return, some substantial token of appreciation for their long-suffering and forbearance, to help them now in the hour of their dire distress."

We trust that this appeal will meet with a hearty and immediate response, and that something practical may be done to relieve the sufferings of these poor and deserving people.

RELIGIOUS INTELLIGENCE

HARPER'S WEEKLY
May 17, 1879, p. 387

The Rev. Dr. R. S. Rust, the secretary of the Methodist Episcopal Freedmen's Aid Society, reports that he has held frequent personal interviews with the freedmen who have reached Kansas from the South, and has found them determined to take no backward steps. They said to him "that death in almost any form would be preferable to their return." About seven or eight thousand have left; several thousand more are on the banks of the Mississippi waiting for transportation. Very foolishly, the white people at some points on the river are trying to detain the blacks by threats and the show of force. The meetings for relief are becoming more numerous every week, but the relief measures are as yet very imperfectly organized.

At a recent exhibition of a school for colored children, held in the court-house of Edenton, North Carolina, the stage gave way, and the building took fire from the overturned lamps. A frightful panic followed; the house was densely packed, and there was a rush for the doors. Many children were crushed, had limbs broken, or were severely burned—some so badly that they can not survive. By the efforts of a few brave, self-possessed persons the building was saved, and hundreds rescued from a terrible death.

DOMESTIC INTELLIGENCE

HARPER'S WEEKLY
May 24, 1879, p. 403

Congress: In the House, on the 5th inst., Mr. Ladd (Greenbacker), of Maine, introduced a bill to prevent military interference at elections. It was referred to the Judiciary Committee. The text is as follows: "*Whereas,* The presence of troops at the polls is contrary to the spirit of our institutions and the traditions of our people, and tends to destroy the freedom of elections; therefore, *Be it enacted, etc.,* That it shall not be lawful to bring to or employ at any place where a general or special election is being held in a State any part of the army or navy of the United States, unless such force be necessary to repel the armed enemies of the United States, or to enforce Section 4, Article 4, of the Constitution of the United States, and the laws made in pursuance thereof, on application of the Legislature or the Executive of the State where such force is to be used; and so much of all laws as is inconsistent herewith is hereby repealed." A similar bill was introduced in the Senate, and referred to the Judiciary Committee. On the 6th, the new bill was reported in the House, without amendment, and passed, by 124 to 90. No debate was allowed, and a substitute offered by Mr. Robeson was voted down.—On the 7th, the Senate resolved to re-open the question of Mr. Kellogg's title to his seat in that body.—On the 8th, the House laid the bill to enforce the eight-hour law on the table.

SOUTHERN REFORM

HARPER'S WEEKLY
May 24, 1879, p. 406

The Southern political leaders who call an extra session of Congress excite public attention of no favorable character, force themselves into an unpleasant publicity, can have no just cause of complaint if they find their own conduct and the affairs of the section of the country they profess to represent become subjects of severe criticism. And what an unfortunate retrospect do they bring up before the people! The twenty or thirty Confederate generals who would shake anew the whole fabric of government, the whole prosperity of the nation, are as unlucky in the present as in the past. They are destined to be beaten. Their careers are only the forerunners of misfortune to their own people and to themselves. The Southern States have been badly led in war and peace. They have sunk rapidly even in relative importance. They are surrounded by an immense chain of more liberal communities, full of vigorous life and progress, but the whole section of country from the Potomac to the Rio Grande has been condemned by its political leaders to a hopeless decay. Its reformers in 1865–66 forced upon it a system of free schools that might well have given it a new life; the Democrats from

1870 have left their schools to languish, and only out of shame suffer some of them to flourish imperfectly; they begin to fear even their own depressed people, and sometimes dole out a scanty subsistence to the common-school teacher. From 1865 to 1870 the Republicans gave to the Southern States a system of railways that might well have enriched and cultivated their waste or neglected lands; they have built Atlanta, revived Charleston. When the Democrats came in power again, they kept the railways, sometimes refused to pay for them, and checked the progress of the system. Under the Republican rule immigration had begun; the people of the North and of Europe formed colonies in Alabama or Louisiana; even Kentucky was invaded by some ardent Republicans, and Virginia showed some trace of advance. Massacre, insecurity, death, drove away the honest settlers, and after Coushatta, Vicksburg, the dark deeds in Kentucky, no stream of immigration has been turned toward the South. Labor and capital fly from the unquiet land. Since 1873 the only kind of emigration known there has been a destructive one. Texas has drawn in as swarm of Southern whites, who have gone thither from the more eastern States, only to find want, starvation, disappointment; and the Mississippi is covered with its gangs of workmen escaping Northward, as they declare, from a new slavery.

The reformers introduced to the Southern States the conception of a free press, free speech, a free suffrage. It need not be told how perfectly the Democratic leaders have eradicated even the ideas. The period from 1865 to 1870 brought with it lessons that have never been wholly forgotten, taught to Charleston and New Orleans the sanctity of human life, the necessity of reform, the barbarity of the duellist, the odious cruelty of the street fight, the supremacy of the law. For a time Republicanism and reform softened the manners of the people, checked the progress of crime. Street fights became rare in Louisiana and Mississippi, and duelling was discountenanced even in New Orleans. But since 1870, and wherever the Democratic leaders have renewed their rule, the savage practices of the past have been revived. The duellist once more lifts his murderous front even in the halls of Congress, and escapes unpunished. Murder once more stalks abroad in Atlanta and Vicksburg. The barbarous contempt for human life that marked the days of slavery and isolation has nearly returned, and a united South seems resolved to repel every trace of progress. There is not a liberal newspaper in all Georgia—a State as populous as Switzerland. There is no one in Alabama who dares to denounce the secret or open tyranny of its reactionary chiefs. South Carolina has fallen into the hands of its old oppressors, and the men who fired upon Sumter rule in its decaying borders. The reactionary party has seized upon the control of the South. Knowledge perishes, civilization retrogrades, the manners of the community become barbarous. A surveillance more rigid than that of Russia over its Nihilists represses the progress of the reformer.

Free speech is forbidden. In dreadful silence men watch the advance of the party of revolution and disorder. It is the silence before the storm.

This is the picture the Southern leaders have brought before the nation; this the strange revolution they have caused. They flaunt their crimes even in Washington. The duellist sends his challenge, and is not expelled, not even rebuked—nay, is applauded. To argument they reply by threats of violence; to reason they oppose the scorn of brutal insolence. We are to be ruled at the North, it seems, as they are ruled in South Carolina, and the laws of a great nation enacted at the pistol's mouth. "Your money or your life!" is the highwayman's cry. It is the burden of almost every Southern harangue in Congress. This peculiar mode of ruling will, no doubt, produce a united opposition in all the Free States. No large section of the people will consent to accept the Confederate politicians as their leaders, or go to the polls side by side with the noisy autocrats of South Carolina. But a still more important question arises as to the effect of the reactionary rule upon the people of the Southern States themselves. Will they suffer their best interests to be disregarded, their lands laid waste by emigration, see their trade decay, their population even decline, while the savage politician rules them by force, checks free speech, free thought, the press, the school, and exercises an espionage over the opinions of men more severe than that of Russia in its mortal terror, France under its Bourbons and Napoleons? There is one agent the Francias of the South have to fear—they are environed by a free and active press; they are exposed every where to a keen scrutiny; they are pursued, even to the most secret retreats of violence and crime—to Kemper County and to Caddo Parish. Their conduct can no longer, as in the time of slavery before 1860, be hidden in darkness. The accomplished correspondent tracks them where he can not punish. The telegraph relates the latest encounter on the streets, or paints the flight of the pilgrims of the Mississippi. Knowledge is slowly encircling the Southern section. Reform is already invading it. It is possible that it can always be ruled by terror?

The measures of the reformers of 1865–70 have not been without their lasting effect. The railroads they built, the school systems they founded, the freedom they gave to labor and intelligence, are the elements of a progress that are indestructible. They have borne already a vigorous fruit. It is stated that the number of small farmers, white and colored, in the Southern States has greatly increased, that intelligence has made considerable advances, that there is a large party of thoughtful merchants, laborers, mechanics, all the industrious and frugal, who see in the politics of Messrs. Butler and Blackburn only a presage of their own ruin, who would gladly enter into any projects of reform. This class of the people naturally demands education and free speech, the liberal newspaper, the advocates of progress. They are not satisfied with the dead past of reaction and decay; they still hope to see their native land filled with the highest results of modern cultivation. It is said that in Texas there is a large German population often capable of checking the action of extremists, insisting upon the preservation of good order and the supremacy of the law. Eastern Tennessee stands like a beacon of loyalty, unconquerable and unintimidated, the land of free speech, free newspapers, honesty, and reform. It is destined probably to have a large share in the regeneration of all its section. It is said that in Virginia there are honorable men who are ready at a moment to take the lead in the cause of popular progress; that in all parts of the South the men of blood and violence may soon be supplanted by a generation of the tolerant and humane.

It is, in fact, quite time for the industrial and mercantile classes of the South to compute how much they have already lost by the needless agitation of an extraordinary Congress, and the disloyal, threatening harangues of the politicians who profess to represent them. It is safe to say that every valuable interest has suffered by the violence of these self-chosen Representatives. The sum the Southern States have already paid within a few years for the folly of their political leaders must reach hundreds of millions of dollars. How many contracts have been laid aside! how many business engagements revoked! how carefully the foreign capitalists avoid investments in Southern lands! how rigidly the tide of immigration turns away from Charleston and Savannah because Messrs. Blackburn and Chalmers are thought to represent the people of the South, and the party of violence and agitation have seen fit to force themselves into power! Under a tolerable administration of their affairs, the Southern States would long ago have been covered with railways and filled with busy life; under a Democratic rule of oppression, land is almost valueless, and nearly every project of internal communication fails. In the price of their lands the Southern States have paid for the savage cruelty of their politicians in millions of money, in a general decay. The industry of its colored laborers has alone saved the South from the utter ruin invoked by the madness of its white oppressors. To the honest labor of its colored population the Union and the Southern States owe a ceaseless debt of praise. Colored farmers already thrive in the outskirts of Savannah, and substantial colored men in the neighborhood of Charleston have been the favorite objects of the cruelty and fraud of Democratic politicians.

It is the hope of every humane and intelligent thinker that the reign of political violence at the South will end at last. It seems plain that it can not forever resist the power of the press, the example of the free and progressive States, the discontent of its own people. The Confederate generals who have summoned an extra session of Congress, and rule over their Democratic slaves of the North with no gentle hand, can not forever be permitted to destroy the material welfare of a great nation, the hopes of their own section, the peace of an advancing country. The welfare of the working classes demands their complete overthrow; the hopes of the capitalist must rest upon their utter destruction. We may well look forward to the time when the whole South shall proclaim its adhesion to free speech, free thought, a free press, and, when relieved from political agitation, the Southern States shall become rich in prosperity and ease.—Eugene Lawrence.

RELIGIOUS INTELLIGENCE

HARPER'S WEEKLY
May 24, 1879, p. 407

The idea has taken possession of many minds that the exodus of the freedmen from the South will help the solution of one of our most difficult political problems. The demonstration of the fact that the negroes, if ill treated, will migrate, it is thought, will insure hereafter their good treatment. It may be doubted if even that will secure in the South a tolerance of their political ascendancy. On this side Southern prejudice is ineradicable. Meetings in behalf of the freedmen continue to be called. A large one has been held in Faneuil Hall, Boston. Appeals to the churches are made, and should not be made in vain. A convention has been in session at Vicksburg, Mississippi, to devise means of arresting the exodus. It opened May 5, with an attendance of four hundred delegates. The resolutions adopted by the convention reveal the alarm created in the minds of the Southern planters. They declare that "errors have been committed by whites and blacks alike; that the interests of planters, laborers, landlords, and tenants are identical; that the colored race has been placed on a plane of absolute legal equality with the white race; that they shall be assured the practical enjoyment of all rights, civil and political, guaranteed by the Constitution and laws; and that the members of the convention pledge themselves to protect the colored race against all dangers in respect to the fair expression of their wills at the polls which they apprehend may result from fraud, intimidation, or bulldozing on the part of the whites." The colored men present spoke, but did not vote.

The National Conference of Colored Men, which has long been announced to be held at Nashville, was opened May 6 in the Hall of the House of Representatives. In Kansas a State Central Freedmen's Committee has been organized and incorporated by law. From all these facts the conclusion may be drawn that the strenuous efforts of the churches and religious societies to educate the freedman have already given him sufficient intelligence to protect himself. Philanthropy has here proved to be the highest statesmanship.

THE "NEGRO QUESTION" IN VIRGINIA

HARPER'S WEEKLY
May 31, 1879, p. 423

We considered last week the letter of a Louisiana planter upon the "negro question." We have also a line from "A Virginia Scalawag" upon the same subject from another point of view. He incloses some suggestive statements about the colored people as real-estate owners, from the *Public Ledger,* of Norfolk, which he describes as one of the fairest Democratic papers in Virginia:

> "In 1870 there were the names of twenty-six colored owners of real estate on the land book, the value of their property being placed at $21,150. In 1878 the number had increased to one hundred and forty-one, and the value to $114,530. Most of those who are assessed have only one house and lot, valued at from $500 to $800, but there are several who own two and even three houses. The largest owner of real estate is assessed for $5325, and is the happy possessor of eight pieces. The result of the investigation shows that the surplus earnings of many of the colored people are used to provide homes for their families, and that they are also placing their money in real estate for safe investment. The improvement of the negroes in the matter of education keeps pace with their desire to accumulate wealth, and there are now hundreds of colored families in Norfolk where the daily papers are regularly taken and eagerly read. It must be borne in mind that between the years mentioned the failure of the Freedmen's Bank occurred, and that a large number of those people lost their all by that catastrophe. There are, however, a number of colored persons who at present have various sums of money deposited in the city banks. In addition to other improvements of the colored people, we noted that they are more tolerant toward each other in political matters than formerly. At the meeting held a few nights since sentiments were uttered which a few years ago would have caused the speakers to be hooted at, and probably violently dealt with."

The "scalawag" adds:

> "In view of the fact that this statement has reference only to property within the corporation, and ignores the large quantity owned in like manner just outside the corporate limits, and the like large amount which they are accumulating on the installment plan, but which will not appear in their names on the records till fully pain for, it is not a bad showing for a population of, say, 9000, and that, too, where the industries in which they can engage are very limited. This statement is but a small concession of their great steps forward."

These are the facts which prove what we have often alleged, and what seems to us to be undeniable, that, upon the whole, and in consideration of all the circumstances, bulldozing, tissue ballots, etc., all conceded, the present situation in the late Slave States is very much better and more encouraging than could have been anticipated. It is simply amazing, therefore, when it is so plainly demonstrated by experience that the peace and prosperity of these States are assured the moment that they win the confidence of the new citizens, that such an order as the following should be issued, and, so far as appears, not revoked, in New Orleans. It has been served upon fifty colored clergymen.

> *To the Preacher of* ——— *Church, on* ——— *Street:*
>
> Your attention is called to the following order:
>
> "Office Chief of Police, April 22, 1879.
>
> > *"To all Stations:*
> > "Commanding officers are hereby instructed to notify the preachers of the various colored churches in your precinct that services whenever held must terminate at 10 o'clock P.M. Under no circumstances must they be allowed to hold services after that hour. Affidavits must be made against preachers violating this order for disturbing the peace. By order of the Mayor. T.N. Boylan, Chief of Police."

Our correspondent, the Louisiana planter, may see in this order, and not in the reconstruction laws, the real spirit from which the "misery" of the situation springs. It does not need "superstition and credulity" to read in such an order the spirit of a tyranny which naturally produces an "exodus" of its victims.

PERSONAL

HARPER'S WEEKLY
May 31, 1879, p. 423

—The New York *Tribune* says: "The negro exodus now in progress was not unforeseen by careful and intelligent observers of events in the Southern States. So long

ANOTHER STEP TOWARD CIVILIZATION.

Mr. Solid Brutus. "Why, Mr. Exode Cæsar, you are a Man and a Brother after all. So step into my parlor."

Harper's Weekly, May 31, 1879, p. 421.

ago as 1871 President Grant, in conversation with the Hon. Andrew D. White—who, it will be remembered, was a member of the commission appointed to visit San Domingo and inquire as to the desirability of the purchase and annexation of the island—expressed the opinion that the course pursued by the Southern whites toward the negroes would eventually drive the latter to emigration; and the principal argument in his mind in favor of annexation was the advantages San Domingo would offer in such a case for colonization. President Grant was very positive in his belief that the social and political condition of the South made such a result

RELIEVING ("BAYONET") GUARD.

U. S. A. "Keep the Peace at the Polls."
C. S. A. "We'll keep it!"

Harper's Weekly, May 31, 1879, p. 432.

inevitable, and also that nothing short of a general movement of the blacks such as he anticipated, and as has apparently recently begun, would bring the people of the South to their senses, and teach them the necessity of cultivating amicable relations with the class upon whose labor they are so dependent for their own prosperity and comfort."

RELIGIOUS INTELLIGENCE

HARPER'S WEEKLY
June 7, 1879, p. 447

The more accurate information upon the causes of the negro exodus which has now been obtained proves that it is not a sudden freak. To tell the truth, the negroes have been trying for several years to get away from the South. The scheme of migration to Africa was an effort to find a way of escape. Two ideas have taken deep root in their minds—one the desirableness of the possession of property, the other the value of the ballot. The several hundred who reached Kansas this spring have now obtained work as laborers. The colonies planted in that State several years ago are prosperous, and this fact will have influence on the minds of their brethren in the South. A Convention of colored men was held in Richmond, Virginia, on May 19, in which the following resolution was introduced: "That we recommend to our race throughout the State to organize themselves into emigration societies, for the purpose of leaving the State, provided our condition is not bettered by the authorities of the State." The discovery that the freedman can take his hat—or, rather, his fragment of a hat—and walk off, completely changes the situation for his oppressors.

THE FLIGHT TO KANSAS

HARPER'S WEEKLY
July 5, 1879, p. 522

There have been two interesting and important recent contributions to the story of "the negro exodus." One is the appeal of the cotton planters of Washington County, Mississippi, to "the business men and benevolent societies of the North," and the other is the letter of ex-Senator Alcorn, of Mississippi, to J. L. Berry, of Atchison, Kansas. The Washington County planters apprehend that the appearance of boats upon the river to convey laborers to some Northern point would be cruel to the negroes and ruinous to the planters. They assert that the colored laborer has no peculiar cause for dissatisfaction, and that it is often forgotten that his protection is secured by laws more powerful than any legislative enactment—the absolute dependence of the planter upon his labor, and its inadequate supply. But the planters upon their part forget that self-interest is by no means an adequate guarantee for justice. The drayman who is absolutely dependent upon his horse, when he gets angry will kick and beat him, and his interest will not restrain him.

Ex-Senator Alcorn's letter is very interesting and instructive, and may be regarded as one of the few intelligent and candid accounts of the situation. Farming in the Mississippi Delta is conducted upon the contract system, as it is in Florida and upon all the great estates in "the South." The crop is cultivated on shares, the planter supplying land, houses, mules, forage, tools, and a garden spot, the tenant clothing and feeding himself and supplying the labor. The corn or cotton crop is equally divided. But food and clothing are supplied to the tenant by the planter or his merchant, always with a lien upon the crop. Here is the point of friction, as we have known it to be in Florida. The tenant is illiterate and careless and dependent. The accounts are kept by the planter or his agent, and the laborer is forced to take his word for the amounts and cost that have been supplied to him. "The absolute dependence of the planter upon his [the tenant's] labor and its inadequate supply," of which the Mississippi address speaks, does not prevent the enormous swindling and injustice possible under such a system and such circumstances as those that actually exist. Granting that the cheating is by no means universal, yet such as there [is] naturally greatly magnified in the morbid imagination of an ignorant and suspicious class of persons, naturally making them restless and easily inclining to emigrate. The distrust and hostility produced by this situation would readily explain a migration. It might be, however, ameliorated by a general consciousness of good treatment and regard for fair play. But that is made impossible by the actual situation.

Senator Hampton says that the colored people are satisfied in South Carolina. But if that be so, ex-Senator Alcorn is quite as good a witness for Mississippi, and his testimony ought to be carefully pondered. He says that nowhere does unskilled labor command higher prices than in the Mississippi Delta, and he thinks that he could find employment in his own county for five hundred laborers at from twelve to twenty dollars per month. He is a planter, not an agitator, and all his interests are involved in retaining the colored labor. But this is what he says:

"Competition for labor guarantees to good negroes on plantations the best of treatment. When they go out to vote they meet with roughs, and generally come out second best. The ballot-box in this State has been, and is to-day, thoroughly prostituted. Ballot-box stuffing in this State, while equally effective, is more humane than the bulldozing shot-gun policy of the past. In this I take pleasure in recording an improvement.

"Outside the voting places, aside from politics, the negro is kindly treated. Before the courts, on the plantations, in the family, I doubt if in all the broad land the negro can find more tender and sympathizing whites.

"The cause of the present hegira may be traced to the politicians. The present unwise agitation in Congress has been seized upon to rob the South of its labor. The negro is a volatile, impulsive, emotional creature. I mean the plantation negro. His fears are easily excited. He is made to feel that he represents God's chosen people, the children of Israel; that the wicked Southerners—Egyptians—are contriving for his practical re-enslavement; that he must shake the dust of Egypt from his feet, and hasten to the land of Canaan.' Out of the South the poor negro seems determined to go. He will consume with a relish the good things supplied him by the liberal hand of the plentiful North; but when the 'manna' ceases to fall, when the buttered parsnips shall be no longer supplied, but bread must be supplied with labor, mark my prediction—the negro will yearn to return to his native South."

This, we have no doubt, is the key of the situation, and it suggests the only possible remedy. If Mr. Conway should send a steamer up the Hudson, and invite the laborers upon its banks to go with him to El Dorado or Arcadia, they would laugh him away, because they are satisfied that their rights are respected. Let the Mississippi planters and all other white men in "the South" make the colored laborers equally sure, and there will be no exodus. "The South" was torn to pieces by war because of its injustice. So long as injustice continues in the industrial treatment of the colored people, "the South" will be disturbed and restless. Justice and justice alone— such justice and fair play as prevail in the Northwest and New England—will give "the South" and the Union peace. Is it not a policy worth trying; and is it not worth while to show that it is tried? The testimony confirming that of ex-Senator Alcorn is universal, and if instead of denouncing "the army at the polls," Southern leaders should take care to secure perfectly fair elections, not by rifle clubs and red shirts and terror and bulldozing, but as fair elections are secured in every county in other States, those leaders would instantly "take the negro out of politics."

THE COLORED EXODUS

HARPER'S WEEKLY
July 5, 1879, pp. 533–534

Our readers will remember that in the *Weekly* of May 17 we published a striking illustration relating to the movement of the negroes of the Southern States toward Kansas, and showing their principal point of embarkation at Vicksburg. In most cases the objective point of the poor fugitives is Topeka, on the Kansas River, and on page 532 of this issue will be found a series of sketches showing the arrangements that have recently been made at that place for their reception. All the negroes who are not previously assigned to specified localities, when landed at the Kansas ports on the Missouri River are forwarded to Topeka, where the Central Committee has its headquarters. Certain buildings in the Fair Grounds have been secured for the negroes, and transformed into barracks, where lodging and food are provided until some disposition can be made of them. They come and go constantly, so that the committee rarely have more than two or three hundred, out of the thousands that pass through the city, to care for. The able-bodied are quickly disposed of, the main source of difficulty being the sick and helpless that persist in attaching themselves to the emigrant bands.

Past experience shows that the emigration of Southern negroes toward the West has not resulted unfavorably. Whatever cause for alarm there may be in the vast proportions assumed by the present exodus, there can be no doubt that small bands have profited by their removal from the scene of their late bondage. One or two instances will show that as Western pioneers and colonists the negroes have proved themselves possessed of energy, endurance, and ability to provide for their own maintenance. Thirty miles northwest of Kinsley, and twenty-five miles north of Dodge City, on the Atcheson, Topeka, and Santa Fe Railroad, is a flourishing negro settlement. The location is 280 miles from the east line of the State of Kansas, and 120 miles from the western border. It is far out upon the great plains, which until lately were supposed to be uninhabitable. This colony was formed near Lexington and Harrodsburg, Kentucky. Its location was selected in 1877, by a committee of their own number sent out for the purpose.

The colony arrived at Kinsley March 24, 1878, 107 in number, and immediately commenced their settlement. Additions have since been made to the number of about fifty. About fifty homesteads have been taken, besides a few timber claims, and all have been improved. But one has been abandoned—that in the case of a young man who left and came to Topeka. Their houses are chiefly of sod and dug-outs. There are one stone house and two frame houses. Some of the colonists have teams, and such ploughed and planted last spring, raising a little corn and considerable of garden vegetables—potatoes, beans, onions, melons, etc. Sorghum and millet were raised for feed for stock. A large proportion of these colonists, as they came with little or no means, have had to earn their own living at the same time that they were making their homestead improvements. Being clear out on the frontier, this has been difficult. They have had to go to the railroad towns, or near them—in some instances fifty miles or more away—for work. In the wheat harvest they found the best time for employment. But work has been scarce, as much time having been spent in searching for employment as was given to labor when obtained. Wages have ranged from seventy-five cents to $1 50 per day, the latter price being paid only in harvest. The people have, however, been healthy, two deaths only having occurred. They make no complaint of the climate, enduring all the hardships that fall to their share bravely.

In Graham County, Kansas, is located a negro colony called Nicodemus. It consists of about 125 families, comprising about 700 souls, scattered over an area twelve miles in length by six in breadth. Nicodemus has its post-office, store, hotel, land-office, etc., and, like nearly all new towns, aspires to the possession of the county seat. The colony had its first start in August of 1877, a few families locating at that time. In October and November of the same year large accessions were made by the arrival of new immigrants, who, with the usual want of forethought of the race, pushed out to the then extreme frontier at the commencement of winter, in almost utter lack of the means to shelter, feed, or clothe themselves during the winter. With the opening of the spring of 1878 more came. They were mainly from the farming regions of Kentucky and Tennessee. In the beginning the colonists, as a rule, were nearly destitute of means, a few only bringing either teams or money. They located on government homesteads, and set about to provide themselves with shelter, which was easily and cheaply secured by building dug-outs and sod houses, roofed with poles and brush, with a covering of earth sufficient to keep out the rain. As board floors were regarded as an unnecessary luxury, all the lumber required was for a door and its frame and one window. A fire-place at one end in most cases takes the place of a stove, and serves the double purpose of heating and cooking. Coming as most of them did in the autumn, but one resource was open to them in order to support life during the winter, and that was an appeal to the charity of the people of the State. This was resorted to, and agents of the colony, duly authenticated, canvassed the older-settled portions of the State for aid, which was freely given in provisions, seed grain, clothing, etc., the Kansas Pacific Railroad generously transporting all such contributions without charge. Many of the men and women sought and obtained work in the towns along the line of the railroad and in the settled counties east, and by their labor aided to carry the colony through the winter. With the spring of 1878 every effort was made to put all the ground possible under cultivation; but the great practical difficulty was that they had but few teams, and these not in good serviceable condition, for want of proper feed during the winter. But every body went to work. Those who had teams broke for themselves and others. Some were able to get a little breaking done for them by outside parties. Those who could do no better went to work digging up the ground with the space and grub-hoe, determined to make a crop in some way; and some families (the women helping) got two or three acres in crop by this slow and laborious process. At the present time the land under cultivation will average about six or seven acres to every family. The solicitation for aid has continued all along to some extent, but recently a public meeting was called, and after full consideration of the subject it was decided to discontinue the colony organization. A series of resolutions was passed thanking the people of the State for the aid that had been so freely given, and stating that henceforth no further aid would be solicited, as it was believed that from that time the colony, with proper effort and industry, could be self-supporting.

One of the most important features of the movement of the negroes toward Kansas, and the proofs given that they have found a suitable asylum for their wretchedness in that hospitable State, is the effect had upon the agricultural interests of the South. A thorough feeling of alarm has taken possession of the white population. In many cases, it is said, the planters have declined to make arrangements for raising crops during the ensuing season on account of the uncertainties that attend the situation, and the doubts whether there will be laborers enough to take care of the harvest. In certain sections public sentiment is actually aroused against the modern amusement of "bulldozing," and mass-meetings have been held denouncing it as an unworthy practice. At Caseyville, Mississippi, a gathering of the citizens to consider the difficulties of the present situation resulted in the following resolutions, which forcibly suggest the sudden reformation of a culprit who finds that his next meal depends upon his good behavior:

> "*Whereas*, That for two years or more certain citizens of this and adjoining counties have been committing acts of lawlessness disgraceful to the civilization of this age; and *whereas,* this community, hitherto peaceful, has been thrown into the utmost consternation by an act of certain lawless characters acting in the night-time, and unknown to the good citizens of this community, to wit, the burning of Mr. Thomas Erwin's gin, to his great damage; and *whereas,* within a short time after the committal of said act, this community was shocked by a grosser act of violence (seeming in retaliation of said act), to wit, the whipping and otherwise ill treating certain colored citizens, and the assassination of another at the dead hour of night—the assassin's chosen hour; and *whereas,* divers burning, whipping, and ordering of colored citizens in various parts of this county to leave their homes and

crops have occurred, to the great injury of the country at large; and *whereas,* it is the sense of this meeting that those lawless characters are citizens of adjoining counties who invade this county at night, and commit these lawless acts, and return to their homes before daylight, leaving the stigma of their acts to rest on the good citizens of this county; and *whereas,* we admit those citizens (styled bulldozers) may have had some cause for acts hitherto committed, by being deprived of their homes by a system of extortion under the lien laws of this State, which are erroneous and bad as class legislation, favoring one class of citizens and utterly ruining another greatly in the majority, yet this is no justification for acts of punishing and assassinating unoffending colored citizens; and *whereas,* we have waited patiently for the courts to bring to condign punishment those lawless characters, and having been sadly deceived by seeing them, instead of being visited by swift justice, turned loose on straw bonds or no bonds at all, at great expense to the county, already nearly bankrupt; therefore, be it

"*Resolved,* 1. That it is the sense of this meeting that such acts must be stopped.

"2. That we look with indignation on all lawless acts by any and all citizens who have not the fear of the law before their eyes.

"3. That it is the sense of this meeting that all such lawless persons be requested to desist from such lawless acts in the future.

"4. That it is the sense of this meeting that we look with contempt on the party or parties who wrote the notice posted at this place, near Caseyville, warning the good citizens of this community from doing their duty."

Action of this kind on the part of the citizens of Caseyville or other communities unfortunately comes too late to stop the progress of the negroes toward their land of promise. Threats and arguments are without efficacy, and the exodus goes steadily on. Even the Southern newspapers, which have been doing their best to induce people to believe that the tide of emigration is stayed, have finally concluded to abandon their policy of profitless mendacity. The New Orleans *Times* says:

"Our newspapers all through the lower valley, our Washington, St. Louis, and Kansas correspondents, for a month past have been repeating that the exodus has ceased; that the negroes are miserable in Kansas, and are coming home; that every body now admits the movement was induced by land speculators, and such twaddle and nonsense. The truth is that the threatened departure of the great body of the colored laborers from several portions of the State is still impending. The truth is that there were more who left this city last week than have returned to the entire South from Kansas. Why in the world can we not be honest and truthful to ourselves about this matter? Why not recognize the evil, acknowledge its causes, appreciate its seriousness, understand the necessity of averting and checking the movement which threatens to impoverish the fairest portions of the State?"

At the same time, while the Southern planters are uttering their wail, and the Southern newspapers alternately denying and acknowledging the fact that their industrial population is rapidly passing away from them, Kansas is holding out her hospitable arms, and making the best arrangements she can for the reception of the poor fugitives who launch themselves upon her in such overwhelming numbers. A certain amount of alarm is naturally felt at the approach of such a vast horde of suffering and impoverished human beings; but as yet the opposition to their coming has taken no decided shape, and Senator Ingalls undoubtedly expressed the sentiments of the people of his State when he said: "I do not think there is any class prejudice or any feeling of hostility to the colored people that would prevent their being cordially welcomed as an element of our population. We have an area of about 81,000 square miles, comprising 55,000,000 of acres of arable land, not more than one-tenth of which has been reduced to cultivation. The remainder is open to settlement under the Homestead Act, requiring five years' residence before title can be secured, and I am inclined to think we could absorb 100,000 of these people without serious injury or inconvenience."

A SURVEY OF THE FIELD

HARPER'S WEEKLY
July 19, 1879, p. 562

. . . The Republican party is accused of fostering sectionalism and of arousing perpetually the slumbering animosities of the war. But who have done most to revive sectional feeling, those who proposed to retain the laws securing fair elections, or those who struck at the army, and tried to make bulldozing and electoral cheating easy? Those who urged the repeal compelled a statement of the reasons of the laws and the consequences of their repeal. This necessarily involved allusions to the situation in the Southern States and to the notorious suppression of the colored vote. In the heat of debate, of party spirit, and of the weather, this took excited rhetorical form. We repeat the question. If this was waving the bloody shirt, who waved it? Who was responsible for it?

That wrong was done by the laws was not asserted. Nobody was so silly as to say that it was the army that interfered with freedom of elections in the Southern States. It is not the honorable officers of the little army, it is the midnight riders, the Rifle Clubs, the Red-Shirts, that are notoriously guilty of coercing voters, and when the political allies of the Red-Shirts and the Ku-Klux began to agitate the repeal of salutary laws, which no court has condemned as unconstitutional, and which Democratic reports have commended as most serviceable, they deliberately unfolded the bloody shirt of sectionalism, and shook it madly in the wind. It was in the power of leading Democrats from the Southern States to frustrate this policy of the party that they rule, and they have not done it. Every Northern State Convention of Republicans begins by affirming, what the war seemed to settle, that States are not sovereign, and that the Union is in practical fact a nation. This will be, and by the acquiescence of Southern Democrats, apparently, the question of the election of 1880. The discussion will necessarily involve that appeal to sectional feeling and reminiscence which patriotic men wished to avoid. The fact that men like the more prominent Southern leaders have yielded to what they must feel to be a fatal folly shows their consciousness of the real forces that control their party. But neither they nor their Northern followers must hope to raise successfully the cry of sectionalism against the Republicans. It is they who have appealed to that jealousy, and who have consequently fired the dormant feelings of the war, so that as the extra session ends and Congress disperses, it is impossible to point to one great reason, either in wisdom of policy or in details of method, for preferring Democratic to Republican ascendancy. If a man desires tranquillity with justice in the different States, or commercial confidence so far as it is affected by politics, or that reasonable steadiness of administration and legislation which is most conservative of the general welfare, or intelligent and sincere movements of reform, or, indeed, any great object which patriotic Americans ought to desire, can he honestly say—whatever his disgust with individual Republicans—that there is a fairer promise of any one of them under Democratic supremacy?

THE BLOODY SHIRT

HARPER'S WEEKLY
August 16, 1879, p. 642

The Republican speeches and platforms of the summer are notable for their strong statement of the sectional question. That this question should be prominent is greatly to be regretted. But however the fact may be deplored, no fair man will say that the responsibility rests with the Republican party. The Administration certainly has not fostered the agitation, and if the Democrats had not made it of such vital importance, the Republican friends of the Administration would have prevented its playing the part in 1880 which it did in 1876. The sectional question ought to be disappearing, and its present prominence is due to two things, for which Democrats exclusively are responsible—the suppression of the colored vote, and the tone in which those who suppress it demand State rights. The suppression of the colored vote in the Southern States, of which the evidence is incontestable, is equivalent to a forcible seizure of power which may easily control the government. That is a wrong which the intelligent "North" will not tolerate. All classes of voters are here protected in their electoral rights, and the strongest Democratic authority agrees that the national supervision in New York has secured the most peaceful and honest elections. The sectional question is kept alive by the Democratic treatment of equal citizens in the Southern States, not by the Republican protest against it; and to reproach the Republicans because of that protest with shaking the bloody shirt is to reproach them for maintaining the fundamental principle of the government—free and fair elections. Nor is it surprising that the cry of State rights in the mouths of those who are responsible for this suppression should arouse apprehension. In the States where the colored vote is suppressed there seems to be no local redress. One of the most trenchant public papers that we have recently seen is the address to the colored people of Texas, adopted by the Colored Conference at Houston on the 2d of July of this year. It is a very strong but perfectly temperate statement of the situation of the colored population. The crimes of every kind against them "have never been indicted or punished in any manner by the judiciary of the South, yet we have never attempted to take the laws into our own hands in order to vindicate or right our wrongs." And believing that neither time nor any sacrifice upon the part of the colored people will remove the ill-will with which they are regarded—in proof of which the address submits forcible considerations—the Conference proposes emigration as the only resort. When those who are responsible for this wrong raise the cry of State rights, their demand means only greater impunity in criminally seizing political power. As we write we receive a letter from "a Southern Union man," who would give his name except that he "does not mix with politics." The writer says that there can never be peace and prosperity at the South until there is a different voting population. He adds that he himself, who "stuck to the party until Grant got so many thieves around him, has put in money knowing it was to go for paying to stuff the ballot-boxes, and did right; it was the easiest and best way to protect my property, and you would have done the same thing under the same circumstances." Here is one citizen confessing to another that he and his friends send Representatives to Congress by fraud, and asking the other to hold his tongue about it. What the "thieves" around Grant stole he does not say, but he owns that he and his friends steal seats in Congress and the control of the government. Now if exposing and opposing this flagrant, forcible, and confessed attempt at usurpation is shaking the bloody shirt, the bloody shirt has become again the banner of American liberty, and he who does not wave it is a contemptible coward. The position of such men as our correspondent in the Southern States is undeniably hard. We have admitted it always. The whole situation there is extremely difficult. Calhoun, whose instincts upon the subject of slavery were remarkable, uniformly said that slavery could be abolished only by war, and that the same force which freed the slaves would enfranchise them, but that there could be no social or political fusion of the races. However, that may be, the course pursued by the whites in those States is naked revolution. It is the complete overthrow of all legal rights, and an overthrow in which the rights of those who do not live in those States are also involved. When our correspondent pays money to stuff a ballot-box to protect his property, he commits our property to the care of a man who has no more right to such care than the next tramp. Do he and his friends really suppose that we shall submit?

The difficulties of the Southern States are great. But the intelligent whites of those States must see that they can not settle them without a good understanding with the controlling sentiment of the North, which, politically, is Republican. That good understanding, therefore, should be the first aim of Southern politics, for no difficulty of situation would justify the rest of the country in conniving at a general disregard of vital constitutional principles and guarantees, which is the present policy of the Southern whites under Democratic auspices. Our correspondent proposes there shall be a different voting population, and insists that if this is "a nation with a big N," it shall pass a national election law prohibiting voting except to those who can read and write. Here there would be a question, but he can have another voting population without such a law, and without any question whatever. Any State may require an educational qualification for voters. Why, then, do not he and his friends urge such a qualification in his State? It would reduce its Congressional representation. Undoubtedly it would; but is not such reduction better than anarchy? The whites control many of the Southern States. They complain of the ignorant black vote. But the legal remedy is in their own hands. Why do they not use it? For two reasons: they know that it would greatly reduce the white vote as well as the colored, and they prefer to suppress the colored vote, and still count it with the white in the basis of representation, and to accuse citizens elsewhere who expose and denounce the iniquity as cherishing sectional hate. Really our Southern brethren have learned our courage, and they ought now to credit us with some commonsense. There is not the slightest vindictive feeling in this part of the country toward Southerners, whatever the fervor of platform rhetoric may be. But the only way to a good understanding and to the disappearance of the bloody shirt is plain proof that Southerners seek to remedy their undoubted difficulties by just, legal, and constitutional means. At present the Democratic plan is to obtain complete control of the national government by fraudulent and forcible suppression of the colored vote wherever necessary. This is the overthrow of popular government and sheer usurpation, and it is this that the Republican party unitedly opposes.

A NATIONAL QUESTION

HARPER'S WEEKLY
August 23, 1879, p. 662

We have been reminded that the principle of State rights has been invoked for the protection of liberty more than once, and that our statement of the contrary was too sweeping, as it certainly was. The fact, however, remains that the distinctive State-rights party was the party of slavery and disunion, and that the cry is now raised again by those who count upon fraud and violence to carry elections, and upon so great a scale that it is a matter of national importance. The Springfield *Republican* thinks that to call attention to an immense electoral wrong, which involves possible civil convulsions, is to show an anxious desire to help the stalwart plan of a sectional campaign. If the statement of such a wrong be untrue, the *Republican* very properly deprecates its repetition. But if it be true, it ought to be emphasized, whether it helps the stalwart plan or any other. A sectional campaign resulting from suppression of the colored vote would be one for which "the North" would be in no sense responsible. Such a campaign arising from such a cause would be deplorable. But it would be much more deplorable if sensible men, seeing such a situation, should play that it did not exist, because to recognize it, and to deal with it by an appeal to the country, might be called a stalwart programme. That such is the situation is incontestable, and it is not to be dismissed with the remark that there are always irregularities at the polls. We quoted last week from a letter addressed to us by a Southern Union man, in which he says that he gives money to stuff the ballot-boxes, and that he does it in self-defense. Sir George Campbell, in his *White and Black in the United States,* says that he was in the South during the elections of 1878. He describes the cheating in detail as practiced in South Carolina. There was no concealment, and no pretense that anything but fraud was intended; and he states that there was matter enough within his own knowledge to have vitiated such elections in England a hundred times over. The result was, he adds, that "South Carolina returns a solid Democratic representation to the next Congress." The question raised by such elections Sir George frankly admits to be whether the amendment of the United States Constitution securing equal electoral rights to the blacks is really to be enforced, or whether it may be set aside in practice by the action of individual States—"Is, in fact, the settlement at the end of the war to be maintained or surrendered?"

Sir George is not a stalwart shaker of bloody shirts, but an exceedingly sensible and shrewd observer, who sees the situation without party spirit or sectional prejudice, and his testimony is of the highest value. It is precisely the situation that he describes which keeps alive the sectional aspect of politics, and which renews the discussion of State rights. The Louisville *Courier-Journal,* with the amusing truculence of the old fire-eating epoch, remarks in effect that the condition-of-the-negro question is not a national question. But even that journal will not deny that a party majority in Congress or a party President secured by an elaborate, open, and general system of fraud is a matter in which even voting mud-sills may rightfully interest themselves. The puerility of the effort to set off against the suppression of the colored vote the influence of large proprietors in Northern and Western States over their laborers is merely contemptible. Instances of sporadic cheating and unfair influence at the polls are always possible. But does any well-informed man allege that in any other than certain Southern States there is deliberate coercion of the vote of an immense voting class? In the election of 1844 that eminent Louisiana politician John Slidell, by his Plaquemine frauds, secured a Democratic majority of 970 in a parish in which the whole Democratic vote of the previous year was 306; and this fraud gave the electoral vote of the State to the Democrats, whose whole majority was only 690. Would anybody pretend to put against such systematic and wholesale electoral swindling at one point, the cases of farmers and proprietors in other States who may have threatened to dismiss their hands if they did not vote as they were told?

It is both to facilitate and to conceal this enormous wrong that the cry of State rights and of soldiers at the polls has been raised. What invasion of State rights is alleged? The supervision of national elections in the States by national agents. If that be a danger to just local right, it is in pursuance of a law whose constitutionality has not been questioned by the courts. The cry of military interference is raised to confuse the real question, which is usurpation by forcible and fraudulent suppression of the colored vote. It is a dismal prolongation of the politics of the war, which is to be regretted on every account, but which can not be avoided by shutting our eyes. The instant that any Southern white party insists that the legal colored vote shall be protected, or that it shall be reduced by any equable qualification, the national question arising from it will vanish. But so long as the Southern whites forcibly and fraudulently suppress the colored vote, lest by an honorable and legal reduction they should lose in the basis of representation, it will be necessarily a national question.

YAZOO POLITICS

HARPER'S WEEKLY
September 13, 1879, p. 722

The Yazoo trouble is not a riot merely, or a breach of the peace; it is a system of suppressing political opposition by murder and terror, and when it has been carried a little further, it will be time to inquire whether Mississippi has a Republican form of government. Meanwhile, even if Mississippi chooses to tolerate the assassination and outrage of her citizens for political reasons, the United States will hardly consent to see a President elected by such means. In 1871 the vote of Yazoo County was 2966 Republican and 997 Democratic. In 1875 its vote was 7 Republican and 4044 Democratic, and it has so remained. In 1876 there were 3 Republican votes, and 2 in 1877. Two or three months ago Captain H.M. Dixon—a Democrat, ex-Confederate, a prominent citizen, and planter—announced himself as an independent candidate for Sheriff. Other candidates were placed upon his ticket, and as the registry was made, it was clear that they would be elected. An order was issued from the Democratic headquarters in Yazoo City, and an armed and drunken mob compelled Dixon to withdraw. Some time afterward, upon going into Yazoo City, he was met by James Barksdale, the Democratic candidate for Chancery Clerk, who hailed him, and stepped into the street armed with a double-barrelled shot-gun. Dixon drew a pistol, but Barksdale fired and killed him, and has been bailed for $15,000.

In the same way in 1880, in such districts as Yazoo, of which there are many in the Southern States, Republican candidates and voters will be menaced, driven from the polls, and outraged, and there will be plenty of Democrats to write pamphlets proving that the vote as cast must be regarded as conclusive. Have the United States really no remedy? Is the will of the honest majority of intelligent citizens in the country to be set aside by such methods without recourse? Does a just interpretation of the Constitution and a fair regard for State rights require that the country shall acquiesce in an election decided by terror and crime? These are questions not to be summarily disposed of; and it was to provide some kind of defense against such results that the national election laws were passed which those who are to profit

HARPER'S WEEKLY.
JOURNAL OF CIVILIZATION.

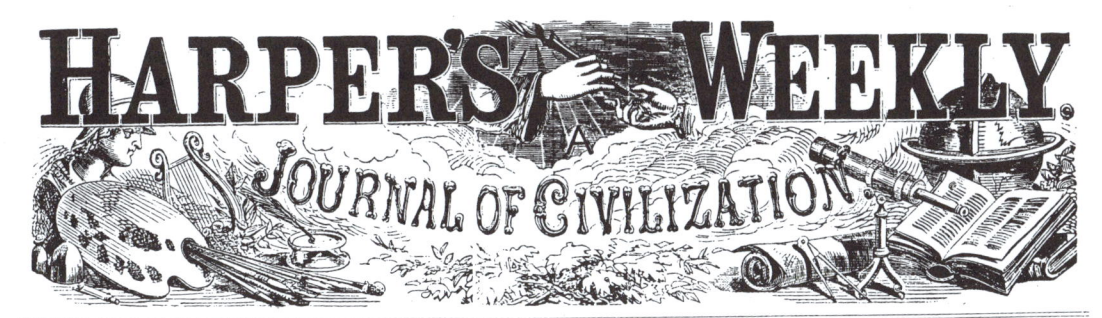

Vol. XXIII.—No. 1183.] NEW YORK, SATURDAY, AUGUST 30, 1879. { WITH A SUPPLEMENT. PRICE TEN CENTS.

Entered according to Act of Congress, in the Year 1879, by Harper & Brothers, in the Office of the Librarian of Congress, at Washington.

"TIME WORKS WONDERS."
WHEN SOLID SOUTHERN BULLDOZERS FALL OUT, THEN THE NEGRO GETS HIS DUE.

by the Yazoo system have made such desperate efforts to repeal, sustained by the Democratic majority in Congress, and baffled only by the President's veto. The United States say by these laws that they do not propose, without an effort at resistance, to allow men who suppress political opposition by the shot-gun and bowie-knife to take possession of the national government by the same weapons. The voters of the State of Mississippi are made voters for members of Congress not by the laws of Mississippi, but by the national Constitution. Except for that authorization, they could not vote for such officers, and the same authority is supreme as to the time, place, and manner of holding such elections, with the sole exception of the places at which Senators are chosen. The electoral power which the United States thus confer, the United States may rightfully protect. If the State, under the Constitution, chooses to reduce by stringent qualifications the total number of voters for the most numerous branch of its Legislature, the United States have consented that it shall thereby reduce the number of voters for members of Congress. But they have also provided that such reduction shall diminish the basis of the Congressional representation of the State. The Democratic position is that the State alone makes voters. That is true only so far as the State is concerned. No State can make a voter for members of Congress, and if any State should try to paralyze the national power by an absolute disqualification of voters, the United States would at once establish for it a republican form of government. Except in the way we have mentioned by which the number of voters may be reduced, elections for members of Congress are wholly national elections, and the power which confers the authority can protect its exercise. It must be remembered that a voter in New York votes for a member of Congress not by authority of the State, but of the United States, and this is true whether the number of voters be larger or smaller.

The opposition to this exercise of the national authority springs from the desire to extend the Yazoo system, and by means of it to secure control of the national government. This is a plan which must be opposed at once and resolutely by a cordial support of the Republican party. There may be Republicans who hold extreme and dangerous views of the national power. It is evident also that the national care of national elections may be abused. But nothing can be plainer than the constitutional duty of such care and its expediency under existing circumstances. In view of the danger of the exclusion of that care under the plea of State rights and the palpable consequences, Mr. Hill's professed fear of "centralization" is ridiculous; and if Mr. Lamar be correctly reported as saying that the Dixon murder is a personal affair, when he knows, in common with the whole country, the fact of Dixon's compulsory withdrawal from his candidacy, Mr. Lamar must be content to take a place among the timid demagogues of his party.

A NATIONAL SUFFRAGE LAW

HARPER'S WEEKLY
September 13, 1879, p. 722

The Southern correspondent who recently informed us that he had helped stuff ballot-boxes to defeat the colored voters, although he had been a Republican, and that all intelligent Northern men would do the same thing if they were exposed to the danger of colored rule, insists that the only remedy for the Southern trouble is "a national suffrage law." Relief by an educational qualification self-imposed by the States, he says, is not to be expected, because, as we have suggested, it would reduce the basis of representation. Military enforcement of national election laws, he asserts, will be unavailing, because, of his own knowledge, one white regiment sent into a certain Southern town "to a man" took the side of the white as against the colored citizens. Republicanism, he informs us, is considered in the Southern States to be a system of "negro control." The real situation, he thinks, is not political; it is social, and one of race. He reminds us that Mr. Botts said, when the reconstruction legislation was adopted, that in ten years the Democrats would control every Southern State. The only way, in our correspondent's judgment, to build up nationality is by a national suffrage law. "The present condition will go from bad to worse, and if it should continue, trouble has but begun." It is known where the colored majorities are throughout the South, and there "the elections are carried by fixing the ballot-boxes, and you can't stop it except by a national law."

We suppose the writer to mean by this a national law prescribing the qualifications of voters for members of Congress. But he forgets that the Constitution already determines these qualifications. "The electors [of members of Congress] shall have the qualifications requisite for electors of the most numerous branch of the State Legislature." This provision is not essentially affected by the Fourteenth or Fifteenth Amendments, which ordain only that no citizen shall be disfranchised by reason of race, or color, or previous condition of servitude, and that if any other disqualification be imposed, the State shall suffer in the basis of representation. This clause, indeed, does not make the State the creator of the national voter; it is the manner in which the United States appoints its own voters. But it is a constitutional appointment, and it can be changed only by a change of the Constitution. No law requiring other qualifications than those which the State exacts of its own voters would be of any avail. We assume, of course, that our correspondent does not suppose that Congress could impose qualifications upon the State suffrage; and if not, it could not touch the constitutional qualifications for national suffrage.

Meanwhile the course pursued and justified by our correspondent of stuffing the ballot-box will not

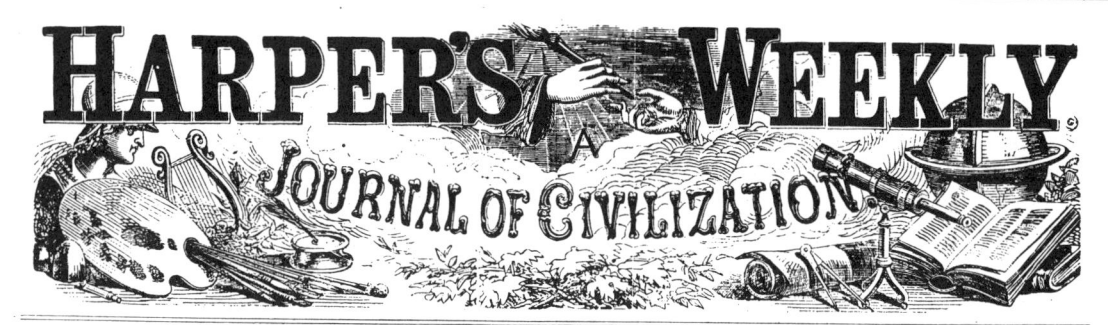

Harper's Weekly, September 13, 1879, p. 721.

mend the matter. It will merely consolidate the North against the South as an anarchical and barbarous community, and delay indefinitely the recuperation of the Southern States. There is no short road out of the difficulty. The work must be done mainly within the States. The first and paramount necessity of the Southern States is a spirit of obedience to law, and a public opinion which will enforce it. If a political crime is committed at the South, or a crime against colored citizens as a class, there seems to be no effective body of public men, or newspapers, or private citizens, which has the wish or the pluck to denounce and punish it. There are single papers, like the Vicksburg Herald, which speak out with manly indignation, but there is apparently no responsive public opinion. Both Northern and Southern Democrats fail to apprehend the great change of situation which has been produced within two years. While the "carpet-baggers" and "Federal bayonets" were in the Southern States, and the governments were Republican, it was easy to say, as it was said, that the anarchy and the "prostration" were due to the suppression of the whites, who were the real intelligence of the section. But now for two years, and in some quarters for a much longer time, the whites have been in supreme and unquestioned ascendency, and the chief results thus far are the ballot-stuffing in South Carolina and the Yazoo system. The consequence is that Northern opinion is naturally and strongly settling into the conviction that the Southern situation was not due to scalawags and carpet-baggers, but to a widely spread semi-barbarism, largely the result of slavery, and that no catastrophe would be so great as any further dominance of this spirit in the national administration. If men like our correspondent do not see that open cheating at the polls fosters that lawlessness which is now the chief danger of the South, and that the first duty of good citizens in the Southern States, instead of dreaming of national suffrage laws, is to foster a State opinion which will summarily and legally punish murderers and Ku-Klux and bulldozers and ballot-box stuffers as public enemies, they will have to be taught the lesson at greater cost. They wish to control the administration, but the liberty-loving and law-abiding people of this country have paid a tremendous price for the salvation of their government, and they do not mean to surrender it to the assassins, bulldozers, and ballot-box stuffers who evidently control certain districts in the South unchecked by good citizens.

THE VIEW OF A SOUTHERN REPUBLICAN

HARPER'S WEEKLY
October 11, 1879, p. 803

Since the Southern question has been reopened by the Democrats, there is one aspect of it which deserves attention. It is presented to us very earnestly by a Southern Republican, who, writing from Ohio, declares that no man living is more anxious for Republican success in the North than he, and that he is delighted to say that he believes Ohio will go for Foster by thirty to fifty thousand majority. But he says, frankly, that "this will not relieve us of the 'solid South,'" because, in his opinion, the root of the trouble is "unlimited uneducated negro suffrage." The explanation of the general apathy and indifference toward political crimes against Republicans in many parts of "the South" he holds to be impatience of negro ascendency, that is, of ignorance and semi-barbarism. He does not hesitate to say that he and other white Republicans in the South willingly stuff ballot-boxes to avoid that ascendency, and he advocates a national suffrage law as the only practicable remedy. His words are emphatic, and they are worth considering: "You can not make a Republican party in the South as the question stands now, simply because it means negro control and carpet-bag thieves. The North is opposed to this, and every soldier in the service is opposed to it."

But we have already shown that the Constitution authorizes every voter in a State who is qualified by the State law to vote for members of the most numerous branch of the State Legislature to vote also for members of Congress. This is a constitutional provision which no national or State law can change. Voters for members of Congress are created by national authority in the Constitution. They derive all their right for such voting from the Constitution, and not from the State, and there is no power in a State to authorize any citizen to vote for members of Congress, except by making him a voter for members of one branch of the State Legislature. By prescribing the qualification for this last function the State affects the number of national voters. The nation adopts as its voters, and for its own purposes, a certain class of citizens which the State has qualified for another purpose. Obviously, therefore, under the Constitution, the State may restrict national suffrage by limiting State suffrage. This is implied in the second section of the Fourteenth Amendment, which provides that if such restriction shall be made, the State shall suffer in the basis of representation. The limitation which our correspondent desires can proceed, then, only from the State, or from a new constitutional amendment; for it will not be denied that the State may define the qualification of voters for the most numerous branch of its Legislature, and the people of the United States have already declared in the Constitution that these, whether they be few or many, whether they are required to own land, or to pay a poll-tax, or to be able to read and write, or to satisfy certain conditions of residence, shall be also voters for Representatives in Congress. Judge West, to whom our correspondent refers, says nothing inconsistent with this. He is very far from saying that Congress could authorize any resident of New York who is not qualified to vote for a member of Assembly in that State to vote for a member of Congress, or that it could prevent any person who is so qualified from voting at a national election.

If the Southern Democrats who, with the aid of our Republican correspondent and those who agree with him, control their States, were really so opposed to colored suffrage as they declare themselves to be, they would unite to restrict it by a land qualification, as in Rhode Island, or by an educational qualification, as in Connecticut, or by some other limitation. We know, of course, why they do not. What the Democrats who control the elections want is not relief from colored suffrage, but control of the national government, so they restrict the colored vote in districts where it is controlling, as in the Yazoo district, not by law, which would reduce their representation in Congress, but by fraud and violence. If we correctly understand our correspondent's proposition, we reply that a national suffrage law is not a practicable remedy for what he feels to be the intolerable wrong of the situation. Relief must be sought in State action. But while the laws providing for general suffrage remain as they are, he can not expect that the people of other States will quietly see their votes nullified by fraud and terror. He asks how we propose to stop it. In the first place, by that appeal to public opinion which is the beginning of all redress for wrongs in this country; and in the second place, in consequence of that appeal, by the constant defeat of the party which aims to secure the benefit of the suppression of the colored vote. The rest must be left to time and local action. The first thing for our correspondent to do is to clear his mind of the idea that, whenever a grave difficulty of this kind arises, he and his friends must at once invoke the aid of the national government.

SHOT-GUN CIVILIZATION

HARPER'S WEEKLY
October 11, 1879, p. 803

A correspondent in Georgia, who supposes that, as a Georgian, he is in our opinion but a semi-civilized barbarian, writes to us commenting upon certain events in this part of the country. Our correspondent states that he once heard a father say that "he had witnessed personal violence offered to his daughter at the hands of her husband, and I was shocked to learn that he had not slain the brute on the spot." He adds that he thinks our Northern civilization false and monstrous if we do not share his views. Now it is not as a Georgian that we should consider our correspondent to be imperfectly civilized, but as a man, whether of Georgia or of Massachusetts, who prefers the ways of barbarism to those of civilization.

When a Feejee islander or a Sioux Indian thinks that he has been wronged, he takes his club, or gun, or tomahawk, and proceeds to slay the offender upon the spot. Every such man makes himself the judge of the offense and of the penalty, and enforces his own decision. This is barbarism. It is the practice of all uncivilized people, whether in New York, or Georgia, or the isles of the sea. In the lower stages of civilization there is a modification of this practice, called the duel. It prevails among people who, without the virtues which are known as Christian, call themselves "men of honor." They do not shoot without warning those who offend them, but they invite the offender to seize his gun or toma[h]awk, and take the chance of killing or being killed. This practice has also disappeared before the advance of civilization.

There are fellow-citizens of our correspondent in certain districts of the country who think that the voting of colored citizens is an offense to those who are not colored, and the uncolored peremptorily punish such offenders with the shot-gun. This also seems to us a low form of civilization. That those persons in this part of the country who think that they are offended by other persons do not slay the brutes at once, far from seeming to us proof of pusillanimity, seems to us to show that kind of self-restraint and intelligent comprehension of law which alone make high civilization possible.

THE AVERY INSTITUTE

HARPER'S WEEKLY
November 1, 1879, p. 867

The Avery Institute is a colored Normal School of a high grade, located in Charleston, South Carolina. It received its name from the noted Pittsburgh philanthropist Charles Avery—a man whose name deserves the grateful love of the whole race for whom he did so much. Charles Avery was born in Westchester County, New York, in 1784. For many years he was a cotton manufacturer, which business was the basis of his great wealth, although he subsequently increased it very much by investments in the copper regions of Lake Superior. Indeed, he was among the first to perceive the wonderful richness of that district, and in company with Messrs. Howe, Hussey, and others sunk the first shaft for copper in all that region.

His wealth rapidly increased, and the most of it was dedicated to the elevation and education of the negro race, although he was a large and constant giver to the poor of all sections and all races. He erected in Alleghany City, on his own grounds, and exclusively at his own expense, the commodious college for negroes which now bears his name, the design of which was to furnish a complete college course to the colored students. He left a fortune of nearly eight hundred thou-

AFRICAN AMERICAN HISTORY IN THE PRESS, 1851-1899

HARPER'S WEEKLY.
JOURNAL OF CIVILIZATION.

Vol. XXIII.—No. 1190.] NEW YORK, SATURDAY, OCTOBER 18, 1879. [WITH A SUPPLEMENT. PRICE TEN CENTS.

Entered according to Act of Congress, in the Year 1879, by Harper & Brothers, in the Office of the Librarian of Congress, at Washington.

DEATH AT THE POLLS, AND FREE FROM "FEDERAL INTERFERENCE."

Harper's Weekly, October 18, 1879, p. 821.

Harper's Weekly, November 1, 1879, p. 861.

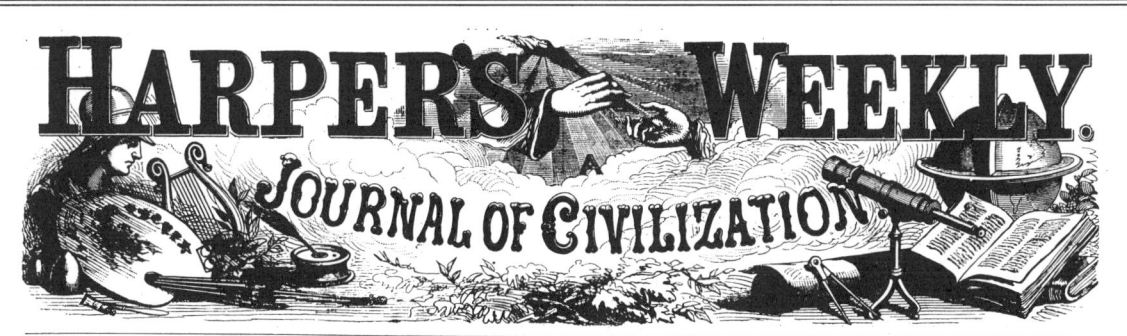

THE AVERY INSTITUTE, CHARLESTON, SOUTH CAROLINA.—[See Page 867.]

Harper's Weekly, November 1, 1879, p. 864.

sand dollars, almost all of which was given to benevolent objects; and he certainly disbursed an equal sum in public and private charity while living.

The institute in Charleston to which he gives the name was first opened in October, A.D. 1865, General Rufus Saxton assigning for its use the State Normal Building of Charleston. It commenced with one thousand pupils and a corps of twenty teachers, four-fifths of the pupils being freedmen who had never been to any school, and who were quite ignorant. The end of the first scholastic year showed a progress which was highly encouraging to the friends of the freedmen. But in spite of the support of some of the most intelligent citizens, the opposition to it was so powerful that the building was taken away from the projectors, and the children turned adrift.

They were soon regathered in the Military Hall, and the spacious building that had hitherto only heard the clash of weapons, and the drill of soldiers intended to perpetuate slavery, now heard daily the patient efforts of freedmen, women, and children striving to acquire the knowledge which would make them worthy of the great boon the Union had bestowed upon them.

In Wentworth Hall the school remained two years, steadily raising its standard of excellence and widening its curriculum, and on May 1, 1868, it was transferred to a large and handsome building on Bull Street, and its name changed from the "Saxton School" to the "Avery Institute." On page 864 will be found a picture of the building.

At first there was a corps of twenty teachers—ten Northern whites and ten Southern blacks; but the second year these were reduced to eight white and eight black; and the third year, the school having quite assumed the condition of a Normal School—which was the object and hope of its organization—the principal had but eight assistants. These, however, were all Northern teachers of very superior attainments and large experience. Its first principal was the Rev. F. L. Cardoza, but in 1868 Mr. Cardoza was elected Secretary of State, and resigned the charge of Avery Institute. He was succeeded by Mr. Warren, of Connecticut, who in 1874 was elected principal of the State Normal School of South Carolina, and retired from Avery. Since then its principals have been selected by the American Missionary Association of New York city; for it is to be noticed that the institute is supported mainly by this association. They pay three-fourths of its expenses, the deficiency being met by the charge of one dollar per month from those pupils who are able to pay it; and there is no expense the Charleston negro meets with greater pride and pleasure than his school fee.

The school contains a Primary Department of two divisions, a Grammar Department of three divisions, and a Normal Department, consisting of Junior, Middle, and Senior classes, the latter including a classical course. Those who desire it, or who show special talents, have also competent instruction in modern languages, music, and drawing.

The graduating class of 1879 consisted of nine young women and five young men, all of whom, excepting two, are among the group resting after the dumb-bell chorus. It is worthy of remark that Avery Institute has lived down prejudice and opposition, and that this year the Commencement exercises were witnessed with a pleasant enthusiasm by the most prominent white and black citizens of Charleston. The hall in which they were held was beautifully decorated with flags and flowers, and the musical efforts of the different classes were received with great delight and astonishment.

Zeline M. Mitchell, a young girl who took four prizes, and whose scholarship ranked ninety-five per cent., delivered an excellent valedictory address. Next to her was Charles J. Smith, who ranked eighty-eight per cent., and who delivered the salutatory. In Latin, Edward Corbett and Beulah Gibbs received diplomas.

Through bitter opposition, passive scorn, and cold indifference, Avery Institute has won its way to local recognition and respect. This is a good sign for the future, and the founders of Avery may hopefully expect the day when the communities blessed with these educational safeguards and advantages will not only give them their respect, but also the weight of their social influence and the aid of their pecuniary support.

A MILD SLAVE-HUNT

HARPER'S WEEKLY
November 1, 1879, p. 867

Mr. John T. Butler, of Hamburg, South Carolina, has come North with a pack of hounds, with which he proposes to show the manner in which runaway slaves were formerly hunted, and convicts are still pursued in the South. He asserts that an exaggerated impression prevails at the North respecting the cruelty of this practice, and his exhibitions are intended to make money, and also to illustrate his claim that the purpose of using the hounds was simply to find and detain the fugitives, without injuring them. He has brought with him a negro named Sam, who is willing to play the runaway, and a sturdy little sorrel mare, whose speed is to give him an advantage over the hounds.

His first exhibition was given recently at Fleetwood Park. Sam mounted the mare, and rode down the hill on which the spectators sat, to the judges' stand, where he dismounted, and started to run at a pace that would win him a place in a short-distance foot-race. He ran about a quarter of a mile just inside the race track, and then rushed in behind some bushes. Mr. Butler called his hounds by sounding an old cow-horn, and started them in pursuit by a kind of "cat-call." Catching the scent quickly, they followed, baying loudly, and were lost to sight. The negro re-appeared from the bushes, and running quickly to the fence, remounted the mare, and galloped around the course. The dogs came behind, at a considerable distance, taking his exact course; but when they came to where the negro had remounted, they were puzzled. In trying to recover the scent, they got across the former trail, and gave up the hunt. Mr. Butler had said before the trial that the high wind and dry ground would make it difficult to give a satisfactory exhibition on that day.

Sam then came up with the pack, and again started, mounted from the beginning this time, with the pack at his heels, and an exciting chase took place around the course, with odds in favor of the mare. She increased her lead all the way around. Reaching the gate, Sam consented to be "treed," and mounting the high gate-post, awaited the hounds. When they found him, they redoubled their noise, and leaped high into the air, trying to reach the negro, who beat them off with his whip, until Mr. Butler came up and sounded his horn, at which the barking ceased as by magic, and the fugitive came down. Mr. Butler said the dogs would have bitten the negro, well as they knew him, had he descended before the horn sounded, unless he had a club with which to beat them off. The moral seemed to be that a runaway slave must be careful to have a tree handy when the dogs overtake him, or, if he is caught in a swamp, he should be able to cut a hickory stick in season.

The absurdity of this exhibition as an illustration of a real slave-hunt is well hit off in Mr. Nast's cartoon on our first page.

FIGHTING THE UTES

HARPER'S WEEKLY
November 1, 1879, p. 870

Our Indian sketches of last week are admirably supplemented in this issue by a spirited cartoon by Reinhart, and a sketch of the charge in which Major Thornburgh lost his life.

The origin of the difficulties with the Ute Indians seems to have lain in the fact that this tribe, like the Cheyennes, could not content themselves upon their reservation. The country north of the Colorado Reservation is said to be very desirable for farming and grazing purposes, and is thickly settled. For three or four years past the Indians have been in the habit of intruding into this district, which practice has caused considerable annoyance to settlers, particularly on Snake and Bear rivers. There are many lawless persons in the vicinity, it

THE UTE WAR—THE COLORED TROOPS FIGHTING THEIR WAY INTO THE BELEAGUERED CAMP.—Drawn by C. S. Reinhart.—[SEE PAGE 870.]

Harper's Weekly, **November 1, 1879, p. 868.**

is said, who for years have carried on a brisk trade with the Indians, supplying them with whiskey and ammunition, causing constant complaints to the Indian Office. Depredations have also been committed by the Indians along the valleys of the rivers referred to. In the fall of 1877 Agent Danforth visited that country, together with Lieutenant Parke, of the Ninth Cavalry, United States army, with a view to the adoption of measures to protect the settlers and break up this unlawful traffic. They reported in September, 1877, that it would be necessary to establish a military post there, that this would keep the Indians on their reservation, serve to protect the settlers, and break up the unlawful trade referred to. The recommendation was never complied with.

At about this time a gentleman named Meeker, not unknown in the newspaper world, received the appointment of agent among the Ute Indians. He found them refractory, and entirely unwilling to abandon their old habits and settle down to anything resembling agriculture. Mr. Meeker, however, was determined that the soil should be cultivated, but the first ploughman who turned the sod was shot by Chief Douglas's son. The agent still persisted in his resolution, and secured the services of a rival chief, and presently order was restored. This occasioned a terrible animosity between a certain portion of the Indians and the agency, and Mr. Meeker felt that at any time an outbreak might take place. The state of affairs was one that justified considerable apprehension, yet a general uprising on the part of the Indians, though constantly threatening, seemed not to occur, and a feeling of comparative security was finally entertained.

In July last the Utes showed unusual symptoms of discontent, and Governor Pitkin telegraphed to the Secretary of the Interior that the Indians were burning timber. He also stated that if they were not immediately stopped by the government, the citizens of Colorado would take the matter in their own hands. The Secretary immediately directed Agent Meeker to call in the Indians engaged in these depredations, and, if necessary, to secure military assistance. The idea of the Indians in burning the timber, it is said, was to concentrate game, in order that it might be killed with less difficulty. Agent Meeker, however, succeeded only temporarily in stopping the destruction of woodland. Subsequently, in the same month, a party of Utes destroyed, in the vicinity of Middle Park, some property, together with a tract of timber. For the purpose of arresting the party engaged in the work of destruction, Governor Pitkin dispatched the sheriff with a posse to the White River Agency. Chief Douglas, of the White River Utes, protested against the entrance of the posse to the agency, which fact was reported to the Indian Bureau. Agent Meeker was then instructed to cause the arrest of the guilty parties. In attempting to carry out this order he incurred the ill-will of the Indians.

By the beginning of September matters were in such an inflamed condition that the agent determined to

IF, LOCKED BY KEY.

FIRST CITIZEN (S. C.). "The Federal Government thinks to punish *us* by stopping the mail!"
SECOND CITIZEN. "It's only those cussed ignorant niggers that care so much for reading and writing."

Harper's Weekly, November 1, 1879, p. 876.

hesitate no longer about sending for troops. It was impossible to go on with the farming operations, and violence was not only offered to the employes of the agency, but even to Mr. Meeker himself. He accordingly wrote as follows to the Governor:

> "White River Agency, September 10, 1879.
> *"To Governor Pitkin:*
>
> "We have ploughed eighty acres. The Indians object to any more being done; shall stop ploughing. One of the ploughmen was shot at last week. I was assaulted Monday in my own house by Chief Johnson, forced out doors, and considerably injured. The employes came to the rescue. The Indians laugh at my being forced out of the house. I feel that none of the white people are safe, and I want United States troops to protect me. They are positively needed at this time.
>
> "N.C. Meeker, Agent."

In response to this demand from the agent, gallant Major Thornburgh, whose portrait and a sketch of whose life were given in the last Weekly, was sent upon the expedition wherein he met his fate. In command of three companies of cavalry and one of infantry he made his way from Rawlins to the northern boundary of the Ute Reservation. The wagon road from the former place to the White River Agency crosses this boundary at about the point where Milk Creek is met. Milk Creek is a narrow, shallow stream, which here flows in a southwesterly direction through a narrow canon. Through this canon, after making a detour to avoid some very difficult ground, the wagon road passes for three or four miles. Along the stream is a growth of cottonwood-trees; but its great advantage as an ambuscade lies in the narrowness of the canon, which is confined by steep hills rising on either side, those on the west being 500, 600, 800, and, lower down, 1000 feet high. On the night before reaching this point, Major Thornburgh had been urged by two Ute chiefs, Coloral and Ute Jack, to go forward with but five men. This he refused to do, and the Indians left the camp in an angry mood. The advance was resumed in the morning, and caution seems to have been observed. So great were the advantages offered by the close-together cliffs of Milk Creek Canon to a lurking foe, that every precaution was taken to see if the Indians were in ambush there without exposing the command of 160 men. A reconnoissance proved that the hills on either side were covered by Indian warriors, who doubtless had expected the troops would advance to certain slaughter. At this point a trail practicable for horses and light wagons breaks off from the main road, to rejoin it below Milk Creek Canon. Corralling the wagons, Major Thornburgh, under the guidance of the scout Rankin, advanced with a detachment of his men along this trail. The Indians at once saw that their ambush was discovered, but with boldness and cunning at once changed their tactics. They saw that Thornburgh had divided his forces. Accordingly, those in ambush nearest to the trail crossed the hills and appeared suddenly in Thornburgh's front, while the remainder dashed down between him and the wagon train. Thornburgh waited, it seems, for the Utes in his front to open fire, and then replied. He was about to make head against them when he discovered that the Indians had outflanked him, and were already in his rear. Wheeling about, he ordered a charge back to the wagons, about three-quarters of a mile off. The Indians poured a murderous fire into the retreating force, and the troops, on coming near the wagon train, met the second body of Indians, who were already raining bullets upon the corral, killing and running off the horses. Through these it was necessary to force a way, and here, within four hundred yards of the wagons, the commander fell.

Captain Payne, now in command, at once set about having the wounded horses shot, to be used for breastworks, dismantling the wagons of boxes and bundles of bedding, corn and flour sacks, which were quickly piled up for fortifications. Picks and shovels were used vigorously for digging intrenchments. While this was being done, the fire from the Indians was galling, but the gallant troops stood it well, and by evening Captain Payne found leisure to prepare the following dispatch, dated Milk River, September 29, 8.30 P.M.:

> "This command, composed of three companies of cavalry, was met a mile south of Milk River by several hundred Ute Indians, who attacked and drove us to the wagon train with great loss. It becomes my painful duty to announce the death of Major Thornburgh, who fell in harness, the painful but not serious wounding of Lieutenant Paddock and Dr. Grimes, the killing of ten enlisted men and a

wagon-master, with the wounding of about twenty men and teamsters. I am corralled, near water, with about three-fourths of my animals killed, after a desperate fight since 12 M. We hold our position. I shall strengthen it during the night, and believe we can hold out until reenforcements reach us, if they are hurried. Officers and men behaved with the greatest gallantry. I am also slightly wounded in two places."

As soon as this dispatch was received by Brigadier-General Crook, who was at that time in Chicago, orders were sent to General Merritt, at Fort Russell, to go with 550 men to the relief of Captain Payne. As soon as possible these troops were under way, and reached the vicinity of Payne's camp on Monday, October 6. After a brief engagement with the Indians, who were compelled to retreat, General Merritt succeeded in relieving Captain Payne.

The welcome given to the troops by the camp was rapturous. They had been six days under the fire of the Indians, and relief had not come too soon. Before their arrival, however, Payne had been most gallantly succored by a colored company of forty-five men of the Ninth Cavalry, under Captain Dodge. His company had come down Bear River, past Steamboat Springs, the preceding Friday and night, and learning of Thornburgh's fight and Payne's situation, resolved to get to Payne's side at every hazard. In their attempt they were met by the besieging Utes, who turned upon them with a fire so hot that they were compelled to dismount. In the course of the subsequent engagement this brave colored company lost every horse but two.

General Merritt advanced on the agency Saturday, October 11. On his way he encountered many dead bodies. The agency itself presented a most appalling sight. All the buildings except one had been destroyed by fire, and the ruins still smouldered. The stockade surrounding the place was a blackened line of upright charcoal. Not a living thing was in sight except the command. The Indians had taken everything except the flour, and decamped. The women and children were missing, and nothing whatever could be found to indicate what had become of them. A hundred yards or so from his late residence lay Mr. Meeker's body, having on it every evidence of having been beaten and dragged about the grounds by chains for some time before his death. A blow had been given him on the head, and he was stripped of clothing. The corpses were almost unrecognizable. The dead body of Mr. W. H. Post, Agent Meeker's assistant, was found between the building and the river, a bullet hole through the left ear and another under the ear. He, like Mr. Meeker, was entirely naked. Another employe, named Eaton, was found dead. He was stripped naked, and had a bundle of paper bags in his arms. His face was badly eaten by wolves. There was a bullet hole in his left breast. There were other bodies lying near, but these examples serve to show how the savages had treated their victims.

At the time of writing it is supposed that the Indians have retreated southward, and it is expected that small bands will drop into the various agencies, and thus covering themselves, preclude all possibility of finding out who were the warriors who began the battle upon Major Thornburgh. In the mean time the government is making every effort to punish the Utes. General Sheridan telegraphs from Chicago that when all the troops now *en route* between Rawlins and the White River Agency join General Merritt, he will have a force of 1500 men. Instructions have also been sent from Washington to the effect that nothing must be left undone to punish the Indians who attacked the troops and killed the agent and his employes, and that only their unconditional surrender shall be accepted.

"THE NEGRO EXODUS."

HARPER'S WEEKLY
December 6, 1879, p. 950

There have been many good accounts of the great emigration of laborers from the Southern States, but we have seen none which is more complete and satisfactory than that of the Rev. Dr. Hartzell, the editor of the *Southern Christian Advocate*, at New Orleans. His account is published in the *Methodist Quarterly* Review for October, 1879, and it is wholly in accord with the report of Colonel Frank H. Fletcher, the agent appointed by the St. Louis Commission to investigate the subject in Kansas among the colored emigrants, much of whose testimony he publishes in his report. The colored emigration, as Dr. Hartzell points out, is not a recent movement, although its immense proportions are a late phenomenon. Its older form was the escape of the fugitive slaves to Canada, and in 1869 there was an organized movement in Tennessee and Kentucky to colonize in Northern and Western States. But in the early spring of 1879, in certain parts of Louisiana and Mississippi, the emigration became a stampede. In May, 1879, a colonization organization among the plantation laborers in the cotton belt of Louisiana, Mississippi, Texas, and Arkansas contained 92,800 men, women, and children more than twelve years old. Such organizations are now universal throughout the Southern States. In New Orleans there are three, and in the month of July of this year two hundred families left that city and vicinity. Between February and September 7000 emigrants went to Kansas alone. How serious a matter this is, appears from a few figures. The value of the combined cotton, sugar, and rice crops for the year 1878 was $256,000,000, made almost entirely by negro labor. Whatever seriously af-

DOES NOT A MEETING LIKE THIS, ETC.
"Hello, Niggy man! Youlee golee West—Melee golee East."

Harper's Weekly, November 22, 1879, p. 923.

fects such production touches the interests of the whole country.

Dr. Hartzell says that "the causes of the negro exodus may be grouped under a single head, namely, the conditions of financial, political, and social distress in which the negroes in the South find themselves after fifteen years of freedom; and the conviction that their former owners, who with their allies now control every Southern State, have in the past opposed their advancement, and do not now give sufficient evidence of good desire toward them to insure their present and future welfare." This view is confirmed by the statements made to Colonel Fletcher by the most intelligent colored leaders in Kansas. One such from Mississippi said: "I don't believe that all the colored people are coming from the South. They will prefer to stay South if they can have peace there. I would prefer to live South if I was not afraid of my life there. To get away I sold six thousand dollars' worth of property for a nineteen-hundred-dollar note. I had bargained for a five-hundred-acre tract of land, which I was to pay for the day of the riot. Instead of closing the trade, I hid in the woods for four months, and finally got away. It is just as impossible for a colored man to get justice in Mississippi as it is to fly." Another, from Louisiana, said: "One man offered me fifty dollars to stay. I didn't stay, because I know'd I wouldn't get the fifty dollars. We have lost confidence in the Southerners. We don't believe anything they tell us, they have deceived us so often."

Dr. Hartzell reviews briefly the legislation in the Southern States since the war, and says that the spirit which dictated the Black Codes has prevailed almost universally. "The South" is an agricultural region, and the contract system of labor is very general, and the

VOTING POWER OF THE SOUTH.

Mr. CHANDLER dwelt at some length upon the Election Laws, and claimed that the Southern end of the republic didn't want any safeguards put upon the purity of elections, because they would interfere with the operations of the Ku-Klux at the polls. Said Mr. CHANDLER, "Give them permission to perpetrate the same kind of fraud and violence in New York city and Cincinnati as has been perpetrated in the South, and those two cities, with the solid South, will give them the Presidency of the United States, and by fraud and violence they would hold it for a generation."

THE ROUGH IS READY.
THE SOUTHERN EPIDEMIC WILL SPREAD NORTH IF NOT CHECKED.

Harper's Weekly, November 22, 1879, p. 925.

contracts are drawn so as easily to entrap an ignorant and docile class of laborers. The argument of Mr. Randall and others, therefore, drawn from the large crops, is valueless to show the content of the laborers. Dr. Hartzell does not deny a slow improvement in some quarters. There has been some acquisition of property by the colored laborers, but the masses of them are poor, and after fifteen years of freedom the outlook is gloomy, and multitudes are discouraged. The general view of the white class is that the negroes are a dependent race, which must be rigidly kept dependent. The colored vote is practically suppressed. In no State office, nor in the controlling element of a single State legislative branch, can there be found any trace of the 887,348 negro voters. Public opinion, as Governor Nicholls, of Louisiana, and Governor Stone, of Mississippi, agree, does not protect the colored people, and Dr. Hartzell thinks that by no ordinary process of law can the United States protect them in the exercise of their political rights. His conclusion is the one which we have often stated—that it is vitally important to the Southern section of the Union to stop the exodus which is draining its life-blood away. Labor, and with it wealth and power, are flying from the Southern States. The white people of those States alone can stop the exodus, and they can do it only by justice, by absolutely preventing bulldozing of every kind, by fostering a friendly feeling, by education and moral and religious training. It is especially a local State work, but until there are signs of its honest beginning, intelligent and patriotic men in those States will understand that no mere professions of good feeling will avail. It is for them to take the Southern question out of politics, for in the rest of the country, while by no means the only question, it is the one upon which the public mind is most easily excited.

1880

The year 1880 commenced with Republican tirades on the lack of free voting and fair counting in all elections—national and regional—in the South. Charges abounded on how Democrats used intimidation, violence, and fraud to control the African American voter. Such behavior secured the desired results, the return of white supremacy via the Democrats, but it also contributed to the increase in the number of African Americans who were now beginning to support territorial separation and emigration. Editorials called for the resurrection of national election laws that would protect the black vote, hence guaranteeing the return of Republican victories in the South.

The treatment of African American cadets at West Point Academy in New York was the focus of the coverage of the brutal beating of Cadet Whittaker. Whittaker, the only black cadet at this national institution at the time, was the victim of a savage beating. He testified that three young men entered his room late one night and attacked him severely, even mutilating his ears as a mark of triumph. Though unable to identify the assailants, Whittaker believed them to be fellow cadets. While fleeing, they warned Whittaker what other actions were possible due to his presence at the school if he disclosed this incident.

Since this incident followed closely the removal of Lt. Henry Flipper, West Point's first black cadet, journalists seemed disturbed that the school was not addressing the issue of racism. How was it, it was asked, that a federally supported institution, located in former abolitionist country, opened to all qualified citizens without regard to race, could tolerate such treatment of one of its students by fellow students? Though clearly not supporting legislative or forced social equality, the editorials questioned the discriminatory conditions that Whittaker had endured prior to this incident. How could those officials, sworn to uphold the Constitution of *the United States, allow such gross injustice? Did their silence imply consent? How much scrutiny had the institution given in finding the truth in the accuser's facts and the fellow cadets' version? Testimony that Whittaker had self-inflicted his wounds to avoid taking an examination were decried. Congress was asked to intervene, and if civil rights had been violated, the coverage called for the removal of the officials and the guilty students.*

The authors seemed especially disturbed that such prejudice existed in the "legendary antislavery North" by possibly sons of this movement. The issue of racism was seen as "a perpetual menace to the peace and order of the country." The national government had the responsibility to suppress such injustice by law. For surely the country expected the cadets of West Point, future national leaders, to be "decent...innocent, well behaved comrades."

The presidential election of 1880 pitted Republican Union veteran James A. Garfield against Union veteran, Winfield S. Hancock, the Democratic candidate. Charging that the Solid South had become Democratic by destroying the free ballot, the editorials delineated the variety of corruptive practices implemented. Such elections guaranteed Democratic success even in black Republican majority districts. So, the question was, why would the country now support a party that fought for its dissolution? Why would it now place a Democrat in the nation's highest office? How would the party justify its past in order to raise the country's confidence? The viable option was the election of Republican James A Garfield, who would support national elections laws and hard money.

Democrats charged that such rhetoric appealed to hatred, sectionalism, as it continued to "wave the bloody shirt." A lengthy Republican response centered on the need for a free and fair popular vote. The urgency of the elections demanded that questions be raised about the history and current practices of the party in the areas where it was in control. The suppression of black voters was common knowledge, the editors proclaimed. For the Democratic control of the South was accomplished by coercion and cheating. Where blacks had voted the Democratic ticket, they did so due to force and bribes. Still, the Republicans argued, southern Democrats would not be deterred. Warnings were issued to prospective voters: whites voting for the Republican party would be treated as enemies of the race to be socially ostracized. Black Republicans would face eviction, loss of jobs, loss of credit, loss of favors from whites, and the defamation of leadership before the entire race.

By the close of the year, there was an interest in ascertaining how the freedmen had progressed under emancipation. A journalist decided to visit the southern states of South Carolina, Georgia, and Alabama Though confronted still with abject poverty and only the rudiments of life's necessities, in sum, these southern blacks believed that future generations would be able to "uplift" the race. Towards these goals, they sacrificed to provide educational opportunities for their children. Schools— day, night, and Sunday—all became centers of knowledge for all ages.

The southern African Americans had also developed an extended community where work loads and responsibilities were shared. Non-kin members, particularly the elderly, became vital forces in the community. Values, traditions, and beliefs were passed on via stories, songs, group meetings, and religious activities. Though confronted with limitations and restrictions, journalists had to reluctantly acknowledge the levels of success the freedmen had secured in their transition from slavery to freedom.

Jacqueline A. Rouse
Georgia State University

A SOUTHERN REPUBLICAN VIEW

HARPER'S WEEKLY
January 17, 1880, p. 34

A Southern Republican, the only white man in his precinct who voted for Hayes and Wheeler, sends us a very interesting and instructive letter in reply to our assertion that if the intelligent whites in the Southern States do not now lead the colored vote, they have themselves to blame for it. He points out the kind of antagonism, not necessarily unfriendly, which often exists between employer and employed, each side overvaluing what he supplies, and which leads to a positive independence of action. In the Southern States the colored race as slaves lived in opposition

or in abject subjection to their masters. The slaves were practically freed by the Northern soldiers, who remained and befriended them, rightfully or wrongfully, against their old masters, and became bound to the freedmen in a friendship which no business bargains or disputes disturbed. The government appointed officers to administer State and county affairs, and they effected the party organization, from which the defection of the colored man seemed to his fellows a crime against nature. The colored people were bound together in the militia, the school, the church, and the party, and the latter bond was riveted by the vague fear of a restoration of slavery. This various and all-embracing organization united the colored people against the old master class and the whole white population. The fear of re-enslavement is disappearing, but it was a great reason of the exodus; for when bulldozing or fraud nullifies their votes, the colored people feel themselves to be helpless in the hands of their old enemy. The course of President Hayes was misrepresented to them as a total withdrawal of protection, and a panic seized them, which quickened the emigration.

Mr. Lamar has said more than once that except for the carpet-baggers no ill feeling would have existed between the races after the war. But Mr. Lamar forgets the black codes, which were the very first action of the whites at the close of hostilities. Our correspondent says that in 1868, at the end of the Johnson era, the plantation hands were full of suspicion and defiance, while the planting class regarded the laborers as their property of which they had been robbed. This was the key to the situation. Without protection the colored people would have had no political rights whatever. It is, in our correspondent's view, nobody's fault that they found other leaders than their old masters. It was perfectly natural. Industrially, like all other laborers, they are now treated both well and ill by their employers and suppliers. But injustice is not universal, nor due to their color. The Irishmen who build the levees are much worse treated and more heavily charged by contractors than the colored plantation laborers. Three-fourths of the traders are Hebrews, and the dishonest among them cheat white and black with absolute impartiality. When a planter supplies his own hands, they are generally fairly treated, because hands are scarce and land plenty. A large class of laborers are constantly becoming closer traders and more thrifty spenders, and on the whole our correspondent—a singularly fair-minded man, and himself a Republican planter—says that the colored laborers of his section, in Arkansas, are the best paid unskilled laborers in the world. The last year, indeed, has been an exceptionally good one; but he knows

ANOTHER INVESTIGATION COMMITTEE.

SELF-APPOINTED GENT. "An' what right have you, sure, to be afther laving your native place an' coming here? Spake!"

Harper's Weekly, January 31, 1880.

many colored families which, after paying rather extravagant bills, and even in some cases old debts, will have a balance of some hundreds of dollars. Few will clear less than $100, while the most economical of the colored people would be considered extravagant by Germans of the same class.

The Southern whites are mainly Democrats, and anxious to see their party in power. But they are much more interested in local than in national politics. This arises from the fact that their most material interests depend upon the result of the local elections. The power of taxation has been used to the great injury of property-holders; and in some counties the carpet-baggers have argued that the imposition of high taxes would bring estates to the hammer, and the colored people could ultimately become owners of all the land. The colored people had no interest in low taxes, and their leaders wished to handle high ones. In Arkansas the Constitution limits taxation, and in general the colored people exercise their full political rights. In our correspondent's own county the officers are both white and colored, Republican and Democratic, the magistrates mainly colored. In Mississippi, where there is no restraint upon taxation, the vote, if honestly cast, would be undoubtedly Republican. But four or five years ago the taxation was about five per cent. on a high valuation, which brought much property into market. Violence is generally the result, as our correspondent thinks, of some spoliation of this kind, and is intended to baffle it. His opinion, like that of most sensible men, is that the only way to manage the matter is to leave it to work itself out. There is a steady, if slow, improvement, and there is no doubt that the colored people have been better treated since the withdrawal of the troops than before. Our correspondent's glimpse of the late election in Washington County, in Mississippi, is interesting and suggestive when it is added that the Vicksburg *Herald*, the paper of largest circulation in the State, is in favor of cutting loose from the Bourbon Democrats:

"In one sense there was no election at all. There were no regular Republican candidates, and no regular Democratic candidate. They had what they called the People's ticket, a fusion of parties, managed by prominent Democrats and some of the Republicans. The Democrats got the most important offices, but many negroes were elected to other positions. The Representatives were a white Democrat and a negro Republican, the prosecuting attorney an old carpet-bagger, and there were conciliation, whiskey, and apparent good feeling on every side. This could not be called a natural state of affairs. Neither party, if unrestrained, would have allowed the other anything; but the fusion was arranged by men who did not care much for party, and was perhaps as well as was practicable. The best men here are not much interested in politics except when they have a direct bearing on business."

GENERAL TELEGRAPH NEWS
Lynched for an Outrage.

NEW-YORK TIMES
March 3, 1880

A One-armed Colored Ruffian Hanged by a Mob
Charleston, S. C., March 2.—A one-armed negro named Louis Kinder committed an outrageous assault, on Saturday, upon a white woman named Byrd, residing near George's Station, Colleton County, about 50 miles from the city. A hunt was organized, and the villain was captured about four o'clock Tuesday morning by a mixed white and black posse. He was taken to the scene of the outrage and identified by his victim. A vote of the posse was taken and it was decided not to lynch him, but to allow the law to take its course. Kinder was then taken to George's Station, and placed in the guard-house under a strong guard. On Monday morning he was sent to Walterboro to jail, still strongly guarded. On their way to Walterboro the guard were over-powered by an armed force, consisting, it is said, largely of the relatives of the outraged woman, and the éprisoner was conveyed to a secluded spot in the woods, where he was kept until night. About 9 o'clock last night he was again confronted with the woman whom he had outraged, and again identified. He was again taken to the woods, where preparations were made to hang him. While denying this crime, he confessed to a similar outrage upon a colored woman in Newberry six years ago. He further acknowledged the killing of a colored girl near King's Tree last April, and confessed to four burglaries and innumerable thefts. At 10:30 o'clock he was hanged, and after firing a volley of pistol shots into the body, the crowd quietly dispersed.

A gentleman arrived in this city to-day from the vicinity of George's Station, on the South Carolina Railroad, the scene of last night's tragedy. He reports that Kinder showed no fear or resistance when taken from two constables yesterday by the lynchers, while on their way to Walterboro Jail. He stubbornly denied his guilt, so far as Mrs. Byrd was concerned, but confessed complicity in other outrages and robberies. He watched the preparations for his killing with stolid indifference. The rope, attached to a strong limb, gave him a drop of about three feet from the buggy on which he was placed, and he seemingly died without a struggle. The body was cut down this morning by colored men living near by, and

Harper's Weekly, February 21, 1880, p. 124.

turned over to the Coroner, who was holding an inquest when the gentleman went away. Kinder's reputation was exceedingly bad, and the action of lynchers, though a violation of the law, is generally approved by white and colored.

THE CIVIL RIGHTS CASES

HARPER'S WEEKLY
March 27, 1880, p. 194

The Fourteenth Amendment to the Federal Constitution declares that all persons born in the United States, and subject to its jurisdiction, are citizens. It then prohibits every State from denying to any citizen the equal protection of the laws. The amendment does not mention race or color; but its great and well-known purpose was to give to colored persons the common rights of citizenship, and to empower Congress to protect those rights against the hostile action of any State. One of the laws passed for this purpose is the act of March, 1875, which provides for the trial and punishment by a heavy fine of any officer who shall exclude a colored citizen from a jury on account of his color. Congress has further provided, by Section 641 of the Revised Statutes, for the removal of a case to the Federal court whenever a citizen is denied, or can not enforce, in a State court, "any right secured to him by any law providing for the equal civil rights of citizens of the United States." Despite the Fourteenth Amendment, however, and the laws passed by Congress to give effect to it, colored citizens have been unlawfully excluded from the jury-box in more than one State. In West Virginia this wrong has been done by express legislation. A statute passed in 1873 declares that no colored person shall sit on a jury, and the Supreme Court of that State affirmed the constitutionality of the act in the case of the negro Taylor Strander, who had been convicted by a white jury, and sentenced to death, for the murder of his wife. In Virginia colored citizens are not disqualified for jury service by the Constitution or laws. But they have been purposely and effectively excluded from the jury-box by the studied action of the county judges charged with the summoning of jurors. This state of affairs was brought to the attention of Judge Rives, of the United States court, about a year ago. A negro named Reynolds, indicted for killing a white man, was tried and found guilty by a white jury. On appeal, the Supreme Court of Virginia held that the total exclusion of colored persons from the jury was not a violation of the Fourteenth Amendment or any act of Congress. Judge Rives then granted an application for the removal of the case to the United States court, pursuant to Section 641 of the

Revised Statutes. At the same time he caused a number of county judges to be indicted, under the act of Congress of 1875, for making an unlawful discrimination against colored citizens; in the summoning of jurors.

The Strander and the Reynolds cases, and the case of Judge Coles (one of the indicted county judges), were carried to the Supreme Court of the United States. They were argued together last October, and they are now decided together. In each case there were special points not directly involved in the other two. But the great fundamental question in all was whether the Fourteenth Amendment secures, or empowers Congress to secure, to colored citizens the privilege of sitting as jurors in a State court, or the right to demand that a jury for the trial of grave questions of life, liberty, or property shall be chosen without discrimination as to color. Two States at least has solemnly denied that such was the purpose or the effect of the amendment. Nor was it by any means certain what view would be taken by the Supreme Court. That tribunal had not yet interpreted the meaning of the amendment in any political controversy, or any case directly involving the question of color. In every one of the three or four cases decided under the amendment the judges had divided. The judgment in the slaughter-house cases—the leading authority on this subject—rests on the bare majority of one. Four of the nine justices dissented, and Chief Justice Chase was one of the minority. This marked diversity of opinion among the judges, as well as certain doctrines affirmed by the court, left in no little doubt questions relating to the civil rights of colored persons under the amendment.

The court has now spoken, and spoken well. With a unanimity not found in any previous opinion concerning the amendment, it declares that the purpose of this great constitutional guarantee, and of the acts of Congress for its enforcement, "was to place the colored race, in respect of civil rights, upon a level with whites. They made the rights and responsibilities, civil and criminal, of the two races exactly the same." The court declares that trial by a jury chosen without discrimination as to color is a right secured to every citizen by the Fourteenth Amendment. "The very idea of a jury," says the opinion, "is a body of men composed of the peers or equals of the person whose rights it is selected or summoned to determine." A statute like that of West Virginia is pronounced a brand upon the colored race. It denies to one class of citizens that equality of protection which is guaranteed by the Constitution to all, and deprives of a valuable civil right every colored person tried under it. It is, therefore, unconstitutional. A new trial was accordingly ordered in the case of Strander. In the Coles case and in that of Strander the judgment of the Supreme Court is against the State. But the case of Reynolds was ordered to be returned from the Federal to the State jurisdiction. This was done on technical grounds. Under Section 641 of the Revised Statutes the application for removal to the Federal courts should have been made before trial in the State court. The Supreme Court admits that Congress has full power to pass a more effective statute, but the act now in force is not as broad as the Fourteenth Amendment. Moreover, Reynolds had claimed the right of trial by a mixed jury. But this is not one of the rights secured by the Fourteenth Amendment. The law requires not that colored jurors shall be expressly summoned, but that they shall not be purposely rejected. Both the letter and the spirit of the law are observed when the jurors are selected without distinction as to color. There is, then, no ground for complaint whether the jury be black, white, or mixed. On the main question involved as to the meaning of the Fourteenth Amendment the opinions in the three cases are in harmony, and are concurred in by six of the eight justices now sitting.

THE NATIONAL ELECTION LAWS

HARPER'S WEEKLY
March 27, 1880, p. 195

We speak elsewhere of the late decisions of the Supreme Court of the United States in the Civil Rights cases. The court has now decided, with but two dissenting justices, the complete constitutionality of the National Election Laws. The court affirms the power of Congress to regulate the election of Representatives in such way as it deems wisest; to appoint Federal officers to enforce such regulations, and to punish those who violate them. This opinion is undoubtedly the deliberate judgment of the country, and it was the perception that its principle was not acknowledged by the Democratic party, as the extra session showed, which largely explains the Republican victories of last year.

This decision is of great importance, and is very satisfactory. The great purposes which it was the object of the new amendments to secure have been opposed by the Democratic party upon constitutional grounds, and the Supreme Court, as in the Civil Rights opinions, has happily decided the amendments to be effectual for the purpose designed. The present decision, however, meets the Democratic attempt to nullify by indirection Republican voting in the Southern States, not upon one of the amendments, but upon the constitutional provision that Congress may make or alter regulations for the election of Representatives.

As the court has thus decided the laws under which marshals and deputies are appointed to be constitutional, it remains to be seen whether Congress will still withhold appropriations for their payment. Should it do so, should the enormous folly of the extra session be repeated, the Democrats will invite a verdict at the polls which will amaze them.

THE FATAL TRAP
The Noose from All Points.
Special Dispatch to The Constitution.

ATLANTA CONSTITUTION
April 3, 1880

Three Negroes Hanged in Mississippi—A Head Jerked from the Body in Washington—A Vermont Woman-Murderer Goes Through Protesting Innocence

Macon, Miss., April 2.—Andrew Macon, James Brown and Samuel Boler, all negroes, were hanged here at half-past two this evening. Macon and Brown for the murder of Tarleton Macon, father of Macon and father-in-law of Brown in January last, Boler for the killing of Frank Reed, a white man, in 1876. Brown and Macon confessed, assigning whisky the cause. Boler has always claimed he was justified. In consequence of the rain only about eight thousand were present, which number is verified by old soldiers. All of them asserted on the gallows their assurance of heaven. Governor Stone was petitioned by telegraph an hour before the execution to grant a respite in the case of Boler, but replied that he could not interfere. They were pronounced dead in ten minutes by W. C. Yarnigan, M. D. Three men never died gamer or met death with more ease.

Washington, D.C., April 2—James Madison Wyatt Stone, colored, was hanged here today for the murder of his wife in 1878. Stone was a large man, weighing about 200 pounds. When the drop fell his head was severed from the body. The body fell to the ground, and the head, after adhering to the noose a few seconds, fell to the ground a few feet from the body. Dr. Cook picked up the head, and as he did so noticed the lips move. The features were calm. It is supposed that the fatness had weakened the muscular tissues, and the neck was unable to bear the weight of the body.

New York, April 2—A special from Louisville, Ky., gives the following: Robert Anderson, white, and Charles Webster, colored, were hung privately in the jail yard this morning at 9. Webster, who was convicted on circumstantial evidence, asserted his innocence to the last. Anderson denied any knowledge of what occurred when he murdered his wife. Governor Blackburn has resisted the most urgent appeals to commute both sentences. The men went to the scaffold coolly without bravado and met their end courageously. Webster's death was instantaneous by the dislocation of his neck. Anderson was strangled. There was not much excitement, as the execution was held three hours before the people generally expected it.

New York, April 2.—A special from Winchester, Kentucky, says: "Ben Johnson, the young negro who was arrested on Wednesday for an attempt to outrage a respectable young lady, had an examining trial yesterday and held to answer to the circuit court and sent to jail. He had caught the bridle of the young lady's horse at a lonely place along the road, and made desperate efforts to get her off of the horse, but she struck him with her whip and escaped. It was with difficulty that the negro was taken to jail. About one o'clock this morning a crowd of thirty armed men overpowered the guard at the jail, took Johnson, and, after trying in vain to get a confession from him, hung him to a tree in the jail-yard, where his body was found this morning."

THE WHITTAKER ASSAULT
Much Testimony Taken and Little News Obtained.

NEW-YORK TIMES
April 28, 1880

Excitement Over the Arrest of Ryan—Another Expert in Handwriting Called—Testimony of Drummers and Others Who Have Been Used as Messengers

West Point, April 27.—The arrest of Ryan excited great surprise here, as it had been kept a secret from the officers and everybody connected with the post. The news arrived from Highland Falls early this morning and threw the development before the court of inquiry quite into the shade. Ryan's perjury is even more glaring than specified in the affidavit of Detective Newcome, as he swore at length and in detail to material points on which every Cadet examined, and even his own wife and daughter, contradicted him point-blank. There are various speculations as to the upshot of the matter, the most prominent one being that, whatever the findings of the court of inquiry, the investigation will not stop there, but be continued in a much more impartial and exhaustive manner before the criminal courts. Officers and others who have been loudest in their expressions of belief of the corps's innocence looked decidedly grave at the news of Ryan's arrest.

Mr. Townsend was on hand bright and early, but says that he has nothing to communicate in regard to Ryan's intentions. The letter mentioned as being written by Ryan to him proves to have been, in reality, written by Detective Newcome. The venerable ex-Congressman comes back greatly refreshed by his Sunday in Troy, where he had the pleasure of attending the session of the Bible class of the First Presbyterian Church, of which he is a member. The lesson for the day was the passage of Scripture referring to Philip and the Ethiopian eunuch of Queen Candace, who invited Philip to get upon this chariot and ride with him. Mr. Townsend remarked that there seemed no hesitation on the part of these Christians about getting up and riding with an Ethiopian when they, the aforesaid Christians were traveling on foot, and his recent experience at West

Point had impressed him more strongly than ever with this belief.

D. T. Ames, the third expert, has made an examination of the Cadets' handwriting in reference to identifying the author of the anonymous note, and will submit his report at the end of the week. He would have done so to-day, but he was called to New-York to testify in an important case. At the morning session, John E. Hagen, a mechanical and chemical expert brought from Troy by Mr. Townsend, took the stand. The court have hitherto never questioned experts as to their previous records, but on this occasion Mr. Townsend's expert was subjected to a searching examination as to experience, &c. Recorder Sears then confided to him the 250 specimens of Cadets' handwriting to compare with the anonymous note. The Recorder added that he would give the witness 50 or 75 more specimens in the afternoon.

John Mahr, a Highland Falls saloon-keeper, swore that a man named Powell, while in his saloon on the night of Sunday, April 11, said that they [the authorities] would never find out who committed the outrage, but that he [Powell] could pick them out. The witness supposed Powell referred to the Cadets. Two fishermen heard Powell say this; also, a man whom the witness knew as "Charley," who, he thought, works in West Point. Powell had had two glasses of beer at the time, but did not appear at all intoxicated. The witness considered him a trustworthy man.

The Recorder stated that he would now summon drummers, bandsmen, and other [hangerson] around the barracks, to see if any of them had carried the anonymous note to Cadet Whittaker's room. Several of these persons were called, but without result. One admitted carrying notes from Cadets to ladies, whereat there was a sympathetic stir among the fair spectators.

William H. Brooks, engineer of the boiler-room had a supposition which involved Whittaker's having an accomplice he had heard Louis Simpson say in the boiler-house that the affair would create a big sensation in the country, and would probably end in Whittaker's graduating. A person might enter the boiler-house and throw something into the furnace. If two or three suits of citizens' clothing had been thrown in, they would have been entirely consumed, with the exception, possibly, of metal buttons; he had not looked for any remants of the kind. To Mr. Townsend the witness said he left the boiler-house the night of the outrage at 9:15 P.M. He was not around when ashes were drawn; his men had to keep awake to tend the fires. A nervous person, well on in years, a quartermaster and policeman, swore that he had received instructions to take three men and search around the grounds for concealed disguises; he and his men searched around the post, and looked all over the rocks to find clothing, or traces of clothing, but did not find any.

In the afternoon the post surgeon, Dr. Alexander, was recalled, and testified as to the position in which Cadet Whittaker's knife was found. The knife was picked up while Whittaker was dressing; it was found on the floor of the alcove; it was lying about one foot away from the foot of the bed and close to one of the Cadet's legs—the leg nearest the bedstead; the large blade was open when picked up.

Clerk McEnany, of the Quartermaster's Department, counted with a glass the threads in the border of one of the ordinary commissary handkerchiefs and those in the cut one found in Whittaker's room and reported that there was one thread difference. In every other respect, size, pattern, material, &c., the handkerchiefs were the same. The court endeavored to draw out of him that the absence of the single thread proved the [cut handkerchief] to be of a different kind, but the attempt failed.

Recorder Sears said that as there had been some unfavorable comment in the papers in respect to Cadet Whittaker's letter to his mother, referring to the lobes *of* his ears having been cut "off," he would state that the court was in possession of the letter, and that Cadet Whittaker had not written the word "off" but "of;" that his assailants had "cut the lobes of his ears." Mr. Whittaker had therefore not exaggerated the extent of his injuries.

Cadet Carter, of the second class, swore that Whittaker had always been treated with uniform kindness; had not been "deviled." The witness tried to remember when he had seen any white Cadet talking to Whittaker; he knew of one speaking to him last January. The Cadet was Mr. Peck. The witness afterward said that he knew of Mr. Peck speaking to Cadet Whittaker many times; Mr. Peck confided the fact to no one else but himself. The witness afterward defined "treating kindly" to mean not hazing or deviling.

A DANGER TO BE AVOIDED

HARPER'S WEEKLY
May 1, 1880, p. 274

There was never more political independence than now, and one of the most striking phenomena of the situation is that differences within the parties are more decided and bitter than those between the parties. This, which is undeniable, forecasts a kind of voting next November which demands the most careful consideration. This will be the seventh Presidential election in which the Republican party has taken part. In the first two the issue was plain and momentous. It was not merely a choice between the parties with a vague doubt as to probable policies, it was a sharply drawn contest between the restriction and the extension of slavery. No

Harper's Weekly, May 1, 1880, p. 285.

man who desired to see slavery curbed had any question about his action. The issue of the third election—that of 1864—was still simpler. It was the maintenance or overthrow of the national government, and voters took their parts accordingly. The elections of 1868 and 1872 involved reconstruction and its settlement; and despite the powerful leading of a Republican schism in the latter year, the party was strongly sustained. In 1876 the Republican party narrowly escaped defeat. Its popular vote was 4,033,950, against a Democratic vote of 4,284,757. These figures were undoubtedly largely the result of terrorizing the new voters in the Southern States; but only after a doubtful and alarming contest over the electoral count was the Republican candidate declared elected by one electoral vote. Such was the acrimony of feeling, however, within the party lines that had Republican success depended upon the vote of the only Republican Senator from New York, Mr. Conkling, who evaded voting upon the Louisiana return, the Republicans would have been defeated, and the Democratic candidate would have been seated.

The situation this year involves no distinct issue like that of the restriction of slavery, the prosecution of the war, or reconstruction. It is mainly an appeal to the country by both parties upon their general character and traditions. This is a situation in which personal considerations regarding candidates will have necessarily great weight. When a vote meant the restriction of slavery, or the vigorous prosecution of the war, the candidate was lost in the issue. But when the issue is less clearly defined, the candidate rises into importance, and the practical objections to candidates become vital considerations. It is at this point that the first condition of a prosperous campaign appears, and that condition is a perfectly free deliberation and choice of the candidate. Here one of the most serious possible mischiefs of instructions appears. All the States are represented in the nominating Convention. But some of the States can by no possibility cast a Republican majority. Kentucky and Missouri, for instance, will give their electoral vote to the Democratic candidate, whoever he may be, as certainly as they will vote. It is of the utmost importance, therefore, that the nomination should be made by the really Republican States, which alone can elect the candidate. A nomination made by an alliance between States that can give no aid to the candidate, and an artificial representation, such as instructions produce, from one or two Republican States, would be a disaster, because it would misrepresent Republican sentiment at a time when its honest representation is indispensable. The instructions given by the New York and Pennsylvania and Iowa and Kansas Conventions have plainly not increased the chances of Republican success. They show a doubt of the real condition of party sentiment with a determination to force a particular expression. Now the object of every Republican should be to ascertain the real preference of the party, and this is possible only upon a perfectly free and fair comparison of views and patriotic deliberation at the Convention.

We have heretofore shown—and we are glad to see the position maintained by the ablest Republican papers in the State—that the State Convention has no authority to instruct district delegates, because it does not appoint them. This point was brought directly before the late New York Convention by a motion to substitute for the district delegation one that coincided in opinion with the apparent majority of the Convention. Mr. Conkling voted loudly for the motion, but it was lost by an immense majority, and that decision renounced every shadow of right to instruct. This was in accordance with the uniform practice of New York Republican Conventions, and with the whole spirit and tradition of the Republican party. Twice this question has been raised in the National Republican Convention, and twice the final tribunal of the party has decided that the instructions of a State Convention can not bind the action of the delegates. Should this decision be reversed, it would only show how much more stringent, and consequently how much more dangerous, the mere organization of party has become.

THE AFFAIR AT WEST POINT

HARPER'S WEEKLY
May 1, 1880, p. 274

The consequences of the Whittaker incident at West Point will not end with the investigation, even if it shall establish beyond question that Whittaker tied and cut himself in order to get a better chance at a later examination. If this shall be proved, it will be seen that the young man was a foolish fellow, but it will be seen also that the form which his folly took is a severe reflection upon the authorities and cadets of the institution, because it would show that the general treatment he had received made such an assault upon him a probable and plausible assertion. Indeed, whatever the result of the inquiry, whether Whittaker cut himself or not, it is evident that during all his course this young American, at a national school where he is entitled to precisely the same rights with all his companions, has been practically proscribed and avoided and despised, like a leper or a pariah in a semi-civilized community. Apparently, also, this has been done with the tacit connivance, or without the protest, of the officers in charge of the school.

Now our view of American equality does not require that our choice of social companions should be regulated by law. But our view of manhood does hold that there is nothing more unspeakably mean than to indulge the prejudice of race and color; and to proscribe a comrade because African blood flows in his veins is as unworthy a gentleman as to despise him because he is poor. The number of West Point cadets is limited, we believe, to two hundred and fifty; and according to the uncontradicted and repeated statements, since the Whittaker affair, not one of these scions of the "superior race," with every advantage and feeling and tradition in favor of his color, has been even decently courteous to the one youth whose only offense was a darker skin, and who was sprung in some degree from the most unhappy and most wronged race in history. If, as is alleged, Whittaker has endured this treatment throughout his course, and has personally done nothing to justify any kind of ostracism, he has shown a moral pluck and a genuine manliness which any of his white comrades might be proud to have displayed, and of which their treatment of him shows no sign whatever. We must all await the decision of the board of inquiry as to his specific guilt in the incident which has aroused public attention. But the whole weight of presumption, based upon his treatment hitherto, and increased by the alacrity of the Superintendent to discredit his story, is in favor of its truth. It may appear incontestably that Whittaker tied and wounded himself, but what will dispose of the fact, as yet uncontradicted, that the cadets have shown a spirit toward him which justifies the impassioned criticisms of Senators in Congress of both parties?

There is one aspect of this matter which deserves attention. Whenever we have argued that the white citizens in the Southern States are really responsible for the wretched political condition of those States, and for the whole shameful catalogue of Ku-Kluxery in every kind and degree, we have been told that the colored citizens were generally well treated, and that the mischief was all made by carpet-baggers and Northern political tramps. We have cited the most impartial witnesses, like Sir George Campbell, and observers who could have no political bias of any kind, but we have been told that strangers knew and could know nothing. We have pointed to the colored exodus and its unanswerable significance, but the reply has been that its cause was anything but ill treatment. Now if here in the State of New York, in a public school which must count many sons of antislavery parents and Republicans among its members, trained all of them in communities whose antislavery sentiment has been intensified by the war, the race prejudice still exists in its most odious form, as this event at West Point shows, it is useless to assert that it does not affect the welfare of the colored citizen in the old Slave States in the way that has been constantly alleged. The corollary is obvious. This spirit is a perpetual menace of the peace and order of the country, and if it is not to be suppressed by law, still less will it be suppressed—on the contrary, it will be greatly stimulated—by committing the government to those who cherish the prejudice. It is useless to say that the antipathy of race is stronger in the Northern than in the Southern States. The Black Codes, the Ku-Klux, bulldozing, and the tissue ballot are the answer. West Point is a public school. The government which sustains it recognizes no distinction between the pupils whom it admits. The officers in charge are morally bound to represent this disposition in their official conduct, and no pupil should ask to be instructed there at the public expense who will not honorably conform to the understanding upon this subject. The cadets are not bound to choose as associates those whom they do not like, but they are bound, as gentlemen and Americans, to treat innocent and well-behaved comrades, who, like themselves, are public beneficiaries, with decent courtesy. And if the officers do not require such treatment, they should be replaced by officers who will.

THE WEST POINT OUTRAGE

HARPER'S WEEKLY
May 1, 1880, p. 286

Early on the morning of April 6, Johnson C. Whittaker, a colored cadet at West Point, was found by the guard lying, apparently unconscious, on the floor of his room, with his feet tied to the iron bedstead, his hands bound together, and his head resting on a pillow that was saturated with blood. His face, head, and night-shirt were also bloody. Lying about the room were pieces of burned paper, locks of hair, a knife, and an Indian club. An alarm was given, and when the officer of the day came in, the cadet was released from his fastenings and laid upon the bed. The surgeon who examined him found that a small portion of the left ear had been cut off, and that the right ear, the left hand, and one of the toes were also cut.

When able to talk the wounded man told the story of the outrage, as follows:

"Last night, immediately after tattoo, I retired, and had been to sleep some time when I was awakened, I think shortly after 2 A.M., by the moving of the latch on the door of my room. The door is never locked. At first I thought the noise might have been occasioned by the wind against the hall window. I listened for a moment, and then fell into a doze, when I was again suddenly awakened by some one jumping right on me. I looked sharp, and there were three men in all. Two of them were attired in dark clothing, and the third had on a light gray suit, and all wore black masks.

"I drew back my arm to strike the man who had jumped on me, and I partially raised in the bed in the struggle, when I was seized by the throat, and choked till I was almost suffocated; and I was also struck a heavy blow on the left temple and also on the nose with something hard. The man who dealt the blow shouted to me, 'If you don't be still, you will be a dead man; don't you holler.' I was completely overpowered.

"One of the men then said, 'Let's mark him like they do hogs down South.' And then, with what I think was a knife, they cut off the lower end of my left ear, and slit the lobe of my right ear once or twice. Next they began to tie my feet, and I kicked as hard as I could, when one exclaimed, 'Don't you kick, or I will cut you,' and he did stick my feet twice.

"At this time the small man dressed in gray said to one of the others, 'Look out, don't hurt him; see how he bleeds; take my handkerchief, and put it around his wounds;' and the handkerchief was taken and applied as suggested, but afterward taken away. They then tied my feet and my hands with strips of white cross-belts, and then laid me on the floor with my feet toward the bed in the little alcove you see there, and my head toward the wall. Next they tied my feet to the iron bedstead.

"I asked them if they would place a pillow under my head, and they did. Again they told me not to holler, and one said, 'Now let's leave,' and they passed quietly out of the room. After they left, I tried hard to gnaw the straps from my hands with my teeth, without success. I cried, but not very loud, 'Help! help!' but got no answer. I did not dare to shout loud, for fear of more harm from them. I think I must have lain there three hours before reveille, and was in a stupor from blows received. I don't know who could have done this thing. I didn't know that I had an enemy. I think I could recognize at least one of the men by his clothing. I tried to pull his mask off, but he jerked back.

"About a year ago I got a note on which was written: 'Look out!' I don't know where it came from. Last Sunday I found a sealed envelope in my room, and opening it found a note inside which read as follows:

"'Look out; keep awake; you will be fixed.

"'A Friend.'

"I paid no attention to the first note of a year ago, nor did I pay any attention to the warning of Sunday. I felt bad this morning, but am better now. I guess I will come out all right."

When asked afterward if he knew who committed the assault, he said he did not, but thought they were cadets. He had no special enemies, he added, but there was a general feeling against him. The statement that he had done the deed himself, he characterized as a gross outrage. Giving some further details of the affair, he said that one of his assailants suggested that they shave his head, and a few locks of his hair were cut off. The short man, who seems to have been the tender-hearted one of the three, held aloof from the struggle, but at the close offered to put his handkerchief under his ear, so as to stop the bleeding. "Then," continued Whittaker, "one of the men said, 'Get a glass, and let him see himself.' They brought a glass, and after pressing it against my nose, broke it over my head. When they were about to go away, I asked them to put a pillow under my head, and they did so."

Whittaker is twenty-one years of age, and has a complexion so light that he could not be identified as a colored man while parading with his corps. His hair is not very kinky, but his face is covered with freckles. He has handsome eyes, and is very retiring in his manner.

A Court of Inquiry, appointed by General Schofield to investigate the matter, began to take testimony April 9. The members were: Major Mordecai, President; Captain Raymond and Lieutenant Tillman, members; and Lieutenant Sears, Recorder. Lieutenant Knight was appointed to represent Whittaker. Later on, United States District Attorney Martin I. Townsend appeared as the representative of the War Department. Our illustration on page 285 was made at the point when Mr. Townsend, in examining the surgeon, Dr. Alexander, held up the bloody bed-quilt, and asked him to measure the stains. Behind the questioner sits Professor R. T. Greener, of Washington, the friend of Whittaker. To the left of the doctor, whose back is toward us, is the cadet's counsel, Lieutenant Knight, and on the right is the Recorder, Lieutenant Sears. The two officers at the other end of the table are also members of the Court. In the upper left-hand corner is a portrait of Whittaker himself.

REPUBLICANISM IN GEORGIA

THE ATLANTA CONSTITUTION
May 4, 1880

We have already alluded to the differences of opinion that exist between the white republicans of Georgia and the colored voters in regard to the proper distribution of offices, but the situation is so unique—so full of the native humor for which the negro is famous—and the amazed whites take the matter so seriously to heart, that we are tempted to return to the subject not only on account of the interest which we feel in the political future of our colored fellow-citizens, but because the discussion of the question affords and agreeable diversion from the graver topics that are either worn threadbare, or that are not sufficiently developed to require editorial treatment.

We might be tempted to sympathize with the afflicted white republicans in this their hour of bereavement if they meet the emergency with any display of tact or with any suggestion of manliness; but in these respects, they display a most lamentable lack of nerve and of discipline. They pretend, in the first place that their recent meeting, under the auspices of Mr. Jonathan Norcross, was not a movement in opposition to the colored men, and in the same breath admit that the great majority of white republicans in Georgia are so bitterly opposed to the negro that they will not even go to the polls and vote the republican ticket because, to that extent they would be compelled to associate with colored men. What effect the cool announcement of this remarkable fastidiousness will have upon the negroes remains to be seen. But it is to be borne in mind that they have not betrayed any undue sensitiveness with respect to the attitude of white republicans heretofore, and as likely as not they will [treat the] whole matter in that spirit of rollicking good humor which is an excellent disguise for subserviency. The truth is, the recent declaration of independence by the colored leaders was a piece of pardonable buncomb, and it is a little surprising that the whites were not inclined to view it as such. The negroes have become so accustomed to fetch and carry at the beck and nod of the white republicans that they are not yet prepared to take charge of their own affairs. They are competent to do so, but they cannot at once throw off a habit which the white leaders have taken care to nurse and foster until it has become one of the most prominent characteristics of negro citizenship. The interest THE CONSTITUTION takes in this matter is not by any means political, but in the interest of the welfare and development of the negroes themselves, and with a view to hastening the day when their hopes and desires as citizens of the state may in some sort assimilate with the purposes of the white people in all matters pertaining to the political and material prosperity of the commonwealth. For this reason, and for no other, we have been tempted to applaud the recent movement of the colored men.

But at the same time, it was and is perfectly apparent to us that the negroes are not prepared to carry out the designs of the more thoughtful of their leaders. The movement in the convention was a mere wholesome hint of what may take place at some period in the future. In no other way can we account for the aggressiveness of the white republicans; in no other way can we account for the boldness with which the statement is made that there are republicans in Georgia whose prejudices against the negro are so violently unreasonable that they will not go to the polls and vote for fear that the act might in some way compel them to associate with him. Mr. Norcross is evidently convinced that he and his friends possess the means of coercing the negro voters, for he knows that without their aid and support the white republicans would never have the smallest opportunity of tasting the sweets of office.

A remarkable fact in this connection that has not previously been alluded to, is, that during the proceedings of the recent convention when Bryant thought he was weakest, he was really strong. When he was nominated for the chairmanship of the executive committee, he could have carried the convention by a large majority. This was apparent to any close observer. A colored man named White was nominated in opposition, and in the midst of the clamor that ensued, Bryant became demoralized for the first time, and stampeded his friends by withdrawing his name. If he had stood his ground, he would have carried the convention. Even as it is, he accomplished his purpose, and it has been hinted that he will still remain the de facto chairman of the committee. It is to be observed, moreover, that in the meeting at which Mr. Norcross flung down the gauntlets of the high-toned republicans, Bryant was conspicuous by his absence.

We refer to these things merely as matters of desultory interest. They have no sort of bearing upon the campaign. So far as Georgia is concerned, the republican party is a thing of the past. Mr. Jonathan Norcross and his fastidious republican friends may stay away from the polls on grounds of social propriety, or they may venture out; the colored men may attempt to control their own affairs, or they may allow Bryant to control them by proxy; but the democratic party will retain control of state affairs, and if the white republicans hold any offices they will have to depend upon the not very hopeful contingency of a republican victory in the presidential election. And even in that event, they will be asked if they have any other claim beyond the fact that they managed to organize sufficiently to make a feeble attempt to support an electoral ticket.

WEST POINT AND FAIR PLAY

HARPER'S WEEKLY
May 15, 1880, p. 307

A correspondent in Georgia, referring to our recent article upon the colored cadets at West Point, asks whether we really mean that, because some sons of Northern Republicans will not associate with colored classmates, therefore "the South can not be trusted." We certainly mean no such thing. Our argument was that if here in the old Free States the color prejudice is still so strong, it is useless to assert that in the old Slave States it does not injuriously affect the political rights of the colored citizens, and that consequently the assertion that such citizens freely enjoy such rights is presumptively untrue.

The existence of the prejudice we no more deny than the fact of difference of color. But in a public institution of a government which has proclaimed the equality of the races before the law, it is the duty of the government to see that its agents do not suffer any innocent inmate to be treated as if he were a leper or a moral outcast. Cadet Flipper told the story of the treatment to which he was subjected at West Point, and its accuracy is not denied. It is a reproach to Americans and to honorable men. Senator Saulsbury says, in his place in the Senate, that it was cruel to send Whittaker to West Point, because the interests of both races require that there should be distinctions between them in their associations. The Senator says that of color which he would not dare to say of sect or of nativity, and he furnishes another argument for distrusting the control of the government by a party whose leaders deliberately justify—for that is what it comes to—the ostracism of a colored cadet.

We repeat what we have said before, that cadets, like the rest of us, must choose their social companions for themselves; but the inhuman and unmanly treatment of Flipper and Whittaker is not to be dismissed upon any such ground. If the officers of the institution did not sympathize with it, it would not be permitted. As the agents of the government, they are officially bound to see fair play. But whether the colored cadets have had fair play, let the record show. The white cadets may well ponder the words of John A. Andrew: "I know not what record of sin awaits me in the other world; but this I do know, that I never was so mean as to despise any man because he was poor, because he was ignorant, or because he was black."

THE VETO

HARPER'S WEEKLY
May 22, 1880, p. 323

. . . The Election Laws were not originally intended to protect the new vote in the Southern States; they were designed to restrict such frauds as Tweed practiced in New York in 1868. They authorize the appointment of a supervisor in chief, who is a United States Commissioner, selected by the Circuit Judge; two supervisors of election for each election district, appointed by the Circuit or District Judge; and the Marshal with his general and special deputies. In cities of more than 20,000 inhabitants, but not elsewhere, the supervisors may act as special deputies, and summon the *posse comitatus*. They must watch the registration and voting, and see and count every vote that is canvassed. They may satisfy themselves of the right of the voter to cast his ballot, and if any fraud is attempted, they may at once lay the evidence before the courts. These are not laws to which citizens who desire honest elections ought to object. They may be, of course, abused and perverted, like all laws, but that is not an argument against them. They must be guarded against abuse so far as practicable, and that is the object of the amendment recently adopted

"SUNDAY MORNING IN VIRGINIA."—From the Painting by Winslow Homer, in the National Academy of Design.

Harper's Weekly, May 22, 1880, p. 324.

requiring that both political parties shall be represented. Any reasonable amendment offered in good faith is not likely to be vetoed.

RACE PREJUDICE

HARPER'S WEEKLY
May 22, 1880, p. 323

A graduate of West Point who was a classmate of Mr. Flipper, and who writes from a well-known military post, wishes to say a word for the cadets. He takes us to task for censuring the conduct of boys at an academy, and omitting to comment upon the similar conduct of men which might be much more reasonably supposed to be restrained by principle or policy. The best representatives of the colored race, the most intelligent, and the least pronounced in difference from the white race, are nevertheless not treated by the latter as natural and agreeable associates. It is true, he admits, that West Point is a public school, but it is no more a public arena than Congress, and the prejudice of race is just as observable, socially, in Congress as at West Point, and ought to be quite as severely rebuked. "Official discourtesy," he asserts, has been seldom shown to the colored cadets; and although Mr. Smith, who was at the school with Flipper, "early gained for himself the sobriquet of 'Nigger Jim,' he was never so addressed."

The prejudice of race we do not deny. No regulation can make cadets at West Point or members of Congress in Washington associate socially with those who are distasteful to them. A civil rights bill can do no more than secure equal rights before the law, and the regulations at West Point can secure to the cadets only the equal privileges and equal benefits of the school. But when that is said, all is not said by any means.

The abolition of slavery and the elevation of the colored race to equal political and civil rights with the whites was a national declaration that as fast as possible all factitious differences arising from mere prejudice shall be done away. The national authority is pledged to that result, and if at any place under its control its agents tacitly connive at the indulgence of the prejudice, they betray the national purpose, and ought to be removed. If members of Congress, however, treat a colleague as an inferior because of his color, and not of his qualities or habits, it is a meanness for which there is no remedy; and if they choose to encourage the same disposition in a public school under their complete control, there is nothing to be done except to point out the baseness of such conduct and appeal to public opinion.

WEST POINT

HARPER'S WEEKLY
July 3, 1880, p. 419

The report upon the case of Whittaker has been submitted to the Secretary of War, but his decision is not yet announced. Should he disapprove it, it is fair to conclude that the guilt of Whittaker is not as evident as has been assumed. Should he approve it, it is, we suppose, not improbable that Whittaker will demand a court-martial, in which it is to be hoped that the *exparte* evidence and the expert testimony will be thoroughly tested by able counsel.

It is obvious that from the first Whittaker was really assumed to be guilty, and was placed upon trial before an unfriendly court, which had no proper knowledge of the rules of evidence. The one authority upon which his guilt has been generally accepted was the testimony of the experts about the torn edges of the paper. That testimony, however, has not been subjected to the examination of an expert in legal evidence, and, however damaging, it ought not to be received as absolutely conclusive until it has been so tested. Meanwhile there is great emphasis laid upon the fact that Whittaker has been "plucked" in astronomy and philosophy. It is only surprising that he is not plucked in every study, and in heart and hope, by the prejudice which pursues his color and his race.

At the late examination at West Point the Hon. Alexander Ramsay, Secretary of War, made a short speech to the cadets, in which he said, impressively—and he spoke for the American love of justice and fair play:—

"It is peculiarly the duty of all officers of the government by their action to demonstrate the truth of our theory of true national life. It is pre-eminently the duty of all graduates and under-graduates of this Academy, who are the beneficiaries of all our people, to symbolize their faith in the vital source of our national strength, the equality of manhood, by recognizing the right of every person, of whatever condition, to strive for the attainment of such positions as their abilities and desires may warrant. It is an ignoble thing to be governed by an imaginary superiority over any of our less fortunate fellow-citizens, born of adventitious circumstances, and thrice ignoble to make active exhibition of so unworthy a sentiment by oppressing those whom we may deem beneath us. A true manhood dictates the extending of a helping hand to lift up the lowly, and kind words of encouragement to those who are struggling to elevate themselves. I ask you, my young friends, to give some thought to these suggestions, and to cultivate, not only love of country, but as well a love for the sentiment of which our country was born."

The cadets listened in profound silence, and after a moment they burst forth in loud and long applause.

PERSONAL

HARPER'S WEEKLY
July 3, 1880, p. 419

... John Brown's old fort at Harper's Ferry—the engine-house to which he retreated after he could no longer hold the United States Arsenal—was among the Harper's Ferry property the government recently offered at auction, but only one bid of $10,000 was offered, whereas the government holds the premises at $55,000, and the sale was adjourned. The water privilege at Harper's Ferry is considered one of the most valuable in the country, but neither business nor sentimental considerations made a demand for the property, though its intended sale was widely advertised.

A PRACTICAL JOKE

HARPER'S WEEKLY
July 24, 1880, pp. 466–67

A free ballot, we are told by the Democratic platform, is the right preservative of all rights. That was the Garcelon Democratic view, we presume, and the bulldozing Democratic view, and the White League and Ku-Klux Democratic view, and the tissue-ballot Democratic view, and the Tweed and McCunn naturalization Democratic view. If the right of an American citizen, black or white, to vote freely, and to have his vote honestly counted, is anywhere imperiled, it is in the Democratic "solid South," made Democratic by destroying the free ballot. Nobody can have the least doubt that if all authorized voters of every complexion were allowed to vote unconstrained, and if the votes were honestly counted, there would be an enormous Republican majority.

Sir George Campbell, who was in "the South" during the last Congressional election, says that there was not only no question of the tissue-ballot frauds, but that they were openly defended as the best practicable means of securing the ascendency of the whites. Indeed, this particular Democratic form of destroying the right preservative of all rights is also defended by Democratic experts as a much less disagreeable method than the equally familiar Democratic method of the shot-gun. The Returning Boards for which Republicans have been so warmly denounced by Democrats were devices of the law to annul Democratic overthrow of the right preservative of all rights. When in certain districts which were known to have large Republican majorities the entire Republican vote was kept from the polls by Democratic violence, and a loud Democratic demand was heard to have the vote counted as fraudulently cast, the Republicans determined to do something to preserve the right preservative of all rights, and they established Returning Boards with authority to reject the votes of districts in which the rights of the majority, or of large minorities, had been overthrown. Doubtless the Returning Board authority was abused, but that was no reason for permitting Democratic fraud and violence to destroy the rights of voters.

And what remedy has the Democratic majority proposed for this fundamental wrong? It has insisted that the national authority shall have no power to protect its voters, if necessary, by armed force, and it has refused to prohibit armed force to those who threaten such voters. The intelligence and the humor of the country will be equally entertained by a declaration that a free ballot is the right preservative of all rights, proceeding from a party which for many a year has been a conspiracy against free voting and honest counting.

GENERAL GARFIELD'S LETTER

HARPER'S WEEKLY
July 31, 1880, p. 482

General Garfield's letter of acceptance cordially approves the Chicago platform, and elaborates some of its points. His position in regard to the nature and extent of the national power is that which he has always maintained, and which is undoubtedly that of the country. His expression of it is unequivocal, and is in no way inconsistent with what he has said in Congress. While he heartily sustains national election laws, he thinks them capable of amendment. But in this letter it is the principle, not the detail, that he naturally considers. The question of free elections, of the right of every voter to be protected by the government in which he is discharging his part, is fundamental. It is one of the great results of the war, but it is not yet acknowledged in many parts of the Southern States, and it is a question quite as vital as commercial prosperity and industrial enterprise. The "Southern Question" exists so long as there is a general and systematic suppression of the colored vote. It is by that suppression, which is the permanent overthrow of the most essential political right, that the South is made solid; and the South is solid for no national and patriotic purpose that has been as yet disclosed. The attitude of the Democratic party toward the new citizens in the Southern States is essentially hostile to the government itself by constantly casting doubt upon the honesty of the vote of a large section. While this condition of things endures, the Republican party can not be divided.

General Garfield being in himself a hard-money platform, all that he says upon the finances is sound, although he might have said more as to future policy. There are still important problems before us, and one great advantage of General Garfield's candidacy is that his clear convictions are so well known as to assure the country that his administration would take no backward steps. His remarks upon the tariff imply a leaning to protection, which he has always shown. But this is a point upon which neither party is agreed. General Garfield's treatment of the Chinese question shows that he hopes much from the Angell commission, and that he favors some kind of restriction of that immigration. . . .

THE DEMOCRATIC PLEA

HARPER'S WEEKLY
August 7, 1880, p. 498

All the preliminaries of the campaign have been arranged as we write, except the letter of General Hancock. That has not yet appeared; but it is understood, as the play-bills say, to be in active preparation. We may be very sure, however, that it will not differ materially from the Cincinnati platform and the letter of the committee announcing to him the nomination. If he had been known or supposed to hold views seriously different from those declarations, General Hancock would not have been nominated. His only "record," apart from his service in the field, is that of military Governor of Louisiana; and if that had not been interpreted as favorable to the Democratic view of the situation at that time—if, in a word, it had not been so favorable to those lately in rebellion as to suggest that he was even then contemplating the nomination—he would not have been nominated now. As a Union general merely, however loyal and brave and successful, he would not have been selected or supported. We have looked carefully to see upon what general policy or leading question the Democratic party asks the confidence of the country. The presumption, of course, is against it. It went out of power twenty years ago as a party seeking the extension of slavery, and threatening disunion if it could not have its way. For the next four years, actively at the South, and passively at the North, it aimed at the overthrow of the government. Since the war it has perplexed and obstructed the general plan of reconstruction approved by the country. This is its general history, and it is this which creates the presumption against it. What argument does it now offer?

The Cincinnati platform declared that the "fraud issue" "precedes and dwarfs every other." The New York *Sun,* while the Convention was in session, said, "If the Democrats do not nominate Mr. Tilden, they do relinquish the fraud issue—the strength of their canvass." But the Convention immediately rejected Mr. Tilden. General Hancock plainly does not represent the issue which in Democratic judgment precedes and dwarfs every other. Indeed, the letter of the committee of the Convention is ludicrously at variance with the platform, and justifies the remark of the Sun that the fraud issue has been abandoned. Instead of saying that General Hancock represents the issue which "precedes and dwarfs all others," the letter says:

> "That which chiefly inspired your nomination was the fact that you have conspicuously recognized and exemplified the yearning of the American people for reconciliation and brotherhood under the Constitution, with all its jealous care and guarantees for the rights of persons and of States."

This is in accord with the general tone of the Democratic press. Thus the serious pleas are two: that the Democratic party is the party of the Constitution, and that General Hancock stands for reconciliation. But as the armed overthrow of the Constitution was attempted by the controlling force of the Democratic party, under the plea of traditional Democratic principles of State rights, this argument is not powerful. The party which claims to be that of constitutional liberty is the party which has sought, by destroying the liberty of speech and of the press, to annihilate the personal liberty of millions of our fellow-countrymen. The Democratic party is historically that of slavery, not of liberty. Its respect for the Constitution was shown from the first shot at Sumter down to the last shot of Lee's army. The theories upon which those Democratic shots were fired were urged by Democrats in the extra session as a plea for starving the government. It is surely not this party, but the one which was formed to protect liberty assailed by Democrats, which was loyal to the Constitution, and which saved the Union from Democratic arms, which, as against the Democratic party, is the party of liberty, of the Union, and of the Constitution.

And how does General Hancock, as a Democratic candidate, represent "reconciliation"? Because, we are told, although a Union soldier, "the South" is willing to support him, while, if he should be defeated, reconciliation would be postponed. But General Hancock is no more a Union soldier than General Garfield, and if reconciliation is to be postponed should General Garfield be elected, the argument amounts only to saying that if "the South" can dictate the President, it will be "reconciled." This argument disposes of itself. "I am the most amiable of men, my dear," said the young husband to his bride; "I ask only to have my own way." By this kind of reasoning we might say that the loyal States will be reconciled to the South if "the South" will vote for General Garfield. What is the meaning of this word "reconciliation"? Why is "the South" not "reconciled"? Is "the North" to be forgiven? Is "the South" gravely to play in the Union the part of John Kelly at Cincinnati, and pardon the loyal country? The Democratic tactics are the very madness of sectionalism. Here is a section of the country which has plunged the Union into a sanguinary contest, in which the section was worsted, and after fifteen years, during which all that has been asked of it is no penalty, but the acceptance of equal liberty for all citizens, it is seriously announced that the section will be "reconciled" upon condition that the control of the government is placed in its hands. As an argument for the support of General Hancock, this is simply silly. The only ground upon which "reconciliation"—that is to say, sectional harmony—is possible, is the acquiescence of every section in equal civil and political liberty. The parties of the war continue because that equality is denied in the old slave-holding section, and the last reason that would persuade a loyal American to vote for General Hancock is that his election, by giving the government to those who practically deny constitutional equal rights, would "reconcile" or pacify them.

FREE VOTING

HARPER'S WEEKLY
August 7, 1880, pp. 498–99

A Western correspondent asks for the evidence that free voting is prevented in the Southern States. He will find it in all the Congressional reports upon elections since 1865, especially in the Stevenson Louisiana report of 1869, and the Mississippi reports, and in letters from Louisiana after the disputed election of 1876. The terror in certain parishes of that State is as well established as any other accepted fact of history. The evidence of Democratic tissue-ballot frauds in the South Carolina elections is the ballots themselves, many of which we have seen as prepared for use. They could have had no other object than fraud, and that there might be no question, the intention of fraud was frankly confessed.

The best—because wholly non-partisan—witness to this last fact is Sir George Campbell. During a journey in this country two or three years since, he was in many of the Southern States, and he reports that there was no concealment whatever, and that the tissue ballot, or fraud, was considered a preferable method of suppressing the colored vote to the shot-gun, or violence. There is no more reasonable doubt of Democratic electoral fraud in many of the doubtful districts in the Southern States than there was of the Tweed frauds in New York. The election law of Louisiana creating the Returning Board, with its extraordinary powers, was adopted in 1870 because of the virtual violent destruction of the right of free voting in many parts of that State.

A few figures will be useful to our correspondent. In the year 1868 the official registration of Republican voters in various parishes in Louisiana was as follows: St. Landry, 3069; Bossier, 1938; Caddo, 2894; Jefferson, 3562; St. Bernard, 679. In September, October, and November, 1868, the number of political murders in thirty-five parishes of the State, including those we have mentioned, according to official returns, was more than 1000. At the election in 1868 the actual Republican votes in the parishes of which we have mentioned the registration were as follows: St. Landry, none; Bossier, 1; Caddo, 1; Jefferson, 672; St. Bernard, 1. It was to prevent the practical annihilation of the Republican vote that the new election laws were passed. It was also because of this annihilation by terror that the Democrats in 1876 insisted that the vote should be counted as cast. Thus, in the two noted parishes of East and West Feliciana, the registered colored vote, which was mainly Republican, was 3046. The Republican vote as cast was 781. It is thus that "the right preservative of all rights" has been destroyed by Democratic force in parts of one Southern State. It is for our correspondent to decide whether freedom of voting is as secure in "the South" as in "the North," and whether, under a Democratic national administration adopting and enforcing the Democratic views of the extra session, a free vote and a fair count in those States are more probable than they are now.

"THE SOUTH."

HARPER'S WEEKLY
August 28, 1880, p. 546

Whenever a Republican speaks of "the South," except to pity or to praise it, he is denounced as an apostle of hate. If he asks why "the South" should be intrusted with the government, he is reviled for shaking the bloody shirt. If he appeals to history to show what "the South" means, and what the dominance of "the South" portends, he is stigmatized as wickedly sectional. But "the South" can be no more left out of this campaign than slavery out of that of 1860, or the war from that of 1864, or reconstruction from that of 1868. The primary Democratic allegation is that "the South" is solid for the Democratic candidates, and Wade Hampton pledges its 138 electoral votes to them. This is generally conceded. The electoral vote of "the South" will be cast for them, because the popular vote will not be cast freely nor counted fairly. The only way in which the Democratic party can succeed is by obtaining the 138 electoral votes of "the South" in the usual Southern way, and by picking up 47 votes in "the North." Democratic success, therefore, is the success of "the South," and that fact is the most important in the canvass. There is no use in calling such a result Democratic, not only because it has nothing to do with Democracy, but because it is best to call things by their right names. The election of Hancock would be the control of the government by "the South." Is it desirable that "the South" should control the government? That is not a question of Republican choosing. It is raised by the facts of the case.

If to state the facts and to ask the question is to show hate, and to shake the bloody shirt, and to be sectional, we are certainly and gladly guilty of all those offenses. Since the question whether "the South" shall control the government is unavoidable and paramount, we shall consider it, and we naturally ask what "the South" means. How can we estimate probable action except by experience? The Democratic party is rigorously and unscrupulously testing the Republican party by its record. But when the Republicans retort, "Very well, since you wish to control, what are your credentials?" The Democrats burst into a whining chorus, "Oh, by-gones must be by-gones; don't let us fight the war over again; don't be sectional; don't shake the bloody shirt; don't talk about fiat money, or the extra session, or Garcelon, or the alliance of Northern slums and Southern bulldozing and tissue-ballot stuffing; don't fan the fires of hate, but let us be brethren, and dwell in amity." In other words, they insist that the Republican party shall be tried by its deeds, and the Democratic party by its promises. To ask to see the credentials of the party that would control the government is to preach the gospel of hate, and to thrive by sectional prejudice.

This is nonsense which deceives nobody. Since Democratic success in 1880 means Southern domination as plainly as Republican success in 1860 meant Northern supremacy, the relevant inquiry is whether the objects which good citizens desire will be attained more probably under Southern control. That question can be answered intelligibly only by inquiring what "the South" means. It can not be answered by not asking. If a man seeks to be trusted with a ship, the owner will certainly inquire who he is and what he has done. If the traditions and principles and spirit and tendency and acts of "the South" have been such as to promise sounder financial policy, surer correction of the corruption of patronage, wiser taxation, greater security of equal rights, diminution of sectional feeling, and vigorous suppression of fraud and violence at the polls than are probable under Republican ascendency, then "the South" may be safely called to administer the government, but not otherwise. How is this to be ascertained but by inquiry? And what is more absurd than to call such inquiry preaching hate and shaking the bloody shirt? If anybody supposes that a general election can take place in this country, while a "solid South" continues, without reference to the war and to political and national history, he is strangely mistaken. Sectional politics are dangerous politics. Our own can not be normal and sound so long as there is a "solid South." Why is it solid? Why does it not feel the

PARADE-DAY.—Drawn by H. P. Wolcott.

Harper's Weekly, August 14, 1880, p. 517.

currents and influences that divide the country elsewhere? As the little "Half-hour" book, *Republican or Democrat?* of which we spoke last week, truly says, the South is solid either for a sectional purpose or because of resentment. It is made solid not by conviction, but by coercion and cheating. In three of the Southern States at least there are more colored than white citizens. That the colored citizens are Democrats the marines or Judus Apelles may believe. That their votes are largely bought is not alleged. That they are bulldozed is known. It was not at all necessary for Mr. Randolph Tucker to tell us how the South is made solid. It is "familiar knowledge." Now the fact that the South is solid is no reason for supposing that a Southern-Hancock administration would secure the objects which we have mentioned more certainly than a Republican administration, and that "the South" would be appeased or conciliated by Democratic success is no reason for giving it the government. If any reason can be found in the tone of Southern sentiment, in the traditional political theories of that section, or in its history before, during, or since the war, for supposing that American principles and civilization and progress would be more assured by Southern supremacy in public affairs, we do not know what it is nor where to look for it. The Democratic party by suppressing the colored vote makes a "solid South," and we are asked to give the government into the hands of that "solid South" because to do so will conciliate it, and not to do so is sectional hate. In this situation, which is that offered to us by the Democratic party, we are glad to recall the sententious wisdom of a village philosopher— "The American people are not a fool."

THAT WICKED RETURNING BOARD

HARPER'S WEEKLY
August 28, 1880, p. 547

The Democrats have denounced the Louisiana Returning Board as the most iniquitous of institutions, a mere legal device for monstrous fraud, unconstitutional and wicked. There are a great many persons who have been persuaded by Democratic declamation that the Louisiana Returning Board was the means of defrauding the country of a rightful result at the last election. But the Democrats have been in complete possession of Louisiana for three years. They have, of course, repealed this wicked law? Far from it. They were in power in the State in 1872, and they made the law more stringent. They are in power now, and the law is unrepealed. Like many laws passed to protect the oppressed, it may be enforced so as to increase oppression. The Louisiana Returning Board was a Republican device to protect bulldozed districts. It will now be used by Democrats to

GENERAL HANCOCK'S NEW COMMAND.

Harper's Weekly, August 21, 1880, p. 540.

annul Republican majorities. The virtuous horror affected by Democrats was a campaign trick. The Democratic Returning Board will do its share in making the South "solid" by throwing out Republican majorities wherever they shall seem to throw doubt upon the result. We shall hear no more from Democrats of the appalling wickedness of the Returning Board.

"SOLIDIFYING" ALABAMA

HARPER'S WEEKLY
September 11, 1880, p. 578

The report of the Republican State Committee of Alabama upon the frauds of the late election recites nothing unfamiliar, but it describes in detail the method by which "the South"—that is, the Democratic vote—is made "solid." The report should be generally circulated and read, because it treats of one of the ways in which popular government is overthrown by the Democratic party, and of the means by which Hancock's electoral vote is to be obtained. The Democrats in Alabama, when they came into power in 1874, changed the excellent electoral laws, so as to make fraud easier. The changes are fully described in the report, and their purpose is obvious. One of the changes enables inspectors to "cook" the returns without difficulty, and another forbids distinguishing ballots by any kind of mark or number. It is curious to remark that the opposition to registries and every other method of preventing fraud and securing an honest election proceeds from the Democratic party. Naturalization frauds in New York, repeating in Connecticut, the Ku-Klux and bulldozing, the shot-gun and the tissue ballot, in the Southern States, are familiar Democratic devices for "a free vote and a fair count."

The Alabama report mentions one incident to which "the thoughtful patriot"—who is much satirized, but who is still the true American—should direct his attention, and meditate a Presidential election carried by such means. At one polling place in Montgomery County the Republicans received their tickets from one man, giving him their names, and going directly from him, holding the ballot in full view, and dropping it in the box. By actual count they polled 672 votes, and at the close of the poll one of the Republican inspectors demanded that the vote, as the law directs, should be counted immediately. The Democratic inspectors, one of whom was under indictment for "stuffing" ballot-boxes, objected under various pretexts. Presently a military company appeared, under orders from the Governor of the State, and "bayonets" surrounded the poll, summoned by Democrats to protect the accomplishment of their intended fraud against what they

AFRICAN AMERICAN HISTORY IN THE PRESS, 1851-1899

UP-HILL WORK.

Harper's Weekly, September 4, 1880, p. 561.

supposed would be the indignation of the swindled voters, under the plea that the inspectors were threatened. The "count" was then begun. After 116 Republican and 59 Democratic ballots had been counted, the candle was blown out, and the ballot-box vanished. When the candle was lighted, the box was found to be full of tickets, and the colored Republican inspector protested. His associates resented the imputation upon their integrity in so demonstrative a way that he retreated. Re-assured by his friends outside, the inspector attempted to return, but was told that having voluntarily abandoned his post, he could not resume it; and the other inspectors completed the count, making a return of 132 Republican and 540 Democratic votes. It thus appears that while of the 175 votes taken from the box when the Republican inspector was present 116 were Republican, of the 500 taken out when he had left his post only 16 were Republican. But if there were but 132 colored Republicans, how could they have terrorized 540 colored and white Democrats so as to require an armed military company to protect them?

This is the Democratic respect for what the party platform calls "the right preservative of all rights." It is open, undeniable, and undenied fraud. It is the method by which the Democratic party intends to carry "the South," and while it is doing so, it denounces exposure of the crime as shaking the bloody shirt. It is the most deadly crime against popular government and national peace; but if any Republican chooses to call attention to it instead of discussing the currency or reform, he is accused of fighting the war over again. It is gravely asserted that if we lived in the Southern States we should all do the same, and that under no circumstances should we submit to "negro rule." That is merely to say that intelligent citizens would not tolerate the government of the ignorant. It is untrue. The greatest city on the continent tolerates it. Hundreds of communities everywhere in the country tolerate it. Popular government always takes that risk. But the man, or the party, or the community, that attempts to prevent it by fraud or force, overthrows popular government and invites anarchy. The white voters in Alabama and Mississippi and South Carolina, when they stuff ballot-boxes to prevent "negro rule," cheat New York, New England, the Northwest, and the whole Union of its honest and legal will. Reform of this infamous outrage upon the central principle of our institutions is the most urgent of all reforms. The systematic destruction of the honest vote of large districts is a peril which necessarily takes precedence of all other issues in a popular government.

SECTIONALISM AND NATIONALISM

HARPER'S WEEKLY
September 18, 1880, p. 594

The only document that we have seen which is in any proper sense a Democratic argument in this election is a letter of Mr. John Pool's, of North Carolina, an old Henry Clay Whig of that State, and more recently a Senator in Congress "in affiliation with the Republican party." Mr. Pool says that in his judgment the great issue is that of nationality against sectionalism, and that now when there are two candidates, "the one striving to be elected by a sectional vote, and the other basing no hopes of an election except upon votes from both sections, one

THE ALABAMA PLAN WORKS LIKE MAGIC.
ALABAMIAN. "Put up your shot-gun, Mississippi: this way is better, and *looks more civilized;* and, besides, it don't reduce the census."

Harper's Weekly, September 11, 1880, p. 592.

seeking a sectional triumph, the other a national," he will, in short, vote for General Hancock. This extract is an illustration of the want of candor in the letter. The fact is that the only hope of General Hancock's election lies in a perfectly solid section, and a section made solid by fraud and violence. Without that fraud and violence which after fifteen years have finally suppressed a large part of the Republican vote in Mr. Pool's section of the country, General Garfield's election by a national vote would be overwhelming. Mr. Pool's argument is absolutely futile, unless he can show that the vote in the Southern States is freely cast and honestly counted, and that neither he nor anybody else can show. The proof of the contrary is conclusive. What he says now was said in 1860. It was urged that Mr. Lincoln was not a national candidate because he had no support in the Southern States. But he had no support in the Southern States because the Democrats would have murdered his supporters. Nor can Mr. Pool and his Democratic friends pretend to parallel the alleged coercion of his workmen by some proprietor in a Northern State with the wholesale violent repression of an entire vote in the Southern States. Mr. Pool is, we hope, unjust to himself, as he certainly insults the common-sense of intelligent Republicans who are no more vindictive or sectional than he, when he assumes that the solidity of his section, which is the basis of Democratic hope in this election, is legitimate or honest.

From the passage of the Black Codes, including the vagrant and contract laws—codes enforced by the vast and efficient terrorism known as the Ku-Klux Klan—down to the bulldozing of 1876, and the still more recent tissue ballots, the policy of Mr. Pool's section has been to establish the old Democratic slave-holding dogma that this is a white man's government. As Mr. Marten, a Southern Democratic orator in Vermont, recently said, the Southern whites having obtained some forty electoral votes and votes in Congress upon the basis of the colored population, propose to hold those votes, that is, to nullify the colored suffrage. This has been the steady policy of "the South"—that is, the white Democrats in the Southern States—since the war. The Ku-Klux Klan, the organized system of terror, has largely accomplished its purpose. We do not now hear of many "outrages," in the old sense. Naturally not. Order reigns in Warsaw, and by the familiar methods. The terror has done its work. The short-gun has yielded in due order to the tissue ballot. But the shot-gun stands within reach; the Ku-Klux could be rallied again at once upon the least pretense, and "the South" is solid only because of the general system known as Ku-Klux, and not, as Mr. Pool says, because of Republican oppression. He knows, undoubtedly, that Republican reconstruction was not vindictive, but equitable. He knows, or ought to know, that to abandon the freedmen to the Black Codes, the vagrant laws, and the contract laws, without the ballot, would have been a national crime second only to slavery. He knows certainly that the Republican settlement of the war was unprecedented in history for mildness and equity. There were no executions or confiscations. Nothing whatever was required but a guarantee of justice; and if the suffrage was prematurely conferred, it was because the white Democrats who complain of it made it indispensable. That they have nullified it by force and fraud only shows how deep and vital and malignant was the spirit which confronted Republican reconstruction. Even Mr. Pool, however, is compelled to do homage to the patriotism of that policy. He admits that it was "the triumph of the more moderate over the more extreme sentiments of Congress," and he says that he vainly tried to persuade "the South" to accept it "promptly and in good faith." Had "the South" done so, he says, the sorrows that followed would have been avoided.

Mr. Pool, of course, here "gives away" his whole case. The white Democrats of the Southern States did not accept in good faith the measures that they pretended to accept. The basis of reconstruction was equal suffrage, and equal suffrage they have prevented and destroyed. In other words, by illicit and inhuman means, and despite the law, they have done all that they possibly could do to nullify and reverse reconstruction upon a fundamental point while the national Government was Republican, and they now complain because it is feared that they might attempt to nullify and reverse other essential points if they should obtain complete control of the executive and legislative power. It is this perfectly logical and legitimate apprehension which holds the Republican party together, and makes a practically solid North, not by crime and terror, but by intelligent perception and conviction. If the white citizens of the Southern States had shown that they accepted in good faith—as Mr. Pool admits that they did not, and as some amiable and loyal men, like the late General Bartlett, in this part of the country, assumed that they did accept—the principle of reconstruction, both of the war parties would have disappeared. We do not think, indeed, that it was to be expected, and we have never been surprised at the result. But nothing could be more unfounded than the assertion that the Republicans have compelled the solidity of "the South," that is, of the white voters. If, indeed, they had left the freedmen to the Black Codes, the old Democratic leaders who made those codes, instead of calling Republicans sectional because they insisted upon an equal ballot, would have called them sectional because they would not compensate slaveowners and pension rebel soldiers. There is no greater treachery to the principles established by the war—and not less treachery because it is the act of well-meaning but shallow persons—than the assertion that to alarm the country against the control of the government by those who have nullified the right of suffrage in the Southern States is to revive old hates and agitate settled issues. The only sectionalism which threatens the country is not that of a party which demands that the right of every citizen to vote freely shall be everywhere respected and protected, but that which makes the States lately in rebellion against the government "solid" by force and fraud and indescribable crimes, in order to obtain control of the government. If Mr. Pool wishes to abate sectionalism, let him and his friends continue their efforts to persuade "the South" to accept in good faith the principle of reconstruction, and to cease to suppress the colored vote.

MAKING A "SOLID SOUTH."

HARPER'S WEEKLY
October 2, 1880, p. 626

Extensive preparations are making to secure a "solid South," and "a free vote and a fair count." Readers of the newspapers will have observed ex-Governor Perry's exhortation in South Carolina:

> "Every true Democrat and every honorable man should rise up in the majesty of his strength, and swear on the altar of his country and his God that this [Republican success] shall not be, let the consequences be what they may. The poor, miserable, unprincipled white man who tries to restore the Radical party to power in South Carolina should be socially ostracized, and not even spoken to on the streets. He should be treated as an enemy to his race. 'Hostis humani generis.' The colored man should be told that his leaders are making tools of him only to gratify their pitiable ambition, and have a chance of stealing

1880

THE GREAT DEMOCRATIC MORAL SHOW.

Harper's Weekly, September 25, 1880, p. 616.

his hard earnings. He should be told, too, that if he will vote to place rogues and scoundrels in office and power, no honorable Democrat will employ him in any way. This should be resolved on and adhered to throughout the State—social ostracism for the white man, and no employment for the colored man."

The Aiken *Journal and Review* remarks:

> "The negroes are forming all over the county. It then behooves the Democrats to go to work at once and forestall the plans of the Radicals. The first thing to be done is to reorganize the red-shirt mounted clubs. Let every meeting, Democratic or Radical, be fully attended by them."

The Greenville *News* deprecates nailing anybody's ears to the pump:

> "We do not advocate the use of the short-gun or the 'bull-whip.' We do advocate full use of such means as we can use lawfully. We mean that the white-skinned man who joins with the corrupt remains of the party of corruption in this State should be a social leper—shunned, despised, and hated. We mean that the white-skinned man or negro who deliberately enters the fight for a Radical State ticket will do so with the understanding that he will hereafter receive no favors or recognition from white men. Let them understand that there will be no employment for them where it is possible to avoid it; that there will be no credit given them; that from them the last farthing will be relentlessly exacted; that the kindness of masters will cease."

The Red Shirt clubs and the general white Democratic attendance at Republican meetings are the present form of the Ku-Klux. The more active and heroic methods of midnight hunting, harrying, scourging, and ear-cropping of Republicans, the flagrant terror of "the Mississippi plan" and the shot-gun, have largely subdued and suppressed the Republican voters in the districts where they are a majority, so that tissue ballots and false counts will now generally secure the desired result. But the Democrats are still obliged to take some trouble, as appears from this recent special dispatch to the Columbia *Register,* describing a Republican meeting at Abbeville:

> "The Radicals are in session, nominating delegates to the State Convention. There was a slim turn-out. The stores are closed, and the Democrats will attend.
>
> "Later.—The meeting was captured by the Democrats. Colonel Cothan, and Wallingford, an elector on the Greenback ticket of Indiana, made speeches, and the Rads dispersed."

The usual Democratic treatment of these facts is either to sneer that to allude to them is to wave the bloody shirt

THE LONG-SUFFERING AND PATIENT RACE.

COLORED POLITICIAN. "So, Uncle Tom, I hears you's a-goin' ter vote fer Gen'l HANCOCK?"
UNCLE TOM. "No, sah; I votes fer Massa GARFIELD straight, and will be counted out. But, young man, don't laugh, I's waited long for Freedom, and now I'll wait till my Vote *is* counted, and de good Lord knows it *will* be."

Harper's Weekly, September 25, 1880, p. 617.

and to foster a wicked sectionalism, or else to dismiss them with the remark that if a majority permits a minority to impose upon it, there is nothing to be done....

THE QUESTION

HARPER'S WEEKLY
October 23, 1880, p. 674

The question of the election, we are told, is, which of the two parties is more likely to govern the country wisely and well; and again, whether the present prosperous and contented public situation will be more disturbed or more surely maintained by a change of administration. This is substantially the question of the campaign. It is with this debate that the country rings. All the gentlemen who are announced in the papers to speak every day and every night, upon one side or the other, are speaking upon this question. Mr. Evarts, at the Cooper Institute, brilliantly shows that a change would be unwise from every point of view. Mr. Seymour, at Chickering Hall, argues that such a change is most desirable. This, indeed, is always the question of a Presidential campaign; and the necessary point of departure of the debate is the principles, professions, history, and character of the parties. How, indeed, can we tell whether a ship is likely to carry us safely, until we have investigated ship and crew? and how absurd it would be if we were told, when we wished to look into the hold, that we ought not to do that, because it would be sure to excite unpleasant feeling. Yet that is precisely the manner in which Republicans are accosted when they propose to consider what the antecedents and spirit and tendency of the Democratic party are. The one great glaring fact in the history and present situation of that party is that it is a Southern party. Deduct "the South," and the Democratic party practically disappears. Yet to inquire into this fact, to try to ascertain what it means and what it promises, is declared to be a kind of wickedness, proving a bad heart, and showing a ferocious disposition to alienate brethren, and foster a hateful sectionalism.

This is exceedingly droll. Mr. Wade Hampton, for instance, comes into the State of New York. He denounces the extravagance, the corruption, the centralization, of the Republican party. He complains of its distrust and hostility toward his own part of the country, and insists that its present administration was born of fraud, and that it is, in a word, the enemy of the peace, prosperity, and progress of the country. He then asserts that his own region has heartily acquiesced in the results of the unpleasantness, that it cheerfully recognizes the changed conditions of affairs, and the equality of all citizens; that it is overflowing with brotherly love and good-will to man, especially the colored man, and that the only serpent in the paradise is that monster, compact of every crime, the Republican party. But if in the same State Mr. Evarts, or Mr. Depew, or any other eminent Republican, proposes to look into the nature of this hearty acquiescence, and at this overflow of brotherly affection for everybody, especially the colored voter, and to ask whether a free vote and a fair count are to be secured by Mr. Hampton and his friends, and if, still prosecuting these perfectly legitimate inquiries, he proceeds to ask what is this party of Mr. Hampton's, what has it done, what views has it held, and how and why, with its history and character and spirit, it is more likely to administer the government more wisely for all citizens and all interests than the Republican party, he is assailed by Mr. Hampton's party presses and fellow-orators as thirsting for blood, and rekindling old embers of strife, and preaching the devil's gospel of brotherly hate. And while this is the fate of Mr. Evarts and Mr. Depew and their Republican associates in New York, if a Republican club holds a meeting in Mr. Hampton's own State, the Democratic Rifle Clubs and Red Shirts and Regulators of every kind shut up their shops, attend the meeting armed, and insist upon sharing the time with the speakers or silencing them altogether.

But if in one part of the country to inquire what the Democratic party has done, in order to determine what it probably will do, is wicked sectionalism, and in another part not to be a Democrat is to be silenced by hook or by crook, how is the debate to proceed? It is apparently proper, in the estimation of Democratic journals, for Democrats to show what Republicans have done, but it is something in the nature of a crime for Republicans to show what Democrats have done. It is perfectly legitimate, by Democratic standards, to hold Republicans responsible for the Whiskey Ring four years ago, but altogether devilish to hold the Democrats responsible for the massacre and murder and harrying of colored voters at the same time, and for the systematic and organized cheating of the tissue ballots. In a word, unable to deny the flagrant crimes intended to seize the government by force and fraud at the polls, the Democrats try to distract the public eye and mind by insisting that it is unbrotherly to allude to the crimes, while apparently it is not to be thought wrong and wicked and bloody and sectional and unfraternal to commit them. For the crimes themselves not a Democratic orator or paper has a word of condemnation. But they unite in decrying as stirrers up of fraternal strife and assassins of union those who expose them, and who warn the country against the domination of a party which seeks power by such means. The Democrats would prefer speculations about finance and the tariff; but the one natural, logical, inevitable question of the campaign, namely, Does the Democratic party show by what it did when it had the national power, and by what it does where it has the local power to-day, that it would probably adopt a wiser financial policy, more surely protect the equal rights of all citizens, and more certainly promote administrative reform?—this is the question

AFRICAN AMERICAN HISTORY IN THE PRESS, 1851-1899

HARPER'S WEEKLY.
JOURNAL OF CIVILIZATION.

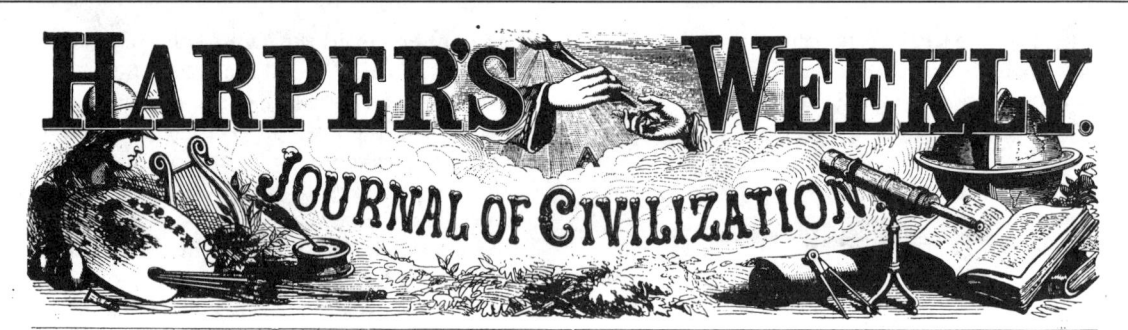

Vol. XXIV.—No. 1243.] NEW YORK, SATURDAY, OCTOBER 23, 1880. [SINGLE COPIES TEN CENTS. $4.00 PER YEAR IN ADVANCE.

Entered according to Act of Congress, in the Year 1880, by Harper & Brothers, in the Office of the Librarian of Congress, at Washington.

"FREEDOM OF SUFFRAGE TO THE BLACKS MEANS FREEDOM OF SUFFRAGE TO THE WHITES."—EVARTS.
SOLID SOUTH. "Hurry up, dough-face, and shut up your side. Mine is *solid*."

Harper's Weekly, October 23, 1880, p. 673.

970

which they declare no true lover of his country can ask, while, in fact, no true lover of his country would ask any other.

A SOUTHERN VIEW

HARPER'S WEEKLY
October 30, 1880, p. 690

The Republican administration of President Hayes has unquestionably fulfilled the Republican demand of the Cincinnati platform, upon which he was nominated, for the permanent pacification of the country. The administration, as we have constantly said, is one of the most powerful arguments for Republican success, not only because of an ability which is not questioned, and of a purity which even scandal does not assail, but because of the feeling which it has produced among quiet and intelligent business men in the Southern States. There is no doubt that there is a moral coercion in those States like that which preceded the war. At that time the suspicion of sympathy with Northern or antislavery sentiment was fatal to business success. The tyranny of opinion was absolute and remorseless, and would have been impossible except in an aristocratic or oligarchic society like that of "the South" before the war—a society composed of a few great proprietors monopolizing the wealth and the political power, a large multitude of ignorant and poor citizens subject to this class, and of slaves owned by it. This was as un-American a society as could be imagined, and the conflict between it and real American principles and instincts was inevitable. The maintenance of slavery was the common object of the two white classes in the Southern States, and there was a total suppression of freedom of speech and action hostile to slavery. This disposition went so far as to denounce merchants at the North who sold goods but not principles, and any Southern trader who dealt with any such merchant whose name was posted upon the black list was renounced by the community in which he lived.

This kind of moral coercion still survives. Slavery has been abolished, but the Southern white who is supposed to favor what General Hancock calls "nigger domination" is suspected and marked. There is the same old Bourbon terrorism, as may be seen in the columns of the Charleston Courier, and in the advice of ex-Governor Perry. In communities, like many in the Southern States, full of bitterness following the war—like that which recently made two ladies in a Southern city step into the muddy street rather than pass under the American flag—full, also, of the mingled antipathy and contempt for the race whose freedom is a memorial of defeat, and with all the old ignorance and hot passion and prejudice of ante-bellum days, the force of this coercion is evident. To be known as a Republican, or friendly to Republican success, is to be in favor of "nigger domination," and that is punished by social ostracism and hatred, and by business loss and injury. The great mass of persons engaged in business in the Southern States, therefore, however they may "leave politics alone," and regret this degrading tyranny of Bourbonism, are included in the Democratic party, acquiesce in the fraud and violence of the Democratic managing politicians, and will vote for the Democratic candidate. They do so because they do not dare to do otherwise. But there are many among them who see as clearly as any intelligent man at the North that to intrust the government of the Union to the class which makes and enforces this tyranny is a most dangerous madness. These men give no sign at home. They subscribe to pay Democratic expenses. They are enrolled in Democratic clubs. They will vote for General Hancock. They do not dare to do otherwise, but they hope and pray for the election of General Garfield.

The reason is obvious. The administration of Mr. Hayes has pursued a policy of constitutional non-interference. While it has been perfectly ready, and has been known to be ready, firmly to enforce the whole extent of constitutional authority, its friendly and pacific disposition has been equally known, and its freedom from the control of questionable Republican counsels. During this administration, and despite the practical violent and fraudulent suppression of the colored vote which had been accomplished before President Hayes came in, the business interests of "the South" have greatly increased and flourished. They share the general prosperity of the country, and there is a class of business men in those States who are as little desirous of a change which can by no possibility help them, and may very easily and very probably injure them, as the great mass of business men in other parts of the country. Such Southern men have unconsciously, yet naturally, experienced a change of heart which they had not thought possible. They have come to associate prosperity, success, and content with the Republican name. They do not, indeed, like the name, and they do not take it. But they see that Republican success would assure and confirm their prosperity, and while, for the reasons we have stated, they will vote for Hancock, they hope that Garfield will be elected. Four years of a Republican administration which would continue the equable and just policy of the administration of President Hayes—and such would be the course of the Garfield administration—would tend to the dissolution of the solid South. The class of which we speak, taking advantage of local contentions, would break with the Bourbons, and secure at least a freedom of discussion and action which would be fatal to the tyranny under which the intelligent and business circles in the Southern States still lie. It is in this way, as in so many others, that the Republican cause is that of the country, and breaks that sectional bondage which has been always the curse of "the South."

THE FRIEND OF THE FREEDMEN.

"Now, that we have made them free, we will stand by these black allies! We will stand by them until the sun of liberty shall shine with equal ray upon every man, black or white, throughout the Union!"—GENERAL GARFIELD, August 6, 1880.

WHAT HANCOCK SAID.

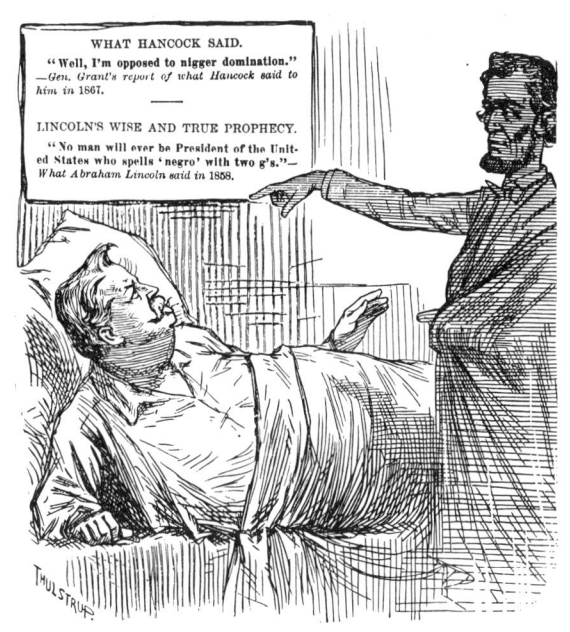

"Well, I'm opposed to nigger domination."
—*Gen. Grant's report of what Hancock said to him in 1867.*

LINCOLN'S WISE AND TRUE PROPHECY.

"No man will ever be President of the United States who spells 'negro' with two g's."—*What Abraham Lincoln said in 1858.*

HANCOCK AND LINCOLN.

Harper's Weekly, November 6, 1880, p. 719.

INSIDE SOUTHERN CABINS
Georgia.—No. 1.

HARPER'S WEEKLY
November 13, 1880, pp. 733–34

The following facts and incidents relating to the true life of the emancipated negro in South Carolina, Alabama, and Georgia I have gathered in a visit to these States, extending over a period of nine months. I shall attempt no idealization, and shall leave, as far as possible, all moralizing and deduction to my readers. The simplest language will best befit my homely tale of ignorance and oppression; and if the facts can not speak for themselves, I have neither the power nor the wish to give them any advantage from sentiment or fiction.

It must be understood, first, that the negroes of different States vary as much in character as do the white men of those States. The gentlemanly, indolent Carolinian is not more unlike the keen, alert Georgian than is the careless, polite Carolinian negro to his Georgian brother. The first thing, indeed, that struck me with regard to the Georgian negro was his insolence, and his open aversion to white people. It was some time before I could gain their confidence; all kindnesses were accepted suspiciously, and they looked at a gift as cautiously as a bird looks at an open snare.

This suspicious coldness is of itself a veil that few white people care to lift; and there is still another reason why the negro, as he really is, remains a misconception to the casual observer—a reason which an intelligent colored man thus defined to me: "We have been accustomed to look upon white people as beings to be conciliated at any cost, and so we hide ourselves behind a mask that reflects their moods and opinions." This I found to be very true. It was only after many weeks of familiar visiting in their cabins that I discovered a shrewd thoughtfulness about public events, and an anxious carefulness about the future of their families and their race, which no one would have suspected to exist beneath the mask of jest or indifference worn outside their homes.

The Georgian negroes are physically finer men and women than the Carolinians, and although they lack the suave, jovial manner of the latter, I think they wear better—that is, if you can penetrate the I-don't-trust-anybody air that repels you at first. Indeed, it is only necessary to see what they will go through to procure an education to feel sure that there is an amount of mental grit in them that can not but make its mark sooner or later. I have known boys and girls work hard all summer, either teaching, or at service, or in the fields, to earn enough for three months' tuition, going out again at the end of that time to make the fee for another quarter.

There is nothing the Georgian negro values above knowledge, and there are few sacrifices he will not make to obtain it. And it must be remembered also that even when he has painfully saved his tuition fee, he will most likely have to walk five or six miles to the nearest school. Those who can not go to school generally manage, with the help of some friend, to pick up a little learning while at their work. In this way Bishop Holsey laid the foundation of his by no means contemptible acquirements. I had the pleasure of meeting this colored bishop, and found him a native gentleman, with a great deal of both practical and acquired information.

The colored public schools in Atlanta are a libel on the name. I found the Wheat Street School in a wretchedly ventilated basement. It consists of two rooms divided by such a flimsy partition that the two rooms are virtually one. There were four teachers, each having from fifty to sixty scholars to attend to, though they had little or no assistance from blackboards or any of the necessary aids of a school-room.

I do not know that I can give any more forcible example of the value put upon education by the Georgian negro than the fact that during last summer Storr's Chapel—a little colored congregation in Atlanta—sent out *fifty-seven* of its partially educated members into the dark places of Houston, Greene, and Pulaski counties to help their degraded people in those almost barbarous districts. When these teachers returned I had many interesting conversations with most of them; and if the half of what they told me is true, we certainly need not send our missionaries across the ocean. In these counties the men pin bits of bright-colored cloth down their pants and sleeves, and cut their hair close to the head, except just in front, where they leave a "forelock." On working-days this forelock remains unplaited and bushy, but on Sundays and election days it is carefully braided with bits of colored flannel, tied with a ribbon, and allowed to fall over the forehead and face. They also carry a short, thick club, and use it with a wild cry in a very singular dance, wherein, at intervals, the men fall upon one knee, and strike with violence the clubs of the men opposite. They have no ideas of life beyond their own isolated plantations, and speak of persons even from the neighboring cities as "foreigners." Their religion is vague and full of gross superstitions, and yet if approached by one of their own color, or even by a white person in whom they have confidence, they are eager to learn the truth, and accept it with the docility and faith of a child.

"You done made me grow two inches while you bin talking to me," said one man, when he first heard of the love of Christ. Another, after listening to the same story, exclaimed, "Arter this, the debil kin come to my house and smoke awhile, but he can't camp dar obernight no more." They whip chickens for straying from home, and are altogether so far behind the colored people in the cities that these latter pray for their "benighted brethren" very much as we pray for the heathen of Ashantee.

Undoubtedly Georgia is raising up the future teachers of the colored race; and yet I never conversed on this subject with any of them that they did not deplore the one-sided character of the education placed within their reach. "We want something besides preachers and teachers," said an intelligent leader among his people to me. "We are systematically robbed in the stores, and lawyers, except in cases of old family ties, or for some political interest, refuse to take a civil case up for us."

As to doctors, I know their need is very urgent. The ward physicians told me many times that they "never doctored a nigger with anything but castor-oil or rhubarb." In one very bad case of sickness I went *nine times* for a ward doctor before I could get him to attend to it; and even when he did so, his treatment of the patient was so brutal that I do not wonder they prefer their charms, herbs, and "wise-women." Lawyers and doctors are as urgently needed by the colored race as preachers, and in my humble opinion, if the colored universities taught boys and girls less Greek and Latin and theology, and turned out more merchants, tradesmen, and tradeswomen, it would be for the real advantage of the people whose interests they profess to study.

I was often struck by an apparent preference of the Southern white man to the Northern, although the latter were among them as their special friends. And when I spoke of this, I got invariably one answer: "The Southerners don't acknowledge any possibility of equality between us; we know just what we have to expect from them; while our Northern friends talk about our perfect equality, and yet if we attempt to pass the equality line they draw, the check-rein is shortened in a hurry." I am convinced that the efforts the present negro-teachers are making to conciliate the Southern whites are a great mistake. No one can serve two masters. They lose the confidence and respect of the negro entirely, and they gain nothing from the whites but contempt. The only possible way to enlist Southern favor for colored colleges is to put them under the care of Southern white teachers, instead of bringing teachers from the North. Yet, as these colleges are nearly altogether supported by Northern charity, it seems reasonable to employ Northern teachers. I am only indicating a possible way to that social favor negro-teachers seem so very anxious to attain.

While on the subject of the equality of the races, I will mention a well-known case that forcibly illustrates the Southern view of it. In Atlanta I knew a young mulatto, the son of one of Georgia's most prominent citizens. There was no attempt ever made to deny or even conceal his parentage; he went by his father's name, and his resemblance both to his father and his white half-sisters was an ordinary subject of remark. Yet though the relationship was fully acknowledged, this boy cleaned his father's office, and always waited on his father's table when he had any special entertainment. This white gentleman also professed to be a friend of the negro, and often preaches in their churches.

To the colored man, home is not home unless he shares it with a dog—*dogs*, I should say, for their name in every house is legion. Some of them are splendid animals; the greater number are detestable, barking, mangy little curs. I saw, at a respectful distance, some magnificent specimens of the bull-dog, which is the favorite species with negroes. It struck me as a significant fact that though they will give almost any little ugly brute a home, I never anywhere saw a hound among them.

The places they call homes are, as a general thing, squalid and miserable beyond description; and any stranger, looking at the hovels in which Georgia's working classes live, would draw a most unfavorable—and erroneous—opinion as to her intelligence and resources. Many of them are scattered all over the hills surrounding Atlanta—miserable huts into which wind, rain, and sunshine find easy access through the multitude of crevices in walls, roof, and floor. They have no windows, and however wet or cold the weather, they must keep the door open, unless they are so fortunate as to possess a lamp. I saw but one candle among the colored people the whole time I was in the South; generally light is obtained by putting some grease in a saucer, and laying a lighted wick in it.

The floors are usually very dirty, but whenever I found a hut with a clean floor, I found also that the walls had been chinked with bits of rag or cotton, and the walls covered with newspapers. Harper's Weekly was a great favorite for this purpose, and they begged it eagerly from me, because, I suspect, it served the double purpose of wall-paper and pictures. Cheap prints of the Virgin Mary, of Catholic saints, and of the Crucifixion—such as are favorites in the shanties of New York—are highly valued by them, and I have often been much amused at their horror and indignation when I told them they were Roman Catholic pictures. "I ain't no Roman Catholic; I belong to Big Bethel, I do," was the usual answer, and that in a very resentful tone.

Most of these huts are occupied by two families, and the furniture of all is similar. One or two dirty ragged beds, a common table, some broken chairs or empty soap boxes, two or three wooden chests piled one upon another, a few pieces of broken crockery, and the old time covered skillet, pot, and kettle, complete the inventory of household furniture. In the few huts that are chinked and papered the beds are usually special objects of pride, and those who possess feather ones, and a few colored quilts, will part with anything rather than relinquish them. Some of their quilts are, indeed, of great beauty, exhibiting much taste in design, and great skill in needle-work.

Economical people would be shocked to see every comer-in, no matter whether kin or stranger, made welcome to the corn-bread, bacon, and coffee, which are the regular food of the negro throughout the South. I must confess this indiscriminate hospitality struck me as very improvident, until I discovered its motive—a tacit understanding that any one out of food is to be supplied by some one in better luck, the obligation to be faithfully returned when called for. I was told that this national relief system extended all over the South, and that it was rarely abused.

A still nobler hospitality is quite as prevalent. I was in hundreds of cabins in the South, and in the large majority I found some gray-headed old uncle or aunty, too old or too ill to work, who had been taken in to share the rough kindness of people on whom they had no claim whatever but that of race, age, or helplessness. It was after conversing with many of these old people I began to understand how it is that the feeling of hostility between black and white remains so deep and bitter. Sooner or later their conversation always drifts backward to the days of their slavery. They tell tales that make you cry out and stop your ears, and the young men and women and the little children sit listening to them with souls all on fire. To the children these tales are what Cinderella and fairy-land are to our happier boys and girls; and the young men and women take them into hearts already chafing and sore under wrongs they daily feel, and yet which they know not how to alter or redress.

I have seen many an old woman sitting among a dozen young people showing the marks of the cruel iron bands by which they were "belled" for running away, or exhibiting scars left by fiendish dogs and not less fiendish men and women. I have seen many women who bore on their arms and faces the mark of a hot flat-iron. Others have shown me the very windows in which they stood all day with "For Sale" pinned on them. I never shall forget the story of one old woman who had sat quietly listening to such memories for a long time. Raising herself up suddenly, she said, in a husky voice:

"When I warn't no older nor Mandy sitting thar, my three little chillen were sold 'way from me, all at once; and thar warn't one of 'em big enough to pull t'other out of the fire if it fell in. Them was sorrowful days, so them was. 'Bout a week arterward, while I was cooking dinner, I heerd some chillen singing, and I went out to defence to see who dey was. Thar was two big wagons going 'long, and a heap of little chillen running by de road-side, playing and singing, and never knowing how dey was every minute going furder from their mammies. I sez to one ole woman, who kind had charge of them, 'Whar dem chillen come from?'

"'Kansas,' sez she.

"'Whar dey going to?' sez I.

"'God knows,' sez she.

"I went back to my kitchen, but, O my Christ, dinner was full of tears that day."

"Did you ever see your children again?" I asked her.

"No, nor never heerd tell on them," she answered, as she leaned forward again, and stretched her trembling hands before the blazing pine log, which was our only light. I know an old woman who has had twelve children sold away from her, and who, ever since Emancipation, watches through Christmas week for some of them to come and see her; and I know an old man who goes all Christmas week to meet every train, in the confidant hope that some of his children will be sure to come and see him at the holidays. For Christmas is the negro's happy date; they expect everything good to come at Christmas.

The homes in the city are no better than those on the hills. A description of one block will give a very fair idea of the colored quarters in Atlanta. A square built round with windowless cabins of one room each, all opening into a court, in the centre of which is a wash shed and a well. All day long, and late into the night, this court is full of crying children, quarrelling dogs, loafing men, women washing, women smoking, women dipping snuff. And yet, if I took a Bible into one of the cabins, and offered to read a chapter, those very women would gather round me, as eager as little children for a story. Wash-tubs and idle husbands would be forgotten, and after I had finished, they would very probably, by some spontaneous impulse, begin in a low, almost whispered monotone, the old slave song,

"Steal away, steal away,
Steal away to Jesus," etc.

This habit of singing *sotto voce* originated in slavery, and it is one of the most thrilling things imaginable. "You see," said a negro woman to me, "that's de way we used fur to hab a prayer-meeting in old Uncle Wash's cabin. We sot round just as still, and then we'd start some hymn just so"—here she leaned forward, softly clapping her hands together, and patting one foot, as she sang, in a scarcely audible tone,

"Steal away—steal away to Jesus."

And the other women present, quite familiar with the form, immediately took it up. "Then," she said, "we done prayed in de same low voice, but dat ole nigger Wash he allays got so full he'd have to jam his head under de bed-tick and shout, 'case, you see, we warn't 'lowed to 'noy de white folks."

As a general thing these women live with one another very peaceably, using tubs, brooms, crockery, and all household utensils in common. They are very desirous of being called "good neighbors," and if a readiness to lend food, clothing, and even money, when they have it, makes a good neighbor, I know of no one more worthy of the name. Domestic quarrels are also much less frequent than one would expect among a people whose ordinary language is very coarse and brutal, and who, while performing almost impossible tasks to keep their husbands or children at school, very rarely show their affection in words of tenderness or praise.

The women accept it as a settled fact that they are to support their husbands, and many of them work almost day and night in order to send him to school, because, perhaps, he imagines himself a born preacher. This sacrifice is always accepted as a lawful tribute to his superiority, and he generally has an extempore sermon on hand from some of Paul's dicta about women.

Almost the only domestic quarrel of which I was made a confidante was the following:

Away up on the hill-side, in a pigeon-hole of a room, lives a Mrs. Chappel, one of those merry little women who rejoice over a crumb as though it were a fortune. Her husband drinks a great deal too much, and one day I found her ruffled over a little domestic trouble. "You see," she said, "Chappel he got cross yesterday morning, so sez I to myself, it takes two to make a quarrel. I went round kinder singing to myself, when, sez he, 'Whar's dem taters gone dat was in dis box?' 'I lent 'em to Mrs. Smith,' sez I, and goes right on singing. Well, he rowed round 'bout dem taters, and I sung on like I never heerd him. I was singing 'Over Thar,' and sez I, 'Chappel, why don't you jine in and gib de words back to me? When I says "Over Thar," you should sing up "Over Thar," dis way,' and I showed him how. 'Taters! Taters!' sez he." And as Mr. Chappel was blacking his shoes to go to Sunday-school, and continued the altercation in a way which made the brushes handy, I think I had better leave the rest of the story to individual imagination.

Children are brought up not only under the mother's eye and lash, but also under the eyes and lashes of all the mothers in the neighborhood; and they have a habit, which I shall notice more particularly with reference to the Carolinian negroes, of *giving* their children away to sisters and friends. The life of a colored child is often a very hard one, and this is especially so in regard to the girls, who are introduced to the wash-tub and hard work generally at a pitiably early age.—B.

INSIDE SOUTHERN CABINS
Georgia.—II.

HARPER'S WEEKLY
November 20, 1880, pp. 749–50

I found the negro women, almost without exception, full of superstitions; one of the most singular is the supernatural power which they attribute to May water; that is, the first rain that falls in May. All of them bottle a large quantity of it, and they assured me it kept quite sweet for a year. They use it to make lotions, salves, tonics, etc., and they confidently affirm that any one caught accidentally in the first rain of May is safe from all contagious diseases for that year. If possible, they have a sunflower patch, and they attribute all kinds of miraculous powers to this plant; and there is an amount of attention paid to the moon and stars that is not altogether free from actual worship. For some reason or other, however, they are very chary of speaking about their superstitions.

Their power to endure pain struck me as one of their most remarkable traits. They not only endure it, but do so with a patient cheerfulness that seems miraculous. To one old woman, who had not known a moment's freedom from suffering for years, I said, "Aunt Mary, you are a wonder; I am going to write a story about you."

"I'd be powerful glad if you would," she said, delightedly; "I do want to be heerd of outside Georgia." This same old woman had a very funny habit of quoting King George the Fourth as her authority or reference.

The rising generation are apt to speak slightingly of the old slave spiritual songs, but I noticed that they could all sing them; and that they were quite as easily enthused by them as were the generation from whose toil and travail they sprung. No music moves them as this does. The Jubilee Singers give no idea, or rather they give a very false idea, of them; all the *native* power is lost in their too artistic rendering. They want no music but the emphasized clapping of hands to which they are naturally sung, and performers in full dress in some fashionable concert hall are a travesty on the original singers.

Instead of these accessories, imagine an unchinked cabin, with a fire of pine knots, and seated round it a group of grave, almost mournful, men and women, clad

A GREENE COUNTY NEGRO.

Harper's Weekly, November 13, 1880, p. 733.

in rough brogans and scanty homespun. After a total silence, sometimes of long duration, some one begins in a low voice:

> When I was down in de Egypt land—
> Love, love, for me,
> I heerd some talk of de promised land—
> Love, love, for me;
> Yes, 'twas love—yes, 'twas love,
> Love, love, for me.
> As I walked on de heavenly road—
> Love, love, for me,
> De elements opened and de love came down—
> Love, love, for me;
> Yes, 'twas love—yes, 'twas love,
> Love, love, for me.

During the progress of the hymn, the soft clapping grows more emphatic, the dark drooping faces are gradually lifted, and the enthusiasm gains with every repetition.

I have often stood in the dark outside the cabins, and watched a group of young girls sitting in a circle on the floor, singing these native songs. One of their number always sits in the middle of the ring, and gives the opening line, thus:

> *Leader*. Old Satan is a liar, and a conjurer too—
> *Rest*. Oh, my Lord!

READING THE BIBLE.

Harper's Weekly, November 13, 1880, p. 733.

> *Leader*. If you don't mind, he'll conjure you—
> *Rest*. Oh, my Lord!
> *All*. Oh, my Lord is a lily in the valley,
> A lily in the valley;
> Oh, my Lord!
> *Leader*. Old Satan wears one iron shoe—
> *Rest*. Oh, my Lord!
> *Leader*. If you don't mind, he'll slip it on you—
> *Rest*. Oh, my Lord!
> *All*. Oh, my Lord is a lily in the valley,
> A lily in the valley;
> Oh, my Lord!

These songs are almost the only ones sung in country churches, and some of them are of a much wilder character than those just cited. Many are impromptu, and to no one but their composers could express any religious feeling. Still, however ridiculous, I never found it possible to laugh at them, the intent was so sincere. Their manner of singing them in church is quite as effective in its way as their fireside singing. Imagine a building of unchinked logs, standing perhaps in a pine wood, and lighted by great torches of fat pine held in the hands of negro men, who are often singularly tall, black, and uncouth-looking.

They stand around a crowd of women, who keep up a constant half-step swaying motion, exactly like the uneasy movement of a camel. These women probably begin in a low, soft voice, but the clapping grows wilder, the time quicker, and they are cheered into a frenzy of excitement by the constant ejaculations of "Shout, sisters!" from the "Amen Corner," where the elders of the church sit. The flickering, flaring, smoky light, the wild

A DOMESTIC QUARREL.

Harper's Weekly, November 13, 1880, p. 733.

dark faces, the noise, and the excitement make a scene which brings Central Africa startlingly near to us.

While in Atlanta I attended a "revival" in the Big Bethel Colored Church. Several women were lying before the altar in a kind of trance, others were standing around them singing and shouting. Before the service began the minister said: "Brethren, I've got a very bad cold, so I sha'n't address you at length. I want to say that all the mourners will give their hats to Deacon ———, and their bonnets to Sister ———. Last night a mourner gave his hat to a person to keep while he proceeded to the altar, and that person took that hat plumb away, and I had to lend that mourner a hat to go home in."

A few minutes afterward a woman took off her bonnet deliberately, jerked wildly round for a minute or two, and then jumped up and down, clapping her hands and shouting. During this paroxysm it took two women to hold her; but she stopped in a few moments as suddenly as she had commenced, picked up her bonnet, tied it on, and walked out of church as quietly as possible.

One little girl converted at this time said that while her soul was on its "travels" she had met her mother, who was a shining angel of light, and who told her that her step-mother (just deceased) was wallowing in fiery brimstone. The child had to be strictly concealed after this revelation, or she would have fallen a victim to the vengeance of the step-mother's relatives.

The louder the shouting, in the opinion of this class, the better the Christian. They have no faith in the conversion of any one who has not lain in a trance for two or three days, and whose soul has not been on its travels; while the wilder and more improbable the stories told on "coming through," the more positive is the salvation.

This class of negroes also considers noise the grand element of preaching; and a good loud voice is often considered a very positive call to the ministry. One man, who was preaching with all the eloquent noise he could possibly make, suddenly stopped, and after a moment's reflection said, "Dar, now! I had a thought, but de debil's done got him under his foot." Another talked about God raining down whales in the wilderness, and called himself "doctor" during his sermon a great many times. A preacher in Atlanta who professes to be an educated man said in one of his discourses that "God, in the concatenation of His wisdom, caused the angels to swing rapidly round His throne"; and was continually, and in the most absurd connections, alluding to what he called "the hecatombs."

Still, this is but one side of colored worship; there are many very orderly congregations, although this order and silence is a great trial to most of the older negroes. I heard an old woman say, after listening to a white minister who would not permit shouting, "Lord bless the man! it was a powerful good sermon, but it 'most killed me to hold in them shouts."

During the cotton season the streets of Atlanta are wonderful. They are blocked up everywhere with cotton, the coarse brown sacking beautifully relieved by the snowy staple torn out from the heart of the bale by the sampling hook. Cotton is the panacea for a Southerner's inertness. I have seen them passing up and down on the top of the bales as if they were thoroughly alive, using "big, big D's" as prodigally as if some other person's tongue had to coin them. The negro also is in his element among cotton; he is never so happy in any other labor, and his brisk "Yes, sahs" are heard above all the noise of clattering wagons, cracking whips, shouting men, and barking dogs.

I never wearied of this animated, bustling scene, and I never was at a minstrel entertainment half as comical as the continual little disputes between the negro drivers on the streets of Atlanta. "Look yar, boy," replied one, indignantly, in reply to some passing impudence; "don't you know 'tain't safe to tickle a mule's heels?"

"Your'n ain't no good fur kicking," was the ready response.

But Atlanta has, alas! other street scenes besides these amusing ones. Go into any street where repairs are being made, and you will see how shamelessly Georgia wears her disgrace. Men, women, and children—for very young boys and girls are put in her chain-gang—are mending roads, loading carts, or shovelling dirt; the women and girls chained together with the men, and often for first offenses. This chain-gang is Georgia's training-school for her penitentiaries, for since she has leased out her convicts to licensed slave-drivers, it pays her well to have criminals. I have heard that white men and women are put in the chain-gang; I only know that during the four months I was in Atlanta I never saw a white man, woman, or child in the gang, though I was informed that a white woman gave birth to a child while at work in it. I never saw this chain-gang without a shudder, and I do not believe that it would be tolerated in any Northern city, nor, indeed, in any place in America where slavery had not first prepared the way for it; and how chivalrous Southern gentlemen can permit their wives and daughters to daily see such sights is a problem they alone can solve.

This is but the beginning of the wrong. Men who can daily bear this sight have found it easy and very profitable to lease the lives of their fellow-creatures for long terms of years. These lessees are irresponsible private people, whose only interest is to get as much labor out of their slaves for as little outlay as possible. While in Georgia I paid a visit to the Dade coal mines, where three hundred convicts are worked by a lessee who is an ex-Confederate Governor. The stockade in which the men are kept covers an acre, and is fenced with great rails fifteen feet high. The gates are guarded by armed men, and by fierce blood-hounds. The houses in which the convicts sleep are built of logs with apertures of about an inch wide between them. The logs stand perpendicular, and are not laid in the usual horizontal fashion, and none but those who have lived in log-houses can understand the difference this makes. Logs laid horizontally suggest the home, the church, or the school-house; huts made of upright logs, the calaboose and the slave-pen.

The room of this convict house is about one hundred feet long, and the doors and windows are of grated iron. They have no bedsteads; a shelf the length of a man, and raised a few feet from the floor, answers that purpose. The filthy condition of the wretched beds on these shelves is beyond description; something of it may be understood from the fact that the miners sleep in the clothes in which they work. As far as cleanliness and comfort are concerned, a hole in the coal seam would be preferable. At the foot of each shelf is a chain, to which at night the chain which the convict wears is fastened.

The floor of this stockade is also of logs, and there is the usual opening between them, except under the beds, where it is boarded; but I can not see what great comfort is gained in this partial flooring, because the whole stockade is raised several feet from the ground, and the freezing mountain winds find entrance through the whole centre of the floor. In the winter months this place, though boasting of five stoves, must be a cold hell. Even in summer, rain-storms will drive right through the unchinked walls, and deluge the wooden shelf which serves as the sleeping-place of the convicts. They claim that the walls are left open for ventilation, and by order of the doctor, but I noticed that his own house was not ventilated after this fashion. The hospital is a room built on the same plan, excepting that the floor is wholly boarded, the walls being all open as in the stockade.

I noticed a large quantity of books and papers in the commissary department, covered with dust and cobwebs; and I was told they had been sent by charitable societies in the North for the use of the convicts. I offered to clean and arrange them, but my offer was refused. "You see," said an official, "we don't wish the men to have such publications, on account of their objectionable political stand-point." The greater portion of this reading matter was *Harper's Monthlies* and *Weeklies* and *The Independent*. There were also many volumes of a miscellaneous character. I was told here that a majority of the negro convicts could read, and that it was the educated negroes who filled the penitentiaries. I beg leave to doubt the latter statement.

I saw no means of cleanliness anywhere about the stockade, although I was told that there was a tub at the entrance of the mine, where the men could wash themselves as they came out—over one hundred men to a tub! There is no excuse for this shameful neglect, for Captain Evans, who has charge of the mine, and who is a practical miner, told me, when I pointed out the filthy condition of the men and the stockade, that "by the loss of a very little time to the company, morning and evening, the men and the stockade could be kept as clean as either he or his own house was"—and I never saw a man more scrupulously neat for his position, nor a sweeter, cleaner home than the one he inhabited. The men are, however, compelled to bathe on Sundays, when it is no loss to the company.

There are sixty acres of ground under cultivation for the use of the convicts, and, as far as I could judge, they got plenty to eat, but it was served in the filthiest little tin buckets it has ever been my lot to see, and yet when I examined them they had been just washed for the men's dinners.

Both Captains Reese and Evans asked me to lay before the public the case of a colored boy called Charles Davidson. They told me he had been in the mine for five years, and *was then fifteen years old*—his sentence being a term of forty years for burglary. Brown, the lessee, has since claimed that "he is serving out a sentence for three distinct crimes," although I was told by a famous Georgian lawyer that a man could not be sentenced for more than one crime at a time; that is, he would have to be re-arrested, tried, and sentenced for each separately. Brown also claims that this boy of ten years old was a confirmed desperado. Reese and Evans spoke highly of the boy's docility and general good behavior.

The mines, as a matter of course, are dark, damp, dreadful places. Each man is required to fill five car-loads a day; and I should think this is not very hard work, for many do it in less than the prescribed hours. The injustice comes in here, that they can not leave the mine until six at night, and for the extra work they do they get no money, but simply an order on the commissary for extra food, clothing, or tobacco. But of what use is extra food and clothing to men who ought to have sufficient from the lessee? And if he paid them for their extra work in money, they could buy their tobacco.

"We used to pay them so much money an hour, and some men sent as much as thirty dollars a month home to their families," said Captain Evans to me; "but we have stopped that now."

The three hundred men leased by Brown are divided into three camps. I really can not decide which of these three is the nearest to the Infernal City. I think it would take an expert devil to do that. At Castle Rock the stockade was cleaner than at Dade, and the beds viler, and the dogs more vicious. At Cole City I found a man who was a very old convict, and who had been leased out to Grant and Alexander while they were laying the Air-line Railroad with convict labor. He told me stories of floggings and cruelties which I should hesitate to repeat, although Captain Evans, who was at that time with Grant, said "he had seen men flogged until it made him sick"; and it certainly must have been a devilish punishment which could have so moved this experienced man. While laying this route the men were not always put under cover at night; very frequently both men and women were chained by one leg to a tree. This man had just come to Cole City from a convict camp known as "Smith's Camp," and he said that all the time he was there he had never once had enough to eat.

It is something to know, however, that public sentiment is slowly awakening to a sense of shame regarding these inhuman prison-houses. Last summer Senator Boyd laid before the Senate reports of atrocities, which, if they desire it, my readers can refer to for further information on the subject. This is the second chapter of slavery in the South, and I have no hesitation in saying that in some respects it is more terrible than the first. Its victims are prejudged; they are kept in far-away, desolate places; their masters have no interest whatever in treating them mercifully, or in even caring for their lives; they have no friends and no helper, unless it be in heaven; and "heaven," as one poor fellow said, despairingly, "is so far away."

I have written of these convict camps in connection with negro life in Georgia with a purpose; it is this: *I think they exist because free negroes exist*. When the negro was a slave, his master punished him as he thought proper; even if he committed murder, he was "sold away," to avoid loss, if possible. I know this, for I remember many such cases, having lived ten years in a Slave State before emancipation. Now, as a free man, the negro comes before the law, and I fear the law is made to suit the circumstance.

Yet the Georgian negroes, without being the most interesting of their race, are perhaps the most progressive. As I said before, the teachers of their people will spring from them; and I think the white Georgian scornfully misconceives and undervalues the power with which he will yet undoubtedly come in collision. However, I have only told what I have seen; if there is any lesson, moral, social, or political in it, my readers will easily find it, each for himself.—B.

INSIDE SOUTHERN CABINS
III.—*Charleston, South Carolina.*

HARPER'S WEEKLY
November 27, 1880, pp. 765–66

The Charleston negroes are the aristocracy—so far as I have seen—of their race. They copy the whites, and that very fairly, in courtesy, hospitality, and especially in that air of "we are the cream of humanity" which the white Charlestonian is sure to inform you is the case, if he or she thinks you have failed to make the discovery for yourself.

The division between the rich and poor negroes is far more decided here than in any other place I visited. The colored upper-ten include a great number who have never been slaves; and the majority are of very light color—indeed, all but white. This social division line is, however, a slight one compared with the *color line,* which among Charleston negroes is of the most intense and prejudiced character. In talking with the wife of a white Northern minister, pastor of a colored church there, she told me that several of her husband's light—or, as they prefer being called, "bright"—members called upon her, and requested that she would not be so familiar with the black members of the congregation. "There is no necessity for you to shake hands with them when you meet them on the street," was the monition given her. In the colored boarding-schools the "bright" girls make indignant protests against occupying the same room with the black girls. This color line I found to exist both in Georgia and Alabama, but in a much less pronounced way. Still, there is undoubtedly among very light colored people a persuasion of their superiority; yet, singularly enough, this feeling is generally blended with an intense dislike to white people.

One of the most prominent traits of negro character here is their readiness to adopt children. It is almost impossible to find a home in which there are not one, two, or more adopted children. Perhaps a neighbor dies, leaving three or four little ones. Some nursing woman instantly claims the baby, "because she can 'tend best to it," and the rest are taken readily by others on equally satisfactory grounds, and I believe they receive just as much love and care from the adopting mother as they did from their own; at any rate, I never saw any difference in the treatment of natural and of adopted children—both were made equally welcome

NEGRO DRIVERS.

Harper's Weekly, November 20, 1880, p. 749.

to the ragged bed and the corn-dodger, even in the poorest house.

The universality of this custom implies that negro women still regard their interest and right in their children as paramount, the father's being really as small as it was in the days of slavery, for I never once heard of a father objecting to this partition of his family.

They have also another custom that savors strongly of slavery—that of *giving* children away. A mother, when her eldest daughter marries, will frequently give her as a wedding present a younger brother or sister, and this gift is as complete and real as a sale was twenty years ago. The child given belongs to the daughter, to the sister, or friend, as absolutely as if it was an inanimate object, and henceforward transfers its regard and obedience solely to its new protector, looking entirely to him or her for food, clothing, and education. This ownership of brothers, sisters, nephews, and nieces is one of the most significant remnants of slavery. I saw it in South Carolina, Georgia, and Alabama, and was told that it existed all over the South.

The affection between brothers and sisters is often a singularly tender one, and in Charleston many beautiful instances of it came under my notice; one especially of a young man who worked almost night and day at his trade—shoemaking—in order to give his sister a fine education, he himself spelling out, while at his work-bench, such lessons as with her help he was able to manage.

I doubt if it would be possible to find a colored home in Charleston in which Solomon's little remark about sparing the rod and spoiling the child is not practically illustrated by the most unmerciful use of the strap, or "lash," as they call it, and oftener, I fear, to the spoiling than the saving of the child. This is the more remarkable because many of these mothers must retain a very lively memory of their own floggings; and even the younger ones, born after emancipation, have all listened to the stories of the old uncles and aunties, and sympathetically shared their sufferings.

For here, as in Georgia, every little cabin shelters some gray-headed man or woman "who ain't got no folks to care for them." They have a corner for their chest and comforters, and not only share the coffee, corn-bread, and bacon, but are also, in some way or other, supplied with their beloved tobacco or snuff.

In Charleston there are many beautiful residences owned by colored men, and I shall always remember with pleasure my entertainment by Mr. Hall, a prominent colored cotton merchant, who owns a fine house on Rutledge Street. It is surrounded by a lovely flower garden, and handsomely and appropriately furnished throughout. No dining-room could have been better appointed; the silver, the china, the cooking, were all in the best taste and of the most perfect quality; the servants were dressed in clean white linen suits.

Both Mr. and Mrs. Hall had been slaves, and have educated themselves since they were set free. They talked intelligently and grammatically of the events commented on in the newspapers, and were people whose sympathies stretched out to all suffering wrong or oppression, no matter what their creed or nationality. Still, I noticed that the majority of his books referred to his own race and to slavery. They had no children, but, following the usual custom, had adopted three, and were educating them for useful and honorable lives.

Among the higher class of Charleston negroes the fashion of wearing mourning for deceased friends is carried to such a ridiculous pitch that I wonder it has not caused its entire disregard among white people. For the death of relatives of the most remote consanguinity, for infants which have scarcely breathed, they assume the deepest trappings of woe; and even babies may frequently be seen dressed in black. That they have never seen these relatives, or that they have been in life on the very worst terms with them, does not alter the conditions. As soon as they are dead, they are deemed worthy of the longest crape veil that can be procured.

Turning from the higher class of Charleston negroes to the laborers, one stands appalled before the mass of poverty, ignorance, and superstition that is apparent on all sides. From most of the streets in Charleston lanes and alleys branch off, and these lead into courts full of vice and misery—places which almost any one who had no knowledge of negro character would refuse to enter.

But push open the doors, and in every cabin you will find a welcome. The best chair or soap box will be carefully wiped off for you. Everywhere black babies, dogs, cats, and dirt are so mixed up that it is impossible to say which is the dirtiest. Everywhere you hear the same pitiful story of hard work, miserable pay, high rents, hunger, nakedness, and sickness.

The women, as a rule, are ragged and dirty, and rarely seen without the snuff-stick in their mouths. Their language is coarse and brutal, and the most trifling offenses will elicit terrible threats—not in anger, but just from habit. I have often been interrupted in the middle of a chapter by, "I'll stomp the life out ob you, you little debbil, ef you don't git that water on," and then in the same breath, "Go on, miss; that's a powerful good chapter." The woman had not the slightest intention of "stomping the life" out of any one; it was only her way of telling her child to put the kettle on.

These very women are probably members of some colored church, and can pray in the most intense language for the conversion of their "dear partners," as they call their husbands, and their "beloved children." Yet I don't remember ever hearing a single word of love or praise given to a child, no matter how well it had done its task; and when I asked a woman why they refused such encouragement to their children, she answered, "Lord, chile! you ken't praise niggers; ef you do, they git the big head so bad that heaven ken't hold 'em."

The immorality of this class is a common subject of remark, and I have frequently had it pointed out to me as a complete settlement of the negro question. "What can possibly be done for such men and women?" is asked. I think the answer is very easy. Give them proper places to live in. As long as parents and children, young men and young women, sometimes even two families, are crowded into one room, the ordinary rules of decency are almost of necessity disregarded. I did not discover any unusual immorality among the higher class of Charleston negroes, and with regard to the laboring class, everywhere and among all races, we see

"Evil effects from evil causes spring."

Still, even in these wretched courts, I met with some singularly beautiful characters—men and women who, hungry, suffering, bent with ill-usage and toil, have told me with radiant faces how "de Lord Jesus come and sot right down on dat chair" and talked with them; men and women who, in the beauty and simplicity of a wonderful faith, have had visions, and seen the "golden chariots swing low," and Jordan shine like the river of God.

"Yes, ma'am," said one of these women to me, "I am de richest woman in Charleston."

I looked round at the few pennyworths of peanut-candy, the can of milk, and the half-dozen sticks of green wood which composed her whole stock in trade, and then at the bright black face bound round with a white kerchief, and asked, "How is that, Ellen?"

"Well, chile," she answered, her face brightening all over, "I don't know A B C, but I know de Lord Jesus Christ! Let me tell you how, chile. Four years ago I buried my dear partner, and when I came back from de funeral, thar was jist bread 'nough for supper, and no more. Well, 'bout five o'clock next morning I riz up from my bed, and I got down on my bendings [knees] right thar, and I battled with de Lord fur breakfast fur me and de chillen. By-'n'-by comes a boy fur a nickel's worth ob milk. I gib it to him, and then down I knelt ag'in, and I says, 'Thank you, Lord, thank you; but 'tain't 'nough, Lord; send some more, good Lord, send some more, Lord.' Pretty soon a boy come 'long, and he buys twenty cents worth ob wood. Den I goes and wakes up de chillen. 'Come,' says I, 'git up now, chillen; Jesus done sent de money for de breakfast; and I's gwine to git it.' Ebery day since He's gi'en me 'nough; and some days more 'an 'nough. I don't know A B C, miss, but I know de Lord Jesus Christ—and I'm de richest woman in Charleston."

Incidents of simple faith as remarkable as this are abundant in these wretched hovels, and setting aside the religious aspect of the question altogether, I could not but regard with wonder the influence of this intangible comforter. St. Paul has told us what faith was to the early Christians; if he stood among these Charleston negroes to-day, I think he would give a still broader definition. He would say, "Faith is a faculty of the soul which enables men who have nothing to possess everything."

Hid away in a dark hot little room in one of the inner courts I found a woman utterly destitute, blind, and helpless, yet as calm and content as a child. "The Good Master"—a favorite name for the Lord—she said, "He saw I was so much taken up wid what was a-gwine on by de wayside, and didn't gib 'tention 'nough to what was a-doing in my soul's house, so He sent His angel *to draw de curtains ober my eyes.*"

"De Lord is mighty curious 'bout de way He does wid His chillen," answered another woman.

Religion is, indeed, so much a part of these negroes' lives that it is impossible to speak truthfully of them without giving it an apparent predominance. Yet if there is any place in this world where mountains could be moved by faith, I should say that these are the people who could work the miracle.

Generally the woman is the provider for the whole family, and even when the man works, the wife takes in washing or sewing, or goes out to day's work, it being an understood thing that she is to provide clothing, while he undertakes for the rent and food. In most cases, however, the woman takes care of the whole family.

The most picturesque and interesting class of Charleston negroes are, I think, the licensed venders. Some of them, both men and women, are very handsome, and all of them seemed to be endowed with the most amusing eloquence. If the vender was of a religious turn of mind, he mixed up Scripture and vegetables, fish and fruit, in a style which could hardly fail to attract attention. I have heard them with an intense solemnity inform the inhabitants of a street that this was their last chance to buy vegetables, the last time they were going through the street that day, and that no more beans or potatoes were to be bought, though perhaps a stout handsome negress, with large gold hoops and bright turban, and a great flat basket on her head, was crying "Beans and potatoes" a block behind him.

Sometimes their local and political hits are very clever, and elicit hearty laughs. Again, their peculiar use of any long, fine-sounding word that they have caught is very amusing. I once heard an old man crying: "Strawberries, superfine strawberries gwine by; strawberries, *supernoctial strawberries* gwine by."

Charleston market, to an epicure, would be a place to loiter in and dream of dinners. Every delicacy that can tempt the eye and the palate is there. The place is sweet and fresh, with a marvellous wealth of flowers, and there is a never-ending free entertainment in the piquant and comical invitations to buy from the negro women, seated, not on the ground, but up among their wares. One thing detracts from the idyllic charm of this really picturesque market—the number of buzzards that abide there, seemingly quite at home, and on the most familiar terms with all the habitues of the place. They are, however, the scavengers of the city, and are protected by law, a fine of five dollars being imposed for injuring them.

There is hardly anything the colored men and women dread so much as going to the hospital. Yet the Roper Hospital, a portion of which is open to them, is a beautiful building, admirably ordered, and scrupulously clean. I visited it very often during a stay of nine weeks, and I believe that the colored patients were kindly and intelligently treated.

But the negro is a born herbalist; his faith is in weeds and roots, and it was really pitiful to see their anguish of disappointment when I refused to smuggle in their beloved plantain leaf. One man suffering with acute rheumatism begged me in the most impassioned manner to get him some rattlesnake oil to rub himself with, assuring me that it would cure him. After some search I succeeded in getting it from some country negroes. It was clear, not unlike olive-oil in appearance, and had a faint indescribable smell. It was extracted, so the negroes told me, by hanging the snake before a slow fire, the oil dropping from between the body and the skin. Whether the oil or his faith in it worked the cure, I know not, but certainly he was immediately relieved by its use. I must not forget to state that the head of the rattlesnake is cut off before it is subjected to the fire process.

The negroes' fear of the poor-house is still greater than his fear of the hospital, and I must say that this terror has a just foundation. There is one comfortably sized building and numerous rows of cabins, but into every room three or four paupers are crowded. Gaunt poverty, decrepit old age, terrible deformities, consumption, dropsy, paralysis, and disease in some of its most loathsome forms hold here a delightful carnival.

From statistics given me by the ward physicians it is evident that consumption and dropsy make great havoc among the colored race since their emancipation—the dropsy, I believe, in most cases the result of insufficient or improper food. The slightest bruise, in nine cases out of ten, if not attended to at once, becomes in negroes an ugly eating ulcer. During my short stay in Charleston I knew six women with ulcers of from two to three years' standing.

One of these women I thought I could cure, and I went every day to attend to her. She had a large brindle dog called Prince, that had received a very ugly bite from a neighbor's dog. When I first attended his mistress, he regarded me with the utmost suspicion, and, standing close by me, watched everything I did with a critical eye. After three days' consideration of my ways, he seemed to have satisfied himself that I was no quack, for after I had finished with his mistress, he came and lay down at my feet, licked his own sore, and looked rather authoritatively in my face. After a little hesitation I bathed and dressed his wound, he standing perfectly still during the operation. Every morning, when he saw me coming, he followed me into the house, and waited until I had dressed his wound, and this he repeated until he was quite well, when he never noticed me again. I was disappointed at his want of gratitude, but that is exactly how Prince treated me. I can only suppose that his instinct taught him that in my heart I hated and dreaded dogs, and that therefore, though he was willing to take advantage of my charity, he felt no more kindness to me for it than the patients in a hospital feel for its supporters. And though I did not gain his affection, I gained his confidence, for he never afterward barked at me, and he suffered me to go into his mistress's room without following and watching me.

I saw a class of negroes in Charleston who greatly interested me, but whom I had not time enough to visit, because they live far out of the city, and their speech is so barbarous that it would require some little time to establish an intelligent communication with them. Some of this class work in the rice fields; others, still more picturesque, live on the sand-bars and islands adjacent, and are the fishermen of this locality.

I think, from what I saw of them, that their lives would afford very distinct traits, songs, and traditions; and I hope at some future day to touch it below the surface. I tried to talk to them, and understood enough to feel sure that, as far as their religion is concerned, they need a missionary as much as any tribe in Central Africa.

There is among the Charleston negroes, as elsewhere, a kind of religious aristocracy. The *élite* of colored society go to St. Mark's Episcopal Church, the well-to-do middle class to the Centenary Methodist Church. Here, as in Georgia and Alabama, there exists many congregations of "shouters." I was present at one of their services. The women crowded about the altar, keeping up a constant half-step dance to a really beautiful song, of which I only remember one line:

"Let us walk in the light of God."

The sermon was nearly an hour long, and consisted only of these words, "David, the son of Jesse; shout, brudders, shout!" Evidently this was a mere word of command or encouragement, the real worship consisting in the dance, the singing, and the shouting. I can not say that as a service it commended itself to my spiritual nature, but in some inscrutable way it really did seem to comfort and satisfy the poor creatures who participated in it.

The Baptists are the strong body among the Southern negroes. The Roman Catholics can not gain any permanent hold upon them, mainly, I believe, because they dearly love to have a voice in the church services themselves. They have intensely religious natures, but they are actively, not passively, religious; and they like to do their own singing and praying—yes, and their own preaching likewise.—B.

"SHOUT, SISTERS!"

Harper's Weekly, November 20, 1880, p. 749.

PERSONAL REMINISCENCES OF LUCRETIA MOTT

HARPER'S WEEKLY
December 4, 1880, p. 779

At the age of seventeen, Lucretia Coffin married James Mott, who, like herself, was a member of the Society of Friends. Even at this early age she gave evidence of a taste for oratory, which made her prominent in Quaker meeting, and her husband, a strong, wise man, had the good judgment to put no restraint upon her in this respect, though he himself was reserved and retiring, seldom taking any active part in the services of the meeting. As a young girl, Mrs. Mott was very beautiful. Her face had the charm of delicate and regular features combined with great strength of character; her eyes were peculiarly bright and intelligent, and ordinarily seemed gray. When she became animated in conversation, however, they would deepen and darken until they appeared to be almost black. By the side of her husband, who was an unusually tall and muscular man, she appeared like a sprite, so small and slight was she of stature and figure; and in the simple dove-colored Quaker dress, with the crossed white muslin kerchief at the neck, and the prim little Quaker cap, she made a picture which was very pleasing to look at.

On many subjects her views were in advance of the times. Long before the abolition of slavery her sympathies were enlisted for those in bondage, and she lectured at the North and at the South on the subject. Many a runaway found refuge and protection in her home until he could be passed on to others waiting to receive him, and so get beyond reach of the law. Her convictions on this question made her many enemies, and during a great riot in Philadelphia, years ago, the furious mob fixed upon her house for one of its acts of outrage. They were rushing madly on, shouting, "To Lucretia Mott's! Lucretia Mott's!" when a friend of hers rushed to the front, and assuming command of the crowd, joined in the cry, "On to Lucretia Mott's!" leading them on through street after street, getting them farther and farther away, until finally, when they had reached a distant part of the city, he fell back, and left them in confusion. Unfortunately they gave vent to their fury by burning the Colored Orphan Asylum, which was near. All colored people know the name of Lucretia Mott; many a colored child has been called after her, and indeed this distinction belongs not to the colored class alone. When Lord and Lady Amberley were in this country they visited Mrs. Mott, and the daughter born to them on their return to England was named Lucretia Mott Amberley.

When the question of women's rights came up, Lucretia Mott advocated the theory, but neither in the words she uttered on this subject, nor, in fact, on any other, was there anything but what was suggestive of the highest refinement and modesty. No one ever heard, for no one ever breathed, a word in contradiction of the gentle womanliness of Lucretia Mott. She spoke in public because she was conscious of a power which impelled her to do so. Like the noble Methodist woman in *Adam Bede,* it was "as if speech came to her without will of her own, and words were given to her that came out as the tears come, because our hearts are full, and we can't help it." This was the secret of her eloquence, and possessing this gift, she never made use of notes. Of all the prominent American women of this century, there is probably not one so little associated with that which is disagreeable in publicity, and yet there is none who has been more prominently before the public....

INSIDE SOUTHERN CABINS
IV.—Alabama.

HARPER'S WEEKLY
December 4, 1880, pp. 781–82

Agricultural Negroes

The negro life I came in contact with in Alabama was mainly agricultural, and it was a very pleasant change from the city life of the race that I saw in Charleston and Atlanta. Physically the Alabama negroes are very large and strong, and in this respect resemble those of Georgia, though mentally and morally I doubt if they are quite equal to them. At any rate, they are more inclined to treachery, not, perhaps, to the whites, but among themselves. For this reason all the secret societies formed to protect their labor rights have hitherto been failures. Many have been organized, but in no single case have the members been faithful to their obligations.

But this is true only of the men. A finer race of *working-women,* and one more loyal to their people and cause, does not exist. Indeed, the women are the real stamina of this locality, and all efforts to combine for mutual protection must fail until the women take the direction of such efforts. For they are the workers and the providers; they can keep a secret, and they can fulfill a promise. There is another reason why no organization excluding women could succeed here, namely, if all the men in this neighborhood refused to work for the wages offered them, it would make little matter as long as the women did not strike. "They would step in," said a white citizen of Talladega to me, "and do any kind of work, except barbering, better than their husbands."

I met a woman who lived a few miles from Talladega, and she showed me $98, the receipts from her own little cotton patch, and, said she, "I ploughed, and I sowed, and I hoed every lick of it myself; and I picked it, and got it baled, and sold it too."

This is no extraordinary case. I met everywhere in the neighborhood of Talladega women not only able but eager and willing to do more than a man's work, if by it they could only send their children to school. I noticed, also, as a result of this predominating female energy, that here the girls as well as the boys are sent to school. In Georgia even there was a feeling that a girl's education was rather a luxury, or a secondary matter. They have the same hard struggle here to obtain a little learning; what opportunities there are are dear for their means, and often far away, and they make large sacrifices for the purpose, and generally at pitiful odds. They are noble mothers, fighting life in a terribly narrow arena.

Ambrose Hedden, a colored man of high standing in Talladega, and universally respected by the better class of citizens, told me a very interesting incident about the Baptist College in Talladega. "I sawed," he said, "the first plank and knocked off the first shaving for the white Baptist College in 1852. I was a slave then, and I put $900 worth of work on the building—my master's donation to the college. Many a time when I was busy there I used to wonder what I and my people had done that we could not be educated also. The Lord was better to me than I trusted. I lived to see my sons and daughters, every one of them, graduate from its halls."

Mr. Hedden's house is one of the most comfortable homes in Talladega, and while sitting in its pretty parlor he told me the story of the sale of his wife and the same four children who have since graduated. As this story shows one of the most kindly and amiable sides of slavery, I think it only just to tell it.

"One morning," said he, "old Aunt Mary came to me, and after making me promise not to say a word to anybody, she told me she had overheard Mr. Hunt—that was my wife's master; I belonged to Mr. Hedden—making arrangements to sell my wife and four little children. I had promised to say nothing, and for several days I carried this grief on my heart; and never had my work seemed so hard and hopeless. One morning I was sent to Lawyer ———'s office with a message.

"'All right, Hedden,' said the lawyer, when I had delivered it.

"There was a man sitting there, and when the lawyer said 'Hedden,' he kind o' looked up, and pulling a paper out of his pocket, read aloud, 'Mary Hedden' (for in Alabama the wife took her husband's name), 'Ambrose Hedden, Andrew Hedden, Kate Hedden, Alice Hedden—why, them five will be my property soon,' says he.

"'Yes,' I answered, 'and they are my wife and children. Oh, Mr. ———, it is dreadful when a man has to sit still and bear all this.'

"'Come, Ambrose,' said the lawyer, 'don't take on so hard; perhaps they won't be sold far away.'

"Now I could speak of it without hurting any one, and I went that night to see Mr. Hunt, and he promised me he would not sell them until I had tried to get some one in Talladega to buy them."

"Why did you not ask your own master, Mr. Hedden, to buy them?" I inquired.

Harper's Weekly, December 4, 1880, p. 780.   PREPARING THE THANKSGIVING DINNER.—Drawn by S. G. McCutcheon.

"Because my wife had never done field-work, and she wasn't able for it, either, and Mr. and Mrs. Hedden were people who did not like to keep a woman round the house for nothing but house-work. But next day, when I was at my work, old master he came down where I was, and says he—you know he talks with a lisp, and very slow—says he, 'Well, Ambrose, you are wading through deep waters, boy, ain't you, Ambrose?'

"'Yes, sir.'

"'Yes, yes, just so. Why didn't you come to old master about it, now, Ambrose? Eh, Ambrose?'

"I didn't answer, and says he, 'Come, now, Ambrose, why didn't you come to old master about it?'

"So I just up and told him; and when I got through, he said, 'Yes, yes, Ambrose, I see. Now you go hitch up, and take old misses down to see your wife and children, Ambrose, and if she likes them, I'll buy them, and I'll promise you your wife shall never go into the field, Ambrose.'

"Then I asked him if he would promise me one thing more—that if ever he wanted to sell my wife and children, he would sell us all to-together. And he promised me that wherever one went, the others should go too. Well, old misses was delighted with my wife and the children, and after a little trouble about the price, old master bought them; and he kept his word, both he and old misses, and no one in bondage was ever more kindly dealt with than they dealt with me and mine."

With the exception of Mr. Hedden's and a few other houses, the homes of the colored people are miserable as can be. They are usually log-huts of one room, with a chimney of mud and logs, and a rickety door that answers both for door and window. Yet nearly all these one-roomed cabins shelter some homeless, friendless old man or woman, whom freedom left without a protector, aged, sick, and decrepit. I think this universal and kindly care of the old victims of a dead wrong is one of the most beautiful traits of humanity I ever saw.

Outside Talladega there are two suburban settlements of negroes, called Needmore and Knoxville. The huts here are usually surrounded by rail fences, not of the open zigzag form, but of stakes driven into the ground close together. Every hut is guarded by the biggest and most ferocious dogs I ever saw. I became convinced here that I bore a charmed life, or else I certainly should have been either torn to pieces or frightened to death. Curiosity led me into yards which seemed to be safe enough, but before I could reach the door, I had to retire against the fence, and defend myself with a stout cane, which I carried for the purpose, while I shouted aloud for help. This usually alarmed all the dogs in the neighborhood, and by the time the mistress appeared—quite as often from her neighbor's house as her own—I had made a vow, which I always broke, never to go inside a negro's fence again.

The aggravation was nearly always increased by the smiling information that "the dog wouldn't bite me." One woman told me that I must call upon her between meals, and then her dogs—four immense ones—would not hurt me, but that they would tear any one to pieces, black or white, who opened the gate while the meals were on the table. They profess to keep these brutes to protect their chickens—a very unnecessary amount of protection, it struck me; and I strongly suspected that dog-fighting was a prevalent amusement among them, though all denied it.

I found the women here a little more careful as to their appearance than the same class were in Georgia, and their homes were not quite as filthy. I do not mean that they were clean, but only that they were a little above the average dirt line—that is all. Homespun and the white or colored head-cloth, or turban, are more worn here than in Georgia, for the Alabama women seem to have a natural aptitude for the loom. They do all their own spinning and dyeing and weaving; and I have seen designs which they have drawn and worked out, of which the least praise that can be given them is that they were exceedingly pretty.

I went once to another colored settlement, called Lawson, and Mrs. Lawson showed me some of the most beautiful white counterpanes I have ever seen. From the sowing of the cotton to the knotting on the handsome fringe that finished them, all was her own work. This woman had taken the prize for two years at the State Fair, not only for her fine work, but also for her beautiful designs. When I called on her, she was drawing a pattern for the quilt she purposed sending to the next State Fair.

The patches of ground around these cabins are generally sown with corn and vegetables, the cotton patches being further away. But the fields of both black and white, with few exceptions, are disgracefully cultivated. Most of them are full of old stumps, or of trunks of great trees that have either been killed by burning, or else by cutting a gash all round the roots, through which the tree bleeds its life away in streams of amber resin. The planting is of the most primitive kind: the briers are cut down, the seed scattered over the ground, and then ploughed in. "We do dat way 'count ob de lan' being so rich," said an old man to me. And even with this scanty labor the crops are abundant.

The question naturally rises, How does it happen that the colored people are so poor in such a rich country? Mainly because they are so shamefully cheated when they work a farm on shares, and very few of them have the little capital necessary to work on any other plan. "Why," said a prominent man in Talladega to me, "you can get a nigger to put in a whole year's work on your place, give him some corn and bacon to feed himself and family, take the crop to town, sell it, and put the money in your pocket, and if you clap the nigger on the shoulder, give him a quarter, and say, 'Well, John, we ain't made much this year, but we'll do better next, maybe,' he's satisfied." Yes, satisfied, just as a child who knows it is wronged, but has neither the skill nor strength to right itself, is satisfied.

As a usual thing, the agreement is to work the farm for a third of the cotton and a fourth of the wheat and corn; and I have known instances where they have been told that "the crop didn't make any third or fourth," and the negroes were so ignorant as to believe this a reasonable excuse. It is a very common trick to get one or two colored families on plantations, and agree to provide for them food, shelter, and clothes from spring to harvest, the negro to pay the planter interest for such provision out of the proceeds of his share of the crop. The shelter is the ordinary miserable cabin; the food corn meal and bacon; the clothing is usually that cast off by the white family. Yet all the time the negro is paying interest to the planter, who is supposed to be providing real comforts for his family, and not only to the planter, which is perhaps just, but also to the store-keeper who is supposed to be lying out of the interest on the goods supposed to be provided. I tried in several cases to explain to them the folly of paying interest twice over on the same bill, but the whole interest question is a puzzle to them over which they shake their heads in hopeless despair.

Then, again, the negro has a mule, horse, or ox to provide, and this has to be bought and fed on the same principle; still, the crops are generally so large that the colored partner believes himself perfectly safe. Then comes the harvest; the white partner sells the cotton, corn, and wheat, and without thinking it necessary to render a bill of totals, let alone items, he tells the negro that it has taken everything to pay what he owed him and the store-keeper, and that in fact he is twenty, forty, or fifty dollars in debt, and must remain and work it out.

This information, and much more of a similar kind, was given me both by black and white men whose truthfulness I have not the slightest reason to doubt; besides, it agrees exactly with what most of the colored women told me, and with much that I myself observed. Still, though this robbery is very general, there are honorable exceptions, and the plan of working on shares has been frequently proved to be good and fair for the negro laborer, if he falls into honest hands, or if he is clever enough to understand what rightly belongs to him, and to insist on having it.

The negroes here are very good farmers, and from such rich land ought to draw at least comfort and respectability; but they are as ignorant as little children, and *it is so easy to rob them that* the temptation to do so is irresistible, except to very honest men. Besides, either through ignorance or carelessness, they neglect the most obvious means of protecting themselves, as the following instance will show.

Quite a number of colored families went some miles away from Talladega, and settled a little place, which they called after their leader—Lawson. (This Lawson was the husband of the woman whose fine designing and weaving I have spoken of.) They cleared the land, and made such improvements as a colony so humble could afford. But they neglected to enter their land, and a white Baptist minister went to Montgomery, entered the land as his own, and turned out the colonists almost at an hour's notice. It said something for their perseverance that instead of going back to town, they struck deeper into the pine forest, cleared new ground, and began again.

For such wrongs as these there is practically no redress: except at election times the negro has few friends and little influence. A few here and there are sufficiently educated to know their rights, and morally strong enough to insist on having them. But I am not speaking of these exceptions, but of a great nation of poor, helpless, ignorant *children*—children in everything but physical strength, for they have in a remarkable degree a child's bitter sense of injustice, a child's secret, futile anger, and perhaps a child's foolish dream of some future revenge.

I am not making these statements without being sure as to what I say; even such a man as Ambrose Hedden, whose natural intelligence is of a high order, can not always protect himself. He told me that when a certain building was to be erected he had the offer of the work. Having inquired carefully of many prominent gentlemen in Talladega as to the responsibility of the party building, he took the contract, the payment to be in three installments. The contract was drawn out by a lawyer who never gave Hedden a copy of it, and who refused to allow the one drawn out to leave the office. When the last payment of $200 was due, the contract could not be found, and the man who had employed Hedden told him that he did not owe him anything, and bid him "go to the devil."

When I was in Talladega a wealthy planter deliberately shot a colored man, wounding him severely, because he accidentally dropped his gouty foot as he lifted him from his carriage. There was no action of any kind taken in the matter, and no more severe comment made than that "the Blanks were all *very high spirited*." At the same time I saw in Talladega jail a colored man whose crime was carrying concealed weapons.

I have often heard it said, even by their Northern teachers, that negroes have no sense of gratitude or of honor. For gratitude they have little opportunity, and whenever they received an honest kindness, I have rarely known them slow to acknowledge it. I remember, almost with tears, little "widows' mites" of offerings, whose very poverty made them almost sacred. As for their sense of honor, I could give instance after instance of scrupulous regard to contracts, when ruin to themselves was the consequence.

I knew a colored man who was studying for the ministry, and who got into debt for his tuition. This seemed to be a case where the end might have excused the fault. But he never thought of shirking his obligation on that ground. His wife, though she had been raised as a house-servant, and was a slight, delicate-looking woman, went up to Alabama Furnace, took up ground, and worked in the fields herself, to pay his missionary teachers. I spent a night at the pretty home she had made among the pines, and she showed me with honest pride a fine cow, a pretty mare, some pigs and chickens, all of which she had bought with her own labor. When I called on her she was in the field sowing rye. As a rule I found the negroes afraid of debt, and willing to give the one thing they had to give—their labor—in payment of any bill, just or unjust, that is urged against them.

They are much more quiet and decorous in their religious services than I expected to find them; but this is quite natural, for they are not under any circumstances as demonstrative as the Charleston, or even as the Georgia negro. For two or three weeks after I went to Talladega I could not think what it was I missed in their homes; finally I discovered it was the want of music. *They don't sing.* In Carolina and Georgia every cabin had some singer, and very often the songs were impromptu, and referred to events just happening. In Alabama I never heard an impromptu verse. They indeed sing in their churches, but they don't break into song over all the joys and sorrows of their simple life as I have heard other negroes do.

Still, they are not wanting in a humble kind of imagination. When under spiritual excitement their similes have a kind of natural flavor about them that shows them to be at least genuine and heart-felt. I heard one old man pray, "Good Master, when our heads are like de cotton, all white, do Thou gather us into Thy keeping." A woman very seriously asked the "Lord Jesus to start at de back ob de house, and if thar war any rusty knives laying round, to help 'em to rub 'em up bright." Another, who had probably had that day a long and dirty walk to church, prayed for a heart "to choose de cleanest stepping-stones."

At one prayer-meeting at which I was present—for it is in these gatherings the negro character reveals itself—I witnessed the following amusing scene. Two women, Aunt Lucy and Aunt Phoebe, had had a bitter quarrel. After it Aunt Phoebe fell ill. On the night of which I speak, Uncle Bill, the husband of Aunt Lucy, led the prayer-meeting; and in the warmth of his exalted position he forgot all about the quarrel between his wife and Aunt Phoebe, and began praying fervently for the sick woman. The injured wife bore it but a very few minutes, ere she called out in great anger:

"Dar, now, Bill, dat'll do fur you! Dat prayer don't go no higher nor de roof!"

I am compelled to say that Bill and his prayer subsided before the furious woman, and that a hearty hymn scarcely concealed the general laugh against him.

In the outside churches the congregations are collected by blowing long tin horns, it being understood that at the third horn service begins. But no people can have less conception of the importance, or of the flight, of time, and I have seen them come in as the benediction was being pronounced. All during service they go in and out, get a drink, or a smoke, and come back whenever they please.

Their churches are little log-huts in the pine forests, and I have some very pleasant and very funny memories connected with them. One day I was met as I was coming out of one by a little old woman as black as a crow. She took firm hold of me, and insisted that she had made a fine dinner for me, and I must go home with her and eat it. I looked at her, and I thought I should like to go home with her very much. So I followed her down the cone-covered hill-side, and over half a dozen rail fences, till we came to the very smallest house I ever saw in my life. An old man, with a white night-cap tied under his chin, made his appearance from out a dense smoke, as the little old woman called, "Here we are, pap; whar are you?"

Then it appeared he had been smoking his bacon, and he dived back into the smoke, and brought out an iron pot half full of burning corncobs. "Go inside, ma'am," he begged, and bowed, and that with such an expression of pride and delight that it would have been a sin to refuse the invitation. When the room was cleared, I saw that the rafters were hung with half-smoked bacon, and the rude table was laid with three forks, four knives, and two or three coffee-cups.

The dinner consisted of three pieces of chicken—very small—some bacon and greens, four little sausages, some corn-dodgers, a small indescribable pie, and the best coffee the dear old soul knew how to make. My seat was in danger of falling to pieces, and the two prongs of my fork were so wide apart that it required some careful guiding to get the food safely as far as my mouth. But what of that? I could see nothing but the childlike delight of the old couple, whose life-long poverty had been so great that they honestly thought they had spread for me quite a noble feast.

"Eat all you kin," cried my hostess, piling on my plate the greens and bacon—"eat eberything on de table. 'Tain't often I go on a spree, *but when I do, I go it.* Don't I, pap? I tell you, I don't often entertain; but once in a while I jist break loose, and den I sprees roun'. Don't I, pap? Hev some more. Do, now. Hev all there's on de table. Do, now;" and the dear old creature's smiles and nods were wonderful.

The negroes here light their houses almost altogether with fat pine; and I have spent many happy hours about these blazing hearths, listening to histories which had far more of romance in them than what usually goes by that name. For instance, sitting one night by the comfortable fire-side of a very excellent house, the proprietor of it told me that he had been a wretched slave in that very house, and that he had determined, on being set free, to become master where he had once been a slave. Between the determination and the realization lay a heroic story, too long to tell here, but he had compassed the utmost of his wishes.

I am aware that these little incidents touch only one or two points of a many-sided nationality; but, as far as they go, they truthfully index a wide and interesting chapter, which either as good citizens of a great republic, or as good children of a common Father, we can not read too soon or too carefully.—B.

WHY YOUNG AMERICANS ARE REPUBLICANS

HARPER'S WEEKLY
December 11, 1880, p. 787

A young man in Indiana writes that he personally knows thirteen families in his city of which the fathers have voted the Democratic ticket, from scavenger to President, since 1852, but the oldest son in each family, casting their first Presidential vote in 1880, gave it to Garfield. He believes that three-quarters of such ballots were thrown for the Republicans this year, and he naturally claims for this vote the credit of the result in Indiana, and proudly signs himself "one of 'em." His view is singularly confirmed by the striking article in the Chicago *Times,* which has been universally copied, and which might have been one of Mr. Ingersoll's speeches. This article asserts that "the youth of this republic is not Democratic," and proceeds in a forcible and picturesque strain to give the reasons.

The Democratic party is identified with slavery and slave-holding; the Republican party with emancipation and the war. "The curse of slavery has poisoned the blood and rotted the bone of the Democratic party." After a very eloquent description of the way in which the war and its events and separations and sorrows weaned the children that were born from the Democratic party, the article proceeds:

> "The children go to school. There is not a Democrat on its benches. The first Reader contains a portrait of Abraham Lincoln: that kind and sturdy face never made a Democrat. On its simple pages, in words of one or two syllables, is told the story of his birth and death: that story never made a Democrat. In the pranks of the play-ground the name silences the frolicsome, and makes the jolliest grave: that name never made a Democrat. In

"YOU ARE WADING THROUGH DEEP WATERS, BOY, AIN'T YOU?"

Harper's Weekly, December 4, 1880, p. 781.

the pictures that light up the geography are the firing on Fort Sumter and the death of Ellsworth: those pictures make no Democrats. The first page of the History contains a representation of the surrender of Ler at Appomattox: no boy gazes on that and ever after avows himself a Democrat. In the higher grades the same subtle and unresisted influence is at work. The text-books contain extracts from patriots' speeches during the war: those speeches make no Democrats. The great battles are briefly described: the narrative has no Democratic listeners. The strain of martial music runs through the Readers, and that music makes no Democrats. Sketches of the great generals are given: their brave deeds arouse the enthusiasm of the lads, but there is no Democrat among them. The horrors and sufferings of the slaves are told: the maddened blood that mounts the boys' cheeks is not Democratic blood. The curse of slavery has pursued the Democratic party, and has hounded it to its death. Therefore let it die, and no lip will be found to say a prayer over the grass on its grave."

This is both forcible and true. It is seen as plainly, and more plainly, across the ocean, for distance in space is like the lapse of time in giving an accurate point of view. The London *Spectator*, in commenting upon the result of our late election, says that the great majority of the people outside the old slave-holding region lived through the war, and are still unwilling to trust power to the Democrats again. It thinks that it is to defend "State rights" that the solid South supports the Democratic party, and to defend the national right that the solid North adheres to the Republicans. They are the theories of two civilizations. Finally it sums up the situation, and in a manner curiously accordant with the view of the Chicago *Times,* which is indisputably the view which history will approve. The root of the feeling which has controlled the decision by the election of General Garfield the *Spectator* believes to be the conviction of intelligent and patriotic Americans that the Republican party, with many faults, stands for "human freedom, equality before the law, and open careers for all, independent of color, creed, or caste." That this is the historical significance of the party can be no more denied than that the Sons of Liberty in the Revolution stood for American independence. Until the Democratic party ceases to be, as the late election shows it to be now, a political organization whose force and control lie in the hands of those who tried to destroy the Union to save slavery, and who now destroy liberty to seize control of the Union, it can return to power only by successful bulldozing or forgery. Some Democrats ask for an end of sectionalism and a return to decent and normal politics. Does anything prevent but the Democratic party?

VICIOUS TEXT-BOOKS

HARPER'S WEEKLY
December 18, 1880, p. 807

An old Virginia correspondent, not a "carpet-bagger," who voted for Garfield "with as much pleasure as for any candidate I ever supported," says that he does not wish to see the Republicans locally successful in his town, and a correspondent in Arkansas says exactly the same thing. They are both very earnest and very intelligent Republicans, and their feeling is well worthy the attention of our Louisiana correspondent, of whose letter we speak elsewhere. The Virginian holds that the first step to be taken to remedy the evil at the South is to attack the ignorance of the voters, both white and colored, which is the real source of difficulty. This, he thinks, should be a national work, and such is his faith in the efficacy of national action that he would gladly see the government wholly centralized.

President Hayes has pointedly called attention to the subject of education as a political solvent in our situation, and it is very possible that he may make some recommendations upon the subject in his annual message. But we remind our Virginian friend, who can see "no use in two sets of laws in this country," that the political distinction between his county and his State is very valuable, and that the same kind of distinction between the State and the Union is most serviceable. The speculative cast of the Southern political mind will long cause it to talk of "the sovereignty" of the State—of

Florida, or Oregon. That is a phantasm, however, which will gradually disappear. But so long as it is honestly believed to be more than a pointless speculation it will, and for good reason, radically injure the section which fosters it.

One of the most copious sources of mischief and of prolonged sectional estrangement is the State system of education. No interest is more essentially national, and none demands more stringently a national care, than education. Some of the States actually teach in the common schools a feeling of hostility to the Union. That is to say, text-books pervert the facts of history to the discredit of the national government, and to the perpetuity of angry feeling. No text-book known to us in any Northern State does this. Its narration of fact does not necessarily foster ill feeling. The story of slavery is told, indeed, as it should be, but not with party acrimony or personal crimination. Our correspondent may be sure that there is the utmost disposition in this part of the country to support any wise national aid for education in the Southern States.

EDUCATION OF THE COLORED RACE

NEW-YORK TIMES
December 29, 1880, p. 3

The action of the School Board of Baltimore in refusing to appoint as teachers in schools for colored children persons of their own race who were proved on examination to be entirely competent, and in going directly back on a promise to try the experiment of placing two new schools for colored children in charge of colored teachers, shows that race prejudice is still one of the great obstacles in the way of educating the largest class of illiterate persons in the States where slavery formerly existed. The question of educating the enfranchised race is one of vast importance to the country, and especially so to the section where it constitutes a considerable part of the population. The movement in favor of national aid to popular education in the States is based mainly on the great need of stimulating the intelligence and informing the minds of the negroes, who are henceforth to exercise the functions of citizens. That they are ill-fitted in some respects for the duties and responsibilities of citizenship must be admitted, and the consequences are inevitably such as to interfere either with the wisdom and efficiency of local government or with the free exercise of their rights. Their ignorance and incapacity to understand fully their recently acquired relations to the State are to a large extent the cause of the disorders from which they suffer, and of the difficulty of securing for them the benefit of their enfranchisement. These are made the excuse for efforts to keep them in political subjection even where they constitute a majority of voters, and are the source of the weakness of the race for political self-defense.

The civic rights of the negro race in this country are the result of irresistible events, and they are, beyond question, to be securely established by one means or another. The whole Nation is pledged to see that they are not taken away or rendered of no effect by indirection. Most assuredly, the best and surest method of solving the problem involved is to endeavor to raise the colored citizens to the capacity of citizenship by education rather than to be continually plagued with the difficulty of protecting them in their incapacity. Many of the more liberal-minded people of the South profess to have no other objection to the free exercise of the suffrage by negroes than the ignorance that prevails among them. It is, in fact, very generally admitted that the great necessity of the race is education, and if its members can be improved in intelligence and put in the way of understanding public interests and the duties pertaining to them, it is believed that the obstacles placed in their way will gradually disappear. The Southern States, where they exist in great numbers, plead that the task is too much for them. They profess to be willing that the negroes should be put to school, that their children should have every opportunity and advantage for instruction, but the organizing and maintaining of the necessary school system is a work of difficulty and expense too great for them to cope with. We prefer to believe that these professions are in the main true, though beyond doubt there still remains much of the old prejudice against educating negroes. There is a sort of unworthy jealousy of any increase in their capabilities and a desire to keep them in the position of hewers of wood and drawers of water, content with menial functions.

But assuming the professions of willingness to have them better fitted for the exercise of the duties of citizenship, and to allow them freedom in that exercise so far as they are fitted for it, to be genuine, we have a right to expect that no obstacles shall be put in the way of their acquiring education. They should have their full share in the benefit of such schools as exist, and those who rise to the capacity of good teachers should be gladly welcomed to the task of helping on the work. There is one thing to be said of the enfranchised blacks generally. They are eager to learn; they are ambitious to place themselves on an intellectual level with the whites, so far as they can, and they are anxious to exercise their rights intelligently and honorably. It cannot be said that as a class they are vicious or depraved, turbulent or disorderly, or disposed to be intractable. They are remarkably docile, and all things considered they show a disposition to become good citizens that is altogether surprising. They may have been misled and used by unscrupulous leaders for purposes inconsistent with good government, but there is every reason to believe that education would make excellent citizens of them, far better than many whose favor is courted by politicians of all parties through a display of special solicitude for their rights and claims. One of the first steps in the great work of educating the colored race must be the discountenancing of such perverse Bourbonism as that so conspicuously displayed in Baltimore. The negroes must be allowed to do all they can for their own advancement. The States should do all that can reasonably be regarded as within their power to provide for their instruction, and then there will be no grudging of national aid for the work. But national aid should be a help to efforts earnestly and honestly undertaken by State and local authorities and in no sense or degree a substitute for them, and it should be understood meanwhile that the protection of all citizens in the exercise of their rights is not held in abeyance. Such exercise is in itself an important part of education and should be secure while its results are improving under the process of making all classes of citizens better qualified for it.

1881

Coverage for 1881 continued to reflect the lingering sectional animosity and the role political parties had in promoting the sovereignty of the federal government and the states. Critics charged and countercharged that the appropriate party to run the country was the one that had long term loyalty to the Constitution. Both parties, however, saw each other as dangerous to the final unification of the country. Yet rising from the mayhem one heard faint voices of reconciliation from both regions.

Will the Solid South ever allow for free and fair elections? Will black voters be allowed to vote without intimidation? Will attempting to vote bring economic reprisals and physical harm to African Americans? The Bourbons/Redeemers loudly proclaimed that true democracy—one man, one vote—was in operation across the South. Yet, cautious Republicans continued to remind the public of the atrocities committed against blacks in the name of white supremacy. In fact questions of fairness and equality abound in the 1881 coverage of African Americans. Editorials continued to address the prejudicial foundation with which West Point handled the Whittaker case—the overt racism at a national institution like West Point. The call for public disclosure of the charges against the black cadet, the credibility of his white accusers, and the enforcement of the Fifteenth Amendment in states where loopholes, i.e., poll taxes, grandfather clauses, and white primaries, were reducing African American voter eligibility.

But sketches of southern progressivism are evident in editorials that call for the abandonment of the "lost cause" and the creation of a new industrialized region. A few economic opportunities had given the rising merchant class of the South reason to believe that sectional prejudices and divisions were beginning to disappear. It was this new generation of southerners, now coming of age, that Republicans believed would be *freed from blind loyalty to a bygone era and now would seek mutual alliances in bringing forth a fair and diverse South. Otherwise, like their ancestors, the critics declared, this group of young men would be locked into a preoccupation with the return of Black Reconstruction, i.e, "Negro ascendency."*

By fall, bipartisan politics had to confront the emergence of third parties like the Greenbacks and address how these parties would benefit from the schisms in the Democratc and Republican parties. Each of the two traditional parties had to face a reduction of strength as the two party system began to be challenged by persons no longer concerned with the bickering between the two.

Jacqueline A. Rouse
Georgia State University

THE WHITTAKER COURT-MARTIAL

HARPER'S WEEKLY
January 22, 1881, pp. 50–51

General Howard has been appointed to the Superintendency of West Point, and a court-martial has been summoned for the trial of Whittaker. These two facts show very clearly that the Administration was not satisfied that Whittaker had had fair play. This impression was widely diffused, and it was not removed by General Schofield's report, the tone of which was that of ill-concealed indignation with the policy of equal rights at West Point. We do not mean that the General used language which could be verbally cited to this effect. But it certainly seems to us impossible to read the document without perceiving the old, bitter, aristocratic prejudice which was so long associated with West Point. It is undoubtedly true, as General Schofield says, that social preferences and the choice of friendly companionships can not be controlled by law. No law can make men fond of each other, or compel them to associate upon friendly terms. No law can destroy the distaste of race, where it exists. No law can force the white and the colored people in this country to mingle upon unconsciously equal terms.

All this is true. But something else is true of which these assertions take no account. When a nation has decided that in a national institution there shall be absolute equality of right in all things to which the national authority properly extends, it is possible to place the institution either under a control which is perfectly friendly to that policy, or under a direction which acquiesces in it because it can not help itself, but which regards the policy itself as fanatical and moonstruck folly. It is evident that, under the first, there will be a disposition to secure fair play, which will of itself go far to secure it; and under the second, a feeling that every protest and outbreak against the established order is precisely what might be expected. At a school like West Point, if there be a prejudice among the pupils against the equal association in a public school of white and colored students, and this prejudice is known to the pupils to be shared by the authorities of the school, the condition of the students against whom the prejudice lies will be very much more uncomfortable, and demonstrations of the prejudice will be very much more probable, than if it be known that the authorities heartily and honestly despise the prejudice. It is possible, of course, that a homopathic hospital may be administered according to the principles of that school by allopathic managers, but if the trustees would secure that result beyond question, they would place it in homoeopathic hands.

In regard to Whittaker, there is no doubt that the evidence seemed to be very unfavorable to him; but there is no doubt, also, of a general feeling that the atmosphere of the court was unfriendly. General Schofield declared his own impressions plainly at the outset, and they were very hostile to Whittaker. The gentlemen who compose the new court are beyond suspicion and reproach. We certainly intend no insinuation against the first board of inquiry; and if their conclusion is confirmed by the present board, there will be no further question. There can be no valid objection against a trial conducted with all the authority of a court in a case of which the preliminary inquiry was far from satisfactory to many minds. Meanwhile, whatever the final judgment upon this case may be, the spirit disclosed by General Schofield's letter and report, and by the work of the colored cadet Flipper describing his residence at West Point, and by all that is known of the state of things at the school, is such that if the country really intends that the kind of equality which it has guaranteed shall be maintained at West Point—by which, we repeat, we do not mean the regulation of social preferences and companionship—the change of superintendency which has been made is most desirable and commendable.

SENATOR EDMUNDS AND WEST POINT

HARPER'S WEEKLY
February 5, 1881, p. 83

Senator Edmunds tells the truth in his West Point report, and in his usual pungent way. Of the Whittaker inquiry he says that the young man was placed in a false position from the first, and he asks why, if the mere word of the white cadets acquitted them of all complicity, the same theory did not apply to the colored cadet. We hope that Mr. District Attorney Townsend's experience in this case will be made public. He is a man of ardent feeling, but his sympathies are no warmer on one side than the military authorities showed theirs to be upon the other.

Senator Garland says that there is every reason that the colored boys should receive full and equal advantages at West Point, but that no regulation of law can control the terms of social equality. He adds, tentatively, that "if it be deemed expedient to continue further this co-education," the matter must be left to time and experience, "which may result in its mitigation, or the complete separation of the two races in their military education."

Upon this point Senator Edmunds remarks that there is no insurmountable objection to the correction of existing evils at the Academy. The wise influence and example of the instructors and officers could do much to secure justice of feeling and treatment. If such a result is really not to be attained, Senator Edmunds thinks that it should be a matter of serious consideration whether the school should not be abolished. If in an institution supported by the country the equal rights of citizens can not be maintained, the mischiefs of such an example are very much greater than any technical advantages to be gained by a certain class.

THE INAUGURAL ADDRESS

HARPER'S WEEKLY
March 19, 1881, p. 179

President Garfield's inaugural address appears just as we go to press. The President speaks strongly and

BOWING TO THE POWERS THAT BE.
"What, not gwan ter keep Thanksgivin'? Don' you know de President ob dese United States has made a proclamation to dat effect?"
"Shoo! is dat so? Wal, I s'pose I's a law-abidin' citizen."

Harper's Weekly, March 5, 1881, p. 371

temperately of the great question of free suffrage, which is the real dividing line of parties; but his tone, while perfectly firm, is entirely unexceptionable, while his reference to old issues shows that he believes their day to have ended. He re-affirms his predecessor's views upon the wisdom of national provision for education, and he restates his uncompromising fidelity to hard money, expressing his confidence that the metals may be so adjusted that the purchasing and debt-paying power of the dollar shall be equal. President Garfield quotes the decided expressions of President Hayes in regard to the isthmian canal projects as indicating his own conviction and policy. He speaks strongly against the toleration of polygamy in Utah, and would prohibit it rigorously. . . .

PERSONAL

HARPER'S WEEKLY
March 19, 1881, p. 179

The Papyrus people had a pleasant time at their monthly meeting, a few evenings since, at the Revere House, and many good things in prose and verse were said and read. Mark Twain was very amusing. His experience in endeavoring to obtain a berth in a sleeping-car, the rough discourtesy of the gentlemanly conductors, and his final triumph in getting the big family stateroom through the benign attentions of the colored porter, are very well told. "Law bless you, sah, I knowed you in a minute! I told de conductah so; I knowed you de minute I sot eyes on you." "Is that so, my boy?" (handing him a quadruple fee); "well, who am I?" "General McClellan," replied the man and brother, and disappeared.

A NEW "SOUTH"

HARPER'S WEEKLY
March 26, 1881, p. 194

The pleasant reception of the New York Seventy-first Regiment in New Orleans, and the incidents recorded by the reporters, are signs of that awakening of a new South which every good citizen is glad to observe. Among these signs is the recent article of the Hon. A. H. H. Stuart, of Virginia, in the *Southern Planter and Farmer*. It is an appeal to the young men of Virginia, and these are among the sensible remarks of Mr. Stuart:

"The overthrow of slavery has destroyed the foundation on which the old system rested, and the time has come when we must conform our methods of instruction and our pursuits in life to the changed condition of our social and industrial organization. What Virginia now needs is not closet men, learned scholars, or brilliant orators, but 'men of affairs'—earnest, practical business men, men competent to deal with and push forward the material interests of the State—such as skilled engineers, geologists, mineralogists, miners, machinists, and mechanics. Slavery is dead, and many of the sectional jealousies and prejudices which it engendered are dying out with it. Sagacious Northern men had their attention drawn to the vast sources of undeveloped wealth which exist in the Southern States. . . . Our people are beginning to take more common-sense views of questions connected with business and politics. They are beginning to see the policy of 'kicking against the pricks.' They have found out that, under our system of government, the majority of the States are not in accord with those of Virginia, and that true policy requires that they should no longer wage a fruitless contest, but accept the situation, and secure for themselves all the benefits to which they are justly entitled. . . . There are but two sources from which danger is to be apprehended: first, habits of indolence and self-indulgence, and prejudice against manual and mechanical labor, which is the last legacy of slavery; second, a mistaken system of education, which has given too much attention to the ideal, and too little to the practical. A determined and manly spirit can vanquish the first, and a change in the course of instruction, by which more prominence will be given to physical science and mechanics and the construction and uses of machinery, will overcome the last."

SOUTHERN REPUBLICANS AND REPUDIATION

HARPER'S WEEKLY
May 7, 1881, p. 294

In another column we print a very timely and instructive Republican letter from Alabama, written by the chairman of a Republican District Committee, in reply to one which we recently published from a Democratic correspondent in the same State. We commend the letter to careful attention, because it throws indirectly a great deal of light upon the Mahone controversy in Virginia, showing why Southern Republicans who, like our correspondent, are "hard-money, national-bank" men, vote with Greenbackers and Re-adjusters rather than with Bourbons. The reason, as the letter states, is that the paramount question in Southern politics is a free vote and a fair count, and that the Bourbons, whether they are anti-repudiators, as many in Virginia are, or rank paper-money repudiators, like many in Alabama, are still the party of fraud at the polls. Exceptions to the rule there doubtless are. But it is those who are known as Bourbon Democrats who suppress the colored vote. The Independents, Greenbackers, and anti-Bourbons of Alabama met at Montgomery, and denouncing Democratic tampering with the election laws, which had produced fraud and perjury, demanded a fair election and an honest count. Republicans, who regarded that as the most vital issue, naturally voted with its friends, and against its enemies.

This is the clew, also, to the Virginia situation. The colored Republican voters in that State are doubtless very poor and very ignorant. But, as we said when Mr. Mahone was elected, he captured the colored vote, not because it knows anything of finance or of "re-adjustment," but because he declared for a free vote and a fair count, and, so far as has appeared, he has kept his word. Mr. Mahone's personal character is not pertinent to the discussion. In Mr. Hill's first violent speech he assumed that Mr. Mahone was a Democrat who was elected by Democrats, and who was morally bound to vote with Democrats. Mr. Hill knew Mr. Mahone then as well as he knows him now. He knew that he was a repudiator, and if he was a man of bad repute, he knew that also. But, repudiator as he was, Mr. Hill evidently did not think that his repudiating heresies disqualified him as a Democrat. Democratic denunciation of Mr. Mahone as a repudiator, therefore, evidently does not arise from any unwillingness to have his vote. Hard-money Democrats would say that his re-adjustment is his own affair, but if he chooses to vote for Democratic candidates and measures, they would not object. That is precisely what Southern Republicans say. If, indeed, Republicans have bought his vote, and have not merely accepted it, it is an infamous bargain; and if in Virginia Republicans vote for repudiation in order to secure a free vote and a fair count, they play a desperate game, because those who would cheat creditors would not hesitate to cheat allies. So far, however, as Mr. Mahone is supported in Virginia by intelligent Republicans, it is in spite of his repudiation, and in order to break down Bourbonism, which is regarded as a greater evil. It is alleged that his cry of a free vote and a fair count is insincere, that he has heretofore done as much cheating at the polls as any man in Virginia, and that he did not declare for honest elections until his prospects as a Democratic politician were ruined. If this be true, he is an unprincipled politician, but it is certainly not strange that the colored voter prefers the unprincipled politician who is on his side to the same kind of politician on the other side. Let the reader mark the Democratic resolutions in Alabama quoted by our correspondent, and he will see that to be a Democrat, at least in that State, is to be also a wholesale Greenbacker. To secure his great end of a fair election in an overwhelmingly Democratic State, the Republican, white or colored, will generally take the course which our correspondent has taken.

So in Virginia, if Mr. Mahone be the worthless character that his Democratic opponents declare him to be, do they not see that he has acquired his ascendency because of their own conduct? Why did not they long ago win the colored vote by a wise and friendly policy? Mr. Mahone has captured it, not by his repudiation, but by his manifesto for a fair vote. Granting that elections are tolerably fair in Virginia, the declaration was a sign of friendship, which, had the Bourbon Democrats made it, would have gained them the vote. If, therefore, the Mahone party triumphs, and the debt of Virginia is repudiated, it will be because the Bourbon Democrats, who pride themselves upon their honest-money views, were yet not so anxious for success as to secure it by guaranteeing honest elections. They are more opposed to what is called negro ascendency than to re-adjustment. But they have no right to be surprised and indignant that while their party in other Southern States is quite as unsound financially as Mahone, and resolutely hostile to free elections, it should be opposed in Virginia, although in that State there is a large element which holds financial good faith. If to good faith at the Treasury such Democrats had added good faith at the polls, Mahone would not have succeeded. All this, however, is no reason that Republican Senators should bargain with Mahone for the minor offices of the Senate. It is, however, an obvious reason for the Southern political situation. In Virginia the Bourbon Democrats, who hold to honest money, pay the penalty of the dangerous attitude of their party at large upon a paramount question. In Alabama, if honest money gains nothing by the success of either of two Greenback Democrats, honest elections gain much by the defeat of one of them.

POLITICS IN THE SOUTH

HARPER'S WEEKLY
May 7, 1881, pp. 302–3

Huntsville, Alabama
To the Editor of Harper's Weekly:

I find a letter from Francis P. Ward, Esq., of this city, published in Harper's Weekly of March 19th, and I beg leave to submit a statement in reply. I am a Republican, and chairman of the Republican Committee for this Congressional District. I supported Colonel Lowe for Congress in 1878 and in 1880 against the regular Bourbon candidate, and would feel bound to do so again under like circumstances. Why? I did not then and do not now indorse Colonel Lowe's wild and impracticable financial views. I am a hard-money, national-bank man. Why, then, did I and the mass of Republicans here support the Greenback-Labor candidate? Let me frankly tell you. There are questions of more vital importance in Southern politics than banking and currency or any phase of the money question. They are issues such as fair elections, an honest count, free thought, free speech, free government itself. Upon these Colonel Lowe and the Greenbackers were with us; upon these I felt impelled, as a Republican and as a man, to act with my best judgment and conscience.

As to the financial question, there was professedly no difference between the Democrats and Greenbackers. In order that you may judge for yourself, I submit the following platform, unanimously adopted two years ago by the Democracy of this county, and indorsed *nemine contradicente* by the entire Bourbon press and party of this district.

Platform

> *Resolutions adopted by the Democratic Party of Madison County, in Convention, August, 1878.*
>
> *The committee on resolutions reported as follows, and their report was adopted without dissent:*
>
> "*Whereas,* Throughout our entire country the value of real estate is greatly depreciated; industry paralyzed; trade depressed; enterprise destroyed; unparalleled distress inflicted upon the middle and poorer classes; millions of honest laborers thrown out of employment, reduced to want, and compelled to beg, steal, or starve; the country filled with fraud, bank-

ruptcy, and crime; and *whereas,* this state of things has been brought about by legislation in the interest of capitalists, corporations, bankers, and bondholders, who have purchased members of Congress, and dictated the legislation of the country, whereby the honest tax-paying people have been defrauded of untold millions, and now desire to perpetuate their fraud and power by reducing the great masses of the people to a state of poverty, ignorance, and slavery; and *whereas,* no relief can be given to the suffering millions until this class legislation is repealed, and the financial policy of the government is changed; and whereas, we believe that the government was established for the benefit of the people, and not exclusively for the capitalists, corporations, bankers, and bondholders; and whereas, we believe the true principle of Democracy is to adopt measures which bring the greatest good to the greatest number;

"*Therefore, be it resolved,* by the Democratic and Conservative party of Madison County:

"1. We re-affirm the time-honored principles of the Democratic party.

"2. We demand the immediate and unconditional repeal of the Resumption Act, the unlimited coinage of silver, and that as a legal tender it be put upon the equal footing with gold.

"3. That all national banks be abolished, and a paper currency be issued directly by the government, which shall be a legal tender for all debts, public and private.

"4. There shall be no privileged class of creditors, but official salaries, pensions, bonds, government dues, and all other obligations, public and private, shall be discharged in the legal money of the United States, strictly according to the stipulations of the laws under which they were incurred.

"5. To counteract and remedy the existing evil, we demand that the government shall issue a full legal tender paper money adequate in volume to the requirements of commerce, the revival of business, employment of labor, and the just distribution of its products.

* * * * * * *

"7. That we do not believe a public debt to be a public blessing, but a great public evil, and we are, therefore, in favor of the extinction of the public debt as rapidly as may be consistent with the interests of the great masses of the people; and to this end, that the government shall be required to pay the bonds due with greenback currency, wherever the bonds were originally payable in greenbacks, and we regard the substitution of gold bonds for bonds originally payable in greenbacks a violation of the original contract, and a gross fraud, injustice, and oppression perpetrated upon the tax-paying people."

General Garth accepted this platform and nomination, and declared everywhere that he was a better Democrat than Colonel Lowe, and a better Greenbacker than Peter Cooper. I believed him, took him at his word, and voted for Colonel Lowe as the least of evils. Mr. Ward then supported General Garth upon this platform, and subsequently General Wheeler upon a like platform. He now inveighs against "repudiation and Communism." He now proposes an alliance, offensive and defensive, between the Northern bondholder and the Southern Bourbon? He now says, "Could not the Northern Republican and Southern Democrat both be twisting separate strands that might yet be laid in an anchor cable?"

What sort of "separate strands" was Mr. Ward's party "twisting" when they adopted the above preamble and resolutions in 1878? What sort of "anchor cable" was he laying when he supported General Wheeler upon a like platform in 1880? Let the following letter from General Wheeler to the editor of our Greenback organ answer for itself:

"Wheeler, Alabama, June 17, 1880.
"Colonel A.H. Brittin, Editor 'Advocate':
"Dear Sir,—In your paper of the 16th I observe an editorial which in substance contains the following, viz.: 'That I owe it to myself and to those people in North Alabama to whom I have often asserted that the Democracy was a good enough Greenback party, and that a new Greenback party was not necessary, to state if it is true or false that the committee on resolutions, at any time during the session of the State Convention, presented resolutions on the subject of finance which might be called Greenback resolutions. If so, were they passed upon by the Convention? If so, how? And why does not the action of the Convention appear in the proceedings as published?' In reply to the above I will state that such a resolution was introduced and read from the Speaker's stand by my eloquent young friend Colonel Sam Blackwell to a full representative Convention, consisting of 575 members, nearly every member being in his seat. The resolution was received with great enthusiasm, and was unanimously adopted, not a single objection being made thereto. I think, Colonel, that this most abundantly proves my assertion that 'a new Greenback party is not necessary'; and I hope and trust you will agree with me, and in future exert your energy and ability in our most glorious cause.

"Five hundred and seventy-five representative delegates, including members from every county except Winston, voting in one voice for the resolutions, proves beyond question that the resolution expressed the sentiments of the entire Democratic party of Alabama. I hope this will so impress you that on my return from Cincinnati I will find our entire ticket, State and national, at the head of your columns. . . . Join our columns, Colonel; seize one of our banners, and march with us to victory.

"With respect, your obedient servant,
"Jos. Wheeler."

The Republicans, under these circumstances, had to choose between the Greenbackers and the Bourbons. If we ran a ticket of our own in this overwhelmingly Democratic district, it was tantamount to taking sides against the Greenbackers, and securing to that extent the victory to the Bourbons. Under ordinary circumstances, we could and perhaps would have done so, but the circumstances were not ordinary. They were most extraordinary. The Bourbons had enacted election laws that practically disfranchised the Republicans, especially in local and State elections. These laws exist to-day, and are executed in the same fraudulent spirit in which they were enacted. Our elections are, in fact, a fraud and a farce. The boasted right preservative of all rights—a full, free, fair vote and an honest count—has been wantonly and wickedly destroyed throughout the State. A shameful cloud of popular suspicion and distrust broods over the sanctuary of the ballot-box. Elections are no longer believed to elect. They are decided, not by the people at the polls, but by partisan inspectors after the polls are closed and the elections over. Fraud has taken the place of force. The ballot-box stuffer has taken the place of the Ku-Klux to accomplish, perhaps with nimble fingers and perjured conscience, the nefarious but necessary work. In view of this condition of the community, the Greenbackers, Independents, and anti-Bourbon Democrats in the last election assembled at Montgomery, Alabama, and adopted the following platform:

"1. In view of the pending State election, this Greenback-Labor Conference hereby denounces the action of the present Democratic State administration in changing the time-honored election laws of the State, so as to open the door to fraud and perjury, and close the door to detection and punishment. We demand the repeal of said laws, and a restoration of the honest and simple provisions under which the people have heretofore enjoyed the sacred right of the elective franchise. We demand a fair election and an honest count."

The Republicans felt bound, under the circumstances, to stand by the Greenbackers upon this issue. We had a common grievance, and we made a common cause against it. We antagonized a common enemy on Bourbonism, and felt impelled, first and last, by every law of nature, to fight together as one man for the right of political existence. The country knows the result of last August's election in Alabama, the Bourbon victory (by inspectors) being about ninety-seven thousand majority, with several counties to be heard from. In November we had United States supervisors, and under the intrepid leadership of Colonel Lowe, who is a rare organizer and leader of men, we rallied again for a bold, aggressive canvass. We had in this district a full, free, fair vote at the election, and a plain, square, dead open and shut "count out" afterward. Everybody here knows these things. We hope that even Mr. Ward will find, when this contest comes up in Congress, new sources of information.

In the mean time Mr. Ward has appointed himself ambassador extraordinary and minister plenipotentiary from the Bourbons of the South to the hoodwinked heathen of radicalism in the North. He seeks an alliance offensive and defensive. He deplores the "extension of suffrage to the freedmen, and the admission of the Southern States into the Union under the amended Constitution," but fondly hopes that "the adoption of a clear and consistent theory of government, and an honest and fearless application of it, might greatly lessen the difficulties that have arisen from the premature adoption of these measures." He does not favor us with the specific remedies he would apply to the case or the country, but leaves us to infer that as the South was legally right in secession, and the North was morally wrong in reconstruction, the State-rights theory of government, enforced by appropriate legislation, would leave the suffrage of the freedman subject to the local despotism of fraudulent elections, without hope of relief from the nation. This is notoriously the present condition of the South, and Mr. Ward does not seem to object to it. He is as silent as the grave upon the subject of suffrage, although he knows that this paramount right is the question of questions upon which parties here are now divided. Mr. Ward's reference to the first war between Russia and France as illustrating the relations between the North and South betrays the vice of his position and the condition of his mind on this subject. He fails to comprehend, or refuses to realize, that we are not to be considered as two foreign powers engaged in mortal conflict with each other, but as one people living under one government, with a common Constitution and a common destiny.

Mr. Ward is an accomplished gentleman, an able advocate, learned in the law and literature, but irregularly developed in politics. As slave-owner, secessionist, Confederate, and Bourbon, he represents every extreme phase of Southern sectionalism in the past, present, and future. He belongs to a school of thought that sees nothing wrong in slavery but its abolition, nothing shameful in secession but its defeat, and nothing to be regretted in Southern politics or society but its purblind fight against fate, and its inherent weakness and failure.

What have the relations between Augustus and Herod, to which Mr. Ward refers, to do with the union of the hard-money Republicans of the North with the soft-money Bourbons of the South? Which is Augustus, and which is Herod? And who, except Mr. Ward, will personate the daughter of Herodias dancing before this Bourbon Herod for the head of our Greenback John the Baptist in a charger? If we have read history aright, Augustus was an invading Roman despot, and Herod, whether father or son, was a native Jewish sycophant. If Mr. Ward refers to the Herod who murdered his wife, children, and relatives generally, his wicked name is one of the most repulsive in history. If he refers to Herod the Tetrarch of Galilee, he must recollect that he was not the friend but the parasite of Augustus. He was the friend of Pontius Pilate, and made his infamy Scriptural by slaughtering John and James, and persecuting the early Christians. We are told in the good Book that for his insolence and pride "the angel of the Lord smote him, and he was eaten of worms, and gave up the ghost." If this is the Herod to which Mr. Ward compares the Bourbons of the South, may we not hope, without blasphemy, that history ere long will repeat itself?

However this may be, back of all this historical reference and Scriptural subterfuge, back of this screen of casuistry and special pleading, I find Mr. Ward's distinct proposal for a political alliance between the Northern Republicans and Southern Democrats. If Colonel Lowe and the Greenbackers have done nothing else, we must credit them at least for whipping the Bourbons of the South into something like respect for the Republicans of the North. But Southern Republicans can not accept Mr. Ward's overture. They can not join the Bourbons until the leopard shall change its spots. They can not war upon the only native white organization in this section that demands honest elections and equal laws for the whole people. We are bound by the first law of self-preservation to unite with anybody, whether it be Mahone of Virginia, or Lowe of Alabama, or Felton of Georgia, to beat down the lawless and intolerant spirit of Bourbonism, and to regain for ourselves as American citizens the essence of free government. Respectfully,

A.W. McCullough.

POLITICAL BOURBONISM

HARPER'S WEEKLY
May 21, 1881, p. 326

The Charleston *News,* which is the leading organ of Southern Bourbon sentiment, admits with Senator Hampton that there have been "irregularities" and frauds in the elections in that State, but it boldly justifies them by the right of revolution. It says that what was done in 1876, in 1878, and in 1880—that is, the violence and fraud by which American citizens were deprived of their fundamental right—was necessary. But it holds it to be no longer necessary. The Democratic party having resolved, as it says, "to carry the elections by hook or by crook," and having succeeded, the colored vote being disciplined and suppressed, the process is no longer necessary. The colored voters were not murdered and harried, and the boxes filled with tissue ballots, says the *News,* in effect, merely to give the offices to one set of men rather than to another, but to assure the very existence of the people. The plea is not new. "I," said Louis Napoleon, as he shot down the Parisians in crowds, and shipped them by thousands to Cayenne—"I am the savior of society." That imperial worthy continued the salvation of society in similar ways for some years. When one body of citizens announce that the destruction of the equal rights of another body is indispensable to the peace of the community, it is mere anarchy, and not bloody anarchy only because there is no resistance.

The Charleston *News* says that this suppression of equal rights is no longer necessary. But certainly it can not expect that its word will be taken upon the subject. Mr. Frye's illustrations of the frauds upon electors were not drawn from old documents, but from the records of the last election. So the reports of the examination of witnesses in the Fifth Congressional District of South Carolina show by uncontradicted testimony that at Edgefield Court House nearly 2000 colored Republicans were not allowed to vote; at Johnstone's, in the same county, 400 or 500 colored voters were prevented from voting, and one colored man was killed, and no effort has been made by the authorities to bring the criminals to justice. At other places in the district cannon were planted, barricades erected, and the voters assaulted with Cayenne pepper thrown in their eyes, and driven from the polls; the supply of Republican tickets for certain polls was seized and destroyed; one poll was closed in the middle of the day; one was not opened at all. These facts are more significant than the assertion of the *News* that such proceedings are no longer necessary. They show that what was thought to be necessary four and five years ago is thought to be necessary now, and that nothing can be more unmanly than the denials of Southern Democratic Senators, except their assertions that Maine and Massachusetts are as bad as South Carolina. There were great electoral frauds of the Southern kind in New York in 1868, in Tweed's palmy day, and they led to the passage of laws which insure honest elections so far as the ballot-boxes are concerned.

We are not unmindful of the plea for the suppression of the colored vote. It is the assertion that intelligence and property and character can not submit to be ruled by ignorance and dishonesty, and that the most conservative and patriotic Northern community would do just what the whites in South Carolina do if it were turned topsy-turvy by election laws. To this, however, the reply was made by the President in his inaugural address. He admitted the danger that arises from the ignorance of the voter, and that bad local government is an evil which ought to be prevented. But he truly added that suicide is not a remedy. The violation of the freedom of the ballot is a crime which, if continued, will destroy the government itself. The Southern Bourbon policy is the correction of ignorance and vice by fraud and corruption. Sensible men in the Southern States can not expect that sensible men in the Northern States will submit to the consequences of such a policy. The plea is to purify local government. But the suppression of votes equally affects the national government. The Charleston *News* confesses that the procedure is revolutionary, but justifiable. If, then, the vote of the solid South had elected the Democratic candidate, the result, by this admission, would have been revolutionary. It would have been due to what the leading Bourbon paper calls justifiable irregularities, that is, violence and fraud. Since Senator Hampton and the News both admit the fact, there need be no further Democratic denial of it; and when South Carolina or any other State takes the same energetic course in pursuing and punishing such "irregularities" as Congress took in dealing with those in New York, the cry of free vote and fair count will have lost its force. Until then a "solid South" will be opposed as the great national danger, not vindictively, but simply because it will mean government by force and fraud.

MAHONISM IN MISSOURI

HARPER'S WEEKLY
May 28, 1881, p. 343

An ex-Confederate soldier in Missouri writes us that "Mahonism," not as repudiation, but as independence and overthrow of Bourbonism, is "breaking out and ready to break out all over the South." He says that the old middle class in the Southern States, which owned few slaves, and which was kept in thrall by the great slave-holders, furnished the fighting rank and file of the Southern army; but neither during the war, nor since, was this class properly considered by "the aristocrats," who commanded the "courts" of Richmond and Montgomery.

Our correspondent heard Humphrey Marshall, in a speech to a Kentucky cavalry brigade, near Abingdon, in 1864, declare the cause to be lost unless "the fine-haired and kid-gloved young gentlemen" who shirked behind substitutes were forced into the ranks. These gentry, he says, are the leaders of "Yazooism," and "the terrors of the South." It is not the old soldiers, but the indolent youth who shunned service, who have since commanded rifle companies, and harried negroes. There will be "tens of thousands of Mahones" at the next Presidential election, is his confident prediction, and he finds reasons for it in his own State of Missouri.

The great Democratic majority of that State has been reduced. St. Louis, a Democratic city, has elected a Republican government; Kansas City, St. Joseph's, Jefferson City, Warrensburg—indeed, all the chief towns except Sedalia—were carried against the Bourbons. The intelligent citizens see that during ten years of Democratic supremacy nothing has been done for the public schools, "except to tolerate them." There are thousands of Democrats in Missouri, he avers, who are "worn out with this slow coach," and are resolved to have a change. "Mahonism" is mainly this tendency, in his judgment. It is shaking, and it will presently break, the solid South. Then he anticipates the break of the solid Republican party in the North, and the union of the people upon new issues. It is not an unreasonable view, and the tone of the letter in its assertion that the independence of the individual voter is the most important of present questions, is an augury of beneficent change.

THE VIRGINIA READJUSTERS

HARPER'S WEEKLY
June 25, 1881, p. 406

The general interest in the Readjusters' party and movement in Virginia is not surprising. The Bourbon rule throughout "the South" is virtually a mere dogged resistance to the influences which would restore the prosperity of that part of the country. The primary and essential condition of sectional harmony is fair play, and especially a free vote and an honest count in the Southern States. As long as it is known that "the South" is kept "solid" by Democratic fraud and violence in order to control the 138 electoral votes, which, with those of two or three Northern States, would give the Southern Democrats control of the government, so long our national politics must be reactionary and sectional. This situation also injuriously affects all minor politics by necessitating strict party discipline to insure success in the general election. How to change this situation, therefore, has long been the problem. The reasons why citizens of the Southern States do not care to ally themselves with the colored citizens under the Republican name has been obvious. Yet it was plain that the color line must mark the division between the parties so long as dishonest elections were the Democratic policy. But whenever a party of white native citizens should appear in any State honestly resolved to protect and befriend the colored vote, instead of ostracizing and suppressing it, a chance for a political break-up would be opened.

This is precisely the chance which the Readjusters' party in Virginia offers. It takes its name from a proposition to re-adjust the old State debt by assuming two-thirds of it, and leaving the other third to West Virginia, providing for the payment of the interest equally to all holders, at a rate which the revenues of the State will warrant. This is repudiation just so far as the rate which the revenues will warrant differs from the rate pledged. The duty of the State is to make the revenues warrant payment according to the pledge. This can be done only by taxation; but the Bourbon party, while denouncing the Readjusters, does not propose the necessary increase of taxation. In this situation, and to secure the support of the colored voters, and Readjusters propose to repeal the capitation tax, which has disfranchised great numbers of the poor colored citizens, to defend a free vote, and to secure a fair count. In other words, the party proposes to give the colored citizens fair play. As the Readjusters are composed largely of "the plain people," they are naturally very strong, and the attraction which they offer to Republicans, especially colored Republicans, is very powerful. It is an alliance of the kind which has been long foreseen as the only kind under which the "solid South" is likely to dissolve, offering an alternative which has been presented to Republicans in many Southern Congressional districts, of foregoing the honest financial policy of the Republican party in order to secure other advantages which seem to many such Republicans much more pressing.

The Readjusters' platform contains a cordial and liberal resolution to strengthen the general good understanding of the country by honestly maintaining equal rights, and by promising a hearty welcome and perfect liberty of every kind to all who choose to throw in their fortunes with those of Virginia. It is a frank and significant declaration, which no Democratic platform in the Southern States has contained, and the conduct of the Readjusters has not belied their words. They are Democrats who voted for Hancock, but who have broken with the regular State organization of their party; and while there is undoubtedly the usual proportion of self-seeking and hypocrisy among them which are familiar in all parties, they show a practical sympathy with the fundamental Republican policy of honest elections which contrasts most favorably with the action of the Bourbon Democrats, who are certainly no less selfish, and infinitely more reactionary. The letter of a late correspondent in Missouri, an ex-Confederate soldier, says plainly that the essential significance of the Readjuster movement is not financial, but political. It is the insurrection of the younger Southern voters, who are weary and impatient of a domination which paralyzes "the South," and as the debt question has become subordinate, it can hardly be doubted that the Readjusters who welcome colored delegates to their Convention, and nominated an old Union man and Republican as Lieutenant-Governor, will have a strong Republican support as the best practicable policy in the actual situation.

OLD DAVE.
"I wouldn't tell no lie for a *hundred* mules. He's jest eight year ole next July, and as gentle as a lamb; dat I knows, for I tended him sin' I was a boy!"

Harper's Weekly, July 9, 1881, p. 451.

THE FOURTH IN ATLANTA
A Motley Gathering of the Colored Element.

ATLANTA CONSTITUTION
July 5, 1881

Yesterday was not as big a Fourth of July as Atlanta has had, and yet it was hardly big enough for the people that was in town.

Early in the morning excursion trains began to arrive, and until after two o'clock additions were being constantly made to the immense throng that came to Atlanta.

The West Point road alone brought in sixty-two car loads. The Central, State, Georgia and Air-Line roads also inducted their full quota and the town was packed. Our visitors were mostly of the colored persuasion but that did not affect the sale of lemonade, ice cream and goobers. In fact it made a corner on the market and a huckster's stand was to be seen on every corner in the business portion of the city. Near the car shed there were no less than forty-two of these vending booths that add so much to the colored race's happiness. Wheelbarrows, wagons and carriages were converted into goober stands and lemonade counters, and the loud voice of the negro gave evidence of his thrift and enterprise.

The big influx had only a slight effect upon the trade in the city. The retail stores kept open doors, and the clerks rushed to and fro with unusual rapidity. Only a few houses were decorated, and these not very profusely.

In the afternoon Captain Bentley's company gave a parade and exhibition drill, which attracted a large crowd. The streets were packed and jammed and the neighborhood of the carshed was one seething mass of colored individuals.

The crowd was variously estimated at from 5,000 to 7,000, but in all probability there was more.

For the size of the throng there was but little unpleasantness, yet a few cases were made by the police.

Fifty-eight city cases were entered. These were for drunks, disorderly conduct and quarreling.

For concealed weapons the day was good. That the fifteenth amendment is devoted to firearms is proven by the following arrests: Joe Thomas, George Stokes, Watty Pinkert, Stephen Reed, James Akeis, James Dalton, John Price, Lowe Callaway, Waverly Jackson, Israel Sanford, Jacob Slaughters.

Joe Thomas was booked for suspicion and John Jones for burglary.

The number of arrests filled the station-house, and to-day Recorder Glenn will make his debut with a full court.

The big arrest of the day was made by Captain Connoly and Officers Veal and Brenning. Soon after the arrival of an excursion train on the West Point road Officers Veal and Brenning were notified by the conductor in charge of the train that a man, who was wanted in Alabama for cattle stealing, had been a passenger on his train until it arrived at the Peters street crossing where he jumped off and came up town.

The conductor also furnished the officers with the name of and description of the party. He also said that from conversation had with the man while aboard the train he was induced to believe that he was an Atlanta man.

Taking this as his cue, Captain Connolly, the officer in charge of Policemen Veal and Brenning, made an investigation of the city directory and was rewarded by finding the name, which was James Spiers, whose residence was 29 Stonewall street.

Accompanied by his men the captain repaired to that locality, where he found Spiers's mother, but the wanted man was not in. Instructing Officers Veal and Brenning to go one way Connolly went another, and finally came upon the man. An arrest was at once made and Spiers taken to the station-house, where he now is.

In his possession was found a razor and knife. To Captain Connolly Spiers plead ignorance of any cause for the arrest until he was told that he had stole some cattle. He then remarked that he had sold some cattle, but that he had bought them from a negro.

Previous to Spier's arrest Captain Connolly learned that the charge against him was cotton stealing, and

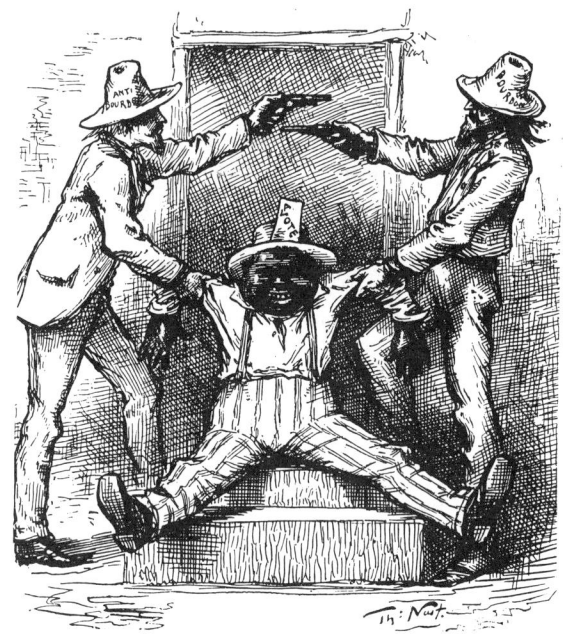

THE NEXT POLITICAL CONDITION—SOUTH.

Harper's Weekly, July 9, 1881, p. 452.

soon after calaboosing him the captain telegraphed to LaFayette, Alabama, the place designated by the conductor at which the crime was committed.

The telegram was received by Mr. Henderson, the party who bought the cattle from Spiers. To the dispatch Captain Connolly received the following answer:

LaFayette, Ala, July 4.—A. B. Connolly, Captain of Police: The dollars for Spiers delivered to marshal at West Point.
J. W. Henderson.

After receiving the above reply Connolly telegraphed to the sheriff at LaFayette, Alabama, asking for a charge against Spier, and was answered as follows:

LaFayette, Ala., July 4.—A. B. Connolly, Captain of Police: The charge against Spier is grand larceny. Deliver him to the marshal of West Point, Georgia. H. W. Finney, Sheriff.

Friends of Spier's intervened and employing Mr. Hoke Smith, caused a writ of habeas corpus which will be tried to-day at 10 o'clock before Judge Clark.

The following circular was secretly printed in the city last week and distributed in the small towns. It doubtless caused many a colored brother to turn his eyes wistfully in this direction. It is hardly necessary to say that the circular "basely fabricates:"

To the Colored People of Georgia: Rally to the capital and see the father of freedom. President Grant has consented to speak to the colored people of Georgia in Atlanta, on July 4th, at one o'clock, p.m. Extra trains will leave

THE REV. DR. GARNETT.—[SEE PAGE 542.]
PHOTOGRAPHED BY J. U. STEAD.

Harper's Weekly, August 6, 1881, p. 541.

Marietta, Jonesboro and Conyers at 9 o'clock, a.m., and will arrive in Atlanta at 11 a.m. Will return at 5 p.m. Round trip 50 cents. Come one, come all and see and hear the great man who gave us our liberty.

Among the various covers which adorned the refreshments stands one had painted on it: "Johnston the Bill Poster has exclusive right to fair grounds, railroad trains, street cars, and opera house." Many read it and thought of the tragic death of the unfortunate bill poster.

OUR MINISTER TO LIBERIA

HARPER'S WEEKLY
August 6, 1881, p. 542

The Rev. Henry Highland Garnett, who has been appointed United States Minister to Liberia, was born a slave on the estate of Colonel William Spencer, of Maryland, in 1816. At the age of eight years, on the death of his master, he succeeded in making his escape to the Free States. He graduated from the Oneida Collegiate Institute in 1839, and from the Troy Theological College in 1842. It is a singular circumstance that his grandfather was brought from the country which is now Liberia, about a hundred years ago, by slave-dealers, and that the Doctor's daughter, Mrs. Barboza, a missionary, now resides with her family in the same place whence their ancestor was torn.

Dr. Garnett has long been known as an eloquent and able minister of the Presbyterian Church, and he goes abroad with the best wishes of his countrymen.

POLITICS IN VIRGINIA

HARPER'S WEEKLY
August 20, 1881, p. 562

The political situation is strikingly illustrated by the platform of the Virginia Democrats. The Convention cheered old Confederate soldiers, and the orators recounted with enthusiasm the Confederate services of candidates, but it also passed a hearty resolution of sympathy for the President, hoping for his speedy restoration "to the discharge of his important duties for the welfare and honor of our common country," and it declared general principles which are the very creed of republicanism. Indeed, the Virginia Democracy surpasses even that of Ohio in its unconditional assertion of republican principles. In North Carolina the Democrats adopted the Prohibition instead of the Republican creed, and they have been overwhelmed at the polls. In Maine some Democrats proposed a fusion with the Greenback party, but they were overborne, and the Convention reaffirmed the Hancock platform, sympathized with the President, and adjourned.

All this shows that the two great parties are no longer divided by the old issues, and that they have not yet taken position upon new questions. This is the situation in which elections will be decided by the traditions of party, and by the personal character of candidates. In Virginia, for instance, the Democrats declare generally for exact justice, freedom of the press and of the person, free voting and fair counting, trials by impartial juries, respect for State rights, and preservation of the national authority. Nothing could be better. But the voter will naturally consider whether the Democratic party has proved its sincere regard for all these great rights, and whether they are probably safer under Democratic than under Republican ascendency. The Virginia Democrats declare specifically for maintaining the public-school system for white and colored children, against increasing the present rate of taxation, and for settling the State debt upon the basis of a three-per-cent. bond. Here, again, experience will decide. The Democrats have been long in power. The voters know whether they have honestly maintained the school system, whether they have taxed equally, and how zealously and effectively they have labored for an actual settlement of the debt. Those voters know also the position of the Democrats upon the repeal of the capitation tax, the

NEGRO LABORERS AT WORK UNDER THE "STORM KING," HUDSON RIVER.—Drawn by John Alexander.—[See Page 574.]

Harper's Weekly, August 20, 1881, p. 572.

LIEUTENANT FLIPPER.—Photo. by Pach.

Harper's Weekly, September 17, 1881, p. 637.

abolition of the whipping-post, and the petty larceny laws. As the party in power, they will be tried by their performances, not by their professions. If their policy has been plainly a policy of equal justice, of protection of an honest vote, of equality in the school management, of opposition to a mean, petty, teasing tyranny intended to work practical injustice, if they have vigorously and successfully addressed themselves to the settlement of the State debt, they have a right to expect the continued confidence of the voters. But if they have done nothing of all this, and the decision is to be made upon the results of experience, fine professions ought not to save them. . . .

A PICTURESQUE SCENE

HARPER'S WEEKLY
August 20, 1881, p. 574

A large number of negroes from the South have been engaged to work in the construction of the West Shore Railway, along the Hudson River. Our artist visited the scene of their operations a few days ago, and gives the results of his observations and notes in the sketches printed on page 572. These men are employed in the gravel banks and rock cuts of the Highlands, and will eventually be distributed all along the line. Many of them are scantily clothed, working with bare feet and bare heads. It is a curious sight to see the brawny blacks bending over their work, busily plying shovel and pick,

CAPTAIN HOWGATE.—Photo. by Bell.

Harper's Weekly, September 17, 1881, p. 637.

and a more cheerful company of laborers it would be difficult to find anywhere. There are no dissensions among them, and all day long they join their melodious voices in some refrain.

In some places the banks are so steep that the men are let down by ropes from above, as shown in the sketch, and held suspended in mid-air until they can pick out a foot-hold from the mass of crumbling rock.

CAPTAIN HOWGATE AND LIEUTENANT FLIPPER

HARPER'S WEEKLY
September 17, 1881, p. 637

A few weeks ago the country was astounded by the charge of embezzlement brought by General Hazen against Captain H.W. Howgate, who had been for five years connected with the Signal Service Corps, for a large part of that time as disbursing officer. As the *Evening Post* remarked at the time, the charge was "especially startling from the fact that it affects a branch of the service whose purity is so customary as to be taken almost for granted. In times of wide-spread corruption, when the looseness and vice of a speculative age produced their effects upon civil administration, when gross scandals of whiskey rings and other swindling combinations brought reproach upon the country, the army was not convicted of misconduct of this kind, General Belknap's crime being connected with the performance of a civil duty. While politicians, and even men who passed for statesmen, were believed to have grown rich in the patriotic service of their country at comparatively small salaries, the army seemed to exhibit modest but proud content with the moderate support of their regular pay."

The amount of embezzlement charged against Captain Howgate was at first stated to be from fifty thousand to eighty thousand dollars. Subsequent investigations swelled the sum which he is charged with stealing from the government to more than four hundred thousand dollars; and as the amount appropriated for the Signal Service last year amounted to about fifty thousand dollars more than that sum, it would appear that, if the charges are true, he must have made away with about one-quarter of the money which passed through his hands during the five years of his connection with the corps. Captain Howgate and his friends asserted that he had a perfect defense. He did not, however, choose to await a trial. It is also charged that Captain Howgate has misappropriated funds intrusted to him by a clerk in the Signal Corps for the purchase of mining stock.

About the same time that these charges against Captain Howgate were made public, it was reported that Lieutenant Flipper, the only colored officer in the United States army, stationed at Fort Davis, Texas, had been detected in defrauding the government. For several months he had been Acting Commissary of Sabsistence, and the charge was that since the 9th of July last he had not transmitted his funds to the Chief Commissary at San Antonio. On an explanation being demanded no reply was received, but on further inquiries being made Mr. Flipper stated that he had sent the funds by mail, but had kept no record of the fact, and consequently could not prove it. The funds which he reported to have been sent by mail consisted in part of checks on different banks, given him by the officers of the fort in payment of their monthly bills. A description of them was forwarded to the banks, and it was learned that they had not been presented for payment. Lieutenant Flipper was now placed under arrest, and a search set on foot, which resulted in the discovery of what are said to be the missing checks upon the person of a woman-servant.

Lieutenant Flipper is to be tried by court-martial on the charges made against him. His side of the story has yet to be made public, and it is useless to speculate on the probability of his guilt or innocence. With the assistance of some friends, pending the result of the trial, Lieutenant Flipper has made good the deficit in his accounts, amounting to a few hundred dollars; and it is to be hoped that the first impression of his brother officers, that the seeming crime may be a case of carelessness instead of deliberate dishonesty, may prove to be correct.

1882–1883

Would the assassination of President James Garfield unite sectional differences? Would his desire to restore "friendly feelings" in the Union be continued under the administration of President Chester Arthur? The consensus was that the country was beginning to heal. "Clear intelligent and patriotic citizens of (the) southern states must believe that there is no longer a 'bloody shirt' in politics." Yet, even with the rising anti-Bourbon movement in the South, the region still had not risen above its national and international image of racism and violence. Labor and industry sectors still preferred to omit the South from consideration for future growth.

Yet, several examples of new trends in the South would give some credence to the journalists' belief that moderate Democrats would be the ones to move the region forward. Such was evident in the 1882 gubernatorial election in Georgia. Former vice president of the Confederacy Alexander Stephens was elected governor by a large majority of voters, implying a crossover of black and Republican voters. Editorials saw this election as the emergence of a movement in the South.

During the 1880s the Supreme Court ruled that the Civil Rights Acts of 1864, and most of the legislation of Reconstruction, was unconstitutional. In establishing the difference between state and federal citizenships, the Court ruled that the Fourteenth Amendment could not protect the civil rights of individuals when such violations were authorized by the state. Otherwise, such charges were under the purview of state laws. For the author, the new interpretations of those legislations showed the "wisdom of the constitutional system." The return of strict constructionalism was lauded as protecting the soveregnities of both state and national governments.

The major attraction of this period was the new voices in African American male leadership. The national convention movement reconvened after the Civil War as African Americans began to establish specific agendas for their communities. The black press, led by the New York Globe, *began to call on blacks to abandon the Republican party, for it had deserted them since 1876. Instead blacks needed to be available to advance an independent agenda. The* Globe *advised blacks not to throw "away votes upon a party which does not appreciate them."*

While the paper acknowledged racial prejudice, it concluded that to ask for special favors or to expect prejudice to be controlled by the law was unjust. The way to overcome exclusion was to participate freely in the electoral process. To organize around the issue of race only opened the group to collusion and bribes. While protest may be of service to the race, many journalists saw it as deterring racial harmony. An example of respectable leadership for the papers was Frederick Douglass. A former slave, international abolitionist, diplomat, ardent Republican, Douglass continued to be the most recognized race leader following the antebellum and Civil War eras.

Race relations contributed to many African Americans' decision to emigrate or to support territorial separation. Douglass called for blacks to work toward full citizenship in America. To colonize outside of the country or to separate racially would be detrimental to blacks. Blacks demanded full citizenship, not preferential treatment. To appeal to division based on class, race, or ethnicity was essentially anti-American, decreed Douglass. "We cannot adopt for ourselves a political creed apart from the rest of our fellow citizens.... The Constitution knows no boundary (for) all citizens are equal regardless of color, faith, etc." For many journalists, these were "wise words." People of similar views were called to organize and to secure "the passage of laws embodying their views."

Douglass was also asked to review the condition of the recent freedmen. "Have former slaves made any sensible degree of progress" since freedom? Douglass asserted that the question should be if former slaveholders had made any sensible degree of progress in civilization since the emancipation of their slaves. In the age of racial violence, are the "slaveholders more industrious, honest and humane than when they bought, sold and flogged their fellow men to toil for them without wages?" Considering the freedmen's recent history, the more appropriate query would be how far the freedmen had risen considering their slavery past. Douglass continued by exploring various areas of growth. Of all, the most impressive, in spite of limited resources, was in the field of education. Blacks of all classes sacrificed in order to provide educational opportunities for their children.

This sacrifice is evident in an editorial on the white and black public schools of Richmond, Virginia. Though the schools were limited by poor physical facilities, the writer could not escape the passion that blacks of all ages had for education. After being assured by a black administrator that black children were also human, the writer wondered how such poor people could concede so much of these meager resources to such a luxury, education.

With age, the learning patterns altered. In the early years, the children excelled. The higher the grade level, the more the students fell behind. However this did not deter their dreams of becoming teachers and educating the race. But the lack of home support handicapped the students. Learning was limited to the classroom. By the end of 1883, critics of black higher education were now recommending that mathematics and languages be eliminated from the black schools' curriculums and instead, the school year should be shortened and focused more on industrial instruction.

Jacqueline A. Rouse
Georgia State University

GARFIELD AND "THE SOUTH"

HARPER'S WEEKLY
March 18, 1882, p. 162

The anti-Bourbon movement in Kentucky, of which we speak elsewhere, is one of the most encouraging signs of the times. The friends of President Garfield know how anxious he was that his Administration should see a thorough restoration of friendly feeling in the Union, and how hopeful he was of its accomplishment. Mr. Blaine alluded to this purpose in one of the most interesting passages of his recent discourse, and stated that it was the intention of the President to go into the Southern States and to declare his views frankly. He expected to be a guest at the Yorktown celebration, at the Atlanta Cotton Exposition, and at the meeting of the Army of the Cumberland at Chattanooga, and he was even considering the general character of the speeches that he would make, believing that the three occasions offered him precisely the scope and variety of opportunity that he desired. The frustration of this plan is one of the great misfortunes consequent upon his death. Of all conspicuous Republicans, General Garfield was incomparably the best fitted for such a duty, and speaking as President, his words would have been events. His complete familiarity with the subject, his power of clear and eloquent statement, his admirable tranquillity of temperament, and the candor which had always retained the respect and friendship of his political opponents, his strong convictions, earnestness, patriotism, and generous, simple Americanism, would have enabled him, among those who are peculiarly susceptible to effective oratory, to have knit more closely the bonds of union.

This general purpose of acknowledging no other "Southern question" than that of a constantly more friendly understanding was maintained by President Arthur in his Message, and it must be now clear to intelligent and patriotic citizens of the Southern States that there is no longer a bloody shirt in politics. The most absurd of Democratic orators would hardly shout that "hatred of brethren" is the sole Republican principle. But the disagreeable fact for the Southern States remains that immigration is not eager to pour into them, and that capital does not greedily seek Southern investment. Yet industry revives in those States, and they are generally as peaceful and orderly as any others. They have, indeed, a larger poor and ignorant class, and race distinctions are more obvious and troublesome, than in other States. But it is singular that the intelligent citizens of that part of the country do not more generally see and weigh the disastrous influence of one familiar fact, or that if they see it, they are so silent. The Southern States, since the "carpet-bag" era, have been unitedly and constantly opposed to the National Administration. As that Administration since the war has represented the party which maintained the Union and the government, the conclusion is natural

THE QUEEN OF INDUSTRY, OR, THE NEW SOUTH.

Harper's Weekly, January 14, 1882, p. 17.

and obvious that the real sentiment of the Southern States is unfriendly to the Union. That this is not so is undoubtedly true. But it is not surprising that labor and capital should both prefer those parts of the country in which there can be no such impression. The adherence of the Southern States to this apparent hostility certainly has been of no advantage to them. The Bourbon Democratic alliance has been of no service, and so far as national principles and local policy are concerned, there is no reason why they should not be as solidly Republican as they are Democratic. . . .

A MONUMENT IN THE NATION'S HEART.

Harper's Weekly, June 3, 1882, p. 349.

JOHN TYLER AND TEXAS

HARPER'S WEEKLY
July 8, 1882, p. 418

A paper in the current number of the *Magazine of American History* makes the unexpected claim for the Administration of John Tyler that, measured by the importance of the results achieved by it, no Administration, "from Washington's down, can compare with it." The paper is written by Lyon Gardiner Tyler, a son of the President, and its object is to claim for Mr. Tyler the glory of the annexation of Texas as well as that of the Ashburton Treaty, the latter of which achievements is usually supposed to have been the work of Mr. Webster, and the former of Mr. Calhoun. The article insists that the President was the actual head of his cabinet. Officially he certainly was so; but Mr. Tyler can not be justly represented as the head of Mr. Webster or of Mr. Calhoun. The writer says that Mr. Calhoun perplexed and prejudiced the Texas negotiation by insisting upon making the question of slavery prominent, and representing the possession of Texas as essential to the protection of slavery, and he asserts that Mr. Tyler regarded annexation from a much broader and more national point of view.

But there was never any doubt of the object of the annexation of Texas. All the facts and the situation are familiar, and it is too late to produce a new theory. Long before Mr. Tyler was President, Mr. Webster, at Niblo's Garden, called attention to the scheme of annexation, and pointed out that it contemplated a territorial extension of slavery. It was frankly acknowledged by Mr. Wise, who is evidently an authority with the author of the paper in the *Magazine,* that "the South" must obtain more territory or be overpowered. There was no concealment of the object. Mr. Van Buren lost the Democratic nomination because he was not unqualifiedly in favor of annexation, and Mr. Clay lost his election because he was not unqualifiedly opposed to it. It was the policy of the slave power which controlled the government, and of which Mr. Tyler was a faithful devotee, to secure its permanent ascendency by acquiring territory for four or five new Slave States. Mr. Calhoun knew perfectly well the real object of annexation, and he did not conceal it from the French Government at least.

The reason for annexation assigned by President Tyler himself, as quoted in the paper we are considering, does not clash with the well-known facts. Mr. Tyler wished to acquire Texas, he said, because it would give us the command of cotton, and cotton, as he and the other slave leaders believed, was king. But cotton was simply slavery. To say that Texas was annexed to control the cotton supply is only to tell the truth, that Texas was annexed in the hope of protecting and perpetuating slavery. Mr. Tyler was a Virginian. But a great Virginian, George Mason, said that Providence punishes national sins by national calamities; and another Virginian, whom Mr. Tyler held in high reverence, Thomas Jefferson, declared that he trembled for his country when he reflected that God was just. The story of the annexation of Texas belongs to the darkest annals of the American republic, and no good service is done to the memory of any public man by recalling the fact that he was its conspicuous advocate.

THE GEORGIA ELECTION

HARPER'S WEEKLY
October 14, 1882, p. 643

Among the political signs of the times the Georgia election must not be overlooked. Alexander H. Stephens has been chosen Governor by a majority of 50,000 or 60,000, in which, according to the accounts, must be included many Republican and colored votes. It is stated also that there was no intimidation, and that party feeling was greatly relaxed. Mr. Stephens, of course, is a Democrat, but an independent kind of Democrat, and his election shows rather release from iron party dictation than a mere Democratic victory.

Indeed, while national issues are somewhat in abeyance, the question of party reorganization and assimilation is working itself out in the different States. The contest is apparently intended to determine what party names shall mean. Both parties are plainly struggling to be first in the race of declarations for reform. The voters, meanwhile, knowing the relative value of words and deeds, are looking sharply to see which party actually undertakes reform.

When in a Southern State Democrats and Republicans, white and colored, unite in voting for the Vice-President of the Confederacy, it is very clear that the political situation is full of pleasant possibilities.

PERSONAL

HARPER'S WEEKLY
November 18, 1882, p. 723

Mr. Francis G. Shaw, who died in West Brighton, Staten Island, on Tuesday, November 7, was one of the early leaders in the antislavery movement, and took a prominent part in the agitation of the question, with William Lloyd Garrison, Wendell Phillips, and Gerrit Smith, at a time when to advocate freedom for the slave was dan-

THE WATCH ON THE RIND.—From a Sketch by Michael Hottes.

Harper's Weekly, August 4, 1883, p. 484.

gerous in the North as well as in the South. He was active in the formation of the Republican party, and supported the government heartily in its measures to crush the rebellion. When the Freedmen's Bureau was established, Mr. Shaw became its President, and conducted its affairs with signal ability. His philanthropy was not confined to the colored race. He was always ready to contribute liberally to any cause which he thought to be deserving. His genial character, fine culture, and high intellectual qualities gained him the warm esteem of all who knew him.

INCREASE OF ILLITERACY

HARPER'S WEEKLY
January 6, 1883, p. 3

In a late address in New York, Mr. Eaton, United States Commissioner of Education, stated some interesting and suggestive facts:

"The colored persons ten years of age and upward unable to write, as returned by the late census, number 3,220,878, or a number equal to the entire population when the original thirteen States were united under one form of government. The foreign white population of ten years of age and upward unable to write numbers 763,620, and the number of native white persons of the same age unable to write is 2,225,460. The total number of persons of ten years and over in all the States unable to write is 6,239,958, showing, as compared with similar figures from the census of 1870, relatively a gain of three per cent. in intelligence, but an absolute gain in the number of illiterates of 581,814, in spite of all the educational activities of the intermediate ten years.". . .

SOJOURNER TRUTH

An Effort to Indicate Her Age by What She Claims to Remember.

NEW-YORK TIMES
January 27, 1883

One of Sojourner Truth's friends, writing from Ball's Creek, Mich., to the *Christian at Work,* claims that she never thought of being put forward as a candidate for honor because of her age, and gives a "few facts" to enable partial readers to draw their own conclusions. The correspondent writes:

"She says there is no person living who knows her exact age. Long ago her contemporaries were all numbered with the dead, leaving no record of her age behind them. When the little book was written and published in 1850, called the 'Narrative of Sojourner Truth,' no effort was made to find historical proofs of her age. She knew nothing of dates then, neither does she know now, but she remembers circumstances, and history gives the date of their occurrence. Sojourner—Isabella she was called in her slave life—was born, she says, 'if she was born at all'—for it seems to her that 'she had been here ever since the world began'—in Ulster County, N.Y., near Kingston. Kingston was burned by order of Sir Henry Clinton, in 1777. She saw Kingston many times, when it was a blackened ruin, before any attempt was made to rebuild it. Of course she does not know how long a period elapsed from the time of its destruction to the commencement of its renovation. It was common in her young days to see the disabled revolutionary soldiers limping about on their mutilated, bandaged limbs. She distinctly remembers the dark day of 1780. 'The candles were kept burning throughout the day, and the family was terrified by the unusual gloom;' but little Isabella thought it was pretty, and ran about, jumping up to catch the undulating clouds. The incidents of that day are fresh in her memory. She was a full-grown woman when the Ulster *Gazette*—edited by Sam Freer & Son—came out dressed in mourning for the death of Gen. Washington. This was in 1799. She says she was as tall as she is now, when, standing on the banks of the Hudson, she saw the steam-boat Fulton go up the river for the first time. How angry the Dutchmen were, because it frightened away the fishes. This was in 1807. The act of 1817 in the State of New-York emancipated all slaves who were 40 years old and upward. Horace Greeley says in his 'Great American Conflict,' that 10,000 slaves were then set at liberty. All younger than 40 were retained in servitude till 1887, when all were freed. Sojourner was freed by the first act. All her children were retained in bondage, except the younger, Sophia. Isaac Von Wagner bought her for $5 and gave her to her mother. Sojourner was the mother of five children, but this was the first one she had ever owned. It was Sophia's son, who enlisted in 1863, fought at Fort Wagner, and was taken prisoner and kept in a Southern slave pen 19 months. The work of digging the Erie Canal was in progress at the eastern extremity when Sojourner left her old master, John I. Du Mont. On her way to Isaac Von Wagner, as stated in her book, she stopped to see Levi Rowe, one of the laborers. This canal was begun in 1817. Diana, Sojourner's oldest child, says she was a large girl when her mother was freed, and that she, with her brother Peter and sister Elizabeth, were held as slaves several years longer."

SUPREME COURT REVIEW

NEW-YORK TIMES
January 30, 1883

The court also decided the miscegenation case of Toney Pace vs. The State of Alabama, which was a criminal proceeding under a State law against a colored man for living in sexual relations with a white woman. The court holds that the law of Alabama prohibiting miscegenation is not in conflict with the fourteenth amendment to the Constitution, or with the civil rights legislation founded on it, for the reason that it applies the same punishment to both offenders, the white and the black, without discrimination.

THE CIVIL RIGHTS DECISION

HARPER'S WEEKLY
February 3, 1883, p. 66

The Supreme Court has pronounced the conspiracy clause of the Ku-Klux law, section 5519 of the Revised Statutes, to be unconstitutional. At the time of its passage it was held to be authorized by the Fourteenth Amendment, which lays certain restriction upon State action. The substance of the decision is that under that amendment the United States can protect the civil rights of individuals only when violated by State authority. But for a simple conspiracy against such rights the remedy must be sought under State law.

The sound opinion of the Court, which commends itself to every intelligent mind, shows the groundlessness of the fear expressed by ex-Governor Seymour in his late article in the *North American Review,* that there is a dangerous centralizing tendency in the government. The loose, vague, and perilous Jeffersonian—Virginia—and—Kentucky—resolution theory of the Union has been happily discredited by the war. Of that theory Calhoun was the logical advocate in asserting the superior sovereignty of the States. But the declaration of the true doctrine of national supremacy, with distinctly defined State authority, is one of the great traditions of the Supreme Court, and its present decision is in strict accordance with it.

The long and terrible civil war sprang from the dogma of State sovereignty invoked to protect and perpetuate slavery. It was natural that at its close the tendency to magnify the national authority should have been very strong, and especially to defend the victims of slavery. That tendency was in every way preferable to the disposition to connive at the crimes of the old slavery spirit under the same old plea of State sovereignty. In a calmer time the laws passed under that humane impulse are reviewed, and when found to be incompatible with strict constitutional authority, they are set aside. It is another illustration of the singular wisdom of our constitutional system.

TISSUE BALLOTS AVOIDED

NEW-YORK TIMES
April 6, 1883

The approaching prosecution of persons accused of having violated the election laws in South Carolina directs attention to the Bourbons' new device for suppressing a part of the colored vote. The dark history of election frauds in that State shows that, while the object sought has always been the same, the means have changed from year to year until brutal force and bloodshed have been succeeded by schemes which have taxed the brains of unprincipled legislators and have not depended for success upon the bull-dozer and the shotgun. Murderous attacks upon peaceful voters and the open intimidation of negroes by red-shirt clubs aroused too much criticism and opposition in the North, and the leaders of the dominant party, wiser than some of their followers, labored to secure a plan by which "white supremacy" could be maintained without attracting so much attention. An attempt was made to shelter ballot-box frauds under forms of law, by delays at the polls, and in many other ways with which the country has become familiar. Tissue ballots played their part in the work, and for a time seemed to furnish just what was wanted by the party. The new device may serve the purposes of those who designed it more satisfactorily than any of the old ones, and it has the advantage of being sanctioned by a law of the State.

The new law provides that at each polling-place there shall be a certain number of ballot-boxes, each one for an officer or group of officers to be voted for, and only one voter is allowed at a time in the inclosed place where the ballots must be deposited. The election Managers are there, and are required to read the names on the boxes to those voters who cannot read. The perils which surround the negro voter who does not know how to read can easily be seen. The Manager may point out the right box for a certain ballot—the ballot for Governor, for example—but if the voter can read neither the name on the box nor the names on the ballots in his hand, he is utterly at sea, and the distribution of his ballots is governed by chance. There is no friend at hand to guide him. He is alone, and no one who is acquainted with election methods in South Carolina can suppose that the Democratic Managers will waste any time on him. They will simply enjoy his discomfiture. He can be sure, however, that if any of his ballots get into the wrong boxes they will not be counted. It is said that the negro vote was cut down one-half by this arrangement of boxes in the last election. Colored men were either discouraged by the obstacles in their path, and did not vote, or many of their votes were thrown away because they got into the wrong boxes. It is the illiterate voter who suffers, and the illiterate colored voter for the illiterate white Democrat can rely upon the assistance of the Managers, who will not allow his ballots to go astray. This law applies only to State offices; the voter can easily distinguish, it is said, the box in which ballots for members of Congress must be put. It will be seen that the law is a much better thing for the dominant party than tissue ballots, but it also appears that the law must be unconstitutional, because it indirectly, but effectively, restricts suffrage by requiring an educational qualification. So long as it remains in force, however, the old methods of the bull-dozer and ballot-box stuffer can be laid aside.

The possible effect of an educational qualification in South Carolina is shown by the census tables. Very nearly half of the inhabitants 10 years old and upward cannot read. There were in 1880, in the State, 86,900 white males of voting age, and 118,889 colored males of voting age, and probably two-thirds of the latter cannot read. "When our pleasant vices are likely to become whips to scourge us, we are in a humor to mend our ways," said the leading Democratic newspaper of South Carolina two years ago, after Democrats had stuffed the boxes against Democrats. It was this statement, read in the United States Senate, that led Mr. Hampton to admit that there had been frauds in his State, and to declare that he would prevent them in the future, if possible. It may be that this law, very plainly intended to disfranchise illiterate Republican voters, is regarded by Mr. Hampton and his friends as a step in the direction of reform.

SOUND ADVICE

HARPER'S WEEKLY
April 28, 1883, p. 259

Frederick Douglass is still a wise counsellor of the colored men. In an address in Washington upon the anniversary of emancipation he said that three solutions have been offered of the problem of the fate of the colored man in America. The first was colonization, which was certainly not worth talking about. The second was extinction by poverty and disease. But it appeared that in the Southern States the increase of the colored people is ten per cent. greater than that of the whites. The third solution was assimilation and unifica-

Frank Leslie's Illustrated Newspaper, July 21, 1883, p. 353.

tion with the rest of the population, and this seems to Mr. Douglass the natural course.

> "There is but one destiny, it seems to me, left for us, and that is to make ourselves and be made by others a part of the American people in every sense of the word. Assimilation, not isolation, is our true policy and our natural destiny. Unification for us is life; separation is death. We can not afford to set up for ourselves a separate political party, or adopt for ourselves a political creed apart from the rest of our fellow-citizens."

This is simple good sense, and may well be pondered by every American. The demand of "recognition," that is to say, of patronage, upon the ground of color or previous nationality, is as foolish as to demand it upon a sectarian ground. The Constitution and the laws do not know German, or English, or French, or Irish, or colored, or Baptist, or Jewish, or pagan, or atheistic, Americans. They know only equal citizens, who, if they are white or black, may have been born anywhere in the world, and may hold any religious faith, or none. Consequently any body of citizens who, as citizens, try to separate themselves into a class upon grounds of race, or nativity, or religious opinion, are essentially anti-American.

Citizens who hold similar views of public policy will naturally and properly organize to secure the passage of laws embodying their views. But this is very different from organizing to secure advantages as colored, or Baptists, or Catholic, or German, or English, American citizens. Mr. Douglass's words, like all wise words, are timely and suggestive.

RICHMOND PUBLIC SCHOOLS

FRANK LESLIE'S ILLUSTRATED NEWSPAPER
July 21, 1883, p. 354

At the courteous suggestion of Mayor Carrington, the Superintendent of Public Schools placed himself at my disposal, during my recent visit, for the purpose of making a tour of inspection of the various abodes of learning in "gallant Richmond." My interest centred in the colored schools, and thither we hied, taking in en route the mansion occupied by Jefferson Davis when President, now the (white) Normal School. Its many-pillared portico suggested memories of the fateful past, when it was the busy headquarters of the "lost cause." At the Normal School (colored) the same standard of study and discipline is maintained as at the white. The lady superintendent, on my expression of surprise that the standard was the same, remarked with grim humor that colored people were "very human." In the primary

EDUCATIONAL PROGRESS IN VIRGINIA.—THE SCHOOLS FOR COLORED CHILDREN IN RICHMOND.
FROM SKETCHES BY C. UPHAM.—SEE PAGE 354.

Frank Leslie's Illustrated Newspaper, July 21, 1883, p. 353.

first room I found fifty-eight little scholars diligently at work. The grammar school during the war was the office of that dread functionary, the Provost Marshal. There are 3,000 negro and 4,000 white children registered at the Normal Schools.

In the primary, secondary and grammar colored schools the teachers are all blacks—graduates of the Normal School. They evince great interest in their work, and nearly all seek to labor among their own people.

I was glad to learn that the blacks show intense appreciation of educational privileges, and willingly make the greatest sacrifices that their children may acquire learning. They are contented to labor and endure the uttermost privation in order that their offspring may become "real ladies and gentlemen." They scarcely know how to define precisely what this means, but possess a vague notion that education is what constitutes the difference between whites and blacks.

Apropos of this, a young lady told me that in her father's family was a slave who continued to work for them with the same fidelity during and after the war, and whose wages were principally devoted to his daughter's comfort and toilet. The girl was sixteen years of age and well advanced in her studies. So my friend suggested to the father that she would take her as a maid and thus economize his wages, while the daughter would be earning her own livelihood. To this the old darkey indignantly replied, that he intended his daughter to be "a lady," which meant that she should be educated and never work. There is something quite pathetic in the idea of a poor old darkey's laboring so hard for what he himself stood so greatly in need of.

Another strange feature in the character of the negro is his devotion to his old master wedded to his unwillingness to vote for him. He will work, beg, borrow, steal for him, if need be, but his votes cannot be commanded or purchased at any price!

Mr. Garnett observed that insanity and *mania a potu* were entirely unknown among the colored people in Richmond until after the emancipation. Even in the primary school we found the children neatly dressed, as a rule—much more so than the children in the New York schools (of the poorer districts), and very well conducted and quite anxious to learn. I put some questions to the most diminutive among them, and asked that those who were capable of answering should put up their hands. They manifested great interest, and all seemed desirous of replying, holding up the little black fists with apparently the greatest delight in order to claim an opportunity for speaking.

They sang in that sweet minor key peculiar to their race, but musical exercises are not so general in the schools of the South as with us.

We learned that the whites and the blacks keep quite *pari passu*, the latter frequently exhibiting greater anxiety and quickness of apprehension, until the higher classes are reached, when the negroes fall behind in a most notable manner. Their highest ambition is to become teachers—the one calling to which they eagerly aspire.

The colored children labor under the disadvantage of having no home education to supplement the school training—to one with whom to study or have their lessons explained. Unlike the whites, they learn during school hours *only*.

The advisability of eliminating the higher branches of mathematics and languages from the schedule of study and substituting industrial instruction, is now said to be under consideration.

I was deeply interested in all that I beheld and with all that I learned during my visit, and inexpressibly gratified to find the wheels of progress moving with such celerity with the children of the Sunny South.

THE COLORED PATRIOTS
A Resolution to Indorse Arthur Raises an Oratorical Storm.

ATLANTA CONSTITUTION
September 27, 1883

Louisville, September 26.—The only point of importance in the colored convention this morning was a resolution by W. S Wilson, of Louisiana, indorsing the administration of President Arthur. The resolution raised a great stir, and much oratory was indulged in, which was only quieted when L. D. Herbert, also of Louisiana, moved to refer it to the committee on resolutions, which was adopted. Nothing of note has been accomplished.

Strong feeling exists in favor of adopting Fred Douglas's speech as the expression of the sentiments of the colored people of the union, and having the same transmitted to congress. A Kentucky delegate moved the following resolution, which created great uproar. Resolved, that we, the colored people of the United States in convention assembled, do affirm our devotion anew to the republican party, and will use our utmost endeavors for its continued ascendency, and control of the national government, believing it to be for the best interest of the whole people." The chair rendered a decision sending the question to the committee on resolusions, and saving the convention from a spilt.

At the Exposition

The convention visited the exposition this afternoon in a body. To night a long list of speakers is named to address the convention, and its business will for a time be held in abeyance. The chances are fair for an adjournment being taken without further actual results.

THE CIVIL RIGHTS LAW
Manager L. De Give Arrested for Its Violation.

THE ATLANTA CONSTITUTION
September 28, 1883

The Outcome of an Ejectment During the Last Theatrical Season at DeGive's—W. D. Moore Causes the Arrest of Manager DeGive for Having Him Fired from the Hall.

On yesterday Mr. L. DeGive, proprietor of DeGive's operahouse, was arrested on a warrant sworn out before Commissioner Conley.

The cause of the arrest was as follows:

During the last theatrical season, a negro man named W. D. Moore, who is in the service of the internal revenue department, entered the gallery of the operahouse and walking over to the left hand side seated himself. As is well known the right hand side of the gallery is reserved for colored people and the left hand for whites. A small uproar was created among the negro's white neighbors as soon as he sat down and a policeman asked him to move into the colored side of the gallery. He declined to do as he was asked and the policeman then appealed to Mr. DeGive for instructions. Mr. DeGive said if he did not move out to eject him from the operahouse. The policeman acted under these instructions and put Moore out. Moore now begins a suit against Mr DeGive for damages and for his rights under the civil rights bill. The penalty under this bill is $500 fine or hard labor for a certain time in the penitentiary, and $500 indemnity to the injured colored man, provided he makes out his case and gets a verdict.

When the warrant was presented to Mr. DeGive he stated that he was not ready for trial, but would be in a few days, and the case was set for next Wednesday, when it will be tried before Commissioner Conley.

A Talk with Mr. DeGive

A Constitution man sought Mr. DeGive yesterday and found the genial Belgian wearing something less than his usual urbanity and in the conversation that ensued, applying his finger to his forehead with something more than his usual energy and frequency. He said in answer to a query:

"WHAT DE OLE WOMAN SAY NOW?"

Harper's Weekly, August 25, 1883, p. 541.

"I have done everything possible to avoid any issue of this sort. It goes without saying that the theatre cannot be acceptable to either whites or blacks if they are seated together. Such a course would keep the best white people from attending the theatre, and those white men who did go would go for the purpose of making it warm for the colored people. Every theatrical manager in the south and in the north, too, for that matter, understands this perfectly well. I provided a section of the gallery for the colored people and one for the whites, and it has been my determination to keep each race on its own side."

"Was the colored section of the gallery as good as the other?"

"Just as good. In fact the seats were identical, the price, was the same and there was not one iota of difference."

"Did you keep the whites from the colored side?"

"Yes. I have frequently had white men to move out of the colored gallery and make room for colored men and women. The trouble in this particular case was that the colored gallery was not crowded. Moore entered the gallery late with some colored women, the play was already in progress and two men that he says were white, occupied some front seats that he wanted. There was plenty of room in the rear of these men and they were entitled to the front seats as they had taken them, seeing them vacant after the play began. I did not know, however, that there were any white men in the gallery and I don't know it yet. I only know that there were plenty of comfortable and choice seats vacant on the colored side of the gallery and that Moore could have had no object in crossing over to the white side of the gallery, except to force an issue. When the policeman reported to me that there was about to be a row over it I though best for all parties to have Moore ejected from the house just as any man who was inciting disorder whether he was white or black, would have been."

"You will stand by the case in the courts?"

"I certainly will. I think it is best that this issue should be settled definitely, and I do not believe that any court of justice will decide that, considering I provided equally good seats for the colored and white people, that I should be punished for insisting on their taking the sections allotted to them. It has been my aim to conduct the theatre so that there should be no disorder and every man should have exactly what his ticket called for, and an equal chance to see and enjoy the performance. If it is decided that the colored people can invade the white gallery there is nothing to keep them from occupying seats in the parquet or dress circle."

"Have there been any ejectments from your theatre before this?"

"None by my order. Just after the passage of the civil rights bill in 1875, three young colored men entered the theatre and took seats on the white side of the gallery, for even before this bill was passed the gallery was divided into a white and colored side. As soon as they were seen there were hisses and calls in the house and a number of young men arose from the parquet and walked up stairs, where they were joined by others and forcibly ejected the colored boys, throwing them down the stairs. It was to avoid just such another scene as this and just such violence that I asked the policeman to invite Moore to take a seat in the colored gallery or to leave the house, and in failing to do either to eject him. I believe I have done best for both white and colored people and I am willing to stand by my action."

THE COLORED COMPLAINT

The Freedman's Bank, Civil Rights and Other Topics.

THE ATLANTA CONSTITUTION
September 28, 1883, p. 2

Louisville, September 27.—The national colored convention late last night adopted the following address: The national convention of colored men assembled, respectfully present the following as embracing and presenting their views and sentiments:

1. That we are gratified for and rejoice in the miraculous emancipation that came to our race twenty years ago. The shock of embattled arms was the lullaby of a nation born in a day. We cannot forget the great sacrifice of the women and heroic men who made possible the struggle in which treason and slavery were consigned to a common sepulchre, nor would we be unmindful of the measure of devotion and patriotism that the white and colored soldiers rendered the nation.

2. That we are not insensible to the fact that the congress of the United States has spread the statute books many laws calculated to make us secure in our rights as citizens, nor would we be forgetful of the magnificent amendments to the constitution intended to render for ever impossible the crime of human slavery.

3. We do not ask for any more class legislation. We have had enough of this. But we do believe that many of the laws intended to secure to us our rights as citizens are nothing more than dead letters. In the southern states, almost without exception, colored people are denied justice in the courts, denied the fruit of their honest labor, defrauded of their political rights at the ballot box, shut out from learning the trades, cheated out of their civil rights by innkeepers and common carrier companies and left by the state to an inadequate opportunity for education and general improvement.

4. We regard the labor question, education and sound moral training, paramount to all other questions, We believe that these questions, especially in the south, need recasting, and that the plantation, credit and mortgage system should be abolished, so that honest

DA CAPO—WITH A DIFFERENCE.
(SATURDAY NIGHT REHEARSAL.)
LEADER OF CHOIR (*with a weakness for First Voice*). "Now, den! ober agin, an' dis time de Tenner needn't come so close to de Soapranner; an' Brer Gustover, we doan' need so much base in de 'soap-fat!' tone. Dat's too much like ebery-day work."

Harper's Weekly, September 29, 1883, p. 623.

labor should be remunerated, so that the landholders of the south should recognize that this question is to be solved by encouraging the negroes to industry, to frugality, and to business habits, by assisting them to acquire an interest in the soil by paying them honest wages for honest work, and by making them content and happy in the land of their nativity. The white men and owners of the soil in the south can settle the question of labor and capital between white and black.

5. We believe in a broad comprehensive system, looking towards the education of young colored girls, so that they may become intelligent and faithful women, and of young colored boys that they may learn trades and become useful men and good citizens. The religious and moral training of the youth of our race should not be neglected. The hope of every people is in an adherance to sound social logical and ethical principles. The moral element in character is of greater value than wealth or education, and this must be fostered by the family and encouraged by the pulpit.

6. The failure of the freedmans Saving Bank and Trust company, is the marvel of our time. It was established to receive the earnings of persons heretofore held in bondage and the descendents of such persons. It was established by the government, and thought to be solvent. In changing its charter the trustees transcended their authority, and thereby made themselves liable. The government, in appointing the machinery to close the insolvent institution violated the United States statutes in bankruptcy, and should therefore reimburse the creditors of the bank.

7. The distinction made between white and black troops in the regular army is un American, unjust and ungrateful. White men can enter any branch of the service, while colored men are confined to the cavalary and infantry service, and in the appointment of civilians to the regular army all believe it the duty of the president to consider the claims of colored men. This distinction is carried into the navy as well.

8. It is not our province to dictate the policy of the government, or the action of our fellow citizens in the several states. It is a matter that their services, patriotism and needs should shape.

9. As a race struggling and contending for our political and civil rights, we are not unmindful of the efforts of Ireland to gain her rights, and we extend to our Irish friends our profound sympathy and best wishes.

10. We earnestly desire the abolition of the chaingang system, and the admission to trade unions of men of our own race, and to their employment in commercial pursuits.

11. In nearly every state of the union both north and south, our race are not allowed to enter freely into the trades of gain or employment in the higher walks of life. This is unworthy of our institutions and hurtful to the reputation of our country at home and abroad.

After adopting the above address, the convention adjourned and the members dispersed to their homes.

CIVIL RIGHTS

The Supreme Court Declares the Bill to be Unconstitutional.
A Radical Relic Rubbed Out.
Special Rights for None but Equal Rights for All.
A Triumph of Law and Sense.
Which Strengthens the Decree That the Republicans Must Go.

THE ATLANTA CONSTITUTION
October 16, 1883

Washington, October 15.—The most important decision rendered by the supreme court of the United States to-day, was that in the five cases, commonly known as the civil rights cases, which were submitted to the court on printed arguments about a year ago. The titles of these cases, and the states from which they came, are as follows:

No. 1. The United States against Murray Stanley, from the United States circuit court for the district of Kansas.

No. 2. The United States against Michael Ryan, from the United States circuit court for the district of California.

No. 3. The United States against Samuel Nichols, from the United States circuit court for the western district of Missouri.

No. 26. The United States against Samuel D. Singleton, from the United States circuit court, from the southern district of New York.

No. 28. Richard A. Robinson and wife against the Memphis and Charleston railroad company, from the United States circuit court for the district of Tennessee.

These cases were all based on the first and second sections of the civil rights act of 1875, and were respectively prosecutions under that act for not admitting certain colored persons to equal accommodations and privileges in inns or hotels, in railroad cars and in theatres.

The Defense Set Up

The defense set up in every case was the alleged unconstitutionality of the law. The first and second sections of the act, which were the parts directly in controversy, are as follows;

Section 1. That all persons within the jurisdiction of the United States shall be entitled to the full and equal enjoyment of accommodations, advantages, facilities and privileges of inns, public conveyances on land and water, theatres, and other places of public amusements, subject only to the conditions and limitations established by law, and applicable alike to citizens of every race and color, regardless of any previous conditions of servitude.

Second section provides that any person who violates the first section shall be liable to a forfeit of five hundred dollars for each offense, to be recovered in civil action, and also to a penalty of from five hundred to one thousand dollars fine, or imprisonment from thirty days to one year, to be enforced in criminal prosecution. Extensive jurisdiction is given to the district and circuit courts of the United States in the cases arising under this law. The rights and privileges claimed by and denied to colored persons in these cases were full and equal accommodations in hotels, in ladies' cars on railroads, and in the dress circles in theatres.

The Holding of the Court

The court in a long and carefully prepared opinion by Justice Bradley, holds 1st,—That congress had no constitutional authority to pass the sections in question under either the 13th or 14th amendment of the constitution; 2d, that the 14th amendment is prohibitory upon the states only, and that the legislation authorized to be adopted by congress for enforcing that amendment, is not direct legislation on matters respecting which the states are prohibited from making or enforcing certain laws or doing certain acts, but is corrective legislation necessary or proper for counteracting and redressing the effect of such laws or acts. That in forbidding the states, for example, to deprive any person of life, liberty or property, without due process of law, and giving congress power to enforce prohibition, it was not intended to give congress power to provide due process of law for the protection of life, liberty and property, which would embrace almost all subjecs of legislation, but to provide modes of redress for counteracting the operation and effect of state laws obnoxious to prohibition. Third, that the 13th amendment gives no power to congress to pas section referred, because that amendment relates only to slavery and involuntary servitude which it abolishes, and gives congress power to pass laws for its enforcement; that this power only extends to the subject matter of the amendment itself, namely: slavery and involuntary servitude, and the necessary incident and consequences of these conditions; that it has, nothing to do with different races or olors, but only refers to slavery, the legal equality of the different races and classes of citizens being provided for in the fourteenth amendment, which prohibits the states from doing anything to interfere with such equality; that it is no infringement of the thirteenth amendment to refuse to any person the equal accommodations and privilege of an inn or place of public entertainment, however it may be violate of his legal rights; that it imposes upon him no badge of slavery or involuntary servitude, which imply some part of subjection of one person to another and incapacity incidental thereto, such as inability to hold property, to make contracts, to be parties in court, etc., and that of the original civil rights act, which abolished these incapacities might be supported by the 13th amendment. It does not, therefore, follow that the act of 1875 can be supported by it. Fourth—That this decision affects only the validity of the law in the states, not in the territories or the district of Columbia, where the legislative power of congress is unlimited, and it does not undertake to decide what congress might or might not do, under the power to regulate commerce with foreign nations, and amongst the several states, the law not being drawn with any such view. Fifth—That therefore it is the opinion of the court that the first and second sections of the act of congress of March 1st, 1875, entitled "an act to protect all citizens in their civil and legal rights," are unconstitutional and void, and judgment should be rendered upon the indictments accordingly.

Judge Harlan's Dissent

At the conclusion of the reading of Judge Bradley's opinion, which occupied more than an hour, Justice Harlan said that under ordinary circumstances and in ordinary cases he should hesitate to set up his individual opinion in opposition to that of his eight colleagues, but in view of what he thought the people of this country wished to accomplish, what they tried to accomplish, and what they believe they had accomplished, by means of this legislation, he must express his dissent from the opinion of the court. He has not had time since hearing that opinion to prepare a statement of the grounds of his dissent, but he should prepare and file one as soon as possible. In the meantime he desired to put upon record this expression of his individual judgment.

Another War Case

Another interesting case, involving war legislation, was also decided by the supreme court to-day, namely the case of the United States against Edward T. Gale and William S. Gibson, which was brought here on certificate division from the circuit court of the United States for the district of Florida. This was a suit against the supervisor and clerk of election district No. 8, in Marion county, Fla., on the occasion of the election of congressional representatives in 1878. The indictment charged the defendants with misconduct as election officers, in stuffing the ballotbox with randulent tickets, and abstracting tickets which had been voted. The defense was that sections 5512 and 5515 of the revised statutes, upon which the indictment was based, and section 820, under which was chosen the grand jury by which the indictment was found, were unconstitutional and void. The court disposes of the first part of the defense very briefly, by saying the question of the validity of sections 5512 and 5515 has already been decided by this court in the case of Siebald and Clarks 100 United States, 371–390, and was determined in favor of their validity. Section 820, upon which the second part of the defense was based, contains the statement of causes for disqualification and challenge of grand and petit jurors in the courts of the United States as follows: "Without duress and coercion, to have taken up arms or to have joined any insurrection or rebellion against the United States; to have had adhered to any insurrection or rebellion, giving it aid and comfort," etc. In empanelling the grand jury which found the indictment against the defendant, four persons otherwise competent were excluded from the panel for the causes mentioned in this section. The court, after a review of the circumstances as shown by the record, declines to decide whether section 820 is valid or not, for the reason that the objection to the constitution of the grand jury under that section was not raised in due time.

A History of the Law

The court, however, gives a brief history of this law, excluding from juries persons who took part in the late insurrection, and comments upon it as follows: "It may be proper to call attention to the singular position of this section, (section 820.) It was originally enacted as section 1 of an act passed June 17th, 1862, entitled "an act defining the different causes of challenge, and prescribing an additional oath for grand and petit jurors in United States courts. 12 Statutes, 430," At that time—1862—it was no doubt a very proper and necessary law, but after the rehabilitation of the insurgent states, the proclamation of a general amnesty and the adoption of the fourteenth amendment, guaranteeing equal rights to all citizens of the United States there would seem to have been no just reason for a continuance of the law, especially as by far the largest portion of the citizens in the states lately in rebellion would be disqualified under it. Accordingly, by the fifth section of the act commonly called the enforcement act, passed April 20, 1871, 17th statute, 15th congress, after providing that in prosecutions under that act no person should be a grand or petit juror who should, in the judgment of the court, be in complicity with any combination or conspiracy punishable by the provision thereof repealed. The said first section of the act of 1862 and the law remained in this state until the adoption of the revised statutes. For some unexplained reason the revisers imported the section back again into the revised statutes as section 820, although it had not been in force for more than two years. It is probable that the fact of its repeal was overlooked by congress when the revision was adopted, and it is to be hoped that their attention will be called to it.

The Questions Answered

The questions certified by the court below, are answered by this court as follows: "It is the opinion of this court, and it so decides, that the question whether 5,512 and 5,515 of the revised statutes of the United States are repugnant to and in violation of the constitution of the United States, should be answered in the negative, that the question as to the validity of section 820 of said revised statutes is unnecessary to be decided, in-as-much as objection to the constitution of the grand jury, under that section, was not raised in due time, and that the remaining question, namely, whether the judgment of this court could be rendered against the defendants on an indictment found by a grand jury empanelled and sworn under the sections aforesaid, and whether the indictment aforesaid charges any offenses for which judgment could be rendered against the defendants in this court, under the constitution and laws of the United States, should be answered in the affirmative. Opinion by Justice Bradley.

CIVIL RIGHTS AT DEGIVE'S
How an Immense Audience Received the Supreme Court Decision.

THE ATLANTA CONSTITUTION
October 16, 1883

Above will be found the report of the decision rendered yesterday in the supreme court of the United States on the famous civil rights cases. This decision, adverse to the right of congress to legislate upon the question of civil rights in the states, takes on considerable interest in Atlanta, from the fact that two notable efforts to enforce the act of Congress have recently agitated the public. One of these was the case of Moore, the colored man who had Manager DeGive arrested and bonded for ejecting him from the white people's portion of the gallery at the opera house. The other was the action of Professor Chase in introducing three negroes into the white people's cars upon the Air-Line railroad.

Civil Rights in Georgia

In Georgia the operations of the civil rights bill have been invoked but sparingly, and almost entirely in cases where the colored people have been refused the right on railroads to enter and occupy any portion of the cars of a railroad train. Several cases of that character have been started in the United States courts, but for one cause and another have never reached a definitive issue and decision. The railroad officials have prevented much complaint upon this line by affording good and sufficient accommodations to colored passengers and keeping them free from the presence of white passengers.

An Early Decision

The temper of the Georgia courts was tested early in the era of the civil rights act in a case made by the intermarriage of a white and a colored person. There is a penal law, in this state against such intermarriages, and this law was violated. The parties thereto were indicted and convicted, and the case was taken to the supreme court of the state. That court was then organized by the republican administration of Governor Bullock and now United States Senator Brown was the chief justice of the court. It was argued by the counsel for the convicted parties that the civil rights bill and the amendments to the constitution protected the parties and that no law of the state could affix a penalty to and make a crime of the exercise of the rights thus established and guaranteed by congress.

Chief Justice Brown delivered the judgment of the court in an able and exhaustive opinion, upholding the state law making such marriages criminal and denying the applicability of the act of congress to these internal police regulations of the states.

Since the rendition of the above decision all grievances upon the plea of civil rights have been carried to the United States courts, and as stated above none of these that can now be recalled have reached an issue. The case of Manager DeGive was expected to be made a complete test case in this state.

A Singular Coincidence

It is notable that in the DeGive case the prosecutor, Moore, was ejected from the opera house on the occasion of the second night's performance of the Haverly troupe last season. Moore took a seat in the part of the gallery assigned to the white people and refused to "shinny on his own side," as it were. The consequence was that the police forcibly assisted him to take the fresh air on the pavement of the street below. Last night the Haverly troupe again occupied the boards for their first performance here since the night of the ejectment in question. While the end man was convulsing the audience with his latest conondrums, the wires from Washington were busily ticking to The Constitution the summary of the text of the decision above given. Word was given to Manager DeGive that the decision had been rendered, and he was naturally greatly elated over this sudden and complete stoppage of his civil rights troubles.

A Lively Demonstration

Manager Gulick, of the Haverly troupe, went on the stage during the final act and got the attention of the vast audience by a wave of his hand. He then announced, in appropriate language to the audience, the facts in the DeGive case above recited and concluded by stating that a dispatch to The Constitution had just brought the welcome news that the supreme court of the United States had decided against the civil rights cases from the states, involving the equal rights of the races to the same privileges in all hotels and theaters and on railroad trains.

The audience instantly grasped the full purport of the announcement and burst into such a thunder of applause as was never before heard within the walls of the operahouse. This was no sooner subsided than it was repeated and prolonged with even greater unction. The people smiled at each other with beaming faces and congratulations were exchanged all through the audience. It was welcome news to every one, excepting only the dusky occupants of the colored galleries. These were silent and evidently smitten with dumb-founded consternation. Not a note of applause came from those solemn rows of benches, and their occupants evidently believed that the decision meant the total abrogation of the chief blessings that are involved in the facts of their emancipation and citizenship.

The scene in the theater was an inspiriting one and exhibited the lively interest which all the people have felt in the matter of the legal effect of the provisions of the civil rights act. Many expressions of approval of the decision were made by those present and after the performance the subject was everywhere discussed with interest and animation.

Senator Brown's Views

When asked through the telephone what he thought of the decision, Senator Brown replied:

"I think it is right decision, because I have never doubted the unconstitutionality of the act. I do not see how the court could have made any other decision and I have always felt a certainty that when the question came squarely before them they would make the decision they now have made, It will have a good effect upon the country, and result in the adjustment by natural methods of many questions that have been vexatious and irritating to the public peace."

What Mr. DeGive Said

When The Constitution courier delivered the news to Manager DeGive that gentlemen was surprised into the unusual act of suspending the count of the evening's receipts. He was supremely gratified and said:

"I would not, for a thousand dollars, have been beaten in the case made against me, but I am glad that I shall not have to pursue the fight. I believe myself that the law was unconstitutional. My lawyers said so and I was determined to carry the matter to the last court of resort—to the same supreme court of the United States."

"If the decision had been the other way, what would have been the effect upon your business?'

"It would have been ruined. You know the white people would not have brought their wives and sisters to a place where they were liable to be seated for hours next to colored people of all grades, from the lowest even to the best of them. As it is, we have given them good places in the theater and protected them always in their rights in such places. They should be contented there, and now I believe they will be."

Interview with Judge H. B. Tompkins

When the suit was brought against Mr. DeGive, he determined to make it a test case. He employed Judge Henry B. Tompkins as his counsel. A Constitution reporter found Judge Tompkins last night and asked him what he thought of the decision?

"It is what I knew it must be when the issue was fairly presented to the supreme court. When Mr. DeGive put his case in my hands I thought it best to get it before the highest tribunal without delay. We therefore gave bond to the commissioner's court without a hearing and decided to take the case to the circuit court, if necessary, and from there to the supreme court, if the decision had been against us."

"You have kept very quiet about it?"

"Because we thought it best. The danger in all these cases has not been so much the effect of any finding of the courts as the danger of mischievous agitation of the question involved. I thought it best to keep the case out of the newspapers and carry it quietly to a final conclusion. While it remained unsettled it was a menace to every hotel keeper, theatrical manager and railroad company in the country—in fact, a menace to the peace of society itself."

"But the decision of the court does not surprise you?"

"Not at all. I was satisfied that the court would decide that congress had no right delegated to it by, or suggested in, the constitution to legislate upon such questions. There is nothing in the constitution that justifies the interference of congress in the police regulations of sovereign states. I am glad the decision has been reached, for while I was perfectly confident of what the decision would be when made, much mischief might have been done while the country was waiting for it. Of course this decision settles all cases now pending, and our suit with the others."

COLORED INDIGNATION
The Effects of the Supreme Court Decision.

THE ATLANTA CONSTITUTION
October 17, 1883

The Colored People of Washington to Hold a Meeting of Protest Next Monday—Fred Douglas, Ex-Senator Bruce, and Others Expressing Their Views on the Situation.

Washington, October 16.—The decision of the supreme court declaring the civil rights act of 1875 an unconstitutional invasion of the rights of the states, has been the subject of much comment here to-day. Several of the most prominent colored men of the district have been interviewed, and have given their opinions as to the moral effect of the decision. Naturally a majority of them express regret that the supreme court has rendered such a decision, and are inclined to regard it as an obstacle to the progress of the colored race. Ex-Senator Bruce, from Mississippi, and present registrar of treasury, declares it a most unfortunate decision, one which will carry the county backwards fifteen years; also that it does not reflect the sentiment of the people of the United States, and is a revival of the theory of states rights. Fred Douglass says the decision places the colored people again outside of the law, and places them, when on steamboats or railroads, or in the theater, restaurant or other public place, at the mercy of any white ruffian who may choose to insult them. Professor Greener says, in view of this decision, every colored man with any self-respect must continue to demand the fullest protection of the law, both as a man and as an American citizen, and that he does not think the civilization of the age can be turned back, even by the supreme court of the United States. At a conference of the colored people of the district to-day, it was decided to hold a meeting on Monday night to express the sentiment of the colored race with respect to the decision, and to consider what course to pursue in view of that decision. Among those who are to be invited to address the meeting are several prominent white lawyers and clergymen, and such colored speakers as Fred Douglass and Professor Gregory.

THE LATE COLORED CONVENTION

HARPER'S WEEKLY
October 27, 1883, p. 674

The late National Convention of colored citizens at Louisville was a very interesting and pathetic assembly. It naturally made Frederick Douglass, the most noted representative of the colored citizens in the country, its President, and his address was a vigorous plea for self-reliance and united action. The object of the Convention apparently was to give formal and impressive expression to the feelings and demands of the colored citizens. But it proposed no definite scheme to secure the fulfillment of its wishes, and distinctly disclaimed the desire of class legislation, while it protested strongly against certain laws and customs which it holds to be injurious to the interests of the colored people. The Convention refused to approve the Republican party or the Administration. Mr. Douglass, who has always been a Republican, and, as has been sometimes thought, too blind a Republican partisan, exhorted the delegates to follow no party blindly, and "to compel the world to receive us as equals."

The New York *Globe,* which is the chief paper of the colored citizens, heartily commends the speech of Mr. Douglass, and the address and acts of the Convention, but agrees that it is not yet ready to advise the formation of a colored party. It asserts, however, that so far as colored men are concerned, the law countenances violence by not protecting them against it at the polls, and it advises its friends to defend their rights when assailed by force, and, presumably, to defend them by force. That is, it would have the colored voters in the Southern States refuse to be cheated or to be driven from the polls, and to fight if necessary to secure their right of voting. It thinks that the Democratic party still follows toward the colored race the course "indicated years ago by that archvillain Chief Justice Taney." It holds that the Republican party also is unfriendly, and that since 1876 the colored people have made no advancement in the party except the appointment of Mr. Bruce as Register of the Treasury. The *Globe* advises its friends not to throw away votes upon a party which does not appreciate them.

No one will deny that the situation is extremely trying for the colored citizens. The real obstacle in their way is expressed in the word colored. Charles Lenox Remond, a very intelligent and highly educated colored man, said forty years ago that he would willingly be flayed alive if he could emerge from the torture with a white skin. Mr. Douglass exclaimed, with energy, "Down with prejudice!" That, indeed, is the enemy. There is no discrimination in law against colored citizens, but prejudice and the usages that spring from it are not controllable by law. Prejudice may affect the honest enforcement of the law, and make it practically a dead letter. There is an unjust criticism current upon the recent demand of colored men for "recognition." They are accused of a willingness to sell their principles for place. But this is not the true explanation of their demand. As their general exclusion is doubtless due to the prejudice against their color, their election and appointment to office would show that the prejudice was declining. There could be no test so conclusive, and this is the meaning of the remark of Mr. Douglass that they will know the prejudice to be disappearing when a colored man is made Vice-President or called into the cabinet. If any other class of citizens in the country lay under the kind of ostracism that rests upon the colored people, they would naturally and justly urge that their demand for equal consideration in appointment to public office was a sign of proper self-respect and not of venal desire of place. The fact of the meeting of the Convention, and its dignified and serious protest and appeal, will be of undoubted service to the colored citizens. Those citizens need not regret the fate of the Civil Rights Bills. The wrongs under which they suffer are not to be remedied by law.

FREDERICK DOUGLASS

HARPER'S WEEKLY
November 24, 1883, p. 743

Frederick Douglass is the most conspicuous American of African descent, and his career is a striking illustration of the nature of free popular institutions. Born a slave, he is to-day, by his own energy and character and courage, an eminent citizen, and his life has been a constant and powerful plea for his people. Over infinite disadvantage and prejudice, his patience, intelligence, capacity, and tenacity have triumphantly prevailed, and in himself he is a repudiation of the current assertions against the colored race. Mr. Douglass's address at the late Colored Convention showed a comprehension of the situation of the colored people in this country which justified the regard in which he is held, and which explains the leadership that he has held so long. Its tone toward his people is not that of flattery and sentimentality, but of rebuke and exhortation; and he understands, if no other colored man perceives, the immense and crushing power of that prejudice which overwhelms a race whose color is an ineffaceable sign and suggestion of prolonged servile bondage.

The story of Mr. Douglass's early life has been told by himself with a simplicity and power which make his autobiography one of the most striking and unique books in our literature. There is no closer and more intimate view of slavery as it was fifty years ago, and it is impossible to read it to-day as a tale of recent American life without incredulity. No man who directly or indirectly, by sophistry, or evasion, or resolute refusal to know the truth, sustained the system of slavery, can read the narrative of Frederick Douglass without sorrow and remorse. Three books contain the most complete and vivid picture of American slavery in its details, in its spirit, and in its influence upon master and slave, and upon industry and society. These are Douglass's narrative, Olmstead's *Sea-board Slave States,* and Mrs. Stowe's *Uncle Tom's Cabin*. Careful study of these reveals the nature of the malign power with which good men at the South as elsewhere were called to contend.

Frederick Douglass was born in Talbot County, Maryland, sixty-five or sixty-six years ago. Like all slaves, he was not permitted to know his age, but he supposes, from the conversations of his master which he overheard, that he was about seventeen years old in 1835. His master was probably his father, and he was at different times a field hand and hired out to mechanical work in town. He was partially taught to read by a kind mistress, whose husband "stopped the nonsense" as soon as he knew it, and he taught himself by stealth to write. He was undoubtedly a very clever boy, and it was perhaps an instinctive apprehension that his cleverness might make his fellow-slaves troublesome which caused him to be frightfully flogged and abused in the hope of breaking his spirit. Fortunately the savage treatment stimulated rather than subdued his manhood, and when living near Baltimore in 1835 he organized a party of his comrades to attempt to escape. The scheme was betrayed, and he expected to be sent to Alabama; but this doom was averted, and, waiting patiently a little while, on the 3d of September, 1838, he quietly left Baltimore by a railroad train, and soon after reached New York, at two o'clock in the morning.

He was working in a ship-yard at the time, and observing a sympathy for his race among the sailors, he thought that he could disguise himself as a sailor and so escape. He had caught the air and the vocabulary of sailors, and carefully dressing himself and carrying a "protection," which he does not say how he procured, and knowing that if he offered to buy a ticket he would be exposed to a searching examination, he jumped on the train after it was in motion. The disguise was so good that men who knew him did not recognize him. The conductor, passing through the cars, asked for his free papers, and Douglass, with a sailor's air, showed his protection, and said that he did not carry his papers to sea, from which he had just returned. So the slave became a freeman, and the most powerful witness against the woes of the house of bondage found his tongue.

In 1841, at an antislavery convention at Nantucket, Mr. Garrison first saw Mr. Douglass, who had vaguely heard of the abolitionists, and was curious to know what they proposed to do. He was persuaded to address the convention, and after apologizing for his ignorance, the slave of three years before spoke with such force and eloquence that Mr. Garrison said that he had never hated slavery so intensely as at that moment. From that time Mr. Douglass was one of the most popular and powerful of the antislavery orators, and his life was devoted to arousing public sentiment, that the liberty which he had gained for himself might be secured for his fellow-victims of slavery. He shared the fate of all the antislavery pioneers. He was denounced, mobbed, and pursued, and the very fact that he was a living example of the abuses of his race seemed to give peculiar malignity to the hatred with which he was regarded. If such men were slaves, how unspeakable was the wrong of slavery to humanity! Isaiah Rynders, who says in a recent statement that he "got mad with Garrison because he was an infidel," replied to a speaker in one of the antislavery meetings who cited Douglass as evidence of the equality of the races, "That won't do; he is half white, and that accounts for him." "Oh," retorted Douglass, "then I am only your half-brother," which, Captain Rynders adds, was "as good a shot as ever I got in my life."

In later years Mr. Douglass has been an editor, a popular lyceum lecturer, and a devoted Republican orator. He was a Republican Presidential Elector in New York, and he has been Marshal of the District of Columbia. His address, of which we have spoken, at the late Colored Convention, was the wisest word that has been spoken for his race for many a year. He is still a Republican, but he exhorts his brethren to subordinate party attachment to their own welfare. Mr. Douglass is one of the most interesting figures in the country, and no American career has had more remarkable and suggestive vicissitudes than his.

George William Curtis

THE CIVIL RIGHTS BILL

NEW-YORK TIMES
November 29, 1883

Columbia, S. C., Nov. 28.—A bill was introduced in the State Senate to-day to repeal the Civil Rights bill passed by the State Legislature in 1870 under the reconstruction regime. The feeling was very generally expressed through the leading newspapers of the State immediately after the Supreme Court decision adverse to the civil rights law passed by Congress, that the State law should be allowed to remain upon the statute-books, and it is thought that the General Assembly will stand to this and reject the bill which was introduced to-day.

AFRICAN AMERICAN HISTORY IN THE PRESS, 1851-1899

HARPER'S WEEKLY.
JOURNAL OF CIVILIZATION.

Vol. XXVII.—No. 1405.
Copyright, 1883, by Harper & Brothers.   NEW YORK, SATURDAY, NOVEMBER 24, 1883.   TEN CENTS A COPY.
WITH A SUPPLEMENT.

FREDERICK DOUGLASS.—[See Page 743.]

Harper's Weekly, November 24, 1883, p. 737.

1030

Harper's Weekly, December 1, 1883, p. 768.

THE CONDITION OF THE FREEDMEN

HARPER'S WEEKLY
December 8, 1883, pp. 782–83

Whether the lately emancipated slaves in the Southern States have made any sensible degree of progress since they obtained their freedom is a question often put to me in a tone of doubt and denial. Another question, equally pertinent, and even more momentous in view of the history of Yazoo, Hamburg, and the recent slaughter at Danville, is this: Have the recent slave-holders made any sensible degree of progress in civilization since the emancipation of their slaves? Are they more industrious, honest, and humane than when they bought, sold, and flogged their fellowmen to toil for them without wages? These two questions, like the two sides of a horse, should go together, since they are largely dependent upon each other. Plainly enough the recent bondsmen can make little progress without the consent and co-operation of the ruling class among whom they live, and who own the land upon which they live. Nobody seems to doubt the progress of the masters, but everybody is curious to know how the freedmen are getting along.

Well, it is not for me to speak for the late slave-holders. They have never been in want of defenders. It is mine, by your leave and magnanimity, to speak for the class less favored. The answer to the question now put to them is of vital importance. If it shall be found that the freedmen are progressive and improving, that they only need time, patience, and a fair chance in the race of life to become useful citizens, making the nation prosperous in peace and powerful in war, there is, I believe, justice and generosity enough in the American people to supply the needed conditions of success. If, on the other hand, they are found to be non-progressive, worse masters to themselves than their old masters were to them, that liberty neither improves their character nor condition, they are sure to be treated in the end as cumberers of the ground, and will in due season perish from the earth. Civilization is all love and tenderness toward whatever accords and co-operates with it, but implacable, cruel, and remorseless to all obstacles. It spares neither forest, mountain, nor ocean, and it will not spare Indian, Mongolian, or Ethiopian. All must go along with it, or be crushed beneath its swift-flying wheels.

Before answering *pro* or *con* concerning the progress of the freedmen, candid men will see the justice of another inquiry, namely, what these people were before they were emancipated, under what conditions they were emancipated, and what have been the means of improvement within their reach since they were emancipated? All will admit that it would be manifestly and grossly unfair to judge the freedmen without taking their antecedents into account. They should be measured, not from the height yet to be attained, but from the depths from which they have come.

My relation to these people does not make me close my eyes against facts favorable or unfavorable to them. I know no race in my regard but the human race. The same feeling that led me to risk my life to save that of a white boy in my boyhood made me espouse the cause of the slave as soon as I was able to think.

The question asked at the beginning of this article includes mental, moral, and material improvement. What the American people want to know, and have a right to know, is whether the lately enslaved lead better lives and have made for themselves more comfortable conditions of existence than in slavery—whether during these twenty years they have advanced, stood still, or retrograded.

Let us first compare their mental condition of twenty years ago with what it is at present. Prior to emancipation the colored intellect of the South made no visible sign—and could make no sign—of life or power. It was suppressed and shrouded in darkness. Letters were unknown. The law made fine and imprisonment the penalty for teaching one of these sable children to read. So far down were they in the scale of intelligence that they were deemed by many incapable of mastering the rudiments of an English education. Even in religion nothing more than oral instruction was allowed them. "Servants, obey your masters, and be contented with your lot," was the most they got of this, but of this they got abundance, both by arguments from the pulpit on Sunday and by the rhetoric of the lash in the field on Monday. In those days a colored man who could read was a curiosity, and was generally set down in the estimation of the white people as a dangerous character. It would be easy to enlarge upon this mental midnight darkness, but I will leave something to the reflection of the intelligent reader.

I affirm that in nothing have these illiterate and benighted people made more progress than in the acquisition of knowledge. There are now in the Southern States, according to statistics in the Bureau of Education at Washington, between two and three hundred thousand colored children attending schools during some portion of the year. Of course this is but a small proportion of the children there of school age, and for whom there is no provision. The amount of illiteracy is therefore still great and deplorable. The indisposition inherited from slavery to allow the States to be taxed for the education of the laboring classes is still strong, and the general government, which had no hesitation in crossing State lines to catch slaves, has thus far too much respect for the sovereign dignity of the States to cross their lines to secure civil rights or education to its citizens.

It may be adduced as a fair argument that the freed people have made some progress in the matter of education, that now nobody can be found to deny their capacity for education. If any such could be found, they would only need to visit the public schools here in Washington, and witness the qualifications of the colored teachers and the aptitude of the colored pupils to have their doubts and denials made ridiculous. Colored children, to the credit of the statesmen of twenty years ago, have commodious school-houses, competent teachers, and are pursuing the same course of study that white children pursue, and with almost equal success.

With respect to the moral progress of the lately enslaved class I am sorry to speak in a somewhat lower tone. But the same rule of judgment should be applied here as elsewhere. They are in this respect, as well as others, the legitimate results of their antecedents. The sense of right and the voice of conscience had little chance of cultivation in the relation of master and slave. Conduct in that relation was guided by force and fear. Mutual interest and common welfare were excluded from that relation. Its corner-stone was composed of the blood-cemented fragments of the moral constitution of human nature. Each party to it found himself impelled to do that which was not to the advantage of the other. They were mutual enemies on the same territory, and in daily unfriendly contact. In his notes on Virginia Mr. Jefferson says, "The whole commerce between master and slave is a perpetual exercise of the most boisterous passions, the most unlimited despotism on the one part, and degrading submission on the other." In such a state of society the moral sense was blunted, and the voice of conscience suppressed. The attributes of a manly character such as liberty now demands had no chance of development. The master forced what he could and all he could from the slave, and the slave in turn stole all he could from the master, his only restraint being the fear of detection and punishment. He was born into a society organized to defraud him of the results of his labor, and he naturally enough thought it no robbery to obtain by stealth—the only way open to him—a part of what was forced from him under the hard conditions of the lash. I do not pretend to deny that there was ever a generous slave-holder or honest slave, for I know the contrary, but I equally know that the system made tyrants of one class and thieves of the other.

As to social relations, the system was even more destructive and deadly. Its victims were herded together like horses, sheep, and swine, without the restraints of moral instruction or decency. The master was made more important by every addition to his slaves. Marriage did not exist; the family was abolished. The young had no reputation to gain, and the old had none to lose.

Let it be remembered in respect to the morals of these people that streams are not easily diverted from well-worn channels; that the moral character formed under the conditions thus feebly described is not easily or speedily reformed. There is not only much to learn, but much to unlearn. It is sad to think of the multitude who only dropped out of slavery to drop into prisons and chain-gangs, for the crimes for which they are punished seldom rise higher than the stealing a pig or a pair of shoes; but it is consoling to think that the fact is not due to liberty, but to slavery, and that the evil will disappear as these people recede from the system in which they were born. From what has been now said it must not seem that I have conceded that there has been no improvement in the manners and morals of the freedmen since emancipation. I do not admit any such thing, for in morals, as in mental power, according to my knowledge, obtained from many sources of information, there is a visible and growing improvement both as to honesty and chastity. What was once done among these people not only with impunity, but with mirthful boasting, and without apparent sense of wrong or shame, does not now escape the rebuke and reprobation of a large and growing class of their own color. There is everywhere among them a dawning recognition of the new order of life and society into which freedom has brought them, and they are gradually adjusting themselves to the requirements of a higher civilization. Churches, preachers, teachers, Sunday-schools, night schools, day schools, singing schools, and other schools, societies for mutual aid, debating societies, libraries, and literary clubs, lawyers, doctors, editors, and newspapers, have sprung up and have multiplied with wonderful rapidity. These come not from immorality. Sin is death to such effort. They show an upward tendency which may well invite patient and benevolent effort in their behalf, and justify Mr. Slater in his magnificent donation to the cause of their elevation.

It is noticeable, too, that the old camp-meeting emotional religion is subsiding among them, and that thought is taking the place of feeling. In the dark time of slavery, when this world held only toil, stripes, and pain for them, they were easily wrought into paroxysms of momentary joy by the painted and promised glories of another world. They are now beginning to see that something can be made of this world as well as of the other. Of course some of them are still wearing the old cast-off theological hats and coats of fifty years ago, but the young people who have learned to read and write have no further use for these old garments. They now demand an educated, chaste, and upright ministry. This spirit of improvement has cost the old-time preachers many sighs and groans. They see in it only decline of true religious feeling. However that may be, it is evident that morals and manners have gained by the change, and will continue to gain as the lamp of knowledge grows brighter among them. No doubt that even the wild incoherent Sambo sermons were a help in time of slavery. It was something to be told that their suffering time would soon be over, and that for stripes on earth they would have stars in heaven, even though it was clumsily and wildly told; but the rant of those days will not do for these. These old-fashioned preachers minister to passion, decry the intellect, and induce contentment in ignorance and stupidity, and are hence a hinderance to progress. The effect aimed at by their preaching is to excite feeling, and raise a shout—a thing which can be as well done by an eloquent stump-speaker as by any modern Whitefield.

Among the instrumentalities which have been most effective in lifting up these people to a higher plane of life none is more worthy of mention than the American Missionary Association. While it has taken the church among the freedmen, it has not forgotten to take the school-house. But nearly all denominations, Catholic as well as Protestant, have rushed into this vast field, each after its kind, to labor for the salvation of the late slaves. This is the more surprising in view of the long years during which our churches could more easily see the heathen thousands of miles over the wide waste of waters than at home. But let the dead past bury its dead.

I now come to the question as to what was the physical condition of these people before emancipation; and in referring to it I bear in mind that I am speaking to many of a generation to whom slavery is little more than a name, and who have no adequate idea of what that name covered. I have had this class of readers in mind in all I have said, and I deem it fortunate that you have allowed me to speak my word on this subject through your respected journal. With the exception of a few highly favored house servants, the physical condition of the slaves was indescribably wretched. A bushel of corn and eight pounds of salt pork per month were considered a large allowance for a full - grown man. The huts in which they lived left them largely exposed to the mercy of the elements. Their beds were boards, and their covering a miserable blanket, with which they were served not even once a year. Much of the time they were worked under the lash in all weathers. Want, exposure, and cruelty brought to them bodily ills and general physical deterioration often to the extent of repulsive deformity. That physical well-being is essential to physical perfection is easily demonstrated both in the case of man and beast. Men laugh at the irregular make-up of the negro, but forget that no people, white or black, could preserve the finer attributes of physical manhood subjected to two hundred and fifty years of slavery. The woes of the slave mother can be read in the faces of her children. Slavery has twisted their legs, flattened their feet, and imparted a depressed and cowardly aspect to their features. Let those who laugh rather be ashamed of the crime against human nature which has produced the deformity over which they make merry.

Looking at the freedmen to-day, in that class which remains on the old plantation, we see but little improvement in food or raiment, in form or feature. Twenty years are but a speck in the life of a race. Still, even here there is improvement. Many have managed to get a few acres and a little home of their own. In the State of Louisiana colored people pay taxes on more than twenty millions' worth of property, and in Georgia, according to the late Senator Hill, of that State, they paid taxes five years ago on six millions. I doubt not of a showing equally creditable in North Carolina, Virginia, and other of the old Slave States. The manner in which these people were set free should never be overlooked. No people were ever emancipated under conditions more unfavorable for good results. The Israelites had spoils of the Egyptians; the serfs of Russia had three acres of land given to each head of a family; the West India slave was permitted to remain upon the old plantation; but the American slave was turned loose to the open sky without money, land, or friends, and, worst of all, under the fierce resentment of those who owned the land from which he must obtain his bread. These in the heat of momentary wrath drove him away; and away he went, free, but free only to want, hunger, and pain; free to the chilling blasts of winter, free to starve. Off he went with his sick and well, young and old, and the infant in arms. Many died, and the mortality for a time caused the belief that the race would speedily die out. From the gallery of the United States Senate I heard an able Senator from the North answer Mr. Sumner's plea for suffrage with the remark that it was useless to legislate for these people, since they were sure to die out in a short time. But the old masters who thus resented emancipation relented, if they did not repent, and after a time called back the freedmen to their old fields and quarters. They saw that they had sent away the hands, but had left the mouths, and that they still needed the negro to work their fields—a fortunate discovery for both. Instead of dying out, as predicted, the census tells us these people have increased ten per cent. faster than the native-born white people of the South.

In conclusion:

When I consider that these people have only been free during the last twenty years, and that this freedom has been more in name than in fact; when I consider the manner in which their emancipation was brought about, not with the consent, but against the consent, of the masters; when I consider the fact that it was born of blood boiling over on the battle-field, the wounded pride and sullen determination it left in the old master class smarting under defeat, and the many obstacles thrown in the way of the progress of these people—I am far from discouraged or dissatisfied. On the contrary, I see the colored people steadily rising, and I believe they will ultimately fully justify all the endeavors made in their behalf, and fulfill the highest hopes of their friends.

Frederick Douglass

THE SITUATION IN VIRGINIA

HARPER'S WEEKLY
December 15, 1883, pp. 794–95

The "Re-adjusters" and the "Bourbons" in Virginia, or the Mahone party and the Democrats, have each published a document describing the political situation in that State. One of the original and ostensible objects of the formation of the Mahone party, and that which gave it its distinctive name of Re-adjuster, is disposed of by the acquiescence of the Democrats in the decision of the Re-adjuster Legislature and the opinion of the Supreme Court of the United States. This leaves each organization to be tried by its general character and the results of its administration. The Democratic address asserts that the question of the debt having been settled, the real reason for the new party has disappeared, and that the late election shows that the voters are returning to the Democratic fold. The Mahone charges of systematic murder and bloodshed in certain counties and in Danville are met by the Democratic address with the assertion that in those counties the Re-adjuster or coalition vote was increased, showing that the disorder arose from individual quarrels. The address retorts the accusation by the declaration that the only intimidation was that of non-coalition colored voters by coalition colored voters. The general Democratic arraignment of the coalition party is this:

"A Legislature pledged by its majority in advance to obey every mandate of a party caucus, that caucus sitting only to register and transmit the decrees of its master; the executive and judicial offices greedily seized by the dictator's personal adherents; blind loyalty to one man set up as the sole test of fitness for positions of trust; the asylums for the insane, those touching monuments of the public charity, and the free-school system, that nobler monument of the public wisdom, thrown in to swell the dirty heap of party spoils—so much of this wild revel of mock statesmanship has passed into history. What was threatened—re-arrangement of Congressional districts and judicial circuits, repeal of municipal charters, usurpation of the powers long vested in chancery courts to control through their own commissioners judicial sales of lands—all this was intended to fix, confirm, and perpetuate the power of the autocrat, this new Dr. Francia."

To all this the Mahone manifest offers a powerful counter-statement, the chief allegations of which, so far as they regard administration, do not seem to be challenged. The coalition claims more successful financial management, and charges the Bourbons with hostility to the colored voters and to the school system:

"The Funders by their unfriendly legislation and administration reduced the number of public schools from 3087, of which 709 were colored, to 2491, of which but 89 were colored. They reduced the pupils from 131,088, of whom 38,076 were colored, to 108,074, of whom but 5208 were colored. They reduced the teachers from 3084, of whom 504 were colored, to 2504, of whom but 94 were colored. They reduced the expenditures from $587,472 for the year to $511,902. On the other hand, in their three years the Re-adjusters have increased the number of schools from 2491 to 5587, the number of colored schools from 89 to 850; the pupils from 108,074 to 257,362, the colored pupils from 5208 to 49,560; the teachers from 2504 to 4538, the colored teachers from 94 to 644. The expenditures from $511,902 were increased to $1,157,142."

The coalition also insists that it has greatly improved the care of the insane, removing them from prisons to asylums with kind and skillful attendance, and that it has abolished the whipping system, which was made "a disfranchising machine" against the colored voters. The cost of the State government previously averaged $1,084,664 annually; under the Re-adjusters it has averaged $802,234. The rate of taxation has been reduced from sixty to forty cents on the one hundred dollars. Within the last three years the floating debt of the State, which was nearly two millions, has been reduced to less than three-quarters of a million ($715,000), while the balance of cash in the treasury has increased from twenty-three thousand dollars to over a million and a half.

The coalition claims, therefore, that while it has truly respected the spirit and purpose of the equal citizenship conferred by the Constitution of the United States, it has administered the government of the State more wisely and prosperously than the Bourbons. There is no question that its manifest is much the stronger of the two. But the coalition movement has failed to command general favor among intelligent and patriotic men, because its original purpose was *quasi* repudiation, and because it resorted to the bribery of patronage. Had it proposed the security of colored citizens in their rights, the improvement of the school system, and more efficient and economical administration as its great objects, it would have been sustained by the best and strongest Republican sentiment in the country. But handicapped as it was, it has not had united Republican sympathy, as Butler has not been supported by reformers, despite his profuse professions of reform. The massacre at Danville, according to the careful report in the New York Times, was not preconcerted, but it revealed a state of feeling which seems to make fair play for the colored voters very uncertain. The assertion that Mahone ought to have been supported by all Republicans, whatever his financial plans and his political methods, because of his efforts for the colored people, seems to us extremely ill-judged. It is only another form of the Jesuit doctrine that the end justifies the means.

INSISTING ON THEIR RIGHTS
The Colored Citizens' Convention of the State of Connecticut.

NEW-YORK TIMES
December 31, 1883

Norwich, Dec. 30.—The convention of colored citizens of the State assembled in this city yesterday to discuss the question of civil rights as affected by the decision of the Supreme Court declaring the Civil Rights bill unconstitutional was largely attended by influential delegates from all parts of Connecticut. Walter H. Burr, of this city, was chosen Chairman. Mr. Burr, in a ringing speech, said: "The colored people have the balance of political power in this State, and the dominant party must walk straight or the parties will change. We must accord the present Democratic Governor the union of the State militia, a movement which is in advance of any movement ever before made in behalf of this people. The sincerity of the next Legislature is to be tested upon the question of civil rights for the colored people. The intention of this organization is to arouse the colored citizens of this State to a realization of their strength, and to a united effort for their rights." After speeches by Major Delaney, of South Carolina; Mr. Cleggett, of Hartford, and George Jeffries, of Meriden, the following resolution was passed:

> *Resolved,* That the fourteenth amendment of the Constitution confers the right of citizenship upon all persons born or naturalized in the United States and subject to the jurisdiction thereof. It was the special purpose of this amendment to insure to members of the colored race the full enjoyment of civil and political rights. Certain statutory provisions intended to secure the enforcement of those rights having been recently declared unconstitutional by the Supreme Court, any legislation by which the Legislature may lawfully supplement the guarantee which the Constitution affords for the equal rights, privileges, and immunity of citizenship will receive our hearty approval.

Mr. Jeffries made the speech of the meeting, declaring that the colored people had been accorded full political rights. "The Legislature may pass laws till doomsday," said he, "telling the people to respect you, but it cannot enforce such laws, for the virtue within you must command for you respect. The success of civil rights is within you. We are holding a position to-day I never expected to see—a position the world never before witnessed—the raising of a people so low as our people were to be the equal of every man. We have representatives in Congress, in the Legislature, in law, in religion, in literature. I have no objection to the placing of such a law on the statute books, but if you cultivate thrift, intelligence, and virtue you will lift yourself to the position you covet. It is impossible for the Legislature to legislate you into the heart of a single citizen. You are a civil rights law to yourselves; by growing in the best elements of manhood you can make your neighbor respect you, and at the same time elevate your race.

Before adjournment it, was decided to from an Executive Committee composed of a representative from each town in the State.

The colored people here were not, as a rule, in sympathy with the convention, not believing in the efficacy of legislative action.

1884

The presidential election of 1884 gave the country the first Democrat to occupy the White House since the antebellum period. Grover Cleveland was characterized as a moderate Democrat who would be fair to all the country's citizenry. Still, many Americans were not prepared to exonerate the South for past sins. Fair and free elections were still not realities in the Solid South. Directly or indirectly, violence and exploitation guaranteed the destruction of true democracy. But in this election year, most voting Americans were willing to return the Democrats to the White House. Industrialization and the New South superseded the "race question."

The election of President Cleveland represented a significant shift in the editorial tone of the papers reviewed. Significant distinctions were now discernible between national obligations and state privilege. This demarcation reflected the Supreme Court's revisiting the legislation of Congressional Reconstruction. As the Court redefined national versus state citizenship, state rights versus individual actions, new coverage now mirrored the rising tide of national conservativism. Declaring the new president an intelligent and patriotic individual, journalists assured their readers that "no race of people had anything to fear from this administration." Race relations, once a national preoccupation, were deferred to the sphere of state and regional jurisdictions. Editorials stressed the national government's duty of noninterference in local issues.

The Republicans did not leave the discussion of race unscathed either. The party's abandonment of the black southerner cleared the way for the Solid South's control over blacks. Northerners' records showed how they were also guilty of denying their black neighbors their civil rights. Still, black voters remained "friendly" to the party that had secured their freedom. The race question was an American dilemma, not merely a party or sectional concern.

Believing that President Cleveland's election was free of special interests, the public trusted the new chief executive's administration would "enforce and direct the laws for the protection of all of its citizens." Cleveland was not to be feared by any group because of his political affiliation. His election offered the long-awaited chance for genuine political reorganization and patriotism.

Jacqueline A. Rouse
Georgia State University

THE SHERMAN RESOLUTIONS

HARPER'S WEEKLY
February 9, 1884, p. 87

The Democratic Senators did very wisely in not debating Mr. Sherman's resolutions. There is no doubt of the current and general rumor of organized political intimidation at Danville, in Virginia, nor of the extraordinary action of citizens of the county of Copiah, in Mississippi, after the murder of Matthews. These undeniable facts were the allegations of the preamble, and *prima facie* there was reason for an investigation. The purpose of introducing the resolutions may have been as wholly partisan as that of Mr. Hewitt's O'Donnell resolution. But it would have been very unwise to oppose an inquiry into events so undeniable.

When the committee reports some measure for adoption by Congress, the whole question will be opened for debate. The Democrats must then remember the real point of the question in the public mind. It is not whether Congress has the constitutional power to do anything to prevent such conduct, and to punish such crimes as those which are alleged at Danville and in Copiah, but whether public opinion in Virginia and Mississippi really condemns such lawlessness, and if so, what steps have been taken by the State or the community to prevent its recurrence and to punish the criminals.

Politically the question is whether, if those States and communities do nothing, and thereby practically condone and tolerate—that is, protect and promote—such conduct, it is desirable that the government of the country should be intrusted to a party whose chief strength lies in the public opinion of such States. If it should be shown that these events are exceptional in the States concerned, that they are condemned by public opinion, and that the perpetrators are rigorously pursued, prosecuted, and punished, the result of the inquiry will be most favorable to those States. Due allowance will be made by every sensible man for the situation in those States arising from the great numbers of freedmen, and from old traditions of the relation of the races. But the argument that the national government can do nothing about it, and that there are crimes in other States, will not persuade the intelligence of the country that it would be wise to renounce the supremacy of a party which seeks to defend the political equality of all citizens for that of a party which either directly or indirectly, by overt acts or by indifference, opposes and tries to destroy it. The essential reasonableness and force of this view is not to be overcome by decrying the bloody shirt.

WENDELL PHILLIPS

HARPER'S WEEKLY
February 16, 1884, p. 102

In the death of Wendell Phillips the greatest of American orators passed away. But to call him an orator is not to suggest a rhetorician, a maker of phrases, a mere elocutionary artist. It is to speak of an effective force in the state; of a man whose words were things, and whose speeches were events. The service of his oratory to the early antislavery cause in this country was incalculable. It drew the great multitude, who were charmed while they cursed. The resistless logic, the appeal to manliness and morality, the fiery indignation, the remorseless hail of wit and epigram and invective, the undaunted courage, the scornful defiance, yet all invested with superb suavity, with matchless grace, with penetrating music, could no more be eluded than in the clear sunshine the tree can escape its shadow. Wendell Phillips was as integral a part of the antislavery cause as John Bright of the Corn Law reform in England. Emancipation was not wrought in his way, but he quickened the conscience that compelled emancipation. His oratory vindicated the claim of oratory to a rank among the fine arts. Alone among all the famous orators which Puritanism has produced in Old and New England, Phillips blended the sturdy conviction and rugged earnestness of the Puritan with the exquisite refinement and simple elegance of the Greek. . . .

THE FUNERAL OF WENDELL PHILLIPS

HARPER'S WEEKLY

February 16, 1884, p. 111

The funeral services over the remains of Boston's great orator were simple but impressive. As the body was borne from the house to Hollis Street Chapel, hundreds of people, including many aged co-workers with Mr. Phillips in antislavery times, lined the streets, and the old chapel was surrounded by throngs of men and women. The services in the church were private, and consisted of singing, a reading from Isaiah, and a prayer by the Rev. Samuel May.

The body was afterward removed to Faneuil Hall, where the casket was placed on a catafalque in front of the rostrum, and for the first time opened to public view. The face of Mr. Phillips wore a placid, half-smiling expression, and was very natural in appearance. A great crowd of people passed through the hall to take a farewell look at the familiar features. Late in the afternoon the remains were interred in the Old Granary Burying-ground, on Tremont Street. The coffin was placed, without formal ceremonies, in the Phillips family tomb, which is in close proximity to the graves of John Hancock, Samuel Adams, and Crispus Attocks, the latter a colored victim of the Boston Massacre, to whom Mr. Phillips often referred in his public speeches. It is understood that this disposition of Mr. Phillips's body is only temporary, and that it will soon be transferred to the burial-place of his wife's family, in Milton, Massachusetts.

A GLIMPSE OF "THE SOUTH"

HARPER'S WEEKLY

April 26, 1884, p. 262

A correspondent in Arkansas writes us that the agents who are busy in that State in securing for the National Convention supporters of particular candidates are mainly working for General Logan, while there are no signs of activity for the President upon the part of those who enjoy the patronage of the Administration. This seems to our correspondent a very pleasing contrast with the usual situation, and extremely creditable to the President. In justice to the President also it should be said that while it may be true that a large proportion of the officeholders in this State favor his nomination, yet the old familiar organization of patronage, with its headquarters in the Custom-house and Post-office, is now unknown. This is a state of things due to the reform of the civil service, the law for which the President has honestly enforced, and for that enforcement he has been abandoned by many of the most notorious managers of the old machine, who have transferred their allegiance to Mr. Blaine. It is certainly highly creditable to the President that Mr. Platt and Mr. John F. Smyth, for instance, are ardently opposed to him. In a general survey of the political situation in the Southern States our correspondent says that Copiah and Danville are illustrations of the familiar methods by which Mississippi, Louisiana, and South Carolina are kept Democratic States, which, under a system of free elections, would be Republican because of the preponderating colored vote. The same situation is observable in Alabama, Florida, and Louisiana.

In Arkansas the system is somewhat milder and less obtrusive than "the Mississippi plan," except in Phillips County, where more stringent methods are adopted to maintain Democratic ascendancy. The Legislature has generally seated members from the strong Republican counties who were fairly elected, but last year Democrats who were counted in by the Pulaski County Returning Board were admitted. The court of

A VALENTINE BY PROXY.

"Oh, you jes' say de same 's if 'twas yous own, Miss Katie."

Harper's Weekly, February 16, 1884, p. 112.

last resort in the State, however, has dealt a heavy blow at fair elections by reversing the decision of a lower court which seated a Republican upon the evidence of Democratic witnesses alone that he had been elected by nearly six hundred majority. This decision is supposed to mean that "no Republican need apply."

The undoubted fact that the electoral vote of many of the old Slave States is not a free or fair vote, and that the result is therefore fraudulent, makes it especially incumbent upon the Republican Convention not to hazard Republican success by action which will endanger any important Northern State. It would be very unfortunate if a candidate should be declared elected by means of a vote which, like that of several Southern States, is known to be due to intimidation and fraud. This is the bloody shirt, which is perpetually waved by those who countenance the frauds, not by those who point out the peril of such a situation.

LYNCH-LAW

HARPER'S WEEKLY
April 26, 1884, p. 271

The summary disposal of alleged criminals by volunteer judges and executioners is a practice more known in the United States than in any other land, and is sometimes referred to as an American "institution." But its name is very generally derived from one James Fitzstephen Lynch, whilom Mayor of Galway, Ireland, who hung from his own window, with his own hands, the body of his son, guilty of robbery and murder, whom the legal processes of the time had failed to reach. The legend, if it be at all credible, shows that it was a Welshman in Ireland who set the example which so many Americans have since followed. Lynch law has a curious history in the United States, which shows that it has not always, or necessarily, served bad ends, though it is essentially fit for circumstances that happily can but rarely happen, and even these tend to disappear pretty rapidly. The most noted instances of its application occurred in California between the years 1849 and 1856, and these have probably given tone to the general opinion of it more than any others. Yet so far as the facts are known from trustworthy sources, that opinion is much mistaken, for the vigilance committees of San Francisco, Sacramento, and Marysville, in California, possessed about all the virtues that Lynch-law can have, and none of its vices, except the single and unavoidable one of illegality. They were made up of responsible and peaceable citizens; the great body of them men of property and repute; they were known where the work was done, and as they could at any time have been called to account, had public sentiment permitted, they could not be called irresponsible. They had a comparatively permanent organization; they made their arrests and held their trials and inflicted their penalties openly, and the survivors of them are still known and respected in the place where they enacted their extraordinary parts. These committees were, in fact, simply unions of citizens to protect life and property and public order where the regular and official means for that end had failed. They hanged not more than a score of desperadoes, deported perhaps five times as many, and frightened away many more; but their known determination, steadiness, coolness, and rapidity of action made them irresistible.

They are not, however, fair examples of Lynch-law administration as it has been known in the United States, or as it is from time to time known now. The curious situation which gave rise to them has never occurred elsewhere. Lynch-law has generally been a gross violation not only of the forms but of the purposes of law. In a few instances, in the mining camps, or among the scattered settlements of the frontier where there is little law and less police force, mob justice has a wild sort of excuse for existence. But these are now, and have for years been, very rare instances, and even in these it is probable that it protects property in horseflesh much more adequately than it does other property or human life. In general, as now known, it is only the outbreak of passion, with no guide to its cruel course, quite as likely to destroy the innocent as the guilty, and wholly needless. There are very few places in this country at the present moment where the courts and the Executive, sustained by public sentiment, can not be relied on to secure more justice, and more quickly and surely, than can the mob. Usually lynching nowadays is done in a way which shows the practical efficiency of the real law by the fear of it manifested by the lynchers. They assemble in secret, they disguise themselves with masks and grotesque clothing, they make their assaults by night, and hurriedly hang or shoot or flog their victim, and then disperse. In the main their conduct is as cowardly and cruel as it is unjust and opposed to the real interests of law and order in the community. But their judgments, once reached and carried out, are irrevocable. The life they have taken in anger can not be given back, though they may learn that they were in error. Such action, in this country and in these times, is revolting to all sense of fairness and decency, to all respect for human life and human rights.

Obviously it is an evil which tends to steadily disappear, because it is at war with civilization and the spirit of organized and orderly society. It is a rude survival of the time when each man was the defender and to a great extent the judge of his own rights, and when there was no recognized standard of common rights, and no adequate means of enforcing such a

JUDGE LYNCH.—Drawn by R. F. Zogbaum.—[See Page 271.]

Harper's Weekly, April 26, 1884, p. 269.

standard. It is a curious fact that such survivals in the midst or on the outskirts of organized society are frequently more savage than was the life from which they sprang in the past. It seems that when the conventional bonds which hold the passions of men who live together in restraint once give way, these passions burst out with an explosive force. And this fact undoubtedly increases the obligation of sober and right-minded men in communities where such outbursts are liable to occur—an obligation that is generally only dimly recognized, especially in the South and West of the United States. It rests on the fact, which is the basis of all orderly society, that no man can safely be the judge of the rights of another, unless clothed with authority delegated by his fellow-citizens, and exercised with responsibility for its use. The rash zeal for justice which leads men to take the law in their own hands would be an effective and powerful influence if rightly exerted, in the support of proper authority, and holding to account those to whom such authority is intrusted.

THE RACE PROBLEM

HARPER'S WEEKLY
May 24, 1884, p. 326

A correspondent in Alabama takes us to task for the tone of hostility which he finds in the allusions of the Weekly to Southern politics and society, and he especially designates our assertion that several Southern States, except for fraud and intimidation of the colored citizens, would be Republican in politics. Our correspondent says that Mississippi, Louisiana, and South Carolina are the only States in which, according to the last census, there is an actual colored majority of the population, and he holds that, according to his own observation, it is unfair to say that all the colored citizens vote the Republican ticket, while the colored Democratic vote is steadily increasing, although there is intimidation of colored Democrats by colored Republicans. On the other hand, an original Union man in Arkansas asserts that throughout the war the colored people were in perfect concord with the Union men in their own States and with the Union soldiers, and that from 1862 the colored people were unshaken in the faith that the war would emancipate them, although the white Union men could not see it. Our Arkansas correspondent affirms that there can be no doubt of the Republicanism of Louisiana, with two thousand more colored than white people; of Mississippi, with sixty-two thousand more; and of South Carolina, with one hundred and twenty-six thousand more;

and he thinks, although he makes no claim, that with the large Republican vote in Alabama and Florida, those States, with fair play, would also be Republican. The reason of the case certainly seems to be with him, nor can any man who knows the facts and considers human nature doubt that the great body of the colored voters in the Southern States are Republican, and that Mississippi and South Carolina, in a free and fair election, would be certainly Republican. But this is not the point of our Alabama correspondent. He asks whether intelligent Republicans in the Northern States will not candidly consider the race problem in the Southern States, although he says plainly that "pretty much all the moral sense and integrity, the high and lofty purpose, and noble aim," of the Republican party are gone with its great leaders and fathers; and, indeed, in his sharp arraignment of the party, he forgets to state how the race problem is to be treated, except by the abandonment of the Republican party by its more honest and intelligent members.

This would hardly solve the problem properly, although we fully agree that the question is one of the utmost gravity and importance. Our correspondent, however, will not forget that in the Southern States, where the Democratic party holds undisputed control, it has made no effort whatever to solve the problem upon any other basis than that of the subordination of the colored people as a kind of Pariah class. If we are mistaken in this, and if there has been any sincere Democratic endeavor to deal with colored citizens as politically and civilly equal—as, for instance, all citizens of whatever national nativity are treated in the rest of the country—we shall willingly acknowledge our error. Our correspondent's own party is plainly unequal to the task, and while we concede that it is unpatriotic and ungenerous to slander any section of the country, we can not admit that the dominance of the Democratic party would bring us nearer to the result which our correspondent desires.

THE OTHER SIDE

HARPER'S WEEKLY
July 26, 1884, p. 475

A correspondent in Florida denies the accuracy of the statements of an Arkansas correspondent, to which we referred some weeks ago, in regard to the position of the slaves and colored people in the Southern States during the war, and he wonders whether the Weekly will be fair enough to publish the substance of his rejoinder. We are

AFRICAN AMERICAN HISTORY IN THE PRESS, 1851-1899

RAID À LA MODE ON A GAMBLING HOUSE.

SOLOMON SNOWBALL (*to inquiring Detective*). "Yes, Boss, de gemmen got de note sayin' you was comin', an' am out ob de city to-day; an' de imple'nts was tuk dis mornin', sah, to de Safe Decloset Cump'ny."

Harper's Weekly, June 21, 1884, p. 403.

sorry that he should wonder, because he can not justly have found any hostile disposition upon the subject in these columns. The question is not to be decided by individual testimony alone, but by the general consent of evidence, and by "the nature of things," including human nature. Our Florida correspondent asserts that the slaves were faithful to their masters who took them to the army, that they were perfectly loyal when left at home among old men and women and children, and in camp demanded to be armed against the Union soldiers, until the Union army obtained possession of certain points. Yet the slaves knew that the war was waged for their liberation.

Our correspondent then questions whether the colored men are Republican at heart, and denounces the frauds of Northern elections, insisting that so long as the Southern States were held by military power, and "Moses's negro militia" ruled the roast in South Carolina, and a kind of Union terrorism prevailed in the Southern States, there were no Republican complaints of unfair elections, although every honest Republican in the country knows what a parody of free government the Southern situation was. To our remark that the Democrats have made no effort to settle the race problem upon any basis but that of making the freedmen a pariah class, our correspondent replies that he and others hold the white race to be superior, and that intelligence and honesty ought to prevail over ignorance and dishonesty; and he asks why Republicans should complain of the efforts of intelligent white men in the Southern States to prevent the ascendency of an ignorant, demoralized, and lately servile class, which is in some States actually a majority, when Republicans themselves prohibit by severe penalties the entry into the country of a few thousands of a race superior to the African, simply because they will work more cheaply than native Americans. He also alleges that the denial of civil rights to the colored people is even more frequent in the Northern than in the Southern States, and that Northern judges have sustained the denials.

The weight of testimony, it seems to us, shows what would be only natural—that the slaves, while peaceful, were friendly to the Union cause, but they naturally kept quiet until actual occupation by the Union army made them less cautious. Even our Florida correspondent will admit that slavery is not a condition which inspires gratitude in the heart of the slave or antipathy to his rescuer. For the same general reason that the slaves were friendly to the cause of their own emancipation, the freedmen have been naturally friendly to the party that secured it. Our correspondent also would agree that the Moses *régime* under a Republican name is no excuse for similar offenses under Democratic auspices, and that the "superiority" of the white race can not be pleaded in extenuation of any kind of injustice to other races. As for his retort about the Chinese exclusion, although it is true that it is commended in the Republican platform, it is none the less opposed to the views of the best Republicans. It is as Americans and men, not as Republicans and Democrats, that intelligent and patriotic men everywhere in the country should consider the question of race.

A COLORED WEIGHER

HARPER'S WEEKLY
August 16, 1884, p. 529

A colored weigher has just made his appearance upon the wharves of Philadelphia, where he is viewed with surprise by the general public, and with apprehension and alarm, as is reported, by his Caucasian colleagues. There are two noteworthy facts about this appointment. One is that the new weigher won his place after a competitive examination, in which he passed third, with an average of eighty-five per cent.; and another is that he is a full-blooded African, so that the hypothesis by which believers in the ineradicable intellectual inferiority of the negro have striven to account for the ability of persons of mixed race can not here be applied.

The appointment is not only highly creditable to the appointee, Mr. Tucker, but it is full of encouragement both to believers in democracy and to believers in civil service reform. It is an indication of that equality which Senator Bayard well described as "the equality of opportunity," which lies at the base of our political and social system. A white weigher or other functionary who resents the appointment of a black man to a place which he has fairly won is not a good American, because he is not a good man.

FACTS OF INTEREST

FRANK LESLIE'S ILLUSTRATED NEWSPAPER
August 30, 1884, p. 23

It is said that negroes scarcely ever commit suicide. They may be hard up from the day of their birth to the day of their death, but they rarely become melancholy. Notwithstanding their complaints of hard times, the give-me-a-nickel expression on their faces and general hungry appearance, they hang on to life with the tenacity of a mud-turtle. They do it not for the hope of something better, but simply for the fun they will have.

THE COMING ADMINISTRATION

HARPER'S WEEKLY
November 22, 1884, p. 764

It is the good fortune of Mr. Cleveland that he has been elected upon an issue and by a vote which enable him to enter upon his great office with singular freedom and independence. It is evident that upon a simple party issue he would not have been elected. The result was decided by New York, and in New York his plurality is small. But the independent vote fortunately outweighed the Democratic defection. Mr. Cleveland owes his election to no party wing, faction, squad, or hall. He is no man's man. He is bound by no personal pledges or engagements. The wildest whims were urged as arguments against his election. We ourselves heard it stated that slavery would be restored, that the rebel debt would be paid and rebel soldiers pensioned, and all kinds of rebel claims allowed. It was gravely argued that enterprise would be paralyzed and labor ruined. In other words, it was contended that if the candidate whom, as it proves, the constitutional majority preferred, should be elected, the country was delivered up to its remorseless enemies. When party madness had reached this point, it was evident that a party change of administration was desirable, if for no other reason than to prove that a constitutional majority, or half of the nation, is not a public enemy....

The rights of no man, no State, and no section, of no vested interest and of no industry, are threatened by the election of Mr. Cleveland. The organ of the colored citizens promptly declared that if feared from him no

POLITICS IN VIRGINIA.—FIRST APPEARANCE OF A HUSBAND AND FATHER IN THE ROLE OF A PLUMED KNIGHT AFTER A PARADE.—SEE PAGE 103.

Frank Leslie's Illustrated Newspaper, **October 4, 1884, p. 101.**

injustice for the colored race, nor does any man doubt that every law and all lawful power which protects any citizen, white or black, at home or abroad, will be enforced and directed by President Cleveland with perfect honesty and impartiality. When a Republican Administration properly withdrew the army from the Southern States, it practically and wisely announced that the internal difficulties of the States were now remitted to their own settlement, and that the relations of the races, beyond the provisions of existing laws, could not be adjusted by the national government. In what way has any Administration recently attempted to adjust them? The congratulations of Mr. Vanderbilt and Jay Gould do not indicate alarm upon their parts of business disturbance, while the remarkable and enthusiastic support which Mr. Cleveland received from the business men of New York was the most significant and conclusive answer of the most responsible representatives of business interests to the assertions of the professional campaign orators. The task before the new President is, of course, prodigious. But we believe that his administration will be wise, moderate, and conservative. That it may lead to political reorganization and to party changes is very probable. That there will be disappointment of various kinds within his own party ranks is inevitable. But that the patriotic purpose of the administration will be plain, and that it will commend itself to the approval of all good citizens, we see no reason to doubt. We shall treat Mr. Cleveland's administration as we should have treated Mr. Blaine's, not as partisans, but with candor, without prejudice, and with a clear perception both of its great opportunities and its great difficulties.

MR. BLAINE'S SPEECH AT AUGUSTA

HARPER'S WEEKLY
November 29, 1884, pp. 780–81

Mr. Blaine's bitter, unpatriotic, and mischievous speech shows what a misfortune the country has escaped. Such a revelation of the spirit that he would have brought to the Presidency must go far to reconcile to his defeat the honorable Republicans who at first deeply regretted it. The speech can serve no possible purpose but to rekindle the fires of old animosities, and to delay and perplex the solution of one of the most difficult of public problems. It is addressed to the worst passions, and its plain purpose is to array section against section, the colored citizen against the white, and the white laborer against the colored. It is the last desperate endeavor of a defeated politician, whose candidacy has rent his party,

A DISTINGUISHED GUEST.
"Come out to Orate in de Canvass."

Harper's Weekly, October 11, 1884, p. 674.

to confuse public sentiment, to exasperate the country, and to produce such evil results as may be wrought by the words of a disappointed and unscrupulous partisan.

The burden of the speech is the suppression of the colored vote in the Southern States, the low wages of colored laborers as degrading white labor at the North by competition, and the assertion that Southern whites are enemies of the government, and that they will now control it to base ends, as they did in the days of slavery. But there is no suggestion of any remedial measure; not a word nor a thought of statesmanship. Mr. Blaine knows perfectly well that the first signs of any such result as he professes to anticipate would sweep away the party which was responsible for them, and he ought to know that the solution of the peculiar problems which are offered by the condition of the Southern States is impossible so long as the white citizens of those States are regarded and treated as public enemies.

Unfortunate as the situation in many parts of the Southern States may be, every intelligent American must rejoice that it was not made by the country a pretext for electing a Presidential candidate whom many of his own supporters frankly declared to be a dishonest man, whose candidacy for such reasons enormously reduced his party vote, whose election was desired by jobbers and speculators of every degree, and whose administration would have been surrounded and swayed by the most demoralizing and corrupting influences. The patri-

otic good sense which has prevented his election will deal both with the questions that now demand attention and settlement and with any party which should viciously obstruct such settlement. If any doubt had remained of the unworthiness of Mr. Blaine as a candidate of the Republican party, it would be totally dispelled by this speech.

THE ELECTION AND EQUAL RIGHTS

HARPER'S WEEKLY
December 6, 1884, p. 796

The situation in the Southern States arising from the emancipation and enfranchisement of the colored race is one that presents a difficult problem. But undoubtedly it has been long the general conviction that little more

AFRICAN AMERICAN HISTORY IN THE PRESS, 1851–1899

ONE OF THE FIRST-FRUITS OF THE VICTORY.
PRESIDENT-ELECT CLEVELAND. "Shake heartily, boys!"

The Atlanta (Georgia) *Constitution* (Democratic) says: "The negro will find that his best friend is the Southern Democrat. President Cleveland is his friend. The Southern people are his friends. Every right that they have as freemen and citizens will be jealously protected by the white men of the South, who have been their neighbors for years. In their schools, at the ballot-boxes, everywhere, they have their full rights. That man is the best Southerner and the best Democrat who stands by this doctrine and shows the negro that we are his true friends."

Harper's Weekly, November 22, 1884, p. 763.

can be done by means of law, and that the harmonizing and healing influence of time, with the steady pressure of sound sentiment and of the obvious interest of both races, would gradually complete the good work which, at least, is begun. It was this feeling which led to the withdrawal of the troops by a Republican Administration—an act which was denounced by many Republicans as a surrender of helpless freedmen to the fury of angry ex-slave-holders. But nobody now would seriously doubt the wisdom of the course that was pursued in 1877, nor would any intelligent man gravely allege that the colored people in the Southern States are in

AN UNEXPECTED THANKSGIVING VISITOR; OR, TOO SMALL TO GO ROUND.
VISITORS (IN CHORUS): "WE THO'T YOU'D BE KIND O' LONELY, EATIN' DINNER ALL ALONE, SO WE JEST COME OVER TO KEEP YOU COMPANY AND MAKE THINGS KIND O' CHEERFUL LIKE!"

Frank Leslie's Illustrated Newspaper, November 29, 1884, p. 236.

greater danger of ill treatment because of the election of Mr. Cleveland. The testimony upon this point is very general and significant. From Wisconsin a correspondent writes: "I am a young Democrat of the most pronounced abolition antecedents, and I glory in the fact that our national victory is due so much to the sentiment. . . .that he who serves his country most serves his party best." A New-Yorker writes: "If any such dire results follow a Democratic administration as are predicted by Mr. Blaine, especially as to the negroes, thousands of Simon Pure Democrats like myself will hereafter vote the opposition ticket." The colored chairman of the Republican Executive Committee of Georgia alleges that he and the most prominent colored Republicans in the Southern States made every effort for Mr. Blaine. But he denies any apprehension among the colored people, and says that there is no reason that the colored vote should be solidly Republican. If the new administration be half as conservative as he anticipates, he says that it will divide the colored vote. The *Gazette* of Cairo, Illinois, an organ of the colored people, says very plainly and truly that nothing can disturb the equal citizenship of the colored Americans, and that they "are not victimized by the office-seeker who, under the guise of Republicanism, would make us believe that the wolves are in our secret chambers and about to devour our vitals."

From Michigan a Republican says: "I am a Republican, and love for that party and dislike of the Democratic party were so strong that I could not bring myself to break with the former and support the candidate of the latter, although I disapproved of the nomination of Mr. Blaine. I find myself now, however, not only acquiescing in Mr. Cleveland's election, but for several days past, as the official count progressed, actually hoping

CUTTING MISTLETOE IN THE SOUTH.

Harper's Weekly, December 20, 1884, p. 846.

that it would not change the apparent result. I begin to realize that success under Mr. Blaine would have been more damaging to the fair name and to the future of the Republican party than failure." A voice from Virginia says: "Now that the people of Virginia are rid of Mahone and his followers, we hope to bring about the kindest feelings between the two races." In Louisiana, Surveyor Pinchback and other colored leaders who voted for Mr. Blaine deny absolutely that there is any general apprehension among the colored citizens of the State, and anticipate a disappearance of the colored political line. This is not an unreasonable expectation. The Southern Democrats have regarded Republican ascendency as a standing menace to the Southern whites. This was a very mistaken view, but it served to hold them firmly united upon what they regarded as the chief issue, and against the colored voters who represented Republican supremacy. The change will show the colored citizens that a President of another party is perfectly friendly to them, and it will lead to the distribution of both the white and colored vote according to local and general interest and preference.

The daily papers have pointed out some misapprehensions in regard to the vote in the Southern States. In only three States are the colored people a majority, and in one of them, Louisiana, they are only a small majority. In that State the colored vote is divided, and even if the other two States, Mississippi and South Carolina, had given their electoral vote to Mr. Blaine, he would not have been elected. In other words, the colored vote is so distributed that it could not have changed the result. If in certain communities in the Southern States the colored vote is suppressed by intimidation, it is not to that intimidation, which would not affect the general majority, that Mr. Cleveland owes his election. And if the national government can intervene to protect the voter beyond the existing laws, there is no reason to fear that Mr. Cleveland will not protect it. Congress certainly has power to defend itself, and if it can be shown that any member owes his seat either to corruption in the Northern States or to actual violence or intimidation in the Southern, he could be unseated. To any general attempt to arouse the alarm of the colored people in the Southern States, Mr. Cleveland's words are the emphatic and conclusive reply. They are the words, moreover, of a man who never talks for effect, and whom everybody believes. "The whole country can be sure that the lawful power and jurisdiction of the Executive will be so exercised that the rights of all citizens, white or black, under the Constitution and the law, will be preserved and protected, and all the advantages to which they are entitled by reason of their citizenship will be secured to them.... It seems to me that our efforts...would be aided if mischievous croakings and dark imaginings should give place to an earnest endeavor to inspire confidence, and to make universal a cheerful hope for the future."

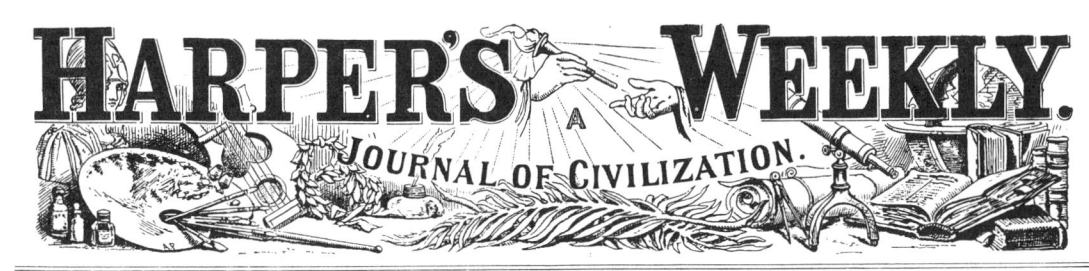

"ON EARTH PEACE, GOOD-WILL TOWARD MEN."

Harper's Weekly, December 27, 1884, p. 851.

MORAL BULLDOZING

HARPER'S WEEKLY
December 27, 1884, p. 852

The efforts of supporters of Mr. Blaine to stigmatize and injure the Independent Republicans who opposed his election is a futile imitation of the old pro-slavery methods before the war, and of the bulldozing and Ku-Kluxery in the Southern States that followed the war. It shows all the viciousness of the old slavery spirit, and betrays a thorough ignorance and contempt of the essential principle of the Republican party. Blaine church officers refuse to speak with the Independent church pastor, and some such pastors have been practically forced to resign; country merchants are boycotted; Blaine combinations have been attempted—but wisely abandoned—to boycott Independent newspapers; lyceums largely composed of Blaine supporters boycott Independent lecturers; and the Morristown *Jerseyman*, a Blaine organ, publishes the following remarks in regard to a lecture which Mr. Nast consented to deliver in aid of one of the churches of the town: "It is possible some self-respecting Republicans may be found among his audience, but we hope they are not many. Mr. Nast is not a person for whom they can have a very warm affection at the present time." Mr. St. John has been burned in effigy, and it is stated that the countenance of Blaine supporters has been withdrawn in some places from the prohibition cause. . . .

1885–1886

Westward expansion of the post–Reconstruction period was triggered by lands opening, by railroad expansion, and through Homestead Exemption Acts. Ranchers and herders were attracted to the wide open plains. Wagon trains of easterners moved west seeking riches of the frontiers.

Native Americans restricted the encroachments on the lands theirs by birthright and those federally set aside for reservations. But public opinion held that all lands not occupied by American citizens were public properties. Futile attempts by a few conscientious officials did not deter the fervor of Manifest Destiny. Such was the case of the Oklahoma bloomers. These white settlers were determined to occupy federal territories once given to migrating tribes who were forced from the southeast during the infamous Trail of Tears.

Southern African Americans relocated to the Midwest and established all-black towns. At times these expeditions were assisted by emigrant relief societies of New England. These societies also sponsored expeditions into the Mormon territory of Utah, to "purify" the religious group's practice of polygamy.

As Republicans sought to understand the election of Cleveland, southern blacks who voted with the Democrats, and the failure of their campaign charge—that the country would be destroyed if the Democrats returned to national power—to materialize, they reconsidered the desirability of an all-white party. The success of the Democrats, it was determined, was due to the African American voter dividing his loyalty. Interviewed blacks no longer felt indebted to the party of freedom; instead, they felt "led to vote for their own Interest." In retrospect, there was a sense that the removal of these voters paved the way for the party to become lily *white. A new "moral force based on conviction and intelligence could stimulate the party and would gain for it greater local respectability...."* It was suggested that the "misfortune" of the South, e.g., mob rule, was due in part to the solidarity of the African American vote. By defusing black voting strength, the race would really be exercising real citizenship. The black community was no longer a political threat to white males of either party. Thus, blacks' political demise became common ground for white male solidarity.

In 1885 the Protestant Episcopal Church of South Carolina welcomed the membership of two black clergy. Considering the church's role in tolerating slavery, some believed that this step could mark equality in every Christian sect in the South. Acceptance into the flock did not imply race mixing or social equality—only that the church was a common ground for all saints.

Readers were assured that kneeling in humble submission would not lead to racial amalgamation. Some writers sought to revisit the presidency of Abraham Lincoln and the issue of black suffrage. Former Secretary of Treasury McCulloch supported Lincoln's reconstruction plan. On the issue of suffrage, McCulloch did not believe that any action of Lincoln's indicated that he would favor immediate or full enfranchisement of former slaves, whom both believed to be unfit for the ballot. In fact, there was no provision in Lincoln's plan for black suffrage. For Lincoln, consideration was a congressional issue, addressed via amendments, when the country deemed necessary. Concerning former citizens, McCulloch predicated that Lincoln would not have viewed the entire southern population as traitors. Nor would he have given federal positions to those who sought to enrich themselves or to perpetuate sectional discord. Dedicated to national union, Lincoln would have given new life to southern industry by binding regional ties.

The 1880s hosted the partitioning of the continent of Africa in the 1884 Berlin Conference. But coverage of the continent seemed limited to African American ministers' sojourns to Christianize the populace. This mission to Christianize Africa was prevalent in the careers of contemporaries Reverend Alexander Crummell and Bishop Henry McNeal Turner. Even educational institutions and individual educators incorporated the redemption of Africa as a mission incumbent upon the African American community.

As congressional elections in the fall of 1886 approached, the time was appropriate to examine the process of campaigning and the role of recent history in the support and direction of the two political parties. The appeal of politics and parties based on mudslinging had been altered by the election of Grover Cleveland. What had become obvious, the journalists revealed, was that the immediate disaster for the country did not happen; in fact, there was a restoration to normal procedures in a *constitutional government. Now the public had matured. It knew now that the election of neither political party was essential to the country's safety. So, in the congressional elections, personal character became tantamount. Flaws would no longer be overlooked because of the necessity to elect one party. Political parties could no longer control the public by appealing to the party line.*

Tribute is paid to the role of the Tenth Cavalry in policing the Southwest. With few tents, scanty provisions, and inadequate clothes, these black soldiers honorably discharged their duties as peacemakers. Editorials praised their gallantry and patriotism in such deprived and disgraceful surroundings.

Yet racial organizing around the interests and needs of the African American community, led by black men, was viewed with caution and grave concern. African American men had assembled in conventions throughout the nineteenth century. Following the Civil War, the tradition revived. In 1886 black men in Boston, led by James Trotter, father of activist William Monroe Trotter, called for African Americans to increase their participation at the polls by electing candidates who were committed to the interests of the race. To their critics, such a call was unwise, for it would ultimately lead to bribes and not solve the question of injustice. For the editors, to ask for special favors or differentiation based on race would surely produce more prejudice. Equal rights came through the group gaining self-respect, industry, energy, and intelligence. Such actions on the part of black leaders were interpreted as irresponsible and provocative.

Jacqueline A. Rouse
Georgia State University

THE CREOLE PATOIS

HARPER'S WEEKLY
January 10, 1885, p. 27

Although the pure creole element is disappearing from the *Vié faubon*, as creole children call the antiquated part of New Orleans, it is there nevertheless that the patois survives as a current idiom; it is there one must dwell to hear it spoken in its purity, and to study its peculiarities of intonation and construction. The patois-speaking inhabitants—dwelling mostly in those portions of the quadrilateral furthest from the river and from the broad American boundary of Canal Street, which many of them never cross when they can help it—are not less *bizarre* than the architectural background of their picturesque existence. The visitor is surrounded by a life motley-colored as those fantastic populations described in the *Story of the Young King of the Black Isles;* the African ebon is least visible, but of bronze-browns, banana-yellows, orange-golds, there are endless varieties, paling off into faint lemon tints, and even dead-silver whites. The paler the shade, the more strongly do Latin characteristics show themselves; and the oval faces, with slender cheeks and low broad brows, prevail. Sometimes in the yellower types a curious Sphinx visage appears, dreamy as Egypt. Occasionally, also, one may encounter figures so lithe, so animal, as to recall the savage grace of Priou's "Satyress." For the true colorist the contrast of a light saffron skin with dead-black hair and eyes of liquid jet has a novel charm, as of those descriptions in the Malay poem "Bidasari," of "women like statues of gold." It is hard to persuade one's self that such types do not belong to one distinct race, the remnant of some ancient island tribe, and the sound of their richly vowelled creole speech might prolong the pleasant illusion.

It must not be supposed, however, that the creole dialect is the only one used by these people; there are few who do not converse fluently in the French and

English languages, and to these acquirements many add a knowledge of the sibillant Mexican-Spanish. But creole is the maternal speech; it is the tongue in which the baby first learns to utter its thoughts; it is the language of family and of home. The white creole child learns it from the lips of his swarthy nurse; and creole adults still use it in speaking to servants or to their own little ones. At a certain age the white boys or girls are trained to converse in French; judicious petting, or even mild punishment, is given to enforce the use of the less facile but more polite medium of expression. But the young creole who remains in Louisiana seldom forgets the sweet patois, the foster-mother tongue, the household words which are lingual caresses.

Now the colored inhabitants of the *carré* regulate the use of the creole after the manners of their former masters, upon whose time-honored customs they base their little code of urbanity. Let us suppose you are dwelling in one of the curious and crumbling houses of the old quarter of the town, and that some evening while dreaming over a pipe as you rock your chair upon the gallery, the large-eyed children of the habitation gather about you, cooing one unto the other in creole like so many yellow doves. Invariably you will then hear the severe maternal admonition, "Allons, Marie! Eugène! faut pas parler créole devant monsieur; parlez Francais, donc!" Creole must not be spoken in the presence of "monsieur"; he must be addressed in good French, the colonial French of Louisiana that has been so much softened by tropicalization.

The general purpose of these little sketches will not admit of any extended linguistic dissertation, otherwise it would be a pleasant task to follow the foot-prints of many philological harvesters, and glean something in fields where French, English, and American scholars have reaped so well. It would be interesting to trace back the origin of the creole to the earlier ages of Latin-American slave colonies, showing how the African serf softened and simplified the more difficult language of his masters, and made to himself that marvellous system of grammar in which philologists have found material for comparison with the tongue of Homer and the speech of Beowulf. But the writer's purpose is to reflect the spirit of existing things rather than to analyze the past, to sketch local peculiarities and reflect local color without treating broadly of causes. It will be sufficient, therefore, to state that the creole patois is the offspring of linguistic miscegenation, an offspring which exhibits but a very faint shade of African color, and nevertheless possesses a strangely supple comeliness by virtue of the very intercrossing which created it, like a beautiful octoroon.

That word reminds one of a celebrated and vanished type—never mirrored upon canvas, yet not less physically worthy of artistic preservation than those amber-tinted beauties glorified in the Oriental studies of Ingres, of Richter, of Gérôme! Uncommonly tall were those famous beauties—citrine-hued, elegant of stature as palmettos, lithe as serpents; never again will such types re-appear upon American soil. Daughters of luxury, artificial human growths, never organized to enter the iron struggle for life unassisted and unprotected, they vanished forever with the social system which made them a place apart as for splendid plants reared within a conservatory. With the fall of American feudalism the dainty glass house was dashed to pieces; the species it contained have perished utterly; and whatever morality may have gained, one can not help thinking that art has lost something by their extinction. What figures for designs in bronze! what tints for canvas!

It is for similar reasons that the creole tongue must die in Louisiana; the great social change will eventually render it extinct. But there is yet time for the philologist to rescue some of its dying legends and curious lyrics, to collect and preserve them, like pressed blossoms, between the leaves of enduring books.

The creoles of the Antilles seem to have felt more pride in the linguistic curiosities of their native isles than the creoles of Louisiana have manifested regarding their own antiquities. In Trinidad fine collections of creole legends and proverbs have been made, and an excellent grammar of the dialect published; in Martinique, hymn-books, *paroissiens,* and other works are printed in creole; the fables of La Fontaine and many popular French fairy tales have found creole translators in the West Indies, while several remarkable pamphlets upon the history and construction of the West Indian dialects are cited in Parisian catalogues of linguistic publications. But it was not until the French publishers of *Mélusine* showed themselves anxious to cull the flora of Louisiana creole that the creoles themselves made any attempt to collect them. Happily the romantic interest excited throughout the country by George Cable's works stimulated research to further exertion, and even provoked the creation of a Franco-Louisianian novel, written by a creole, and having a considerable portion of its text in patois. Nevertheless nothing has yet been attempted in Louisiana comparable with the labors of MM. Luzel and Sebillot in Bretagne; no systematic efforts have been made to collect and preserve the rich oral literature of the creole parishes. The inedited creole literature comprises songs, satires in rhyme, proverbs, fairy tales—almost everything commonly included under the term *folk-lore*. The lyrical portion of it is opulent in oddities, in melancholy beauties; Alphonse Daudet has frequently borrowed therefrom, using creole refrains in his novels with admirable effect.

Some of the popular songs possess a unique and almost weird pathos; there is a strange naive sorrow in their burdens, as of children sobbing for lonesomeness in the night. Others, on the contrary, are inimitably comical. There are many ditties or ballads devoted to episodes of old plantation life, to surreptitious frolic, to description of singular industries and callings, to commemoration of events which had strongly impressed the vivid imagination of negroes—a circus show, an unexpected holiday, the visit of a beautiful stranger to the planter's home, or even some one of those incidents indelibly marked with a crimson spatter upon the fierce history of Louisiana politics. Of these lyrics I shall speak in another paper.

Lafcadio Hearn.

THE CREOLES

HARPER'S WEEKLY
January 24, 1885, p. 379

The average Northern visitor to New Orleans at this time seems to have come principally to see the creoles, and, incidentally—if time permits—to do the Exposition. Scarcely has he reached his hotel before he inquires where the creole beauties are to be seen—being apparently under the impression that they are on exhibition at certain street corners, or are displayed somewhere in glass cases at so much per head. Exactly what a creole is he doesn't seem to have much idea, but he evidently has a vague notion that a creole is a being of surpassing beauty, full of grace and elegance and dignity, and all that sort of thing, who moves through life in an atmosphere of perpetual sunshine and perfume, and who is to be found only in New Orleans. There is just a dash of African blood, he fancies, in the veins of the creole; and she—for to his mind the creole is always of the feminine sex—dances divinely, dresses exquisitely, converses in French with the fluency of the Parisian, and speaks English with the musical accent made familiar to his ears by the traditional full-dress foreign villain of the stage. Determined to learn all that is to be learned on this subject, the stranger orders creole eggs for breakfast, and finds that they taste exactly like other eggs; calls for a creole cocktail at the first bar, and discovers no peculiar effects; lights a creole cigar and saunters down Canal Street to look for creole beauties. He doesn't find them. He passes Englishmen and Frenchmen, and Germans and Italians, and Spaniards and Mexicans, and no end of Africans; but the rare and radiant beings whom he seeks do not materialize. In an indignant mood he ends his stroll, and returns to his hotel with the firm conviction that "this creole business is all humbug," and that he has been made a victim of false pretenses.

But if he looks into Webster's dictionary he will find that the creole is "one born in America or the West Indies of European ancestors." If this definition is correct New Orleans is full of creoles, and so, for that matter, is the city council of Chicago. But, as to their beauty. Ah, well, that is a matter of taste. There are different standards of beauty. The Piute chief sees in the dusky maiden, besmeared with grease and filth, covered with gaudy trinkets, and redolent with the pungent odors of the tepee and the wigwam, a being

"—fairer than the evening air,
Clad in the beauty of a thousand stars."

But the unpoetical Anglo-Saxon would have the dusky maiden abated as a nuisance.

Webster's definition of the word "creole" is pronounced by a local authority of high repute to be in every way inaccurate. The term, he declares, "has a more restricted and special application." The creole proper is the descendant of the original French settlers who, by intermarrying, has preserved the type of his ancestors, which, though modified by time and association, still retains, in a great measure, their traits and manners. The creoles, then, are the true Louisianians; all others are simply imitations. When the Northern visitor once discovers that the creole is not a "nigger" of any shade or degree, is of both sexes, and is not necessarily beautiful, he loses, to a great extent, his interest in the general subject of creoles, and is ready for a visit to the Exposition.

Of recent years the creole element in New Orleans society has lost, to a considerable extent, that prominence which it formerly possessed. The old creole families have been slow to adapt themselves to the changed conditions of life in the Crescent City. Tenacious of old ways and forms, clinging with characteristic French fondness to the homes endeared to them by a thousand tender associations and pleasant memories, they have retired more and more within themselves as the waves of modern progress have swept with ever increasing force across the familiar paths they and their ancestors had trod for many generations, and gradually obliterated the landmarks which told of the luxury and splendor of the ante-bellum period. The loss of their slaves and the ravages of the war reduced most of these old families from affluence to comparative poverty. Most of the creole mansions in old New Orleans are fallen into architectural decrepitude; but the occupants are still as stately, as dignified and as courteous as in the days of their prosperity. They are, if anything, more exclusive than before, and general society knows them less and less as the years pass by. Some of them of advanced age have never, I am told, crossed Canal Street, the line which separates the old city from the new.

There are splendid types of female beauty among the creoles, but they are not on exhibition for the benefit of curious strangers. They are to be seen of a Sunday morning at the cathedral, or at the French opera upon some special occasion, or perhaps at the annual reception of the Pickwick Club. Their complexions are olive; their hair black and lustrous; their eyes large, dark and expressive; their hands and feet small; their figures slender and graceful; their carriage stately and dignified; their taste in dress exquisite. These types are by no means rare, but as a class it may be doubted whether the creole women can be really pronounced handsome.

PERSONAL GOSSIP

HARPER'S WEEKLY
January 24, 1885, p. 379

The Moody revival meetings held in Richmond, Va., have been largely attended. So great was the desire to hear Mr. Moody that many persons remained in the building from one meeting to another, afraid to leave the hall lest they should be unable to get in upon their return. Some took their lunches with them, and partook of them before the services opened. On one day the revivalist preached to the colored people exclusively, when the largest gathering of colored worshipers ever seen in that State was present.

JOHN BROWN AT CHARLESTOWN

HARPER'S WEEKLY
January 31, 1885, p. 74

The story of John Brown is one of the possessions of which mankind will never grow tired. In peaceful and commonplace times, to peaceful and commonplace citizens, the dash upon Harper's Ferry has become absolutely unintelligible. It is only those who remember the stress of excitement which lay upon the whole community, after the preliminary skirmish in Kansas of the war for freedom had been fought, who can dimly imagine what an impulse this excitement must have given to a man like Brown—one of Cromwell's Ironsides born out of due time, or still more a belated Covenanter. The "rabid philanthropy" of John Brown was a recrudescence of the fierce Christianity of Balfour of Burley. Mad and hopeless as the raid into Virginia was, it was one of the attempts which, like the equally mad and hopeless charge of the Light Brigade, will be remembered and admired beyond the most sober and scientific feats of arms. Three years in the New York wilderness as a teacher and leader of fugitive slaves, and two years in Kansas as a leader in the guerrilla warfare between freedom and slavery, had constituted an experience singularly fitted to temper Brown's iron nature even to so desperate an undertaking as that of outlawing himself in order to strike a blow at slavery in its intrenchments. Everybody remembers the story of the hopeless attack and the hopeless resistance of the party of zealots who had carried the fiery cross to a people which could not be inflamed to insurrection. Everybody remembers, too, the one visible softening of the rugged nature, when leaving the jail for the gallows, "with a radiant countenance and the step of a conqueror," as an eye-witness told, he "paused for a moment by the door to kiss a negro child held up to him by its mother." Though his enterprise must then have seemed to him utterly without result, it was one of the loosening pebbles which together set the mountain-side in motion. He was hanged December 2, 1859, and on September 22, 1863, Lincoln issued the Emancipation Proclamation.

OKLAHOMA

HARPER'S WEEKLY
March 28, 1885, p. 199

The "Oklahoma boomer" has come to be a familiar name of late. At present there are one thousand or more Oklahoma boomers. They are encamped on Cheeota Creek, six miles from Arkansas City, on the southern border of Kansas. To the south of them lies the Indian Territory. Nearly in the centre of that Territory stretches the Oklahoma country, an exceedingly fertile and attractive area. The boomers wish to march upon it, to settle in it, and to possess it. The United States government says that they must not do this; that the land is pledged to the Indians. The boomers declare that they will do it. United States troops are posted opposite the camp of the boomers, on the opposite side of Cheeota Creek. They have orders not to permit the boomers to set foot in the Indian Territory. Other United States troops are posted in the Territory—in the Oklahoma country—to guard it against the boomers. From the accounts that come to us there is likely to be an outbreak and bloodshed at any moment.

In November last died Captain David L. Payne, known better as Oklahoma Payne. He was the originator and first leader of the Oklahoma boomers. He was a man of obstinate convictions. He contended that the Oklahoma lands were public property, upon which he and his followers had the right to settle....

Captain Payne made his first raid into the Oklahoma country in July, 1880. President Hayes had issued a proclamation declaring an invasion of Oklahoma an offense against the law, and ordering interlopers out. Payne and his party were arrested by United States troops. He was tried civilly at Fort Worth, Texas; the court decided against him, and he was warned by Secretary Teller to keep out of the Indian lands. In 1882, with twenty-nine followers, he again pushed across the border, and settled in Oklahoma. The troops again

"PROCLAIM LIBERTY THROUGHOUT ALL THE LAND UNTO ALL THE INHABITANTS THEREOF."
LISTENING TO THE SOUND OF LIBERTY, AND REJOICING THAT THERE IS NO MORE SLAVERY.

Harper's Weekly, January 24, 1885, p. 49.

drove him out. Again he went back, and in August last two squadrons of the Ninth United States Cavalry (colored) arrested him and the whole community which he had established at Rock Falls, and escorted them, with their personal property, to the Kansas line. It is said that Payne at his death was worth $60,000.

Captain Couch succeeded to the command of the boomers on the death of Payne in November last. On the 15th of January last, General Hatch, in command of the United States forces opposing the boomers, sent word to Couch from his head-quarters at Camp Russell, Indian Territory, warning him not to proceed in his

AFRICAN AMERICAN HISTORY IN THE PRESS, 1851-1899

JOHN BROWN ON HIS WAY TO EXECUTION.—Drawn by T. Hovenden.—[See Page 74.]

Harper's Weekly, January 31, 1885, pp. 72–73.

EJECTING AN "OKLAHOMA BOOMER."—Drawn by T. de Thulstrup from a Sketch by Frederic Remington.—[See Page 199.]

Harper's Weekly, March 28, 1885, p. 193.

scheme of colonization. Captain Couch, then at the head of 400 men, defied the United States officer. On January 23, General Hatch sent Lieutenant Day, with forty-two soldiers, to Captain Couch at his encampment at Stillwater. Lieutenant Day requested the boomers to quit. Captain Couch ordered them to prepare for battle, and Lieutenant Day retired. On January 25, General Hatch visited Couch's camp in person, and offered him twenty-four hours in which to retreat. The general had at hand four companies from Fort Leavenworth, one from Forth Gibson, Indian Territory, one from Fort Lyon, Colorado, three from Forth Wingate, and three troops of cavalry from Forth Riley. After a parley, Couch made a conditional surrender, and on January 26 left the Territory with the honors of war. Troops and boomers fraternized immediately after the surrender.

The troops escorted the boomers to Arkansas City. There the boomers were received with applause by the citizens. A public meeting passed resolutions condemning the action of the government, and declaring the intention of an early renewal of the attempt to colonize the Oklahoma country. Captain Couch, H. H. Stafford, George W. Brown, and Colonel S. E. Wilcox were imprisoned in Arkansas City on a charge of conspiracy and rebellion against the United States government. They were arraigned at Wichita, Kansas, before United States Commissioner Sherman, and bound over in $1000 each for a hearing on February 10. While awaiting trial, Captain Couch presided at the boomers' convention at Topeka, which assembled on February 3. Delegates from sixteen Oklahoma colonies were present. They declared that they represented twenty thousand boomers. A committee was appointed to prepare and publish an address to the people of the United States defining the position of the boomers, and also to present the case to President Cleveland, and to protest against interference with American citizens who contemplated settling on such lands in the Oklahoma country as did not belong to any Indian tribe. Arrangements were also made to send Sidney Clark, an ex-member of Congress, and S. N. Wood, an editor, of Topeka, East to present the case of the boomers more clearly to the President.

There was not sufficient evidence to convict Captain Couch and his associates at the trial on February 10. They are now at liberty, and Captain Couch is in command of the encampment of boomers on Cheeota Creek. It is said that many of the boomers are old soldiers, and that most of them are frontiersmen accustomed to arbitration by bullet.

On March 13, General Hatch telegraphed from Caldwell, Kansas, to the Secretary of War that there were then no trespassers upon the Indian Territory, though the boomers on Cheeota Creek were threatening to go over the line. Troops, he said, were stationed in the Territory, and would drive out any invaders.

On the same day President Cleveland issued a proclamation warning the boomers that they would be met by the troops if they attempted another raid upon the Oklahoma country.

The boomers again protested when they heard of this proclamation. They passed resolutions declaring that "a large number of cattle men and cattle syndicates" were occupying the Oklahoma country with permanent improvements for farming and grazing purposes. The resolutions were telegraphed to the President. On the same day Captain Couch announced that he would break camp on Monday, March 16, and move south into the Indian Territory. He called upon those who would follow him to be prepared with agricultural implements and sixty days' rations, as he was going to stay. On the same day General Hatch announced that the boomers could not get through his line. He had six companies of the Ninth Cavalry (colored) directly opposed to the boomers, and plenty of other troops near by. He said they could successfully contend with 3000 or 4000 men.

The government at Washington says that the whole of the Indian Territory is guaranteed by the United States to the use of friendly Indian tribes forever. Squatters may not light upon it. If there are cattle men there, they are not permanent, and may be driven off at any moment.

PERSONAL

HARPER'S WEEKLY
April 4, 1885, p. 211

Professor James A. Harrison, of the Washington and Lee University, Lexington, Virginia, has recently contributed to *Anglia* (the well-known German *Zeitschrift für Englische Philologie*) an elaborate paper on the "Negro English" of the Southern States. This is the first attempt made by any scholar to treat the subject systematically, and it is astonishing to find how interesting it becomes in the hands of a trained philologian. After a brief outline of some of the salient features in negro character which have exerted the most powerful influence in shaping their dialectical peculiarities, Professor Harrison presents an extended scientific register of the varied phenomena of "Negro Phonetics," and follows this up with a skeleton grammar of negro language as it exists to-day south of the Potomac. To this is finally appended "Specimen Negroisms," which occupy eighteen closely printed crown octavo pages, forming a most interesting and diverting collection, which ought to be simply invaluable to novelists undertaking to portray the humors of negro character. The paper is altogether very good reading, and could only have been written by a trained scholar whose whole life has been spent in the old Slave States.

SOMETHING WORTH THINKING OF

HARPER'S WEEKLY
April 11, 1885, p. 122

The part played by the Emigrant Aid Societies of New England in delivering Kansas from the grasp of the slave power has not been forgotten; and now some of the very men who organized and led that movement propose to operate upon the Mormon Territory of Utah by the same means; in other words, to overwhelm the Polygamists by filling the Territory with emigrants opposed to their uncleanness. Amos A. Lawrence, the veteran millionaire of Boston, the Rev. Edward Everett Hale, and Eli Thayer, have asked the Legislature to grant them an Act of Incorporation for this purpose, with liberty to acquire $1,000,000 as capital. A Bill for this purpose has already been reported to the House, and is not likely, we suspect, to meet with much opposition. The corporators are said to have examined the subject, and to believe the scheme practicable, and it is thought the desired capital may be easily obtained. . . .

THE BLACK VOTE DIVIDING

FRANK LESLIE'S ILLUSTRATED NEWSPAPER
May 30, 1885, p. 234

Mr. Carl Schurz was among the very first Republicans to predict the Presidential disaster that befell that party, and he pointed out some time in advance of the public perception the inevitable growth and force of the Civil Service Reform movement. He has, therefore, very fairly earned some right to the claims of a political prophet, and what he says about future policies and parties in a time of such political quiet and scarcity of definite issues as this deserves consideration.

In the pamphlet which Mr. Schurz has just published about "The New South," in which he expresses the conclusions that he drew during his recent journey through the Southern States, he points out the important political fact, that the black vote is already beginning to divide, and gives reasons why a further division will take place. This is of very great importance, because it means the breaking of the "Solid South"—at least, the disappearance of the color-line in politics. Mr. Schurz reports that he found the opinion prevalent among many of the most intelligent freedmen, that they had already paid their debt to the Republican Party for giving them their freedom, and that they felt now at liberty to vote as their interest distated. Hitherto their political life has been a blind life, for they voted in herds and voted for Republican candidates for all offices, from constable to President, merely because they were Republican candidates. The Republican Party will gain incalculably in moral force and usefulness in the South when all its members vote from conviction and with intelligence. By losing a portion of the negro vote that it has hitherto had, it will gain a greater local respectability, which will attract white voters whom it has never had. On the other hand, when a portion of the freedmen become Democrats, the professional machine-manager of the negro vote will lose his vocation; the freedmen will not go in droves, politically, but, for sensible reasons, being divided intelligently into parties, their political privileges will become what they were meant to be—a power to be used intelligently, and not a halter to be led or hanged by.

The danger of ignorant citizenship is at its greatest when the body of ignorant citizens is herded on one side. If it is divided, one portion has a tendency to correct the evil of other portions. It is the concentration of the ignorant, or of any other more or less dangerous class, that makes it threatening. The most of the recent political misfortunes of the South, if not all, have been caused by the solidity of the black vote. Mr. Schurz's prediction of its division, therefore, is as cheerful a prophecy as has recently been made by anybody. There is abundant evidence, too, to confirm Mr. Schurz's judgment. The new Democratic Administration can scarcely do more useful service to the country than it is doing in emancipating the freedmen from political solidity, so that they may, through an intelligent exercise of their rights of citizenship, really become free men.

DECORATION DAY MEMORIES

FRANK LESLIE'S ILLUSTRATED NEWSPAPER
May 30, 1885, p. 242

In this number we present interesting illustrations *apropos* of Decoration Day, which, during the last twenty years, has been the most honored of our patriotic holidays. Every old soldier into whose hands this paper comes will have his blood stirred anew by the pictorial reminiscences of the march and the bivouac, the fight and the truce.

The sombre picture in the centre will recall to many memories the saddest incidents of the war—the culprit kneeling on his coffin, the long lines of military spectators, the unhappy executioners, with rifles at shoulders, compelled to slay a comrade, but unable to banish from their hearts some sense of pity for the wretch whose hardships instigated his crime. It was a scene witnessed more than once by the army around Petersburg, where most of the sketches were taken which form the basis of our page to-day.

Still more familiar to the seasoned soldier will be "Winter Quarters," with its possession of snow and slush, of fun and discomfort, its daily dole of rations and of medicine, and the well-remembered song, "Come, get your quinine! Come, get your quinine! Come, get your quinine! Come, get your pills!" See the enlarged woodchuck's hole, where three or four comrades manage to make themselves comfortable, with no ventilation except through the stovepipe sticking out at top! See the tent where the uncanny weather intrudes from every

AFRICAN AMERICAN HISTORY IN THE PRESS, 1851-1899

"Ain't dis a slam on de Niggah? Dis fule dog has lost his boss, an' has tuk me fur one ob dem dudes! Ha! haw!"

Harper's Weekly, April 4, 1885, p. 224.

quarter, and its inflammable chimney of flour-barrels set up end to end! To the active mind of the veteran soldier no feature comes back oftener through the mists of twenty years than the grotesque camp architecture, and the multifarious comforts and miseries of Winter quarters.

Another scene—the memory of which gives the old soldier a shudder, and sends a very cold chill creeping down his back—is, "Sleeping in the rain after a hard march." Every soldier that was *really* a soldier had the common experience, and the man who, under those circumstances, could get a pile of rails to sleep on, with their triangular, sharp edges where the mattress ought to be, had reason to feel that he was, indeed, a lucky fellow. A very large proportion of our dead owed the ailments which proved mortal to the exposures which were generally inevitable after a long day's march.

The novel punishment, adopted in the camp of a negro regiment, we have illustrated from a sketch taken on the spot. The colored persons had been detected in the act of prosecuting their profession of alienating chickens from the neighboring farms against the orders of the general commanding; and the punishment allotted to them was compelling them to "roost" like the poultry of which they were so fond. They liked it for awhile, and laughed and sang and played cards; but a few hours of the difficult balancing was enough, and then it became an extremely distasteful pastime.

The "arrival of the wash-lady in the camp" in those days was an event that almost ranked in importance and jubilant interest with the coming of the mail-carrier. Some of the boys, indeed, did not patronize the sable goddess of cleanliness, renovating their washable clothing at the nearest brook; but even these were

OUR ULYSSES.
APRIL 9, 1865—A NEVER-TO-BE-FORGOTTEN DEED.

Harper's Weekly, April 11, 1885, pp. 232–33.

REMINISCENCES OF A WAR ARTIST.—SCENES AND INCIDENTS IN GRANT'S PETERSBURG CAMPAIGN AGAINST LEE.

Frank Leslie's Illustrated Newspaper, May 30, 1885, pp. 240–41.

PREACHING VERSUS PRACTICE.

"Elijah Vanderbilt, what's you doin' all dressed up, er loafin' on de street an' foolin' 'way your time? If dar am one thing I 'spise more'n anoder it am laziness. Go straight home, sah!"

Harper's Weekly, May 30, 1885, p. 351.

interested to find out the sum-total of the luxurious belongings of their fellows. So her arrival and departure were always the signal for rejoicing.

In the picture of "Avoiding Shells in the Dutch Gap Canal," the work for that futile excavation is going forward in the background to the left, and the alarmed laborers have rushed into one of the artificial retreats in the bank on hearing the alarm, "Look out! shell coming!" That was a familiar shout along the picket-line, when all in range generally sought shelter behind a tree or rock, or comparative safety by lying down.

One of the pathetic scenes of this part of the frontier was Grant's commissary feeding the remnant of Lee's starving army after the surrender near Appomattox. It is illustrated in our page. Nothing has ever done more to enhance the fame of the chief hero of the War than the liberal terms he granted to Lee on that occasion, the attention he gave to the comfort of the vanquished soldiers, and the energy with which he afterwards insisted that the terms he had made should not be violated.

The study of "Politics in Camp" will recall to our great army of citizen-soldiers a scene that has never been witnessed in any other army in the world, when the men laid aside their weapons and their knapsacks and assembled around the ballot-box in 1864, and cast their vote for President. There was, that day, excitement all over the North, somewhat akin to the excitement of the battle, and the soldiers spoke their mind with no uncertain voice.

The allegory, which is set as a caption to these Decoration Day memories, needs no description—Father Time, glancing over his War-diary, and jogging the memory of Dame Columbia as to that famous but melancholy combat of brothers.

"Dat's er eel foolin' roun' dat hook; I kin tell from de way he pull."

Harper's Weekly, May 30, 1885, p. 351.

THE COLOR LINE IN THE CHURCH

FRANK LESLIE'S ILLUSTRATED NEWSPAPER
June 6, 1885, p. 251

The enrolment of two colored clergymen as members of the South Carolina Convention of the Protestant Episcopal Church, with the cordial concurrence of the Bishop, marks a new era in the history of that Church in the States that once tolerated slavery. In not one of those States is what is usually called "the prejudice of color," or the pride of superiority on the part of the whites over the blacks, stronger than in South Carolina. The Episcopal Church there, moreover, is led by the wealthiest and most aristocratic citizens, and we must, therefore, regard this action as a prophecy of the time, when, in every Christian sect at the South, the religious equality of the negro will be recognized. True, a minority of the South Carolina Convention indignantly protested against the affirmation, "that persons of color, and not belonging to the white race, are entitled to seats upon the floor and to participate in the government of the Church"; but the Bishop and the majority of the Convention were in no degree disturbed by this fact, and the future belongs to them, and not to the dissenters.

This recognition of the doctrine asserted by Paul, that in the Church "there is neither Greek nor Jew, circumcision nor uncircumcision, barbarian, Scythian, bond nor free, but Christ is all, and in all," has nothing to do with what is called the "social question." It does not imply a mixture of races, as so many will be ready to

RT. REV. SAMUEL DAVID FERGUSON.—PHOTOGRAPHED BY FREDERICKS.—[SEE PAGE 432.]

Harper's Weekly, July 4, 1885, p. 424.

assert, nor require whites and blacks to invite each other to their parlors and dining-tables in a promiscuous fashion. It simply makes the Church common ground for all orders and conditions of men, and divests "the communion of saints" of the hateful oppugnancies of race. The oldest Christian Church, to its credit be it said, has always recognized this principle. Its altars and aisles are free to worshipers of every shade of complexion, who may kneel upon her floors side by side without offense. This has never led to amalgamation among Catholics, and will not among Protestants.

[UNTITLED]

FRANK LESLIE'S ILLUSTRATED NEWSPAPER
June 6, 1885, p. 251

The very latest discovery is that the United States is doomed to be an African republic. A clergyman named Allen has discovered that the colored population of the country doubles once in twenty years, and the white population only of once in thirty-five years; and from this superior fecundity he deduces the broad conclusion that in 1985 there will be 96,000,000 white folks in this republic and 192,000,000 colored folks. Mr. Allen's method of figuring is faulty. Of course, it is true that all of the ignorant races are more prolific than the intellectual and refined races; but it is equally true that a far greater proportion of the former die in childhood, and that number of whites and blacks living to the adult condition is about the same. Of a hundred white male children born, something like fifty may be expected to grow to manhood; but it will take at least one hundred and fifty male black children to produce the same number of men. As races become enlightened and educated, they have fewer children; but the sanitary conditions are improved, and the death-rate is correspondingly reduced. So there is no danger that Dr. Allen's bugbear will ever become dangerous.

THE BLUE AND THE GRAY

HARPER'S WEEKLY
June 6, 1885, p. 354

In the midst of the echoes of the eloquence of Union orators on Decoration Day it is pleasant to hear an answering strain from a Confederate orator upon the Confederate Memorial Day, which occurs a month before our own. Mr. W.H. Fleming delivered an address at Atlanta at the close of April, in which he considers the probable judgment of history upon the Confederate soldier and his cause. He holds that the essential question was the nature of the government. It was a conflict between the doctrine of State rights and centralization. There was undoubtedly a question of the exact nature of the dual system of the Union. But, in our opinion, that was not, as Mr. Fleming thinks, the moving cause of the war. Except for slavery, the exact nature of the government would have been a point of casuistry.

We may concede, however, that the national sentiment was stronger in the non-slave-holding States, and history will take account of that fact. But the interest of the discourse is its frank and manly statement of truths, which is of itself, under the circumstances, an evidence of high character and courage, and which fully justifies Mr. Schurz's report in his *New South*. Thus the orator says—and we beg him to remember that "the South" is an undesirable political term—

> "But, however well justified the South may have been, according to human nature, to custom, and the Constitution, in taking the steps she deemed wisest for self-preservation, nevertheless it is a solemn fact that this great country, in the onward march of events, had grown out of the institution of slavery, and, if you will pardon the seeming sacrilege, had grown out of the written Constitution as it bore

THE "PRACTICAL" POLITICIAN'S LOVE FOR THE NEGRO.

Harper's Weekly, July 25, 1885, p. 473.

upon that subject. . . .Slavery at last was doomed, and, amid the tempest of war, God in his providence laid the axe at the root of the tree, and it fell. . . .

"Without abating one jot or tittle of loyal devotion to the memory of our Confederate dead, we can here, in the presence of their graves, turn our eyes to heaven and exclaim: Thank God! slavery, that material curse and moral incubus, has been lifted from our land. Thank God! that black cloud has vanished from our sky. Yes, even though it could spend

CONDITION PRECEDENT.
POMPOUS COLORED DOCTOR AND FORLORN PATIENT.
DOCTOR (*loquitur*). "Yo' know I larnt my 'fession from my ole marster, en I used to hyar him say, 'Hit's more easier to kyo 'em dan it is to git de money,' sez he. Dat's *my* principle, an' I'd like to see de color ob yo' money 'fo' I looks at yo' tongue."

Harper's Weekly, July 25, 1885, p. 483.

DRESSED UP FOR SUNDAY.
POLICEMAN. "See here, you young Hottentot, you'll have to put on more clothes before you can bathe here—do you hear?"
YOUNG HOTTENTOT. "Why, boss, I isn't thinkin' 'bout gwine in dis water; but uz I wuz dressed up fur Sunday, an' had nothin' to do, I jist came down to see dem oder fellers swim."

Harper's Weekly, August 29, 1885, p. 575.

its fury only in the lightning and thunder of war."

The orator anticipates the continuance of the conflict between centralization and State rights. But he says:

"No State will ever again resort to secession from the Union as a remedy for wrongs, present or prospective. That much is settled forever. Mr. Webster's prayer is answered, for the sun will never again shine upon 'the broken and dishonored fragments of a once glorious Union, upon States discordant, dissevered, belligerent.'"

Contrast with the manly and honorable tone of the speech of Mr. Fleming the following remarks from the *Freeman,* a Republican paper published at Kingston, in New York, which, in our judgment, most grossly misrepresent the feelings of the truest Republicans, and which the Pratt Post of the Grand Army of the Republic at Kingston strongly denounced. The Post with the civic authorities had invited among the orators two Democrats, one of whom was Mr. Schoonmaker, and this is the comment of the *Freeman:*

"The memory of the dead soldiers is not in the thoughts of the men who have now got control of the arrangements. Two peculiarly despicable creatures will address the crowd in the evening, it being presumed that by the time it will have become so drunk as to be unable to discriminate between the talk of a traitor and that of a patriot. Now the rebels are in control at Washington, and these men are coming forward to tell you that they are the patriots and you the rebels of the new dispensation. Remember your manhood. You have fought better men—men who were not like them, cowards and sneaks as well as traitors—with bullets and bayonets. Now fight the miserable scoundrels with the overwhelming weapon of your contempt."

Mr. Fleming, we understand, is a young man, and his speech shows a spirit in the young men of the Southern States, a patriotism and generosity of feeling, which are very far removed from a sullen and stupid Jacobite devotion to a lost cause. It merits from honorable men in the Northern States something else than sneers at Confederate brigadiers and the rebellion in the saddle. As it was long ago observed that the constant appeal to the cries and passions engendered by the great antislavery conflict and by the fiery struggle of the war came, not from the soldiers on either side, but from those who staid at home, so it is the mere politicians and dull partisans who can see no difference between '50 and '60 and the war, and '85 with slavery abolished twenty years ago. There are those in the Northern States who still feel toward the citizen of a Southern State as in the dark days of the Fugitive Slave Law and the border ruffians of Kansas we used to feel toward the Southern slaveholder and the fire-eating bully in Congress. Devotion to a glorious cause achieved has become a kind of sectional hatred. But it must not be mistaken for patriotism. We do not suppose that slavery and the war have left no baneful results in the Southern States. But we do suppose that the interests of liberty and good government do not require that citizens of the Southern States shall be treated as rebels and enemies lying in wait for vengeance.

A DEAD ISSUE.

SOUTH. "I should like to oblige you by killing a few negroes, Mr. Tribune, but I am too busy."

Harper's Weekly, August 29, 1885, p. 576.

MR. McCULLOCH ON PRESIDENT LINCOLN

HARPER'S WEEKLY
July 4, 1885, p. 423

Mr. McCulloch, late Secretary of the Treasury, has contributed to the *Tribune* a very interesting paper upon Mr. Lincoln, under whose administration he was called into service at Washington. The ex-Secretary is an admirable critic of public men and measures, because of the calm and generous tone of his mind, and his freedom from party passion and prejudice. His paper is delightful in many ways, but it is especially timely for its view of Mr. Lincoln's probable conduct in the reconstruction of the Union after the war. Mr. McCulloch does not doubt that he would have dealt as wisely with all questions then as he did during the conflict. He had obtained a leadership which Mr. Johnson could never hope to win, and he would have influenced the legislation of reconstruction. In regard to the fundamental question of suffrage, Mr. McCulloch says:

"There is nothing in his record to indicate that he would have favored the immediate and full enfranchisement of those who, having been always in servitude, were unfitted for an intelligent and independent use of the ballot. In the plan for the rehabilitation of the South which he and his Cabinet had partially agreed upon, and which Mr. Johnson and the same Cabinet endeavored to perfect and carry

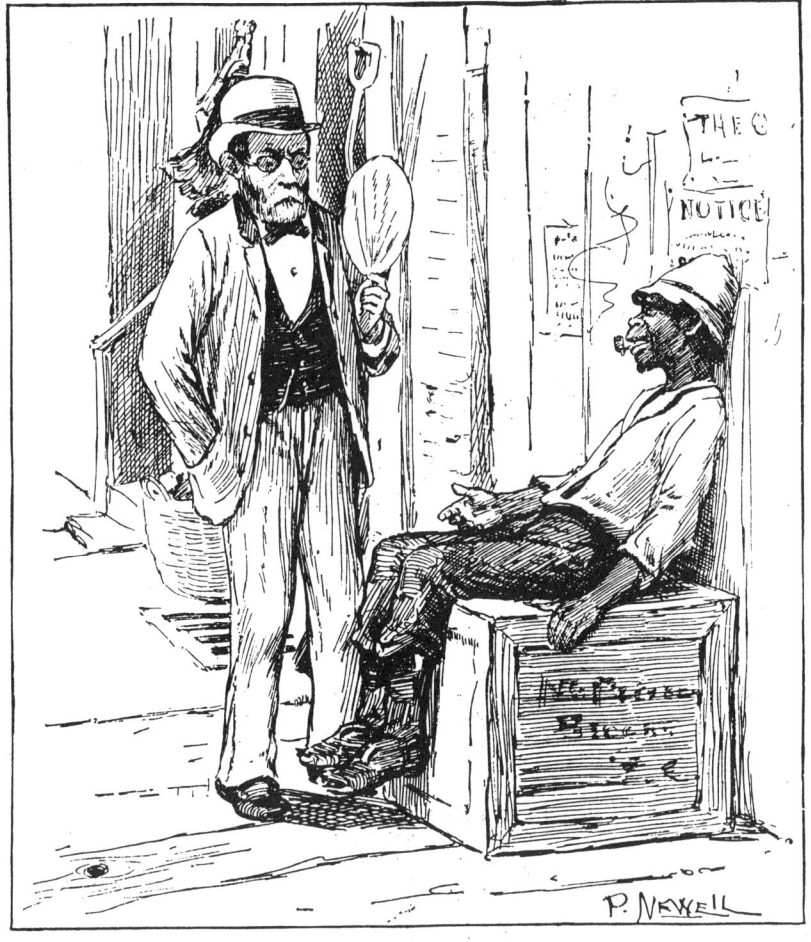

A GENTLEMAN OF LEISURE.

Mr. B. (*former master*). "Jim! Jim! what do you mean by loafing around in this manner, with a wife and seven children at home?"

Jim. "Well, Massa John, I's makin' 'bout a dollah settin' yer in de shade."

Mr. B. "How so?"

Jim. "Well, yo' see, I made two yisterday, an', strikin' a av'age, I's makin' 'bout a dollah ter day; so yo' see, sah, I's like a gem'an jes settin' 'roun' takin' it easy an' de money a-comin' in."

Harper's Weekly, September 5, 1885, p. 591.

out, no provision was made for negro suffrage. This question was purposely left open for further consideration and for Congressional action, under such amendments of the Constitution as the changed condition of the country might render necessary. From some of his incidental expressions, and from his well-known opinions upon the subject of suffrage, and the States to regulate it, my conclusion is that he would have been disposed to let that question remain as it stood before the war, with, however, such amendments of the Constitution as would have prevented any but those who were permitted to vote in Federal elections from being included in the enumeration for Representatives in Congress, thus inducing the recent Slave States, for the purpose of increasing their Congressional influence and power, to give the ballot to black men as well as white."

If to this view it should be objected that the black codes which followed the war showed a spirit which upon its revelation Mr. Lincoln might have concluded could be encountered hopefully only by general enfranchisement, it must be remembered that the black codes were the natural consequences of Andrew Johnson's apparent desire to restore his old Southern political relations, and that they would not have been adopted had Mr. Lincoln lived. In saying that Mr. Lincoln would not have been vindictive against the masses who had been in arms against the government, and that he would have regarded as "traitors" only those who while holding national offices, and drawing money from the national Treasury, used the influence of their positions to destroy the government, Mr. McCulloch says what is undoubtedly

"JOHNNY WISE'S BOYS" MAKING TROUBLE FOR THE REAR OF THE DEMOCRATIC PROCESSION.

VIRGINIA.—THE RECENT POLITICAL CAMPAIGN—GENERAL FITZHUGH LEE, THE DEMOCRATIC CANDIDATE FOR GOVERNOR, AND HIS ESCORT, ENTERING PETERSBURG, OCTOBER 24TH.
FROM SKETCHES BY A STAFF ARTIST.—SEE PAGE 178.

Frank Leslie's Illustrated Newspaper, November 7, 1885, pp. 184–85.

SAMBO'S TESTIMONIAL

PEARS' SOAP

I have found matchless for the complexion — Adelina Patti

"MATCHLESS FOR UM COMPLEKSHUN."

Specially drawn by H.S.MARKS, R.A. for the Proprietors of PEARS' SOAP

Frank Leslie's Illustrated Newspaper, December 5, 1885, p. 256.

true. But these persons were few. The actual leaders were revolutionists, not traitors. They were so treated during the war, and they have been so treated by Republican administration since the war. We know that Governor Andrew, of Massachusetts, when the war ended, was of opinion that the hope of successful reconstruction lay in concert and co-operation with the real leaders in the Southern States who had been the chiefs of the Confederacy.

In what Mr. McCulloch describes as the probable policy of Mr. Lincoln, undoubtedly Mr. Lincoln would have had Governor Andrew's earnest and efficient support.

"Nor would Mr. Lincoln have appointed to Southern offices such men as, unfortunately, were appointed, whose chief mission seemed to have been to enrich themselves, overload the States with debt, and perpetuate the sectional discord which had always, to some extent, existed, and which had been aggravated and intensified by the war. His sympathy was as broad as his patriotism, Devoted to the Union—not merely a geographical union, but a true national Union—his aim would have been to build up the waste places, give new life to Southern industry, and bind together North and South, the people of the country and the whole country, by ties of mutual respect, brotherhood, and interest."

These reminiscences, we say, are timely. They recall the time when, at the close of the actual strife of civil war, and amid passions still fiercely burning, Mr. Lincoln saw his country and not his party, and knew that primary truth of statesmanship in a free country, "He serves his party best who serves his country most."

A COLORED BISHOP

HARPER'S WEEKLY
July 4, 1885, p. 432

The first colored member of the American House of Bishops was consecrated in Grace Church, New York city, on the 24th of June, by Bishop Lee, of Delaware, the Presiding Bishop of the Protestant Episcopal Church in this country. The new Bishop is the Rev. Samuel David Ferguson, his birth-place Charleston, South Carolina, and his age forty-three. His destination is Cape Palmas, Africa, where he will preach the Gospel to his brethren of the same color, and will be the fourth Missionary Bishop of that region.

When six years old, Bishop Ferguson went with his parents to Liberia, and his education was received entirely in the mission schools of that state. He has been a teacher and preacher there for more than twenty years. The services at his consecration were very impressive, and his clear replies to the questions propounded to him were heard distinctly in every part of the vast and crowded edifice. Several bishops publicly assisted him in donning his robes of office, while the choir sang the anthem of investiture. Bishop Stevens, of Pennsylvania, who preached the sermon on the occasion, expressed in hearty and eloquent terms the esteem felt for Dr. Ferguson by his co-laborers in the Church, and their sincere wishes for his happiness and usefulness in Africa. The Doctor's official title is "Missionary Bishop of Cape Palmas and adjacent parts." He will proceed to his new field in a few days.

THE CONGO AND ITS FREE STATE

HARPER'S WEEKLY
July 11, 1885, p. 439

The very handsome book of Mr. Stanley's which is just issued in two fully illustrated volumes by the Harpers is one of the most important works of the year. It is a

WILFUL SLAVERY MAKES WOFUL SUFFERING.

COLORED LABOR TO WHITE LABOR. "No sooner am I really set free than you enslave yourselves, and at the expense of your families, too."

Harper's Weekly, April 17, 1886, p. 253.

AN EXPANSIVE HEAD.

"Dare, dot schust feels like id growt on you."
"Yes, boss, it's too neat a fit, cuz I's 'feard when I gits to 'xspandin' on de trombone I bus' de ban', shuah. Guess yo' bettah gimme a little mo' roomy one."

Harper's Weekly, July 24, 1886, p. 475.

thorough and exhaustive account of all the aspects of life in the heart of the "Dark Continent," the valley of a river larger than the Nile, which until now has been wholly hidden from human knowledge. The author recognizes this fact. He is aware that his subject is invested with no charm of poetic association or historic renown. It is not a region of which old travellers tell their "idle tales" for "fools at home" to believe, and almost the sole information in regard to it is that it is the chief seat of the most inhuman traffic in the world, the slave-trade.

The opening of such a realm not only to general knowledge, but to civilization and the arts of industry and peace, is an enterprise which marks the humanity of the time. To this great project the services of Mr. Stanley are inestimable. He has explored the vast Congo Valley with the zeal and the talent of the born traveller, and his record is indispensable to those who would understand its resources, opportunities, and possibilities. The book is the narrative of a practical discoverer and explorer, but it is also a cyclopaedia of the Congo.

The descriptions of the slave traffic which are given in detail are pictures most painful and revolting from their truth. Nothing could prove more conclusively that essential "barbarism of slavery" upon which Charles Sumner used strenuously to insist. This crime will disappear in the free state of the Congo which has been formed by the great states of Christendom, and which Mr. Stanley describes as a region of singular fertility, with a vast variety of products, the most valuable forest trees, coffee, peltries, ivory, copper, with a soil friendly to cotton, maize, rice, tobacco, sugar, and wheat, while the climate is generally healthful. The book is a glimpse into a new world which humane and civilized energy and skill will rapidly transform into a better world.

MRS. MARIA WESTON CHAPMAN

HARPER'S WEEKLY
August 1, 1885, p. 487

The death of Mrs. Maria Weston Chapman removes one of the most familiar figures of the earlier antislavery contest. Her name is probably little known except among those who knew the women who in that time were among the most courageous and unshrinking assertors of the fundamental American principle, and to whom a late number of the Philadelphia *Ledger* pays a most trustful and eloquent tribute.

An excellent story is told of one of these women, Mrs. Lucretia Mott. During one of the Rynders riots in New York, when he and his gang were engaged in breaking up one of the antislavery meetings, Mrs. Mott was asked, in the height of the tumult, how she expected to escape. "Oh," she replied, quietly, laying her hand upon the shoulder of one of the most active rioters, "this gentleman will see me to the door." And "this gentleman" was so overwhelmed with amazement at her serene self-possession that he escorted her safely through the mob to the street. . . .

TIME'S CHANGES

HARPER'S WEEKLY
September 26, 1885, p. 627

A recent diplomatic appointment shows the marvellous changes of the time. The President is a Democrat. He belongs to the party which, a few years since, was absolutely controlled by the power of slavery. But he has just nominated as Minister-resident to Liberia a man who was born a slave in North Carolina, the Reverend Moses A. Hopkins.

When he gained his freedom Mr. Hopkins fitted himself for college, graduated at the Lincoln University in Pennsylvania and at the Auburn Theological Seminary, and he was for some years the principal of the State Colored Normal School in Franklinton, North Carolina. For the appointment to Liberia he was warmly recommended by the Democratic Governor of North Carolina and by other prominent citizens, including many of his own color in various parts of the country.

In view of such facts and of all the other signs around us, it is hopeless and puerile to insist that nothing is changed, that our politics are still those of 1850 and 1856, and to suppose that intelligent Americans, lovers of liberty and of fair play, are to be startled

AFRICAN AMERICAN HISTORY IN THE PRESS, 1851-1899

THE STREET-CAR READER.

Mr. Bang hands out his fare to an advancing shadow under the impression that it is the conductor, while his eye remains fastened on his paper.

THE SHADOW. "Tank yo', boss; you's a berry kine gemmen."

Harper's Weekly, September 25, 1886, p. 627.

and controlled by the cry that we are still practically fighting with slavery.

REV. MOSES A. HOPKINS, A.M.,

U.S. Minister and Consul-General to the Republic of Liberia.

FRANK LESLIE'S ILLUSTRATED NEWSPAPER
October 10, 1885, p. 124

In the selection of Rev. Moses A. Hopkins, of North Carolina, as United States Minister to Liberia, Secretary Bayard displayed a sagacity and superiority to old prejudices which have been only too rare in his official action. Mr. Hopkins is not only a colored man, but he was a slave, and the first of the enslaved race to receive an appointment under any Administration, since their freedom was declared, to a ministerial or diplomatic position.

Moses Aaron Hopkins was born a slave in Montgomery County, Va., on Christmas Day, 1846. In 1850 he was taken to near Newbern, Pulaski County, Va. During the late war he made his escape, and served in the Union Army as a cook, on the Ohio and Mississippi Rivers. Upon the disbandment of the Union forces, he went to Pittsburg, Pa., in October, 1865. There he secured employment and learned the English alphabet, in November of the same year. He worked to maintain himself, and studied during his spare moments, attending night-school and using other opportunities, and in this way prepared himself to enter Avery College, in Alleghany

1078

FUN-ATIC SPELLING.

"Mistah Borey, what yo' tink of de projected refo'm in spellin' dat's bein' agitated?"

"Doan b'lieve I jis un'erstan' de nater on it."

"Waal, yo' see, for instance, in de place of spellin' hoss h-o-r-s-e, in dat roun'bout way, yo' jes cut it sho't an' spell it h-o-s, like it soun's, 'liminatin' all de silent soun's."

"Ugh—hugh—seems to me dat's sensable."

Harper's Weekly, September 25, 1886, p. 628.

City, Pa. To sustain himself while attending college, he worked from four until a quarter to nine A.M., and from a quarter past three until nine P.M., daily. In 1870 he entered the Freshman Class of Lincoln University, and graduated valedictorian of his class in 1874. Choosing divinity as his profession or calling, he was stated supply of Hope Chapel in Utica, N.Y., and while so acting pursued his theological studies under Dr. Herrick Johnson in the Theological Seminary at Auburn, N.Y., and graduated with honor in the Class of 1877.

After finishing his education, he was ordained an Evangelist by the Presbytery of Baltimore. He went to Franklinton, N.C., June 14th, 1877, and built a church at White Hall, and while the church was in course of erection, conducted the largest revival ever witnessed in Louisburg. In the Fall of 1878-79 he visited Mount Pleasant Church at Franklinton. In the new church he organized Albion Academy with just six scholars. He closed its fifth annual session with *three hundred and thiry-five* pupils. Having secured the location of one of the State Normal Schools for colored teachers in Franklinton, by his untiring zeal in the cause of education for the colored race, a commodious building was erected, which is a credit to the town. He erected a school and church-building, valued at ten thousand dollars, in Franklinton, in eight years; all the churches—with one exception—with which he has been connected, have more than doubled their membership, and over two hundred persons have been converted under his ministry. He is one of the leading spirits of his Presbytery, and is well known to the General Assembly of the Presbyterian Church of the United States.

In politics, Mr. Hopkins always voted for the best man for office, and in the cause of good government,

MAINTAINING HIS SHINE.

"William Heneree! Yo' scoundred, come right out heah an' han' me my rubber outen de mud. Yo' tink I's a crane ter stan' a hour on one leg a-hollerin' for yo'? I's jest nigh tuckered out a-balancin' heah like a akerbat."

Harper's Weekly, October 9, 1886, p. 659.

CRUMPLED.

DRUSILLA (*to Cousin Miriam, down from Little Rock*). "Why, Mir'm, yo' dress is all crumpled up in de back whey yo's set on't. Trabellin' ha'd on clo'es, any—"

MIRIAM. "Laws, hain' yo' folks eber been out de woods? Dat's draped like de style is, yo' know."

Harper's Weekly, October 9, 1886, p. 659.

which of course made him enemies among his own people, but many more friends among all classes throughout the Old North State. Mr. Hopkins will sail for his post of duty on the 21st of October.

THE AUTUMN ELECTIONS

HARPER'S WEEKLY
August 14, 1886, p. 514

There is one significant aspect of the elections of this year. They will be practically uninfluenced by the consideration which has been most powerful at elections for a generation. The chief Republican reliance from the beginning has been less the argument against Democratic policy than distrust of the Democratic party. The Republican orator has recalled its traditions as the party of slavery, the Copperhead party of the war, the obstructive party during reconstruction, the party of the liquor interest and of the more ignorant and dangerous classes of the population, and his final appeal has been the question whether the obvious danger of placing the control of the government in hands which had been so recently raised against it, and of intrusting the protection of the freedmen to the residuary legatees of all the un-American and inhuman prejudices of slavery, was not wantonly to risk the safety of the country. This has been the cogent Republican appeal. For ten years the party has asked the confidence of the country upon its traditions and its illustrious services rather than upon any general and defined policy. In the language of English party contests, it has asked the country to sign a blank check in its favor. This appeal was fair, and it was usually successful until the Presidential election of 1884. The party action then raised the question whether the great and undoubted services of the party were to be held to justify the support of whatever might be proposed, including party nominations however unworthy. The Republican protest of that year was the answer. It showed that the original Republican impulse and principle survived. But its great service was not in contributing to the defeat of a particular candidate, but in showing that the election of a Democratic President did not necessarily mean disaster to the country.

This fact has now been demonstrated, and the demonstration disposes of the powerful argument of vague distrust, and restores the normal situation of a constitutional election. No man in his senses would gravely say to an intelligent audience that Mr. Cleveland, Mr. Bayard, Mr. Manning, Mr. Endicott, Mr. Whitney, Mr. Lamar, and Mr. Vilas, are less to be trusted with the honorable administration of the government than any cabinet of their predecessors. Some parts of their policy, some measures, some views, may be disapproved. That would be a matter of course, because they are Democrats. But the notion of their disloyalty, of their secret purpose to pay the rebel debt, to pension rebel soldiers, or to pursue any policy but one which is perfectly patriotic, is absurd. Not only has this more radical ground of distrust entirely vanished, but the general course of the Administration has invited public confidence. Its financial policy on all important points is cordially sustained by the most intelligent Republican as well as Democratic opinion. Its course in regard to the

WHAT THE COLORED RACE HAVE TO BE THANKFUL FOR.

"We are thankful for PRESIDENT LINCOLN'S Emancipation Proclamation, issued by his pen.
"We are thankful for GENERAL GRANT'S enforcing it by his sword.
"And we are thankful for PRESIDENT CLEVELAND'S freeing our minds from the belief that we would be enslaved again under a Democratic Administration."

Harper's Weekly, November 27, 1886, p. 769.

civil service has been more considerate of sound principle than any administration since that of John Quincy Adams, although, like that of all administrations, it has been inconsistent and illogical. Its general domestic policy in regard to the Indians and the public lands has been agreeable to public sentiment, and its foreign policy has been pacific. All this is the record of an Administration whose possible possession of power was denounced as a catastrophe to be averted at the cost of political honor and of the individual conscience. And it is this fact which has changed radically the aspect of the elections of this year.

"A MAN AND HIS BROTHER."

Harper's Weekly, December 11, 1886, p. 820.

The same fact explains the general public indifference. The intelligent voter sees that the success of neither party is essential to the safety of the country. But he sees also that the success of neither promises the enforcement of a special policy. Neither party wishes seriously to disturb the tariff, nor to change the general course of financial administration, while the best opinion of both coincides in regard to the currency and coinage, and upon the true principles of maintaining the civil service. The conclusion is that while there is no definite conflict of national policy, it is a matter of indifference whether the Congressional majority calls itself Republican or Democratic. The chief Republican argument in the campaign will be probably the infidelity of the Administration to reform, for which the speech of Senator Hoar gives the cue, and the Southern crime against a free vote and a fair count. But neither appeal will greatly disturb the general indifference, because the Republican record of administrative reform is no whiter than that of the Democratic Executive, and because Republican control of every branch of the government did not secure free voting and honest counting. The Senate is Republican, but it has not proposed any measure to correct the evil, nor thrown upon the Democratic House and Executive the responsibility of defeating or of vetoing it. Moreover, the scandals of the Payne election in Ohio, and the general consciousness that election frauds are not confined to any part of the country, will have their influence upon the voter. Whatever a man's party sympathies may be, he will concede that it is a time of personal politics. The party appeal, as such, was never so weak, and so properly weak. More than ever parties will be estimated by the personal character of candidates. That character will not be disregarded because of the supposed vital necessity of party success. In Massachusetts, for instance, the Republican party is divided upon the question of selecting Mr. W. W. Crapo or Mr. Oliver Ames as the candidate for Governor. Mr. Crapo is one of the "cleanest" and ablest of Republicans, and Mr. Ames is known mainly as a rich man, a "good fellow," and an ancient "pal" of General Butler. It is an epoch of personal politics, and if Massachusetts Republicans should decide that Mr. Ames is a better representative of Republicanism than Mr. Crapo, it is fair to assume that personal considerations, not the conviction of the importance of party success, will materially affect the result. It is a situation also in which a question like that of temperance will have a great influence upon the election. The autumn campaign will open immediately in Maine, where Mr. Blaine is announced as the chief speaker, and we shall now see the general drift of the argument.

THE SENATE

HARPER'S WEEKLY
August 14, 1886, p. 515

Senator Hoar recently said that the Senate was never of higher character than it is now, and Senator Hawley denounced as "infamous" the constant attacks of the press upon public men. Both of these Senators very properly favored an inquiry into the scandal of the Payne election in Ohio. The scandal of the Thomas confirmation might be also investigated with advantage. The character of the Senate greatly suffers from all such acts, and it is good neither for the Senate nor for the country that its conduct should seem to justify statements which are constantly made both in public and in private. Respect for the Senate is certainly not increased by such conduct as confirming Mr. Dement, whose unfitness was known, upon the ground of "Senatorial courtesy," then reconsidering the confirmation and rejecting the nomination because the plea of "Senatorial courtesy" was withdrawn, nor by rejecting Mr. Matthews, a colored Democrat, because, as Senator Ingalls is reported to have said, it would be "bad politics" for a Republican Senate to consent to confer good offices upon colored Democrats.

The Senate's reputation is in its own keeping. Such action as we mention properly diminishes public respect. There is no doubt of the existence of a general feeling that it is becoming a club of rich men, and that Senators are not sensitive to the charge of voting upon questions in which they have a pecuniary interest. To mention the fact of such feelings is not to insult Senators, but to warn them, and we have seen no more definite and temperate statement of them than the following from a correspondent of the Springfield *Republican:*

> "The fact that the millionaires on both sides voted to sustain Mr. Payne has given new force to the complaints which are so often heard now about the Senate. It is growing more and more aristocratic, more and more regardless of public opinion, more and more separate from the House, and some people say more and more corrupt. Each Senator has his personal clerk, besides all the pages and messengers of the Senate-chamber; they do not condescend to receive cards, even from the most distinguished private citizens, before two o'clock; they go into secret session and make virulent attacks upon private character, and the majority decides for itself when it will make public the reports upon contested nominations in the way to help the party. Senator Ingalls, in the debate on the legislative bill, the other day, said that the House had no right to question the appropriation for Senators' clerks. The clerks were officers of the Senate, and the House had no right to dictate how many officers the Senate should have, or what they should be paid. The indifference of the Senators to popular clamor gives them a strength in some situations which is beneficial to the country; but when this indifference goes so far that the Senate is not sensitive to charges against its own honor, and the members capable of purchasing seats (if not guilty of it) coolly refuse to investigate grave charges, people begin to ask if there is not need of some reform. The "courtesy of the Senate" made Senators almost the bosses of their State patronage during the Republican administrations, and though Cleve-

land's energetic independence has somewhat shaken the traditions, Senators are still able to stand by each other in the matter of confirmations."

OUR SOLDIERS IN THE SOUTHWEST

HARPER'S WEEKLY
August 21, 1886, p. 535

If the present or any other controversy of our government with Mexico should ever bring our soldiers in the Southwest prominently and critically into public attention, they would have no need to fear judgment of their bravery. But their manner of life would not excite envy. Their uniform would attract attention, but it would hardly be regarded as a model of military dress. Whether or not they do "thirteen dollars' worth of fighting" every month, no other men in the government's service so well earn their pay. The military service done by General Miles's troops in the Southwestern border is as onerous and as barren of opportunities for achieving renown as ever fell to soldiers in any land. They cannot attack the enemy, whip him, and be done with it. They seldom have the pleasure of a battle, but they may at any time suffer an attack. They have to do a sort of police service, which may on a sudden become warfare over a large area. The marauding Indians have no homes, no base of operations, no supplies to be cut off, no military code, no purpose or plan more definite than to wander about the mountains, to take their revenge, and to gratify their passion for cruelty. But while the Apaches can desist from fighting at any time, and retreat to renew their supplies by plunder, the soldiers must be always on guard, must subsist on scanty fare, must camp without tents, where there are no trees, and are as far removed from the luxury of life in the least attractive garrison as an explorer is from civilization.

The individual troopers that Mr. Remington presents in the accompanying illustrations are men who are never safe from death by an Apache surprise. Their camp may any night be their burial-place. But they can never be surprised out of a heroic mood. Their personal careers may have been uneventful except for their fights, but they are as far from being commonplace men as they are from being refined. . . .

The personality of many of these soldiers never passes beyond the sergeant's knowledge, and many deeds of heroism in this fitful and long war with the Apaches is never heard of beyond the camp fires of their comrades. The brave conduct of Lieutenant Clark, of the Tenth (colored) Cavalry, in rescuing, under fire, the wounded Corporal Scott, was such conduct as makes military history interesting. But for Corporal Scott's telling of the story, while he lay in the hospital, it might never have been heard outside General Miles's camp. One of Lieutenant Clark's troopers, who saw him expose himself to the fire of the enemy in an open space to rescue the wounded man, then found expression for his admiration in the most vigorous language of the camp vocabulary: "De Injuns jes fairly ploughed up de groun' wid bullets, when he run, an' never tuk no notice what was gwine on no more'n if de man 'd jes fell down in a fiel' anywhar. He'd 've fairly dusted 'way fum dar to save he own hide whole if he wa'n't a—fightin' man—fightin' man, I tell you, an' it jes do 'im good ter see a—Injun. An' he don't forgit a man in his 'stress." It is deeds of unselfish bravery like this, when done on battle-fields that whole armies are watching and war correspondents see, that make heroes of men for all the world to admire. But the admiration of his comrades is as sweet to the trooper as praise in print could be; and sweeter than either is the feeling of having done a soldier's duty. The love of such service and the satisfaction that comes of doing a dangerous duty bravely and generously are the same to the born soldier in the Southwestern mountains as on a battle-field that will become historic; and this must be why these men love this hard life.

THE COLOR LINE

HARPER'S WEEKLY
October 2, 1886, p. 631

The colored men of New England recently held a conference in Boston to protest against the injustice done to them in society, business, politics, etc., and Mr. James M. Trotter, who presided, said:

> "These conferences and conventions have ceased to do any good toward ameliorating the lot of the colored men by acting upon the sentiment of the white people of the country. The fault," he continued, "is our own more than that of any other race in the country that we are not free and independent men. The time has come when the negro should demand a whole loaf and nothing else. He has played the half-loaf game long enough. The only place to affect the politicians is at the polls."

Charles Lenox Remond, a cultivated and accomplished colored man, used to say forty years ago that he would willing be flayed alive if he could be remade with a white skin, and an intelligent colored farm laborer—the cleverest hand in the field—said that it was of no use for him to be skilful or honest or intelligent or industrious, because he was always accounted "a d—d nigger."

1084

There was never a race whose fate was so tragic, because their color is accepted as a proof of inferiority. Happily it has ceased in this country to be also the badge of a servile race. But it will be long before the prejudice—for it is nothing more—disappears.

The advice of Mr. Trotter means apparently that the colored men should vote for the party which will "recognize" them most fully. This means the party that will give them offices. That, however, is a course which would not raise them in their own respect nor in that of the community. It would be merely a price paid for votes—a bribe. It would not correct the injustice which colored men feel to be done to them in society, business, politics, etc. This is a relief which no protest or law or office or any other device can suddenly remove. There must be, of course, perfect equality before the law. The State, as such, must make no discrimination. But the prejudice, which is the real grievance, will disappear only before the fact of self-respect, energy, industry, and intelligence. The same course which is best for all other citizens in this country is best for colored citizens, so long as the laws do not discriminate against them, namely, not to insist upon any distinction or difference of race, but to regard themselves as equal American citizens, and "live down" prejudice.

CHESTER ALAN ARTHUR

HARPER'S WEEKLY
November 27, 1886, p. 767

Ex-President Arthur was one of the many men of distinction born in the United States of Irish parentage. His father, the Rev. William Arthur, came in early youth to this country from the County Antrim. He was a clergyman of the Baptist denomination, a man of much learning, and by taste and research an antiquarian. Chester Alan, his eldest son, was born October 5, 1830, in Fairfield, Franklin County, Vermont, and was educated at the schools of various places in or near which the father was pastor. He entered Union College, at Schenectady, New York, at the early age of fifteen, and graduated four years later, though he was two winters absent teaching school. He was a good student, and took the highest honors in his class, being, moreover, a "popular" man in college, and already an ardent politician of the college type. The next four years were spent in the study of law and in teaching, and in 1853 young Arthur, then just twenty-three, became a partner in the law firm of Culver, Parker, & Arthur, in the city of New York, of which the Hon. E.D. Culver was the chief. This gentleman is still well remembered for his ability as a lawyer, and for his zeal in the antislavery cause. Mr. Arthur found in the office when he entered it, the "Lemmon slave case," which was afterward to become one of the most noted of the time, and in some regards one of the most important, and in which he was destined to take an active part. It was the case of one Lemmon, of Virginia, who brought eight slaves with him to this city *en route* to Texas, and lost them by a writ of *habeas corpus,* which Mr. Culver, with Mr. John Jay, secured. Virginia was, of course, intensely excited, and took measures to carry the case to the higher courts. The State of New York took up the defence, and Mr. Arthur was made State's Attorney in the proceedings. He continued his connection with it to the end, when the Court of Appeals confirmed the action of the lower court. But by this time—1862—the matter was merged in that dread arbitrament to which the slave power had appealed, and Mr. Arthur was supplying arguments for freedom in the shape of a regiment a day, equipped and armed and sent to the front.

It was while in the firm with Mr. Culver, also, that Mr. Arthur undertook the case of Lizzie Jennings, a colored woman who sued for damages for ejection by force from a Fourth Avenue street car. He won the case, and from that time colored people enjoyed rights that had been previously almost wholly denied them. . . .

He was elected, and succeeded to the Presidential office September 20, 1881, on the death of President Garfield. His career as President is too familiar to need recital. It was marked by a very conservative and candid tone in foreign affairs, which was of great service to the country in matters in which a dangerously zealous policy had been previously pursued, and by great firmness and integrity in financial policy. It was also distinguished by his signature of the Civil Service Reform Act, January 14, 1883, and by the establishment of the Civil Service Commission. The President's health, which had been severely strained by the death of his wife in 1880, never permitted him to enter very actively into politics or business after the close of his term, and he lived in dignified retirement. He died on the morning of November 18, at his residence in New York city, leaving a son aged twenty-one and a daughter aged fourteen.

1887

The remaining years of the 1880s marked a significant turning point in the ideologies of traditional allies on race relations and racial accountability. As the Solid South matured, it appeared to be no longer tasteful to conduct sectional tirades, for the national public dialogue on regionalism had become more conservative and accommodative. The urgency of the race question had been eliminated as the issue was removed from the country's overt consciousness.

By 1887 the Democratic party had assumed home rule in the South and was preparing to convene statewide constitutional conventions to legally recognize discrimination and segregation. The ascendancy of the Democratic power was evident in national campaigns as former confederates crisscrossed the country stump speaking for northern Democratic candidates. Liberal Republicans joined with southern industrialists to create a New South full of new wealth and promise. In return each section sought common ground to develop trust and unity.

Military heroes of both parties campaigned for offices that were local, state and national, including the White House. Prominent Republicans like William T. Sherman lectured on the financial crisis of the nation—taxation, protective tariffs—while calling for a new look at the southern question. All debates on the black male's readiness for the ballot were deferred to southerners as the center of the Republican party moved. Now Republicans saw voting by blacks as empowering an ignorant and an unintelligent class of people, who were always opened to collusion and corruption. The situation in the southern region, they maintained, should be completely deferred to the states, for past efforts to "assure freedom and citizenship [to African Americans] had proven that these were not national issues, but state ones." In defending the South's constitutional right to restrict the ballot, Republicans called on blacks to *accept this reality but to remain hopeful that ultimately the South would produce a new leadership who would initiate inclusion of all southerners into the body politic. It was essential that blacks be prepared for this futuristic opportunity through manual and industrial arts education. For those black leaders who demanded immediate, full equality, the party offered emigration as the most logical option.*

Emigration was an option many blacks were eagerly choosing, minus any nudging from their former allies, the Republicans. Limited economic opportunities and the prominence of mob violence augmented the numbers who migrated west to create all black towns or others who supported missionary emigration to Africa under the auspices of Bishop Turner. These decisions to separate physically from their native lands were options conceived by African Americans in addressing the color line. Nuvovo Republicanism was never a variable in this equation.

African American institutions came under seige. Buffoons, sapphires, and ignorant philosophes were overused stereotypes in belaboring the race's inferiority. This inferiority became one of the reasons the Republicans deferred to the strategy of "waiting"—waiting until local public opinion would become enlightened on the constitutional rights of all U.S. citizens. This process also served to underpin the policy of non-interference by federal officials, even to protect its citizens whose civil rights were known to be violated.

Secondly, organization within the African American community was not only scrutinized, but viciously attacked. Such activism, the papers chastised, openly invited corruption and class division within the race. The black middle class had established the African American League specifically to confront racism. Like other interest groups, the organization's agenda was disseminated to politicians who sought the black vote and those who represented districts heavily populated by blacks. Blacks were warned that such protest for change was "extreme folly." The black community had to grasp that such actions were for personal patronage only. Collusion with unscrupulous partners would only agonize southern whites, possibly escalating into more violence. Instead, the papers called on the more sober race leaders of the South to console and convince their race to adopt the realistic policy of "watching and waiting."

The papers do condemn the Georgia General Assembly for a proposed bill concerning Atlanta University. The institution's white faculty violated the state's segregation laws by permitting integration. The state's annual appropriation of $8,000 gave the legislature the right to propose that teachers and others should be fined, imprisoned or placed on the chain gang for violating the law. The writers were stunned. Atlanta University was an admirable institution, providing the "best technical, agricultural, and industrial education," producing students who be-

came leaders, who then trained other leaders. The papers feared that the proposed drastic measure would only stimulate more racial hostility.

Again, we travel with white adventurers as they track across the South, mesmerized by some facet of African American culture. One journalist visited a voodoo ceremony in New Orleans. As chronicled, the ceremony allegedly entailed "human and animal sacrifices and scenes of indecent license." The writer soon abandoned the narrative when he became overwhelmed by the presence of many whites. Struck by the presence of a lone young white female, he decided to serve as her guard from possible magical obsession. One leaves this expose re-enforced with familiar stereotypes of black life and culture, even among the race's intelligence.

The year does not conclude before the "southern question" is again revisited. In this continuous diatribe—black suffrage—the northern papers now understand the need for the Solid South—"the solidification of the white vote in the southern states was due to the instinct of self preservation against a government based upon ignorance and corruption." For the author, the only way to restore unity is to guarantee that the region would not suffer national interference. White southerners resisted because of the solidarity of the African American vote for one party. This collective vote ensured the election of candidates who supported black issues, opening the possibility of the return of black ascendancy. Such a threat to white supremacy ignited mob violence. Such "extreme difficulties," the authors stated, "can be avoided with cordial cooperation with the sentiment of the region; southern white Democratic sentiments which aim(ed) at the most friendly possible relations [among] the races."

Jacqueline A. Rouse
Georgia State University

TWO PIONEERS

HARPER'S WEEKLY
January 29, 1887, p. 71

The newspapers recently announced on the same morning the death of two of the conspicuous pioneers in the antislavery agitation—Henry B. Stanton and Abby Kelley Foster. They were both old, and both had seen the emancipation for which they labored with an eloquence that aroused and directed public opinion. Abby Kelley was one of the earliest and most effective of the antislavery women who went upon the platform. She married Stephen S. Foster, who was no less earnest in his convictions and speech, and who indeed was a figure of the sternest Puritan epoch appearing in a later day. Their reputation was limited to the antislavery circle, and their names would be little known beyond the line of the abolition tradition. But within it they are very familiar.

Mr. Stanton was one of the first and one of the most eloquent and effective of the antislavery orators. But he had a taste for politics which was not shared by Garrison and many of his friends, and which with the woman question, and especially the church question, and the "isms" which abounded and were adopted by many of the early abolitionists, led to the "new organization," which was the great schism in the abolition ranks. Mr. Stanton approved political action, and he passed through the various degrees of antislavery politics, the Liberty party, and the Barnburners, into the Republican party. . . .

THE INDUSTRIAL SOUTH
Atlanta, Georgia.

HARPER'S WEEKLY
February 12, 1887, p. 111

The "Gate City," the "Capital City of the Empire State of the South," the "Chicago of the South," the "Phoenix City," the "Progressive City," the "City of Men and Ideas." These names, and many more equally significant of the position held by the city, and of its wonderful progress and prosperity, are bestowed upon Atlanta by its inhabitants, and are generally accepted as well-deserved titles by strangers who have familiarized themselves with its history. In the year 1835 the people of Georgia determined to build a trunk line of railway to the Northwest. After much opposition a bill was adopted by the Legislature, and signed by Governor Schley, authorizing the construction of a railroad from the Tennessee line, near the Tennessee River, to the southwestern bank of the Chattahoochee River, at a point most eligible for the running of branch roads thence to Athens, Madison, Milledgeville, Forsyth, and Columbus. This road was the Western and Atlantic, which now connects Atlanta with Chattanooga, and the engineer in charge of its construction selected a site among the breezy uplands, seven miles from the Chattahoochee River, as the most suitable place from which to build branch railroads to all parts of the South. The point thus selected was named Terminus—a name which, in 1844, was changed to Marthasville, and in 1847 to Atlanta. In 1836 Mr. Hardy Ivy built a log shanty, which was the first house erected within the present city limits. The first store was opened in 1843, and during the same year the first locomotive made its appearance on the new railroad. The branch roads from the trunk line were built as rapidly as the resources of the country would allow, and from 1846 to 1864 the growth of Atlanta was steady and prosperous, though by no means remarkable....

The Atlanta of to-day is a city of over 60,000 inhabitants, who are as full of life, energy, and progressive ideas as any community in the North or West. Eight railroads centre in its Union Depot, which has indeed become a gateway to the South. It is a city of well-paved, well-lighted, and well-drained streets, handsome public buildings and business blocks, and, above all, of beautiful private residences. On both sides of Peachtree Street these are being built in such numbers that it is rapidly becoming to Atlanta what Euclid Avenue is to Cleveland....

Atlanta was the first Southern city to prohibit the sale of intoxicating liquor within its corporate limits, and its experiment in this direction is being watched with the greatest interest by the whole country. Its sixty thousand people support seventy-one churches, and send six thousand children to its public schools, which are model institutions of their kind. The city has expended more than a million of dollars upon free colored schools, which are upon exactly the same basis as those for white children. Clark University, the colored college of the city, receives an annual appropriation of eight thousand dollars from the State, which also allows the State University for white students the same amount, and no more. The State Technological School has been located in Atlanta, the city giving $150,000 toward its buildings and equipment. It will be maintained by the State, and be conducted upon the most approved models of similar schools throughout the country. The tendency of the negro schools and colleges of the city is also toward practical education and manual training, in which subject the citizens of Atlanta take a most lively interest....

SCENE IN A GEORGIA VILLAGE DURING THE COTTON SEASON

HARPER'S WEEKLY
February 12, 1887, p. 111

Nothing could be more characteristic of the rural South than a view during the cotton season such as is shown on the front page of our Supplement. During the month of October the season fairly begins, and continues through the winter months. Early in the morning the different avenues leading into town are alive with little caravans of varied and picturesque teams. The wagons of the more prosperous are drawn by healthy mules and horses, pulling five or six bales of cotton; while the "turn-outs" of the poorer classes often show a strange combination of oxen and mules, harnessed side by side, struggling in friendly rivalry—with two or three bales—to reach their destination. The negro farmer generally brings up the rear with a rudely made cart, pulled either by a dyspeptic mule or a contrary "gentleman cow," whereon is placed the hard earnings of the year, in the shape of one bale of cotton, besides eggs, butter, chickens, and other barter. As this amusing procession slowly winds its way over the road of red clay soil, fringed with rail fences, all are happy alike in the anticipation of bargain and sale.

Before mid-day the square in front of the county court-house is reached, and there the countrymen are met by the cotton buyers, who sample the staple, classify it, and soon effect a trade. The bales are then taken to a warehouse, weighed, the farmer receives his pay, and immediately becomes a favorite with the proprietors of the village stores, where various wares and goods are displayed in profusion. Possibly last year's guano bill has to be paid, or a supply of bacon procured, but the purchase generally includes a little of everything that can be bought, including calicoes and ribbons "for the old woman and the gals." Those who fairly represent the New South, however, are able to place the bulk of their receipts in bank, or invest part of the money in new and improved farming implements.

The farmer of to-day is more progressive than formerly, and is experimenting with diversified products. The time has been when only cotton was cultivated, but the younger men, instead of buying Western meat, are raising their own pork and all produce necessary for home consumption. In many instances the colored farmer tills his own land, and though his acres are few and the yield small, yet his needs are in proportion, and by industry and good management at the end of each succeeding year he makes plenty to eat and wear, after having contributed his "one bale" among the millions.

MR. SHERMAN AT NASHVILLE

HARPER'S WEEKLY
April 9, 1887, p. 250

Mr. Sherman's speeches are always worthy of attention. He is a public man of great experience, of acknowledged ability and sagacity, and of a fortunate temperament for public life. His recent speech at Nashville is an important event, because it was evidently very carefully considered, because it is the first speech in that part of the country by a Republican leader of Mr. Sherman's eminence, and because its tone shows a profound change in the temper of political controversy. The "bloody shirt" has disappeared. Mr. Sherman says, "No man in the North questions the honesty of purpose or the heroism with which the Confederates maintained their cause, and you will give credit for like courage and honorable motives to the Union soldiers North and South." He admits that "it is conceded that under the limitations of the Constitution the rights of the citizen of a State can only be enforced through State or national tribunals," and that the national enforcement has thus far failed; and he trusts that the wrongs which are still practised in "the black counties" will be speedily redressed by the people of the States in which they are perpetrated. The tone and significance of all this are very different from those of Mr. Blaine's speech at Augusta in the bitter moment of his defeat in 1884. The first part of Mr. Sherman's address is conceived and expressed with very great sagacity and skill. Tennessee was an old Whig State. Mr. Sherman was an old Whig. He treats the slavery debate and the war as an honest difference which is now happily passed. Those disturbing questions are settled, and the questions of the hour

AN ECONOMIST OF LIFE.
UNCLE ABRA'M (*reading*). "'De brack murd'rer ob Jer'miah Johnsing pays de oxtreme pendlety ob de law.' Now, dat's what I nebber could onderstan' nowhow. Why'd 'ey wait till de murderin's all dun 'fo' dey hang 'im? 'Pears like 't 'ud be pow'ful sight better to hang de murd'rer b'fo' he kill sumbody; den dey save *one* nigger, sho'."

Harper's Weekly, February 19, 1887, p. 139.

can be most satisfactorily solved by the old Whig policy of the Republican party.

After his careful and temperate treatment of the situation since the formation of the Republican party, and his expression of admiration of the rapid development of the various industries of the Southern States, Mr. Sherman proceeds to unfold his policy, which he commends with great art to the changed condition and sentiment of the Southern States. It is in substance a general policy of protection and paternalism. Mr. Sherman holds that the national questions which should be alone discussed are taxation, currency, public debt, foreign and domestic commerce, education, internal improvements, and, chief of all, the mode of national taxation. It is not a free vote or the Confederacy in the saddle, but the mode of levying duties on imported goods, which is "the main issue between the Republican and Democratic parties." He says that "the Republican idea is practically embodied in the tariff laws as they now exist." But these laws now produce an enormous surplus, and Senator Sherman condemns a Democratic House for practically defeating the Blair educational bill. His policy, then, for reducing the surplus is that of distribution among the States, and not revision of the tariff. Indeed, the Senator's exhortation to Tennessee and to the Southern States is, in brief, "Let us be friends, and maintain a high protective tariff." His speech discards all sectional appeal, leaves the question of the rights of colored citizens to the several States, while frankly asserting that the Republican party is pledged to

A SPENDTHRIFT IN KILLING.

"An' yer brudder's done got drown' in de pond skatin', is he? Well, dat nigger 'll be de deaf of me yit! He's forebber an' etarnally gittin' killed some way er udder. Jes let me git my han's on him once and I'll knock de life outer him, de triflin' rascal!"

Harper's Weekly, February 19, 1887, p. 139.

the maintenance of these rights in every constitutional way, and declares the tariff to be the great issue of the hour.

This is exceedingly adroit, because it presents Mr. Sherman as the one prominent Republican leader who concedes that the negro question is not an actual issue, and who urges the national fostering care of the new industries which are everywhere arising in the Southern States. At the same time it forces the Democratic party to a declaration upon the tariff for which it is not prepared, and upon which, if made, it could not act in concert. But while Mr. Sherman's speech shows that he apprehends clearly the situation in the Southern States, it shows with equal clearness that he does not fully understand the Northern situation. He leaves wholly out of account the currents of opinion which have thrown the Republican party out of power: the change of sentiment in regard to high protection; the demand for administrative reform; the hostility to the political ascendency of the liquor interest; the belief that liberal national expenditures for every kind of purpose under the head of the general welfare necessarily involve enormous corruption and extravagance. These opinions played a great part in the defeat of Mr. Blaine, and Mr. Sherman, with all his sagacity and ability, has never shown himself to be in sympathy with the progressive impulse of his party. In 1884, he treated the significant bolt which defeated the party only with petulance and irritation, as a whimsical, ill-tempered, and outrageous folly. It was not creditable to a man of Mr. Sherman's ability to misconceive so

totally a movement of which he now undoubtedly perceives the importance. The same want of perception is shown in his present sneers at the President. Mr Sherman misstates the fact when he says that the Administration has made no proposition to reduce the surplus, and he is evidently unaware of the strong hold that the President has taken of "the plain people," by the obvious good sense and intelligent uprightness of his course. His vetoes of the dependent pension bill, and of individual pension bills, and of the Texas seed bill, and his appointment of the Inter-State Commerce Commissioners, are recent illustrations of an independent and able and patriotic discharge of public duty which have impressed the country in a way which no passing sneer even of so distinguished an opponent as Mr. Sherman can affect. None the less, the Senator's speech is a very significant manifesto, and it is sustained by a public confidence in his personal integrity which makes him a very conspicuous figure in view of the approach of the "Presidential year."

JEFFERSON DAVIS AT MERIDIAN

HARPER'S WEEKLY
June 4, 1887, p. 399

The recent speech of Jefferson Davis at Meridian, in Mississippi, was remarkable for his apparent adhesion at last to "accomplished facts." He was greeted with the usual enthusiasm, and in his speech at the dinner he said that "the army and navy of the South" were composed of patriots who "bared their breasts to bullets in defending constitutional rights," and he recalled the scenes, familiar to all parts of the country during the civil war, of partings with brave sons, husbands, lovers, marching away to war.

The speech was short, and ended with these words:

"But now these scenes and incidents have passed, and they only live in minds and history. United you are now, and if the Union is ever to be broken, let the other side break it. The army of the South will shine forever around the camp fires, and will still shine to our children and our children's children. The truths we fought for shall not encourage you to ever fight again; but keep your word in good or evil. God bless you all!"

From Jefferson Davis these are certainly remarkable words. Following those of Mr. Lamar at Charleston, they

As Different as Black from White.

As different as black from white are the CUTICURA REMEDIES from all other remedies for the treatment of diseases of the skin, scalp, and blood, with loss of hair.

CUTICURA, the great Skin Cure, and CUTICURA SOAP, an exquisite Skin Beautifier, prepared from it, externally, and CUTICURA RESOLVENT, the new Blood Purifier, internally, are a positive cure for every form of skin and blood disease, from pimples to scrofula.

CUTICURA REMEDIES are the greatest medicines on earth. Had the worst case of Salt Rheum in this country. My mother had it twenty years, and in fact died from it. I believe CUTICURA would have saved her life. My arms, breast, and head were covered for three years, which nothing relieved or cured until I used the CUTICURA RESOLVENT, internally, and CUTICURA and CUTICURA SOAP, externally. J. W. ADAMS, Newark, O.

Your CUTICURA REMEDIES performed a wonderful cure last summer on one of our customers, an old gentlemen of seventy years of age, who suffered with a fearfully distressing eruption on his head and face, and who had tried all remedies and doctors to no purpose.
J. F. SMITH & CO., Texarkana, Ark.

CUTICURA REMEDIES are absolutely pure, and the only infallible skin beautifiers and blood purifiers.

☞ Send for "How to Cure Skin Diseases," 64 pages, 50 illustrations, and 100 testimonials.

PIMPLES, blackheads, chapped and oily skin prevented by CUTICURA MEDICATED SOAP.

I have been afflicted since last March with a Skin disease the doctors called Eczema. My face was covered with scabs and sores, and the itching and burning were almost unbearable. Seeing your CUTICURA REMEDIES so highly recommended, concluded to give them a trial, using the CUTICURA and CUTICURA SOAP externally, and RESOLVENT internally, for four months. I call myself cured, in gratitude for which I make this public statement.
MRS. CLARA A. FREDERICK,
Broad Brook, Conn.

I must extend to you the thanks of one of my customers, who has been cured, by using the CUTICURA REMEDIES, of an old sore, caused by a long spell of sickness or fever eight years ago. He was so bad he was fearful he would have to have his leg amputated, but is happy to say he is now entirely well — sound as a dollar. He requests me to use his name, which is H. H. CASSON, merchant, of this place.
JOHN V. MINOR, Druggist,
Gainsboro, Tenn.

H. E. Carpenter, Henderson, N. Y., cured of Psoriasis or Leprosy, of twenty years' standing, by CUTICURA REMEDIES, the most wonderful cure on record. A dustpanful of scales fell from him daily. Physicians and his friends thought he must die.

Sold everywhere. Price, CUTICURA, 50c.; SOAP, 25c.; RESOLVENT, $1. Prepared by the POTTER DRUG AND CHEMICAL CO., Boston, Mass.

BABY'S Skin and Scalp preserved and beautified by CUTICURA MEDICATED SOAP.

Harper's Weekly, April 9, 1887, p. 263.

---

show how completely the war is passed, and that even its Confederate chief now relinquishes the useless contention. The "Southern question" really disappears from practical politics. There are great wrongs undoubtedly which still survive, but they are not remediable by national laws, and cannot therefore be made the basis of national parties until some party proposes a remedial policy. The Supreme Court, which cannot be supposed to sympathize with injustice toward the freedmen, declares that the remedy lies in the State or national courts, and Senator Sherman adds that if these fail, emigration alone remains.

ABSTRACTION NOT SUBTRACTION.

Friend who has been laboring to supply deficiencies in his fellow-porter's arithmetic—subtraction is under consideration.—*Loq.*: "Well, now, s'pose you wuz to len' Harris Jones fif'—"

PUPIL. "*Naw*, sah! naw, *sah!* I ainter gwine to s'pose to len' Harris Jones fif' dollars 'bout nuttin."

INSTRUCTOR. "Well, den, s'pose he wuz to borry fif' dollars from *me*, and arter I done count 'em out, I diskivers dat I done give him *three* twenty-dollar notes. How much is dat too much, an' how much must he give me back?"

PUPIL. "Well, sah, ef you wuz fool enough to len' dat sassy darkey money, you wouldn' get none of it back, *nevar*."

Harper's Weekly, May 14, 1887, p. 355.

But there are sagacious and intelligent colored leaders in the Southern States who hold that the course of events will develop political differences among the white citizens which will open a way to the free but divided vote of the colored citizens. Such leaders agree that Congress can do little to affect the situation, and that the States, like South Carolina, where the colored population, although in the majority, has not the intelligence or the power of leadership, must leave to time and the good influences of increasing mutual confidence the final adjustment of the relations of race. This result will be hastened by the disappearance of sectional animosity, and to that end no surrender of principle upon either side is necessary.

PERSONAL

HARPER'S WEEKLY
June 4, 1887, p. 399

Bishop W.H. Hillery, of the African Methodist Church of Tennessee, is in San Francisco, engaged in raising funds for the education of the colored people of the South. . . .

The King of the Tonga Islands dresses in well-made European clothes which set off his handsome figure, but he can get no civilized shoes to fit him, because his feet are so large and have so enormous a development of heel. His subjects have recently been worrying the Wesleyan missionaries, who have long exercised a controlling influence on the islands. They tried to assassinate the Premier, who is a missionary, and they have looted some of the mission stations.

THE SOUTHERN QUESTION

HARPER'S WEEKLY
June 18, 1887, p. 434

The speech of Mr. Sherman at Springfield brings forward prominently as an issue of the election next year the question of colored suffrage in parts of the Southern States. In his speech at Nashville Mr. Sherman treated this question as follows:

> "Both sides felt that the abolition of slavery was the necessary result of the war, and it seemed to us, if the slaves were to be free, they must be armed with the privileges of freemen, and these were secured to them by constitutional amendments. The attempt to enforce these rights by national authorities has thus far partially failed, and it is now conceded that under the limitations of the Constitution the rights of the citizen of a State can only be enforced through the State or national tribunals, and where public opinion is intolerant, and jurors will not do their duty, a citizen, either white or black, may be without remedy for the grossest wrong, except the right to migrate where his rights will be respected. Our institutions are based upon the idea that such denial of rights is impossible, and I trust that the time is not far distant when the people of every State will feel it to be both just and expedient that every citizen of the State shall be protected in the free and equal enjoyment of every right and privilege conferred by the Constitution of the United States. The Republican party is pledged to this policy, and though it will use no unconstitutional means to secure it, would be false to its principles if it does not use all its moral and legal power to that end."

Mr. Sherman quoted a remark of Senator Vest that a Southern white man who would wrong the colored citizen deserved "to be blotted from the roll of manhood"; and Mr. Sherman added that if this were so, we might appeal to the manly spirit of our own race to protect the freedmen. And having said this, Mr. Sherman proceeded: "And now, fellow-citizens, I gladly turn to those questions of national politics which alike affect all parts of our country, and which alone ought to be the subject of political discussion." He went on to mention them, and he held the question of national taxation to be the most important of all, but he did not even mention protecting colored suffrage.

At Springfield, however, such wrong and protection against it seem to him one of the most vital and pressing of public questions. In his Springfield speech Mr. Sherman admits that the Republicans did not deal with the question under General Grant's administration, and that the Force Bill was not passed by a Republican Congress because of Republican sentiment in the Northern States against it. Moreover, President Arthur treated the question as practically settled, so far as the national government was concerned, and a Republican Supreme Court could not sustain the constitutionality of the acts that were passed to protect the rights of the freedmen in the States. All these facts show, not that these were not wrongs, but that the remedy for them was not national, and could not therefore be made a subject of national politics. Mr. Sherman was a member of the cabinet of President Hayes. Did that Administration urge any positive or restrictive policy upon the subject? Was not the Administration virtually denounced by Mr. Blaine as even discriminating in favor of the "rebel" side in certain questions of the election in Southern States? Are the Republicans prepared to define in the campaign of next year a measure which they will sustain to redress the wrongs mentioned by Mr. Sherman? If the situation be, indeed, as he described it at Nashville, if the only constitutional remedy lies in the courts or in emigration, and in the enlightenment of local public opinion, is the Springfield speech an illustration of the manner in which local public opinion can best be influenced to right the wrongs?

What is the Southern question? It is essentially one of the gravest and most vital that can concern any community, for it is substantially the question whether where the colored vote is largely in the majority, and is cast all together, the community shall be placed under the government of its most ignorant class, recently emancipated from a dehumanizing slavery, and led by unscrupulous chiefs. The pitiless cruelty of slavery was not a good school for the exercise of political supremacy in an otherwise highly civilized community, and the situation in some parts of the Southern States is one which, could it be reproduced in the Northern States, would not be tolerated. Relief would be sought and found under law or over law, and that is what is done in such communities in the Southern States. There is plainly a deprivation of rights conferred by law. But would any humane and intelligent Republican say that the power of the United States should be employed to compel submission to an endless rule like that of Moses in South Carolina? Republicans could not and would not say so, and therefore the Force Bill was not passed, and it is to the credit of Mr. Blaine that he opposed it, although he insisted afterward that if Mr. Hayes was elected, so was the Republican Governor. The most intelligent colored citizens in the Southern States do not look to national interference to secure their complete political rights, but to the differences that will spring up among the dominant voters in the State when they are not united by fear of colored ascendency. And one point is clear and conclusive: either the power to correct an acknowledged deprivation of legal political rights in the State should be given to the national government, if it does not now possess it, or if such power cannot be constitutionally given, and if its exercise, should it be conferred, would not be justified by the rest of the country, the demand for such power should cease, and with the relegation of the subject to the State and to the control of its public opinion the action of all good citizens elsewhere should be directed to affecting that public opinion toward practical relief. Calling Southerners rebels and the Democratic party the left wing of the new Confederate army will neither help the colored citizens nor redress any wrong, and if that kind of rhetoric did not rally Republicans a dozen years ago to support the Force Bill, it will hardly carry an election now.

THE AFRO-AMERICAN LEAGUE

HARPER'S WEEKLY
June 25, 1887, p. 450

The New York *Freeman* is a journal earnestly devoted to the interests of colored citizens, and its editor urges strongly a national defensive and protective organization of such citizens, which he proposes to call "The Afro-American League." The reasons that he states for the formation of such a league are, first, the suppression of the colored ballot in the Southern States; second, "the universal and lamentable reign of lynch and mob law," of which in the Southern States the colored citizens are the victims; third, the unequal distribution of school funds; fourth, "the odious and demoralizing penitentiary system of the South"; fifth, "the almost universal tyranny of common carrier corporations in the South"; sixth, the distinction of color in hotels and places of amusement.

The object of the League will be to procure a repeal of all laws which support any of these abuses, and to correct public opinion where that is the basis of the wrong. But all the wrongs alleged are remediable only by the States, unless a State can be shown to authorize the denial or abridgment of the right to vote on account of color. The editor of the *Freeman* therefore says that the stronghold of the proposed League should be in the Southern States, while in the North and West its object must be to correct the public opinion which in those States still disregards the fair claims of colored citizens. This situation, however, he says, is very much worse in the Southern States. The methods of the League are not defined in the statement, but they are plainly implied: "We have controlled a million of votes annually for twenty years, and what have we to show for them? Where are the colored men who have been honored above their fellows by the men we have placed in high position?" This would seem to mean, as we recently stated, that the colored vote is to be thrown with the party that promises to carry out the several purposes of the League. Among those purposes, however, office-holding is not specifically mentioned, but election and appointment to office would be regarded probably as evidence of the change of public opinion which is held to be essential to secure the objects sought. Could this general plan be carried into effect, the result probably would not be what the editor of the *Freeman* anticipates. It would end in the organization of a large body of voters of African descent offering their votes in consideration of benefit to them as a class. Would it not necessarily result, in the Northern States, in the purchase of a few offices, and so stigmatize such voters as a mere mercenary class, whose conduct would necessarily produce immense and perilous corruption? This would neither foster the self-respect of colored citizens nor heighten the estimation in which they are held by white citizens.

The laws of the Northern States make all citizens equal, except women. If injustice were done by those laws to any class of citizens, nothing could be more natural and proper than their union to procure a change in the laws. But that is not the case, and political union to cope with prejudice would be unavailing. In the Southern States, however, a union of colored voters to secure the change of laws which discriminate against colored citizens is the American method of redress. But such voters must distinguish between legal wrongs and wrongs which are due to prejudice and which are not remediable by law. The suppression of the colored vote, wherever it occurs, is now accomplished, not by violence, but by the contrivances of law. The cause of the suppression is two-fold—traditional class prejudice, and the instinctive unwillingness of intelligence to submit to the domination of ignorance viciously and corruptly controlled. It is a very grave and difficult problem. But it is one which cannot be solved by national action. It is, indeed, not so bad as slavery. But even slavery was declared by the Republican party to be the concern of the State, not of the nation, and it attempted no direct interference. Meanwhile, however, we suppose that the situation is understood by the colored leaders in the Southern States, who feel that, under the actual circumstances, their policy is watching and waiting. Practically, in the only part of the country where a league is desirable it exists already. It seems to us that the real evil which produces the situation that the League would aim to remedy is not amenable to political treatment, and that such an organization would disappoint its founders.

A VOUDOO DANCE

HARPER'S WEEKLY
June 25, 1887, pp. 454–55

There was nothing mysterious about it. The ceremony took place in broad day, at noon, in the upper chambers of a small frame house in a street just beyond Congo Square and the old Parish prison in New Orleans. It was an incantation rather than a dance—a curious mingling of African Voudoo rites with modern "spiritualism" and faith-cure.

The explanation of Voudooism (or Vaudouism) would require a chapter by itself. It is sufficient to say for the purpose of this paper that the barbaric rites of Voudooism originated with the Congo and Guinea negroes, were brought to San Domingo, and thence to Louisiana. In Hayti the sect is in full vigor, and its midnight orgies have reverted more and more to the barbaric original in the last twenty-five years. The wild dance and incantations are accompanied by sacrifice of animals and occasionally of infants, and with cannibalism, and scenes of most indecent license. In its origin it is serpent worship. The Voudoo signifies a being all-powerful on the earth, who is, or is represented by, a harmless species of serpent (*couleuvre*), and in this belief the sect perform rites in which the serpent is propitiated. In common parlance, the chief actor is called the Voudoo—if a man, the Voudoo King; if a woman, the Voudoo Queen. Some years ago Congo Square was the scene of the weird midnight rites of this sect, as unrestrained and barbarous as ever took place in the Congo country. All these semi-public performances have been suppressed, and all private assemblies for this worship are illegal, and broken up by the police when discovered. It is said in New Orleans that Voudooism is a thing of the past. But the superstition remains, and I believe that very few of the colored people in New Orleans are free from it—that is, free from it as a superstition. Those who repudiate it, have nothing to do with it, and regard it as only evil, still ascribe power to the Voudoo, to some ugly old woman or man, who is popularly believed to have occult power (as the Italians believe in the "evil-eye"), can cast a charm and put the victims under a spell, or by incantations relieve them from it. The power of the Voudoo is still feared by many who are too intelligent to believe in it intellectually. That persons are still Voudooed, probably few doubt; and that people are injured by charms secretly placed in their beds, or are bewitched in various ways, is common belief—more common than the Saxon notion that it is ill luck to see the new moon over the left shoulder.

Although very few white people in New Orleans have ever seen the performance I shall try to describe, and it is said that the police would break it up if they knew of it, it takes place every Wednesday at noon at the house where I saw it; and there are three or four other places in the city where the rites are celebrated, sometimes at night. Our admission was procured through a friend who had, I suppose, vouched for our good intentions.

We were received in the living-rooms of the house on the ground-floor, by the "doctor," a good-looking mulatto of middle age, clad in a white shirt with gold studs, linen pantaloons, and list slippers. He had the simple-minded shrewd look of a "healing medium." The interior was neat, though in some confusion; among the rude attempts at art on the walls was the worst chromo print of General Grant that was probably ever made. There were several negroes about the door, many in the rooms and in the back yard, and all had an air of expectation and mild excitement. After we had satisfied the scruples of the doctor, and signed our names in his register, we were invited to ascend by a narrow, crooked stairway in the rear. This led to a small landing where a dozen people might stand, and from this a door opened into a chamber perhaps fifteen feet by ten, where the rites were to take place; beyond this was a small bedroom. Around the sides of these rooms were benches and chairs, and the close quarters were already well filled.

The assembly was perfectly orderly, but a motley one, and the women largely outnumbered the men. There were coal-black negroes, porters, and stevedores, fat cooks, slender chamber-maids, all shades of complexion, yellow girls and comely quadroons, most of them in common servant attire, but some neatly dressed. And among them were, to my surprise, several white people.

On one side of the middle room where we sat was constructed a sort of buffet or bureau, used as an altar. On it stood an image of the Virgin Mary in painted plaster, about two feet high, flanked by lighted candles and a couple of cruets, with some other small objects. On a shelf below were two other candles, and on this shelf and the floor in front were various offerings to be used in the rites—plates of apples, grapes, bananas, oranges; dishes of sugar, of sugar-plums; a dish of powdered orris root, packages of candles, bottles of brandy and of water. Two other lighted candles stood on the floor, and in front an earthen bowl. The clear space in front for the dancer was not more than four or five feet square.

Some time was consumed in preparations, or in waiting for the worshippers to assemble. From conversation with those near me, I found that the doctor had a reputation for healing the diseased by virtue of his incantations, of removing "spells," of finding lost articles, of ministering to the troubles of lovers, and, in short, of doing very much what clairvoyants and healing mediums claim to do in what are called civilized communities. But failing to get a very intelligent account of the expected performance from the negro woman next me, I moved to the side of the altar and took a chair next a girl of perhaps twenty years old, whose complexion

A VOUDOO DANCE.—Drawn

BY JOHN DURKIN.—[SEE PAGE 454.]

Harper's Weekly, June 25, 1887, pp. 456–57.

and features gave evidence that she was white. Still, finding her in that company, and there as a participant in the Voudoo rites, I concluded that I must be mistaken, and that she must have colored blood in her veins. Assuming the privilege of an inquirer, I asked her questions about the coming performance, and in doing so carried the impression that she was kin to the colored race. But I was soon convinced, from her manner and her replies, that she was pure white. She was a pretty, modest girl, very reticent, well-bred, polite, and civil. None of the colored people seemed to know who she was, but she said she had been there before. She told me, in course of the conversation, the name of the street where she lived (in the American part of the town), the private school at which she had been educated (one of the best in the city), and that she and her parents were Episcopalians. Whatever her trouble was, mental or physical, she was evidently infatuated with the notion that this Voudoo doctor could conjure it away, and said that she thought he had already been of service to her. She did not communicate her difficulties to him or speak to him, but she evidently had faith that he could discern what every one present needed, and minister to them. When I asked her if, with her education, she did not think that more good would come to her by confiding in known friends or in regular practitioners, she wearily said that she did not know. After the performance began, her intense interest in it, and the light in her eyes, were evidence of the deep hold the superstition had upon her nature. In coming to this place she had gone a step beyond the young ladies of her class who make a novena at St. Roch.

While we still waited, the doctor and two other colored men called me into the next chamber, and wanted to be assured that it was my own name I had written on the register, and that I had no unfriendly intentions in being present. Their doubts at rest, all was ready.

The doctor squatted on one side of the altar, and his wife, a stout woman of darker hue, on the other.

"*Commencons*," said the woman, in a low voice. All the colored people spoke French, and French only, to each other and in the ceremony.

The doctor nodded, bent over, and gave three sharp raps on the floor with a bit of wood. (This is the usual opening of Voudoo rites). All the others rapped three times on the floor with their knuckles. Any one coming in to join the circle afterward, stooped and rapped three times. After a moment's silence, all knelt and repeated together in French the Apostles' Creed, and still on their knees, they said two prayers to the Virgin Mary.

The colored woman at the side of the altar began a chant in a low, melodious voice. It was the weird and strange "Dansé Calinda." A tall negress, with a bright, good-natured face, entered the circle with the air of a chief performer, knelt, rapped the floor, laid an offering of candles before the altar, with a small bottle of brandy, seated herself beside the singer, and took up in a strong, sweet voice the bizarre rhythm of the song. Nearly all those who came in had laid some little offering before the altar. The chant grew, the single line was enunciated in stronger pulsations, and other voices joined in the wild refrain,

"Dansé Calinda, boudoum, boudoum!
Dansé Calinda, boudoum, boudoum!"

bodies swayed, the hands kept time in soft pat-patting, and the feet in muffled accentuation. The Voudoo arose, removed his slippers, seized a bottle of brandy, dashed some of the liquid on the floor on each side of the brown bowl as a libation, threw back his head and took a long pull at the bottle, and then began in the open space a slow measured dance, a rhythmical shuffle, with more movement of the hips than of the feet, backward and forward, round and round, but accelerating his movement as the time of the song quickened and the excitement rose in the room. The singing became wilder and more impassioned, a strange minor strain, full of savage pathos and longing, that made it almost impossible for the spectator not to join in the swing of its influence, while the dancer wrought himself up into the wild passion of a Cairene dervish. Without a moment ceasing his rhythmical steps and his extravagant gesticulation, he poured liquid into the basin, and dashing in brandy, ignited the fluid with a match. The liquid flamed up before the altar. He seized then a bunch of candles, plunged them into the bowl, held them up all flaming with the burning brandy, and, keeping his step to the maddening "Calinda," distributed them lighted to the devotees. In the same way he snatched up dishes of apples, grapes, bananas, oranges, deluged them with burning brandy, and tossed them about the room to the eager and excited crowd. His hands were aflame, his clothes seemed to be on fire; he held the burning dishes close to his breast, apparently inhaling the flame, closing his eyes and swaying his head backward and forward in an ecstasy, the hips advancing and receding, the feet still shuffling to the barbaric measure.

Every moment his own excitement and that of the audience increased. The floor was covered with the debris of the sacrifice—broken candy, crushed sugar-plums, scattered grapes—and all more or less in flame. The wild dancer was dancing in fire! In the height of his frenzy he grasped a large plate filled with lump-sugar. That was set on fire. He held the burning mass to his breast, he swung it round, and finally, with his hand extended under the bottom of the plate (the plate only adhering to his hand by the rapidity of his circular motion), he spun around like a dancing dervish, his eyes shut, the perspiration pouring in streams from his face, in a frenzy. The flaming sugar scattered about the floor, and the devotees scrambled for it. In intervals of the dance, though the singing went on, the various offerings which had been conjured were passed around—bits of sugar and fruit and orris powder. That which fell to my share I gave to the young girl next me, whose eyes were blazing with excitement, though she had remained perfectly tranquil, and joined neither by voice or hands or feet in the excitement. She put the conjured sugar and fruit in her pocket, and seemed grateful to me for relinquishing it to her.

Before this point had been reached the chant had been changed for the wild canga, more rapid in movement than the chanson *africaine:*

> "Eh! eh! Bomba, hen! heu!
> Canga baflo te
> Canga moune de le
> Canga do ki la
> Canga li."

At intervals during the performance, when the charm had begun to work, the believers came forward into the open space, and knelt for "treatment." The singing, the dance, the wild incantation, went on uninterruptedly; but amid all his antics the dancer had an eye to business. The first group that knelt were four stalwart men, three of them white laborers. All of them, I presume, had some disease which they had faith the incantation would drive away. Each held a lighted candle in each hand. The doctor successively extinguished each candle by putting it in his mouth, and performed a number of antics of a saltatory sort. During his dancing and whirling he frequently filled his mouth with liquid, and discharged it in spray, exactly as a Chinese laundryman sprinkles his clothes, into the faces and on the heads of any man or woman within reach. Those so treated considered themselves specially favored. Having extinguished the candles of the suppliants, he scooped the liquid from the bowl, flaming or not as it might be, and with his hands vigorously scrubbed their faces and heads, as if he were shampooing them. While the victim was still sputtering and choking he seized him by the right hand, lifted him up, spun him round half a dozen times, and then sent him whirling.

This was substantially the treatment that all received who knelt in the circle, though sometimes it was more violent. Some of them were slapped smartly upon the back and the breast, and much knocked about. Occasionally a woman was whirled till she was dizzy, and perhaps swung about in his arms as if she had been a bundle of clothes. They all took it meekly and gratefully. One little girl of twelve, who had rickets, was banged about till it seemed as if every bone in her body would be broken. But the doctor had discrimination, even in his wildest moods. Some of the women were gently whirled, and the conjurer forbore either to spray them from his mouth or to shampoo them.

Nearly all those present knelt, and were whirled and shaken, and those who did not take this "cure" I suppose got the benefit of the incantation by carrying away some of the consecrated offerings. Occasionally a woman in the whirl would whisper something in the doctor's ear, and receive from him doubtless the counsel she needed. But generally the doctor made no inquiries of his patients, and they said nothing to him.

While the wild chanting, the rhythmic movement of hands and feet, the barbarous dance, and the fiery incantations were at their height, it was difficult to believe that we were in a civilized city of an enlightened republic. Nothing indecent occurred in word or gesture, but it was so wild and bizarre that one might easily imagine he was in Africa or in hell.

As I said, nearly all the participants were colored people; but in the height of the frenzy one white woman knelt and was sprayed and whirled with the others. She was a respectable married woman from the other side of Canal Street. I waited with some anxiety to see what my modest little neighbor would do. She had told me that she should look on and take no part. I hoped that the senseless antics, the mummery, the rough treatment, would disgust her. Toward the close of the séance, when the spells were all woven and the flames had subsided, the tall, good-natured negress motioned to me that it was my turn to advance into the circle and kneel. I excused myself. But the young girl was unable to resist longer. She went forward and knelt, with a candle in her hand. The conjurer was either touched by her youth and race, or he had spent his force. He gently lifted her by one hand, and gave her one turn around, and she came back to her seat.

The singing ceased. The doctor's wife passed round the hat for contributions, and the ceremony, which had lasted nearly an hour and a half, was over. The doctor retired exhausted with the violent exertions. As for the patients, I trust they were well cured of rheumatism, of fever, or whatever ill they had, and that the young ladies have either got husbands to their minds or have escaped faithless lovers. In the breaking up I had no opportunity to speak further to the interesting young white neophyte; but as I saw her resuming her hat and cloak in the adjoining room there was a strange excitement in her face, and in her eyes a light of triumph and faith. We came out by the back way, and through an alley made our escape into the sunny street and the air of the nineteenth century.—Charles Dudley Warner.

THE DISADVANTAGES OF COLORED CITIZENS

HARPER'S WEEKLY
July 16, 1887, p. 499

An intelligent and thoughtful correspondent writes us from Baltimore that there are five or six thousand colored children in the public schools who are taught by white teachers. A colored man himself, our correspondent perceives the wrong of such system. The moral influence upon the children of seeing teachers of their own race and color would be good. It would spur their ambition and foster their self-respect. Moreover, the general care of the children would be very much better than it is. The reason of the selection of white teachers is that the appointments are matters of patronage, and not only the teachers in the colored schools, but in all the others, are the parasites of patronage.

As for industrial training, says our correspondent, the colored children are equally unfortunate.

"There is a manual training school for white boys, supported by the city, but none for colored. The various trades-unions block him out, and will not permit a colored youth to learn a trade. The stores are all closed, and will not permit any of them to become salesmen or saleswomen; and how in the world are colored people here to advance morally, intellectually, and industriously when every avenue is nearly closed to them? There is a force inherent in many which has exerted itself, and notwithstanding all opposition they have and now making themselves felt in the community. While we as colored people appreciate highly the philanthropy which has caused such marked changes in the South, yet in a Border State we are helpless; we have not the means, and the city or State will not furnish us the means, whereby our youths may become skilled in the various trades of our city. It requires, as Mr. Warner states, $3000 per year to support an industrial training school in a Southern city, and no doubt an equal if not larger amount would be required here. Where are we to obtain it? Echo answers, Where? How can people take a rose-colored view of the progress of colored people in the South when they have so many barriers to overcome?"

Undoubtedly there is much yet to do, and very much to suffer. A race which is the victim of prejudice, and with the sad traditions of the colored race in this country, can advance but slowly. Yet the first great step is gained in emancipation. The rest can be gained only gradually, and by the character of the colored citizens themselves. There is no short and easy way. But our correspondent may be sure of a constantly increasing sympathy and respect for those on whose behalf he speaks. If the proposition to form an Afro-American League shall be carried out, the result will be watched not only curiously, but with the most friendly disposition among the most intelligent citizens to aid any judicious course that may seem to promise speedier progress.

A COLORED HERO

HARPER'S WEEKLY
July 23, 1887, pp. 527–28

Arthur Robertson, to whose heroic efforts was due the saving of seven lives from the drowning mass of humanity thrown into Canarsie Bay by the capsizing of the sloop *Mystery* on Sunday, the 10th of July, was born in Quire Creek, Virginia, ran away to sea, and followed the water since he was about ten years of age. He is a man of thirty-five years, looking much younger, of deeper than mulatto tint, and of the wiry, well-knit texture of build and unconsciousness of attitude which bespeak the healthy man at ease in all his movements. Being asked as a test question, in the course of a long interview, how he felt when he got "among them," and especially when the gunwale dipped, under one clinging person's pressure from without, so far that much water was taken into his boat, and everything was in jeopardy, he said: "I am one of them fellers that it takes a heap to make up my mind, but when I do, I mean to do or die, and I never lose my senses. I see my wife at home; I see *them* struggling and screaming in the water; I see myself, and knows as all depends on me; and I put my feet firm on the keel when I got among 'em, stooped down summat, reach over the gunwale careful, and has them in". The heavy woman who nearly swamped him and his freight he nevertheless succeeded in saving, and he avers he had to use more bad language on that occasion than he ever did in his life—"language as I'm ashamed of ever since".

Did he like the sea life? He had rather inclined to it before he got married, but since then the feeling was very different, and he would have left the business long ago except for his devotion to Captain Collins, of the *Reaper,* who, with his (the captain's) father, had befriended him all his life. He has been in their service about seven years, two months of which have been put in on board the *Reaper.* The idea of so much "fuss" being made about him seems quite ridiculous to him; chaffing, promises, the wiseacre predictions of his friends, seem to slide of him harmlessly. His common-sense and modesty are evidently ingrained.

This man saved seven lives. How did he do it? He had been taking a nap in the cabin, got up to get fresh air, met a colored friend, and entered into conversation with him on the deck and around the dock as he lay at Barren Island. Suddenly, while remarking to one another that *that* sloop seemed to be carrying too much sail, he saw her topple over. The distance from him was about fifteen minutes' row. The sea was rolling with white-caps over a swelling tide, and to use his own words, "I had grabbed my line when I saw her going, and was off." There came first a little boy; then a little baby; then Mr. Sweitzer, who had jumped and swum from the *Christina* to save his wife and child struggling

LIFE AMONG THE TENEMENTS.—Drawn by F. Barnard.—[See Page 523.]

Harper's Weekly, July 23, 1887, p. 529.

in the water; he made for them, took them up in the same iron-bound way, nearly getting his gunwale pulled under, as before recorded. Then, seeing nothing moving that was floating, pulled off for the *Deane,* "landed" them, as he says, and seeing something moving about sixty feet in the wake of the *Deane,* now near the wreck, pulled furiously for that; and now he puts his hand to his forehead in the relation, and asks: "What color of dress had she on?—was it red or dark red, John?" "Dark red, Arthur," said a witness. "I got her on—got her on the *Deane*"—here the poor fellow actually broke down—"and then I saw what broke my heart far more than all the rest. When the woman had been put on board she was alive," he groaned; "and if a doctor had been there he could have saved her; but there were no barrels on the poor little willing tug-boat, and she had to be rolled on the rails, and that killed her."

Arthur Robertson makes two voyages a week to Canarsie in the service of the steam-boat company of that name. The relations between him and his employers have plainly been so cordial all along that there is no possibility of maladjustment; and the best that can be hoped for is that in some way or other the sense of the public's appreciation of his splendid daring and coolness, joined to his honest unconsciousness of any heroism whatever, may be fittingly brought home to him.

THE ATLANTA UNIVERSITY

HARPER'S WEEKLY
August 6, 1887, p. 554

The "raid on the Atlanta University," as a correspondent of the *Evening Post* calls it, and to which we alluded last week, is a more serious question than it may seem to many readers. The great danger in the Southern States for whites as well as blacks as the correspondent points out, is an ignorant leadership of the colored people. The white vote cannot long remain solid; and when it breaks, the colored vote will be too important to be suppressed, and the object of each white side will be to secure it. The more rapid and general the education of the colored people, therefore, the better for the whole Southern community. The Atlanta University was founded in 1867 by the American Missionary Association for the education of colored youth, but not to the exclusion of any proper person who might desire admission. The money to establish and to maintain the school was contributed by persons in the Northern States, and a correspondent of the New York *Tribune* states that the aggregate sum thus contributed is now not less than $350,000. There have been a few white pupils in the university, chiefly the children of professors.

The State of Georgia receives an annual sum of about $16,000 as interest upon its share of the grant of public lands in aid of education. This sum the State appropriates to the benefit of the white university at Athens; but it appropriates from the State Treasury $8000, or half of the sum, for the colored university at Atlanta. Having ascertained, however, that there are a few white pupils, some very foolish person has introduced a bill prohibiting the reception of white pupils in colored schools and of colored pupils in white schools, under penalty to the teacher or manager of fine, imprisonment, or work on a chaingang. This is a blow at the Atlanta University, which is not only an admirable institution, but which is of the highest value in providing the best technical, agricultural, and industrial education for colored youth—an education which is indispensable if they are to become useful citizens. About five per cent. of the Atlanta students pass on to higher studies, and they are the men who will naturally become leaders. Many others finish an excellent normal course, and pursue advanced grammar-school studies. Boys and girls all work under skilled instruction, and they learn the inferiority of the stupid unskilled labor which is the chief obstacle to agricultural progress in the Southern States.

Such leaders as this school provides for their race cannot be trained elsewhere in the State. The maintenance of the university in full vigor is therefore for every reason, for the common interest of the 817,000 white and of the 726,000 colored citizens, one of the most vitally desirable objects in the State. The proposition to send the teachers and managers to the chaingang unless they expel their own children from their schools is preposterous. The good sense of the State should prevent the further prosecution of the scheme. Every sensible citizen of Georgia would admit that nothing could be more unwise than to stimulate hostility of race in the same population by means of penal laws. Each race in Georgia undoubtedly prefers separate schools for the present, but to punish and disgrace the few persons who are indifferent to the separation, and by that course to retard the indispensable education of half the population, would be an unspeakable folly.

THE "REBEL INVASION" OF OHIO

HARPER'S WEEKLY
November 19, 1887, p. 834

By a curious coincidence the Democratic plan of the late campaign brought into Ohio, on the Democratic side, Governor Gordon, of Georgia, who was a conspicuous Confederate officer, and who had recently spoken in a very extravagant strain of Jefferson Davis. His arrival gave new fury to the canvass. It was announced as a "rebel invasion" of Ohio, and whatever could influence

HIS CHOICE.
MAGISTRATE. "It's ten dollars or thirty days, Uncle Rastus. You can take your choice."
UNCLE RASTUS (*after some contemplation*). "Well, yo' kin gimme de money, sah."

Harper's Weekly, August 13, 1887, p. 588.

angry feeling was invoked to secure a Republican victory. In the light of today and of the actual condition of the country the Republican campaign was exceedingly comical. It was an *ópera bouffe* canvass. But the essential question suggested by the phrase "rebel invasion" to describe the appearance of a political orator from another State is very significant. Nothing is more common than such an appearance. In the year of a Presidential election distinguished speakers are summoned into the doubtful States from every part of the Union, and even in what is called an off year their services are often solicited. In the late campaign in New York Senator Allison made speeches, and Senators Sherman and Hale were invited to speak. If all the Republican Senators in the country had traversed the State it would have been nothing new or remarkable, nor would the Democrats have been surprised, nor would they have complained.

The invitation of noted Democrats from other States to speak in Ohio was therefore not an unusual proceeding. But it was resented as in some way an outrage upon the citizens of that State. And why? General Gordon was Governor of one of the States of the Union. He had been recently a Senator of the United States. He lay under no kind of disability. But he had been a Confederate officer, a rebel. Yes, and so Mr. Orr and Mr. Key and Generals Mosby and Longstreet had been rebels. But they were all honored and trusted by Republican administrations, and one of them had sat in a Republican cabinet. If to have been a rebel disqualified a man from taking part in an election campaign in Ohio, how was it that to have been a rebel did not disqualify him from making laws in the Senate and executing them in the cabinet? Simply because the Republican party wisely declared, at the end of the war, that a man may have been a rebel, and still a man of honor and worthy of confidence. Because the party wisely held that, notwithstanding his part in the civil war, he could be trusted to sit in Congress and to advise the President, and because the Republican party did not believe that to have been a rebel was to be permanently an enemy of the Union and an unwearied conspirator against the national welfare. If there has ever been, in the sense in which the words were lately used in Ohio, "a rebel invasion," it captured the Republican President Grant when he appointed Mr. Orr Minister to Russia, and the Republican President Hayes, of Ohio, when he appointed Mr. Key Postmaster-General. If rebels are in office anywhere, it is because the Republican party permitted it. If public officers who were rebels come to Ohio to speak, it is because the Republican party opened the way. If rebels are in the saddle, it is because the Republican party knew that they had ceased to be rebels, and were as good citizens as any others. For if such be not the fact, nothing could have demonstrated such complete incapacity to administer the government as to have made it possible for its enemies to control it.

The cry of rebel invasion because a Democrat from Georgia comes to address Democrats in Ohio is the last desperate effort to carry an election by an appeal to passions which have no longer any reason and are fast expiring. It is a cry totally unworthy of a patriotic party and of honorable American citizens. One great need of the country is, not a sectional and traditional prejudice, which would keep orators from the Southern States out of Northern States, and Northern orators from speaking in Carolina and Mississippi, thus fostering and prolonging the old and perilous sectional alienation, but the freest discussion of all public questions everywhere in the country by orators from every State. The effort to maintain this alienation and to profit by it is one of the worst aspects of the Republican policy. On the eve of the election an Ohio Republican, who proposed to support the whole ticket because the State administration had been honest and efficient said publicly in print of the sectional and free-whiskey national policy of the Republicans:

> "The excuse for this is that in places South the negro is not permitted to vote. These leaders know perfectly well that under like circumstances they would not let the negro vote in Ohio. The presence of a few mulatto children in the schools in Ohio has evoked an explosion of the meanest form of race hate. What would take place if the black children were as two to one of the whites? What would take place in this State if two-thirds of a county were ignorant field hands? Would they be permitted to rule? The abolitionist sought the freedom of the black man, not to make him master. The race problem is a difficult one. Many wise and good men in the North thought that the two races could not live in peace together, both free. This problem the South is

THANKSGIVING MORNING IN THE "JOHNSING FAMBLY."
"Dar, Binilee Johnsing! Didn't I tole yer all 'long you dun feed dat turkey too much veg'table diet?"

Harper's Weekly, September 26, 1887, p. 863.

solving better than any one anticipated. I lived in the South with slavery. In recent years I have spent my summers in an old Slave State. I have travelled extensively in the South. And in my opinion the negro laborers South are better off than the white laborers in Cincinnati. The negro in most respects is treated better South than he is in Cincinnati. In the South I see whites and blacks playing base-ball together. Do you do that in Cincinnati? As an old abolitionist I rejoice to see the South doing so well with the negro. The Union and abolition are secure; so, in my opinion, this outbreak of sectional resentment in Ohio is as weak in policy as it is unpatriotic and wicked in principle. . . .

"Now, Mr. Editor, a leadership that makes the Republican party the representative of sectional hate or free whiskey shocks the moral sense. I protest against it. I hope the Republican party, as the representative of honest administration, may win; but I protest in advance against the claim that such a victory is an endorsement of either sectional hate or free whiskey. If this misguided leadership fastens next year these atrocious principles upon the Republican party, it will and ought to be defeated."

THE SOUTHERN PROBLEM

HARPER'S WEEKLY
December 10, 1887, pp. 894–95

The Republican success in Ohio, where the chief speaker was Governor Foraker, whose chief topic was the wrongs of colored voters in the Southern States, naturally suggests to the party managers a policy for the campaign next year. Mr. Sherman thinks that great stress should be laid upon the suppression of the colored vote, and Mr. Sherman is one of the ablest of Republican leaders. This opinion is undoubtedly based upon what he has observed of the party feeling. In his speech at Nashville last March he said of the rights secured by the new constitutional amendments: "The attempt to enforce these rights by constitutional amendments has thus far partially failed, and now it is conceded that under the limitations of the Constitution the rights of the citizens of a State can be enforced only through State or national tribunals," and where public opinion is intolerant, and juries fail in their duty, the only remedy, he said, is emigration. He added that he had been happy to learn in the Southern States that in many quarters public sentiment revolted at the suppression of such rights, and if this were so, he thought the citizens of other States might appeal to the manly spirit of our own race to protect the colored citizen against the white men who would oppress him. He then turned to questions which, he said, should alone be subjects of political discussion. All this was unmistakable. It meant that "the Southern question" should be left to settlement in the Southern States as now beyond national adjustment. But a few weeks later, at Springfield, in Illinois, his tone was wholly changed. He denounced "the cruel and barbarous atrocity of the controlling elements of the South in their treatment of Republicans," and declared that Mr. Cleveland owed his seat to crimes against the elective franchise.

Such a change upon the part of a cool and wary public man signified that he was alarmed by the response of his party to his Nashville speech, and that he perceived his error. If forecast the late Republican campaign in Ohio, and Mr. Sherman now announces that his platform is simple, consisting of high protection and Congressional control of national elections in the Southern States. The result of the elections this year leaves little doubt that both the issues he mentions will make part of the Republican platform next year. In regard to the Southern question, Republican leaders should be careful. The general conviction is that whatever injustice may be done to the colored voters, the remedy is neither simple nor summary. As early and as stanch and as constant a Republican as Mr. Sherman is a citizen of Ohio whose views we published the week after the election. He speaks of "the meanest form of race hate," which is expressed in Ohio by the refusal to admit mulatto children to the public schools, and states his opinion, after extensive personal observation in the Southern States, that "the negro laborers South are better off than the white laborers in Cincinnati." This is the feeling in one of the most enlightened and progressive of the old Free States, the home of Chase and Giddings, which has a population of 3,118,344 white and 79,665 colored. This original antislavery Ohio Republican touches the very heart of the Southern question when he asks, even of Ohio: "What would take place in this State if two-thirds of a county were ignorant field hands? Would they be permitted to rule?" Among intelligent, reasonable Americans what would be the prospects of a party which should propose to enforce that rule by the whole power of the national government? Would not the general and just conviction be that it was a question which for every good reason in the nature of our government should be left to the adjustment of the State? And if that were true in Ohio, what is the truth in Mississippi, where the population numbers 479,371 white and 650,337 colored, or South Carolina, where there are 391,258 white and 604,325 colored people? Would the intelligent Republican majority in the old Free States deliberately support a proposition to restore and maintain by the national arm the Moses regime in South Carolina? Is it not true that the solidification of the white vote in the Southern States was due to the instinct of self-preservation against a government based upon ignorance and corruption? The whole Southern situation sprang chiefly from the tragical misfortune of Andrew Johnson's administration, which compelled the adoption of a policy which without that immense misfortune would probably have been different.

Can any sagacious and patriotic statesman believe that the peremptory interference of Congress and the Executive with elections in the Southern States will have any other result than the bitterest hatred of the government and a vast and helpless increase of the suffering of the colored citizens? The intelligent white vote of those States will be solid just so long as this apprehension exists, and the only way to remove the color line and to restore a normal political condition is to prove to every Southern State that it is in no more peril of this kind of interference than any Northern State. The moral weakness of the policy of interference lies in the consciousness that, under the circumstances which exist in the Southern States, every Republican State would resent it. The feeling that the question is a profoundly complicated one, which can be best adjusted by the States concerned, and that time and education and the natural play of different interests will gradually divide the colored vote and dissolve the color line, is so general and so increasing that the Republican party could not be strengthened by the adoption of the policy of interference. It is not because Republicans like our Ohio correspondent have grown indifferent to human rights and have lost sympathy with the colored race that they condemn so warmly what they call a policy of sectional hate. It is because they regard the Republican party, and have always sustained it, as a wiser, more patriotic, more humane, and more truly American party than the Democratic that they would see it seek a more reasonable and permanent solution of the Southern question than the one now proposed. That solution will be found, not in national interference, but in a frank acknowledgment of the extreme difficulties of the situation, and in cordial co-operation with the Southern sentiment to which Mr. Sherman alluded, and which aims at the most friendly possible relation of the races.

1888

Voting and electoral politics dominated this presidential election year. As a new generation of voters came of age, what would be their interests? Born after the 1860s, they did not have the legacies of slavery or abolitionism as controlling factors in their politics. The media then sought to watch them carefully to see how the Republicans and Democrats would be effected. Journalists predicated a more exciting, less corruptive era in politics.

Yet the country would not soon forget the "southern question." Volumes of editorials recounted the domination of the South by "African Americans and Republican ascendancy." The empowerment of "ignorant and illiterate masses" of men gave rise to the unification of southerners around white supremacy. These editorials stood in sharp contrast to those of earlier years. Now serving as revisionists on the question of southern race relations, editors were determined to justify or at least to understand the violent reaction to black freedom and suffrage. Such actions were committed in self-defense, it was declared. Such action also proved that social and political equality could not be legislated. Plus, the papers stated, responsible black leaders shied away from encouraging black voting, sensing the physical repercussions. Even if federal troops were to return or if the National Elections Laws existed, blacks would not risk going to the polls considering the economic reprisals afterwards. This reluctance eliminated a major strain in southern race relations. Federal officials were asked to remain out of this issue in order to allow local communities, full of people of good will, to honorably settle this complex situation.

As the editors sought to convince the American public, especially African Americans, that the "wait and watch" policy was the most effective for all, they could not conceal the growing anxiety a new group *of men invoked. Independent of Republican loyalty and undaunted by the Solid South's trickery and travesty, new voices advocated direct action to destroy segregation and the establishment of organizations to guide and generate the budding racial protest tradition. Speaking to blacks, this class of educated blacks called on the race to stand up for immediate justice and equality. The editors saw such rhetoric as inflammatory and a threat to the status quo. Such demands were codes for racial amalgamation. So the papers attempted to appeal to the Talented Tenth's logic. Surely such radical demands could not be operational overnight. Such change demanded patience, time, faith and resignation on the part of both races. Such delicate issues must be left to wise, just, and rational minds. Some writers sought to defame the reputations of these men and women by warning the black community that these alleged leaders were after personal patronage and did not have the genuine interest of all blacks as a priority. Even in trying to establish a motive of self-centeredness, these whites could not overlook or underestimate the potential power this new generation of mostly northern blacks had accumulated. The only viable option for the editors was to try to censure or diminish the message of these leaders, as more accommodative and conciliatory black leaders were held up as the true champions of racial and sectional harmony.*

Ironically, the institution that had produced such voices, Atlanta University, was strongly defended during this year. In the summer of 1887 the state of Georgia had passed the Glenn Bill, which made it illegal to teach in mixed schools. Violations called for fines and/or imprisonment, even on the infamous chain gang. Since the founding of Atlanta University (during Reconstruction) the state had appropriated an annual supplement of $8,000. The school could retain its funds if it complied with the bill. The president, Horace Bumstead, relinquished the annual monies. The papers praised him for taking the only sensible action. While calling on friends and supporters to fill this financial void, the editors wondered why the issue of integration at Atlanta University had became so germane? The school had always had a mixed faculty and student body and had received state funds from its inception. Yearly monitoring reflected the make-up and objectives of the school. There were never any attempts to conceal the obvious. The school had produced outstanding teachers and leaders for the race. National recognition validated the school's excellence. Atlanta University, they stated, "shows what excellent and useful citizens of a proscribed race may become." For this reason alone, the papers called on northern philanthropists to come to the institution's aid.

But, then, saving Atlanta University and defying independent black leadership were probably unrelated in the papers' new attitude about "cordial cooperation on the race question." Equating unpatriotic feelings to racial protest would be a constant refrain over the upcoming twentieth century. Racial justice would come from compromise and conciliation.

Patience and long suffering would be necessary in this long and deliberate process.

Jacqueline A. Rouse
Georgia State University

THE VOTERS OF 1888

HARPER'S WEEKLY
January 14, 1888, pp. 22–23

A Western Democrat has prepared an interesting and suggestive table of the male population between the ages of twenty and forty-one years, according to the census of 1880, with race and nativity. It is perfectly accurate except as to colored voters, under which head Chinese, Japanese, and civilized Indians are included. But as these three races number less than 175,000 in all, of voting age, the table is sufficiently accurate for its purpose. A very large portion of the Chinese are in California, and as the Chinese and Indians are almost the only "colored" population in California, Nevada, and Oregon, they are all omitted in those three States. The increase of young voters is unquestionably greater for the seven years since the census, by reason of the larger aggregate population and of the increased distance from the war period. The table is prepared by States, and its summary is as follows:

Native white males	5,220,213
Foreign white males	1,545,522
Colored males	918,325
Total	7,684,060
Total voting population	12,302,810
Majority of young voters	3,055,310

The figures shown by the table indicate that seven years ago there was not a State in the Union, except Vermont, where the young men were not a clear majority of the voting population. In the New England States their majority was smallest, naturally, as the young men very generally leave those States early for the West. Vermont shows a majority of 401 voters over forty years of age; New Hampshire follows with a majority of only 1128 young men; Maine had a majority of 5535 young men. In Massachusetts the majority of young men, in a total voting population of 502,648, was 75,974. When the Western States are reached the other extreme appears, though the prolific negroes hold the Southern States well in line. Colorado shows a majority of young men of 52,954 in a total vote of 93,608; Nebraska had a majority of 51,030 young voters in a total of 129,042; Minnesota had 115,979 young voters in a total vote of 213,485; Wisconsin had a majority of 44,152 young voters in a total voting population of 340,482. The significance of these figures lies in the fact that the party appeals based upon the traditions and feelings of the war fall with comparative indifference upon the ears of the majority of voters. The mass of the voters and tax-payers and active citizens of the country look upon the civil war largely as they look upon the Revolution. They are engrossed and interested in the questions of to-day, as their fathers were devoted to the question of slavery, which overshadowed the politics of their time. it was natural that the antislavery party and the party of the war should have seemed to the voters of twenty and thirty years ago the true American and progressive party, and its opponent a reactionary and essentially un-American party. But both parties have changed. The young Republican is now something else than an antislavery Whig; the young Democrat detests slavery as heartily as Sumner detested it.

Neither party, however, is yet controlled by its newer blood and views. But the Democrats in nominating Mr. Cleveland fortunately found a modern Democrat, while the Republicans in nominating Mr. Blaine, and in now appealing once more to the war, and even to the *ante bellum* feeling, show a reactionary rather than a progressive tendency, which can have little influence upon the new voters. The boy who was eighteen in 1860 will be a man of forty-six—past the age of compulsory military duty—when he votes for President this year; the boy who was born in 1860 voted six years ago; the boy who was born two years after the war will vote for President this year; and those who have become voters since 1860 will this year be in a majority of nearly five millions of votes. These are very suggestive facts. There is no reason to doubt that the active voters of to-day are quite as intelligent as their fathers, and their fathers voted upon the questions of 1856, '60, '62, and '64, and not upon those of 1830 and '34.

THE SOUTHERN QUESTION

HARPER'S WEEKLY
January 21, 1888, p. 38

The catastrophe of Mr. Lincoln's assassination lay chiefly in its effect upon the policy of reconstruction. Had he lived, there would have been none of the black codes in the Southern States after the war, and the apparent necessity of enfranchising those who were notoriously and absolutely unfit for political responsibility would not have existed. The view of Mr. Lincoln, of Governor Andrew of Massachusetts, and of other wise and devoted Republicans, was that the work of reconstruction, to be effective, must be the result of the cordial co-operation of the leaders upon both sides. It was worse than idle, they thought, to leave out of the account the intelligence, the property, the experience, the ability, the actual leadership, the Anglo-Saxon and American element, of the South, and to attempt reconstruction without them. The course which would have been taken in accordance with this wise, comprehensive and patriotic view of the situation was frustrated by the assassination of Mr. Lincoln, and the succession to him of Mr. Johnson, a Tennessee Democrat whom Republicans distrusted, and in whom the Southern leaders supposed they had providentially found an ally to enable them to save all that could be saved of the old order.

The rupture between Mr. Johnson and the Republican party, and the mad legislation of the Southern States in regard to the freedmen, with the unwillingness of the Northern States to maintain a Territorial or temporary condition in the South, led to the scheme of reconstruction including the enfranchisement of the freedmen as the best guarantee of their rights. This was followed by military occupation and the carpet-bag epoch, ending in the solid and supreme ascendency of the white citizens, secured at first by violence, and now maintained by election laws and by the large abstention of the colored vote in some districts, although elsewhere, as in Virginia, it is divided and freely cast, or is not large enough to menace the general result. The situation is one of extreme difficulty, but Congress saw the impracticability of trying to subject intelligence and civilization to ignorance and barbarism led by local knavery, and decided that the solution of the question could be most wisely left to the communities themselves. That was the conclusion of a Republican Administration, and it has been generally approved. Without denying the fact that the colored vote in some Southern communities is not free, the conviction of intelligent Northern citizens undoubtedly is that the remedy does not lie in national interference.

The reason is obvious. If the national government should assume the supervision of elections in the Southern States, and assure the colored voters of armed protection, what would be gained? There would be no considerable increase of the colored vote because of the relations of the two races, which would not be changed by such a law. The relations of the races in the Southern States are determined by causes which could not be affected by enabling colored citizens to vote under guards of United States soldiers, and every colored man would consider how the national supervision of the polls would affect his comfort and his advantage tomorrow and all the rest of the year. There is little doubt that the more intelligent colored citizens in the Southern States would greatly regret the passage of laws which, however well intended to secure to them the free exercise of the suffrage, must necessarily deepen the difficulties of their position. A return to the policy of fifteen years ago in the Southern States would be as unwise as the English policy in Ireland seems to most Americans. The trouble is one which cannot be settled peremptorily by legislation or by force. Undoubtedly the general situation has been greatly improved in the Southern States since the change of policy which was wisely made by the Administration of Mr. Hayes. It is constantly improving, and if left to time and to the communities which are vitally and immediately concerned, the difficulties will be naturally and happily adjusted as they cannot be adjusted by the violent interference of national authority.

THE ATLANTA UNIVERSITY

HARPER'S WEEKLY
February 11, 1888, p. 91

The question of the Atlanta University in Georgia was very generally discussed last summer in connection with the Glenn bill, which made it a penal offence to teach in mixed schools of white and colored pupils. There was such a vehement national condemnation of the bill, and it was so warmly opposed by a certain sensible opinion in the State, that a modification was adopted withholding State appropriations from any such schools. This measure forced the Atlanta University to the alternative of abandoning its policy and violating certain obligations upon which money had been received from benefactors of the school, or relinquishing the State appropriation. The latter course was honorably and bravely adopted. This involved an annual loss of $8000, to replace which the institution must look to its friends. The university was founded in 1869 as a private institution, the American Missionary Association of New York, the Freedman's Bureau, and private friends furnishing the money to establish it, but not a fund for its support. It was designed for the education of all, without regard to sect, race, color, or nationality. It comprehended a primary school, a preparatory school, and a college course, with the alternative of a normal-school course following the grammar-school course. But besides this it provides an efficient industrial training, the boys in the elements of wood-working, iron-working, and printing, and the girls in plain sewing, cutting, dress-making, cooking, and nursing the sick. In a community where the population is colored in the proportion of seven to eight, such an institution is of the highest service, because it teaches teachers and trains leaders.

There are convenient and pleasant buildings, and there are now 236 boys and 264 girls as pupils. The great

TABLE TALK BELOW-STAIRS.

Dinah. "Lord-a-massy, 'Liza, be perpared for great 'sturbance in de heabens, chile. Dey'z been talking at de dinner-table 'bout no mo' protection. Massa he say de *world* gwine one way, and de *son* gwine de odder, and dat it's all got to be fixed next fall at de poles."

Harper's Weekly, January 28, 1888, p. 71.

object is to provide the trained leadership of which we speak, and an illustration of the practical value of the institution is found in the fact that of the twenty-eight colored teachers engaged by the city of Atlanta in the public schools twenty-three are graduates of the university, and similar facts are observable in other towns and cities of Georgia. The support of the institution has been derived hitherto from the State appropriation of $8000 and a similar sum contributed by friends in the Northern States and elsewhere. The relinquishment of the State grant compels an application for making up an equal sum by the friends of the university. The institution is charged with violating the law and long-settled policy of the State. But there was no concealment of the purpose of the school, and if the presence of white pupils was overlooked in 1874, when the appropriation was made, it has been constantly observed since that time, and no objection was made. The excellence of the institution and its advantage to the State have been frankly and fully acknowledged, and the technical objection under which the appropriation is with-held is unworthy of a great American State.

Professor Bumstead, of the university, is now in New York, and appeals to the generosity of those who comprehend the immense value of such an institution in the community in which it is planted. His mission is on behalf of what seems to be one of the most efficient and hopeful of the enterprises which are among the most necessary and beneficial to which aid can be given, and a permanent fund for it would be a great and humane public service. A State like Georgia, with a population of 817,000 white and 726,000 colored citizens, one of the most prosperous and intelligent of Southern States, might well consider whether it is desirable for the common interest to deepen and exacerbate the color line, instead of accepting so excellent an opportunity as the Atlanta University offers of intelligently elevating the colored race. Experience shows that the feeling of race is more wisely left to settle itself, like sectarian feeling, and that what nature has separated or joined, nature is capable of maintaining. But the best way to soften a feeling of this kind is to do just what the Atlanta University is doing, namely, to show what excellent and useful citizens the members of a proscribed race may become. The liberal support of the institution, therefore, is a helpful service toward the practical solution of one of the most important of our public problems.

THE OUTRAGE AT JACKSON

HARPER'S WEEKLY
February 18, 1888, p. 111

The statement of Mayor McGill, of Jackson, Mississippi, may be taken as a fair account of the facts in regard to the late election in that city. Mr. McGill has lived for forty-two of his forty-nine years in Jackson. He was a Confederate soldier through the war, and "when the surrender took place," he says, "I also surrendered." He was first elected Mayor in 1874, and was re-elected annually until this year, and the facts which he mentions about the reduction of the rate of taxation for general improvement under his administration are exceedingly creditable. Mr. McGill is a Republican. Of the six aldermen, five have been white Democrats and one a colored Republican. Of the other five chief city officers, three were white Democrats, and one a white and one a colored Republican. Of the six members of the police force, four were white Democrats and two colored Republicans. This was certainly not a "negro-ridden" government. On Christmas Eve, during a meelée, a young white man was killed by a colored man, who was in turn immediately killed. This occurrence led to a bitter attack upon Mayor McGill and his administration, and to an inflammatory appeal to race prejudice. An anonymous circular in the old Ku-Klux vein was issued, professedly from the young white men of Jackson, denouncing the city government as the rule of negro butchers, and warning the colored citizens not to attempt to run for office at the pending election, nor by their votes to foist upon the city again "the black and damnable machine miscalled a government."

The colored citizens thereupon resolved not to attempt to take any part in the election—a determination which, the Mayor thinks, alone prevented riot and bloodshed. Such an incident, as we said, so far as appears, and upon the statement of the Mayor, is due to the old Ku-Klux spirit. It is the suppression of a vote by mysterious, and therefore more effective, terrorism. It is an incident, like the cheating at the polls in Cincinnati and Indianapolis, like the old Tweed frauds in the New York elections, and the Plaquemine frauds in Louisiana, greatly to be deplored by all good citizens, and to be corrected as summarily and effectively as possible. But it is not an offence to be distorted in the account, and attributed to a whole community. The Democratic *Daily Advertiser,* published in Jackson, at once denounced the outrage, and Judge Wharton called the attention of the Grand Jury to the statements. This was not reassuring, as the Judge is said to have opposed bitterly the exercise of their rights by colored citizens, and the jury rather rebuked the *Advertiser,* and declared that, with the exception of the circular, they knew of no intimidation. The Democratic journal was not abashed, however, and reiterated its statements. Meanwhile the subject had been called to the attention of the President, and hearing that Mr. Harris, the United States District Attorney of Mississippi, had been implicated in the transaction, the President summoned him to Washington. His explanation was unsatisfactory, and he was removed. The interview is said to have been warm, and the President to have declared that such proceedings would not be tolerated.

The special committee of the Senate to investigate the facts will, we hope, proceed without delay. But the action of the President is very significant, and the course of the *Daily Advertiser* shows that the outrage cannot be turned wholly to party account. The purpose of the inquiry is undoubtedly to furnish "campaign material." But the wrong is of a kind which is to be corrected by just such local opinion as that which the *Advertiser* represents, and by such vigorous and unmistakable conduct as that of the President. The protest of the *Advertiser,* and the removal of the attorney, and the universal attention drawn to one such incident of a kind which is now infrequent, show the great advance since the days of the Ku-Klux. The gradual change of public opinion wrought by many influences, and not force bills and similar legislation, is the remedy for such wrongs. If the committee should recommend stringent legislation of the kind contemplated by the Chandler resolution, the best judgment of the country, as it seems to us, would not sustain them.

THE COLORED VOTE

HARPER'S WEEKLY
April 14, 1888, p. 262

There is no doubt or denial of the fact of a suppression of the colored vote in some districts of the Southern States. Even Mr. Henry Watterson, in the current number of the *Forum,* in a trenchant paper upon "The Hysteria of Sectional Agitation," of which he thinks Mr. Murat Halstead to be the most conspicuous victim, does not deny it. He holds that the situation is due to the inevitable failure of the Republican scheme to perpetuate the power of the party by erecting a black oligarchy in certain Southern States, to be controlled by the party chiefs in Washington. This, he says, was a preposterous and hopeless scheme, dependent wholly upon force, and consequently it was totally ruined when the army was withdrawn. But even during its continuance there was, according to Mr. Halstead's reasoning, a suppression of the vote. Mr. Halstead takes five to one as the fair ratio of population to ballots, which in thickly populated, but not in rural States, Mr. Watterson holds to be fair. Yet upon this ratio he calculates the Presidential vote of 1872 in ten Southern States, "in the heyday of Republican domination," and according to the census of 1870 there was, on Mr. Halstead's reasoning, a suppression of more than 60,000 votes out of 245,032 in Virginia, of nearly 74,000 out of 257,704 in Tennessee, and of nearly 94,000 out of 236,821 in Georgia. Yet the polls were absolutely under Republican control. Such figures show the impossibility of inferring suppression from failure to vote.

But Mr. Watterson does not evade the point. He says frankly that he should be entitled to no respect or credit if he

> "pretended that there is either a fair poll or count of the vast overflow of black votes in States where there is a negro majority, or that in the nature of things present there can be. There was not when the ballot-box was guarded by Federal bayonets. There is not now. There can be only when both races divide upon other than race lines, and when, with the disappearance of old antagonisms, new issues, involving differences of opinion among the whites and blacks alike, remove from each the dangers of by-gone conflict."

These words are certainly worth considering. Ex-Senator Harrison, in a recent speech before a Republican club in Chicago, says that although the Republican party be unable to apply a direct remedy, it can at least protest, and prevent the Democratic party from enjoying the usufruct of the wrong. But that is a feeble and futile policy. A great party, addressing itself to an admitted evil, must be able to do something more than protest. If the national government can deal with the evil, such a party should appeal to the country to sustain it in applying a remedy. But even in that case what remedy would there be? The States could not be deprived of their proportional representation in Congress, for the wrong is not a State act. If they could be, the wrong would not be remedied, and only bitterness and wrath would ensue. If, again, Congress should take charge of national elections in those States, probably not a suppressed voter would appear at the polls. Actual relief, being, then, within the control of each State, and not of Congress, do not humanity and justice and patriotism demand that the conditions under which alone the color line can be effaced shall be produced as soon as possible?

It is a public wrong to take a course, for the sake of a possible partisan advantage, which perpetuates a lamentable situation that confessedly cannot be remedied by national legislation. The first duty of good citizenship is to seek relief in the way which promises to secure it. That can be done by encouraging, wherever the vote is suppressed, the normal political situation in an American State, the free play of differing interests, the development of parties, the legitimate operation of the causes which divide at the polls the citizens of New York and of the New England States. External pressure of any kind, where nothing else can be wisely done, merely destroys parties and forces a union of voters for common protection. A solid Republican North would be no remedy for a solid Democratic South, and between the two the political and the social advantage of the colored citizens would be pulverized. The situation is plain. But it is one with which the Republican party, in all the plenitude of its power and all the flush of feeling that immediately followed the war, found itself unable to deal. The remedy is not mere protest, as ex-Senator Harrison suggests. It can be found only in the wisest, most temperate, and most fraternal thought and statesmanship. The mere excitement of partisan passion will only deepen the difficulty. One good suggestion is that of ex-Mayor Low, that the Republican party, by their ablest representatives, shall show to the intelligent people of the Southern States in what way their interests and sympathies coincide with the Republican spirit and purpose, and prove to them, as ex-Governor Bullock, of Georgia, says, that Republicanism does not mean the subjugation of the intelligence of a State to its ignorance, which is the present general impression in the Southern States.

PATRIOTISM

HARPER'S WEEKLY
May 19, 1888, p. 350

The disposition to revive the war feeling as a part of the political campaign is very evident, but it is both a blunder and a crime. Honorable and intelligent men are bound to know the feelings and views of the leaders and representatives of sentiment in the Southern States, and to treat the question of suffrage not in a formal and technical, but in the most generous and sympathetic spirit. The proposition is indisputable that every legal voter has the right to vote freely and to have his vote counted. But when that right is violated in a jurisdiction over which other communities and citizens have no control, a remedy must be sought by the most careful consideration of all the circumstances. In our situation mere obloquy and denunciation can have but one result, and that is to perpetuate the conditions which are to be mitigated. We have already indicated the general course which seems to promise the best results, namely, to abolish the color line by promoting the normal conditions of party government, division according to opinions and interests, and not as a defensive league against presumed external interference.

The recent foolish tirade of Senator Ingalls served one excellent and wholly unexpected purpose. It was of no possible avail to array the evidence of a fact so notorious as that Mr. Voorhees was a Copperhead during the war. It was a performance like that of demonstrating the same fact in regard to Fernando Wood. But the intention to discredit all Southern Democrats as disloyal—the "Confederacy in the saddle" trick—was admirably rebuked and frustrated by Senator Randall Gibson, of Lousiana. Those Republicans who are still apprehensive of rebel brigadiers may well ponder these words of Senator Gibson:

"What was the issue put at arms by the Southern and Northern sections? It was, in the first place, the institution of slavery. Every one knows that slavery was the occasion of the war, and every one understands perfectly well that the principle of secession was invoked by the Southern people as the only safeguard to protect their property and liberty, their public peace, their social and political systems, from violent overthrow. Those two questions were settled, and settled finally, by the amendments of the Constitution, which we have sworn to support, the thirteenth and fourteenth amendments. What Southern man, what Southern State, has attempted to revive the institution of slavery? What Southern statesman has since the arbitrament of arms agitated the doctrine of secession? Not one. We all admit to-day that if any one were to take up arms, whether under State authority or not, against the United States, he would be guilty of treason, because the constitutional amendments declare that 'all persons born or naturalized in the United States, and subject to the jurisdiction thereof, are citizens of the United States.' Citizenship and allegiance are correlative. Southern members have voted for years with a lavish hand nearly a thousand millions in pensions to the soldiers of the Federal army and their families. We have freely voted supplies to the army and navy of the Union, from which we ourselves are excluded. We have done what we could to establish a sound currency for the people of the country, to diminish the public expenses, to improve the rivers and harbors, and to maintain the credit and honor of the flag in every land and on every sea under the sun."

Senator Gibson concluded this branch of his remarks by quoting the famous concluding passage of Webster's reply to Hayne, as the sentiment of the people that he represents. Could there be a manlier statement of the perfect good faith of our old foes than this; and in comparison with the vituperation of Senator Ingalls, can there be any question whatever of the nobler patriotism of such a speech as Senator Gibson's?

Another significant sign of the same kind occurs in the article contributed by Senator Wade Hampton, one of the most fiery and apparently implacable of Confederate leaders, to the new Chicago weekly journal, *America,* which publishes admirable and noteworthy papers upon important current topics. Senator Hampton, in discussing immigration and the results of the war, holds the experiment of incorporating in the body-politic a large mass of inexperienced and ignorant voters not to be so promising as to encourage a great and careless extension of such suffrage. Turning to the people of the Southern States, he says that no brave man who once opposed them would respect them if they did not honor the memory of their old comrades who are dead, and respect those who are living and have earned such regard. They do not confess that they were guilty, because they were wholly sincere, and gave the highest proof that men can give of entire sincerity. Senator Hampton says that he has never seen a man in those States who would be glad to see slavery restored, and that he is the enemy of both races who would seek to array them against each other. They are naturally interdependent, and when forced into collision, the weaker will necessarily suffer. The Senator adds:

"Most of the vexed and irritating questions which unhappily distracted and divided the country have been permanently settled by the late war. The South has accepted this settlement in absolute good faith, without reservations of any sort. She recognizes the supremacy of the Constitution, with all its recent amendments, as the supreme law of the land, and she regards the integrity and perpetuity of the Union as an established fact—one irrevocably fixed by the arbitrament of war, and the unanimous verdict of the people of the United States. To emphasize these statements, let me say farther that the Southern people, recognizing fully the results brought about by the war, feel that they have now but one country—one and indivisible—and that it is the duty of every patriotic man to strive to make that country powerful, respected abroad, honored at home, the fit abode of freemen for all generations to come, the home of Americans, who owe no allegiance, in fact or in feeling, to any foreign government, and who feel a sincere desire for the maintenance of our republican institutions; who, whether they are native-born or adopted citizens, wish to promote the prosperity, the honor, and the glory of the great republic."

There is nothing which can be cited to disprove the general truth of this statement. The relation between the races is indeed a problem of the utmost importance. But to say that it can be settled at once, or that settlement is obstructed only by the outrageous conduct of the whites, is to show a very imperfect comprehension of the situation. Before embarking in a campaign of which Mr. Ingalls's speech shall be the key, every well-meaning citizen, not as a Republican or Democrat, but as a man and an American, may profitably consider the honest words that we have quoted.

THE UNIVERSITY OF ATLANTA

HARPER'S WEEKLY
May 19, 1888, p. 351

We are glad to know that the effort of Professor Bumstead, of Atlanta University, to raise the $16,000 to replace the $8000 withdrawn from the institution by the State, and to make up the $8000 needed for current expenses, has been largely successful. Eleven thousand dollars have been subscribed by those whose names are a guarantee of the great worthiness of the enterprise, and we hope that the $5000 yet remaining to be raised will be soon obtained.

The University is in its nineteenth year of successful operation, with five hundred students from the primary school to the college course. Its religious training is Christian, but unsectarian. Its industrial training is adapted to the more probable needs and opportunities of the boys and girls. More than two-thirds of its graduates are teaching in Georgia, eleven of them being principals of city schools. Its property consists of sixty acres of land, four large brick buildings, a library of 6000 volumes, apparatus and industrial equipment, all free from debt. Its invested funds are mostly for scholarships, and besides these it has no endowment.

At a meeting in Boston Rev. Phillips Brooks, Edward E. Hale, Henry W. Foote, George A. Gordon, and J. F. B. Marshall were appointed a committee to further the project of completing the sum required. There is no enterprise of the kind which more richly merits confidence and assistance.

UNIVERSAL SUFFRAGE.

FIRST SABLE SON OF THE SOIL (*resting on his hoe*). "Aber'am, what's yo' 'pinion ob dis hyah women's sufferage?"

SECOND SABLE SON (*gloomily*). "Waal, I don' know; looks pow'rful jubious. Ain' dar ol' Sis' Cl'rindy done got de aiger agin? 'n' ain' po' Aunt Chloe laid onto de she'f wid a strike ob de appleplexy? an' Sis' Bijah Johnsing's gal, M'rindy, done bruk her juggler bone plumb off'n; 'n' yo' ol' woman wus'n ebber long o' the rhomatics; 'n' my ol' woman mos' daid wid de misery en her back. I d'know—I d'know, Br'er. 'Pears likes 'sif 'twel *end up'n Universalist Sufferage.*"

Harper's Weekly, June 16, 1888, p. 439.

THE FOURTH OF JULY IN A SOUTHERN TOWN

HARPER'S WEEKLY
July 7, 1888, p. 490

In the South, as far as colored people are concerned in the celebration of the Fourth of July, it is something novel, and on that account has an especial charm for them. The present growing generation of negroes from Virginia to Louisiana were born in a state of freedom, whereas their fathers and mothers, living before emancipation, knew of the Fourth of July only by hearsay. The old slaves paid little or no attention to it. The Fourth—the glorious Fourth—was for the white people, and not for the black ones. Following in the wake of French or Spanish customs rather than of English ones, as far as related to those noisy demonstrations which are supposed to be in unison with religious ceremonies, the colored folks shot off their fire-crackers on Christmas. Little white boys, with their colored playmates, rather ignored the "poppers," as fire-crackers are called South, on the Fourth of July, and exploded them on the 25th of December.

These things are changed now, and nowhere is Independence Day more thoroughly kept than in the South, and by the colored people. Whether our patriotic fathers had any idea of issuing the most important paper on human rights the world ever read during watermelon time nobody can tell. It may, however, be considered in the light of a happy coincidence.

The local colored military organization has looked forward to the Fourth as the day when they were to exhibit themselves arrayed in their best, and the wives and sweethearts of the soldiers have been wild with excitement for months beforehand. A great many colored people, the old men and women, as purveyors of lemonade, gingerbread, and other refreshments, turn an honest penny on this gala-day. The consumption of water-melons on the Fourth is enormous. No economic statistician has ever figured up melons and colored people, but perhaps not quite two melons per head on the Fourth would be a computation not very much out of the way. Under the cake-seller's table in the picture is a jug, just such a one as "Uncle Remus" would have chuckled over; but there is no reason to suppose that that jug does not contain lemon juice or syrup, because a drunken negro is by far a more uncommon sight than a tipsy white man. A more decent and well-behaved crowd it would be impossible to find, for the colored people South are naturally polite and considerate. Acquaintances greet one another, and kindly words are interchanged. The new era South admits of a personage never seen in former times of slavery, and that is the ambulant white peddler. He may be seen in the background of the picture proclaiming the excellence of his wares.

It is getting to be more and more the habit for some colored man to address an assembly of his own race on this momentous occasion. Certainly his bird of freedom soars and swoops in an eccentric manner. As far as eloquence goes, he is the rival of the white speaker; but he invariably shows good judgment, for he tries to teach his hearers that a colored man, to be a free man, must call into play that higher mental quality common to all humanity.

Sensible white people in the South encourage the celebration of the Fourth, for to understand why the day is to be held in reverence is to educate the negro of the duties he owes his country.

THE COLOR LINE

HARPER'S WEEKLY
August 18, 1888, p. 606

Some time ago, in speaking of the Southern question, by which we meant that of the colored vote, we pointed out that the remedy for such wrongs as existed is not national or political, but lies in the erasure of the color line and the encouragement of the normal division of parties by differing opinions upon great national policies. The situation in those districts where the colored vote is in the ascendant is due to the dread of negro domination—a dread founded, as is held by the white citizens in those districts, upon reason and experience. The feeling toward a peaceful, intelligent, and industrious colored minority, even in a peculiarly enlightened community, is shown by the fact that the unequal laws against negroes have been only recently modified in Ohio, and that in parts of that State the mixed schools authorized by law are still repugnant to the whites. In such communities it is fair to presume that if the majority vote were that of recently emancipated slaves, some means would be devised directly or indirectly to escape its control. The wrong and the danger of refusing to respect the rights of a majority of legal voters in a community are indisputable. They cannot be confined to that community, and patriotic and intelligent men will therefore not content themselves with decrying them, but by a careful and sympathetic study of causes and circumstances will seek practical measures of relief. The actual situation is plainly stated by Judge McClure, of Arkansas, in a recent speech to the Lincoln Club at Little Rock. The Judge has been one of the chief Republican leaders in the State for twenty years. He says that "the white element of the South will never submit to negro rule," seeing in it only a promise of the horrors of San Domingo. As long as the negro vote is solid, every other question and interest will be postponed to that of opposing it.

In Jefferson County, in Arkansas, where there is a Republican or colored majority of 2800, a bargain is made between the Republicans and Democrats to divide the offices. The reason is that the minority wills that it shall be so, and the majority does not dare to resist. Judge McClure says that in Phillips County, in Arkansas, 400 Democrats hold 3600 colored Republicans in subjection, and less than 100 Democrats in Crittenden County have overborne the colored Republican organization and expelled the colored officers from the county. He says that they are asking the Governor for redress, but that it will be in vain. Negro domination, he thinks, once overthrown by revolution, has never been restored. This situation, he says as a Republican, cannot be changed until the negro vote is divided. While it is simply black against white, "the law is powerless, the Governor is powerless, the courts are powerless." Judge McClure advises the dissolution of the alliance between the Republican party and the negro vote as the only way of promoting natural and normal party relations, and consequently of giving the Republican party a chance of growth and influence in the State. The Republican platform, he says, is acceptable to large interests and bodies of voters in Arkansas and other Southern States. But while Republican success means negro domination there can be no other question. When, however, the vote is determined, not by color, but by conviction and preference, as in Massachusetts of New York, then the fear of black domination will disappear, and the white voters will take sides according to their interest and belief.

Judge D. L. Russell, an equally prominent Republican leader in North Carolina, an ex-member of Congress, in recently declining a nomination for the Chief-Justiceship of the Supreme Court, speaking as a Republican, says:

> "I would rise to remark that, while as a rule the South does not treat its colored people with the same liberality and justice which they receive in the North, there is yet defence for the deep and dire determination of the Southern white man to never submit to negro rule. The negroes of the South are largely savages. We, with Northern aid and sanction, kidnapped them, enslaved them, and by most monstrous wrong degraded them so that they are no more fit to govern than are their brethren in African swamps, or so many Mongolians dumped down from pagan Asia. In North Carolina, Tennessee, Virginia, and other frontier States there is not the slightest danger of negro government, nor has there ever been. But in South Carolina and most of the cotton States there was negro rule, which was as much a parody upon civilized institutions as is the present Bourbon dominion in South Carolina a travesty upon free government."

Judge Russell proceeds to say as strongly as possible that he does not say that all negroes are savages, and that he has the deepest sympathy with the race, for which, through hatred and obloquy, he has contended for twenty years. An intelligent and prosperous African citizen is as agreeable to him as the Southern Bourbon Democrat is disgusting. But he feels that the identification of Republicanism with negro domination keeps "the South" solid. The movement for a division of the colored vote, of which the Indianapolis Convention is a sign, is therefore to be warmly welcomed. The remarks of its President, Mr. Peter H. Clark, a former principal of the colored high-school in Cincinnati, from which position it is stated that he was dismissed by the Republicans solely because he ceased to be a Republican, show great intelligence and shrewd perception. Judges McClure and Russell would apparently seek to dissolve the alliance of Republicanism and the colored vote by repelling it from the Republican organization. But the method of which Mr. Clark's course is an illustration, the resolution of colored voters to cast their ballots according to their convictions upon current public questions, is the natural and better way. As Mr. Clark truly says, few of the evils under which the negroes suffer are political in their nature or can be remedied by political means. Experience since the war shows clearly that a situation which merely arrays the colored voters against the white is for every reason to be deplored. The responsibility and the fault are not to be charged exclusively to either party. But it is evident that mere persistence in recrimination will not solve the problem; and as the maintenance of the color line will remedy no abuse, its disappearance in a natural difference of opinion upon public questions will be the earnest of the solution of a serious problem.

A QUESTION ANSWERED

HARPER'S WEEKLY
September 8, 1888, p. 667

A correspondent asks if we approve "the Democratic doctrine" contained in some remarks of Mr. Z. N. Estes, of Memphis, as reported in the Chicago *Times*. He spoke very contemptuously of colored citizens, and said that "it was a great mistake when they were given the ballot," and that all they were fit for was to labor. Our correspondent also asks our attention to the views of Major Pettit, of Shelby County, in Tennessee, who holds that trouble with the negroes is sure to come, and who prefers that it should take place during his life than afterward.

Both these gentlemen, if correctly reported, forget that a colored American citizen, however ignorant and degraded, has precisely the same rights as a voter that they have. In their remarks, as reported, they express an ignorant Bourbon sentiment, and if that be a Democratic sentiment it is one which we certainly do not approve. But it certainly cannot surprise our correspondent that such feelings and views survive in the old Slave States the extinction of slavery, and he would hardly assert that the problem presented by emancipation and by the political enfranchisement of the freedmen is one which admits of a summary solution, or that it is not one of the most perplexing that was ever submitted to a nation.

It is to be solved, probably, indirectly rather than directly, and one of the most suggestive signs of the probable solution that we have recently observed is the visit of Mr. McKinley to Georgia. He went to state the position of the Republican party upon a great public question, and it is by the natural division of public sentiment upon such questions that the political color line is to be erased. This result will be promoted by the perception that Republicanism does not mean negro ascendency, and a speech like that of Mr. McKinley's tends directly to that conviction. In the degree that the conviction grows, a happy solution becomes more probable. Men who think and talk as Mr. Estes and Major Pettit are reported to have talked will do nothing toward a settlement of the situation, and if they represent the controlling spirit of their part of the country, the solution is still very distant.

PERSONAL

HARPER'S WEEKLY
September 8, 1888, p. 667

The Rev. Nathan Smith, a colored preacher at Macon, Georgia, has learned the Bible by heart, from Genesis to Revelation.

PERSONAL

HARPER'S WEEKLY
October 13, 1888, p. 771

The colored Methodist church up at Putnam, Connecticut, is to have the Rev. Thomas Sunrise, a full-blooded Indian, for pastor, Brother Sunrise is declared to be an impressive orator. His devotion to his calling is proved by his proposal to work without pay.

THE GIFT OF DANIEL HAND

HARPER'S WEEKLY
November 10, 1888, p. 847

The American Missionary Association has received from Mr. Daniel Hand, of Clinton, Connecticut, a noble gift of one million of dollars, to be devoted to the education of the colored people in the Southern States. Dr. Streeby, the secretary of the Association, in presenting the gift, said that it was the largest public gift ever bestowed by a living person upon any benevolent society in the country. Mr. Hand is now eighty years of age, and made his fortune in the Southern States, mainly in Augusta, Georgia, and Charleston, South Carolina. When the civil war began he returned to the North, where he has since resided. All his immediate family have been long dead, and he has been nursing his property with the purpose of consecrating it to some benevolent use.

The conditions of the fund are simple. The Association is to invest the money as it thinks best, and the expenditure of the income is limited to one hundred dollars a year for any individual, which may be paid either to him or to the school. A scholarship of seventy dollars, together with industrial work, will support a colored or Indian pupil at Hampton Institute for a year, so that the provision of the Hand fund is adequate for its purpose.

The humane spirit of such a gift is one of the strongest bonds of national union, and the gift itself is addressed to an object of the most vital importance. The race problem in the Southern States is one which cannot be safely neglected, and which in its bearing is not limited to any part of the country. But whatever its wisest solution may be, the one indispensable thing is that the colored people shall be educated. Self-respect comes with mental and moral enlightenment, and whoever contributes to it effectively is not only a benefactor, but a patriot.

THE BOSTON MASSACRE

HARPER'S WEEKLY
November 17, 1888, p. 867

The monument commemorative of the Boston massacre of March 5, 1770, which will be unveiled on the 14th of November on the Common in that city, recalls an event which was held at the time to be of such importance that the recurrence of the day was annually celebrated and a patriotic oration delivered. It is one of the Revolutionary legends, and the contemporaneous feeling in regard to it has been transmitted without examination and as a part of the great tradition of the contest. A British sentry was insulted and assailed. He raised an alarm. A squad of soldiers appeared, and after enduring taunts and attacks from the crowd, they fired, and five Americans were killed. The leader of the Americans in the affray was Crispus Attucks, probably a half-breed Indian, and his name leads those of the five who fell. The memorial therefore is regarded as especially honoring the colored race, and prominent colored citizens will take a chief part in the ceremonies. . . .

DANIEL HAND'S GIFT

HARPER'S WEEKLY
November 17, 1888, p. 870

Mr. Daniel Hand, who has given one million dollars for the education of colored children of both sexes in the South, has had an interesting career. Before the war he was widely known in the South as a prominent and prosperous business man. Fifty years ago he was already established in Augusta, Georgia, and by the time the war broke out he had acquired large interests as a merchant in that city, in Charleston, and elsewhere. One of his partners of that time, who had grown up to affluence from a clerkship under him at a salary of fifty dollars a year, still lives in Charleston, and has a romantic story to relate of the method by which Mr. Hand's fortune was saved from confiscation by the Confederate government. When the war began, Mr. Hand was in this city purchasing supplies for his various business houses in the South. He was not in sympathy with the secession movement, and hence concluded to remain in New York. But when the sequestration acts were passed he was alarmed for the safety of his property, all of which was in the South. He was advised to return, and attempted to do so, but at Washington and Baltimore he failed to get through the lines, and on trying to enter by way of New Orleans he was arrested for a spy. Through the good offices of his partner in Charleston he was soon released, and allowed to proceed to Augusta, his former home. Here a howling mob called for his punishment as a spy from the North, and the Mayor, who was his friend, had to put him in jail as a protection from violence. Released from this confinement, he was then taken to Richmond under suspicion, and confined there for several weeks in Libby Prison. During this time a suit for the sequestration of his property in Charleston was pressed, but it ended in his favor. When finally he secured a release from Libby Prison he decided to go North again, and remain until matters took on a brighter look. Meanwhile his Southern interests were confided to the care of his old partner, who was to hold and manage them as his own. In case of further attempts at confiscation they were to be regarded as the partner's individual property. The real estate stood in the partner's name. This partner was the banker George W. Williams, now of Charleston, and a man of large fortune.

Mr. Hand's entire possessions are estimated at more than $2,000,000. The $1,0000,000 which he gives for the education of colored children represents, generally speaking, the amount saved for him through the intervention of Mr. Williams. There is a kind of poetic fitness, therefore, in the disposition now so generously made of this large sum of money. About a year ago it was known that Mr. Hand expected to bequeath the sum for this purpose, but he changed his plan. Like Peter Cooper, Ezra Cornell, and other wise and sane philanthropists, he has made the gift in his own lifetime. He has chosen the method of turning the money over to the American Missionary Association, and it is expected that no time will be lost in making use of it. It is in the form of securities bearing interest in part at six per cent., the total present income from them being placed at between $50,000 and $60,000. The $1,000,000 given represents the face value of the securities. Their market value is now something more. Mr. Hand lives at Guilford, Connecticut, and is said to be a bachelor between seventy-five and eighty years of age.

AN EDUCATIONAL QUALIFICATION AND WHITE SUPREMACY

HARPER'S WEEKLY
December 22, 1888, pp. 978–79

The result of the election has obviously again directed public attention in the Southern States to the question of the suffrage. The feeling which Mr. Charles Dudley Warner describes in his delightful *On Horseback in Virginia, North Carolina, and Tennessee,* and which is known through myriads of private channel, and in public speeches like that of Mr. Grady in Texas, and generally in the press of the Southern States, is undoubtedly the dominant sentiment of the intelligent and naturally controlling society in that part of the country. It is not unfriendly to the colored race. It favors education and industrial opportunities for colored citizens, but its fundamental conviction and purpose is white supremacy. To secure this fairly is the problem; that is, how to divide the colored vote so that it will aid this supremacy, or how to reduce it equitably below a threatening point. Devices like the eight-box system, which labels every box at polls, and requires all votes to be deposited in the right box without hints or aid to the voter, and which, of course, practically disfranchises the voter who cannot read, are now felt to be unworthy methods, and the proposition of an educational qualification is openly advocated by some of the leading Southern journals, even at the cost of some Representatives in Congress. But it does not seem to us that this would necessarily follow, because it is very questionable whether a qualification applicable to all voters could be regarded as an abridgment of the right in the sense of the Constitution. The doubt of the wisdom of an educational qualification under the circumstances springs from a different consideration.

The larger part of the colored voters and considerable number of white voters in the Southern States cannot read, and the qualification would disfranchise both classes so long as the disability should continue. But it would have another result. It would probably retard education in those States where education is of the most vital importance. If the main object be white supremacy, whatever menaced that supremacy would be instantly covered with suspicion. But education, by practically enfranchising the colored voters, would increase the chance of colored supremacy in such States as South Carolina, Mississippi, and Louisiana. To encourage education, therefore, would be to foster that chance, and under such circumstances an honest and resolute policy of instruction for the colored people could not be anticipated. Thus this simple and legal solution of the problem, even accompanied by a surrender in some States of a degree of representation in Congress, and honestly sought as a fair measure of

A NECESSARY PRECAUTION.

Rev. Jer'bo'm Johnsing (*ruminating on the backslidings of his flock*). "Now dere's dat Poleyun Jones 'n' dat Ne'miah Sawbuck! Dey ain't no more'n got started on de narrer road ter glory dan dey flops ober on ter de debil's bro'd highway and done gets cotched a-stealin' chick'ns! Dey is sech eberlastin' onsartin' critters, dat when dey once gets 'ligion, 'pears like dey ought to stay right in de church de plumb while, 'n' *hab dere dinners fotched to 'em!*"

Harper's Weekly, September 22, 1888, p. 719.

relief, would probably paralyze the movement which is essential to the general and peaceful prosperity of that part of the country, which is the movement for education. It is alleged, and we believe with good reasons, that since the war the mulato is disappearing and the distinctive color line is deepening, while the black population increases decidedly faster than the white. Under these circumstances an educational qualification for the suffrage in the States where the colored population is in the majority would tend not only to disfranchise, but to keep in ignorance, the large majority of the people of those States.

An educational qualification is always desirable, but always upon the condition that there is not only ample provision of free instruction, if not compulsory laws, but also that general perception of the value of education which will keep the schools full. Now in a community where the two races live together, but at great disadvantage to the colored race because of its previous enslavement, because its color is perpetual ban, and because the white race proposes to maintain supremacy at any cost, it is evident that the white race, which is undoubtedly in the actual situation the master race, would not favor any change in the conditions which menaced its supremacy. The real solution of the problem lies, of course, in the simple and natural relation among all citizens in the Southern States which prevails in general in the Northern States. But the method of reaching the solution—that is, how to produce that relation—is not clear. If what we have said be correct, it would not be produced by an educational qualification for the suffrage. That would be justly regarded as a measure intentionally inimical to the colored race, and that belief would of itself deepen the sense of unfriendliness. One of the surest methods of

Harper's Weekly, November 10, 1888, p. 852.

dispelling that feeling would be a careful abstention from any policy plainly hostile to equality of political or civil rights. Social relations, as everywhere, must regulate themselves. The problem is one of very great importance, in which all good American citizens in all the States are interested, and its great difficulties, especially to those who are immediately and locally concerned, are fully appreciated. We shall watch with great care and the most friendly disposition the manner in which the advocates of white supremacy at all costs, who are also advocates of an educational qualification for the franchise, dispose of the argument that the one must necessarily conflict with the other.

PERSONAL

HARPER'S WEEKLY
December 22, 1888, p. 979

—Among the most respected citizens of Canada are fugitive slaves from the United States, who found their way over the border by way of the "underground railroad." They have made their mark in the trades and even in the professions, and some of them are successful farmers. Hamilton, Ontario, has the largest negro population in Canada, and the colored people own some of the handsomest dwellings in the place. One of the men, Henry Brown, while escaping from Virginia was shipped to Philadelphia in a box two feet wide and three feet deep. He had a fearful ride, the caution on the outside of the box, "This side up with care," being but little regarded by expressmen during the journey. Montreal has a negro notary, and one of her white churches a colored assistant pastor. . . .

—The hair of a farmer living in Fulton County, Georgia, is so much like the wool of a sheep that several pairs of stockings and mittens have been made from it. It is brown in color, and soft and thick.

A LETTER FROM SOUTH CAROLINA

HARPER'S WEEKLY
December 29, 1888, p. 999

"Greenville, South Carolina.
"To the Editor of Harper's Weekly:

"You recently printed a letter I had the honor to receive from President-elect Harrison, and spoke briefly of the indications that letter gave of the policy likely to be used in the Southern States by the next administration. I ask of you the opportunity to put before the thoughtful and conservative people among whom your journal goes some facts which are generally unknown or forgotten.

"There is a 'Southern situation,' an abnormal, unusual political condition, demanding from wise statesmanship political methods different from those used in other parts of the country where the conditions are natural and wholesome. The South was the scene of one of the most sudden and violent revolution in history. Within five years a rich and arrogant people was made poor and beaten, and millions of men who had been held by those people as slaves were made freemen and voters and the political rulers of their former masters. The statement of the event must carry with it conviction that it left distortions on the surface and dangers beneath it, as surely as a volcanic explosion must leave earth cracks above and heat below. More by the teachings of instinct and the guidance of nature than by definite plan or with purpose, the Southern people have to a degree restored the conditions so violently reversed. The whites, owners of the soil and property, descendants of generations of freedom and civilization, again rule, and the negroes, newly freed slaves, representing only muscular labor, and descendants of generations of barbarism and slavery, are agained ruled. Heredity has asserted its power.

"These two races are on the same territory, nominally the same people, with legal rights and positions in all respects equal, with the color line dividing them politically and socially. The mass of the negro race in the South is composed of farm and day laborers, whose intelligence varies over a scale from that of the average white mechanic to a barely perceptible remove from actual barbarism. They are all Republicans. They believe the Republican party made them free; they know the little lease of political power that they had was under the patronage of the Republican party, and that in that party is their only hope of return to power. They also know that the white men who fought to keep them in slavery, and who have taken their power from them, are called Democrats. They know nothing of political creeds, principles, and platforms, or of the characters or purposes of candidates, and care nothing for them. They reason by what they see and know within their own observation, and from their point of view they reason properly and wisely. Much more wisdom and intellectual training than they have is required to induce men to accept the belief that power is sometimes a curse to its possessor. The more intelligent, educated, and well-to-do negroes are naturally in sympathy with their race. Aside from that, the more highly developed the colored man is, the more bitterly he must chafe under the restrictions put upon him by the enveloping conditions. Every hour of the day he has to realize that he is thought of as an inferior by the poorest white man he meets. Merchandise, independent manufacture, law, and medicine are closed against him, because the patronage of his own race is rarely enough to support him in any of them. His social life is confined to those he feels to be beneath him, or to the very small circle of his race equal to him in acquirements. His resentment against the race holding itself above him, and keeping him down while he feels the power and the impulse to rise, intensifies the tendency created by instinct and interest to stand with his color, to look to it and to the Republican party for the fulfilment of his hopes and ambitions.

"How is it with the white man? He may be a descendant of old Whig or Federalist stock, all his impulses and opinions may be with the Republican party and its principles; yet if he votes the Republican ticket and becomes a member of the Republican party in the South, he is part of and helping an organization the local bulk and strength of which is the unreasoning, ignorant, irresponsible negro vote. He cannot know who will direct that vote or receive its power in municipal, State, or district politics, but he knows the chances will always favor the most unscrupulous, cunning, and reckless leader, the man who will promise most to a people unable to measure promises, and pander most diligently to prejudices where they are most easily aroused. If a violent demagogue can sometimes carry with him hosts of your reading, thinking, self-respecting Northern working-people, what can he not do with such material as he will have to work with here? Let it be remembered that this is not theory. In some States of the South the governments resting on the solid negro vote in a short time piled up bonded debts, for which there was no occasion or actual return, which we will not finish paying in twenty years; in some the militia companies, fully armed and equipped, were composed entirely of negroes, subject to be inflamed to any atrocity by accident or design, incapable of understanding the results of their own acts, no more fit to be trusted with weapons than so many children. These are serious facts and considerations with the Southern white man. They involve his business, his tax rates, the development of his country, and the peace and safety of his family. They not only keep him away from the Republican party; they keep him inside the Democratic organization as the one power between his State and black rule, and make him as much the servant of that organization, and as prompt and zealous in action with it, as utterly debarred from freedom of thought and act, as if he was a soldier of an army marching through a hostile country.

"The white people and the Democrats of the South are as eager as any for the relief of the situation, and for freedom from the stain of keeping the negro vote down, and the fear of having it regain control and force blight and ruin on the country. Our condition is not wholesome for the republic or for us as States and individuals. A large Southern vote is represented in the Electoral College and the House of Representatives, but never cast; it is here, repressed, gathering strength perhaps from its repression, threatening always. Suppose the white men stay away from the Federal boxes and allow the black half of the population to send the Representatives now sent by the white half, will that improve the position? No power can give assurance that the black vote would be confined to the Federal boxes. If there could be such assurance I believe two-thirds of the whites would be glad to barter their rights of representation in the Federal government for undisputed control of their States, counties, and cities, for the power other people have to divide among themselves on questions of local policy.

"The educational qualification is prescribed for our troubles. Its first practical effect is to add to the mass of sullen, resentful, disfranchised negroes a smaller but more active and aggressive mass of sullen, resentful, disfranchised white men, the two together making a majority of the men of each State, and offering a standing inducement to politicians and parties to obtain permanent power by bringing about the restoration of the manhood franchise. Without that consideration would it be wise or humane to establish by law what would be practically a race difference, to leave the negro, at this late day, entirely powerless, at the mercy of the white man, without his former value as property or his present strength as a political factor? He would be as prey inviting aggression, and the utmost efforts of the vast number of white Southern Democrats who wish to see him have fair play could not secure it for him when the interests or sentiment of the time opposed it. He would receive the same fair play the all-mastering, eager white man, unrelenting in acquisition, has given the Indian and the Chinaman.

"If what I say is accepted as truth, the failure of the plan for dealing with the South indicated by General Harrison is sure. The Southern white people do not ask to be either petted or driven, because the two policies are equally powerless in releasing them from the hard political obligations to which they are bound by necessity. They will not divide on the tariff question. They are already divided on that and other issues in sentiment, but they dare not divide in action.

"To leave the situation undisturbed will not be statesmanship, good morals, or good politics. If every Democratic office-holder in the South should be left unmolested during the coming four years, the end of that time would find the relations and membership of the parties unchanged. Every negro would be a Republican, and not a white man would have become one. The differences and lines between the parties in the South are deeper than any questions of policy or principle or patronage. They are the differences and lines between Anglo-Saxon and Ethiopian, between former master and former slave, between aggregated capital and aggregated labor, between a race kept down by sentiment, custom, inheritance, and necessity, and a race forced by sentiment, custom, inheritance, and necessity to keep it down. The evils will increase with time. As the two races increase they will crowd each other within their territory, and the struggle for place and foothold will become stronger and harder; as the educated class increases among the negroes, its pressure against the confining, repressive forces above will be more serious, and the friction will be more irritating to both sides.

"Any scheme which contemplates the amalgamation of the races may be rejected instantly. It is an impossibility, because it is abhorrent to every nerve and sentiment of white men. Those of them who can bring themselves to cool thought upon that subject are convinced that the practical result of amalgamation would be the merging of both races in a mongrel, useless to itself, and an everlasting weight upon the country.

"The situation is told here as it appears to one who is part of it and in it, and who has tried to give intelligent thought to its realities, stripping away the pretences with which it is covered by the politicians and political writers of the respective sides as sentiment, interest, and ignorance suggest.

"As the personal position of the writer may give some light to those who think of the subject as it is here presented, I venture to give the information that I am the editor of a South Carolina newspaper and a Democrat, believing with the Democratic party in its every principle and theory, and loving it, hoping to vote always in the future, as always in the past, a straight Democratic ballot.

"As I love and believe in the Democratic party, I love and believe in this Republic and its people, and in my heart there is an earnest, enduring faith that the American people, at the right time and in the right way, will find and use the solution of the problem presented to them here, as they have solved the many dangerous and puzzling questions which they have had to consider in the past, and will dispose of these troubles wisely and justly. I have written with the hope of humbly helping to that end by directing public thought to the two facts that (1) there is a distinctive 'Southern situation,' and (2) that it is not to be dealt with or disposed of by a single expedient or plan devised and executed off-hand, and will demand careful study, mature thought, patience, and mutual forbearance, that right may be done on all sides.

"A. B. Williams."

THE AFRICAN SLAVE-TRADE

HARPER'S WEEKLY
December 29, 1888, p. 1006

Cardinal Lavigerie, the venerable Archbishop of Algiers, in preaching his crusade against the Arabic slave-hunter and slave-trader of Africa, has succeeded in arousing a public interest throughout western Europe that is as significant as it is encouraging. He has spoken amid great applause in Paris, London, Lisbon, and other great cities. The Pope has become interested in his projects, and has sent him a handsome sum of money. The Protestant Evangelical Alliance in Berlin and the Catholic Congress at Freiburg have both adopted resolutions aiming to create public sentiment in favor of aggressive measures. In the last week of October a great meeting was held in Cologne in the interest of this work, at which the principal speaker was Lieutenant Wissmann, of the German Army, who had only a few months ago returned from eastern Africa. The German and the English governments have entered into a special agreement to enforce rigidly the sixth article of the Congo Conference, which makes it obligatory upon all participants to cooperate in the suppression of the slave horror, by blockading against the slave-ships those portions of the east and southeastern coast of Africa which have not been sufficiently protected in this regard, chiefly on account of the weakness or weak will of the Portuguese, who there lay claim to a vast stretch of debatable land. The King of Belgium, the leader of the Congo enterprise, naturally is heart and hand in the movement. None, however, are more strongly aroused in the matter than the Germans, who, in their new colonial policy, rightly consider it a high aim to introduce European civilization into their new possessions, and in the interest of this aim to suppress, as much as possible, the trade in human beings. The result of all this has been that, even if Lavigerie will not be able, like a modern Peter the Hermit, to conduct a crusade to Africa and realize his wish of direct military attack on the traders, the interest aroused has certainly exceeded all expectations. Prominent individuals, societies, and organizations of various kinds, and even the governments, are fully enlisted in the cause.

And the suppression of the nefarious business will need the earnest and continued co-operation of all these forces. Institutions that are the growth of tens and tens of centuries cannot be easily eradicated. Slave-hunting and the slave-trade have almost from prehistoric times been the curse of the Black Continent. In old Egyptian hieroglyphics, and on wall-paintings in the temples, the story of ancient African slavery is told. There never was a time when slavery was not carried on to an almost unlimited degree throughout the continent. It is decidedly a historical African institution. To make the problem all the more difficult to solve, the various Mohammedan governments of Africa, from the smallest to the greatest, sanction and aid the inhuman business. The Koran encourages slavery, and approves of inhuman treatment of those not of the faith. The raids often partake of a religious character. Schweinfurth narrates that he repeatedly saw at the head of the procession of unfortunates, the fakirs, or Islam priests, marching with the Koran in their hands.

Nor had the attitude of the European nations in former centuries been such on that continent as to make the task now an easy one. It is less than a century since even civilized western Europe began to abolish slavery, and in the centuries before that these same peoples were the leaders in African slave-traffic. None have a worse record in this regard than has England. Of Liverpool it has been said that "its streets were paved with the skulls of slaves"; and in the flourishing period of the trade no less than one hundred slave-ships landed each year in that metropolis. On the eastern African coast there were formerly seventy harbors from which European vessels drew their cargoes of human freight. In the latter years of the Middle Ages, Italy, France, and England had their regular slave markets; Portugal and Spain sent thousands of stolen Mohammedans to their American possessions. As late as 1770 the Christian Knights of Malta had their galleys manned with Mohammedan slaves. It was not till 1807 that Wilberforce succeeded in persuading England to abolish slavery in her possessions. But for three hundred years and more Christian nations and Christian peoples had grown fat on the profits on the slave-trade. Even religious sanction was not wanting. Pope Nicolaus V. in a special bull permitted the Christians to keep non-Christians as slaves.

At present the trade is entirely in the hands of the Arabs, although it is claimed, with a good show of reason, that the Portuguese government is for mercenary reasons derelict in its duty of fighting the great wrong. The well-known method of procedure is to organize, either under the leadership of such chiefs as Tippoo Tip, or as a private robber band, and then make raids into the negro districts of inner Africa. Both the trade and the raids have for many years been effectually stopped along the whole western coast. Within the last few years, since Germany, England, and others have divided up among themselves the unclaimed districts on the east coast, the exportation has almost been stopped there too; only recently, however, an English gun-boat captured a trading vessel with eighty-six slaves on board. The vessels have frequently adopted the ruse of sailing under the French flag, as France has only within the immediate past decided to take aggressive measures in this matter. The slaves are exported to Turkey, Persia, and the Mohammedan East.

Egress with slaves is now practically possible only through the lands controlled by the Mohammedans, that is, Egypt and some North African states. And it is to these that the slave caravans are led, although some still go eastward to the Zanzibar coast and the adjacent islands. Since the failure of the English Soudan expedition, Khartoum has again become the chief distributing-point for the tens of thousands of slaves annually brought there; while south of Ethiopia, through the wild Galla country, vast hordes reach the coast at Obok, on the Gulf of Aden. The states nominally under influence of Western nations, such as Egypt, do not, of course, officially sanction the trade, nor do they suppress it. At most, it is not carried on where European visitors may see it. Cairo is not a slave market. The principal routes of the slave-robber lie through the Great Desert of Sahara, through which the caravans go to Fez, Wadan, Ghadamis, Mursuk, and Aujila, and also to Siout on the Nile.

Travellers, old and new, agree that the horrors of the slave-trade do not lie in the condition of the slaves when once sold, but in their sufferings when being stolen and transferred to the markets. Livingstone, Stanley, Schweinfurth, Nachtigal, Wolf, Cameron, Wissmann, Crawford, and others are a unit on this point. The Mohammedan master as a rule is easy on his slave. Wolf, in describing the slaves on the Congo, says the average status of those in servitude throughout Africa is this: "The slaves are compelled to do a part of the labor in the field, but they are never overworked. They enjoy a good and gentle treatment, and even may eat with their masters. The muluba (leader) has only the ambition of possessing many wives and many slaves, because his social station is conditioned by these. He does not think of overloading his slaves with work, and were he to ill-treat them he would suffer in the eyes of his neighbors. But still the Damokles sword constantly impends over both women and slaves of being sold into another land."

But of the sufferings on the long marches to the markets the African travellers report only tales of terror and horror. They all agree in this, however, that for every man or woman brought to the journey's end alive, no less than four perish on the way. In other words, eighty per cent, of those that are captured die a wretched death before reaching the markets. Of course it is impossible to even approximate the number of slaves taken each year. One writer goes as far as to say that "at least 400,000 negroes are annually carried into bondage, and that thus the lives and liberty of upwards of 2,000,000 are each year sacrificed on the altars of lust and mammon." The lowest figures given are those of the careful German statistician, the Mission Inspector, Dr. Fabri, who calculates that at least 100,000 lives are lost each year in these murderous expeditions.

It would be a very superficial way of looking at this problem to think that it involves only the one feature of an abolition of a crime of centuries. It involves the question of the future civilization of Africa. If the slave-trade falls, then Arabic aggression and dominion too falls in Africa. It is a question of life and death for the future of the Black Continent. Or, in the words of the famous geographer Andree: "The abolition of slavery and of slave-robbing in Africa signifies a contest with Islam and a regeneration of the Orient. When Islam has once been crowded out by the Christian nations of the West, then the African slave problem will solve itself, and Africa will, in its own way, take an active part in the world's work. But there are immense perspectives, the work for future generations. We are standing only at the beginning; we can only lay a few foundation-stones; the completion of the edifice this generation will not see."

Charles - Martial - Allemand Lavigerie is now in his sixty-third year, having been born at Esprit in 1825. Early in life he showed a singular aptitude for theology and the classics, and was, above all, distinguished for piety and honesty of purpose. Before he was thirty he filled various ecclesiastical functions at Rome, and occupied the position of French Auditor. He was one of the prelates attached to the service of the Pope. In 1863 he was made Bishop of Nancy. During the late Napoleonic regime he was a member of the Imperial Council and a leading member of the Board of Public Instruction. In 1867 he left Paris and took the highest ecclesiastical position in Algiers. In this French colony he became familiar with Islamism, its habits and customs, and though slavery had long been abolished in this French possession, the prelate must have been struck with the moral disturbances such an institution had left there. In Algiers M. Lavigerie played a distinguished part in ecelesiastical and municipal matter. His endeavors toward the conversion of the Algerians brought him into conflict with Marshall Macmahon, and in 1868 the subject was one which played an important part in the politics of the time. After the fall of the Empire the Archbishop paid further visits to Africa, and was for some time in Tunis. Before this he had given frequent indications of his abhorrence of slavery, and had been outspoken as to the efforts civilized nations should take in order to break it up. A very touching incident just recorded is that of Cardinal Sanfelice, who, having had sent him a valuable golden cross for his care of the sick during the cholera in Italy, has just sent this cross to Cardinal Lavigerie for the use of the anti-slavery fund. His creation as Cardinal dates from 1882.

1889

This year marked one of the first elections of a Republican to Congress from the South: H. Clay Evans was elected to represent the state of Tennessee. Such an election was seen as "exceedingly interesting" and held much promise for the New South. For too long, some said, the South had been focused on the race problem. Now this Republican protectionist had been elected on a platform to industrialize the South, bringing labor and capital into an untouched region. The South yearned for the trade and Clay could attract millions of dollars to the "fertile fields and rich mineral lands of the 'sunny Southland.'" The editors believed the time was favorable for recent actions had demonstrated the declining power of the Bourbon class and the reduction of mob violence. New men of the South had the moral courage to "proclaim their real principles and vote for their honest convictions in defiance of social ostracism, not affrighted by the spook of negro (sic.) domination."

Other new voices of the South began to question if racial harmony could be accomplished without fair treatment on the race question. Some southerners believed the only way to maintain their institutions, their wealth, and their "civilization," i.e., segregation, while keeping seven million African Americans content, was by giving them "a fair chance in the race for life." These southerners were calling for some regional answer to the race problem, an answer left entirely to local authorities, white people of good-will and conscious, upon whose shoulders the problem rested. The interference of the federal government would not bring more blacks into politics nor would it foster any affinity towards kindness. Therefforth, white southerners wanted the nation to realize that they held the answer to the African Americans' future in the South. Any other option would probably prove disastrous.

Soon racial violence rapidly reappeared in the South. Some feared that the climate would give way to federal interference. The new president, Benjamin Harrison, was expected to make the southern question a major focus of his administration. Some southerners offered two solutions to solve the problem. Some wished for the repeal of the Fifteenth Amendment, which would eliminate the black male voter, and others wished blacks would leave the South. They envisioned a "Negro Territory" similar to Native American reservations. The editors felt both "solutions" were fancies. What the papers did call for was for black and white southerners to befriend each other and to mutually work together. The establishment of such a relationship would allow for free and fair elections. Even with fair elections, the papers realized that not all southerners would respect the law. The editors warned that this was not a local problem. Regional terrorism reflected on the national and international images. Local communities had to find realistic solutions that would foster productive racial relations.

More attention was given to the acceleration of violence in the South, i.e., lynchings, race riots, burnings, and shootings. Such constant disturbances disturbed the "sagacity of American statesmanship," warned the papers. No longer is it a question of local concern or concern of the state where the violence occurred. The question concerned American democracy and constitutional rights. Sober and intelligent citizens had to establish order and civility back into the region and realize that equality of the races by free elections and fair votes were guaranteed to all citizens by the Constitution. The papers recognized that this must be done within the region itself and it would not mean the total dissolution of Southern Society as it was known. Allowing for free elections and a fair vote would not restore black domination. Various strategies could be used that would divide the black vote, as a multi-party region now vied for their support. For the editors, allowing for black inclusion would be far more tolerable than the threat posed by the emerging "semi-civilized negroes" (sic.) who were "becoming aware of their rights and their superior forces." The editors assured the southern public that the servile Negro was rapidly disappearing. These new voices would not be controlled and would bring established agendas with them for negotiations. The papers were afraid that if the black community was impressed with the race rhetoric of this group, the balance of power could be forever changed or altered. Hence, it was imperative that some overtures be made to include some segment of the black population in the political process. Ironically, these concerns would prove true before the decade of the 1890s concluded. Prominent race leaders would meet in Louisville, Kentucky, for the first annual meeting of the Afro American League, later Afro American Council. The tradition of racial protest would continue across the first two decades of the twentieth century in the creation of additional race and gender protest organizations like the National Association of Colored Women Clubs, The Niagara Movement, the National Association for the Advance-

ment of Colored People, the National Equal Rights League and many local councils and committees.

Jacqueline A. Rouse
Georgia State University

THE ATLANTA UNIVERSITY

HARPER'S WEEKLY
January 5, 1889, p. 3

The statement that Governor Gordon, of Georgia, has recommended the Legislature of that State to restore the appropriation of $8000 to Atlanta University is entirely incorrect. On the contrary, the Governor stated that the money could not be legally given to the university, and recommended that it be appropriated in succession to several institutions supported wholly for and by the colored people. Mr. Glenn, the author of the well-known bill of 1887, has introduced a bill to devote the sum to the establishment of a State colored normal school.

Dr. Bumstead, the president of Atlanta University, who makes this statement, adds that the announcement of the State grant seriously interferes with the efforts to raise money for the university. Upon this point he says:

"With no State aid and no endowment, with five hundred students in all grades of study and all kinds of industrial training, under twenty-six officers and teachers, whose salaries must be paid from donations, in four large brick buildings, to be kept constantly heated, lighted, repaired, and insured, the university must receive $18,000 from its friends to meet its expenses for the current year. And it must renew this appeal every year until an endowment of at least $250,000 can be secured. The work of the institution has been developed too far, and it has become too important a factor in the problem of Southern education, to admit of any curtailment. Nor do we believe that our friends at the North will allow so great a calamity to happen through any failure to respond to our present appeal with the same liberality that they have manifested in the past."

PERSONAL

HARPER'S WEEKLY
January 5, 1889, p. 3

The oldest Free-Soiler in the country, and one of the few remaining members of the antislavery band to which William Lloyd Garrison belonged, Hon. Samuel E. Sewall, has just passed away at Boston in his ninetieth year. He was counsel for several fugitive slaves who were arrested in Boston, helped obtain the famous decision in the Dred Scott case, and prepared the arguments and assisted at the trial of John Brown. Mr. Sewall was the lifelong friend of Whittier, who dedicated to him the prelude to "In War Time." Of late years Mr. Sewall has distinguished himself by his persistent efforts to obtain legislation for the benefit of women in the Bay State. He was a member of the famous class of 1817 at Harvard.

—Among the gifts which Whittier invariably receives on his birthday is a barrel of pitch-pine kindlings from the Whittier colored school at Tuscaloosa, Alabama. The kindlings were accompanied this year by two photographs—one of the two hundred children composing the school, and the other of the children in the act of voting their thanks to the poet.

IN THE SOUTHERN STATES

HARPER'S WEEKLY
January 19, 1889, p. 42–43

On the last night of the late year there was a Republican banquet at Chattanooga in Tennessee to celebrate the election of Mr. H. Clay Evans, a Republican Representative to Congress. The chief interest of the occasion was a letter from General Longstreet. If not the ablest leader of the Confederate armies, he was second to none in the best soldierly qualities. At Gettysburg, if any Confederate general could have prevailed, it was Longstreet. There was no doubt of his ability, his courage, and his devotion to the Confederate cause, as there has been none since the end of the war of his complete and honorable acceptance of the great result.

The views of such a man, when the election has restored to power the party which has been held to be inimical to "the South," are exceedingly interesting and suggestive, because they must be held to express a feeling which is shared by others. General Longstreet would seem to be of opinion that the minds of Southern citizens are fixed too exclusively upon the race problem, and as a pendant to the very interesting letter of Mr. Williams, of South Carolina, which we recently published, we quote the essential part of General Longstreet's letter. He is a Republican and a protectionist. But his views, expressed with great plainness, reveal a spirit in the "New South" which must be reckoned with seriously in any just estimate of the situation:

> "Chattanooga is the centre or pioneer of the 'New South,' and being one of the first cities, if not the first, of any size in our section to elect a Republican Congressman, pledged to the protection of American labor and American industries, she has blazed out a path to industrial supremacy that her sister cities would do well to imitate. Had it not been for the 'Morrill tariff' of 1861, with its strong protective features, your flourishing city might have still been in its swaddling-clothes, instead of the vigorous specimen of robust municipal manhood that gladdens the eye of the laborer and the capitalist. It may be taken for granted that men who have the sense to amass wealth have also sense enough not to risk their investments among a people who are unfriendly to their interests, and where a community yearn for free-trade it is but natural that labor and capital should give that community a wide berth. Nothing is so timid and cautious as capital, and to get it in your midst it must feel that it is safe and welcome. Thousands and millions of dollars are locked up in government bonds or hoarded in bank vaults that would be gladly released from its 'prison bounds' and seek the fertile fields and rich mineral lands of the 'sunny Southland' if the conditions were believed to be favorable. Two recent events in our midst will conduce to this end: first, the heroic action of the Birmingham sheriff in defending his prisoner against mob violence; and second, the visit of the Birmingham delegation to General Harrison. The one showed the world the supremacy of law and order, and that lynch law will soon be a reminiscence only with us; and the other was notice to the Bourbons that their party shackles are broken, and that hereafter men will have the moral courage to proclaim their real principles and vote their honest convictions in defiance of social ostracism, not affrighted by the spook of negro domination.

> "I trust that General Harrison will meet with no factious opposition from the South, for our people owe him more than we now can discern, so close are we to the smoke of the battle of the 6th of November. The approval of Mr. Cleveland's policy would have been a calamity, notably to our section; for it would have retarded our industrial growth and arrested the development of our material resources. Although General Harrison will not get a single electoral vote from the South, yet history will record that the Southern people received greater benefits from his election than those States that voted for him. Let our old boys in gray meet General Harrison on half-way ground, and take the outstretched hand of the patriot and statesman, and co-operate with him in his efforts for the upbuilding and glory of our common country. Help him and hold up his hands, that he may be the stronger to help you."

The Charleston *News and Courier,* in considering at length the letter of Mr. Williams, of Greenville, South Carolina, which we recently published, admits it to be candid and strong, but wonders that we should suppose it to represent the view of a great part of the intelligent and earnest people in the Southern States, denying emphatically that it does so. This view it holds to be much more truly expressed in a speech of Mr. Breckinridge, of Kentucky, prepared for delivery at the late New England dinner in Charleston. Mr. Breckinridge states the question to be, How the people of the Southern States can preserve the control of their affairs and the preservation of their institutions, their civilization, and their wealth consistently with the contentment of the seven millions of colored people? He thinks that this can be accomplished by a kindly spirit, by Christianizing and civilizing them, and giving them a fair chance in the race for life. The Atlanta *Constitution,* commenting upon some remarks of the Weekly, says that "the South is striving to find some solution of the negro problem," and ex-Governor Bullock thinks that it will be certainly found. All these authorities agree that the question must be left entirely to local adjustment, because the future condition of the colored race in the Southern States must depend, as Mr. Breckinridge says, upon the good-will and the conscience of the white people among whom it is placed. Of this there can be no doubt. The most stringent national interference which the Constitution would permit would not necessarily bring another Southern vote to the polls, and would certainly not foster greater kindliness of feeling. If the well-nigh universal sentiment in this part of the country, where the colored population is very small, does not even entertain this suggestion of a representative of it in the cabinet, it cannot be difficult to understand the feeling in communities which have seen a Moses administration and a carpet-bag Legislature.

A BAD REPUTATION.

BRER SARGENT (*reading of the conviction of a fellow-citizen of color*). "No, sah! ef I'd 'a ben on dat jury I wouldn't 'a brung in no verdic' ob 'guilty.'"

BRER MOSES (*in surprise*). "But, brer, don' you see de paper say how as he done plead 'guilty' 'for' de jedge and de jury?"

BRER SARGENT (*scornfully*). "What diff'rence dat goin' make? He lie so like de debbil, yo' 'spec' I gwine b'lieve w'at he say? No, sah!"

Harper's Weekly, February 9, 1889, p. 115.

SUBTROPICAL GLIMPSES

FRANK LESLIE'S ILLUSTRATED NEWSPAPER
February 23, 1889, p. 27

It is only thirty hours from "lands of snow to lands of sun," as represented respectively by New York and Florida. Such is the degree to which air-line railroads and fast trains have annihilated distance. In other respects, however, such as climate, scenery and popular customs, the North and the South are as far apart as ever. To be whisked from one to the other in hardly more than a day's time is certainly a curious and bewildering sensation. These fast trains are vestibule trains, and they are provided with spacious "observation platforms," which afford the flying tourist every opportunity for seeing whatever can be "taken" by such instantaneous mental photography. A most interesting series of these rapidly shifting impressions is given in the drawings on pages 28 and 29. . . .

Jacksonville finally reached, it is difficult to recognize the but lately helpless and plague-stricken city in the bright, bustling, ambitious port and metropolis which now welcomes the stranger from the North. The place has emerged from the clutches of Yellow Jack more hopeful and enterprising than ever. The Subtropical Exposition enterprise has received a new lease of life, and everything is being done to offer the tourist as strong inducements for coming to Jacksonville as six months ago he had for staying away.

The scene here chosen by the artist for illustration, however, relates to a different phase of life in the South, which is as significant as it is striking. Here is a negro justice rebuking and passing sentence upon a riotous young white man—a scion of one of the "first families," it may be—who has been arrested by a negro policeman, and has passed the night in "durance vile" amongst "drunks and disorderlies" of all shades of complexion. This is not an uncommon sight in the Jacksonville police court, where Judge Lee (colored) presides with learning, tact and dignity enough to make his authority respected in any similar court, North or South.

AT HOME AND ABROAD

FRANK LESLIE'S ILLUSTRATED NEWSPAPER
February 23, 1889, p. 27

A delegation of colored men, headed by ex-Minister J. M. Langston, called on General Harrison last week, and asked the appointment of a man as Attorney-general who will enforce the election laws in the South. Although they suggested no names, Mr. Langston told a reporter afterward that Governor Foraker, he thought, would fill the office well.

THE QUESTION OF RACE

HARPER'S WEEKLY
March 2, 1889, p. 162

The inaugural address of President Harrison will throw light, perhaps, upon what is called the Southern question, which it is clear is to be made prominent in some way under the new administration. Events like the assassination of Mr. Clayton tend to deepen impatience with a "solid South." It is not, however, the solidity that is the source of trouble, but the methods by which it is believed to be effected. We have received from correspondents in the Southern States many suggestions looking to a solution of the question of the relation of the two races in those States. One view, which seems to be quite common, contemplates the repeal of the Fifteenth Amendment, and another the creation of a negro Territory, to which negro emigration from the Southern States should be directed. But such schemes are fancies merely. The repeal of the Fifteenth Amendment is impossible. No wilder proposition could be made. It stands for one of the great results of the war, and a practical abandonment of the colored race in the Southern States by the rest of the country is as absolutely out of the question as the abandonment of the war would have been. Had it been possible at any time, the experience of the black codes and the revelation of feeling during Andrew Johnson's administration removed the question from the range of practicable suggestions.

The proposition of a Territory especially devoted to the colored race, like the Indian Territory to the Indians, is equally fanciful. As Mr. Mayo remarks in the article to which we recently alluded as one of the most sympathetic and sensible treatments of the subject, the colored race in the Southern States is inseparably attached to the soil, and could not be removed except by force. Such a scheme to resolve the difficulty would be as futile as colonization would have been to abolish slavery. One such consideration is final. But it must be remembered also that the colored race furnishes the labor of the Southern States, and its exodus, upon reflection, could not be urged seriously as a practical solution of the situation. Yet in a recent speech in the Senate Mr. Morgan, of Alabama, said that if he could expel every negro from the State he would gladly do it. He regards the colored race as a burden and incubus, and holds it to be impossible that it should ever supply the thrifty, intelligent, and effective industry which the development of the State demands. The Birmingham *Age-Herald*, confirming this statement, remarks that "the South" wants every kind of white immigration, but it wants negro emigration. Such views, held by representatives of Southern opinion and feeling, when considered in the light of the universal assertion in the Southern States that white supremacy must be maintained at all costs, show the scope and the gravity of the question. This is but deepened by the fact of the character of much of the local colored population, and by the limitations of the national power over the subject. The moderate tone of Senator Evarts's recent speech in introducing the report upon the election outrages in Texas shows his conviction of the extreme difficulty of a remedy by national legislation, even if supported by the national arms. A file of soldiers at every poll would not increase the vote; but even if it should do so, the hostility of race and the public disorder would only deepen, and the solution of the question would be even more indefinitely postponed.

The Southern problem is not a free vote and a fair count, but the establishment of that relation of the races which makes a free vote and a fair count possible. To say that all that is necessary is general obedience to the laws does not advance the solution, unless it be also shown how such obedience can be secured. Senator Evarts's report recommends the revision of the Congressional election laws with a view to such security. But neither the Senator nor any one else has yet intimated the way in which, under the circumstances, it can be done. The question is of a gravity which entirely transcends party schemes and passions. It is by no means a local question in its effects. Without efforts for its solution it remains a constant and dangerous menace, and the very first step toward a solution seems to us to lie in the local cultivation by white citizens of such relations with the colored race as would naturally produce a normal distribution and division of their votes. Toward such good feeling

ON THE OBSERVATION PLATFORM OF A VESTIBULE TRAIN, ENTERING CHARLESTON, S. C.—MUSIC BY THE "BOTTLE BAND."

Frank Leslie's Illustrated Newspaper, February 23, 1889, pp. 28–29.

the prompt action of the Governor and Legislature and many communities in Arkansas, and the strong and sincere denunciation of the press, in the case of the Clayton murder, are promising signs. Without consciously friendly understandings and relations between the races, no legislative or military scheme can avail to solve the real problem.

HON. H. P. CHEATHAM

HARPER'S WEEKLY
March 2, 1889, p. 165

The successor of Congressman F. M. Simmons, of the Second North Carolina District, is H. P. Cheatham, who will be a conspicuous member by reason of the fact that he will be the only negro in Congress. He was born near the town of Henderson, North Carolina, thirty-two years ago. He is a graduate of Shaw University, of Raleigh, which institution conferred on him the degree of A.M. Immediately after graduating he was chosen Superintendent of the Colored State Normal School at Plymouth, North Carolina, where he remained until 1885, when, with little or no opposition, he was elected to the office of Register of Deeds of Vance County. He per-

formed the responsible duties of this position with very general satisfaction up to his election to Congress in November last. He has read law, and would have obtained his license but for the duties of his office interfering. The Congressman-elect is a bright mulatto of good address. He is an effective stump-speaker, and is very popular with his race, while enjoying the friendship of many white people in his district. He is very ambitious to do something toward elevating his race, and he will be pretty sure to be heard from when the new Congress assembles.

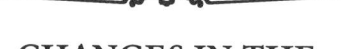

CHANGES IN THE CONSTITUTION

HARPER'S WEEKLY
April 27, 1889, p. 326

During the last nineteen years, according to Mr. McMaster, three hundred and ten amendments to the Constitution have been proposed in Congress. But three only have been adopted. These prohibit slavery, and the restriction of the right of voting on account of race, color, or previous condition of servitude. They define citizens of the United States, and the basis of enumeration for

A JACKSONVILLE (FLA.) POLICE COURT—THE NEGRO JUSTICE REPROVES A DISORDERLY WHITE BROTHER, AND DISMISSES HIM WITH A FINE.

Frank Leslie's Illustrated Newspaper, **February 23, 1889, pp. 28–29.**

Representatives, state certain disqualifications for the offices of Senator and Representative in Congress, and affirm the validity of the public debt. That after the great civil convulsion, and in the natural and powerful drift toward national centralization which succeeded the war, so little change should have been made in the organic law, and that little so wisely comprehensive of the essential and fundamental results of the war, is singularly illustrative of the moderation and good sense of the people. The same calm intelligence has been shown in the judicial interpretation of these amendments by the Supreme Court. The Richmond *Despatch* has argued recently, however, that the three amendments were not constitutionally adopted. Its general ground is that the Thirteenth Amendment, prohibiting slavery, "paved the way for the Fourteenth and Fifteenth," that this was ratified by the casting vote of West Virginia, that this State never had constitutional existence, because it was formed and erected wholly within the jurisdiction of Virginia, and that, according to the properly punctuated constitutional clause relating to the subject, such creation was not permissible.

But the *Despatch* states that it argues only for the truth of history, and not with the expectation of changing the fact that the amendments are now part of the Constitution. It is what is called an academic argument—for the pleasure of dialectics, and not practical results—an exercise which used to be thought characteristic of what was called the Southern school of politics. But it has an illustrious precedent in Mr. Webster's argument in favor of the assent of the Senate to removals, which, even against the authority of Madison, he held to be the true constitutional doctrine. He agreed, however, that the contemporary decision of Congress and the long and uniform practice had practically settled the

H. P. CHEATHAM, THE ONLY COLORED MEMBER OF THE NEW HOUSE OF REPRESENTATIVES.
FROM A PHOTOGRAPH BY THE RICHMOND ART GALLERY.

Harper's Weekly, March 2, 1889, p. 165.

question. This conclusion is equally sound in regard to the amendments that followed the war. By the action of every branch of the government and the acquiescence of the country their validity is placed beyond question, and the discussion belongs really to the realm of casuistry. To consider either their validity or their repeal as bearing upon the question of suffrage in the Southern States is useless. They are the fundamental law of the land, and they will not be repealed.

The race question, as it is called, must be settled in other ways, and it is time lost to agitate the validity or repeal of the amendments. In the general discussion of the subject, which is certainly a very serious one, we have seen nothing truer or more worthy of consideration than a remark of President Decker, of Roanoke College, in Virginia. He describes himself as a "Southern man" "by birth, education, and residence, an ex-Confederate soldier, whose home was in the track of Sherman's march through South Carolina." Such a man of course speaks for others, and when he says that the negro "is naturally docile and peaceable, and if we treat him as a man, with the same fairness, justice, and consideration we claim for ourselves as men, the less we shall hear of race antagonism in the future." It is by the light of such primary and simple principles as these that the question must be settled, and this is undoubtedly as clear to intelligent citizens of the Southern States as it is to their fellow-citizens elsewhere. Senator Eustis, of Louisiana, makes a serious mistake in regarding the interest in this question which is felt in other States as an interference with the "local affairs" of his own State and other Southern States. He will agree certainly that it is not necessary to live in Louisiana or Mississippi to understand that the perpetual practical disfranchisement of half the legal voters or more is a condition of which President Decker says truly, "For if we deprive any class of citizens of their lawful participation in the choice of law-makers and rulers, we repress or remove the most powerful incentive to the growth of that patriotic devotion to country which lies at the foundation of our national welfare, and gives the only sure promise of the perpetuity of our free institutions." This is surely a better point of departure from which to approach the subject than discussion of the validity of the amendments.

RACE FEELING

HARPER'S WEEKLY
August 24, 1889, p. 679

The disturbance in Atlanta in regard to the appointment of a colored clerk in the post-office shows not only the feeling against the negro, but also the existence of a sound conservative sentiment, which must be the reliance of the Southern communities for the adjustment of all such outbreaks, and for the moderation of the feeling from which they spring. The newly appointed postmaster was obliged to fill two vacant clerkships, and to fill them according to law. His choice was limited to two persons, one of whom was white and the other colored. In deference to the prevailing prejudice against the negro, he decided to place the white clerk at a desk where he would be in frequent contact with the public, and the colored clerk at a desk more retired from public view.

It was alleged that this desk was next to that of a white woman, who immediately resigned, it was said, in consequence of her colored neighbor. But the postmaster says—and there is no reason to doubt—that the desk of the colored clerk was in another and adjoining room, but separated by a wall. Nevertheless the incident produced great excitement, and the postmaster and a prominent Republican politician were hung in effigy. In the disturbance a colored offender was shot by a white policeman, and a race conflict was apparently imminent, which was averted by the good sense of Governor Gordon and other sensible citizens. This interference, together with the fact that a woman of excellent character and standing immediately accepted the clerkship which the other woman had resigned, shows that the better sentiment of the Southern community perceives the danger of acquiescing in disorders arising from race prejudice.

Such excitement over the employment of a colored clerk reveals a situation which involves one of the

WANTS THE EARTH.

"What's the matter, Uncle Rastus?" inquired a citizen. "You look gloomy."

"I is gloomy, sah. I'se jess had a business transaction wif 'Dolphus Johnson, an' he expec's de roas' beef, an' wan's ter giv me nuffin but de gravy. Dey calls us de sons ob Ham, sah; but dat yaller rascal is wuss, he's de son ob de hull animile."

Harper's Weekly, April 6, 1889, p. 271.

most serious of public questions. It is not to be paralleled by the prejudice against negroes in States where they are few, and it must be dealt with by local courage. It is unfair to generalize against the whole Southern community from such an incident. Those who are disposed to think that no negro can expect fair-play in any of the Southern States may well ponder the fact that John Yeldell, the colored clergyman who was recently taken from Pennsylvania to South Carolina to be tried on a charge of murder, was vigilantly protected by white citizens, upon his acquittal, against a threatened attack from friends of the murdered man, and he left safely by a special train on his return to Pennsylvania. If it be said that an attack upon a person legally acquitted of crime does not argue very advanced civilization, it is none the less plain that the facts of Yeldell's trial and departure show the successful determination of good citizens of South Carolina that a colored man under such circumstances shall be treated as fairly as in Pennsylvania or Massachusetts.

A GREAT QUESTION

HARPER'S WEEKLY
August 31, 1889, p. 698

Recent incidents in Southern States, the lynching of the negro assailant of a white girl in Georgia, the riot and murder at Richmond in Texas, the lynching of a negro prisoner by Louisiana "regulators," the burning in effigy of the postmaster at Atlanta for appointing a colored

A CHANGE OF MANŒUVRE.

GUIDE TO BATTLE-FIELDS (*sure of his party, he thinks*). "Yes, sah; hit were jest hyah dat de rebels 'gin to run, an'—"

TOURIST (*bantering him*). "Come, now! *run?* I was a reb myself, and don't believe that they ran."

GUIDE. "Hole on, boss; you ain' let me git through. I did'n say *which way* dey wuz runnin'; 't wuz *to'ards* de enemy."

Harper's Weekly, April 20, 1889, p. 311.

clerk, the circumstances of the trial of the colored preacher Yeldell in South Carolina, the shooting of a chief of police in Tennessee by colored men, and other constant disturbances and troubles, are all signs of a situation which will soon challenge the utmost sagacity of American statesmanship. The problem presented in the Southern States is wholly unprecedented, and ought to be fully comprehended and considered. It will not be settled by the remark that it is a local question which concerns only the States in which it exists, that the Supreme Court has decided that the United States have no authority to intervene, and that every State, under the same circumstances, would do what South Carolina and Louisiana and Mississippi do. Nothing was literally truer than that slavery was sectional, and existed only by State law. The antislavery movement was denounced as culpable meddling with the rights of States. But however all that might have been, the event proved, as had been foreseen by the most thoughtful and intelligent Americans, that the national interest in the question of slavery was vital. It is equally true that the question of the relation of the white and colored races as equal citizens in States of a population equally divided between the two, and where the colored race is much more rapidly increasing, involves the interests of the whole Union, and tests the principles and institutions of the American government more severely than they have yet been tested.

It is a fact of the highest significance that the great multitude of the most intelligent and substantial citizens of the Southern States, the leaders of their education, industry, and prosperity, who are neither Jacobites nor Bourbons, who rejoice that slavery is at an end, and who cherish no aims or desires apart from the Union and the national welfare, are firmly persuaded that the political equality of the races, the unrestricted exercise of the rights of equal citizenship, is impossible in those States. Look, for instance, at the feeling and situation in a county of North Carolina, one of the quietest of the Southern States, where the colored population is about one-third of the whole. Just after the war, during the negro dominance, the County Commission was composed of a negro chairman and three negro members who could not write their names, and one white man. They levied high taxes, and the financial situation was such that when they were driven from power the county paper was hardly worth ten cents on the dollar, and the colored sheriff, one of "the ring," absconded with nearly thirty thousand dollars. There was universal and complete misgovernment. But under "white rule" the county has paid the debt, the taxes are low, and schoolhouses are open everywhere for black and white. There is general content and prosperity, except that the negroes are represented as even more ignorant and superstitious than when emancipated. There is, however, no ill feeling toward them upon the part of the whites, and no disposition whatever to re-enslave them. But the new generation, which never held slaves, and is perfectly loyal to the Union, is determined to prevent what it considers the lapse of their community into barbarism under negro ascendency. Yet this determination contemplates, if necessary, the destruction of the right of the majority, the overthrow by the whites of the law of suffrage, from which alone they derive their own right to vote. It contemplates a State living in constant violation of its own fundamental law, and securing by that violation political advantages over those citizens in other States who obey it. That is to say, it contemplates an intolerable and impossible condition. It is in the highest sense an overthrow of the most sacred right of every State in the Union, which is to enjoy constitutional equality. It contemplates a result by individual action in a State which is constitutionally forbidden to the State itself, namely, the suppression of a vote—in many districts a majority vote—on account of race and color.

It is, however, undeniable that the reasons for this course are of the most powerful kind. It has been demonstrated that any other course in many districts abandons them practically to the control of those who are absolutely unfitted for civilized government. Apparently it must lead to their abandonment by the whites, and to their total occupation by semicivilized negroes. Yet, again, the negroes are acquiring a certain degree of instruction, which will reveal to them their rights and their superior force, while the habit of servility sprung from slavery is rapidly disappearing. And all the while the negroes are increasing in numbers more rapidly than the whites, while the instinct of social self-preservation naturally welds the whites together, and what they hold to be the safety of society itself is with them necessarily the paramount public issue. This compels the intelligence of the Southern communities to oppose any party which by favoring negro ascendency seems to them to threaten civilization among them. In this grave situation something more is necessary than to say that a free vote and a fair count will settle the question. Nobody has yet proposed to show either how, under the circumstances, a free vote and a fair count can be secured, or how they would settle the question. A free vote and a fair count might restore the North Carolina county of which we have spoken to the condition from which it has escaped. Is that a result which the country desires, or which it would wish to employ the army to maintain? The truth is that the question, which we have merely stated, is one of the most serious, and certainly the most difficult, which confronts the American people. We are very far from saying or thinking that they are unequal to its wise settlement. But nothing will be gained by denying the existence of the question, or by belittling it, or by ostrich statesmanship which shuts its eyes. Its treatment must be approached in a larger spirit than that of a desire to secure a party advantage. It appeals to patriotism, not to party, like the question of slavery and the war.

1890

The 1890s continued what historian Rayford Logan termed the nadir in the history of African Americans. Political and human rights were jeopardized, and in many cases destroyed, as white southerners created a Democratic "Solid South." These turbulent times brought about racial, class, and gender conflicts that resulted in a call for major reform at the national and local levels. Just three years before the decade began, the Republican Party, through the compromise election of President Rutherford B. Hayes, abrogated its responsibility to the black citizenry of the South. But in 1890, after winning the presidency by a narrow margin of votes cast primarily by northerners, Republican leaders sought to re-establish a solid base in the South—and key to the party's plans was the continuing support from African Americans. In January 1890, Senator Henry W. Blair (R-New Hampshire) proposed federal aid to public schools, with an underlying motive to render illiteracy tests ineffectual by educating the black populace. The possible impact of the bill on the South polarized many southern senators. Some believed the bill would assist in maintaining the desired dual educational system for whites and African Americans; others argued it would open the door for federal interference and most likely lead to an increase in the number of black voters. Though the bill was defeated, it awakened white southerners' fear of a return to Radical Reconstruction.

Then in June 1890, Senator Henry Cabot Lodge (R-Massachusetts) caused greater consternation among white southerners by introducing a federal supervision bill to protect the African American's right to vote in congressional elections. The "Force Bill," so labelled by its opponents, passed the house, but did not reach the Senate in time for consideration.

The Lodge (Force) Bill prompted quick action from white Mississippians who wished to maintain political control of the state—a constitutional *convention was called to pass an amendment that would disfranchise African Americans. Before the convention, African Americans from forty counties issued an appeal to President Benjamin Harrison, but he refused to intervene. In violation of the Fifteenth Amendment and terms under which Mississippi had been readmitted to the Union, the new amendment legalized a two-dollar poll tax, a literacy test, residence requirements, and denial of voting rights for those convicted of minor crimes. Soon, disqualifying tactics and acts of terrorism were commonplace as southern whites devised and implemented strategies to eliminate the black vote. When Congress reconvened in December, Republican interest in protecting the voting rights of African Americans waned again. On January 22, 1891, the Lodge Bill died; it never left a Senate committee.*

The Colored Farmers' National Alliance and Cooperative Union, founded in 1886 as an affiliate of the Southern Farmers' Alliance, supported the Lodge Bill although the Southern Alliance itself opposed it. The platform of the parent body addressed a myriad of economic, political, and social issues, paramount among them a federal subtreasury system which, if adopted, could end the farmer's annual indebtedness to the "furnishing merchants." Because of its large membership base, 1.5 million in 1890, most southern politicians were reluctant to arouse the ire of the Southern Alliance's leadership. Nevertheless, noted Democrats refused to support the subtreasury plan.

It was, however, lack of executive support for the Sherman Silver Purchase Act of 1890 that spurred leaders of the regional farmer alliances to discuss the formation of a third party. Apprehensive that a split in the white vote would restore political power to African Americans, white southerners balked at the idea of a third party. Because of past efforts by the Republican Party to defend the civil rights of African Americans, the leadership of the Colored Alliance was wary of shifting its loyalty from the party. Even so, the agrarian reform movement offered a ray of hope, though short-lived, to the Colored Alliance's 1.3 million members.

According to a 1890 U.S. Bureau of the Census report, the majority of African Americans and whites in the South were agricultural workers. Conservative southern leaders proclaimed that the growing importance of industry and business in the region pointed to a "New South." Contrary to their pronouncement, most African Americans were tied to the land as sharecroppers, tenant farmers, or hired help. Some were slowly establishing a land base; 120,000 owned their own farms but also had to weather adversities, lack of capital for equipment and supplies, declining crop prices, poor harvests, and the national depression of 1893-97. The second largest group of wage earners was domestic or service workers, also primarily in the South. The large number of women employed as domestics is significant commentary upon gender and racial restrictions placed upon them. The trend toward northern women working primarily as domestics reveals that, in spite of the highly industrialized economic base of the North, women who had to work to sustain themselves or their families found it extremely difficult to secure employment even in factories engaged in "traditional women's work." Manufacturing and mechanical industries employed the third largest group of African Americans, primarily males, as unskilled workers. Although the majority of the three million black wage earners, ten or older, resided in the South, significant numbers were in the North and West.

Fleeing from spiraling oppression in the South, African Americans were settling in the West and in northern urban areas. Rediscovered records reveal a much larger black population than previously believed; by 1890, 518,986 lived west of the Mississippi River. Primarily attracted by the possibility of meaningful employment, the number of black residents in Chicago more than doubled by 1890 to 14,271. However, as was true for the majority of their southern kinsmen, most were relegated to the bottom of the economic ladder as they encountered the rigid color line William Edward Burghardt DuBois would write about in his 1903 classic, Souls of Black Folk. *De facto segregation was fast becoming the norm in housing, public accommodations, and education. In spite of efforts to limit their advancement as a group, there were clear indicators that Chicago's black populace was not content with its status. It was also apparent that if change were to occur, they, like African Americans in communities throughout the United States, would have to assume direct responsibility.*

In 1890, the concept of self-help was central to the founding of the Afro-American League by T. Thomas Fortune. During the League's first meeting in Chicago, more than 100 black men developed strategies for combatting segregation and discrimination. Other protest groups formed and held national conventions. J. C. Price, president of Livingstone College in Salisbury, North Carolina, and vice-president of the League, chaired the Citizen Equal Rights Association in Washington, D.C. Although both organizations were beset by internal conflicts and eventually rendered ineffectual, the League did reorganize as the Afro-American Council in 1898. The Council issued a proclamation in 1899 that condemned lynching and called upon African Americans to demonstrate their outrage by fasting and praying for a day. It also recommended citizens to seek assistance through the judiciary system; the primary charge was action, not silent acceptance. Toward the end of the 1890s, a struggle to control the ideological foundation of the Council ensued between factions critical of and supportive of Booker T. Washington, recognized after 1895 as the spokesman for the race. After 1900 the Washington accommodationist school of thought gained dominance in the Council. With periods of inactivity, the Council existed until 1908.

As 1890 drew to a close, the challenges facing African Americans were numerous and varied. The renewed hostility of many white south-

erners, the withdrawal of federal support, and the lengthening shadow of segregation threatened to erase all the gains achieved during the reconstruction era. Although much of the overt oppression would occur in the South, the indifference of the federal government and citizens throughout the nation silently sanctioned discriminatory practices and policies. Believing that race relations would always hinder black progress, African Americans and whites advocated emigration from the United States in a Back-to-Africa Movement. Some African Americans proposed the establishment of all-black communities as the best defense against the racist onslaught. However, the majority of African Americans did not support separatist concepts. Instead, they advocated self-help, racial solidarity, the establishment of a sound economic base coupled with support for black businesses, and the expansion of the middle class and its value system as ways to gain full equality and acceptance in the American society.

Thus, cooperative businesses and mutual-benefit fraternal organizations boomed during the decade. The Masons, the black Knights of Pythias, the Independent Order of St. Luke, and the Grand Fountain of the United Order of True Reformers in Virginia were just a few of the organizations paving the way for the development and growth of businesses in black communities; additional jobs for African Americans and the stimulation of the production of goods and services were two desired outcomes. By 1898, John Merrick had transformed a quasi-religious fraternal society, the Royal Knights of King David, into the North Carolina Mutual Insurance Company. The company was reorganized in 1899 under the leadership of C. C. Spaulding.

Inextricably linked to the development of a viable economic base was a quality educational system. During the 1870s, the thousands of schools established by the Freedmen's Bureau were replaced by public schools. For African Americans, the public school system was often inferior; this was particularly true in the southern region of the nation. Even the southern land-grant higher educational institutions for African Americans, authorized by the Morrill Land Grant Act of 1862 for training related to agriculture and mechanical arts, received fewer operational funds. Private schools, especially those founded by religious denominations, including the Methodists and Baptists, were thought to provide the better education, and Howard University, founded in 1867 in Washington, D.C., was still considered the premier black institution of higher learning. Although African Americans found it increasingly difficult to obtain skilled jobs in the trades, industrial education and vocational training were in vogue, with Hampton Institute in Virginia and Tuskegee Institute in Alabama serving as model institutions.

In spite of the growing structural discrimination, there were impressive achievements in education, the arts, the sciences, and business. However, the vast majority of African Americans were not the direct beneficiaries of those achievements. Drawing upon the church, collective enterprises, and cultural traditions, African Americans would seek ways to provide greater opportunities for a more inclusive racial advancement.

Cynthia Neverdon-Morton
Coppin State College

A QUESTION AND AN ANSWER

HARPER'S WEEKLY
February 15, 1890, p. 119

The Charleston *News and Courier* replies with perfect courtesy to our late question. The *News and Courier* having said that in all the Southern States a reasonable and intelligent ballot would be counted whether cast by a white or colored voter, we asked who shall decide what is a fair and reasonable ballot? The *News and Courier* answers, "The white race of the South is going to decide for itself, unaided and unhindered by any others." But as the postulate of this answer, as given in the same article, is that "negro rule cannot and will not be borne," the answer means that if the majority of ballots at any election should be those of colored voters, they would for that reason be rejected by the white voters as not fair and reasonable. The answer, therefore, as the *News and Courier* will see, does not vindicate its original remark, which was that ballots, even if from colored voters or presumably for colored candidates, would be counted if fair and reasonable. The conclusion now is, plainly, that fair and reasonable ballots would not be counted if they resulted in what is called negro rule; and this, unquestionably, is the position of the white voters in the Southern States.

It is at least a frank and intelligible position. The resources of the national government are exhausted. The question has become one for the people of every State to decide for themselves. The Supreme Court has interpreted the Fourteenth and Fifteenth amendments in accordance with this view. But there are yet two points which so intelligent a journal as the *News and Courier* cannot neglect. The first is that its declaration, "negro rule," however intelligent, "cannot and will not be borne," is in direct contravention of the purpose and spirit of the declaration of the Constitution that the right to vote shall not be abridged by any State on account of color. Technically and literally it is not abridged by the State, but it is abridged in fact, and confessedly on account of color, by citizens of the State. The *News and Courier* will not deny that in such abridgment the moral purpose of the amendment is defied. Does the *News and Courier* think that a community can wisely and safely live in constant, confessed, and intentional contempt of the provision of its fundamental law upon the most vital power of a popular government—the suffrage? This is not a question of color, because it is equally applicable to any similarly disfranchised class.

The other point is of another kind. The Fourteenth Amendment provides that if the right to vote is denied to any lawful voter because of any reason except for crime, the basis of representation shall be proportionately reduced. This again contemplates State action. But there is no moral or honorable doubt of its purpose. When, therefore, the right to vote of half the voters in a State is denied by the other half, although there may be no national remedy, does the *News and Courier* think it fair or safe for that other half to enjoy the share of representation which is based upon the suppressed vote? Granting that the negro is incapable of intelligent voting, and that the whites are justified in annulling his vote, are they also justified in securing by that course a representation which in some cases is double that of their fellow-citizens in New York and elsewhere? These are questions, as we think the *News and Courier* will agree, not of mere sentiment, but of national harmony. They are asked in no spirit of dispute, but for information. They must have occurred to honorable and patriotic citizens of the Southern States. To the direct inquiry of the *News and Courier* what we should do in the same situation, we answer that before abandoning the fundamental principle of popular government and the purpose and provisions of the Constitution, we should certainly attempt a legal restriction of the suffrage, and we should insist that the State should relinquish the representation which she enjoys solely because of the assumption that the vote is actually cast which is in fact suppressed.

CONGRESS AND THE ELECTIONS

HARPER'S WEEKLY
April 5, 1890, p. 254

The reception of the Lodge bill by the press and by such members of Congress as have expressed themselves shows fortunately little disposition to question its constitutionality. Objection, however, is justly made to its general expediency and to some of its details. The unbroken tradition of usage is the regulation of Congressional elections by the States, except in regard to the time and manner of electing Senators. This tradition should be disregarded only in extreme cases, where the end can be gained in no other way. The argument for the Lodge bill is that in certain districts a class of citizens are deprived of their votes, not by law nor technically by the State, but either by local terrorism or by ingenious election devices which are approved by public opinion. The assumption is that the proposed law will remedy this situation, and enable such citizens to vote freely and without fear. But is this a fact? Are the colored citizens in the districts contemplated so desirous of voting that because of the kind of protection afforded by this law they will defy those who are now believed to prevent them from voting?

In other words, do they now abstain from voting because they are outwitted, or because they are afraid? Do they abstain because they cannot read the labels on the boxes, as in South Carolina, or because they know that they are "spotted," and will be made to suffer? The white voters, as a class, are the more intelligent, masterful, and powerful, and they are the property owners. They are convinced that negro ascendency would be fatal to society itself, and they say frankly that while they wish to live at peace with the colored people, and will gladly do what they can for their education and cultivation, and do not object to their filling small offices, yet they will resist at all hazards colored control of the State governments, and generally colored representation in Congress, for reasons which, they allege, would lead Northern communities similarly situated to do precisely the same thing. This is their contention, with the justice of which we are not now concerned. Is not this conviction and determination, which is perfectly well known to the colored people, and which occasionally manifests itself in the most unmistakable manner, and not the inability to read, the real reason of the abstention of the colored vote? It is a moral reason. It is the persuasion of the colored voter in certain districts that he will vote at high cost to himself which keeps him at home; and from this original conviction presently arises an indifference to voting—an act which, in any case, he comprehends imperfectly. This is the secret of the suppression of the colored vote.

If now five hundred such voters can procure a United States judge and clerk, inspectors and marshals, to manage the election, will those voters, or any considerable number of their race, for the privilege of voting by allowing an inspector to mark their ballots, be willing to take the risk of incurring the hostility of those who now really prevent their voting? This is the practical question. The Lodge bill assumes that they will, and that the sense of protection at the polls will cause such voters to forget that when the polls are closed the protection ends. This we do not believe. Unless Congress can provide protection for the colored citizen all the time, it does not seem to us probable that protection of his vote, only with the certain result, under the circumstances, of deepening the hostility of race, will greatly increase the colored vote, although it will unquestionably increase difficulties and disorders in the communities affected. Those difficulties, including voting, are of a kind which by the nature of the case and of our government is not summarily remediable by law and the marshal's posse. The practical suppression of the votes of lawful voters is unquestionably an immense evil. It is an evil for the local community in which it is tolerated as well as a wrong to the whole country, and that truth should be constantly shown. But it is a wrong which can be remedied only by time, by experience, by agitation, and changes of local feeling and opinion, but not by a law of Congress. In this part of the country also the negro as a man and equal citizen is greatly wronged. But the wrongs are of a kind which laws do not and cannot relieve. The Lodge bill is, we believe, constitutional, but should it become a law it will be futile. It subverts a tradition which has almost the sanction of fundamental law, and does not offer in compensation any reasonable prospect of relieving any wrong or removing any difficulty.

A SOUTHERN VIEW OF "THE SOLID SOUTH"

HARPER'S WEEKLY
May 24, 1890, p. 399

The Birmingham *Age-Herald*, in Alabama, says of the late book *Why the Solid South?* that while it is useful and timely as a history of the facts of carpet-bag and negro domination, it really does not touch the chief point at issue. The *Age-Herald* says that the work does not answer the Republican complaint that the negro is a constitutional voter prevented from voting by those who are allowed full representation for his vote. The book, it thinks, while approving the fifteenth amendment, attempts to justify its nullification.

This is an important and very suggestive criticism from a leading journal of opinion in its part of the country. It deprecates the tone of appeal to "Northern sympathy" which it finds in the work. The remedy for the trouble, the *Age-Herald* thinks, lies solely in the action of the States interested. "There is but one way in which the South can ward off the danger of negro rule, and in so doing put itself on secure ground and square before the country. That is, to provide such qualification for suffrage as will disfranchise the illiterate and irresponsible." This should have been the course pursued, it says, as soon as the rule of the carpet-baggers was overthrown. It must be adopted, it adds, before there will be honest and satisfactory politics in the Southern States, and immunity from Republican federal interference.

APPEARANCES ARE DECEITFUL.
"See here, my boy, what do you use to kill alligators with down here? I've fired ten shots at that chap, and he won't budge."
"'Tain't likes as he will, sah! 'Twould keep yer shootin' fo' de nex' ten yeah ter make a 'pression on dat ole cypress stump, sah."

Harper's Weekly, April 26, 1890, p. 331.

Whether the vote of the States in which the negro vote is largest could be procured for such a disfranchisement, the *Age-Herald* does not say. But that the suggestion is of great importance is undeniable. The division of the colored vote between the white parties seems to be conceded to be contingent upon open bribery, which would not promote the honest politics of which the paper speaks. The fact of the suggestion made by the *Age-Herald* as a solution of the problem is, however, very interesting as a sign of the disposition to look at the question practically, and to consider it in a candid spirit.

PERSONAL

HARPER'S WEEKLY
May 24, 1890, p. 399

Another colored man has come to the front in the Senior Class at Harvard College. He is William Edmond Burghardt Du Bois, and he divided the Boylston prize of $120 for declamation with a white competitor the other evening. He was born at Great Barrington, Massachusetts, was fitted for college there, and after being graduated with high honors at Fisk University, in Nashville, he entered the Junior Class at Harvard. He is fitting himself to be a teacher in the South, and supports himself by teaching, lecturing, and mining scholarships.

AN ANGRY WOMAN'S WORK

One of St. Louis's Suburbs Involved in a Sensation. Mrs. Cairns's Valuable Property in an Aristocratic Neighborhood Sold to a Body of Negroes.

NEW-YORK TIMES
July 21, 1890

St. Louis, July 20,—Kirkwood, just thirteen miles from this city, is the ultra aristocratic suburb where a large number of the wealthiest merchants, bankers, and business men of St. Louis reside. Mrs. Anna Sneed Cairns has for nineteen years conducted there a female seminary that draws patronage from all over the United States. She is a strong-minded woman, well known in the ranks of advanced thinkers, and well to the front in all movements for the advancement of her sex. Her husband is one of the best known architects in St. Louis.

Two years ago Mrs. Cairns got into a quarrel with the Town Board of Kirkwood over a trivial complaint about a drain pipe that was declared a nuisance, and which she refused to remove. The matter was taken into a Justice's court, and was carried up through all the courts until it reached the State Court of Appeals, where it now is. In the meantime the Town Board persecuted her in many small ways and she fought back. Finally she determined to take her seminary away from Kirkwood.

When she announced this the people laughed, for they thought she would not do it, as she owned the property. She bought property elsewhere and began the erection of a new seminary, which will be ready for occupancy in October. Then she sought a purchaser for her Kirkwood property. It was reported that she was going to sell to negroes and a negro school was to be established. To stop this Kirkwood people offered her $20,000 and advanced the price to $27,000. She refused to sell to them, but has sold for $32,000 to a syndicate of wealthy negroes.

J. Milton Turner, ex-Minister to Liberia, engineered the deal. He induced Henry Bridgewater, a negro worth $200,000, to give $10,000, and this check was given to Mrs. Cairns yesterday. Milton Turner is now in Boston, where he went to raise money. He telegraphed to-day that the Peabody fund would give $5,000. This $15,000 is the first payment, and the property passes into the hands of the negroes. Work will be at once commenced to convert the beautiful seminary into a manual training school, and it will be called the Bridgewater Manual Training School for Colored Boys.

The people of Kirkwood would not believe the sale was really made until informed to-day by your correspondent that Bridgewater's check had been given, and now they are simply speechless with indignation. The property is right in the heart of the beautiful little town. Bridgewater, the man who thus becomes the

AFRICAN AMERICAN HISTORY IN THE PRESS, 1851-1899

CHANGE.

TOURIST IN THE SOUTH. "You must have seen lots of change down here the last few years, uncle."

UNCLE. "Dey say dere's been lots, boss, but de mos' I's seen ob it ha' been a dime or a nickle ebery now an' den, explainin' to folks dat it wa'n't safe to trabel roun' here 'mong de scrub palmetters, on 'count ob de rattlers an' moccasins."

Harper's Weekly, April 26, 1890, p. 336.

founder of the first and only manual training school for negroes in the world, is the proprietor of two big negro saloons and "dives crap." He has grown very rich selling whisky to his race and keeping gambling houses for them. It is an almost nightly occurrence for the police to raid his place and haul off from five to twenty-five inmates and frequenters. He has been a figure in politics for the last ten years.

Mrs. Cairns smiles serenely when questioned, and says she simply sold her property for the best price and a very laudable purpose. She denies that there is any spite work in it. She says: "This trade has been going on for some time past. The Peabody fund sent a committee to St. Louis some months ago to look into the matter, having for four years been trying to decide upon a location for the establishment of a manual training school for colored boys. The committee was, I believe, under charge of Prof. P. H. Murray, and on returning to Boston strongly recommended the seminary purchase. I have myself been on to Boston and have conferred with those interested in the movement. There is great surprise felt in the East that the Kirkwood people should object to having such a school in their midst. It is for a noble purpose—that of enabling colored boys to become skilled artisans in place of forever condemning them to perform menial labor—and I am glad and proud to sell my seminary to be used as the home for such a great work. The colored people all over the country are stirred into great enthusiasm over the matter, and I am myself in receipt of letters asking for terms of scholarship in the school, and am told that Mr. Turner has been assured of support, in the enterprise by many well-to-do colored families in St. Louis alone who are anxious to give their children the benefit of such a training." The Kirkwood people to-day, when con-

A COMFORTABLE REFLECTION.

REV. BRO. JUDKINS. "Well, Aunt Sally, we's gittin' pooty old, yo' an' I is, an' hev to be tinkin' soon 'bout leavin' dis hyar worl'."
AUNT SALLY (*who clings tenaciously to life*). "Don' know 'bout dat, br'er—don' know 'bout dat; I'se noticed dat plenty sight mo' young folks die dan ol' ones!"

Harper's Weekly, May 3, 1890, p. 343.

vinced that the sale had been made, sent a formal communication to the Commissioners of the Peabody fund asking what they intended to do.

MORE TROUBLE FOR MRS. CAIRNS

Her Friends Object to Her Entertaining a Colored Liquor Dealer.

NEW-YORK TIMES
August 8, 1890

St. Louis, Mo., Aug. 7.—The sale of the Cairns Seminary property in the aristocratic suburb of Kirkwood to negroes for a manual training school has developed another curious feature. The rumor comes from Kirkwood that there is trouble between Mrs. Anna Sneed Cairns and the Women's Christian Temperance Union. The cause ascribed is a dinner at the Kirkwood seminary which was given when the sale of the property was consummated. The report says that the dinner was given by Mrs. Cairns, and among those who sat at the table was Henry Bridgewater, the negro saloon keeper who contributed so largely to the manual training school for negroes.

Now it is said that many of the ladies of the union are very much put out because Mrs. Cairns entertained a negro saloon keeper. They did not see why a member of the union should have shown any such consideration for a liquor dealer, simply because she had sold him a house and lot. It is said that the union reprimanded Mrs.

THE RECRUIT AND HIS TRAINING AT DAVIDS ISLAND.—Drawn by E. W. Kemble.

Harper's Weekly, June 28, 1890, p. 511.

Cairns, and that in response to the reprimand she withdrew from both the central and district unions of which she was a member. Members of the union decline to affirm or deny the story.

A MURDERER LYNCHED

NEW-YORK TIMES
August 22, 1990

Midway, Ky., Aug. 21.—John Henderson, who murdered Gilbert Satterwhite, a prominent white farmer, near here night before last, was taken from jail about 2 o'clock this morning by a mob and strung up to a tree in the edge of the town. The negro confessed the killing, but he said he did not know why he did it. His crime was particularly atrocious. He assaulted Mr. Satterwhite while that gentleman was driving along the road after dark, shooting him first and afterward butchering him with a razor. When found Mr. Satterwhite's head was almost severed from his body and he had seven other terrible gashes on his body, any one of which would have proved fatal.

Testimony indicates an accessory to the murder, and upon it another negro was arrested at noon to-day. The chances are that he will be hanged to-night. The negroes killed Satterwhite because of their being discharged by him from a thrashing machine gang a few weeks ago. Negroes are reported as greatly incensed at the hanging and threaten to avenge it on the whites. Trouble is feared.

THE NEW MISSISSIPPI CONSTITUTION

HARPER'S WEEKLY
September 13, 1890, p. 714

The final action of the Mississippi Constitutional Convention will be watched with great interest to see if its provisions in regard to the suffrage offer any reasonable and practical restriction of ignorant voting. The Committee on the Elective Franchise has agreed to abolish the general property qualification, and retains an educational qualification limited to the understanding of the Constitution when read. This is not a very lucid proposition. It is evident by the constant necessity of a judicial interpretation of the Constitution of the United States,

A VERY NATURAL CONCLUSION.

UNCLE PETE (*having been landed upside down and his load strewed for a quarter of a mile along the road*). "B'rer Jonsing say w'en he sol' me dat anemil dat he hed one fault, but he couldn't remember w'at it was. I shouldn't be soaprized ef dis was de berry one."

Harper's Weekly, September 6, 1890, p. 707.

after long and able debates by learned counsel, that that venerable instrument is by no means always understood when read by trained wits. Who is to determine in the case of the Mississippi document whether the voter understands it or not, is not stated. If the inspectors of election are to decide, they will have conclusive control of the vote. A modified form of the Australian system, called the Dortsch law, is recommended; proper residence also, and a poll-tax. An important and surprising provision is that of qualified woman suffrage based on the possession by her, if single, or, if married, by her husband, of real property to the value of $200.

That such a proposition should be made in Mississippi would be extraordinary but for the colored voters. In Wyoming it is constitutional, but elsewhere, as in New York, although the proposition may reach a vote sometimes in the Legislature, it is always regarded as a joke, even by some who support it. Upon all such questions of political method and reform the Southern States have been generally extremely conservative, as it is called, that is to say, unprogressive. Civil service reform is a question which has excited little attention or interest in the Southern States, so that provision for ballot reform and for woman suffrage in Mississippi may well arrest attention. The explanation, however, is simple. The purpose of the provision is to offset the colored vote. As the number of white husbands owning property is much larger than that of colored husbands, the white vote would be largely re-enforced. But whatever the object of the provision, its practical operation would demonstrate the advantage or disadvantage of the vote. If, as in Wyoming, it should be found entirely satisfactory, Mississippi in one political reform, without the least sympathy with it, would have taken precedence of Massachusetts.

There are other important propositions in the Mississippi Convention. Last week we described the wretched system of leasing convicts. The statement of the facts was the strongest argument. The committee on the subject has reported in favor of the abolition of the system on and after January, 1895, and for the establishment of a prison farm in place of the penitentiary; also for a reformatory school, with constant separation of the sexes, and of juvenile offenders from association with hardened criminals. The long postponement of the abandonment of the convict-leasing system is inexplicable. The lease to the Gulf and Ship Island Railroad Company was cancelled two years ago. There are a few convicts in the State-prison at Jackson well cared for. But the mass of them, some 400 in number, are leased in squads of ten to thirty to persons in various parts of the State. There are thus twenty or thirty convict camps, which are the seats of great wretchedness. It is not easy to understand why a system of suffering which has been thoroughly exposed, and which is so bad that the Convention proposes to abolish it utterly, should be continued for five years. But the general work of the Convention will command universal attention.

COLORED STUDENTS RULED OUT

No More Will be Admitted to the Maryland Law School.

NEW-YORK TIMES
September 15, 1890

Baltimore, Sept. 14.—The Maryland Law School has determined that it will admit no more colored students. Last year two colored students, Cummins and Johnson, the first who ever attended lectures there, were graduated with high honors. After their graduation two more colored students, W. Ashbie Hawkins and John L. Dozier, applied for admission and were received. They have been at the university one year, and have been notified by Mr. John P. Poe, on the part of the Regents, that they cannot return.

The white students of the Law, Medical, and Dental Departments of the university sent a petition to the Faculty protesting against the admission of any colored students to the Law School. Mr. Poe says that some time last Winter a petition against the admission or retention of colored students was laid before the Faculty, signed by nearly all of the ninety-nine students. The matter had been [continuously] agitated since that time, and this Summer the Regents, in whose hands the question was left for adjudication, had held several meetings, and considered it very carefully in all its bearings. They had finally resolved that it would be unwise to endanger the school or jeopardize its interests in any way by any longer allowing colored students to attend the school in the face of such manifest opposition. A number of students had left the school and others had refused to enter because of the presence of the two colored men, and the school was continually liable to those losses so long as that state of affairs lasted. That was the chief consideration influencing the action of the Regents, and, in view of their exceedingly low record, they did not feel it incumbent upon them to force an issue on their account.

Hawkins is the Principal of a public school at Towson. Dozier will go to the Howard University in Washington. Hawkins states that the action of the Faculty practically shuts him out of all possibility of entering the legal profession. He is so placed, being a married man, that he cannot leave his present position to study elsewhere.

UNDER THE CIVIL RIGHTS LAW

Two Colored Stenographers Sue a Restaurant Proprietor.

NEW-YORK TIMES
October 2, 1890

George William Lattimore and Richard B. Ross have begun a suit against Proprietor Currier of a Fulton Street restaurant for $5,000 damages. Lattimore and Ross are colored men. They are both stenographers, the former being employed in the Detective Agency of Robert Pinkerton and the latter in the law offices of Clapp & Mason at 50 Broadway.

Last Saturday Lattimore and Ross entered Currier's restaurant at 144 Fulton Street and took seats at a table near the entrance. They were proceeding to order dinner when a waiter informed them that they could not be served at that table. They protested against moving and appealed to Currier, who corroborated the statement made by the waiter. Currier, however, offered to serve the two colored men at a table in the rear of the dining room. They consented to go to this table, but after having seen its location they declined to remain there on the ground that it was not as comfortable or desirable a place for dining as the first table at which they sat. They then left the place.

Their action for damages is brought under the civil rights law.

MR. WATTERSON'S SPEECH

HARPER'S WEEKLY
October 11, 1890, p. 787

In his recent speech at Boston Mr. Henry Watterson depicts with great vigor what he holds to be the mistaken views of "the South" which are expressed by Republicans like Senator Hoar and Speaker Reed, and he condemns them as absolutely false. There is apparently, he says, a belief in the Northern mind that the people known as "the South" are radically and essentially different from those of "the North." On the contrary, he asserts that "body and soul they are exactly alike"; and they have done nothing which in their places the Northern people would not have done. "The sin of slavery was in the beginning a divided sin, but the cost and curse of it have fallen solely upon us, and we have expiated it." He protests strongly against the misapprehension of the character and conduct of Southern citizens, and states plainly the race problem as it appears to them.

Mr. Watterson holds that the separation of races is practically as absolute in Boston as in Charleston, yet that the separation in the South is even more natural, because the "average black man" in Boston is as different intellectually from the "average black man" in Alabama as Frederick Douglass from Topsy in *Uncle Tom's Cabin*. But if the colored man's right of civil equality should be asserted by an act of Congress, and enforced in Boston under pains and penalties by a complex array of officers, and finally by the army—how then? In the "black belt" the negroes generally, he says, have no conception of the meaning of a ballot. But it is proposed to organize them as voters, under the most irresponsible partisan leaders, and "vote them" at the polls in blocks of five or five hundred. Left to himself the negro cares little for the franchise, but hitched to a political machine he becomes a terrible because unintelligent force. Mr. Watterson thinks that only the pressure from without to unite the negro vote for a party makes the solid South, and that the withdrawal of that pressure would at once divide both the white and the colored vote, and with that natural division eight-box laws and tissue ballots and the shot-gun policy would disappear. This, in his judgment, is the only solution of the problem.

But in considering the question it must be remembered that the explanation of the fact that after the war the suffrage was not left to the decision of the Southern States is that they showed such a disposition toward the freedmen that the country had no moral right to abandon them altogether. Mr. Blaine compares the process of moulding the reconstruction policy to the Sibyl's books. Speaking sectionally, that policy was determined less by the feeling of the North than the conduct of the South. The suffrage was conferred upon the colored citizens mainly to protect them against a treatment for which there seemed to be no other practicable remedy. This must not be forgotten when it is urged that the settlement of the question should be left to the communities which are most concerned. This is unquestionably true, but much of the old doubt and distrust, renewed by frequent incidents, still lingers, and explains the support of such a bill as that of Mr. Lodge. Mr. Watterson is undoubtedly right, and Mr. Mayo is evidently of the same opinion, that the settlement must be finally intrusted to the communities directly interested. But acquiescence in that conclusion would be much more general and willing if those communities showed plainly a determination not only to treat the colored citizen kindly as an inferior, but to protect his political equality under the law.

HARRISON WILL NOT BE THERE

The Negroes' Efforts to Celebrate the Emancipation Proclamation.

NEW-YORK TIMES
October 14, 1890

Richmond, Va., Oct. 13.—The negroes are meeting with many obstacles in carrying out the programme of celebrating the twenty-eighth anniversary of Lincoln's emancipation proclamation. This is to take place here on Oct. 15 and continue for three days. The most extensive arrangements have been made for making this event the most notable known to the colored people of the South. The first obstruction the Committee of Arrangements met with was the failure to get the Governor to order a crack white artillery company here to fire salutes on the day the exercises open. Now it is asserted that President Harrison, who had promised to be here, cannot come. Mr. Harrison had assured the Committee of Arrangements that he would certainly be here, "even if he could not remain more than an hour." His extensive tour through the West and Northwest, it is said, will preclude the possibility of his being here.

Gov. McKinney, who declined an invitation to be present at Col. Archer Anderson's house, to be presented to the Count of Paris, was asked to deliver an address on the day of the celebration. The Governor, however, will visit his old home in Farmville on that day.

A COLORED PREACHER

HARPER'S WEEKLY
November 1, 1890, p. 852

With the freedom which the colored people of the United States possess, and a higher educational standard obtainable in theological schools, the colored clergymen of a newer generation offer marked differences from those of the past. Half a century ago the power of impassioned prayer, with but a slight acquaintance with the Bible, sufficed the negro preacher. The class-leader owed somewhat of his position to his years. There were reverence for the old man, respect for his attainments, [meager] though they might have been. It was not always necessary that the leader should know even how to read. The primitive church in the Southern States was in a measure isolated. A congregation might consist of the hands on one or more plantations, meeting, according to their degree of fervor, several times during the evenings of the week, with a marked observation of the Sabbath. On large plantations there was always a church. This might have been modest in its construction, but it was built and kept in good order by the master. The "brother," or parson, was always a slave, often a field laborer, rarely a mechanic, sometimes a taskmaster or "driver," but he was invariably held in high respect by his owner as an honest and truthful man. Certain small privileges were allowed him and his family. The "brother's" wife held a leading position among the servants at "the gre't house," as the slaves called the master's mansion. If on a Sunday the distance to be travelled by the colored preacher was great, it was the custom to let him have a mule or a horse, and sometimes a buggy.

In this system of country service no emolument was received by the leading brother. It was a labor of love, and dictated by piety alone.

In the large Southern cities the pastor held a higher position in the estimation of both whites and blacks. As often as not he was the butler in some well-to-do house. He could not only read and write, but knew his Bible by heart. The master took no small pride in the preacher, and cared for his personal appearance in the pulpit. If he were a family servant, he was released from all house duties on a Sunday. A good deal of respect was always paid them, even by the younger children in the white family, and they were invariably addressed as "father." When Northern strangers were on a visit South they were sometimes taken to these colored churches in the city, and were pleasantly received by the elders, and the best seats were given them. Invariably the good influence of these colored fathers was recognized by the whites, and innumerable instances could be shown of these pious men who by their teachings and by their own sinless example redeemed from a career of crime men of their own race.

It is so difficult even to-day, when the highest culture is supposed to be necessary for the equipment of a clergyman, to establish whether a man preaching the word of God is more effective when armed with logic, philosophy, and all the resources of art, than the simple brother who takes his text from the promptings of his own heart, and carries away his hearers by means of that most powerful of all motors, true human sympathy. Preachers do not learn from books how other men feel. That is something only gained by experience. Illiterate, then, as may have been most of these colored fathers of the past, they were admirably fitted for their surroundings. They taught the word of God as they understood it; and simple as it might have been, it was at once absorbed by the hearers. Suppose it was of an emotional kind? Would these field hands on the plantations, or cotton-press laborers, or draymen in the cities have taken away with them the faintest impression of the goodness of God had it been imparted to them in any other way? The faith of the colored man was limitless. Blessed are those who believe as do children, for then their troubles are so readily healed. Some great philosopher has said that religions were made for peculiar capacities; and what the colored fathers taught in their honest way was exactly adapted to the wants of their congregations.

But was there any true eloquence among these illiterate ones? There was much of it. The language had some little of the grotesque about it, but the words were musical. If hell was painted in its most fiery colorings, there never was so blissful a rest as that of their own special heaven. Life was toil, but the hereafter was one of joyful repose. The main points always dwelt upon were to be found in the commandments. Strict observance of them, punishment when there was the least deviation from them, was the every day text. It may be said in defence of the South that all the stock stories of the past, rendering the old colored preacher ridiculous are of Northern origin. It might have been that thoroughly accustomed to the negro's ways there was nothing strange to the Southern man in the negro's manner of thought or method of expression. Mr. Reinhart in his sketch presents the negro preacher of the middle period, where the past and present overlap, as it were. The man holds the Psalter in his hand and reads the verse, and on the big velvet cushion before him lies his Bible. The head is broad and massive, the hair is grizzled. He intones the service well and clearly, with due reverence for the sacred words. His sacred calling is the pride of his life. He is not unconscious of its responsibilities. A man of sixty, he knows what was the condition of his race in the past, and what is to be expected of them in the future. Education must come to them as to the whites. But what will it profit his people unless religion and morality be their guides? Freedom is useless, he knows, unless all its responsibilities are understood.

1890

A COLORED PREACHER.—DRAWN BY C. S. REINHART.

Harper's Weekly, November 1, 1890, p. 852.

In the United States, according to the information furnished by the Rev. Rufus L. Perry, the various religious sects to which the colored Christians belong are Baptists, Methodists, Congregationalists, Presbyterians, Episcopalians, and Catholics. There are fully 1,200,000 Baptists, and perhaps as many as 800,000 Methodists. The Catholics are in the minority, found mostly in Maryland and in Louisiana. Today, due to that higher education, there are many colored men who fill the pulpit who preach to their brethren the words of God with elegance of diction, perfection of pronunciation, and who are thorough masters of theology. The more thorough are these leaders the more cultured ought to be the congregation; but whether this be the case, cannot be asserted. It is not to be expected that a colored church should present any features which do not find analogies in white churches.

A COTTON PICKER

HARPER'S WEEKLY
November 15, 1890, p. 887

This year completes a century since Dr. Franklin signed the first petition that was presented to Congress for the abolition of slavery, and two years hence will end the century since Eli Whitney invented the cotton-gin. The machine enabled the grower to clean for market a thousand pounds of cotton daily instead of five or six. In 1791 the export of cotton was 189,500 pounds. In 1803, by means of Whitney's gin, it had risen to more than 41,000,000. The machine was the great ally of slavery, and the Warwick of King Cotton. No industrial invention ever wrought so much wrong and did so much mischief. It was the chief of the causes that arrested the antislavery movement that followed the Revolution, and was more persuasive than the efforts of Dr. Franklin and his society.

Whitney's gin cleaned the cotton. A new invention will pick it. The other day, at the Memphis Cotton Exchange, a bale of cotton was placed on exhibition which was the first ever picked by machinery. The inventor asserts that it will do the work of fifty-men. And if he be correct, the Memphis *Avalanche* says that "the negro question is solved, and he will have to seek for employment elsewhere." The popular valid objection against the colonizing of the negro has been that he was essential to the gathering of the cotton crop. It would be a remarkable fact if the century that began with an invention which doomed the negro to slavery should end with another that makes his labor valueless.

The conclusion of the *Avalanche,* however, is too sweeping a generalization. Laborers will still be wanted in the cotton States, even if cotton picking should be done by machinery, and there is the other fact that the attachment to the soil on the part of this particular laborer is very close and clinging. The deportation of a great and unwilling free population is not a reasonable proposition. Since the war there has been no obstruction to the exodus of the negro from his home if he desired to go. But there has been no such exodus, and no sign of a general disposition to go. Poverty has, of course, detained him, but not against his will. Nevertheless, the fact recorded by the *Avalanche* is very interesting and suggestive.

THE ELECTION BILL

HARPER'S WEEKLY
December 20, 1890, p. 986

The condition of public feeling is such that it may be predicted safely that the election or force bill will not pass the Senate, unless, as we said last week, the rules are changed to admit some form of the previous question. This can be done, however, only by the consent of all the Republican Senators, and the prevention of the passage of the bill depends, therefore, upon a few such Senators. The Republican opposition to the bill, manifested less in the newspapers than in private conversation, is such that it is not unreasonable to suppose that it may be proportionably represented in the Senate, and find expression in a refusal to consent to so extraordinary a measure as a fundamental change in the rules in order to pass a particular bill, which cannot be said to be generally demanded by the Republican party, and which some eminent Republican leaders warmly disapprove. The party caucus might practically compel Republican Senators to support the bill if it were brought to a vote. But the power of the caucus to compel them to agree to change the rules is by no means the same. The right of the majority to enact laws after adequate debate is undeniable. But that the majority of the Senate approve this bill may be justly doubted.

The true ground of opposition to this legislation was not laid down by Mr. Turpie in his opening speech. The superiority of the white race is not disputed, and the constitutionality of the act cannot be successfully contested, and there is practical ostracism of the negro at the North. But the real opposition to such a law lies in the fact that it disregards the situation, is essentially partisan, and that it must necessarily fail of its object. The true motives of proposing the law are not probably avowed, and the alleged motives may be wisely distrusted. No American would say that any citizen should be deprived of his vote. But if there were a county in Massachusetts in which the large majority were composed of men in the lowest stages of ignorance and moral irresponsibility, whose ascendency under the most reckless leadership could ruin, under forms of law, every interest of the community, some evasion of the law might be expected, not for partisan benefit or the gratification of personal ambition, but to save the interests of property and civilization itself. Immense interests of every kind are held in the Southern States by Northern owners of every party. They are in constant communication with the most intelligent citizens of those States, who have no hostility whatever to the colored people, and who know that their labor is indispensable. But while acknowledging that the colored people have been bitterly wronged and degraded, such citizens cannot agree that the wrong and degradation have fitted their victims for the proper discharge of the duties of government. The most earnest

A GOOD CATCH.—Drawn by Caran d'Ache for Harper's Weekly.

Harper's Weekly, November 1890, p. 880.

and intelligent friend of the negro in any part of the country could not contemplate with composure, in the interest either of the white or colored race, a return of the carpet-bag rule. That the colored citizen is a voter is true, and that acquiescence in the deliberate neglect of law is to be deprecated and must be ended is conceded. But where law is evaded for reasons which commend themselves to intelligent and conscientious men, evaded, as is honestly and not unreasonably believed, in the best interests of society, some other remedy than the bald and strict enforcement of the law at all hazards will be sought by those who are really bent upon the peace, harmony, and welfare of the whole community.

Thirty years ago slavery was as wrong in Alabama as in Kansas, and a man had the same right to personal liberty in South Carolina as in Massachusetts. But not for that reason did the Republican party insist upon immediate and absolute emancipation. It took counsel of the actual situation, and sought the destruction of slavery by confining it within its State limits; that was the wise and patriotic course. Today the right of the colored citizen to vote is practically denied in some parts of the Southern States. But a law which will embitter the feeling against him a hundredfold, although it may assume to protect one of his rights, will not relieve him. Doubtless, there should not be such a feeling, but can legislation prevent it? In dealing with offences against the suffrage, does statesmanship take no account of facts and circumstances? Time and education and more friendly feeling on both sides are aiding the solution of an immensely difficult question. Such suffrage provisions as those of the new Constitution of Mississippi show the disposition to make the local law conform to the situation. However honest the support of the pending bill may be, however plausible the President's statement that it aims only to protect the acknowledged equal right of every citizen, we doubt whether a great majority of intelligent Americans do not believe that the law would be a public misfortune.

1891–1892

In 1891, disfranchisement of the black populace and agrarian reform, two movements that appeared on the surface to be diametrical opposites, converged to produce hope for southern African Americans. Interracial cooperation as a means of improving conditions for black and white farmers was touted by members of the National Farmers' Alliance. However, white southerners clearly were unwilling to let go of discriminatory practices in support of coalescence. At the 1891 National Farmers' Alliance convention in Cincinnati, southern white representatives recommended segregating the National Colored Farmers' Alliance delegates. Though not accepted, the recommendation helped widen an existing schism. At the 1892 National Farmers' Alliance convention in St. Louis, an African American was elected assistant secretary; the one dissenting vote was cast by a white delegate from Georgia.

Cooperative endeavors were further jeopardized by the Colored Alliance's support of a cotton pickers' strike. Leonidas L. Polk, president of the National Farmers' Alliance, argued that a strike might benefit African Americans, but would surely harm white farmers. Soon after the black cotton pickers were defeated, the Colored Alliance dissolved. Nevertheless, the momentum of the radical agrarian reform movement, which would briefly reconfigure race relations between black and white farmers in the South, could not be stopped. In an 1892 magazine article, Thomas E. Watson, a Georgia lawyer and organizer for the newly formed Populist's Party, appealed for unity among black and white farmers, based on common economic needs and goals:

> You are kept apart that you may be separately fleeced of your earnings. You are made to hate each other because upon that hatred is rested the keystone of the arch of financial despotism which enslaves you both. You are deceived and blinded that you may see

how this race antagonism perpetuates a monetary system which beggars both.

Black and white farmers gathered in Texas in support of the Populist, sometimes referred to as the People's Party. White solidarity and the Democratic Party's southern wing's espousal of a "Solid South" lost their footing for a time as the populist ideology prevailed. Included on the Populists' national platform were social, economic, and political reform initiatives which, if accepted, would have dramatically transformed the United States—election of U.S. senators by popular vote; concepts of initiative, recall, and referendum; abolition of national banks; and the creation of a postal savings system. At the local level, Populists called for an end to the convict lease system and lynching.

Bloc voting by black Populists enabled the party to win many state and local offices. In order to halt the developing loyalty to the Populist Party, Democrats resorted to violence in Georgia, Virginia, and North Carolina. A new reign of terror emerged with the hasty addition of Jim Crow laws to state statutes. H. S. Doyle, a black preacher, ignored threats of lynching and continued to deliver speeches in support of the party and Watson's ideas. He finally fled to Watson to escape a lynch mob.

During the 1890s, Ida B. Wells' direct actions against lynching were at times unparalleled. She also spoke out against other practices that made life in the South unbearable for millions of African Americans. Born in 1862 in Holly Springs, Mississippi, Wells was orphaned at the age of sixteen and assumed responsibility for her five siblings. After graduating from Shaw University (later named Rust College,) she accepted a teaching position near her home, but soon relocated to Memphis, Tennessee. She purchased a one-third interest in the Memphis Free Speech and Headlight *and became its editor.*

Earlier, Wells had assumed the editorship of the newspaper Living Way *and regularly contributed articles to other publications designed for a black readership. Fired from her teaching position because of what some considered inflammatory articles about education for African Americans in Memphis, Wells devoted her time fully to* Free Speech. *She successfully extended the influence of the newspaper by selling subscriptions in the surrounding states.*

When three black males were lynched after a white business competitor spread false rumors of their involvement in a conspiracy, Wells used the press to become the most militant anti-lynching advocate, as well as a voice for full equality for African Americans. She strongly urged black citizens of Memphis to leave if their civil rights weren't protected. She also challenged one of the underlying assumptions of the cult of true womanhood by daring to suggest that white women might be attracted to black men. While travelling to Philadelphia for a conference of the African Methodist Episcopal Church, Wells learned that the newspaper's office had been destroyed by angry whites; she decided not to return to Memphis. Instead, she joined the staff of the New York Age, *edited by T. Thomas Fortune, and achieved national recognition in 1892 with the publication of "Southern Horrors: Lynch Law in All its Phases."*

The New York Age *was one of fifty-five major black newspapers and journals, thirty-seven of which were in southern states, committed to keeping African Americans abreast of issues affecting the race. As the literacy rate among African Americans increased, a growing audience of readers for other mediums emerged. Anna J. Cooper published what has been labelled the first black feminist publication,* A Voice from the South: By a Black Woman of the South. *In the book, she clearly identified the double burden—race and gender—faced by black women in the United States. Other black women also narrated aspects of the uniqueness of the black female experience.*

In addition to their efforts to help shape national thought regarding issues and concerns facing African Americans, black women also organized self-help organizations to improve the quality of life for the race. Victoria E. Matthews and Marchita Lyons founded the Woman's Loyal Union of New York and Brooklyn; the Colored Woman's League was organized by influential women in Washington D.C. In 1895, the League was instrumental in organizing the most productive national body, the National Association of Colored Women (NACW).

Most of the women's clubs emphasized the necessity of education for racial advancement by actively supporting educational institutions. In spite of limited resources, the desire for improved and greater educational opportunities resulted in a valiant effort at the common school level to reduce illiteracy. In addition five major black institutions of higher learning were founding in 1891 and 1892: North Carolina Agriculture and Technical University (Greensboro, N.C.); West Virginia State College (Institute, W.V.); Delaware State College (Dover, Del.); Elizabeth State University (Elizabeth City, N.C.); and Winston-Salem State University (Winston-Salem, N.C.).

During this time period, Daniel Hale Williams incorporated Provident Hospital and Training School in Chicago. The Crusader, *a Chicago black weekly newspaper, publicized Provident as an "interracial venture of great significance, where white and colored work together for the benefit of mankind." The hospital also gained distinction from its training school for nurses and for Williams' accomplishment of the world's first open heart surgery. Williams would later become chief surgeon at Freedmen's Hospital, an affiliate of Howard University in Washington, D.C., and hire an interracial staff, as he did in Chicago.*

Education figured prominently in the rise of a black professional class that included doctors, nurses, teachers, lawyers, journalists, and entrepreneurs. Real property owned by African Americans in Montgomery, Alabama, Washington, D.C., and Baltimore, Maryland, was used as an indicator of economic and social progress. The property value of several Baltimore residents reportedly ranged from $15,000 to $100,000.

Still, the majority of African Americans suffered the absence of well-paying jobs, and found urban life—whether in the South or North—difficult. Lack of training for skilled industrial jobs precluded many from membership in the newly formed unions. Until 1900, the American Federation of Labor's (AFL) anti-racial discrimination policy permitted a few African Americans to join; most were not eligible for membership because the organization primarily consisted of craft unions. In time, the AFL admitted unions with exclusionary clauses in their constitutions. Yet, it was inventions by African Americans that aided the industrialization of the nation and revolutionized certain domestic functions. These included Granville Woods (numerous electrical inventions), Elijah McCoy (automatic lubricators for machines), and Jan Matzeliger (shoe lasting machine). Seldom cited, but in many ways as significant, were the patents received by J. Standard (refrigerator), G. T. Sampson (clothes dryer), Sarah Boone (ironing board), and S. R. Scottron (curtain rod).

Between 1865 and 1900, the nation's population doubled from 36 million to 76 million. Recent immigrants, many unskilled, clustered in the cities near the factory jobs. Limited and restrictive industrial employment opportunities, inadequate housing, legal exclusion from the political process, Jim Crow laws, lynching, a projected decline in the cotton market, and the peonage land system convinced many African Americans to flee from the North and South to the West. The largest flights of the Exodusters, 1879-1880, were to Kansas and other areas in the Great Plains. Travelling in groups of 50 to 600 persons, individuals and families went West by wagon trains and foot. Due to their skills, resources, and reduced racial prejudices, it is claimed the majority of the 50,000 Exodusters were self-supporting within a year. Between 1891 and 1910, nearly twenty-five all-black towns were established in Oklahoma, known as Indian territory until Oklahoma's designation as a U.S. territory.

A series of military skirmishes and battles ended the Native American's control of the Great Plains. During the Plains War, the all-black Ninth and Tenth Cavalries and the Twenty-fourth and Twenty-fifth Infantry Regiments were scattered across the western frontier. The duties of the black units included protecting the settlers and railroad workers, guarding the mail delivery and posts, and suppressing the Native Americans. Nicknamed "Buffalo Soldiers," the men received hundreds of medals, including the Congressional Medal of Honor, for their valor during the Indian Campaigns.

Noted African Americans and whites participated in a national debate over African Americans' right to migrate to the West. Richard T. Greener, the first African American to graduate from Harvard College and the dean of Howard University's Law School from 1879 to 1880, argued that migration was one of the viable solutions to problems faced by southern African Americans. At the other end of the continuum, Frederick Douglass, noted orator, author, and former abolitionist, believed that African Americans must remain in the South and confront the obstacles blocking access to equal rights. The debate, and the exodus, continued through the 1890s.

It is against the backdrop of innumerable social and legal barriers facing those who remained east of the Mississippi that the unifying force of the black church becomes most evident. Independent black churches were established during the colonial era, but following Nat Turner's rebellion, most in the South lost their autonomy until after the Civil War. In addition to spiritual development, churches and religious denominations were responsive to other needs of the people. Particularly in urban centers, the church served as a welfare agency, establishing child-care centers and homes for the elderly and infirm, supporting orphanages, and founding kindergartens. The church also served as the center of community life, hosting social activities and political meetings.

Steeped in traditional theology and practices, some black ministers were not as progressive as members of the emerging black intelligentsia. The resulting tension forced some black progressives from the Methodist and Baptist denominations to turn to churches more supportive of their ideas. Strife between white and black Baptists had led to the development of the National Baptist Convention in 1886 and later escalated when Richard Henry Boyd, organizer of the first Negro Baptist Association in Texas, founded the National Baptist Publishing Board in Nashville, Tennessee, in 1896. Boyd's Sunday school materials, reflective of the black experience, were deemed more appropriate by some black churches. Others continued to purchase their materials from the white American Baptist Publication Society.

In spite of internal problems, the influence of the black church was positive during the 1890s. The black minister, regardless of professional training and educational background, was generally seen as a leader, accorded respect, and granted privileges that often extended beyond the black community. With few exceptions, black churches assumed principal positions in the struggle for equality.

Cynthia Neverdon-Morton
Coppin State College

SOME OPINIONS OF CLEVER PEOPLE

Some Black Females I Have Known.

ATLANTA CONSTITUTION
January 25, 1891

Once upon a time, some eighteen months ago, upon first going to housekeeping, I essayed to air my callow wisdom concerning the management of servants, going so far as to assert that the virtue and docility of a servant lay entirely in the hands of the mistress.

Pardon me, my sex. I have been humbled, through experience. And the knowledge of my mistakes hath reached me through many channels.

The widest and most varied experience has reached me through my acquaintance with washerwomen.

My first was a creature recommended me by one whose judgment I had every reason to trust—although he did declare with a lightness of spirit that I wondered at afterwards that she did keep his clothes awfully long sometimes. She came—a pale, gray-eyed mulatto of forty, very weakly in her back and full of complaints. The clothes she consented to return to us each week were beautifully laundried. We parted many months ago; she has still as souvenirs of our acquaintance a number of my daintiest garments.

After her came one black, big, impudent and execrable as to laundrying. Then came a line of others—good-natured ones who did bad work; bad-natured ones who did good work—not one satisfactory in the lot.

Has any one ever found a good small negro girl?

I had one recently who wasn't good. She came to me in full viciousness of her black childhood—voracious of appetite and light of finger. What she didn't eat she carried home. She was beaten nightly by her mother, and she told of it every morning in a stubborn, unconverted way that gave little hope of reformation. She used napkins for dish rags and wiped up my floors with towels. Upon many an article of food lay the print of her fingers. Custards disappeared like magic; a dish of preserves was put on the table once and then was no more. I never looked up food in my house, and I remonstrated with her upon her evil conduct, begging her to apprise me of her hunger and I would gratify her always. She apprised me, but continued her unlawful eating just the same. I thought to give her a pleasure, and sent her to the circus. She returned wild and impertinent, and left without doing her afternoon's work. I filled for her a Christmas stocking to overflowing. She spent the day in utter idleness, when there was most urgent need of celerity in her movements.

I lectured her kindly upon becoming slow and dazed whenever any company chanced to drop in for luncheon. The next day, when a friend came to lunch, she tore madly to and fro, and shattered many dishes.

She has departed, and she tells my nurse she loves me still; but her charity is greater than my own.

My next and last experiment thank, heaven, was—but how can I describe her? When I say that she was of a form most ungainly, with the walk of an elephant and a countenance ebony in hue, squint-eyed, a visage much resembling that of a vicious black horse. I have but dimly pictured her attractions. When you looked and saw that she moved on feet it made you ashamed of being a human creature.

She said she was accustomed to hiring herself as a house servant, but never told how long she stayed hired.

The fires she made never burned, the rooms she swept were full of dust, the dishes she washed were sticky, the table she set was awry. Everything she did would have been better undone—and there was no health in her. I discharged her with some broad language upon Sunday, and felt so elated from the relief of her aggravating presence that I wrote three poems in consequence.

Poor, ignorant, trifling creatures! It is a wonder any of them amount to anything. Their homes are hovels. They are taught to have no pride or decency.

Carrie Steele is going to train children for servants in the orphan asylum she is building. Heaven bless her work! It is a worthy one.

Despite this history of African woes, I'm sure we southern people couldn't get along without them. When they are good, they are the best servants on earth—patient, kind, humble. The best nurses and the best cooks come from the negro race. And I cannot leave my theme without a tribute to that servant who has made my life a comfort from the time I went to housekeeping nearly two years ago. She is clever in all things, a beautiful cook, brisk, honest, full of pride in her work and the mother does not take more care of and pride in the small inmate of the house than this young woman. During all these months I have never seen a sulky look on this girl's face, or heard an unpleasant word from her to any one. Verily, such a servant is a blessing and, for the sake of many suffering sisters, I wish there were more of them.

ARP ON THE EXODUS

*Every Race Has Its Own Sir Oracle.
And the Colored Race Seems to Have Been the Most
Unfortunate of All—What the Present Movement
Means.*

ATLANTA CONSTITUTION
January 25, 1891

Of course it was a trick—somebody's trick—this gathering of the negroes to go to Africa. The mystery about it all is that $1.2. They could have gotten $2 just as easy—maybe 5$. But it wasn't the trick of our people. The credulity of the negro is amazing. One would think they had learned something since freedom came—something about trusting strangers. The idea of going to Africa for $1 and a postage stamp would convict anybody of lunacy. Two thousand of the dupes in Atlanta with their tickets and as many more all along the line to Washington—all waiting for the agent and the ships. Some went from Cartersville, and are on the road somewhere. They won't talk. They are bound to secrecy. They have been houdood. Education does not seem to rid the negro of the superstitions and vagaries that belong to the race. Every community has its oracle, its conjurer, its fortune teller. There is one over on the hill back of us. The women and the girls have more faith in her than in their preacher. If one of them loses anything she goes to the old woman, who listens to her story and floats some coffee grounds in a saucer and tells the name of the thief, and generally tells the truth, for she is smart and knows her nabors. My daughter's nurse went to her yesterday to have her fortune told, and said the old woman told her she would get a present before night from the good lady she was nursing for. Well, of course that was a compliment, and my daughter dident go back on the colored oracle. Her good will is worth something when nurses are scarce.

But I was ruminating about the exodus to Africa—not about the going, but about the desire to go. Is it a sign of anything? Ever since I was a boy there has been talking and writing about the Jews going back to Jerusalem, and sometimes the signs of it are pretty good, but they have never made a start. And now the wise men say that Providence planned the slavery of the negro for his good and waited 100 years for his civilization, and then sent Stanley to Africa to get the Dark Continent ready, and now that same Providence is inclining his mind to go there, and this is the beginning of the great exodus that is to come. Well this may be so or it may not be, but it is all right if it is. Our people are willing and waiting. But the negroes can't swim and they can't be floated over for $1.02. One thing is certain—they will go when their time comes and not before. This thing was tried half a century ago and it was too soon and [didnt] work. The Colonization Society meant well and spent lots of money. They built ships and sent agents over to Liberia to prepare the country for the colony. They took over thousands and thousands of negroes who had been set free by their masters in Maryland and Virginia, but they died like cattle with the murrain. Most of the states had laws which forbade slaves from remaining in the state after they were set free. They had to go north or go to Liberia. But still there was a great many free negroes in the south—negroes who were born free—and they were a middle class between the slaves and the white folks. They were not up to the one nor down to the other. Like the Irishman's definition of a fairy, "They are the spirits of folks who are not quite good enough for heaven, but are a leetle too good for hell." And so when freedom came to the slaves, the old-fashioned, high-toned free negro was in a fix. His middle station was knocked out and he felt it keenly and was mad. He was either down to the level of the "common nigger" or they were brought up to his. Most of them were respectable mulattoes and had trades and occupations in the towns like white folks. From that class all our southern barbers came, but as one of them said to me not long ago: "I was always a democrat, sir, and mixed with southern gentlemen, sir. I was in the Mexican war, sir, and I was intimate with General Henry R. Jackson and Governor Colquitt, and all the blooded stock. I associated with gentlemen, sir, before the war, but one day Mr. Lincoln took his pen in his hand and set all these black niggers free, and, before we knew it, there was about 40,000 new barbers jumped up with a brush in one hand and a razor in the other, and we old-fashioned free niggers hain't had any comfort since."

I knew one of these high-strung mulattoes who got rich, and owned a plantation, and bought some slaves and worked them. He never forgave the yankees for taking his property without paying him for it, and what was worse, they raised up the other negroes to be his equals.

About fifty years ago an old gentleman died in our county leaving a large estate and over 100 slaves. He left a will in which he set free thirty-seven of them, and directed that his executors should send them to Liberia. He charged that they should be provided with abundant clothing, and when they embarked they should be given $200 apiece in gold. These negroes were his favorite household servants and their parents and their children—they had been raised by him and treated with care and humanity and he was attached to them. They were reluctant to go but finally consented and old William, who was the trusted and confidential agent of his master, made preparations to go with them, as his master had directed. Their departure was prevented by a bill of injunction that was sued out by one of the heirs and the case had to go to the supreme court, where the will was sustained and the executor ordered to proceed with its provisions. Those negroes were sent from Savannah to Liberia on the ship Elizabeth. Three years after their departure the old man, William and six others very unexpectedly made their appearance in our town and delivered themselves to the executor. They reported all the others dead and asserted that they had tried for a year to get back but were refused transportation by every vessel that came.

Finally they hid themselves in the hold of a trading vessel one night, and kept hid until the ship had been three days at sea. Their rations gave out, and they came on deck and begged for favor from the captain and got it, for he was a kind-hearted man, and brought them safely to Philadelphia. The abolitionists of that city tried very hard to keep them from coming south, and would give them no money to pay their travelling expenses. William was well acquainted with Howell Cobb, who had been his master's guest in the old times, and who was then a member of congress, and so he wrote to him at Washington, and Mr. Cobb sent them money and they came to him, and he gave them enough to come home on, and the old darky's face fairly shone with illumination as he told of their trials and sufferings, and how happy he was to get back to his old home, where he could live with Mas' Tom, and die and be buried in the old family graveyard.

Mas' Tom soon heard of their return and hurried in to meet the old darky who had taken care of him from infancy to manhood, and they wept and sobbed upon each others' shoulders and there never was a more touching, loving scene than that. This is not much of a story, but it is a true one, and my father was that executor. Some of our southern writers who knew nothing of slavery, caught the infection from northern literature, and have pandered to the northern appetite, and thereby found an easy admission into northern magazines. Perhaps they were sincere, but it is a dirty bird that fouls its own nest.

The attachments that bound together the great majority of martyrs and their slaves were strong and beautiful; but they have passed away, and now it seems that the negro wants to go. The two races are living together merely by force of circumstances over which neither has any control. How long they can live together depends upon their good sense and forbearance. I feel sure that I can live with them and keep their respect and their friendship, but perhaps it is because I used to own slaves and still feel and maintain my love and my superiority. Our class will soon pass away, and so will the old slaves who love to do us honor. How the coming generations will harmonize I cannot foresee nor foretell, but from the signs I fear there will be less forbearance from the one and less humility from the other. The problem not solved, and such political measures as force bill will only make it more complicate not that the force bill will ever be enforced our injury, but the animus of it is bad. If conflict comes it will not be precipitated by or our negroes, but it will be the same strife that still rankles between us and northern enemies.

From that enmity I k[ ] of no discharge unless we fall back upon scripture which says: "If a man's ways pl[ ] the Lord, even his enemies shall be at [peace] with him."

Bill Arp

A PATRIOTIC PENSIONER
Gives Some Friendly Tips to Another [ ] Would Be Likewise.

ATLANTA CONSTITUTION
January 25, 1891

Washington, January 22.—To Jim Shuff Foxes Retreat, Kansas: Here i am in Washi[ngton] a lokin' arter mine and your penshun interest particular, and Skitters and Joe Workshirks gen'l. I'm gettin' on purty well, thou I don't Raum by no means as wel as Tanner, he's [ ] afraid. i find Hon. Mr. Annanias Wisdom is of the good ca?s. he sez he means to git as [ ] money fer his konstitents as eny other non [ ] ber dus fer his deestric, fur he expecs the [ ] penshunner tu stan by him at lection time. has giv me ful liberte to use his inflooens [ ] Rums at the penshun ofis, and he sez Raum go his de'th on him. i tel him the boys allus lers me anyew 'lection times.

Now i find, Jim, its ne'sary tue be si'k, or abeld tu git the best penshuns, and if a [ ] hes loss a leg—no matter when or how—he [ ] in front ranks, if he has frens te stan' by [his] certin rite, as too its ampitation from wo[ ] rece'ved in akshun. If you ken git up evid[ ] nuf, yew can co[ ] in top sawyer fer tew or thousan' dollers ba'k pay. So yew mus'[ ] lay 'round and sythe, and find mittee hard tew git up an' down, special when strangers is rown. The [ ] will be that when yew listed in February, 1865, lade round Washinton it wus kinder swampy yew cot the myrasma, which yew hev never wel of ever sense. No konsekense ef yew never in danger, or never went too the front, wus patriotick in cummin' promp'ly in line git yer pay, fer goin' to Washin'ton and ba[ ] long and fatiging car rides, wastin' yer [ ] servin' yer kentry in them air Washinton bari 'twant yer falt yer didn't git inter a fite, smel powder, but yer misfortin', for [ ] yer reely oter git more of a [ ] shun fer not havin' eny confedrits tew [ ] Yew needen't say anythin' 'bout [yuwr] bein' off, and able tew tak' car' er yerself and fam[ ] that you hev er good trade and plenty er [.] Yew air tew delapidated tew doe any more [ ] livin' when guverment is so anxush to sup[ ] yew, and by which y?w must be full supported.

Sense I've ben heir i has went down south, the southern state, with some guvment office so it didn't cost me anything; and [ ]e be da[ ] ef I can understan' it, but there town[ ] growin' up and lookin' more fluris than Foxes retreat. The land is hier price, boomin' more than it dus in our state, the queerest in all is the niggers, i men?

our lerd feller sitizens, is as hapy as clams, aller singin' and a grinin', an' su[ ] uv 'em is git rich, and these carpenders, an' brick layers we rite along side uv the white men 'thout cuy k[ ] fus; darned if I ken understand it, but nausen't giv' up the ery of persecution of our [ ] lerd feller-citizens, by the white, tho' i didn't [ ] may uv 'em as complained of bad usage, wh[ ] made me mad at ther damed fools. But wunderfull fernomenom, as Hon. Mr. Wis[ ] sez, is, that while the suthern people had ne[ ] as mony men wounded and disabled an' sicken an' brok' down, as we had; an' the country [ ] ruin', with no [money] or wurk sho[ ] they hev' growed up so fast, while at Foxes retreat hev' ben spend stil, waitin fur our penshuns to live on. While i wus at the south i didn't se eny old soldiers that ware not gittin on comfortable without penshuns, or gittin eny. it sorter puzeled me tu onderstan how them air critters git along so wel an prosperus like, with little or no penshuns while we nothern sojers is gittin poorer en poorer with um, and a strivin and a wantin more an more penshuns to prevent suferin, but I opose it grows out er the fact thet we air better edicated then they air an ken git fer the askin of we play our cards wel and make out our papers rite. No more at present.

Ammidab Packer

THE EXODUSTERS

Orange Davis Has Gone to Investigate the Matter. The Congo-American Emigration Movement Is Likely to Come to a Focus in a Few Days.

THE CONSTITUTION
January 25, 1891

The Congo-American emigration scheme is likely to come to a focus.

And that in a very few days.

The exodusters are growing restive under the hope long deferred, and begin to want some satisfactory information.

Friday night Orange Davis, the treasurer of the Atlanta African band, left for Washington to investigate.

He did not say what time he would return, but promised to write back as soon as he secured any definite information in regard to the matter.

The Waiting Planters

Planters from Louisiana, Mississippi and even Arkansas, are as thick as blackbirds in the spring time, around the railroad offices.

Pegleg Williams's emigration agency is headquarters for them, and make things pretty warm in their solicitude for laborers.

Mr. Williams left yesterday with a party of thirty negroes for Brinkley, Ark.

There is another party of eleven on the way to Arkansas, but none of them are of the Georgia exodusters. The latter are still here, and cling tenaciously to the hope of crossing the water.

Watching and Praying

The negroes are pretty badly off in the way of lodging, and none of them have any cash to spare.

But what they lack in means they make up for in faith.

Tonight they will hold a religious meeting to watch and pray. There will be the usual amount of exhorting and hymn singing, but no business.

Tomorrow night they will hold a business meeting, and it is possible that Orange Davis will be heard from by that time.

BISHOP GRANT AROUSED

NEW-YORK TIMES
February 9, 1891

New-Orleans, Feb. 8.—At the African Methodist Conference at Tangipahoa yesterday Bishop Grant made a severe attack on Bishop Newman of the Methodist Episcopal Church, who recently gave publicity to the charge that great immorality existed among the colored clergy. Bishop Grant pronounced the charge unfounded, and denounced Newman for bearing false witness.

Says Bishop Grant: "This is the kind of talk from men of his section of the country, misleading the negroes, representing that which is false, which has done more to cause dissatisfaction between the races in the South than anything else. His class of men come down here when they want to hold a conference, after which they return and tell the Northern people how we are getting along; that we are on the verge of starvation, and all about to go to the devil. Bishop Newman appealed to the prejudices and passions of a few men because he thought he could receive their applause. Bishop Newman spoke to a crowded house of people of African descent and misled them because he could mislead them by appealing to their prejudices and passions. It was a sin before God, and he may have something to repent of before he goes to heaven."

THE NEGRO IN WASHINGTON

*Conditions Favorable to His Development.
He Is in the Departments and the Professions,
Making Money in Some Instances but Not
Amalgamating with the Whites.*

NEW-YORK TIMES
February 15, 1891

The Census Office has recently announced the statistics of population for the city of Washington. Of the total population of 230,392 persons 75,927 are colored. In 1880 there were 118,006 whites and 55,596 colored; 1870, 88,728 whites and 43,404 colored, and in 1860 60,763 whites and 14,316 colored. The white population in the last ten years has, the figures show, increased 30.80 per cent., whereas the colored population has increased only 27.40 per cent. There is, then, no prospect of Washington becoming a colored city, but, nevertheless, one-third of the residents are colored. It will be seen that the large influx of negroes occurred between 1860 and 1870. During the war they came in from the surrounding country, and even from more distant points, for safety, and immediately after the war many of them were attracted to the Capital by the allurements of holding office under the Government. Others followed because their friends had preceded them.

Because of the liberal distribution of Government offices among the better educated negroes, Washington came to be the centre of the most intelligent men of the race, and it has continued to be so up to the present time. What advancement they can make, what capacities they possess, are illustrated here under the most favorable conditions. They have suffered from no such repressive influences from the white population of the city as they have encountered in the large cities of the South. Every political and civil right that the law confers upon them has been carefully guarded by the Government.

Most favorable circumstance of all, they have had no opportunity to engage in local politics, because in Washington there are no local politics. Thus they have not been exposed to the temptation of devoting their time to ward elections. They have had no opportunity to become the tools of unscrupulous politicians or to discredit themselves by mismanaging the City Government. The prejudice of the white population has not been excited by their participation as a political body in city affairs. Only once every four years does the District of Columbia assert itself in politics, and then it is to send delegates to the conventions which nominate candidates for the Presidency and Vice Presidency. On the occasion when these delegates are chosen by the Republicans the colored population comes out in force, and the Republican City Convention is, to say the least of it, a disorderly assemblage, reflecting no credit upon the city. But these conventions occur at such distant intervals that their ill effect upon the colored population is slight and immaterial. If the conditions for the development of the colored people have been favorable anywhere, they have been favorable in Washington. It is interesting to see what they have done.

In the different offices of the Government nearly all of the messengers are colored men. If anybody has occasion to go to one of the departments, he is thrown upon their tender mercies. Somebody has said that they recognize but two classes of persons who frequent the departments. The first class is composed of those who have rights of free ingress everywhere. These are Cabinet officers, Senators, and members of Congress. The second class comprises those who are not Cabinet officers, Senators, or members, and who have no rights at all. To high Government officials the negro messenger is most obsequious; to all ordinary people he is highly independent. He is not prone to exert himself; in short, he is lazy. As a matter of fact, the negroes in the Government offices who are clerks are far more efficient than those who are messengers. Frequently an intelligent negro rises from the latter place to the former, and from having been an indifferent messenger becomes a good clerk.

In all the departments, with one or two exceptions, there are colored clerks. Some of them are ex-members of the Legislatures in the Southern States, some are men with political ambition who regard any Government office as higher than a private business; some are self-educated young men who have obtained their places by competitive examination, entirely through merit. It cannot be denied that until recently many of the colored clerks were inefficient, but these have been weeded out to a great extent and the colored clerks in the departments at the present time are, generally speaking, capable. In the Pension Office, for instance, where there are quite a number of them, there are several of marked ability. An example may be cited in Osborne Hunter, Jr., of North Carolina, an examiner, a young man who was in his youth a slave, who is a good officer as well as one of the most promising and conservative of the rising generation of colored men. There are also several colored chiefs in the departments who are most useful and faithful officers. The Surgeon General's office, in the War Department, has more colored clerks than any other Government office, and they have given satisfaction; indeed, the finest clerical record in that office was made by a colored clerk.

It is a fact that is well worth noting that the better class of colored clerks are in full sympathy with the Civil-Service Commission. Under the old régime of partisan appointments colored men of inferior ability were provided for, and simply because they were colored their superior officers were afraid to recommend their discharge. When one was dismissed the cry of race prejudice was raised, and the public forgot to ask whether he was a capable clerk. But now the competitive examinations that the law requires give an opportunity to any colored man to take his chances of appointment with the rest, and a considerable proportion of the colored clerks owe their places solely to their merits, and when they are promoted it is because they deserve it.

They do not complain of ill treatment on account of their color. Government clerks come from every quarter of the country, and race prejudice is as slight among them as it well can be. Many of the colored clerks who have been appointed on competitive examination were formerly school teachers, and most of them may be said to represent the most intelligent and progressive portion of the race. An evidence of this may be found in the fact that, while they hold department places, nine-tenths of them study a profession. Some qualify themselves to be dentists, others pursue theological studies, but by far the larger proportion studies medicine or law.

"Once a Government clerk always a Government clerk" is a saying which cannot fairly be applied to the negroes. A fair proportion of those who study professions, having saved up sufficient money to support themselves for a limited period, resign. Those who have been admitted to the bar do not find Washington a good field. There are colored lawyers around the police court and there are a number of colored claim agents, but the former do not enjoy a lucrative practice and the latter hardly rise to the dignity of lawyers. The colored lawyer finds it to his interest to leave Washington, and it is greatly to be feared that not a few of them become politicians in the South.

In medicine, on the other hand, they find a considerable practice among the colored people of the city. Their patients being for the most part poor, they do not, as a general thing, charge the regular fees, but content themselves with more moderate compensation. It would seem that in this field there should be a really good opening, but, unfortunately, not all colored people are willing to employ colored doctors, and the honors of the medical profession are not so fascinating to the ambitious colored man as are the honors of the law. As a consequence more become lawyers than physicians. Among the highest class of negroes in Washington there is a growing disposition to rely upon themselves, but among the masses there is a distrust of the ability of their own race in the professional walks of life.

Probably the most important and widespread interest pervading the negroes is their interest in the Church. Any person who has been thrown with colored people must have noticed their intense religious feeling. Among the farm hands of the South—the "cornfield darkies," as they are called—religious belief is strong and universal. It is seldom that one is found who has not "got religion". The old "mammies" and "uncles" on the plantations are constantly singing hymns, and they attend revivals and immersion baptisms and camp meetings with great regularity. With the younger generation there is the same enthusiasm. Their religion enters into their daily life and is a genuine comfort to them. The superior intelligence and education of the higher-class negroes has merely given to them more civilized forms of worship. They are all connected with one church or another. They, like the lower-class negroes, devote a great deal of their time to church work. Church building, church ornamentation, church sociables, and church fairs are constantly exciting their activity, and are, it must be admitted, frequently the cause of serious dissensions. Just as among the whites, there are "swell" negro churches and select negro congregations.

Perhaps the most highly-cultivated colored men in Washington are the rectors of these parishes. They number among them several university, graduates. Alexander Crummel, for example, rector of the colored Protestant Episcopal church, is a graduate of Cambridge College, England, and his sermons are logical and scholarly. They would compare favorably with the discourses of any white clergyman in the city. His congregation is small, however, and the colored people themselves confess that he preaches above them. A large Methodist congregation is presided over by the Rev. Mr. Bowen, a graduate of Harvard, and the select Presbyterian congregation that meets in the church next to John R. McLean's big hotel, the Normandie, has for its pastor a decidedly able man, the Rev. Mr. Grimke of South Carolina. As everybody knows, the favorite religious sects of the negroes are the Baptist and Methodist, but in Washington, strange to say, many negroes have changed their religion and become Roman Catholics. St. Augustine Church, one of the largest Catholic churches in the city, is given up to the colored people—not exclusively, however, as the excellence of the colored choir attracts large numbers of white people every Sunday. The priests of this parish are, however, white. As for the inferior colored churches, they are scattered freely over the city, and one may, if he choose, hear the shouting and thundering preaching of the plantation negro on any Sunday.

The Christianity that carries into the house of worship the class distinctions of the parlor and drawing room is prevalent among the negroes. They are clever imitators, and the class distinctions of the churches are even more carefully applied in their social life. It is a very common mistake for white people to suppose that in social life all negroes rank equally among themselves. Nothing can be further from the real state of the case. They have their swell set, their old-fashioned set, their exclusive set, and the set that Mr. Ward McAllister has termed "smart." They give parties and balls, not only of the plantation style, with the banjo for the music, but entertainments very similar to those of the white people. The standards of excellence of colored society in Washington are the same as those of white society. They have a great respect for money and prosperity, and their adulation of office holders is extreme. There are two select young men's clubs, the Manhattan and the Acanthus. The latter is generally considered the more fashionable. Its members are for the most part department colored men, but a few stewards and others of equal consequence are admitted.

All this is very different from the lime-kiln clubs and crap-shooting societies with which one is apt to associate thoughts of negro amusement. Such leading lights of the race as Bruce, Douglass, Pinchback, and Purvis give dinner parties. There would be no valid excuse if the entertainments of the higher-class negroes were not elegant, for some of them are men of considerable wealth.

The increase in the value of city property in Washington has been the cause of the acquisition of large fortunes by a number of persons who had the good sense to buy building lots years ago. Property in some localities has doubled in value in five years; in others the increase since the war has been a hundredfold. In this accession of wealth the colored population has had a full share. Many of the finest building lots in the northwestern section of the city are owned by colored men, and more were until recently their property. Sixteenth Street, rapidly becoming one of the most fashionable places for building fine residences, is largely owned by colored men, and parts of Connecticut Avenue, the Fifth Avenue of Washington, also belong to them. Several colored women are among the wealthy property owners. Of course, this property was as a general thing acquired when its cost was insignificant, but the negroes have shown considerable shrewdness in disposing of it to their advantage.

That there are many of them who have money is shown by the existence of a bank. The Capital City Bank, in F Street, near Eighth, is an institution run exclusively by colored men. The President, Directors, cashier, all are colored, and the clientage of the bank is drawn from the colored population. The bank is represented as being prosperous, and its depositors have full confidence in it. The Land and Building Association is another entirely colored concern. These are merely some of the indications of a number of capitalists among the colored people.

In the slight sketch that has been given here of the colored people of Washington it will be observed that only the highest class has been considered. The laborers, servants, hawkers, and others are classes that may be found in any Southern city in numbers and under conditions similar to those that exist at the capital, but the Government officials, professional men, and capitalists flourish here more favorably than elsewhere. The criminal class of Washington, composed so largely of negroes, is not unique. The "blameless Ethiopian" sometimes gets drunk sometimes is brutal, and is very fond of gambling. His children snatch pocketbooks occasionally, and the women of the race are often dangerous when their jealousy is aroused. But they are not a dangerous set taken all in all.

It cannot be denied that there has been no amalgamation of races in Washington. Men may live here year after year and know nothing directly of the colored people. They are thrown into contact with them at every turn, but it is the contact of two distinct peoples who do not enter into one another's daily lives with mutual sympathy. As the colored people are improving they are marking out for themselves occupations and amusements similar to those of the whites, but entirely separate from the whites. Yet the two peoples dwell in the same city side by side without antagonism and with hardly any friction. A white man would as soon buy from or sell to a colored man as not. It is his money or his commodity that he wants. There is no jealousy on the part of the whites because of the advancement of the negroes. Perhaps the chief reason for this peaceful state of affairs is found in the fact, already alluded to, that there are no local politics in Washington to stir up strife between the races.

THE NEGRO AS A SOLDIER
His Brilliant Record on the Field of Battle.

NEW-YORK TIMES
February 22, 1891

Employed in Military Service in Ancient Times—Andrew Jackson's Call for Colored Troops—Valor in the War of the Rebellion

The general impression seems to prevail that the employment of negroes as soldiers in war is of quite recent date in the world's history, and dating back no further than the war of the rebellion. Very many of the citizens of this Republic to-day have never seen a military organization of negroes, though we have had four regiments in the regular army for nearly twenty-five years, and many officers of the army have never served with them, as the entire service of those troops has been on the Western frontiers, extending from the British possessions on the north to the Gulf of Mexico and west of the Mississippi.

Ancient history affords ample evidence of the fact that the negro was placed in military service many hundred years prior to the Christian era, and participated in many wars. He appears in military history in Egypt, commanded by Una, under King Pepi, in the course of the sixth dynasty. King Pepi in the second year of his reign placed his army in the field, and, being successful against the Mentu, he turned his victorious arms against the Amu and Herusha, tribes inhabiting the desert to the east of Lower Egypt. The nucleus of the King's army were native Egyptians, but, encountering strong resistance from these inhabitants of the desert, he soon turned his attention to the negro tribes to the south, and from them received thousands of black levies. Una says: "His Majesty placed me at the head of the negroes from Kau, from Amau, from Uauat, from Nam, and the negroes from the land of Takam. The chief men of Egypt, the Chancellors, the friends of the palace, rulers of the Nomies of the north and south, held positions and drilled the negroes of those lands."

King Pepi evidently had confidence in these negroes or he would never have recruited them for service in his [Egyptian] army, and to show that his confidence was not misplaced, after the work of drilling this vast negro contingent was completed, it was moved into the enemy's country. Five battles were fought in this campaign, in which the negroes were victorious. Una, the commander and historian of the campaign, furnishes this account: "The warriors came and destroyed the land of the Herusha; they came again and took possession of the land and demolished the fortresses, cut down the vines and fig trees, set fire to the houses, killed the chief men by tens of thousands, and returned fortunately home. And the warriors brought back with them a great number of living captives, which pleased the King more than all the rest. Five times did the King send me out to set things right in this land of Herusha and to subdue their revolts by force; each time I acted so that the King was pleased with me."

Military paintings connected with campaigns of the Egyptians in the Eighteenth Dynasty represent negro troops as numerous in King Shishak's armies, nearly one thousand years before Christ. They were also found in large numbers in the armies of Sesostris and Xerxes. For many hundreds of years before the Christian era there is an unbroken chain of historical evidence of the military employment of negroes but subsequently the fierce conflict of war was succeeded by a spirit of repentance, hope, and charity, which changed the tone of the empty formalism of the age.

While the vast negro army appeared upon the pages of Egyptian history, brilliant successes flashed forth upon its records like meteors, yet disappearing almost as suddenly from view. The carnage of war did not cease, but was transferred from the Orient to the Occident. Christianity turned its march westward, leaving all behind in darkness and ignorance. Again for fifteen hundred years the negro's hands were empty of weapons.

Not until after the discovery of the Western Hemisphere was he again viewed with interest, which took the form of traffic in human flesh by robbing Africa of her natives with seemingly little resistance on their part. During the ages which elapsed after his former brilliant achievements under the ancient Egyptian Empire the negro seemed to have lost both the art and taste for military glory and prowess. While both docile and submissive, with 800 years of servitude under the dominant races of the world, he became as clay in the hands of the potter, to be molded to their liking—passed from the dark night of savage barbarism into the dawn of civilization. Listening to the voice of the people against the oppression of the British toward the colonies of North America, he was neither deaf nor did he evince stupidity in regard to the efforts of the colonists to free themselves from the mother country, but showed a willingness to aid in the struggle.

In Nubia, in Brazil and Peru, South America, negroes may be found in military organizations. The army in Hayti is composed almost entirely of negroes and officered by their own race. During the century they have successfully defended themselves against the French, Spanish, and English, and unaided established a negro republic. Several black Generals came to the front in these conflicts, the most prominent being Toussaint l'Ouverture, a native of the Island of San Domingo. The fame of this negro reaching France, the great Emperor resolved upon his destruction. An expedition was fitted out under Gen. Leclerc, brother-in-law of Napoleon, and when landing in San Domingo was met by their forces under Gen. Christophe, who set fire to his own house and the city and fought Gen. Leclerc's forces with an impetuosity almost unparalleled in history. In the heat of the battle Gen. Toussaint l'Ouverture appeared on the scene, and, taking in the situation, shouted out: "Burn the city children, poison the wells, flee to the mountains, and make this island the hell the white man comes to." Failing in this expedition, an honorable peace was capitulated, after which Toussaint was induced to go to France, where he was seized by Napoleon's order and placed in confinement, where, after several years, he died in prison, neglected and almost forgotten. Not many years ago a young Prince, the only lineal male descendant of the Napoleonic line, was killed in Africa by the Zulus, from whom Gen. Toussaint l'Ouverture descended.

Negroes participated in the war for independence of Mexico both as officers and soldiers. These were the descendants of the negroes brought from Africa by the Spaniards to work the mines of that country some years after its conquest by Cortez, the great Spanish conqueror.

France has in Algiers two regiments of negroes composed of four battalions, each of 1,000 men. They served in Mexico under Maximilian and in the Franco-German war of 1870. England has employed negro troops for more than a hundred years, and has several colored regiments in British India composed of West African negroes. The English Government has never commissioned negroes as officers, as no foreigner is ever intrusted with a commission in the British Army.

In the early battles of the Revolution, at Lexington, Concord, and Bunker Hill, we find the negro sharing with spirit the perils of the white race. He was there in a servile capacity. One of the decisive events of the battle of Bunker Hill, as recorded in Washburn's history, was the killing of a British officer, Major Pitcairn, at the hands of Private Peter Salem of Col. Nixon's regiment of the Continental Army. Another negro of Col. Frye's regiment so distinguished himself in the battle of Charlestown that fourteen American officers commended his valor to Congress, saying: "He behaved like an experienced officer as well as an excellent soldier." It was agreed, at a council of war held at Gen. Washington's headquarters, to reject all slaves, and, finally, to reject all negroes. This seemed to settle the military status of the negro.

Soon after this came the coup d'etat of Lord Dunmore, Governor General of the colony of Virginia, who issued a proclamation declaring "all indentured servants, negroes or others, appertaining to rebels, that were willing to bear arms and would join his Majesty's troops as soon as may be, free." This in a very short space of time wrought a wonderful change in the minds of many of the colonists, for in less than two months after the issue of Lord Dunmore's proclamation the commander of the colonial army authorized in general orders the enlistment of free negroes. An official report made soon after the battle of Monmouth showed 755 negroes under Washington's command.

On the 21st of September, 1814, Gen. Andrew Jackson, commanding the Seventh Military District, issued an appeal to the free negroes of Louisiana to join his army. He said a mistaken policy had hitherto excluded them from the army; it should be so no longer. New-York, in October, 1814, enacted a law authorizing two regiments of free negroes. The recruiting officers of the United States Army accepted negro recruits under authority given to them, and up to July, 1815, over three hundred had been mustered into service.

The guiding hand of a Divine Providence seems to have foreordained that the largest negro army of modern times should be that engaged in a war that resulted in their freedom, after a period of over three hundred years of slavery, and where in all probability a larger body of negroes participated than in any other, ancient or modern. In all probability the first overt act committed by the friends of the freedom and liberation of the slaves was that of a negro, aided by twenty-one others, who on Sunday night, Oct. 16, 1859, captured the United States arsenal at Harper's Ferry, Va., and gave to the South the most stupendous fright it had ever experienced up to that date.

The election of Abraham Lincoln, in 1860, seemed to have been regarded by the South as a casus belli. It was followed soon after his inauguration by the attack on Fort Sumter, in Charleston Harbor, which opened the war of the rebellion. The fearful carnage that followed caused both contending parties to resort to every means available to gain the vantage point. The Confederate Army quite early in the conflict began using the slave in aid of their forces in constructing breastworks, forts, and fortifications, making them equivalent to soldiers. Gen. B. F. Butler, with his usual perspicacity, knowing that slaves were recognized as property, and being used in aid of a rebellion against the Government, were consequently contraband of war, ordered that when captured or found within our lines they should be set at work. Soon after the President's emancipation proclamation went into effect, in 1863, orders were issued for their enlistment and organization into regiments, to be officered by white men. They were soon afterward enlisted in all the Northern States and credited as part of their quota.

There were organized in the course of the rebellion more than 150 regiments of infantry, several of cavalry and artillery, in all about 180,000 soldiers. By way of explanation as to the writer's opportunity to know the efficiency and bravery of the negro as a soldier, the statement may be made that his services in connection with regiments composed entirely of colored men extended over a period of twenty-one years. He has seen the negro tested under every phase of a soldier's life, in battle, charging the enemy's works under a deadly fire of cannon and musketry, lying wounded on the field of battle, writhing in the agonies of death, in the bivouac, on the march amid driving storms of sleet and snow, with frozen ears, fingers, and feet, and in all circumstances has found him the equal of his white comrade in arms.

In the early organization of negro troops it was a serious question in the minds of many whether the negroes had sufficient moral courage to stand up in battle array against their late masters and owners, but there are many living witnesses to testify to the fact that they had that courage, even in so early a dawn of their freedom, knowing, too, that if captured they would not be treated as prisoners of war, but murdered, as in the case of the capture of Fort Pillow. The negro troops participated in many of the battles of the rebellion, around Petersburg, Mine Run, Fort Fisher, Nashville, and in many other engagements, they were found with the white race sharing the perils and hardships of war. At Fort Pillow they were ever ready for the fray, and, though surrounded by superior numbers and compelled to surrender, met death at the hands of murderers.

There was a division of ten regiments of negroes in the battle of Nashville, one brigade of which, commanded by Gen. T. J. Morgan, the present Commissioner of Indian Affairs, made the opening attack and charge on the morning of Dec. 15, 1864. Col. Benjamin Harrison, Seventieth Indiana Volunteers, commanded a brigade on the right of Morgan's and witnessed that charge, and I am credibly informed that the President speaks in very complimentary terms of the action of the negro troops. The casualties that day in one regiment amounted to eighty-two, nineteen of which were in the company commanded by the writer. The negroes fought nobly, this being the first test of the regiment under fire.

As further proof that the services of the negro were recognized in the war of the rebellion, the fact may be cited that, in the reorganization and increase in the regular army of thirty regiments in 1866, Congress directed that four regiments of infantry and two of cavalry of the increase should be composed of colored men. At the present time one-tenth of the regular army (four of the forty regiments) consists of negro soldiers, and they are fully equal to any others. A company of the Tenth Cavalry, (colored,) under the command of Col. Carpenter, now commanding Fort Myer, Virginia, was the first to reach the beleaguered command of Col. G. A. Forsyth on the Arrickaree Fork of the Republican River in Kansas in 1868, when he was surrounded by Indians, living on mule meat and almost dead. A company of the Ninth Cavalry Capt. F. S. Dodge, was the first to reinforce the command of Major Thornburgh, who had been ambushed by the Ute Indians.

Only about one year ago the President gave certificates to ten negro soldiers of the Twenty-fourth Infantry for gallant conduct in their efforts to protect a Paymaster who was attacked by robbers in Arizona. These are only a few of the many instances of negro valor and gallantry, even in the regular service.

About ten years ago a Lieutenant Colonel in the regular army, and a graduate of the Military Academy, after inspecting two companies of negroes, (Twenty-fourth Infantry,) said that one of them was in the finest condition as to arms, equipments, cleanliness, clothing, &c., of any company of the regular army he had ever inspected, white or black, and he had then served over thirty years in the army, and had been a Brigadier General of volunteers.

The desertions from the negro regiments are very much fewer in proportion to those from the white regiments. There is less complaining, less drunkenness, and the negro soldiers are more easily controlled.

Visit the national cemeteries at Petersburg, near Richmond, Beaufort, Fort Pillow, Chattanooga, and Nashville, and many others, and you will find among the silent graves of the heroic dead those of the colored men "who made their breast a barricade between our country and its foes, whose soldier lives were the reveille of freedom to their race in chains and their death the tattoo of rebellious tyranny in arms." They have one consolation—that while the balmy Southern breeze sighs a requiem over their last resting place it will never fan a slave.

A NEGRO MURDERER LYNCHED

NEW-YORK TIMES
March 27, 1891

Middlesborough, Ky., March 26.—A terrible tragedy took place this morning at Cumberland Gap, Tenu., a few miles from here, in which J. A. Burke, the telegraph operator at that place, was shot and instantly killed by Thomas Hunter, a negro. Reports are conflicting as to what caused Hunter to commit the deed, but from what can be learned it seems that Burke and Hunter fell out over some trifling matter in a saloon. Hunter then left, and procuring a shotgun lay in ambush for Burke. The latter was on his way home when the negro discharged the contents of both barrels at him, tearing out his eyes, cheeks, and teeth. Burke died instantly.

The murderer then fled, but was captured here this morning, and on the way back to the Gap the officers were met by sixty armed men, who took Hunter from them and hanged him. His body was then riddled with bullets.

A CASE OF RACE PREJUDICE
How an Educated Colored Girl's Path Is Made Difficult.

NEW-YORK TIMES
April 19, 1891

New York, Thursday, April 16, 1891
To the Editor of the New-York Times:

May I call the [attention] of your readers to an instance of shameful race prejudice, in the hope that the sympathies of some one will be roused either to aid the present sufferer or to prevent a similar occurrence in the future?

A young woman of a well-to-do colored family is ambitious to obtain a good education, with the ultimate object of qualifying herself to be a physician. Whether or not she encountered difficulties in her early education I do not know. Suffice it to say, she matriculated at a well-known Eastern college for women, from which she graduated with honor, and with the respect of her instructors and classmates. She then went to a Western university to begin her medical studies. After pursuing them for a year she was compelled by ill health to suspend work for a time. She returned to her Eastern home, bringing with her from the university authorities excellent testimonials as to the quality of her work.

This year, being restored to health, she determined to complete her course at a woman's medical college in this city, where by her work she has shown herself fully equal to her white associates. Wishing to have more practical experience than can be derived from the course of a medical school, she decided to enter a training school for nurses, where she might have the advantages of hospital practice. But at this point she has found her progress completely barred. Applications made to a number of places where the training she seeks is to be gained met with the same result. Not daunted by her first repulse, she has tried channel after channel, only to find that the world has still so little practical Christianity in its workings that the fact of color renders it impossible for her to be admitted as pupil into any training school for nurses, or into any hospital for regular practice.

Some of the answers which she has received written by supposed Christians, are cutting and cruel in the manner of their refusal, it being probably unnecessary for their writers to consider the feelings of one to whom her Creator has given a colored skin. Is it any wonder that she feels desperate and says: "Of what use is it to allow me to receive an education when I am absolutely shut out from the practice which can alone perfect my knowledge."

She says, too, that in Europe she could find ready admittance to nursing and hospital practice, while here in her native country there seems to be no sphere open to her beyond that of domestic service. Why is our Christianity so much less advanced than that of our brothers on the other side of the Atlantic? If the United States is the "land of the free," why should one of its own children be forced to find in a foreign land her only opportunity for advancement in her chosen line of noble work?

H. S.

A COLORED SCHOOL COMMISSIONER

NEW-YORK TIMES
April 22, 1891

T. McCants Stewart, a colored lawyer, was yesterday appointed a member of the Brooklyn Board of Education by Mayor Chapin. He succeeds the late Philip A. White, also a colored man.

Mr. Stewart is thirty-six years old, a native of South Carolina, an ardent Democrat, and a popular political speaker. He was educated at the Howard University and at the University of Edinburgh, Scotland. He studied for the ministry for a time and was professor in a college for negroes in his native State. Afterward he was pastor of the Sullivan Street Methodist Episcopal Church, in this city, and then he went to Sierra Leone on missionary work. On his return he studied law and has built up a profitable practice.

THE BODY IN THE TREE

A Problem that Puzzles the People of Milledgeville. A Mystery [ ] to [Shroud] the Finding of the Negro's Body—How Did It Got in the Tree?

ATLANTA CONSTITUTION
May 1, 1891

Milledgeville, Ga., April 30.—[Special.] Our citizens have not ceased to wonder at the ghastly discovery of that negro fisherman, to-wit, a dead human body lodged in the forks of a tree, where it was supposed to have been left by the high waters of January last. The wonder is that a body, and especially a human body, could remain in an exposed position to sun, to rain and to the general elements, without corroding, or putrefaction. The verdict of the coroner's jury was: "We, the jury, empaneled to hold an inquest over the dead body of a colored man (name unknown), find to the best of our knowledge and belief, the said person came to his death from accidental drowning." In commenting on this remarkable case The Milledgeville Chronicle says that the fact that the unfortunate was found by the coroner in the forks of a tree, and amid the debris and flotsam of high water, is conclusive evidence that the body was placed there by high water. It could not have been placed there by the hand of man. The high character of Mr. Gause and the gentlemen jurors precludes the possibility of doubting the statement that the uncorroded body of a negro who had been exposed to the elements, twelve feet above the river's present measurement, had been found, and that the negro's body must have been placed there by the high waters three months ago. Is it possible in the natural order of things for such a body to remain there for that length of time without the birds finding it? And if, the birds failed to find it, would not the worms have taken hold and destroyed the body? These are speculative queries and are thrown out simply because of inquiry.

The verdict of the coroner's jury, the statement of Mr. Gause himself, the facts, circumstances and surroundings—all show that this is a most extraordinary case.

There are parties who think that there is some mystery connected with the finding of the body, and the circumstances certainly do partake of the mysterious. The body could not have remained in the tree for so long a time without decaying. But it was certainly found in the forks of the tree. How did it get there?

PERSONAL

HARPER'S WEEKLY
June 27, 1891, p. 475

General Armstrong, founder of the Hampton School for Indians and negroes, is the son of a missionary, and was born in the Sandwich Islands, where his father was stationed. He is to visit his birthplace this summer. When he began his work among the negroes in the South, both himself and his wife were absolutely ostracised by the whites.

INCREASE OF THE COLORED POPULATION

HARPER'S WEEKLY
July 11, 1891, p. 510

General Francis A. Walker contributes an interesting article to the *Forum* on the census and the colored race, pointing to the conclusion, contrary to the general impression, that the colored population shows but a relatively slight rate of increase by means of a very high birth rate, just a little in excess of a very high death rate. The colored race was brought to this country by force, and except for the slave-trade between 1620 and 1808 there would not be 75,000 Africans in the United States, instead of 7,500,000, who are substantially descended from the 700,000 African women who were here in 1810. Naturally the race would not have been diffused widely in the country, but the interests of the master class and the effort of the slave for freedom have carried the colored people into regions naturally alien or hostile to them. By the first census, in 1790, they are estimated at 757,208. By that of 1890, partly estimated, they are 7,500,000. The increase per cent. in thirty years varies from 133.97 in 1820 to 68.85 in 1890. In ten years the increase per cent. varies from 37.5 in 1810 to 13.9 in 1890. The total population during the century has increased sixteenfold, but the colored element only tenfold. In 1790 it was one-fifth of the population, in 1890 less than one-eighth; and by thirty-year periods its decline has been continuous from the beginning.

General Walker finds that these figures establish a strong probability that the reduction of the relative importance of this element in the population will continue. Comparative study of the census taken at different periods—and there is no more competent student than General Walker—shows a disposition on the part of the colored people to abandon the higher, colder, and drier lands, to which they were carried by the will of the master class. Dividing the old slave States into two groups, the middle southern belt, in which slavery was maintained as a political and social, quite as much as an economic, institution, and the more southern group, the increase in the first during the last decade has been but five and a half per cent., while in the other it has approximated 19 per cent. Still further, within the second group the tendency is marked to a concentration of the colored element upon the lower lands. In Georgia in 1880, 48.43 per cent. of the colored population lived less than 500 feet above the sea. In 1890 the ratio had increased to 51.87.

The general conclusion drawn from such observations is that the vast increase of the colored race here, which has been anticipated by political seers, is wholly improbable. The natural field for the colored race is circumscribed by climate and industrial conditions, and a race which is limited in its range becomes by that fact subject to important restrictions upon its capabilities of sustained increase within that range. "If the growth of the colored race is hereafter to take place mainly within the cotton belt, it is safe to say that it will never reach fifty millions, or a third of that number." General Walker is of opinion that the natural tendency of the colored race is toward the hot regions bordering on the Gulf of Mexico. In the Northern States, in the high lands of the old slave States, and even in the upland cultivation of the cotton crop, the greater vigor and ability of the white race will assert themselves; and assuming the proximate correctness of his views, General Walker attributes the probable relative decline of the colored population throughout the United States partly to the more rapid growth of the white element, partly to migration southward, under the imperious demand for labor in the cotton fields, and partly to the high rate of colored mortality in Northern latitudes, and even in Southern cities.

ON THE ROLL OF HONOR

Enlisted Men Whose Names Appear in General Orders.

HARPER'S WEEKLY
July 11, 1891, pp. 518-19

By Barnet Phillips.
The order designated as "No. 109" was issued by command of Major-General Schofield, December 10, 1888, and as promulgated by the Adjutant-General, R. C. Drum, is as follows:

"Announcement is made to the army that it is in contemplation to publish annually hereafter, at the close of each year, commencing with 1889, an order making mention of gallant or specially meritorious acts or conduct in service, on the part of either commissioned officers or enlisted men of the army, and contain-

JAMES SETTLERS, OF TROOP E, NINTH CAVALRY.

Harper's Weekly, July 11, 1891, p. 519.

ing the names of those who have received medals of honor and certificates of merit. . . ."

On May 11, 1889, Major Wham, paymaster of the United States army, left Fort Grant, Arizona, to pay off troops at certain other forts. He had $28,345 in the boot of an ambulance. Major Wham knew what he was about, and had with him an escort of two non-commissioned officers and nine privates—and that was two more than the usual number. All, the soldiers were of the Twenty-fourth Infantry and Tenth Cavalry, and were colored men. Everything went pleasantly until, about twenty-six miles from Fort Grant, down the rugged road a peculiar obstruction was seen. It was an uncommonly large bowlder in the middle of the cañon. Had it rolled down the mountain-side of its own volition, or had somebody put it there? It had to be removed, no matter how it got there. There is nothing that ought to stop a paymaster. Off got the sergeant and the men, and began laboring with that big bowlder, when crack went a rifle from the rocks above, followed by a volley of shots; an enemy ensconced in a natural fortress was pumping lead on the soldiers. Then came a pretty fight—that is "pretty" in an Irish sense; but the Committee on Military Affairs, who sifted out the whole thing, state that Major Wham and his party "made a stubborn and efficient resistance." The men in blue showed no fear, and they rallied and stuck to their arms until eight of them were wounded. Major Wham and his escort did not seem to care about the risks they were running. The case of a paymaster with government funds in his keeping is a peculiar one. It carries with it great responsibilities. He must not lose the money, or the accounting for its disappearance is a state affair, rigidly examined. Major Wham rallied his men, and fought them to a stand-still; all were wounded excepting the officer and one man. The corporal, who was not touched, told how impossible it was to fight any more. "He did not think it plausible"; that was his testimony. At last Major Wham, with his wounded, had to retire behind some mesquite brush. The rascals kept up a desultory fire for about an hour afterward, sweeping the place of action. They understood their business. Then they got to the ambulance, broke open the treasure-box, and looted it. The money was lost, to the last penny, but not a shred of the honor of that plucky major and his gallant colored escort. When the ground was carefully looked over afterward by military experts it was seen that the robbers knew exactly what to do, and had arranged their plans long before. They could throw in a galling fire whenever they pleased. It was believed that there were from thirteen to twenty bandits, with all the advantages of a surprise. "The robber chief"—so testified an infantry officer—"had evidently foreseen that if the soldiers resisted they would retreat to the particular position which they did occupy, and he had therefore placed part of the outlaws to the right and rear of the rock to flank them." For that good fight with robbers, for gallant and meritorious conduct, medals of honor were given to Sergeant Benjamin Brown, Company C; Corporal Isaiah Mays, Company B; and certificates of merit to Privates George Arrington, Benjamin Burge, Julius Harrison, Hamilton Lewis, Squire Williams, James Young, Thornton Hams, and James Wheeler.

Here is the pleasant face of another colored man. It is Private James Settlers, of Troop E, Ninth Cavalry, and a soldierly like young man is he. The army roll of honor is brief about James Settlers, but tells the whole story. He was distinguished for special meritorious conduct, "saving, at the risk of his own life, his commanding officer from drowning while crossing the Wind River, Wyoming." Having, through correspondence relative to Private James Settlers, made at least an epistolary acquaintance with the officer who is indebted to his soldier for existence, Lieutenant-Colonel Burt's reply to me was properly brief, but it spoke volumes: "I have to say that as to Private James Settlers, it was my life he saved. I do not know how to give you a statement of the affair without dragging myself into it, which would appear more like how I was drowned than how gallant Private Settlers, my orderly was. Moreover, it has become one of my stock stories, and I don't know how I could write out of that groove. At best it doesn't work into much of an incident, except as far as it gives the lie to the popular belief that there is unkindly feeling between the enlisted man and his officers. . . . Men do not trisk their lives unhesitatingly for those who oppress them." Certainly Colonel Burt, of the Seventh Infantry, has the good of the service at heart, and true pride in his calling, and the liveliest interest in the welfare of those who, through his own brilliant services, he has been called on to command.

NEGRO KILLED NEAR SELMA

Shot from Ambush by Unknown Parties—Lived Only an Hour.

ATLANTA CONSTITUTION
July 26, 1891

Selma, Ala., July 26.—(Special.)—Jack Davis. a negro living on the plantation of William Weaver, a few miles from the city. was killed early this morning. It seems that some weeks ago, a woman who had been living with Jack for the past few years, tired on him and became the companion of another negro living at Orrville. On Sunday last the lover of the woman went to Davis's house to get something belonging to her. These Davis refused to give up. A quarrel ensued, though no damage was done. That night while Davis was going home he was shot at but not hit. Last night, however, while passing through a dark piece of woods he was shot from ambush, receiving wounds from which he died about an hour later. He stated before dying that he had seen two negroes shoot him, but refused to give their names. Davis and Dr. Whitts Stuart had a falling out about two weeks ago and the doctor whipped him. Since then the negro has been very surly and had threatened vengeance. It was reported at first that the negro came to his death at the hands of a white mob, but the particulars are given as above.

PERSONAL

HARPER'S WEEKLY
September 19, 1891, p. 703

Ex-Senator Blanche K. Bruce, of Mississippi, has held the highest official position ever attained by a colored man in this country, having at one time, by Vice-President Wheeler's request, presided over the United States Senate. Mr. Bruce's son was named after Roscoe Conkling, in recognition of a courtesy which the New York Senator showed him when he first entered the Senate. It was time for Mr. Bruce to be sworn in, but his Republican colleague, Senator Alcorn, instead of escorting him to the Vice-President's desk, according to custom, quietly ignored him. Then Mr. Conkling quickly arose, and gracefully performed the service.

AN APPEAL TO WHITE AMERICANS

HARPER'S WEEKLY
November 28, 1891, p. 935

The wrong of which Mr. Downing speaks in the subjoined paper is universally known, but the feeling of those whom it most deeply affects is little considered. It will be but slowly corrected, because of the conditions from which it springs. But one such fervent appeal will be of some service to a righteous end.

108 Bellevue Avenue,

Newport, R. I., November 6, 1891.

Respected Sir,—The colored man's struggle, lately dubbed "The Negro Problem," has a side seldom discussed. White friends at the North who talk of freedom and equality before the law read of the wrong done the colored people of the South, and justly appeal to Heaven. They exclaim, "My God! my God!" but do not seem to realize that great injustice is being done the colored man daily in the North, and that this injustice encourages abuses in the South against which they protest. In fact, the outraging in question differs in the North from that of the South only in degree.

The colored man in the North is almost invariably discriminated against; his life is made miserable; his is a soured and embittered existence. It matters not if he be industrious, educated, and scrupulously law-abiding. The contempt manifested discourages, depresses, and embarrasses. I am under the harrow, and know whereof I affirm. This crushing iniquity shuts the colored man out from thrifty and elevating pursuits; from your factories, your workshops, sales-rooms, from dignified callings, from positions in political parties that command respect. Professing followers of the meek and lowly Jesus proscribe him invidiously. It is seen in their holy sanctuaries. Let me impress upon you that all of this outraging stimulates to the abuse of colored men in the South. It is held up by the South as an offset to the North's invocations and exclamations denunciatory of the South. Let the North wash its hands of the too general iniquity, and the South would sooner fall into line.

Education and refinement, with the consequent sensitiveness that go along therewith—both of which are possessed by the colored man of to-day—cause him to realize painfully, acutely, the injustice he encounters at every turn. He does so with feelings that should have no place in the breast of any human being.

TRAINING HORSES TO LEAP OBSTACLES, TENTH UNITED STATES CAVALRY.—Drawn by Frederic Remington.—[See Page 710.]

Harper's Weekly, September 19, 1891, p. 709.

This is to me a keenly felt reality. It would not be so hard if the colored people were completely degraded and debased. But is it not cruel to throw open your schools and colleges to them, to inspire them with your daily talk as to rights and entitlements, unless you intend to have regard for the resultant feelings upon their part?

I can see the bosoms of a hundred thousand men and women of the North swell and heave. I can hear a hundred thousand and more voices exclaim, "Mr. Downing, you speak correctly; great injustice is being done to the colored man in the North and in the South." But here they rest. I feel that they are thus moved, for I am persuaded that deep down in the breast of my fellow-countrymen a sense of justice has its abode. Let me appeal to that sense of justice, to that hundred thousand and more, and entreat the multitude, in the name of fair play, of justice, of the genius of our institutions, of the character and laws of our government, of the professed Christianity of the land, not to rest, but to be troubled about the injustice, to be aggressively active in efforts to free the North from the deep disgrace that dishonors her, that assists in making outrages decent in other parts of the country.

George T. Downing.

PERSONAL

HARPER'S WEEKLY
November 28, 1891, p. 935

Among the Freshmen at Williams College is Prince Besolow, the son of an African chief, who is fitting himself for missionary work in his native land.

MR. BRYCE ON THE NEGRO PROBLEM

HARPER'S WEEKLY
December 19, 1891, p. 1011

The opinion of no foreigner upon an American political question could be more friendly and intelligent than that of Mr. James Bryce, to whom we owe the *American Commonwealth*. He is so heartily in sympathy with the truest American spirit and tendency, and is so familiar with our political system and the movement of American public opinion, that his views cannot fail of decided influence. Many readers of Republican political sympathies, we are sure, will agree with us that there has been no more thoughtful and wise treatment of the Negro Problem in this country than Mr. Bryce's recent article in the North American Review. He states the familiar situation and the gravity of the question with entire candor, and he is naturally free from the unconscious bent of party predilection.

After stating fairly the alleged party purpose in the force bill, Mr. Bryce says:

> "Under the Constitution the negro has the suffrage. He is—this nobody denies—in many districts practically excluded from the enjoyment of it. Two courses are open. If the law cannot be enforced, it ought to be repealed. If it cannot be repealed, it ought to be enforced. No one supposes it can be repealed. Those, therefore, who advocate its enforcement by that very authority which made it have a weighty *prima facie* case. Whatever may be their secret motives, they come forward as the protectors and vindicators of law, of orderly government, of democratic principles."

He mentions the constitutional objection, but he thinks that most lawyers would hold that the letter of the Constitution covers the proposed legislation. But the practical objections, he thinks, are of the greatest weight. Having described the actual social separation between the races which exists everywhere—and of which Mr. George T. Downing, a colored man, recently spoke in these columns with the utmost feeling—and after a survey of the whole field, which no Democrat or Republican would condemn as unjust or unreasonable, Mr. Bryce proceeds to his conclusion:

> "Assuming, as one may safely assume, that neither the commixture of the two races nor the elimination of the negro by removal to Africa can be carried out, the question remains whether the federal power must intervene, or whether it will be better to let things take their natural course. It is from no blindness to the evils of the situation as it stands, nor from any want of sympathy with the negro, that I conceive the latter policy to be the safer one. The maxim that the physician who doubts whether to administer a drug or not had better refrain, is applicable to legislative interference. Where the reasons for and against such interference are nearly balanced, where success, though possible, is quite uncertain, non-interference is to be preferred, because in politics, as in the human body, there is a tendency similar to that which used to be called the *vis medicatrix naturae*. Things find their level and readjust themselves according to their natural affinities and the balance of actual forces, not, perhaps, in the best way, but in a way which has elements of stability. The reconstructors after the war disregarded the balance of the local forces they found in the South, too readily believing that federal law would prevail against the purposes or passions of the whites. Events have proved that they erred; and another error of the same kind might turn out as ill."

This is precisely the ground of the intelligent and wholly unpartisan opposition in this country to the force bill. It is really an effort to accomplish by law what law cannot accomplish, and it is in the interest of the colored race, of the white race, of respect for law, and regard for the true welfare of the Union that the force bill is opposed as futile legislation. Should it appear again for discussion, no better comment upon it could be presented to the country than this paper of Mr. Bryce.

THE SLAVE-TRADE

HARPER'S WEEKLY
January 30, 1892, p. 118

Civilized Europe has frowned upon the African slave-trade, and the British are continually fighting over it. Strong efforts are being made to stamp out this awful traffic, and Christian is arrayed against Mohammedan. Death, except so far as self is concerned, is regarded lightly by the Arab slave-trader, and the consolations of his religion are such that he can even look upon his own death with equanimity. Where his savage black brother is concerned, an Arab seems to exercise about as much humanity as would be looked for in a tiger of the jungle. The religion of the Prophet is decidedly selfish, and was probably moulded to fit just such men as make up the bands of slave-hunters.

Picture a little village in Darkest Africa. Whatever may be the condition of life, it is certainly as the inhabitants choose to make it; and however savage the people are, there is no question but that they must enjoy a certain freedom of existence, and hold family ties that even the beasts are not bereft of. They know of no better life; but there is the possibility of a worse state always before them. Their creed is war, their virtues few; but for this they can hardly be held to blame, for the pall of darkness is over them at all times. Suddenly a horde of Arabs sweeps down upon them. The village is demolished; every one of the inhabitants is captured by the hunters. To resist means torture and death. The life of each Mohammedan must be paid for by the slaughter of the young and old, which is accomplished with the most terrible exhibitions of cruelty; and even if the Arabs make their captures without loss, there is no pity felt for the poor negro. Those who are unfit for slaves are told that they may go; but as they sneak off, they are run and shot down by the brutal captors. The Arabs have no regard for life. They will tie a rope around the ankles of one of the helpless ones, and fastening it to the saddle of a horse, compel the lesser brute to drag the victim across the desert until life is extinct, or nearly so; the latter suits their devilish taste much better. The slaves on the line of march bear round wooden yokes, and are linked in pairs, with their hands often tied. Any murmur against their captors or refusal to eat—in fact, the slightest act of insubordination—means instant death. Crossing the Great Desert these slaves suffer the agonies of thirst—a suffering that we cannot appreciate. Scores fall by the wayside, and are left to die as best they may; for, in the height of their exquisite cruelty, the Arabs deny unto these men the merciful bullet. When the wells are reached, these poor slaves expire within reach of the water that they are unable to drink, and the robbers of the desert show no sign of pity. It is hard to think of these Arabs as men and human beings; yet they are men who glory in their religion, and often show themselves worthy of higher influences. They regard life as lightly as possible, and it is said of the great number of captives that begin the march across the desert, very few ever reach the markets. The route of a slave caravan is marked by the dead that lie upon the sand.

The outlook is one of promise. Already these bands of slave-traders have been diminished, and earnest men are engaged in the suppression of the traffic. England has been deeply interested in the subject, and it will probably be but a short time before this horrible trade is a thing of the past. The world progresses, and the gentler influence of Christianity or civilization—call it what you will—may soon extend to Darkest Africa, and wipe out the scourge of the poor native.

THE PROBLEM OF THE RACES

Talk by the Rev. Samuel J. Barrows on "Afric-Americans."

NEW-YORK TIMES
February 15, 1892

The Brooklyn Ethical Association discussed the race problem last night at the Second Unitarian Church, Clinton and Congress Streets, Brooklyn. The Rev. Samuel J. Barrows of Boston, Mass., editor of the *Christian Register,* spoke on "The Evolution of the Afric-American and His Relation to the Race Problem."

"The negro originally came to America," said Mr. Barrows, "on the invitation of the white man, and he came involuntarily. He has come to stay, but not as a negro. The Afric-American race is being merged into the Caucasian stream. After being 200 years in slavery in this country, the negro was emancipated, and his progress in the subsequent quarter of a century has been marvelous. Shall the races mix[?] They have mixed, and probably they will continue to mix. In the South the negro has become a land owner and tiller, and has made rapid progress in education and in industrial welfare. The amalgamation of the white and black races ought to be left to the instincts of those races, unhindered by laws. The American negro of to-day has a better sense of English than the peasant of Great Britain. The colored man's future is largely in his own hands."

Lawyer T. McCants Stewart, the colored member of the Brooklyn Board of Education, replied to Mr. Barrows. He quoted history to show that the negro and the white man had a common origin, that the negro originally led the world, and that his degeneracy had been due to his long exile in a tropical clime.

"When the Romans took the Britains back home as slaves," said Lawyer Stewart, "they were so dull that nobody wanted them. They were a drug in the market. The negro does not want to leave America, and, what's more, he won't leave, and you can't make him leave. The solution of the race problem depends on justice, liberty, and education."

T. Thomas Fortune also spoke.

MUSTN'T GO TO LIBERIA

So Declares the Colored Mass Meeting as to the Stranded Ones.

NEW-YORK TIMES
February 26, 1892

A mass meeting of colored people was held at the Bethel African Methodist Episcopal Church, in Sullivan Street, last night, to consider the predicament of the negroes who, coming to this city expecting to sail from here for Liberia, found that the means of transportation on which they had counted were not provided.

Resolutions were adopted protesting against the movement to help the would be emigrants on their way to Liberia, and a collection was taken up to provide food and homes for them here, or to send them back whence they came if they desired to return. About $75 was contributed.

The emigrants seem pretty well satisfied with New-York, and some of them, though still possessed with the idea of making Liberia their home, are pretty well content to remain by the wayside for rest and refreshment, preparatory to their long trip. The Cherokee people, who are at the Merritt Mission, are getting three square meals a day, and as long as that lasts they are not likely to see any good reason why they should bother about the future.

"Wants mo' brade, does you, to gib to white trash an' lower yo'self? Now git out fo' I slap de face offin you!"

Harper's Weekly, April 16, 1892, p. 384.

One of them said yesterday, after eating his dinner, "Doan I tell yer, dis am de lan' ob Beulah, on de way to de promus lan'."

Mr. Merritt, however, is troubled, not on account of the expense of feeding his guests, but because yesterday he received a notice from the Health Department stating that he was violating the law by allowing his cellar to be used as a sleeping place. Mr. Merritt said that he did not know where else he could put the negroes, but he would try to find a resting place for them. He would see that they were fed as long as they remained under his care.

The negroes from Arkansas are quartered [in] Thompson and Sullivan Streets, and their money is rapidly giving out. Some tried to find work yesterday, but were unsuccessful. The Rev. Thomas Addison and Mr. Reginald Fendall of the American Colonization Society went back to Washington yesterday to report to the Executive Committee what they saw while here. One of them will probably return within a few days and look out for the negroes.

THE MASS-MEETING OF COLORED CITIZENS IN NEW YORK

HARPER'S WEEKLY
April 16, 1892, p. 363

The late demonstration of feeling at the largest meeting of colored citizens ever held in the city of New York was an interesting illustration of the public situation. The treatment of negroes in some parts of the Southern States has usually been exposed and denounced by white Republican journal and orators. But a meeting of citizens of their own race to protest against the frequent wrongs practised upon them is unusual. The assembly was very large, and very emotional. But the chairman, the Rev. Dr. Derrick, is a man of discretion and of great influence among his brethren, who, however, in moments of excitement, was unable to control the crowd.

An address was read, and enthusiastically approved, which said, among other things:

> "We recommend that the race in the South maintain their trust in God, but we also recommend that they unite for mutual protection; that they seek to bring to their support and into public expression the opinion of that part of the white people in the South who are disgusted and who feel compromised by the lawless elements among them.
>
> "We urge Afro-Americans in the South to keep always within the law, to bring, as far as practicable, actions for damages against cities and against counties in which these lawless acts are allowed to occur by public officers, who are sworn to execute the law and to protect life and property.
>
> "We urge organization; we urge agitation; we urge the prosecution of every peaceful remedy; but we also advise our brethren to protect to the extent of their ability their defenceless fellows charged with crimes against the lynchers and midnight marauders, who are always brutal outlaws, and we advise our brethren to let it be known that endurance has a limit, and that patience under some conditions may cease to be a virtue."

And when, at the conclusion of a long list of outrages, Mr. Fortune asked, "What are you going to do about it?" the answer, "Fight!" burst in a tremendous shout from the whole multitude, and there was immense uproar for some minutes. Ex-Representative John R. Lynch, of Mississippi, denounced the new Constitution of the State, and said that those who supported the party that framed it sustained the wrongs that were done to colored citizens.

Mr. Fortune attempted to interrupt Mr. Lynch, and the excitement for some time threatened to end in a fight. After the combined efforts of the chairman and the band, the chorus of "My Country, 'tis of Thee," composed the meeting, which adjourned after hearing the rest of Mr. Lynch's speech, and appointing a committee to lay the address before the President, and to ask him to appeal to Congress to correct the personal wrongs of which complaint is made. The feeling of the meeting is not surprising, and although Congress and the laws can do little to assure a remedy, the perpetrators of the crimes complained of are not beyond the reach of public opinion acting upon the communities in which they live. What is called "the South," cannot be held responsible for the crimes. But a strong and urgent local protest and the prompt application of the local law to the criminals would soon restrain such outbreaks.

COLORED MEN'S CONVENTION

NEW-YORK TIMES
April 21, 1892

Cincinnati, April 20.—A national convention of the colored people of the United States is to be held here on July 4 and 5, to enlist sympathy for the recent lynchings of colored men.

Each State will have one delegate for every 10,000 of colored population. It is not intended that this convention shall be in any sense a political one.

COMBINED AGAINST NEGROES
A Society to Uphold White Supremacy in the South.

NEW-YORK TIMES
July 3, 1892

Chicago, July 2.—A special from Birmingham, Ala., says: "An organization has been formed here known as the 'Knights of the White Shield.' About 250 were initiated into the order. The oath is iron-bound and rock-ribbed. The constitution narrates the troubles with the negroes and proposes to form alliances for the preservation of white supremacy.

"Nothing will be done in violation of United States and State laws, but steps are to be taken to spread the order and rid the country of the negro race. Some of the prominent men of the city are members of the organization.

"It is proposed to organize lodges all over the South as fast as possible, and to form them as soon as feasible into a political party. The meetings will be held weekly, but sessions will be secret."

COLORED MEN IN CONVENTION

Race Interests Discussed and Resolutions Adopted.

NEW-YORK TIMES
July 5, 1892

Cincinnati, Ohio, July 4.—A national convention of colored men of the United States to consider the interests of the race convened to-day at Zion Baptist Church. Mr. Daniel A. Rudd of this city, who has been the leader in the matter, announced that it was changed from a delegate convention to a mass meeting, and that no credentials were required. There were a hundred or more men in the church and a few women. Mr. Rudd called the meeting to order, and on motion of Col. Robert Harlan, Mr. Rudd was chosen temporary Chairman.

Mr. Rudd eulogized the patriotism and fidelity of his race, saying the starry flag had nowhere truer friends than among the negroes, whose blood had been spilled for its existence.

He counseled moderation, and especially culture of hand, head, and heart, to the end that the race might command respect and deserve fair treatment.

The afternoon session was opened informally by George W. Clark, an aged white man, who years ago was an "abolition vocalist."

The Committee on Permanent Organization [reported] for Permanent Chairman Daniel A. Rudd; for Vice Chairman, J. F. T. Carr; Secretary, S. G. Hunter.

A speech made by Mr. Merrywether of Arkansas, now a refugee in this city, told of horrors which he had witnessed in that State which, he said, were not told by the newspapers. He predicted that in time the negroes would turn and the Caucasian race would receive a baptism of blood. Mr. Merrywether was so full of breathings of vengeance that when his time expired the convention refused to extend the limit.

J. T. Robinson of Kentucky read a paper. He referred mildly to the poor comfort given to the representatives of the race by President Harrison. After reading he formally voted to commend Dr. Tourjees's National Civil Rights Association. The Committee on Resolutions then reported resolutions, among which were the following:

"We ask nothing of you in behalf of colored people, except the right to eat the bread our own hands have earned, to dwell safely in our own homes, to pursue our vocations in peace, to be granted a fair and equal opportunity in the race of life, to be protected under the law, and to be judged according to the law.

"We appeal to you against murder and violence, against robbery and extortion, against hasty and cruel judgments, against fierce mobs that outrage our people and desolate their homes."

OUR COLORED POPULATION

Africans Not Increasing So Rapidly as Has Been Supposed.

NEW-YORK TIMES
July 15, 1892

Washington, July 14.—The Census Office today issued a bulletin on the subject of the colored population of the United States in 1890.

The bulletin shows that the total colored population is 7,638,360. Of this number 7,470,040 are persons of African descent, 107,475 are Chinese, 2,039 are Japanese, and 58,806 are civilized Indians.

Considering persons of African descent, it is seen that there has been an increase during the decade from 1880 to 1890 of 889,247, or 13.51 per cent., as against an increase during the decade from 1870 to 1880 of 1,700,784, or 34.85 per cent. The Bulletin says:

"The abnormal increase of the colored population of the South during the decade ending in 1880 led to the popular belief that the negroes were increasing at a much greater rate than the white population. The present census has shown, however, that the high rate of increase in the colored population, as shown by the census of 1880, was apparent only, and was due to the imperfect enumeration of 1870 in the Southern States.

"There has been an increase in the number of Chinese in the United States during the decade from 1880 to 1890 of only 2,010 or 1.91 per cent., the number returned in 1880 being 105,46[5] and the number returned in 1890 being 107,465. The Chinese increased 66.88 per cent. from 1870 to 1880 and 80.91 per cent from 1860 to 1870.

"In 1880 the Japanese in the United States numbered only 148. While in 1890 they numbered 2,089. In 1870 there were only 55 Japanese returned under that census.

"The civilized Indians have decreased during the past ten years 7,601, or 11 45 per cent., the number returned in 1880 being 66,407, as against 58,806 returned in 1890."

FRED DOUGLASS TO HIS RACE
He Knows That Mr. Cleveland Will Guard Their Rights.

NEW-YORK TIMES
November 22, 1892

Washington, Nov. 21.—Fred Douglass has received so many inquiries since the late election from members of the colored race who are anxious to hear his views as to the probable effect of Democratic accession to power that he has put his answer in the form of a printed circular to save the labor of replying to each by letter.

In this circular he expresses the opinion that those persons who have apprehended a violent change for the worse, both in the general condition of the country and in that of the colored people North and South, will find themselves agreeably surprised by the little difference which the change of Administration will make. There will, he thinks, be made by the new Administration no disastrous assault upon the enterprise, industry, and welfare of the country.

The Democrats will, Mr. Douglass believes, endeavor to overhaul the tariff, and in some cases changes will be made, but the principle of protection will be neither ignored nor abandoned. As to the effect of the election of Mr. Cleveland upon the condition of the colored people of the South, Mr. Douglass says he is free to say that he has his fears as well as his hopes.

"It is hard," he says, "to tell what will happen. One thing I may with safety say. It is this: It will be very hard to make the condition of the negro in the South much worse than it is now and has been during the present Administration. I believe that the President-elect will see and act upon the wisdom of justice, peace, and good-will, alike to the white and the colored people in the South. I am sure that he will give no support or encouragement to lawless violence anywhere. I say this because I know the man and that he stands high above the meanness that would strike down any because they are weak, unpopular, and defenseless."

TO WIPE OUT THE NEGRO VOTE
A Unique Scheme To Solve a Troublesome Problem in Alabama.
Special to The Associated Press.

NEW-YORK TIMES
November 23, 1892

Montgomery, Nov. 22.—A bill was introduced in the Legislature to-day which is bound to attract a great deal of attention throughout the country. If it becomes a law it will practically do away with the negro vote in Alabama.

Th[e] bill was introduced by Representative Brewer of Lowndes County, who has been in the Legislature for fourteen years, and who was State Auditor four years. He is looked upon as the financial authority of the State, and has written a history of Alabama. The bill provides that "all persons whose State and county taxes as assessed do not amount to $5 shall not be required to pay the same if it be shown that such person failed to vote at the August and November elections of the previous year."

This is the first attempt in the history of Alabama to legislate against the negro vote. Ther[e] are not 20 per cent. of the negro voters who pay taxes exceeding $5 a year. At the lowest calculation 50 per cent. of the negro voters would take advantage of the opportunity of saving $5. The negro vote of the last election was 136,000 out of a total of 300,000. It can be seen that the effect of this bill will be widespread. Those most competent to judge think it will do away with the trouble which so vexes the white people.

The bill was a surprise. Few of the members expected anything of the kind. It was the most talked-about matter during the day. The opinion seemed general that the bill will pass.

NEGROES LEAVE THE SOUTH
A Great Exodus from Tennessee in Progress.
Special to The Associated Press.

NEW-YORK TIMES
November 24, 1892

Colored Laborers Making for the West and North in Large Numbers—Driven from Their Homes by Want of Work—The Southern Problem to Settle Itself

Chattanooga, Tenn., Nov. 23—Public attention here has been called to the large number of negroes who are leaving this section of Tennessee in search of work and homes in Northern and particularly Western States. The railroads are carrying away scores of negroes, women and children, every week, and it is said that about 700 colored people have left this city alone within the past month, the greater portion since election day. The first person to remark the extent of this negro exodus was Capt. J. L. Prince, a well-known real estate dealer in Chattanooga, who, in the matter of rents, &c., has constant dealings with the colored population.

"I was struck," said Capt. Price, "by the number of negro cottages which were being vacated, and I began to make inquiries. From all sides I got the same answer: 'We are going away because we can't live here. We only just keep from starving, but out West they promise us good wages.'"

Pushing his investigation still further, Capt. Price learned that Richard Cleag, who has been a Post Office official here under Harrison, but who now apprehends removal, is at present in Kansas making arrangements with the railroads to bring out a colony of negroes on terms which will be mutually advantageous. Charles Stanley, who has been for years a sort of patron saint to the colored population of Chattanooga, and who built up "Stanleytown," which is the negro quarter, is interested in this emigration scheme, and has hundreds of families ready and eager to start as soon as they get the word and the necessary tickets. Referring to the causes and conditions which lie at the bottom of this movement out to Kansas and Colorado—for these are the States chiefly under consideration—Capt. Price said:

"The fact is, the business enterprises and the manufacturing concerns of Chattanooga have been doing so badly during the past year that they have been obliged to cut down their force, of employes, or in many cases to close up altogether. This has thrown hundreds, I may almost say, thousands of men out of employment, the majority of them being negroes. The result has been that these poor fellows have not been able to pay their rents, and scarcely to find food for their families. Here are some of the works to which I refer: Within a few months the Lookout Rolling Mills found itself unable to stand the depression and the heavy taxes and moved away from Chattanooga altogether. That threw 300 men out of work. About a month ago the Roan Iron Works, which employed 800 men, shut down, and the City Coal Furnace also shut down temporarily. Several lumber companies have failed recently, and an army of laborers was thrown out of employment not long ago when the last of the five-hundred-thousand-dollar appropriation for city improvements was spent. Facts like these tell the whole story."

Another man in a position to speak with authority on this subject is J. G. Burg, an ex-Justice of the Peace of Chattanooga and one of the most intelligent colored men in the city. This evening, discussing the question of a negro exodus, he said:

"You ask me if there is going to be a negro exodus from here. I answer without hesitation, Yes, and I will go a step further and tell you that there is going to be a negro exodus from many parts of the South. Why do the colored people want to leave their homes? For two reasons. First, because the present business and industrial depression makes the labor market so overcrowded that the negro workman has no chance of making a living here, whereas he can get plenty of work and good pay if he will go North or West. I know hundreds of such cases not a mile away, and they are beginning to see the foolishness of trying to carry a burden which is altogether too heavy when it is so easy to throw it off. Then there is a second reason why the colored men are tending more and more to move their families away from the South, and that is the fact that the further North or West they get the better and more fairly they are treated. Oh! it won't be long before there will be ten negroes going away where there is one now. I know what I am talking about, and I tell you it is bound to come."

"But what will be the ultimate result of such an exodus?" was asked.

The ex-Chief Justice of the Peace lifted his eyebrows significantly. "The result will be that the South will have solved what the Yankees call its negro problem in a very simple though unexpected way. I mean by sending enough of its negroes to the North so that both halves of this country will be in the same boat. That's what the result will be, and you won't have to wait so very long for it either."

Squire Burg rather chuckled as he concluded this novel expression of opinion.

LOOKS LIKE A SWINDLING SCHEME

NEW-YORK TIMES
December 11, 1892

In the opinion of Messrs. Yates & Porterfield, who are in the African shipping trade, with an office at 19 William Street, the plan of colonizing negroes in Arkansas, with the view of sending them to Liberia, as has been told in The Times, is probably part of a scheme to obtain money under false pretenses, which has already been attempted by the so-called agents of a colonization society.

Last February a number of ignorant and unsuspecting colored people from the South came to this city under inducements to send them to a land of promise. They were stranded here, and in the end sent back to their former homes or put in the way of getting work.

The Arkansas plan, it is suspected, is being carried out much upon the same misrepresentations.

ARKANSAS NEGROES ALARMED

Preparing to Emigrate in Large Numbers from the State.

NEW-YORK TIMES
December 12, 1892

Little Rock, Ark., Dec. 11.—The assassination of Lightfoot, the Jackson County (Ark.) negro preacher and agent of the Liberian Emigration Society of New-York, has created great excitement among the negroes of this city and vicinity. The question of emigration was discussed in the colored churches here to-day, and the impression seems to prevail that emigration is the only thing left for the negroes of the back counties, where it is claimed by the leaders of that race the black man will stand no show of getting his rights hereafter.

Negroes of Lightfoot's stripe are operating in every county of the black belt in this State, and the killing of the preacher will only serve to hasten the blacks to pick up and leave for some other county than Arkansas. It is also said that Lightfoot was murdered by white men and the crime charged against negroes.

There is, however, a strong sentiment among many colored people of this community against the blacks leaving Arkansas.

TAKEN FROM A DETECTIVE AND LYNCHED

NEW-YORK TIMES
December 12, 1892

Wheeling, West Va., Dec. 11.—Police Officer James Dillon was killed and Constable Burton mortally wounded near Bluefield yesterday by a colored man named Cornelius Coffee. Coffee made his escape and boarded a Chesapeake and Ohio train, but was arrested at Pocahontas, Va., and held until the arrival of Detective Eugene Robinson of Elkhorn, who brought his prisoner over the line into West Virginia. At Keystone, a little hamlet a few miles from the State line, a band of men stopped the train, entered the car, quietly relieved Robinson of his prisoner, and proceeded to the nearest tree, where Coffee was strung up and his body riddled with bullets.

1893–1894

While fairgoers were enjoying the many exhibits at the World's Columbian Exposition in Chicago, Illinois, many urban dwellers and farmers were facing extreme hardships resulting from the devastating depression of 1893. As the economic downturn worsened, more than 15,000 businesses failed, the unemployment rate soared from nearly 3 percent to over 18 percent by 1894, and social unrest rose throughout the nation. There was a direct correlation between the economic depression and violence directed against African Americans; as cotton prices declined in the South the number of lynchings rose. Congressman Thomas E. Miller (R-South Carolina), an African American, stated in 1891: "The first and dearest rights the Negro of the South wants are the right to pay for his labor, his right of trial by jury, his right to his home, his right to know that the man who lynches him. . . .shall be convicted." In the year 1892 alone, 235 persons were lynched. From 1882, the first year records were available, to 1900, more than 3,000 persons were lynched, and the majority were African American. Historian Rayford Logan identifies the typical victim as an African American male unjustly accused of a crime, usually the rape of a white woman, or economic competition with a white.

At a convention in Georgia on January 25, 1888, 300 African Americans unanimously adopted a resolution against lynching. They appealed for every true citizen to assist in ending the infamous practice of lynching. Unfortunately, wide-spread silent acceptance of lynching as a control mechanism left organizations, abroad and in the U.S., unable to influence the passage of anti-lynching legislation.

After the 1880s, lynching shifted from death by hanging or shooting to slow, tortuous murder. Often the participants created a carnival-like atmosphere with picnic baskets, photograph sessions, and the hunt for *souvenirs. Another radical change occurred in 1894 with the lynching of an African American woman; fourteen others were lynched before the end of 1898.*

The fact that African American women were also victims underscored the negative perceptions many whites held of them. Dating from the era of slavery, most African American women were regarded as objects of property inferior to whites. The cloak of protection afforded white women because of their gender was not extended to African American women. In 1893, Chris Rutt capitalized upon the prevailing beliefs regarding African American women. As a pancake mix marketing concept, Rutt hired Nancy Green to dress in costume and flip pancakes. The concept proved successful—five years later it became the Aunt Jemina trademark. The caricature epitomized the boundaries established by whites for African American women, domestic servants who cater to their needs.

Recognizing that these negative beliefs were not confined to any one region of the country, and that they had a responsibility as educated, middle-class women to refute the stereotypes and chart a positive direction for members of their race, African American women accelerated their involvement in the club movement. The growing influence of women was also evident in organized religion. In 1893, the African Methodist Episcopal Church established its second club specifically for women, the Women's Home and Foreign Missionary Society. The next year, Julia A. J. Foote, evangelist and missionary, became the first woman ordained a deacon in the African Methodist Episcopal Zion Church.

The literature and art of the period glorified the strengths and cultural traditions of African Americans, but also reflected the despair felt by many African Americans. Paul Lawrence Dunbar's first collection of poetry, Oak and Ivy, *received national acclaim. The multi-talented George Washington Carver was invited to exhibit his paintings at the Colombian Exposition in Chicago, Illinois. Henry Ossawa Turner unveiled his painting titled "The Banjo Lesson" at the Chicago Exposition. Discouraged by racial prejudice, Turner had moved to Paris in 1891, where he remained until his death in 1937. The talent of Sissieretta Jones reached a broad crossover audience in the U.S., but was more appreciated in Europe. Jones performed for Benjamin Harrison at the White House in 1892 and enjoyed a grand tour of Europe in 1893. Upon returning to the U.S., rather than submit to discriminatory practices of the Metropolitan Opera, Jones organized her own company in 1896. Sissieretta was the featured soloist in the all-African American company, "Black Patti's Troubadours." Colleagues praised her efforts to instill racial pride and self-esteem in her work and in the work of younger African American performers.*

For most of the nation, the color line separating whites from African Americans was ever present; so much so that the idea of colonization resurfaced as a viable alternative to harsh treatment in the U.S. The return to Africa was seriously considered, and some sought assistance from the American Colonization Society (ACS). Fearful of losing a cheap labor force with knowledge of the land, whites, by force or by promises of higher wages and better working conditions, attempted to keep African Americans in the South. For many reasons, the idea of colonization never attracted a large number of African Americans during this time. In 1896 the Laurada *set sail from Savannah, Georgia, with 321 persons bound for Liberia, West Africa, founded by the American Colonization Society in 1821. At the time of its origin, prominent slave owners were listed among the members of the Society. Although the intent of the Society to send free and enslaved African Americans to the colony was opposed by free African Americans, 12,000 would settle there.*

The anti-colonization sentiment was the greatest in the North. In 1817, James Forten and Bishop Richard Allen of the African Methodist Episcopal Church led an oppositional meeting of 3,000 African Americans in Philadelphia. In their entreaty to the Humane and Benevolent Inhabitants of Philadelphia, they declared the colonization movement was designed to benefit the slaveholding interests of the nation. The movement to reject colonization was swift and successful—until a new "Back to Africa" campaign was energized after the Civil War. Under the leadership of Marcus Garvey and the Universal Negro Improvement Association, the concept was revived yet again in 1916, but died with the end of the association in 1925.

Nothing seemed to curtail the slow but continuous erosion of race relations and civil rights in the United States. The trend toward complete exclusion from the political process was evident even at the federal level where only a few African American men remained in Congress; George Murray (R-South Carolina) was elected in 1893. The repeal of the Enforcement Act made it easier for states to disenfranchise African American voters. No longer could states receive direct appropriations for hiring special federal marshals and supervisors of elections. Virginia, more so than other states at the time, framed an extensive election code in 1894. Poll registration certificates, time limitations for voting, and a poll tax were a few of the requirements effectively eliminating poor, illiterate African Americans and whites from the vote.

Cynthia Neverdon-Morton
Coppin State College

A PLEA FOR COLORED MEN

The Rev. Joseph C. Price before the Nineteenth Century Club.

NEW-YORK TIMES
January 13, 1893

The Rev. Joseph C. Price of Livingston College, North Carolina, received a hearty welcome last night at the meeting of the Nineteenth Century Club at Sherry's, Fifth Avenue and Thirty-seventh Street. Mr. Price is a noble specimen of the negro. He is six feet tall and of massive frame, and his face, although bearing the full stamp of the characteristics of his race, suggests a man of marked intelligence. He was to have taken part, with George J. Winston, President of the University of North Carolina, in a discussion of "The Future of the Colored Race in the South," but Mr. Winston was stormbound, as President Horace E. Deming announced, somewhere between here and North Carolina, and therefore Mr. Price presented his views on the problem with no one to urge different views.

Mr. Price's address was frequently interrupted by applause, and some particularly apt stories—which might be old in North Carolina, but were new to his Nineteenth Century Club audience—with which he illustrated points that he made, were greatly appreciated. Among those who listened to the address were Gen. Stewart L. Woodford, Alfred R. Conkling, S. H. Nichols, Mrs. H. M. Field, Mrs. Ethan Allen, Prof. Brander Matthews, Mrs. Charles J. Gould, Mr. and Mrs. T. C. Williams, C. A. Van Santvoord, Mrs. Robert Abbe, Daniel G. Thompson, William Travers Jerome, Mrs. Henry Draper, and Walter Page.

The treatment to which colored men and women were subjected, Mr. Price said, in beginning his address, followed the theory that all colored men and women belonged to the same class. It seemed to be forgotten that there could be different classes of colored men and women as well as different classes of whites. The race question, Mr. Price said, was merely how long men could be denied their inalienable and constitutional rights without a serious rebound and conflict, involving not only the section in which the colored race was strongest, but also the whole Nation.

The prejudice against the negro was generally supposed to be due to his color, Mr. Price said, but this was not the fact. It was against color only as it stood for a condition. If ignorance was the real cause, then intelligence must be the remedy. In education must be found the response to all the leading objections raised against the colored man.

Another remedy would be found in the division of the negro vote. White or black political solidarities on racial lines were unwise and unpatriotic. Such a division had already begun to be marked in the South, and good results could but follow.

Mr. Walter Page, editor of the *Forum,* was asked by President Deming to take Mr. Winston's place in the discussion, but could not be induced to do so. At the conclusion of Mr. Price's address the members of the club crowded to the platform to shake his hand.

ANOTHER NEGRO BURNED

Henry Smith Dies at the Stake.

NEW-YORK TIMES
February 2, 1893

Drawn Through the Streets on a Car—Tortured for Nearly an Hour with Hot Irons and Then Burned—Awful Vengeance of a Paris (Texas) Mob.

Paris, Texas, Feb. 1.—Henry Smith, the negro assailant of four-year-old Myrtle Vance, has expiated, in part, his crime by death at the stake.

Every since the perpetration of his crime this city and the entire surrounding country has been in a frenzy of excitement.

When the news came last night that he had been captured, that he had been identified by B. B. Sturgeon, James T. Hicks, and many others of the Paris searching party, the city was joyful over the apprehension of the brute.

Hundreds of people poured into the city from the adjoining country, and the word passed from lip to lip that the punishment should fit the crime, and that death by fire was the penalty that Smith should pay for the most atrocious murder and outrage in Texas history.

Curious and sympathizing alike came on trains and wagons, on horse and on foot, to see what was to be done.

Whisky shops were closed, and unruly mobs were dispersed. Schools were dismissed by a proclamation from the Mayor, and every thing was done in a business-like manner.

Officers saw the futility of checking the passions of the mob, so the law was laid aside, and the citizens took into their own hands the law and burned the prisoner at the stake.

The story of the crime is as follows: On Thursday last Henry Smith, a burly negro, picked up little Myrtle Vance, aged three and a half years, near her father's residence, and, giving her candy to allay her fears, carried her through the central portion of the city to Gibson's pasture, just within the corporate limits.

En route through the city he was asked by several persons what he was doing with the child. He replied that she was Mr. Williams's little girl and he was carrying her to the doctor.

Arriving at the pasture, he first assaulted the babe, and then, taking a little leg in either hand, he literally tore her asunder. He covered the body with leaves and brush, and lay down and slept through the night by the side of his victim.

About 7 o'clock Friday morning Smith awakened, went home, and compelled his wife to cook him breakfast. She asked him what had become of that white child. He replied, "I ain't seen no white child, and don't have nothing to do with no white folks." After eating his breakfast he left, and was not seen until his capture.

At 2 o'clock on Friday a mass meeting was called at the Court House, and captains were appointed to search for the child. She was found. As soon as it was learned upon recovery of the body that the crime was so atrocious, the whole town turned out on the chase.

The railroads put up bulletins offering free transportation to those who would join in the search. Posses went out in every direction, and not a stone was left unturned. Smith was traced to Detroit on foot, where he jumped on a freight train and left for his old home in Hempstead County, Ark.

To this county he was tracked, and was yesterday captured at Clow, a flag station on the Arkansas and Louisiana Railway, about twenty miles north of Hope.

Upon being questioned, he denied everything. He was kept under heavy guard at Hope last night, and later on confessed the crime.

This morning he was brought through Texarkana, where 5,000 people awaited the train. Speeches were made by prominent Paris citizens, who asked that the prisoner be not molested by Texarkana people, but that the guard be allowed to deliver him up to the outraged and indignant citizens of Paris.

Along the road the force gathered strength from the various towns, the people crowding upon the platforms and on top of coaches, anxious to see the lynching and the negro who was so soon to be delivered to an infuriated mob.

Arriving here at 12 o'clock, the train was met by a surging mass of humanity 10,000 strong. The negro was placed upon a carnival float, in mockery of a king upon his throne, and, followed by the immense crowd, was escorted through the city so that all might see.

The line of march was up Main Street to the square, around the square, down Clarksville Street to Church Street, thence to the open prairie, about three hundred yards from the Texas and Pacific depot.

Here Smith was placed upon a scaffold six feet square and ten feet high, securely bound, within the view of all beholders.

Here the victim was tortured for fifty minutes by red-hot irons being thrust against his quivering body. Commencing at the foot, the brands were placed against him inch by inch until they were thrust against the face.

Then, being apparently dead, kerosene was pored upon him, cottonseed hulls placed beneath him, and he was set on fire. Curiosity seekers have carried away already all that was left after the memorable event, even to pieces of charcoal.

The cause of the crime was that Henry Vance, when a deputy policeman, in the course of his duty was called to arrest Henry Smith for being drunk and disorderly. The negro was unruly and Vance was forced to use his club. The negro swore vengeance and several times assaulted Vance.

The father is prostrated with grief and the mother now lies at death's door.

The negro for a long time after starting on the journey to Paris did not realize his plight. At last, when he was told that he must die by torture, he begged for protection. He was willing to be shot, and wanted Marshal Shanklin of Paris to do it.

Scarcely had the train reached Paris when his torture began. His clothes were torn off and scattered in the crowd, people catching the shreds and putting them away as mementos. The child's father, her brother, and two uncles then gathered about the negro as he lay fastened to the torture platform and thrust hot irons into his quivering flesh.

Every groan from the fiend, every contortion of his body was cheered by the crowd. Before burning, the hot irons, plenty of fresh ones being at hand, were rolled up and down Smith's stomach, black, and arms. Then the eyes were burned out, and hot irons were thrust down his throat.

The men of the Vance family having wreaked vengeance, the crowd set the fire. The negro rolled and wriggled and tossed out of the mass only to be pushed back by the people nearest him. He tossed out again, and was roped and pulled back. Hundreds of people turned away, but the vast crowd still looked calmly on. People were there from Dallas, Fort Worth, Sherman, Dennison, Bonham, Texarkana. Fort Smith, Ark., and a party of fifteen came from Hempstead County, Ark., where he was captured.

When the news was flashed over the wire at every town, anvils boomed forth the announcement.

THE NEGRO PROBLEM
It Can Be Solved Only By a Line of Steamships to Africa.

NEW-YORK TIMES
February 12, 1893

Atlanta, Ga, Feb. 11.—Bishop Henry M. Turner of the African Methodist Church, who is about to start on his visitation of the missions in Africa, makes a strong appeal for the return of the colored race to the African continent. He says:

"The negro cannot remain here as a permanent factor and occupy his present 'ignoble status.' The negro problem has only one solution, and that is for the negro to return to Africa in sufficient numbers to build up a civilized country of his own, develop the resources of that continent, establish commerce with the civilized nations of the world, and impart his civilization and Christianity to his brethren in heathen Africa, and thus answer the ends for which God tolerated his temporary enslavement and contact with this giant white race.

"That is the only solution of the negro problem; anything else is humbug and nonsense. All the negro wants is a line of steamers between the South and Africa, and he will solve his own problem and at the same time enrich the South beyond the conception of imagination. No injustice, oppression, railroad discrimination, denial of the ballot, ruling off the jury, or species of lynch law will ever solve the negro problem. A line of African steamships alone can do it, and until that line is established the self-reliant and manly negro, as well as the mean and vicious black man, will be a thorn in the flesh of the country.

"You may send negroes to the pen until half of them are convicts, but it will do no good. They will still be a menace to the country. For God has a purpose to serve in the negro, and the white man must help him to serve it, and any subterfuge is simply bosh. Europe can keep a hundred and seventy odd ships, nearly all steamers, hugging the shores of Africa the year round, and this country can keep but two little old sailing schooners, going once in six months, except a whisky craft, which goes out of Boston occasionally laden down with hundreds of gallons of the most deadly drug, commonly called whisky—a stuff that never saw the stillhouse, and as destructive to life as is possible."

THE CHARLESTON NEGRO
Some Observations of a Northern Man Among Them.

NEW-YORK TIMES
February 13, 1893

Their Importance in the Social Structure of the City—How They Are Regarded by the Whites—Children Who Are Glad When There Is No Work for Them.

Charleston, S. C., Feb. 11.—The total population of Charleston is about 62,000 persons, and it is said that of these 32,000 are colored. To say that every other person one meets in the streets is colored may seem a purely general statement, yet it is susceptible of proof.

One afternoon a Northern man sat in the reading room of a hotel in Meeting Street and counted the persons passing by within the range of the view from one window. In ten minutes there were 121 men, women, and children. Of these 61 were negroes—not merely colored, but black—and 60 white. The term white is used here to mean those not indisputably African. That some of those classed as white had negro blood in their veins is beyond question. A second count a few minutes later for the same period showed 60 whites and 58 negroes.

There does not seem to be any distinctively negro quarter in the city proper. They are everywhere, either as tenants or servants. There are practically no white servants in Charleston. The negroes work for less. A gentleman told the writer on the train coming down that he had a negro woman in his house as cook and paid her $6 a month. A young girl came to his house every day and made the beds and did work of that sort. She had two meals at the house, as the writer remembers it, and for her services received 50 cents a week. Other Charleston men said that this was below the average, but it shows that the average is very low. It should be noted, too, that few of the servants sleep in the houses where they work, going to their own homes, or even to rented rooms, for the night.

All the hard labor in Charleston is performed by negroes. Employers say that a white man cannot do hard work in this climate. Negro carpenters are paid $1.50 a day; if skilled workmen perhaps $1.75. Not only is all the heavy work done by negroes, but they fill most of the trades. The barbers, of course, are negroes, but so are the shoemakers, the tailors, the painters. In fact, almost every avenue of employment is not only open to them, but if they were not there the work would not be done. One cannot escape the belief that if every negro should move out of Charleston to-day the city would starve to death in a week. Personally the writer has seen only one place where they were not. There are no negro clerks in the shops owned by white men.

It follows, then, that the negro has a place in the social structure of Charleston difficult for a Northern man to understand. It is certain that there is no such aversion to him as is often seen is in the North. It is not that the necessities of the situation bring about a forced toleration. His presence is not an irritation. He gets his half the sidewalk as readily as the white man.

The fact seems to be that he is not regarded at all—except politically. The white people know he is there in the same way we know the sun rises and sets. If the sun should fail to rise or should remain in the sky when it should set it would attract our attention. If the negro should disappear from Charleston, or should suddenly turn white or do anything else very unusual, the white people would begin to think about him; but as he is to-day there is no more reason for thinking about him than about the color of the leaves or the saltiness of the sea—except politically.

It follows again that the negro in Charleston has his place, as the white man has his. Each keeps pretty close to the path custom has assigned to him. It is speaking within bounds to say that good feeling exists on both sides when this distance is observed. A recent incident shows what happens when it is not. President Harrison nominated a negro for Postmaster of Charleston. A protest so strong, so significant, went up from the white people that the nomination was withdrawn and the Democratic Postmaster appointed by Mr. Cleveland is still holding the office. On the other hand: A Charleston man bred and born, whose father and more remote ancestors were slaveholders, took the writer to see some quaint old houses with histories. The only tenants were negroes of the lower classes. The gate into the yard stood open and not a soul was in sight. Yet he rang the bell until he finally roused somebody, and then asked, as a favor, that the callers might be permitted to enter the yard. And this he did at every place visited.

The blacks do not as a rule go to the whites' churches. There are separate churches, schools, and cemeteries. Very few institutions are used in common.

It is rather unusual in New-York to see a negro very badly dressed. We are accustomed to consider them—the young men at least—as tremendous dandies, and the gaudy extravagance of their apparel confirms that belief. The chances are that of an equal number of whites and blacks in a surface car or elevated train in New-York or Brooklyn the latter will be the better dressed—better dressed as far as show is concerned and often as to material and cut.

If one could imagine a room strewn with cast-off clothes of every conceivable color, style, and size, and all so utterly worn out that he would be afraid of hurting the feelings of an Italian ragpicker by offering them to him, and could fancy half a dozen men put into the room and in some way magnetized so that the clothes would fly to them without choice on their part or reason in the clothes—if one could imagine such a thing as that, he could get some idea of the astonishing garments worn by the male negroes, big and little, one meets in the streets of Charleston.

It does not seem as if any two of the pieces going to make up these suits of clothes bear any sort of relation to each other, or ever did bear, or to any other pieces. Speculation as to the origin and adventures of these garments would be as interesting as it would be idle. They are as far apart as a fossil shark and a "milk shake." They are literally "things of shreds and patches." It is doubtful if anywhere in the world is darning so near a science as among these negroes. A "log-cabin" bedquilt is a simple bit of sewing compared with the mosaic work done on these clothes.

Like everything in this many-sided world, there is a reason for this; indeed, there are several reasons.

"The negroes are poor," said a Charleston man, who was asked to explain this, "poorer than you can comprehend, perhaps. It is true that many of them when they work earn as large wages as the Northern laboring man who brings nothing to his task but brute strength, but he spends it in a different way. The Northern laborer is fond of dress for himself and his wife, and the latter wants her children well clad. With the negro it is different. The women are fond of dress that makes a show, but the men don't care for it and the children take the cast-off clothes."

"That may be an explanation," said the manager of one of the great phosphate fields or "mines," as they are called, "but I think a truer one is that the negroes will not work any more than they are obliged to. If a Northern man in charge of a Northern industry should announce to his men that the works would be closed for two or three days for repairs or 'taking stock,' the faces of the men would show that they regarded it as a blow. They wouldn't like it because it would make a difference on pay day.

"But tell that to a gang of negroes! Faces brighten, there is unconcealed joy, shouts of merriment, and every other indication of intense satisfaction. One would think you had done them a favor and you have. There is nothing in the world the negro likes as well as a holiday."

"Therein lies the strongest characteristic and the weakness of the negro," said another man. "He is a child, a careless, irresponsible child. He doesn't understand an obligation, and he doesn't want to understand it. If one promises to come to work for you at a certain time, you have no reason to feel confident that he will come. The chances are that he won't unless his necessities are pressing, and as soon as they are satisfied he begins to see excuses for quitting. No schoolboy ever lived who could devise better excuses for a holiday than a negro."

"That characteristic of irresponsibility is a curious one," said another man. "A member of my family was suddenly taken ill one afternoon, and mustard was needed. A negro boy who works around my stable was sent for it, and, to expedite him, he was told that it was a case of life and death. He didn't come back, and another messenger was sent. He found the boy lying flat on his back in the middle of the sidewalk, reading a story paper, with the mustard by his side."

A Northern man naturally writes and says "negro," but here very few persons use the word. It is likely that every one of the men quoted said "nigger." That is practically the only word used. It is not a term of disrespect or contempt; it is the common term, and nobody hesitates to use it. They say that a Northern man can always be spotted because he says "negro" or "colored man."

We think we know something about poverty in the North, and we do, but the poverty one sees here among the negroes is—to the eye—appaling. The qualification of "to the eye" has a great deal of meaning, for, except in such almost unheard-of cold weather as the South has experienced in the last month, there is very little suffering among the negroes. Their food is of the simplest kind, but it sustains life, and life itself is happiness to a negro. The lines of Longfellow, in which the poet sings of a perfect day,

> "Whereon is enough for me
> Not to be doing, but to be."

fit the negro exactly. He works when he has to, not because he wants to.

Just here it may be well to say that these observations are necessarily superficial. They are simply those of a man whose business it is to keep his eyes open and to ask questions. They are not intended to "settle," or even to aid in settling, the mighty "negro problem." That there is such a problem no man can doubt who comes into the South with his mind free from prejudice. That, as Major Hemphill of this city told a reporter of The New-York Times in New-York a year ago, it is a problem that the South can work out—if it can be worked out at all, which Major Hemphill did not seem to doubt—is equally beyond question. There is no evidence that any outside aid is needed.

It seems to be the fact that most of the crimes in this city are committed by negroes. In Judge Frazer's court one day not long ago thirty-one prisoners were presented for sentence. Of these, one was a white man, who had been convicted of murder. All the others were negroes. There were two or three boys not more than twelve or fourteen years old, and the oldest prisoner was perhaps fifty. The crimes ranged from gambling to assault with a deadly weapon. The sentences were from one to five years in the State Penitentiary. There is no reformatory in the State, and the boys and men have to go to the same institution. "I wish there was something else I could do with you," said the kindly-faced old Judge to the boys, "but there isn't."

As far as outward appearances indicated, no one of the prisoners was in the least distressed by the fate that had overtaken him. Life in the penitentiary is not as hard as on the local chain gang, to which the police court sentences offenders.

DELUDED NEGRO PILGRIMS
Over 400 of Them on Their Way to an African Paradise.

NEW-YORK TIMES
February 18, 1893

Atlanta, Ga., Feb. 17.—Seven carloads of negroes—410 souls—passed through the city yesterday bound for Brunswick, where they say that they will be met by a steamer which has been chartered to take them all the way to Africa.

For some time a pair of negro preachers have been out in Arkansas working up a party for the African home most negroes think they are to have. The white people of the county in which the preachers were working called the negroes together and advised them not to go, but the preachers had too much away and the negroes disposed of everything they had and invested the money in tickets to Brunswick, where they were informed that a ship would be in readiness to transport them to the land for which they were bound. The party chartered a train of seven cars, and for the train paid $3,000. The train met them at Duval's, and upon it they reached the city.

When the train arrived it presented a pitiable sight. The coaches were crowded with living freight. There were many old men and children. A great many women were also on board, while the absence of able-bodied men was noticeable.

The passengers were so worked up by religious frenzy that it was impossible to engage any of them in rational conversation. They prayed and sang and shouted with such lung power as to suggest the wildest orgies of a lunatic asylum. They were carried away with the idea that they were going back to the promised land, where they were to meet all their ancestors who had died in the centuries gone by. They knew that they were penniless and without resource of any kind, but declared that the Lord would provide for them as He had provided for the children of Israel in the wilderness.

When these people get to Brunswick they will find that there is no ship there for them unless they can raise a large amount of money. As it is a small town, quite overrun with a local supply of negroes, these people will be in a state of destitution as annoying to the citizens of that place as it will be cruel to themselves.

THINGS TALKED OF

HARPER'S WEEKLY
April 10, 1893, p. 295

One of the most interesting publications of the year bears the imprint "Hampton Normal School Press, 1893." Its title is *Twenty-two Years' Work of the Hampton Normal and Agricultural Institute at Hampton, Virginia*. It is not easy to give an impression of its contents, for besides a most clear and engaging introductory explanation by General Armstrong of the purpose and methods of the Hampton School, there are brief biographical notes of the lives of some hundreds of the graduates of the school. It is in these that the value, and we may add the charm, of this remarkable volume is to be found. The notes are very simple and direct, in the words, often, of the subject of them. They tell the career of the graduate, his success in his occupation, the work he is doing for his race, and thus indirectly disclose the influence of this noble school. Take this case at random: A negro boy, born in slavery on the eve of the war, separated from his mother until after emancipation, goes to Hampton, pays his way, from there to be a doctor's "boy" in this State, studying in the evenings, works his course through a medical school, becomes a physician, and now has a large practice and a drug store in a Georgia town. He writes: "I have worked hard for the cause of education, and have contributed liberally—labor and money. As to church and Sunday-school work, I have done very little, my time being so completely occupied, and there are so many who can do that who cannot do what I am doing." This tells the story of many—a quiet, strong, persistent, spreading influence from year to year, from generation to generation. We should say that a dollar could not be better spent than for this book, which can be had from Hampton; but the sympathetic reader should be warned that it will surely lead to spending more. The appeal is irresistible.

A SHERIFF'S SUIT DISMISSED
He and His Colored Prisoner Were Ejected From a Railroad Car.

NEW-YORK TIMES
April 27, 1893

New Orleans, La., April 26.—Judge Theard, in the Civil District Court, delivered a decision to-day in a Jim Crow car case. Sheriff Broussard of Lafayette Parish sued the Illinois Central Railroad for $10,000 damages for ejection from one of the trains of the company. The court decided against him.

He bought two first-class tickets for the purpose of taking a crazy negro prisoner to the State Asylum at Jackson, La. He placed his prisoner in the smoking section of the white car, and the Sheriff, who was ill, went into the non-smoking section. The conductor told him he would have to take his prisoner into the colored car or else sit with him in a smoking section common to both races. Mr. Broussard objected, and he and his prisoner were ejected.

The court held, with the conductor, that the law did not discriminate, except in favor of colored nurses of white children, and as the railroad company was subject to penalty if it violated the law, the conductor's action was justified. The question of inconvenience was one for the Legislature and not for the court, and the Sheriff's suit was dismissed.

THE COLOR LINE AT LUNCHEON
This Railroad Club on Wheels Is Said to Discriminate.

NEW-YORK TIMES
June 19, 1893

The colored porters who look after the comfort of the patrons of the Wagner cars running into the Grand Central Station declare that the color line has been drawn against them. What makes the offense worse in their eyes is that the offender is the Railroad Branch of the Young Men's Christian Association.

A few months ago the Railroad Branch of the Young Men's Christian Association, which has a handsome house in Madison Avenue, near the station, made arrangements with the Wagner Company to take three of its cars, which had grown rather rusty in the service, and place them in the yards at Mott Haven as a sort of branch headquarters. A great many of the members have to spend much of their time in the Mott Haven yards, and it was thought that they should have some place of resort there.

The company liked the idea and lent the cars to the association for the small amount of twenty-five cents a month each. One of the cars was turned into a lunch room, another was fitted out as a reading room, and the third was allowed to remain as a sleeper. Standing on side track, well out of the way, the railroad employes had a club on wheels.

It was evident that the association want[ed] the lunch car patronized, for in the departments of the service placards were posted inviting patronage. In the room where the Wagner car porters go one of these notices was tacked up, calling attention to the lunch, showing the cheap rates and the bill of fare, and inviting the porters to patronize it. And patronize it they did, as did the trainmen, the engineers, the firemen, the yard employes, and nearly all in the service whose duties called them to the Mott Haven yard at a time when they wanted to eat. The lunch car became an immediate success, and the enterprise was highly praised.

There was never any complaint from the engineers, firemen, and other white employes in regard to eating in the car with the colored employes, the porters of the Wagner cars. In fact, the lunch car being patronized mostly by men who had just finished a trip and showed signs of travel, the porters, in their natty uniforms and with the white linen that they are required to wear, had all the best of a comparison of appearances with their white brethren, especially with the grimy engineers and firemen.

All went well until last Wednesday. Then George A. Warburton, Secretary of the Railroad Branch of the Young Men's Christian Association, went to the lunch car to regale himself with a piece of pie and a cup of coffee. There were several trainmen, engineers, and firemen eating there, but at the time there were none of the colored employes at the tables.

Porters Dixon and Craven, two of the finest looking negroes in the service, happened to enter while Secretary Warburton was at the table. When they took seats, after bowing pleasantly to him, he stared at them for a moment, laid down his knife and fork, and went to the colored cook in the kitchen. He asked the cook if the colored porters were in the habit of eating in the car, and when he was told that they were the largest consumers of the highest priced dishes on the menu he hastily left the car.

The next day, and since that day, all the colored porters who have gone to the car for lunch have been told that the orders were that only coffee could be served them there. Some of them have made inquiries as to why the privilege of the lunch car has been denied them and have been told that it is because they are not members of the association. They declare that this statement is only a blind to conceal the real color line which has been drawn, as many white employes who are not members of the association use the lunch car regularly.

MISS PUTNAM IS WORRIED
More Annoyances for the Colored School Teacher.

NEW-YORK TIMES
June 29, 1893

T. McCants Stewart, the Colored Member of the Brooklyn Board of Education, May Again Seek to Replace Her—Colored Society Considerably Excited Over the Matter—Stewart and Miss Putnam Were Formerly Friends—No Explanation of the Change.

There is a serious schism among the Afro-Americans in Brooklyn caused by the opposition of T. McCants Stewart to the appointment of Miss Georgiana F. Putnam of 37 Fort Greene Place as head of department in Public School No. 83. Miss Putnam, who is colored, has been a teacher of colored children for twenty years in the public schools of Brooklyn. At a recent meeting of the Brooklyn Board of Education, when Miss Putnam was appointed, Lawyer T. McCants Stewart, the only colored member of the board, unexpectedly opposed her, and voted for Miss Beck, the white candidate for the position.

Knowing Miss Putnam's ability to be of a superior order, and knowing her long service and experience as a teacher, and that she held a certificate of the first grade, granted not more than five years ago, a majority of the white members of the board voted for her, but Lawyer Stewart was arrayed against one of his own race.

When he was asked why he had opposed Miss Putnam, Stewart said he voted as he did solely because he deemed her opponent more competent. He did not criticise Miss Putnam's ability, but simply declared that, no matter how competent she might be, he considered the other candidate more so. This aroused considerable talk in colored society in Brooklyn, as Mr. Stewart and Miss Putnam both moved in the most select colored social circle. They had also been the most intimate of friends, and, therefore, his motive in opposing her appointment was, naturally, quite generally discussed.

In an article printed in The New-York Times June 8, Mr. Stewart gave extended reasons for his actions, based upon his assertion that he voted for the person he considered most competent. This the friends of both parties declare to be utter rubbish, and they express the belief that he had hidden his real motive.

Fresh fuel was added to the flames last week when it was announced that at the meeting of the Board of Education to be held on July 11 Mr. Stewart would move for a reconsideration of Miss Putnam's appointment. In consequence of this, all of her friends, most of whom were formerly Stewart's friends also, are up in arms. Last Friday night a number of them met at the residence of Mrs. S. J. S. Garnet, widow of the clergyman, Henry Highland Garnet, at 205 De Kalb Avenue, and held an indignation meeting.

The Rev. A. M. Freeman, Brooklyn's venerable colored preacher, presided over the meeting, which he stated had been called to approve of the appointment of Miss Putnam by the Board of Education, and to express their disapproval of the conduct of T. McCants Stewart in opposing her.

Lawyer Alfred C. Cowan and Samuel R. Scottron expressed themselves as in favor of absolutely ignoring Mr. Stewart in the matter, as he had proved recreant to the interests of his race.

George E. Wibecan, a clerk in Post Office Station E, East New-York, said: "Let the contempt of his people fall silently upon him, for he has called down upon his head the contempt and hatred of every person in Brooklyn, without regard to color."

A committee, composed of Samuel R. Scottron, Mrs. Garnet, and Mr. Wibecan, drew up the following resolutions, which were adopted, and will be presented to the Board of Education, after having been circulated among the colored citizens of Brooklyn for signatures:

To the Honorable Members of the Board of Education:

The undersigned, citizens of the City of Brooklyn, respectfully beg leave to present resolutions of approval of the action of the board in the case of Miss G. F. Putnam, who was lately appointed to the position as head of department in Public School No. 83.

The action of the board in this particular case claims our attention because of its exceptional character, marking a new era in the history of our schools and proof of the fact that color shall not be a bar in the future to promotion among the teachers in our public schools.

We believe Miss Putnam to be a competent teacher, and that her past years of service entitled her to the marked consideration.

Mr. Stewart was seen yesterday at his office in Cedar Street by a New-York Times reporter and said: "I have nothing further to say about the matter than what was published in The Times of June 8. I decline to say whether I will ask for a reconsideration of Miss Putnam's appointment at the next meeting of the board or not. I will say this, however: I form my opinions with deliberation and caution, and, after I have formed them, stick to them with courage. I speak for the masses, not for a coterie of social 'nincompoops.'

"If you desire to know my standing among my own people, I will say that I have recently been re-elected, by a unanimous vote, President of the Brooklyn Literary Union, a body composed largely of wealthy colored people and wholly of those of education and refinement. The leader of these protests against my action is Mrs. Henry Highland Garnet, a lifelong friend of Miss Putnam and herself the Principal of the colored public school in West Seventeenth Street, New-York. That is all I have to say upon the subject except that I shall stand by my convictions."

Mrs. Garnet was not at home when the reporter called, but her sister, Dr. Susan S. McKinney, said:

"We cannot find any excuse for Mr. Stewart's action in the premises. He has been a most intimate friend of our family and of Miss Putnam for many years. We all admire him and feel proud of him, but cannot understand his motive in opposing Miss Putnam's appointment. It surely cannot be because she is incompetent, for she is not. On the contrary, she is a finely educated and highly-cultured woman. She has been like a sister to Mrs. Garnet and me, and taught with my sister twenty years ago in Williamsburg."

Mrs. McKinney exhibited Miss Putnam's certificate, granted by Superintendent of Public Instruction Patterson five or six years ago, in which he certified that he had examined her and found her capable in every way to hold a certificate of the first grade.

"Mr. Stewart could not have been ignorant of the fact that she held this certificate," Mrs. McKinney said, "and therefore, while we think a great deal of him, we think he has gone out of his way to do an injustice to one of his race. We hope he will go no further with this matter. We are at a loss to understand his motive."

She said the meeting held on last Friday night in her sister's parlors was conducted with the utmost decorum. Efforts had been made to get Mr. Stewart to attend, but the committee could not reach him. She denied that her sister was the leader in the revolt against him, and said they were only protesting against an injustice to Miss Putnam.

Miss Putnam was ill when the reporter called at her home and could not be seen.

NEGRO SOLDIERS OF THE WAR

Massachusetts's Part in Mustering Them into Service.

NEW-YORK TIMES
January 21, 1894

Though Credited to Her Quota, Few Members of the Fifty-fourth and Fifty-fifth Ever Saw the Old Bay State—First Enlisted by Gen. Butler in 1862 at Camp Parapet—

His Attempts to Officer Them with Men of Their Own Race.

The interest with which everything relating to the war of the rebellion is read twenty-nine years after its close shows how lasting was the impression it made on those who were witnesses of many of the events of that stirring epoch. That some mistakes should be made in its history might naturally be expected, but the more important incidents should be easy to remember. These observations are made because the other day it w[as] stated in a Boston journal that the first negro regiments ever recruited and mustered in the United States service were known as the Fifty-fourth and Fifty-fifth Massachusetts, commanded by Cols. Higginson and Shaw, respectively. Though credited to the quota of Massachusetts, in reality these regiments had not twenty men in them who ever saw that State.

The very first negro troops ever mustered as United States Volunteers were enlisted at Camp Parapet, about six miles above the City of New-Orleans, in August, 1862, long before the emancipation proclamation was issued, and almost two years before the two regiments mentioned were organized. They were recruited from an immense camp of "contraband" fugitives that had gathered in the wake of the Union Army, and, in order that they might be kept under some kind of discipline and control, they were directed to go into camp pending the orders to Major Gen. Butler from Washington respecting the disposition to be made of them. The force recruited there consisted of three regiments of 1,000 men each and two batteries, and they were completely organized within three weeks after the order for their recruitment was issued.

A grave difficulty arose concerning them in the beginning. Gen. Butler had determined that they should be colored regiments in fact as well as name, and he therefore temporarily directed colored line and field officers to command them, not doubting that the President and Secretary of War would commission them. The most aristocratic colored men in Louisiana—and there was then, and still is, a very curious colored aristocracy, educated and rich, living in and near New-Orleans—were among the officers thus acting pro tem. The Major of the first colored regiment was a young mulatto named Dumas, born in New-Orleans, who had had a thorough military training at the Polytechnic School in Paris. His family had always been free, were people of handsome fortunes, owning numbers of slaves, some whiter than their owners, and the younger members were educated in France. A brother of B. F. Joubert, who held a prominent Federal appointment under Grant's Administration in Louisiana, was a field officer. P. B. S. Pinchback, afterward Governor of the State, was a Captain, as was Massicot, Criminal Sheriff under Gov. Warmoth's regime, and Aristide Marie, who is the richest of all the type mentioned in Louisiana.

The Government was not favorably disposed toward Gen. Butler's startling proposition. It was admitted that, as enormous numbers of fugitive slaves would gather in the trains of the Union armies, it might be better if they could be somehow utilized. One thing was certain, they had to be fed. It was not the intention of Gen. Butler at first to equip them as regular combatants. They were to be used only as sappers and miners and in the construction of heavy fieldworks. But the organization of the army then did not admit of any such non-combatant corps, and they all had to be armed—even working parties—for self-defense. This was a small matter compared to what happened when Gen. Butler's recommendation of colored men for commissions came up at army headquarters. Then the row began in real earnest.

So strong was the feeling among the white volunteers against association with the negro upon any footing of direct or implied equality that Mr. Stanton was obliged to inform Gen. Butler that negroes could not be commissioned; that if his colored regiments were disposed to remain in the service they might do so, but they must have white officers and be brigaded by themselves. So the colored officers quietly retired, whites were substituted for them, and the next year the colored brigade was put in the advance line at Port Hudson, and when the assault was ordered they were literally blown away. As far as can be learned, they behaved well enough at first, and if they had been properly officered, might have stood the shock. But it was their first fight. Against them were their old white masters, and the hereditary instincts of twenty generations cannot be drilled out of a man, be he black or white, in six months. So they got the worst of it.

When these regiments were finally mustered in some of them were credited to Massachusetts. A story is told illustrative of New-England thriftiness by a former officer on Gen. Butler's staff. They had several negro regiments ready to muster. The rank and file neither knew nor cared to what State they were credited, so each man made his mark on a piece of paper when he was being mustered in. That was not part of the process, though the man did not know it. He was credited on the quota of a New-England State, and the bounty of $450 per head, amounting to $450,000, was then divided by—who knows? This is one of the romances of the "flush times" in the Department of the Gulf in the years 1862–3.

A prominent citizen of Louisiana, who has held many important positions in his time under Republican rule, made a fortune during the war in an unexpectedly sudden way. In the year that turned the scale of the war a draft was ordered in many of the Northern and Eastern States, and enormous bounties were offered to procure enlistments or substitutes. One New-England State was very much behind in her quota, and certain towns were called upon to furnish 1,000 men. In desperation their agents wandered around among the contraband camps trying to fill the contract. The Southern Louisiana negro speaks French, and his characteristics were all colored by his association with his American-born master, to whom French is the mother tongue. The southwest part of the State, which is almost purely French—the Lafourche and Teche country—had first been occupied by the Sixteenth Army Corps, under Gen. William B. Franklin, and the usual contraband army came out along with it.

The New-England agent was invited over to the camp of a division of this corps, and as he traveled on, thought how he should fill up the quota of the God-fearing town of ———, whose people had sent all the Dutch and Irish they had to the war, and were ready to send more, when the stock ran out. On his way he went through the contraband camp. Never in his born days had the New-Englander beheld such a picturesque mass of color. There were giant, coal-black negroes whose blood had not been tainted since their African forefathers left the banks of the ancestral Congo 200 years before, and there were soft-eyed, graceful mulattos, with the courtesy of the "house servant," from the haughty creole planter's home, and a hundred intermediate shades between the types, all speaking the soft bastard French, unchanged in word or accent for 150 years.

The Yankee had never dreamed of such a scene as this. He tried to talk to some of them, but, for the most part, they shook their heads and said: "No spik 'Merican, me mo parle creole," while others, speechless, ran away. By chance he came across a man he had seen before, an officer in the ——— Connecticut, and told him of his trouble. "I think I know the man who can help you," the Captain said. "He is neither black nor white, but a mixture of the two in such a way that I do not know which race predominates in him. He speaks all these dialects, and can pull you through. I will send for him." Directly the man came. He was a tall, straight mulatto, ready, alert, and full of energy. It was agreed between them that the colored assistant was to have $250 per head for each recruit he procured, the person enlisted $50, while the thrifty recruiting agent kept the rest.

The colored tout knew his business. He went among the ragged, dirty contrabands, told them the Government would give every man who wanted them new clothes and a new gun and "a big handful of money," and he would not have to work and would have plenty to eat besides. He dressed one or two of them in uniforms to show them how they would appear when a beneficent Government had clothed them as it would if they wanted clothes. The agent got his quota filled, the sagacious colored citizen got $250,000 in cash in seven days, and the United States got a great many parti-colored warriors named Jean, Francois, and St. Jean Baptiste, who staid with their commands until they heard of the emancipation proclamation, and then they drew their pay and cut out. Soon, disguised in their usual picturesquely-dirty garments, they would never have been recognized as the smart Corporals or Sergeants of the late New-England regiment of infantry.

Not long ago a Washington pension agent said to a Louisiana friend: "In looking over the rolls of the ——— regiment I find ever so many French names. I can't get any clue to the whereabouts of their owners. Some of them must be still alive. If they are dead, they should have heirs. The towns they enlisted in, a part of whose quota they were, know nothing about them. Where do you suppose they are?"

"My friend," said the one addressed, solemnly, "these people never saw Massachusetts or Connecticut. They were enlisted in the Opelousas and Attakapas country of Louisiana. Those who are living are somewhere between the Gulf and Red River on the north and from the Bayou Chacala, in the Parish of Terre Bonne, or on the Lower La Fourche on the east, to the Cote Gelee hills on the west. They could not speak to you if you met them, for they parle the creole dialect alone. Then they would tell you forty lies about their enlistment, and deny, probably, that they were ever in the volunteer army at all if pressed, for they would believe your questioning them was a scheme of the Government to catch and punish them for some unknown offense. The less intelligent, having been told by Republican statesmen that if the Democrats ever did get into power the first thing they would do would be to kill all those who had been in the Union Army, would believe a list was being made up for the purpose of giving the killers the proper names of persons upon whom they were to operate, and would die before they would own to their military experience. You can't do any business there."

"Well," said he, with a groan, "you may be right. You ought to know. But just think of such an unworked mine as there is in Southwest Louisiana for a pension agent absolutely untouched. Why, some of those people have $1,000 in back pay, pensions, &c., due them. There are not less than $1,500,000 of good claims for pensions and bounty, the proper owners of which are Louisiana negroes in the region you speak of, who can't be got at. By the Lord, this is hard!" added the enterprising gentleman, almost overcome to tears by the thought.

THOMAS WENTWORTH HIGGINSON TELLS OF THEIR FIRST ENLISTMENT

NEW-YORK TIMES
January 28, 1894, p. 3

To the Editor of The New-York Times:

My attention has been called to your issue of Jan. 21, containing a paper on the enlistment of colored troops. This paper is valuable, as correcting some frequent errors, but it also makes some very serious errors, which you will pardon me if I correct. You are quite right, for instance, in correcting the mistake often made in the newspapers of regarding the Massachusetts Fifty-fourth and Fifty-fifth as the first colored regiments mustered into the United States service.

On the other hand, you err in speaking of them as having been "commanded by Cols. Higginson and Shaw." As a fact, they were commanded respectively by Cols. Shaw and Hallowell. Col. Higginson had been already six months in the field as commander of the First South Carolina, afterward Thirty-third United States Colored Troops, and never was connected with any Massachusetts colored regiment.

Neither of the Massachusetts colored regiments was formed until 1863, but five colored regiments were recruited in 1862, one in South Carolina, one in Kansas, and the three of which you speak, in Louisiana. Of these, the First South Carolina had clear and unquestioned priority in its original formation, having been recruited by Major Gen. Hunter in South Carolina, his order dating May 7, 1892, (G. O. 84, Dept. South.) The muster of Col. Stafford of the First Louisiana Native Guards was dated Sept. 27, 1862, more than four months later, and only six months (instead of two years, as you say,) earlier than that of Col. Shaw of the Fifty-fourth Massachusetts, which was dated April 17, 1863. The first enlistment of the First Kansas colored was on Aug. 2, 1862.

It is true that the First South Carolina, as first organized, was never recognized or paid by the Government, and was ordered to be disbanded, but it is also true that it was not disbanded, inasmuch as one company was allowed to remain in service, under Capt. C. T. Trowbridge, now of St. Paul, Minn., and did duty on St. Simon's Island, Ga., until it became the nucleus of a revival of the regiment under Brig. Gen. Rufus Saxton, who appointed me to its command, on Nov. 10, 1862. His orders from the War Department, authorizing him to recruit colored troops, were dated Aug. 25, 1862. It is safe, therefore, to say that the First South Carolina had a double distinction, (1) in that one of its companies had been four months earlier in service than any other colored regiment, slave or free; and (2) that it was, at any rate, the first slave regiment mustered into the United States service, Gen. Butler's New-Orleans regiments having been recruited, as he himself said, mainly from free colored men, "the darkest of whom," by his own statement, "was about the complexion of the late Daniel Webster."

Let me say, in conclusion, that the impression conveyed by you that some of these colored recruits found their way North and enlisted in the Massachusetts colored regiment seems absolutely without foundation. I have before me the roster of the Fifty-fourth Massachusetts, worked out with uncommon thoroughness, and giving the whole military and civil history of every man, with birthday, occupation, and place of abode. Not a single man was enlisted in Louisiana, nor is there a French name in the whole list of 1,268, with the possible exception of Toussaint L'Ouverture Delaney, and he was from Chatham, Canada. The same is equally true of the Fifty-fifth Massachusetts.

That you have not examined this part of the subject in detail is obvious from the fact that you say that "these two regiments had not twenty men in them who ever saw that State, (Massachusetts.)"

As a matter of fact, they almost all saw it, inasmuch as they were encamped and drilled there; and I find that there were in the Fifty-fourth Massachusetts alone, by actual count, 277 men who were, at the time of their enlistment, resident in Massachusetts towns. No claim was ever made that the majority of the men were from that State. Col. Shaw said expressly in his speech on departure, "The greater number of men in this regiment are not Massachusetts men." The honor claimed by Massachusetts is that of having sent all over the country to recruit colored soldiers, at the time when the attempt was derided on every side, and the Confederate Congress had passed an act (May 1, 1863,) that every white person enlisting or commanding colored soldiers should be put to death as a felon; and President Davis (Dec. 23, 1862,) had threatened similar punishment to the black soldiers themselves.

That Massachusetts should have gone with such energy into this enterprise, in the face of these threats, certainly did her some credit. And as the excess of troops furnished over her quota was 7,635—the quota being 139,095, and the whole number furnished being 146,780—it is evident that she might have gone without every colored man she enlisted and still have had a good balance to her credit.

Thomas Wentworth Higginson,

State Military and Naval Historian.

Boston, Jan. 23, 1894
To the Editor of The New-York Times:

In your last Sunday's issue there appeared an article under the caption: "Negro Soldiers of the War—Massachusetts' Part in Mustering Them Into Service." In this article it is stated that though the Fifty-fourth and Fifty-fifth Massachusetts colored regiments were credited to the quota of that State, in reality not twenty men in them ever saw the State. This statement is grossly erroneous. I have the roster of the Fifty-fourth Massachusetts Infantry before me at this writing, and I find every town, city, and hamlet in the State represented in this regiment alone by native-born colored men, and in the Fifty-fifth Massachusetts Infantry there is even a larger percentage of Massachusetts colored men upon its roster.

It is stated that these regiments were recruited from Louisiana. I have gone carefully over the rosters, and cannot find ten names in the roster of the Fifty-fourth Massachusetts of persons natives of Louisiana. The members of the Fifty-fourth Massachusetts (Col. Shaw) came principally from Massachusetts, New-York, Ohio, Rhode Island, and some few of the other Eastern

States, as the official roster of that regiment will show, and not from any of the Southern States, and it was about the first regularly-organized negro regiment in the service. Those organized prior to the enlistment and muster in of the Fifty-fourth Massachusetts had not the full legal status and authority at the time of their organization as did the Massachusetts negro regiments, and hence many of them were disbanded and re-organized. My brother and myself were members of the Fifty-fourth, and are natives of the State of Massachusetts.

Charles R. Douglass.

Washington, Jan. 24, 1894.

A BRITISH ANTI-LYNCH LEAGUE

HARPER'S WEEKLY
August 10, 1894, p. 891

It seems that American sympathy for down-trodden Ireland is reciprocated by British sympathy for the persecuted Southern negro. An Anti-Lynch League has been formed in England, the officers of which include the Duke of Argyll, the Archbishop of Canterbury, Justin McCarthy, Sir John Lubbock, and others, with a Woman's Auxiliary Committee, of which Mrs. Humphry Ward is president, and Lady Henry Somerset and the Countess of Aberdeen are active members. Five thousand pounds has been raised by this league to be used in agitating against the murdering of Southern negroes, in which purpose the society expects to co-operate with a similar organization to be formed in America. Among the Americans whose aid has been successfully bespoken by the league are said to be Carl Schurz, R. W. Gilder, Archbishop Ireland, Dr. John Hall, Archbishop Jannsens of St. Louis, and Bourke Cockran, three of the Protestant Episcopal bishops of the South, and many others. Another auxiliary society, having the same purpose, is the Afro-American Anti-Lynch League, of which T. Thomas Fortune and Frederick Douglass are leaders.

It cannot be said that the benevolent efforts of our cousins to amend the penal methods of the South have been received with much cordiality in the region most concerned. The Governors of Georgia, Virginia, West Virginia, Arkansas, and North Carolina have been heard from on the subject, and are agreed that so far as the movement is British it is a piece of impertinent intermeddling, and can do no good. Governor Tillman, of South Carolina, alone gives a more courteous answer, and says that if the Englishmen come to his State they will be welcome, and shall have every opportunity to get at the facts.

"MASSY'S SAKES! WHAT AM DOSE CHILLUN AT?"

Harper's Weekly, December 29, 1894, p. 1252.

The organization of these societies emphasizes what was fully realized before, that the lynching of negroes in the Southern States has become a very serious national reproach. It is true enough that not much can be done directly to check it except by the law-abiding element of the Southern people, which resists it already with energy and occasional success. But it is possible that rousing public opinion everywhere against the lynching of negroes may help to strengthen the hand of this element in the South, and stir them to greater exertions still to have all criminals, black and white, dealt with by legal processes. Aside from all considerations of justice or humanity, a reputation for lawlessness is exceedingly detrimental to the commercial interests of the South. That this aspect of the lynching epidemic is appreciated appears from the action taken by merchants and business men of Memphis in relation to the lynching of six negroes near Millington, Tennessee, on the 31st of August. On the 7th of September an indignation meeting was held at Memphis, at which the outrage was denounced, and a fund started for the relief of the families of the murdered men. Three men concerned in the lynching have been indicted and are in jail, and there is a good prospect that all the others implicated will be caught and tried. As soon as the punishment of lynchers really begins in the South, lynching will stop. The temper shown by the people of Memphis is most encouraging.

1895

The death of Frederick Douglass on February 20, 1895, ended a personal quest for the rights of African Americans—a quest that had inspired and garnered support from many people, regardless of their race. African American Congressman George Murray's (R-South Carolina) request that Douglass' body lie in state in the rotunda of the capital was indicative of the high esteem many had for Douglass. Although, Charles F. Crisp (D-Georgia), speaker of the House, denied the request, the list of those who publicly mourned Douglass' passing through their letters to editors, articles, essays, and speeches was a veritable who's who of African American and white leaders from every aspect of life.

Almost seven months to the day after Douglass' death, another African American, with a different message and proposing a new approach, ascended to the position of national Negro leader. On a sweltering day in September, the Cotton States and International Exposition opened in Atlanta, Georgia, featuring Booker T. Washington, principal of Tuskegee Institute, as one of the speakers. Washington's message of racial cooperation in matters economic, but accommodation to the racial policies of the day, touched a responsive chord in white America. President Grover Cleveland publicly thanked him, and in 1897 Harvard University conferred upon him an honorary Master's degree, the first ever awarded to an African American.

Washington's strategies for the progress of African Americans focused on industrial education, vocational training, and the development of African American entrepreneurship. But it was his commitment to industrial education that generated the most criticism. These questions were central to the debate: What was the most appropriate curriculum to meet the goals of African Americans? Should that curriculum be different from that of white Americans? How would historically African American colleges and universities acquire the funds necessary to maintain the institutions?

Many African American colleges and universities, including those founded in 1895—Fort Valley State College in Fort Valley, Georgia, and Natchez Junior College in Natchez, Mississippi—and those founded earlier, like Atlanta University, offered some industrial courses. The difference for some critics was that the kind of industrial education and industrial training favored by Washington would equip African Americans with skills already becoming obsolete, relegating them to the lower-paying jobs in an industry that required more highly-trained technical workers. Some historians argue that the real tragedy enveloping Washington was his ascendancy to power at a time when every effort to improve the lives of African Americans was met with open hostility and opposition from whites at various strata of the society.

Ida B. Wells-Barnett documented one mode of retaliation in the pamphlet The Red Record: Tabulated Statistics and Alleged Causes of Lynchings in the United States, 1892–1894. *Henry McNeal Turner, Bishop in the African Methodist Episcopal Church, well aware of the violence African Americans faced in the U.S., championed a return to Africa where he believed: "One thing the black man has here and that is manhood, freedom, and the fullest liberty." Turner lost faith in both Democrats and Republicans after he was expelled from the Georgia legislature so that whites could resume control. In 1870 his disenchantment with the U.S. led him to propose emigration to Africa in order that a select group of skilled African Americans could build a model nation there. He affiliated with the American Colonization Society (ACS), which sent approximately 100 settlers each year to Liberia. Interest in the ACS was linked directly to periods of extreme oppression in the U.S. Turner visited West Africa for the first time in 1891, and wrote glowing reports of what he saw, resulting in thousands of requests for passage abroad a ship set to sail in March 1892.*

When the ACS could no longer send settlers to Liberia, Turner encouraged African Americans to unite and finance their own travel. Turner's views were spread through the dissemination of a monthly newspaper he created, the Voice of Missions. *Late in 1893, after a second visit to Liberia, Turner called a national convention and attempted to interest middle-class African Americans in his ventures. His appeals were not successful.*

Still convinced that thousands of poorer African Americans would emigrate if funds were available for transportation, Turner supported the establishment of the International Migration Society (IMS) by a group of businessmen in Birmingham, Alabama. By March 1895, 200 persons from Arkansas, Mississippi, Alabama, Tennessee, and Texas arrived in Savannah, Georgia, awaiting transportation to their new homes in West Africa. A second group of 321 left in March 1896 but encountered difficulties prompting many to seek return to the U.S. As the economy of the U.S. improved following the 1893–1897 depression, the idea of returning to Africa waned.

Turner's black nationalism was not favorably received by most middle-class African American women who were also seeking ways to end white oppression. Washington's wife, Margaret Murray Washington, was regarded as one of the leading club women of the 1890s. Through her affiliation with the National Federation of Afro-American Women (NFAAW), she was invited to the Women's Congress held in conjunction with the Atlanta Exposition. Margaret had founded the Tuskegee Woman's Club earlier in the year.

Many thought the most meaningful way to address women's concerns was to develop an educated populace. Those most suited for the task, they believed, were formally educated African American women. Most African American teachers in the U.S. were women trained at African American institutions. Depending upon the school district and focus, teachers were responsible for instructing students in a wide range of subjects, including but not limited to English, Latin, history, algebra, housekeeping, cooking, biology and dressmaking. Because of their location, inferior facilities, and inability to pay competitive salaries, rural schools often had to hire inexperienced teachers.

The Plessy v. Ferguson Supreme Court decision of 1896 exacerbated the problems, serving to justify decreased funding for African American public schools at all levels. Not only was the per child allocation less for African American schools, rarely were African American teachers equitably compensated. As a rule, African American teachers were paid less than their white counterparts in the same school districts. Still, the commitment of the educators to assist in providing options for African American youth was demonstrated in many ways.

To enhance their skills, many teachers attended summer institutes held by African American colleges and universities. Hampton Institute's summer programs were so popular they were extended to six weeks in 1903. Teachers, seen as leaders and role models, were also instrumental in establishing community-based programs. Although the women's role as teachers and nurturers of children was preferable during this period, men were not excluded from the profession. While it would have been easier for teachers to see only the obstacles to quality education, they generally chose instead to focus on such positive factors as community involvement, community progress, and opening the doors of opportunity for African American children.

Cynthia Neverdon-Morton
Coppin State College

THE COTTON STATES AND INTERNATIONAL EXPOSITION

HARPER'S WEEKLY
January 19, 1895, p. 59

When at a banquet a few days ago Mr. Clark Howell was introduced as "the man who invented the map which showed that anybody starting from any point in this hemisphere to go to any other point must pass through Atlanta," everybody said the laugh was on Mr. Howell. But that map, which appeared in the Atlanta *Constitution* during the early days of exposition talk, unquestionably had a good deal to do with shaping the scope of that which has become the Cotton States and International Exposition.

The South had no exhibit at Chicago—at least there was none from Georgia and from most of the Southern States. Perhaps the people of the Southern States did not realize what a magnificent thing the World's Fair was to be, and perhaps their negligence was due entirely to inability to make the necessary appropriations; but however that may be, it is certain that when the fair was over the progressive men of this section did realize that an opportunity had been lost, The leadership of Atlanta in the progressive movement throughout the South is universally recognized, and it was natural, therefore, that Atlanta should be the first to see the great benefits which could be obtained right at this time from proper display and advertisement of the resources of these States. . . .

In some respects the exposition managers believe that they will be able to eclipse all former expositions. One of these is in the display of the progress of the negroes of the South. Not since their emancipation have the colored citizens of America had an opportunity to show what they have accomplished. A special building, to be designed by a colored architect, to be erected by colored workmen, and to be filled with specimens of the handiwork of the members of their race in all lines of life, will be one of the prominent features of the exposition. The leading men of that race throughout the South have this in their direct charge, and the enthusiasm with which they have entered upon their work, and the results already attained, show that in completeness this will exceed even the most sanguine expectations of its projectors. . . .

LET THE WOMEN VOTE

And Disfranchise the Illiterate Negro, Says Lucy Stone's Husband.
Says He Has Studied "the Southern Question," and That Is the Only Solution of the Subject.

ATLANTA CONSTITUTION
February 4, 1895

Mr. Henry B. Blackwell, of Boston, the husband of Lucy Stone, and an ardent suffragist, says that the only solution of what he calls "the southern question" is to enfranchise the educated women and disenfranchise the negroes who are uneducated—which would mean nearly all—and the illiterate whites. In short, he is in favor of the educational qualification for voters.

Mr. Blackwell is a striking figure. His hair is white as snow and fine as silk. He has a massive brow, a strong, thoughtful face of an English type, and is very direct in conversation. He only reached the convention Friday, having been detained in Boston to appear before the committee of the Massachusetts legislature which had in hand the bill to allow women to vote in municipal elections.

He, Lady Somerset, Mrs. Julia Ward Howe, Mrs. D. H. Livermore and several other suffragists made argument before the committee on Thursday. According to the newspaper accounts, he made an able speech.

He left Boston Thursday, immediately after appearing before the committee, reaching here Friday night. He will remain until Wednesday at the Aragon. He regretted very much that Lady Henry Somerset could not attend the convention here, and said that it was because her time was entirely filled with engagements.

Mr. Blackwell has devoted a great deal of time to the consideration of the situation in the south as it relates to suffrage. He says the only thing that will make the south secure is to take away the right of franchise from the many uneducated negroes and place it in the hands of the educated and intelligent white women.

"Take it in your own state. Georgia," he said, "there are 149,895 white women who can write, and 143,471 negro voters, of whom 116,516 are illiterates.

"The time has come when this question should be considered. An educational qualification for suffrage may or may not be wise, but it certainly is not necessarily unjust. If each voter governed only himself, his intelligence would concern himself alone, but his vote helps to govern everybody else. Society, in conceding his right, has itself a right to require from him a suitable preparation. Ability to read and write is absolutely necessary as a means of obtaining accurate political information. Without it the voter is almost sure to become the tool of political demagogues. With free schools provided by the states, every citizen can qualify himself without money and without price. Under such circumstances there is no infringement of right in requiring an educational qualification as a pre-requisite of voting. Indeed, without this suffrage is often little more than a name. 'Suffrage is the authoritative exercise of rational choice in regard to principles, measures and men.' The comparison of an unintelligent voter to a 'trained monkey,' who goes through the motion of dropping a paper ballot into a box, has in it an element of truth. Society, therefore, has a right to prescribe, in the admission of any new class of voters, such a qualification os every one can attain and as will enable the voter to cast an intelligent and responsible vote.

"In the development of our complex political society we have today two great bodies of illiterate citizens; in the north people of foreign birth; in the south, people of the African race, and a considerable portion of the native white population. Against foreigners and negroes, as such, we would not discriminate. So far as male citizens are concerned, we cannot recall an existing political equality. But, in every state save one, there are more educated women than all the illiterate voters, white and black, native and foreign."

DEATH OF FRED DOUGLASS

The Negro Leader Dies Suddenly in His Own Hallway.
Apparently in Perfect Health.
He Attended the Convention of the Women's National Council and Was to Have Spoken Last Night.

NEW-YORK TIMES
February 21, 1895, pp. 2, 5

Washington, Feb. 20.—Frederick Douglass dropped dead in the hallway of his residence on Anacostia Heights this evening at 7 o'clock. He had been in the highest spirits, and apparently in the best of health, despite his seventy-eight years, when death overtook him.

This morning he was driven to Washington, accompanied by his wife. She left him at the Congressional Library, and he continued to Metzerott Hall, where he attended the sessions of the Women's Council in the forenoon and the afternoon, returning to Cedar Hill, his residence, between 5 and 6 o'clock. After dining, he had a chat in the hallway with his wife about the doings of the council. He grew very enthusiastic in his explanation of one of the events of the day, when he fell upon his knees, with hands clasped.

Mrs. Douglass, thinking this was part of his description, was not alarmed, but as she looked he sank lower and lower, and finally lay stretched upon the floor, breathing his last. Realizing that he was ill, she raised his head, and then understood that he was dying. She was alone in the house, and rushed to the front door with cries for help. Some men who were near by quickly responded, and attempted to resaore the dying man. One of them called Dr. J. Stewart Harrison, and while he was injecting a restorative into the patient's arm, Mr. Douglass passed away, seemingly without pain.

Mr. Douglass had lived for some time at Cedar Hill with his wife and one servant. He had two sons and a daughter, the children of his first wife, living here. They are Louis H. and Charles Douglass and Mrs. Sprague.

Mr. Douglass was to deliver a lecture to-night at Hillsdale African Church, near his home, and was waiting for a carriage when talking to his wife. The carriage arrived just as he died.

Mrs. Douglass said to-night that her husband had apparently been in the best of health lately, and had shown unusual vigor for one of his years. No arrangements, she said, would be made for his funeral until his children could be consulted.

It is a singular fact, in connection with the death of Mr. Douglass, that the very last hours of his life were given in attention to one of the principles to which he has devoted his energies since his escape from slavery. This morning he drove into Washington from his residence, about a mile out from Anacostia, a suburb just across the Eastern branch of the Potomac, and at 10 o'clock appeared at Metzerott Hall, where the Women's National Council is holding its triennial. Mr. Douglass was a regularly-enrolled member of the National Woman's Suffrage Association, and had always attended its conventions. It was probably with a view to consistency in this respect that he appeared at Metzerott Hall.

Although it was a secret business session of the Council, Mr. Douglass was allowed to remain, and when the meeting had been called to order by Mrs. May Wright Sewall, the President of the Council, she appointed Miss Susan B. Anthony and the Rev. Anna H. Shaw a committee to escort him to the platform, where most of the delegates, not more than fifty in number, were sitting. Mrs. Sewall presented Mr. Douglass to the Council, and contenting himself with a bow in response to the applause that greeted the announcement, he took a seat beside Miss Anthony, his lifelong friend. Nothing to indicate that he was not in his usual good health was remarked at the time, and to-night, after his death was made known, nobody could recall anything in his appearance or actions out of the ordinary, except, according to the statement of a lady present, that he rubbed his left hand constantly with his right, as though it were benumbed.

The morning session lasted until after 12 o'clock, and just before that hour an informal discussion was started on the proposition that has been mooted for some time, to divide the National Council into an upper and a lower house. Mr. Douglass became much interested in this discussion, so much so, in fact, that when the council reconvened at 4 o'clock to give further consideration to the matter, he was again present, although it had been his intention to return to his home earlier in the day. He left the hall on the adjournment of the session, about 5 o'clock, and had been at his home but a short time when his death occurred.

When Miss Susan B. Anthony heard of Mr. Douglass's death, at the evening session of the council, she was very much affected. Miss Anthony has a wonderful control over her feelings, but to-night she could not conceal her emotion. Despite her seventy-five years, she immediately announced her intention of going to the Douglass homestead, near Anacostia, and had actually started, when some of her friends, fearful that the journey, with its quota of bad roads, and the excitement of a visit to the presence of death would have a bad effect on her used persuasion to such an extent that she finally consented to defer the trip until to-morrow. She was very much averse to returning to the stage in Metzerott Hall, contending that it would appear unfeeling for her to do so, but as a number of the more distinguished members of the council were absent, she agreed to take her accustomed place to the right of the presiding officer.

Miss Anthony and Mr. Douglass formed an intimate friendship when both resided in Rochester, N. Y., and that friendship had continued for many decades. One incident in connection with her relations with Mr. Douglass was recalled by Miss Anthony. During the early days of the anti-slavery agitation Miss Anthony and her venerable associate, Elizabeth Cady Stanton, appeared at an anti-slavery meeting in which Frederick Douglass was taking a prominent part. Women were not welcome as public speakers in those days, and Mr. Douglass had agreed to read an address prepared by Mrs. Stanton. His rendition of her written remarks did not suit that lady, and, stepping forward, she took the paper from his hands with the remark, "Here, Frederick, let me read it." And she did so, thus marking the initiative in the appearance of women as actors in public gatherings.

At to-night's meeting of the Women's Council Mrs. May Wright Sewall announced the death of Mr. Douglass. There was a murmur expressing surprise and sympathy, and then the council settled down to the business of the evening.

THE SLAVE WHO RAN AWAY
Career of the Most Representative African America Has Produced.

NEW-YORK TIMES
February 21, 1895, p. 5

Frederick Douglass has been often spoken of as the foremost man of the African race in America. Though born and reared in slavery, he managed, through his own perseverance and energy, to win for himself a place that not only made him beloved by all members of his own race in America, but also won for himself the esteem and reverence of all fair-minded persons, both in this country and in Europe.

Mr. Douglass had been for many years a prominent figure in public life. He was of inestimable service to the members of his own race, and rendered distinguished service to his country from time to time in various important offices that he held under the Government.

He became well known, early in his career, as an orator upon subjects relating to slavery. He won renown by his oratorical powers both in the northern part of the United States and in England. He had become known before the civil war also as a journalist. So highly were his opinions valued that he was often consulted by President Lincoln, after the civil war began, upon questions relating to the colored race. He held important offices almost constantly from 1871 until 1891.

Mr. Douglass, perhaps more than any other man of his race, was instrumental in advancing the work of banishing the color line.

Mr. Douglass's life from first to last was filled with incidents that gave to it a keen flavor of romance.

The exact date of his birth is unknown. It was about the year 1817. His mother was a negro slave and his father was a white man. Mr. Douglass's birthplace was on the Eastern Shore of Maryland, in the Tuckahoe district. He was reared as a slave on the plantation of Col. Edward Lloyd. He was sent, when ten years old, to one of Col. Lloyd's relatives in Baltimore. Here he was employed in a shipyard.

Douglass, according to his own story, suffered deeply while under the bonds of slavery. His superior intelligence made him conscious of his wrongs and rendered him keenly sensitive to his condition. The manner in which he acquired the rudiments of his education has become a familiar story. He learned his letters, it is said, from the carpenters' marks on planks and timbers in the shipyard. He used to listen while his mistress read the Bible, and at length asked her to teach him to read it for himself. All the while he was in the shipyard he continued to pick up secretly all the information he could.

It was while here, too, that he heard of the abolitionists and began to formulate plans for escaping to the North. He made his escape from slavery Sept. 3, 1838, and came to New-York. Thence he went to New-Bedford, where he married. He supported himself for two or three years by day labor on the wharves and in the workshops.

He made a speech in 1841 at an anti-slavery convention, held at Nantucket, that made a favorable impression, and he became the agent of the Massachusetts Anti-Slavery Society. He then traveled four years through New-England, lecturing against slavery.

He went to England in 1845, where his lectures in behalf of the slave won a great deal of attention. He also visited Scotland, Ireland, and Wales. Mr. Douglass's friends in England feared that he might be captured and forced back into slavery, and so they raised (L)150, by means of which he was afterwards formally manumitted.

Mr. Douglass often met with many unpleasant experiences while traveling about, owing to the prejudice that was felt against his race. On one occasion, when the passengers on a boat would not allow him to enter the cabin, his friend, Wendell Phillips, refused to leave him, and the two men spent the night together on deck.

William Lloyd Garrison had also become interested in young Douglass, and before Douglass went to England had done all he could to assist him in gaining an education. Throughout the anti-slavery agitation, Mr. Douglass's efforts in behalf of the slaves was unflagging.

DEATH OF FREDERICK DOUGLASS

HARPER'S WEEKLY
February 23, 1895, p. 198

Whenever the long agitation in America against negro slavery is recalled the name of Frederick Douglass will also be remembered, and his shade will be conspicuous in the ghostly company made up of William Lloyd Garrison, Wendell Phillips, John Brown, Henry Ward Beecher, Oliver Johnson, and Owen Lovejoy. Among

FREDERICK DOUGLASS,
Died February 20, 1895.—[See Page 198.]

Harper's Weekly, February 23, 1895, p. 196.

these Douglass was the only man with negro blood in his veins, the only one who, in his own person, had suffered the penalties and experienced the pains of slavery. Born in Maryland in 1817, a slave, his mother being a negro woman and his father a white man, he conquered opportunities and achieved distinction in the face of extraordinary difficulties. Lloyd, the owner of Douglass, perceiving that this lad was bright and enterprising, and that he was learning to read and write, did what he could to put a stop to this sort of advancement. But Douglass had already achieved the alphabet by studying the carpenters' marks on the lumber that he handled on the wharfs at Baltimore, and he had received some instruction from the lady with whom he lived.

Douglass has related that so early as he could remember he realized to some extent the degradation of slavery. The stop to his studies deepened this feeling, and he determined to win his freedom as quickly as possible. But it was not till he was twenty-one years old that he managed to escape, by way of New York, to Connecticut. He supported himself on the wharfs of New Bedford, and studied hard. In his efforts at self-education he was aided by William Lloyd Garrison. In 1841 he attended an antislavery convention at Nantucket, and made a speech which excited the enthusiasm of those who heard it. His description of slavery and its horrors was no fanciful sketch, but plain realism colored somewhat by the warmth of an inherited Orientalism. The convention offered him the agency of the Massachusetts Antislavery Society, and he accepted the post.

For several years he travelled through New England, speaking and organizing.

At the invitation of a committee headed by the famous philanthropist, Lord Shaftesbury, in 1845 Mr. Douglass visited England, and staid there two years, telling of the inhumanity of slavery and assisting in the awakening of opposition to it on the part of the working and middle classes of the people. When he returned to this country, in 1847, he went to Rochester to live, and there began the publication of *Frederick Douglass's Paper,* the name of which was soon changed to *The North Star,* and as such issued weekly for several years. During his residence at Rochester Mr. Douglass was consulted by the antislavery leaders, and it has often been said that it was at the house of Mr. Douglas that John Brown made his plans to raid Virginia by way of Harper's Ferry. Douglass always insisted that he did not approve of Brown's project, though he admired his zeal and earnestness. But Governor Wise, of Virginia, made a requisition for Douglass's arrest and removal to Virginia as a conspirator with Brown. This requisition was on the Governor of Michigan, where Douglass then was. Douglass, however, did not wait to be arrested, but went to England, where he remained for many months. He then returned to Rochester and continued the publication of his paper.

When the war broke out he urged upon Mr. Lincoln the emancipation of the slaves and their enlistment in the army. When this was done Mr. Douglass was active in his aid of enlistment, and his assistance in forming the Fifty-fourth and Fifty-fifth Massachusetts regiments has been generally recognized.

After the abolition of slavery he discontinued his paper and began lecturing. This was his profession so long as he lived. It proved so remunerative that when he died, on the 20th of February, in Washington, he left a fortune of two or three hundred thousand dollars. In 1870 he founded in Washington a paper called *The New National Era,* which was conducted by him for several years, and then transferred to his sons. He held several public offices. In 1871 he was Assistant Secretary to the Commission to Santo Domingo, in 1872 he was Member of the Territorial Council of the District of Columbia, in 1872 he was Presidential Elector for the State of New York, in 1876 he was Marshal of the District of Columbia, in 1881 he was Recorder of Deeds for the District of Columbia, and in 1889 he was Minister of the United States to Haiti.

He wrote several books. They include *Narrative of My Experiences in Slavery, My Bondage and My Freedom,* and *Life and Times of Frederick Douglass.*

Mr. Douglass was twice married. His first wife was a negress. His second wife, now his widow, is a white woman. There was something strikingly noble in Mr. Douglass's appearance, and whoever beheld him felt immediately sure that the man before him was one of note—a personage. And yet he was in no sense a poseur. His last public appearance was on the day of his death, when he attended a meeting of women suffragists—a reform which he advocated with characteristic zeal.

HONORS TO FREDERICK DOUGLASS

His Body to Lie in State Tuesday in the City Hall by Permission of Mayor Strong.

NEW-YORK TIMES
February 24, 1895

The body of Frederick Douglass, the distinguished negro leader, will lie in state in the City Hall Tuesday forenoon, from 8 until 10 o'clock.

A committee of five colored men, appointed at a meeting of the members of St. Mark's Methodist Episcopal Church, 139 West Forty-eighth Street, on Friday night, and consisting of William R. Davis, S. J. Stokely, Pierre Baguet, Waverley E. Scott, and the Rev. Granville Hunt, called at the Mayor's office yesterday morning and asked the necessary permission. Secretary Hedges at once communicated with Mayor Strong, at his home, and the permission was granted.

The body will reach this city early Tuesday morning, and will lie in state in the centre of the large vestibule of the City Hall, in the same spot where Gen. Grant's catafalque rested in 1885. People desiring to view the remains will enter by the main entrance and pass out by the rear doors. In the afternoon of Tuesday the body will be taken to Rochester, N. Y., for burial in Mount Hope Cemetery.

WASHINGTON, Feb. 23.—Representative Murray of South Carolina, the only negro member of the House of Representatives, endeavored unsuccessfully to-day to secure favorable action upon a resolution permitting the body of Frederick Douglass to lie in state to-morrow in the rotunda of the Capitol. The matter was brought to the attention of Speaker Crisp too late to be presented to the House before the execution of the special order, the delivery of eulogies upon the late Senator Vance, was entered upon. He informed Mr. Murray that had he given notice of his desire to present the resolution earlier in the day, he would have given him an opportunity to offer it for the action of the House.

Later in the day Mr. Pettigrew offered a resolution reciting that in the person of Frederick Douglass death had borne away a most illustrious citizen, and permitting the body to lie in state in the rotunda of the Capitol to-morrow and he asked for its immediate consideration. Mr. Gorman, (Dem., Md.,) objected, and the resolution went over.

"THE MOST PICTURESQUE HISTORICAL FIGURE IN MODERN TIMES."

Eulogized by the Rev. Dr. Banks.
His Lofty Ideals Alone Made It Possible for Him to Achieve the Great Triumphs of His Life.

NEW-YORK TIMES
February 25, 1895

The Hanson Place Methodist Episcopal Church, Brooklyn, was well filled last evening when the pastor, the Rev. Dr. Louis A. Banks, delivered an excellent sermon on "Frederick Douglass, the Eloquent, the Most Picturesque Historical Figure in Modern Times."

Dr. Banks took for his text these words: "Know ye not that there is a prince and a great man fallen?"

"If I were asked," he said, "what person in the present century had fought against the greatest odds and won in the struggle of life at most points, I should answer, Frederick Douglass. There is a great deal of talk about self-made men in our time, and we have had an abundance of eloquence concerning Abraham Lincoln's rise from the place of railsplitter to the Presidency; concerning Gen. Grant's career from the tannery to the position of first American citizen, and concerning Garfield's, from the tow path to the White House; but none of these men, nor all of them put together, had to make life's race with such a handicap or facing such odds as had Frederick Douglass.

"Here is a man who learned to read and write by studying out the characters made by the carpenters in the Baltimore lumber yards, who comes by his own devoted effort to speak the English language with an eloquence equal to Charles Sumner, or Henry Ward Beecher, in their best days.

"Here is a man who did not know who his father was, who never saw his mother but a few times, and then by moonlight or by glimpses caught by a tallow dip, in a log cabin; who came to be a bosom friend of John Bright, the intimate of Abraham Lincoln, the boon companion of Daniel O'Connell; who came to be loved by Wendell Phillips and William Lloyd Garrison, and was held in highest honor and most tender regard by many of the noblest women of both continents; came to be the undisputed leader of his race; known wherever the English language is spoken, and to be respected by the whole civilized world.

"The story of his life is the most romantic of all modern times. No man began so low and climbed so high as he.

"Frederick Douglass had many elements of greatness, and one of the greatest was his power of grim perseverance. He had the power to patiently, ploddingly, whip himself through any hard work that must be done. It was once said by an opponent of Sir Walter Raleigh: 'He can toil terribly.' Frederick Douglass had in a remarkable degree that terrible, irresistible power of the toiler. Whether it was learning to read by the carpenters' marks on strips of building timebr, or plodding, after he was a grown man, through the grammar of the English language, or setting himself, in middle age, to acquire that information and knowledge necessary to make him a skillful friend of his people, he had the perseverance and the pluck and the devotion to toll mercilessly until his task was accomplished.

"Frederick Douglass had great ideals. He never compromised with himself for anything less than the best that was possible. Nothing short of being the very best type of man and the most noble orator that it was possible to produce out of his circumstances and gifts satisfied him for a moment.

These lofty ideals alone made it possible for him to achieve the great triumphs of his life. For, after all, the greatest triumph of Douglass's life is not to be found in his glorious success as an orator, nor in his triumphs as a political leader, but in the splendid moral fibre of the man, that enabled him to live a life which is not only a precious heritage to his own race, but an inspiration to men of all races, throughout all time. Think of the fearful odds he had to fight against in order to produce such a moral character.

"Milton says: 'It is a long way out of hell up to light.' Think of the hell of iniquity into which he was born. He was born in the midst of that enforced tendency to every vicious passion and unholy appetite that springs from the world, the flesh, and the devil; but in spite of it all, he developed a strong, robust manhood, which he kept clean and spotless throughout half a century lived in the public gaze. Frederick Douglass did no greater thing for his race than that.

"Douglass's oratory gained much of its power from the superb manhood that was behind him. I once heard him deliver his great address on John Brown. His discussion of the law of retribution was the strongest I ever heard. As he stood there on the platform, giving us the evolution of John Brown, he filled one's ideal of the old Hebrew prophets. He reached the climax in these words:

"'The cry that went up from the startled and terrified inhabitants of Harper's Ferry was but the echo of that other cry which began two hundred years before, when the man hunter first set foot in the quiet African villages. The raid on Harper's Ferry was contracted for when the first slave ship landed on these shores.'

"'The question has been often asked,' said Douglass, in that great address, 'why Virginia, with a grand magnanimity, did not spare John Brown? But they had a thing down there, and that thing could not stand the life of John Brown. Her own Patrick Henry loved liberty for the rich man and the great; John Brown loved liberty for the poor and lowly. It was not white man dying for white man; it was white man dying for black man. He came down from the heaven of New-England liberty to the hell of African slavery. He gave his life as the best gift he could lay on the altar of human liberty.'

"Frederick Douglass was a broad-spirited, public man. He was too large a man for any bitter, bigoted partisanship. His declaration about some public affair, not long ago, in a letter which has been printed, in which he says: 'I am a Republican, but I am not a Republican right or wrong,' shows the breadth of the man. And it is well to notice in connection with this fact the marvelous growth in Frederick Douglass's time in toleration of freedom of principles and speech which is illustrated in the House of Representatives of the North Carolina Legislature, adjourning in honor of Frederick Douglass, on receiving the news of his death last Thursday.

"It is very appropriate that his last appearance in public should have been on the platform of the Woman's Council, on the very day of his death. To no other cause had he given more sincere devotion than to the equality of rights and privileges between man and woman.

"I heard him, one time, in an address on woman's suffrage, in reply to the suggestion that the pool of politics was too dirty to allow women to come into it, ask, with stinging sarcasm, 'Who made the pool dirty? No woman has been playing in it.'

"The fact that a bill now before the New-York Legislature to punish by flogging certain classes of human brutes has been so amended by that august body as to permit a man to beat his wife without danger of punishment, very clearly indicates that there is great necessity that Frederick Douglass's mantle shall fall upon younger men, and that his position, that a disfranchised class will always be an oppressed class, was well taken.

"No man doubts for a moment that if equal suffrage had been granted by the last Constitutional Convention the wife-beater would have had to take his dogging along with the other brutes.

"A career like that of Frederick Douglass is at once an honor and an inspiration to humanity. In such a man the kinship of all races is demonstrated."

A DEGRADED STATE

HARPER'S WEEKLY
June 1, 1895, p. 505

The decision of Judge Goff on the registration law of South Carolina is a remarkable judicial event. Judge Goff is known as an intense Republican partisan, who, like all Southern Republicans, holds that the welfare of the Southern States may be best promoted by Federal control and interference. His opinion, therefore, is not as convincing as a like opinion by a judge who is less of a partisan would have been, and this view of the matter is strengthened by the judge's own confession that in rendering this decision "duty mingles with inclination." It is so much a judge's duty to suppress his inclination that this confession of entertaining one is suggestive that inclination may have controlled the judicial mind.

Judge Goff has decided that the registration law of South Carolina is unconstitutional; that it offends against both the Constitution of the State and the Constitution of the United States. There seems to be no doubt that the registration law of South Carolina was designed to cheat the ignorant and the unwary, and that the Tillmanites expected by rascally manipulation of it to control the coming Constitutional Convention of the State. It is a new departure in the history of Federal jurisprudence, however, for the Federal court to set aside a State law by injunction in order to protect the State's own citizens. It may be that this question will be decided finally by the Supreme Court at Washington. In the mean time lawyers will doubt the validity of Judge Goff's decision, notwithstanding the good results that may be expected to flow from it. The Federal government obtains jurisdiction over a State law affecting the suffrage under the Fifteenth Amendment, which provides that the right of a citizen to vote shall not be "denied or abridged by the United States or by any State on account of race, color, or previous condition of servitude." Judge Goff, therefore, must have held that the registration law of South Carolina offended against the Federal Constitution by discriminating against the negroes. The statute itself, however, is general, and applies to whites as well as blacks. Indeed, the white Democrats of the State, of the respectable sort, who sustain Judge Goff, say that the registration law is aimed at them as well as at the negroes. If this contention is true, then whatever discrimination there may be in the registration law cannot be based on "race, color, or previous condition of servitude," and any other discrimination but that, even although it might include the negroes, would not bring the law within the meaning of the Fifteenth Amendment, unless the Supreme Court is ready to carry the Federal power much further than it has yet done.

Judge Goff's decision, however, gives partial expression to the desires of all who have the welfare of South Carolina at heart. Through the instrumentality of Populism or Tillmanism the State has been degraded. It is in the power of its meanest, most ignorant, and most vicious classes. Its government is a disgrace to the country. It is itself lawless and barbarous. Its officials have no respect for the law. Its judges are on the bench not to administer justice, but to carry out the narrow, dangerous, and communistic policy of the ignorant whites who have "captured" the State government. If the law does not sustain that policy, so much the worse for the law. The Governor and the courts vie with each other in riding rough-shod over it. South Carolina's government is republican in form, but not in substance. This very registration law, for example, was enacted for the purpose of fastening on the State the rule of the base and ignorant mob that made Tillman first Governor and then Senator, and has now placed in the Executive chair one Evans, a young man of uncertain mind and bad principles, with a large talent for revolutionary boastfulness, without the courage to abide by his threats. And although the law is clearly against the State Constitution, Tillmanite judges cannot be trusted to protect the citizens of the State and to declare it so. Such a state of things is unexampled, except in a smaller degree in this State. In New York police corruption has been authorized by Platt's Legislature; in South Carolina the statutes and the courts unite to put the State in control of the worst men of the commonwealth. It is in consequence of this terrible degradation that the extraordinary interference of the Federal court has been invoked.

SOUTH CAROLINA

HARPER'S WEEKLY
August 10, 1895, p. 937

South Carolina is in a pitiable condition. The majority of its population and of its voters are blacks. The majority of the whites are weak and ignorant enough to be the tools of such demagogues as the Tillmans, Irby, and Evans.

The rule of these men is a gross travesty on republican institutions. It makes the State conspicuous by reason of the strange antics that go by the name of government. Its laws are the crude experiments of the ignorant or the bold devices of the corrupt. Its executive department has been administered in a manner that is sometimes pitifully absurd, and sometimes grossly tyrannical. Its bench was once an honor to the whole country; it is now contemptible.

Under a good Constitution such a government as that under which South Carolina suffers might be endured, in the hope that the people would some day rise up against it and overthrow it. But Senator Tillman and his associates are now holding a convention for the purpose of framing a Constitution that will establish the rule of ignorant and corrupt whites. The best element of the State, now known as conservative, is hardly represented in this Constitutional Convention. It has no influence and no leader. The man who might have been its leader, Senator Butler, courted the favor of the Tillmanites, and was justly spurned and degraded for his mean surrender. The educated men of the State will have little to say in the framing of the new fundamental law, and the control of the Tillmanites over the electoral machinery is so complete that whatever instrument they submit to the people is likely to be adopted.

The first great problem in the minds of the men who have seized upon the government of the State concerns the suffrage. They are trying to adopt a provision which will disfranchise the negroes without violating the Constitution of the United States, and yet that will not disfranchise the ignorant whites. An educational qualification will not do this, unless the inspectors of election are the judges of the voter's intellectual qualification in each case. But an educational and property qualification may effect the desired result. Whatever will give to white ignorance and corruption the control of South Carolina will be adopted by Senator Tillman's convention. If he and his followers fail in this, it will be because they are not cunning enough to make their instrument declare their will. And besides the perversion of the suffrage, we may expect to see in this Constitution provisions for the establishment of every communistic contrivance that the brains of the half-informed, the vicious, and the weak have invented. At present, and for a generation to come, South Carolina promises to be an object lesson to other commonwealths of what a democracy can become when its worst elements obtain absolute control. And one sad phase of the whole business is that there seems to be no light in the dark cloud which is overhanging the State. There are thousands of good men in South Carolina, but in the hands of the Tillmanites they are as powerless as the negroes have been since the day when Wade Hampton became Governor, and the State started on what was hoped would be a career of good fortune. Then the rule of the whites began; but at last the cleavage has come in the ranks of what is called the dominant race itself, and the division is between ignorance and corruption on one side, and intelligence and character on the other. The Tillmanites stand between the best of the whites and the negroes, hating and fearing both, and for the time at least South Carolina takes its place as the most backward of the States in the art of government.

GOLDEN BUTTON PRESSED

Pres Cleveland at Gray Gables Opens the Cotton States' Exposition.

BOSTON DAILY GLOBE
September 18, 1895, p. 2

The City of Atlanta Alive with Strangers, and the Fair Grounds Aflame with Flags—Northern Veterans Warmly Greeted—The Buildings Marvels of Beauty and Utility, and the Industrial and Amusement Features Novel and Numerous.

The negro building will probably attract more attention than any other, because this is the first opportunity of its kind offered to the negro in freedom and civilization to demonstrate the progress he has made and the liberty he enjoys.

The exhibit in this building will be interesting and unique, and will probably prove a source of great surprise to southerners and northerners alike.

Mr. I. Garland Penn, a highly educated colored man from Virginia, has charge of this exhibit, and is doing much to elevate and advance his race. An album of views of the negro building is in course of publication. It will be of great interest, and will reflect credit upon Mr Penn, while it will materially aid in educating the negroes.

A PLEA FOR HIS RACE

Booker T. Washington Tells About the Efforts of the Negro.
His Speech a Thoughtful One.
He Was Given a Splendid Reception and His Speech Was Frequently Interrupted by Applause.

ATLANTA CONSTITUTION
September 19, 1895, pp. 2–3

The colored race had a representative on the programme of the opening exercises of whom they have great reason to be proud.

Booker T. Washington, president of the Tuskegee Normal and Industrial school, spoke for the negro. It was the first time a colored orator had even stood upon a platform before such a vast audience with white men and women. It was an event in the history of the race.

No one expected such a speech from Washington as he made. His speech could not have been excelled. There was not a superfluous word in it. It was in the very best of taste and there was not a jarring note in it. It made a magnificent impression and was frequently interrupted by applause.

Washington said:

"Mr. President, Gentlemen of the Board of Directors and Citizens: One-third of the population of the south is of the negro race. No enterprise seeking the material, civil or moral welfare of this section can disregard this element of our population and reach the highest success. I but convey to you, Mr. President and Directors, the sentiment of the masses of my race, when I say that in no way have the value and manhood of the American negro been more fittingly and generously recognized than by the managers of this magnificent exposition at every stage of its progress. It is a recognition which will do more to cement the friendship of the two races than any occurrence since the dawn of our freedom.

"Not only this, but the opportunity here afforded will awaken among us a new era of industrial progress. Ignorant and inexperienced, it is not strange that in the first years of our new life we began at the top instead of the bottom; that a seat in congress or the state legislature was more sought than real estate or industrial skill; that the political convention or stump speaking had more attractions than starting a dairy farm or truck garden.

A ship lost at sea for many days suddenly sighted a friendly vessel. From the mast of the unfortunate vessel

PROFESSOR BOOKER T. WASHINGTON
The Talented Representative of the Negroes, Who Made Such a Brilliant Speech Yesterday.

Atlanta Constitution, September 19, 1895.

was seen the signal, 'Water, water, we die of thirst!' The answer from the friendly vessel at once came back, 'Cast down your bucket where you are.' A second time the signal, 'Water, water, send us water,' ran up from the distressed vessel, and was answered, 'Cast down your bucket where you are,' and a third and fourth signal for water was answered, 'Cast down your vessel where you are.' The captain of the distressed vessel, at last heeding the injunction, cast down his bucket and it came up full of fresh, sparkling water from the mouth of the Amazon river. To those of my race who depend on bettering their condition in a foreign land, or who underestimate the importance of cultivating friendly relations with the southern white man who is their next-door neighbor, I would say cast down your bucket where you are, cast it down in making friends in every manly way of the people of all races by whom we are surrounded. Cast it down in agriculture, in mechanics, in commerce, in domestic service and in the professions. And in this connection it is well to bear in mind that whatever other sins the south may be called upon to bear, when it comes to business pure and simple, it is in the south that the negro is given a man's chance in the commercial world, and in nothing is this exposition more eloquent than in emphasizing this chance. Our greatest danger is, that in the great leap from slavery to freedom we may overlook the fact that the masses of us are to live by the productions of our hands, and fail to keep in mind that we shall prosper in proportion as we learn to dignify and glorify common labor and put brains and skill into the common occupations of life; shall prosper in proportion as we learn to draw the line between the superficial and the substantial, the ornamental gewgaws of life and the useful. No race can prosper until it learns that there is as much dignity in tilling a field as in writing a poem. It is at the bottom of life we must begin and not at the top. Nor should we permit our grievances to overshadow our opportunities.

"Cast Down Your Buckets"

"To those of the white race who look to the incoming of those of foreign birth and strange tongue and habits for the prosperity of the south, were I permitted, I would repeat what I say to my own race: 'Cast down your bucket where you are.' Cast it down among 8,000,000 negroes whose habits you know, whose loyalty and love you have tested in days when to have proved treacherous meant the ruin of your firesides. Cast down your bucket among these people who have without strikes and labor wars, tilled your fields, cleared your forests, built your railroads and cities and brought forth treasures from the bowels of the earth and helped make possible this magnificent representation of the progress of the south. Casting down your bucket among my people, helping and encouraging them as you are doing on these grounds, and to education of head, hand and heart, you will find that they will buy your surplus land, make blossom the waste places in your fields and run your factories. While doing this you can be sure in the future, as you have been in the past, that you and your families will be surrounded by the most patient, faithful, law-abiding and unresentful people that the world has seen. As we have proved our loyalty to you in the past in nursing your children, watching by the sick bed of your mothers and fathers and often following them with tear-dimmed eyes to their graves, so in the future in our humble way we shall stand by you with a devotion that no foreigner can approach, ready to lay down our lives, if need be, in defense of yours, interlacing our industrial, commercial, civil and religious life with yours in a way that shall make the interests of both races one. In all things that are purely social we can be as separate as the fingers, yet one as the hand in all things essential to mutual progress.

Where Security Lies

"There is no defense or security for any of us except in the highest intelligence and development of all. If anywhere there are efforts tending to curtail the fullest growth of the negro, let these efforts be turned into stimulating, encouraging and making him the most useful and intelligent citizen. Efforts or means so invested will pay a thousand per cent interest. These efforts will be twice blessed —'blessing him that gives and him that takes.'

"There is no escape through law of man or God from the inevitable:

"'The laws of changeless justice bind
Oppressor with oppressed,
And close as sin and suffering joined
We march to fate abreast.'

"Nearly sixteen millions of hands will aid you pulling the load upward or they will pull against you the load downward. We shall constitute one-third and much more of the ignorance and crime of the south or one-third of its intelligence and progress; we shall contribute one-third to the business and industrial prosperity of the south, or we shall prove a veritable body of death, stagnating, depressing every effort to advance the body politic.

"Gentlemen of the Exposition: As we present to you our humble effort at an exhibition of our progress, you must not expect overmuch; starting thirty years ago with the ownership here and there in a few quilts and pumpkins and chickens (gathered from miscellaneous sources), remember that the path that has led us from these to the invention and production of agricultural implements, buggies, steam engines, newspapers, books, statuary, carving, paintings, the management of drug stores and banks has not been trodden without contact with thorns and thistles. While we take just pride in what we exhibit as a result of our independent efforts, we do not for a moment forget that our part in this exhibition would fall far short of your expectations but for the constant help that has come to our educational life not only from the southern states, but especially from northern philanthropists who have made their gifts a constant stream of blessing and encouragement.

Labor's Social Equality

"The wisest among my race understand that the agitation of questions of social equality is the extremest folly, and that progress in the enjoyment of all the privileges that will come to us must be the result of severe and constant struggle, rather than of artificial forcing. No race that has anything to contribute to the markets of the world is long in any degree ostracised. It is right and important that all privileges of the law be ours, but it is vastly more important that we be prepared for the exercise of these privileges. The opportunity to earn a dollar in a factory just now is worth infinitely more than the opportunity to spend a dollar in an opera house.

"In conclusion, may I repeat that nothing in thirty years has given us more hope and encouragement, and nothing has drawn us so near to you of the white race, as the opportunity offered by this exposition; and here bending, as it were, over the altar that represents the results of the struggles of your race and mine, both starting practically empty handed three decades ago, I pledge that in your effort to work out the great and intricate problem which God has laid at the doors of the South you shall have at all times the patient, sympathetic help of my race: only let this be constantly in mind—that while from representations in these buildings of the product of field, of forest, of mine, of factory, letters and art, much good will come, yet far above and beyond material benefits will be that higher good that, let us pray God, will come in a blotting out of sectional differences and racial animosities and suspicions, and in a determination, even in the remotest corner, to administer absolute justice, in a willing obedience among all classes to the mandates of law and a spirit that will tolerate nothing but the highest equity in the enforcement of law. This, this, coupled with our material prosperity, will bring into our beloved south a new heaven and a new earth."

WASHINGTON'S GREAT SPEECH

ATLANTA CONSTITUTION
September 19, 1895

Professor Washington is a representative of his race, and stands in the foremost ranks of those who have elevated the negro, both intellectually and morally. His life work has been spent in working reforms, and today he is without a peer among his race. His address yesterday afternoon proved his depth of thought and the deep study he has given the living issues of the day. His address was loudly applauded and his effort was most happy. He said that the negro had risen with equal proportion with the white people from the ashes of the war; that his race began life anew when Sherman passed through, and that both races had but very little as a basis left them on which to lay the foundation of their new lives. The negroes were poor when the chains of slavery were broken and they started out in life with but little of worldly goods. They had a few quilts, a mattress or two and a few chickens they had obtained from miscellaneous places. His reference to chickens brought down the house, and for several minutes he was unable to proceed with his speech. The audience was worked up to a high pitch when the speaker told of the heroism of the negro during the war, and how at times when treachery would have given the south a death blow, the negroes were true as steel. He said that the negro had been the friend of the white man through thick and thin, and that for the future the same friendly relations would exist. He told the story of a foundering ship at sea, whose crew were dying for the want of water. A signal of distress was sent up to a friendly vessel that had been sighted. The signal said: "We are dying for water." The other ship answered: "Let down your buckets where you are." Again and again the same signals were exchanged, and finally driven to desperation, the captain of the waterless ship let down the buckets and found in the depths a cooling draught from the waters of the Amazon's mouth. The speaker said that the great fault the negroes were about to make was they wanted to let down their buckets in foreign soil. His advice was for them to let their buckets down in the soil of the south among the people who knew their habits and appreciated their circumstances. The same advice he said applied to the white people and he thought no good could be the result of the importation of foreign labor. He wanted the white people to rest assured that in the negroes' heart the welfare of both races was most sacred and that nothing would ever occur to make the white people regret the existence of the colored race. He said that the time was coming when the two races would be as separate as the fingers, but one as the hand.

He tendered the negro exhibit as the gift of the colored people to the world, showing what they had accomplished in material things and the lines of progress made since the days of the war. He said that the negroes had been blessed of God and he believed the blessings of the Eternal would hover about the negro's head and under His guiding hand a long period of success, hope and constancy was in the future.

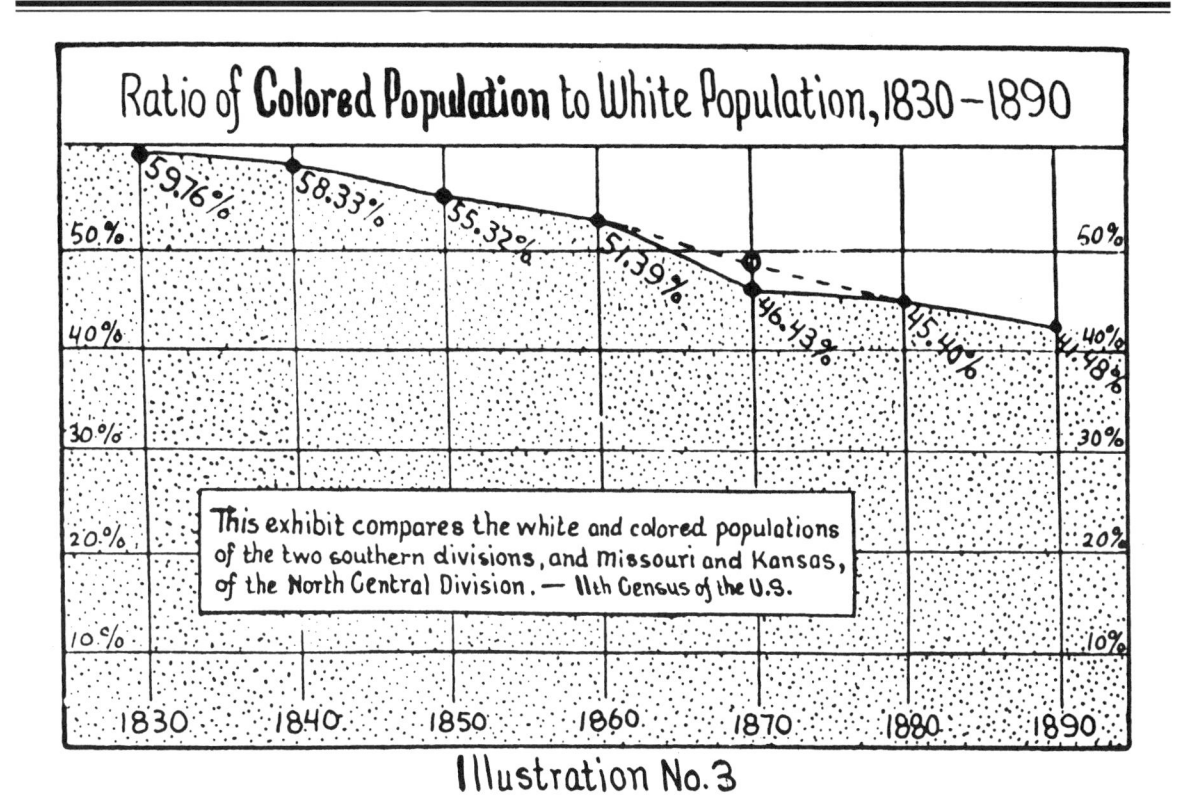

Ratio of Colored Population to White Population, 1830-1890

This exhibit compares the white and colored populations of the two southern divisions, and Missouri and Kansas, of the North Central Division. — 11th Census of the U.S.

Values: 59.76% (1830), 58.33% (1840), 55.32% (1850), 51.39% (1860), 46.43% (1870), 45.40% (1880), 41.48% (1890).

Illustration No. 3

Harper's Weekly, November 16, 1895, p. 1093.

THE PUBLIC SCHOOLS OF THE UNITED STATES

Fourth Paper.—Pupils.

HARPER'S WEEKLY
November 16, 1895, p. 1093

It is worth while to study the influence of women, as teachers, on the educational development of the country. It is also worth while to consider the remuneration of both male and female teachers in the various parts of the country, and to understand the attitude of the people of the various sections of the United States towards the public-school system, as evinced by their expenditure for its support. These subjects have been discussed in the previous papers of this series. An equally important question is, are as many persons reached by the instruction provided as should be?

In the study of food-supply it would be worth while to begin with an examination of the kinds of agricultural implements employed, and to follow with an inquiry as to their cost, but more important questions would be. What parts of the country are adapted to raising wheat? and, How much wheat is produced?...

Colored Population.—The increased school element of the South naturally raises the question as to whether this increase is proportionately or disproportionately divided between the white and colored population. Fortunately the increase of total population in the South is due almost wholly to the natural increase of the native population. Of all the multitude of foreigners that come annually to this country the South receives next to none. So true is this that the foreign-born population of the South is less than three per cent of the total, while in many of the Northern and Western States it ranges from twenty to forty per cent.

A study of the historical proportions of the white and colored populations of the South will therefore show whether the increase in the proportion of school population is due to the increase of the white or colored element of the population. That study is provided in illustration No. 3.

While this exhibit may surprise many readers, it simply reveals what careful students of population have for many years known to be the fact. In spite of the largely prevailing opinion that the colored people are increasing more rapidly than the whites, the facts prove that since 1830 they have increased less and less rapidly, and that, too, at a very uniform rate. The irregular rate indicated at 1870 has been proved to be due to faults of that census in enumerating the colored population of the Southern States. If, therefore, the census of 1870 had been correctly made, the dot for that date would have been higher up in the diagram, and the line of decrease would have been very uniform.

It seems impossible, therefore, to avoid the conclusion that the increase of the school element in the South is more largely apportioned among the white than among the colored population. The South, then, is naturally adapted to receive a larger proportionate benefit from a full application of the public-school system than any other part of the country because it has a larger school element. Not only so; the adaptation is steadily changing in favor of the South, so that each year is increasing the natural advantage possessed by the two Southern divisions, and that increasing advantage falls more largely to the white than to the colored population. This latter feature may, however, be of small importance, for reports of the progress of real intellectual development in the schools of the South show little if any difference between the attainments of the white and colored pupils. . . .

By F. W. Hewes

1896

With few exceptions, historians agree that the most momentous event of 1896 was the U.S. Supreme Court's reinforcement of the Jim Crow Movement. On May 18, the court upheld the concept of separate but equal facilities in the case of Plessy v. Ferguson, a dispute over transportation facilities in Louisiana. Distinguishing between political and social equality, the court decision ruled that states could pass laws to enforce "the customs and traditions of the people." Jim Crow laws, regulating discriminatory practices against African Americans from "cradle to grave," would remain sanctioned policy for more than fifty years. In a prophetic assertion, Justice John Harlan stated segregation laws fostered ideas of racial inferiority and helped increase violent attacks against African Americans and denied them their basic rights as American citizens.

The earliest Jim Crow law regulating travel on a railroad was passed by Tennessee in 1881. Ida B. Wells, African American educator and journalist, challenged the law in 1884 by refusing to sit in a smoking car designated for African Americans. Her suit against the Chesapeake and Ohio Railroad was successful at the lower court, but was overturned by the Tennessee Supreme Court. As of 1891, the majority of the southern states, following Tennessee's example, had "separate but equal" railroad legislation. Uniform application of the law in all of the southern states would not occur, however, until after 1896. States extended the concept after 1900 by segregating Pullman cars and waiting rooms. Segregation, on streetcars, in parks, in residential areas, in schools, in the work place, and in most places where whites and African Americans might meet outside of their homes, became the rule.

African Americans did not quietly accept the patterns of disfranchisement, segregation, and racial subordination spreading throughout the United

States. In addition to seeking legal remedy, other resistance strategies were employed. As early as 1894, African Americans in Georgia boycotted the Atlanta streetcars in an attempt to overthrow a recently passed segregation law; their success was noted and applauded even by Booker T. Washington, labelled an accomodationist after his 1895 speech at the International Cotton Exposition in Atlanta.

Another watershed event in 1896 was the collapse of the Populist Party in the South, ending efforts to unite black and white farmers. Prior to the decline of the party, there were last-ditch efforts to fuse Populists and Republicans. Historians August Meier and Elliott Rudwick assert that the fusion did not always include African Americans. Broadly speaking, they posit, the Populists and the Lily-white Republican faction, rather than Populists and the Black and Tan faction, joined forces. The Lilywhites were the white southern members of the Republican Party who wished to remove African Americans from key party positions. The Black and Tan Republican faction included African Americans and their white allies. Nevertheless, cooperation between the two parties in 1896 resulted in the election of Populists to most state and congressional offices in North Carolina, white Republicans to the offices of Governor and senator, and George White, an African American, to the U.S. House of Representatives. It was the inability of the Populists to influence the outcome of the 1896 presidential election that ultimately led to its demise.

Between 1896 and 1915, thirteen southern states legalized white primaries. Rather than nominate candidates for public office at party conventions, party members would nominate them through a special election. It was argued that the primary was a more democratic method of selecting candidates. Even so, it virtually eliminated African American participation in the political process. Because African Americans were barred from membership in the Democratic Party, the controlling party in the South, the primary guaranteed white voters would nominate white candidates to become the public officials. The impact of the white primaries was dramatically felt in Louisiana: of the 130,334 African Americans registered to vote in 1896, 5000 were eligible to vote in 1898, and only 1342 could vote in 1904.

Prior to the ruling, the consequences of the primaries were also evidenced by the sharp decline in the number of African American elected officials at the state and national levels. White (R-North Carolina) was elected to the U. S. Congress, but the number of African American males elected to the House of Representatives decreased from eight in 1875 to one in 1899; Oscar de Priest, (R-Illinois) was the next elected in 1928. After Blanche K. Bruce left the U.S. Senate in 1881, no African American would serve in that body until the 1966 election of Edward Brooke, (R-Massachusetts). Bolstered by the political and social reversals reminiscent of the pre-reconstruction era, the overt racist stance of

Governor James K. Vardarman of Mississippi was emulated throughout the South.

Turning inward again, African Americans initiated programs and activities to minimize the devastating legal reverberations. In July, African American women from various regions met in Washington, DC, and organized the National Association of Colored Women (NACW) with Mary Church Terrell as president. The year before, Terrell had gained national recognition because of her appointment as the first African American woman to the DC Board of Education. She would lead the NACW as it developed kindergartens, day care centers, mothers' clubs, and other self-help projects. The NACW membership also addressed key political issues of the day; suffrage and lynchings were given top priority.

In her role of president, Terrell became the spokesperson regarding gender issues. Her privileged position as a college-educated woman married to a attorney/educator did not preclude her understanding national and international issues facing African American working class women. Terrell knew the majority of African American women had to earn a wage and was disturbed when white immigrant women were hired for positions traditionally held by African American women.

At Atlanta University, W. E. B. DuBois inaugurated the Conference on Negro Problems. Held annually under his direction until 1914, the conference encouraged the study of African American life. DuBois' insistence that the problems facing African Americans be examined within a sociological framework added to the value of the published conference proceedings.

Also in 1896, Booker T. Washington convened the Fifth Tuskegee Negro Conference, with the goal, "to show the masses of Colored people how to lift themselves up in their industrial, educational, moral and religious life." George Washington Carver was hired that year to teach and conduct research at Tuskegee Institute. Much of his research would serve as the basis for agricultural reform in the rural South. By 1896, use of the conference to promote thrift, hard work, and community development among African Americans was prevalent in the South. Hampton Institute in Hampton, Virginia held its first conference in 1897. In 1899, 150 farmers' conferences, utilizing the Tuskegee model, were held. On the instructional and curriculum development levels, the line dividing African American educators in their thinking regarding the most appropriate ideology to undergird black education was forming.

Cynthia Neverdon-Morton
Coppin State College

FOR BLACKS AND WHITES
The Louisiana Law Providing Cars for the Races Sustained.

ATLANTA CONSTITUTION
May 19, 1896

Washington, May 18.—The supreme court of the United States today, in an opinion read by Justice Brown, sustained the constitutionality of the law of Louisiana, requiring the railroads of the state to provide separate cars for white and colored passengers. There was no interstate commerce feature in the case for the railroad upon which the incident occurred giving rise to the case. Plessy vs. Ferguson, the East Louisiana railroad, was and is operated wholly within the state.

The opinion states that by analogy to the laws of congress and of many of the states requiring the establishment of separate schools for children of the two races and other similar laws, the statute in question was within the competency of the Louisiana legislature, exercising the police power of the state, upholding the law was therefore affirmed.

Justice Harlan announced a very vigorous dissent, saying that he saw nothing but mischief in all such laws. In his view of the case no power in the land had the right to regulate the enjoyment of civil rights upon the basis of race. It would be just and reasonable and proper, he said, for states to pass laws requiring separate cars to be furnished for Catholics and Protestants or for descendants of those of the Teutonic race and those of the Latin race.

HEATED HOT
Supreme Court Decision is Denounced.
Colored League Indignant at Action on "Jim Crow Car" Law.
One is Teaching His Children to Speak Spanish.
"United States is no Place for Black Men."
"South Will Receive Pay for Slaves Freed by War."

BOSTON DAILY GLOBE
May 20, 1896

For about three-quarters of an hour, last evening, at the meeting of the Colored national league in the Charles st A. M. E. church, there was a hot debate.

It was over the recent decision of U S supreme court on the Louisiana separate car law, which decision was denounced as "infamous."

The evening had been set apart for a memorial service to the late Dr James T. Still, the first and only colored man to occupy a position on the Boston school board.

I. D. Barnett called the attention of the organization of the recent decision of the supreme court of the United States in regard to the separate car law of Louisiana by moving that this matter be referred to the executive committee and that the colored lawyers be called upon to write their opinions of it.

This motion brought George T. Downing to his feet, who said:

"That the way things seem to trend today; all appears to be against us. You younger people should become more jealous of your rights.

"The supreme court of the United States has decided that separate case against us. Out of the nine judges only one, a democrat at that, Judge Harlan, dared stand up and say that the decision was wrong, and that the state has no right to discriminate against a person on account of his race or religion or color.

"I want some of the younger men of the race to stand up and assert their rights. I want to call your attention to the fact that five of the nine judges are republicans, the other four are democrats, and all profess to be Christians, six of whom are of one church."

Rev W. H. Scott followed. "It is useless for a colored man to aspire to be anything in this country. I am now training my boys to speak Spanish, so that they can go to South America or some other country, where ability and not color is a test for advancement.

"The south is again getting the upper hand in this country, so that in less than 10 years the south will have so won the north and west around that she will receive, upon demand, $300 for every slave which she lost as the result of the last war, and so too for her benefit will the fourteenth and fifteenth amendments to the U S constitution be repealed."

Edwin G. Walker said: "If I had a boy or 40 children I would not send one from this country, but I would educate them to remain in America and fight it out.

"The great trouble is remedied not in sending your children out of America, but in preparing them to arraign any judge or man of either party who commits an outrage on the race.

"I belong to neither party. I am independent, and just as long as the colored people declare for the republicans, just so long will that party treat you as meanly as they have during the past 20 years.

"What has the republican party done for the race during the last five years, when colored people have been murdered and lynched in cold blood, and the platform of the party has been as silent as the tomb."

Rev S. C. Grice: "I believe after all that the democrats are truer to the republican party than the republicans are. The republican party is a wolf dressed in sheep's clothing, and acts when the time comes like a snake to the negro."

Ex Representative Robert T. Teamoh said: "I am a republican because I believe the party to be better than the democratic party. I believe that it has done more for our race than the democratic party. It was the members of the democratic party in those southern states that made these 'jim crow car' or separate coach or school laws possible."

Dr Samuel F. Courtney said: "I think, like the former speaker, that this is not a question of parties, but one of right. I believe that this is a question of personal liberty, and we should do all we can toward having our people all over the country more united."

Mr Downing said: "That man is not a fit man to represent the race at St Louis."

Clifford H. Plummer, Johnson Ramsay and others also spoke.

Following this came the exercises in memory of the late Dr James T. Still, M D. The chair was occupied by Pres W. O. Armstrong. Prayer was offered by Rev J. Francis Robinson. The oration was by Dr Wm. C. Lane, M D. Other addresses were made by Edwin G. Walker, R. T. Teamoh and Samuel F. Courtney, M D.

THE SUBJECT DISCUSSED AT THE ATLANTA UNIVERSITY

Professor Cummings, of Harvard University, Writes an Interesting Letter on the Subject.

ATLANTA CONSTITUTION
May 28, 1896, p. 2

The conference at the Atlanta university on the investigation of the city problem as it relates to the negro race, and the mortality rate among the negroes in cities and its causes, held its first session at Atlanta university Tuesday. The conference was called to order by President Bumstead, of the university, who spoke upon the value of such investigation and the necessity for patient and painstaking work.

The plan of the work was outlined by Mr. George G. Bradford, of Boston, who said:

"In 1860 only 4.2 per cent of the colored population of the United States was living in the cities. By 1880 the number had increased to 8.4 per cent of the whole colored population, while by 1890, it had increased to 12 per cent. This process of concentration in the cities has been relatively much more rapid among the colored people than among the whites; the figures for whites during the same period being 10.9 per cent in 1860, and 15 per cent in 1890, or an increase of 4.8 per cent, as against 7.8 per cent for colored.

"How rapid this increase in the city population really is may be illustrated by the growth of the colored population in the city of Atlanta, where the increase has been at a rate three times as great as for the country at large.

"For the decade, 1870 to 1880, the increase was 64 per cent; from 1880 to 1890, 72 per cent, while the average increase of colored population for the whole country during the same period was only 20 per cent in each decade.

"In taking up the study of city problems we feel that we cannot do better than begin by an inquiry into the physical and moral condition of the people. It is a line of inquiry which has not been previously pursued on any systematic or extensive scale. Up to the present time students and investigators of the problems confronting the colored race have confined themselves principally to the study of problems of country life, or directed their attention toward economic or educational questions. Of the physical condition of the negro under the trying conditions of city life, we have little accurate information.

"Many of the southern cities have not had, until within a few years, any city boards of health, and as a result there has not been hitherto sufficient official data from which any broad generalizations could be drawn, and such data as have been obtainable have not yet been brought together into available form. We have, however, some few data that are sufficient to prove the necessity of the inquiry upon which we have begun.

"The death rate among the whites in five of our largest cities ranged from 17 to 22 per thousand, and among the colored, from 32 to 37 per thousand, or from 63 to 106 per cent greater among the colored than among the whites. In the city of St. Louis the death rate among the colored was more than twice that among the whites.

"The significance of this excessive mortality can be appreciated only when we come to study the causes of destitution in our great cities.

"There are some very valuable figures on this point in a comprehensive treatise by Amos G. Warner, Ph. D., entitled "American Christians." In his analysis of causes of destitution among the colored people of Baltimore, we find 38 per cent of all cases of destitution are due to sickness. We have no official figures on this point, for Washington or any other southern city. But a similar report for New York shows 37 per cent from sickness and for Boston 45.6 per cent. These are among cases of destitution of which there is official record. The result might be different, could we obtain the facts for all cases.

"Among the whites, also, sickness is one of the chief causes of destitution, but the percentage is much smaller, averaging about 20 per cent, while the average among the colored people is 39 per cent, or nearly twice as great."

The following letter from Professor Edward Cummings, of Harvard college, was read:

"Permit me to express my interest in the contributions which graduates of Atlanta university are making to the vital statistics of city life. Such inquiries are everywhere commanding the attention of sociological students: and it is a gratfying tribute to the spirit of your university that her students are so prompt in entering this field. It is in cities that the great problems of life and labor press most earnestly for solution; and anything which throws light upon the commonplace but obscure conditions of every day life must help us better to understand the progress which has been made and the evils which have still to be overcome. The home is the unit of our civilization: it is the nursery of social virtues, the source from which must flow those regenerating moral influences which help society at large to realize that ideal of fraternity which has always been the goal of civilization. Whatever strikes at the integrity of the home strikes at the integrity of our civilization.

"Whatever ministers to the health and beauty of family life tends to sweeten the fountains of our social life. Sound economic and sanitary conditions are the only environment in which social virtues may thrive. Industry, economy, cleanliness, plain living and high thinking are the source no less of individual happiness than of social welfare.

"It is specially gratifying to observe the promptness with which the recent call for information has been met in the city of Atlanta. If the same spirit of enterprise and co-operation can be relied upon to carry on the work in other places there is every reason to hope that these investigations may prove not only a valuable contribution to our knwledge of the progress which has been made, but an incentive and a guide to future effort.

"All who are interested in our common welfare will await with interest the results of these investigations by men and women who are so well acquainted with the conditions and are so well equipped for the work I shall consider it a privilege to be of assistance in any way that I can. Very truly yours, Edward Cummings."

Professor Frank S. Churchill, of Chicago, then read a most interesting paper on infant mortality and the meeting adjourned until tonight, when the following papers will be read:

"Causes of Mortality"—

"Ignorance as a Cause"—Professor W. B., Matthews.

"Intemperance as a Cause"—Georgia S. King.

"Poverty as a Cause"—Rosa M. Bass.

"Negligence as a Cause"—Henry R. Butler, M. D.

"General Conditions"—Lucy Laney.

"Infant Mortality"—Professor F. S. Churchill, M. D., Chicago.

Report of committee on resolutions.

NEW ORLEANS

HARPER'S WEEKLY
July 25, 1896, p. 727

The negroes of New Orleans, who number 75,000, or about one-fourth of the whole population, have filed petitions with the several railroads to provide them with some park or picnic-grounds where they can go of an evening. The public parks are legally open to them, but the race prejudice is so strong that very few venture to go there. For the past few years Spanish Fort, where General Jackson entered New Orleans, has been their chief resort; but this summer it was thrown open to the whites, and consequently closed to colored people. "Little Woods" has followed suit, and the negroes have now nowhere to go. They point out that even in slavery days they had their special park set apart for them by the whites, and which still bears the name of "Congo Square." It has been rechristened Place d'Armes and Beauregard Place, but all in vain. It is still "Congo Square," in spite of all the city ordinances, and the fact that the Congo negroes were crowded out a half-century ago. One of the railroads and some leading negroes are now looking for a quiet, secluded spot that can be used as a colored Coney Island.

N.W.

THIS BUSY WORLD

HARPER'S WEEKLY
September 8, 1896, p. 942

The State of Kansas is fast becoming the most notable curiosity in Uncle Sam's museum. In Leavenworth, in that State, on September 12, Lieutenant Charles Young, of the Ninth Cavalry, a colored officer, and the only one at present in the service, was refused admission at the hotels, and had to go on to Kansas City and spend the night in the State of Missouri. Lieutenant Young was ordered to Leavenworth to be examined for promotion. The Secretary of War might properly consider whether it is not inexpedient to have examining boards sit in cities where colored officers are excluded from hotels.

NEW ORLEANS

HARPER'S WEEKLY
September 8, 1896, p. 943

Up in Alabama, not far from Birmingham, is a negro colony unique in the South. Its post-office address is Vance, and the colony is settled on the former plantation of Marion Banks, a slave-owner of old days, who left his land to his negroes when he died. There were eleven heads of families among the negroes at the time, and each got a farm of 209 acres, but they have preferred to live together in community, working together and helping each other when it was necessary. The settlement has been a prosperous one, and is now self-supporting, and has over 300 members, nearly all of the pure African type. But what the negroes want more than anything else are better school facilities, for they are beginning to appreciate the fact that only with education can they "keep up with the procession"; and they are now going to work to add the necessary school, and thus secure educational advance as well as material prosperity. There are dozens of negro settlements in the South, but this is perhaps the only one which has been thoroughly successful without the advice, assistance, or guidance of white men, and where the principle of co-operation, believed to be so difficult in the negro, has been carried out thoroughly.

NEW ORLEANS

HARPER'S WEEKLY
November 14, 1896, p. 1119

There has perhaps been no more enthusiastic gathering of colored people in New Orleans than that held on the last day of October to inaugurate the Phyllis Wheatley Training-School for Nurses. The school is for the education of colored girls as hospital and professional nurses, and the enthusiasm of the colored people over its success was largely due to the fact that they themselves organized the charity without the usual assistance from their white brethren. All the negro charities in the South have been organized and established by the whites, and the progress of the colored race was never better illustrated than in its organization of this school. It is connected with the medical department of the New Orleans University, a college for colored youth supported by the Methodist Church. The college is of recent origin, and has already done good work in instilling some ideas of sanitation in the minds of the negroes; and, in connection with the Phyllis Wheatley School, it is expected largely to improve the sanitary condition of the negroes and reduce the death rate among them, which, in New Orleans, is nearly twice as great as that of the whites.

ADVENTURES OF AMERICAN ARMY AND NAVY OFFICERS

IV.—A Sioux Indian Episode.

HARPER'S WEEKLY
December 26, 1896, pp. 1273–75

While seated in my office at Fort McKinney, Wyoming, on the 19th day of November, 1890, the following telegram was handed me:

"Move out as soon as possible with the troop of cavalry at your post; bring all the wagon transportation you can spare, pack-mules and saddles; extra ammunition and rations will be provided when you reach the railroad.—By order of the Department Commander."

What possible cause for this interruption of our peace and happiness, and the breaking up of our homes, settled for the long and usually trying winter, and the leaving of our families could not be imagined. A distance of nearly 200 miles from the railroad, uncertain mail and telegraphic facilities, or at least much delayed news, kept us ignorant of outside troubles.

Preparations were at once made, and the following day I marched out of Fort McKinney with Troop D, Ninth Cavalry, Captain Loud, Lieutenants Powell and Benton. Turning the point of a hill, after crossing the beautiful Clear Fork of the Powder River, the post and our families were soon lost to sight. Little did we suspect at the time that we were never to return to Fort McKinney as a station. This is a peculiarity of army life—to leave, on twenty-four hours' notice, a place possibly never to be seen again, or maybe only when, after a lapse of years, a similar notice may as suddenly return you to your old station. Nearing the railroad, we began to hear all sorts of rumors of the Indians being on the warpath—the murder of settlers, the starting of a party of Indians in the direction of Fort McKinney, so as to obtain a refuge in the Big Horn Mountains; these and other reports found us mentally prepared for a winter's campaign, so that on reaching the railroad we were not surprised to find cars in readiness to carry us to Rushville, the nearest point to the reported place of trouble—Pine Ridge Agency, South Dakota.

We arrived at Rushville at night, and immediately detrained, and started early the following morning on our march to the agency, where we arrived early in the afternoon of the same day. Contrary to expectations, we met with no hostile Indians or resistance.

"REVEILLE FOUND THESE JOLLY FELLOWS STILL LAUGHING."

Harper's Weekly, December 26, 1896, p. 1274.

We found all the troops camped close about the agency, and made our own camp in the bottom, about half a mile away, on White River. The next day we were joined by Troops K, F, and I, with Captains Wright and Stedman, and Lieutenants Guilfoyle, McAnaney, and Perry, Dr. Keane being the medical officer; the four troops constituting the Ninth Cavalry squadron. Our time was fully occupied in daily drills and in getting our pack-mule train in order, for upon this we depended for rations and forage when absent from our wagons.—Rumors came often to us that the Indians were keeping up their ghost-shirt, or Messiah dances; that they considered these shirts; when worn, to be impervious to the bullet; of their desire to clean out the whites and to occupy the promised land; of their having occupied an impregnable position in the Bad Lands, so fortified and difficult of approach that an attempt to dislodge them would result in the annihilation of the whole army—these and many other rumors gave the Indian, who is a great braggart, an abundant opportunity to air himself, and left us plenty of leisure to prepare ourselves for our future state.

The afternoon of December 24 an order reached us to move out at once to head off Big Foot—an Indian chief—and his band, who had escaped from our troops, and, it was supposed, would join the hostiles in the Bad Lands; and this we were to prevent. So at 2 P.M. the "general" sounded—a signal which meant to strike our tents and pack our mules and wagons. The latter were to follow us, escorted by one troop. Soon "boots and saddles" rang out, when horses were saddled, line formed, and then, with three troops and with two Hotchkiss guns of the First Artillery, under Lieutenant Hayden, we commenced our march of fifty miles, expecting to reach our goal before daylight. Only a half-hundred miles! It does not seem far on paper, but on the back of a trotting horse on a cold winter's night it is not to be laughed at. On we dashed through the agency, buoyed by the hearty cheers and "A merry Christmas!" given us by the comrades we were leaving behind to revel by the camp-fires, while we rode on by moonlight to meet the foe. Every heart went out in sympathy with us, every one waved his hat and cheered as we rode out on the plains—perhaps to glory, perchance to death. Proud and gallant the troopers looked, more as if going on parade than like men riding forth, it might be, to meet a soldier's death. It made one's heart beat quicker, and brought to mind the words—

> To sound of trumpet and heart-beat
> The squadron marches by;
> There is color in their cheeks,
> There is courage in their eyes;
> Yet to the sound of trumpet and heart-beat
> In a moment they may die.

Little did we think at that time that within less than one week some of the gallant men we were leaving behind would be killed by the very band we sought, while we should be saved. After riding for two hours, alternately at a trot and a walk, a short halt was made for the men to make coffee and to give the horses a feed. Then the march was continued, and on and on we sped, that cold, moonlight Christmas eve. The words, "Peace on earth, good will toward men," rang in our ears as we pushed on with hostile intent toward the red man. The night was beautiful with the clear moon, but so cold that water froze solid in our canteens, notwithstanding the constant shaking. Crossing a narrow bridge, a pack-mule was shoved off by its crowded comrades, and falling on the ice of Wounded Knee Creek, broke a hole, smashed a box of hardtack, but gathered himself together, and ambled off, smiling serenely at having received no damage to his body.

Here we passed abandoned ranches, the owners driven off by threats or fear of the Indians; here we were at the scene of the ghost-dances, where the Indians were taught that the Messiah would appear, rid the country of the white man, and bring plenty to the Indian; that the common cotton ghost shirt worn was bullet-proof; while in every other possible way the medicine men worked upon the fanaticism of the deluded creature. We saw at a distance stray cattle, whose spectral appearance almost led us to believe in ghosts, if not in ghost shirts, and an examination was made to see whether or not they were Indians waiting on their ponies to attack us.

To cross White River we had to take a plunge from solid ice to mid-channel water, and then rode to Cottonwood Springs, at the base of the position of the Indians in the Bad Lands. We reached this place at 4 A.M., and threw ourselves on the ground for rest, knowing that to obtain wood and water for breakfast Christmas morning we should have to march eight miles. And this is the way the Ninth Cavalry squadron spent Christmas eve of 1890. Christmas day we proceeded to Harney Springs, a place where I had encamped during my winter's march of seventeen years before, and finding wood and water, we made our breakfast. We scouted the country for several days to find Big Foot's trail, but he had passed east of us. We discovered the tepees of the Indians, but finding no trace of the former occupants, we returned to White River. The next day we made a reconnoissance of the Bad Lands. Instead of narrow trails or defiles of approach accessible only in single file, where we could have been shot down by the Indians at will, we found a broad open divide; instead of impregnable earth-works, only a ridiculously weak pile of earth existed, here and there, filled in by a dead horse. The Indians occupied a narrow position, from which they could easily have been shelled. They had taken one military precaution, however, that of preparing for retreat, and had cut openings in the bluffs, which on their side were abrupt, so that they could slide down and escape. The reality, as compared with the reports of Indian guides and interpreters, was greatly exaggerated, all brag and bluster, and but for the existence of high hills, little more than a "bluff" on the part of the Indians. I had spent many a moment, when I supposed we should have to make an assault on this position, thinking how it could be done, and worrying over the probable loss of life, such perhaps as had occurred in the Lava Beds when troops were opposed to the Modoc Indians; but when I saw this burlesque I could only laugh, and I made up my mind that it was best not to cross Fox River till it was reached.

On returning to camp that night, while the weary but light-hearted troopers were singing negro melodies after supper, a scout who rode a pony steaming and flecked with foam dashed into camp, bringing information of the Seventh Cavalry's fight at Wounded Knee, of the death of Captain Wallace, of the flight of 5000 Ogalala Sioux, and of the probable chance of an attack on the agency. For the second time that day trumpets rang out "boots and saddles." There was not a laggard; tents went down like a flash; wagons were packed; every man sprang to his horse, and in less than forty minutes after the news had been received we were off for Pine Ridge, nearly fifty miles away.

It was now ten o'clock at night; the wind was cold, and as it howled out of the canyons and swept over the valley, it carried with it the crystals that had fallen the day before. There was no moon; the night was inky dark, even the patches of snow which lay here and there on the ground gave no relief to the eye. Muffled in their shaggy buffalo overcoats, and hooded by the grotesque fur caps used by our Western troops, the negro troopers looked like meaningless bundles that had been tied in some way to the backs of their horses. Through canyons whose black walls seemed to be compressing all the darkness of the night, over buttes whose crests were crowned with snow, and across the rickety bridges which span Wounded Knee and Porcupine creeks the command sped at a pace which would have killed

A PLANTATION CHRISTMAS AS 'FO E

"DE WAR."—Drawn by W. T. Smedley.

A DIFFICULT CHRISTMAS PROBLEM.
"Tek you' choice, sah, fo' fifty cents."

Harper's Weekly, December 26, 1896, p. 1288.

horses that had not been hardened by practice, as ours had been. Nothing could be heard but the clatter of hoofs and the clanking of the carbines as they chafed the metallic trappings of the saddle; silence had been ordered, and the usual laugh and melodious songs of the darky troopers were not ours to beguile the march. Now and then came the reverberation of the mule-whacker's whip as he threw his energy and muscle into a desperate effort to keep the wagon train near us; figures could be seen flitting across the road and on the bluffs, and we knew not at what moment we might be fired upon; accordingly, the effort was made to reach the agency before daybreak, in the hope that darkness and the Indians' superstition would protect us from attack in the mean time.

As we neared the agency the country became more open, hills easy of occupation commanding the road if the occasion required. So, in order to enable us to get our horses into camp, and the riders and saddles off our weary animals, we left the wagon train a short distance in the rear, guarded by one troop, and the column moved on, entering the agency at daybreak, men and horses much tired after our long day and night ride of about one hundred miles. Reaching our old camp, we all sought rest at once by throwing ourselves on the ground; but we had been resting only a short time when Corporal Wilson, of the wagon-train guard, who had volunteered at the risk of his life to reach us, rode rapidly into camp, and reported that the train beyond the agency was surrounded, and one man already killed. In a moment the command, many not waiting to saddle, galloped to the front and quickly occupied the hills, whereupon the Indians retreated, and the train moved in.

Scarcely had we returned to camp, when orders were received to proceed to the Mission, the smoke from whose buildings indicated Indian depredations. By request, owing to tired men and horses, we were allowed to rest longer, the Seventh Cavalry going out. Later we went to the Mission as rapidly as our wearied horses could carry us, and after accomplishing the purpose for which we had been urgently called, returned, reaching our camp about dusk. We had marched some 108 miles in 22 hours, and although one horse had died, there was not a sore-backed horse in the outfit; men and horses were fatigued, but all were in good condition. The following day, December 31, we remained in camp, with a howling snow-storm prevailing, and amid these gloomy surroundings the Seventh Cavalry buried its dead. January 1, again under orders, we left the agency to combine with other troops in forming a cordon to drive back the hostiles who had fled from the agency, or to follow them if depredations upon the settlements were commenced. Finally the Indians were forced back to the agency, not, however, until Lieutenant Casey had been killed by them, nor before they saw that resistance was useless, and that the ghost shirt was not impervious to the bullet.

Preparations were then made for a final review of troops. We were encamped in line of battle, extending nearly three miles, which made a great impression upon the Indians, many of whom looked on from a distance in amazement and distrust, fearing that our arrangements might mean an attack instead of a peaceful march in review previous to the return of the troops to their posts.

The morning broke with a pelting flurry of a combination of snow and dirt. A veil of dark clouds hung suspended above the hills, which surrounded the camp-ground like a coliseum, and a piercing breeze swept from the north, making the contrast with the previous Messiah weather we had been having anything but agreeable. We were fearful that a Dakota blizzard might strike us, meaning death to our animals in their exposed position, and probably serious results to the soldiers. Accordingly, we all were anxious that the review ordered by General Miles be not postponed.

General Miles, after passing along the line, took position opposite the centre, so that the troops, all of whom had participated in or rendered service during the Pine Ridge troubles, might march past him. They moved in column of companies, troops, or platoons, and by infantry, cavalry, and artillery corps, respectively, and in order as above. General Brooke and staff headed the column, followed by the band of the First United States Infantry. When opposite General Miles, the band wheeled out of the column, playing, or attempting to do so, during the passage of the troops—a difficult matter, as the fierce wind almost prevented any musical notes being made or heard.

Then came 100 mounted Ogalala Indian scouts, commanded by Lieutenant Taylor, of the Ninth Cavalry. Their precision of march was noticeable, and in various ways they had rendered valuable service during the campaign. General Wheaton, as a brigade commander, followed with his staff. The first regiment of his command was the First United States Infantry, under Colonel Shafter, whose martial appearance and indifference to the cold—the men not wearing overcoats—suggested blood warmed by their California station. Then came the Second United States Infantry, under Major Butler. Their marching showed service, and they had recently lost Captain Mills, whose sad death in his tent, as reveille sounded, was fresh in the minds of his comrades. Next followed six companies of the Seventeenth Infantry, under Captain Van Horne, who marched well; then two companies of the Eighth Infantry with a Gatling gun, under Captain Whitney; then Captain Capron with his light battery of the First United States Artillery, which had distinguished itself at the battle of Wounded Knee Creek during the fight with Big Foot's band on December 29, and afterwards at the Mission. Next in order came General Carr, commanding the cavalry brigade, followed by the historic and veteran Sixth Cavalry, and the Forth Leavenworth cavalry squadron, composed of one troop from each of the First, Fifth, and Eighth regiments of cavalry, followed by a Hotchkiss battery; then came the scowling black faces of the Ninth Cavalry Squadron, with three other troops, A, C, and G, of the same regiment, who passed at "advance carbine," and whose gallant and hard service is of official record; then the Seventh United States Cavalry, whose fine appearance attracted attention, and whose losses in action were attested by the vacancies in the ranks made by the gallant men killed or wounded. The ambulance, wagon, and pack-mule trains brought up the rear, making a total in passing of about 3000 men and 3700 animals.

The column was pathetically grand, with its bullet-pierced gun-carriages, its tattered guidons, and its long array of cavalry, artillery, and infantry, facing a pitiless storm which caused the curious Indians who witnessed it to seek protection under every cover and butte which could be found. It was the grandest demonstration that had ever been seen by the army in the West, and when the soldiers had gone to their tents the sullen and suspicious Brules could be seen going to their tepees in ill-disguised bad humor. The forces disbanded in a few days, the First Infantry remaining at the agency for one month, while the Ninth Cavalry squadron was ordered to select a comfortable winter camp, and to remain till spring.

Our comfortable camp was located on a small stream, under cover of a high bluff, which, like a snow fence, secured and held the drifting snow from the plain above, and caused a bank of snow twenty feet high and ten thick to form beyond and near our camp. The men had stoves in their tents, but their beds were on the ground; the officers were a little better off. The animals had canvas-blanket covers. But with all this there was suffering in various ways. There were damp, cold nights; many had colds and pneumonia; there were few comforts. But yet our soldiers did not complain. On the contrary, it would have been difficult to find a more truly happy lot than those colored troopers.

Each of the big Sibley tents held fifteen or sixteen men, and when supper was over (bread and coffee, and sometimes a little bacon), these little communities settled down to have a good time. Song and story, with an occasional jig or a selection on the mouth-organ or the banjo, with the hearty laugh of the darky, occupied the night hours till "taps" sounded for bed; and the reveille, or awakening, seemed to find these jolly fellows still laughing. The Indians seem to hold the darky in reverence, if not awe. The doctrine of the Messiah religion is that all the whites are to be cleaned off the earth—and this leaves the negro. The Indians have a superstition that the bullet cannot kill the darky; but this, as with the ghost-shirt "not kill" theory, had been dispelled by actual experience.

The negro is not easy to scalp—I have never heard of one being scalped, their wool not giving so good a hold as the hair of the white man—and the theory is that only those who are scalped are kept from the "happy hunting - grounds," where the fighting unfinished on earth is continued. It is certain that the treatment of the black by the Indian is different from that given to the white, and when thrown together the red man seems to hold the black in greater respect. I recall an instance in my youth, when a band of Indians attacked a party of whites, killing the men and children, but keeping a white woman and a colored woman nurse. The two women were obliged to change clothes, showing the greater respect for the black, who was treated then and afterward with consideration, while the white woman was killed when on the eve of recapture by our troops who had pursued the Indians.

The colored troops make excellent soldiers; in garrison they are clean and self-respecting, and proud of their uniform; in the field patient and cheerful under hardships or deprivations, never growling nor discontented, doing what is required of them without a murmur. Arriving in camp after hours in the rain or cold, they will sing and be happy; an enforced reduction of rations is received with good humor. The peculiar owl-like character of the negro, who apparently does not need so much sleep at night as the white man, makes him a good and vigilant sentinel.

If properly led will fight well; otherwise, owing to his habit of dependence upon a superior, he is more liable to stampede than the Caucasian; nor has he, as with the white, except in exceptional cases, the same individuality or self-dependence—he goes rather in a crowd, and you seldom see a negro himself. He is generous, to a fault, and has but little regard for the care of United States property, for which neglect he pays; but in this respect he is much improved over former years. He is like a child, and has to be looked after by his officers; but will repay such interest by a devoted following and implicit obedience. It would not be safe to suggest to some of these black troopers your desire that one of their comrades, whose conduct had not met with approval, should be hung before daylight, for it would very likely be an accomplished fact. Drunkenness is not one of his vices—it is seldom you see one under the influence of liquor; his loyalty to the flag is unquestioned, and the desertion of one is almost unknown.

The above are some of the virtues of the black trooper, all necessary attributes of a good soldier. Card-playing—and he is an inveterate gambler, as is also the Indian—is one of his vices, if such it may be called. His defective education leads him to indulge in it largely as a means of whiling away the time.

Our service with such men made the disagreeable camp surroundings endurable, even pleasant, and imparted to the white officers a more contended feeling, or at least an acceptance of the situation in a more equable manner than would otherwise have been the case.

Spring came, and with it our orders to march to Fort Robinson, a station where I had been seventeen years before, when on my winter's march to the Black Hills. I was now to return to it under very different circumstances. Leaving our winter camp, and marching through deep snows, we made the town of Chadron, on the railroad, the first day, our men sleeping in a building loaned by the citizens. The second day we marched nearly forty miles through deeper snows up to the girths of the saddles, in drifts much deeper, and, as the snow began to melt, through lakes of slush and bog, many of the men and animals becoming snow-blind. As the retreat gun fired, with the band playing a welcome, we entered Fort Robinson, thus ending the duties of the Ninth Cavalry squadron in the Pine Ridge Sioux Indian campaign.

By Brevet Brigadier-General Guy V. Henry, U.S.A.—Illustrated By R. F. Zogbaum.

1897

The writings of noted historian Benjamin Quarles remind us that African Americans often viewed their participation in the military history of the U.S. as a way not only to assist their country but also to prove that they were deserving of full citizenship rights. Symbolic of their efforts is the monumental frieze on the Boston Commons of Robert Gould Shaw and the men of the Fifty-fourth Massachusetts Infantry. Soon after President Abraham Lincoln issued the Emancipation Proclamation in 1863, the governor of Massachusetts authorized the formation of the Fifty-fourth Massachusetts Colored Volunteer Infantry Regiment. The U.S. War Department established a Bureau of Colored Troops in May 1863 to oversee the recruitment and structuring of black regiments. In addition to the Fifty-fourth, three other volunteer regiments were quickly mustered, all from New York. At the end of the war in April 1865, there were 166 black regiments: 145 infantry; seven cavalry; twelve heavy artillery; one light artillery; and one engineer.

The black units fought in more than 250 engagements, earning distinction at Hudson and Millekins Bend in Louisiana; Fort Wagner, South Carolina; and at the Crater near Petersburg, Virginia. African Americans suffered heavy casualties during the two years they fought—over 37,000, or 25 per cent of those who served in combat, died by 1865. Originally, there was no intent to commemorate the participation of African Americans in the Civil War. However, when it was decided to honor Col. Shaw, white commander of the Fifty-fourth, his compassion and respect for the black men he led was noted. Thus, the concept for a memorial statue of Shaw was expanded to include other officers and the men of the Fifty-fourth, though the African Americans on the frieze remained nameless. Even Sgt. William H. Carney who, while dying, uttered the words, "The old flag never touched the ground, boys!," words *which became the rallying cry for thousands of other black troops, was not depicted on the statue.*

Lincoln wrote, "I was opposed on nearly every side when I first favored the raising of colored regiments, but they have proved their efficiency." Opposition would surface again and again as the nation, in later years, moved toward war. At times, military exigencies necessitated the inclusion of African Americans in the military, but widespread resistance to their utilization as officers remained. The U.S. Military Academy at West Point, New York, and the U.S. Naval Academy at Annapolis, Maryland, were particularly reluctant to train black officers. Early graduates from West Point were Henry O. Flipper in 1877, and Charles Young in 1889. Although a few African Americans were admitted after 1931, in 1936, Lt. Benjamin O. Davis, Jr. was the first African American to graduate from the military academy in the twentieth century. In his autobiography, Benjamin O. Davis, Jr: American, *Davis writes of the efforts by his fellow cadets to discredit him and force his dismissal from the academy. As at West Point, few black men were admitted to the Naval Academy. The Naval Academy commissioned its first black graduate, Ensign Wesley R. Brown of Washington, DC, in June 1949.*

The belief that African Americans were incapable of leadership was conveyed in many ways to the general society. Caricatures and editorial cartoons illustrated, even for the illiterate white American, the notion that African Americans were infantile, ignorant, and deservingly the subjects of ridicule and amusement. The use of blackened faces, distorted features, and dialect language created powerfully negative images of African Americans.

Noted black intellectuals of the period believed that the behavior and lack of education on the part of some African Americans contributed to the perpetuation of these negative stereotypes. To combat the images and model the desired appropriate deportment, W. E. B. DuBois and Howard University professor Kelly Miller, among others, founded the American Negro Academy on March 5, 1897. The national organization included in its membership many of the noted scholars of the era and those labelled the elite of the black populace. The larger goal of the Academy was to effect change by molding "the opinions of the crude masses." The members published papers, collected materials relating to the black experience, and lobbied for the creation of research centers and repositories that would focus on aspects of the black diaspora. The members of the academy met annually for thirty-one years exchanging ideas, developing initiatives to encourage promising black youth, and at times, formulating protest strategies. Robert Adger, who was also concerned about the collection and preservation of records relating to the black experience, founded the Afro-American Historical Society in Philadelphia, Pennsylvania, in the same year.

White southerners in particular feared the unifying and elevating potential of black educational institutions and the black church. Each year during the decade of the 1890s, new colleges and universities were founded, or existing colleges and universities expanded their curricula to reflect the changing needs and aspirations of African Americans. In 1897, Elizabeth Evelyn Wright, aided by Jessie Dorsey, established the Denmark Industrial School in Denmark, South Carolina, later renamed Voorhees Industrial School and then Voorhees College.

Spelman Seminary, with an all-female student body, serves as an excellent example of those institutions redefining their mission. In 1897, Spelman, founded in 1888 in Atlanta, Georgia, opened a college department with courses offered on the campus of the Atlanta Baptist College (later Morehouse College).

Anna Julia Cooper and other educated black women were encouraged by the expansion of curriculum offerings for women. Many educational institutions provided specialized training for women in fields designated most appropriate for them, such as nurse's training and teacher education. The Cannon Hospital and Training School for Nurses (later McClennan-Banks Hospital) was started by leading black citizens in South Carolina, including Lucy Hughes Brown the first black woman physician in the state.

Langston University in Langston, Oklahoma, had a strong teacher education component as reflected in its original name, The Colored and Normal University. The name was changed in honor of John Mercer Langston, soldier, educator, diplomat, U.S. Congressman, and great uncle of Harlem Renaissance poet and author Langston Hughes. Prior to his death in November 1897, Langston had achieved many distinctions including the fact that he was the first African American to win an elective political office in the U.S.— clerk of Brownhelm Township in Lorain County, Ohio. Representing Virginia from 1889 to 1891, Langston was one of the last African Americans elected to the U.S. Congress in the nineteenth century. Before his tenure in Congress, he served as the president of the Virginia Normal and Collegiate Institute from 1885 to 1888.

Cynthia Neverdon-Morton
Coppin State College

THIS BUSY WORLD

HARPER'S WEEKLY
May 1, 1897, p. 434

Congressman Shattue, of Ohio, has appointed D. J. Bundy, a colored lad, to a cadetship at the Naval Academy. There have been sighs and expressions of displeasure at the appointment. The Congressman is quoted as saying that it had been intimated to him that if the colored cadet was entered at Annapolis the other cadets would resign, but that he had replied: "Let them resign. The boy earned his appointment fairly, and I'm going to see that he goes to Annapolis and receives fair treatment if it is in my power to do so." It seems that young Bundy did earn his appointment fairly, since he won it in a competition. Bundy himself has been quoted as saying that he feared nothing at Annapolis but physical violence. The examinations he thinks he will be equal to. It ought to be and doubtless is matter of course that the colored cadet will receive perfectly just treatment at Annapolis from instructors and cadets. It seems to be pretty hard work for any lad to go through the Naval Academy. Even if young Bundy is equal to the intellectual labor of it, it will be a greater strain on him than on a white boy, because he will inevitably have to sustain a certain amount of social isolation, which will be a tax on his endurance. He is not likely to be happy under it, and if he bears it and graduates, it will indicate that he is an exceptionally hardy person, or possibly that he is a lad of unusually strong character. If he goes to Annapolis he ought certainly to have just as fair a chance as can be given him, and no doubt he will.

Still, the expediency of sending colored boys either to Annapolis or to West Point seems very questionable. All army and navy officers and all cadets at the army and navy academies live in theory, and to a very large extent in practice, on terms of social equality. But white people and black people do not live on terms of social equality in this country. They enjoy equal political rights, and to some extent equal social rights, but they do not enjoy equal social consideration. Bundy's comrades at Annapolis will not consider him their social equal, and will not treat him as such. They will probably let him alone, and if they do better by him than that it will be because they have kind hearts. If he graduates he will not be welcomed by white officers into the service. Is it wise, then, to start a colored lad in a profession where his preparation must necessarily be painful, and in the practice of which, after he has learned it, he will have peculiar obstacles and embarrassments to contend with? General Shattuc has thought it his duty to do this for young Bundy, but he has not made it clear that his action is either kind or wise. He sends to the academy a lad who at best will have a hard and lonely time there, and who, if he graduates, will be an embarrassment to the service.

* * * * * * *

A paper called *Dixie*, which is published in Atlanta, Georgia, says that 30,000 negroes have been graduated, at a cost of one hundred million dollars, from colleges for negroes which are supported by Northern money in the South. It also says that there are many thrifty, prosperous negroes everywhere in the South who are doing well; but it declares that very few of these 30,000 college graduates are to be found among them. It says the college graduates find it very hard to make a living, because in trade and in the professions for which higher education might be supposed to fit them they have to contend with race prejudice and to compete with educated white people. It finds that they do not succeed (except in rare cases) as lawyers or doctors, and it thinks it would be "an unspeakable boon" for the Southern negroes if the money that supports colleges for them were devoted to the establishment of industrial training-schools in which they might learn to work to advantage at industries in which they would have a fair chance.

Dixie may be prejudiced, and very possibly it under-rates the good that the colleges do, but it speaks very positively, and assumes to know whereof it speaks, and its opinions seem, on the face of them, to be pretty sensible. To fit negroes for professions in which they will surely be greatly handicapped by their color may be excusable on grounds of sentiment, but it certainly seems to lack practical justification. There are excellent chances for colored men in this country, but they are not as yet to be found in the army or navy, and only to a very limited extent in the professions of law and medicine.

E. S. Martin

THE SHAW MEMORIAL

HARPER'S WEEKLY
May 29, 1897, p. 546

One fine day in the early spring of '63 the Fifty-fourth Massachusetts, the first colored regiment raised in New England, tramped on its way to the front through the city of Boston, and as the line turned the corner into Beacon Street it marched by the reviewing-stand that stood between the two elms fronting the State House. At the head of the column rode Colonel Robert Gould Shaw, a young citizen-soldier who had seen more than one battle, and whose early military training had been gained in the Seventh Regiment of New York city.

Many thousands watched that dusky line tramp down the hill; no holiday soldiers these, no careless, laughing body of recruits, but free men, facing almost certain death to relieve from bondage their brothers of

Harper's Weekly, January 2, 1897, p. 24.

the South. None knew the fate that was to befall them and their leader; of their test of flame and carnage at Fort Wagner there is not time to tell. "He is buried with his niggers," said the Southerners, when, under a flag of truce, the officers of the regiment sought their colonel's body. With them he had marched and fought and fallen; with them he lies in the deep trench below the ramparts.

When the work of perpetuating the memory of Shaw and his officers was given to Augustus St.-Gaudens, it was known that something fitting the place and the occasion would be forth-coming. For years St.-Gaudens wrought upon his masterpiece, and gradually it took shape and form—a deep bass-relief some eighteen feet in length by ten in height.

The mounted figure of the young colonel stands boldly out life size. He rides beside his troops—for here they are, black men sprung from the many scattered tribes of Africa, negroes from the Nile and the Congo, and from the eastern coast. In the rough uniform that made them part of the great blue-clad army that was spread from the Mississippi to the sea, here they are hurrying forward, silently hurrying in their creaky army boots. No pomp or magnificence, no trimly fitting tunics or bright accoutrements, mark them. The heavy knapsacks hang from their sturdy shoulders; the coarse, ill-fitting trousers flap about their dusty feet; the black, sinewy fingers grasp the heel-plates of the muskets with an eager determination.

On they come, on they go, file upon file, in column of fours, and at their head two little drummer-boys. One can see the peculiar drummer's swing of hip and shoulder, and can almost catch the excited tremble of the lips as their faces twitch to the time and excite-

Harper's Weekly, February 6, 1897, p. 144.

ment of their music. Back in the ranks a low-browed, thick-featured soldier, with a surly countenance, marches beside a lad whose good-humored face reflects a merry nature. Those lips were made to whistle with; there is a restless twinkle in his eye; he slouches a little in his walk, with the dragging gait of the darky.

Here is the well-studied, heavily bearded face of an older man, a natural soldier, the Libyan of the upper desert; here is the soft-spoken, ease-loving dweller of the plains and river valleys. And beside his troops rides the colonel. No vainglorious expression on his face, no mark of the man who lives by fighting; here is the citizen-soldier going to the war, with the full responsibility of his position marked in his calm, grave face. Though erect his attitude, no aggressive military swagger or dominant pride marks him. His eyes are straight ahead, and one might think that he was looking without a tremor down the long path of duty to that bloody, yawning trench.

Above the marching column there floats an allegorical female figure, hard to name at a first glance. It seems no more out of place than were it a realistic adjunct of the scene. The flowing draperies make the clouds, the palms carried in the hand might be the reaching branches of a tree. It is the essence or the spirit of a thought embodied in the bronze. She is not Fame, nor Destiny, nor Glory, nor Victory, with onward-pointing finger and courageous visage. Nor is she Fate exactly. Pityingly, lovingly, and with full sympathy, this figure

AFRICAN AMERICAN HISTORY IN THE PRESS, 1851-1899

MEMORIAL TO COLONEL ROBERT GOULD SHAW AND THE OFFICERS AND MEN OF THE FIFTY-FOURTH MASSACH
AUGUSTUS ST.-GAUDENS, SCULPTOR —[SEE PAGE 546.]

USETTS REGIMENT, TO BE UNVEILED ON THE BOSTON COMMON, MAY 31.

Harper's Weekly, May 29, 1897, pp. 540–41.

looks down upon the marching men—the men who were never taken prisoners, the men who were to fill the trench at Fort Wagner, who were to lead the charge against the Confederate line. It is Humanity watching without urging on; it is the embodiment of Sympathy.

The scope of the memorial has been enlarged from its original object. It is no longer a monument to Colonel Shaw alone, but to the officers of the Fifty-fourth Massachusetts (and to the men in the ranks also it must be, for here they are). At the unveiling, which takes place on the 31st of this month, there will be present Colonel Shaw's old regiment, the Seventh. The few survivors of those who served with him will attend, and the fact must impress itself upon the mind that the grizzled and time-furrowed handful of colored men, standing there bare-headed, with little bronze buttons in the lapels of their coats, thirty-four years ago marched with their regiment from this same spot one bright April day.

As a work of art and an ornament to Boston Common, the Shaw Memorial can be noticed but as in a class of its own. In dignity, in realism, and art of grouping, construction, and method, it is unsurpassed in this country, and Augustus St.-Gaudens has made for himself a lasting monument also, for the value and greatness of his work shall here be recognized by succeeding generations of his countrymen. There has not been a detail that he has not studied thoroughly. Texture as well as atmosphere has been produced. Dramatic action as well as motion has he succeeded in imparting. Without the aid of any trickery he has suggested sound. This is art that serves no other ends than those of its own.

The work itself may be said to have a northern and a southern exposure. On the north side, fronting the Capitol, is the great brass-relief with inscriptions beneath it. From either flank project two long stone wings, or, better, walls of granite. A stone bench is in front of the bass-relief, and two others at the angles of the wall. On the southern side, fronting the Common, are a number of tablets bearing various inscriptions, and wreaths with the names of the officers of the regiment. The design for the pedestal and the plans of the architectural surroundings are the work of Charles F. McKim.

A drinking-fountain occupies the centre, and on each side of it are two more stone seats.

As the Common slopes abruptly from the roadway upon which the monument faces, the walled space is high and wide, affording a good chance for mural decoration. Viewed from in front, the monument stands midway between two tall elms that are embraced by the arms of the low stone wall. It occupies the space where the old reviewing-stand once stood.

The location is a most happy one in many respects. Here Shaw started for the front; from under these very elms his regiment was reviewed, and in the shade of their branches he and his brave black men in bronze will continue marching, and their memory will never perish.

James Barnes

THIS BUSY WORLD

HARPER'S WEEKLY
June 5, 1897, p. 559

Allusion was made some time ago in this department of the Weekly to statements made in the periodical called *Dixie*, published in Atlanta, about the colleges established in the South for the education of negroes. *Dixie* thinks that the educational opportunities which Northern philanthropists have provided for Southern negroes are not such as are most profitable to them. It does not find that the college-bred negroes are the most prosperous, and it believes that if the colleges now maintained for negroes in the South were devoted to manual training, the benefit to the colored race in the South would be much greater. *Dixie* says that there are now as many as 30,000 graduates of the negro colleges, but that the more prosperous negroes of the South are not of their number.

Mr. T. Thomas Fortune does not at all agree with *Dixie's* conclusions. He says (in the *Sun*) that there are no high-schools for negroes in the South, and that it is only in the schools and colleges maintained by Northern money that they can get higher education. He declares that the idea that the 30,000 graduates of the negro colleges have not prospered is preposterous. Twenty thousand of them, he says, are school-teachers; 1500 are employed in the higher schools; 5000 are preachers; 2000 are lawyers or doctors. He declares that every one of the hundred schools for higher education of negroes in the South has justified its cost, and is as much needed to-day as it was twenty years ago.

It would seem that *Dixie* and Mr. Fortune are not quite agreed in their statement of facts, but the chief disagreement between them is in their conception of a prosperous negro. *Dixie's* idea seems to be that a negro is prosperous when he is making and saving money; Mr. Fortune's notion is that a negro is prosperous when he is preaching or teaching school. *Dixie's* sentiment is that the negro would better get money first and learning afterwards; but Mr. Fortune clearly dissents from that view, and does it forcibly, and with a good showing of argument on his side.

SUNDAY MORNING IN THE VIRGINIA PINES —Drawn by W. A. Rogers —[See Page 571.]

Harper's Weekly, June 5, 1897, p. 560.

SUNDAY MORNING IN THE VIRGINIA PINES

HARPER'S WEEKLY
June 5, 1897, p. 571

The old colored woman who handed me an envelope with "Bide by the Lilly Baptist Piscopal Christian Church" written across it couldn't tell me, she said, "zackly" what "bide" meant, only it was "'speckfully to 'quest 'sistance for de church."

"De 'Lilly' Church," she said, "war mile down de road, an' gen'leman been kind to 'scribe might stop when he git dar."

The "Lilly" Church proved to be a small shanty built of odds and ends from the wrecks of old buildings in the neighborhood. In the doorway stood the good old minister, Bible in hand.

A black broadcloth suit and white choker assisted him somewhat in looking conventionally solemn, but the black man's religion has more enthusiasm than solemnity about it, and all the gravity of the minister and his flock had a suspicious air of being a trifle histrionic.

At one side of the door a group, whom I took to be the trustees, were earnestly discussing some question—probably the church finances. Other members of the congregation were gathering in, some on foot, and others in carts drawn by undersized, scraggy-looking oxen or mules.

The Virginia darky is a happy creature. His brother in other parts of the country may suffer from ambition, discontent, desire to better himself, riches, or other evils, but here, whether he is "ketchin' oysters" in the James River, raising a few rows of goobers and a razor - back pig or two, or hauling "shadders" (pine needles), he and his dog are well pleased with the world and themselves. Having enjoyed himself over the ordinary affairs of life for six days, he proceeds on the seventh to enjoy his religion.

The morning service in a negro church is really a sort of concession to the surrounding white civilization. It is in the evening that the negro's own idea of religion manifests itself. When the interior of the little church is dark, with only a glimmer of light from a smoky kerosene-lamp on the pulpit, the weird imagination of the black man takes the place of the white man's doctrines and dogmas. Then the old spirit of the tropical forests invades the pines, breaks through the thin crust of white folks' manners, and the Virginia darky is once more an African.

W. A. Rogers.

THIS BUSY WORLD

HARPER'S WEEKLY
June 19, 1897, pp. 606–7

The Southern editors are duly scandalized, as all law abiding citizens should be, at the deplorable lynching incident at Urbana, Ohio; but most of them, while they condemn the crime, find occasion to point out that human nature is about the same in one State as in another, and that illegalities which have been common in Southern States might, under similar provocation, be just as common in States lying farther north.

No one concerned in the Urbana disaster seems to have come out of it with any sort of credit. The mob killed the negro, but any satisfaction they might feel in that must be offset by the knowledge that their turbulence cost several comparatively innocent citizens their lives. The captain of militia who ordered his company to fire at the mob is, at this writing, still profoundly dismayed at the results of his own efforts to support the law, and is afraid to go home; the sheriff is in retirement too, and very low in spirits; Governor Bushnell is mortified; Adjutant-General Axline is disgusted; the Mayor of Urbana is still uncertain what will happen next, and many members of the militia company that did the shooting are keeping away from home for fear of their neighbors.

The predicament of Captain Leonard of the militia company, and of his men, seems entirely undeserved. He and his company simply tried to do their duty—a very disagreeable duty at that. Whether the captain's judgment was at fault or not, the State of Ohio will have to back him and his men if it hopes to maintain the efficiency of its quota of the National Guard. To have militiamen driven from home for acts done under orders in defence of law won't do, as perhaps the Urbana people themselves will understand when they cool down and get their bearings again.

* * * * * * *

A bit of news that is of much interest, especially to every one who is concerned with the development of the negro race, comes in the form of a report that the French government has bought for the Luxembourg Gallery a large picture, representing "The Raising of Lazarus," painted by Henry O. Tanner, an American negro, born in Philadelphia about thirty-five years ago, and a pupil in the Pennsylvania Academy of Fine Arts. We have grown used to musical talent in negroes, have seen them win signal distinction as orators, and recently have heard one of them highly praised as a poet of true merit, but to most of us the news of this success of Mr. Tanner will be as much a surprise as it is a gratification. To have a picture bought for the Luxembourg is no small honor, and any young painter who wins it ought to have a bright future before him.

E. S. Martin

FURTHER BARBARISMS

HARPER'S WEEKLY
September 4, 1897, p. 870

The stories of lynchings continue to constitute an important feature of the news of the day. Barbarism seems to be prevalent in all parts of the country. It is certainly not confined to the South; nor is the offence for the punishment of which the mob has been murdering its victims always what some of the defenders of lynching denominate the "crime against the hearth-stone." So long as the whites of the South pleaded in defence of their murders that they were punishing, in the only way impressive to the negro imagination, savage blacks for assaults on white women, there was a seeming exception in some minds to the general rule of civilization that a community ought to be ruled by law and not by passion. But some recent cases indicate that the general spirit of mob murder is abroad. A few days ago the farmers of Cook County, Illinois, killed a white tramp for an assault on a woman. It is true that it was still a case of assault; but there was no race passion in the case, no immediate need of impressing so-called savage imaginations and repressing so-called savage instincts. It ought to have been presumed that the law and the courts were sufficient for the punishment of this villain. We have also the news of the turning out of a whole community in Michigan with the avowed intent of lynching the bankrobbers who had murdered a cashier. We have had a mob in Albany pursuing with murderous intent a kidnapper who was in the hands of the police. We hear from Georgia of the brutal killing of a drunken negro, who had not outraged a white woman, but who had killed a black woman in an effort to shoot his own wife. Nor is all the killing done because the administration of the law has failed, for we learn that in Kentucky a mob has taken from prison and hanged a white man who had been convicted and sentenced to imprisonment for twenty years.

Finally, as if in grim irony of all this hand-to-mouth justice, this contempt for delay and investigation and for regular trial, it is discovered that the Louisiana mob that last year killed two Italians for the supposed murder of a Spaniard in St. Charles Parish made a grievous mistake, the real murderer having recently confessed.

There is only one meaning to all this, and that is that there is no respect for the criminal law in many parts of the country, North and South. And we may rest assured that while we have Governors and judges like him of West Virginia and him of Kentucky, respect for the law will diminish; and that while criminals continue to enjoy so many opportunities to escape not only immediate but ultimate punishment, the temptation to the mob to take the law into its own hands in cases arousing popular passion will be very great. And in this phase of the subject it becomes the duty of lawyers to reflect deeply as to their own responsibility, both for the evils that the law permits and for those other evils which professional acumen has created.

THE NEGRO IN POLITICS

HARPER'S WEEKLY
September 4, 1897, p. 871

Emancipation has brought to the colored people of the United States, with its blessings, also many disappointments. It was very natural that those who had been born and grew up in slavery should, when they heard the word "freedom" pronounced, have pictured to themselves with their naive imagination something very like the life of their masters, which was to them a subject of constant admiration and envy. When emancipation came, freedom struck them, after the first paroxysm of joy was over, in the shape of burdensome responsibilities. For the first time in their lives they were confronted by the stern necessity of taking care of themselves, and this, too, surrounded by a white population which, immediately after the civil war, was exasperated by its defeats and losses, and harassed by its own wants, and therefore by no means in a state of mind to take kindly to the new order of things, and to help the negro over the first bewilderments of his free state. Many of the negroes of the South had then to suffer much for their liberty, which brought to them persecutions and struggles for life unknown to their former condition. Then came the endowment of the former slaves with the right of suffrage, and with it dreams of power, which were artfully stimulated and turned to their own personal advantage by the more unscrupulous of their white leaders. The scandals of the so-called carpet-bag governments during this reconstruction period could not fail to provoke a sweeping reaction, and then the negroes found themselves thrown upon their own resources, face to face with their white neighbors, who, greatly their superiors in intelligence, wealth, and energy, compassed and maintained, sometimes by very high-handed means, their ascendency over the blacks even in those States in which these were largely in the majority. At the same time the efforts to establish the negroes by law in their social position on a footing of equality with the whites— efforts made partly by colored men themselves, partly by white philanthropists—met with exceedingly slim success. The privileges that were conceded to them here and there remained confined to matters of comparatively small moment, while, on the whole, in spite of their advance in education as well as in the possession of property, they continued to be treated as an inferior race. Even those persons of color who have distinguished themselves by extraordinary cleverness have so far rather been looked upon as curiosities, instead of being generally recognized as entitled to that social position which, did they belong to the white race, would be readily yielded to them as their due.

Their ambitions, that had naturally been excited by emancipation, having thus been foiled on the social field by the stubborn resistance of race feeling on the part of the whites—a resistance, perhaps, not now as general or as virulent as it was a quarter of a century ago, but still positive and obstinate enough to forbid all hope of its disappearance in the near future—it is not surprising that the negroes should wish to make that power on the political field, which they exercise through the ballot, tell to the utmost for their benefit. It would be too much to expect that they should do so with great discretion. Like other classes of citizens who are in one way or another different from the rest and form a distinct force in politics, which may be of more or less use to this or that political party, the negro politicians demand, "recognition for the colored vote" wherever that vote appears to have contributed to party success. This is by no means extraordinary, and it would be unjust to reproach them for it more than we reproach the patronage hunters who demand recognition for the Irish vote or the German vote or the Norwegian vote. On the contrary, the colored people are, on account of their scanty opportunities and of the peculiar difficulties they have to contend with, entitled to far more lenient judgment.

But owing to the race feeling against them they are as politicians laboring under disadvantages of a serious nature. When organizing for political action and the eventual attainment of political reward in the shape of public employment, they are apt to fall under a leadership which may not be, morally and intellectually, very much inferior to that representing and guiding other organizations of spoils politicians, but which usually, although sometimes unjustly, strikes the general public as much less deserving of respect. The colored politician, unless he be a man of acknowledged ability and character, ordinarily fails to be taken seriously. When pressing his "claims" for recognition with energy, he produces not seldom the impression of a droll forwardness, which is calculated very greatly to weaken the influence which he otherwise might possess. Worse still is the inclination now and then shown by negro leaders or clubs of colored voters to compel attention to their wishes by the threat that unless the "claims" of the colored vote be sufficiently recognized by the party which they have supported, that vote will be transferred

THE HEIGHT OF ORATORY.

MRS. JOHNSON. "Am parson Jackson ve'y eloquent?"

MRS. WITEWASH (*ecstatically*). "Am he *eloquent?* Oh, my!—I wish yo' could hab heard his sermon las' Sunday 'bout Balaam an' de ass—yo' could almost 'magine yo' heard de ass a-talkin'."

Harper's Weekly, October 23, 1897, p. 1068.

to the other side. Such threats cannot but strengthen the apprehension already widely entertained that the colored vote is, or at least is apt to become, a generally venal vote. The more this apprehension grows into an accepted belief with party managers, and the more it is acted upon by them, the more will the colored citizens as a class be regarded and treated as a band of mere mercenaries in politics, and the more demoralized and degraded will the negro politicians and the great body of colored voters inevitably become. It is, therefore, as to their character and the respectability of their standing, of the highest importance to them that their political leaders should not be mere spoils-hunters or patronage-mongers, but men of principle, genuine public spirit, and true self-respect. At the same time, it must be admitted that so long as spoils-hunting and patronage-mongering play a great part in politics, there is no class of voters more apt than the colored people to fall under the influence of persons who promise them the distinction of public employment with good pay for easy work, or for no work at all, as the prize of political activity.

Although the time when the rights and welfare of the colored race were especially cared for, not only by hosts of philanthropists, but also by one of the great political parties, has passed away with the abolition of slavery and the reconstruction period, the negro does not by any means lack sincere and solicitous friends among the white people. Those friends have perhaps become somewhat sober and discriminating, but they are none the less earnest and faithful. They generally believe that the social and political advancement of the colored race cannot be accomplished by legal enactments or in other ways by rapid strides, but by gradual development, and especially by judicious and steady efforts on the part of the colored people themselves.

BOWING TO THE POWERS THAT BE.

Harper's Weekly, November 27, 1897, p. 1188.

While they observe with the warmest satisfaction that not a few colored men in public office have acquitted themselves with great credit, and that, even in the South, the prejudice against colored persons holding public place has somewhat abated, and while they recognize that under the Constitution the right of the black citizen as to holding office is in no way inferior to that of the white citizen, yet they have to admit that so far the negro in politics has, in point of success, not come up to the expectations of the colored race, and that especially the pursuit of public employment or station by negro politicians has, as a rule, not served to raise the colored people in the esteem of their white fellow-citizens, but that, on the contrary, the manner in which that pursuit has frequently been carried on has made the negro vote an object of increasing distrust and dread as to the uses that may be made of it.

On the whole, the wiser heads among the colored people themselves can hardly fail to see that their political preferment must not precede but follow their advancement in the other walks of life. A goodly number of negroes achieving distinction as lawyers, or as physicians, or as ministers, or as educators, or as business men, will, by the impression produced upon public opinion, effect far more for the political advancement of their race than ever so many negro politicians getting themselves elected to Congress or appointed to other offices, and infinitely more than the horde of colored place-hunters who besiege party committees for "influence" or appointing-officers for favors in the name of the colored vote, and who thus intensify the repulsiveness of one of the most baneful features of our political life. In this respect nothing more helpful can happen to the colored people than that all the government employments be put under civil service rules, so that every colored citizen who gets an appointment be known to have obtained it on account of his own individual merit, in free competition on an equal footing with other citizens, white or black, and that he is therefore fairly and honorably entitled to it. Places so won will indeed be marks of real proficiency and distinction, and raise the colored people in that public esteem which above all things they need.

Carl Schurz

THIS BUSY WORLD

HARPER'S WEEKLY
November 6, 1897, p. 1099

Mr. Schurz's article on "The Negro in Politics," published in the Weekly of September 4, has brought out from the Rev. J. M. Henderson, of the African Methodist Church on West Twenty-fifth Street, in New York, an acknowledgment which there is not room here to quote in full, but of which, he says, the purpose is to help readers to see the negro in a new light, and consider him from the true stand-point. He writes:

> The colored "political leader," the silver-tongued "colored orator," the irrepressible "solicitor of funds," the ever-present "caller of conventions," the bumptious "representative men interviewed," and the wretches who may commit heinous crimes against society are all obnoxious relics of a sad and dark past, from which the colored people of to-day have emerged, and back upon which they look with horror. Read the inner life, the soul of the negro in the thousands of humble efforts he is making to be like the best of the people who surround him. Do not take the cries for charity as the voice of the progressive colored people. Those who have become men are struggling silently, and beg no pity, seek no charity; they contend as men should, with closed lips, bared arms, and an unfaltering trust in Almighty God.

This is the expression of the spirit of manhood and resolution. Many negroes seem like children, though they show childhood's attractive side as well as its limitations. There can be little of that in those Mr. Henderson speaks for. Their ideas are sentiments of men grown up.

THE CONFERENCE AT OPELIKA
Colored Methodists Hold Their Fourth Day's Session.

ATLANTA CONSTITUTION
November 20, 1897

Opelika, Ala., November 19.—(Special.)—The fourth day's session of the African Methodist Episcopal Zion conference on Saturday was presided over by Bishop Lomax, who delivered a sermon on man's good deeds.

The Tuskegee district, through Joseph Gomez, presiding elder, made a report. Total collections, $2,421. Wetumpka district reported $2,807.41.

At the evening session fraternal greetings from Florida were received through Rev. S. Derry, messenger.

The bishop gave a lucid and comprehensive statement of the organization of the church.

Action upon the report of the committee on holy orders was postponed indefinitely.

Memorial services on three deceased ministers—W. W. Talbert, Rigdon Harris and R. Wilcoxon—were held.

1898

The year 1898 marked a volatile time for the nation in general and African Americans in particular. Early in the year, Blanche K. Bruce, the first African American to serve a full term in the U.S. Senate and the second to be elected from Mississippi, died in Washington, DC. While in the Senate, Bruce introduced a number of bills to advance the cause of African Americans. After leaving office, Bruce was appointed as the register of the U.S. Treasury.

The political realities of the South in 1898 underscored the impossibility of African Americans securing an elected position at any level. Louisiana passed the first grandfather clause, worded to allow poor whites to vote while curtailing black registration. By 1910 Georgia, North Carolina, Virginia, Alabama, and Oklahoma had adopted the clause which, while finally declared unconstitutional by the Supreme Court in 1915, effectively eliminated many African Americans from the voting process in the South.

Despite continuing disfranchisement, African Americans sought to prove their loyalty and demonstrate their worthiness for inclusion in the American Dream by volunteering to serve during the Spanish-American War. United States involvement in the war had its roots in national economic goals dating back to the 1840s and 1850s. Trade made the U.S. an active participant in world affairs and the industrial revolution boosted her image as a world leader. The decision of President William McKinley's administration to secure a world empire for the U.S. directed the attention of the nation to external affairs. At that time, the European powers in their search for colonies and new markets were extending their involvement in Asia and Africa.

The partitioning of Africa, with its many resources, at the international Berlin Conference in 1884–1885 had not gone unnoticed by African Americans. George Washington William, historian and author of the 1883 classic volume History of the Negro Race in America from 1619 to 1880, *protested Belgium's colonizing policies in the Congo. Because of their natural link to the continent, African Americans had been actively involved through their religious institutions in bringing relief to the indigenous Africans. The African Methodist Episcopal (AME) Church, organized by Richard Allen, would have a sustaining interest in developing missions and schools in various parts of Africa. Bishop Henry McNeal Turner visited South Africa in 1898 to consolidate a new branch of the church. While there he was said to have imbued the indigenous people with a nationalist spirit that spread rapidly. By the 1890s the Baptist churches also had a missionary arm. The Lott Carey Baptist Home and Foreign Mission Convention of the U.S. opened its first mission in Brewersville, Liberia, in 1898.*

The owners of the New York Journal *and the New York* World *focused the attention of all American citizens on Cuba. As arguments escalated between the imperialists and the anti-imperialists, African Americans were vocal members of both camps. The explosion of the battleship* U.S.S. Maine *in the Havana harbor provided the spark the Republicans needed to convince McKinley to request a congressional declaration of war against Spain. Of the more than 250 officers and men on board the* Maine, *twenty-two were African Americans. Several states, including Virginia, Alabama, North Carolina, Ohio, Illinois, and Kansas, organized volunteer units for African Americans. The Third North Carolina Infantry was commanded by all-black officers. West Pointer Charles Young was promoted to brevet major and placed in charge of the Ninth Ohio. Congress authorized the creation of an additional ten black regiments, but only four were organized after African Americans protested the assigning of whites to all grades above second lieutenant.*

Because the war lasted a mere ten weeks, only the Ninth and Tenth Calvary and the Twenty-Fourth and Twenty-Fifth Infantry Regiments were involved in combat. The Tenth Calvary participated in the Battle of Las Guasimas and fought at El Caney; the Twenty-Fourth Infantry assisted in the famous charge up San Juan Hill. Approximately, 10,000 African Americans served in the military during the war. About 4,000 were in special "immune" units so called because it was believed that African Americans possessed a genetic immunity to tropical diseases. Regardless of their placement, the men's valor was acknowledged by the awarding of six Medals of Honor. Even after their display of bravery and commitment, black men in the military remained a highly controversial issue.

As a result of the Spanish-American War, the U.S. assumed control of many nations in the Caribbean and in the Pacific. The acquisition of territories populated by peoples of darker races fueled resentment against African Americans. Black soldiers, returning home, were met with hostile reactions from whites.

The year 1898 also saw the most violent of the race riots erupt in Wilmington, North Carolina. Racial tensions, often involving employment issues, were also evident in northern states. For example, the use of African Americans from the South as strike breakers by Illinois coal companies precipitated hostility between white and black members of the United Mine Workers.

The black nationalist Henry McNeal Turner again proposed emigration as the best solution for the "Negro Problem." His rationale for emigration had been given earlier in an 1895 statement, "I believe that the Negroid race has been free long enough now to begin to think for himself and plan for better conditions than he can lay claim to in this country or ever will. There is no manhood future in the United States for the Negro." Most African Americans were not persuaded by Turner's argument, and subsequently rejected emigration as a viable alternative.

Playwright and lyricist William Marion Cook successfully satirized the anti-emigration sentiments held by most African Americans in his 1902 Broadway show "In Dahomey." However, it was his musical-comedy sketch "Clorindy, the Origin of the Cakewalk," which opened on Broadway in 1898. The operetta was based on lyrics by Paul Lawrence Dunbar, and featured a company of twenty-six performers. "Clorindy" brought the cakewalk to national attention—a high-stepping dance originally performed by slaves as they mimicked plantation owners.

Middle-class Americans expressed concern that riotous urban living was corrupting citizens and leading to the moral decay of the nation. Members of the Women's Christian Temperance Union (WCTU), led by Frances Willard from 1879 until her death in 1898, agreed. Because black women were not permitted to join the southern branches, they formed "colored" divisions of the WCTU to alleviate problems caused by drunkenness and poverty. Only one black woman, Frances Ellen Harper, ever served on the WCTU's executive council and board of superintendents. This lack of support from white women contributed to the increasing effectiveness of black women's church organizations and clubs as they were forced to operate in a separate sphere. Challenged by their exclusion, African Americans, both male and female, worked at forging alliances across gender and class lines.

Cynthia Neverdon-Morton
Coppin State College

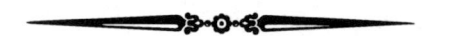

NEGRO OUTLAW IS BURNED AT STAKE

Mob Metes Out Punishment to a Desperate Character.
Great Crowd Is Present.
Would Be Murderer Is Tied to Post and Wood Saturated with Oil Piled On.
Lawyers Make Speeches to Throng.
Before Death Came the Negro Confessed the Crime for Which His Life Was Taken—His Victim's Life in a Precarious Condition.

ATLANTA CONSTITUTION
June 18, 1898

Shreveport, La., June 3.—A thousand people gathered at Doyline, which is situated on the Vicksburg, Shreveport and Pacific railroad, about eighteen miles from here, to witness the burning at stake of William Street, a negro, who attempted the ruin and murder of Mrs. Parish. The crime was committed on the night of May 30th.

The people erected a post beside the railroad track near the town, quietly laid the lightwood and kindling, saturated with coal oil, preparatory to chaining Street to the post. Street was a gingerbread colored man of about twenty-eight years. He confessed the crime to a colored minister, but said a negro minister named John Rhodes was implicated.

When going to the stake he looked frightened and refused to have anything to say. He was tied to the stake and uttered not a word as the great crackling flames shot up in succession above his head. The flames were started at 1 o'clock.

It was a sickening sight which lasted ten minutes, when Street was a charred mass. Well known lawyers made speeches warning the crowd of negroes that such crimes would not be tolerated in a civilized community.

The woman whom Street assaulted is in a most critical condition and could not identify Street when caught until a doctor held open her eyelids.

Arkansas Mob Hangs a Negro
Crowd Stops an Iron Mountain Train To Complete Its Work

Texarkana, Ark., June 3.—Yesterday morning little Jesse Scott, daughter of the late circuit clerk, J. V. Scott, was assaulted by a negro named Bud Hayden, near Fairview. He was arrested and lodged in jail last night. A short while before noon to-day a committee of seven of the best men in this city took Hayden to Mrs. Scott's residence and placed him in the barn where the crime was committed. The young girl was taken to the scene and upon entering the barn said:

"That's the man."

He was handed over to the mob. A rope was placed around his neck and the crowd began moving. An opening was made, and through the lines the negro was dragged, and everybody hit him as he went.

The rope was fixed so it would not choke him and a run made for a tree. Finally the crowd halted at the Iron Mountain crossing and the rope was thrown over a limb of a tree which stood within a few feet of where Ed Coy was burned for a like offense a few years ago. He was then jerked into the air, the rope tied and as the body swung in the air he was riddled with bullets.

THIS BUSY WORLD

HARPER'S WEEKLY
July 9, 1898, p. 662

At Commencement (May 26) at Tuskegee Institute, Mississippi, this year, Principal Booker T. Washington, A.M., reported an enrolment during the year of 712 boys and 335 girls. The income of the year was $114,469, of which $52,000 was expended on the permanent plant. The pupils paid in work towards their personal expenses $52,000. The institute has many departments, in which are taught agriculture, truck-gardening, and various trades and industries, besides which it carries on the general business of education. Its deserts are widely known and appreciated. It needs an endowment of half a million dollars, and should have it. In its aims, scope, and methods it has proved itself one of the best machines that exist for promoting self-help and intelligent industry among the colored population of the South. It is starting on its eighteenth year. Its pupils last year came from twenty-four States and two foreign countries. Three thousand of its former pupils are at work.

THIS BUSY WORLD

HARPER'S WEEKLY
August 20, 1898, p. 815

"Hell's Kitchen," the scene of recent disturbances in New York, is the name applied to Thirty-ninth Street near the North River, a region of unenviable repute, which has of late years become a residence quarter for negroes. So far as appears from the deliverances of the local historians, negroes have been received there as tenants of tenement-houses because they were the only decent people who were willing to live in a neighborhood that bore so bad a reputation. It is not they who have given the quarter a bad name, but it is because the bad name already existed that property-owners made negroes welcome there. The original inhabitants do not view the negro immigration in the same favorable light that the house-owners do, and hence much jealousy and friction, culminating from time to time in such outbreaks as that of three weeks ago.

CAMP WIKOFF

[*Special Correspondence of "Harper's Weekly."*]

HARPER'S WEEKLY
September 10, 1898, p. 890

On the Monday after the memorable flood at Johnstown, a man dropped into the press headquarters in the old plaster-mill at the end of the stone bridge over the Conemaugh, who said he had witnessed the whole catastrophe, and would tell us all about it. He said, as we newspaper men crowded around him, that he was a man who did not get excited like other people, he always kept cool, and he would tell us just how it happened. Before he had said a dozen words he went all to pieces, overwhelmed by the vivid memories of that day, and his story was never told.

I have been asked to write my impressions of our army just back from its glorious campaign in Cuba, and after three days spent at Camp Wikoff I am free to confess that the sight of those poor starved boys has put me in pretty much the same condition as that citizen of Johnstown.

When the Secretary of War arrived in camp he was agreeably disappointed, we are told, that things were no worse; but other visitors, not having the same opportunity for knowing the details of official delinquency in his department beforehand, were so shocked that the tears streamed down their cheeks—even the furrowed cheeks of old men hardened to life's blows, and of young men careless ordinarily to the hardships of others....

It is, of course, impossible for the regimental surgeons to talk, except in confidence, about the lack of medicines and food before and after the fight at Santiago, on the voyage home, and here in camp, but it is also just as impossible for them to keep still about it in talking privately. The one cheerful feature of the camp is the

9TH U.S. CAVALRY (COLORED) DETRAINING AT PORT TAMPA.

Harper's Weekly, May 21, 1898, p. 496.

black soldier; he, as a general thing, came through but little the worse of the pestilent climate of Cuba, and coming of a race used to privations, stood the starvation rations better than his white brother.

He is looked upon by the white soldier with positive affection and pride.

The gallant conduct of the black man, his hunting out and exterminating the sharp-shooters and guerillas who were picking off the officers and wounded from the trees, is a story that every white soldier will tell you with kindling eyes. To see the colored troopers bringing a hundred horses down to the water, singing and laughing as they swing along at a canter, is a sight pleasant to remember. Not one good word is to be heard in the whole camp for the Cuban. "Cubans! Well, if I have to go back to Cuba, I hope it'll be to lick those horse-thieves.

The Spaniards are all right; I haven't a word to say against them. In fact, we all liked the Spanish boys when we got to know them." This was what you might hear all over the camp....

"THE CONSENT OF THE GOVERNED."

HARPER'S WEEKLY
September 17, 1898, p. 907

Nothing is more bewildering, in the present bewildering state of a public feeling which cannot be said to have

Harper's Weekly, May 28, 1898, p. 508.

crystallized into public opinion, than the fact that the authors of our political failures at home should be the chief advocates of "expansion" abroad. The Jingoes are the incompetents. "We have been unfaithful over a few things," they say; "make us rulers over many things."

Now nothing is clearer than that the agencies of government we have are ill adapted to their present limited uses, and that, if we mean to undertake larger problems, we must have a very different set of tools. The House of Representatives, we have to admit, whether we like it or not, is a house of representatives—that is to say, it is composed of average American citizens who know no less than the average of their constituencies about trade, finance, currency, foreign politics, and all the other subjects upon which they are called to legislate, and whose pride it is to know no more. The Senate is not even a house of representatives—and that for a manifest reason. The House of Representatives is immediately responsible to the people. Every member of it is aware that his course must meet the approval of his district, or of his party in his district. He is constantly held in check by the necessity of obtaining the consent of the governed. A Senator feels no such responsibility. It is only when his term is drawing to its close that he inquires how the people of his State will regard his official course. Even if he is aware that it is disapproved, he hopes, by the favor of the boss, unless he himself is the boss, to circumvent public disapproval. Unless his misbehavior has been so scandalous as to "lose the State," as in Gorman's case, he is very apt to succeed. Now in governing distant territories, in which "the consent of the governed" is not required, the member of the Lower House is freed from the one influence that steadies him. The representative will be as bad as the Senator. Since the Constitution puts the whole matter in the charge of Congress, have we the least guarantee that our government of colonies will be honest or intelligent? Our solution of our Indian problem by extermination, our solution of our negro problem by lynching, our solution of our Alaskan problem by apathy—these achievements scarcely indicate that we are prepared to shine in an "Imperial" capacity.

"Imperialism" seems likely to become the watchword of the Republican party. That party asks the people to intrust it with the destinies of some millions of foreigners of whose needs it knows nothing, and by whose desires it does not even profess to be guided. The answer of the people to this demand ought to be an insistence that the party should purge itself of its abuses, and set its own house in order, before reaching out after new dominion; that it should show itself much more faithful over a few things before asking to be intrusted with rule over many things. The Republican party does at least profess to be guided by public opinion in domestic politics, and to "derive its just powers from the consent of the governed." But it is perfectly well known that in those States which are governed by bosses not even this condition is fulfilled. The boss is not guided by the opinion, we will not say of the voters, but of the voters even of his own party. His machine enables him to defy their will, up to the point where their exasperation will induce them to turn on him and defeat him at the polls.

We have already pointed out instances in which the Republican party might vindicate itself by showing that "the consent of the governed" was an integral part of its rule, that the opinion of the voters was, in fact, taken and not defied in the selection of candidates for the governorship of American States. In our newly acquired dependencies nobody pretends that "the consent of the governed" will be requisite to our government. But what the most unbridled Jingo theoretically admits is that our government ought to be satisfactory to the people of the United States. It is the one responsibility that all the Imperialists admit. Our government of Hawaii may not be, and in fact we know it is not, satisfactory to the Hawaiians. Our government of the Philippines may not be satisfactory to the Filipinos. It remains to be seen whether the Puerto-Ricans will like our way of governing after they have had a fair trial of it, while as for the Cubans, we no longer pretend to care whether they are satisfied with our proceedings preliminary to the condition in which we shall acknowledge that their own government is "stable," and evacuate the island, leaving them to their own devices. But we do pretend that the governments we establish, whatever may be the opinion entertained of them by "the governed," will meet the views of the people of the United States, who are not to live under them. The only way of making that pretence good is to make sure that the people of the United States are governed in accordance with their own desires; that here, at least, governments "derive their powers from the consent of the governed." But in boss-ridden States even this is notoriously untrue. Before the boss can decently appear as an "Imperialist" he must abdicate as a boss, and give the people of New York and Pennsylvania and Connecticut some evidence that they are governed in accordance with their own opinions, before he presumes to assure them that Hawaii and Puerto Rico and Cuba and Luzon will be governed in accordance with their opinions.

THIS BUSY WORLD

HARPER'S WEEKLY
September 24, 1898, p. 935

Mr. Booker T. Washington, of the Tuskegee Institute, at Tuskegee, Alabama, believes that the new responsibilities which we have incurred in Cuba and Puerto Rico include an obligation to promote the education of the negroes of those islands. Both in Cuba and in Puerto Rico the negroes form half of the population. No one disputes that they need training—intellectual, industrial, religious—such as is given at Hampton and Tuskegee. In the present state of Cuba industrial education is especially necessary. By way of making a beginning Mr. Washington proposes to bring to this country a few promising young Cuban negro men and women and train them at Tuskegee, so that they can go back and begin the work of industrial training on the island. To bring them to Tuskegee and teach them will cost $150 apiece for each year's instruction. Mr. Washington wants to hear from persons who are disposed to help in defraying the costs of this work.

E. S. Martin

THIS BUSY WORLD

HARPER'S WEEKLY
October 15, 1898, p. 1006

Hampton (Virginia) Institute has been raising its standard of admission, and has started its thirty-first year with an entering class slightly smaller than last year's, but of unusually good material. The class includes about seventy negro boys and fifty-five girls, and twenty Indian boys and eighteen girls. About one-third of all the applicants were accepted. All the Indians in the present entering class have had primary instruction in the reservation schools. The work at Hampton now is altogether a work of secondary education. This term, for the first time, the institute uses its new building for the agricultural and domestic science courses. It is described as one of the finest school-buildings in the country, admirably provided with class-rooms and laboratories, with a model kitchen, laundry, and bedrooms for the domestic-science department at one end, and, at the other, a creamery and dairy and arrangements for the study of the use of farm machinery and the care of live-stock.

E. S. Martin

THIS BUSY WORLD

HARPER'S WEEKLY
October 22, 1898, p. 1030

Mr. T. Thomas Fortune, who is known to newspaperreaders as a frequent contributor to the *Sun* of articles about our colored brethren and their interests, is a representative colored citizen, and is president of the Afro-American League, and editor of the *Age*. In a speech made in Rochester the other day, at the time of the dedication of the monument to Frederick Douglass, he said:

> "The management of the colored people of the South has been a conspicuous failure. The race has been educated, but race prejudice has not abated. I see other black and yellow peoples about to come under the care of this government. If you rule the black and yellow people in Cuba, Puerto Rico, and the Philippines as the South has been and is being ruled, you will have revolution upon revolution, and you ought to have it."

It is the open season for prophets, and Mr. Fortune's forebodings are worth recording.

The summer brought many examples of the friction between blacks and whites in the South. One of the most interesting cases was that of the Second Texas Volunteers, who refused for a time to accept their pay from Major Lynch, a colored paymaster, but presently relented, and found by a practical test that the money lost none of its value in passing through a negro's hands. A few days ago there was a clash in color lines at the camp at Huntsville, Alabama, which cost three lives; and in Illinois there has been serious fighting over a question of negro labor, as elsewhere told.

A great many persons besides Mr. Fortune feel that the future of the negro in this country is a problem that is yet to be solved, and many minds are busy with it all the time. Bishop Turner of Georgia is strongly in favor of negro emigration, and believes that there will presently be a great exodus of American negroes to Africa, where, he thinks, the black men will have a fairer chance, and will prosper better than will ever be possible for them here. An obstacle to the exodus is that few of our negroes have any inclination to go to Africa, but much prefer to stay at home. A correspondent of the New York *Evening Post*, who writes from Birmingham, Alabama, believes that relief for such of the Southern negroes as are not content with their social condition will come presently in the form of countries here and there in the South which shall be owned, populated, and administered exclusively or almost altogether by negroes. This reasoner objects strongly to a negro State, but thinks that negro counties would be very useful in providing refuges for negroes who dislike contact with the whites, and want to get out of the shadow of the dominant race. The suggestion is interesting, though its originator admits that it will be long before it is put into practice, as the transfer of the property of any Southern county into negro hands would necessarily be a slow process.

[UNTITLED.]

HARPER'S WEEKLY
November 5, 1898, p. 1074

In the midst of our concern about distant islands of the sea, the defective government which Spain has given the Philippines, and the incompetency of the Cubans and the natives of the Philippines to govern themselves, parochial politics in this country are lively, and, in our view, important. Race wars are going on in North Carolina, Alabama, and Mississippi. In Mississippi eleven negroes have been killed, and the whites in the neighborhood of Forest seem to be out gunning for blacks as if they were game. The reign of law was suspended for several days, until Sheriff Stephenson came to aid her outraged majesty, and with the help of fifty good citizens carried five of the negroes in safety to the jail at Meridian. In North Carolina the fighting between the whites and the blacks seems to spring from politics. Owing to Mr. McKinley's appointment of black politicians to office, the whites there appear to dread the return of negro rule. Now, although Sheriff Stephenson is engaged in the vindication of the right of the blacks to live, and in also vindicating the majesty of the law, he is, according to the expansionists, simply performing narrow duties in the sphere of parochial politics. We nevertheless, for our part, regard his conduct in the performance of his duty as heroic and useful as was the conduct of any of our heroes at Santiago or at Manila. In fact, we are inclined to think his conduct essentially more heroic than the bravery of the soldiers in battle, because he stood up against public opinion in his own community, and invited persecution, and perhaps ostracism, while the soldiers who fought in the war were sure of praise and honors. These events in the South are symptomatic, and until the country meets and settles properly the conditions thus presented to it, democratic government here cannot be said to be wholly successful. This is the plain truth, and we cannot escape it by deriding those who are for civilization at home, or by shouting for more savages to govern—white or black—in the islands of the Pacific.

THIS BUSY WORLD

HARPER'S WEEKLY
November 5, 1898, p. 1078

"Race wars" continue to be unusually prevalent in the South. One curious explanation of the unusual number of them is that a strong impression has been made on the minds of the more ignorant and isolated Southern ne-

FORGOTTEN

TROOP C, 9TH U. S. CAVALRY, CAPTAIN TAYLOR, LEADING THE

HEROES.
CHARGE AT SAN JUAN.—DRAWN BY FLETCHER C. RANSOM.

groes by the stories of the exploits of the colored regulars at San Juan. It will be remembered that the colored soldiers and the Rough Riders fought side by side, and very valiantly. Everything that concerned the Rough Riders was thoroughly narrated and printed, and the colored regiments, by reason of their fortunate propinquity, got fuller and more general credit for their work than others of the regulars. Perhaps their gallantry and its renown had their effect on the other colored brethren; perhaps not. At any rate, last week there were race riots near Harpersville, Scott County, Mississippi, in which, up to October 24, eleven negroes and one white man had been killed and one negro and three white men seriously wounded, and the situation was such as to make more casualties probable. Near Ashpole, Robeson County, North Carolina, on October 23, a band of negroes shot and wounded three white men, who were part of a guard left after a recent riot to prevent further disturbance. Four of the negroes were captured.

On the same day a negro was lynched at Lafayette, Alabama, for the murder of a white farmer; a white boy was killed in Dallas, Texas, by three negroes, and a lynching was expected, and a white man was shot by a colored soldier in a street row at Chattanooga, Tennessee.

THIS BUSY WORLD

HARPER'S WEEKLY
November 19, 1898, p. 1126

Election brought out very serious rioting between negroes and whites in North and South Carolina. It is still difficult to get at the correct details of these occurrences, or to discover all the immediate causes of them, but the gross results in dead men are conspicuously considerable. As the results of election riots near Greenwood, South Carolina, about a dozen negroes and half as many white men are reported dead, and many others are wounded. Some of the negroes were shot; others were hanged. Still more serious, if possible, were the proceedings in Wilmington, North Carolina. In that city a newspaper, the *Record*, edited by a negro, published an article derogatory to white women. A mass-meeting of white citizens, called on November 9, ordered his expulsion from the city within twenty-four hours and the removal of his press. A committee of twenty-five appointed by the meeting called in fifteen prominent negroes and gave them notice of the meeting's edict. It appears that they agreed to try to comply with the demands of the committee, but their letter to that effect, being mailed instead of personally delivered to the committee's chairman, was not received in time. The editor of the *Record* ran away; but no action being taken about his press within the specified time, a mob of white citizens, led by former Congressman Waddell, proceeded, on November 10, to destroy the *Record's* press and gut its printing-office. Incidentally the mob burned the building. These proceedings agitated the negroes of the town, who feared a general massacre and began to get together. Fighting soon ensued between negroes and whites, and continued briskly during the day. About a score of negroes were killed and several whites. In the evening the Board of Aldermen resigned, one by one, the place of each being filled by his colleagues. When the board had thus been renewed the Mayor and Chief of Police resigned, and their places were filled by the new Board of Aldermen. Then 250 special policemen were sworn in, and with their help and that of three militia companies the new government hopes to restore order.

[UNTITLED.]

HARPER'S WEEKLY
November 26, 1898, p. 1146

The white mobs of South Carolina and North Carolina may in the end bring about a peaceful state of things in the communities lately the scenes of violent outrage. It all depends upon the amount of killing which they can accomplish. The negroes have been overpowered, and many of them have disappeared. The war between the races, which appears to have reached a climax in Wilmington, in Greenwood, and in McCormick; is a natural result of the bestowal of political power upon the blacks. The war has been going on ever since the negroes were enfranchised. In Mississippi and in South Carolina enfranchisement has been practically abolished by constitutional provision. Nevertheless, the war between the races is not over even in those States, and it has been aggravated by the appointment of negro Federal officials, much to the disgust of the whites, who resent what they call "negro rule." There is no good reason that can be given by those who are responsible for the appointment of negroes for thus inciting disturbance of the peace. They are to blame, as all men are to blame who do not deal tactfully with the situations confronting them. It is no more right to appoint a distasteful negro as postmaster in the South than it is right to appoint a distasteful white man to be postmaster in the North. But, all this barred, so long as the government is within its right—that is, the right of its power and its jurisdiction—it should have the strength and the firmness, and its Chief Executive should have the courage, to maintain peace and order everywhere within its borders. The riot in North Carolina seems to have been entirely beyond the Federal jurisdiction; but the riot in South Carolina involved an assault upon a Federal official, and therefore invited and demands Federal interference. More serious still than either one of these riots in Southern States is the conduct of Governor Tanner of Illinois in making war upon Alabama negroes who were seeking work in Illinois, and who, as citizens of the United States, had the right to the protection of the State. The riots in the South and in Illinois are a blot upon our civilization and an impeachment of our government. The immediate duty of the country lies here and with these offenders. To distract the attention of the country from these domestic crimes and this weakness at Washington is to invite a continuance of bad government at home. The one thing that the politician of today most desires is a means by which he may distract the attention of the American people from his sins at home. He is just now seeking that means in the Philippines and in the West Indies, and if he succeeds, we may expect that the days of bad government will be lengthened in this land.

A SABLE HERO

HARPER'S WEEKLY
November 26, 1898, p. 1151

George Berry, Troop D, Tenth Cavalry, with the rank of First Sergeant, was retired at Camp Forse, Huntsville, Alabama, November 1, 1898. That the man is alive today seems nothing short of a miracle, because of his conduct at San Juan Hill, where, under heavy fire, fifty feet in advance of his comrades, he waved aloft two flags, the stars and stripes of the Tenth and the Third Cavalry.

This hero did not burst upon his commanding officers as first distinguished for gallantry in the war with Spain. He had long before won his laurels, having, during his thirty years' service in the army, actively participated in six separate campaigns, against the Cheyennes, Kiowas, Arapahoes, Comanches, Apaches, Utes, in Colorado, Kansas, Texas, and New Mexico.

Sergeant Berry, who, after the manner of all real heroes, is modest of his own achievements, in speaking of his action at San Juan Hill, where he successfully planted the colors of his own regiment upon the works from which the Spaniards were even then running away, said:

"Where did my courage come from? It came from our 'war chief,' Captain Ayres. When I saw him leading his men, waving his hat in the air, shouting out like a trumpet to the soldiers to follow, I took the two sets of colors and ran, calling as I ran: 'Dress on the colors, boys! Dress on the colors!'"

During the recent peace celebration in Philadelphia, as this sable hero, bearing the tattered battle-flags he had carried so gallantly at Las Guasimas, San Juan, and Santiago, marched in the procession with the Tenth

COLOR-SERGEANT GEORGE BERRY, TROOP D, 10TH U. S. CAVALRY,
Who carried the Colors of the 10th and 3d Cavalry in the Charge at San Juan Hill, Santiago.
[See Page 1151.]

Harper's Weekly, November 26, 1898, p. 1150.

Cavalry, he was pelted with roses from the balconies and stands crowded with people.

The picture on the opposite page shows Sergeant Berry standing near Captain Ayres's tent at Huntsville, Alabama. In his left hand he holds his regimental national colors, while in his right is the regimental flag ribboned by the Spanish bullets in the three great land battles of the Spanish-American war.

Katherine E. Thomas.

THE PRESIDENT AT ATLANTA AND TUSKEGEE

HARPER'S WEEKLY
December 31, 1898, pp. 1299–1300

President McKinley's faith and interest in the elevation of the negroes were very firmly registered when, on the 16th of this month, he spent the greater part of a day in visiting and addressing the teachers and students of the Tuskegee Normal and Industrial Institute in Alabama. His visit South was primarily to participate in the Peace Jubilee at Atlanta, Georgia, and a journey of eighteen hours along the eastern slope of the lower Alleghanies brought the Southern Railway's special train of the

PRESIDENT McKINLEY REVIEWING THE PROCESSION TUSKEGEE.

Harper's Weekly, December 31, 1898, p. 1284.

President and party to Atlanta early Wednesday morning, December 14. In the accompanying party were Mrs. McKinley, Secretary and Mrs. Gage, Secretary and Mrs. Alger, Secretary and Miss Long, Postmaster-General and Mrs. Smith, Secretary and Miss Wilson, Secretary and Mrs. Porter, Assistant-Secretary Cortelyou, General and Miss Wheeler, General Shafter, General and Mrs. Lawton, and Captain Scherer, press correspondents, messengers, and maids. Wednesday and Thursday, 14th and 15th, were given over to the programme of the civic and military parades, addresses, and demonstrations in Atlanta, closing Thursday night with a banquet, in which veterans of the gray wove laurels of good cheer for a reunited blue, in response to President McKinley's magnanimous utterance that "we should share with you in the care of the graves of the Confederate soldiers." After which the party passed from Atlanta into the "Black Belt," *en route* to Tuskegee.

The distance of a hundred and forty miles into this "Black Belt" furnishes an ample study and evidences of the seriousness of the negro problem in this country. Near one station a negro owns a plantation of eleven hundred acres, well stocked and managed. Half a dozen others own small farms of less value. On the other hand, hundreds in this community and thousands in the section are tenants living in one-room cabins, with families as high as thirteen to fifteen in number. In one settlement there are nearly thirty of these cabins, made of logs, with large apertures between the logs, permitting draughts that mean consumption and pneumonia. There is scarcely a picture on the wall, save an occasional advertising chromo, and patent-medicine almanacs seem the only excuses for books to furnish mental food to families, whose kitchen, dining, bed, and sitting room, for all ages and sexes, is a single four-wall enclosure. On the other hand, there are clocks worth five dollars which have cost fourteen dollars from smooth-tongued agents, who collected the money by instalments. Likewise there are sewing-machines with no evidence of their need from the scanty clothing to be seen. With no mule or horse to draw them, some of these people own buggies. The fact is every where apparent that the first principle of "getting on in the world" has not been learned. These people, who as slaves were fed and clothed by a master, find it a hard lesson to learn the white man's economy for future wants and the necessity of owning land. Their crops even are mortgaged before planting, in order to draw from the merchant rations and clothing, which the merchant sells to them at a profit of from 12 to 180 per cent, over usual retail prices. Mules are rented to cultivate crops: an old man told me that he has paid $14 a year rent for a mule for seven years, when the mule might have been bought in the first place for $50. The moral status is as unsatisfactory as the industrial. The camp-meetings prove attractions for lewdness, drunkenness, and gambling, the preachers often winking at these evils if financial returns are increased. Men who have gone to coal-mines, public works, and large

SOME OF THE TUSKEGEE INSTITUTE FLOATS IN THE PARADE—TUSKEGEE.

Harper's Weekly, December 31, 1898, p. 1284.

commercial centres to get better wages have learned the games of dice and cards, and returning, have taught them to their fellows, who revel by night amidst the fumes of cheap whiskey and tobacco, while women and children are half clothed and half fed.

It is significant, however, that everywhere the people are at work, practically all the unskilled labor and much of the mechanical work done in the South being performed by negroes. But the difficulty seems to be that the people do not know how to utilize the results of their labor. They are anxious to learn, and will always seek the school-house. Last year 27,435 negro teachers enrolled 2,816,340 negro children in the public schools of the South, and 1795 teachers instructed 45,402 negro boys and girls in 169 normal, industrial, and collegiate schools. Of these the Tuskegee Institute is one of the best known. Founded by Booker T. Washington, July 4, 1881, in a frame church and cabin, with one teacher and thirty pupils, and no property, the school has grown during the seventeen years to the large proportions of 90 teachers, 1000 students, 2267 acres of land, 37 buildings, 26 industries, the equipment, with land and buildings, reaching the value of $300,000. The students, of both sexes, are from 21 States, Cuba, and Puerto Rico, and receive an education in English, with religious and industrial training.

The visit to this institution of the President and most of the cabinet was an event of tremendous interest to teachers, students, and citizens, white and black, in the community. After the party had breakfasted on the train a start was made at half past eight o'clock for the institute through the streets of Tuskegee, whose score of large columned mansions bespeak the magnificence of *ante bellum* living in this "Heart of the South." As the carriages approached the school campus, a mile away, the thirty-seven buildings, erected by students in carpentry and brick masonry in their self-help education, were a welcome sight in happy contrast to the fields of waste and decay surrounding the town. Upon entering the gate the grounds were observed to be beautifully arranged, and ornamented by students in horticulture. The buildings, plans for most of which, including the largest, were drawn in the architectural and mechanical-drawing department of the institute, were well arranged and strikingly commodious. Bricks, of which students in the brick-yard have made this year a million, were being put into the Armstrong Slater Memorial Industrial Building. Logs, cut by students, were being sawed in the saw-mill into lumber by other students. The wheelwright, blacksmith, and harness shops exhibited beautiful and substantial buggies and wagons constructed by these black boys. Still other students exhibited well-fitting suits of clothes made by them in the tailor shop; circulars, books, etc., printed by them in the printing-office; shoes produced by them in the shoe-shop; steam-engines, etc., manufactured in machine, foundry, and plumbing shops; while all tin vessels used are made by students in the tinning department, and the painting and plastering are done by students in those trades. Handsome dresses

GIRLS MARCHING IN REVIEW—TUSKEGEE.

Harper's Weekly, December 31, 1898, p. 1284.

and fancy articles were seen representing the work of girls who are students in plain sewing, dress-making, and millinery shops, while other girls are being taught nurse-training, housekeeping, cooking, and laundry-work, the last being carried on in a three-story brick building devoted wholly to hand laundry-work. A farm of 700 acres is cultivated by students in agriculture, whose instructor is a graduate of Iowa Agricultural College, and crops of corn, oats, pumpkins, etc., have been harvested for food. Fifty acres are planted in grape-vines and fruit trees, partly from which three thousand gallons of fruit have been canned during the past summer and are stored in the cellar of the boarding department. Sixty Jersey cows furnish milk, butter, and cheese, the creamery being handled by students.

Each of the various industries has as its head a teacher who is skilled along the special line, and when it was learned that President McKinley was to visit Tuskegee, the faculty decided to prepare floats which, passing in review before the visitors, would show the literary and industrial phases of the school. Hence for three weeks plans were wrought into beautiful floats, consisting of a frame-work of lumber dressed in cedar, moss, pine, and ivy. The broad platform gave the opportunity to exhibit innumerable devices of student handicraft. A reviewing-stand was arranged for the President's party, and for the Governor and Legislature of Alabama, who attended in a body. When President McKinley, with Governor Johnston of Alabama on his right, and Principal Booker T. Washington on his left, stood in the front row to view the parade, the appearance was an evidence of the present achievement in the solution of the racial problem and a prophecy of hope and ultimate success.

Promptly at nine o'clock seven hundred young men in double file, bearing each a sugar-cane surmounted with a palm leaf, began to pass in review, keeping step to the students' brass band, and following were four hundred girls, each with a sugar-cane, on top of which was a boll of cotton. Every face in this long procession was a ray of hope, in every eye was the sparkle of purpose, and both in form and feature did the lessons of life's seriousness show their imprint. Then began the magnificent pageant of forty-five floats drawn by horses, mules, and oxen, each float representing a different phase of the institute. While a pen picture is impossible, it is safe to say that no tableaux were ever more effective in conveying to a vast audience a concrete vision of the aims, methods, and results of an institution's work. From floats contrasting old and new methods of butter-making to the artistic floats of physics, electricity, and architecture, every feature of the institute was exhibited in an entertaining style. But to those who have watched and aided the transition from the rude cabin homes and ignorant and crude farming to the skill and training displayed, the tableaux were an inadequate exhibition of the manhood and womanhood awakened in those young men and women.

At ten-thirty o'clock the large brick chapel was filled with the full Senate and House of Representatives of the Legislature of Alabama, white and black citizens of the community, teachers and students. There were about two hundred white ladies in attendance, who, with their escorts or alone, had mingled on the grounds freely and promiscuously during the parades, and now struggled good-naturedly for seats. There was no repulsiveness anywhere apparent, and any one who may have thought the races are living here in perpetual enmity was amply convinced otherwise. The troubles which recently occurred in the Carolinas are not possible in such an atmosphere of tolerant disposition as at Tuskegee. A few of these white people are contributors to Tuskegee Institute, and others, as trustees of the school and officers of the State, are contributing their influence to its success.

In the audience was one man who, as an owner of 400 slaves, was reared in all the convictions of his section. A few years ago a negro boy left his plantation, came to Tuskegee, completed the course there, and returning, exhibited such a marked improvement as to convince the planter of the value of negro education, and to turn his life into one of perfect sympathy and co-operation, so that he now gives annually his money and still more largely gives his influence.

Of such remarkable composition was the audience to which President McKinley spoke, and no audience ever welcomed him more warmly. While his speech was mainly of a congratulatory nature upon the aims and methods of the institute, in which he remarked that it "is ideal in conception," he thus touched the negro problem, already overshadowing the South, and destined to more largely tax the American people:

"One thing I like about this institution is that its policy has been generous and progressive; it is not so self-centred or interested in its own pursuits and ambitions as to ignore what is going on in the rest of the country or make it difficult for outsiders to share the local advantages. I allude especially to the spirit in which the annual conferences have been here held by leading colored citizens and educators, with the intention of improving the condition of their less fortunate brothers and sisters. Here, we can see, is an immense field, and one which cannot too soon or too carefully be utilized. The conferences have grown in popularity, and are well calculated not only to encourage colored men and colored women in their individual efforts, but to cultivate and promote an amicable relationship between the two races—a problem whose solution was never more needed than at the present time. Patience, moderation, self-control, knowledge, character, will surely win you victories and realize the best aspirations of your people. An evidence of the soundness of the purposes of this institution is that those in charge of its management evidently do not believe in attempting the unattainable, and their instruction in self-reliance and practical industry is most valuable."

The general awakening of the negro masses referred to by the President as being made through the Tuskegee Institute, and which the visit of himself and cabinet will immensely stimulate, is a special work of national value. The last week in each February a farmers' conference is held, and the people are urged to improve their homes, buy land, cease mortgaging their crops, lengthen their school terms, demand good moral character and fitness in their teachers and preachers, etc. This agitation has spread from this centre to all the South, and the results are already to be seen.

Principal Booker T. Washington has received many words of praise and endorsement, more than any other living man of his race, but it is doubtful if any man has ever received a higher testimonial from the Executive of the nation, speaking as its representative, and fully aware of the significance of his utterance, than when he said in his address:

"To speak of Tuskegee without paying special tribute to Booker T. Washington's genius and perseverance would be impossible. The inception of this noble enterprise was his, and he deserves high credit for it. His was the enthusiasm and enterprise which made its steady progress possible and established in the institution its present high standard of accomplishment. He has won a worthy reputation as one of the great leaders of his race, widely known, and much respected at home and abroad as an accomplished educator, a great orator, and a true philanthropist."

By Thomas J. Calloway, Vice-Principal of Tuskegee Institute

1899

President William McKinley's willingness to appoint African Americans to federal positions, twice as many as any president before him, was seen as cause for hope by black leaders. In most cases, the appointments were in exchange for support given to the Republican Party and did not hold any special significance for African Americans. However, McKinley's tour of Tuskegee Institute during a scheduled visit to the Alabama legislature would have far-reaching implications for many African Americans, and directly influenced the level of funding afforded Tuskegee and the institutions that adopted it as a model. McKinley's visit not only reaffirmed Booker T. Washington's position as the "Negro leader," but also conveyed McKinley's support for the type of curriculum offered at the Institute.

During the 1890s, higher education underwent a transformation that emphasized university education as preparation for a career. By 1900, more than 2,000 students had graduated from black colleges. Some of the institutions had specific curricula emphases: Wilberforce University in Wilberforce, Ohio, trained men for the military; Shaw University in Raleigh, North Carolina, established one of the first medical schools; and Livingstone College in Salisbury, North Carolina, trained men for the ministry.

Philanthropists, primarily white, contributed large sums of money for the education of African Americans living in the South. Through direct and indirect taxes and religious organizations, African Americans also supported the improvement of education. Of particular note were the fund-raising efforts of black higher educational institutions, like Fisk University's Jubilee Singers. Still, one-third of African Americans over the age of ten could neither read nor write in 1910, a time when only 7.7 percent of Americans were illiterate. Yet, it was evident that great gains had been made; the number of African Americans who could read in 1910 was more than twice the number who could read in 1863. Over 1,700,000 African Americans were attending public schools, most taught by black teachers, numbering 35,000 in 1910.

An educated populace was desirable for many reasons, the primary being the maturation of an entrepreneurship base to foster community development. In the antebellum period, free African Americans established or operated businesses. After the reconstruction era, numerous small black-owned businesses were established in segregated urban areas of the South. However, the number of businesses was still small, and involved a minute percentage of the population. Physical isolation from white communities reduced patronage from white clientele and adversely affected service businesses such as catering and barbering.

On the other hand, isolation assured the black professional of black customers he might have lost to whites. Even in northern and western areas, segregation of the races became customary as Jim Crow laws were passed in nearly every state. Some exceptions were noted—Douglass Hospital in Kansas City, Kansas, was opened in 1899, becoming the first hospital west of the Mississippi River without racial barriers for admittance.

How to strengthen existing businesses, establish new ones, and extend economic stability in the black community posed a true challenge for African Americans in 1899 and beyond. Because banks and insurance companies could provide financial services sorely needed by African Americans, much attention was given to their formation. Of the two, banks, as repositories for funds and as lending agencies, had the best potential to effect the greatest economic progress in a community. Stellar examples of the positive multiplying effect banks could have were the True Reformers Bank and the Consolidated Bank and Trust Company, both in Richmond, Virginia. Of special note are the innovative approaches utilized by Maggie Lena Walker to transform the Independent Order of St. Luke into a financial complex in Richmond—the Consolidated Bank and Trust Company.

Booker T. Washington also touted black entrepreneurship as an essential component of the black community. As the new century unfolded, he launched the National Negro Business League, another aspect of his economic integration plan. The organizational meeting was held in Boston, and was attended by 115 delegates representing twenty states. However, charges that the various branches were simply extensions of Washington's accommodationist philosophy, without concrete programs and initiatives, triggered the decline of the league in Chicago and other northern urban centers. The development of a viable economic base for the black community, although never fully successful, would remain a priority throughout the twentieth century.

A hunger for words about the black experience motivated many African Americans to share their research and thoughts with a growing educated populace. After the July 1899 publication of the collection of stories, The Conjure Woman, *Charles Waddell Chesnutt was considered the foremost black novelist of the times. The book was based on superstitions held by blacks in North Carolina and gained the attention of literary critics, both white and black. Racial conflicts encountered by African Americans of mixed ancestry was another theme explored by Chesnutt as evidenced in* The House Behind the Cedars *and* The Marrow of Tradition. *For his outstanding contribution to the field of black literature, Chesnutt was given the Spingarn Medal in 1928, the highest honor awarded by the National Association for the Advancement of Colored People (NAACP).*

Also published in 1899, Sutton Griggs's Imperium and Imperio *detailing the efforts of a black militant to create an anti-white society is now considered the first black power novel. The plot's central focus, the creation of an all-black republic in Texas, contributed to an ongoing debate among African Americans. Other literary achievements were not as controversial; librarian Daniel Murray prepared an exhaustive bibliography of every title and pamphlet written by persons of African ancestry. The listing grew out of an earlier project as Murray prepared a display on Negro literature for the American Exhibit at the 1900 Paris Exposition. In time, Murray was recognized as the leading authority on black works.*

W. E. B. DuBois influenced the growing research on African Americans with the release of the pioneer sociological study, The Philadelphia Negro: A Social Study. *The study is most helpful in analyzing the development of a black urban community, residential pattern shifts, the decline and growth of black neighborhoods, and the formation of black religious, social, and civic institutions.*

African Americans also documented and celebrated their heritage in the visual arts and entertainment. Scott Joplin, "king of the ragtime," published the "Maple Leaf Rag" and elevated piano-rag-music to a new level. The composition, drawing upon black dance-music popular during the antebellum period, was the first piece of sheet music to sell a million copies. The success of "Maple Leaf Rag" furthered Joplin's goal of gaining the acceptance of ragtime as a legitimate musical form. Scott also composed ballet music and a folk opera, "Treemonisha," which advocates education as fundamentally essential for the social advancement of African Americans.

As the decade drew to a close, the struggle for the ascendancy of the most appropriate philosophy to undergird racial advancement was well underway. Although black women were marginal figures in the national social reform movement effecting changes in the status of women, they were active participants in identifying strategies to eliminate racial prejudice. Ida Wells-Barnett, married to Ferdinand L. Barnett, a prominent Chicago journalist and businessmen in 1895, took an uncompromising stance against lynching and segregation—a stance that placed her solidly within the camp of the "militants." In addition, she was extremely outspoken in her rejection of Booker T. Washington's accommodationism as a viable option for racial advancement. Even so, she was able to garner enough support within the Afro-American Council to be elected secretary, and later chairperson, of the Council's Anti-Lynching Bureau. When the Tuskegeean political viewpoint finally dominated the Council, Wells-Barnett resigned and Mary Church Terrell became chair of the Anti-Lynching Bureau.

Wells-Barnett's repudiation of the Washington philosophy led to a major schism in the National Association of Colored Women (NACW). At the 1899 NACW convention in Chicago, Wells-Barnett worked against the re-election of Mary Church Terrell as president of the body. All knew that Wells-Barnett supported DuBois while Terrell was loyal to Washington and Wells-Barnett's campaign had as much to do with Terrell's support of Washington as it did with the NACW's two term limitation for the presidency. Mary Terrell insisted that the two year NACW constitutional clause should not apply to her because her first term occurred prior to the writing of the constitution. Terrell's supporters were able to override Wells-Barnett's objections and have their candidate elected.

The NACW election dispute captured the attention of other women's groups, and was used to support white suffragists' claims that black women were not yet ready for the vote. As early as 1894, white suffragists had begun eliminating the inclusion of black women. Susan B. Anthony, fearing negative reactions from the southern white suffragists, asked Frederick Douglass, a long-time agitator for the right of women to vote, not to attend the National American Women's Suffrage Association's (NAWSA) meeting in Atlanta, Georgia, the first in the South. White women's interests were clearly judged more important than the "Negro Question" in 1899, when Anthony successfully blocked a resolution calling for a NAWSA pronouncement against the railroad policy of segregated seating for black women. The NAWSA, like other national women's groups, was most concerned that its southern white members not withdraw their support.

The African American's quest for the coveted prize of full equality in the United States was not realized during the decade of the 1890s; yet, the lives of many underwent drastic changes resulting in relocation, an *acquisition of a formal education, the ascension to the middle-class, and the development of self-help organizations.*

Cynthia Neverdon-Morton
Coppin State College

PEOPLE TALKED ABOUT

LESLIE'S WEEKLY
January 19, 1899, p. 43

One of the most interesting incidents connected with the recent journey of President and Mrs. McKinley through the South was the visit they made to Tuskegee Institute, the great school for colored young men and women, of which Booker T. Washington is the principal. This school, which is located at Tuskegee, Alabama, in the very heart of the "Black Belt," was established about fifteen years ago in an abandoned church, into which thirty untaught negro boys and girls were gathered for the opening session. Now it has a thousand pupils and forty buildings, all but the first three of which have been built by the pupils themselves, even to the making of the bricks, as a part of their industrial education. Booker T. Washington, who had not long before been graduated from Hampton, went to Tuskegee when the school was opened, and the remarkable growth and success of the institute have been very largely due to his energy and ability. Mr. Washington, who is now about forty years old, was born a slave in Virginia. After the war he learned to read while working as errand-boy for a Northern woman then living in the South. Hearing of Hampton he worked his way over the mountains to that school, and stayed until he was graduated. No small amount of his success at Tuskegee is due to the efficient assistance of his wife. Mrs. Washington's work among the neglected wives of the poverty-stricken negro farmers on the plantations has been specially notable. The most unique feature of Tuskegee, and one which President McKinley commended publicly while there, is the famous "farmers' conference," which every February assembles there, and when 2,000 negro farmers and their wives meet under Mr. Washington's leadership to "talk over things."

PEOPLE TALKED ABOUT

LESLIE'S WEEKLY
March 23, 1899, p. 223

The name of a colored man appears on every piece of paper currency issued by the United States government.

MRS. BOOKER T. WASHINGTON

Frank Leslie's Illustrated Newspaper, January 19, 1899, p. 43.

That man is the register of the Treasury, Judson W. Lyons. He was born in 1858, in Georgia, was sent to school in Augusta, by his mother, and afterward to the Augusta Institute, teaching school at night to obtain means of support. In 1878 he was elected a delegate to a Congressional convention meeting at Crawfordsville, Georgia, and made a fiery speech, which infuriated the Democrats and led to threats of lynching. Young Lyons did not know of these threats, and was greatly surprised when he was invited by the Hon. Alexander H. Stephens the ex-Vice-President of the Confederacy, who lived at Crawfordsville, to become his guest. At three o'clock in the morning Mr. Stephens's secretary and valet accompanied Lyons to the depot and saw him safely off for Atlanta. Some time afterward Mr. Lyons asked Mr. Stephens the reason for his entertainment, and then learned, for the first time, that his life had been saved by the thoughtfulness of his friend. Mr. Lyons was a member of the Republican National Convention in 1880, and served in the internal-revenue service of Georgia. In 1884 he was graduated from Howard University, at Washington, and was admitted to the Bar in Augusta. He was a Presidential elector on the Republican ticket in Georgia in 1892, and in 1896, as a delegate to the Republican National Convention, voted for McKinley. In 1898 he was appointed register of the Treasury. He is president

EVERYBODY WANTS HIS AUTOGRAPH.

Frank Leslie's Illustrated Newspaper, March 23, 1899, p. 223.

of the board of trustees of Haines College, Augusta, and is one of the leading colored men in the United States.

THIS BUSY WORLD

HARPER'S WEEKLY
March 25, 1899, p. 281

On March 11 one hundred volunteers, drawn from four companies of the Twenty-fourth Infantry (colored), started out from Fort Russell, Wyoming, to dig out a train on the Cheyenne and Northern Railroad, which at that date had already been snow-bound for two weeks. These volunteers are from one of the regiments that made so fine a record last July on San Juan hill. From fighting Spaniards in Cuba in July to fighting snow in Wyoming in March is a considerable change, and the story of the attack of these veterans on the snow-drifts at Iron Mountain, fifty miles from Cheyenne, ought to be worth reading. Moreover, to be snowed up in a railroad train for three weeks and dependent for food on stray cattle is a severe experience, and the forty-two passengers on the Cheyenne and Northern who at this writing have just reached Cheyenne will have stories to tell too when their powers of narration are restored. They finally abandoned their train, and walked ten miles to meet the rescue-party.

E. S. Martin

THE PLAIN TRUTH

LESLIE'S WEEKLY
April 6, 1899, p. 262

The action of Governor Candler, of Georgia, in publicly denouncing the recent murder, by a mob, of half a dozen negroes, while the latter were bound with ropes and penned in a jail at Palmetto, will not lessen the feeling of great indignation which this outrage has aroused. The murdered negroes were accused of incendiarism, and it is said that some of them had confessed; but, as Governor Candler says, "the outrage was inexcusable, as the men were in the hands of the law and the law was amply able to punish them, and conviction and punishment were absolutely certain if the proofs were at hand." Much sympathy has been expressed with the South in the past, by those who believed that the predominance of a vicious element among the blacks endangered the welfare of unprotected women. The one partly-accepted excuse for the lynching and shooting of negroes has been that it was made necessary in order to protect defenseless women throughout the South. But in the Palmetto case women were not concerned, and the murder was a cold-blooded, cowardly outrage. A mob of armed men, masked, as cowards always are, rode to the warehouse in which the helpless culprits were incarcerated, compelled them to stand up, bound as they were, and shot them to death. The negroes pleaded for a chance to fight for their lives, but even a moment in which to prepare their souls to meet their Maker was refused them. The Southern press and Southern leaders denounce this outrage in unmeasured terms. It should not be charged to the people of the South. It was the work of criminals, whose punishment, we trust, will be swift and certain.

A BENEVOLENT NEGRO

LESLIE'S WEEKLY
May 4, 1899, p. 358

It is seldom that a negro leaves a large estate, and very seldom that he leaves any part of it to public or benevolent institutions. The unfortunate conditions which surround colored people in the United States are largely responsible for this. An exception to the rule, however, is to be noticed in Boston. The will of Frederic G. Barbadoes, a wealthy negro, who died in that city several weeks ago, was recently filed for probate, and it was found that the bulk of the estate was distributed in bequests of from $250 to $1,000 each, to various colored homes, asylums, and churches, mostly in Washington.

He made thirty or forty personal bequests to relatives and friends, and left the residue of the estate to the Tuskeegee University, of Alabama, the Lincoln University, of Pennsylvania, and Manassas Institute, Virginia.

THIS BUSY WORLD

HARPER'S WEEKLY
May 13, 1899, p. 473

Whatever any Northern reader may feel about the burning of the negro Sam Hose and the lynching of the negro preacher Strickland, in Georgia, one thing he should always bear in mind, that there is no vital difference between the white man in the South and the white man in the North, and that what white men do in Georgia white men from New York, or Massachusetts, or Minnesota would probably do in Georgia under similar circumstances. A county in Georgia went stark crazy over Sam Hose. Northern readers cannot understand it. A letter has come to the Weekly from a Georgia woman which tells a story of Sam Hose's crime as Georgia understands it. It is hardly a letter that the Weekly may print, but it may all be believed, and it helps to an understanding of what has happened. No man who believed what this woman believes and has written about Hose and Strickland and negroes of their class in the South would be surprised at anything that might follow such a crime as Hose committed. It may be that nothing can justify such an orgy as was held over Hose, but there is plenty that can explain it. The men and women of the South believe that certain unruly negroes can only be restrained from horrible crimes against white women by swift and terrible punishment. We of the North have little experience of these crimes, but our blood circulates, and we know what sort of dispositions such crimes arouse. To read the story of Sam Hose's crime as our Georgia correspondent has written it begets absolute indifference to that negro's sufferings or fate. It fills the mind with horror, and makes one feel that any means that is effectual to prevent such crimes is justified. One forgets the monstrousness of the Sam Hose lynching, and only wonders whether it was expedient.

E. S. Martin

ONE OF THE EXCUSES

HARPER'S WEEKLY
May 20, 1899, p. 492

One of the excuses made for lynching in rape cases in the South is that women who have suffered violence will not appear in court and testify against their assailants. A letter which recently came to the Weekly from a correspondent in Georgia speaks of a case, apparently well known in Georgia, of the wife of a prominent clergyman, who received injuries from a negro, from the effects of which she eventually died. Her husband would not allow the man to be lynched, and the wife would not testify against him in court, consequently he escaped punishment altogether.

The unwillingness of women to appear in court against such assailants is entirely natural and comprehensible. To get over this difficulty and still avoid the counter-evil of lynching, it has been proposed to establish drum-head courts, which will deal out sudden and summary punishment to authors of crimes against women. Mr. Archibald Hopkins, of Washington, who has taken some thought on this idea, suggests that, in States where lynching is common, the Governors be authorized to appoint an officer in every township, who, on the day an assault becomes known, shall summon six citizens who live conveniently near, constitute them a special jury, preside over them himself, hold a summary trial, and, if guilt is proved, give sentence, and execute it without further delay. Such a trial would be better than none, in that the accused would have a chance to demonstrate his innocence, and because the responsibility for the proceedings would be openly borne by known men.

A curious supplementary reason given for favoring these drum-head courts is that negro criminals of the sort these courts would deal with do not greatly object to being hanged, provided they have plenty of time to get ready, and especially to repent and get religion. Where the criminal, after a life of vice ending in some hideous crime of violence, is given time to become a happy convert, so that he steps confidently from the gallows trap into eternal bliss, the effect of his punishment upon other evil-doers is almost nullified. When he is sped into the unknown with unwashed hands, the example is held to be more salutary.

Here is what a Georgia woman writes about how the children in the country districts in that State go to school:

> You know Georgia is distinctly an agricultural State. The greater part of her people live on farms and plantations. The only labor employed is black, and the blacks outnumber the whites in the rural districts. Well, the white children go to school by the ringing of the plantation bells. At a place where there are large boys in the family the bell rings first; then the girls and small children on the farms within hearing flock to the call. They start off, and when they reach the next plantation that bell rings, and another band joins them, and so they go, gathering strength until they reach the school. Thus, you see, Southern boys early learn that they are our protectors. In the busy

season, when the large boys are needed to help with the crops, the schools close, because the girls and small children cannot with safety go alone. If our land was infested with wild beasts, there could not be a greater fear in the breasts of parents when their girls and little ones start for school on a lonely country road.

That is interesting. All that concerns the relations of blacks and whites in the South is of surpassing interest just now. But as we read the tales of the insecurity of women, and the need of drum-head courts for their protection, we must recall that four-fifths of the lynchings in the South last year were for crimes other than violence or attempted violence to women.

A REMEDY

HARPER'S WEEKLY
May 20, 1899, p. 492

In trying to devise a remedy for affairs in the South, it must be remembered that the proportion of criminals among the negroes of the South is about three times as great as among the white people; that mere secular education seems not to be effective in improving the negroes' manners or morals; and that lynching as a remedy for crime in the South is a failure. Crime increases under it, and it scares away prosperity.

The worst enemy of the negro race seems to be the negro criminal, and especially the criminal who assails a white woman. The worst enemy of Southern civilization seems to be the lyncher. The most vigorous opponents of Southern lynching are white people in the South, who know that the lawlessness which it begets is ruinous to society. The worst crimes of Southern negroes are crimes in which lust and revenge are combined, but lust and revenge are not allayed, but incited, by such an orgy as was held over Sam Hose.

Our Southern brethren have a very difficult and perplexing problem in making law and order prevail in their borders. The North has always recognized its large responsibility for the condition of the Southern negroes, and has been more than willing to do its share in looking after them. It is not enough for the North to be willing. It must be wise also. It gave the negroes the suffrage long before they were fit to exercise it. Has it proved a useful gift? Booker Washington, that great and noble negro leader, the most honored man of his race, counsels his people to keep out of politics and leave government to the whites, and to concentrate their energies upon improving their condition by learning better methods of work and acquiring property.

It is not enough for the North to denounce lynching. It must be prepared to uphold the best people in the South in the execution of any sound measures that can be devised to train the young negro in the way he should go, secure the restriction and punishment of crime by legal methods, and put lynching down.

Cruelty begets cruelty. Terror leads naturally to violence. So long as the whites in the South are afraid of the negroes the negroes will doubtless have reason to be afraid of the whites. No intelligent white person in the South defends lynching except as a desperate remedy, the need of which ought to be removed by some better means of restricting crime.

THIS BUSY WORLD

HARPER'S WEEKLY
May 27, 1899, p. 517

In the Weekly of last week was given an extract from the letter of a Southern woman, telling how white children go to school in Georgia. In a later letter this same correspondent writes:

> What I wrote of the way white children go to school is only one out of many illustrations that could be given of "life behind the scenes" on a Georgia plantation to-day. My own little nephews and nieces go to school by the ringing of the plantation bells. Think of these children, scarce knowing what it all means, yet listening for the sound of the bells to tell them that the big boys are coming to protect them from the dark shadow that hides in the bushes! This thing has not come about in a day. It has not started since the Sam Hose lynching. It is the slow and steady growth of thirty years of negro outrages on white women and girls.
>
> It is said that education at the South is increasing faster among the negroes than among the whites. Is it any wonder? The negro children go to school in perfect freedom and safety all the year round, while the white schools are closed half the time because of a lack of sufficient protection for the children. Is it any wonder that the white men of the rural districts, the landlords and property-owners, who are taxed to educate these negroes, are beginning to fight free schools? and that the Georgia Legislature at its last session cut down the appropriate for education?

* * * * * *

The injustice that is done the South is that the outrages committed by negroes cannot be described in print nor discussed in public, while the lynching of negroes for crime is given in all its horrible details.

The letter from which these extracts are made is, of course, the letter of a partisan, speaking for her own side, yet speaking truthfully as far as she goes. Her words are quoted not to excite animosity towards negroes, nor to excuse lynching, nor to justify oppression, nor to disparage the education of negroes, but to show that there are two sides to the race question in the South, and that the negroes are not the only people who live in apprehension and insecurity. Of course the very bad negroes who are dangerous to women and children are a small minority of their race, but it is averred that when these men commit outrageous crimes the other and better negroes hide them from justice.

There the misery of lynching comes in. Of course negroes hide black criminals from mobs and lynching parties.

About the strongest thing in the world is human nature. It is stronger than law, stronger than argument, stronger than self-interest. In the relations of blacks and whites in the South it shows at every turn. The problem in the South is how to make two races, almost equal in numbers, but unequal in capacity and force, live together in peace on equal terms without merging. If negroes and whites could intermarry, the problem might settle itself faster. The Southern white man says that a black man shall not marry a white woman. That prohibition is, no doubt, at the bottom of most of the cases of negro violence to white women. It is the prohibited thing that unruly passions demand. If the black woman was prohibited to the white man with the same determination that the white woman is prohibited in the South to the black man, no doubt we should oftener hear of white men in Georgia taking to the woods with blood-hounds on their trail.

But of course nothing in these reflections must be interpreted to favor a mixture of blacks and whites as a solution of race troubles. It is a true instinct of self-preservation that leads the Southern white to keep his race separate. It is obviously demoralizing for Southern whites to live with negroes as they do, but if the two races began to merge, what would the end be?

It is all a very big and intricate problem—too big to be settled by mass-meetings in Boston, too big to be settled by emigration or colonization. It will have to be settled in the South, where it is best understood. The best people in the South are the people most competent to deal with it.

In one particular at least the present position of the Southern negroes is more advantageous than that of the negroes before the war. They can leave the South if they wish to. There is no need of an underground railroad. All that is necessary is for each negro to learn of some place where he will be better off, and provide himself with the money to take him there. If the seven million negroes of the South could be distributed through-

out the United States, lynchings would probably cease, for the negro element would not be strong enough anywhere to cause race jealousy or disturb politics. Of course such a distribution is impracticable, but it can be attempted, at least on a small scale. The newspapers tell of the plan of Mr. Perry, a colored lawyer of New York, to start a colored colony on the Peconic River on Long Island. His plan is to buy 3000 acres of land, bring up a picked lot of negroes, and establish a negro community, governed by special rules, and run by negroes for negroes. If such a scheme should be carried out it would be very interesting to watch its progress, but no one who knows anything about the history of attempts to establish exclusive communities of working-people can be very sanguine of its success.

E. S. Martin

THIS BUSY WORLD

HARPER'S WEEKLY
June 3, 1899, p. 541

Persons who have sympathy to spare are invited to bestow some of their surplus on the people of Lake City, South Carolina. There are about five hundred persons in Lake City, and they are much inconvenienced because there is no post-office in their village, and they have to send several miles to get their mail and post their letters. They had a post-office, but it got them into trouble. The readers of the Weekly may remember about it. The postmaster was a negro named Baker. He was not satisfactory for some reason, and instead of bothering the department with complaints about him, some of the neighbors surrounded his house one evening and set fire to it, and shot and killed him and his wife and baby. Since then the department has not employed any postmaster at that village, but has been trying to find out who was responsible for killing Baker. It got together a good deal of evidence and tried several persons for the murder, but the jury stood seven to five for acquittal. The trial was about a month ago. Since then the Congressman from those parts, Representative Norton, has been to Washington to try to have a new postmaster appointed, but the department feels that Lake City has been too careless about its postmaster, and is too indifferent about bringing his murderers to justice. It seems to feel that a town that has not public spirit enough to catch and convict any one for murdering its postmaster in a conspicuous and public manner cannot really care whether it has a post-office or not. Representative Norton is quoted as holding that the inaction of the department is "infamous," but that will not be the general sentiment about it. The more reasonable feeling is that if the man who carries the mail for Lake City is one of the men who shot Baker, it serves him right to be put to that trouble, and if he is not one of the men who shot Baker, he ought to be thankful to have an errand that takes him out of Lake City and away from the murderers of Baker at least once a day. The simplest way for the Lake City people to escape the annoyance of not having a post-office is to move out and go somewhere else to live. But if they insist on staying on where they are, they ought to use their influence with the mob that killed the Bakers to induce some of them to come forward and be tried and convicted and hanged, for the general convenience of the community. The chances are that if one or two men could be lawfully hanged by the sheriff in memory of Baker, the post-office would be reopened.

E. S. Martin

THIS BUSY WORLD

HARPER'S WEEKLY
June 10, 1899, p. 565

On May 20 a meeting of women was held in Boston "to protest against the barbarism of lynching." A great deal of vigorous language was used. Mrs. Richard P. Hallowell, who opened the meeting, said that the majority of the people of the North were shamefully indifferent to the rights of the colored people in the South; Mrs. Florida Ridley declared that the thinking people of America must arouse themselves; Mrs. Julia Ward Howe, venerable and honored, called for Federal troops to see that the negro votes are counted; Mrs. Alice Freeman Palmer said, very justly, that lynching led to anarchy; Lucia Ames Mead lamented "the cessation of rebuke, which the South needs at this time"; Mrs. Mary Clement Leavitt said that the alleged cause for most lynchings is not the true one, and that "the real truth is that lynching is only one link in the chain the whites of the South are forging to bind back into actual, though not nominal, slavery the colored population." The meeting included some of the best known and most respected women of Boston. They spoke their minds freely and were carefully reported. Several of them laid stress on the statement, which has not been as yet successfully contradicted, that while the chief excuse made for lynching was that it was necessary for the protection of Southern women, four fifths of the lynchings were for offences in which women were not concerned.

The Boston women did ample justice to the side of the question which appeared to them. It seems only fair that women who speak on the other side should be heard too.

A woman who went years ago from New York to Florida, but who still has in New York many acquaintances who respect her judgment, says, in a letter to the Weekly:

I have now lived in the South for fourteen years, in a lonely house. A loaded pistol has for all these years been an unobtrusive article of furniture, and for the last few years a huge and faithful dog has given me a delightful feeling of security. My intimate friends have tried to keep the local papers of the South out of my sight. It would surprise you to read how often lynching seems the whole duty of man. The fact that it is an inevitable punishment under certain conditions is no doubt a far more valuable protection than the weak, procrastinating arm of the law. Fancy, after such crimes, the delays, the appeals, the horrors of the witness-stand, the probable release of the criminal on some technicality! One does not think of reasoning over a mad dog.

The law has cut adrift too many murderers in my part of the country. There is no doubt that the certainty of hot-footed pursuit and sudden death does much to restrain men whose glimmering of human cunning makes them more dangerous than the fiercest brute. I have never, until I read something lately written in Harper's Weekly, known any Northern paper that could look at the question from the point of view of the man or woman who knows. If you could understand the daily fears I have struggled against for years, you would understand also, perhaps, the curious feeling of gratitude that I have to a journal that has put it in print for the North to read that lynching may, after all, be at least expedient. May the Fates forbid that, until at least our American criminal law is radically changed, the women who live in the South should know that they must wait while the lawyers adjust the scales of justice!

Those words were surely as warmly felt as any spoken at the woman's meeting in Boston. Yet they are spoken by a Northern woman, whose mind is as clear and her heart as kind as those of her sisters in Boston.

Another correspondent, a Southern woman this time writes from Georgia in a strain that might make even Mrs. Howe doubt if it would help matters much in Georgia to send soldiers there to count the negro vote. After speaking at some length of the idiosyncrasies of negro morality as observed in her neighborhood, she says:

In Atlanta, Georgia, two years ago, six hundred colored children presented themselves at the public schools who were without parents, guardians, or homes. Major Slaton, superintendent of public schools, investigated these cases, and found that these children had been abandoned by their parents, and left on the streets of Atlanta practically homeless. What the negroes need is not education, not voting privileges, but fathers, mothers, homes. They have houses to live in; they have bread to eat; there are men and women who are responsible for their being; but they are a fatherless, motherless, homeless race. This would not have been so but for outside interference—for the mistaken efforts of those who thought they were working for the good of the negroes.

It is to the interest of Southerners that the negroes become good citizens, and the way to make them good citizens is to encourage them to buy homes and farms. Land is cheap. We would have been glad to have sold every colored family in Georgia a little farm, and let them pay for it in labor; let them become taxpayers as well as voters. Representation without taxation is worse than taxation without representation. But no. The negro must be educated, and he must vote. Too much *free* education is as bad for the masses as too much free charity, free bread, or anything else that God intended they should earn by the sweat of their brow. It is too late now. Our cities are filled with colored professional men out of work. Our prisons and chain-gangs are overflowing with criminals who can read and write. Our farms lie idle, or else are stocked with a restless, roving, disquieted multitude.

* * * * * * *

It may surprise you to know that I am one of the best friends of the colored people in this community; one of the first persons they come to in times of sickness and trouble. But it is not true friendship to hide the truth. It is for the good of the negroes that both they and the world should look facts squarely in the face.

The only time that my heart ever burns with indignation against them is when I consider that they have divided the greatest nation on earth. That our white brethren of Anglo-Saxon blood have turned against us, and hate us, because of these dark people from the Dark Continent. Oh, my God!

"It isn't the shame and it isn't the blame
That stings like a white-hot brand:
It's coming to know that *you never can know;*
You never can understand."

So it seems that women of the South and women of the North who live in the South have views about the Southern race problem that are quite as pronounced as those of the Boston women who live in Boston. The readers of the Weekly may safely be left to form their own conclusions as to which of the ladies whose opinions have been quoted speaks most intelligently, and out of the fullest knowledge of the subject.

A gentleman who had been to Cuba was asked, the other day, if the Cubans could manage their own concerns. "Not yet," he said. "Give them time to learn. Teach the young ones. There are admirable men in Cuba who can do anything; but the mass of the folks there have had no chance to learn any sort of administration. They have never so much as managed an orphan-asylum. The Spaniards managed—and mismanaged—everything."

The Southern negroes, as we all know, were invited to vote and govern, not only before they had had a chance to learn how to run an orphan-asylum, but while most of them had no experience of independent family life. The theory was that if they had a vote they would rise miraculously to the level of it. They have voted for thirty years, and some have risen, and others have sunk. The wonder is, all things considered, that so many of them get on so well.

E. S. Martin

THIS BUSY WORLD

HARPER'S WEEKLY
June 17, 1899, p. 589

Such negro leaders as Booker T. Washington and T. Thomas Fortune do not advise their brethren to meet violence with violence in the South. Mr. Fortune insists that the lawless men in the South are not the black men, but the poor white men, and he says he is willing to contribute a dollar a year towards the elevation of the poor whites. Mr. Fortune's appeal in behalf of the Southern negro is an appeal to law, and practically it is an appeal to public opinion in the South itself; for if the white men of the South, the natural leaders, are not able to put down lynching, it is likely to go on.

But let us examine Mr. Fortune's assertion that the lawless men in the South are not the negroes, but the poor whites. There is obviously this much truth in it, that the lynching is done by whites, and not by blacks. But crime is lawless as well as lynching, and the excuse made for lynching is that there is a stronger tendency at present towards violent, outrageous crimes, like murder and rape, among the present younger generation of Southern negroes than can be restrained by legal process. Lynching is rarely defended as being right, but it is sometimes extenuated as being necessary.

An idea of how some Southern white men regard some Southern negroes may be had from this extract from a recent letter from a Southern correspondent:

> I do believe (though how can I prove it?) that you have been misled into the publication of a statement that four-fifths of the lynchings in the South during the past year were for crimes other than rape or attempted rape. Lynchings for rape are so lamentably numerous that, if I were to admit that they constitute only one-fifth of the total number, I must confidently expect to see a dead negro hanging at every country cross-road. I simply cannot believe it, and I regret that you should.
>
> My opinions on the negro question have been formed from personal observation. My grandfather was the owner of many negroes, and I know all of his servants who are now living. I know some of them well. My dry-goods bill last month was divided between my wife's purchases and those for the benefit of an old woman who was my mother's "mammy." I sat up many a night at the bedside of my own nurse, and helped bury her, but I would see the *children* of either of these a long way into trouble before I would lift a hand. Why? Because the utter corruption, degradation, filth, loathsomeness of this generation of negroes is the scourge of the South.

That is very strong language. It was not written to be printed, and perhaps it is not quite fair to print it. But it has its value as expressing one phase of Southern opinion. It is evident that this writer, though he speaks so harshly of negroes, does not hate a black man because he is black. His objections to him are based on conduct. He believes that the Southern negroes of the rising generation are worthless—not *all* worthless, of course, but very many of them. He explains his sentiments by telling of individual cases of worthlessness, degradation, and crime that have come to his notice. He says further in his letter, after telling about a bad negro who was hanged for rape by due process of law, and after making a written confession, "We deal so patiently with these creatures, in view of the temptations to do otherwise, that it *hurts* us to be misunderstood."

That is the same cry that found expression in an extract from a Georgia woman's letter printed in the Weekly last week. She too insisted that the situation in the South is not understood in the North, and that it drives Southern white people desperate to be criticised and preached to and condemned by Northern critics who do not understand whereof they speak.

Practically the Northern papers preach about the same doctrine as to lynching as the best of the Southern papers do, but they fail to preach it acceptably to the South. Perhaps the reason is partly because they preach from knowledge that is not, and cannot be, familiar and comprehensive.

Incidents come often to notice which show a determination among the law-abiding Southern whites to stand between their more impetuous brethren and the negroes. The determined attitude of the Governor of Georgia towards the White Caps of Griffin, Georgia, who lately undertook to drive the negro mill-hands out of town, is an encouraging case in point, and a fine example to the Governor of Illinois and sundry folks in that State. So was the verdict given on the 5th of May in Louisville in the case of Dinning against Moore and others. That case was widely noticed in the newspapers last month. The story of it, as told by a correspondent of the Weekly, is that Dinning, a negro farmer, with twelve children, who lived in Simpson County, Kentucky, was roused in the night of January 21, 1897, by a gang of white men led by Moore, who accused him of stealing chickens, and warned him to leave within ten days. He said he had stolen nothing, and would not go. He then exchanged shots with the regulators and killed one of them. He escaped to the woods, and next day gave himself up to the sheriff. He was tried at Louisville, and sentenced to seven years' imprisonment. Public opinion did not approve the sentence, and the Governor promptly pardoned him. He then went to Colonel B. H. Young, a Confederate veteran, and Mr. St. John Boyle, son of General Boyle, a Federal soldier. They brought suit for him against seven of his assailants for trespass, asking $50,000 damages. The case was tried, and the jury brought in a verdict for the whole sum asked for. "The most despicable of men," said Colonel Young, in his address to the jury, "is one who would impose upon another because his skin is black, and the conduct of these marauders shows them to be as cowardly as they are ignoble."

Of course to get a verdict of $50,000 against seven night-riding scalawags is not quite the same thing as getting the money, but still the verdict is a credit to Kentucky, and an honor to the lawyers who undertook the negro's cause. In Kentucky the whites outnumber the negroes six to one, a condition much more favorable to peaceful relations between the two races than that which obtains in the States farther South. In Louisiana, Mississippi, and South Carolina there are more negroes than whites. In Alabama, Georgia, and Florida there are nearly as many blacks as whites.

E. S. Martin

THIS BUSY WORLD

HARPER'S WEEKLY
June 24, 1899, p. 613

One of the customs of the South which usually excites disapproval in the minds of Northern readers is that of pursuing fugitive criminals with hounds. The newspapers always say "blood-hounds," but doubtless any dog with a good nose answers the purpose, and as the object is merely to catch the criminal, probably smaller and less savage dogs than blood-hounds are usually used. Putting "blood-hounds" on the trail of a man sounds bad. But let us see. Near Stratford, Connecticut, on June 3, an elderly widow was found bound and gagged in a farm-house. She had been assaulted by a strange negro. The neighbors immediately wanted him, and turned out to beat the woods for him. They hunted all day for him, and continued at night with torches. If there had been dogs handy to put on his trail, would there have been any humane disinclination to do it? Who can think so? The man was finally caught, was arraigned, pleaded guilty, and was locked up in the jail at Bridge-port, much to the disappointment of a crowd which had other views about his disposition. Let us record our obligations to Connecticut for one good example set.

It is with regret that the Weekly records the impulsiveness of its neighbors of Cherry Hill, a stone's-throw from its front door, 500 of whom, on June 10, the papers say, chased Andrew Vera, a colored sailor, with sticks and stones across the Fourth Ward. He had done no wrong whatever, but our near neighbors here, under some misapprehension as to his conduct, clamored urgently to kill him. A policeman saved him.

Negroes may commit atrocious crimes, and innocent negroes may be chased by mobs, in the North as well as in the South. Here is the record of something that could hardly have happened in the North. A Georgia newspaper of recent date says: "Judge George Hillyer talked interestingly about the proposed lynching convention this morning. He remarked that public burning for the crime of rape, by the legal authorities, is not, in his opinion, too severe a punishment, and it may be that some effort will be made by the convention to have a law enacted to that end."

The convention which the judge speaks of will probably be held at Atlanta, and of course there is not the slightest chance that it will advocate public burning as a legal punishment for anything. But the suggestion is very interesting. Considering the effect of public burnings on the reputation of Georgia, and the damage they do, the fact that a citizen can advocate them in the newspapers and not be in danger of being lynched speaks very well indeed for Georgia's self-restraint and belief in free speech. What an example of the intellectual mastodon Judge George Hillyer of Georgia must be!

E. S. Martin

THIS BUSY WORLD

HARPER'S WEEKLY
July 19, 1899, p. 689

It does not take profound study of the race problem in the South to discover that the penal system in many of the Southern States seems only too well adapted to make unruly negroes bad and bad negroes worse. Chain-gangs are pretty generally criticised as being schools of vice, yet they are maintained in the South because they provide a cheap way of disposing of criminals, and because the proportion of criminals to tax-payers being in some States very large, a cheap provision for them is urgently needed. Any reader of race-problem literature is likely to ask himself whether Northern philanthropists who want to help the South in working out its problem might not do well to consider whether the need of reformatories is not even more urgent than the need of more schools. Report says that young persons—lads and girls—and especially young negroes, are sent to the chain-gangs for slight offences, to their great detriment, because there is nowhere else to send them. At present the only reformatory for young negroes in the South is at Birmingham, Alabama. It is good news that another is to be started in Hanover County, Virginia, and that Mr. C. P. Huntington has bought 1300 acres of land which he expects to devote to it. Among the promoters of the scheme are Dr. H. B. Frissell, of the Hampton Institute, and President J.H. Smith, of the Reformatory Association.

General Funston, whose graphic use of language leads to his sentiments being quoted more, probably, than he would approve, is reported as saying that though not on general principles an expansionist, he believes that, being in the Philippines, we should stay there to the bitter end, "and rawhide these bullet-headed Asians until they yell for mercy." That sounds somewhat savage, although the general sentiment it expresses is very widely held; but much of the sting is taken out of it by the general's supplementary declaration, that "after the war I want the job of Professor of American History in Luzon University, when they build it, and I'll warrant that the new generation of natives will know better than to get in the way of the band-wagon of Anglo-Saxon progress and decency."

It is certainly an interesting combination of purposes to rawhide the Tagals until they are ready to quit fighting and then to give them prompt and thorough instruction in American history. No doubt General

Funston feels, as we all do more or less, that it is ignorance of the American character and American intentions that makes the Filipinos so intractable at present. The suggestion that Funston, for his part, would like to stick to Manila when the schoolmaster's turn comes shows an interest in the islands which it is an encouragement to note. It ought not to be possible—probably it is not possible—to fight a brave people (even though they are bullet-headed Asians), who are ready to die for what they call liberty, without becoming interested in their future welfare. Exchange of hard blows is apt to breed respect on both sides.

E. S. Martin

NEGRO KILLED NEAR SELMA

Shot from Ambush by Unknown Parties—Lived Only an Hour.

ATLANTA CONSTITUTION
July 26, 1899

Selma, Ala. July 25.—(Special.)—Jack Davis, a negro living on the plantation of William Weaver, a few miles from the city, was killed early this morning. It seems that some weeks ago, a woman who had been living with Jack for the past few years, tired of him and became the companion of another negro living at Orrville. On Sunday last the lover of the woman went to Davis's house to get something belonging to her. These Davis refused to give up. A quarrel ensued, though no damage was done. That night while Davis was going home he was shot at but not hit. Last night, however, while passing through a dark piece of woods he was shot from ambush, receiving wounds from which he died about an hour later. He stated before dying that he had seen two negroes shoot him, but refused to give their names. Davis and Dr. Whitts Stuart had a falling out about two weeks ago and the doctor whipped him. Since then the negro has been very surly and had threatened vengeance. It was reported at first that the negro came to his death at the hands of a white mob, but the particulars are given as above.

THIS BUSY WORLD

HARPER'S WEEKLY
July 29, 1899, p. 737

Apropos of a recent paragraph in the Weekly about Mr. C. P. Huntington's gift of land in Hanover County, Virginia, for a reformatory for negroes, and of the accompanying statement that at present the only reformatory for negroes in the South is at Birmingham, Alabama, a Georgia correspondent writes:

> There is a reformatory at Milledgeville, Georgia. It is called "The State's Farm," but it was established for the purpose of separating young criminals and women from the more hardened and desperate kind. It is splendidly managed, and one of the institutions our State takes most pride in. It is likely that other Southern States have the same thing, but, like Georgia, not under the name of a reformatory. If Northern philanthropists will spend their money on reformatories instead of colleges, the South will co-operate with all her heart, soul, mind, body, and strength.
>
> It is a mistaken report that you have heard that "young lads and girls, especially negroes, are sent to the chain-gang for slight offences." Young criminals are rarely sent to chain-gangs, and never for small offences, unless so often repeated as to make it necessary. Young criminals (under sixteen years) are usually whipped—with their parents' consent—or fined, or made to "knock rocks" for a short while on the county's roads.
>
> In all my experience I have never seen nor heard of a young *girl* being sent to the chain-gang.

This correspondent, like many other dwellers in the South, believes that the Southern negroes need training in conduct rather than free education. The Northern idea is that education quickens intelligence, and that increased intelligence surely, though perhaps slowly, makes for a higher plane of conduct. That may be true, and yet the first fruits of education may be disappointing and far from satisfactory to observers close at hand. This much at least it is safe to say, that, though there may be dispute about the usefulness of colleges for negroes, there will be none as to the great value of good reformatories and penal institutions. They are needed everywhere, but especially in the South, where the burden of misbehavior falls heavier on the tax-payer than with us.

E. S. Martin

THIS BUSY WORLD

HARPER'S WEEKLY
August 5, 1899, p. 761

There has been another extensive negro hunt in Georgia. A woman is said to have been assaulted by two negroes at Saffold on July 20. Up to July 25 five negroes had been lynched on account of this crime, and several other deaths were likely to follow. The custom in these cases seems to be to extort confessions from the perpetrators of the crime when caught, and then to hunt down and kill all negroes implicated by the criminals' testimony. Heaven knows what degree of justice or injustice is done! At such times the wildest and most improbable tales seem to find credence, and when the killing is all over, and denial is made that any of the men killed were guilty of anything, it is impossible to disprove the denial. There is no machinery for proving a man's guilt after you have killed him. It has been asserted repeatedly, and is very widely believed, that Sam Hose, who was roasted in Georgia last spring, was guilty of no worse crime than killing a man in self-defence; and as for Strickland, the old negro preacher who was killed at the same time, the charges against him were improbable, to say the least. Now it will be asserted that there was no assault committed at Saffold, and that the gang of negroes who were said to be accessories were innocent. There will be no record of their guilt, no recorded testimony, nothing to show for their taking off but pistols, ropes, and scalps. Lynching is surely very unsatisfactory. There is a strong feeling against it now in the South, and here's hoping that it will grow. The papers said last week that a Georgian named Cardell, who captured Mack, one of the principals in the crime at Saffold, secreted his prisoner with intent to get him to jail, and only gave him up when a rope had been put around his own neck and hanging threatened.

E. S. Martin

THE RACIAL TROUBLES IN THE SOUTH

HARPER'S WEEKLY
August 19, 1899, p. 817

Newberry, S. C.
It was the ambition of Robert Toombs, the great antebellum fire-eater of Georgia, to call the roll of his slaves at the foot of Bunker Hill Monument. An equally distinguished son of Georgia, in our day, more fortunate than General Toombs, is accorded a most attentive and respectful hearing before a highly cultured, religious, and "moneyed" audience in Boston while for two long hours he palliates and extenuates, if he does not defend outright, recent brutal lynchings of negroes in his own and other Southern States; for that is what the recent address of ex-Governor Northen amounts to, however he may seek to obscure its real purpose.

I have often thought that the Southern people were, to say the least, remiss in their duty and unjust to themselves in not deputizing representative men of the highest standing and culture, and of unblemished personal and political character, to go North on suitable occasions and to explain to the Northern people the position of the law-abiding and cultured white people of the South on our most difficult and troublesome race question. It is not wise to leave the Northern people to infer our position from our lynching mobs, from our fire-eating politicians of the Tillman stamp, or from our very one-sided partisan press. These do not by any means fairly represent the better public sentiment of our people, but too often the very opposite.

Had I been called upon, however, to suggest the most suitable person to send upon such an important errand to Boston, the very seat of learning and of culture and of strict obedience to law, there is but one man from the entire South that I would probably have suggested in preference to Governor Northen. I refer, of course, to Rev. J. L. M. Curry, D.D., the able and scholarly manager of the Peabody Fund at the South, who has unquestionably contributed more to the cause of the education of both races than any other living man, and whose teachings would always lead to peace and harmony between them. Governor Northen is a man of unblemished political and religious character. And yet, after a careful reading of his impassioned address at Boston, I cannot but feel disappointed, and fear that he has missed the key-note, and done that better sentiment of our section harm rather than good. He has been led away by his zeal and his ardent desire to screen his own people, the white people of the South, against severe and often unjust outside criticism, into drawing the line rather between the races than between crime and lawlessness on the one side and virtue and obedience to law on the other. No one, North or South, will be found to defend or even to palliate the fiendish crime of Sam Hose, and certainly no one ought to be found anywhere to justify or extenuate his worse than brutal lynching. Governor Northen's address has, I fear, too much the appearance of an attempt to palliate the crime of lynching, and to throw the chief blame for our unfortunate condition at the South on the shoulders of others, instead of where it properly belongs. He even goes back to the early days of slavery, and attempts to throw the chief blame for the existence of that institution on the Yankee slave-dealer of over a century ago. One hardly sees the purpose of this historical retrospect. No well-informed person questions the fact that the sin of slavery was national, and not alone Southern. It was this writer's pleasure to be on very friendly personal terms with Charles Sumner, the great antislavery agitator, during the latter part of that gentleman's life, and on various occasions to discuss with him reconstruction and the race question, on some points of which we differed very materially. On one occasion I recall Mr. Sumner's avowing most emphatically that he had never regarded slavery otherwise than as a national crime, and not alone a sectional one, and that he had therefore always been ready to vote any amount of money to purchase the slaves, and to liberate them gradually as they became prepared for their new position. But the insuperable obstacle to this was that the South had come to regard slavery as a good to be perpetuated at all hazards, rather than as a national and local evil to be got rid of. The voice of reason and of argument on the subject of "our peculiar institution" was no longer tolerated at the South; and on the mere election of that very conservative antislavery man, Mr. Lincoln, as President in 1860, without awaiting his inauguration or an overt act against slavery, several Southern States made haste to raise the standard of rebellion; for such of course was the act of secession. Who, then, was responsible for the war and its dire results?

It is no doubt quite true, as Governor Northen informs us, that some New-Englanders did engage in slave-stealing in Africa—a most heinous crime certainly. There are unworthy people to be found in all countries and at all times. But had there been no slave-markets at the South these Northerners would perhaps have been engaged in some more legitimate business. If I remember aright, however, the last cargo of slaves from Africa was brought to Georgia by a distinguished Georgian, Major Lamar, and distributed there and in South Carolina but a short time prior to the outbreak of the rebellion.

Governor Northen dwells upon and emphasizes the absolute necessity for the rule of the white man at the South. This presumably every intelligent man admits. The writer certainly does, and quite as decidedly perhaps as Governor Northen. Intelligence and virtue, and the material interests in any country, ought always to rule. The white people of the South are entitled to rule, not on account of the color of their skin, but because they possess at least a largely predominant part of these qualifications in our section. Dr. Curry, in an able address along this line before the Georgia Legislature a few years ago, told that body distinctly that if the time ever came that the negro race took the lead in intelligence and virtue and the material interests of the State, it *would* rule and *ought* to rule. But this right to rule does not at all imply the right to trample under foot the constitutional, civil, and political rights of the inferior race, as is being done in several Southern States, nor the right to commit lynchings by wholesale, as has recently been done with so appalling frequency, especially in Governor Northen's State. Laws and governments in civilized countries are supposed to be for the protection of the poor and the weak and the helpless, and not for their oppression and murder. In Georgia and South Carolina, however, our Chief Executives seem to entertain a different idea as to the proper functions of government.

The grave errors and blunders of reconstruction are now fully admitted on all sides. The Republican as well as the Democratic party fully admits them, or it would not tacitly acquiesce in the enactment of constitutions like those of Mississippi, South Carolina, and Louisiana, which completely annul both in letter and spirit the Fourteenth and Fifteenth amendments to the Constitution of the United States—amendments enacted by the Republican party especially for the protection of the ex-slaves. These two amendments are complete dead letters, not only in these three States, but virtually also in several others. The uneducated negro has fully demonstrated his complete failure as a political factor, except for evil, as ought to have been foreseen by the legislators of the reconstruction period. From the very outset he showed a decided tendency to follow blindly the shrewdest demagogue, or to sell out to the highest bidder. Hence the saturnalia of the reconstruction period all over the South, which brought the Republican party into well-merited disrepute, from which it has not yet recovered. Had the principle of gradual enfranchisement on an intelligence and perhaps also a low property qualification been incorporated by Congress in the original reconstruction law, applicable alike, of course, to both races, this writer was then and is still of the opinion that very many of the evil results of reconstruction might have been avoided, and that the relations between the races might never have become so strained. But it may be well to recall that the North was not alone, and not primarily, responsible for the reconstruction measures. It will be remembered that under the so-called "my policy" plan of reconstruction of President Andrew Johnson, the "Black Code" had been enacted in South Carolina, and more or less similar measures in other States, making of the ex-slave a sort of serf of the soil. Of course the North, after having liberated the slave, could not permit a kind of Russian serfdom to take the place of slavery. This unwise legislation of the white people of the South was then primarily responsible for the later reconstruction measures, with all their blunders and resulting evils. Governor Northen ought not, in his zeal, to forget such important points of recent history. This writer urged on Mr. Sumner and other Republican leaders at the time the grave danger of granting suffrage to the negro without at least a minimum educational qualification. But it was urged, in reply, that it was necessary to grant universal suffrage to enable the negro to protect himself by his ballot. How utterly this idea has failed is now matter of history.

But the most serious objection, perhaps, to Governor Northen's address is its utter failure to suggest any remedy for our existing race troubles. On the contrary, he complacently informs us, in closing, that the relations between the races "are in no sense alarming." A condition of affairs which makes certain sections of the South a byword of reproach for lawlessness and brutality in all civilized countries is, to his mind, "in no sense alarming." That such a man as Governor Northen should so regard our situation, and try to palliate instead of remedy it, is perhaps the most alarming feature of all. I am glad to know, however, that there are other good and eminent men at the South who take a more serious view of the subject, and who have a rational and practical remedy to suggest. Here, for instance, is Colonel Julian S. Carr, a millionaire banker and manufacturer of North Carolina, who is a most liberal supporter of the education of both races and an earnest advocate of harmonious relations between them. In an address before the Colored Agricultural and Mechanical College at Greensboro, North Carolina, about the time Governor Northen was speaking to a Boston audience, Colonel Carr was urging the law-abiding negroes of the South to combine with law-abiding white men to put a stop to the present deplorable and alarming condition of affairs. He told them, in the way of encouragement, how the negro population of ten years old and upwards has progressed from an illiteracy of over 85 per cent. in 1870 to 60 per cent. in 1890, and less than 50 per cent. now; how it has accumulated over $226,000,000 in property, and has over 30,000 teachers in the field. Then he warned them that North Carolina "will never again submit to the government of ignorance"—note he did not say "government of the negro," but of "ignorance." Next he took up and invoked their most serious attention to what he properly termed the "living and burning question" between the races—that is, the question of lynching and the crime that usually provokes it. He warned the colored race that all white men "hold the homes and virtue of pure women sacred, and that the wretch who invades the one or assaults the other shall die." There is no division, he said with truth, among honorable men on this question. The only division is as to the method of inflicting the death-penalty. The advocate of lynch-law insists that an angry mob is the best medium, because its promptness and brutality act as a deterrent to the commission of the crime by others. Colonel Carr says, in reply to this idea, that "lynch-law, to say nothing worse of it, has proved a horrible failure." He might have gone a step further and said, with entire truth, that, instead of being a remedy, it rather tends to provoke and incite to the very crime it is intended to prevent. In brief, Colonel Carr's plan is to combine the intelligent and law-abiding elements of both races for the purpose of putting a stop to both the crime of rape and the crime of lynching, and for the promotion of peace and harmony between the two races. This plan seems to be practical, and should be satisfactory to all good citizens at the South; and it is one which ought to enlist the hearty support of the Northern press, pulpit, and people in carrying it into effect.

B. Odell Duncan.

STREET FAIRS IN OHIO CITIES

HARPER'S WEEKLY
August 19, 1899, p. 829

When the Chief of Police in Jersey City suggested recently that certain blocks of asphalted streets be roped off at night and given up to dancing by the populace generally, it was thought that he had hit upon a novel and unique method of giving pleasure to the masses in our cities. Chief Murphy got the idea from watching children dance on the asphalt to the tunes of street pianos, and it occurred to him that if wagon traffic could be stopped for several hours of an evening on certain blocks, not only the children, but the older folks would come out and pass a pleasant evening in dancing and promenading. He even suggested that bands could be hired, by subscription or otherwise, and that the monotony of city life could be brightened by an evening carnival on the street, with lights and music, and dancing by all who cared to join. The moral side of the question appealed to him. He said such open-air dancing would be less harmful by far to young people, conducted in the sight of all who cared to look on, than dancing in obscure halls or in gloomy picnic-grounds. . . .

It is customary to place freaks of various kinds, real and made-up, on exhibition, and among the attractions frequently are public weddings. When the bride and bridegroom are negroes there is general hilarity at these ceremonies. Merchants vie with one another, for the sake of the advertisement involved, in a competition of donating wedding outfits to the happy couple. Recently one negro couple received enough furniture to start a boarding-house. They also received three "honey-moon railroad passes." The bridegroom received sufficient clothing to last him for two years or more. The household goods included supplies of every sort that might be useful, and the bride and bridegroom willingly submitted to the notoriety for the sake of the material prosperity that came to them. On this occasion it was advertised that the wedding ceremony would take place in a lion's cage. The bridegroom objected to that at the last moment, and the knot was tied on a platform in view of thousands, after which the couple were escorted to their home by a brass band and a great crowd. That was a wedding to delight a happy negro pair, and it far surpassed the joys of being married in a balloon—one of the commonest diversions in the Western county fair.

THIS BUSY WORLD

HARPER'S WEEKLY
August 19, 1899, p. 833

Miss Lillian Clayton Jewett, described as a young woman of twenty-four years, with blue eyes and brown hair, recently a schoolgirl in a Virginia institute, has come to public notice in Boston as an agitator against lynching in the South. She conceived the idea of bringing to Boston the family of Postmaster Baker, the negro who was murdered at Lake City, South Carolina. This plan she has carried out, and at last accounts was exhibiting the widow Baker and her children at public meetings, to which a small admission-fee was charged. Her efforts have by no means met with unqualified approval in

AFRICAN AMERICAN HISTORY IN THE PRESS, 1851-1899

STREET FAIRS IN THE MIDDLE WEST.—[SEE PAGE 829.]

Harper's Weekly, August 19, 1899, p. 814.

1282

Boston, and the expediency of bringing the Bakers there is questioned by the judicious with considerable unanimity. Boston, as it is, is very much alive to the evils of lynching in the South. What is needed is not so much to stir her up further as to strengthen and encourage in the South the conviction, already strong among the best people and best newspapers there, that lynching is ruinous to the States in which it prevails, and must be stopped as matter of public policy. Dr. Broughton of Atlanta, a Baptist minister, said, the other day, in a sermon preached in Brooklyn:

> The best people in our community are not in sympathy with lynching. They believe in upholding the law. The best among the blacks are trying to prevent it. It is only the low-down, immoral element that keeps the thing alive. The trouble is that we allow such things to go on without trying to arrest the men who do it. What is needed is real men in official positions, from Governor down.

Lynching in the South must be stopped by Southern men. It is to their interest to stop it. It is their duty to stop it. No one else can do it. How much agitation in Boston, or generally in the North, will help them to do it is a question. It costs something for Southern men to fight lynching. It is troublesome, and doubtless dangerous. The Vicksburg papers have denounced the abominable lynching of Italians at Tallulah. It won't make them any more popular in the Tallulah district, but that has not influenced them. Governor Candler of Georgia seems to be in earnest in his efforts to put down mob law and make the courts do their work in his State. With the aid of militia companies he has foiled one or two gangs of lynchers, and he has appealed to the people of Georgia to stand by him and uphold the courts.

It would seem likely to have a wholesome effect if some one should sometime be punished for lynching. It would help to make the impatient realize that to hang or shoot a man on suspicion and without trial is a crime. There has been an extraordinary story in the newspapers about a most brutal lynching that occurred at Alexandria, Virginia, on August 8, where the victim appears to have committed no crime, and where the lynchers were a mob largely recruited from the slums and saloons of Washington and its neighborhood. The details of this outrage, as given at length by a correspondent of the New York *Evening Post,* are such as to leave the impression that the taking of human life by a mob is coming to be regarded by certain classes in this country as a legitimate diversion. If such things can happen in the shadow of the Capitol and no one get hurt except the man murdered, Miss Jewett or any one else can claim fair excuse for being agitated.

We have all been following the Dreyfus trial from day to day, and some of us have doubtless been telling ourselves what a bad pass the administration of justice had come to in France, when a man could be condemned of so serious an offence on such evidence as was used against Dreyfus. We have probably congratulated ourselves that Anglo-Saxon methods are better. For our minds' health we ought to remind ourselves to what an extent our system of trying accused persons and punishing criminals has broken down in this country. Trial by jury is a grand thing when it works, but when the difficulty of making it work is so great that too many criminals who are tried escape justice, and mobs usurp the functions of courts, it is no longer a thing to brag of.

E. S. Martin

PAPER ON NEGRO EDUCATION

HARPER'S WEEKLY
September 16, 1899, p. 925

The paper on negro education read by William H. Baldwin, Jr., at the annual meeting of the American Social Science Association on September 5, at Saratoga, seems better worth attention than any other recent discourse about the problems of the South. Mr. Baldwin is the president of the Long Island Railroad. He grew up and was educated in New England, and what he knows about negroes and their needs is the result of three years of active work in the South, and of six years of service as a trustee of the Tuskegee Institute. The gist of what he says is that industrial education, such as is given at Hampton and Tuskegee, is the solution of the negro problem. The army of white traders that went to the South after the war with spelling-books and Bibles to educate the negro began at the wrong end, for though Bible and spelling are necessary, the negro must first be taught to use his hands. Incidentally he will learn to use his head, but to teach him to hope that through books he may learn to live from the fruits of a literary education was a mistake. It is a crime, says Mr. Baldwin, for any teacher, white or black, to educate the negro for positions which are not open to him. His opportunity is in the South, where his labor is needed, and where he can get not only into agriculture, but into the principal trades, which are not open to him in the North. Mr. Baldwin tells him to hurry and learn to work hard and skilfully before the foreigner crowds in and drives him out of the trades. He tells him to buy land, keep out of politics, live a moral life, and learn to work. Mr. Baldwin is not at all concerned about social equality for the negroes. It does not trouble him that in many Southern States the negro is practically disfranchised. He should be disfranchised if he is not qualified to vote, but his qualifications should be determined by the same tests as a white man's are.

With the idea of deporting the Southern negroes Mr. Baldwin has no sympathy. The South needs them, he says, and they are better off there than they would be elsewhere. He abhors lynchings and Whitecap outrages, and discusses measures for abatement of them, but he says that thirty years is a short time to work out such a problem as the war left, and that the last two years have done more to bring out the truth of the situation than all the years previous since the war.

Mr. Baldwin wants better organization of industrial education in the South. The North, he says, is tired of giving indiscriminately to a multitude of colored schools in the South. He wants more concentration of money and effort, and suggests a system of secondary schools modelled after Hampton and Tuskegee, and in charge of a properly organized educational board.

The need of education for Southern whites was not Mr. Baldwin's theme, but he said the South could not rise unless the negro was educated, and that the negro could not rise unless the whites rose too.

THE RACE QUESTION

HARPER'S WEEKLY
September 23, 1899, p. 932

As to the deplorable race quarrel in the South, he [Theodore Roosevelt] believes that Booker T. Washington is pointing out the right path to his race. Lynchings and rapings are co-ordinate forces of evil. The negro must grow in grace before the white man will hold his hand from vengeance. The two must improve together before justice and law can prevail. No one doubts what Governor Roosevelt would do with a lyncher if he had the power over him, but no one will ever find him telling the negro that he has no part to play in the necessary regeneration of social conditions, or that he can play his part by turning his back to the light and merely being loyal to the Republican ticket. Fundamentally he believes that each locality of the country must work out its own salvation.

THIS BUSY WORLD

HARPER'S WEEKLY
November 18, 1899, p. 1158

Booker Washington's report of the Tuskegee Institute is interesting and highly satisfactory. What the institute does has come to be very well known, but readers cannot be too often reminded of what its needs are. Mr. Washington wants a new heating system, a water-works, a lighting system, $10,000 for the Industrial Department, $4000 for a hospital, $15,000 for a library, $5000 to rebuild a barn, $15,000 for a dormitory. He has now an endowment fund of $68,000; he wants to increase it to $500,000. There is a remarkable concurrence of opinion that the greatest and most effective work that is being done in behalf of the Southern negro, and consequently in behalf of the whole South, is being done at Tuskegee.

The trustees of the Hampton Institute are also making known the needs of their institution. As most people know it was the pioneer in the field that it now shares with Tuskegee. It educates Indians as well as negroes. Its deserts and usefulness are undisputed. It wants to add a million dollars to its endowment-fund. Its present endowment is $742,000. Its treasurer is George F. Peabody, Esq., 27 Pine Street, New York.

E. S. Martin

Appendix A

Newspaper Histories

Atlanta Constitution

The first edition of the *Atlanta Constitution* was published June 16, 1868, by Carey W. Styles. A single copy sold for ten cents; a one-month subscription sold for three dollars; a six month subscription, six dollars; a year subscription, ten dollars.

According to *A History of the Atlanta Journal and the Atlanta Constitution,* the paper's name was suggested by President Andrew Johnson as one "fitting for a Democratic newspaper seeking to fight for the restoration of constitutional government in the South." The paper was strongly opposed to the Radical Republicans and the Reconstruction.

Six months after founding the paper, Styles sold his interest to G. H. Anderson and William A. Hemphill; Edward Y. Clarke served as editor. In 1876 Evan P. Howell became editor-in-chief after acquiring a half-interest in the paper. Under the leadership of Howell the *Constitution* became one of the largest daily papers south of Baltimore and Louisville and east of New Orleans. In 1876 folklorist Joel Chandler Harris joined the *Constitution.* As associate editor, Harris edited the "Roundabout in Georgia" series which featured sketches in Black dialect. Harris was also responsible for creating the Uncle Remus character which appeared in numerous stories.

In 1879 Henry Woodfin Grady purchased a fourth interest in the paper for $20,000. As managing editor, Grady changed the paper's format and increased the number of pages. Editorials during Grady's reign were more liberal and advocated social, economic, and political reform in the South. Grady was responsible for coining the term "The New South" in 1886, which he felt crystallized the idea of salvation for the South and reconciliation with the North. Grady was convinced that racial issues in the South should be solved without interference from the North and was an advocate of separate accommodations but equal opportunity for blacks.

Clark Howell succeeded Grady, serving as managing editor and publisher until 1936. Staff included Henry Woodfin Grady and Joel Chandler Harris. By 1889 the *Constitution* had a weekly circulation of 140,000—at the time the largest in the United States.

Boston Daily Globe

Maturin Ballou issued the first edition of the *Boston Daily Globe* on March 4, 1872. The morning paper sold for four-cents. When Charles Taylor joined the paper as managing editor in 1873, he cut the price to two cents. In 1877 the price was raised to three cents, and an evening edition was added. As a result, the *Globe*'s circulation increased from 8,000 to 30,000 within three weeks; within three years the circulation had increased (for the two editions) to over 150,000.

Taylor believed that the *Globe* "should help men, women and children to get some of the sunshine of life, to be better and happier because of the *Globe*"; this idea became known as the cornerstone of the paper.

Charleston Daily Courier

The first issue of the *Charleston Courier* was published

on January 10, 1803 by Loring Andrews of Hingham, Massachusetts. The paper consisted of four, four-column pages, measuring 20 inches by 12 inches; a one-year subscription sold for seven dollars.

In 1808 "The wreath as the rod" was adopted as the paper's motto and the subtitle "Mercantile Daily Advertiser" added. The word "Daily" was added to the title in 1852, and on February 23, 1861, the words "Confederate States of America" were added to the title.

From November 21 to November 30, 1863, the paper suspended publication due to the bombardment of the city by Union troops. In 1865 the paper was published as a single sheet, measuring 10 inches by 15 inches, with the title *Daily Courier*. Although the war was still in progress, little war news was reported.

Charleston capitulated to Federal forces on February 18, 1865, and the words "Confederate States of America" appeared for the last time on the masthead. During the Federal occupation, the paper was managed by George Whittemore and George W. Johnson, who were authorized to issue a newspaper loyal to the Union. The title was changed back to *Charleston Daily Courier* and the format enlarged to five column, 12 inches by 18 inches.

In 1873 the *Charleston Daily Courier* was sold at auction and consolidated with the *Charleston Daily News*. The General Assembly of South Carolina incorporated the News and Courier Company in 1881.

Charleston Mercury

The *Charleston Mercury*, founded in 1822, was purchased by Henry Laurens Pinckney in 1823. The paper espoused the free trade and states' rights ideals of the Democratic party. In 1832 John Stewart joined the paper as editor. Under his leadership the paper became one of the most influential dailies in the South. Considered a mouthpiece for southern leaders, the *Mercury* was an advocate of secession and proslavery ideas. Stewart, himself, advocated the idea of every white person owning at least one slave.

During the Civil War the *Mercury* was owned and edited by Robert B. Rhett, Jr, whom many considered "the father of secession." As a member of the United States Congress, he was known for delivering emotional speeches; as a journalist he was known for his fiery editorials. In a November 29, 1862, editorial, Rhett claimed that "slavery is the best condition for the African; for he is incapable of rising pupilage and, in his master, he obtains a permanent and interest guardian."

The *Mercury* was credited with boosting morale in the South. During the blockade of Charleston, the paper was reduced to a single two-page sheet, and each issue of the *Mercury* was headed by the number of the day of the siege. On the 589th day the paper recorded the burning of Charleston by the Confederate troops.

Daily Phoenix

The first edition of the *Daily Phoenix* was published July 31, 1865, by Julian A. Selby who served as the paper's editor and proprietor. Its motto was "Let our Just Censure Attend the True Event." (The *Phoenix* was a continuation of the *Columbia Daily Phoenix*.) A one-year subscription sold for eight dollars. In 1875 the paper was purchased by the owners of the *Columbia Register*. The paper ceased publication in 1879.

Detroit Free Press

The *Democratic Free Press and Michigan Intelligencer* was first published on May 5, 1831, as a weekly political sheet, providing world news and information on the local arm of the Democratic Party. Sheldon McKnight was publisher, John P. Sheldon served as editor, and Joseph Campau and John R. Williams provided the capital. The first edition consisted of four, five column pages. The *Free Press* had the largest morning circulation in Michigan; 38,000 copies were printed the first year.

According to Frank Angelo in his book, *On Guard, A History of the Detroit Free Press*, McKnight printed the paper's philosophy on page two as:

"The democratic citizens of this territory having found the two newspapers (*the Journal* and *the Courier*) already established in Detroit completely under the control of the city aristocracy have been compelled to set up an independent press. Forming as they do a large majority of the electors of the Territory, they have found no medium with which to communicate to the public.

"This dilemma was presented to them either tamely to suffer a knot of politicians, in whose patriotism they have not confidence . . . or to establish a press that should be guided by the wishes of the majority.

"Our appeal is made to the people of the outer counties, and by their verdict we 'sink or swim.'

"We shall endeavor to merit the favor of our fellow citizens of the interior, by giving them a newspaper conducted on true democratic principles, and with such industry and judgement in the selection and arrangement of foreign and domestic news. . . ."

Aided by the growth of Detroit and its surrounding areas, the *Free Press* became the first daily paper published in the Michigan Territory on September 28, 1835. The paper dropped "and Michigan Ingelligencer" from the title and expanded to six columns November 28, 1832. Subscribers were charged two dollars per year in advance or two dollars and fifty cents at the end of a year; advertisers were charged one dollar and twenty five cents per square.

In accord with the Democratic Party, the paper did not support freedom for slaves, but supported the right of each state to allow or not allow slavery within its borders.

Wilbur Fish Storey became editor and publisher of the paper February 2, 1853. Story believed "It's a newspaper's duty to print the news and raise hell." He attacked abolitionists and denounced Negroes. Among Storey's editorial standards was for the Republican Party to always be referred to as the "Black Republican Party." Another was that no obituaries were to be published for prominent Detroit Whigs or Republicans. Storey was opposed to states seceding from the union and emancipating slaves.

By 1884 William E. Quinby was chief editor of the *Free Press,* which cost three cents daily or 15 cents per week. Throughout the 1800's the paper remained loyal to the ideals of the Democratic Party. The paper had a circulation of 2,420 issues daily by 1856.

Frank Leslie's Illustrated Newspaper

English engraver Henry Carter emigrated to New York in 1848 and soon thereafter legally changed his name to Frank Leslie. *Frank Leslie's Illustrated Newspaper,* a 16-page weekly that sold for 10 cents a copy, was launched December 15, 1855, and was the first newspaper to emphasize current news events with pictures and text. *Leslie's* was also the first newspaper to use a voluminous number of illustrations and, along with *Harper's Weekly,* was not matched in this capacity by other publications until after the Civil War. The paper was illustrated using large woodcuts; photographs by Mathew Brady were the primary basis for many of the linecuts and engravings. Frank Leslie employed Thomas Nast at age 15 to sketch for the paper for four dollars a week.

Writers such as Wilkie Collins and Walter Besant were contributors to the paper. William Waud sketched for the paper before joining his brother Alf at *Harper's Weekly* in 1864. *Leslie's* included features such as the "Great West" on the American frontier, and the "Housewife's Friend" department.

After the Civil War the paper became a "scandal sheet." News in the paper was usually sensational and published approximately two weeks after the fact. During the 1880's journalistic emphasis around the country focused on crusades. In 1881, for example, Leslie's campaigned against contaminated milk in New York. *Leslie's* was published until 1922, although in later years it was known as *Leslie's Weekly.*

Gleason's Pictorial Drawing-Room Companion and *Ballou's Pictorial Drawing-Room Companion*

Gleason's Pictorial Drawing-Room Companion, a weekly newspaper published out of Boston, Massachusetts by Frederick Gleason and edited by Maturin Ballou, first appeared in 1851. The paper sold for four-cents; a one-year subscription sold for two dollars. Gleason also published *The Flag of Our Union,* as a weekly miscellaneous family journal.

Modeled after the *London Illustrated News, Gleason's* covered national and international news and contained woodcuts, stories, poems, marriage and death notices, serial stories, travel epilogues, and short book reviews of new publications. The "Joker's Olio" column featured jokes; "Sands of Gold" column, pearls of wisdom; the "Foreign Miscellany" column, international trivia; and the "Wayside Gatherings" column, national trivia. Artists for the paper included William Waud, who sketched the "Gleason's Weekly Line-of-Battle Ship" in 1859, and Winslow Homer.

Between 1854 and 1859 Maturin M. Ballou served as editor and proprietor, and in 1855 the name of the paper changed to *Ballou's Pictorial Drawing-Room Companion. Ballou's* prided itself on being "The Cheapest Weekly Paper in the World"; a one-year subscription sold for two dollars. In 1855 the paper claimed that its 170,000 copies in circulation were not enough to meet the demand of subscribers.

Harper's Weekly

Harper's, a weekly, Republican-oriented newspaper, was established in 1857 and published in New York City. It sold for six cents per copy or three dollars per year. Later the paper increased its cost to ten cents per issue or four dollars per year. During the civil War, *Harper's* had a circulation of 100,000 readers; by 1872 circulation had grown to 160,000.

Fletcher Harper managed the weekly, which was published by one of the largest publishing houses in the United States, Harper Publishing. George W. Curtis wrote the "Easy Chair" column for the paper starting in October 1863. Curtis served as political editor for *Harper's* from 1863 to 1892.

The artist and political cartoonist Thomas Nast had illustrated John Brown's funeral for *Harper's* before becoming a staff artist. Nast's cartoons were a favorite feature with *Harper's* readers; his drawings in the paper were credited with helping to stimulate patriotism in the North during the Civil War. President Lincoln described Nast as "our best recruiting sergeant." Nast created the donkey and elephant as symbols for the Democratic and Republican parties. Notable sketches in the paper focused on the Civil War era, including: Condemnation of guerrilla warfare in the border states; the January 24, 1863 drawing of Emancipation depicting Black life past and present (see the 1863 chapter); and a sardonic drawing titled "Compromise with the South," a triumphant Southerner clasping hands with a crippled Northern soldier over the grave of Union heroes.

Painter and graphic artist Winslow Homer was a free-lance illustrator for *Ballou's Pictorial Drawing-Room Companion* and *Harper's* in the 1850s. *Harper's* sent Homer to Virginia several times to sketch battles on the front.

Alfred Rudolph "Alf" Waud was a "special artist" with the paper during the war. Waud spent most of his time with the Army of the Potomac. His brother William, illustrated for *Frank Leslie's Illustrated Newspaper* until joining *Harper's* in 1864. Photographs by Mathew Brady were the primary bases for many of the linecuts and engravings in the paper. Later the paper employed artists such as Theodore R. Davis, Edwin A. Abbey, William T. Smedley, and Howard Pyle.

In the 1870's *Harper's* and *The New York Times* fought to expose corruption in New York City by Tammany boss William Tweed. Nast's cartoons depicted the tiger as the emblem of Tammany Hall, the Democratic organization in New York. Tweed and his gang were eventually accused of misappropriating $200,000,000 for the city of New York.

Cartoonist A.B. Frost illustrated for the paper in 1876. Illustrator, painter, and sculptor Frederick Remington sketched the Southwest for two years for *Harper's* beginning in 1886. The paper carried serial fiction and short stores by writers such as Charles Dickens and Conan Doyle. Other journalists who worked for the paper included Eugene Lawrence, T.B. Thorpe, and Charles Dudley Warner, who wrote *The Guilded Age* with Samuel Clemens (Mark Twain).

The New York Times

George Jones, Henry J. Raymond, and Edward B. Wesley started *The New York Daily Times* on September 18, 1851, and charged a penny for the four pages and six columns. Jones and Wesley each put up $40,000, Raymond served as editor and Jones served as business manager for the paper. In the first ten weeks circulation jumped to 20,000. The second year the cost of the paper jumped to two cents for eight pages and the circulation of 26,000 dropped by a third temporarily. "Daily" was dropped from the title in 1857.

The New York Times was considered a well-balanced, well-edited newspaper. *The Times* began as a Whig paper then turned Free-Soilers, and then to Republican. In 1856 Raymond wrote the Republican Party platform.

Initially, in 1860 *The Times* opposed Lincoln for the Republican presidential nomination. After his nomination, however, the paper gave Lincoln its full support. The paper advocated conciliation when the issue of secession arose. At the beginning of the Civil War *The Times* published the editorial "Wanted—A Policy" accusing the Lincoln administration of inactivity and blindness.

Along with *Harper's Weekly*, *The Times* crusaded against official corruption headed by Tammany boss William Tweed. According to *The Times*, Tweed and his cohorts robbed New York City of $200,000,000, including paying a plasterer $50,000 a day for an entire month while working on the courthouse.

Between 1876 and 1891 circulation for *The Times* varied from 30,000 and 45,000. Louis J. Jennings and John Ford were editors in the 1870s and in 1883 Charles R. Miller became editor.

Richmond Enquirer

With the encouragement of Thomas Jefferson and others, Thomas Ritchie published the first issue of the *Enquirer* in 1804. The paper was a Democratic biweekly with a circulation of 1,500; by 1830 the circulation had jumped to 5,000. Ritchie edited the paper for forty-one years before turning it over to his sons. One of his sons, Thomas Ritchie, Jr., killed the publisher of the *Richmond Whig*, John Pleasants, in a duel. Ritchie Jr. accused Pleasants of abolitionist tendencies.

In his earlier years, Ritchie favored some form of emancipation. However, when slavery became a North-South issue Ritchie was proslavery. In the 1850s the paper chastised northern opponents of slavery and southern advocates of separation.

The *Enquirer* was considered a national newspaper rather than a regional newspaper. The *Enquirer* and the *Richmond Whig* expressed themselves as against slavery in 1831 but were quieted by the southern taboo against antislavery. During the Civil War the *Enquirer* favored secession and states' rights, and was supportive of Jefferson Davis's administration.

James Southall became editor in 1868. The paper was published as the *Enquirer and Examiner* between 1867 and 1870. From 1870–1877, when the paper ceased publication, it was known as the *Enquirer* once again.

Richmond Whig

Founded by John Pleasants in 1824. The *Whig* and *Richmond Enquirer* were political rivals in Virginia. Until the Confederate forces fired upon Fort Sumter in 1861, the *Whig* had been opposed to secession. The paper criticized war policies of the Confederate government and the leadership of Jefferson Davis. Pleasants was killed in a duel with Thomas Ritchie, Jr., editor of the *Richmond Enquirer*. Ritchie Jr. accused Pleasants of abolitionist tendencies.

General William Mahone acquired the paper in 1879 and made it an organ for the Virginia Readjuster Movement until it ceased publication in 1888. The Virginia Readjuster Movement was a political revolt in the commonwealth during the 1870s and 1880s. Strongest support for the movement came from the economically deprived and politically-disaffected—mountaineers, African Americans, poor whites, and small businessmen. The "Readjusters" won commonwealth elections in 1879 and proceeded to reduce taxes on the poor, liberalize voting requirements, and increase school and asylum expenditures. Mahone was elected to the U.S. Senate in 1881 as a Republican.

Appendix B

Newspaper Index

Atlanta Constitution

1880
April 3, 1880
May 4, 1880

1881
July 5, 1881

1883
September 27, 1883
September 28, 1883, p. 2
October 16, 1883
October 17, 1883

1891
January 25, 1891
May 1, 1891
July 26, 1891

1895
February 4, 1895
September 19, 1895, pp. 2–3
September 19, 1895

1896
May 19, 1896
May 28, 1896, p. 2

1897
November 20, 1897

1898
June 18, 1898

1899
July 26, 1899

Ballou's Pictorial Drawing-Room Companion

1855
January 20, 1855, p. 43
March 17, 1855, pp. 84–85
March 20, 1855, p. 101
May 15, 1855, p. 173
September 20, 1855, p. 318

1856
July 21, 1856, p. 255
September 17, 1856, p. 319

1859
September 10, 1859, p. 170
September 24, 1859, p. 208

Boston Daily Globe

1895
September 18, 1895, p. 2

1896
May 20, 1896

Charleston Daily Courier

1867
January 10, 1867
February 7, 1867
March 4, 1867
April 2, 1867

1868
June 12, 1868
June 13, 1868
June 15, 1868
June 16, 1868
June 17, 1868
July 6, 1868
July 7, 1868
July 28, 1868
July 29, 1868
July 31, 1868
September 22, 1868
September 23, 1868
September 24, 1868
September 26, 1868
September 28, 1868
October 26, 1868
October 27, 1868

1870
February 2, 1870
February 3, 1870
June 2, 1870

1871
April 5, 1871
April 7, 1871
April 8, 1871
April 15, 1871
April 20, 1871
April 22, 1871
May 19, 1871
May 22, 1871

1872
November 2, 1872
December 11, 1872
December 13, 1872
December 16, 1872

Charleston Mercury

1861
April 13, 1861, p. 13
April 15, 1861, p. 14

1862
April 26, 1862, p. 102
August 15, 1862, p. 131
December 23, 1862, p. 156

1291

1863
January 6, 1863, p. 159
April 13, 1861, p. 13
April 15, 1861, p. 14
August 14, 1863, p. 207

1864
April 23, 1864, p. 226
May 21, 1864, p. 229

1865
January 26, 1865, p. 281

Daily Phoenix

1865
December 20, 1865

1866
May 3, 1866, p. 1
September 25, 1866, p. 3

Detroit Free Press

1867
April 2, 1867, p. 1
April 2, 1867, p. 4

1870
February 2, 1870
February 25, 1870

Frank Leslie's Illustrated Newspaper

1857
March 21, 1857, p. 239

1858
March 13, 1858, p. 227
March 13, 1858, p. 234
July 24, 1858, p. 123

1859
February 12, 1859, p. 160
April 2, 1859, p. 272
October 29, 1859, p. 335–36
October 29, 1859, p. 344
November 5, 1859, p. 351
November 5, 1859, p. 351–52, 359
November 5, 1859, p. 360
November 12, 1859, p. 368
November 19, 1859, p. 394
December 10, 1859, p. 20
December 17, 1859, p. 34
December 17, 1859, p. 35
December 31, 1859, p. 66

1860
January 21, 1860, p. 117
March 3, 1860, p. 209
March 3, 1860, p. 210
March 3, 1860, pp. 211–12
March 31, 1860, p. 275

1861
June 8, 1861, p. 55
July 13, 1861, p. 131
September 21, 1861, p. 290

1862
June 14, 1862, p. 171
December 20, 1862, p. 194
December 20, 1862, pp. 199–200

1863
January 24, 1863, p. 275

1864
January 16, 1864, p. 267
March 5, 1864, p. 369
March 5, 1864, p. 370
March 5, 1864, p. 371
March 26, 1864, p. 7
April 9, 1864, p. 34
May 7, 1864, p. 99
May 7, 1864, p. 109
May 21, 1864, p. 132
July 9, 1864, p. 242
July 9, 1864, p. 247
August 20, 1864, p. 349
September 10, 1864, p. 386

1865
April 22, 1865, pp. 65–66
April 29, 1865, pp. 81–82

1866
April 28, 1866, p. 81–82

1869
March 6, 1869, p. 393
March 20, 1869, p. 13??
April 17, 1869, pp. 75–77
April 24, 1869, p. 92
May 15, 1869, p. 131
July 24, 1869, p. 295
September 25, 1869, p. 27
October 30, 1869, p. 115
December 4, 1869, p. 187
December 25, 1869, p. 247

1870
February 26, 1870, p. 401
March 12, 1870, p. 431
May 21, 1870, p. 157
July 16, 1870, p. 277
July 30, 1870, p. 311
October 15, 1870, pp. 69–70
December 31, 1870, p. 261

1883
July 21, 1883, p. 354

1884
August 30, 1884, p. 23

1885
May 30, 1885, p. 234
May 30, 1885, p. 242
June 6, 1885, p. 251
October 10, 1885, p. 124

1889
February 23, 1889, p. 27

Gleason's Pictorial Drawing-Room Companion

1851
May 3, 1851, p. 4
May 3, 1851, p. 5
May 21, 1851, p. 28
July 28, 1851, p. 63
October 4, 1851, p. 175
December 4, 1851, p. 271

1852
January 8, 1852, p. 15
January 21, 1852, p. 63
February 13, 1852, p. 111
February 13, 1852, p. 112
February 27, 1852, p. 123
February 27, 1852, p. 127
March 13, 1852, p. 165
April 3, 1852, p. 223
May 1, 1852, p. 287
May 21, 1852, p. 335
May 28, 1852, p. 351
June 5, 1852, p. 367

1853
January 5, 1853, p. 13
January 8, 1853, p. 15
February 16, 1853, p. 47
February 25, 1853, p. 95
March 18, 1853, p. 127
April 3, 1853, p. 157
June 5, 1853, p. 213
September 21, 1853, p. 332
October 3, 1853, p. 351

1854
March 3, 1854, p. 95
April 3, 1854, p. 157
September 16, 1854, p. 223
September 23, 1854, p. 239
December 2, 1854, p. 336

Harper's Weekly

1857
January 10, 1857, p. 22
March 7, 1857, p. 145
March 14, 1857, p. 161
March 14, 1857, p. 162
March 14, 1857, p. 166
March 21, 1857, p. 182
March 28, 1857, p. 193
April 4, 1857, p. 209
April 18, 1857, p. 241
April 18, 1857, p. 246
April 18, 1857, p. 246
May 2, 1857, p. 273

Newspaper Index

May 2, 1857, p. 278
May 23, 1857, p. 326
July 18, 1857, p. 454
July 25, 1857, p. 470
August 22, 1857, p. 534
August 29, 1857, p. 550
September 5, 1857, p. 566
September 12, 1857, p. 582
December 19, 1857, p. 802

1858
January 2, 1858, p. 6
January 9, 1858, p. 22
January 16, 1858, p. 38
February 6, 1858, p. 82
February 13, 1858, p. 102
February 20, 1858, p. 118
March 13, 1858, p. 162
March 13, 1858, p. 166
April 3, 1858, p. 214
April 24, 1858, p. 262
September 11, 1858, p. 582
November 30, 1858, p. 335
December 11, 1858, p. 790
December 18, 1858, p. 808

1859
January 29, 1859, p. 72
February 5, 1859, p. 86
September 17, 1859, p. 598
October 29, 1859, p. 690
October 29, 1859, p. 694–95
November 5, 1859, p. 712–14
November 19, 1859, p. 742
November 26, 1859, p. 758
December 24, 1859, p. 822

1860
January 21, 1860, p. 38
March 17, 1860, p. 167
May 12, 1860, p. 295
May 26, 1860, pp. 321–22
May 26, 1860, p. 326
July 14, 1860, p. 439
November 17, 1860, p. 726
December 15, 1860, p. 787
December 15, 1860, pp. 790–91

1861
February 2, 1861, pp. 70–71
March 9, 1861, p. 146
March 16, 1861, p. 167
March 30, 1861, p. 194
March 30, 1861, p. 199
April 13, 1861, p. 231
April 27, 1861, p. 258
June 8, 1861, p. 354
June 29, 1861, p. 413
July 13, 1861, p. 447
August 10, 1861.
August 17, 1861, p. 515
August 24, 1861, p. 530
August 24, 1861, p. 531
August 31, 1861, p. 546
September 14, 1861, p. 578

September 21, 1861, p. 594
September 28, 1861, p. 610
September 28, 1861, pp. 620–21
November 2, 1861, p. 690
November 9, 1861, p. 719
November 16, 1861, p. 732

1862
January 25, 1862, p. 50
February 15, 1862, p. 108
March 1, 1862, p. 130
March 8, 1862, p. 150
March 22, 1862, p. 178
May 10, 1862, p. 290
April 12, 1862, p. 226
May 10, 1862, p. 299
May 31, 1862, p. 338
June 7, 1862, pp. 354–55
June 7, 1862, p. 363
June 7, 1862, p. 355
June 14, 1862, p. 371
June 14, 1862, pp. 372–73
June 14, 1862, p. 373
June 28, 1862, p. 403
July 26, 1862, p. 467
August 2, 1862, p. 482
August 9, 1862, p. 499
September 6, 1862, p. 562
September 6, 1862, p. 563
September 13, 1862, p. 578
September 20, 1862, p. 595
October 4, 1862, p. 626
October 4, 1862, p. 627
October 18, 1862, p. 658
October 25, 1862, p. 675
November 8, 1862, p. 718
December 13, 1862, p. 786

1863
January 10, 1863, p. 17
January 17, 1863, p. 35
January 24, 1863, p. 55
January 24, 1863, p. 61
January 31, 1863, p. 67
February 7, 1863, p. 87
February 14, 1863, p. 98
February 21, 1863, p. 114
February 21, 1863, p. 119
February 28, 1863, pp. 130–31
February 28, 1863, p. 131
February 28, 1863, p. 142
February 28, 1863, p. 143
March 7, 1863, p. 147
March 7, 1863, p. 150
March 14, 1863, p. 162
March 14, 1863, p. 174
March 21, 1863, p. 179
April 4, 1863, p. 219
April 18, 1863, p. 243
May 30, 1863, p. 838
June 20, 1863, p. 386
June 27, 1863, p. 402
July 4, 1863, p. 418

July 4, 1863, p. 418
July 4, 1863, p. 427
July 4, 1863, p. 429
July 18, 1863, p. 459
July 25, 1863, p. 466
August 1, 1863, p. 482
August 1, 1863, p. 482–83
August 1, 1863, p. 494
August 15, 1863, p. 514–15
August 15, 1863, p. 526
August 22, 1863, p. 530
August 22, 1863, p. 531
August 29, 1863, p. 546
August 29, 1863, p. 551
September 19, 1863, p. 595
September 19, 1863, p. 603
November 28, 1863, p. 755
December 12, 1863, p. 787
December 12, 1863, p. 796
December 19, 1863, p. 803
December 26, 1863, p. 818

1864
January 16, 1864, p. 84
January 23, 1864, p. 51
January 23, 1864, p. 54
January 30, 1864, p. 66
January 30, 1864, p. 71
February 13, 1864, p. 98
February 20, 1864, p. 117
March 5, 1864, p. 147
March 12, 1864, p. 163
March 12, 1864, p. 173
March 19, 1864, p. 178
April 2, 1864, p. 211
April 9, 1864, p. 227
April 23, 1864, p. 258
April 30, 1864, p. 283
April 30, 1864, p. 274
May 7, 1864, p. 294
May 7, 1864, p. 302
May 14, 1864, p. 306
May 21, 1864, p. 334
June 11, 1864, p. 370
July 2, 1864, p. 422
July 9, 1864, p. 445
July 30, 1864, p. 482
August 6, 1864, p. 498
August 20, 1864, p. 531
September 17, 1864, p. 594
December 31, 1864, pp. 834–35
December 31, 1864, p. 835

1865
January 21, 1865, p. 34
January 28, 1865, p. 50
January 28, 1865, p. 51
February 11, 1865, p. 82
February 11, 1865, p. 83
February 18, 1865, p. 98
February 18, 1865, p. 99
February 25, 1865, p. 124
March 11, 1865, p. 146

March 18, 1865, p. 164
March 18, 1865, p. 172
March 25, 1865, p. 179
April 8, 1865, pp. 210–11
April 29, 1865, p. 259
May 6, 1865, p. 274
May 6, 1865, p. 275
May 13, 1865, p. 290
May 20, 1865, p. 306
May 20, 1865, p. 307
May 27, 1865, p. 322
June 3, 1865, p. 338
June 3, 1865, p. 339
June 10, 1865, p. 355
June 17, 1865, p. 370
June 24, 1865, p. 386
July 1, 1865, p. 403
July 8, 1865, p. 418
July 8, 1865, p. 419
July 29, 1865, p. 466
September 30, 1865, p. 610
September 30, 1865, p. 611
September 30, 1865, pp. 613–14
October 7, 1865, p. 626
October 28, 1865, p. 674
October 28, 1865, pp. 674–75
November 4, 1865, p. 690
December 2, 1865, p. 754
December 2, 1865, p. 755
December 16, 1865, p. 786
December 23, 1865, p. 811

1866
January 13, 1866, p. 19
January 20, 1866, p. 34
January 27, 1866, p. 51
February 10, 1866, p. 82
February 10, 1866, p. 83
February 10, 1866, p. 92
February 24, 1866, p. 115
March 3, 1866, p. 130
March 3, 1866, p. 131
March 3, 1866, p. 142
March 10, 1866, p. 146
March 10, 1866, p. 147
March 17, 1866, p. 174
March 24, 1866, p. 179
March 24, 1866, pp. 180–81
March 31, 1866, p. 194
March 31, 1866, p. 195
March 31, 1866, p. 206
April 14, 1866, pp. 226–27
April 14, 1866, p. 238
April 28, 1866, p. 259
May 5, 1866, p. 274
May 12, 1866, p. 300
May 19, 1866, pp. 317–18
May 19, 1866, p. 318
May 26, 1866, pp. 321–22
May 26, 1866, p. 322
May 26, 1866, p. 323
June 2, 1866, p. 338
June 2, 1866, p. 339

June 30, 1866, p. 411
July 14, 1866, p. 446
July 28, 1866, p. 477
August 4, 1866, pp. 485–86
August 18, 1866, p. 514
August 25, 1866, p. 531
August 25, 1866, pp. 534–35
September 1, 1866, p. 547
September 1, 1866, p. 556
September 15, 1866, p. 579
September 15, 1866, p. 581
September 22, 1866, p. 594
September 22, 1866, p. 598
November 24, 1866, p. 739
December 1, 1866, p. 754
December 8, 1866, p. 770
December 15, 1866, p. 790
December 22, 1866, p. 803
December 29, 1866, p. 819

1867
January 5, 1867, pp. 2–3
January 5, 1867, p. 3
January 5, 1867, p. 13–14
January 12, 1867, pp. 18–19
January 12, 1867, p. 19
January 19, 1867, p. 34
January 19, 1867, p. 35
January 26, 1867, p. 62
February 2, 1867, p. 66
February 9, 1867, p. 83
February 9, 1867, p. 94
February 16, 1867, p. 99
February 23, 1867, p. 114
February 23, 1867, p. 115
March 9, 1867, p. 146
March 16, 1867, p. 162
March 23, 1867, p. 179
March 30, 1867, pp. 193–94
March 30, 1867, p. 195
April 6, 1867, p. 210
April 6, 1867, p. 211
April 6, 1867, p. 218
April 13, 1867, p. 238
April 20, 1867, p. 242
April 27, 1867, p. 258
April 27, 1867, p. 259
May 18, 1867, p. 306
May 18, 1867, p. 307
May 18, 1867, p. 318
May 25, 1867, pp. 321–22
June 1, 1867, p. 339
June 1, 1867, p. 341
June 8, 1867, p. 354
June 8, 1867, p. 355
June 22, 1867, pp. 397–98
July 6, 1867, p. 418
July 20, 1867, p. 451
August 3, 1867, p. 492
August 10, 1867, p. 499
August 24, 1867, p. 530
August 24, 1867, p. 531
September 7, 1867, p. 563

September 7, 1867, p. 564
September 14, 1867, p. 577
September 14, 1867, p. 579
September 21, 1867, p. 606
October 12, 1867, p. 643
November 30, 1867, p. 755
December 14, 1867, p. 786
December 14, 1867, p. 787
December 21, 1867, p. 803

1868
January 11, 1868, p. 18
February 8, 1868, p. 82
February 8, 1868, p. 94
February 22, 1868, p. 115
February 29, 1868, p. 130
March 21, 1868, p. 178
March 28, 1868, p. 195
April 4, 1868, p. 211
April 11, 1868, p. 227
April 18, 1868, p. 243
April 25, 1868, p. 258
June 13, 1868, p. 370
June 13, 1868, p. 371
June 20, 1868, p. 387
June 20, 1868, p. 387
June 27, 1868, p. 403
June 27, 1868, pp. 404–5
July 18, 1868, p. 450
July 18, 1868, p. 451
July 25, 1868, p. 466
July 25, 1868, p. 467
August 15, 1868, p. 514
August 22, 1868, p. 531
August 29, 1868, p. 546
August 29, 1868, pp. 546–47
August 29, 1868, p. 547
September 19, 1868, p. 594
September 26, 1868, p. 610
September 26, 1868, p. 611
October 3, 1868, p. 626
October 3, 1868, pp. 626–27
October 3, 1868, p. 627
October 10, 1868, p. 642
October 10, 1868, pp. 642–43
October 10, 1868, p. 643
October 24, 1868, p. 674
November 14, 1868, p. 722
November 21, 1868, p. 738
November 21, 1868, p. 739
November 21, 1868, p. 740
November 28, 1868, p. 755
December 5, 1868, p. 770
December 5, 1868, p. 771
December 5, 1868, p. 780
December 12, 1868, p. 791
December 19, 1868, pp. 813–14

1869
January 16, 1869, p. 34
January 23, 1869, p. 53
February 6, 1869, p. 81
February 13, 1869, p. 99

Newspaper Index

February 20, 1869, p. 115
March 13, 1869, p. 163
March 20, 1869, p. 189
April 3, 1869, p. 211
May 1, 1869, p. 274
May 1, 1869, p. 283
June 26, 1869, p. 403
August 14, 1869, p. 514
August 14, 1869, p. 518
September 11, 1869, p. 579
September 25, 1869, p. 610
October 2, 1869, p. 626
December 4, 1869, p. 771

1870

January 1, 1870, p. 2
January 29, 1870, p. 67
January 29, 1870, p. 77
February 5, 1870, p. 82
February 19, 1870, pp. 114–15
February 19, 1870, pp. 116–17
March 5, 1870, p. 151
April 2, 1870, p. 211
August 20, 1870, p. 530
September 3, 1870, p. 563
September 24, 1870, p. 611
October 1, 1870, p. 627
November 5, 1870, p. 707
November 19, 1870, p. 739
December 17, 1870, p. 810

1871

February 18, 1871, p. 139
April 1, 1871, p. 282
April 15, 1871, p. 330
April 22, 1871, p. 354
April 22, 1871, p. 355
April 29, 1871, p. 378
April 8, 1871, p. 306
May 20, 1871, p. 450
May 20, 1871, p. 451
May 27, 1871, p. 474
May 6, 1871, p. 407
July 29, 1871, p. 690
August 5, 1871, p. 715
August 19, 1871, p. 762
September 2, 1871, p. 811
October 28, 1871, p. 1005
November 18, 1871, p. 1074
December 23, 1871, p. 1194
December 30, 1871, p. 1219

1872

January 6, 1872, p. 2
January 20, 1872, pp. 50–51
January 27, 1872, p. 73
January 27, 1872, pp. 73–74
February 24, 1872, p. 155
February 24, 1872, p. 157
March 16, 1872, p. 203
March 16, 1872, p. 203
March 9, 1872, p. 187
April 20, 1872, p. 308
May 11, 1872, p. 363

May 18, 1872, p. 391
June 8, 1872, p. 443
June 15, 1872, p. 467
June 22, 1872, pp. 482–83
June 22, 1872, p. 483
July 20, 1872, p. 562
August 3, 1872, pp. 593–94
August 10, 1872, p. 623
August 17, 1872, p. 634
August 24, 1872, p. 651
August 31, 1872, pp. 666–67
August 31, 1872, p. 667
September 14, 1872, p. 714
September 21, 1872, p. 730
September 28, 1872, pp. 757–58
October 12, 1872, p. 798
October 19, 1872, p. 803
October 19, 1872, pp. 805–6
November 2, 1872, p. 843
November 23, 1872, p. 910
December 7, 1872, p. 947
December 14, 1872, p. 971
December 14, 1872, p. 974
December 7, 1872, p. 951

1873

January 4, 1873, p. 1
March 22, 1873, p. 219
May 3, 1873, p. 362
May 3, 1873, p. 368
May 10, 1873, p. 396
May 24, 1873, p. 434
May 24, 1873, p. 435
June 7, 1873, p. 482
June 14, 1873, p. 498
June 14, 1873, p. 504–5
July 26, 1873, p. 643
August 23, 1873, p. 738
September 13, 1873, pp. 794–95
November 8, 1873, p. 985
December 6, 1873, p. 1085
December 27, 1873, p. 1158

1874

January 10, 1874, p. 27
February 14, 1874, p. 150
March 14, 1874, pp. 240–41
March 14, 1874, p. 242
April 4, 1874, p. 289
April 11, 1874, p. 310
April 18, 1874, p. 330
April 25, 1874, p. 359
May 9, 1874, p. 391
May 16, 1874, p. 411
May 23, 1874, pp. 430–31
May 30, 1874, p. 451
June 13, 1874, p. 490
June 27, 1874, p. 534
June 27, 1874, p. 545
August 1, 1874, p. 630
August 22, 1874, p. 690
August 29, 1874, p. 710
August 29, 1874, p. 715

October 3, 1874, p. 811
October 3, 1874, pp. 813–14
October 10, 1874, p. 831
October 10, 1874, p. 842
October 17, 1874, p. 858
October 24, 1874, p. 871
October 31, 1874, p. 890
October 31, 1874, pp. 901–2
November 14, 1874, p. 930
November 28, 1874, p. 971
November 7, 1874, p. 911
December 12, 1874, p. 1015
December 19, 1874, p. 1038

1875

January 9, 1875, p. 26
January 9, 1875, pp. 37–38
January 16, 1875, p. 50
January 2, 1875, p. 3
January 23, 1875, p. 70
January 23, 1875, p. 71
January 30, 1875, p. 90
January 30, 1875, p. 99
January 30, 1875, pp. 101–2
February 6, 1875, p. 110
February 6, 1875, pp. 110–11
February 6, 1875, p. 111
February 13, 1875, pp. 147–48
February 20, 1875, p. 150
February 27, 1875, p. 170
February 27, 1875, p. 171
March 6, 1875, p. 190
March 13, 1875, p. 210
March 13, 1875, p. 211
March 20, 1875, p. 230
March 27, 1875, p. 254
April 10, 1875, p. 295
April 17, 1875, p. 315
April 17, 1875, p. 316
April 24, 1875, p. 334
April 24, 1875, p. 335
April 24, 1875, p. 336
July 24, 1875, p. 595
July 31, 1875, p. 629
September 11, 1875, p. 734
October 2, 1875, p. 795

1876

January 15, 1876, p. 51
February 26, 1876, p. 162
March 4, 1876, p. 182
March 18, 1876, p. 222
April 8, 1876, p. 294
June 3, 1876, p. 443
June 24, 1876, p. 510
July 15, 1876, p. 575
August 5, 1876, p. 630
August 5, 1876, p. 631
August 12, 1876, p. 651
August 19, 1876, p. 671
September 2, 1876, p. 715
September 9, 1876, p. 731
September 23, 1876, p. 770

October 21, 1876, p. 846
November 4, 1876, p. 886
November 18, 1876, p. 938
December 9, 1876, p. 987
December 9, 1876, p. 988
December 16, 1876, p. 1006
December 16, 1876, p. 1011

1877
January 27, 1877, p. 62
February 17, 1877, p. 122
February 17, 1877, pp. 122–23
February 24, 1877, p. 142
March 17, 1877, p. 202
March 31, 1877, p. 242
March 31, 1877, p. 253
April 14, 1877, p. 282
April 21, 1877, p. 302
April 21, 1877, p. 306
May 12, 1877, p. 362
July 7, 1877, pp. 518–19
July 7, 1877, p. 519
July 14, 1877, p. 539
September 22, 1877, p. 739

1878
April 20, 1878, p. 309
May 18, 1878, p. 397
July 6, 1878, p. 527
July 27, 1878, p. 586
September 21, 1878, p. 747
October 5, 1878, p. 787
November 16, 1878, p. 906
November 23, 1878, p. 926
December 14, 1878, p. 986
December 21, 1878, p. 1006–7
December 21, 1878, p. 1015

1879
January 25, 1879, p. 71
March 29, 1879, p. 247
April 26, 1879, p. 322
April 26, 1879, p. 326
May 10, 1879, p. 363
May 17, 1879, p. 386
May 17, 1879, p. 387
May 24, 1879, p. 403
May 24, 1879, p. 406
May 24, 1879, p. 407
May 31, 1879, p. 423
May 31, 1879, p. 423
June 7, 1879, p. 447
July 5, 1879, p. 522
July 5, 1879, pp. 533–534
July 19, 1879, p. 562
August 16, 1879, p. 642
August 23, 1879, p. 662
September 13, 1879, p. 722
October 11, 1879, p. 803
November 1, 1879, p. 867
November 1, 1879, p. 870
December 6, 1879, p. 950

1880
January 17, 1880, p. 34

March 27, 1880, p. 194
March 27, 1880, p. 195
May 1, 1880, p. 274
May 1, 1880, p. 286
May 15, 1880, p. 307
May 22, 1880, p. 323
July 3, 1880, p. 419
July 24, 1880, pp. 466–67
July 31, 1880, p. 482
August 28, 1880, p. 546
August 28, 1880, p. 547
August 7, 1880, p. 498
August 7, 1880, pp. 498–99
September 11, 1880, p. 578
September 18, 1880, p. 594
October 2, 1880, p. 626
October 23, 1880, p. 674
October 30, 1880, p. 690
November 13, 1880, pp. 733–34
November 20, 1880, pp. 749–50
November 27, 1880, pp. 765–66
December 4, 1880, p. 779
December 4, 1880, pp. 781–82
December 11, 1880, p. 787
December 18, 1880, p. 807

1881
January 22, 1881, pp. 50–51
February 5, 1881, p. 83
March 19, 1881, p. 179
March 26, 1881, p. 194
May 7, 1881, p. 294
May 7, 1881, pp. 302–3
May 21, 1881, p. 326
May 28, 1881, p. 343
June 25, 1881, p. 406
August 6, 1881, p. 542
August 20, 1881, p. 562
August 20, 1881, p. 574
September 17, 1881, p. 637

1882
March 18, 1882, p. 162
July 8, 1882, p. 418
October 14, 1882, p. 643
November 18, 1882, p. 723

1883
January 6, 1883, p. 3
February 3, 1883, p. 66
April 28, 1883, p. 259
October 27, 1883, p. 674
November 24, 1883, p. 743
December 8, 1883, pp. 782–83
December 15, 1883, pp. 794–95

1884
February 16, 1884, p. 102
February 16, 1884, p. 111
February 9, 1884, p. 87
April 26, 1884, p. 262
April 26, 1884, p. 271
May 24, 1884, p. 326
July 26, 1884, p. 475
August 16, 1884, p. 529

November 22, 1884, p. 764
November 29, 1884, pp. 780–81
December 6, 1884, p. 796
December 27, 1884, p. 852

1885
January 10, 1885, p. 27
January 24, 1885, p. 37
January 31, 1885, p. 74
March 28, 1885, p. 199
April 4, 1885, p. 211
April 11, 1885, p. 122
June 6, 1885, p. 354
July 4, 1885, p. 423
July 4, 1885, p. 432
July 11, 1885, p. 439
August 1, 1885, p. 487
September 26, 1885, p. 627

1886
August 14, 1886, p. 514
August 14, 1886, p. 515
August 21, 1886, p. 535
October 2, 1886, p. 631
November 27, 1886, p. 767

1887
January 29, 1887, p. 71
February 12, 1887, p. 111
April 9, 1887, p. 250
April 21, 1887, pp. 305–6
June 4, 1887, p. 399
June 18, 1887, p. 434
June 25, 1887, p. 450
June 25, 1887, pp. 454–55
July 16, 1887, p. 499
July 23, 1887, pp. 527–28
August 6, 1887, p. 554
November 19, 1887, p. 834
December 10, 1887, pp. 894–95

1888
January 14, 1888, pp. 22–23
January 21, 1888, p. 38
February 11, 1888, p. 91
February 18, 1888, p. 111
April 14, 1888, p. 262
May 19, 1888, p. 350
May 19, 1888, p. 351
July 7, 1888, p. 490
August 18, 1888, p. 606
September 8, 1888, p. 667
October 13, 1888, p. 771
November 10, 1888, p. 847
November 17, 1888, p. 867
November 17, 1888, p. 870
December 22, 1888, pp. 978–79
December 22, 1888, p. 979
December 29, 1888, p. 1006
December 29, 1888, p. 999

1889
January 5, 1889, p. 3
January 19, 1889, p. 42–43
March 2, 1889, p. 162

REF E 185.2 .A25 1996